• At the dinner table. Discussing characters in old Westerns. They wore those long, droopy mustaches. What's that word? Quick! WORD MENU™! The Index! Look up "mustache" and turn to that page. There's what you want—*handlebar mustache*!

• The deadline is at hand. You're writing a magazine piece about tending bar at an upscale cocktail party. You need to mention some colorful drinks. Quick! WORD MENU™! The Table of Contents! Here, under Chapter Seventeen, Leisure and Recreation, you find the section on Mixed Drinks, replete with terms for lovely liquid concoctions such as *kamikaze, godfather, velvet hammer,* and *salty dog,* clearly grouped together with each one defined.

"One of those rare inventions that creates a legitimate niche for itself. WORD MENU™ is unlike any other word reference book you've seen, and may replace some you have."

—Digby Diehl

Prodigy Computer Network Daily Book Columnist

Published by Ballantine Books:

RANDOM HOUSE WEBSTER'S DICTIONARY
RANDOM HOUSE ROGET'S THESAURUS
RANDOM HOUSE GUIDE TO GOOD WRITING
RANDOM HOUSE POWER VOCABULARY BUILDER
RANDOM HOUSE WEBSTER'S SPELL CHECKER & ABBREVIATIONS DICTIONARY
RANDOM HOUSE WORD MENU™
RANDOM HOUSE LATIN-AMERICAN SPANISH DICTIONARY
RANDOM HOUSE SPANISH-ENGLISH ENGLISH-SPANISH DICTIONARY
RANDOM HOUSE JAPANESE-ENGLISH ENGLISH-JAPANESE DICTIONARY
RANDOM HOUSE GERMAN-ENGLISH ENGLISH-GERMAN DICTIONARY
RANDOM HOUSE FRENCH-ENGLISH ENGLISH-FRENCH DICTIONARY

Random House WORD MENU™

by Stephen Glazier

BALLANTINE BOOKS • NEW YORK

 Published in the United States by Ballantine Books, a division of Random House, Inc., New York, and simultaneously in Canada by Random House of Canada Limited, Toronto. This is an abridged edition of a work originally published by Reference & Information Publishing, Random House, Inc., in hardcover in 1992.

http://www.randomhouse.com

Library of Congress Catalog Card Number: 97-93875

ISBN 0-345-41441-1

Manufactured in the United States of America

First Ballantine Books Edition: August 1997

10 9 8 7 6 5 4 3

In memory of my father, Bill Glazier,
and for Anna, *sine qua nihil.*

Brief Table of Contents

Staff and Consultants

Conceived and Created by Stephen Glazier in Association with Karen Pedersen
Editors: Sol Steinmetz, Enid Pearsons
Managing Editor: Jennifer L. Dowling
General Editors: Carol Braham, Robert B. Costello, Joyce O'Connor
Contributing Editors: Barry Koffler (Life Sciences), Penny Marienthal, Terence Mulry (Religion), Roger Packard (Chemistry), Michael Rich (Medicine), Roberta Rubin-Dorsky, Georg Zappler (Life Sciences)
Copy Editors: James Gullickson, Judy Johnson, Felice Levy, Linda Massie, Jesse T. Sheidlower, Alice Kovac Somoroff
Production Director: Patricia W. Ehresmann
Designer: Steve Kennedy
Publisher: Charles M. Levine
Revision and Updates: Frank R. Abate, Elizabeth J. Jewell
For the Ballantine Edition: Barbara Ann Kipfer, Megan R. Schade

Consultants

Lisa Andreini (Photography)
Karen Atkinson (Computers)
Harriet Balkind (Advertising)
Paula Biran (Classical Music)
David Black (Publishing)
Christopher Blunden (Law)
Michael Bunyaner (Securities)
Angus Cameron (Fishing/Hunting/Firearms)
Carl P. Carrigan (Theater)
Dan Del Col (Advertising)
Stephen Donaldson (Prison/Eastern Religions)
Wayne Dynes (Homosexuality)
Peter R. Feuche (Theater)
Andrew Field (Real Estate)
Gary Fleisher (Medicine)
Carl Giordano (Sports)
Donald Goldstein (Economics)
Sharon Goldstein (Linguistics/Grammar/Phonetics)
Jeff Grambs (Weapons/Military)
Lee Greathouse (Telecommunications)
Elizabeth Greenberg (Theater)
Ruth Gross (Psychology)
Joan Keener (Ballet)
Verly Klinkenborg (Literature)
Denise Marika (Sculpture)
Bob Merlis (Rock Era Dances)
Joyce O'Connor (Fashion)
Joan Pancoe (New Age)
Jan Paradise (Medicine)
Enid Pearsons (Computers)
David Peters (Graphic Design)
Alison Postman (Hair Styles)
Bruce Postman (Cinema)
Charles Pye (Taxation/Accounting)
James Rader (Birds/Prefixes and Suffixes)
Anna Raviv (Theater)
Jon Resier (Anatomy)
Kurt Richards (Aircraft)
Deane Rink (Physics)
Jon Rubin (Popular Music)
Carol Sacks (Geology)
Roger Scorcio (Building Materials/Structural Components)
Simon Sheridan (Tools and Hardware)
Martin Smith (Television)
Zachary Smith (Basketball)
Alice Kovac Somoroff (Geography)
Jeff Spurrier (Journalism)
Ann Summa (Photography)
Emanuel Thorne (Mathematics)
Richard Van Dorn (Electricity and Electronics)
William Van Dorn (Ships and Boats)
Antoinette White (Ballet)
Wendell Williams (Automobiles)

User's Guide

The *Random House Word Menu*™ organizes the English language by subject matter. Subject categories are listed in the Table of Contents. The categories are arranged in a logical structure that runs from the general—The Human Body, or Leisure and Recreation—to the specific—the Reproductive System, or Stringed Instruments. The lowest level of the structure contains nearly 800 individual lists, each with 50 to 200 defined terms.

The logical structure and its word associations are designed to make it easy to find the group of words one is seeking. In technical and institutional areas this logic is virtually absolute—*Parts of Ships, Sails, and Equipment* must lie within *Ships and Boats,* which must lie within *Transportation.* In nonconcrete areas like *Language, Cognition,* or *Faith,* users will quickly become familiar with the structure so that they can locate *Judgment and Criticism,* or *Magic and the Occult,* or *Exclamations,* or *Verbs of Motion.*

Thus, to find a verb that describes disagreement or opposition, turn first to the category *Judgment and Criticism,* where you will find the subcategory *Opposition, Disagreement, and Attack.* There you can compare definitions and choose from among such terms as "niggle," "nitpick," "quibble," "repudiate," and "take issue with." If these do not seem strong enough, move on to the next subcategory: *Blame, Censure, Ridicule, and Contempt.*

Or to find the difference between a davenport, a divan, an ottoman, and a settee (perhaps you need the word to describe a room in a story, or you plan to talk to a furniture salesperson), turn to the subcategory *Chairs and Sofas* in the list of *Furnishings* under *The Home.*

Or, if you can't remember the word for "a close-fitting academic cap with flat, square top and tassel," look under *Hats* (in the category *Hats, Headgear, and Hairpieces*) to find the word "mortarboard."

The reverse-dictionary function can also be useful in solving crossword puzzles, where the clue is a definition and leads to the appropriate subject. For example, a seven-letter word beginning with *m* for "a large, broad-bladed knife" would lead you to the list of *Blades, Clubs, and Projectiles* under the category *Weapons and Armaments,* where you would find the word "machete."

Conversely, if you know the word and wish to learn its spelling, definition, or part of speech, look up the word in the Index at the back of the book. Or, if you don't know the word but do know a synonym or related word, look up the latter in the Index. Chapters and categories are also listed in the Index, in boldface. The Index leads you directly to the page where the word you are looking for is listed.

Another quick way to find information in the book is by checking the Guide Words above the black line at the top of each page. The Guide Words indicate the chapter number, chapter name, and subclass.

Most words listed under a category have concise definitions, except where they form a long list defined by its heading, as the list of *Pet Names* under the category *Terms of Endearment and Respect* or the list under *Meats and Cuts of Meat.*

Many entry words are followed by italicized labels that describe the level of usage of a word. The commonest of these restrictive labels are *Slang* and *Informal.* These labels are often very specific, as, for example, *Vulgar Slang, Yiddish Derogatory Slang.* Labels serve to warn you that using the labeled word in formal contexts may be inappropriate. Trademarks are indicated by the italicized label *Trademark* before the definition.

Though this book includes definitions, it is clearly not intended to replace a standard dictionary. Pronunciations of words, etymologies, and usage notes are not included in this book, and users should consult a standard college-level dictionary, such as the *Random House Webster's College Dictionary,* to obtain this and other more detailed lexical information.

Again, unlike a standard dictionary, this book does not provide all the meanings of a word in one place. Instead, each meaning or usage of a word appears as a separate entry in the appropriate place in the structure. For example, the word "mole" appears in eight places: *Animals; Chemistry; Medical Problems; Machinery; Ships and Boats; Foods; International Relations; and Strategy, Intrigue, and Deception.*

Definitions of the same word appearing under different categories (for example, *Trinity,* appearing under two categories) may differ in wording in order to focus on the distinctive use of the word in each category.

All listed words, defined and undefined, are arranged in alphabetical order. Example: *solar, solar corona, solar eclipse, solar flare, solar nebula, solar wind, solstice.*

With few exceptions, nouns and noun phrases are listed without a part-of-speech label. Verbs, adjectives, and adverbs are given an abbreviated part-of-speech label after the entry word. The labels appear in italics within parentheses, thus: (*vb*) for verbs, (*adj*) for adjectives, (*adv*) for adverbs. Defined entries whose headings indicate exclusive verbal use (e.g., *Eating Verbs*) do not show the (*vb*) part-of-speech label.

Derivatives of words, as those ending in *-ed, -ing, -ly, -ness,* and *-ation,* are usually not listed separately from the base word. We thus enter "abjure" but not abjuration, "indict" but not indictment, "relative" but not relatively, "paradox" but not paradoxical or paradoxically.

The following abbreviations occur in the book:

adj	=	adjective
adv	=	adverb
arch.	=	archaic
Brit.	=	British
c.	=	century
etc.	=	et cetera
esp.	=	especially
lit.	=	literally
n	=	noun
opp.	=	opposite
orig.	=	originally
pl.	=	plural
sing.	=	singular
usu.	=	usually
vb	=	verb

The best way to become familiar with this book is to use it, especially as a quick reference for certain types of information: a list of the world's currencies (Chapter 12 - THE ECONOMY, *Finance, World Currencies*); or a list of medical prefixes and suffixes (Chapter 4 - THE SCIENCES, *Medicine, Prefixes and Suffixes*); or a list of cyclical events (Chapter 3 - THE EARTH, *Weather and Natural Phenomena, Forecasting and Meteorology/Cyclical Events*).

Or you might use the book to find a Latin, French, or other synonym for an English word (Chapter 21 - FOREIGN EXPRESSIONS); or to find a list of titles and ranks (Chapter 11 - SOCIAL ORDER, *Titles of Rank*); or to find the correct name of a particular tool (Chapter 5 - TECHNOLOGY, *Tools and Hardware, Common Tools and Tool Types*).

You can find all of these and many other types of information by any of the three routes described above: the Table of Contents, the Guide Words, or the Index. Before long you will find this volume to be a useful and indispensable reference book.

Outline

Random House WORD MENU™

Chapter One
The Human Body

ANATOMY

Head and Neck

head bony topmost portion of body, containing brain and sense organs
neck top of spinal column
Adam's apple (thyroid cartilage), adenoids
brow
cheek, cheekbone, chin
eardrum, ears, eyeball, eyebrow, eyelash, eyelid, eyes
face, forehead
gums
hair
jaw
larynx, lips
mouth
nape, nasal cavity, nose, nostril
scalp, skull
temple, throat, thyroid cartilage, tongue, tonsil, trachea
vocal cords
voice box (larynx)
windpipe (trachea)

bridge bony portion of nose where it joins brow
buccal cavity hollow formed by mouth containing tongue, teeth, and salivary glands
cranial cavity hollow formed by skull, containing brain
cranium bone enclosing brain; skull excluding lower jaw
epiglottis flap of cartilage covering windpipe to prevent food from entering lungs
esophagus tube through which food passes from pharynx to stomach
larynx muscles and cartilage at upper end of trachea holding vocal cords
mandible bone of lower jaw
mastoid process projection of skull behind ear
maxilla bone of upper jaw
nares nostrils, nasal openings
occiput back portion of skull
orbital cavity bony hollow containing eyeball
pharynx top of alimentary canal leading from mouth and nose to larynx and esophagus
philtrum vertical groove on surface of upper lip, below septum of nose
proboscis snoutlike nose
sebum oily secretion of sebaceous glands that keeps hair and scalp soft and waterproof
septum dividing wall or membrane, esp. between nostrils of nose
sinus hollow air cavity beneath skull connected to nostrils

Eyes

aqueous humor jellylike fluid that fills eye chamber in front of lens
blind spot point where optic nerve joins retina that is insensitive to light
bony orbit framework of bones surrounding eye socket
ciliary body smooth muscle and its connection to suspensory ligament of lens
conjunctiva protective layer of mucous membrane lining inner surface of eyelid over cornea
cornea transparent covering over iris that produces refraction needed to focus image on retina
epicanthic fold epicanthus
epicanthus long fold of skin on upper eyelid; epicanthic fold
eyeball globe of the eye containing nervous tissue stimulated by light
fovea centralis small depression at back of retina that is point of sharpest vision
iris colored circular muscle in front of eye that controls amount of light entering eye
lens transparent, biconvex element between iris and vitreous humor that focuses light rays on retina
optic nerve nerve that sends sight impulses from eye to brain
orbital cavity bony hollow containing eyeball
pupil round contractile aperture in iris of eye
retina inner layer of eye wall composed of nervous tissue stimulated by light to send impulses to brain
sclera tough, white, fibrous membrane forming protective outer wall of eyeball except area of cornea
twenty-twenty (*adj*) having normal visual acuity
vitreous humor jellylike material that fills eyeball and forms its shape

Ears

auditory nerve either of pair of cranial nerves, consisting of sensory fibers that conduct impulses from ear to brain
cerumen ear wax; yellow, waxlike secretion of external ear
cochlea spiral tube in inner ear filled with liquid

that senses loudness and pitch and sends nerve impulses to brain
concha shell-like structure of external ear
ear wax cerumen
Eustachian tube canal from middle ear to pharynx
helix curved fold along rim of external ear
incus anvil-shaped ossicle of middle ear
inner ear receptor for sound and sense organ of balance
lobe fleshy lower tip of outer ear
malleus hammerlike outermost ossicle of middle ear
middle ear part of ear with eardrum and bony adjacent cavity; tympanum
organ of Corti part of ear in cochlea that hears sounds
ossicle small bone in middle ear that passes vibrations from eardrum to oval window: incus, malleus, or stapes
outer ear short, protective tube leading to eardrum
oval window thin membrane that passes vibrations from middle ear to labyrinth of inner ear
pinna structure of skin and cartilage fixed to head forming visible portion of outer ear; auricle
semicircular canal one of three curved tubular canals in labyrinth of ear, serving to maintain equilibrium
stapes stirrup-shaped innermost ossicle of middle ear
tympanic membrane eardrum
tympanum middle ear
vestibule hollow forming approach to inner ear

Mouth and Teeth

alveolus socket within jawbone in which roots of teeth are set
bicuspid premolar tooth with two-pointed crown
buccal cavity hollow formed by mouth containing tongue, teeth, and salivary glands
canine sharp, pointed tooth behind incisor
crown enameled portion of tooth above gum line
cusp pointed projection on crown of tooth
cuspid canine tooth with single-pointed crown
dentine hard, bonelike substance forming main part of tooth
enamel hard substance forming outer cover of tooth
gingiva gum
incisor tooth with cutting edge at front of mouth
molar flat-surfaced grinding tooth at rear of mouth
occlusion fitting together of teeth of lower jaw with teeth of upper jaw
overbite occlusion in which upper incisor teeth overlap lower ones
palate roof of mouth, separating it from nasal cavity
premolar bicuspid tooth in front of molar
pulp soft tissue at center of tooth containing nerves and blood vessels
rictus opening of the mouth
root part of tooth embedded in and attached to gum
saliva mucus-containing liquid secreted by glands in mouth to lubricate passage of food through alimentary canal
soft palate posterior, muscular portion of palate
taste bud receptor of taste on surface of tongue that responds to bitter, sweet, sour, or salt
underbite occlusion in which lower incisor teeth overlap upper ones
uvula pendent fleshy lobe in middle posterior of palate
velum soft palate
wisdom tooth third molar at rear of mouth

Trunk

abdomen part of body lying between thorax and pelvis and containing digestive organs; belly
abdominal cavity hollow within abdomen containing digestive organs
appendix narrow, blind tube three inches long in lower right part of abdomen; vermiform appendix
back rear part of body from neck to base of spine
backbone spinal column
belly midriff; abdomen
breast front upper portion of chest; either of two milk-secreting glands in upper chest of female; corresponding undeveloped gland in male
breastbone sternum
buttocks rear of hip forming fleshy seat for body
chest part of body enclosed by ribs and sternum
clavicle bone linking sternum and scapula
coccyx end of spinal column beyond sacrum that represents vestigial tail
collarbone clavicle
crotch point where legs fork from base of trunk
dorsal (*adj*) on or near the backside
groin juncture of lower abdomen and inner thigh
hipbone either of two bones forming sides of pelvis
ilium broad upper portion of hipbone
ischium lower portion of hipbone
loin region on either side of spinal column between hip and ribs
midriff front of torso between abdomen and chest
navel small scar in middle of abdomen where umbilical cord was attached to fetus
nipple small protuberance of breast where milk duct discharges in female; teat
paunch flabby midriff
pectoral girdle arch formed by scapulae and clavicles
pelvic girdle arch formed by ilium, ischium, and pubis
pelvis basin-shaped skeletal structure formed by pelvic girdle and adjoining bones of spine
pericardial cavity thin, membranous sac enclosing heart
perineum area between anus and male scrotum or edge of vulva in female
pleural cavity thin, membranous lining of chest cavity that encloses lungs

pubis part of hipbone forming front of pelvis
rib paired curved bones protecting entire viscera, ten fixed and two floating
sacrum compound bone forming back of pelvis
scapula large triangular bone lying in each dorsal lateral part of thorax; shoulder blade
shoulder blade scapula
solar plexus nerve complex at pit of stomach
spinal column series of joined vertebrae forming axial support for skeleton and carrying nerves; backbone; spine
spine spinal column
sternum flat bone of upper chest connecting ribs to shoulder girdle; breastbone
teat nipple
thoracic cavity hollow in trunk containing heart and lungs
thorax part of body between neck and abdomen, containing thoracic cavity
torso trunk containing organs
trunk central portion of body apart from head, arms, and legs
tummy *Informal.* stomach
umbilicus navel
ventral (*adj*) abdominal; located on lower front surface of trunk, opposite back
viscera organs in thoracic and abdominal cavities, including heart, lungs, stomach, liver, and kidneys

Limbs and Extremities

ankle joint between foot and leg
arm upper limb between shoulder and wrist
armpit axilla
axilla hollow under shoulder where arm joins trunk; armpit; underarm
ball rounded portion at front of bottom of foot, behind the toes
biceps lateral muscle along inside of upper arm
big toe largest toe, on inner edge of foot
calf fleshy hind part of leg below knee
carpus wrist, esp. bones of wrist
crazy bone *Slang.* elbow
crook inside bend of elbow or knee
cuticle hardened epidermis that accumulates at base of fingernail
digit finger or toe
elbow hinge joint at mid-arm
extremity limb, esp. hand or foot
femur proximal bone of upper leg; thighbone
fibula outer, smaller bone between knee and ankle
finger any of five terminating digits of upper forelimb: thumb, index finger, middle finger, ring finger, little finger
fist hand clenched with fingers curled inward
foot terminal part of leg upon which person stands
forearm half of arm between elbow and wrist; forelimb
funny bone *Slang.* elbow
hamstring long muscle down back of thigh
hand grasping extremity, with fingers, at end of arm
haunch hip, hindquarter
heel rear portion of foot below ankle
hip region on each side of lower part of trunk, formed by pelvis and upper femur
hollow pit beneath shoulder
index finger finger closest to thumb
instep arched middle portion of foot
knee joint where upper and lower leg meet
knuckle protuberance at joint of finger, esp. large joint at middle of finger
leg lower limb used to walk and support body
limb arm or leg
little finger smallest finger, farthest from thumb; pinkie
middle finger second finger from thumb, usu. longest finger
pinkie *Informal.* little finger
ring finger third finger from thumb, next to little finger, traditionally finger on which engagement ring or wedding band is worn
shank part of leg between knee and ankle
shinbone tibia
shoulder joint that connects arm to upper trunk
tarsus ankle, esp. bones of ankle
thigh segment of lower limb from hip to knee
thighbone femur
thumb short, thick digit of hand nearest wrist, in opposition to other fingers
tibia long, inner bone of leg between knee and ankle; shinbone
toe one of five terminal digits of foot
triceps lateral muscle along back of upper arm
ulna bone on little finger side of forearm
underarm axilla
upper arm portion of arm between elbow and shoulder
wrist ball-and-socket joint between hand and lower arm

Brain and Central Nervous System

alpha wave long, slow brain wave of relaxation
axon long, threadlike part of neuron that conducts impulses away from cell body
beta wave short, fast brain wave of activity
brain seat of nervous system controlling neural coordination and thought
central nervous system CNS; portion of nervous system comprising brain and spinal cord
cerebellum part of brain that regulates coordination of voluntary muscle movement
cerebral cortex gray matter covering forebrain
cerebral hemisphere either of the rounded halves of the cerebrum
cerebrospinal fluid liquid that fills space in middle of spine and cavities in brain
cerebrum left and right hemispheres at front of brain that send and receive stimuli to and from voluntary muscles, perceive sensory input, and control memory and thought
CNS central nervous system
corpus callosum mass of nerve fibers connecting two hemispheres of cerebrum

cortex outer layer of gray matter covering most of brain
dendrite short, branching, threadlike part of neuron that carries impulses to cell body
frontal lobe anterior portion of each cerebral hemisphere
ganglion solid mass of neural cell bodies that serves as relay center for impulses
gray matter nervous tissue forming inner part of spinal cord and outer part of brain
hypothalamus basal part of third ventricle beneath thalamus that regulates pituitary gland, body temperature, and sleep
impulse traveling wave of excitation that sends message through neuron
limbic system ringlike section in midline of brain, concerned with emotions and memory
medulla part of brain joined to spinal cord that controls sense organs, respiration, and cardiac muscle
meninges *sing.* meninx; three membranes covering spinal cord and brain
meninx one of three meninges
motor (*adj*) designating nerve that stimulates muscle or organ to move or act
myelin protective sheath around peripheral nerve fibers
neocortex outer layer of brain, center of intellect and imagination
nerve bundle of neurons supported by connective tissue, conveying impulses of sensation or motion
nervous system nerve tissue that coordinates all activities and receives all sensory stimuli, consisting of brain, spinal cord, axons, dendrites, and synapses, and composed of the following major nerves:
brachial nerve nerve in upper arm
cervical nerve nerve in neck and shoulder
coccygeal nerve nerve at base of spine
digital nerve nerve in fingers
femoral nerve nerve in thigh
intercostal nerve nerve between ribs
lumbar nerve nerve in groin
mandibular nerve nerve in lower jaw
maxillary nerve nerve in jaw
median nerve nerve in middle of arm
ophthalmic nerve nerve in eye
peroneal nerve nerve in lower leg near fibula
radial nerve nerve around lower arm
sacral nerve nerve from spinal cord in sacrum
sciatic nerve nerve running down spinal cord and back of each thigh
thoracic nerve nerve in thorax
tibial nerve nerve in lower leg near tibia
ulnar nerve nerve in forearm and elbow

neuron single cell consisting of axon and dendrites in system of nerves that conducts impulses
occipital lobe most posterior portion of each cerebral hemisphere
olfactory lobe anterior portion of each cerebral hemisphere, responsible for sense of smell
parietal lobe middle portion of each cerebral hemisphere
pons band of nerve fibers through which impulses pass between various parts of brain
sciatic nerve largest nerve in body, running down spinal cord and back of each thigh
sense organs eyes, ears, nose, and taste buds, the organs containing nervous tissue that responds to particular external stimuli
sensory receptors sense organs and other tissue that respond to external stimuli, recording temperature and sensations such as pain and heat
spinal column series of jointed vertebrae forming axial support for skeleton and carrying nerves
spinal cord cylindrical mass of nervous tissue running through spinal column
synapse meeting place of axons and dendrites along which impulse travels from neuron to neuron
temporal lobe lateral portion of each cerebral hemisphere, in front of occipital lobe
thalamus lower anterior portion of brain above pituitary gland that acts as main relay center for impulses to cerebrum
ventricle any of four cavities within brain filled with cerebrospinal fluid

Heart, Circulatory, and Lymphatic Systems

aorta main artery leaving heart
arteriole small artery with walls of smooth muscle that controls blood supply to capillaries
artery blood vessel conducting blood from heart to tissue
atrium auricle
auricle upper chamber in heart that receives blood from veins; atrium
blood liquid of circulatory system containing dissolved digestive products and conveying oxygen to tissue: plasma, red and white blood cells, and platelets
bloodstream flow of blood through circulatory system
blood vessel artery, vein, or capillary
capillary very small blood vessel with thin, permeable walls
capillary network arrangement of branching capillaries in tissue
cardiac muscle muscle in walls of heart with action that is automatic, regular, and faster than that of involuntary muscle
carotid artery one of two principal arteries on either side of neck that conveys blood from aorta to head
circulatory system network of vessels through which blood is pumped by heart
clot network of fibrin fibers that trap red blood cells and platelets to form solid mass
coronary artery either of two arteries that originate in aorta and supply heart with blood
corpuscle free-floating blood or lymph cell

diastole stage of relaxation in action of heart muscle
erythrocyte red blood cell
fibrin insoluble protein that forms fibers in blood clotting
heart hollow organ with muscular walls that pumps blood through circulatory system
heartbeat pulsation of heart, including one complete systole and diastole
hematic (*adj*) of, pertaining to, or contained in blood
hemoglobin oxygen-carrying substance in red blood cells which gives them red color
homeostasis state of maintaining constant blood composition
leukocyte white blood cell
lymph colorless fluid that bathes body cells and contains lymphocytes
lymph node small organ that produces lymphocytes to filter foreign bodies and bacteria from lymph
lymphocyte white blood cell of the immune system that attacks foreign substances directly or by producing antibodies
pericardial cavity thin, membranous sac enclosing heart
phagocyte white blood cell that defends against bacterial attack and digests tissue debris
plasma clear, colorless liquid left after blood cells are taken out of blood
platelet minute disk of cytoplasm formed in bone marrow that assists in blood clotting; thrombocyte
pulmonary artery artery that conveys blood from right ventricle of heart to lungs
pulmonary vein vein that conveys blood from lungs to left auricle of heart
red blood cell elastic blood cell formed in bone marrow and containing hemoglobin; erythrocyte
Rhesus factor antigen present on surface of red blood cells of most people; Rh positive blood
serum liquid obtained from clotted blood; form of plasma
spleen organ that produces lymphocytes and stores red blood cells
systole stage of contraction in action of heart muscle
thrombin enzyme in blood serum that promotes production of fibrin
thrombocyte platelet
vascular system circulatory and lymphatic systems of vessels for conducting blood and lymph through body
vein blood vessel conducting blood from tissue back to heart
vena cava main vein entering auricle of heart with blood from upper and lower parts of body
ventricle lower chamber in heart that receives blood from auricle and pumps it back through circulatory system
white blood cell phagocyte or lymphocyte blood cell without coloring material that fights bacteria in body; leukocyte

Digestive and Excretory System

alimentary canal long tube, running from mouth to anus, for digestion and absorption of food
anus excretory opening at end of alimentary canal
ascending colon portion of colon rising from cecum
bladder urinary bladder
bowel any of divisions of intestine; gut
cecum small bag at start of the large intestine
colon main absorptive part of large intestine, running from cecum to rectum
descending colon portion of colon leading to rectum
digestive system organs causing chemical decomposition of food into substances that body can absorb or excrete
duodenum part of small intestine joined to stomach, with ducts leading to liver and pancreas
enzyme complex protein substance produced by cells to catalyze metabolic processes such as digestion
esophagus long muscular tube from pharynx down neck to stomach
excretion discharge of waste products from body
gastric juice liquid secretion produced by walls of stomach to aid digestion
gastrointestinal tract portion of alimentary canal from esophagus to rectum
gullet esophagus; throat
gut portion of alimentary canal between pylorus and anus; bowel; intestine
ileum last division of small intestine, opening into large intestine
intestine part of alimentary canal between stomach and anus for absorption of food into body
jejunum middle portion of small intestine between ileum and duodenum
large intestine broad tube with muscular walls, consisting of colon and rectum, that absorbs water, leaving feces
peristalsis wavelike muscle movement in alimentary canal that pushes contents along
pylorus opening between stomach and duodenum
rectum storage area for feces in last part of large intestine, ending with anus
sigmoid flexure curving final portion of colon that ends in rectum
small intestine long tube between stomach and large intestine where absorption and digestion of food occur
sphincter annular muscle that closes and opens rectum
stomach baglike part of alimentary canal below esophagus with muscular walls that mix food with gastric juice
transverse colon portion of colon running from ascending colon to descending colon
ureter tube leading from kidney to urinary bladder
urethra tube from urinary bladder to outside of

body for discharge of urine; in males, also used to discharge sperm through penis
urinary bladder baglike structure for storing urine prior to its discharge from body; bladder
urinary tract system of tubes that conducts urine from kidney through ureter, urinary bladder, and urethra
villus small, fingerlike structure growing out of mucous membrane of small intestine that absorbs and carries off food material

Respiratory System

alveolus tiny, blind-ended cavity in lung that receives carbon dioxide from blood and gives back oxygen
bronchiole small air passageway in lung; division of bronchus
bronchus tube leading from trachea to each lung
cilium hairlike fringe on walls of trachea and bronchus that flaps to drive dust from lungs back up to mouth
diaphragm cup-shaped muscle between thorax and abdomen that flattens when air is drawn into lungs
intercostal muscle muscle between two ribs that contracts when air is inhaled
lung either of two organs for breathing that takes carbon dioxide from blood and returns oxygen to it
pleura membranous, baglike outer covering of lung
pleural cavity thin, membranous sac that lines chest cavity and contains lungs
respiration process by which oxygen is conveyed to tissues and carbon dioxide is given off in exchange
respiratory system organs involved in exchange of carbon dioxide and oxygen between body and environment: nose and mouth, pharynx, larynx, trachea, bronchi, and lungs
sputum saliva ejected from respiratory passages
trachea tube leading from mouth and nose down throat to lungs for in-and-out passage of air

Endocrine System and Glands

adrenal gland either of two endocrine glands lying above the kidney
adrenalin epinephrine
apocrine (*adj*) designating glands in which part of secreting cell goes into secretion, as in mammary gland
bile green, alkaline liquid produced by liver that forms emulsion with fat to assist enzyme action
bile duct tube that conducts bile from liver to duodenum
duct short pipe through which secretions leave gland
eccrine (*adj*) designating glands that secrete externally, as certain sweat glands
endocrine gland any gland that secretes a hormone into the bloodstream
epinephrine hormone secreted by adrenal glands that increases heartbeat, sends blood to brain and muscles, increases perspiration, and enlarges eye pupil; adrenalin
exocrine gland any gland that discharges a secretion through an opening on epithelial surface
follicle small cavity or gland
gallbladder small vessel near liver for bile storage
gland organ that selectively removes materials from blood, chemically alters them, and secretes them for further use in body or discharges them from body
holocrine (*adj*) designating glands in which cells disintegrate entirely to form secretion, as in sebaceous glands
hormone organic substance, such as insulin, prolactin, adrenalin, estrogen, or testosterone, produced by endocrine glands and carried by bloodstream to produce a metabolic effect
islets of Langerhans insulin-producing cells in pancreas
kidney either of a pair of bean-shaped glands in upper abdominal cavity that control amount of water in blood, maintain homeostasis, and excrete waste water as urine
lacrimal gland either of two tear-secreting glands located at top of eye
lactation production of milk in mammary glands
liver large gland that secretes bile and stores glycogen
mammary gland either of two milk-producing glands on female upper chest
melatonin hormone secreted by pineal gland, important in regulating biological rhythms
ovary female reproductive gland that produces ova
pancreas gland that produces digestive juice and insulin
pancreatic juice digestive juice secreted by pancreas and passed to duodenum
parathyroid gland one of four small glands on or near thyroid
pineal body small endocrine gland in brain that secretes melatonin
pituitary gland endocrine gland beneath floor of brain that controls action of all other endocrine glands
prostate gland muscular gland surrounding male urethra at base of bladder
renal (*adj*) designating artery supplying blood to kidneys
salivary glands three pairs of glands in mouth that secrete saliva: parotid, sublingual, submaxillary
sebaceous gland gland in dermis, opening onto hair root, that produces oily sebum
sublingual gland one of a pair of salivary glands located below the tongue
submaxillary gland one of a pair of salivary glands located on each side of and below the lower jaw
sweat gland small, coiled, tubular gland that regulates body temperature by secretion of perspiration
testis male reproductive gland that produces sperm
thymus gland in neck that produces lymphocytes

and becomes vestigial after puberty
thyroid gland endocrine gland that controls rate of metabolism and growth and production of body heat
urea soluble organic compound formed from ammonia in liver

Reproductive System

afterbirth placenta and fetal membranes
cervix short, narrow tube leading from uterus to vagina
clitoris small, sensitive organ at anterior part of vulva
embryo developing human in womb during first eight weeks after conception
epididymis long tube that receives and stores sperm
fallopian tube tube that conducts ovum from ovary to uterus
fetus embryo that has appearance of fully developed offspring; also, *esp. Brit.* foetus
gamete reproductive cell with chromosomes in nucleus: male spermatozoon, female ovum
genitals external reproductive organs, male or female
glans head of penis or clitoris
gonad reproductive gland that produces gametes: male testis, female ovary
labia folds at margin of vulva, majora and minora
menstruation periodic discharge of blood, secretions, and tissue due to shedding of uterine lining when ovum is not fertilized
mons veneris rounded eminence of fatty tissue on female pubic region
ovary female reproductive gland that produces ova
ovum female gamete or unfertilized egg cell
penis erectile male organ with many blood vessels, through which sperm passes for internal fertilization of ova, also used for urination
placenta vascular organ that surrounds fetus and unites it with uterus for nutrition
reproductive system organs and structures concerned with production of gametes and conception of new individuals of a given species
scrotum external pouch containing male testes
seminal vesicle either of two glands on each side of male bladder that add nutrients to sperm passing through vas deferens
smegma cheesy secretion by sebaceous glands at genitalia
spermatozoon male gamete with flagellum that allows it to swim toward female gamete; sperm
testicle male gonad; baglike structure that produces sperm
testis male reproductive gland that produces sperm; testicle
umbilical cord cord connecting fetus with placenta
urethra tube in males used to discharge sperm through penis
uterus muscular hollow organ in female in which embryo and fetus develop; womb
vagina canal leading from cervix to outside of body in female that receives sperm and acts as birth passage
vas deferens long tube that passes sperm from testes to urethra
vulva external portion of female genital organs
womb uterus

Skeleton

backbone spinal column
ball-and-socket joint round end of one bone that fits into hollow of another, allowing movement in any direction
bone hard, largely calcareous substance of skeleton
cartilage tough, elastic, whitish tissue that forms skeleton of embryo, most of which later turns to bone
flex (*vb*) bend joint so angle between two bones becomes smaller
Haversian canal small tube in bones containing nerves and blood vessels
hinge joint joint such as knee or elbow, in which round end of one bone turns on flat surface of another in one direction only
joint structure that joins two bones so they can move
ligament strong band of fiber that holds bones of joint together
marrow soft, fatty material that forms inside of bone
ossification hardening of cartilage into bone
process bony outgrowth on larger structure
skeleton hard internal structure that supports organs and tissue, composed of the following major bones:
acetabulum hip socket
calcaneus heel bone
carpus wrist bones
clavicle collarbone
coccyx base of spine
coxa hip joint
cranium skull bone
femur upper leg bone
fibula lower leg bone
frontal front of cranium
gladiolus sternum, breastbone
humerus upper arm bone
ilium upper portion of hipbone
ischium lower portion of hipbone
lacrimal forehead
lumbar vertebrae five vertebrae of middle back
mandible lower jawbone
manubrium upper breastbone
mastoid bone behind ear
maxilla upper jawbone
metacarpus bone in fingers
metatarsus bone in toes
nasal nose bone
occipital back of cranium
orbit eye socket
parietal top of cranium
patella knee bone
pelvis bone forming pelvic cavity

phalanges bones at ends of toes and fingers
pubis groin bone
radius lower arm bone
ribs twenty-four curved bones around chest cavity
sacral vertebrae five vertebrae of lower back
sacroiliac joint between sacrum and ilium
sacrum bone forming back of pelvis
scapula shoulder blade
skull bones covering brain
sphenoid base of skull
sternum breastbone
tarsus foot bone
temporal side of cranium
thoracic vertebrae twelve vertebrae of upper back
tibia shinbone
ulna bone in forearm
vertebrae thirty-three bony segments of spinal column
xiphoid process point of lower breastbone
zygomatic cheek bone

spinal column series of joined vertebrae forming axial support for skeleton and carrying nerves; backbone; spine; vertebral column
vertebra hollow bone with large central mass and fingerlike pieces of bone standing out from core
vertebral column spinal column

Muscles

abductor muscle that moves from median axis of body
adductor muscle that pulls toward median axis of body
constrictor muscle that contracts cavity or opening or compresses organ
coordination muscles acting together to produce same effect
erector muscle that erects body or body parts
involuntary muscle muscle tissue in sheets around hollow organs that contracts slowly without conscious control
muscle tissue consisting of long cells with power to contract, causing all movements of body parts
muscular system system of muscles that cause all bodily movements, composed of the following major muscles:
abdominal stomach muscle
biceps muscle at front of upper arm
deltoid shoulder muscle
erector lower back muscle
extensor forearm muscle
fascia lata hip muscle
flexor forearm muscle
gastrocnemius calf muscle
gluteus buttocks muscle
hamstring muscle at back of thigh
latissimus dorsi back muscle
oblique muscle at side of torso
pectoral upper chest muscle
quadriceps muscle at front of thigh
rectus abdominis long muscle in abdomen
rectus femoris long muscle in front of thigh
rotator cuff muscle in shoulder under deltoid
sartorius muscle across front of thigh
soleus muscle down back of lower leg to foot
sternocleidomastoid neck muscle
trapezius upper back muscle
triceps muscle at back of upper arm
tendon band of connective tissue that attaches muscle to bone
tensor muscle that stretches a body part, making it tight
voluntary muscle long muscle able to contract rapidly that moves bones of joints in locomotion by conscious control

Tissue, Fiber, and Integumentary System

adipose (*adj*) designating fat in connective tissue
cartilage tough, elastic, whitish tissue around bones or through muscles; embryonic skeleton that turns to bone
connective tissue fibrous tissue that provides support for other tissue or organs
cuticle epidermis, esp. hardened outer layer of skin
dermis inside layer of skin cells, providing elastic strength
epidermis outside layer of cells
epithelium tissue that forms surface or outside of organism, such as skin, or covers inside of tubes and cavities
fascia thin layer of connective tissue around and between muscles or organs
fat ester of glycerol and fatty acid; tissue of cells expanded with greasy or oily matter
fiber strong, threadlike structure of protein
hair fine, threadlike growth from skin, concentrated on head, in armpits, and above genitals
hair follicle small cavity in epidermis from which hair develops
horny layer tough, protective outer layer of epidermis
integumentary system any of various kinds of tissue covering body or enclosing organs
ligament strong band of fiber holding bones of joint together
lobe portion of an organ separated by fissures
marrow soft, fatty material that forms inside of bone
matrix solid material made by cells and secreted around them
melanin insoluble pigment that gives dark color to skin and hair
melanocyte cell that produces melanin in skin and hair
membrane thin, pliable sheet of tissue that forms covering or lining
mucous membrane lubricating membrane lining organ or internal surface such as alimentary or respiratory canal
mucus sticky, lubricating liquid secreted by some membranes
nail thin, horny plate covering end of top of finger or toe

organ body part with definite structure and particular function
skin outer covering, containing dermis and epidermis
soft tissue muscle, fat, or tissue not part of skeleton or organ
subcutaneous (*adj*) designating tissue situated just beneath epithelium
synovial capsule baglike membrane in joint filled with sticky lubricating liquid
tendon band of connective tissue that attaches muscle to bone
tissue mass of cells and intercellular material which performs specific function in organism
vessel tube for conducting fluids within organism

MEDICAL PROBLEMS

Diseases and Infestations
Afflictions and Conditions
Defects and Disabilities
Injuries and Accidents
Signs and Symptoms
Diagnostic Terminology

Diseases and Infestations

acquired immune deficiency syndrome AIDS
Addison's disease condition marked by weakness, low blood pressure, and dark pigmentation due to inadequate hormone secretion by adrenal glands
adenitis regional inflammation of gland or lymph node
ague malaria; general malaise marked by fever
AIDS acquired immune deficiency syndrome; severe weakening or destruction of body's immune system by human immunodeficiency virus, allowing opportunistic diseases and infections to attack, spread by direct contact of body fluids such as blood or semen: SIDA
AIDS-related complex ARC; chronic enlargement of lymph nodes and persistent fever caused by AIDS virus
ailment physical disorder or chronic disease
Alzheimer's disease progressive dementia and brain degeneration in elderly
amebic dysentery severe dysentery caused by protozoan amebas
amyotrophic lateral sclerosis progressive loss of muscle bulk and control due to nerve disease; Lou Gehrig's disease
anthrax acute infectious livestock disease, transmitted to humans by contact, causing pneumonia or skin ulcerations
aplastic anemia anemia due to failure of bone marrow to produce sufficient leukocytes and blood platelets
apoplexy stroke
appendicitis acute inflammation of vermiform appendix that requires surgical removal
arteriosclerosis deposit of cholesterol on artery walls; hardening of the arteries
arthritis inflammation of joints
atheroma degeneration of artery walls due to fatty plaques and scar tissue; common form of arteriosclerosis
autoimmune disease disorder that permits destruction of tissue by body's own antibodies
basal cell carcinoma common, usu. curable, slow-growing malignant tumor on skin
beriberi often fatal nutritional disorder due to vitamin B_1 deficiency
bilirubinemia excess bile pigment in blood that causes jaundice
Black Death bubonic plague
black lung slow-developing respiratory disease due to regular inhalation of coal dust or asbestos; miner's lung
blackwater fever rare complication of malaria, with massive destruction of red blood cells, that causes hemoglobin in urine
blepharitis inflammation, scaling, and crusting of eyelids
botulism serious toxin-produced bacterial food poisoning
Bright's disease nephritis
bronchitis inflammation of walls of bronchi in lungs due to virus or bacteria, causing coughing and production of sputum
brown lung occupational disease due to inhalation of cotton dust; byssinosis
bubonic plague often fatal bacterial epidemic disease transmitted to humans by rat fleas, with painful swelling of lymph nodes; Black Death
cancer malignant tumor anywhere in body due to uncontrolled cell division, causing disruption of metabolism and invasion and destruction of neighboring tissue
candidiasis yeastlike fungus infection in mouth and moist areas of body; thrush
carbuncle staphylococcus infection of skin that causes boils with multiple drainage channels
carcinoma cancer in epithelium lining skin or internal organs
cardiac arrest cessation of heart pumping, due esp. to fibrillation, that results in rapid brain damage or death
cardiac stenosis abnormal narrowing of heart valve
cardiomyopathy chronic viral, congenital, or other disorder that affects heart muscle and causes heart failure, arrhythmias, or embolisms
carditis inflammation of heart
caries decay and crumbling of tooth or bone; dental cavity
cat-scratch disease viral infection causing fever and swelling of lymph glands, due to scratch of cat
cerebrospinal fever bacterial meningitis; spotted fever
cerebrovascular accident sudden and severe attack of cerebrovascular disease; stroke
cerebrovascular disease disorder of blood ves-

sels in brain due to atheroma or hypertension, causing cerebral hemorrhage or thrombosis and stroke
chickenpox mild, highly infectious viral disease primarily in children with itchy rash of red pimples, blisters, and pustules; varicella
childbed fever puerperal fever
chlamydia sexually transmitted, viruslike microorganism causing conjunctivitis, urethritis, and cervicitis
cholera acute bacterial infection of small intestine causing massive diarrhea, often leading to dehydration
chorea neurological disease of the basal ganglia that causes jerky, involuntary movements and distorted posture of shoulders, hips, and face; St. Vitus's dance
chronic fatigue syndrome persistent, extreme exhaustion and weakness due to unknown causes
cirrhosis progressive liver condition from various causes, esp. alcoholism or hepatitis, in which cells die and the liver turns tawny and knobby
clap *Vulgar slang.* gonorrhea
cold contagious respiratory infection that causes inflammation of mucous membrane and nasal discharge; common cold
colitis any inflammation of colon, causing diarrhea and lower abdominal pain
collagen diseases various diseases characterized by changes in makeup of connective tissue: lupus, rheumatic fever, rheumatoid arthritis, and scleroderma
common cold cold
congestive heart failure inability of heart to adequately supply blood to body tissue, often due to weakening of cardiac muscle, causing body swelling and shortness of breath
conjunctivitis inflammation of mucous membrane covering front of eye, often with discharge of pus; pinkeye
consumption any disease that causes wasting of tissues, esp. pulmonary tuberculosis
contact dermatitis skin inflammation produced by contact with some substance that causes redness, swelling, and often itching
coronary coronary heart disease; heart attack
coronary heart disease serious condition affecting coronary artery
coronary infarction myocardial infarction
coronary occlusion coronary thrombosis
coronary thrombosis formation of a blood clot in coronary artery that obstructs blood flow to heart and causes coronary infarction, usu. due to atherosclerosis; coronary occlusion
cowpox viral infection of cow's udder, transmitted to humans by direct contact, causing mild version of symptoms similar to smallpox
crab louse crablike louse that infests pubic regions, transmitted by sexual contact
crib death sudden infant death syndrome
croup inflammation and obstruction of larynx in young children due to viral respiratory infections, characterized by harsh cough
cystic fibrosis hereditary disease of exocrine glands that produces respiratory infections, malabsorption, and sweat with high salt content
cystitis often infectious inflammation of urinary bladder that causes frequent painful passage of urine
deficiency disease any disease, such as beriberi, caused by nutritional deficiency
dengue viral disease transmitted by mosquitoes in the tropics, causing fever, severe pain in back and joints, rash, and sore throat
dermatitis skin inflammation
diabetes diabetes mellitus
diabetes mellitus common deficiency, possibly inherited, of the pancreatic hormone insulin, causing disorder in carbohydrate metabolism and inability to properly utilize sugars; diabetes
diphtheria acute, highly contagious bacterial infection of the throat that can cause death from respiratory obstruction or carditis
disease physical disorder with specific physiological cause and recognizable signs and symptoms
diverticulitis colonic diverticulosis with inflammation
diverticulosis condition characterized by existence of diverticular sacs at weak points in walls of alimentary tract, esp. intestine
duodenal ulcer ulcer in lining of duodenum caused by excess stomach acid
dysentery infection of intestinal tract that causes severe diarrhea mixed with blood and mucus
dystrophy organ or muscle disorder caused by insufficient nourishment or hereditary disorder
elephantiasis gross enlargement of legs or other body parts due to obstructed lymph drainage, caused by parasitic worm transmitted by mosquitoes
emphysema air in tissues; pulmonary disorder, characterized by increase in size of air sacs due to destruction of their walls, causing shortness of breath
encephalitis viral or bacterial inflammation of brain, also caused by infection or allergic reaction; sleeping sickness
endocarditis inflammation and damage to heart cavity lining due to bacterial infection or rheumatic fever
enteritis viral or bacterial inflammation of small intestine, causing diarrhea
epilepsy one of various brain disorders that cause recurrent, sudden convulsive attacks
Epstein-Barr syndrome infectious mononucleosis caused by herpeslike virus; glandular fever
fibroma usu. benign tumor composed mainly of fibrous or connective tissue
fibrosarcoma malignant tumor of connective tissue, esp. in legs
filariasis disorder that affects lymphatic system, caused by parasite
flu influenza
food poisoning digestive system disorder, usu. from the consumption of bacteria or bacterial toxins in food, causing vomiting, diarrhea, nausea, and fever
functional disorder condition for which no

physical cause can be found
fungus simple parasitic organism that can infect humans and cause disease
gastric ulcer stomach ulcer caused by action of acid on stomach lining
gastritis inflammation of stomach lining from an ingested substance, infection, or chronic irritation
gastroenteritis inflammation of stomach and intestine, due to virus, bacteria, or food poisoning, that causes vomiting
genital herpes infection of genital area by herpes simplex virus
German measles rubella
gingivitis inflammation of gums, sometimes with bleeding
glandular fever Epstein-Barr syndrome; mononucleosis
glaucoma abnormally high fluid pressure in the eye, often leading to loss of vision
gonorrhea sexually transmitted bacterial disease that affects mucous membranes in genital tract, pharynx, or rectum
gout accumulation of excess uric acid in bloodstream and joints that causes joint destruction, kidney stones, and arthritis
grand mal generalized epileptic seizure with flexion and extension of extremities and loss of consciousness
Graves' disease disease characterized by enlarged thyroid and increased basal metabolism, due to excessive thyroid secretion
grippe influenza
heart attack myocardial infarction
heart failure inadequate pumping of heart ventricle due to coronary thrombosis, hypertension, or arrhythmia; congestive heart failure
hepatitis inflammation of liver, due to virus transmitted by food or drink (infectious hepatitis) or blood on needle or in transfusion (serum hepatitis), causing fever and jaundice
herpes herpes simplex; small viral blisters on skin
herpes simplex virus in herpes family; nonvenereal blisters on mucous membrane that can cause conjunctivitis, vaginal inflammation, or cold sores; herpes
herpes zoster virus in herpes family characterized by vesicles, often with severe pain along distribution of nerve; shingles
HIV human immunodeficiency virus
Hodgkin's disease condition marked by malignancy in lymphatic tissue that causes enlarged lymph nodes, fever, and profuse sweating
hookworm infestation of small intestine by parasitic hookworm that penetrates skin and causes diarrhea, debility, and sometimes anemia
human immunodeficiency virus HIV; virus that causes AIDS
Huntington's chorea hereditary chorea with progressive dementia due to widespread degeneration of neurons throughout brain
hydrophobia rabies
hyperthyroidism overactivity of thyroid gland that causes rapid heartbeat, sweating, tremors, weight loss, and anxiety
hypoglycemia glucose deficiency in bloodstream that causes weakness, confusion, and sweating, often in patients with diabetes mellitus who take an insulin overdose
hypothyroidism subnormal thyroid gland activity that can lead to cretinism if present at birth
icthyosis hereditary skin disease causing flaking of skin in large scales
ileitis inflammation of ileum in small intestine
illness disease or condition that causes poor health
impetigo contagious skin infection from streptococcal or staphylococcal bacteria, esp. in children, causing crusty yellow blisters
infantile paralysis poliomyelitis
infectious disease disease caused by a microorganism or parasite and usu. passed by direct human contact; communicable or contagious disease
infestation invasion of body by animal parasites
influenza highly contagious viral infection of respiratory system, transmitted by coughing or sneezing, that causes headache, fever, general aches and pains; flu; grippe
Kaposi's sarcoma cancer of skin characterized by multiple purplish lesions on face and extremities, often associated with AIDS and usu. fatal
kwashiorkor malnutrition due to protein deficiency in diet, esp. in children ages one to three
laryngitis inflammation of larynx and vocal cords, due to bacterial or viral infection, causing coughing, husky voice, or complete voice loss
legionnaires' disease bacterial lung infection that causes malaise, fever, chest pain, and coughing
leprosy chronic contagious tropical disease caused by Hansen's bacilli that results in lumps and patches on skin, thickening of nerves and skin, numbness, and paralysis; Hansen's disease
leukemia overproduction of abnormal white blood cells by bone marrow and other blood-forming organs, usu. causing fatal systemic malignancy
lockjaw tetanus
Lou Gehrig's disease amyotrophic lateral sclerosis
louse small, wingless insect that is an external parasite
lung cancer malignancy in epithelium of air passages or lung, esp. due to smoke or other outside agents
lupus any of several chronic skin diseases, esp. lupus erythematosus
lupus erythematosus chronic inflammation of connective tissue that causes red scaly rash on face, arthritis, and organ damage
Lyme disease spirochetal infection transmitted by a tiny tick that causes skin rash, headache, fever, and sometimes arthritis and heart damage
lymphoma malignant tumor of lymph nodes that is not Hodgkin's disease
malaria infection caused by parasitic protozoa in red blood cells, transmitted by mosquito in tropics and subtropics, causing fever, sweating, and anemia

measles highly infectious viral epidemic disease, mainly in children, that causes high fever and elevated pink rash; rubeola
melanoma malignant tumor of melanin-forming cells, esp. in skin
meningitis inflammation of membranes lining skull and vertebral canal, due to viral or bacterial infection, causing fever, intense headache, muscular rigidity, and sometimes convulsion, delirium, or death; spinal meningitis
miliaria inflammatory skin disease characterized by formation of vesicles or papules about sweat glands; prickly heat
miner's lung black lung
mononucleosis infectious disease that manifests a high number of monocytes in blood, enlarged lymph nodes, prolonged fever, appetite loss, and malaise, esp. in young adults; glandular disease caused by Epstein-Barr virus; glandular fever
MS multiple sclerosis
multiple sclerosis MS; chronic nervous system disease with recurrent symptoms of unsteady gait, shaky limb movements, rapid involuntary eye movements, and speech defects
mumps viral infection that causes fever and swelling of parotid salivary glands, esp. among children
muscular dystrophy inherited muscle disease marked by degeneration of muscle fiber
myasthenia gravis muscular weakness that has its onset with repetitive activity and leads to paralysis
mycosis fungus infection
myeloma malignancy of bone marrow
myocardial infarction death of portion of heart muscle due to interrupted blood supply; heart attack; coronary infarction
myocarditis acute or chronic inflammation of heart muscle
nephritis inflammation of kidney; Bright's disease
neuritis inflammation of nerves; neuropathy
osteoarthritis joint cartilage disease that causes pain and impaired joint function and occurs in later life, due to overuse of joint or as a complication of rheumatoid arthritis
osteomyelitis inflammation of bone marrow and adjacent bone, mostly from infection, esp. after compound fractures where marrow is exposed
osteoporosis loss of bony matrix that causes brittle bones, due to injury, infection, or old age
otitis inflammation of ear, due to viral or bacterial infection, causing severe pain and high fever
pancreatitis inflammation of pancreas with sudden, severe pain
paratyphoid fever bacterial infectious disease, caused by nontyphoidal salmonella and spread by poor sanitation, marked by diarrhea, fever, and pink rash on chest
parkinsonism Parkinson's disease
Parkinson's disease neurological disorder of late middle age characterized by tremor, rigidity, and little spontaneous movement; parkinsonism
pediculosis infestation of body and/or scalp by lice, causing itching and sometimes bacterial infection with weeping lesions
pellagra B-vitamin nutritional deficiency that causes scaly dermatitis, diarrhea, and depression
peptic ulcer breach in lining of digestive tract due to excess acid, occurring in esophagus, stomach, or duodenum
pericarditis acute or chronic inflammation of sac surrounding heart, due to viral infection, uremia, or cancer, often causing fever, chest pain, and fluid accumulation
periodontal disease disease of gums, mouth lining, and bony structures supporting teeth, caused by plaque
peritonitis inflammation of abdominal cavity membrane, often due to bacteria spread in bloodstream or perforation or rupture of abdominal organ, causing pain, swelling, fever, and shock
pernicious anemia autoimmune disease, due to vitamin B_{12} deficiency, that can affect nervous system
pertussis whooping cough
petit mal lesser epileptic seizure characterized by brief spells of sleepiness or unconsciousness
pharyngitis inflammation of pharynx that causes sore throat or tonsillitis
phlebitis inflammation of vein wall, esp. in legs as complication of varicose veins, causing extreme tenderness
pinkeye conjunctivitis
plague acute epidemic bacterial disease of rats, transmitted to humans by rat fleas, causing severe headache, fever, enlarged lymph nodes, and delirium, usu. fatal
pleurisy inflammation of pleura that cover lungs, usu. due to pneumonia or other lung disease, causing painful breathing
pneumonia inflammation or infection of lungs in which air sacs fill with pus, causing coughing and chest pain
pneumonic plague plague bacterium in lungs, usu. fatal
podagra gout of foot, esp. big toe
polio poliomyelitis
poliomyelitis infectious viral disease of central nervous system, formerly epidemic, causing stiffness and sometimes paralysis of muscles, esp. respiratory system muscles; infantile paralysis; polio
prickly heat miliaria
psychosomatic illness disease caused at least in part by emotional state
puerperal fever blood poisoning in mother shortly after childbirth due to infection of womb lining or vagina; childbed fever
rabies acute viral infection of central nervous system, transmitted by bite of infected mammal, causing fever, excitation, painful spasms of throat muscles, paralysis, and death; hydrophobia
radiation sickness acute disease caused by exposure to radioactive emissions, causing nausea, vomiting, diarrhea, bleeding, hair loss, and death

relapsing fever infectious bacterial disease transmitted by tick and lice bites, causing fever, headache, and muscle pain that lapse and then recur
Reye's syndrome acute disorder primarily in children after viral infections such as chickenpox or influenza, associated with aspirin use, causing brain swelling and affecting organs
rheumatic fever delayed complication of upper respiratory streptococcus infection, esp. in young, characterized by fever, arthritis of joints, chorea, carditis, and erythematosus rash
rheumatism any disorder causing aches and pains in muscles or joints
rheumatoid arthritis common form of arthritis that affects extremities, digits, and hips
rickets malformation of unhardened bones in children due to vitamin D deficiency
Rocky Mountain spotted fever disease caused by rickettsial microorganism, transmitted to humans by dogs and wood ticks, characterized by fever, muscle pain, and profuse red rash
roseola rubella
rubella highly contagious viral infection, primarily in children, causing enlarged lymph nodes in neck and pink rash; German measles; roseola
rubeola measles
salmonella poisoning food poisoning caused by aerobic intestinal bacteria
sarcoma tumor of connective tissue
scabies skin infection from infestation of mites that causes severe itching, esp. around groin, nipples, and between fingers
scarlatina scarlet fever
scarlet fever highly contagious childhood disease caused by streptococcus bacteria, characterized by sore throat and widespread rash; scarlatina
scurvy vitamin C deficiency from absence of fresh fruit and vegetables in diet that causes swollen, bleeding gums, subcutaneous bleeding, and death when prolonged
seborrheic dermatitis skin eruption due to excess secretion of sebum, common on face at puberty
serum hepatitis liver inflammation that causes fever and jaundice, transmitted by infected hypodermic needle or blood transfusion
sexually transmitted disease STD; modern term for venereal disease
shingles herpes zoster
sickle cell anemia hereditary blood disease that mainly affects blacks, in which abnormal hemoglobin distorts blood cells and causes anemia
sickness disease, illness; condition of poor health caused by disease
SIDA common name for AIDS outside United States, based on Spanish síndrome inmuno-deficiencia adquirido or French syndrome immuno-déficitaire acquis
SIDS sudden infant death syndrome
sinusitis inflammation or infection of sinus sacs behind and around nose, causing headache and discharge through nose
sleeping sickness condition characterized by presence in blood of parasite from bite of African tsetse fly, causing lethargy, drowsiness, and pain in limbs and joints; encephalitis
smallpox acute viral infection that causes high fever and a scarring rash of blisters, usu. fatal, now eradicated by vaccine; variola
social disease *Informal.* venereal disease
somatogenic psychosomatic disorder disease caused by lowering of immunity to pathogens, due to stress
spinal meningitis meningitis
spotted fever type of bacterial meningitis; cerebrospinal fever
STD sexually transmitted disease
strep throat infection of throat by streptococcus bacteria
stroke sudden weakness or paralysis, often on one side of body, due to interruption of blood flow to brain caused by thrombosis, embolus, or hemorrhage; apoplexy; cerebrovascular accident
St. Vitus's dance chorea
sty acute bacterial infection of gland at base of eyelash
sudden infant death syndrome SIDS; death of baby in its bed due to undetermined cause; crib death
syphilis bacterial sexually transmitted disease that causes a chancre in acute stage and may lead to blindness or paralysis in chronic stage and insanity in advanced stage
tapeworm parasitic flatworm that lives in human intestine
TB tuberculosis
teratoma tumor composed of tissues not normally found at site, esp. in testis or ovary
tetanus acute bacterial infection of contaminated wound with release of toxin that affects central nervous system and causes muscle spasms and rigidity, convulsions, and extreme pain; lockjaw
thrombophlebitis inflammation of a vein and formation of blood clot that adheres to its wall
thrush whitish spots and ulcers on mouth due to parasite, esp. in children; candidiasis
tonsillitis inflammation of tonsils, due to bacterial or viral infection, causing sore throat and fever
Tourette's syndrome neurological disorder characterized by excessive, sudden, violent movements and convulsive noises and thoughts
toxoplasmosis infection of lymph nodes caused by protozoan that can cause blindness and mental retardation in newborn when transmitted to fetus, often acquired from cats
trench mouth respiratory infection caused by bacteria, producing ulcers on mucous membrane of mouth and throat
trichinosis intestinal infestation by worm larvae from undercooked meat that causes diarrhea, nausea, and pain in limbs
tuberculosis TB; infectious bacterial disease characterized by formation of nodular lesions in tissue, esp. lungs and lymph nodes, causing coughing, fever, night sweats, and spitting of blood

tularemia disease transmitted to humans from rabbits by deer flies or direct contamination, characterized by infection with ulcers, fever, aches, and enlarged lymph nodes
typhoid fever bacterial infection of digestive system, transmitted through contaminated food or water, that causes high fever, red rash on stomach, chills, sweating, and sometimes intestinal hemorrhage
typhus one of various infections caused by parasitic rickettsiae that results in high fever, severe headache, widespread rash, and delirium
ulcerative colitis inflammation and ulceration of colon and rectum
vaginitis irritation of vagina, due to inflammation or infection, causing burning pain and discharge
varicella chickenpox
variola smallpox
VD venereal disease
venereal disease VD; any infectious disease transmitted by sexual contact, now usu. called sexually transmitted disease; social disease
whooping cough acute contagious bacterial infection of mucous membrane lining air passages, esp. in children, causing fever and paroxysmal cough with bleeding from mouth and nose; pertussis
yaws tropical infectious disease caused by spirochete in skin, marked by fever, pain, small crusty tumors, and lesions; frambesia
yellow fever infectious viral disease of tropics, transmitted by mosquitoes, causing liver and kidney degeneration with reduced urine flow, jaundice, and death

Afflictions and Conditions

acidosis excess acidity in blood, due to kidney malfunction or diabetes
acne inflammation of sebaceous glands in skin, esp. on face during adolescence
addiction state of physical or psychological dependence due to habitual consumption of habit-forming substance; dependence
affliction painful or debilitating condition, esp. a chronic one
airsickness motion sickness during air flight
alcoholism addiction to alcoholic liquor
allergy hypersensitivity to particular substance or antigen, such as pollens, furs, feathers, mold, dust, drugs, dyes, cosmetics, or foods, causing characteristic symptoms when encountered, ingested, or inhaled
alopecia absence of hair from area where it normally grows, esp. progressive hair loss in men; baldness
amenorrhea absence or cessation of menstruation due to congenital defect, hormonal deficiency, hypothalamus disorder, or emotional problem
amnesia total or partial memory loss due to disease, injury, or trauma
anaphylaxis acute, allergic reaction to substance to which person has been previously sensitized, resulting in faintness, palpitations, loss of color, difficulty in breathing, and shock
anemia reduced hemoglobin in blood, causing fatigue, breathlessness, and pallor
anorexia nervosa extreme loss of appetite, esp. in adolescent females, causing severe weight loss and starvation
asthma paroxysmal attacks of bronchial spasms that cause difficulty in breathing, often hereditary
astigmatism distortion of visual images due to failure of retina to focus light
athlete's foot contagious fungal infection of skin between toes
autism severe psychiatric disorder of childhood that causes inability to speak or form abstract concepts and withdrawal from reality
backache chronic and persistent or recurrent pain in lower back or shoulders, usu. due to tension or injury
baldness alopecia
bedwetting enuresis
Bell's palsy paralysis of muscles on one side of face and inability to close eye, sometimes with loss of taste and excess sensitivity to noise
bends compressed air sickness
binge-purge syndrome bulimia
blood poisoning prolonged invasion of bloodstream by pathogenic bacteria due to infectious disease or skin lesions; septicemia; toxemia
boil tender, inflamed, pustulant area of skin, usu. due to staphylococcus infection; furuncle
bulimia usu. psychogenic syndrome of overeating followed by vomiting, also caused by hypothalamus lesion; binge-purge syndrome
bunion swelling of joint between big toe and first metatarsal
bursitis inflammation of small fibrous sacs lined with synovial membrane, due to injury or infection, characterized by pain and stiffness in joints
cancrum ulceration of lip or mouth; canker
canker cancrum
carpal tunnel syndrome compression of median nerve entering palm of hand that causes pain and numbing in middle and index fingers
carsickness motion sickness in automobile
catalepsy maintenance of abnormal postures or physical attitudes, esp. in catatonia
cataract opacity of eye lens that causes blurred vision, esp. in elderly
catatonia syndrome of motor abnormalities, usu. stupor and catalepsy, due to mental condition
celiac disease hereditary intestinal disorder involving intolerance to wheat and rye
chapping sore roughening or cracking of skin from overexposure to elements
compressed air sickness formation of nitrogen bubbles in bloodstream after experiencing high pressure at great ocean depths or high altitudes, characterized by pain and blockage of circulation; bends; decompression sickness
condition state of ill health, esp. recurrent or chronic, caused by illness, injury, or heredity

corn area of hard or thickened skin on or between toes
cyst any of various abnormal, liquid-filled sacs lined with epithelium, due to blocked duct, tumor, or congenital problem
dandruff small flakes of dead skin on scalp; scurf
decompression sickness compressed air sickness
dehydration deficiency or loss of water in body tissues marked by thirst, nausea, and exhaustion
delirium acute mental disorder due to organic brain disease, causing hallucinations, disorientation, and extreme excitation
delirium tremens dt's; psychosis due to alcoholic withdrawal, causing tremors, anxiety, sweating, and vivid hallucinations
dependence physical or psychological compulsion to consume certain drugs; addiction
diaper rash painful, reddened, raw area of skin around anus, buttocks, and genitals due to irritant stools, urine-soaked diapers, or candidiasis infection
disorder malfunction of normal metabolic or physiological process or part
dropsy former term for edema
ectopic pregnancy state in which fertilized egg implants at site other than uterus
eczema superficial inflammation of skin characterized by itching, red rash, and scaling, due to various causes
edema excessive accumulation of fluid in tissues; dropsy
enuresis involuntary urination, esp. at night, usu. functional in nature; bedwetting
fibrosis thickening and scarring of connective tissue due to injury or inflammation
furuncle boil
gallstone hard mass of bile pigments, cholesterol, and calcium salts in gallbladder that causes pain or passes into and obstructs bile duct
gangrene decay and death of body tissue due to insufficient or absent blood supply, caused by disease or injury
goiter swollen neck due to enlarged thyroid gland
hangnail sliver of cuticle separated along edge of fingernail
hay fever common, usu. seasonal allergy to plant pollen that causes sneezing, runny nose, and watery eyes
heat exhaustion heat prostration
heat prostration fatigue and collapse from low blood pressure due to loss of body fluids after prolonged exposure to heat; heat exhaustion
heatstroke increased body temperature and eventual loss of consciousness without sweating, due to failure of body's heat regulating mechanism after prolonged exposure to heat; sunstroke
hemophilia hereditary deficiency of one blood coagulant that causes slowness in clotting and prolonged or spontaneous bleeding
hemorrhoids enlarged veins in anus walls, esp. due to prolonged constipation or diarrhea, characterized by fissure, painful swelling, and bleeding; piles
hives round, red itching wheals up to several inches across on skin, caused by acute or chronic allergic reaction
hydrocephalus excess of cerebrospinal fluid in brain ventricles that causes enlargement of head in children and pressure and drowsiness in adults
incontinence involuntary passage or leakage of urine
ingrown toenail condition in which toenail grows into surrounding tissue
jet lag disruption of biological and psychological rhythms by lengthy jet travel, causing mood alterations, sleep disturbance, and stress
kidney stone hard, pebblelike mass in kidney that causes pain and blood in urine; nephrolithiasis
liver spot brown, roundish flat spot on skin that results from excess melanin, usu. in elderly
malnutrition insufficient food consumption to satisfy bodily needs over prolonged period
migraine recurrent, intense headache, often accompanied by blurred vision and vomiting, caused by contraction and dilation of arteries in brain
mole flat or raised area of brown pigment in skin
motion sickness nausea, vomiting, dizziness, and headache caused by motion
narcolepsy extreme tendency to fall asleep in quiet circumstances or during monotonous activities
obesity accumulation of excess fat, esp. in subcutaneous tissues, usu. due to overeating or nutritional imbalance
pica abnormal craving for unnatural foods due to nutritional deficiencies
piles hemorrhoids
plantar wart deep wart on sole of foot
pneumonitis inflammation of walls of air sacs in lungs due to virus or unknown causes
premature birth birth of baby before full term of pregnancy
psoriasis condition characterized by chronic, itchy, scaly silvery patches of skin, esp. on elbows, forearms, knees, and scalp, of unknown cause but sometimes due to anxiety
pulmonary embolism obstruction by blood clot of artery that conveys blood from heart to lungs
ringworm highly contagious fungal infection of skin, esp. scalp and feet or under beard
sciatica condition marked by pain down back of thigh, due to disintegration of intervertebral disk, accompanied by numbness and stiff back
sclerosis hardening of tissue after inflammation due to scarring, esp. in spinal cord or brain, causing progressive paralysis
scurf dandruff
seasickness motion sickness on ship or boat
seborrhea excessive secretion by sebaceous glands in face, esp. at puberty
septicemia tissue destruction by disease-causing bacteria or toxins absorbed from bloodstream; blood poisoning
stretch marks whitish streaks, usu. on abdomen

or thighs, due to short-term stretching of skin, as during pregnancy
sunstroke heatstroke
tendonitis inflammation of bands of connective tissue that join muscle to bones and joints, due to physical trauma or hereditary disease
tennis elbow painful inflammation of tendon on outer side of elbow due to overuse
thrombosis formation of clots in blood, potentially causing obstruction of blood vessels
tolerance lessening of normal response to drug or other substance taken over a prolonged period, requiring increased dosages for normal reaction
toxemia blood poisoning caused by toxins formed by bacteria at site of infection
tubal pregnancy pregnancy in which fertilized egg implants in fallopian tube
ulcer open, inflamed, nonhealing sore in skin or mucous membrane, esp. in lining of alimentary canal
varicose veins bulging, distended, sometimes painful veins in legs, rectum, or scrotum due to obstruction of blood flow
vegetative state severe brain damage and deep, persistent coma that cannot be reversed, necessitating maintenance of life functions by machines
vertigo feeling that one's surroundings are in motion, esp. spinning or tilting, due to disease of inner ear or vestibular nerve
wart small, hard, benign growth in skin, caused by virus
withdrawal syndrome of sweating, vomiting, and tremors at cessation of consumption of substance to which one is addicted

Defects and Disabilities

abnormality physical malformation or dysfunction
albinism inherited deficiency of pigment in skin, hair, and eyes
amputation loss or removal of a limb or part of a limb
aphasia speech and language comprehension disorder due to disease in left half of brain
birth defect disability or physical deformity present at birth, either inherited or acquired, that stems from problems during fetal period; congenital defect
birthmark skin blemish present at birth, often diminishing in size over time; nevus
blindness inability or marked reduction in ability to see, due to disease, injury, or birth defect
blue baby infant with congenital malformation of heart in which deoxygenated blood is pumped through body, producing bluish color in skin and lips
bowleg abnormal outcurving of legs that creates gap between knees
bucktooth extreme overbite of teeth of upper jaw over lower jaw
cauliflower ear enlarged and permanently deformed ear due to injury or repeated blows
cerebral palsy abnormal development of brain, usu. due to birth defect, that causes weakness and lack of limb coordination
cleft palate fissure in midline of palate that did not properly fuse in embryonic stage
clubfoot birth defect in which foot is twisted downward and inward so sole cannot be placed flat on ground; talipes
color blindness any of various inherited conditions causing confusion of one or more colors; daltonism
congenital defect birth defect
cretinism congenital dwarfism, mental retardation, and coarseness of skin due to lack of thyroid hormone
crippling birth defect, disease, or injury that severely inhibits movement of limbs, esp. ability to walk
crossed eyes strabismus in which eyes turn inward toward nose
curvature of the spine abnormal deviation in position of spine: scoliosis, lordosis, or kyphosis
deafness partial or total inability to hear in one or both ears due to birth defect, disease, injury, or lesion
debility physical weakness or feebleness
defect abnormal functioning, physical flaw, or blemish
deformity abnormal or disfigured body part
dementia chronic mental disorder or incapacity due to organic brain disease
deviated septum abnormal position of wall or partition in anatomical part, esp. nose
disability condition that makes one unfit, incapacitated, or crippled
double vision vision disorder due to various diseases or drug reaction, causing doubling of perceived images
Down's syndrome chromosomal abnormality that causes oblique slant to eyes, round head, flat nose, small ears, short stature, and reduced mental capacity; mongolism
dwarfism abnormally short stature from pituitary deficiency, genetic defect, or cretinism
dyslexia developmental disorder that hinders the ability to learn to read and write
elephant man's disease neurofibromatosis
farsightedness hyperopia
fetal alcohol syndrome FAS; fetal abnormalities due to consumption of alcohol by mother during pregnancy, leading to retardation and severe behavioral disorders in later life
gigantism abnormal growth to excessive height due to oversecretion of growth hormone by pituitary gland
hammertoe clawlike deformity of toe with permanent flexion of second and third joints
handicap physical malfunction that causes partial or total inability to perform an activity
harelip congenital cleft in upper lip due to failure of embryonic tissue of lip to fuse properly
heart defects congenital anomalies in circulatory system during embryonic development, causing murmurs and hypertension

hereditary defect congenital defect inherited from one's parents through genes
humpback enlarged, rounded deformation of upper back; hunchback
hunchback humpback
hyperopia condition in which parallel light rays focus behind retina, causing blurred appearance of objects closer than 20 feet (6 m); farsightedness
knock-knee abnormal incurving of legs that causes gap between feet when knees touch and leads to degenerative arthritis
lameness condition of having a limb disabled enough to impair normal movement, esp. walking
learning disabilities various conditions, esp. nervous system disorders such as dyslexia, that interfere with the ability to learn to read and write
lordosis accentuation of inward curvature of lower back or neck, causing swaybacked appearance; swayback
malformation physical deformity or abnormality
mental retardation deficiency from birth in some mental functions, often from congenital condition such as Down's syndrome
microcephalic (*adj*) having a smaller-than-normal head
mongolism Down's syndrome
mutation altered inherited characteristic due to genetic change
muteness inability to speak due to congenital condition, disease, or injury
myopia condition in which parallel light rays focus in front of retina, causing blurred appearance of objects farther than 20 feet (6 m); nearsightedness
nearsightedness myopia
neurofibromatosis inherited genetic disorder characterized by bumps and patches on skin and sometimes skeletal deformity; elephant man's disease
nevus birthmark
night blindness inability to see in dim light or at night, due to disorder of cells in retina, caused esp. by vitamin A deficiency
palsy rare term for paralysis
paralysis muscle weakness of varying severity due to injury or disease, total paralysis resulting in motor inability
paraplegia paralysis of both legs due to disease or spinal injury
paresis muscular weakness and mental deterioration, less severe than paralysis, due to neurological disease, esp. syphilitic infection
phenylketonuria PKU; birth defect in protein metabolism that causes damage to nervous system and severe mental retardation
pigeon toes toes with abnormal inward turning, associated with knock-knee
PKU phenylketonuria
presbyopia farsightedness in which lens of eye is unable to focus properly
quadriplegia paralysis of both legs and both arms due to disease or spinal injury
scoliosis S-shaped lateral curvature of spine due to congenital or acquired abnormalities of vertebrae or muscles
senile dementia progressive, irreversible impairment of cognitive function in old age
Siamese twins identical twins joined at birth
speech disorders language defects due to organic or sensory deficiency, poor speech mechanisms, or psychological disorders
spina bifida congenital cleft of vertebral column
strabismus any abnormal alignment of eyes due to muscle imbalance
stuttering speech disorder characterized by blocks or spasms that interrupt normal speech rhythm
subnormality state of arrested or incomplete mental development due to congenital defect, injury, or gross environmental deprivation
swayback lordosis
talipes clubfoot
Tay-Sachs disease inherited disorder of lipid metabolism that causes blindness, mental retardation, and death in infancy

Injuries and Accidents

abrasion wearing away of surface of skin or mucous membrane by rubbing or scraping; scrape
accident unexpected or unintended occurrence that causes physical harm or injury
aneurysm balloonlike swelling of arterial wall
avulsion tearing or separation of part or tissue
black eye bruising of eyelid and area around eye's orbit
blood blister swelling just beneath skin filled with blood, caused by unaccustomed friction
blow sudden, hard stroke against body surface with hard object
break simple or compound fracture of bone
bruise skin discoloration caused by escape of blood under skin following injury; contusion
bump bruising blow to body without breaking of skin
burn first, second, or third degree injury and damage to skin and subcutaneous tissue caused by heat, fire, wind, radiation, or caustic substance
cerebral hemorrhage bleeding from cerebral artery into brain tissue
charley horse injury to arm or leg in which muscles, blood vessels, nerves, and other soft tissues are damaged and cramp up
chilblain red, round, itchy swelling of skin on fingers or toes due to exposure to cold
collapsed lung folding together and contracting of lung due to air in surrounding chest cavity
compound fracture breakage of bone into multiple fragments, sometimes with bone end piercing overlying skin
concussion injury to brain from violent, jarring blow to head, often with limited period of unconsciousness and impaired brain function
contusion surface injury in which skin is not broken; bruise

detached retina separation of retina from layer of eyeball, causing loss of vision
dislocation displacement of bone from proper position in joint
embolism obstruction of artery by lodged blood clot, fat, air, or foreign body carried by circulating blood
first-degree burn reddening of outer layer of skin
fissure crack in bone or thin cleft in tissue
fracture simple or compound breakage of bone
frostbite tissue damage from exposure to intense cold, esp. freezing of tissue and cessation of blood circulation
gash deep, ragged cut through skin
hernia protrusion of tissue or organ outside cavity it normally occupies, esp. in lower abdomen, due to physical strain or coughing
herniated disk slipped disk
injury physical damage to body part by action of external force
laceration tear in flesh, esp. with irregular edges
maiming injury that causes loss or crippling of body part
miscarriage spontaneous abortion and expulsion of fetus, usu. between 12th and 28th weeks of pregnancy
mutilation removal of or severe damage to essential body part
perforation piercing of skin and underlying tissue, or of any hollow viscus, by sharp object; puncture
poisoning condition produced by introduction of natural or synthetic toxic substance into body or sometimes by toxin produced by organism itself
pull strain of muscle or ligament
puncture wound made by sharp object, with small entry hole and little or no bleeding
rupture forcible tearing apart or bursting of organ; hernia
scald burn inflicted by hot liquid or steam
scrape abrasion
scratch superficial lengthwise abrasion
second-degree burn blistering of surface skin and damage to underlying dermis
separation disarticulation of bone from normal joint position
simple fracture clean breakage of bone at one site without piercing of skin
slash long, sweeping deep cut made with blade
slice thin cut through skin and underlying tissue
slipped disk abnormal protrusion of disk between abutting vertebrae, esp. in lumbar region, causing painful pressure against spinal cord; herniated disk
soft tissue damage generalized injury to tissue without damage to bones or organs
spontaneous abortion birth or expulsion of fetus before it has developed enough for independent survival
sprain excessive overstretching of ligament
strain excessive stretching of muscle
stress fracture hairline break, often in bone of lower leg, due to intense physical activity
stub bumping of foot or toe against immovable object
suffocation cutting off of supply of air, esp. by strangling of throat or smothering of mouth and nose
sunburn burn due to overexposure to sunlight, usu. first degree
tear ripping or pulling apart of muscle; ragged cut in skin
third-degree burn total destruction of skin and damage to tissue beneath
trauma physical wound or injury, esp. one causing shock
whiplash damage to ligaments, vertebrae, and spinal cord in neck caused by sudden jerking back of head, esp. in auto accident
wound external injury in which skin is broken, torn, or pierced

Signs and Symptoms

abscess localized accumulation of pus surrounded by inflamed tissue
adhesion union by fibrous connective tissue of two normally separate parts
anesthesia loss of sensation in part or all of body
angina feeling of suffocation; chest pain
ankylosis fusion of bones across joint
anxiety fear neurosis that dominates personality
apnea temporary cessation of breathing
arrhythmia irregularity or deviation from normal rhythm or force of heartbeat
asphyxiation suffocation; failure of oxygen to reach tissues due to respiratory obstruction
asthma difficulty in breathing due to recurrent bronchospasm
ataxia shaky movements and unsteady gait when brain fails to regulate posture or direction of limb movements
atrophy wasting away of normally developed organ or tissue due to degeneration of cells
attrition normal wearing away of surface of teeth
bad breath halitosis
bedsore skin ulceration due to continuous pressure and rubbing on body part
belch audible expulsion of intestinal gas through mouth
bellyache *Informal.* pain in stomach
black-and-blue mark ecchymosis
blackhead black clump of fatty sebum and keratin in outlet of sebaceous gland; comedo
blackout temporary loss of consciousness, vision, or memory
blister external swelling that contains watery fluid and blood or pus, caused by friction
brain damage congenital or acquired injury to tissues of brain, due esp. to inadequate oxygen supply, trauma, incomplete brain development, or disease, manifested by range of symptoms from impaired speech to retardation to vegetative state
burp *Informal.* audible expulsion of intestinal gas through mouth
calculus pebblelike mass, such as gallstone or kid-

ney stone, formed within body; hard tartar layer formed on teeth by plaque
callus hard thickening of area of skin undergoing rubbing, esp. on hands or feet; mass of tissue forming around fractured bone ends
cardiac arrest abrupt cessation of heartbeat, causing loss of pulse, consciousness, and breathing
caries decay of bone tissue, esp. tooth; cavity
catarrh excessive secretion of thick phlegm or mucus by mucous membrane of nose
cavity hollow in tooth produced by carious decay
chancre painless ulcer on lips, genitals, urethra, or eyelid
chills coldness and shivering, esp. during fever
choking obstruction of windpipe, causing partial or complete stoppage of breathing
cicatrix scar
cold sore small swelling or eruption of skin around lips that dries to leave crusty patch; fever blister
colic severe abdominal pain, usu. in waves, due to gas or intestinal obstruction; inexplicable crying in infancy
collapse sudden, severe failure of health; falling down from upright position
coma prolonged state of deep unconsciousness from which patient cannot be roused
congestion accumulation of blood within an organ; clogging of upper respiratory system with mucus
constipation infrequent, difficult, often painful bowel movements with hard feces; irregularity
convulsion involuntary muscle contraction that causes contorted movements of body and limbs
cough violent exhalation of irritant particles or congestive mucus from respiratory system
cramp prolonged painful contraction or spasm of muscle
crick painful muscle spasm or cramp in neck or upper back
cyanosis bluish discoloration of skin and mucous membrane due to inadequate oxygenation of blood
cyst abnormal sac or cavity lined with epithelium and filled with liquid or semisolid substance
decrepit (*adj*) wasted away or weakened by, or as if by, old age
deviation abnormal position, esp. of one or both eyes
diarrhea frequent bowel evacuation, esp. of soft or liquid feces; Montezuma's revenge; runs
dizziness feeling off balance, unstable, confused, as though whirling in place
dyspepsia digestive disorder with abdominal pain and gas after eating, sometimes with nausea and vomiting; indigestion
dyspnea labored or difficult breathing
earache pain in inner ear
eclampsia convulsions, esp. due to toxemia during pregnancy
efflorescence skin eruption, rash, or other lesion
emaciation severe weight loss and wasting of body from malnutrition, cancer, tuberculosis, or parasites
eruption skin irritation, esp. rash
exhaustion extreme fatigue
fainting temporary loss of consciousness due to insufficient flow of blood to brain
fatigue intense, prolonged tiredness
febrile (*adj*) affected with fever
fever rise in body temperature above normal 98.6 degrees F, often accompanied by delirium when over 104 degrees F; pyrexia
fever blister swelling or eruption of skin around lips with high or prolonged fever; cold sore
fibrillation rapid, uncontrolled irregular twitching of heart muscle
fissure crack in membrane lining
flatulence expulsion of intestinal gas through mouth by belching or through anus by passing flatus
flatus intestinal gas
flush reddening of face and/or neck
flux abnormally copious flow from organ or body cavity
gas mixture of swallowed air and fermented contents of stomach; flatus; intestinal gas
goose bumps goose flesh
goose flesh tiny puckers of skin with hair standing on end due to contraction of blood vessels and small muscle attached to base of each hair follicle; goose bumps
granuloma nodule of connective tissue and capillaries associated with tuberculosis, syphilis, or nonorganic foreign bodies
growth abnormal formation on or in body; tumor
halitosis offensive breath, esp. from diseases of gums, teeth, throat, or lungs; bad breath
hallucination false perception of something not there, esp. visual image
headache pain within skull, commonly due to stress or fatigue
heartburn pain rising from abdomen to throat, often accompanied by bitter fluid in mouth
heart murmur blowing or swishing noise produced by blood passing through defective heart valve
hematoma clotted accumulation of blood in tissue forming solid swelling
hemorrhage outflow of blood from ruptured blood vessel, esp. internal bleeding
hiccup characteristic sound made by abrupt involuntary lowering of diaphragm and closing of upper end of trachea
high blood pressure elevation of pressure of blood in main arteries above normal range for age group; hypertension
hyperglycemia excess of sugar in bloodstream, esp. due to diabetes mellitus
hypersensitivity uncommonly strong reaction to stimulus such as sunlight or a chemical, including most allergies
hypertension high blood pressure
hyperthermia exceptionally high body temperature of 105 degrees F or above; fever induced as treatment
hyperventilation abnormally rapid breathing

that lowers carbon dioxide concentration in blood
hypotension low blood pressure
hypothermia dropping of body temperature below normal range
hysteria extreme emotional excitation, sensory and motor disturbances, and outbursts of uncontrolled feeling
illusion false perception due to misinterpreted stimuli; belief in existence of that which does not exist
incoherence inability to produce intelligible, logical speech or thought
incontinence inability to control passage of urine
indigestion dyspepsia
infirmity feebleness, frailty
inflammation immediate defense reaction of tissue to injury or attack, involving pain, heat, redness, and swelling
insomnia inability to fall asleep or remain asleep
intestinal gas gas; flatus
irregularity constipation
ischemia insufficient blood flow to body part due to constriction or blockage of blood vessels
itching minor local skin irritation relieved by scratching; pruritus
jaundice yellowing of skin and whites of eyes from excess bilirubin in blood, often due to obstructed ducts or liver disease
lesion any localized, abnormal structural change in tissue or body part resulting in impaired function, including abscess, ulcer, or tumor
lightheadedness dizziness, mental confusion
low blood pressure dropping of pressure of blood in main arteries below normal range for age
low-grade fever slight rise in body temperature above normal 98.6 degrees F
lumbago lower backache due to injury or sciatica
macule discoloration or thickening of skin in contrast to surrounding area
malaise general sense of being unwell, often accompanied by physical discomfort and weakness
mania excessive activity and euphoria
Montezuma's revenge *Slang.* diarrhea, usu. caused by eating contaminated food in foreign country
mottling blotches, streaks, or spots on skin
mucus viscous fluid secreted by mucous membrane, esp. in upper respiratory tract
nasal discharge drainage of mucus through nose
nausea feeling that one is about to vomit
neoplasm new tumor caused by uncontrolled reproduction of abnormal cells
neuralgia severe burning or stabbing pain along course of nerve
night sweats copious perspiration while sleeping
nit louse egg that attaches to body
obesity distinct, intense accumulation of excess fat in body
pain sensation of strong discomfort in bodily part
palpitation abnormally rapid or violent heartbeat, esp. due to fear, exertion, neurosis, or arrhythmia
papule small, superficial bump or spot on skin, often part of rash
paroxysm sudden, violent spasm or convulsion; abrupt worsening of symptom
perspiration sweating
phlegm sputum
pimple small, pustulant, inflamed swelling on skin, often from bacterial infection
plaque sticky, colorless mixture of saliva, bacteria, and carbohydrates on surface of teeth that causes tartar and caries
pock small pus-filled eruption of skin
polyp benign growth on mucous membrane, esp. in nose, ear, or stomach
postnasal drip draining of mucus from nose onto pharynx
prostration total exhaustion
purpura skin rash due to bleeding into skin from defective capillaries or blood platelet deficiency
pus thick yellow or green liquid containing blood cells and dead cells, formed at site of infection or inflammation
pustule small, pus-containing skin blister
putrescence foul smell caused by decomposition of tissue
pyrexia fever
rash temporary skin eruption characterized by reddening and itching, esp. in form of pimples, hives, or wheals
regurgitation vomiting
respiratory arrest cessation of breathing
rheum watery discharge from mucous membrane of mouth, eyes, or nose
runs *Informal.* diarrhea
scab hard crust of blood, serum, or pus over healing wound
scar mark left on skin by healing wound where connective tissues replace damaged tissues; cicatrix
seizure sudden attack of disease or condition
senility loss of intellectual faculties in old age
shin splint pain in front of shin, usu. caused by running on hard surface
shivers uncontrollable trembling
shock acute, progressive circulatory collapse, with blood pressure too low to maintain adequate blood supply to tissues, causing cold sweat, paleness, weak but rapid pulse, dilated pupils, irregular breathing, dry mouth, and reduced urine flow
side effect incidental or secondary manifestation, esp. of medication
sign physical, psychological, or behavioral manifestation of a disease, injury, condition, or disability
skin eruption swelling, discoloration, or roughening of skin
sneeze involuntary violent reflex expulsion of air caused by irritation of mucous membrane lining nasal cavity
sore ulcer or open wound on skin or mucous membrane from injury or infection
spasm sustained involuntary muscular contraction
sputum mucus coughed up from respiratory tract; phlegm

stomachache generalized intestinal pain, often accompanied by diarrhea, nausea, and vomiting
stridor loud, harsh breathing noise due to partial obstruction of trachea or larynx
sweating secretion of salty, watery fluid by glands lying in dermis of skin; perspiration
swelling growth of body part, curving outward from surface, esp. due to pressure from within; tumescence
symptom indication of disease or disorder, esp. one recognizable by patient
syndrome combination of signs and symptoms
tachycardia rapid heart rate
tartar calcareous deposit and encrustation on teeth
tetany spasm and twitching of muscles of face, hands, and feet
tic uncontrolled muscle twitch, esp. in face
tic douloureux neuralgia of facial nerves
tinnitus ringing in the ears
toxemia accumulation of toxins in blood
toxic shock shock syndrome caused by toxin in body, often associated with tampon use
tremor uncontrollable, rhythmical alternating movement of body part, esp. hands
tumescence swelling, esp. due to accumulation of blood or other fluid in tissue
tumor abnormal growth of tissue in or on body part
tussis cough
unconsciousness lack of awareness of one's surroundings and unresponsiveness to stimuli; state of being asleep
uremia toxic condition due to presence in blood of excess urea and other nitrogenous wastes excreted by kidney
vesicle very small skin blister containing clear serum
vital signs pulse rate, blood pressure, respiration, and body temperature, forming index of essential body functions
welt raised ridge on skin caused by slash or blow
wheal temporary, itching, red or pale raised area of skin due to abrasion or allergy
wheezing high-pitched breathing sounds due to bronchospasm
withdrawal symptoms sweating, anxiety, nausea, vomiting, cramps, and tremors at cessation of addictive substance abuse

Diagnostic Terminology

abnormality malformed part or dysfunctional process
acquired (*adj*) designating condition or disorder contracted after birth, not hereditary
active immunity production of antibodies by body's cells following attack of disease or immunization
acute (*adj*) designating disease with rapid onset, severe symptoms, and brief duration, opposite of chronic
affliction condition that causes pain and suffering
allergen antigen that causes allergy in sensitive person
ambulatory (*adj*) designating patient who is able to leave bed and walk
antibiotic substance derived from a microorganism or fungus that destroys or inhibits growth of other microorganisms
antibody special blood protein synthesized in lymphoid tissue in response to antigen, which it attacks and neutralizes
antigen foreign substance, usu. protein, against which body produces an antibody
asepsis complete absence of disease-causing bacteria, viruses, fungi, or microorganisms
asymptomatic (*adj*) showing no evidence of a disease
autoimmune (*adj*) designating disorder of body's defense mechanism in which antibodies are produced against body's own tissues, treating them as foreign substances
autologous (*adj*) derived from same individual or organism
autonomic (*adj*) occurring involuntarily, controlled by autonomic nervous system
bacillus rod-shaped bacterium
bacteria *pl., sing.* bacterium; primitive microorganisms, usu. unicellular with unique cell wall composition, that reproduce by simple division and often cause disease
bacterial (*adj*) designating disease, condition, or infection caused by bacteria
benign (*adj*) consisting of localized mass of nonmalignant specialized cells within connective tissue that do not invade and destroy tissue or spread throughout body
blood alcohol content measure of alcohol concentration in blood; blood alcohol level
blood pressure pressure of blood in main arteries
breech presentation abnormal position of baby in womb, causing it to be delivered buttocks first
carcinogen substance that may produce cancer in living tissue
carrier individual that harbors pathogen without displaying symptoms
cerebral (*adj*) of the brain
chronic (*adj*) designating disease of long duration with very slow changes and often gradual onset of recurrent symptoms, opposite of acute
clot soft, thickened lump formed in liquid, esp. blood
coccus spherical bacterium
communicable (*adj*) designating disease that can be transmitted from one person to another by physical contact, a carrier, or droplets exhaled into air
condition something causing state of poor health; official status of hospitalized patient, such as grave, critical, serious, poor, guarded, stable, fair, satisfactory, or good
congenital (*adj*) designating condition present at birth, often inherited
contagious (*adj*) designating any communicable

disease, esp. one transmitted by physical contact
coronary (*adj*) of or pertaining to arteries of heart
defect abnormal functioning, physical flaw or blemish
deformity abnormal or disfigured body part
degenerative (*adj*) designating disease or condition growing progressively worse due to deterioration in cell structure or function
deterioration worsening of condition
diagnosis process of determining by examination the nature of a disease or condition
disability condition that makes one unfit, incapacitated, or crippled
discharge liquid or semisolid substance emitted from body
disease particular disorder of organism with specific cause and recognizable symptoms
disorder any bodily abnormality or failure to function
DOA dead on arrival: describing patient's condition on reaching hospital
dysfunction abnormality, impairment, or cessation of bodily function
dystrophy faulty nutrition; disorder characterized by abnormal development of muscle
embolus blood clot, fat, air, amniotic fluid, or foreign body circulated by blood and lodged at some point in cardiovascular system
endemic disease that is constantly present in particular region but generally under control
epidemic contagious disease that spreads rapidly through population of a specific region
etiology cause of specific disease
fatal (*adj*) causing death
fistula abnormal passage that leads from abscess or cavity to skin or to another abscess or cavity, caused by disease or injury
genetic (*adj*) designating condition inherited through chromosomes from one's parents
germ any disease-causing microorganism
hereditary (*adj*) designating condition transmitted from parents to offspring
hypochondria obsession with real and imagined physical ailments
iatrogenic (*adj*) resulting from treatment, esp. of a condition or disease
immunity ability of body to recognize and neutralize foreign matter, either natural or acquired
impairment damage to or weakening of body part or function
incubation period time between entry of disease organisms into body and onset of disease symptoms
infarction death of tissue due to oxygen deprivation
infection invasion of body by harmful pathogen
infectious (*adj*) designating a communicable disease, esp. one caused by invasion of harmful organisms such as bacterium, fungus, protozoan, or virus into body
infestation attack on body by parasitic microorganism
injury physical damage to body part by action of external force
intervention treatment or procedure designed to prevent disease from running its course
intramuscular (*adj*) situated in or administered by entering a muscle, used esp. of injections
life-threatening (*adj*) designating a potentially fatal condition or procedure
malignant (*adj*) consisting of a tumor that invades and destroys tissue in which it originates and can spread to other sites in body through vascular system
metastasis spread of malignant tumor far from site of origin, usu. through vascular system
microbe microorganism
microorganism any organism not visible to naked eye, such as bacterium, protozoan, fungus, and virus; microbe
mold multicellular filamentous fungus
morbidity state of being diseased
moribund (*adj*) dying
mortify (*vb*) cause body tissue to decay
motor (*adj*) designating muscular activity stimulated by impulses from central nervous system
natural immunity inborn lack of susceptibility to specific disease
necrosis death of discrete region of tissue
occlusion closing or obstruction of hollow organ or body part
opportunistic (*adj*) designating disease or infection occurring only under certain conditions, as when immune system is impaired
pandemic (*adj*) designating epidemic disease that spreads to different countries over large region
parasite organism that lives in or on another living organism while contributing nothing to host's welfare, often causing irritation or interfering with function
passive immunity short-term resistance to disease from injection of another's antibodies
pathogen microorganism that produces a communicable disease
pathogenic (*adj*) disease-causing
pathology study of disease processes; course of a disease
plasma liquid in which blood cells are suspended
prognosis assessment of future course and outcome of patient's disease
progressive (*adj*) growing steadily worse, often fatal
psychomotor (*adj*) relating to disorders of muscular activity affected by cerebral disturbances
psychosomatic (*adj*) designating a disease caused by interaction of physical and mental factors
purulent (*adj*) pustulant
pustulant (*adj*) containing and/or discharging pus; purulent
referred pain pain felt in unexpected part of body separate from its source
reflex automatic, involuntary activity caused by simple nervous circuits
rejection immune reaction to transplanted organ or foreign substance
relapse recurrence of disease symptoms after apparent recovery

remission lessening of severity of symptoms, esp. temporary disappearance during course of chronic or terminal illness
resistance measure of body's immunity to disease; degree to which disease is unaffected by antibiotics or drugs
rickettsiae group of parasitic organisms similar to bacteria that infest body through ticks or mites
scabbing formation of hard crust of blood, serum, and pus over healing wound
septic (*adj*) affected with putrefactive destruction by disease-carrying bacteria or their toxins
serum fluid that separates from clotted blood or standing blood plasma
spirochete corkscrew-shaped bacterium
staphylococcus any of several spherical, pathogenic bacteria in irregular clusters, both saprophytes and parasites
stenosis abnormal narrowing of blood vessel or heart valve
streptococcus any of several spherical, chain-forming pathogenic bacteria, mostly saprophytes
stress effect on human body of physical and mental demands and pressures
symptom characteristic indication of disease or disorder
syndrome set of signs and symptoms indicative of particular disease or condition
systemic (*adj*) affecting entire body, not just one part
terminal (*adj*) fatal; in or of final stage of fatal disease
toxin poisonous substance
vector any agent, such as insect or tick, that transmits parasitic microorganisms and infectious diseases from host to host
viral (*adj*) produced by a virus
virulent (*adj*) disease-producing
virus ultramicroscopic, metabolically inert agent composed of DNA or RNA core and protein coating, capable of replication only within living host cells; *Informal*. disease caused by a virus
yeast unicellular fungus that usu. reproduces asexually by budding
zoonosis any infectious disease of animals, such as rabies, that can be transmitted to humans

HEALTH, FITNESS, AND ENHANCEMENT

Activities and Treatments
Equipment and Resources
Martial Arts
Nutrition for Fitness

Activities and Treatments

acupressure massage therapy technique that uses acupuncture points to release tension and promote relaxation and healing; shiatsu
acupuncture Chinese practice of puncturing body with needles at specific points along meridians to relieve pain and cure disease
aerobics vigorous exercise that induces accelerated heartbeat to improve cardiovascular health
aikido Japanese martial art form
Ayurveda ancient Indian medical system of classifying and treating somatic types for optimal health and functioning
biofeedback technique that involves instrument stress readings and training of bodily systems to increase awareness and control of pain and tension
bodybuilding development of muscle layer through program of weightlifting and nutritional supplements
body mechanics science and study of bodily motion, esp. for optimal benefits of exercise
body wrap herbal, steam, or heat weight-loss treatment
breast augmentation surgical silicone implantation in breast for cosmetic enhancement
breast reduction surgical removal of excess breast tissue
breathing exercises practice of deep, regular breathing to increase lung capacity, improve overall health, and relieve tension
buddy system pairing of two individuals for mutual safety in dangerous activity
bulking increasing size of muscles by weight work
calisthenics individual gymnastic exercises
cardiopulmonary resuscitation CPR; procedure to restore normal breathing and heart activity after cardiac arrest, by heart massage and often electrical and mechanical equipment
chemical peel cosmetic chemical burning of facial skin to promote new, smooth skin growth
chiropractic adjustment manipulation of spine to relieve tension, pressure, and imbalances in bones, muscles, and nerves
circuit training system that uses series of weight machines to work all muscle areas
collagen injection implantation of collagen into wrinkles and folds to improve appearance of skin
colonic irrigation treatment involving cleansing of colon with water to flush toxic impurities
cosmetic surgery surgical alteration of face or body for aesthetic enhancement; plastic surgery
CPR cardio pulmonary resuscitation
crunch sit-up in which one reaches out with arms toward bent knees
dancercise system of vigorous dance movements done to music for fitness
dermabrasion process of stripping top layer of facial skin to promote new, smooth skin growth
detoxification program of exercise, nutrition, and cleansing of system to remove pollutants from body, esp. narcotics or alcohol
diet specific program of food preparation and eating to enhance health and appearance
endurance stamina, capacity for prolonged exercise

ergonomics study or practice of adapting working environment to needs of body
exercise physical activity performed to enhance health and appearance
eye tuck cosmetic surgery to remove excess skin folds around eyes
face-lift cosmetic surgery to remove excess facial skin folds and wrinkles
fast period of abstention from food; (*vb*) abstain from eating for prolonged period
first aid simple medical procedures for health and safety
fitness maintenance and improvement of health through exercise and proper diet; condition of being in good health
flexibility degree of movement, rotation possible in body and joints
Heimlich maneuver procedure that involves clearing windpipe of choking victim by sudden upward pressure on abdomen
herbalism use of herbs for healing
holistic health approach that stresses complete system rather than treatment of specific parts and symptoms, based on theory that entity is more than sum of its parts
isometric exercise system that uses muscle groups acting in opposition or against a fixed object
isotonic exercise system that uses normal contraction of muscles
jazzercise vigorous aerobic exercises done to fast-paced music
jogging gentle, medium-slow running gait, esp. as regular program of exercise
jujitsu Japanese martial art based on use of opponent's weight against him or her through leverage and understanding of anatomy
karate Japanese martial art form usu. used for defense by striking sensitive areas of attacker's body with hands, elbows, legs, or feet
kinesiology principles of anatomy and mechanics in human movement
kung fu Chinese martial art form usu. used for defense by striking vulnerable parts of attacker's body with hands and legs
liposuction surgical removal of excess body fat by suctioning it away through a tube
low-impact aerobics gentle form of aerobic exercise, with reduced stress to feet and joints
marathon running long-distance running, traditionally over twenty-six mile course
martial arts Asian forms of exercise and self-defense that emphasize balance and harmony of passive and active motions
massage system of relaxation using hands to knead, rub, stroke, and press body parts
mouth-to-mouth resuscitation method of blowing air directly into victim's mouth for artificial respiration
nose job *Informal.* rhinoplasty
passive exercise machine electronic device that electrically stimulates muscles
physiotherapy massage, heat treatments, and other physical manipulations
plastic surgery cosmetic surgery
power lifting lifting substantial amounts of weight to increase muscle bulk
pulse rate heartbeats per minute; measure of exercise intensity and cardiovascular benefits
push-up exercise done by pushing upper body away from floor with arms to build upper body strength
race walking competitive speedwalking
reflexology massage of specific areas of foot, or sometimes hand, to treat ailments or relieve stress elsewhere in body
regime program or system of exercise and nutrition for better health; regimen
regimen regime
resistance training strengthening exercise incorporating muscle resistance to a sprung lever or similar device
rhinoplasty cosmetic surgery on the nose; nose job
rubdown vigorous massage
shiatsu Japanese massage system that involves bodily points and meridians responsive to pressure; acupressure
silicone implant cosmetic surgery that involves buildup of bodily proportions by addition of silicone, esp. in breasts
sit-up abdominal exercise in which one bends upper body from supine position with legs flat
speedwalking vigorous, quick walking exercise with arms swinging
step aerobics aerobic exercise using a stepping block
steroid any of various hormonal compounds that accelerate increase in muscle bulk from exercise, often with harmful side effects
stress management system of coping with stress and tension using biofeedback, relaxation techniques, and exercise
Swedish massage systematic massage that uses manipulation and gradual soothing of muscles and nervous system
tae kwon do Korean martial art form that resembles karate
ta'i chi chu'an Chinese Taoist martial art form that emphasizes balance, graceful meditative movements, and coordinated breathing
toning firming muscles by moderate weight work without building bulk
tooth bonding cosmetic dental procedure of coating front surface of tooth for improved appearance
tooth capping cosmetic dental procedure of covering entire tooth with white enamel-like cap, for improved appearance
training regular pursuit of athletic activities to build strength and endurance or improve performance
triathletics exercise system that involves swimming, running, and bicycling over significant distances
walking least strenuous, most natural aerobic exercise

warmup brief period of stretching and loosening activity prior to vigorous exercise
weightlifting practice of lifting substantial amounts of weight to tone and strengthen muscles
work out (*vb*) engage in period of strenuous exercise
workout strenuous exercise, esp. aerobic
yoga system of physical postures and meditative breathing to tone muscles and organs, improve balance, flexibility, and strength, and create integration of mind and body

Equipment and Resources

ankle weights weighted straps worn on ankles while one exercises
barbell rod with weighted disks at both ends
bike pants tight-fitting elastic pants or shorts as worn by cylists
compression shorts tight-fitting elastic shorts designed to support thigh muscles
dojo karate or martial arts gymnasium
dumbbell hand-held weight; barbell
earplug piece of soft material inserted in outer ear to keep out noise or water
exercise machine mechanical device that aids weightlifting and muscle-toning exercises
fat farm *Informal.* weight-loss clinic at sanitarium or resort
free weights dumbbells or barbells; weights lifted without weight machines
gravity boots sturdy boots that hold wearer upside down
gymnasium enclosed area for physical activity, training, and contests
health club gymnasium, usu. for members only, with exercise and spa facilities
heating pad electric or water-heated pad for soothing sore muscles or injuries
hot tub whirlpool
hot water bag rubber container filled with hot water, used to soothe injured muscles
ice pack cold compress for sore or injured muscles or ligaments and pain reduction
isolation tank enclosed, sensory-deprivation container in which one floats, without stimuli, for deep relaxation
Jacuzzi *Trademark.* whirlpool spa with turbulent hot water
leg warmers knitted socklike garments that cover and warm lower legs during exercise
leotard tight, lightweight, knitted exercise garment for torso
life jacket buoyant, sleeveless jacket to prevent drowning; life vest
life preserver buoyant vest, jacket, or ring used to remain afloat in water
life vest life jacket
masseur male practitioner of massage
masseuse female practitioner of massage
medicine ball large, heavy ball for exercise and recreation
mineral bath immersion in mineral-rich waters, esp. at spa
mud bath immersion in mud formed by interaction of clay and hot spring water
oxygen mask covering for mouth and nose connected to oxygen tank
parcourse outdoor running and exercise course, esp. in urban areas
punching bag inflated leather bag suspended at eye level for punching
rowing machine device that simulates exercise of rowing a boat with oars
running shoes rubber-soled shoes with good support for running or jogging
sauna Scandinavian steam bath that uses dry heat
spa mineral spring resort; area of health club with sauna, steam room, and whirlpool
sports bra bra designed to give support and comfort during exercise or when playing sports
stationary bicycle exercise bicycle for cardiovascular and muscular toning
steam room tiled room heated with abundant steam, for bathing, refreshment, sweating, and relaxation
sunlamp electric light that produces ultraviolet tanning rays
sweatband headband worn to keep perspiration from dripping onto face during exercise
tanning salon establishment that uses sunlamps to cultivate artificial suntan
track path for runners, usu. oval
treadmill rotary track for running or walking in place
Turkish bath steam bath
weight belt weighted strap worn around waist while exercising; wide leather belt worn as back support when lifting weights
weight machine apparatus with weights suspended over pulleys and connected to handgrips, often with seat or bench
whirlpool tub in which jets or agitator propel current of hot water in soothing, swirling motion; hot tub

Martial Arts

aikido Japanese method of self-defense using various holds to throw one's opponent
atemi the body, especially vital points considered as targets in karate
chagi kick in tae kwan do
dachi stance
dan black-belt ranking in karate
do way of (life, art, etc.), used in combination (karate-do, the way of karate); protective breastplate worn by kendo fighters
dojo training or practice facility
encho-sen extension of a karate match to break a tie
fumikomi stamping kick in karate
geri (or keri) kick in karate
gi uniform for martial arts, consisting of trousers, jacket, and a colored belt indicating the wearer's level of competence in the sport
gohon five-finger strike
gyaku reverse

hadake choke hold
hadan makki low block in tae kwan do
hajime call made by the referee to begin a contest
hidari left side
hiji elbow strike
hosinsul concept of self-defense in tae kwan do
hyong form exercises in tae kwan do
ippon score of one point in a martial arts contest
jigo-tai defensive posture
jimi (*vb*) choke; strangle
jiu jitsu Japanese method of self-defense that emphasizes causing one's opponent to lose his or her balance (also jujitsu, jiu jutsu)
judo East Asian method of self-defense without weapons that emphasizes throwing techniques
judoka practitioner of judo
kamae posture
kareta-ka individual training in karate
karate Japanese method of self-defense without weapons that emphasizes striking the opponent
kata formal competition in aikido; stylized, prearranged forms or formal exercises in karate
katame grappling
katamewaza holding technique used in judo
kekomi thrust
kendo traditional Japanese martial art using bamboo swords
kentsui hammer fist
keri (or geri) kick
ki vital energy
kiai loud cry or shout given by fighters (also kihap, kiap)
kick boxing form of boxing that incorporates martial-art style kicking
kihon basic techniques in karate
kio tsuke call for attention in karate
kumite sparring; competition
kun motto; oath
kung fu Chinese martial art form
kyek pa breaking test (as of boards) in tae kwan do
kyu color belt ranking in karate for ranks under black belt
kyu-sho (or kusho) vital point, such as the temple, windpipe, sternum, solar plexus, groin, shin, back of knee, instep, etc.
makiwara punching board used in karate
matae stop
migi right side
mokuso meditation; contemplation
nage throwing
nagewaza throwing technique used in judo
ninja member of a Japanese society of mercenary warriors skilled in martial arts and stealth
nukite spear finger or spear hand
nunchaku weapon of two rods joined by rope or chain
obi belt tied over the jacket worn by martial arts practitioners
ouse acknowledgment; greeting
randori practice; sparring
ryu traditional system or style of a martial arts school
sanbon winning score in a karate contest
seiza kneeling or sitting position for meditation
sempai senior or advanced student
sensei teacher
shiai contest in martial arts
shiaijo contest area in judo
shihan master instructor
shime choke
shuto knife-edge hand
sogi stances or body position in tae kwan do
sumo Japanese style of wrestling in which two usu. heavy-set contestants vie to force the opponent out of the ring or off his feet
tae kwan do Korean martial art based on karate, literally, "foot-fist-way," or a way of fighting using the feet and fists
t'ai chi (ch'uan) Chinese martial art form emphasizing balance and graceful, controlled movements
taeryon sparring in tae kwan do
tameshiware breaking (boards, etc.) in karate
tettsui hammer fist, a blow with the side of a closed fist
tsuki punch
uchi strike
uchi waza striking techniques
uke attacking position in aikido or jiu jitsu; block in karate
ukemi falling and rolling exercises
ura opposite, reverse, or back
waza techniques
yudansha holder of a black belt in karate

Nutrition for Fitness

additive often chemical substance added to processed food to retard spoilage and improve appearance or taste of food
banting diet without sweets or carbohydrates
basal metabolism basic rate at which body expends energy to maintain itself in resting state
betacarotene isomer of carotene converted by the body to Vitamin A
calorie measurement of energy provided by food
carbohydrate essential nutrient substance in sugars and starches
carboloading *Informal.* ingestion of large amounts of complex carbohydrates to produce extra energy reserves, esp. prior to exercise
cholesterol fatty substance found in foodstuffs, or formed by body itself, that coats and constricts arteries
complex carbohydrate carbohydrate such as sucrose or starch in foods
diet pattern of eating; range of foodstuffs ingested; programmed course of eating to gain or lose weight or improve health
electrolytes dietary components (sodium, potassium, and chloride) essential to fluid retention, nerve impulse transmission, and digestion
empty calories highly caloric foods without significant nutritional value
fad diet eating regimen designed to appeal more

to short-term weight loss goals than to sound nutritional principles
fats saturated, monounsaturated, polyunsaturated, and unsaturated essential nutrient material rich in calories
fiber dietary substance, usu. cellulose, found in plants, that promotes gastrointestinal fitness
folic acid nutrient that facilitates protein synthesis and cell division
food combining system of combining certain food groups in meals for health or weight control
food group basic category of nutritional foodstuffs, including milk, meat, vegetable and fruit, and bread and cereal groups
food guide pyramid chart indicating proportions of food groups for a healthy diet, issued by the U.S. Department of Agriculture
health food any food considered healthful, esp. natural, unprocessed, or organic food
junk food processed food rich in fats and sugars but low in nutrition
lipids class of organic compounds that include fats and fatty acids
macrobiotics restricted diet program, primarily of whole grains, beans, and vegetables, based on balance of yin and yang natural cycles
malnutrition chronic lack of essential and beneficial nutritional foodstuffs
megavitamin therapy use of massive amounts of vitamins to treat illness and promote vitality
minerals chemical elements and compounds necessary in small amounts for health
multivitamin dietary supplement containing several essential nutrients
nutrient dietary substance that provides chemical compounds necessary for growth and replenishment of body
nutrition process by which animals consume and process food; study of dietary requirements
obesity condition of having excess body fat
olestra patented synthetic fat substitute made from fatty acids and sugar
omega-3 fatty acid fatty acid, found esp. in fish oil, that reduces cholesterol levels in blood
organic food foodstuffs grown and prepared without chemical additives, pesticides, or fertilizers
polyunsaturated fat dietary fat, usu. vegetable fat
protein essential nutrient material composed of amino acids
RDA recommended dietary allowance of nutritional elements
roughage foodstuffs rich in fiber
saturated fat dietary fat, usu. animal fat, that increases cholesterol level in blood
sitology science of diet and nutrition
starch foodstuff rich in complex carbohydrates
supplement vitamin, mineral, or protein preparation that boosts intake of nutrients
trace minerals chemical elements necessary in minute amounts for health
vegetarianism practice of eating vegetables, fruits, and grains, and of eliminating animal products from diet
vitamin one of various organic nutrient elements and compounds necessary in very small quantities for health
weight loss reduction in body fat and weight, esp. by consumption of fewer calories relative to calories burned
yo-yo dieting repeated weight loss followed by weight gain

HAIR AND GROOMING

Hair Styles
Beards and Mustaches
Grooming Aids and Processes

Hair Styles

Afro tight, bushy, natural curls, worn esp. by African-Americans
auburn (*adj*) having reddish brown hair, natural or dyed
back combed having hair teased or ratted
bald (*adj*) having no hair, minimal or thinning hair, or a shaved head
bangs fringe of hair above forehead cut straight across
beehive dome of teased hair piled high atop head
blaze streak of contrasting color through hair
bleached blond person with artificially lightened hair
blond person with gold or yellow-toned hair, natural or bleached
bob hair cut all one length, to shoulders or shorter
bouffant hair puffed to large volume, piled high
braid hair plaited singly or in pairs
brunette person with brown or black hair, natural or dyed
brush cut short, bristly haircut
bun long hair pulled into knot or roll at back of head
burr cut *Slang.* extremely short, bristly haircut; crew cut
butch extremely short haircut for men
buzz cut usu. short haircut done with electric clippers
chignon knot or roll of long hair at back of head
close-cropped (*adj*) having hair cut close to scalp
cornrows small, tightly braided rows of hair along scalp, esp. for African-Americans, sometimes with beads braided into rows
cowlick natural whorl or lock of hair standing straight up
crest plumelike tuft of hair
crew cut close-cropped hair, usu. on men; burr cut
crimp tight wave in hair made with crimping iron

curls tight coils or loose waves of hair
DA duck's ass; hair oiled and combed back over ears, dovetailing at rear; ducktail
do *Slang.* hair style, hairdo
dreadlocks long, unbrushed, woolly braids, worn esp. by Rastafarians
ducktail DA
fade *Slang.* modified raised or slanted flattop, sometimes with thin, close-shaven trails through it, worn usu. by African-American men; variations include gumby, slope, high-top, high-low, and tribal
feathercut hair cut to resemble layered feathers
flattop short crew cut with flat, brushlike surface at crown
forelock lock of hair hanging down forehead
French braid braid with three strands pulled back from hairline
French knot long hair rolled into spiral at back of head; French twist; twist
French twist French knot
fringe bangs of hair on forehead
frizz very tightly curled hair that forms a wiry mass
frosting bleached hair ends prelightened to white
henna plant extract used to dye hair red
knot hair rolled or twisted into tight mass
layered cut hair cut in many different layers
locks strands of hair
lovelock long curl of hair hanging alone over shoulder (17th-18th c.)
mane abundant or long, thick hair
mohawk narrow band of bristled, erect hair from forehead to nape of neck, surrounded by shaved scalp
moptop shaggy hair style that partially covers brow or face
natural very curly hair grown long and bushy, esp. by African-Americans
pageboy straight, chin-length hair turned gently under at ends
part separation of hair falling along head, usu. at side of crown
perm *Informal.* permanent wave in hair
permanent wave chemical treatment that curls hair; perm
peroxide blond person with very pale, bleached blond hair
peyes long, uncut side curls worn by Hasidic Jewish men
pigtails hair worn in several braids
pixie short, layered haircut
plait braid of hair
platinum (*adj*) having very pale, esp. bleached blond, hair
pompadour hair fluffed and elevated at forehead
ponytail long hair drawn into single tassel at back of head
pouf hair piled high in rolled puffs
Prince Valiant thick, straight bangs and chin-length, cropped hair around back of head
process chemically straightened curly hair; conk
ratted (*adj*) having hair teased or back combed
razor cut hair cut for layering with razor instead of scissors
receding hairline balding at top of brow, causing hairline to move back on crown
redhead person with reddish orange-toned hair, natural or dyed
ringlets long, spiraling curls of hair
roll hair bunched and held together
set hair styled by curling or waving on rollers
shag usu. long, bushy, layered hair
shingle hair bobbed and cut close in point at nape of neck, gradually longer up back of head, just covering ears
shock bushy or tangled mass of hair
shorn (*adj*) having hair cut short, close to skull
skinhead *Slang.* person with shaved head
spikes hair formed into pointed projections with setting lotion or fixative
spit curl precise curl of hair pressed against face, formed by saliva, water, or fixative
split ends condition in which ends of hair split or fray from abuse or over time
strawberry blond person with light reddish gold blond hair, natural or dyed
streaking contrasting colors in strips through hair
swirl long hair coiled into a circular shape
tail few locks of nape hairs left long with the rest cut short
teased (*adj*) having hair ratted or back combed
thinning early stage of baldness with loss of some hair
tint chemical coloration of hair
tonsure ring of fringed hair around bald crown
topknot tuft, roll, or fluff of hair at crown
tousled (*adj*) windblown, uncombed, or natural in hair style
towhead person with extremely pale, whitish blond hair, esp. a young child
tresses hair, esp. long and luxuriant; plait or braid of hair
twist French knot
updo upsweep
upsweep hairdo in which hair is combed or brushed upward to top of head; updo
wave hair formed into loose curls
widow's peak point formed by hair on forehead
wig artificial hairpiece

Beards and Mustaches

Abe Lincoln thin beard along jaw with mustache shaved
beard man's facial hair, esp. when trimmed into shape, sometimes excluding mustache
burnsides sideburns
down soft, boyish growth of beard
five o'clock shadow growth of heavy beard several hours after shaving, giving unshaven appearance
Fu Manchu thin, delicately trimmed beard and drooping mustache
goatee close-trimmed, pointed beard on chin
handlebar mustache long, full mustache turning up at ends
hirsute (*adj*) having facial hair, esp. rough or coarse

mustache facial hair between upper lip and nose; usu. worn by men
mustachioed (*adj*) wearing a mustache
muttonchops sideburns extending nearly to jaw line
peach fuzz *Slang.* very soft down of facial hair
sideburns beard growth along sides of face below ears; burnsides
stubble growth of beard or mustache shortly after shaving
Van Dyke close-trimmed, pointed beard
walrus mustache extremely long, bushy, drooping mustache covering upper lip
whiskers facial hair, esp. a beard

Grooming Aids and Processes

aftershave scented liquid tonic applied to face after shaving beard
antiperspirant chemical solution used to suppress perspiration, esp. under arms
astringent tonic lotion that tightens pores
atomizer small bottle for spraying cologne or water
balm ointment, lotion, or cream for soothing skin
balsam soothing oil; balm
bath immersion of body in hot water for cleanliness and relaxation
bath salts scented chemicals dissolved in bath water
beautician manager or employee of beauty parlor; hairdresser
beauty parlor business providing cosmetic treatments and hairstyling
bikini waxing removal of stray pubic hairs by coating with hot paraffin and stripping off wax when cooled
blow-dry (*vb*) dry and style hair with electric drying appliance that shoots hot air across hair
blusher rouge
bobby pin small, curved, metal or plastic hair fastener
brush bristles or hairs gathered into handle, used to apply cosmetics or groom hair
bubble bath sudsing, oily powder placed in bath water
clipper small cutting implement for hair and nails
cold cream mineral oil compound used to remove cosmetics and soothe skin
cologne fragrant liquid for scenting body
coloring dyes or tints for altering hair color
colorist hairdresser who alters color of all or some of one's hair with dyes or tints
comb stiff-toothed implement for grooming hair
compact small case holding face powder, puff, and mirror, sometimes also with rouge
conditioner creamy softening lotion applied to hair after shampoo; creme rinse
cosmetician professional trained in application of cosmetics
cosmetics paints, powders, ointments, and lotions used to beautify face and body; makeup; maquillage; war paint
cosmetology art, techniques, or profession of applying cosmetics
cotton swab cotton-tipped stick used to apply or remove cosmetics
creme rinse conditioner
curler small, usu. tubular framework used to set curl in wet hair
curling iron heated metal rod used to curl hair
curl relaxing chemical process that straightens naturally curly hair
dental floss waxed string used to clean between teeth
dentifrice tooth cleaning paste or powder
deodorant chemical solution that neutralizes perspiration odors
depilatory cream that removes facial or body hair
diffuser attachment to blow drier used to dry hair
eau de Cologne dilute solution of cologne
eau de parfum dilute solution of perfume
electric razor electrically powered shaving device, often with many small blades on movable head
emery board abrasive surface used to smooth and shape fingernails
eyebrow pencil colorant stick used to darken and define eyebrows
eyelash curler small, clamping tool for curling eyelashes
eyeliner paint in liquid or pencil form used to outline eyes
eyeliner tattoo permanent dying of eyelash line around eyes
eye shadow colored powder or cream applied to eyelid
eyewash soothing chemical solution used to refresh eyes
face powder cosmetic powder, often talc or cornstarch, applied to face to reduce shine and give matte finish
facial deep cleaning of pores of face
false eyelashes long lashes attached to eyelid
false nails long fingernails attached at natural cuticle
falsies artificial cosmetic aid, esp. breast pads
fragrance perfume or cologne for scenting body
grooming methods, practices, and techniques of creating and maintaining a neat, presentable appearance
hairdresser person trained in cutting, setting, and styling hair; hair stylist
hairdressing grooming of hair; shampoo or conditioner
hair drier appliance that blows hot air to dry hair
hair net fine mesh that holds hair in place
hair spray sticky aerosol used to hold hair in place
hair stylist hairdresser, esp. in cinema and advertising
highlighter cosmetic used to emphasize some feature or portion of face
highlights streaks of hair of different color or shade than rest of head of hair
ice bag small bag that holds ice, for applying to face or eyes
Kleenex *Trademark.* paper tissue
kohl black eyelining pencil

lanolin rich oil used to lubricate skin
lip gloss creamy cosmetic used to give shine to lips, often tinted
lipstick colorant cream for lips
makeover extensive series of beauty and cosmetic treatments
makeup cosmetics
manicure grooming of fingernails
mascara darkening cream for eyelashes
moisturizer cosmetic cream or lotion used to restore softness and moisture to skin
mousse foam or gel that keeps groomed hair in place
mouthwash chemical solution used to rinse and refresh mouth
mudpack facial treatment that uses drying mud
nail polish colored enamel for fingernails and toenails
orange stick small, pointed wooden stick used to groom fingernails
pancake thick cover-up cream for skin, esp. face
pastille breath-sweetening drop
pedicure grooming of toenails
perfume volatile scented oil extracted from flowers or prepared synthetically, applied as fragrance
piercing puncturing hole for earring, as in cheek, navel, or other part of face or body
polish remover solvent for removing old nail polish
pomade fragrant, sometimes medicated ointment for hair and scalp
pomander small ball or box of perfume
powder fine grains of soothing colorant applied to skin, often made from talc
powder puff soft applicator for powder
razor small, sharp blade used to remove body or facial hair
rinse temporary hair coloring
rollers plastic or metal tubes for curling hair
rouge reddening colorant for cheeks; blusher
safety razor handle with protective sheath for razor blade
set (*vb*) style hair while wet so as to retain shape when dry; (*n*) hair thus shaped
shampoo soap for hair, often scented and with various additives for health of hair
shaver razor unit
snood net for holding hair at back of head
sunscreen chemical lotion for preventing or retarding sunburn
swab small, flexible stick tipped in cotton for cleaning ears and applying makeup
talc talcum powder
talcum powder absorbent white powder used to refresh skin; talc
tattoo art and practice of marking the skin with indelible designs and legends by puncturing the skin and inserting pigments; any design or legend so produced
tinting altering natural hair color with dye or tint
tissue thin, soft paper sheet used to clean skin and apply or remove cosmetics
toilet general term for grooming aids and their use
toilet paper tissue paper, usu. in roll, used esp. to wipe anus after defecating
toiletries grooming aids
toilet water scented liquid
toothbrush small brush with handle, used to clean teeth
toothpaste dentifrice in soft, moist form
toothpick small, pointed stick used to clean between teeth
tooth powder dentifrice in dry, granular, gently abrasive form
tweezers small pincer tool used to grasp or remove hairs and other small particles
vent brush brush with air vents used in styling hair
waxing stripping away of body hair with hot wax
witch hazel astringent lotion
zinc oxide ointment creamy white paste for sun protection or soothing burns and rashes

PHYSICAL APPEARANCE

Aspects and Components of Appearance
Physical Attributes
Small/Large
Healthy/Sickly
Beautiful/Ugly

Aspects and Components of Appearance

air manifestation of some personal quality or emotion in one's appearance and bearing
appearance outward, physical look
aspect particular appearance or mien
aura impression given off of one's spiritual or emotional nature
bearing manner in which one stands, moves, and acts
body physical substance of a person; trunk as distinguished from limbs
body language gestures and mannerisms, both intended and subconscious, that communicate one's feelings
brow expression or mien, esp. on forehead
build muscular development and posture; form of one's body
bust torso between neck and waist, esp. woman's breasts
carriage posture and manner of carrying one's body
cleavage area between a woman's breasts
coloring complexion, natural skin tone
complexion color and texture of skin, esp. on face
condition state of physical health and fitness
conduct manner in which one behaves and carries oneself
constitution one's physical makeup, both inherited traits and acquired characteristics

countenance demeanor and expression, esp. on face as indication of feelings
demeanor outward manner, behavior toward others
deportment manner of carrying and conducting oneself; bearing
disposition prevailing mood and emotional makeup as revealed through expressions and actions
expression arrangement of facial features, body posture, and use of vocal intonation to manifest a particular feeling
extremities limbs, hands, and feet
face front of head including chin, mouth, nose, cheeks, eyes, ears, and forehead
features elements of face, esp. mouth, nose, and eyes
figure shape, musculature, and posture of body
form external appearance of body as distinct from face; figure
frame physique or figure, esp. underlying skeletal structure
gait manner of walking
gestures movements of hands and limbs and expressions revealed through these movements
girth size or measure around middle of torso
grin open, wide smile
grooming manner of caring for hygiene, hair, and body hair
hairline point on forehead above which hair growth occurs
hand terminal part of forelimb with five fingers used for manual operations and expressive gestures
height distance from bottom of feet to top of head when standing erect
image impression given off by facial expressions, bearing, posture, deportment, gestures, and voice
impression outward physical appearance
limbs arms and legs, ending in hands and feet; extremities
looks physical appearance and countenance, esp. attractiveness
manner distinct or characteristic air and bearing
mannerism characteristic gesture or peculiarity of conduct
mien expression of mood revealed through demeanor and bearing
nature essential character as shown through physical traits
pate crown or top of head, normally covered with hair
person general image or impression given off by physical appearance and manner
physique form and musculature of body; figure
posture position and bearing of body, esp. when standing erect
presence aura, impression, or sense of personality given off by physical appearance and manner
profile side view of face
proportions relation of parts of body to one another
skin smooth outer covering of body, forming complexion on face
smile facial expression, usu. upward curl of corners of mouth and brightening of eyes
stance posture, way of standing, esp. as expression of feeling
stature natural height in upright position
tic habitual spasmodic movement of facial muscles
tone tautness of musculature
torso trunk
traits form and expression of body parts and facial features
trunk central part of body to which limbs and head are attached; torso
walk posture and manner of moderate forward movement in upright position
weight relative measurement of one's mass

Physical Attributes

almond-eyed, androgynous, aquiline
bald, barefoot, blank, blind, blond, bowlegged, brachycephalic, bristling, brunette, buxom
chip-toothed, clubfooted, cross-legged, curled lip, curvaceous
dark, deadpan, deaf, dewy-eyed, doe-eyed, dolichocephalic, domed, downy
eagle-eyed, erect, exophthalmic
feline, flatfooted, flattened, flossy, fluffy, flushed, freckled, freckle-faced, full-mouthed, goggle-eyed
grimacing, grinning, gummy
hairy, hewn, hirsute, horny
knock-kneed
lambent, lanky, large, leathery, left-handed, life-size, limping, long-faced, loose-jointed, loose-limbed
microcephalic, mongoloid, mute
oblong, open-eyed
pigeon-toed, pinched, poker-faced, popeyed, pouty, puckered, pug-nosed, pursed
rawboned, red-headed, retroussé, right-handed, roundheaded, round-shouldered, rubicund
saurian, scowling, setaceous, sharp-nosed, shorn, shovel-nosed, sinewy, sinuous, skinhead, slanted, slant-eyed, sloe-eyed, slow-footed, smirking, sneering, snub-nosed, speckled, spindle-legged, splayfooted, squinty, straight-faced, stubbly, sulky, swarthy, swivel-hipped
taliped, throaty, toothy
vacuous, varicose veined
wavy, wide-eyed, widemouthed

Small/Large

SMALL, SHORT, OR THIN

bantam, bareboned, bony
compact
dainty, diminutive, dinky, dwarfish
elfin

flat-chested
gangling, gawky
half pint
infinitesimal, insubstantial, itsy-bitsy, itty-bitty
lanky, lean, Lilliputian, little
meager, measly, micro, microscopic, midget, miniature, minimal, minute
narrow, negligible, nipped
peewee, petite, puny, pygmy
reedlike, reedy, runty
sawed-off, scant, scanty, scarce, scraggy, scrawny, scrubby, short, shrimpy, shriveled, shrunken, sinewy, skinny, slender, slight, slim, slinky, small, spindly, spiny, squat, stringbean, stringy, stubby, stumpy, stunted
teensy-weensy, teeny, teeny-weeny, thin, tiny
undersized, underweight
wasp-waisted, wee, weedy, weeny, willowy, wiry, wispy

LARGE, TALL, OR FAT

adipose, amazon, ample
barrel-chested, beefy, behemoth, big, big-bellied, boundless, bovine, brawny, broad, broad of beam, Brobdingnagian, brutish, bulky, bull-necked, burly, buxom
capacious, chubby, chunky, clumpish, colossal, considerable, corpulent, cumbersome, Cyclopean
distended, dumpy
elephantine, elongated, embonpoint, endomorphic, enormous
fat, fleshy, fubsy, full, full-grown
gargantuan, generous, giant, gigantic, goliath, gross
heavy, hefty, herculean, huge, hulking, hunky, husky
immeasurable, immense, imposing
jumbo, Junoesque
large, leggy, leviathan, limitless, long, long-legged, long-limbed, lumbering, lumpish
mammoth, massive, mastodonic, meaty, mesomorphic, mighty, monumental, musclebound
obese, overblown, overdeveloped, overgrown, oversized, overstuffed, overweight
paunchy, plump, podgy, ponderous, porcine, portly, potbellied, prodigious, pudgy, pursy
rangy, roly-poly, rotund
sizable, squat, squdgy, stacked, stocky, stout, strapping, substantial, swollen
tall, thick, thickset, titanic, top-heavy, towering, tremendous, tubby
unwieldy
voluminous, voluptuous
wide
zaftig

Healthy/Sickly

HEALTHY, FIT, BRIGHT, OR STRONG

able-bodied, agile
beaming, blooming, blushing, bouncing, bright, bright-eyed, bursting, bushy-tailed
chipper, clean, clear-eyed
dexterous
elastic, exercised
fit, fit as a fiddle, florid, flush
glossy, glowing
hale, hardy, healthful, healthy, hearty
in fine fettle, in shape, in the pink
light-footed, limber, lissome, lithe, lively, lusty
mighty, muscular
peppy, perky, pink-cheeked, pliable
radiant, red, ripe, robust, rosy, rosy-cheeked, rubicund, ruddy, rugged
scrubbed, shapely, shining, shiny, shipshape, sinuous, sleek, sound, spare, sparkling, spry, square-shouldered, stalwart, staunch, steady, stout, strapping, streamlined, strong, sturdy, sunny, supple, svelte
toned, trim, twenty-twenty, twinkling
vigorous, vital
well-fed, wholesome
youthful

SICKLY, OUT OF SHAPE, DULL, OR WEAK

aged, ailing, amputee, anemic, attenuated
bedridden, bent, blanched, bleary-eyed, blind, bloated, bloodshot
cadaverous, chalky, corpselike, crippled
debilitated, decrepit, delicate, disabled, doddering, droopy, dull
emaciated, enfeebled, etiolated
faint, farsighted, feeble, feverish, flabby, flaccid, flimsy, flushed, fossilized, fragile, frail
gaunt, glabrous, glassy-eyed
haggard, hollow-eyed, humpbacked
ill, incontinent, infirm
lame, limp, lumpish, lurid
mute, myopic
nearsighted
obese, off-color, out of shape, out of whack, overweight
pale, pallid, palsied, paltry, peaked, peg-legged, phthisic, pigeon-toed, pinched, pursy
ravaged, rheumy, rickety, rugose, run-down
scorbutic, shaky, shriveled, shrunken, sick, sickly, skeletal, skinny, slack, soft, sparse, spindle-legged, starved, stone-blind, stone-deaf, strabismic, sunken, swollen
tabetic, tottering, tubercular
underfed, undernourished, underweight
walleyed, wan, washed-out, wasted, waxen, waxy, weak, web-footed, wispy, withered, wizened, wraithlike, wrinkled

Beautiful/Ugly

Beautiful, attractive, or well-formed

adorable, agreeable, alluring, angelic, appealing, appetizing, attractive
beaming, beauteous, beautiful, becoming, beguiling, bewitching, bonny, breathtaking, bright, built
callipygian, captivating, catching, charismatic, charming, classic, clear, clear-eyed, come-hither, comely, coquettish, curvaceous, cute
dainty, dashing, delectable, delicate, delicious, delightful, desirable, devastating, dimpled, divine, doll-like
enchanting, engaging, enticing, entrancing, enviable, exotic, exquisite, eye-catching
fair, fancy, fascinating, fetching, fine, flawless
glamorous, glorious, glossy, good-looking, gorgeous, graceful, great-looking
handsome, hot, hunky, hypnotic
immaculate, intoxicating, intriguing, inviting, irresistible
killer
light, lovable, lovely, luscious, lustrous
magnetic, magnificent, mignon, moon-eyed, mouth-watering
nifty
ornamental
perfect, photogenic, picturesque, pleasing, precious, prepossessing, pretty, provocative
redolent, regular, resplendent
scrumptious, sculptured, seductive, sensuous, sexy, shapely, showy, sightly, silky, slick, smiling, spellbinding, spotless, stacked, statuesque, streamlined, striking, stunning, sublime, sumptuous, symmetrical
taking, tantalizing, tasty, tempting, titillating, toylike
voluptuous
well-built, well-conditioned, well-favored, well-formed, well-groomed, well-made, well-proportioned, well-set, winning, winsome

Ugly, unattractive, or malformed

angular, askew, awful, awkward
bandy-legged, beetle-browed, bent, blemished, blimpish, bloated, blowzy, blubbery, bovine, bucktoothed, bug-eyed
cadaverous, chalky, clammy, cleft, clumsy, crippled, crooked, cross-eyed, cumbersome
defaced, deformed, disfigured, disgusting, disheveled, droopy, dumpy
elephantine, emaciated
farinaceous, fat, foul, frightful, frowzy, fubsy
gap-toothed, gawky, geeky, ghastly, gnarled, goggle-eyed, graceless, grim-faced, grimy, grisly, grizzled, grotesque, grubby, gruesome, grungy
halt, harelipped, hatchet-faced, heavy-footed, hideous, homely, horrent, horrible, hulking, hunched
ill-formed, ill-made, irregular
jagged
leprous, loathsome, lopsided, lumpish
macabre, malformed, malodorous, mangy, marred, mealy, misshapen, moldering, monstrous, musty
offensive, oleaginous
pasty, pendulous, pitted, plain, pocked, ponderous, porcine, putrescent, putrid
ragged, repellent, repugnant, repulsive, revolting, rickety, rumpled, rumply, runty
sallow, scabby, scabrous, scaly, sclerotic, scorbutic, scraggy, scrawny, scrofulous, scruffy, shabby, shaggy, shapeless, sickening, simian, skew-eyed, sneering, splotchy, spoiled, spongy, squat, squinched, stooped, straggly, stumpy, stunted, sunken, swaybacked, swollen
tabescent, terrible, tubercular
ugly, unappealing, unattractive, ungainly, unprepossessing, unsavory, unsightly, unwieldy
walleyed, washed-out, wasted, waxen, withered

Chapter Two

Living Things

BIOLOGY

Branches and Disciplines
Genetics, Heredity, and Evolution
Cell Structure and Function
Physiology
Environment, Ecology, and Animal Behavior
Reproduction and Development
Tools and Techniques
Taxonomy

Branches and Disciplines

anatomy study of structures of organisms
bacteriology study of bacteria
behaviorism study of interaction between organism and organism or organism and environment
biochemistry study of chemical processes necessary to sustain life
biology science that deals with the morphology, physiology, origin, and distribution of living organisms
biometry use of statistical techniques in biology
bionics design of systems that duplicate living organisms
biophysics use of principles and techniques of physics to study biological phenomena
biotechnology recombinant DNA, genetic engineering, cloning, and related applications of genetic research
botany science of organisms of Kingdom Plantae, dealing with life, structure, growth, and classification of plants
bryology branch of botany dealing with mosses and other bryophytes
cell biology study of cell organelles, their functions and interactions
comparative anatomy study of similar structures among organisms
conchology study of shells
cytology study of structure and functions of cells
dendrology study of trees and woody plants, esp. their taxonomy
developmental biology embryology
ecology study of relationships and balance between organisms and their environment
embryology study of development of organism from meiosis to birth; developmental biology
endocrinology study of endocrine glands and hormonal control
entomology study of insects
environmental physiology study of adaptations of living things to environmental conditions
enzymology study of structure and catalytic properties of enzymes
epidemiology study of prevalence and spread of disease in a population
ethology study of animal behavior
evolution study of origin of species as process of development from earlier forms
exobiology study of life beyond Earth's atmosphere
genetics study of heredity
hematology study of blood
herpetology study of reptiles and amphibians
histology study of tissues
ichthyology study of fish
immunology study of how body protects itself from invading organisms and chemicals
life science any of a group of sciences dealing with living creatures and their life processes, esp. biology, zoology, and botany
limnology study of freshwater lakes, ponds, and streams as discrete ecosystems
malacology study of mollusks
mammalogy study of mammals
microbiology study of microscopic organisms and agents, such as bacteria, protists, and viruses
molecular biology study of complex chemistry of biological macromolecules, esp. those involved in genetics
morphology study of physical forms of living things
mycology study of fungi
natural history biology, physiology, origin, and distribution of living things as seen through perspective of time
neurobiology study of nervous systems of animals
nutrition study of foods and how they are used by body
ornithology study of birds
paleontology study of fossil record of living things
phycology study of algae
physiology study of functions and vital processes of living organisms and their parts
phytology former term for botany
protozoology study of microscopic, usu. single-celled, protozoans
systematics study of kinds, diversity, and relationships of living things
taxonomy classification of living things
zoology science of organisms of Kingdom Animalia, dealing with life, structure, growth, and classification of animals

Genetics, Heredity, and Evolution

abiogenesis discredited theory that living organisms can develop by spontaneous generation from inanimate material
adaptation any feature that increases fitness of organism to its environment; process of developing or altering these features by natural selection
adenine one of four nitrogenous bases used to carry genetic information in nucleotides of DNA and RNA
albino organism lacking normal coloration, usu. due to genetic factors
allele form that gene may take at one locus
ameba unicellular, microscopic protist that reproduces by fission

analogy resemblance in structure or function due to evolutionary adaptation rather than common ancestry
anaphase stage in meiosis or mitosis in which chromatids separate and move to opposite poles
autosome any chromosome not carrying sex information
bacteriophage virus that attacks bacteria only, used extensively in genetic research
biogenesis principle that living organisms originate from other living organisms similar to themselves
capsid protein coat surrounding nucleic acid core of virus
character displacement state in which two related species become increasingly different in areas where both occur
chromatid individual strand of double-stranded chromosome in mitosis
chromatin stainable mass of material in nucleus that realigns into chromosomes during cell division
chromosome distinct body in nucleus that appears during cell division, composed of DNA and protein and containing genes
cline pattern of gradual change in character across species' geographic range
clone strain of genetically identical cells; genetically identical organism produced from cells of another
convergence two related species becoming increasingly similar over time
crossing over exchange of segments of chromosomal material between two strands of a tetrad during prophase of meiosis
cytosine one of four nitrogenous bases used to carry genetic information in nucleotides of DNA and RNA
Darwinism Charles Darwin's theory of evolution by variation and natural selection
deoxyribonucleic acid DNA
diploid number chromosome number equal to twice that found in gametes; found in somatic cells
divergence two related species becoming increasingly different over time
DNA deoxyribonucleic acid; nucleic acid that carries encoded message of gene, comprised of double helix ladder of paired nitrogenous bases bonded to phosphate group and deoxyribose sugar
dominant trait allele whose phenotypic trait dominates or prevents expression of recessive traits
double helix intertwining chains of nucleic acid linked by hydrogen bonds that constitutes basic structure of DNA
ecotype locally adapted variant of a species, genetically different from other ecotypes of that species
endemic species found only in limited geographic area
evolution development of species or organism from primitive state to present or specialized state
exon section of DNA that contains information that codes for protein product of gene
extinction dying out of species or population
fitness measure of evolutionary success in terms of contribution to next generation
fossil remains of an organism long dead or direct evidence of it, such as its tracks, usu. preserved in rock
fossil record succession of fossilized living forms, usu. growing more complex, serving as evidence of macroevolution
gene segment of DNA responsible for transmitting hereditary traits
gene pool all genetic variability within a population
genetic code nucleotide triplet sequences in DNA and RNA that encode for protein synthesis
genetic counseling advising people of the probability of their having children with hereditary abnormalities
genetic drift changes in gene distribution due to random effects only
genetic engineering incorporation of new genes into an organism to alter it
genetic isolation absence of genetic exchange between populations due to geographical separation or mechanisms of behavior, anatomy, or physiology that prevent reproduction
genetic map diagram of gene locations on chromosome
genetic recombination change in gene combinations of offspring from that of parents
genetics study of heredity and similarities or differences between related organisms
genome one complete haploid set of chromosomes and their genes for an organism, containing all its inheritable traits
genotype genetic makeup of organism or cell
geographic range area inhabited by population
guanine one of four nitrogenous bases used to carry genetic information in nucleotides of DNA and RNA
haploid (*adj*) possessing only one set of chromosomes, in gametes
heredity transmission of genetic information from generation to generation
heterozygote organism carrying different alleles for the same trait
homologs members of chromosome pair carrying corresponding genes
homology similarity based on common descent that may or may not reflect functional similarity
hybrid offspring from parents of two different species
inbreeding mating of kin
isolation prevention of interbreeding between populations due to factors such as geography or behavior
karyotype form, size, and number of chromosomes of an organism: in humans, forty-six chromosomes, including twenty-two pairs of autosomes and two sex chromosomes
Lamarckism inheritance of acquired characteristics, esp. theory that environmental change causes

structural changes in organisms that are inherited by offspring

law of dominance Gregor Mendel's rule that in certain traits, one allele in a heterozygote can be phenotypically expressed in preference to its alternate

law of independent assortment principle that unlinked genes segregate independently

law of segregation principle that alleles for a trait segregate independently during meiosis

life distinguishing characteristics of organisms, esp. growth capacity, metabolism, reproduction, and adaptation to environment

linkage tendency of genes located near each other on chromosomes to be inherited together

living things organisms distinguished from dead inorganic objects by basic characteristics of life: growth, metabolism, reproduction, and adaptability to environment

locus position of allele on chromosome

macroevolution long-term evolutionary phenomena occurring above level of species

meiosis cell division in which the diploid chromosome number is reduced to the haploid as part of process of gamete formation

Mendel's laws first law: alleles segregate in meiosis; second law: unlinked genes assort independently

messenger RNA mRNA; single strand of RNA that carries genetic information from DNA to ribosome

microevolution small-scale, rapidly occurring evolutionary phenomena in a single species

modern synthesis merging of Darwinism and Mendelian genetics

mRNA messenger RNA

multiple alleles set of genes potentially occurring at one locus

mutagen substance or condition that increases mutation rate

mutation sudden inheritable change to new allelic form of gene

natural selection process that results in survival of those organisms best suited to their environment, based on inherited favorable variations that increase from generation to generation; selection

neo-Darwinism modern synthesis of Darwinism and Mendelian genetics

nucleic acids main component of DNA and RNA, whose arrangement carries genetic code

nucleoprotein protein associated with nucleic acids in nucleus of living cells

nucleotide structural segment of nucleic acid chain, composed of phosphate group, five-carbon sugar, and purine or pyrimidine base

organism any discrete life form belonging to one of the five kingdoms

phage bacteriophage

phenotype observable characteristics of an organism

phyletic group species related to each other through common descent

phylogeny evolutionary history of taxonomic group

polymorphism occurrence in population of two or more distinct forms with no intermediate forms

population interbreeding group of organisms

population genetics study of gene movement and variation among interbreeding organisms

prophase early stage in nuclear division during which chromosomes move toward equator of spindle

protein synthesis transfer of encoded genetic information in DNA from nucleotides to amino acid sequence through initiation, elongation, and termination

purine either adenine or guanine

pyrimidine cytosine, thymine, or uracil

recessive trait allele whose phenotype is not expressed in heterozygous organism

recombinant DNA DNA in which half of DNA double helix has been spliced from each of two different organisms to form new genetic code

recombination change of gene groupings from generation to generation due to independent assortment and crossing over

replication method by which nucleic acids duplicate themselves

ribonucleic acid RNA; usu. single-stranded nucleic acid, characterized by nitrogenous bases bonded to phosphate group and ribose sugar, that acts as genetic material in viruses and as transcriber of genetic information in other cells

RNA ribonucleic acid

segregation assortment of paired alleles into separate gametes

selection natural selection

sex chromosomes pair of chromosomes that determines sex and sex-linked characteristics of organism

sex-linked characteristic any trait whose alleles are found on sex chromosomes

sexual dimorphism distinct differences between male and female in addition to primary sex characteristics

speciation process of genetic diversification through which new species arise by natural selection

splicing separating two halves of DNA double helix and recombining each with strip from another organism

survival of the fittest process of Darwinian natural selection

sympatry populations, esp. species, with geographic ranges that overlap at least in part

telophase final stage of mitosis and meiosis, in which chromosomes form two new nuclei

tetrad four chromatids of pair of replicated homologous chromosomes in prophase of meiosis

thymine one of four nitrogenous bases used to carry genetic information in nucleotides of DNA and RNA

transcription formation of RNA chain complementary to a DNA chain

transduction process in which genetic information in cellular DNA is transferred from one host cell to another by viruses or other filterable agents
transfer RNA tRNA; RNA that carries specific amino acids to messenger RNA
transformation genetic change induced by incorporation of DNA from one bacterial cell into another
tRNA transfer RNA
uracil one of four nitrogenous bases used to carry genetic information in nucleotides of DNA and RNA
variation chance differences among individual organisms, some of them inheritable, that interact with environment to determine which individuals will survive and reproduce
Watson-Crick model double helix structure of DNA, first posited in 1953
X chromosome sex chromosome carrying female traits in mammals
Y chromosome sex chromosome carrying male traits in mammals

Cell Structure and Function

active transport energy-requiring, carrier-mediated transport system in which molecules can be moved across cell membrane against electrochemical gradient
adenosine diphosphate ADP; compound formed by hydrolysis of ATP
adenosine triphosphate ATP; major molecule that accepts energy from nutrients and donates this energy to cell functions
ADP adenosine diphosphate
aerobic (*adj*) living, growing, or occurring in the presence of oxygen
agonist agent that produces a response that enhances the response of another agent
anaerobic (*adj*) living, growing, or occurring in the absence of oxygen
antagonist molecule that competes for binding site with chemical messenger but does not trigger cell's response
ATP adenosine triphosphate
carrier integral membrane protein that combines with specific molecules, enabling them to pass through membrane
catabolism fragmentation of molecule into smaller parts
cell basic structural and functional unit of living organisms; smallest unit into which living thing can be divided and retain characteristics associated with life
cell division process by which cellular material is divided between two new cells, either by meiosis or mitosis
centrioles two small bodies composed of nine fused sets of microtubules, located in cell cytoplasm, which participate in nuclear and cell division
channel passage formed by integral membrane proteins through which certain small-diameter molecules and ions diffuse across membrane
chemosynthesis synthesis of organic material within an organism in which chemical reactions serve as energy source
chloroplast chlorophyll-containing plastid surrounded by two membranes and having complex internal membrane system in which photosynthesis takes place
cilia hairlike projections from surface of specialized epithelial cells that sweep back and forth to propel material along cell surface
citric acid cycle Krebs cycle
creatine phosphate molecule used to store energy in muscle cells, quickly converted to ATP for energy
creatinine waste product derived from muscle creatine
cyclic AMP cAMP; cylic form of adenosine monophosphate that serves as second messenger for many nonsteroid hormones and neurotransmitters
cytokinesis stage of cell division following mitosis, in which cytoplasm divides to form two new cells
cytoplasm entire contents of cell excluding nucleus
cytoskeleton rodlike filaments of various sizes in cytoplasm of most cells, associated with cell shape and movement
diffusion movement of molecules by random motion from region of higher to one of lower concentration
ECF extracellular fluid
endoplasmic reticulum ER; organelle in cytoplasm made up of interconnected network of branched tubules and flattened sacs that assembles or modifies proteins
eosinophil leukocyte involved with allergic responses and destruction of parasitic worms
epithelial cells cells forming tissue that covers body surfaces, lines body cavities, and comprises most glands
ER endoplasmic reticulum
erythrocyte enucleated cell that contains hemoglobin for transport of gases by blood; red blood cell
eukaryote any cell with membrane-bound nucleus containing genetic material in chromosomes and dividing by mitosis or meiosis, including all life forms except bacteria, blue-green algae, and some primitive organisms
extracellular fluid ECF; fluid outside cells that forms environment in which cells live; interstitial fluid and plasma
facilitated diffusion transport system that moves molecules from high to low concentration across membrane until concentrations on both sides of membrane are equal
flagella threadlike organelles used for locomotion and feeding by some eukaryotic organisms
glial cell cell that supports and nourishes neurons
Golgi apparatus cell organelle of membranes and vesicles near nucleus that processes and packages newly synthesized proteins for other organelles or secretion

granulocyte white blood cell containing granules in cytoplasm
histocompatibility antigens antigenic protein molecules on surface of nucleated cells
hypertonic solution fluid whose osmolarity exceeds that of plasma
hypotonic solution fluid whose osmolarity is less than that of plasma
interphase stage between two meiotic or mitotic cycles
interstitial fluid cells between germinal cells in reproductive organs
isotonic solution fluid with same osmolarity as plasma
Krebs cycle stage of cellular respiration and energy metabolism that occurs in mitochondria; citric acid cycle; tricarboxylic acid cycle
leukocyte cell involved with immune response; white blood cell
lymphocyte agranular white blood cell
lysosome membrane-enclosed organelle in which digestive enzymes are confined
macrophage large white blood cell that engulfs invaders such as bacteria
mast cell connective tissue cell containing heparin and histamine
matrix connective tissue ground substance
megakaryocyte large bone marrow cell that produces platelets
meiosis cell division in which diploid chromosome number is reduced to haploid and received by gametes
membrane plasma membrane
memory cell agent of lasting immunity; long-lived lymphocyte that rapidly initiates immune response to previously encountered antigen
microphage neutrophil, esp. one containing granulocytes
mitochondria organelles involved in cellular respiration and breakdown of energy into small units convenient for most cellular processes
mitosis cell division that forms two identical cells with original number of chromosomes
monocyte agranulocytic white blood cell that matures into macrophage
myofibrils contractile elements of muscle fiber
NAD nicotinamide adenine dinucleotide
neutrophil most common white blood cell, which protects body against infection
nicotinamide adenine dinucleotide NAD; coenzyme that accepts hydrogen and transfers it to cytochrome B
nucleolus dense body in eukaryotic nucleus that is site of ribosomal RNA production
nucleus control center for all cellular activities
organelles membrane-bound compartments, nonmembranous particles, and filamentous structures that perform specialized functions and constitute internal structure of cells
osmosis diffusion of water across semipermeable membrane
osmotic pressure difference of solute concentrations on either side of semipermeable membrane
osteoblast bone-forming cell
parietal cells acid-secreting cells of stomach lining
pathway sequence of enzyme-catalyzed reactions by which energy-yielding substance is catabolized by protoplasm
phagocytosis intake of solid particle by cell
photosynthesis process by which chlorophyll in green plant produces organic compounds from radiant light energy
pili rigid, cylindrical rods, comparable to flagella, that attach some prokaryotic bacteria to food sources
plasma cell antibody-producing cell cloned from B cell
plasma membrane outer layer of cell that separates it from environment; membrane
plastid any of various membrane-bound organelles in plants and algae that store starch, contain pigment, or are chlorophyll-containing site of photosynthesis
platelet protoplasmic blood cell fragment involved in clotting
polymorphonuclear granulocytes white blood cells with variable nuclei
prokaryote any cell that lacks distinct membrane-bound nucleus and organelles in its cytoplasm, including bacteria and blue-green algae
red blood cell erythrocyte
respiration process that releases energy by breakdown of complex organic compound
Rhesus factor Rh factor
Rh factor group of antigens that may (Rh+) or may not (Rh-) be present on plasma membranes of erythrocytes; Rhesus factor
ribosome small cytoplasmic organelle and site of protein synthesis
Schwann cells cells forming neurilemma sheath around peripheral nerves
semipermeable membrane membrane that allows only certain substances to pass through
spindle assembly of microtubules responsible for separating sister chromatids during mitosis
suppressor T cell T cell capable of inhibiting activity of B cells and other T cells
T cell lymphocyte originating in thymus gland, involved in cellular immunity; T lymphocyte
T lymphocyte T cell
transport molecule protein molecule involved in active transport and facilitated diffusion
tricarboxylic acid cycle Krebs cycle
vacuole membranous cavity within protoplasm, usu. containing watery fluid
vesicle intracellular membrane-bound sac that is much smaller than a vacuole
white blood cell leukocyte

Physiology

abscess microbes, leukocytes, and liquefied tissue debris walled off by fibroblasts and collagen
absorption passage of water or dissolved substance, esp. nutrient materials, into cell, blood, tissue, or organism
absorptive state period during which nutrients are entering bloodstream from gastrointestinal tract

accommodation adjustment of eye for viewing at various distances by changing shape of lens
acetylcholine ACh; a neurotransmitter
acidosis abnormal state of reduced alkalinity of blood and tissues
ACTH adrenocorticotropic hormone
actin protein located in thin filaments of muscle that, in conjunction with myosin, contracts muscle
action potential electrical signal propagated over long distance by nerve and muscle cells
adaptation decrease in frequency of action potentials fired by neuron despite stimulus of constant magnitude
ADH antidiuretic hormone
adipose fat in connective tissue
adrenaline epinephrine
adrenocorticotropic hormone ACTH; polypeptide secreted by anterior pituitary that stimulates adrenal cortex to secrete cortisol
afferent neuron neuron that transmits impulses to central nervous system and brain
afferent pathway component of reflex arc that transmits information from receptor to integrating center
albumin most abundant protein found in blood plasma
alpha rhythm prominent 8-13 Hz oscillation in EEG of awake, relaxed adult with closed eyes
amino acid any of twenty-five organic acids containing an amino group that link together into polypeptide chains to form the proteins required for life, ten of which cannot be synthesized by the body and must be consumed
amylase enzyme that breaks down starch into disaccharides
anabolism constructive metabolism in which food is changed into living tissue
androgen male sex hormone
antibody protein secreted by plasma cells capable of combining with specific antigen that stimulated its production
antidiuretic hormone ADH; peptide hormone synthesized in hypothalamus and released from posterior pituitary, causing retention of more water in body
antihistamine chemical that blocks action of histamine
antivenin antidote to venom produced by venomous animal
atrophy wasting away of muscle or organ, esp. from disuse
bacteria *pl., sing.* bacterium; ubiquitous, unicellular organisms appearing singly or in chains in spherical, spiral, or rod-shaped form
baroreceptor neural receptor sensitive to pressure and rate of change in pressure; stretch receptor
basal *(adj)* at resting level
basal metabolic rate BMR; metabolic rate when subject is awake but at mental and physical rest, at a comfortable temperature, and without food for at least twelve hours
beta rhythm low, fast oscillations in EEG pattern of alert, awake adult who is actively paying attention or thinking
bile greenish liver secretion that is stored in gallbladder until released to emulsify fats in small intestine
bile salts steroid molecules in bile that promote solubilization and digestion of fats
bilirubin yellow substance that results from breakdown of red blood cells, excreted as component of bile
biological clock internal factors that control innate body rhythms without external stimulation
bioluminescence emission of light produced by living organism
biosynthesis formation of organic compounds from elements or simple compounds by living organisms
blocking antibody antibody whose production is induced by cancer cells or tissue transplants and that blocks the killing of those cells by cytotoxic T cells
blood liquid that serves as an exchange medium between external environment and cells of organism
blood-brain barrier group of anatomical barriers and transport systems that tightly controls types of substances entering extracellular space of brain
blood clot network of fibers and other blood parts that covers wound and prevents additional blood loss
blood pressure pressure exerted by blood on walls of vessels
blood sugar glucose
blood types classification of blood by presence of A, B, O, or AB antigens on plasma membranes of erythrocytes, or presence of anti-A or anti-B antibodies in plasma
BMR basal metabolic rate
breathing movement of air in and out of lungs
carbohydrate any of various organic saccharide sugars, starches, and celluloses that supply energy to body when consumed
cardiac output volume of blood pumped by either ventricle per minute
catabolism destructive metabolism in which living tissue is changed into energy and waste products
central thermoreceptors temperature sensors located in hypothalamus, spinal cord, and internal organs
chemoreceptors afferent nerve endings or associated sensory cells that respond to concentrations of certain chemicals
chemotaxis orientation and movement of cells in specific direction in response to chemical stimulus
chitin tough, horny substance that forms most of outer covering of insects and crustaceans
cholesterol steroid molecule that is precursor of steroid hormones and bile salts, component of plasma membranes, and present in fat and blood
cholinergic *(adj)* pertaining to or acting like acetylcholine
chyme solution of partially digested food in lumen of stomach and intestines

climacteric physical and emotional changes as sexual maturity gives way to cessation of reproductive function in female and testosterone decrease in male
closed circulatory system system in which blood is enclosed in vessels and does not directly bathe organs
coenzyme nonprotein organic molecule that temporarily joins with enzyme during reaction, serves as a carrier molecule, is not consumed in reaction, and can be reused until degraded
collagen extremely strong fibrous protein that functions as structural element in connective tissue, tendons, and ligaments
colloid large molecule, such as plasma protein, to which capillaries are relatively impermeable
command neuron neuron whose activity initiates a series of neural events that result in a voluntary action
compensatory growth type of regeneration present in many organs after tissue damage
complement set of enzymes in bloodstream that work with antibodies to attack foreign cells and bacteria
complex carbohydrate polysaccharide
conducting system network of cardiac muscle fibers specialized to conduct electrical activity to different areas of heart
cone one of two major photoreceptor types in retina that give rise to color vision
contractility force of contraction that is independent of fiber length
contraction tension-generating process of a muscle
core temperature temperature inside of body
corticotropin releasing hormone CRH; hormone produced in hypothalamus that stimulates ACTH secretion by anterior pituitary
cortisol steroid hormone secreted by adrenal cortex that regulates organic metabolism by converting fats and proteins to glucose
cortisone steroid hormone secreted by adrenal cortex that counteracts pain and swelling
CRH corticotropin releasing hormone
dark adaptation improvement in sensitivity of vision after one is in darkness for some time
dead space area of respiratory system in which very little or no respiration occurs
defecation expulsion of feces from rectum
diastole period of cardiac cycle in which ventricles are not contracting
diastolic pressure minimum blood pressure during cardiac cycle
digestion process of breaking down large particles and high-molecular weight substances into small molecules
disaccharide carbohydrate molecule consisting of two covalently bonded monosaccharides
diuretic substance that inhibits fluid reabsorption in kidney, causing increase in excreted urine
dominant hemisphere cerebral hemisphere that controls hand used most frequently for intricate tasks
dopamine catecholamine neurotransmitter, precursor of epinephrine and norepinephrine
ectopic focus region of heart other than sinoatrial node that assumes role of cardiac pacemaker
edema accumulation of fluid in interstitial space
EDV end-diastolic volume
effector cell or tissue whose change in activity constitutes response to stimulus
efferent neuron neuron that carries information away from central nervous system to postganglionic neurons, muscles, or gland cells
electrolyte substance that ionizes in solution and conducts electric current
embolus mass of matter that obstructs blood flow
end-diastolic volume EDV; amount of blood in heart just prior to systole
endocrine gland ductless organ that synthesizes hormones and releases them directly into bloodstream
endorphin neurotransmitter that exhibits painkilling activity
endoskeleton internal bony or cartilaginous supporting structure of vertebrates
end-plate potential EPP; excitatory change in voltage across motor end plate of muscle cell membrane
end-systolic volume ESV; amount of blood remaining in ventricle after ejection
enzyme organic catalyst for physiological activity not used up in reaction
epinephrine hormone released by adrenal medulla that elevates blood sugar and initiates fight-or-flight response; adrenaline
EPP end-plate potential
equilibrium potential millivolts required to oppose movement caused by concentration gradient of specific ion
essential amino acids ten amino acids that cannot be synthesized in body and must be derived from diet
essential nutrients substances necessary for normal body function that cannot be synthesized by body
ESV end-systolic volume
excretion loss of substance through urine, feces, or other material expelled from body
exocrine gland gland that secretes products through duct
exoskeleton hard external supporting structure of invertebrates, such as shell of crustacean
expiration movement of air out of lungs
extension straightening of flexed limb
fat any of various mixtures of solid or semisolid triglycerides in adipose tissue, insoluble in water
fatty acid organic compound whose carbon chain ends in a carboxyl group
feces digestive waste products
feedback change in quantity of substance that initiates either release or suppression of release of that substance
fermentation conversion of complex carbohydrates or other organic substances into other chemicals by enzyme action

fever abnormal increase of body temperature
fibrillation lack of coordination in contraction of muscle fibers
fibrin insoluble protein formed during clotting
fight-or-flight response adrenal-activated mobilization of body for extraordinary exertion
filtration passing of fluid through membrane under pressure
flexion bending of limb at joint
flexion reflex contraction of flexor muscle; withdrawal reflex
flexor muscle muscle that causes bending at joint by contraction
folic acid vitamin in B complex
GABA gamma-aminobutyric acid
gamma-aminobutyric acid GABA; inhibitory neurotransmitter of central nervous system
gamma globulin IgG; globular protein antibody in plasma; most abundant class of plasma antibodies
globulin protein insoluble in water; plasma protein complex comprised mainly of globulins
glucocorticoid adrenal cortex hormone that effects salt and water metabolism and stimulates conversion of noncarbohydrates to carbohydrates
glucose monosaccharide six-carbon sugar in blood; blood sugar
glycerol three-carbon alcohol derived from fats
glycine simplest amino acid, present in most proteins
glycogen white polysaccharide sugar, derived from glucose, that is principal form in which carbohydrate is stored in tissue
Golgi tendon organs sensory nerve fibers that monitor tension between tendons and muscle cells
Hb hemoglobin
HDL high-density lipoprotein
hematocrit percentage of total blood volume made up of blood cells
heme iron-containing pigment
hemoglobin Hb; iron-containing protein that carries oxygen in red blood cells and gives them red color
hemostasis stoppage of bleeding
high-density lipoprotein HDL; lipid-protein aggregate with low proportion of lipid or cholesterol that removes cholesterol from arteries
histamine amine derived from amino acid histidine that is released in allergic reaction, causing dilation of blood vessels and lowering of blood pressure
histone protein that is integral to chromosome structure
homeostasis maintenance of constant internal environment
hormone chemical agent usu. released by ductless gland that has regulatory effect on functions in other parts of body
hydrochloric acid acid secreted by stomach during digestion
hydrolysis splitting of molecules by addition of water
hydrostatic pressure pressure exerted by a fluid
hyperemia increased blood flow
hypersensitivity allergic reaction
hypertrophy increase in size of cells, tissues, or organ
Ig immunoglobulin
IgG gamma globulin
immune responses body's defense reaction through dual modes of antibody and cellular response
immunity resistance to specific disease
immunoglobulin Ig; any of five classes of antibodies: IgG, IgM, IgA, IgD, and IgE
inspiration taking of air into lungs
insulin pancreatic hormone that regulates blood sugar level
interferon molecule that inhibits viral replication in cells
internuncial neuron nerve cell connecting sensory and motor neurons in brain and spinal cord
intrinsic factor glycoprotein secreted by stomach and required for absorption of vitamin B_{12}
ischemia reduced blood supply to organ or tissue
isometric contraction increase of force in muscle whose length does not change
isotonic contraction development of force that remains the same during shortening of muscle
ketone product of lipid metabolism characterized by CO group
kinesthesia sensation of position and movement of limbs
lactase enzyme that cleaves lactose into glucose and galactose
lactic acid three-carbon breakdown product of glucose
latent period elapsed time between stimulus and response
LDL low-density lipoprotein
lecithin phospholipid in nerve tissue and blood
lipase fat-splitting enzyme
lipid fat or fatlike substance insoluble in water, typically serving as energy-storage molecule
lipoprotein molecule combining protein and lipid
low-density lipoprotein LDL; protein-lipid aggregate that is major cholesterol carrier in plasma
lumen cavity within tubular structure
lymph colorless fluid derived from blood and carried in special ducts of lymphatic vessels
lymphoid tissue connective tissue containing lymphocytes
mechanoreceptor sensory cell or organ that receives mechanical stimuli
metabolic rate level of energy expenditure
metabolism sum of all chemical reactions in living cell or organism
microorganism any living organism too small to be viewed by unaided eye, including bacteria, viruses, protists, and some algae and fungi
micturition excretion of urine
mineral naturally occurring inorganic substance required for growth or functioning of organism
mononuclear phagocyte system monocytes and macrophages

monosaccharide carbohydrate, such as glucose or fructose, consisting of a single sugar molecule, generally made up of five or six carbon atoms
monosynaptic reflex pathway involving single junction between two neurons
motor (*adj*) having to do with muscles and movement
motor neuron efferent neuron that innervates skeletal muscle fibers
mucous membrane mucus-secreting membrane lining body cavities and canals connecting with external air
mucus viscid, watery lubricating solution secreted by mucous membranes
muscle fatigue depressed metabolic activity of muscle cells due to increased concentration of lactic acid
muscle spindle modified skeletal muscle cell with stretch receptors that regulate muscle tone
muscle tone condition in which muscles are always slightly contracted
myogenic (*adj*) originating within muscle
myoglobin protein in muscles that binds oxygen
myosin contractile protein that forms thick filaments of muscle
neuron functional unit of a nerve, including cell body, axon, and dendrites
neurotransmitter substance that transmits or inhibits nerve impulses from nerve cell to another cell at synapse
neutrophil exudation release of white blood cells
night vision higher than normal concentration of rods in retina, causing increased ability to see in darkness
nociceptor pain receptor
norepinephrine hormone of adrenal medulla that elevates blood pressure and blood sugar levels
optimal length length at which muscle fiber develops maximal tension
organ collection of tissues joined in structural unit to serve a common function
oxidative (*adj*) using oxygen
pacemaker area of vertebrate heart that initiates heartbeat; sinoatrial node
palpitation abnormally rapid heartbeat
paradoxical sleep sleep with rapid eye movement and intermittent muscular twitching, associated with dream state; REM sleep
parathyroid hormone PTH; hormone that promotes vitamin D synthesis and elevates blood calcium
pepsin stomach enzyme that degrades proteins
peptide compound of two or more amino acids
peristaltic waves successive contractions of tubular wall that move its contents forward
phasic (*adj*) intermittent, as opposed to tonic
phospholipid lipid compound containing water-soluble phosphate group
photopigment colored substance that absorbs light over narrow band of wavelengths
photoreceptor cell or organ capable of detecting light
physiology study of functions and vital processes of organisms and their parts or organs
plasma fluid portion of blood and lymph
polypeptide protein, polymer of amino acid subunits
polysaccharide complex carbohydrate compound of chains of simple sugars, such as cellulose or starch
postsynaptic neuron neuron that conducts information away from synapse
potential voltage difference between two points
potentiation one event making possible the occurrence of another
presynaptic neuron neuron that conducts action potential toward synapse
proprioception awareness of position, balance, and movement
protease protein-splitting enzyme
protein any of a large class of organic nitrogenous substances containing amino acids that occur in all animal and vegetable matter and are essential to diet
prothrombin inactive precursor of clotting enzyme thrombin
PTH parathyroid hormone
pulmonary ventilation volume of air exchanged by lungs per minute
pulse pressure difference between systolic and diastolic arterial blood pressures
rapid eye movement sleep REM sleep
RDA recommended dietary allowance
reactive hyperemia increased blood flow that causes body temperature above normal range; fever
receptor sensory cell or organ
recommended dietary allowance RDA; government estimate of minimal nutrient requirements of vitamins and minerals
red muscle fibers tissues that bind and store myoglobin
reflex involuntary response to stimulus
reflex arc functional pathway of neuron system consisting of at least one afferent and one efferent neuron and usu. one interneuron
refractory period recovery time during which excitable neuron membrane is unresponsive to stimulus
relative refractory period recovery time during which excitable neuron membrane will respond only to stimulus that is stronger than initial stimulus
relaxation time period required for tension in muscle fiber to decrease from peak to zero
REM sleep rapid eye movement sleep; paradoxical sleep
renin enzyme secreted by kidneys
respiration exchange of gases between body tissues and surrounding environment, specifically intake of oxygen by tissues, which give off carbon dioxide and water
respiratory quotient RQ; ratio of carbon dioxide produced to oxygen consumed as food is metabolized
respiratory rate depth and frequency of exhala-

tion and inhalation, related to carbon dioxide levels
rod visual cell of retina of eye sensitive to low levels of light
RQ respiratory quotient
saliva watery, slightly acidic secretion of salivary glands that moistens food and initiates its breakdown
sarcomere structural and functional unit of contraction in striated muscle
saturated fat fat in which carbon chains are bonded by single bonds while simultaneously bound to as much hydrogen as possible
SDA specific dynamic action
secretion synthesis and release of substance by cell or organ; such a released substance
sensor cell that receives signals
serotonin brain neurotransmitter that seems to have calming effect
serum liquid portion of coagulated blood
sinoatrial node pacemaker
slow-wave sleep sleep pattern characterized by slow delta waves for four-fifths of total sleep time
somatic receptor neuron in voluntary nervous system connected directly to central nervous system
specific dynamic action SDA; increase of body temperature and basal metabolic rate after consumption of meal
split brain division of brain into left and right hemispheres, which control different functions
starch complex molecule composed of many monosaccharides; main food storage substance in plants
steroid nonfat lipid characterized by four interconnected carbon rings
stimulus any change or phenomenon that causes response in organism or its component
stress stimulus that causes imbalance in homeostasis
stretch receptor baroreceptor
striated muscle voluntary muscle with cylindrical fibers that controls skeleton
stroke volume milliliters per heartbeat of blood pumped by either ventricle
substrate substance that is recipient of enzymic action
synapse junction between two excitable cells, esp. point at which neurotransmitters send impulses in response to action potential in one neuron
synergistic muscle muscle with additive effects
synthetic reactions anabolic reactions in which food is synthesized into living tissue
systemic circulation movement of blood from heart to all tissues except lungs and back of heart
systole contraction of heart muscle
systolic pressure blood pressure produced when ventricles contract
tetanus continuous contraction of muscle due to fusion of twitches
TH thyroid hormone
thermogenesis production of heat within body
thermoreceptor sensory receptor that responds to temperature changes
thick filaments myosin molecules in muscle cells
thin filaments threads consisting of actin, troponin, and tropomyosin molecules in muscle cells
threshold minimal level at which stimulus excites a response
thrombin enzymatic molecule involved in blood coagulation
thyroid hormone TH; thyroxine
thyroxine active thyroid hormone
tidal volume quantity of air moved during normal, quiet breathing
tissue group of similar cells that performs particular function
tolerance diminished response due to repeated exposure
trace element mineral present in body in extremely small amounts
triacylglycerol neutral fat lipid molecule composed of glycerol and three fatty acids; triglyceride
triglyceride triacylglycerol
tropomyosin cablelike muscle protein in thin filaments
troponin structural muscle protein involved with contraction
T wave electrocardiographic representation of electrical activity just prior to ventricular relaxation in diastole
twitch single contraction of muscle fiber
unsaturated fat fat in which some carbons are linked by double bonds
urea nitrogenous waste product of kidneys
uric acid nitrogenous waste product secreted in urine
vasoconstriction narrowing of blood vessel
vasodilation widening of blood vessel
ventilation movement of air in and out of lungs
vestibular system sensory labyrinth of air in body cavities that responds to balance and movement
vestigial organ body part, such as tonsils or appendix, that no longer functions usefully
virus ultramicroscopic, metabolically inert agent that can reproduce only within a host cell, containing RNA or DNA within protein coat
vital capacity maximal amount of air that can be moved by lungs
vitamin any of various organic compounds necessary for normal metabolic functions
withdrawal reflex flexion reflex

Environment, Ecology, and Animal Behavior

abiotic factors nonliving components that interact with and affect organisms in an ecosystem
abyssal zone deepest part of ocean where light is absent
acclimatization adaptive change in physiological system induced by prolonged exposure to environmental stress or a new environment
acid rain rain with abnormally high acid level, esp. due to combustion of fossil fuels
agonistic (*adj*) displaying any type of fighting behavior

altricial (*adj*) displaying condition in which young are born helpless and remain so for some time
altruism self-destructive behavior performed to benefit or protect others, esp. kin
amphibious (*adj*) capable of living both on land and in water
anaerobe bacterium that lives and grows without oxygen
animal multicellular, heterotrophic, usu. mobile organism
aquatic (*adj*) water-dwelling
arboreal (*adj*) tree-dwelling
autotroph organism that can produce its own food by using inorganic materials as its source of nutrients and usu. photosynthesis as its source of energy
avifauna bird life of particular area
behavior organism's observable responses to environment and stimuli
biodegradable (*adj*) capable of being broken down and absorbed in a natural environment, esp. susceptible to being broken down by microorganisms into simple compounds such as water and carbon dioxide
biohazard life-endangering substance, phenomenon, or activity
biomass total mass of organisms per unit area
biome discrete community and region, such as desert or tropical rain forest, characterized by same major life forms and climactic conditions
bioremediation use of biological means to restore biosphere or solve ecological problems, such as oil-eating microbes on an oil spill
biosphere sphere of life on Earth from crust into lower troposphere
biota flora and fauna of an area
birthrate number of organisms born per unit of time
boreal forest biome of wooded regions with cold, dry climate, sandy soil, and coniferous trees
camouflage any means of blending appearance with environment
canopy top layer of forest, where most food is produced
carbon cycle circulation of carbon in biosphere by plant photosynthesis, animal metabolism, and decomposition
carnivore meat-eating organism; consumer that feeds on other consumers
carrying capacity number of individuals of any species that a particular environment can support
circadian rhythm pattern in which a behavior occurs regularly in twenty-four hour cycle
clear-cutting logging of all trees in an area
climax community final stage in evolution of community
cold-blooded (*adj*) having body temperature that varies with approximate surrounding environment, as in fish and reptiles; poikilothermal
colonial (*adj*) designating species that occupies its habitat in groups
commensalism relationship in which one organism benefits from a host organism without affecting it
communication behavior that influences behavior of another organism in adaptive manner
community naturally occurring group of organisms living in a certain area
competition struggle between organisms of same or different species for access to limited resources
conservation protection and preservation of natural environment and resources
conspecific member of same species
consumer organism that consumes other organisms as food
courtship behavior patterns used to attract potential mate
cryptic coloration type of camouflage in which color of organism blends with environment
death rate number of organisms that die per unit of time
deciduous forest biome with trees that lose their leaves in winter, forming belt through temperate latitudes, including monsoon rain forests of Asia and Africa
decomposer organism, such as bacterium, that causes decay
desert biome of arid regions with sparse, widely spaced vegetation and rainfall under 10 inches (25 cm) per year
detritus substrate litter composed of decaying organic matter
dispersion way in which species uses its habitat, such as colonial or solitary
display behavior or series of behaviors modified by evolution for communication
dominance ability of one member of community to exercise control over other members and their environment
echolocation determination of size, shape, and location of an object by bouncing high-frequency sound waves off it, used by organisms such as bats and porpoises
ecological niche specific role organism plays in community, esp. behavior and position in food cycle
ecology relationship and balance between organisms and their environment
ecosystem all interactions of a community of organisms with its physical environment
ecotage extreme measures, such as destruction of tree-cutting machinery, used in opposition to humanly caused ecological damage
emigration aggregate of movement of animals out of an area
endangered species species of organism in imminent danger of extinction, due usu. to destruction of its habitat, loss of food supply, evolutionary deselection, or destruction by humans
endogenous (*adj*) originating or developing from within the organism
environment all external factors acting on an organism
estuary semienclosed body of water along coast, often brackish
eusociality presence of nonreproductive castes,

such as worker bees, within a species

eutrophication aging and death of lake, esp. due to upset in ecological balance

exogenous (*adj*) originating or derived from outside the organism

fauna animal life of an area

first-order consumer consumer that feeds directly on producer; herbivore

flora plant life of an area

food chain route of passage of energy and materials through community of organisms, with successively larger ones feeding on smaller ones

food web all possible feeding relationships in an ecosystem

global warming increase in Earth's average atmospheric temperature and corresponding changes in climate, esp. due to greenhouse effect

grassland biome of plains regions, characterized by grasses

greenhouse effect increase of carbon dioxide in Earth's atmosphere that prevents radiated heat from dissipating, thereby raising its temperature

grooming manipulative cleaning of body surface

growth basic capacity of all organisms to develop or increase, usu. by assimilation of nutriments

habitat natural environment of an organism

habituation depletion of response to often repeated stimulus

herbivore plant-eating organism, consumer of producers

heterotroph organism that cannot produce food and that requires living or dead organic materials as its principal source of nutrition

hibernation period of dormancy during time of low temperatures when metabolic processes slow to minimum

homing ability of displaced organism to return to its home range or place of birth

homoiotherm warm-blooded organism that maintains relatively constant body temperature

host organism that harbors and provides benefits to another organism

imprinting bonding of newborn, esp. bird, to first organism that mothers it

insectivore animal that feeds on insects

insessorial (*adj*) adapted for perching, as bird's foot

instinct innate behavior genetically keyed for and not learned

jungle dense forest community that results from secondary succession of rain forest

learning process by which responses and behavior of an organism are modified due to experience, as through conditioning and associative learning, imprinting in early life, and imitation

lek area repeatedly used for communal courtship displays

littoral zone area of ocean close to shore and subject to action of tides

marine (*adj*) sea-dwelling

Mediterranean scrub biome with mild winters and long, dry summers, characterized by small trees and spiny, evergreen shrubs, primarily in California and around Mediterranean Sea

migration seasonal movement of populations of animals

mimicry evolution of one species to resemble another for some selective advantage

molting regular shedding of all or part of outer layer of skin, esp. in snakes and crabs; shedding of feathers in birds

mutualism relationship in which two animals live in mutually beneficial, often necessary, association

neritic zone area of ocean along continental shelf beyond littoral zone

niche ecological niche

nitrogen cycle circulation of nitrogen through plants and animals in biosphere

ocean aquatic community covering almost three fourths of Earth's surface

omnivore plant- and animal-eating organism, feeding on both producers and consumers

oxygen cycle circulation of oxygen through biosphere by its release from plants during photosynthesis and utilization by animals during respiration

parasite organism that lives in or on host from which it obtains nourishment

parasitism relationship in which parasite organism is completely dependent on host organism for nourishment and host is usu. harmed

pecking order social hierarchy, dominance

pelagic (*adj*) dwelling in the open sea

pheromones chemicals produced by one organism that influence behavior of another

pioneering stage first stage in ecological succession, usu. consisting of hardy autotrophs

plankton aggregate of microscopic, passively floating or slightly motile organisms in body of water, being primarily algae and protozoans that serve as food for marine animals

poikilotherm cold-blooded organism having body temperature that varies with that of environment

pollutant any substance that makes air, water, or soil unclean

pollution introduction of impurities and contaminants into environment, esp. air and water pollution

population group of organisms that naturally interbreeds, living in same locality

population dynamics combination of various factors affecting the size of populations

population growth changes in size of population with time

precocial condition in which young are able to move about and forage for food shortly after birth

predation feeding of one organism on another

predator animal that feeds on other organisms

primary production energy accumulated and stored in plants through photosynthesis

primary succession ecological succession that begins with lifeless terrain, first succession in an ecosystem

producer organism that can make its own food; autotroph

rain forest tropical rain forest
recycling reprocessing of used materials, esp. nonbiodegradable ones
renewable resource resource that can be replaced naturally
resource anything humans take from environment; anything an organism needs to live
ritualization evolutionary modification of behavior patterns to serve as communication
R selection process that favors rapid population increase, with many offspring and little investment in each
saprophyte organism that feeds on dead and decaying matter
savanna biome consisting of tropical grasslands with scattered clumps of trees, found esp. in Africa
scavenger animal that feeds on dead animals
secondary succession series of ecological changes that occur when species of a climax community are removed
second-order consumer animal that eats a first-order consumer
sedentary (*adj*) not migratory; living in one place
smog fog and mist made heavier, darker, and more toxic by absorption of chemical fumes and smoke, usu. in urban areas
social behavior interactions among animals of one species living in structured, mutually dependent groups
social hierarchy series of dominance-subordination relationships in group; pecking order
sociality conditions and processes of social existence and interaction among organisms of species and among species
solar energy radiant energy of sunlight, an abundant and nonpolluting alternative to fossil fuels
S-shaped curve normal population growth curve
stimulus substance or phenomenon that causes or changes activity of an organism
strip mining laying bare of mineral deposits in earth to extract them, causing erosion
substrate surface on which an organism lives or moves
symbiosis relationship in which two organisms live in close, mutually beneficial association
taiga subarctic biome characterized by coniferous forests
temperate deciduous forest biome characterized by even distribution of rain averaging 39 inches (100 cm) per year; region in which trees periodically shed leaves
temperate grassland biome with flat to rolling terrain, covered by sod-forming grasses and legumes, forming transitional area to deserts, including plains, steppes, veld, and pampas
terrestrial (*adj*) ground-dwelling
territory area defended from intruders, usu. of same species, by organism or organisms
tetrapod four-legged vertebrate such as mammal or reptile
third-order consumer animal that eats a second-order consumer
trophic levels series of steps on food chain
tropical rain forest equatorial biome characterized by constant warm temperature, heavy rainfall, dense, varied, evergreen plant growth, and enormous diversity of life forms
tropism involuntary response of organism to stimulus
tundra arctic biome characterized by low average temperature and rainfall, permafrost, and few large plants
vertical stratification layers of a forest from top to bottom
warm-blooded (*adj*) having relatively constant body temperature regardless of surrounding environment; homoiothermal
warning coloration display of bright colors to announce rather than conceal animal's presence
water cycle worldwide circulation of water molecules throughout atmosphere, powered by sun through evaporation and precipitation
weathering mechanical process of freezing, thawing, and erosion
zero population growth birthrate equal to death rate

Reproduction and Development

allantois membrane for respiratory exchange in embryonic birds and reptiles; part of placenta in mammals
amnion membrane enclosing fluid-filled cavity containing embryo
androgen male sex hormone
bilateral symmetry mirroring of right and left halves of body
budding direct growth of new individual from body of old one
clitoris female erectile organ homologous to penis
coitus sexual intercourse
colostrum thin, milky fluid secreted by mammary glands for several days after birth prior to onset of milk production
copulation sexual intercourse, esp. mammalian
cytokinesis stage of cell division in which cytoplasm divides to form two new cells
deuterostome animal, such as any chordate, in which anus and mouth form separately in the developing embryo
development stages of growth from conception through birth to maturity and death
differentiation development of specialized tissue from nonspecialized tissue
ectoderm outermost germ layer in early embryo that forms nervous system and integument
egg female gamete; protective reproductive structure enclosing ovum and nutrient supply, esp. of birds, fish, reptiles, and insects
embryo organism in early stages of development before birth
endoderm innermost germ layer in early embryo that forms gut and glands
estrogen group of steroid hormones secreted by female reproductive system
estrous cycle repeated series of changes in reproductive physiology culminating in estrus
estrus period of maximum sexual receptivity in

female mammals, usu. related to release of eggs; heat
eutherian (*adj*) designating placental mammals or condition in which mammalian embryo is nourished by placenta
fallopian tube one of a pair of tubes that carries eggs away from ovaries in humans
fertilization union of two gametes that activates development of egg
fetus human embryo after third month
follicle stimulating hormone FSH; anterior pituitary hormone that stimulates maturation of ova and sperm
FSH follicle stimulating hormone
fusion joining of two gametes to form zygote
gamete mature sex cell: egg or sperm
genitalia reproductive organs, esp. external organs
germ cell gamete
gestation developmental period of young in uterus of mammal
GH growth hormone
gonad organ that produces gametes: female ovary or male testis
growth hormone GH; anterior pituitary hormone that stimulates growth
hatching emergence of embryo as newborn from egg
heat estrus
hermaphrodite organism with both male and female reproductive organs
implantation settling of early mammalian embryo into uterine wall
inbreeding mating of closely related individuals within the same species
incubation development of egg by means of body warmth
interstitial cells cells between germ cells in reproductive organs
in utero unborn and developing in uterus
in vitro conceived and developing in isolation from living organism, as in test tube
lactation production of milk by mother's mammary glands
larva immature organism, such as caterpillar, that undergoes metamorphosis to become adult
LH luteinizing hormone
luteinizing hormone LH; anterior pituitary hormone that stimulates testosterone secretion in male and maturation of ovarian follicles in female
maggot larval form of certain insects, esp. flies
maturity stage in development at which organism's secondary sex characteristics and reproductive capacity are functioning
menarche onset of female menstrual cycle at puberty
menopause termination of female menstrual cycle and reproductive capability
menses menstruation
menstrual cycle hormone-regulated changes in uterine lining of human and certain other primate females
menstruation cyclical shedding of lining of uterus with loss of blood and fluid; menses
mesoderm middle germ layer in early embryo that forms muscles and supporting tissue
metamorphosis structural change from larval into adult form
milk letdown hormonal response to suckling of baby that ejects milk from mammarian nipples
monogamy practice of mating with only one partner
myoblast embryonic cell that develops into skeletal muscle
neonate newborn
nest structure in which organisms, esp. birds, lay eggs
nidus nest in which insects or spiders deposit eggs
notocord supporting axis in vertebrate embryo and in lower chordates
nullipara female that has never produced young
ontogeny development and life cycle of single organism or individual
oocyte cell giving rise by meiosis to an ovum, as in humans
oogamy sexual reproduction involving one large nonmotile, female gamete and one small, motile, male gamete
oogenesis origin and development of the ovum
ovarian follicle vesicle in ovary that contains developing egg; Graafian follicle
ovary female gonad
oviduct tube carrying egg from ovary to uterus or outside of body; fallopian tube in humans
oviparous (*adj*) egg-laying
ovoviviparous (*adj*) having membrane-enclosed eggs that remain in female until hatching
ovum egg; female gamete
parthenogenesis production of organism from unfertilized egg
parturition birth process
penis male erectile organ for copulation, esp. in mammals
placenta organ for nourishing embryo and removing waste products in most mammals
polyandry practice of female having more than one mate
polygamy practice of mating with more than one partner
polygyny practice of male having more than one mate
postpartum (*adj*) designating period immediately following birth
progesterone ovarian hormone that promotes continuation of pregnancy
prolactin anterior pituitary hormone that stimulates milk secretion
puberty stage of life at which organism reaches sexual maturity and is capable of reproduction
pupa immobile, nonfeeding stage in metamorphosis of insect from larva to adult
regeneration regrowth of lost parts of organ or organism, as in worms
reproduction sexual or asexual process by which organisms produce new individuals of their species
secondary sex characteristics characteristics that distinguish between male and female of

species, such as facial hair and enlarged breasts, but do not produce or convey gametes
semen male reproductive fluid that carries sperm
sex hormone any hormone that effects secondary sex characteristics or reproduction
sexual reproduction reproduction by fertilization and meiosis
sperm spermatozoon
spermatogenesis origin and development of spermatozoon
spermatophore capsule of sperm passed to female during mating of some species
spermatozoon male gamete; sperm
syngamy point in fertilization at which nuclei of sex cells meet and fuse
testis male gonad
testosterone primary male sex hormone
umbilical cord connection between embryo and placenta
uterus enlarged area of female mammalian oviduct where implantation occurs
vagina canal leading from uterus to outside of body that receives erect penis during copulation and acts as birth passage
viviparous (*adj*) giving birth to live young rather than laying eggs
vulva external genitalia in female mammals
womb uterus
yolk complex nutrient storage material in egg
zygospore cell formed by fusion of two similar gametes, as in certain algae and fungi
zygote cell formed by union of two gametes

Tools and Techniques

agar culture medium for growing bacteria
aquarium glass-sided container for holding aquatic organisms
binomial standard scientific name for organism, including genus and species in Latin, such as *Canis familiaris* for dog
calipers jawed instrument for measuring thickness or distance
cast plaster reproduction
centrifuge machine that removes moisture or separates different densities of substance by force directed outward from center of rotation
chromatography separation of chemical compounds on adsorbent material
cladistics classification of organisms based on lines of descent from common ancestor
control unmanipulated sample used for comparison with experimental group
culture laboratory growth of bacteria, microorganisms, or plant or animal cells in special nourishing fluid or solid
dissection cutting apart of specimen for study
electron microscope powerful optical instrument that uses electron beam to enlarge image of minute object
ether volatile, flammable liquid used as solvent and, formerly, as anesthetic
field glass binoculars; device for observing distant objects
forceps tweezerlike instrument for grasping small objects
live trap device for capturing an animal without harming it
manometer device for measuring pressure of gas
medium material, such as agar, on which a culture is grown
microscope optical device for enlarging images
microtome instrument for cutting very thin slices of tissue for microscopic examination
model simulation of natural event, used for prediction
oscilloscope device that shows electrical pulses as light flashes on screen, used for study of physiological processes
petri dish shallow glass vessel with loose cover, used for growing culture of microorganisms
photomicrograph photograph of enlarged image observed through microscope
preservation any method for permanently storing a scientific specimen
radiocarbon dating method of determining age of fossils by using disintegration rate of carbon-14 isotope
radio telemetry use of radio transmitter placed on organism to monitor its movement or physiological processes
remote sensing obtaining information on biosphere by noncontact method, esp. with satellites
respirometer instrument for measuring gas pressure
scalpel fine-bladed knife used for dissecting specimen
slide flat piece of glass used to hold object for observation through microscope
sonogram sound spectrograph
sound spectrograph visual representation of auditory communication; sonogram
specimen sample of organism for study and experimentation
staining use of various dyes to improve visibility of microscopic structures
synonymy scientific names in different nomenclature systems used to designate same species or genus
syringe device for withdrawing or injecting fluids through needle
taxidermy preparing, stuffing, and mounting of animal skins
terrarium usu. glass-sided container enclosing garden of small plants
type specimen single specimen designated as one on which original taxonomic description and name are based
vivisection experiments conducted on living organisms
zoo parklike facility in which live animals are kept for public exhibition

Taxonomy

taxonomy system of classifying organisms into natural related groups based on shared features or traits, with categories in descending order from kingdom to species, as follows:

kingdom one of the five broadest, principal divisions of living things: Animalia (animals), Plantae (plants), Fungi, Protista (algae and protozoans), and Monera (bacteria)

subkingdom category of related phyla within a kingdom (as: Eumetazoa subkingdom of kingdom Animalia)

superphylum subkingdom (as: Schizomycetes superphylum of kingdom Monera)

phylum principal category within a kingdom, used in classification of animals, protists, and monerans (as: Chordata)

division principal category within a kingdom, used in classification of plants, algae, and fungi (as: Anthophyta, or vascular flowering plants)

subphylum intermediate category between phylum and class or superclass (as: Vertebrata)

superclass intermediate category between subphylum and class (as: Tetrapoda)

class category of organisms ranking below phylum and above order (as: Mammalia)

subclass intermediate category between class and order (as: Eutheria)

order category of organisms ranking below class and above family (as: Primates)

superfamily intermediate category between order and genus (as: Hominoidea)

family category of organisms ranking below order and above genus (as: Hominidae)

genus category of closely related species ranking below family and above species (as: Homo)

species basic unit of biological classification ranking below genus, including structurally similar organisms capable of interbreeding (as: Homo sapiens)

Five kingdoms

Animalia kingdom of multicellular, eukaryotic organisms, usu. motile with ingestion as principal mode of nutrition and primarily sexual reproduction, including all animals: divided into thirty-two phyla

Plantae kingdom of multicellular, photosynthetic, eukaryotic organisms primarily adapted to life on land, including all plants: divided into ten divisions

Fungi kingdom of unicellular or filamentous, multinucleate, eukaryotic organisms, including molds, mildews, and mushrooms, that live by decomposing and feed on dead or living organic matter in which they grow and decompose: divided into four divisions

Protista kingdom of eukaryotic algae, amebas, and protozoans, consisting of photosynthetic autotrophs and heterotrophs: divided into ten divisions and five phyla

Monera kingdom of prokaryotic organisms, or cells without a membrane-bound nucleus and membrane-bound organelles, that reproduce by asexual budding or fission, including bacteria

Major taxonomic subgroups

Note: *Orders of mammals and lists of species appear under Animals, Plants, and Simpler Life Forms. Latin names are used for entries, with English equivalents given in the definition.*

Agnatha class of cold-blooded, aquatic, jawless, boneless fish: about 60 species

Amphibia class of cold-blooded, scaleless amphibians born in water with gills but developing lungs and living on land, including the ancestors of reptiles: about 2500 species, including frogs, toads, and salamanders

Annelida animal phylum of segmented annelid worms with well-defined nervous systems: about 9000 species, including earthworms, leeches, and marine worms

Anthophyta division of flowering plants or angiosperms with ovules enclosed in carpels and mature seeds borne within fruits: about 235,000 species divided into two classes, Monocotyledones and Dicotyledones

Arachnida class of mostly terrestrial arachnid arthropods with four pairs of jointed legs: about 57,000 species, including spiders, mites, ticks, and scorpions

Arthropoda phylum of invertebrate arthropods with paired, jointed limbs, a segmented body, and a hard exoskeleton: over one million species, including insects, arachnids, and crustaceans

Aves class of warm-blooded, egg-laying, two-legged birds covered by feathers, with forelimbs used as wings and an embryo enclosed in an eggshell: about 9000 species

Bryophyta division of multicellular plants with photosynthetic pigments and food reserves similar to those of green algae: about 16,000 species, including mosses, liverworts, and hornworts

Chondrichthyes class of cold-blooded, aquatic, cartilaginous fish such as sharks and rays: about 625 species

Chordata phylum of animal chordates having a notochord at some stage of development, a hollow nerve cord, and a tail, including vertebrates: about 43,000 species

Coniferophyta division of seed plants with needlelike leaves: about 550 species of conifers, including gymnosperms

Crustacea class of mostly aquatic crustacean arthropods with two pairs of antennae, appendages on the thoracic segment, and a hard exoskeleton: about 25,000 species, including lobsters, crabs, crayfish, and shrimps

Echinodermata animal phylum of radially symmetrical, marine echinoderms, having an endoskeleton of ossicles and spines: about 6000 species, including starfish and sea urchins

Eumetazoa animal subkingdom of multicellular organisms with a true digestive cavity, including almost all animals; Metazoa

Eutheria subclass of all mammals other than marsupials and monotremes, broken down into seventeen orders with nearly 4500 species

Insecta class of mostly terrestrial insect arthropods that breathe by means of tracheae and have a tripartite body, one pair of antennae, three pairs of legs, and usu. two pairs of wings: about one million species, including bees, ants, fleas, flies, beetles, butterflies, and lice
invertebrate nontaxonomic grouping of all animals without a backbone or spinal column, comprising all thirty-one phyla of animals other than chordates
Mammalia class of warm-blooded, four-limbed, usu. hairy mammals that nourish their young with milk secreted by female mammary glands: about 4500 species divided into three subclasses
Mesozoa animal subkingdom of fifty species of extremely simple, wormlike organisms that are parasites of marine invertebrates
Metatheria subclass of marsupial mammals whose young are born undeveloped and are carried in the female's pouch: about 260 species, including kangaroos and opossums
Metazoa former term equivalent to Eumetazoa
Mollusca animal phylum of mostly aquatic, unsegmented mollusks with a muscular foot, soft body, and usu. one or more hard shells: about 47,000 species, with major classes being Bivalvia (clams, oysters, mussels, and scallops), Gastropoda (snails and slugs), and Cephalopoda (octopuses and squids)
Nematoda animal phylum of minute, free-living roundworms and plant and animal parasites: over 12,000 species
Osteichthyes class of cold-blooded, aquatic, usu. scaly, bony fish: about 19,000 species
Parazoa animal subkingdom of multicellular organisms without a true digestive cavity, primarily sponges of phylum Porifera
Prototheria subclass of mammals composed of egg-laying monotremes: only five living species
Protozoa nontaxonomic grouping, similar to superphylum, of animallike, eukaryotic organisms belonging to kingdom Protista that are primarily unicellular, colonial, and nonphotosynthetic, formerly categorized as animals
Pterophyta division of primarily homosporous plants: about 12,000 species of ferns
Reptilia class of cold-blooded reptiles with lungs, completely bony skeletons, and bodies covered with scales or horny plates: about 6000 living species, including snakes, turtles, lizards, and crocodiles, and also extinct species such as dinosaurs
Sarcodina phylum of kingdom Protista, including unicellular heterotrophs with pseudopods: about 11,500 species, including amebas
Vertebrata subphylum of chordates whose notochord is replaced by a backbone or spinal column after its embryonic stage, and having a cranium enclosing a well-developed brain: about 41,700 species of mammals, birds, fish, amphibians, and reptiles

ANIMALS

Animal Types and Parts
Animal Groups
Vertebrates
Invertebrates

Animal Types and Parts

alley cat mixed-breed domestic cat, esp. living unowned in city
alter (*vb*) neuter a male animal
animal member of kingdom of living organisms distinguished from plants by their ability to move about independently and to respond quickly to stimuli
antler branched, bony growth on head of deer and some other mammals, usu. shed annually
ass domesticated donkey or similar wild species
avian (*adj*) of or like a bird
baleen horny substance attached along upper jaw of certain whales; whalebone
beak bird's bill, esp. sharp, horny bill of bird of prey
beast large quadruped, esp. domesticated
bill hard jaws of a bird, usu. projecting to point
biped animal that moves on two feet
bitch female dog
boar male pig
bovine (*adj*) of or like an ox
bronco wild horse that resists being ridden
brood offspring from one hatching of bird's eggs
buck male deer, goat, rabbit, or kangaroo
bull male of various large mammals, esp. cattle
calf young of various large mammals, esp. cattle
calico domestic cat marked with black, orange, red, and white, usu. female; horse with similar markings
canine member of family of carnivores including dogs, wolves, and foxes; (*adj*) of or like a dog
cannibal animal that feeds on its own species
capon neutered rooster
carnivore animal that feeds on other animals
caterpillar wormlike larva of certain insects, esp. butterflies or moths
chick young bird, esp. chicken
chordate member of phylum comprising all true vertebrates and animals having a notochord
claw sharp, usu. hooked, horny structure or nail on foot of birds and some reptiles and mammals
cloven-foot mammal with hoof comprising two major toes for support
clutch group of eggs laid at one time by bird
coat natural outer covering of wool or fur
cock male chicken over one year old
cockerel male chicken under one year old
colt male horse before maturity
comb fleshy protuberance on head of chicken
corvine (*adj*) of or like a crow
covert one of small feathers that cover bases of large feathers on wings and tail of bird

cow female of various large mammals, esp. cattle
crest comb or feathered tuft on head of animal, usu. bird
cub young of various large carnivores, esp. bears
cud food regurgitated from ruminant's stomach to be rechewed
cur mixed-breed dog of little value
cursorial (*adj*) having limbs and feet adapted for running
dock (*vb*) shorten tail or ears of animal
doe female deer, rabbit, goat, or kangaroo
domestic animal animal bred and raised in captivity as a pet, to perform work, or for food
draft animal animal used to pull wagon or plow
drake male duck
drone male bee or ant that serves only for reproduction and does no work
duck esp. female duck
duckling young duck
eclipse plumage dull plumage of birds, esp. adult males, that exhibit brilliant nuptial plumage when mating
equine (*adj*) of or like a horse
ewe female sheep
fang long, pointed canine tooth of carnivores, esp. used to tear flesh
fauna animals of a specific region or time
fawn young deer
feather one of horny shafts with soft branching barbs covering body of bird and comprising wing surface
feline member of the cat family of carnivores; (*adj*) of or like a cat
feral wild animal, esp. domestic animal gone wild
filly female horse under four years old
fin winglike membrane on body of fish, used for swimming
fledgling young bird just beginning to fly
flipper limb of pinniped or cetacean, broadened and flattened for swimming
foal young or newborn horse
fowl poultry
gander male goose
gelding neutered male horse
gill respiratory organ of fish and water animals
gilt young female pig
gobbler male turkey
goose esp. female goose
gosling young goose
hand unit of linear measure equal to four inches (10.2 cm), used to determine the height of horses
hart adult male red deer
heat estrus condition
heifer young cow
hen female chicken
hind adult female red deer
hinny offspring of a stallion and a jenny
hoof hard, horny foot of ungulate mammals
horn hard, hollow, bony, often pointed growth on head of certain hoofed animals; hard substance forming horns and other growths
invertebrate any animal without a backbone or spinal column
jack male donkey; jackass
jenny female donkey
joey baby kangaroo
kid young goat
kitten young cat
lamb young sheep
leonine (*adj*) of or like a lion
liger offspring of male lion and female tiger
litter several offspring from one birth, esp. in mammals
livestock domestic animals raised on a farm, esp. for profit
lupine (*adj*) of or like a wolf
mandibles upper and lower parts of bird's bill
mane long hair growing on animal's neck, esp. a horse or lion
manx tailless domestic cat
mare female horse
maw stomach of ruminant, from which cud is regurgitated
minnow any very small fish, usu. freshwater
mongrel mixed-breed dog; mutt
mule sterile hybrid between a horse and donkey, esp. between a mare and jack; any sterile hybrid
mustang wild horse
mutt *Slang.* mongrel
muzzle projecting portion of head of certain mammals, esp. dogs or horses, comprising mouth, nose, and jaws
nag broken-down old horse, esp. female; *Slang.* any horse
nanny goat female goat
nest structure made or place chosen for breeding or laying eggs, esp. by birds
omnivore animal that feeds on other animals and plants
passerine (*adj*) designating any small or medium-sized perching songbird with grasping feet
paw the foot of any quadruped with claws
peahen female peafowl
pelt skin of fur-bearing animal, esp. when stripped from carcass
pen female swan
piebald pinto
piglet young pig
pileum top of bird's head from base of bill back to nape
pinto horse with black and white patches; piebald
piscine (*adj*) of or like a fish
plumage feathers or cluster of feathers on head or body of bird
pony small breed of horse under 14.2 hands high
pooch *Informal.* dog, esp. one of mixed breed
porcine (*adj*) of or like a pig
pouch fold of skin on abdomen of female marsupial in which newborn young are carried
poulard spayed hen
poult young turkey
poultry domestic birds kept for meat or eggs; fowl
predator animal that lives by hunting and feeding on other animals
prehensile tail tail, as of certain monkeys, used for grasping or seizing

prey animal that is hunted and eaten by a predator
proboscis tubular organ, such as elephant's trunk, used for sucking, food-gathering, or sensing
pullet female chicken less than one year old
pup young dog; young seal
puppy young dog
puss any cat
pussycat any cat, esp. one of mixed breed
quadruped four-legged animal, usu. a mammal
queen female cat used for breeding; dominant mother bee in hive
quill stiff wing or tail feathers of bird; spine of porcupine or hedgehog
ram male sheep
roan horse of reddish-brown or black color with thick sprinkling of white
rooster male chicken; chanticleer
ruminant cud-chewing mammal with four-chambered stomach
runt smallest member of litter
saurian (*adj*) of or like a lizard
scales thin, overlapping, rigid plates forming protective covering of most fishes and reptiles and a few mammals
scavenger animal that feeds on refuse and decaying organic matter
seal point cat with pale body and dark brown face, ears, tail, and paws
serpentine (*adj*) of or like a snake
shoat pig under one year old
sire male parent of any quadruped, esp. a horse
snood fleshy appendage trailing from above the beak of a male turkey
snout projecting nose and jaws of various mammals
songbird any common passerine bird that makes musical vocal sounds
sow female pig
spay (*vb*) neuter female animal
spine sharp, stiff projection from body of a porcupine or from a fish's fin
squab fledgling pigeon
stag male deer
stallion male horse
steer neutered bull
stray lost or abandoned domestic animal
stud male horse used for breeding
tabby cat with swirls of dark color on light background, esp. tigerlike stripes
tadpole larval, gilled stage of amphibious frog
tail flexible appendage at rear of animal's body; feathers extending from rump of bird
tetrapod any four-legged vertebrate, esp. mammals, birds, and reptiles
thoroughbred racing horse bred by crossing Arabian or Turkish stallion with English mare
tiger domestic cat with striped tabby markings
tom male cat or turkey
tortoise shell hard, mottled, yellow-and-brown shell of some turtles and tortoises; similar coloration of some female cats
trunk long, flexible snout or proboscis, as on elephant
tusk one of a pair of very long, large, pointed teeth projecting outside of the mouth of some mammals
ungulate hoofed mammal
ursine (*adj*) of or like a bear
vermin destructive, disease-carrying insects or small animals
vertebrate animal with backbone or spinal column, such as mammals, birds, fish, amphibians, and reptiles
vixen female fox
vulpine (*adj*) of or like a fox
wattle fleshy protuberance hanging below the head of chicken or turkey.
whalebone baleen
whelp young of a dog
wing either of the feathered forelimbs of a bird, used for flying; forelimb of a flying mammal, formed by membrane stretched between digits
worker sterile ant or bee that performs work for colony

Animal Groups

bale (turtles);
bed (snakes);
bevy (quail);
bouquet (pheasants in flight);
cete (badgers);
charm (finches);
clowder (cats);
colony (ants, badgers, or frogs);
confusion (guinea fowls);
covert (coots);
covey (partridges, pheasants, or quail on the ground);
drove (animals moving together); (oxen, sheep, or swine);
exaltation (larks);
flight (birds or insects);
flock (birds); (sheep);
gaggle (geese on water or ground);
gam (whales);
gang (elk);
herd (animals grazing together, esp. cattle or sheep); (elephants);
hive (bees);
host (sparrows);
husk (hares);
kennel (dogs);
knot (toads);
labor (moles);
leap (leopards);
murmuration (starlings);
muster (peacocks);
nest (rabbits); (wasps); (vipers);
pace (asses);
pack (wild animals moving together, esp. dogs or wolves); (grouse);
parliament (owls);
plague (locusts);
pod (seals or whales);
pride (lions); (peacocks);
sault (lions);

school (fish);
shoal (fish, esp. bass);
shrewdness (apes);
skein (geese in flight);
skulk (foxes);
sloth (bears);
swarm (insects, esp. bees);
team (ducks in flight); (oxen or horses);
trace (hares or rabbits);
troop (monkeys);
watch (nightingales);

Vertebrates

vertebrate member of the subphylum of chordates whose notochord is replaced by a backbone or spinal column after its embryonic stage, having a cranium enclosing a well-developed brain, including mammals, birds, reptiles, amphibians, and fish

MAMMALS

mammal member of a class of warm-blooded, usu. hairy vertebrates that nourish their young with milk secreted by female mammary glands

Monotremes

monotreme member of the most primitive, egg-laying order of mammals, comprising the subclass Prototheria
duckbill, duckbill platypus
echidna
platypus
spiny anteater

Marsupials

marsupial member of mammalian order whose young are born undeveloped and carried in the female's pouch, comprising the subclass Metatheria
banded anteater, bandicoot, bettong
cuscus
dasyure, dunnart
euro
flying phalanger
glider
kangaroo, koala
marsupial mole, marsupial mouse
native cat, numbat
opossum
pademelon, phalanger, possum, potoroo
quokka, quoll
rabbit-eared bandicoot, rat opossum, ringtail
Tasmanian devil, Tasmanian wolf, thylacine, tree kangaroo
wallaby, wombat
yapok

Edentates

edentate member of mammalian order without teeth or with single-rooted molars only
ant bear, anteater, armadillo
giant ground sloth (extinct)
peba, peludo
sloth
tamandua, tatou, tatouay, tatoupeba

Insectivores

insectivore member of small, primitive, nocturnal order of mammals with weak eyesight that feed on invertebrates, esp. insects
desman
elephant shrew
golden mole, gymnure
hedgehog
mole, moon rat
otter shrew
shrew, solenodon, star-nosed mole
tenrec
water shrew

Dermopterans

dermopteran member of mammalian order of nocturnal, herbivorous gliders that do not actually fly
colugo
flying lemur

Chiropterans

chiropteran member of mammalian order with forelimbs ending in membranes stretched between elongated digits, used for flying
barbastelle, bat, brown bat
chauvesouris
false vampire, fishing bat, flittermouse, flying fox, free-tailed bat, fruit bat
horseshoe bat
leaf-nosed bat, little brown bat
myotis
noctule
pipistrelle
serotine
vampire bat

Primates

primate member of mammalian order with flexible, grasping hands and feet with five digits, usu. omnivorous and arboreal
angwantibo, anthropoid ape, ape, aye-aye
baboon, bandar, Barbary ape, bonnet monkey, bush baby
capuchin, chacma, chimpanzee, colobus, cynomolgus
drill, dwarf lemur
entellus
galago, gelada, gibbon, gorilla, grivet, guenon, guereza
hamadryas baboon, hanuman, hominid, homo sapiens, howler, human being
indri

langur, lar gibbon, leaf monkey, lemur, lion-tailed monkey, loris
macaque, man, mandrill, mangabey, marmoset, monkey, mountain gorilla
night monkey
orangutan
patas monkey, potto, prosimian, proboscis monkey
quenon
rhesus monkey
saki, siamang, simian, snow monkey, spider monkey, squirrel monkey
tamarin, tarsier, titi, tree shrew
uakari
vervet
wanderoo, white-handed gibbon, woolly monkey

Carnivores

carnivore member of mammalian order of flesh-eating predators with prominent canine fangs and shearing molars, having retractable or unretractable claws on toed feet
aardwolf, American lion, Arctic fox
badger, bassarisk, bat-eared fox, bear, binturong, black bear, bobcat, brown bear, brush wolf, buffalo wolf, bush dog
cacomistle, canine, Cape fox, cape hunting dog, caracal, cat (Abyssinian, Angora, Archangel, Balinese, Birman, Burmese, color point, Cornish Rex, domestic shorthair, Egyptian, Havana brown, Himalayan, Korat, Maine coon, Maltese, Manx, Persian, Rex, Russian blue, Siamese, Somali, Turkish swimming, Turkish van), **catamount, cheetah, cinnamon bear, civet cat, clouded leopard, coati, coon, cougar, coyote, cusimanse**
dhole, dingo, dog (affenpinscher, Afghan hound, Airedale terrier, Akita, Alaskan malamute, Alsatian, American foxhound, American pit bull terrier, American water spaniel, Australian cattle dog, Australian heeler, Australian kelpie, Australian shepherd, Australian terrier, badger dog, Basenji, basset hound, beagle, bearded collie, Bedlington terrier, Belgian Malinois, Belgian sheepdog, Belgian Tervuren, Bernese mountain dog, Bichon Frise, black and tan coonhound, bloodhound, bluetick coonhound, boarhound, Border collie, Border terrier, borzoi, Boston bull terrier, Bouvier des Flandres, boxer, Boykin spaniel, Briard, Brittany spaniel, Brussels griffon, bulldog, bullmastiff, bull terrier, cairn terrier, cavalier King Charles spaniel, Chesapeake Bay retriever, Chihuahua, Chinese Shar-Pei, chow chow, clumber spaniel, Clydesdale terrier, cocker spaniel, collie, coonhound, corgi, Coton de Tulear, curly-coated retriever, dachshund, Dalmation, Dandie Dinmont terrier, deerhound, Doberman pinscher, elkhound, English bulldog, English cocker spaniel, English foxhound, English setter, English shepherd, English springer spaniel, English toy spaniel, Eskimo dog, field spaniel, flat-coated retriever, foxhound, fox terrier, French bulldog, gazelle hound, German shepherd, German shorthaired pointer, German wirehaired pointer, giant schnauzer, golden retriever, Gordon setter, Great Dane, Great Pyrenees, greyhound, griffon, Groenendael, harrier, hound, husky, Ibizan hound, Irish setter, Irish terrier, Irish water spaniel, Irish wolfhound, Italian greyhound, Jack Russell terrier, Japanese Chin, Japanese spaniel, keeshond, kelpie, Kerry blue terrier, King Charles spaniel, Komondor, kuvasz, Labrador retriever, Lakeland terrier, Lhasa apso, lurcher, malamute, Malinois, Maltese dog, Manchester terrier, mastiff, Mexican hairless, miniature dachshund, miniature poodle, miniature pinscher, miniature schnauzer, Neapolitan mastiff, Newfoundland, Norfolk terrier, Norwegian elkhound, Norwich terrier, Old English sheepdog, otterhound, papillon, pariah dog, Pekingese, pharaoh hound, Plott hound, pointer, Pomeranian, poodle, Portuguese water dog, pug, puli, rat terrier, redbone coonhound, red setter, retriever, Rhodesian ridgeback, Rottweiler, Russian owtchar, Russian wolfhound, Saluki, Samoyed, schipperke, schnauzer, Scotch collie, Scottish deerhound, Scottish terrier, Sealyham terrier, setter, shepherd dog, Shetland sheepdog, Shiba-Inu, Shih Tzu, Siberian Husky, silky terrier, Skye terrier, soft-coated wheaten terrier, spaniel, spitz, springer spaniel, Staffordshire bull terrier, staghound, standard schnauzer, St. Bernard, Sussex spaniel, terrier, Tibetan mastiff, Tibetan spaniel, Tibetan terrier, toy fox terrier, toy poodle, toy spaniel, toy terrier, Treeing Walker coonhound, turnspit, vizsla, water spaniel, Weimaraner, Welsh collie, Welsh corgi, Welsh springer spaniel, Welsh terrier, West Highland white terrier, whippet, wirehair, wirehaired pointing griffon, wirehaired terrier, wolfhound, Yorkshire terrier)
ermine, eyra
feline, fennec, ferret, fisher, fitch, fossa, fox
genet, giant panda, glutton, gray fox, gray wolf, grison, grizzly bear
hyena
ice bear
jackal, jaguar, jaguarundi
kinkajou, kit fox, Kodiak bear
laughing hyena, leopard, leopard cat, linsang, lion, lynx
maned wolf, manul, margay, marten, meerkat, mink, mongoose, mountain lion
ocelot, olingo, otter, ounce
painter, Pallas's cat, panda, panther, polar bear, polar fox, polecat, prairie wolf, puma

raccoon, raccoon dog, ratel, red dog, red fox, Reynard, ring-tailed cat
saber-toothed tiger (extinct), sable, sand cat, sea otter, serval, silver fox, simba, skunk, sloth bear, snow leopard, spectacled bear, stoat, sun bear, suricate, swift fox, Syrian bear
tayra, tiger, timber wolf
weasel, white fox, white wolf, wildcat, wolf, wolverine
zoril

Pinnipeds

pinniped member of mammalian order of aquatic carnivores that breed on land, with forelimbs adapted as flippers for swimming
eared seal, elephant seal
fur seal
hair seal, harbor seal
ross seal
sea cat, sea dog, sea elephant, seal, sea lion
walrus

Cetaceans

cetacean member of aquatic, nearly hairless order of mammals lacking hind limbs, with forelimbs adapted as flippers for swimming, a flat tail, and nasal blowholes on top of head, having either teeth or baleen
baleen whale, beaked whale, beluga, blackfish, blue whale, bottle-nosed dolphin, bouto, bowhead
cachalot, cowfish
dolphin
finback, fin whale
grampus, gray whale
humpback whale
killer whale
narwhal
orca
pilot whale, porpoise
right whale, rorqual
sea hog, sei whale, sperm whale, susu
toothed whale
whale, white whale

Sirenians

sirenian member of herbivorous aquatic order of mammals lacking hind limbs, with forelimbs modified as flippers for swimming and a flat tail
dugong
manatee
sea cow

Proboscids

proboscid member of mammalian order of large herbivores with long, flexible trunk, incisors modified as tusks, and huge, grinding molars
elephant
imperial mammoth (extinct)
jumbo
mammoth (extinct), mastodon (extinct)
pachyderm
tusker
woolly mammoth (extinct)

Perissodactyls

perissodactyl member of mammalian order of large herbivores with an odd number of toes on each hoof
ass
burro
donkey
horse (American quarter horse, American saddle horse, American trotter, Andalusian, Appaloosa, Arabian, Barbary, Belgian, Cleveland bay, Connemara, Clydesdale, French coach horse, German coach horse, hackney, Haflinger, hunter, jennet, Lippizaner, Morgan, palomino, Paso, Percheron, pinto, Plantation walking horse, polo pony, pony of the Americas, quarter horse, saddle horse, Shetland pony, Shire, Standardbred, Suffolk, Tennessee walking horse, thoroughbred, Trakehner, Turk, Waler, Welsh pony)
jackass
kiang, kulan
mule, mustang
onager
pony, Przewalski's horse
quagga (extinct)
rhinoceros
tapir, tarpan (extinct)
wild ass
zebra

Hyraxes

hyrax member of herbivorous, rodentlike, hoofed order of mammals related to proboscids
cony
dassie
hyrax
klippdach
rock hyrax

Tubulidentates

tubulidentate member of mammalian order of large, powerful diggers that eat ants and termites with a long, sticky tongue and have teeth only in cheeks
aardvark, ant bear
earth pig

Artiodactyls

artiodactyl member of mammalian order of large herbivores, often ruminants, with even number of toes on each hoof, often with antlers or horns
addax, alpaca, anoa, antelope, aoudad,

argali, aurochs (extinct), axis deer
babirusa, Bactrian camel, banteng, barasingha, Barbary sheep, beisa, bezoar goat, bharal, bighorn sheep, bison, blackbuck, blesbok, blue sheep, boar, bongo, buffalo, bull, bushbuck
camel, camelopard, Cape buffalo, caribou, cattle (Aberdeen, Angus, Ayrshire, beefalo, Brahman, Brown Swiss, cattalo, Charbray, Charolais, Galloway, Guernsey, Hereford, Holstein, Jersey, Longhorn, Santa Gertrudis, Scotch Highland, Shorthorn, Texas Longhorn, West Highland, zebu), chamois, chevrotain, chital, cow
dama gazelle, deer, dik-dik, dromedary, duiker
eland, elk
fallow deer
gaur, gazelle, gemsbok, gerenuk, giraffe, gnu, goat (Angora, French Alpine, Kashmir, Nubian, Saanen, Toggenburg), goat antelope, goral, guanaco
harnessed antelope, hartebeest, hippopotamus, hog
ibex, impala, Indian buffalo
javalina
kaama, kob, kudu
llama
Marco Polo's sheep, markhor, mazama, moose, mouflon, mountain goat, mountain sheep, mouse deer, mule deer, muntjac, musk deer, musk hog, musk ox
nilgai, nyala
okapi, oribi, oryx, ox
peccary, Père David's deer, pig, pronghorn, pronghorn antelope, pudu
razorback, red deer, reindeer, river horse, Rocky Mountain goat, roe deer
sable antelope, saiga, sambar, serow, sheep (Cheviot, Corriedale, Dorset Horn, Hampshire, Karakul, Merino, Romney, Scotch Blackface, Suffolk), sika, springbok, stag, steenbok, swine
tahr, takin, topi
urial
vicuna, Virginia deer
wapiti, warthog, waterbuck, water buffalo, whitetail, white-tailed deer, wild boar, wildebeest, wild goat, wild ox, wild pig, wild sheep
yak
zebu

Pangolins

pangolin member of mammalian order Pholidota of toothless, digging insectivores, with whiplike tongue and hairs flattened into scales, that curls into a ball for defense
anteater
pangolin
scaly anteater

Rodents

rodent member of mammalian order of small, gnawing herbivores with one pair of evergrowing, chisellike incisors
agouti, antelope chipmunk, antelope squirrel
bandicoot, beaver, black rat, blesmol, brown rat
capybara, carpincho, cavy, chickaree, chinchilla, chipmunk, cloud rat, coendou, cotton mouse, cotton rat, coypu
deer mouse, degu, dormouse
edible dormouse
field mouse, flickertail, flying squirrel, fox squirrel
gerbil, gopher, grasshopper mouse, groundhog, ground squirrel, guinea pig
hamster, harvest mouse, house mouse, house rat, hutia
jerboa, jird, jumping mouse
kangaroo mouse, kangaroo rat
lemming
mara, marmot, meadow mouse, mole rat, mouse, muskrat
Norway rat, nutria
paca, pacarana, pack rat, Patagonian hare, pine mouse, pocket gopher, pocket mouse, pocket rat, porcupine, pouched rat, prairie dog
quill pig
rat, red squirrel, rice rat, rock squirrel, roof rat
sewellel, spiny rat, springhaas, squirrel, suslik
tree squirrel, tuco-tuco
viscacha, vole
wharf rat, whistle pig, whistler, woodchuck, wood mouse, wood rat

Lagomorphs

lagomorph member of mammalian order of terrestrial herbivores with two pairs of evergrowing incisors and long hind limbs that are used for jumping
Arctic hare
Belgian hare
cony, cottontail
hare
jack rabbit
lapin, leveret
pika
rabbit
snowshoe hare, swamp rabbit

Birds

bird member of a class of warm-blooded, egg-laying, two-legged vertebrates covered by feathers, with forelimbs used as wings and an embryo enclosed in an eggshell, that live on land, shore, or sea

Passerine songbirds

passerine member of the order Passeriformes of land birds having feet adapted for perching, including all songbirds of Oscine and Suboscine suborders
songbird any passerine bird of Oscine suborder

Oscines
oscine member of suborder of passerine songbirds having highly developed vocal organs
Audubon's warbler
Baltimore oriole, bank swallow, barn swallow, blackbird, Blackburnian warbler, blackcap, bluebill, bluebird, blue jay, bobolink, bowerbird, brown thrasher, brown thrush, bulbul, bullfinch, bunting, bush tit, butcherbird
canary, cardinal, catbird, cedar bird, cedar waxwing, chaffinch, chat, chewink, chickadee, chiffchaff, chipping sparrow, cliff swallow, corbie, cotinga, cowbird, creeper, crossbill, crow
dipper, drongo
English sparrow
finch
gnatcatcher, goldfinch, grackle, grosbeak
hermit thrush, honeycreeper, house finch, house martin
indigo bunting
jackdaw, jay, junco
kingbird, kinglet
lark, linnet
magpie, martin, mavis, meadowlark, merle, mistle thrush, mockingbird, myna
nutcracker, nuthatch
oriole, ortolan, ouzel, oxpecker
pipit, purple finch, purple martin
quelea
raven, redbird, redpoll, redstart, redwing, red-winged blackbird, reedbird, reed bunting, ring ouzel, robin, rook
scarlet tanager, scissortail, shama, shrike, siskin, snowbird, solitaire, song sparrow, song thrush, sparrow, starling, sunbird, swallow
tanager, thrasher, thrush, tit, titlark, titmouse, towhee, tree swallow, troupial
veery, vesper sparrow, vireo
wagtail, warbler, water ouzel, water thrush, waxbill, waxwing, weaver, wheatear, white-eye, whydah, wood warbler, wren, wren-tit
yellowbird, yellow finch, yellowhammer, yellow-rumped warbler, yellowthroat
zebra finch

Suboscines
suboscine member of suborder of passerine songbirds having less well-developed vocal organs
antbird
bellbird, broadbill, bush wren
cock-of-the-rock
flycatcher
lyrebird
manakin
ovenbird
pewee, phoebe, pitta
tyrant flycatcher
woodcreeper

Other land birds

American eagle, ani
bald eagle, barbet, barn owl, bee-eater, bird of paradise, black grouse, bobwhite quail, brush turkey, budgerigar, bustard, button quail, buzzard
California condor, capercaillie, caracara, cassowary, cattle egret, chicken (Andalusian, Araucana, Australorp, Barnevelder, Barred Rock, Brahma, Campine, Cochin, Cornish, Dominiker, Dorking, Frizzle, Game, Golden Sebright bantam, Hamburg, Japanese bantam, Jersey Giant, Lakenvelder, Leghorn, Mille Fleur bantam, Minorca, New Hampshire, Old English Game, Orpington, Phoenix, Plymouth Rock, Polish, Rhode Island Red, Rhode Island White, Rock Cornish, Rosecomb bantam, Silkie, Sultan, Sumatra, Sussex, Turken, White Leghorn, Wyandotte), chicken hawk, chimney swift, cockatiel, cockatoo, condor, crane, cuckoo, culver, curassow
dodo (extinct), dove
eagle, egret, emu, erne
falcon, flicker, francolin, frogmouth
goatsucker, golden eagle, goshawk, grouse, guacharo, guan, guinea fowl, gyrfalcon
harpy eagle, harrier, hawk, hawk owl, hemipode, hoatzin, hobby, honey guide, hoopoe, hoot owl, hornbill, horned owl, horned screamer, hummingbird
ivory-billed woodpecker
jacamar, jungle fowl
kea, kestrel, killdeer, kite, kiwi, kookaburra
lammergeier, lanner, lapwing, laughing jackass, lorikeet, lory, lovebird
macaw, mallee fowl, marabou, megapode, merlin, moa (extinct), motmot, moundbird, mound builder, mourning dove
nighthawk, nightingale, nightjar, notornis
oilbird, ostrich, owl
parakeet, parrot, partridge, passenger pigeon (extinct), peacock, peafowl, peregrine falcon, pheasant, pigeon (carrier, fantail, homer, homing pigeon, Jacobin, king, Modena, nun, pouter, roller, runt, trumpeter, tumbler), pigeon hawk, plover, poorwill, potoo, prairie chicken, ptarmigan
quail, quetzal
raptor, red grouse, red-headed woodpecker, rhea, ringdove, ring-necked pheasant, roadrunner, rock dove, roller, rosella, ruffed grouse
sage grouse, sage hen, sapsucker, screamer, screech owl, scrub fowl, secretary bird, seriema, snipe, snow bunting, sparrow hawk, stork, sun bittern, swift, swiftlet
tercel, tinamou, tody, toucan, touraco,

tragopan, trogon, trumpeter, turkey, turkey buzzard, turkey vulture, turtledove
vulture
whippoorwill, whistler, woodcock, wood owl, woodpecker, wood pigeon, wryneck

Seabirds and waterfowl

seabird any bird living on the sea or along the coast and usu. able to swim, esp. gulls and terns
waterfowl swimming water birds, including ducks, geese, and swans
albatross, anhinga, auk, auklet
barnacle goose, belted kingfisher, bluebill, booby, brant, bufflehead
Canada goose, canvasback duck, coot, cormorant
dabbling duck, dabchick, darter, diver, dovekie, duck (Aylesbury, Blue Swedish, call, Cayuga, crested, Khaki Campbell, Muscovy, Pekin, Rouen, runner)
eider, erne
fish hawk, frigate bird, fulmar
gallinule, gannet, garganey, goldeneye, gooney bird, goose (African, Buff, Chinese, Embden, Pilgrim, Sebastopol, Toulouse), graylag goose, grebe, guillemot, gull
honker
jaeger
kingfisher, kittiwake
loon
mallard, mandarin duck, man-o-war bird, merganser, mew, moorhen, murre, mute swan
nene, notornis
osprey
pelican, penguin, petrel, pintail, pochard, puffin
razorbill, razor-billed, redhead, ring-necked duck, ruddy duck
scaup, scoter, sea duck, sea eagle, sea gull, sea raven, shearwater, sheldrake, shoveler, skua, snow goose, stormy petrel, swan, swan goose
takahe, teal, tern, tropic bird
waterfowl, water hen, whooper swan, widgeon, wood duck

Waders and shorebirds

wader any of various long-legged, long-necked, long-billed birds adapted for wading in shallow waters, including bitterns, cranes, flamingos, herons, rails, and storks
shorebird any bird that frequents seashores and estuaries, esp. members of order Charadriiformes, including sandpipers and plovers
avocet
bittern
corn crake, crake, crane, curlew
dunlin
egret
flamingo
godwit, greenshank, gull
hammerhead, heron
ibis
jacana
killdeer, knot
lily-trotter, limpkin
marabou
night heron
oystercatcher
pewit, phalarope, plover
rail, redshank, ring ouzel
sacred ibis, sanderling, sandpiper, shoebill, skimmer, snipe, spoonbill, stilt, stint, stone curlew, stork, surfbird
turnstone
whimbrel, willet
yellowlegs

Birds of prey

bird of prey any of various flesh-eating predator birds having a sharp, downwardly curved beak and talons, that live on land or sea
American eagle
bald eagle, barn owl, buzzard
California condor, caracara, chicken hawk, condor
eagle, erne
falcon, fish hawk
golden eagle, goshawk, gyrfalcon
harpy eagle, harrier, hawk, hawk owl, hobby, hoot owl, horned owl
jaeger
kestrel, kite
lammergeier, lanner
merlin
osprey, owl
peregrine falcon, pigeon hawk
raptor
screech owl, sea eagle, sparrow hawk
tercel, turkey buzzard, turkey vulture
vulture
wood owl

REPTILES

reptile member of a class of cold-blooded vertebrates with lungs, completely bony skeletons, and bodies covered with scales or horny plates, including snakes and dinosaurs
dinosaur extinct herbivorous or carnivorous member of the reptilian orders Saurischia and Ornithischia of the Mesozoic era, including the largest known land animals
snake member of limbless, scaly, elongate reptilian suborder Serpentes, many of which are venomous
agama, alligator, alligator lizard, alligator snapper, anole
basilisk, beaded lizard, blindworm, bog turtle, box turtle, butterfly agama
caiman, chameleon, chicken turtle, chuckwalla, cooter, crocodile
diamondback terrapin, dinosaurs (allosaur, ankylosaur, antrodemus, apatosaur,

archaeopteryx, atlantosaur, brachiosaur, brontosaur, camarasaur, camptosaur, ceratopsian, coelophysis, diplodocus, elasmosaurus, hadrosaur, ichthyosaur, iguanodon, mixosaurus, oligokyphus, ornithiscian, ornithopod, peloneustes, plesiosaur, prosauropod, pterodactyl, quetzalcoatlus, saurischian, sauropod, scleromochlus, scolosaurus, stegosaur, steneosaurus, styracosaurus, tarbosaurus, theropod, titanophoneus, titanosaur, tylosaurus, tyrannosaur)
dragon
false map turtle, fence lizard, flying dragon
galliwasp, gavial, gecko, Gila monster, girdle-tailed lizard, glass snake, gopher tortoise, green turtle
hawksbill turtle, horned toad
iguana
Komodo dragon
leatherback turtle, lizard, loggerhead turtle
marine iguana, matamata, moloch, monitor, mugger
red-ear
sand lizard, sea turtle, side-necked turtle, skink, slider, slowworm, snake-necked turtle, snakes (adder, anaconda, asp, blacksnake, blind snake, boa, boa constrictor, boomslang, bullsnake, bushmaster, cobra, cobra de capello, constrictor, copperhead, coral snake, corn snake, cottonmouth, daboia, diamondback rattlesnake, egg-eating snake, fer-de-lance, garter snake, gopher snake, hamadryad, harlequin, hognose snake, horned rattlesnake, horned viper, indigo snake, king cobra, king snake, krait, mamba, massasauga, milk snake, moccasin, pine snake, puff adder, python, racer, rat snake, rattlesnake, rear-fanged snake, Russell's viper, scarlet snake, sea snake, sidewinder, spectacled cobra, spitting cobra, taipan, tic-polonga, tiger snake, timber rattlesnake, urutu, viper, water moccasin, water snake, worm snake)
snapping turtle, soft-shelled turtle, stinkpot, stump-tailed lizard, swift
tegu, terrapin, tokay gecko, tortoise, tuatara, turtle
wood turtle

Amphibians

amphibian member of a class of cold-blooded, scaleless vertebrates born in water with gills but developing lungs and living on land, including the ancestors of reptiles
anuran, axolotl
blindworm, bullfrog
caecilian, clawed frog, congo eel, congo snake, cricket frog
edible frog, eft
fire salamander, frog
grass frog, green frog
hellbender, hop toad, horned frog
leopard frog
marine toad, midwife toad, mudpuppy
narrow-mouthed toad, natterjack, newt
paradoxical frog, pickerel frog, poison arrow frog
red-eyed tree frog
salamander, siren, spadefoot toad, spring frog, spring peeper, Surinam toad
toad, tree frog
urodele
waterdog, wood frog

Fish

fish any of various cold-blooded, aquatic vertebrates with gills for breathing, fins, and usu. with scales, being a member of any of three classes: Agnatha (jawless, boneless fish), Chondrichthyes (cartilaginous fish such as sharks and rays), and Osteichthyes (bony fish)
albacore, alewife, alligator gar, amberjack, anchovy, angelfish, arapaima, arauana, archerfish, argusfish
balloonfish, barb, barbel, barn-door skate, barracuda, basking shark, bass, batfish, beluga, betta, black bass, blackfish, bleak, blenny, blindfish, blowfish, blueback salmon, blue catfish, bluefish, bluegill, blue shark, bonefish, bonito, bowfin, bream, brisling, brook trout, brown trout, buffalofish, bullhead, burbot, butterfish, butterflyfish
candlefish, capelin, carp, catfish, channel bass, channel catfish, char, characin, chimaera, Chinook salmon, chub, cichlid, cisco, clingfish, clown anemone, clown fish, cobia, cod, codfish, coelacanth, coney, conger eel, corydoras, cowfish, crappie, croaker, cutlassfish, cutthroat trout
dace, darter, devilfish, devil ray, discus, doctorfish, dogfish, dolphin, dorado, Dover sole, dragonfish, drumfish
eel, eelpout, electric eel, electric ray
filefish, flame tetra, flatfish, flounder, fluke, flying fish, flying gurnard, frogfish
gambusia, gar, garpike, giant bass, globefish, goatfish, goby, golden trout, goldfish, gourami, grayling, greenling, grouper, grunion, grunt, gudgeon, guitarfish, gunnel, guppy, gurnard
haddock, hagfish, hake, halfbeak, halibut, hammerhead shark, hatchetfish, headstander, herring, hogfish, horse mackerel, humuhumunukunukuapuaa
jack, jewfish
kelp bass, kelpfish, killifish, kingfish, koi
lake trout, lamprey, lanternfish, lingcod, loach, lumpfish, lungfish, lyretail
mackerel, mako shark, manta, marlin, menhaden, miller's-thumb, minnow, molly, Moorish idol, moray eel, mosquitofish, mudfish, mudskipper, mullet, muskellunge
needlefish, neon tetra, northern pike

oarfish, oscar
paddlefish, panchax, papagallo, paradise fish, parrotfish, pencilfish, perch, permit, pickerel, pike, pikeperch, pilchard, pilotfish, pipefish, piranha, plaice, platyfish, pollack, pollyfish, pompano, porbeagle shark, porgy, puffer, pupfish
rabbitfish, rainbow trout, rasbora, ray, redfin, redfish, red salmon, red snapper, remora, ribbonfish, roach, roosterfish, rudd
sailfish, salmon, salmon trout, sandfish, sardine, sawfish, scad, scat, scorpionfish, sculpin, scup, sea bass, sea bream, sea horse, seaperch, sea trout, sergeantfish, shark, shiner, shovelhead shark, shovelnose catfish, shovelnose sturgeon, Siamese fighting fish, silver salmon, skate, smelt, snapper, snook, sockeye salmon, sole, spadefish, Spanish mackerel, spearfish, speckled trout, sprat, squawfish, squirrelfish, steelhead, stickleback, stingray, stonefish, striped bass, sturgeon, sucker, Sunapee trout, sunfish, surffish, surfperch, surf smelt, surgeonfish, swordfish
tarpon, tautog, tench, tetra, thornback ray, thresher shark, tiger barb, tigerfish, tiger shark, tilapia, tilefish, toadfish, tope, torpedo fish, trevally, triggerfish, trout, tuna, tunny (*esp. Brit.*), turbot
veiltail goldfish
wahoo, walking catfish, walleyed pike, weakfish, whale shark, whitebait, white bass, whitefish, white shark, whiting, wolffish, wrasse
yellowtail, yellowtail flounder
zebrafish

Invertebrates

invertebrate any animal without a backbone or spinal column, including all thirty-one phyla of animals other than chordates

Arthropods

arthropod invertebrate with paired, jointed limbs, a segmented body, and a hard exoskeleton that is molted from time to time, including arachnids, insects, and crustaceans

Insects and arachnids

arachnid any of a class of mostly terrestrial invertebrate arthropods, usu. with four pairs of jointed legs, no wings or antennae, and simple eyes, that have a liquid diet, including spiders, mites, ticks, and scorpions
insect any of a class of mostly terrestrial invertebrate arthropods with a segmented body consisting of a head, thorax, and abdomen, three pairs of jointed legs, usu. two pairs of wings, and one pair of antennae, including bees, ants, fleas, flies, beetles, butterflies, and lice

acarine, admiral butterfly, ant, ant lion, aphid, apple maggot, assassin bug
bark beetle, bedbug, bee, bee fly, beetle, billbeetle, billbug, blackbeetle, black fly, black widow, bloodworm, blow fly, bluebottle, boll weevil, bombardier beetle, bookworm, borer, botfly, bristletail, buffalo bug, buffalo carpet beetle, bumblebee, buprestid beetle, butterfly
cabbage butterfly, caddisfly, cadelle, carpet beetle, caterpillar, cattle grub, cattle tick, Cecropia moth, centipede, chafer, chigger, chigoe, chinch bug, cicada, cicala, click beetle, cockchafer, cockroach, codling moth, Colorado potato beetle, conenose, copper butterfly, crane fly, cricket, crotonbug, cucumber beetle, curculio
daddy-longlegs, damselfly, darkling beetle, deer fly, dermestid, dipteran, dobsonfly, dor, dragonfly, drosophila, dung beetle
earwig, elaterid, elm bark beetle, elm leaf beetle, emperor butterfly, ephemerid
firefly, flea, flea beetle, flesh fly, flour beetle, flour moth, flower fly, fly, frit fly, fritillary, fruit fly, fruit-tree bark beetle
gadfly, gallfly, gall midge, gall mite, girdler, glowworm, gnat, grain beetle, grasshopper, greenbottle fly, greenbug, greenfly, ground beetle, grub, gypsy moth
hairstreak butterfly, harlequin beetle, harlequin cabbage bug, hawk moth, Hessian fly, honeybee, hornet, horn fly, horntail, horse fly, housefly
ichneumon fly
Japanese beetle, jigger flea, June bug
katydid, khapra beetle, kissing bug
lacewing, ladybeetle, ladybug, lanternfly, leaf beetle, leaf-cutting bee, leaf-footed bug, leafhopper, Lepisma, locust, longhorn, long-horned beetle, long-horned grasshopper, louse
mayfly, mealworm, mealybug, medfly, Mediterranean fruit fly, Mexican bean beetle, Mexican fruit fly, midge, miller, mite, mole cricket, monarch butterfly, mosquito, mosquito hawk, moth, mourning cloak
oil beetle
painted lady, pill bug, podura, potatobug, praying mantis, punkie
railroad worm, red admiral butterfly, rhinoceros beetle, roach, robber fly, rose beetle, rose chafer, rove beetle
sawfly, sawyer, scarab, scorpion, scorpionfly, screwworm, shadfly, silkworm, silverfish, skipjack, skipper, snapping beetle, snout beetle, sow bug, spider, spider mite, spider wasp, springtail, squash bug, stag beetle, stink bug, St. Mark's fly, stonefly, swallowtail butterfly, syrphid fly
tabanid, tarantula, tenebrionid, tent caterpillar, tent fly, termite, tettigoniid, thrips, tick, tiger beetle, tiger moth, tiger swallow-

tail, tortoise beetle, tsetse fly, tumblebug, twig girdler
viceroy, vinegar fly
walking stick, warble fly, wasp, water beetle, water bug, water strider, weevil, whip scorpion, whirligig beetle, white ant, wood nymph, wood tick, wood wasp
yellow jacket

Crustaceans

crustacean member of a subphylum of mostly aquatic, invertebrate arthropods with gills, a hard outer shell, a jointed body, appendages on the thoracic segment, and two pairs of antennae
barnacle, beach flea
copepod, crab, crawdad, crayfish
Dungeness crab
fiddler crab
hermit crab, horseshoe crab
isopod
king crab, krill
lobster
prawn
sand hopper, shrimp, soft-shell crab, spider crab
water flea, wood louse

Mollusks and Aquatic Invertebrates

mollusk member of a phylum of mostly aquatic invertebrates with an unsegmented body enclosed in one or more hard shells, with a muscular foot for moving and usu. gills, including clams, mussels, octopuses, oysters, scallops, slugs, snails, and squid
aquatic invertebrates members of any of several phyla of cnidarians, echinoderms, and sponges
cnidarian formerly coelenterate; member of a phylum of invertebrates having a single, internal digestive cavity with tentacles on the oral end, a primitive nervous system, and special protective stinger cells, including jellyfish, sea anemones, and coral
echinoderm member of marine invertebrate phylum having a body wall stiffened by calcareous protruding spines, no head, and tubed feet, that lives on the seafloor, including starfish, sea urchins, sand dollars, and sea cucumbers
sponge member of the chiefly marine invertebrate phylum Porifera having a porous structure and usu. a horny skeleton formed from hard substances that become stuck in its body walls, that lives in large colonies attached to rocks
abalone, acorn worm, amphioxus, anemone, angel's wing
barnacle, bivalve, bloodworm, brain coral, brittle star
cannonball jellyfish, clam, cockle, comb jelly, conch, coquina, coral, cowrie, crown-of-thorns starfish, cuttlefish
dead man's fingers, devilfish
elkhorn coral
gastropod, giant squid
hydra, hydrozoan coral
jellyfish
limpet, lion's mane
mussel
nautilus, nudibranch
octocorallian, octopod, octopus, oyster
periwinkle, polyp, pompano, Portuguese man-of-war
quahog
razor clam
sand dollar, sand flea, sandworm, scallop, scleractinian coral, sea anemone, sea cucumber, sea fan, sea feather, sea hare, sea nettle, sea slug, seasnail, sea star, sea urchin, sea wasp, sea whip, shellfish, shipworm, slug, snail, sponge, squid, staghorn coral, star coral, starfish
tubeworm
whelk
zoanthid

Worms

worm any slender, soft-bodied, legless, symmetrical invertebrate, often segmented, that lives underground, in water, or as a parasite, esp. an insect larva
acanthocephalan, angleworm, annelid, armyworm, arrowworm
bloodworm, bollworm, bookworm
cankerworm, clamworm, cottonworm, cutworm, cysticercus
earthworm, earworm, eelworm
filaria, fireworm, flatworm, fluke
hairworm, hellgrammite, helminth, hookworm, hornworm, horsehair worm
inchworm
larva, leech, looper, lugworm
measuringworm
nemathelminth, nematode, nemertean
pinworm, planarian, platyhelminth, polychaete
red worm, ribbon worm, rotifer, roundworm
sandworm, sea mouse, sea worm, silkworm
tapeworm, teredo, threadworm, tobacco hornworm, tomato hornworm, trematode, tubeworm, tubifex, tussah
vinegar eel, vinegar worm
webworm, wireworm, woodworm

PLANTS

Botany and Plant Parts

algae unicellular organism distinguished from plants by having no true root, stem, or leaf; see under Algae in Simpler Life Forms
angiosperm flowering plant, esp. one having its seeds enclosed in an ovary
annual plant with life cycle of one year or season
anther part of stamen that produces and releases pollen
articulation joint in stem or between branch and leaf
auxin plant growth hormone
axil upper angle formed by leaf or twig and the stem from which it grows
axillary bud bud formed at axil
bark outside covering of stems and roots of trees and woody plants
berry small, fleshy fruit or dry seed or kernel of various plants
biennial plant with two-year life cycle in which the vegetative first-year growth is followed by fruiting and dying during second year
blade broad, expanded part of leaf
botany branch of biology dealing with life, structure, growth, and classification of plants
bract leaflike structure growing below or encircling flower cluster or flower
bryophyte any member of the division of nonvascular plants, including mosses and liverworts, that lack water-gathering roots and tissues to conduct water
bud small swelling on plant from which shoot, leaf cluster, or flower develops
bulb dormant underground bud stage of some plants
bush shrub
Calvin cycle sequence of reactions in second stage of photosynthesis by which carbon dioxide is reduced to carbohydrate
calyx outer whorl of protective leaves on a flower
cambium layer of formative cells beneath bark of tree
cap pileus of mushroom
carpel ovule-bearing leaf or leaflike structure that is primary segment of pistil
chlorophyll pigment in chloroplast, needed for photosynthesis
chloroplast membrane-bound organelle that is site of photosynthesis
club moss any of various small, non-seed-bearing vascular plants with conelike, spore-bearing structures on top of stems
composite one of a large family of herbaceous plants with flower heads of dense clusters of small florets surrounded by ring of small leaves or bracts
cone reproductive structure of certain nonflowering plants with overlapping scales or bracts containing pollen, ovules, or spores
conifer cone-bearing gymnosperm, usu. with narrow, needlelike or small, scalelike leaves
corm underground stem base that acts as reproductive structure
corolla flower petals
corymb flat-topped or convex cluster of flowers in which outer flowers open first
cotyledon first or second leaf of seedling
cuticle waxy layer on outer surface of plants
cycad any of the order of gymnosperms intermediate between ferns and palms, often with thick, columnar trunk crowned by large, tough, pinnate leaves
cyst sporelike cell with resistant, protective wall
deciduous (*adj*) designating any plant that sheds all its leaves once each year
dehiscence splitting open of pod or anther, esp. at maturity to discharge seeds
dicot dicotyledon
dicotyledon angiosperm having two seed leaves or cotyledons; dicot
division major primary subdivision of plant kingdom, comparable to animal phylum
dormancy period of time in which growth ceases
endophyte plant living within another plant, usu. as a parasite
epiphyte nonparasitic plant growing upon another plant for support
evergreen plant that maintains functional green foliage throughout year
fern nonflowering, vascular plant having roots, stems, and fronds and reproducing by spores instead of seeds
fertilization fusion of male and female sex cells, preceded by pollination in seed plants
filament stalklike portion of stamen, bearing the anther
flora plants of specific region or time
floret small flower; one of individual flowers comprising the head of a composite plant
flower seed-producing plant, usu. nonwoody, with shortened stem bearing leaflike sepals, colorful petals, and pollen-bearing stamens clustered around pistils; blossom; plant cultivated for its blossoms; reproductive organ of some plants; (*vb*) produce blossoms
flowering plant any angiosperm that produces flowers, fruit, and seeds in an enclosed ovary
foliage leaves of plant or tree
frond fern or palm foliage
fructose yellowish to white, crystalline, water-soluble sugar found in many fruits

fruit mature ovary of flowering plant, sometimes edible; see list under Foods
fungus unicellular or filamentous organism that lives by decomposing, formerly classified with plants; see under kingdom Fungi in Simpler Life Forms
funicle stalk of ovule or seed
gametophyte gamete-bearing, haploid, multicelled stage of many plants, beginning with haploid spores and ending at fertilization
germinate (*vb*) sprout and start to grow from spore, seed, or bud
gill lamella
grass member of the family of flowering plants with long, narrow leaves, jointed stems, flowers in spikelets, and seedlike fruit
gymnosperm member of the division of seed plants having ovules on open scales, esp. cones
herb nonwoody, seed-producing plant whose stem withers away to ground after one season's growth, often having medicinal or culinary uses
herbaceous (*adj*) designating nonwoody plant
holdfast portion of rootless plant that attaches to a surface
horsetail nonseed-bearing vascular plant with jointed stem, siliceous ribs, and a spore-bearing cone atop its stem
indehiscent (*adj*) not opening at maturity to discharge seeds
inflorescence production of blossoms; flower cluster on a common axis
kernel grain or seed, esp. inside fruit
lamella one of the radiating vertical plates on underside of cap of mushroom; gill
leaf flat, thin structure growing from stem or twig of plant, used in photosynthesis and transpiration
legume any of the family of herbaceous plants, shrubs, and vines having compound leaves, clusters of flowers, and fruit in form of pod
lenticel spongy area of bark on woody plant that permits exchange of gases between stem and atmosphere
lichen fungus in symbiotic union with an alga, formerly classified with plants; see under kingdom Fungi in Simpler Life Forms
ligneous (*adj*) forming or having the nature of wood; woody
lignin organic substance that serves as binder for cellulose fibers in wood and certain plants
liverwort any of various small, flat bryophytes, usu. encrusting logs, rocks, or soil in moist areas
meristem undifferentiated tissue from which new tissue arises
midrib central vein of leaf
monocot monocotyledon
monocotyledon angiosperm having only one seed leaf or cotyledon; monocot
moss any of various small bryophytes without true stems, reproducing by spores, and growing in velvety clusters in moist areas on rocks, trees, and the ground
mycelium mass of threadlike tubes forming the vegetative part of a fungus
nectar sugary fluid in many flowers, which attracts animal pollinators
nonvascular plant bryophyte
nut dry, single-seeded fruit of various trees and shrubs, consisting of kernel enclosed in hard or tough shell
nutation spontaneous movement of plant parts during growth
olfactory (*adj*) affecting, emitting, or having to do with smell
ovary enlarged base of pistil in flowering plants that encloses ovules
ovule female germ cell or rudimentary seed prior to fertilization
palynology study of pollen grains and spores
panicle loose, diversely branching flower clusters; compound raceme
parenchyma soft tissue forming chief substance of leaves and roots, fruit pulp, and center of stems
pectin white, colloidal carbohydrate, found in certain ripe fruits, that has thickening properties
pedicel stalk of single flower, fruit, or leaf
peduncle stalk supporting flower or flower cluster of an angiosperm or bearing the fruiting body of a fungus
perennial plant that lives more than two years, esp. herbaceous plant that produces flowers from the same root structure several years in a row
petal one of the circle of flower parts inside the sepals
petiole stem connecting a branch to a leaf blade
phloem nutrient-conducting tissue of vascular plants
photoperiodism capacity of plants to measure relative periods of daylight and darkness, thus anticipating and accommodating themselves to seasonal changes
photosynthesis production of organic substances from carbon dioxide and water in green plant cells which chemically transform radiant energy of sunlight
phototropism plant growth and movement toward light source
phytochrome light-detecting pigment involved in photoperiodism
phytoplankton aggregate of plants and other organisms in plankton
pileus horizontal part at top of mushroom stalk, bearing gills on its underside; cap
pinna one of the leaflets in featherlike arrangement along axis of a pinnate leaf
pistil central, seed-bearing part of flower, comprised of one or more carpels, each with style and stigma
plankton aggregate of passively floating or slightly motile organisms in a body of water, primarily algae and protozoa
plant member of the kingdom Plantae of multicelled organisms capable of carrying on photosynthesis in their cells, primarily adapted for terrestrial life
pod vessel enclosing one or more seeds, usu. splitting along two sutures at maturity

pollen fine, dustlike grains containing male sexual cells, produced in anthers or similar structures of seed plants
pollination transfer of pollen from stamen to upper tip of pistil
raceme diversely branching flowers lying along common axis
ray any of the flower stalks of an umbel
receptacle modified portion of stem or axis of flowering plant that bears the organs of a flower or flower head; torus
reticulate (*adj*) having veins arranged in netlike threads on leaves
rhizome creeping horizontal stem lying at or just beneath soil surface, which bears leaves at its tip and roots from its underside
root underground part of plant that functions in absorption, aeration, food storage, and as support system
runner long, slender stem growing from base of some perennials; stolon
saprophyte plant or fungus that feeds on dead and decaying organic matter
scale small leaf or bract covering and protecting the bud of a seed plant
sedge any of the family of rushlike or grasslike her-baceous plants growing in wet areas and having solid stems, slender leaves, and spikes of small flowers
seed fertilized plant ovule containing embryo, capable of germinating to produce new plant
self-pollination transfer of pollen from anther to stigma of same flower, another flower on same plant, or plant of same clone
sepal leaflike, usu. green outer circle of calyx
sessile (*adj*) attached at the base or without separate support structure
shrub woody perennial plant with several stems branching off near its base rather than a single trunk like a tree; bush
sieve tube longitudinal tube in phloem of flowering plants that conducts organic food materials through plant
spike inflorescence in which flowers bloom along entire length of single stalk
sporangium organ or single cell producing spores
spore haploid reproductive cell that on germination develops into the gametophyte
sporophyte spore-bearing, diploid, multicelled stage of many plants that begins with fertilized egg and ends with production of haploid spores
stalk stem or main axis of plant; any slender, supporting or connecting part of plant
stamen pollen-producing part of central flower, comprised of filament and anther
stem main upward-growing axis of plant
stigma free upper tip of a flower style on which pollen falls and develops
stipe stalk or slender support, such as petiole of a fern or stem of a mushroom
stolon stem that takes root at intervals along ground, forming new plants; runner
stoma microscopic opening in plant epidermis, esp. one through which gases are exchanged with the environment
style slender, stalklike part of carpel between stigma and ovary
succulent plant with thick, fleshy tissues that store water
taproot deep main root from which lateral roots develop
tendril threadlike, often spiral part of climbing plant which clings to or coils around objects
terminal bud bud growing at end of stem
thallus nonvascular plant body without clear differentiation into stems, leaves, or roots
torus receptacle of a flower
tree tall, woody perennial with single stem or trunk and branches that usu. begin at some height above the ground
tropophilous (*adj*) adapted to climate having marked environmental changes
trunk main stem of tree
tuber fat underground stem from which some plants grow, similar to but shorter and thicker than a rhizome
umbel cluster of flowers with stalks of nearly equal length that spring from the same point
vascular bundle arrangement of xylem and phloem that forms conducting system of a vascular plant
vascular plant any plant, such as the angiosperms, gymnosperms, or ferns, in which the xylem and phloem conduct water and organic nutrients
vegetable any plant, or part of a plant, that is used as food; see list under Foods
vegetative (*adj*) of plants, esp. pertaining to plant growth and nutrition; capable of growing as a plant
veil membrane that covers immature mushroom and breaks open, leaving veillike remnants usu. on stalk; annulus; velum
velum veil
vessel water-conducting tube in xylem
vine plant that grows along the ground or clings to a vertical support by means of twining stems, tendrils, or rootlets
weed vigorous plant of rank growth that tends to overcrowd more desirable neighboring plants; any plant that is unwanted
whorl circular growth of leaves or petals
woody (*adj*) designating a plant consisting of or forming wood; ligneous
xerophyte plant adapted for growth in arid conditions
xylem water and mineral-conducting woody tissue of vascular plants, found in stems, roots, and leaves, that supports softer tissues of plant
zygophyte plant that reproduces by means of zygospores
zygospore cell formed by fusion of two similar gametes, as in certain algae and fungi

Trees

tree tall, woody perennial with single stem or trunk and branches that usu. begin at some height above the ground

acacia, ailanthus, alder, algarroba, allspice, almond, American elm, annatto, apple, apricot, araucaria, arborvitae, arbutus, ash, aspen, avocado
bald cypress, balsa, balsam fir, balsam poplar, banana, banksia, banyan, baobab, basswood, bay, bayberry, bean tree, beech, betel palm, bigleaf maple, birch, black acacia, black alder, black ash, black cherry, black locust, black maple, black oak, blackthorn, black walnut, bombax, bottlebrush, box elder, boxwood, Brazil nut, brazilwood, breadfruit, bristlecone pine, buckeye, buckthorn, bumelia, butternut, buttonwood
cacao, California laurel, camphor tree, candleberry, carnauba, carob, cashew, cassia, catalpa, cedar, cercis, cherimoya, cherry, cherry plum, chestnut, chestnut oak, chinaberry, China tree, Chinese date, chinquapin, cinnamon, citron, citrus, clove, coconut, coffee tree, cork oak, cornel, cottonwood, cycad, cypress
dahoon, date palm, dogwood, Douglas fir, dungon
eastern hemlock, ebony, elder, elm, encina, eucalyptus
fig, fir, frankincense, fringe tree
gardenia, giant sequoia, ginkgo, gleditsia, grapefruit, guava, gum, gumbo-limbo
hackberry, hawthorn, hazel, hemlock, henna, hickory, holly, honey locust, hoptree, hornbeam, horse chestnut
Indian mulberry, ironwood
jacaranda, jarrah, Joshua tree, Judas tree, juniper
kauri, Kentucky coffee tree, kumquat
laburnum, lancewood, larch, laurel, lehua, lemon, lime, linden, litchi, locust, logwood, longleaf pine
madrone, magnolia, mahogany, manchineel, mango, mangosteen, mangrove, maple, mastic, medlar, mescal bean, mesquite, mimosa, ming tree, monkeypod, mountain ash, mulberry
Norway maple, nutmeg, nux vomica
oak, ohia lehua, Ohio buckeye, olive, orange, Osage orange
palm, palmetto, papaw, papaya, paper mulberry, paulownia, pawpaw, peach, pear, pecan, persimmon, pine, pistachio, plane, plum, pomegranate, pomelo, pond-apple, poplar
quince
raffia palm, rain tree, rambutan, redbud, red cedar, redwood, rosewood, rowan, royal poinciana, rubber
sago palm, sandalwood, sandarac, sapodilla, sappanwood, sassafras, satinwood, senna, sequoia, serviceberry, silk oak, silver maple, slash pine, snowbell, soapberry, sorb, sorrel tree, sour gum, soursop, speedwell, spruce, star apple, St. John's-bread, sumac, sweet cherry, sweet gum, sweetsop, sycamore
tacamahac, tamarack, tamarind, tangerine, tan oak, teak, thorn apple, thorn tree, thuja, tolu, tonka bean, toon, torreya, Torrey pine, tree of heaven, tulip oak, tulip tree, tupelo
upas
walnut, Washingtonia, Washington thorn, water elm, wattle, weeping willow, white fir, white poplar, white spruce, willow, willow oak, witch hazel
yellow pine, yellow poplar, yew

Shrubs

shrub woody perennial plant with several stems branching off near its base rather than a single trunk like a tree
alder, allspice, aloe, althea, arbutus, azalea
barbasco, barberry, bayberry, bignonia, bilberry, blackberry, black currant, blackthorn, bladdernut, blueberry, box, bramble, broom, buddleia, buffalo berry, buttonbush
caper, cascarilla, cassia, cayenne, chokeberry, cinchona, clematis, cleome, coca, coffee, coffeeberry, coralberry, cranberry, crowberry, cubeb, currant
daphne, deerberry, divi-divi
elder, elderberry, erica, euonymus
farkleberry, firethorn, flowering maple, forsythia, frangipani, fuchsia, furze
gardenia, genista, germander, gooseberry, gorse, grape, greasewood, greenbrier, guava, guayule, guelder rose
haw, heath, heather, hemlock, hemp tree, henna, hibiscus, holly, honeysuckle, huckleberry, hydrangea
Indian currant, Indian hawthorn, indigo, Italian jasmine
jojoba, Juneberry, jute
kalmia, kat, kumquat
laurel, lavender, leadwort, leatherleaf, lespedeza, lilac, ling
magnolia, manzanita, milkwort, mistletoe, mock orange, mountain cranberry, mountain currant, mountain fetterbush, mountain holly, mountain maple, myrtle
nandina, night jasmine, ninebark
oleander, Oregon grape
partridgeberry, pepper, Persian berry, philodendron, photinia, poison haw, poison ivy, poison oak, poison sumac, prickly ash, privet, pussy willow
quassia
raspberry, rhododendron, rose, rosebay, rosemary, rose of Sharon
sad tree, sage, sagebrush, sand myrtle, scarlet sage, serviceberry, sheepberry, shrimp plant, silverberry, sisal, sloe, smilax, snowberry, spicebush, spirea, staggerbush, strawberry guava, strawberry tree, sumac, syringa
tamarisk, tea tree, titi, toyon

veronica, viburnum
whin, wild hydrangea, winterberry, winter cherry, wintercreeper, wintergreen barberry, wisteria, witch hazel
yaupon, yellowroot
zenobia

Flowering Plants

flower seed-producing plant, usu. nonwoody, with a shortened stem bearing leaflike sepals, colorful petals, and pollen-bearing stamens clustered around pistils
flowering plant any angiosperm that produces flowers, fruit, and seeds in an enclosed ovary
acacia, adder's-tongue, African violet, agave, ageratum, ailanthus, amaranth, amaryllis, American Beauty rose, anemone, arbutus, arethusa, arnica, arrowhead, artichoke, asphodel, aspidistra, aster, atamasco lily, azalea
baby-blue-eyes, baby's-breath, bachelor's-button, begonia, berseem, betony, bird-of-paradise, bitterroot, black-eyed Susan, blazing star, bleeding heart, bloodroot, bluebell, bluebonnet, bluebottle, blue flag, bluet, boltonia, bridal wreath, broccoli, bromegrass, broom, brown-eyed Susan, buttercup, buttonbush
cactus, calendula, calla lily, calypso, camass, camellia, campanula, Canada thistle, candytuft, carnation, catalpa, cat's-paw, cattail, century plant, chamomile, Cherokee rose, Chinese lantern plant, Christmas rose, chrysanthemum, cineraria, clematis, clethra, cockscomb, collcroot, columbine, comfrey, compass plant, cornel, cornflower, corydalis, cosmos, cowslip, crocus, cyclamen
daffodil, dahlia, daisy, damask rose, dandelion, delphinium, dogwood, dragon's mouth, duckweed, Dutchman's-breeches, Dutchman's-pipe
edelweiss, eglantine, erigeron
fairy-slipper, figwort, fireweed, flax, fleur-de-lis, forget-me-not, forsythia, foxglove, foxtail, frangipani, fuchsia
gardenia, gentian, geranium, gladiolus, goatsbeard, golden aster, goldenrod, ground ivy, groundsel
harebell, hawkweed, hawthorn, heather, hepatica, hibiscus, hogweed, hollyhock, honeysuckle, horehound, horsemint, hyacinth, hydrangea
impatiens, Indian cress, Indian fig, Indian hemp, Indian paintbrush, Indian pipe, Indian strawberry, Indian warrior, indigo, iris, Italian aster
jack-in-the-pulpit, japonica, jasmine, jessamine, jonquil
knotweed
ladies'-tobacco, lady's-slipper, larkspur, lavender, lehua, lilac, lily, lily of the valley, lobelia, lotus, love-lies-bleeding, lupine
magnolia, mallow, marguerite, marigold, marsh mallow, marsh marigold, mayflower, maypop, mayweed, mignonette, mimosa, moccasin flower, mock orange, monkshood, morning glory, moss rose, motherwort, mountain laurel, mullein, myrtle
narcissus, nasturtium
ohia lehua, oleander, opium poppy, orchid, Oregon grape, Oswego tea, oxalis
pansy, pasqueflower, passionflower, pennyroyal, peony, periwinkle, petunia, phlox, pilewort, pink, pinxter flower, poinsettia, poppy, portulaca, prickly pear, primrose, pussy-toes, pyrethrum
Queen Anne's lace
rafflesia, ragwort, ranunculus, red fescue, resurrection plant, Rhode Island bent, rose, rose of Jericho, rudbeckia
safflower, saffron, saguaro, sansevieria, santonica, scarlet sage, shooting star, smilax, snapdragon, snowball, snowberry, snowdrop, snow plant, spirea, stock, strawflower, sunflower, swamp pink, sweet alyssum, sweet pea, sweet william
tamarisk, teasel, thistle, tidytips, trefoil, trillium, trumpet flower, trumpet vine, tulip
umbrella plant
vanilla, Venus's flytrap, verbena, vetch, viburnum, viola, violet
wallflower, water lily, wild rose, wisteria, wolfbane, woundwort
yarrow, yucca
zinnia

Grasses, Sedges, and Grasslike Plants

grass member of the family of flowering plants with long, narrow leaves, jointed stems, flowers in spikelets, and seedlike fruit
sedge any of the family of rushlike or grasslike herbaceous plants growing in wet areas and having solid stems, slender leaves, and spikes of small flowers
alfalfa, alfilaria, Australian rye grass
Bahia grass, bamboo, barley, barn grass, barnyard grass, beach grass, beard grass, bengal grass, bent, bent grass, Bermuda grass, blue grama, bluegrass, bluejoint, bog grass, bristly foxtail grass, bromegrass, broomcorn, buckwheat, buffalo grass, bulrush, bunch grass
canary grass, cane, China grass, chufa, cock's-foot, corn, cotton grass, couch grass, crab grass
darnel, durra, durum wheat
eelgrass, English rye grass
feather grass, fescue, finger grass, flyaway grass, foxtail, frog's-bit
gama grass, grama, guinea grass
hair grass, hassock, hay, herd's grass, horsetail
Indian corn, Italian rye grass

Japanese lawn grass, Job's-tears
Kentucky bluegrass, khus-khus, Korean lawn grass
lawn grass, lemon grass, little quaking grass, lovegrass, lyme grass
maize, meadow fescue, meadow foxtail, meadow grass, mesquite grass, millet, myrtle grass
oat, oat grass, orchard grass
paddy, pampas grass, papyrus, peppergrass, pin grass, plume grass, pony grass
quitch
red fescue, redtop, reed grass, Rhode Island bent, ribbon grass, rice, rush, rye, ryegrass
scouring rush, scutch grass, sedge, sheep fescue, silk grass, slender foxtail, sorghum, spear grass, squirrel-tail grass, squitch, star grass, striped grass, sugarcane, switch grass, sword grass
tear grass, timothy, tule, twitch grass
umbrella plant
vetiver, viper's grass
wheat, wild oat, wild rye, windlestraw, wire grass, witch grass, wood meadow grass, woolly beard grass, worm grass
yellow-eyed grass
zebra grass, zoysia

Herbaceous Plants

herb nonwoody, seed-producing plant whose stem withers away to the ground after season's growth, often having medicinal or culinary uses
ajuga, aluminum plant, amaranth, angelica, anise
balm, basil, belladonna, bellwort, bergamot, betony, birthwort, bitterroot, bladderwort, blue-curls, boneset, borage, bugle, bugleweed, burning bush, butterwort, button snakeroot
calamint, calendula, caraway, cardamom, carrot, castor-oil plant, catmint, catnip, cauliflower, celery, chamomile, charlock, chervil, chicory, cilantro, clover, coleus, coriander, corydalis, cowbane, cow parsnip, Cretan dittany, crowfoot, cumin
datura, deadly nightshade, death camass, dill, dittany, dropwort
eryngo
fennel, fenugreek, feverroot, figwort, finochio, Florence fennel, fool's-parsley, fraxinella
gas plant, germander, ginger, glasswort, ground ivy, ground pine
heliotrope, hemlock, hemp, hemp nettle, henbane, henbit, honewort, horehound, horsemint, hound's-tongue, hyssop
leadwort, lespedeza, licorice, lovage, lupine
mandrake, marijuana, marjoram, May apple, mint, monarda, monkshood, mullein, mustard
nutmeg
oregano, Oswego tea
parsley, parsnip, patchouli, pennyroyal, peppermint, perilla, philodendron
rattlesnake weed, rosemary, rudbeckia, rue
safflower, sage, salvia, samphire, sanicle, savory, scarlet sage, sea holly, sesame, sorrel, spearmint, spiderwort, sweet cicely, sweet woodruff
tansy, tarragon, teasel, thyme, tobacco, trefoil, turmeric
water hemlock, wild bergamot, wild marjoram, wintergreen, woodruff, wormwood, wort, woundwort
yarrow

Ferns

fern nonflowering, vascular plant having roots, stems, and fronds and reproducing by spores instead of seeds
adder's-tongue
basket fern, bead fern, beech fern, bladder fern, Boston fern, boulder fern, bracken, bristle fern, brittle fern, buckler fern
chain fern, Christmas fern, cinnamon fern, cliff brake, climbing fern, crested fern, curly grass fern
fern, fragile fern
grape fern
hart's-tongue, hay-scented fern, holly fern
interrupted fern
lady fern, limestone fern, lip fern
maidenhair, male fern, marsh fern, moonwort, mosquito fern
New York fern
oak fern, osmund, ostrich fern
parsley fern, polypody, pteridosperm
rattlesnake fern, resurrection fern, rock brake, royal fern
seed fern, sensitive fern, shield fern, snuffbox fern, spleenwort
walking fern, walking leaf, wall fern, water fern, wood fern, woodsia

Vines

vine plant that grows along the ground or clings to a vertical support by means of twining stems, tendrils, or rootlets
actinidia, Algerian ivy, ampelopsis, Amur grape, asparagus fern
balsam apple, balsam pear, bean, bittersweet, Boston ivy, bottle gourd, bougainvillea, boxthorn, bramble, bryony
cantaloupe, cape plumbago, casaba, catclaw vine, chayote, Chinese wisteria, clematis, convolvulus, coral greenbrier, creeping fig, cross-vine, cucumber, curly clematis
dewberry, dichondra
elephant's-foot, English ivy, everblooming honeysuckle
fleevine, fox grape
gloryvine, golden clematis, gourd, grape, grapevine, greenbrier

Hall's honeysuckle, honeysuckle, hop, horsebrier, Hottentot's bread
ipomoea, ivy
jackman clematis, Japanese creeper, Japanese wisteria, jasmine, jovin clematis
kudzu vine
liana, loofah
matrimony vine, melon, milkweed, monk's hood vine, moonseed, morning glory, muscat
pea, peppervine, poison ivy, poison oak, pokeweed, porcelain ampelopsis, primrose jasmine, pumpkin
rag gourd, rambler rose, Regel's tripterygium, runner bean
scarlet clematis, scarlet kadsura, sevenleaf creeper, silvervine, similax, squash, star jasmine, stephanotis, string bean, summer squash, sweet honeysuckle
teasel gourd, traveler's-joy, trumpet creeper, trumpet honeysuckle, trumpet vine
vanilla, vegetable sponge, vetch, Virginia creeper, virgin's bower
wandering Jew, watermelon, wintercreeper, winter jasmine, winter squash, wire vine, wisteria, woodbine
yam

Weeds

weed vigorous plant of rank growth that usu. reproduces profusely, is difficult to eliminate, and tends to overcrowd more desirable neighboring plants; any plant that is unwanted and interferes with growth of other plants, including many grasses, herbs, and mosses
barren strawberry, bedstraw, beggar-ticks, Bermuda grass, bindweed, bird's-eye pearlwort, bitter nightshade, black bindweed, bluegrass, blueweed, bracken, brake, broad-leaved dock, buckthorn, buckthorn plantain, bugleweed, bull thistle, bur, burdock
Canada thistle, Carolina horse nettle, carpetweed, cat's-ear, cattail, charlock, chickweed, chicory, cinquefoil, clover, cocklebur, corn spurry, cottonweed, couch grass, crab grass, crane's-bill, crazyweed, creeping buttercup, creeping cinquefoil, creeping speedwell, creeping veronica, curled dock
dandelion, devil's paintbrush, dewberry, dock, duckweed
English lawn daisy, Eurasian water milfoil
field bindweed, field chickweed, field horsetail, figwort, fireweed, foxtail
galinsoga, goose grass, goutweed, ground ivy, groundsel
hawkweed, heal-all, hedge bindweed, hemlock, hemp nettle, henbit, hogweed, horehound, horseradish, horsetail, horseweed, hydrilla
ice plant
Japanese fleeceflower, Japanese knotweed, jimson weed, Johnson grass
knawel, knotweed
lace grass, lady's-thumb, lamb's-quarters, liverwort, locoweed
mallow, mayweed, milfoil, milkweed, motherwort, mouse-ear chickweed, mouse-ear hawkweed, mustard
nettle, nut sedge
Oldfield cinquefoil, oxalis, oxeye daisy
pearlwort, peppergrass, pepperweed, pigweed, pilewort, pineapple weed, plantain, poison ivy, poke, pokeberry, pokeweed, prickly lettuce, prostrate knotweed, purslane
quack grass, quitch
ragweed, redroot pigweed, red sorrel, Russian thistle
sandbur, scarlet pimpernel, Scotch broom, self-heal, sheep sorrel, shepherd's-purse, skunk cabbage, smartweed, sorrel, sow thistle, spatterdock, speedwell, spotted lady's-thumb, spotted spurge, spurge, spurry, statice, stinging nettle, stinkweed, St.-John's-wort, strawflower, sulfur cinquefoil, swallowwort
tall buttercup, tansy, tarweed, tassel flower, thistle, thorn apple, tumbleweed
velvetleaf, Virginia pepperwood
water chestnut, water hyacinth, western sage, wheatgrass, white clover, wild carrot, wild garlic, wild lettuce, wild mustard, wild oat, wild onion, wild parsnip, wild radish, wild vetch, witch grass, witchweed
yarrow, yellow foxtail, yellow nut sedge, yellow wood sorrel

SIMPLER LIFE FORMS

Fungi
Algae
Bacteria
Viruses

Fungi

fungus member of the kingdom Fungi, consisting of unicellullar or filamentous, multinucleate, eukaryotic organisms that live by decomposing and feed on dead or living organic matter in which they grow and decompose, formerly classified with plants, consisting of four divisions: Zygomycota, Ascomycota, Basidiomycota, and Deuteromycota
lichen fungus in symbiotic union with an alga

Zygomycota

zygomycota free-living terrestrial fungi, as well as plant and animal parasites, that reproduce sexually by formation of zygospores
black bread mold
dung fungus
zygomycetes

Ascomycota

ascomycota sac fungi, having sexual spores in a sac
ascomycetes
black mold, blue-green mold, bread mold
cup fungus
dead-man's fingers, downy mildew
earth tongue
false mildew, false morel
lorchel
mildew, mold, morel, mushroom pimple
powdery mildew
red bread mold
sac fungus
truffle
yeast

Basidiomycota

basidiomycota club fungi, bearing spores at tips of slender projections on a basidium, including most forms commonly called mushrooms
basidiomycetes, bird's-nest fungus, boletus, bracket fungus, brittlegill
chanterelle, coral fungus, crumblecap
deathcap
earthstar
field mushroom
gill fungus, groundwart
inky cap
jelly fungus
meadow mushroom, milkcap, mottlegill, mushroom
oyster cap
parasol mushroom, pink gill, pore fungus, puffball
ringstalk, roof mushroom, rust
scalecap, sheath mushroom, shelf fungus, shiitake, slime mushroom, smoothcap, smut, stinkhorn
toadstool, tooth fungus, tricholoma
waxy cap, webcap, woodcrust

Deuteromycota

deuteromycota imperfect fungi, mostly parasitic with no sexual stage
aspergillus
blue mold
deuteromycetes
Fungi Imperfecti
green mold
moniliales
penicillium
ringworm fungus
thrush fungus
verticillium

Algae

alga any unicellular, colonial, or filamentous eukaryotic organism belonging to kingdom Protista, with no root, stem, or leaf and having no nonreproductive cells in its reproductive structures, containing chlorophyll masked by red or brown pigment, and growing in water or damp places
Protista kingdom of algae, amebas, and protozoans, consisting of photosynthetic autotrophs and heterotrophs

Photosynthetic autotrophs

photosynthetic autotroph organism capable of self-nourishment by using inorganic materials as its source of nutrients and photosynthesis as its source of energy
brown algae
carrageen, chlorophytes, chrysophytes, conferva, cryptomonads
diatoms, dinoflagellates, dulse
euglenas, euglenophytes
fucus
golden-brown algae, green algae, gulfweed
Irish moss
kelp
olive-brown seaweed
phaeophytes, pond scum, pyrrophytes
red algae, rhodophytes, rockweed
sargasso, sargassum, sea lettuce, sea moss, seaweed, sea wrack, stonewort
wrack
yellow-green algae

Heterotrophs

heterotroph organism requiring living or dead organic materials as its principal source of nutrients
protozoans animallike, eukaryotic organisms of kingdom Protista, primarily unicellular, colonial, and nonphotosynthetic, categorized by means of motility as ciliates, flagellates, or pseudopods
acrasiomycetes, amebas
cellular slime molds, chytrids, ciliates
flagellates
myxomycetes
oomycetes, opalinids
plasmodial slime molds, protozoans, pseudopods
slime molds, sporozoans
water molds

Bacteria

bacteria *pl., sing.* bacterium; ubiquitous, unicellular organisms appearing singly or in chains in spherical, spiral, or rod-shaped form, forming major phylum of kingdom Monera
Monera kingdom of prokaryotic organisms, or cells without a membrane-bound nucleus and membrane-bound organelles, that reproduce by asexual budding or fission

Bacterial form groups

bacilli *pl., sing.* bacillus; rod-shaped bacteria
cocci *pl., sing.* coccus; spherical bacteria
spirilla *pl., sing.* spirillum; long, spiral, rod-shaped bacteria

vibrios *pl., sing.* vibrio; short, curved, or S-shaped bacteria

Eubacteria

eubacteria true bacteria, including most free-living and parasitic bacteria with simple, undifferentiated cells having rigid walls
actinomycetes
blue-green algae
cyanobacteria
endospore-forming bacteria
green nonsulfur bacteria, green sulfur bacteria
lactic acid bacteria
mycoplasmas
purple nonsulfur bacteria, purple sulfur bacteria
spirochetes

Archaebacteria

archaebacteria surviving members of branch of prokaryotes adapted to earliest stages of biological evolution
halobacteria, halophiles
methanobacteria, methanogens
thermoacidophiles

Viruses

virus ultramicroscopic, metabolically inert agent that can reproduce only within a host cell but is partially independent, consisting of nucleic acid enclosed in a protein coat, not fitting into any of the five kingdoms and classified by whether it infects bacteria, plants, or animals

Bacteriophages

bacteriophage any virus that infects specific bacteria; phage
corticovirus, cystovirus
inovirus
levivirus
microvirus, myovirus
pedovirus, plasmavirus
stylovirus
tectivirus

Plant viruses

alfalfa mosaic virus
bromovirus
carlavirus, caulimovirus, closterovirus, comovirus, cucumovirus
hordeivirus
ilarvirus
luteovirus
nepovirus
potexvirus, potyvirus
tobacco mosaic virus, tobacco necrosis virus, tobamovirus, tobravirus, tomato spotted wilt virus, tombusvirus, tymovirus

Animal viruses

adenovirus, arbovirus, arenavirus
baculovirus, bunyavirus
coronavirus
enterovirus, Epstein-Barr virus
herpesvirus
influenza virus, iridovirus
orbivirus, orthomyxovirus
papovavirus, paramyxovirus, parvovirus, picornavirus, poliovirus, poxvirus
reovirus, retrovirus, rhabdovirus, rhinovirus, Rous sarcoma virus
togavirus

Chapter Three
The Earth

GEOLOGY

Branches and Disciplines
Materials, Formations, and Substances
Processes, Phenomena, Events, and Techniques
Geological Time Scale
Mining

Branches and Disciplines

astrogeology geology of celestial bodies in our solar system
chronostratigraphy system of dividing geologic time into eras, periods, epochs, and ages
crystallography study of form, structure, and properties of crystals
earth sciences various sciences dealing with Earth and its nonliving components
ecology study of the relationship between organisms and their environments
environmental geology study of the interaction between human beings and the Earth
geobotany study of the distribution of plant species
geochemistry study of chemical composition and activity in Earth's crust
geochronology study of the age of Earth and dating of evolutionary stages of development
geochronometry measurement of geologic time by radioactive decay
geodesy branch of mathematics concerned with determining size and shape of Earth and position of points on its surface
geodynamics study of activity and forces inside Earth
geography descriptive science that deals with Earth's surface
geology science of Earth's origin, evolution, and structure as recorded in rocks, crust, interior, and fossils
geomorphology study of nature, origin, and development of Earth's landforms
geophysics physics of phenomena occurring on Earth
geopolitics interrelationship of politics and geography
historical geology study of the history of Earth
hydrology study of Earth's water, its distribution and cycles
lithology study of rocks based on megascopic examination of samples
marine geology study of ocean's origin and structure, esp. its floor
metallurgy science and technology of metals and their separation from ores
mineralogy scientific study of minerals
mining engineering applied mineralogy and metallurgy
oceanography science of ocean movement and life
orography physical geography of mountains
paleogeography study of geography of the past
paleontology study of fossils
pedology soil science
petrology study of rocks
physical geology study of material composing Earth
planetology study of the planetary system
seismology study of seismic waves generated by earthquakes or other Earth vibrations
soil science applied study of soil and earth
stratigraphy study of deposition of sediments
structural geology study of structural features of rocks and geographical distributions of these features
tectonics study of movements that shape Earth's crust

Materials, Formations, and Substances

abyssal plain flat plain on ocean floor
abyssal zone lightless depths of open sea, usu. deeper than 12,000 feet (3700m)
agglomerate mass of heat-fused fragments of volcanic rock
aggregate rock composed of mixture of mineral fragments, crystals, and other materials
alloy two or more metals, or a metal and nonmetal, fused together when molten
alluvial fan cone-shaped deposit of earth made by flowing water
alluvium clay, silt, sand, or gravel sediment deposited by running water
alpine glacier valley glacier
amalgam alloy of mercury with another metal or metals
anthracite hard coal that burns almost without flame
anticline configuration of folded, stratified rocks in which rocks dip in two directions away from a crest
aquifer permeable rock that holds groundwater
artesian well well under pressure from weight of water in aquifer column
ash finely powdered volcanic lava
asthenosphere layer of Earth's crust near melting point, almost fluid
atoll coral island remaining after reef sinks below sea level
barrier beach narrow strip of sand and rock separated from coast by channel
batholith large mass of intrusive, igneous rock extending very deep into Earth's crust
bathyal zone ocean area extending beyond continental shelf to depth of about 12,000 feet (3700m)
beach strip of loose, grainy material where land and large body of water meet
bed thin layer of sedimentary rock separating different materials lying above and below it
bedrock solid rock underneath soil layer
berm low ridge built up by storm waves
bitumen naturally occurring asphalt; hard or semisolid tarlike residue of petroleum or coal tar distillation

bituminous coal soft coal
boulder detached, rounded, and worn large mass of rock
breccia rock composed of angular fragments of older rocks
caldera crater formed by explosion and collapse of volcano
calf mass of ice broken off from glacier or iceberg
cast mineral or mud deposited and hardened where body of an organism decayed to form a fossil
cave hollow area in earth with opening at surface
cavern large, roofed-over cave or passageway in rock, often formed by groundwater passing through cracks in limestone
cinder rough piece of solid volcanic lava; slag from reduction of metal ores; intermediate state of burned matter not yet reduced to ash
cirque hollow mountain basin that collects snow, caused by glaciation
clastic rock containing rock particles, minerals, and crushed shells
clay soil composed of fine particles of hydrous aluminum silicates, plastic when wet, and hard when exposed to high temperature and/or pressure
coal black, combustible mineral solid that results from partial decomposition of organic matter under heat and pressure over millions of years
conchoidae fracture fracture that produces curved surfaces similar to those of interior of a shell
cone peak of volcano
conglomerate rock, such as hardened clay, composed of rounded fragments of varying sizes in cement
continent large landmass on surface of Earth
continental glacier large glacier covering major part of a landmass
continental shelf edge of continental landmass covered by ocean
continental slope edge of continental shelf that slopes steeply down to ocean floor
coral reef structure on continental shelf made of shells of colonial marine organisms
core innermost part of Earth
crag steep, rugged rock projecting above rock mass
crater round pit, esp. at summit of volcano
crevasse deep crack in glacial ice
crust thin outer layer of Earth's surface, composed of sial and sima layers
crystal body created by solidification of chemical element or compound into regular atomic arrangement with plane faces; quartz that is close to transparent
delta sediment deposited at river mouth
deposit sediment laid down in new location; pocket of mineral or ore in earth
detritus rock fragments resulting from disintegration by weathering and erosion
diamond mineral of nearly pure crystalline carbon, hardest natural substance known
divide ridge separating two drainage basins
drainage basin area drained by river and its tributaries
dune mound or ridge of sand accumulated by wind
earth soft, granular, crumbly part of land; soil; land surface of the world
eluvium rock debris produced by weathering or disintegration
esker deposit formed by water running under glacier
evaporite rock formed by water evaporating from a mineral mass
extrusive rock igneous rock formed on Earth's surface or seabed, not underground
facies fossil fossil species adapted to limited environment
firn granular ice formed by recrystallization of snow
flint hard quartz that produces spark when struck by steel
fluvial (*adj*) produced by rivers
fossil living thing preserved from previous geologic era in petrified rock form
fossil fuel fuel source, such as coal or petroleum, deposited in earth from organic remains during earlier geologic age
freestone stone, such as limestone or sandstone, that may be cut freely without splitting
gemstone hard mineral, crystal, or petrified material used as jewelry when cut and faceted, designated precious or semiprecious
geode hollow stone nodule lined by mineral crystals growing inward
geosyncline very large, troughlike depression in Earth's surface containing masses of sedimentary and volcanic rock
geyser thermal spring that intermittently ejects water with considerable force
glacier massive, moving ice layer formed in previous geologic era by accumulation and recrystallization of snow
granite very hard crystalline igneous rock found in mountain cores
gravel loose, rounded fragments of rock; stratum of gravel
ground moraine debris remaining from melting of glacier and forming gently rolling surface
groundwater water trapped in underground pores or fissures in earth
hadal zone the deepest trenches of the ocean bottom, usu. deeper than 20,000 feet (6000m)
humus portion of soil made up of decomposed organic matter
hydrocarbon compound of hydrogen and carbon, including fossil fuels
hydrosphere Earth's water environment, including glaciers, oceans, atmospheric vapor, lakes, streams, groundwater, snow, and ice
iceberg mass of ice detached from glacier and floating at sea
icecap localized ice sheet
ice pack expanse of floating ice formed over time due to compaction of ice by wind and currents
ice sheet broad, moundlike mass of glacial ice of considerable extent
igneous rock rock formed by cooling and hardening of magma

index fossil fossil from specific time range, used to date rock layer surrounding it
inorganic material matter that is not animal or vegetable, esp. compounds not containing carbon and derived from mineral sources
intrusive rock igneous rock formed by magma cooling and hardening underground, esp. in cracks or cavities in existing rock
joint break in rock mass with no movement of rock on opposite sides of break
kame detrital mound left by retreating ice sheet, usu. stratified sand and gravel
kettle lake body of water formed by melting glaciers moving over a basin
lava magma reaching surface of Earth, usu. through volcano
lignite low-grade brown coal
limestone calcium carbonate rock formed by accumulation of organic remains of sea animals
lithosphere Earth's crust and upper part of mantle
load soil particles and rock carried by running water, wind, or glaciers
loam rich soil of clay, sand, and organic matter
lodestone rock that possesses magnetic polarity
loess fine, windblown dust particles that are unconsolidated and unstratified
magma hot, molten rock within Earth
mantle solid layer beneath Earth's crust to depth of 1800 miles (2900 km)
mantle rock loose material, residual or transported, resting on solid rock of Earth's crust
marl loose, crumbling earthy deposit of clay and limestone
massif block of Earth's crust bounded by faults and displaced as unchanged unit to form principal mountain mass
meltwater water melted from glacial ice
mesa hill with flattened top of hard sandstone or limestone
metal opaque, fusible, ductile, conductive, lustrous substance, often a chemical element or compound yielding oxides or hydroxides
metamorphic rock igneous or sedimentary rock that has been transformed by heat, pressure, or chemically active fluids
meteorite small particle of matter from space that reaches surface of Earth without being vaporized
mineral inorganic chemical solid naturally occurring in Earth's crust and having definite chemical composition and tendency to form crystals
monadnock resistant rock hill standing well above surrounding peneplain
monolith single large block of stone
moraine rock ridge left after disappearance of glacier, composed of till
mountain natural landform or ridge in Earth's crust, elevated at least to 2000 feet (600 m)
mountain core granite rock at center of mountain, surrounded by metamorphic rock
native metal pure metal, usu. found in vein
natural gas combustible mixture of gaseous hydrocarbons, largely methane, that accumulates in porous sedimentary rocks, used as a fossil fuel
noble mineral precious, pure mineral, esp. corrosion-resistant metal such as gold
nodule mineral lump composed primarily of chert or flint
nonclastic rock sedimentary rock composed of interlocking rock that forms grains
nonfoliated rock nonbanded metamorphic rock
oolite spherical grain of sand size, usu. composed of calcium carbonate, originated by inorganic precipitation
organic material substance derived from living organism
outcropping emergence of rock formation from Earth to surface exposure
outwash material carried by glacier and laid down in stratified deposits
Pangaea hypothetical continent that broke apart to form continents as they now exist
peat partly carbonized decaying vegetable matter; first stage in formation of coal
pebble small stone worn smooth and round
peneplain flat area just slightly above sea level worn down by streams and mass wasting
permafrost permanently frozen subsoil in arctic regions
petroleum oily, flammable hydrocarbon found in rock strata, refined to produce gasoline
piedmont flat expanse of land lying at foot of mountain
plain flat, broad land area slightly above sea level
plate one of huge, movable segments into which Earth's crust is divided and which float over mantle
plateau flat, broad land area at least 2000 feet (600 m) above sea level
playa flat-floored center of undrained desert basin
plutonic rock igneous rock formed by slow crystallization, usu. at great depth
porphyry rock with two or more grain sizes
precious metal rare and therefore valuable metal, such as gold or silver, used in jewelry
precious stone designation for most valuable gemstones, such as diamonds or emeralds
precipitate rock formed from discharge or evaporation of water
quartz common, colorless, usu. transparent mineral of hexagonal crystals or crystalline masses
range system of connected mountains
reef wave-resistant structure composed of sedentary, carbonate-secreting organisms
residual soil with composition similar to that of bedrock below it
rhyolite fine-grained volcanic rock produced by lava flow
rill miniature stream channel carrying sheet wash
rimrock top stratum of plateau that outcrops to form vertical face
rock large mass of stone, concreted mass of stony material, or broken piece of such a mass
rubble rough, irregular, loose fragments broken from larger mass of rock
sand loose granular material formed by disintegration of rocks into particles smaller than gravel but coarser than silt
sandstone sedimentary rock usu. of quartz sand cemented by silica or calcium carbonate

schist metamorphic rock that can be easily split due to effects of heat
scoria loose, cinderlike lava; slag left after smelting
scree loose rock debris; talus
seamount volcanic mountain at bottom of ocean
sediment material deposited by water, wind, or glaciers
sedimentary rock rock formed on Earth's surface from accumulation of material deposited by water, wind, or glaciers
semiprecious stone designation for gems less valuable than precious stones, such as garnets or turquoise
shale consolidation of clay, mud, or silt into finely stratified rock structure of unaltered minerals
silica silicon dioxide that occurs as crystalline quartz, opal, or sand
sill thin layer of igneous rock extruded between layers of sedimentary rocks or volcanic ejecta
silt loose sedimentary material with particles finer than sand and coarser than clay
slag refuse material separated from metal in smelting; lava resembling such refuse
sludge muddy, slushy mass or sediment, esp. on riverbed
slurry water mixture of insoluble mud or lime
soil fragments of weathered rock combined with organic matter
soil horizon layer of soil parallel to land surface
stalactite columnar deposit of minerals hanging from cave ceiling
stalagmite columnar deposit of minerals on cavern floor, caused by accretion of dripping mineral-rich water from ceiling
stone concretion of earthy or mineral matter of indeterminate size and shape; one piece of such concretion
stratified rock rock made up of many different layers
stratum sheetlike mass of sedimentary or igneous rock, usu. lying between other strata beds
syncline fold in rock where strata dip inward from both sides
talus sloping mass formed by pile of loose rock fragments and weathered matter collected at foot of cliff or on slope below rock face
tarn lake formed at bottom of cirque after glacial ice has disappeared
tarpit flat area in which natural bitumens, such as tar or asphalt, collect and are exposed to air so that animals fall in and have their bones preserved
terminal moraine debris piled up at point of farthest glacial advance
terrace flat platform at base of eroded sea cliff
till mix of material dropped from melting glacier
topsoil fertile soil made up mainly of humus
trace fossil imprint left by animal track or burrow
trench long, very deep trough in ocean floor bordering some continents
tufa limestone deposited by springs
tundra polar area soil, composed mainly of peat, whose top layer thaws each spring while base remains frozen year-round
underground rock rock deposits not exposed at Earth's surface
valley glacier glacier formed at high elevation, covering river valley; alpine glacier
vent opening at Earth's surface from which volcanic material is emitted
vesicle small cavity in rock formed by gas bubble, occurring in rock in its molten state
volcanic rock igneous rock that solidified rapidly from molten lava at Earth's surface
volcano cone-shaped mountain that vents hot, molten lava, gases, and rock fragments from Earth's interior

Processes, Phenomena, Events, and Techniques

abrasion wearing away of rock by solid particles carried by wind, water, ice, or gravity
aftershock minor earthquake following greater one and originating at same place
age interval of geologic time shorter than an epoch
antipodes two places at opposite sides of Earth
avalanche expanding mass of loosened material sliding suddenly and swiftly down mountain
belt elongated area, smaller than a zone, characterized by particular features or occurrences
body wave earthquake that moves underground
Brinell hardness measure of hardness of metal or alloy
carat unit of weight for diamonds or gemstones, equal to 200 mg (.007 ounce)
carbon-14 dating radiocarbon dating
carboniferous (*adj*) designating coal-making period of Paleozoic era
cataclysm great upheaval that causes sudden, violent changes in Earth
cleavage pattern of breakage of rock or minerals along flat planes
coalification process by which vegetable matter is transformed into coal
columnar jointing columns of rock formed by slowly cooling lava
comminution particle size reduction by physical processes
compaction reduction in pore space between individual grains due to pressure
compression stress force squeezing crustal rock together
concretion sedimentary rock with succeeding layers of minerals forming around a grain of sand or other nucleus
continental drift very slow motion of major landmasses around Earth's surface
Coriolis effect tendency of any moving body starting from surface of Earth to continue in direction propelled by Earth's rotation
crystallization process in which crystals separate from fluid, viscous, or dispersed structure
decomposition chemical formation of new compounds from elements within rock; chemical weathering
deep ocean current water motion caused by differences in temperature and density

deflation removal of loose particles from ground by action of wind
dendrite branching pattern made by one mineral crystallizing in another
earthquake sudden, violent shaking of Earth's crust
elasticity ability of material to recover from a deforming force
elevation height above sea level
emergent coast land exposed by lowering of sea level
eolian (*adj*) carried, deposited, or eroded by the wind
epicenter point on Earth's surface directly above focus of earthquake
epoch smallest major unit of geologic time; subdivision of period
era largest major unit of geologic time, divided into periods and epochs
erosion wearing down of natural landforms by wind, water, ice, or gravity
eruption sudden, often violent, outflow of lava from volcano
eustasy uniformly global change in sea level, due to change in quantity of water or shape of ocean basins
fault crack in Earth's crust from rock slippage up, down, or sideways
flood plain river valley area flooded at high water
focus underground center of earthquake
fold bend or turn in crustal rock
foliation metamorphic rock banding
foreshock minor earthquake that precedes larger earthquake and originates at its focus
fracture characteristic manner of breakage of mineral
geodetic survey precise description of large land area corrected for Earth's curvature
geologic column layering of rock strata in order from oldest at bottom to youngest at top
geologic time scale convention of viewing geologic history in eras, epochs, and periods, based on fossil data
geomagnetic (*adj*) relating to magnetic properties of Earth
geomorphic (*adj*) pertaining to shape of Earth and its topography
geotectonic (*adj*) relating to structure, distribution, and shape of rock bodies in Earth's crust; pertaining to the conditions within Earth that resulted in movement of crust
geothermal gradient rate of increase of temperature downward into Earth
geothermal power energy from heat of Earth's interior
geothermic (*adj*) relating to heat of Earth's interior
hardness resistance of substance to scratching
horizon specific position in stratigraphic column that identifies stratum with a particular period; soil layer
hydrologic cycle movement of Earth's water from oceans to atmosphere to land and back to oceans
ice age any time of widespread glaciation, esp. Pleistocene glacial epoch
interglacial age historic period between ice ages
isostasy balancing of floating crustal rock on denser mantle
karst topography irregular topography developed by action of surface and underground water in soluble rock such as limestone
landslide collapse of sloped or vertical face of earth or rock
law of superimposition rule that in layered beds of rock, oldest is deepest, youngest is closest to surface
leaching washing away of soluble minerals, esp. alkalines, from upper layers of soil by water
lithification hardening into rock
luster capacity of minerals to reflect light off their surfaces
meander curve formed in riverbed
mold fossil cavity left in rock after body of organism has decayed
normal fault fault formed when one side moves up, the other down
oasis fertile area in desert formed by erosion of surface down to water table
orogeny formation of mountains by folding of Earth's crust
period second major unit of geologic time, subdivision of era, divided into epochs
permeability measure of the ease with which fluid can be passed through pore space of rock
petrified (*adj*) designating organic matter replaced by minerals over time
phase description of minerals present in a rock or soil sample
plate tectonics theory of formation and motion of Earth's crust and its moving plates
porosity percent of total volume of rock not occupied by solid mineral matter
primary waves seismic waves that move fastest through all forms of matter
radioactive decay breaking apart over time of atomic nucleus, with emission of radiant energy
radiocarbon dating dating of fossil remains by measuring ratio of remaining radioactive carbon 14 to total carbon; carbon-14 dating
recrystallization melting and recooling of rock, resulting in larger grain
relief elevation differences among landforms
Richter scale logarithmic scale, ranging from 1 to 10, that indicates magnitude of an earthquake in terms of energy released
rift valley long, narrow valley formed between two faults
rift zone system of fractures in Earth's crust
ring of fire area of earthquake and volcanic activity around rim of Pacific Ocean
rock cycle change in form of Earth materials subjected to geological processes, esp. from magma to igneous, metamorphic, and sedimentary rock, and back to magma
secondary waves seismic waves that pass through solids but not liquids or gases and that move slower than primary waves

seismic wave earthquake wave
seismograph instrument that records magnitude of earthquake as moving graph line
soil layer horizon
soil profile cross section of soil horizons that shows different levels
solfatara volcanic fissure that emits vapors, steam, and sometimes hot mud, but not lava
stack vertical block of resistant rock cut off from mainland by wave action
stratification formation into layers or beds
stress force applied to material that tends to change its dimensions
structural mountain mountain formed from uplift of crust
surface wave earthquake moving on surface of Earth
survey detailed description of tract of land
topography physical features of geographical area
tsunami huge ocean wave caused by underwater earthquake or volcanic eruption
upthrust elevation of part of Earth's surface
vein narrow water channel in rock or earth
vent volcano opening from which lava erupts
volcanism volcanic activity and phenomena
water table level of water saturation into soil and rock; upper surface of zone of saturation below ground
weathering changes in rock produced by heat, cold, wind, precipitation, and living matter
zone large region of Earth's surface with distinctive characteristics

Geological Time Scale

Note: *Entries for geological eras, periods, and epochs have been listed in chronological order, from the earliest to the most recent.*

Precambrian era 3800 million to 600 million years ago; Archeozoic and Proterozoic eras
Azoic era earliest Precambrian era, preceding appearance of life; former term for Archeozoic era
Archeozoic era early Precambrian era, beginning 3800 million years ago; Earth's crust solidifies; blue-green algae and earliest life forms appear
Proterozoic era later Precambrian era, ending 600 million years ago; bacteria, algae, and primitive multicellular life
Paleozoic era 600 to 225 million years ago; Cambrian, Ordovician, Silurian, Devonian, Carboniferous, and Permian periods
Cambrian period 600 to 500 million years ago; age of marine invertebrates, shellfish, and echinoderms
Ordovician period 500 to 425 million years ago; primitive fishes, seaweeds, and fungi
Silurian period 425 to 400 million years ago; abundant shellfish; first land plants and modern fungi
Devonian period 400 to 345 million years ago; age of fishes; first amphibians, insects, and land animals appear
Carboniferous period 345 to 280 million years ago; Mississippian and Pennsylvanian periods
Mississippian period 345 to 320 million years ago; age of amphibians; shallow seas, low lands, and fern forests
Pennsylvanian period 320 to 280 million years ago; first reptiles; warm climate with swamps and cool forests
Permian period 280 to 225 million years ago; conifer forests; extinction of many marine invertebrates
Mesozoic era 225 to 65 million years ago; Triassic, Jurassic, and Cretaceous periods
Triassic period 225 to 190 million years ago; age of reptiles; active volcanoes
Jurassic period 190 to 135 million years ago; age of dinosaurs and flying reptiles; first birds and mammals
Cretaceous period 135 to 65 million years ago; last dinosaurs; modern insects; flowering plants
Cenozoic era 65 million years ago to present; Tertiary and Quaternary periods
Tertiary period 65 to 1.7 million years ago; Paleocene, Eocene, Oligocene, Miocene, and Pliocene epochs
Paleocene epoch 65 to 54 million years ago; age of mammals begins; mild to cool climate; first primates
Eocene epoch 54 to 38 million years ago; modern birds and mammals; warm climate; giant birds
Oligocene epoch 38 to 26 million years ago; browsing mammals and saber-toothed tigers
Miocene epoch 26 to 12 million years ago; widespread grasslands; grazing mammals; apes; whales
Pliocene epoch 12 to 1.7 million years ago; cool climate; mountain uplift; mammals increase in size and numbers
Quaternary period 1.7 million years ago to present; Pleistocene and Holocene epochs
Pleistocene epoch 1.7 million to 10,000 years ago; ice ages
Holocene epoch 10,000 years ago to present; modern humans

Mining

adit almost horizontal passageway into mine
afterdamp mixture of gases left in mine after explosion of fire
airway ventilating passage in mine
assay analysis of ore or alloy to determine proportion and purity of components; (*vb*) make such an analysis
bed layer, stratum, or substance in which minerals or ores are lodged
blackdamp chokedamp
black lung disease caused by inhalation of coal dust
borehole hole drilled in earth to extract core or release gas, oil, or water
borrow pit excavated area from which material has been removed to fill another spot
brattice air passage in mine formed of planks or cloth lining the tunnel

cave-in collapse of mine shaft or tunnel
chokedamp mine atmosphere that is low in oxygen, causing choking; blackdamp
claim piece of land staked out by one person who has exclusive rights to mine it
clinker hard mass of stony matter fused in furnace from coal impurities
coal gas gas produced by destructive distillation of bituminous coal
colliery coal mine and its equipment
continuous cutter machine that takes coal from mine face and loads it onto cars or conveyors
core cylindrical sample of mineral or rock extracted from ground by hollow drill that leaves strata intact
culm coal dust
deposit minerals or ores laid down by nature; location where minerals are found
dig excavation
distillation purification by heating to separate more volatile parts of mixture, then cooling and condensing vapor to produce more refined substance
drift horizontal passageway in mine; gallery
drill (*vb*) bore deep hole into earth, esp. seeking oil
excavation hole or cavity dug into earth to find minerals
extraction removal or separation of mineral from ore
face front or end of excavation and location of mined substance
firedamp combustible gases in coal mine, esp. methane
footwall top of rock stratum beneath vein or bed of ore
gallery small tunnel for inspection or drainage; drift
gangue worthless mineral matter associated with valuable metallic mineral deposits; matrix
gangway primary, level passageway in mine
gold rush large, sudden influx of miners to area where large vein of gold has been discovered
gondola open railroad car with low sides used for carrying coal
gusher high-capacity, flowing oil well
heading road or level leading into coal deposit where mining occurs
horse mass of rock within lode or vein
jack-up rig floating offshore drill rig with retractable legs that lift hull above water level
ledge underground rock layer
lode ore deposit; vein; reef
matrix gangue
mine large excavation in Earth from which to extract metallic ores, coal, precious stones, or salt
mining process of removing ores, coal, and precious metals from Earth
mining engineer designer and builder of mines
mother lode main vein of ore in particular region
offshore drilling sinking of oil wells into ocean bottom from floating platforms
oil well shaft into earth with pump for extracting crude petroleum
open cut designating mine in which excavation is performed from the surface
ore mineral embedded in the earth
panning washing gravel in porous pan when searching for gold
pay dirt spot that can be mined successfully
pinch (*vb*) diminish a vein to nothing
pit man-made cavity in ground for mining
pithead mine entrance and adjacent area
pocket usu. isolated body of ore in ground
portal entrance to mine tunnel
prospect place where mineral deposits are sought; (*vb*) search for ore
prospector person searching for valuable ores
pulp pulverized ore
quarry place where stone is excavated by cutting and blasting
reef lode or vein
refinery facility for purifying crude oil or raw metal
safety lamp lamp designed so as to avoid ignition of mine gases
seam relatively thin stratum or bed
shaft long, narrow, vertical or slanting passage sunk into earth
shoot small tunnel branching off from larger tunnel
sluice sloping trough or flume through which water is run in washing gold ore
smelt (*vb*) melt or fuse ore to separate impurities and extract pure metal
strike discovery of rich deposit of ore, coal, or minerals
strip mining mining, esp. for coal, by laying bare deposits near surface rather than sinking shaft
tailings residue of mining
tram car on rails for conveying loads in mine
trepan heavy boring tool for opening shafts or quarrying
trommel revolving cylindrical sieve for screening ore
tunnel usu. horizontal passageway in mine
vein lengthy, regularly shaped bed of useful mineral matter that fills narrow water channel in rock and earth; lode; reef
wash (*vb*) separate ore or stones by passing water through gravel or earth
well shaft sunk into earth to tap underground supply of oil, gas, or water
wellhead machinery standing above opening of oil or gas well
wellhole shaft of oil or gas well
wildcat oil well drilled in area without known oil deposits

GEOGRAPHY

Branches and Disciplines
Maps and Cartography
Earth's Atmosphere and Topographic Features
Populations and Resources
Nations of the World
States of the United States

Branches and Disciplines

cartography art and practice of making maps and charts
chorography art of mapping and describing a region or district
cultural geography human geography
demography statistical study of distribution, density, and attributes of human populations
economic geography study of how people use Earth's resources and their distribution
geodesy mathematical determining of Earth's shape and location of points on surface
geography study of Earth's surface, physical features, climates, resources, products, and people
geophysics study of materials of which Earth is composed
human geography study of people and their ways of life in different parts of Earth; cultural geography
hydrography science of mapping and describing surface waters of Earth, esp. for navigation
hypsography branch of geography involved with measurement and mapping of Earth's topography above sea level
hypsometry measurement of elevations or altitudes
meteorology study of Earth's atmosphere, climate, and weather
orography branch of physical geography dealing with mountains
physical geography study of nature and history of Earth's surface and atmosphere; physiography
physiography physical geography
soil science applied study of soils
topography science of drawing maps and representing natural surface and man-made features of region

Maps and Cartography

aclinic line magnetic equator
acre unit of area measure equal to 43,560 square feet (4047 square meters)
Africa second largest continent, divided between Northern and Southern hemispheres, between Asia and South America, south of Europe, extending from Atlantic to Indian Ocean
altitude height above sea level; elevation
angle of declination angle between direction indicated by magnetic needle and true meridian
angle of depression angle that descending line makes with horizon
angle of elevation angle that ascending line makes with horizon
Antarctica land area surrounding South Pole, forming fifth largest continent
Antarctic Circle parallel of latitude 66 1/2 degrees south of equator, which is in perpetual daylight in midsummer
Arctic land area surrounding North Pole
Arctic Circle parallel of latitude 66 1/2 degrees north of equator, which is in perpetual daylight in midsummer
arrow symbols map signs indicating motion and direction
Asia world's largest continent, extending from Arctic to Singapore and from Bering Strait to Ural Mountains
atlas bound maps showing different parts of world
Australia island continent, smallest of seven continents, in Southern Hemisphere, between Africa and South America, extending from Indian to Pacific Ocean
axis imaginary line through Earth's center from North to South Pole around which Earth rotates
azimuth angular measurement clockwise around horizon from north or south to location of object or intersection of object's vertical circle with horizon
bipolar (*adj*) involving both North and South poles
border dividing line between countries or other geographical units
cardinal points four principal points of compass: north, south, east, and west
cartogram type of map in which size of nations is based on something other than area
celestial equator great circle of celestial sphere projected from plane of equator
celestial globe sphere on which is depicted map of the heavens
celestial horizon great circle on celestial sphere midway between zenith and nadir
chart outline map, such as weather or resource map, with special information plotted geographically
circumpolar (*adj*) surrounding or near either pole
coastline point at which land meets ocean or sea
compass directional device with magnetic needle pivoting freely and pointing north
conic projection map in which Earth's surface is projected on conical surface which is unrolled to make plane surface
continent one of seven major landmasses of Earth
Continental Divide Rocky Mountain ridge forming North American watershed that separates rivers flowing east and west; Great Divide
contour line line on map that connects all points at same elevation or same ocean depth
coordinates location finders on map, marked by letters or numbers arranged horizontally and vertically along edges
country bounded territory of sovereign nation or state
cylindrical projection map projection of celestial sphere on cylinder that is then unrolled as plane

degree unit of measurement for latitude and longitude
distortion inaccuracies in size and shape of landmasses and oceans on flat map projections
Earth terrestrial globe on which all people live
Eastern Hemisphere half of Earth's surface, lying east of prime meridian
elevation altitude
equator line of latitude halfway between North and South poles at zero degrees
Eurasia landmass made up of continents of Europe and Asia
Europe sixth and smallest continent except Australia, extending from Atlantic Ocean to Ural Mountains
gazetteer geographical dictionary that lists places in alphabetical order
geopolitical map map showing nonphysical as well as physical features
globe spherical model of Earth showing physical features
Great Divide watershed ridge forming continental divide, esp. Rocky Mountains of North America; Continental Divide
Greenwich English city through which prime meridian runs at zero degrees longitude
grid intersections of parallels of latitude and meridians of longitude around globe
hachure one of a series of short parallel lines used on map to represent sloping or elevated surface
hemisphere half of Earth, divided into northern and southern by equator, eastern and western by Atlantic and Pacific oceans
high latitudes areas more than sixty degrees north or south of equator
International Date Line line based on 180-degree meridian that separates one calendar day from another, with west of line twenty-four hours later than east of it
isobar map line that joins places having equal atmospheric pressure over or at a given time
isoclinic line map line that joins points at which magnetic needle has same inclination to plumb line
isogloss boundary on map between places with differing linguistic features or dialects
isogram map line along which there is some constant value, such as that for temperature, pressure, or rainfall
isohel map line that joins points with equal duration of sunshine
isohyet map line that joins places having equal rainfall over a given period
isometric line map line that indicates true constant value for its extent
isotherm map line that joins places having same temperature
key list of map's symbols and their meanings; legend
latitude north/south position of place, measured in degrees from zero to ninety in reference to equator by an imaginary arc passing through both poles
legend key
longitude east/west position of place, measured in degrees from zero to 180 along equator in reference to prime meridian
low latitudes areas less than thirty degrees north or south of equator
magnetic equator imaginary line around Earth near equator where lines of force of Earth's magnetic field are parallel with Earth's surface; aclinic line
map representation, usu. on flat surface, of physical characteristics of whole or part of some area
Melanesia portion of Oceania including Pacific Ocean islands south of equator
Mercator projection conformal map projection that shows meridians of longitude as parallel lines, thus distorting shapes of areas near poles
meridian line of longitude; imaginary line approximating semicircle around Earth through both poles at right angles to equator
Micronesia portion of Oceania including Pacific Ocean islands north of equator
midlatitudes areas between thirty and sixty degrees north and south of equator
minute one-sixtieth of one degree of latitude or longitude
nadir point on celestial sphere opposite zenith and directly below observer
North America third largest continent, extending from Atlantic to Pacific oceans and from Arctic to Panama
Northern Hemisphere half of Earth's surface, lying north of equator
North Pole ninety degrees north latitude; point at northern end of Earth's axis
Oceania Pacific Ocean islands
parallel line of latitude; imaginary line on map or globe parallel to equator, connecting places on same latitude
physical feature land or water form on Earth's surface, esp. as depicted on map
polar projection map centered on one of poles
poles two points at northern and southern ends of Earth's axis; North Pole and South Pole
political feature national boundary or other feature showing how humans have divided Earth's surface
Polynesia eastern portion of Oceania including Hawaiian Islands
prime meridian line of longitude at zero degrees from which other longitudes are measured, running through Greenwich, England
projection one of various ways in which Earth's curved surface is represented two-dimensionally: azimuthal equidistant, conformal, conic, cylindrical, equal-area, homolosine, interrupted, loxodromic, Mercator, Mollweide, polar, polyconic, sinusoidal, and zenithal equidistant
relief elevation differences in land
relief map map showing contour variations of land surface
scale proportion between actual size of place and its representation on map
sea level mean level of sea surface between high and low tides, used as standard for measuring elevations and ocean depths

second one-sixtieth of one minute of one degree of latitude or longitude
South America fourth largest continent, largely in Southern Hemisphere, lying between Atlantic and Pacific oceans south of Panama
Southern Hemisphere half of Earth's surface, lying south of equator
South Pole ninety degrees south latitude; point at southern end of Earth's axis
state geographical and political division of nation
subantarctic (*adj*) bordering on the Antarctic
subarctic (*adj*) bordering on the Arctic
subcontinent major division of continent, often set off geographically
subtropical (*adj*) bordering on the tropics
surveying determining location, form, and boundaries of tract of land through application of geometry and trigonometry
time zone one of twenty-four longitudinal divisions of one hour each that divide Earth
topographic map detailed, large-scale map that shows physical and cultural features of one area
transcontinental (*adj*) reaching from one edge of a continent to the other
transoceanic (*adj*) reaching from one coast of an ocean to the other
triangulation process of determining distance between points on Earth's surface by use of series of connected triangles and angles made by lines to points
tropic of Cancer parallel at 23 1/2 degrees north
tropic of Capricorn parallel at 23 1/2 degrees south
tropics area of Earth closest to the equator, between tropic of Cancer and tropic of Capricorn
Western Hemisphere half of Earth's surface, lying west of prime meridian
zenith point directly overhead on celestial sphere

Earth's Atmosphere and Topographic Features

abyssal (*adj*) pertaining to dark, cold, lifeless ocean depths
acclivity upward slope of ground
alluvial fan fan-shaped deposit of detrital material at place where swiftly flowing water enters plain or open valley
alluvial plain plain formed by deposits of detrital material
anthropomorphic soil soil altered from surrounding environment by human activity
area amount of surface covered by a physical feature or region
atmosphere air forming gaseous envelope that surrounds Earth, consisting of troposphere, stratosphere, mesosphere, thermosphere, ionosphere, and exosphere, which merges into outer space at altitude of several hundred miles
badlands arid area cut by large number of deep gullies and nearly bare of vegetation
catchment area area draining into river or reservoir
chernozem fertile soil, rich in humus, found in temperate zones
climate all weather conditions typical of a specific region
climatic graph combined bar and line graph showing precipitation and average temperature for each month at specific place
coast area where landmass meets body of water
coniferous forests forests comprised of evergreen cone-bearing trees, growing across northern North America and Eurasia
continental shelf relatively flat seabed lying beneath shallow waters bordering continents
cordillera mountain system consisting of several parallel ranges
Coriolis effect change in path of object or fluid moving above Earth's surface due to Earth's rotation
deciduous forests forests with trees that lose their leaves at some point during year, found primarily in midlatitudes
deep zone cold ocean water below thermocline
deserts extremely dry regions with little or no vegetation
diastrophism process that causes movement and reshaping of Earth's surface
doldrums low-pressure region near equator
echo sounding determination of water depth by measuring time required for sound wave to be reflected from bottom
equinox date in spring and fall on which day and night are of equal length
estuary river basin affected by ocean tides, having mixture of fresh and salt water
exosphere outermost portion of Earth's atmosphere, with air density so low that an air molecule is more likely to escape atmosphere than hit other molecules, beginning at altitude of 300 miles (483 km), forming outer portion of ionosphere
fall line line indicating edge of plateau, marked by waterfalls and rapids
flood plain low-lying area subject to flooding by river
horizon point in distance where sky seems to meet curve of Earth; soil layer
horse latitudes areas of high pressure over oceans between trade winds and westerlies
hypolimnion cold layer of water below thermocline in some lakes
ionosphere region of Earth's atmosphere beyond mesosphere, containing ionized layers of thermosphere and exosphere, extending outward from 50 miles (80 km) altitude
island landmass smaller than a continent, surrounded by water
landmass very large area of land, esp. a continent
landscape tract or characteristic aspect of Earth's surface, esp. as viewed extensively from one point
littoral (*adj*) designating intertidal zone along shore, below high-water mark and above low-water mark
mainland principal landmass of continent or country as distinguished from island or peninsula
maritime (*adj*) proximate to and influenced by sea or ocean

massif mountain mass of uniform height broken into individual peaks
mesopause boundary of transition between mesosphere and ionosphere, around 50 miles (80 km) altitude
mesosphere coldest layer of Earth's atmosphere, from 30 to 50 miles (48 to 80 km) altitude
neritic zone ocean life zone from low tide line to end of continental shelf
oasis fertile place with water in middle of desert
ocean great body of water covering almost three-fourths of Earth's surface; one of its four geographic divisions: Atlantic, Pacific, Indian, Arctic
ooze liquid mud, largely of plankton remains, covering deep-sea plains
ozone hole any part of ozone layer that has become depleted by atmospheric pollution, permitting excess ultraviolet radiation to pass through and warm the atmosphere
ozone layer type of oxygen concentrated in stratosphere that blocks much of sun's ultraviolet radiation
peneplain land surface worn nearly flat
peninsula narrow land area almost completely surrounded by water except at point where it connects to mainland
permafrost permanently frozen ground underlying surface soil
planetary winds polars, westerlies, and trade winds; major winds on Earth's surface
polar winds very cold winds blowing from high pressure areas around poles
pollutant harmful substance in atmosphere
pollution contamination of environment with waste
rain forest tropical rain forest
ridge long, narrow crest of elevated portion of Earth's crust
rift valley depression formed by land subsiding between parallel faults
runoff water flowing over Earth's surface after rainfall or spring thaw
salinity amount of dissolved salts in body of water
sea large body of salt water, mainly enclosed by land and usu. connected to ocean
snow line line along mountain slope that represents lower limit of permanent snow
soil layer distinctive layer in a vertical cross section of soil
solstice one of two days each year when period of daylight reaches limit; longest or shortest day of year, June 21 or December 21
stratopause boundary of transition between stratosphere and mesosphere, around 30 miles (48 km) altitude
stratosphere layer of atmosphere from tropopause to inner edge of mesosphere, characterized by little change in temperature with increased altitude, extending from 10 to 30 miles (16 to 48 km) above Earth's surface
subcontinent landmass almost as big as a continent; India or Greenland
taiga extensive, subarctic coniferous forest beginning south of the tundra
temperate (*adj*) without temperature extremes
temperate zone midlatitudes between equator and poles
thermocline zone in body of water exhibiting rapid temperature decrease with increasing depth
thermosphere layer of upper atmosphere above mesosphere with very thin air and temperature that increases continuously with altitude, extending from 50 to 300 miles (80 to 483 km) above Earth's surface; inner portion of ionosphere
tideland land at seashore alternately exposed and covered by normal ebb and flow of tide
timberline boundary marking highest altitude for natural growth of trees
topsoil fertile soil, largely humus, in top horizon layer
trade winds winds blowing from high pressure subtropics toward low pressure at equator
tributary branch stream feeding main river
tropical grassland area between tropical rain forest and desert
tropical rain forest dense evergreen forest of equatorial regions; rain forest
tropopause boundary of transition between troposphere and stratosphere, around 10 miles (16 km) altitude
troposphere layer of atmosphere nearest Earth's surface, extending to altitude of 6 miles (10 km) over poles and 10 miles (16 km) over equator
tundra vast, cold, nearly treeless region north of coniferous forests with permanently frozen subsoil
Van Allen radiation belt doughnut-shaped region of high-energy particles trapped in Earth's magnetic field, extending from 2000 to 12,000 miles (3218 to 19,312 km) altitude
wadi watercourse in arid region that contains water only after heavy rainfall
watershed ridge separating runoff to two different river basins
westerlies winds blowing from subtropical high pressure toward low-pressure midlatitudes
wind erosion removal of powdery topsoil by wind, esp. in areas of prolonged heavy cultivation
woodland forested region of Earth

Populations and Resources

aborigine original inhabitant of area or region
birthrate number of births per year per thousand of population for given region or population
caste one of social groups into which population is divided, esp. among Hindus
census official population count, often accompanied by collection of demographic information
civilization organized society with developing art and technology
clan group of families, often with common ancestor, who live and work together
conservation actions taken to protect, preserve, or replenish natural resources
conurbation group of towns or cities extended to form continuous urban area
cultivation plowing of earth and planting of crops

cultural region geographic area in which most people have common language and customs distinct from other peoples
diversify (*vb*) create and maintain variety of economic forms in one culture
drainage system designation for region from which and means by which water flows off
dynasty series of rulers over generations from single family line
endangered species species of animal or plant in danger of becoming extinct
environment surroundings as they affect living things
ethnic group large group of people with shared heritage and more in common with each other than with other peoples
extended family household or family unit including more than two generations and more than nuclear family
extinct (*adj*) no longer living
extinction fact of being a species no longer living on Earth or no longer capable of regenerating
fossil fuel fuel derived from organic material lying underground for millions of years
greenbelt area surrounding city reserved for parks or farms
heartland central or most important area of nation, esp. agricultural region
homeland region or nation of one's birth
homogeneous population people of one ethnic or cultural group
hydroelectric power power of falling water used to generate electricity
illiteracy inability to read and write
immigration movement of peoples from one area to another
indigenous (*adj*) native to some place
infant mortality percentage of children who die shortly after birth
irrigation process of bringing water for cultivation to area with insufficient rain
landlocked (*adj*) having no border on or outlet to the sea
land reclamation process of making land suitable for cultivation or other use, esp. through irrigation
life expectancy statistical estimate of the number of years an individual is expected to live, based on such criteria as sex, race, health, and occupation
malnutrition chronic, pervasive lack of proper food
mestizo person of mixed Latin American Indian and Spanish descent
metropolitan area urban center and its suburbs
migration movement of peoples from their homeland
minority people people belonging to a different ethnic group than most of nation's population
mulatto person of mixed European and African descent
nation group of people sharing a political system, culture, and territory
natural resource material found on or in Earth and used by people
nomads people who move from place to place as a way of life, with no permanent home
nonrenewable resource useful and irreplaceable material coming from Earth's crust
plantation large farm specializing in one crop with many workers, often slaves
population total number of people in country or region; specific part of people in given region
population profile bar graph showing proportion of different age groups in total population
raw materials substances occurring in nature and used to manufacture goods
reforestation planting of new forests, esp. in areas where trees have been cut down or burned
renewable resource material that can be replaced by nature
resource any useful element of environment
self-sufficiency ability to produce all resources required to meet one's own needs
solar energy energy from sun used as fuel
subsistence farming raising just enough crops to feed one's own family
territory large tract of land under jurisdiction of nation or government
Third World developing nations not allied with superpowers, primarily in Southern Hemisphere
threatened species a species likely to become an endangered species in the near future, within all or much of its range
vegetation plant life on Earth
zero population growth condition in which birthrate equals death rate and population remains constant

Note: *The listings for Nations of the World provide the following information: country name — former name where appropriate; official name; location; capital; area in square miles, population; major language or languages; primary religion or religions; currency. The listings for States of the United States provide the following information: state name — postal code; order of admission, date admitted; location; capital; rank among states in area, population; nickname.*

Nations of the World

Afghanistan Republic of; in central W Asia; capital Kabul; area 250,000 sq. mi., pop. 15,592,000; Pashtu; Sunni Muslim; afghani
Albania Republic of; in SE Europe; capital Tirana; area 11,100 sq. mi., pop. 3,268,000; Albanian; Muslim; lek
Algeria Democratic and Popular Republic of; in N Africa; capital Algiers; area 919,590 sq. mi., pop. 25,714,000; Arabic; Sunni Muslim; dinar
Andorra Republic of; in SW Europe; capital Andorra la Vella; area 191 sq. mi., pop. 51,000; Catalan; Catholic; franc and peseta
Angola People's Republic of; in W Africa; capital Luanda; area 481,352 sq. mi., pop. 8,802,000; Portuguese and Bantu; Catholic; kwanza
Antigua and Barbuda group of islands in Caribbean Sea; capital St. John's; area 170 sq. mi.,

pop. 64,000; English; Anglican; dollar

Argentina Republic of; in S South America; capital Buenos Aires; area 1,068,000 sq. mi., pop. 32,291,000; Spanish; Catholic; peso

Australia Commonwealth of; in S Pacific; capital Canberra; area 2,967,909 sq. mi., pop. 16,646,000; English; Christian; dollar

Austria Republic of; in central Europe; capital Vienna; area 32,375 sq. mi., pop. 7,595,000; German; Catholic; schilling

Bahamas Commonwealth of the; group of islands in W Atlantic; capital Nassau; area 5,380 sq. mi., pop. 251,000; English; Christian; dollar

Bahrain State of; in Persian Gulf; capital Manama; area 250 sq. mi., pop. 512,000; Arabic; Shi"a Muslim; dinar

Bangladesh People's Republic of; in S Asia; capital Dhaka; area 55,126 sq. mi., pop. 117,976,000; Bengali; Muslim; taka

Barbados island in West Indies; capital Bridgetown; area 166 sq. mi., pop. 260,000; English; Anglican; dollar

Basutoland Lesotho

Bechuanaland Botswana

Belgium Kingdom of; in W Europe; capital Brussels; area 11,781 sq. mi., pop. 9,895,000; Flemish and French; Catholic; franc

Belize formerly British Honduras; in Central America; capital Belmopan; area 8,866 sq. mi., pop. 180,400; English and Spanish; Catholic; dollar

Benin formerly Dahomey; Republic of; in W Africa; capital Porto-Novo; area 43,483 sq. mi., pop. 4,840,000; French and Fon; indigenous religions; franc

Bermuda Dependency of; British colony, island in W Atlantic; capital Hamilton; area 20 sq. mi., pop. 58,800; English; Christian; dollar

Bhutan Kingdom of; in E Asia; capital Thimbu; area 18,147 sq. mi., pop. 1,566,000; Dzongkha and Nepalese; Lamaistic Buddhist; ngultrum

Bolivia Republic of; in W central South America; capital Sucre and LaPaz; area 424,163 sq. mi., pop. 6,730,000; Spanish; Catholic; boliviano

Bosnia and Herzegovina formerly part of Yugoslavia; in SE Europe; capital Sarajevo; area 19,741 sq. mi., pop. 4,440,000; Serbian; Eastern Orthodox, Catholic and Muslim; dinar

Botswana formerly Bechuanaland; Republic of; in S Africa; capital Gaborone; area 231,804 sq. mi., pop. 1,218,000; English and Setswana; Christian and indigenous religions; pula

Brazil Federative Republic of; in E South America; capital Brasília; area 3,286,478 sq. mi., pop. 153,771,000; Portuguese; Catholic; cruzeiro

British Honduras Belize

Brunei Brunei Darussalam; in SE Asia; capital Bandar Seri Begawan; area 2,226 sq. mi., pop. 372,000; Malay; Muslim; dollar

Bulgaria Republic of; in SE Europe; capital Sofia; area 44,365 sq. mi., pop. 8,978,000; Bulgarian; Bulgarian Orthodox; lev

Burkina Faso formerly Upper Volta; in W Africa; capital Ouagadougou; area 105,870 sq. mi., pop. 8,941,000; French; indigenous religions; franc

Burma Myanmar

Burundi Republic of; in E central Africa; capital Bujumbura; area 10,747 sq. mi., pop. 5,647,000; Kirundi and French; Catholic; franc

Cambodia formerly Kampuchea; State of; in SE Asia; capital Phnom Penh; area 69,898 sq. mi., pop. 6,993,000; Khmer and French; Buddhist; riel

Cameroon Republic of; in W Africa; capital Yaoundé; area 185,569 sq. mi., pop. 11,109,000; French and English; indigenous religions and Christian; franc

Canada confederation in N North America; capital Ottawa; area 3,558,096 sq. mi., pop. 26,527,000; English and French; Catholic and Protestant; dollar; provinces: Alberta, British Columbia, Manitoba, New Brunswick, Newfoundland, Nova Scotia, Ontario, Prince Edward Island, Quebec, Saskatchewan; territories: Northwest Territories, Yukon

Cape Verde Republic of; group of islands in E Atlantic; capital Praia; area 1,557 sq. mi., pop. 375,000; Portuguese; Catholic; escudo

Central African Republic in central Africa; capital Bangui; area 240,535 sq. mi., pop. 2,879,000, French; indigenous religions and Christian; franc

Ceylon Sri Lanka

Chad Republic of; in N central Africa; capital N'djamena; area 495,754 sq. mi., pop. 5,064,000; French and Arabic; Muslim and indigenous religions; franc

Chile Republic of; in SW South America; capital Santiago; area 292,250 sq. mi., pop. 13,000,000; Spanish; Catholic; peso

China People's Republic of; in E Asia; capital Beijing; area 3,705,000 sq. mi., pop. 1,130,065,000; Mandarin; Taoist and Confucian traditions but officially atheist; yuan

Colombia Republic of; in NW South America; capital Bogotá; area 439,700 sq. mi., pop. 32,598,000; Spanish; Catholic; peso

Commonwealth of Independent States formerly part of the Union of Soviet Socialist Republics; in E Europe and N Asia; capital Minsk; area 8,555,000 sq. mi., pop. 273,307,000; Russian, Ukrainian, and other indigenous languages; Russian Orthodox, Muslim, and others; ruble; republics: Armenia, Azerbaijan, Belarus, Kazakhstan, Kyrgyzstan, Moldova, Russia, Tajikistan, Turkmenistan, Ukraine, Uzbekistan

Comoros Republic of; group of islands in S Indian Ocean; capital Moroni; area 838 sq. mi., pop. 459,000; Comoran, French and Arabic; Sunni Muslim; franc

Congo People's Republic of; in W central Africa; capital Brazzaville; area 132,046 sq. mi., pop. 2,305,000; French; Christian and animist; franc

Costa Rica Republic of; in S Central America; capital San José; area 19,575 sq. mi., pop. 3,032,000; Spanish; Catholic; colon

Côte d'Ivoire Ivory Coast

Croatia formerly part of Yugoslavia; in SE Europe; capital Zagreb; area 21,829 sq. mi., pop. 4,680,000; Croatian; Catholic; dinar

Cuba Republic of; island in Caribbean Sea; capital

Havana; area 44,218 sq. mi., pop. 10,582,000; Spanish; Catholic; peso

Cyprus Republic of; island in E Mediterranean Sea; capital Nicosia; area 3,572 sq. mi., pop. 708,000; Greek and Turkish; Greek Orthodox and Muslim; pound

Czechoslovakia Czech and Slovak Federative Republic; in central Europe; capital Prague; area 49,365 sq. mi., pop. 15,695,000; Czech and Slovak; Catholic; koruna

Dahomey Benin

Denmark Kingdom of; in N Europe; capital Copenhagen; area 16,629 sq. mi., pop. 5,134,000; Danish; Lutheran; krone

Djibouti Republic of; in E Africa; capital Djibouti; area 8,490 sq. mi., pop. 337,000; French and Arabic; Muslim; franc

Dominica Commonwealth of; island in West Indies; capital Roseau; area 290 sq. mi., pop. 85,000; English; Catholic; dollar

Dominican Republic part of an island in West Indies; capital Santo Domingo; area 18,703 sq. mi., pop. 7,253,000; Spanish; Catholic; peso

East Germany former German Democratic Republic, since 1990 part of united Germany

Ecuador Republic of; in NW South America; capital Quito; area 109,483 sq. mi., pop. 10,506,000; Spanish; Catholic; sucre

Egypt Arab Republic of; in NE Africa; capital Cairo; area 386,660 sq. mi., pop. 54,139,000; Arabic; Sunni Muslim; pound

El Salvador Republic of; in Central America; capital San Salvador; area 8,260 sq. mi., pop. 5,221,000; Spanish; Catholic; colon

England largest division of United Kingdom, part of Great Britain with Scotland and Wales

Equatorial Guinea Republic of; in W Africa; capital Malabo; area 10,831 sq. mi., pop. 360,000; Spanish; Christian and indigenous religions; franc

Estonia formerly part of the Union of Soviet Socialist Republics; Republic of; in N Europe; capital Tallinn; area 17,413 sq. mi., pop. 1,573,000; Estonian and Russian; Lutheran; ruble

Ethiopia People's Democratic Republic of; in E Africa; capital Addis Ababa; area 471,777 sq. mi., pop. 51,375,000; Amharic; Muslim and Ethiopian Orthodox; birr

Faeroe Islands Danish island province in the N Atlantic; capital Torshavn; area 541 sq. mi., pop. 46,000; Faeroese and Danish; Lutheran; krona

Fiji Republic of; group of islands in SW Pacific Ocean; capital Suva; area 7,053 sq. mi., pop. 772,000; English and Fijian; Christian and Hindu; dollar

Finland Republic of; in N Europe; capital Helsinki; area 130,120 sq. mi., pop. 4,977,000; Finnish; Lutheran; markka

France French Republic; in W Europe; capital Paris; area 220,668 sq. mi., pop. 56,184,000; French; Catholic; franc

French Polynesia Territory of; French island territory in S Pacific; capital Papeete; area 1,544 sq. mi., pop. 185,000; Polynesian and French; Christian; franc

Gabon Gabonese Republic; in W Africa; capital Libreville; area 103,346 sq. mi., pop. 1,069,000; French and Fang; Christian; franc

Gambia Republic of the; in W Africa; capital Banjul; area 4,361 sq. mi., pop. 820,000; English and Mandinka; Muslim; dalasi

Georgia formerly part of the Union of Soviet Socialist Republics; Georgian Republic; in SE Europe and SW Asia; capital Tbilisi; area 26,872 sq. mi., pop. 5,449,000; Georgian; Georgian Orthodox; ruble

Germany formerly East Germany and West Germany; Federal Republic of; in central Europe; capital Berlin; area 137,616 sq. mi., pop. 77,555,000; German; Protestant and Catholic; mark

Ghana Republic of; in W Africa; capital Accra; area 92,099 sq. mi., pop. 15,310,000; English and Akan; Christian, Muslim and indigenous religions; cedi

Gilbert Island Kiribati

Great Britain England, Scotland, and Wales, three divisions within United Kingdom

Greece Hellenic Republic; in SE Europe; capital Athens; area 51,146 sq. mi., pop. 10,066,000; Greek; Greek Orthodox; drachma

Greenland Kalaallit Nunaat; semiautonomous colony of Denmark in NW Atlantic; capital Nuuk; area 840,000 sq. mi., pop. 55,415; Greenlandic and Danish; Lutheran; krone

Grenada group of islands in SE Caribbean Sea; capital St. George's; area 131 sq. mi., pop. 84,000; English; Catholic; dollar

Guatemala Republic of; in Central America; capital Guatemala City; area 42,042 sq. mi., pop. 9,340,000; Spanish; Catholic; quetzal

Guinea Republic of; in W Africa; capital Conakry; area 94,964 sq. mi., pop. 7,269,000; French; Muslim; franc

Guinea-Bissau Republic of; in W Africa; capital Bissau; area 13,948 sq. mi., pop. 998,000; Portuguese; Muslim and indigenous religions; peso

Guyana Co-operative Republic of; in NE South America; capital Georgetown; area 83,000 sq. mi., pop. 765,000; English; Christian and Hindu; dollar

Haiti Republic of; part of an island in Caribbean Sea; capital Port-au-Prince; area 10,714 sq. mi., pop. 6,409,000; French; Catholic; gourde

Honduras Republic of; in Central America; capital Tegucigalpa; area 43,277 sq. mi., pop. 5,261,000; Spanish; Catholic; lempira

Hong Kong Dependency of; British crown colony in E Asia on South China Sea; capital Victoria; area 402 sq. mi., pop. 5,700,000; Cantonese; Taoist, Confucian, and Christian; dollar

Hungary Republic of; in central Europe; capital Budapest; area 35,919 sq. mi., pop. 10,546,000; Hungarian; Catholic; forint

Iceland Republic of; group of islands in N Atlantic; capital Reykjavik; area 39,768 sq. mi., pop. 251,000; Icelandic; Lutheran; krona

India Republic of; in S Asia; capital New Delhi; area 1,266,598 sq. mi., pop. 850,067,000; Hindi and English; Hindu and Muslim; rupee

Indonesia Republic of; in SE Asia; capital Jakarta; area 735,269 sq. mi., pop. 191,266,000; Indonesian; Muslim; rupiah
Iran Islamic Republic of; on Persian Gulf in Middle East; capital Teheran; area 636,294 sq. mi., pop. 55,647,000; Farsi; Shi"a Muslim; rial
Iraq Republic of; in Middle East; capital Baghdad; area 167,923 sq. mi., pop. 18,782,000; Arabic; Muslim; dinar
Ireland Republic of; part of an island in NW Europe; capital Dublin; area 27,136 sq. mi., pop. 3,557,000; English and Irish; Catholic; pound
Israel State of; in Middle East; capital Jerusalem; area 8,019 sq. mi., pop. 4,371,000; Hebrew; Jewish; shekel
Italy Italian Republic; in S Europe; capital Rome; area 116,303 sq. mi., pop. 57,657,000; Italian; Catholic; lira
Ivory Coast Republic of; Côte d'Ivoire; in W Africa; capital Abidjan; area 124,503 sq. mi., pop. 12,070,000; French; Christian, Muslim and indigenous religions; franc
Jamaica island in Caribbean Sea; capital Kingston; area 4,243 sq. mi., pop. 2,513,000; English; Protestant; dollar
Japan Nippon; in E Asia; capital Tokyo; area 145,882 sq. mi., pop. 123,778,000; Japanese; Shinto and Buddhist; yen
Jordan Hashemite Kingdom of; in Middle East; capital Amman; area 37,738 sq. mi., pop. 3,065,000; Arabic; Sunni Muslim; dinar
Kalaallit Nunaat Greenland
Kampuchea Cambodia
Kenya Republic of; in E Africa; capital Nairobi; area 224,960 sq. mi., pop. 25,393,000; English and Swahili; Christian; shilling
Kiribati formerly Gilbert Islands; Republic of; group of islands in S Pacific; capital Tarawa; area 277 sq. mi., pop. 65,000; English and Gilbertese; Christian; dollar
Korea, North Democratic People's Republic of Korea; in NE Asia; capital Pyong Yang; area 46,541, pop. 23,059,000; Korean; Buddhist and Confucian traditions but officially atheist; won
Korea, South Republic of Korea; in NE Asia; capital Seoul; area 38,023 sq. mi., pop. 43,919,000; Korean; Buddhist, Confucian, and Christian; won
Kuwait State of; in NE Arabian peninsula; capital Kuwait; area 6,880 sq. mi., pop. 2,080,000; Arabic; Sunni Muslim; dinar
Laos People's Democratic Republic of; in SE Asia; capital Vientiane; area 91,428 sq. mi., pop. 4,024,000; Lao and French; Buddhist; kip
Latvia formerly part of the Union of Soviet Socialist Republics; Republic of; in N Europe; capital Riga; area 25,395 sq. mi., pop. 2,681,000; Latvian and Russian; Lutheran; ruble
Lebanon Republic of; in Middle East; capital Beirut; area 4,015 sq. mi., pop. 3,340,000; Arabic; Muslim; pound
Lesotho formerly Basutoland; Kingdom of; within Republic of South Africa; capital Maseru; area 11,720 sq. mi., pop. 1,757,000; Sesotho and English; Christian; loti
Liberia Republic of; in W Africa; capital Monrovia; area 38,250 sq. mi., pop. 2,644,000; English; Christian and indigenous religions; dollar
Libya Socialist People's Libyan Arab Jamahiriya; in N Africa; capital Tripoli; area 679,216 sq. mi., pop. 4,280,000; Arabic; Sunni Muslim; dinar
Liechtenstein Principality of; in W central Europe; capital Vaduz; area 62 sq. mi., pop. 30,000; German; Catholic; franc
Lithuania formerly part of the Union of Soviet Socialist Republics; Republic of; in N Europe; capital Vilnius; area 25,174 sq. mi., pop. 3,690,000; Lithuanian; Roman Catholic; ruble
Luxembourg Grand Duchy of; in W Europe; capital Luxembourg; area 999 sq. mi., pop. 369,000; Luxembourgian, French and German; Catholic; franc
Macao Territory of; Portuguese dependency on South China Sea in E Asia; capital Macao; area 6 sq. mi., pop. 484,000; Cantonese and Portuguese; Buddhist; pataca
Macedonia formerly part of Yugoslavia; in SE Europe; capital Skopje; area 9928 sq. mi, pop. 2,090,000; Macedonian, Eastern Orthodox and Muslim; dinar
Madagascar Democratic Republic of; island in Indian Ocean east of Africa; capital Antananarivo; area 226,657 sq. mi., pop. 11,802,000; French and Malagasy; Christian and indigenous religions; franc
Malawi Republic of; in E central Africa; capital Lilongwe; area 45,747 sq. mi., pop. 9,080,000; English and Chichewa; Protestant; kwacha
Malaysia Federation of; in SE Asia; capital Kuala Lumpur; area 127,316 sq. mi., pop. 17,053,000; Malay; Muslim; ringgit
Maldives Republic of; group of islands in N Indian Ocean; capital Male; area 115 sq. mi., pop. 219,000; Divehi and English; Sunni Muslim; rufiyaa
Mali Republic of; in W Africa; capital Bamako; area 478,764 sq. mi., pop. 9,182,000; French and Bambara; Muslim; franc
Malta Republic of; island in Mediterranean Sea; capital Valletta; area 122 sq. mi., pop. 373,000; Maltese; Catholic; lira
Mariana Islands Commonwealth of the Northern Mariana Islands; group of islands in Pacific Ocean; capital Saipan; area 184 sq. mi., pop. 22,591; Chamorro and English; Christian and indigenous religions; dollar
Marshall Islands Republic of; group of islands in Pacific Ocean; capital Majuro; area 70 sq. mi., pop. 40,609; English and indigenous languages; Christian and indigenous religions; dollar
Martinique Territory of; French dependency, island in Caribbean Sea; capital Fort-de-France; area 425 sq. mi., pop. 336,000; French; Catholic; franc
Mauritania Islamic Republic of; in W Africa; capital Nouakchott; area 397,954 sq. mi., pop. 2,038,000; Arabic and French; Muslim; ouguiya
Mauritius island in Indian Ocean; capital Port Louis; area 790 sq. mi., pop. 1,141,900; English; Hindu; rupee

Mexico United States of; in S North America; capital Mexico City; area 761,604 sq. mi., pop. 88,335,000; Spanish; Catholic; peso

Micronesia Federated States of; group of islands in Pacific Ocean; capital Kolonia; area 271 sq. mi., pop. 86,094; English and indigenous languages; Christian and indigenous religions; dollar

Monaco Principality of; on Mediterranean Sea, surrounded on other sides by France; capital Monaco-Ville; area 0.6 sq. mi., pop. 29,000; French; Catholic; franc

Mongolia Mongolian People's Republic; in central Asia; capital Ulan Bator; area 604,247 sq. mi., pop. 2,185,000; Khalkha Mongol; Buddhist; tugrik

Morocco Kingdom of; in N Africa; capital Rabat; area 172,413 sq. mi., pop. 26,249,000; Arabic and French; Sunni Muslim; dirham

Mozambique People's Republic of; in E Africa; capital Maputo; area 303,769 sq. mi., pop. 14,718,000; Portuguese; indigenous religions; metical

Myanmar formerly Burma; Union of; in SE Asia; capital Yangon, formerly Rangoon; area 261,789 sq. mi., pop. 41,279,000; Burmese; Buddhist; kyat

Namibia formerly South-West Africa; Republic of; in SW Africa; capital Windhoek; area 317,818 sq. mi., pop. 1,372,000; English and Afrikaans; Christian; rand

Nauru Republic of; island in S Pacific; capital Yaren; area 8 sq. mi., pop. 8,100; Nauruan; Christian; dollar

Nepal Kingdom of; in central Asia; capital Katmandu; area 56,136 sq. mi., pop. 19,158,000; Nepali; Hindu; rupee

Netherlands Kingdom of the; in NW Europe; capital Amsterdam and the Hague; area 15,770 sq. mi., pop. 14,864,000; Dutch; Protestant and Catholic; guilder

Netherlands Antilles Territory of; Dutch island dependency in Caribbean Sea; capital Willemstad; area 385 sq. mi., pop. 187,000; Dutch; Catholic; guilder

New Zealand group of islands in S Pacific; capital Wellington; area 103,736 sq. mi., pop. 3,397,000; English and Maori; Christian; dollar

Nicaragua Republic of; in Central America; capital Managua; area 50,193 sq. mi., pop. 3,606,000; Spanish; Catholic; cordoba

Niger Republic of; in W Africa; capital Niamey; area 489,189 sq. mi., pop. 7,691,000; French and Hausa; Muslim; franc

Nigeria Federal Republic of; in W Africa; capital Abuja; area 356,669 sq. mi., pop. 118,865,000; English and Hausa; Muslim; naira

Northern Ireland a division of the United Kingdom

North Korea Korea, North

North Yemen former Yemen Arab Republic, since 1990 part of Yemen

Norway Kingdom of; in N Europe; capital Oslo; area 125,181 sq. mi., pop. 4,214,000; Norwegian; Lutheran; krone

Oman Sultanate of; on SE Arabian peninsula; capital Muscat; area 82,030 sq. mi., pop. 1,305,000; Arabic; Muslim; rial

Pakistan Islamic Republic of; in S Asia; capital Islamabad; area 310,402 sq. mi., pop. 113,163,000; Urdu; Sunni Muslim; rupee

Palau Republic of; group of islands in Pacific Ocean; capital Koror; area 192 sq. mi., pop. 14,106; English and Palauan; Christian and indigenous religions; dollar

Panama Republic of; in Central America; capital Panama City; area 29,208 sq. mi., pop. 2,423,000; Spanish; Catholic; balboa

Papua New Guinea group of islands in SW Pacific; capital Port Moresby; area 178,221 sq. mi., pop. 3,613,000; Pidgin English; Christian; kina

Paraguay Republic of; in central South America; capital Asunción; area 157,047 sq. mi., pop. 4,660,000; Spanish; Catholic; guarani

Peru Republic of; in W South America; capital Lima; area 496,223 sq. mi., pop. 21,904,000; Spanish; Catholic; inti

Philippines Republic of the; in SE Asia; capital Quezon City (official), Manila (de facto); area 115,830 sq. mi., pop. 66,647,000; Tagalog; Catholic; peso

Poland Republic of; in N central Europe; capital Warsaw; area 120,724 sq. mi., pop. 38,363,000; Polish; Catholic; zloty

Portugal Republic of; in SW Europe; capital Lisbon; area 36,390 sq. mi., pop. 10,528,000; Portuguese; Catholic; escudo

Qatar State of; on Persian Gulf; capital Doha; area 4,247 sq. mi., pop. 498,000; Arabic; Muslim; riyal

Rhodesia Zimbabwe

Romania in SE Europe; capital Bucharest; area 91,700 sq. mi., pop. 23,269,000; Romanian; Romanian Orthodox; leu

Russia largest republic within Commonwealth of Independent States

Rwanda Republic of; in E central Africa; capital Kigali; area 10,169 sq. mi., pop. 7,603,000; Kinyarwanda and French; Catholic; franc

San Marino Most Serene Republic of; in Apennines, surrounded by Italy; capital San Marino; area 24 sq. mi., pop. 23,000; Italian; Catholic; lira

São Tomé and Principe Republic of; two islands in E Atlantic off W coast of Africa; capital São Tomé; area 372 sq. mi., pop. 125,000; Portuguese; Catholic; dobra

Saudi Arabia Kingdom of; on Arabian peninsula; capital Riyadh; area 839,996 sq. mi., pop. 16,758,000; Arabic; Muslim; riyal

Scotland a division of United Kingdom; part of Great Britain with England and Wales

Senegal Republic of; in W Africa; capital Dakar; area 75,750 sq. mi., pop. 7,740,000; French and Wolof; Muslim; franc

Seychelles Republic of; group of islands in Indian Ocean; capital Victoria; area 176 sq. mi., pop. 71,000; English; Catholic; rupee

Sierra Leone Republic of; in W Africa; capital Freetown; area 27,925 sq. mi., pop. 4,168,000; English; Muslim and indigenous religions; leone

Singapore Republic of; in SE Asia; capital Singapore; area 225 sq. mi., pop. 2,703,000; Malay and Mandarin; Buddhist; dollar

Slovenia formerly part of Yugoslavia; in SE Europe; capital Ljubljana; area 7819 sq. mi., pop. 1,940,000; Slovene; Catholic; dinar

Solomon Islands group of islands in W Pacific; capital Honiara; area 10,640 sq. mi., pop. 314,000; English and Melanesian; Christian; dollar

Somalia Somali Democratic Republic; in NE Africa; capital Mogadishu; area 246,300 sq. mi., pop. 8,415,000; Somali; Sunni Muslim; shilling

South Africa Republic of; in S Africa; capital Pretoria (administrative), Capetown (legislative), Bloemfontein (judicial); area 472,359 sq. mi., pop. 39,550,000; Afrikaans, English, and Zulu; Christian; rand

South Korea Korea, South

South-West Africa Namibia

South Yemen former People's Democratic Republic of Yemen, since 1990 part of Yemen

Soviet Union Union of Soviet Socialist Republics

Spain Kingdom of; in SW Europe; capital Madrid; area 194,897 sq. mi., pop. 39,623,000; Spanish; Catholic; peseta

Sri Lanka formerly Ceylon; Democratic Socialist Republic of; island in S Asia in Indian Ocean; capital Colombo; area 25,332 sq. mi., pop. 17,135,000; Sinhala; Buddhist; rupee

St. Kitts and Nevis Federation of; twin-island state in Caribbean Sea; capital Basseterre; area 101 sq. mi., pop. 40,000; English; Anglican; dollar

St. Lucia island in W Atlantic; capital Castries; area 239 sq. mi., pop. 153,000; English; Catholic; dollar

St. Vincent and the Grenadines group of islands in W Atlantic; capital Kingstown; area 150 sq. mi., pop. 106,000; English; Anglican; dollar

Sudan Democratic Republic of; in N Africa; capital Khartoum; area 966,757 sq. mi., pop. 25,164,000; Arabic; Sunni Muslim; pound

Suriname Republic of; in NE South America; capital Paramaribo; area 63,037 sq. mi., pop. 408,000; Dutch; Hindu and Christian; guilder

Swaziland Kingdom of; in S Africa; capital Mbabane; area 6,704 sq. mi., pop. 779,000; English and Siswati; Christian and indigenous religions; lilangeni

Sweden Kingdom of; in N Europe; capital Stockholm; area 173,731 sq. mi., pop. 8,407,000; Swedish; Lutheran; krona

Switzerland Swiss Confederation; in W Europe; capital Bern; area 15,941 sq. mi., pop. 6,628,000; French, German, and Italian; Catholic and Protestant; franc

Syria Syrian Arab Republic; in Middle East; capital Damascus; area 71,498 sq. mi., pop. 12,471,000; Arabic; Sunni Muslim; pound

Taiwan Republic of China; island in SE Asia in South China Sea; capital Taipei; area 13,885 sq. mi., pop. 20,454,000; Mandarin; Buddhist and Taoist; dollar

Tanzania United Republic of; in E Africa; capital Dar es Salaam; area 364,882 sq. mi., pop. 26,070,000; Swahili; Muslim and Christian; shilling

Thailand Kingdom of; in SE Asia; capital Bangkok; area 198,456 sq. mi., pop. 54,890,000; Thai; Buddhist; baht

Togo Togolese Republic; in W Africa; capital Lomé; area 21,617 sq. mi., pop. 3,566,000; French and Ewe; indigenous religions; franc

Tonga Kingdom of; group of islands in SW Pacific; capital Nuku'alofa; area 270 sq. mi., pop. 108,000; Tongan; Catholic and Hindu; pa'anga

Trinidad and Tobago Republic of; two islands in West Indies; capital Port of Spain; area 1,980 sq. mi., pop. 1,270,000; English; Catholic and Hindu; dollar

Tunisia Republic of; in N Africa; capital Tunis; area 63,170 sq. mi., pop. 8,094,000; Arabic; Muslim; dinar

Turkey Republic of; in SW Asia and SE Europe; capital Ankara; area 301,381 sq. mi., pop. 56,549,000; Turkish; Muslim; lira

Tuvalu group of islands in S Pacific; capital Funafuti; area 10 sq. mi., pop. 9,000; Tuvaluan; Christian; dollar

Uganda Republic of; in E central Africa; capital Kampala; area 93,354 sq. mi., pop. 17,593,000; English and Swahili; Christian and Muslim; shilling

Union of Soviet Socialist Republics former country, now divided into Commonwealth of Independent States, Estonia, Georgia, Latvia, Lithuania

United Arab Emirates on Persian Gulf on N Arabian Peninsula; capital Abu Dhabi; area 32,278 sq. mi., pop. 2,250,000; Arabic; Muslim; dirham

United Kingdom United Kingdom of Great Britain and Northern Ireland; two islands in NW Europe; capital London; area 94,226, pop. 57,121,000; English; Anglican; pound; comprised of: England, Scotland, Wales, and Northern Ireland

United States United States of America; in central North America; capital Washington, D.C.; area 3,618,774 sq. mi., pop. 250,372,000; English; Christian; dollar

Upper Volta Burkina Faso

Uruguay Republic of; in SE South America; capital Montevideo; area 68,037 sq. mi., pop. 3,002,000; Spanish; Catholic; peso

Vanuatu Republic of; group of islands in W Pacific; capital Vila; area 5,700 sq. mi., pop. 150,000; Bislama and French; Christian; vatu

Vatican City Catholic state within Rome, Italy; area 109 acres, pop. 750; Italian and Latin; Catholic; lira

Venezuela Republic of; in N South America; capital Caracas; area 352,143 sq. mi., pop. 19,753,000; Spanish; Catholic; bolivar

Vietnam Democratic Republic of; in SE Asia; capital Hanoi; area 127,243 sq. mi., pop. 68,488,000; Vietnamese and French; Buddhist; dong

Wales division of United Kingdom, part of Great Britain with England and Scotland

Western Samoa Independent State of; part of an island in SW Pacific; capital Apia; area 1,133 sq. mi., pop. 169,000; Samoan; Christian; tala

West Germany former Federal Republic of Germany, since 1990 part of united Germany

Yemen formerly North Yemen and South Yemen; Republic of; on S Arabian peninsula; capital Sanaa; area 207,000 sq. mi., pop. 11,000,000; Arabic; Muslim; dinar

Yugoslavia Federal Republic of; in SE Europe; capital Belgrade; area 39,449 sq. mi., pop. 10,400,000; Serbian; Eastern Orthodox, Catholic and Muslim; dinar; comprised of: Serbia and Montenegro

Zaire Republic of; in W central Africa; capital Kinshasa; area 905,563 sq. mi., pop. 35,330,000; French; Catholic; zaire

Zambia Republic of; in S central Africa; capital Lusaka; area 290,585 sq. mi., pop. 8,119,000; English; Christian and indigenous religions; kwacha

Zimbabwe formerly Rhodesia; in S central Africa; capital Harare; area 150,803 sq. mi., pop. 10,205,000; English and Shona; indigenous religions; dollar

States of the United States

Alabama AL; 22nd state, admitted 1819; SE United States; capital Montgomery; ranks 29th in area, pop. 4,063,000; Camellia State

Alaska AK; 49th state, admitted 1959; NW of continental United States; capital Juneau; ranks 1st in area, pop. 552,000; The Last Frontier

Arizona AZ; 48th state, admitted 1912; SW United States; capital Phoenix; ranks 6th in area, pop. 3,678,000; Grand Canyon State

Arkansas AR; 25th state, admitted 1836; S central United States; capital Little Rock; ranks 27th in area, pop. 2,362,000; Land of Opportunity

California CA; 31st state, admitted 1850; W United States; capital Sacramento; ranks 3rd in area, pop. 29,840,000; Golden State

Colorado CO; 38th state, admitted 1876; W central United States; capital Denver; ranks 8th in area, pop. 3,308,000; Centennial State

Connecticut CT; 5th state, admitted 1788; NE United States; capital Hartford; ranks 48th in area, pop. 3,296,000; Constitution State

Delaware DE; 1st state, admitted 1787; E United States; capital Dover; ranks 49th in area, pop. 669,000; First State

Florida FL; 27th state, admitted 1845; SE United States; capital Tallahassee; ranks 22nd in area, pop. 13,003,000; Sunshine State

Georgia GA; 4th state, admitted 1788; SE United States; capital Atlanta; ranks 21st in area, pop. 6,508,000; Peach State

Hawaii HI; 50th state, admitted 1959; WSW of continental United States; capital Honolulu; ranks 47th in area, pop. 1,115,000; Aloha State

Idaho ID; 43rd state, admitted 1890; NW United States; capital Boise; ranks 13th in area, pop. 1,012,000; Gem State

Illinois IL; 21st state, admitted 1818; N central United States; capital Springfield; ranks 24th in area, pop. 11,467,000; Prairie State

Indiana IN; 19th state, admitted 1816; N central United States; capital Indianapolis; ranks 38th in area, pop. 5,564,000; Hoosier State

Iowa IA; 29th state, admitted 1846; N central United States; capital Des Moines; ranks 25th in area, pop. 2,787,000; Hawkeye State

Kansas KS; 34th state, admitted 1861; NW central United States; capital Topeka; ranks 14th in area, pop. 2,486,000; Sunflower State

Kentucky KY; 15th state, admitted 1792; SE central United States; capital Frankfort; ranks 37th in area, pop. 3,699,000; Bluegrass State

Louisiana LA; 18th state, admitted 1812; S central United States; capital Baton Rouge; ranks 31st in area, pop. 4,238,000; Pelican State

Maine ME; 23rd state, admitted 1820; NE United States; capital Augusta; ranks 39th in area, pop. 1,233,000; Pine Tree State

Maryland MD; 7th state, admitted 1788; E United States; capital Annapolis; ranks 42nd in area, pop. 4,799,000; Old Line State

Massachusetts MA; 6th state, admitted 1788; NE United States; capital Boston; ranks 45th in area, pop. 6,029,000; Bay State

Michigan MI; 26th state, admitted 1837; N central United States; capital Lansing; ranks 23rd in area, pop. 9,329,000; Wolverine State

Minnesota MN; 32nd state, admitted 1858; N central United States; capital St. Paul; ranks 12th in area, pop. 4,387,000; North Star State

Mississippi MS; 20th state, admitted 1817; S central United States; capital Jackson; ranks 32nd in area, pop. 2,586,000; Magnolia State

Missouri MO; 24th state, admitted 1821; NW central United States; capital Jefferson City; ranks 19th in area, pop. 5,138,000; Show-Me State

Montana MT; 41st state, admitted 1889; NW United States; capital Helena; ranks 4th in area, pop. 804,000; Treasure State

Nebraska NE; 37th state, admitted 1867; NW central United States; capital Lincoln; ranks 15th in area, pop. 1,585,000; Cornhusker State

Nevada NV; 36th state, admitted 1864; W United States; capital Carson City; ranks 7th in area, pop. 1,206,000; Sagebrush State

New Hampshire NH; 9th state, admitted 1788; NE United States; capital Concord; ranks 44th in area, pop. 1,114,000; Granite State

New Jersey NJ; 3rd state, admitted 1787; E United States; capital Trenton; ranks 46th in area, pop. 7,749,000; Garden State

New Mexico NM; 47th state, admitted 1912; SW United States; capital Santa Fe; ranks 5th in area, pop. 1,522,000; Land of Enchantment

New York NY; 11th state, admitted 1788; NE United States; capital Albany; ranks 30th in area, pop. 18,044,000; Empire State

North Carolina NC; 12th state, admitted 1789; SE United States; capital Raleigh; ranks 28th in area, pop. 6,658,000; Tar Heel State

North Dakota ND; 39th state, admitted 1889; NW central United States; capital Bismarck; ranks 17th in area, pop. 641,000; Peace Garden State

Ohio OH; 17th state, admitted 1803; NE central United States; capital Columbus; ranks 35th in

area, pop. 10,888,000; Buckeye State
Oklahoma OK; 46th state, admitted 1907; SW central United States; capital Oklahoma City; ranks 18th in area, pop. 3,158,000; Sooner State
Oregon OR; 33rd state, admitted 1859; NW United States; capital Salem; ranks 10th in area, pop. 2,854,000; Beaver State
Pennsylvania PA; 2nd state, admitted 1787; E United States; capital Harrisburg; ranks 33rd in area, pop. 12,000,000; Keystone State
Rhode Island RI; 13th state, admitted 1790; NE United States; capital Providence; ranks 50th in area, pop. 1,006,000; Ocean State
South Carolina SC; 8th state, admitted 1788; SE United States; capital Columbia; ranks 40th in area, pop. 3,506,000; Palmetto State
South Dakota SD; 40th state, admitted 1889; NW central United States; capital Pierre; ranks 16th in area, pop. 700,000; Coyote State
Tennessee TN; 16th state, admitted 1796; SE central United States; capital Nashville; ranks 34th in area, pop. 4,896,000; Volunteer State
Texas TX; 28th state, admitted 1845; SW central United States; capital Austin; ranks 2nd in area, pop. 17,060,000; Lone Star State
Utah UT; 45th state, admitted 1896; W central United States; capital Salt Lake City; ranks 11th in area, pop. 1,680,000; Beehive State
Vermont VT; 14th state, admitted 1791; NE United States; capital Montpelier; ranks 43rd in area, pop. 565,000; Green Mountain State
Virginia VA; 10th state, admitted 1788; SE United States; capital Richmond; ranks 36th in area, pop. 6,217,000; Old Dominion
Washington WA; 42nd state, admitted 1889; NW United States; capital Olympia; ranks 20th in area, pop. 4,888,000; Evergreen State
West Virginia WV; 35th state, admitted 1863; E central United States; capital Charleston; ranks 41st in area, pop. 1,802,000; Mountain State
Wisconsin WI; 30th state, admitted 1848; N central United States; capital Madison; ranks 26th in area, pop. 4,906,000; Badger State
Wyoming WY; 44th state, admitted 1890; W central United States; capital Cheyenne; ranks 9th in area, pop. 456,000; Equality State

METALS, MINERALS, AND ROCKS

Minerals
Metals
Rocks

Minerals

mineral inorganic chemical solid naturally occurring in Earth's crust and having definite chemical composition and tendency to form crystals

Mineral compounds

acanthite, acmite, actinolite, adamite, alabaster, allanite, alunite, amblygonite, amphibole, analcime, andalusite, anglesite, anhydrite, anthophyllite, apatite, apophyllite, aragonite, argentite, arsenopyrite, asbestos, asphaltum, augite, aurichalcite, austinite, autunite, aventurine, axinite, azurite
babingtonite, barite, bauxite, benitoite, beryl, biotite, bismuth, bismuthite, bixbyite, borax, bornite, boulangerite, bournonite, brochantite, brookite, brucite
calaverite, calcite, cancrinite, carnallite, carnotite, cassiterite, celestite, cerargyrite, cerussite, chabazite, chalcanthite, chalcedony, chalcocite, chalcopyrite, chlorargyrite, chlorite, chromite, chrondrodite, chrysoberyl, chrysocolla, cinnabar, clinozoisite, cobaltite, colemanite, columbite, conichalcite, copalite, cordierite, corundum, covellite, crocoite, cryolite, cuprite, cyanotrichite
danburite, datolite, dendrite, descloizite, diaspore, diopside, dioptase, dolomite, dumortierite
emery, enargite, enstatite, epidote, epsomite, erythrite
feldspar, fluorite, franklinite
gadolinite, galena, garnet, garnierite, gilsonite, glauberite, glauconite, glaucophane, goethite, graphite, gummite, gypsum
halite, hedenbergite, hematite, hemimorphite, heubnerite, heulandite, hornblende, howlite, hypersthene
idocrase, ilmenite, inesite
jadeite, jamesonite, jarosite
kaolinite, kernite, kyanite
laumontite, lawsonite, lazulite, lazurite, legrandite, lepidolite, leucite, limonite, linarite
magnesite, magnetite, malachite, manganite, marcasite, melanterite, mesolite, mica,

millerite, mimetite, mineral coal, molybdenite, monazite, muscovite
natrolite, nepheline, neptunite, niccolite, nickeline
olivenite, olivine, orpiment, ozocerite
pargasite, pectolite, pentlandite, phenakite, phlogopite, plagioclase, polybasite, prehnite, proustite, psilomelane, pumpellyite, pyrargyrite, pyrite, pyrolusite, pyromorphite, pyrophyllite, pyroxene, pyrrhotite
quartz
realgar, rhodochrosite, rhodonite, riebeckite, rutile
scapolite, scheelite, scolecite, serpentine, shattuckite, siderite, sillimanite, skutterudite, smaltite, smithsonite, sodalite, soda niter, sperrylite, sphalerite, sphene, spinel, spodumene, stannite, staurolite, stephanite, stibnite, stilbite, strontianite, sulfur, sylvanite, sylvite
talc, tantalite, tephroite, tetrahedrite, thenardite, thomsonite, thorite, torbernite, tourmaline, tremolite, triphylite, trona
ulexite, uraninite, uranophane
vanadinite, variscite, vivianite
wavellite, willemite, witherite, wolframite, wollastonite, wulfenite
zincite, zoisite

Gemstones

gemstone hard mineral, crystal, or petrified material used as jewelry when cut and faceted, designated precious or semiprecious
agate, alexandrite, almandine, amber, amethyst, amorzonite, andradite, aquamarine, aventurine
beryl, bloodstone
cairngorm, carbuncle, carnelian, cat's eye, chalcedony, chrysoberyl, chrysolite, chrysoprase, citrine
demantoid, diamond
emerald
fire opal
garnet, girasol
harlequin opal, heliotrope, hyacinth
jacinth, jade, jasper, jet
kunzite
lapis lazuli, lazurite
malachite, melanite, milky quartz, moonstone, morganite
nephrite
olivine, onyx, opal
peridot, pyrope
red jasper, rose quartz, rubasse, ruby, rutile
sapphire, sard, sardonyx, smoky quartz, smoky topaz, sodalite, spinel, star sapphire, sunstone
tiger's-eye, topaz, tourmaline, turquoise
white sapphire
zircon

Metals

metal opaque, fusible, ductile, conductive, lustrous substance, often a chemical element or compound yielding oxides or hydroxides

Pure metals

aluminum, americium, antimony, arsenic
barium, beryllium, bismuth
cadmium, calcium, cerium, cesium, chromium, cobalt, columbium, copper
dysprosium
erbium, europium
gadolinium, gallium, germanium, gold
hafnium, holmium
indium, iridium, iron
lanthanum, lead, lithium, lutetium
magnesium, manganese, mercury, molybdenum
neodymium, nickel, niobium
osmium
palladium, phosphorus, platinum, polonium, potassium, praseodymium, promethium, protactinium
radium, rhenium, rubidium, ruthenium
samarium, scandium, silver, sodium, strontium
tantalum, technetium, terbium, thallium, thorium, thulium, tin, titanium, tungsten
uranium
vanadium
ytterbium, yttrium
zinc, zirconium

Alloys

alloy two or more metals, or a metal and nonmetal, fused together when molten
alnico, amalgam
Babbitt, brass, bronze
Carboloy, carbon steel, cast iron, chrome, coin nickel, constantan
Damascus steel, damask
electrum, elinvar
graphite steel
invar
permalloy, perminvar, pewter, pinchbeck, pink gold
solder, spiegeleisen, stainless steel, steel, sterling silver
tombac
white gold, wrought iron

Rocks

rock concretion of earthly or mineral matter of variable size, shape, and chemical composition

Igneous rocks

igneous rock rock formed by cooling and hardening of hot, molten rock within Earth
andesite, anorthosite, aplite
basalt

carbonatite, clinkstone
dacite, diabase, diorite, dolerite, dunite
felsite
gabbro, granite, granite pegmatite, granodiorite
kimberlite
lava
monzonite
nepheline syenite
obsidian
pegmatite, peridotite, phonolite, pitchstone, porphyry, pumice, pyroxenite
rhyolite
scoria, syenite
trachyte, trap, traprock, tuff
volcanic ash

METAMORPHIC ROCKS

metamorphic rock igneous or sedimentary rock that has been transformed by heat, pressure, or chemically active fluids
amphibolite
calc-silicate
gneiss, granulite, greenstone
halite, hornblende schist, hornfels
ironstone
marble, metaquartzite
phyllite
quartzite
schist, serpentine, skarn, slate, soapstone, steatite

SEDIMENTARY ROCKS

sedimentary rock rock formed on Earth's surface from accumulation of material deposited by water, wind, or glaciers
anhydrite
breccia, brownstone, buhr, buhrstone
chalk, chert, coal, conglomerate
dolomite, dripstone
flint
grit, gypsum
hematite
limestone
marl, mudstone
oolite
rock salt, rottenstone
sandstone, shale, stalactite, stalagmite, stinkstone
touchstone, travertine, tufa

LANDSCAPES AND SEASCAPES

Hills, Hollows, and Valleys
Plains and Marshes
Woods and Brush
Inland Waterways and Lakes
Coastal Land, Islands, and the Sea

Hills, Hollows, and Valleys

acclivity upward slope of hill
alp high mountain
arete ridge in craggy mountains with sharp crest
arroyo steep-sided gully in arid region, carved by heavy rains
badlands highly eroded area of hills in fantastic shapes
barrow pile of earth or rocks at location of ancient grave
basin depression in earth's surface, often with lake or pond at bottom; drainage outlet for river
berm narrow shelf at bottom, top, or along side of slope
bluff high, steep, broad-faced bank or cliff
box canyon narrow valley with vertical walls terminating in wall at upstream end
butte sheer-faced, isolated, flat-topped hill with smaller summit than mesa
caldera large basin formed by explosion and collapse of center of volcano
canyon deep, narrow valley with steep sides carved by river
cave underground hollow that opens into a hill
cavern underground chamber, usu. large
cavity hollowed space in rocks, cliffs, or hills
cenote deep limestone sinkhole
chasm deep cleft in earth; gorge
cleft small fissure in earth
cliff tall, steep, vertical face of rock overlooking lower area
col depression in crest of ridge; mountain pass
cordillera series of parallel mountain ranges
coulee dry streambed; shallow depression
crag steep rocks or cliff with sharp outcroppings
crater bowl-shaped depression, esp. at mouth of volcano
crest highest ridge of mountain or hill
crevasse deep cleft in glacier or earth
crevice crack in earth
cuesta ridge or hill with steep face on one side and long gentle slope on other
dale valley, vale
declivity downward slope of hill
dell small, secluded, wooded valley
depression any hollow place or low point in earth's surface
dingle small, wooded valley or dell
divide mountain ridge from which streams drain in opposite directions

donga narrow, steep-sided ravine, dry except in rainy season
draw gully less deep than a ravine
drift glacial deposit of gravel or boulders
dune hill of sand formed by wind
escarpment steep cliff separating two level surfaces
esker elongated ridge of sand and boulders deposited by stream running beneath stagnant glacier
fissure crack or split in earth
foothills low-lying hills at base of mountain range
glacier large mass of moving ice
glacis gentle slope; mound of earth, esp. before fortification
glen secluded, narrow, grassy valley, usu. level at bottom
gorge narrow, steep ravine with rocky walls
grotto cave or cavern, usu. not deep
gulch deep, steep-walled ravine formed by swift stream
gully channel or small valley worn in earth by running water
headland promontory
highland rolling hills in elevated tract of land
hill usu. rounded elevation of land, smaller than a mountain
hillock small hill
hillside one slope of hill
hilltop peak, crest, or ridge of hill
hollow depression, low sunken place
hummock low, rounded hillock
intervale low-lying tract of land along river
kloof deep gorge or ravine (South Africa)
knap summit, hill top
knoll small, rounded hill
massif central, compact portion of mountain range
mound pile of earth or stones; knoll
mountain landmass elevated far above surroundings, higher than a hill
overlook elevated land that affords view of surrounding flatlands
palisade line of steep cliffs, esp. above river
pass low point suitable for crossing mountain range
peak top of mountain with distinct, pointed summit
pinnacle tall mountain peak
piton sharp peak of mountain
precipice vertical or near vertical face of hill or mountain; cliff
promontory point of high land projecting out over water; headland
range series of connected mountains
ravine narrow, steep-sided depression in earth's surface formed by running water, larger than a gully, smaller than a canyon
recess cleft in earth, often concealed from view
ridge range of hills or mountains; long, narrow elevation in earth's surface or ocean floor
rift crack, fissure
rise slope, hillside
saddle mountain ridge connecting two peaks; col
scarp line of cliffs formed by erosion or fracturing of earth
sierra mountain range, esp. with irregular contour of jagged peaks
sinkhole limestone hollow connected to underground passage
spur ridge projecting from mountain or range; projection of elevated land
submontane land at foot of or lying under mountain
summit highest point of mountain or hill
tableland flat-topped, elevated tract of land
talus slope formed by pile of rock debris at foot of cliff
trench long, narrow furrow in ground or deep ocean floor
trough long, narrow, shallow depression between ridges or slopes
vale valley, esp. one hidden between hills
valley long depression in earth's surface lying between hills or mountains, usu. formed by river flowing through it
vista height affording view over large expanse of land
wadi rocky desert riverbed, dry except for rainy season
water gap gap across mountain ridge, cut by and giving passage to stream
watershed area on one side of divide drained by rivers all flowing in same direction; ridge dividing two drainage areas

Plains and Marshes

alluvial plain flat plain where river leaves gorge or joins larger waterway
barrens expanse of flat, treeless land
bog small marsh or swamp; wet, spongy ground
bottoms low-lying area at edge of waterway
clearing tract of land with trees and brush removed
coastal plain flat expanse of land from coast to first range of mountains
delta nearly flat alluvial plain at mouth of river, usu. triangular
desert arid, barren region that may support sparse vegetation
down rolling, open, upland region of grassy land
everglade swampy grassland, esp. in south Florida
fen low boggy land partly covered by water
field open land, usu. without many trees
glade open space in forest; marshy or grassy clearing
grassland plain covered with grasses
heath tract of open land with uncultivated vegetation such as heather and shrubs
mainland primary part of continent, as distinguished from islands
marsh wet, boggy land; swamp
meadow expanse of grassland, often in mountains or along river
mesa small, high plateau; flat-topped, steep-sided, rocky land formation
mire muddy bog, swamp

moor tract of open wasteland often overgrown with low shrubs; heath
morass marsh, swamp
mud flat level area of muddy land, usu. at edge of body of water
paludal (*adj*) marshy, swampy
pampas broad, grass-covered plains in South America, esp. Argentina
peat bog marsh of partially carbonized decomposing vegetable matter
piedmont area lying at base of mountain range
plain expanse of flat or rolling, usu. treeless, land
plateau extensive tract of level land raised above adjoining land
playa sandy, salty, or mud-caked flat floor of desert basin, usu. occupied by shallow lake following heavy rain (western United States)
polder tract of lowland reclaimed from sea or lake and protected by dikes or dams
prairie large tract of rolling grassland
quag quagmire
quagmire marsh, bog; wet ground with difficult footing; quag
quicksand deep bed of loose sand saturated with water that yields underfoot
salt flat level tract of dried salt land left by evaporation of lake or sea
salt marsh marshy tract in stage between saline lake and salt flat
savanna grassy plain with scattered trees; treeless plain in tropics
scabland tract of high, rocky land with no topsoil and dry streambeds
solfatara level area surrounding volcano emitting vapors
steppe vast plain of eastern Europe having few trees
swamp wet, boggy land
sward grassy surface of land; turf, sod and soil with roots
tarpit flat area filled with natural tar or asphalt which is exposed to air
tract any expanse of land
tundra level, treeless plain in arctic region with dark wet soil on base of permanently frozen subsoil
wash bog, marsh
wasteland barren land, desert
wetlands land with nonflowing surface water, such as marsh, swamp, or bog

Woods and Brush

backwoods remote, densely forested region
bosc boscage
boscage thicket or grove of shrubbery; bosc
bracken thicket of large coarse ferns
brake often marshy land overgrown with one plant, esp. ferns
broom shrubbery, esp. with yellow flowers
brush land covered with scrub vegetation
brushwood thicket of shrubs or small trees
bush dense growth of low shrubs; expanse of uncleared area
chaparral dense thicket of stunted evergreen oaks
coppice thicket or wood of small trees; copse
copse coppice
covert thicket giving cover to game
deadfall tangled mass of fallen trees and branches
forest large tract of thickly wooded land
furze gorse
gorse growth of spiny, yellow-flowering shrub; furze
grove small wood or group of trees growing close together
heath shrubby evergreen plants covering tract of open land
hedge row of closely planted shrubs that forms a boundary
jungle wild land overgrown with dense mass of tropical vegetation
motte grove of trees on open prairie
oasis fertile area of vegetation in desert
orchard field of fruit or nut trees
park wooded tract of land, often cultivated
rain forest tropical woods covered by tall, dense canopy of branches in area of heavy rainfall
rush hollow-stemmed marsh grass
scrub growth of low trees and shrubs
sedge tufted marsh plant
shinnery dense growth of small trees, esp. scrub oak
shrubbery growth of shrubs
shrubs short, multistemmed, woody plants
spinney *Chiefly Brit.* small wood with undergrowth
stand group of trees or shrubs growing together or in a line
sylvan (*adj*) covered with woods or groves of trees
thicket dense growth of shrubs and underbrush
timberland forested tract
tussock clump or tuft of sedge or marsh grass
underbrush shrubs, bushes, and small trees growing beneath taller trees; undergrowth
undergrowth underbrush
vineyard field of grapevines
weald forest, wilderness; rolling, upland region of woods; wold
wilderness uncultivated, uninhabited region in natural state
windbreak line or stand of trees affording protection from wind
wold weald
wood dense growth of trees, larger than a grove and smaller than a forest
woodland timberland, forest
woods region covered with trees and shrubs

Inland Waterways and Lakes

bank ground sloping upward from edge of lake, river, or sea
bayou creek or stream that is tributary of larger watercourse; marshy, stagnant body of water
bed bottom of body of water
bend curve in flowing waterway
bight bend in river; curved coast or bay
billabong dry streambed that fills in rainy season; stagnant pool in wilds (Australia)
branch small stream flowing into larger stream; one fork of divided waterway
brook small stream of fresh water

canal artificial navigable waterway that connects bodies of water or is used for irrigation
cascade small waterfall, esp. one of a series
channel bed where natural stream runs; deeper part of river
creek small, usu. slow-moving stream
current swiftest part of stream
distributary branch leading from main waterway and not rejoining it
eddy circular movement of water in pool in stream
falls waterfall; series of waterfalls
feeder tributary leading to larger watercourse
ford shallow part of stream that allows crossing by wading
fork point where river branches into two or more parts
fountainhead source of a stream, usu. a spring; wellspring
freshet stream springing from overflow of melting snow
geyser spring issuing intermittent jets of steam
headwaters small streams and freshets that converge to form source of river, often at high altitude
kill channel, creek
lagoon shallow body of water connected to larger body of water but cut off by atoll or sandbar
laguna small lake or pond
lake inland body of standing fresh water, usu. of considerable size
loch *Scot.* lake
meander curve or bend in river on level ground
mere small lake, pool
millpond pond created by damming of river
mouth point where stream enters lake or sea
narrows portion of stream decidedly less wide than other portions
oxbow U-shaped bend in river
oxbow lake bow-shaped lake formed when river cuts across U-shaped neck of land
pond inland body of standing fresh water, smaller than a lake
pool deep, quiet place in stream; small body of water
race strong current flowing through narrow channel
rapids shallow part of stream with strong current broken by obstacles such as rocks; white water
reach straight portion of river or stream
reservoir artificial, man-made lake, esp. for storing water supply
rill runnel
ripple shallow stretch of rough water in stream; rapids
river natural stream of significant length and volume that follows definite course
riverbank rising ground at edge of river
riverhead source of river
rivulet small stream, brook
run creek
runnel very small brook; rill
runoff rainwater or melted snow flowing down mountain into streams
salt lake body of water in dry region, with no outlet, that has become saline through evaporation
sandbar ridge of sand accumulated by currents in stream
sault waterfall or rapids
shallows portion of stream with slight depth
shoal shallow place in river; sandbar
sink saline lake with no outlet
spout waterspout
spring source of water issuing from ground
strait narrow waterway that passes between larger bodies of water
stream flowing body of water smaller than a river
torrent stream with strong, rapid current
tributary stream leading into larger stream, river, or lake
vortex whirlpool
watercourse any natural stream of flowing water; waterway
waterfall very steep or perpendicular stream of water, often over precipice; falls
water hole small hollow filled with standing water
waterspout geyser; spout
waterway watercourse
well pool filled by spring; flow of water from earth
wellspring source of a stream; fountainhead
whirlpool water spinning rapidly in a circle that produces downward sucking force at its center into which floating objects are pulled; vortex
white water rapids

Coastal Land, Islands, and the Sea

archipelago group of sea islands, esp. in curved row
arm narrow inland extension of sea
atoll ring-shaped coral reef enclosing lagoon
barrier reef coral reef separated from shore by lagoon
bay body of water forming indentation on shoreline of sea or large lake; wide inlet of sea smaller than a gulf
beach rocky or sandy area along edge of sea or ocean
cape point of land extending into water; peninsula
cay key
channel strait of sea between two landmasses
coast land along shore of ocean or sea
coastline boundary between land and sea
côte *French.* coast
cove small, sheltered recess in shoreline
current tidal movement of ocean waters
estuary point where river mouth meets sea's tide; arm of sea at river mouth
firth *Scot.* narrow arm of sea; mouth of river into sea
fjord long, narrow arm of sea with steep cliffs
floe large, flat mass of ice floating on sea
gulf section of ocean or sea that extends into land, larger than a bay
harbor coastal waters protected from open sea and deep enough for anchoring ships
headland high point of land projecting into sea; promontory

high seas open ocean several miles or more from shore
iceberg large mass of ice broken off from glacier, floating in sea
inlet indent in shoreline, esp. narrow passage between points of land or islands, often forming entrance to lagoon
island land area completely surrounded by water, smaller than a continent
isle island
islet small island
isthmus narrow strip of land with water on both sides connecting two larger bodies of land
key low island or reef, esp. coral islet off south Florida; cay
lagoon shallow body of water connected to the sea
littoral (*adj*) of, on, or along the shore
marine (*adj*) of or at the sea or ocean
neck narrow strip of land, usu. between bodies of water
ocean any of vast, connected bodies of salt water that cover almost three-fourths of Earth's surface
oceanfront land directly along seashore
offshore (*adj*) designating area of sea lying a short way from beach
pelagic (*adj*) of or on the open sea
peninsula large land area almost completely surrounded by water, usu. connected to mainland by isthmus
point land projecting into sea and narrowing at end
promontory headland
reach narrow arm of sea that extends inland
reef ridge of rock or coral just under water surface
riviera coastal region of sea used as a resort area
sandbank large deposit of sand that forms a shoal
sand bar underwater ridge of sand formed in coastal waters
sand dune tall mound of sand on beach
sea large body of salt water, generally landlocked and smaller than the ocean; also used as synonym for ocean
seaboard seashore
sea cliff steep slope overlooking ocean
seashore land at edge of sea, esp. beach; seaboard
seaway deep inland waterway connecting with sea
shoal sandbar beneath shallow water, sometimes exposed at low tide
shore land bordering a sea or ocean; coast
shoreline edge of land where a large body of water meets land
skerry reef; rocky island
sound passage between bodies of water; long inlet or arm of sea; water separating island from mainland
spit narrow point of land extending into water; long, narrow reef
strait narrow waterway connecting larger bodies of water
strand land along body of water; beach; tidal land alternately covered and exposed by tides
surf waves breaking against rocks and beach at shore
tidal basin artificial body of water open to river and subject to tides
tidal land flatland at seashore exposed at low tide, covered at high tide; tideland
tide rise and fall of surface of ocean and connected bodies of water due to gravitational pull of moon and sun
tideland tidal land
tide pool tiny lagoon left in rocks along shore by withdrawing tide
tidewater ocean water that overflows land at high tide
waterfront strip of land at edge of ocean or other waterway

WEATHER AND NATURAL PHENOMENA

Storms

anticyclone wind system that rotates around high-pressure center in opposite direction from cyclone
blizzard severe snowstorm with large accumulations of snow
cloudburst sudden, intense rainstorm
cyclone advancing wind system with heavy rain that rotates around low-pressure pressure center clockwise in Southern Hemisphere, counterclockwise in Northern Hemisphere
deluge heavy rainstorm that causes flooding
downpour intense rainstorm
dust storm whirlwind of dust in dry region with hot, electrically charged air
electrical storm storm with atmospheric electrical discharge, thunder, and lightning
gale moderate windstorm, 32 to 63 mph, esp. at sea
hail shower of small lumps of snow or compacted ice pellets, graded by size: pea, marble, golf ball, hen's egg, tennis ball, grapefruit, football
hurricane tropical cyclone at sea with heavy rain and winds over 72 mph, sometimes moving into temperate latitudes; tropical cyclone
ice storm storm with rain that freezes on contact with air
maelstrom powerful, turbulent whirlpool or whirlwind
monsoon seasonal windstorm that brings heavy rains off Indian Ocean
rain water droplets formed by condensation of

atmospheric vapor falling to earth
rainstorm steady, prolonged rainfall
shower mild, brief rainfall
sleet frozen or partly frozen rain
slush partly melted, watery snow
snow precipitation formed into white ice crystals from water vapor at temperatures below freezing
snow flurries occasional windblown bursts of snowfall
snowstorm precipitation of small, dry crystals of water vapor
squall sudden, violent windstorm, often with rain or snow
storm atmospheric disturbance marked by wind and/or precipitation
tempest extensive, violent windstorm with rain or snow
thundershower mild thunderstorm
thunderstorm rainstorm with thunder and lightning
tornado violent whirlwind, advancing over land with funnel-shaped cloud; twister
torrential rain very heavy rainstorm
tropical cyclone hurricane
tropical storm tropical cyclone with winds under 73 mph
twister *Informal.* tornado
typhoon tropical cyclone in China Sea
weather front advancing storm

Winds

anemometer wind-measuring instrument
arctic icy wind from north
austral wind southerly wind
Beaufort scale measure of wind force in miles per hour on scale from one (calm) to twelve (hurricane)
boreal northerly wind
breath wind under 3 mph
breeze relatively gentle wind of 4-31 mph; any light wind
cat's paw light air that ruffles calm water surface
chinook warm, dry wind off eastern Rocky Mountains
downwind (*adv*) in direction toward which wind is blowing
dust devil small whirlwind of sand and dust
favonian wind west wind
foehn warm, dry wind blowing down mountainside
fresh breeze 19-24 mph wind
fresh gale 39-46 mph wind
gale 32-63 mph wind
gentle breeze 8-12 mph wind
gust sudden, sharp burst of wind
headwind wind blowing against course of ship or aircraft
hurricane storm with winds over 72 mph
katabatic wind wind blowing down mountain valley at night
knot measure of wind velocity equal to 1 nautical mile per hour
light breeze 4-7 mph wind
mistral cold, dry, strong northerly wind in southern France
moderate breeze 13-18 mph wind
moderate gale 32-38 mph wind
nor'easter wind from northeast
norther strong wind from north
northerly wind from north
nor'wester wind from northwest
offshore (*adj*) blowing from shore to sea
onshore (*adj*) blowing from sea to shore
prevailing wind general direction of swirling wind
Santa Ana hot, dry wind off desert in southern California
sea breeze moist wind off ocean
sirocco hot, oppressive wind from arid region, esp. on Mediterranean from Libyan desert
southeaster wind from southeast
southerly wind from south
southwester wind from southwest
squall sudden, violent windstorm
strong breeze 25-31 mph wind
strong gale 47-54 mph wind
tailwind wind blowing in same direction as course of ship or aircraft
trade wind wind blowing almost continually toward equator
updraft air pulling upward into atmosphere
upwind (*adv*) in direction from which wind is blowing
violent storm 64-72 mph wind
vortex whirlwind
waft light breath of moving air
westerlies winds from subtropical areas in west toward middle latitudes
whirlwind air current rotating violently upward around vertical axis and moving forward; vortex
whole gale 55 to 63 mph wind; windstorm
wind natural movement of air at any velocity, esp. horizontal relative to Earth's surface
windstorm strong winds with no rain
zephyr gentle breeze from west

Clouds

altocumulus white, globular cloudlets that appear in broken patches at altitudes around 10,000 feet (3048 m), usu. producing rain showers
altostratus dark, drab, thin cloud streaks at middle altitudes
cirrocumulus irregular, small, white sheets of cloud segments at altitudes around 20,000 feet (6096 m)
cirrostratus even layer of translucent, fibrous cloud streaks at altitudes of 20,000 feet (6096 m) or more, indicating that rain is coming
cirrus wispy, white cloud tufts and filaments at high altitudes up to 40,000 feet (12,192 m)
cloud visible mass of water or ice particles suspended at considerable height
cumulocirrus small, delicate cumulus at high altitude
cumulonimbus thunderstorm cumulus that spreads from dark portions at 5000 feet (1524 m) to towers rising upward to 50,000 feet (15,240 m)
cumulostratus cumulus with flat stratus base

cumulus cloud with flat, dark base around 2000 feet (610 m) and rounded, white mountainous outlines to altitudes of 10,000 feet (3048 m), that appears in a broken mass

nimbostratus low, dark gray rain cloud a few hundred feet above ground with ragged tops upward to 3000 feet (914 m), producing continuous precipitation

nimbus rain cloud of uniform gray that covers entire sky

nubilous (*adj*) relating to clouds

stratocumulus large, rounded mass of dark cloud covering the entire sky, esp. in winter, at altitudes from 1500 to 6500 feet (457 to 1981 m), not producing rain

stratus flattened streaks of cloud at altitudes of a few hundred feet, similar to ground fog and producing drizzle

thundercloud electrically charged cloud that produces thunder and lightning; esp. cumulonimbus

Disasters and Phenomena

acid rain precipitation with excess acidity due to industrial pollutants

aftershock smaller tremor following main shock of earthquake

air pollution condition in which toxic substances are in atmosphere, esp. as a result of industrial and automobile emissions

alpenglow reddish glow at sunset and sunrise on mountain summit

aurora australis antarctic version of aurora borealis

aurora borealis streamers and bands of electrically caused radiant emissions that light up arctic night sky

avalanche large mass of snow, ice, and mud moving rapidly down mountain

ball lightning rare, luminous floating ball of lightning

black ice thin sheet of ice, often caused by freezing mist on roadway; transparent coating of ice on the sea

bolt of lightning common, streaking flash of lightning, usu. with thunder

bore tidal flood caused by rapid rise in water in channel

corona discharge storm phenomenon caused by discharge of electricity shaped like flames at surface of conductor; Saint Elmo's fire

dew moisture condensed at night on surfaces of cool objects

dewfall nightly accumulation of dew

dew point temperature at which vapor condenses

drizzle very light, misty rain

drought prolonged period without rain

earthquake volcanic or tectonic crustal movement of Earth resulting in trembling, shaking, and fracturing; quake; temblor

eclipse total or partial obscuring of one celestial body by another

eddy air or water current running against main current; whirlpool

El Ninõ unusually warm Pacific Ocean current that occurs periodically and often causes catastrophic weather conditions

epicenter Earth's surface directly above true center of earthquake

erosion wearing away of topsoil by wind and water

eruption violent release of steam and lava from volcano

eye calm region at center of cyclone or hurricane

fault line fracture in Earth's crust with displacement indicating and causing earthquakes

flash flood sudden, localized, massive rush of water due to heavy rainfall

flood overflow of body of water onto normally dry land; inundation

fog thick mist or vapor suspended in lower atmosphere near ground

freeze drop in temperature below 32° F, or 0° C

frost minute ice crystals that form on surfaces; hoar

greenhouse effect warming of Earth's surface and lower atmosphere when solar radiation is converted to heat and trapped in atmosphere by cloud layers and gases

ground fog low, often dense fog, esp. one through which sky and clouds above can be seen

Gulf Stream warm Atlantic current flowing from Florida to New England and Newfoundland

hailstone pellet of compressed ice and snow

hoar frost

hyperborean (*adj*) of or relating to the extreme north; frozen

hypocenter focus of earthquake; epicenter

ice floe flat, floating mass of ice at sea

ignis fatuus eerie light at night over marshland due to combustion of gas from decomposing organic matter

Indian summer unseasonably hot weather in autumn

inundation flood

Jack Frost personification of frosty weather

jet stream long, narrow, westerly 250 mph air current at high altitude in tropopause

killing frost last frost of spring or first frost of fall, limiting growing season for all but hardiest plants

landslide mass of rock and earth moving rapidly down slope

lava molten rock that issues from volcano

lightning flash of light from discharge of atmospheric electricity between clouds or between clouds and Earth

lunar eclipse condition produced by Earth lying directly between sun and moon so that moon passes through Earth's shadow

meteor shower cluster of falling rocks, incandescent from passage through Earth's atmosphere, generally burned up before reaching ground

midnight sun midsummer phenomenon at arctic and antarctic latitudes, where sun does not sink below horizon during night

mist fine light rain or thick fog

mud slide mass of mud, swelled by rain or flood, moving down slope

natural phenomenon distinct, observable event, fact, or circumstance not caused directly by humans
ozone depletion chemical breakup in stratosphere of ozone layer, which absorbs sun's ultraviolet radiation
pea soup *Informal.* extremely thick fog
pogonip dense ice fog found in mountain valleys of western United States
pollution man-made contamination of Earth and atmosphere
quake earthquake
rainbow arc of prismatic colors in sky, formed by reflection and refraction of sun's rays through water vapor drops
rime frost, esp. coating of tiny granular ice tufts, due to supercooling and exposure to wind
rip current undertow
riptide strong, narrow surface current that opposes another tide and disturbs sea
runoff water from rain or melted snow flowing over land surface and reaching streams
Saint Elmo's fire corona discharge
seismic (*adj*) of or relating to earthquakes
sheet lightning lightning obscured and diffused by clouds so that it appears over a broad area
smog fog augmented by smoke, chemical fumes, and automobile exhausts
snowcap snow covering mountain peak
snowdrift tall bank of windblown snow
snowflake small, tabular, columnar, or otherwise geometrically regular, white ice crystal
snowpack accumulation of winter snow at high altitudes
snowslide landslide of snow and ice; avalanche
solar eclipse condition in which moon passes directly between sun and Earth
spindrift spray swept by wind from waves during storm at sea; spoondrift
spoondrift spindrift
storm surge sudden high tide, 10 to 20 feet (3 to 6 m) above normal, accompanying hurricane
sunburst flash of sunlight through break in clouds
temblor earthquake
thunder sudden, loud, booming noise following lightning, due to expansion of air heated by electrical discharge
thunderbolt single flash of lightning with accompanying thunder
thunderclap booming crash of thunder
thunderhead rounded upper mass of cumulonimbus clouds, signaling thunderstorm
tidal wave unusually high sea wave, often following earthquake; unusually high tide due to high winds and storm; tsunami
total eclipse complete obscuring of one celestial body by another
tremor mild earthquake
tsunami tidal wave
undertow current beneath ocean surface moving forcefully out to sea; rip current
vapor diffuse fog or smoke floating in air
volcano vent in Earth's crust from which steam and molten rock are expelled
waterspout funnel-shaped column of mist and spray reaching from surface of sea or lake to underside of cloud
whirlpool eddy
whiteout severe blizzard condition with low visibility, no shadows, and only dark objects distinguishable
zero-zero condition of zero visibility in vertical and horizontal directions
zodiacal light luminous tract in sky in west after twilight and in east before dawn

Weather Conditions

Clear weather

azure
blue skies
clear, cloudless
fair
high visibility
shiny, sunny, sunshine

Cold weather

arctic
biting, bitter, boreal, brisk
chilly, cold, cold snap, cold wave, cool
freezing, frigid, frosty
gelid, glacial
icy
nippy
subzero

Hot weather

close
dog days
hot, humid
muggy
sultry, sweltering
torrid, tropical

Mild weather

balmy
calm
dry
fair
mild
seasonable
temperate
warm

Overcast weather

cloudy
dark
foggy, foul
half-light, hazy
lowering, low visibility
misty, murky
overcast
partly cloudy
shady, smoggy, soupy, sunless

Wet weather

deluge, downpour, drizzle
freezing rain
inclement
rainy
showers, sleet, slush, snowing, soaking, sprinkles
torrential rains

Windy weather

blast, blow, blustery, breath, breeze
draft
flurry
gale, gusty
swirling
turbulent
windy

Forecasting and Meteorology

air mass body of air hundreds of miles across and extending upward to the stratosphere, with uniform temperature and humidity
air pressure weight of air pushing down on Earth's surface
anemometer instrument for determining wind speed
aneroid barometer barometer in which atmospheric pressure moves pointer
Antarctic region surrounding South Pole, 66 1/2 degrees south of equator
Arctic region surrounding North Pole, 66 1/2 degrees north of equator
arctic air mass cold front moving from frigid to temperate zone in Northern Hemisphere
atmosphere entire mass of air enveloping Earth
atmospheric pressure pressure of air at any given point, equal to 14.7 pounds per square inch at sea level
barometer instrument for measuring atmospheric pressure as indicator of weather change
barometric pressure pressure of atmosphere measured by height of column of mercury in which standard atmospheric pressure equals 29.92 inches (760 mm)
ceiling altitude of base of cloud layer obscuring at least half the sky
Celsius thermometric scale with zero degrees as freezing point of water and one hundred degrees as boiling point, designated C; Centigrade
Centigrade Celsius
chill factor windchill factor
climate prevailing temperature, wind velocity, humidity, cloudiness, and precipitation at given location over period of years
cold front advancing edge of cold air mass
depression area in which atmospheric pressure is lower than surrounding areas, causing unsettled weather; low pressure
equator great circle of Earth, equidistant from two poles, dividing surface into northern and southern hemispheres
Fahrenheit thermometric scale of 180 degrees with freezing point of water at 32 degrees and boiling point at 212 degrees, designated F
forecast prediction of weather based on meteorological data
front advancing edge of air mass
gale warning weather bureau prediction of gale force sea winds
Groundhog Day February 2, day on which legend has it that sunny skies mean six more weeks of winter, cloudy skies, an early spring
high high-pressure air mass
high-pressure (*adj*) designating air mass with barometric pressure exceeding atmospheric pressure
horse latitudes region thirty degrees north to thirty degrees south of equator, characterized by high pressure and relative calm
humidity measure of percentage of moisture in atmosphere
inversion increase of air temperature at higher altitude
isobar map line that connects locations of equal barometric pressure
low low-pressure air mass
low-pressure (*adj.*) designating air mass with barometric pressure less than atmospheric pressure
meteorology scientific study of atmospheric phenomena, used to forecast weather
occluded front air mass forced aloft when cold front overtakes warm front
occlusion cutting off of contact between air mass and Earth's surface
pluviometer gauge for measuring rainfall
precipitation falling to earth of hail, rain, or snow
radiosonde instrument that transmits meteorological data from balloon at high altitude
rainfall measure of total precipitation over specified period in given location
relative humidity ratio of moisture present in air to maximum moisture possible at given temperature
ridge elongated high-pressure area between two depressions
seasonable (*adj*) normal for time of year
seeding producing rain by sprinkling dry ice or silver iodide crystals in stratus cloud layers
semitropical (*adj*) subtropical
small craft warning advisory of gale force winds at sea
snowfall total inches of accumulated snow
stationary front air mass holding fixed position
storm warning weather bureau notice of impending high winds and heavy precipitation
subarctic (*adj*) adjacent to Arctic Circle
subtropical (*adj*) typical of regions bordering the tropics; semitropical
system interacting fronts and air masses that cause weather conditions
temperate zone latitudes between tropic of Cancer and Arctic Circle, or between tropic of Capricorn and Antarctic Circle
temperature degree of hotness or coldness as measured on standardized scale
thermal rising current of warm air
thermometer device used to measure tempera-

ture, esp. by height of column of mercury
torrid zone area surrounding equator, extending north to tropic of Cancer and south to tropic of Capricorn; tropics
tropic either of two parallels of celestial latitude bounding torrid zone and marking sun's southernmost and northernmost declinations
tropic of Cancer latitude 23 1/2 degrees north of equator
tropic of Capricorn latitude 23 1/2 degrees south of equator
tropics latitudes between tropics of Cancer and Capricorn, extending 23 1/2 degrees north and south of equator; torrid zone
troposphere layer of atmosphere nearest Earth, where weather conditions occur
trough elongated low-pressure area between two areas of higher pressure
unseasonable (*adj*) abnormal for time of year
visibility degree of atmospheric clearness; measure of greatest distance at which object can be seen by naked eye
warm front advancing edge of warm air mass
wave period of intense, unseasonable heat or cold
weather state of Earth's atmosphere at specific time with regard to heat, humidity, visibility, pressure, wind speed, and disturbance
weather map chart with meteorological elements shown at specific times and places
weather station installation for recording meteorological measurements and observations
weather vane mounted, rotating object that indicates wind direction
wedge high-pressure area between two depressions, narrower than a ridge
windchill factor temperature felt on exposed skin equal to combination of actual temperature and wind speed; chill factor
wind sleeve mounted cone open at both ends, used to indicate wind direction; windsock
windsock wind sleeve
zone one of five major latitudinal divisions of Earth's surface with respect to temperature: frigid (north and south), temperate (north and south), torrid (equatorial)

Cyclical Events

autumn September 22 to December 20; fall
autumnal (*adj*) occurring in autumn
autumnal equinox first day of autumn, usu. September 22 in Northern Hemisphere
blue moon occurrence of two full moons in one month, taking place approximately every thirty-two months
canicular (*adj*) of or relating to dog days
crepuscule twilight
crescent moon phase of moon between new and first quarter or between last quarter and new
dawn hour during and after sunrise with first light
daylight hours between sunrise and sunset
dog days period of hot, sultry weather from July to late August in Northern Hemisphere
dusk hour during and after sunset with last light
ebb tide diminishing tide
equinox time of year when sun crosses equator, making day and night of equal length everywhere, usu. March 21 and September 22
fall September 22 to December 20; autumn
full moon phase in which entire visible disk of moon is illuminated by sun
gibbous moon phase between full and quarter moon, either waxing or waning
gloaming hour of darkness during and after sunset
harvest moon full moon nearest autumnal equinox
hibernal (*adj*) occurring in winter
high tide highest point reached by tide, usu. twice daily
low tide lowest point reached by tide, usu. twice daily
moonrise hour of moon's appearance in sky
moonset hour of moon's disappearance from sky
neap tide tide of minimum range at first and third lunar quarters
new moon phase in which dark side of moon faces Earth, with thin crescent moon seen a few days thereafter
quarter moon phase midway between full and new moon
seasonal (*adj*) occurring regularly during a specific season
solstice time of year when sun is furthest north or south of celestial equator, June 21 or December 21
spring March 21 to June 20
summer June 21 to September 21
summer solstice June 21, being first day of summer and longest daylight period in Northern Hemisphere
sundown hour of sunset
sunrise hour of sun's appearance in east
sunset hour of sun's disappearance in west
thaw period in spring when snow and ice melt
tide twice daily alternate rising and falling of ocean waters due to unequal gravitational attraction of sun and moon
twilight hour after sunset; crepuscule
vernal (*adj*) occurring in spring
vernal equinox first day of spring, usu. March 21 in Northern Hemisphere
wane tide decreasing tide
wax tide increasing tide
winter December 21 to March 20
winter solstice December 21, being first day of winter and shortest daylight period in Northern Hemisphere

Chapter Four
The Sciences

PHYSICS

Branches and Disciplines
Principles of Mechanics, Waves, and Measurement
Electricity and Magnetism
Nuclear and Particle Physics
Cosmology
Heat
Optics
Acoustics

Branches and Disciplines

acoustics study of production, control, transmission, reception, effects, and nature of sound waves
astrophysics study of physical and chemical constitution of the universe, esp. celestial matter
atomic physics study of the nature of the atom and subatomic particles
biophysics application of principles and methods of physics to biological problems
chaos study of hidden, ordered structures or regularities in seemingly chaotic phenomena
cosmology study of structure, origin, evolution, and probable fate of the universe
cryogenics study of production and application of effects of very low temperatures
crystallography study of form, structure, properties, and classification of crystals
dynamics branch of mechanics dealing with motion of material bodies under action of given forces
electricity study of phenomena and laws governing attraction and repulsion of electrons and other charged particles
electronics study of electron behavior
fluid mechanics hydraulics
geophysics branch of geology dealing with Earth physics: meteorology, oceanography, seismology, magnetism, radioactivity, geodesy
gravitation study of the force of acceleration toward each other of two material particles or bodies
heliology study of sunlight
hydraulics study of mechanical properties of water and other liquids in motion and the engineering applications of these properties; fluid mechanics
hydrodynamics study of fluids in motion and their interaction with their boundaries
hydrostatics study of fluids at rest
kinetics branch of mechanics dealing with all aspects of motion
magnetism study of phenomena associated with magnets and electric currents
mechanics study of energy and forces and their effect on matter
Newtonian physics system based on laws of gravitation and motion developed by Sir Isaac Newton
nuclear physics study of structure, behavior, and radioactive properties of atomic nuclei
nucleonics study of nucleons and practical applications of nuclear phenomena
optics study of propagation, control, transmission, reception, effects, and phenomena of light waves
particle physics study of nature and interaction of subatomic particles
physics study of properties and interaction of matter and energy
pneumatics study of mechanical properties of air and other gases in closed systems
quantum mechanics modern theory of matter which supersedes classical physics and concentrates on atomic and subatomic phenomena in terms of observable quantities
relativity system of thought based on theories of Albert Einstein regarding universal character of propagation speed of light and consequent dependence of space, time, and other mechanical measurements on motion of observer performing measurements
statics branch of mechanics dealing with action of forces on bodies at rest
thermionics study of electron or ion emissions from heated surfaces
thermodynamics study of quantitative relationship and conversion between heat and other energy forms, esp. mechanical energy or work
wave mechanics form of quantum mechanics in which particle motion is described by wave motion

Principles of Mechanics, Waves, and Measurement

acceleration rate of change in velocity with respect to time
acceleration of gravity change in velocity due to gravitational attraction
angular displacement amount of rotation of point, line, or body in specified direction about an axis
angular velocity time rate of change of angular displacement
Archimedes' principle object immersed in a fluid is buoyed up by a force equal to the weight of the fluid it displaces
Bernoulli effect pressure exerted by a fluid decreases as its velocity increases
bond electrostatic attraction between atoms or groups of atoms
calculus system of calculation using symbolic notations, essential to modern physics
capillary attraction tendency of liquid to rise in narrow tube or move through absorbent material, due to greater adhesion of liquid to solid than internal adhesion of the liquid itself
center of gravity fixed point in body through which force of gravitational attraction acts
centrifugal force force that tends to move particles rotating about an axis outward from center of rotation

centripetal force force directed toward the center of a circle that keeps particles in uniform circular motion, assumed to be equal and opposite to centrifugal force
compression reduction in volume of substance due to pressure
concurrent forces forces acting on same point
coordinates numbers that specify position in space and time
correspondence principle laws of quantum mechanics and any other new theory reduce to laws of Newtonian mechanics when Planck's constant is negligible, wavelengths are relatively small, and dimensions are relatively large
crest region of upward displacement in transverse wave
damping reduction in wave amplitude due to energy dissipation
de Broglie principle material particles have wavelike characteristics which can give rise to interference effects and diffraction
deceleration negative acceleration; rate at which motion slows
density mass per unit of volume; distribution per unit of space
distance spatial separation of two points measured by length of hypothetical straight line joining them
Doppler effect amount of decrease or increase in frequency of radiation as source and observer of waves move toward or away from each other
efficiency ratio of machine's useful power output to power input
elasticity ability of object to return to its original form after removal of deforming forces
endothermic (*adj*) referring to process that absorbs energy
energy capacity to do work
energy-matter relationship energy is equal to mass times the velocity of light squared, expressed as e&equal;mc^2
entropy measure of disorder of a system; internal energy of a system that cannot be converted to mechanical work
equilibrium condition in which net force on object is zero and there is no change in its motion
equivalence principle gravitational and inertial masses are equal
exothermic (*adj*) referring to process that releases energy
extrapolation extending of graph beyond measured points to infer values outside known range
field region of space containing lines of force with direction and strength; force that acts through space and time, as opposed to particle existing at one fixed point in space and time
fluid material that flows, such as liquid or gas
force action that results in acceleration or deformation of an object; measure of momentum gained per second by accelerating object
frame of reference coordinate system used to assign positions and times to events in describing motion
friction force resisting motion between two objects that are in contact
fundamental forces four basic forces acting in nature: strong force, electromagnetic force, weak force, gravitational force
fundamental units units of measurement defined in terms of a physical standard, not other units; seven basic units of measurement; International System of Units
gas phase of matter in which substance expands readily to fill any containing vessel, characterized by relatively low density
general theory of relativity Einstein's theory of gravitation, expressed in terms of curved spacetime, which stipulates that the laws of science are identical for all observers regardless of their motion
graph plot on rectangular coordinates showing relationship of two variables
gravitational field region in space in which particles experience gravitational force
gravitational force mutual attraction between particles due to their masses
heat energy resulting from disordered motion of molecules
Hooke's law stress applied to a solid body is directly proportional to strain produced
ideal gas theoretical gas composed of infinitely small molecules that exert no force on each other
implosion opposite of explosion, in which forces are directed inward
impulse product of a force and the time during which it acts
inclined plane flat surface at angle to some force or reference line
inertia tendency of a body to remain at rest or in motion unless acted upon by an outside force
International System of Units SI; system of measurement based on these fundamental units: mass (kilogram), length (meter), time (second), temperature (kelvin), amount of substance (mole), electric current (ampere), luminous intensity (candela)
joule SI unit of work or energy equal to one newton acting through one meter
kinetic energy energy of an object due to its motion
kinetic theory of matter concept that all matter is made of small particles in constant motion whose collisions are perfectly elastic
law verbal or mathematical statement of relationship between phenomena that is always the same under the same conditions
law of conservation of energy energy can be neither created nor destroyed and is constant in a closed system
law of conservation of mass-energy sum of matter and energy in the universe is constant
law of conservation of mechanical energy sum of potential and kinetic energies of ideal energy system is constant
law of conservation of momentum total vector momentum of an object is always constant in a system free of external forces
law of entropy all natural processes tend to increase the measure of disorder in the universe

law of universal gravitation gravitational force between two objects is constant G times the product of the masses of the two objects and the distance between them
length distance between two points
line of flux line whose tangent indicates direction of magnetic field
liquefaction condensation of a gas or solid to a liquid
liquid state of matter in which particles are in proximity greater than that of a gas but less than that of a solid, restricting their random motions to vibrations around moving points
longitudinal wave wave in which vibrations are parallel to the direction of its propagation
mass quantity of matter in an object, measured by its resistance to a change in its motion
mass density mass per unit volume of a substance
matter any substance with mass and inertia
mechanical advantage ratio of resistance force to effort force in a machine
mechanical wave displacement of portion of elastic medium that causes oscillation about an equilibrium position
mechanics effect of energy and other forces on matter
metric system internationally recognized system of weights and measures, based on decimal system
moment tendency to produce motion, esp. about an axis; product of physical quantity such as area or mass and its directed distance from axis
momentum product of the mass of a moving object and its velocity
newton SI unit of force required to accelerate a one kilogram mass at a rate of one meter per second per second
Newton's first law of motion object remains at rest or in motion with a constant velocity unless acted upon by an outside force
Newton's law of universal gravitation force of attraction between any two particles of matter is directly proportional to the product of their masses and inversely proportional to the square of the distance between their centers of mass
Newton's second law of motion the change in motion of an object acted upon by an outside force is directly proportional to the force and inversely proportional to the object's mass
Newton's third law of motion every action force has a reaction force equal in magnitude and opposite in direction
node point in medium or field that remains undisturbed when acted upon simultaneously by more than one disturbance
normal force force perpendicular to a surface
parallax shift in relative position of objects due to change in angle of perspective
parity symmetry property that expresses difference between wave function and its negative mirror image, expressed as +1 or -1
pascal SI unit of pressure, equal to one newton per square meter
Pascal's law external pressure applied to fluid in a closed vessel is transmitted uniformly throughout the fluid
phase number describing wave position within each oscillation or cycle at specific time
Planck's constant fundamental determinant of values in quantum mechanics, expressing ratio of energy of one quantum of radiation to its frequency, equal to 6.624×10^{-27} erg-seconds
plasma high temperature state of matter in which atoms, separated into electrons and positive ions or nuclei, produce conductive gas
potential energy energy based on position of object
power work done per unit of time
precision degree of exactitude and reproducibility in measured data; agreement between two or more measurements of same quantity made in same way
pressure force per unit area
principle of parity for every process in nature there exists an indistinguishable, mirror-image process
projectile motion motion of object moving in two dimensions under influence of gravity
propagation transmission of a wave through material or space
property any measurable aspect of matter
pulse single, nonrepeated disturbance in medium or field
quantum discrete, indivisible, and elemental unit of energy that emits or absorbs waves
quantum jump abrupt transition of system in quantum mechanics from one distinct energy level to another; quantum leap
quantum leap quantum jump
quantum number notation used to characterize discrete value and magnitude that a quantized physical variable may assume
ray line drawn to represent path traveled by a wave front; single line of light from luminous point
relative deviation average deviation of set of measurements, expressed as percentages
rest mass mass of an object not in motion
rotary motion motion of a body about an internal axis
scalar quantity, such as time or mass, that has magnitude only
scientific notation method in which numbers are expressed in the form of $M \times 10^n$, where M is a number between one and ten and n is an integral power of ten
second fundamental SI unit of time measurement, equivalent to 9,192,631,770 emission cycles of cesium-133
SI Système Internationale; internationally recognized metric system of measurement
simple machine lever, pulley, wheel and axle, inclined plane, wedge, or screw
solid state of matter in which particles are close together and in fixed positions relative to each other
special theory of relativity theory formulated by Albert Einstein that physical laws remain con-

stant in inertial reference systems for all freely moving observers, regardless of their speed
state physical condition of matter
strain amount of distortion produced in body under stress
stress distorting force per unit area
sublimation change from solid to gaseous state without intermediate liquid phase
surface tension strong attraction of surface particles for each other due to unbalanced forces; tendency of liquid surface to contract
surface wave surface disturbance with characteristics of both transverse and longitudinal waves
symmetry property that is unchanged by altered operations or reference frames; invariance
Système Internationale *French.* SI; International System of Units
tensile strength maximum stress any material subjected to a stretching load can withstand without tearing
torque force producing torsion or rotation in an object
trajectory curve described by an object moving through space as it is affected by gravitational attraction of other objects
uncertainty principle theory in quantum mechanics, formulated by Werner Heisenberg, that the more accurately the position of a particle is specified, the less accurately its momentum can be known, and that one can never be exactly sure of both
unified field theory principle that gravitational and electromagnetic forces can be expressed within single unified framework
uniform quantity quantity of constant value, such as acceleration or speed
universal gravitational constant constant of proportionality in Newton's law of universal gravitation
vacuum enclosed space out of which almost all matter has been removed
vapor gaseous phase of substance normally a solid or liquid
vaporization change of liquid or solid to gas or vapor by application of heat
vector quantity that has both magnitude and direction
velocity rate of change of position in particular direction
viscosity resistance that a gas or liquid system offers to flow when it is subjected to shear stress
viscous fluid slow-flowing fluid
volatile fluid fluid that is easily evaporated
wave traveling disturbance in a medium that does not create any permanent displacement in that medium
wave equation any of the fundamental equations of quantum mechanics whose solutions are possible wave functions of a particle
wavelength distance between corresponding phase points, such as two adjacent troughs or crests, on two successive waves
weight measure of gravitational force of Earth or celestial body on an object, proportional but not equal to mass
work product of displacement and force in direction of displacement
Young's modulus ratio of stress to strain in a solid

Electricity and Magnetism

AC alternating current
adhesion attraction between unlike particles
alternating current AC; current that periodically changes direction at certain levels, measured in volts
ampere unit that measures rate of flow of charged particles, equal to one coulomb of charge per second
angstrom unit of linear measure used to express wavelengths of optical spectra, equal to 10^{-10} meter
anode positive terminal of electrolytic cell
armature coil of wire that produces current in generator and rotation in electric motor
battery cell two dissimilar conductors that combine with an electrolyte to produce a potential difference
cathode negative electrode in electrolytic cell
conductor material that can transmit charged particles
coulomb SI unit of electric charge, equal to the charge found on 6.25×10^{18} electrons; amount of charge that crosses surface in one second when current of one ampere flows across it
Coulomb's law product of the charges on two objects divided by square of the distance between the charges times constant K equals the force between the charges
DC direct current
dielectric nonconducting medium; insulator
diode solid-state device or tube with anode and cathode which rectifies alternating current and allows current to pass freely in one direction only
direct current DC; current that flows in one direction only and has virtually invariable magnitude
dynamo generator
electric charge property of particle that attracts or repels other particles of opposite or like charge
electric circuit continuous path that can be followed by charged particles
electric current flow of charged particles
electric field space around charged object in which force acts on other charged objects
electric force force created between two objects due to their charges
electricity fundamental physical property caused by movement of electrons and other charged particles, manifested as attraction and repulsion
electrode grid
electrolyte conducting medium in which flow of current leads to movement of charged ions
electromagnet device in which magnetic field is generated by electric current
electromagnetic force fundamental force that exists between electrically charged particles
electromagnetic interaction force that keeps

electrons in orbit and forms bonds between atoms and molecules
electromagnetic wave wave composed of electric and magnetic fields that are perpendicular to each other and that move at speed of light in space
electromagnetism interrelationship of magnetic fields and electric currents
electromotive force EMF; potential difference generated by electromagnetic induction
electron subatomic particle of small mass and negative charge that orbits atomic nucleus
electronics branch of physics dealing with behavior of electrons
electrostatic charge charge at rest, as on an object
EMF electromotive force
farad unit of capacitance equal to one coulomb per volt
Faraday's law mass of an element deposited during electrolysis is proportional both to amount of charge passing through the electrolytic cell and to chemical equivalent of that element
frequency number of vibrations, oscillations, or cycles per unit of time
fresnel unit of frequency equal to 10^{12} cycles per second
galvanic cell battery cell
galvanometer instrument used to measure very small electric current
generator device that uses mechanical energy to produce electric energy; dynamo
grid element of electronic tube; electrode
grounding connection of charged object to Earth or other neutral site to remove object's charge
henry unit of inductance in closed circuit where electromotive force of one volt is produced by current variation of one ampere per second
hertz unit of frequency equal to one cycle per second
impedance total opposition to alternating current by circuit, expressed in ohms
inductance property of electric circuit by which varying current induces electromotive force in that circuit
insulator material that greatly restricts the transmission of charged particles; dielectric
interference combination of two waves or disturbances that arrive at same point at same time
ion charged atom or group of atoms resulting from loss or gain of one or more electrons
Joule's law amount of heat generated in watts when electricity flows through a substance, equal to the resistance of the substance in ohms times the square of the current in amperes
law of conservation of charge electric charge can be neither created nor destroyed
Lenz's law magnetic field generated by an induced current always opposes the field generating the current
line of force imaginary line in field of force positioned so that its tangent indicates direction of electric field
magnetic field region around a magnet in which magnetic forces can be detected
magnetic flux total of all magnetic flux lines through a region of a magnetic field
magnetic flux density number of magnet flux lines per unit area; magnetic induction
magnetic flux line line of force representing magnetic induction
magnetic force force between two objects due to magnetic flux of one or both objects
magnetic induction strength of a magnetic field; magnetic flux density
magnetic moment vector quantity that when multiplied by magnetic induction equals torque of given magnet or current acting on given object
magnetism fundamental phenomena in which magnets and electric currents exhibit force fields
microwave radio wave of a few centimeters' wavelength
ohm unit of electric resistance equal to one volt per ampere
Ohm's law current that flows in a circuit varies directly with the potential difference, or voltage, and inversely with the resistance
oscilloscope instrument with cathode-ray tube in which external voltages deflect electron beam simultaneously along vertical and horizontal axes to form image of wave
phase angular relationship between current and AC voltage
photovoltaic cell device for converting light into electric energy
radio waves electromagnetic radiations produced by rapid current shifts in conductor
reactance opposition of inductance and capacitance to alternating current, expressed in ohms
receiver device used to detect electromagnetic waves and render them perceptible to the senses
rectifier device that changes AC to DC
resistance opposition to flow of electric current; ratio of potential difference across conductor to magnitude of current in it
schematic diagram map of electric circuit using symbols
self-induction production of voltage in a circuit, induced when the current is varied rapidly in that same circuit
siemens SI unit of electrical conductance equal to reciprocal of the ohm
storage cell electrochemical cell that can be regenerated by external reverse currents
superconductivity state of some materials which exhibit zero resistance at very low temperatures; similar state exhibited by ceramic materials at higher temperatures
tesla unit of magnetic induction equal to one weber per square meter
thermionic emission electron emission from surface of heated body
thermoelectric effect production of current in closed circuit composed of two dissimilar metals, in which the junctions are maintained at different temperatures
transformer device used to transfer energy from one circuit to another circuit by mutual inductance across two coils

transistor semiconductor device used as substitute for vacuum tube to control current flow in electronics
triode vacuum tube consisting of grid between anode and cathode
vacuum tube electron tube that contains grids and from which air has been evacuated to highest possible degree
volt SI unit of potential difference between two points of conductor with constant one ampere current when one watt of power is dissipated between them
voltaic cell device that changes chemical into electric energy by immersion of two dissimilar metals in electrolyte
voltmeter device used to measure potential difference between two points in circuit
watt unit of power equal to one joule per second
weber SI unit of magnetic flux, equal to one volt x one second

Nuclear and Particle Physics

accelerator device that uses electromagnets to increase velocity and add energy to moving charged particles; atom smasher
alpha particle helium nucleus that consists of two protons and two neutrons after it is emitted from radioactive atom's nucleus
amu atomic mass unit
antimatter substance composed of antiparticles
antiparticle particle that has the same mass and spin as its subatomic counterpart but opposite charge and magnetic moment
antiquark antiparticle of quark
atom basic unit of matter, composed of protons, neutrons, and electrons
atomic mass unit amu; unit of mass for atomic and subatomic particles, equal to 1/12 the mass of most common isotope of carbon, used to express atomic weight; dalton
atomic number number of protons in nucleus of an atom
atomic theory explanation of various phenomena by theory of properties and interactions of atoms and subatomic particles
atomic weight mass of atom expressed in atomic mass units
atom smasher accelerator
atom-splitting fission
backscatter reflection and reversal of direction of radiation by traversed medium
baryon subatomic particle with large rest mass undergoing strong interactions
beta particle high-speed electron or positron emitted from radioactive nucleus
Bohr theory electrons revolve around nucleus in definite orbits and radiation is absorbed or emitted only when an electron moves from one orbit to another
boson subatomic particle, such as a photon or pi meson, that does not obey exclusion principle
breeder reactor nuclear reactor that produces more fissionable material than is consumed
bubble chamber container of superheated liquid in which paths of ionizing particles appear as strings of vapor bubbles
carbon 14 radioactive isotope of carbon used in radiocarbon dating
chain reaction self-sustaining series of nuclear reactions, in which products of reaction sustain process
charm quantum number assigned the value +1 for one kind of quark, -1 for its antiquark, and zero for all other quarks
cloud chamber closed vessel in which paths of charged subatomic particles appear as trails of liquid droplets
cold fusion hypothetical fusion of atomic nuclei at much lower temperature and pressure than now required
collider particle accelerator in which positively and negatively charged particles circulate in opposite directions and collide head-on
control rods devices in nuclear reactor used to regulate rate of nuclear reaction
core central part of reactor containing fissile fuel and rods
critical mass amount of particular fissionable material required to make fission reaction self-sustaining
curie unit of radioactivity equal to 3.7×10^{10} disintegrations per second of any radioactive nuclide
cyclotron device that accelerates positively charged atomic particles by means of D-shaped electrodes, used to initiate nuclear transformations
dalton atomic mass unit
decay spontaneous radioactive disintegration in which nucleus undergoes transformation into one or more different nuclei and emits radiation, loses electrons, or undergoes fission
deuterium isotope which replaces hydrogen in heavy water
deuteron charged particle equivalent to nucleus of hydrogen isotope deuterium, consisting of one proton and one neutron
dose quantity of radiation absorbed by matter
dynamics study of the motion of particles acted upon by forces
dyne unit of force that produces acceleration of one centimeter per second per second on mass of one gram
elementary particle indivisible particle within atomic nucleus
erg unit equal to work done by force of one dyne acting across one centimeter
exclusion principle no two identical particles in a system can carry the same quantum number
fast neutron neutron with kinetic energy greater than thermal energy
fermion subatomic particle, such as a lepton or baryon, that obeys exclusion principle
fission splitting of heavy nucleus into nuclei of intermediate mass; atom-splitting
fusion reaction in which nuclei of light atoms combine to form nuclei with larger mass numbers
gamma ray electromagnetic wave of extremely high frequency emitted by nucleus of radioactive

atom; high-energy photon
Geiger counter Geiger-Müller tube
Geiger-Müller tube device that detects radiation of subatomic particles by use of ionizing property of radiation; Geiger counter
gluon massless quantum of energy believed to carry force that binds quarks together within subatomic particles
graviton theoretical subatomic particle, without charge or mass, believed to carry gravitational force between bodies
hadron any heavy elementary particle that takes part in the strong interaction
half-life length of time during which one half of a sample of radioactive nuclides decays
heavy hydrogen hydrogen isotope with mass number greater than one; deuterium or tritium
heavy water water in which hydrogen atoms are replaced by heavier deuterium isotopes
isobar one of two atoms that have equal mass numbers but different atomic numbers
isomer any of two or more nuclei with same number of neutrons and protons but different energy states
isotone atom with same number of neutrons as another atom but different atomic number
isotope any of two or more forms of an atom of some element with nearly identical chemical properties, but containing different number of neutrons and same number of protons, therefore having different mass
kaon any of four mesons that are positive, negative, or neutral, with mass 970 times that of electron; k meson
k meson kaon
lambda particle neutral baryon with strangeness number -1 and isotopic spin zero
lepton subatomic particle with small rest mass
mass defect difference in mass between actual atomic nucleus and sum of particles from which nucleus is made
mass number sum of protons and neutrons in nucleus of atom, being integer nearest to its atomic weight
mass spectroscope device used to measure the mass of small, electrically charged particles
meltdown melting of nuclear reactor core due to inadequate cooling of fuel, possibly leading to escape of radiation
meson any hadron or subatomic particle with rest mass intermediate between lepton and baryon, consisting of a quark and antiquark
Mössbauer effect phenomenon in which gamma rays do not lose energy from the recoil of certain radioactive isotope nuclei which are bound in a crystal lattice, resulting in sharply defined wavelength
mu meson muon
muon high-speed lepton, either positive or negative, with mass 207 times that of electron, that decays into electron and two neutrinos with very brief life; mu meson
neutrino chargeless, nearly massless elementary particle affected only by weak force; type of lepton emitted along with beta particles
neutron uncharged subatomic particle of approximate mass comparable to proton, making up half of the particles in all atomic nuclei except those of hydrogen
nuclear force very short-range force that holds protons and neutrons together in atomic nucleus; strong force
nuclear reactor device used to obtain energy from controlled fission reaction; reactor
nucleon proton or neutron in atomic nucleus
nucleus positively charged, dense core of an atom, containing protons and neutrons
nuclide any atom of a particular element
omega particle particle that decays into cascade particle after colliding with pi meson
pair production creation of electron-positron pair from energy
particle piece of matter of negligible size that has both charge and mass
photon massless quantum of electromagnetic radiation or light energy
pi meson meson with mass 270 times that of electron and spin of zero
Planck's law light or other waves can be emitted or absorbed only in discrete quanta whose energy is proportional to their frequency
planetary model model of an atom in which the electrons orbit the nucleus as the planets orbit the sun
positron positively charged antiparticle of electron
proton positively charged subatomic particle of mass one atomic mass unit that is fundamental constituent of all atomic nuclei
quark any of basic, hypothetical particles that, along with antiquarks, constitute all elementary particles: designated up, down, strange, charm, beauty or bottom, and truth or top
rad measured dosage of absorbed ionizing radiation, equal to 100 ergs per gram
radiation energy emitted as electromagnetic waves, gamma or X-rays, or as energetic nuclear particles
radioactive materials substances that exhibit phenomenon of radioactivity
radioactivity spontaneous decay of unstable atomic nucleus with emission of particles and rays
radiocarbon dating determination of age of artifact based on known rate of decay of carbon-14 isotope
radioelement radioactive element occurring naturally or produced artificially
radioisotope radioactive isotope, usu. artificially produced
reactor nuclear reactor
rem measured dose of ionizing radiation whose biological effect is equal to that produced by one roentgen of X-rays
rod control rod in nuclear reactor
roentgen standard unit that measures ionizing radiation from X-rays or gamma rays
Rutherford atom atom in which negatively charged electrons revolve around a small, positively charged nucleus that constitutes nearly its entire atomic mass

scintillation flash of light or charged subatomic particle emitted when substance is struck by radiation
secondary emission emission of electrons due to bombardment of electrode by high-velocity electrons
sigma particle unstable hyperon having strangeness number -1
slow neutron neutron with less kinetic energy than thermal energy
solid state detector device used to detect passage of charged subatomic particles by their ionizing or distorting effects on a non- or semi-conducting solid
spark chamber device used to detect passage of charged subatomic particles by light flashes they trigger
spin intrinsic angular momentum of each kind of elementary particle that exists even when particle is at rest, as distinguished from orbital angular momentum
strangeness number quantum number characteristic of a quark or a strongly interacting particle that is conserved in strong interactions with other fundamental particles, assigned a value of +1, -1, or zero
strange quark quark having strangeness -1 and a charge one-third that of an elementary charge, being more massive than up and down quarks
string hypothetical basic unit of matter, neither wave nor particle but thin, curved string with length dimension only
string theory theory of fundamental physics in which basic entity in four dimensions of space-time is one-dimensional object rather than zero-dimensional point of conventional elementary particle physics
strong force force that holds quarks together with protons and neutrons within atomic nucleus, independent of charge; strongest of four fundamental forces, but with shortest range
strontium 90 deadly radioactive isotope of strontium present in fallout from nuclear explosions and other fission-produced waste
subatomic particle one of several constituent parts of atoms: protons, neutrons, electrons, their component particles, and quarks
supercollider massive, extremely high-speed particle accelerator
superstring theory fundamental theory of subatomic particles in which all matter and energy are derived from vibration modes of one-dimensional strings that control all forces and matter; combination of string theory and supersymmetry
thermonuclear reaction nuclear fusion reaction
tracer radioactive isotope used to follow chemical process or determine physical properties
transuranic element any element that has an atomic number greater than 92
tritium radioactive isotope of hydrogen with atomic weight three, used in thermonuclear devices and as tracer
truth elusive sixth quark, also designated top, believed to have a mass 90 to 250 times that of proton
wave-particle duality quantum mechanics theory that waves and particles are indistinguishable and sometimes behave alike
weak force force involved in decay of atomic nuclei and nuclear particles; second weakest of four fundamental forces, with very short range and no effect on force-carrying particles
weakly interactive massive particle WIMP; small gravitational mass particle, believed to form cold, dark matter comprising ninety percent of universe
WIMP weakly interactive massive particle

Cosmology

antigravity hypothetical force by which one body would repel another; opposite of gravity, never detected experimentally
big bang model theory that universe originated in explosion of hot, dense core that rapidly expanded to cooler, more diffuse states
big crunch singularity at end of universe that reverses big bang effect
black dwarf cold remnant of white dwarf star after thermal energy is exhausted
black hole highly concentrated mass that has collapsed to such a degree that the escape velocity from its surface is greater than the speed of light, so that light and all other energy and matter is trapped in an intense gravitational field
blue shift shift of spectral lines toward shorter wavelengths, observed in celestial objects that are approaching observer
chaos phenomenon of unpredictability and randomness on all scales of physical structures, opp. of cosmos
cold dark matter fundamental particles with no force other than gravity that comprise ninety percent of universe
cosmic background radiation uniform radioactive hiss that fills space, measured at 3 degrees Kelvin
cosmogony study of possible origin and evolution of universe
cosmology study of structure of universe as a whole
cosmos orderly and harmonious universe that follows ascertainable laws, opp. of chaos
event specific point in space-time
expanding universe model of universe based on big bang
grand unification theory theory which unifies electromagnetic, strong, and weak forces
Hubble constant constant that represents rate of expansion of universe
microwave background radiation redshifted radiation from glow of early universe that does not appear as light but as microwaves of extremely high frequency
neutron star cold or collapsed star in which gravitational force has caused combination of electrons and protons to form neutrons
pulsar rotating neutron star whose radio emissions

reach Earth in pulses, usu. at regular intervals

quasar quasi-stellar radio source; powerful source of light and radio energy at limits of known universe, probably a highly luminous galaxy that has violently exploded

redshift shift, due to Doppler effect, in spectral lines of object toward red end of spectrum as it recedes from observer, with degree of shift proportional to object's speed

space-time continuum four-dimensional continuum with coordinates being three spatial dimensions and time; way of representing universe suggested by theory of relativity

space-time curvature conceptual form in which four-dimensional space-time is represented as a curve

spatial dimension any of three dimensions of space-time, other than time

steady state model theory of expanding universe stipulating continuous creation of matter, and stating that universe maintains uniform large-scale structure and constant average density at all times

supernova explosion of massive star near end of its life, possibly due to gravitational collapse, causing greatly increased luminosity and loss of most of star's mass, sometimes leaving behind dense core; white dwarf star in close binary system producing explosions from mass taken from its companion star

unified field theory principle that all forces in universe are part of single concept

universe sum total of potentially knowable objects, matter, and energy, believed to be infinite in space and time

white dwarf very small, faint, cold star that has undergone gravitational collapse

white hole hypothetical time-reversed black hole

Heat

absolute zero temperature at which gas has zero volume and molecular kinetic energy is at minimum, equal to -459.7 degrees F, -273.2 degrees C, or zero degrees Kelvin

adiabatic process thermal process in which no heat is added to or removed from system

advection horizontal flow of atmospheric properties

Boyle's law volume of a fixed mass of gas kept at constant temperature varies inversely with pressure

British thermal unit BTU; quantity of heat equal to 252 calories

Brownian motion (or movement) random motion of colloidal particles due to bombardment of the particles by molecules of the surrounding medium.

BTU British thermal unit

calorie quantity of heat equal to 4.187 joules

Celsius temperature scale with zero degrees equal to freezing point of water and 100 degrees equal to boiling point of water at standard atmospheric pressure; Centigrade

Centigrade Celsius

coefficient of expansion change in area, volume, or length per unit area, volume, or length of a solid per degree change in its temperature

condensation change of state from gas to liquid

convection transfer of heat in a fluid, either by absorption or by rejection once the fluid has moved

convection current current caused by motion of a fluid, caused by differences in density due to thermal expansion

critical constant density, pressure, or temperature associated with critical point of pure element or compound

critical point point at which pure element or compound in one phase, as liquid, has same density, pressure, and temperature as in another phase, as gaseous

cryogenics production and effects of very low temperatures

dew point temperature to which air must be cooled at given pressure to reach saturation

Edison effect emission of electrons from metal when heated in a vacuum

evaporation change of state from liquid to gas or vapor

Fahrenheit temperature scale with 32 degrees equal to freezing point of water and 212 degrees equal to boiling point of water at standard atmospheric pressure

first law of thermodynamics when heat is converted to another form of energy, or vice versa, there is no loss of energy

heat quantity of thermal energy being added to an object, or moved from one object to another, because of a temperature difference

heat capacity quantity of heat required to increase temperature of a body by one degree

heat of fusion energy required per unit mass to change substance from solid to liquid at its melting point

heat of vaporization energy required per unit mass to change substance from liquid to gas at its boiling point

heat sink entity that absorbs heat without significant temperature increase

kelvin SI unit of heat measurement, equal to 1/273 of Kelvin temperature scale

Kelvin temperature scale with zero degrees equaling absolute zero, and 273.16 degrees equaling freezing point of water

kinetic theory of heat theory that particles in a gas move freely and rapidly in straight lines and often collide, causing changes in their velocity and direction

law of heat exchange in any heat transfer system, hot materials lose amount of heat equal to that gained by cold materials

mechanical equivalent of heat conversion factor relating heat units to work units, equal to 4.19 joules per calorie

melting point temperature at which solid changes to liquid

relative humidity ratio of water vapor pressure

in atmosphere to equilibrium vapor pressure at given temperature
second law of thermodynamics heat flows from area of high temperature to area of lower temperature unless work is done to reverse this process
specific heat energy required to change temperature of one kilogram of a substance one degree Kelvin
standard pressure pressure exerted by 760 mm of mercury at zero degrees Celsius
supercooling cooling of substance below normal phase-change point without inducing change of phase
temperature physical quantity measured by the average kinetic energy of particles in matter
thermal energy sum of potential energy and kinetic energy in random motion of particles of a material
thermal expansion moving apart of particles as their temperature rises
thermal unit any of various standard measures of heat
thermometer device used to measure temperature
third law of thermodynamics temperature of a system cannot be reduced to absolute zero in a finite number of operations

Optics

absorption spectrum continuous spectrum of energy absorbed by gaseous atoms of element as white light passes through it
actinic rays light rays, esp. at ultraviolet end of spectrum, that produce chemical changes
actinology study of the chemical effects of light rays
albedo reflecting power of a body, expressed as ratio of reflected light to total light falling on surface
angle of incidence angle between light ray and line perpendicular to surface the ray is meeting
angle of reflection angle between reflected light ray and line perpendicular to the point of incidence
angle of refraction angle between refracted ray and line perpendicular to surface the ray is leaving
beam parallel rays of light considered together
black light ultraviolet or infrared radiation used for fluorescent effects in the dark
candela SI unit of luminous intensity, equal to intensity of a source that emits monochromatic radiation of frequency 540 x 10^{12} hertz
candle former standard unit of luminous intensity, equal to five square millimeters of platinum at 1773.5 degrees C
candlepower measure of luminous intensity
chromatics study of hue and saturation of colors
color property of an object with respect to light reflected by it in particular wavelengths forming a spectrum from red to violet
complementary colors primary and secondary colors that combine to produce white light
concave lens lens that diverges parallel light rays
concave mirror mirror that converges parallel light rays on its surface
continuous spectrum spectrum without dark lines or bands or with uninterrupted changes between colors
converging lens lens, thick in the middle and thin at the edge, that bends parallel rays toward common point
converging mirror concave mirror that causes parallel rays to converge
convex lens lens that converges parallel rays
convex mirror mirror that diverges parallel light rays on its surface
critical angle minimum angle of incidence that produces total internal reflection
diffraction bending of light waves around an object in their path into region behind obstacle
dispersion refraction of polychromatic light into spectrum of its component wavelengths
diverging lens lens, thin in the middle and thick at the edge, that causes incident parallel rays to diverge as though from a common point
diverging mirror convex mirror that causes parallel light rays to diverge
elementary colors seven color regions in spectrum observed by dispersion of sunlight: red, orange, yellow, green, blue, indigo, and violet
emission spectrum spectrum produced by dispersion of light from excited atoms of an element
fiber optics branch of optics dealing with transmission of data or communications in form of light pulses through transparent fibers
first law of photoelectric emission rate of photoelectron emission is proportional to intensity of incident light
fluorescence emission of light by atoms excited during absorption of radiation from outside source
focal length distance from focal point to vertex or optical center of mirror or lens
focal point point of convergence, real or apparent, of rays reflected by mirror or refracted by lens
focus point at which light rays meet, or from which light rays appear to diverge or converge
hertz SI unit of frequency, equal to one cycle per second
illumination rate at which light energy falls on a given area of a surface
image optical counterpart of object formed by lenses or mirrors
incandescence emission of light due to thermal excitation
incident light light rays that fall upon or strike something
infrared light electromagnetic waves longer than visible light and shorter than microwaves
laser light amplification by stimulated emission of radiation; device used to produce coherent light of great intensity
law of reflection angle of incidence is equal to angle of reflection when a light ray is reflected from a smooth surface
light electromagnetic radiation, ranging in wave-

length from 4×10^{-7} to 7×10^{-7} meter, that causes sensation of vision
lumen unit of luminous flux on surface, all points of which are at unit distance from a point source of one candle
luminescence emission of light caused by absorption of radiant or corpuscular energy, not by incandescence
luminous body object visible due to emission of light from oscillating particles
magnification ratio of image distance or size to object distance or size
monochromatic light light of only one wavelength and color
objective lens light-gathering and image-forming lens of microscope or telescope
opaque material material that does not transmit light
optical density property that determines the speed of light, and thus index of refraction, through a transparent medium
optical fiber very thin, flexible, transparent glass or plastic fiber that makes use of total internal reflection to transmit information in form of light pulses
optics study of propagation, control, transmission, reception, effects, and phenomena of light waves
penumbra partially illuminated portion of a shadow
phosphorescence emission of light from atoms excited by outside source that persists for a time after outside source is removed
photic (*adj*) of or relating to light
photoelectric effect ejection of electrons from surface, usu. of metal, exposed to light or electromagnetic radiation
photoelectron electron ejected by photoelectric effect
photometry quantitative measurement of visible radiation emitted from light sources
photon quantum of electromagnetic waves or light energy
photovoltaic cell device used to convert light into electric energy
polarized light light in which vibrations of all waves are in the same or parallel planes in optical region
polychromatic light light composed of several wavelengths and colors
primary color red, yellow, or blue light, from which all other colors may be described or evolved by mixture
primary pigment yellow, cyan, or magenta pigment; complement of primary colors
principal axis radius connecting center of curvature of curved mirror with its geometric vertex, or center of curvature of lens with its optical center
principal focus point at which rays parallel to principal axis either converge or diverge after reflection or refraction
quantum theory of light light is emitted and absorbed in small discrete packets called quanta; the energy in each quantum can be expressed as E &equal; hf, where E is energy, h is Planck's constant, and f is frequency
ray single line of light that radiates from a luminous point
reflection return of light wave from boundary of a medium
refraction bending of wave front as it passes obliquely from one medium to another
saturation degree of purity of a color, measured by absence of dilution by white
secondary color color, such as orange, green, or violet, produced by mixing two primary colors
secondary pigment red, green, or blue pigment; complement of secondary color
second law of photoelectric emission kinetic energy of photoelectrons is independent of intensity of incident light
solar ray ray of sunlight
solar spectrum band of colors produced by dispersal of sunlight through a prism
spectroscope optical instrument used to study spectra
spectrum array of various wavelengths that compose light
speed of light 3.00×10^8 meters per second in a vacuum, or approximately 186,000 miles per second
translucent material material that transmits light but distorts it during passage
transparent material material that transmits light undistorted
ultraviolet light electromagnetic radiations of shorter wavelength than visible light but longer than X-rays
umbra portion of a shadow from which all light rays are excluded
vertex center of curved mirror
white light light, such as sunlight, that is mixture of wavelengths from red to violet
X-ray invisible electromagnetic radiation that has a very short wavelength and great penetrating power

Acoustics

acoustics science of the production, effects, and transmission of sound
anechoic (*adj*) completely absorbing sound waves, therefore free from echoes
audio frequency band of audible sound frequencies between 15 hertz and 20,000 hertz
audiometer device used to measure sharpness and range of hearing
aural (*adj*) received through or relating to the sense of hearing
decibel unit of sound intensity level, one decibel being the smallest change of sound intensity perceptible to human ear
dissonance sound waves perceived as inharmonious noise
echo rebound of sound wave from impenetrable surface that results in repetition of sound
fundamental lowest frequency of sound produced by an instrument or other tone source
harmonics fundamental tone and tones whose

frequencies are whole number multiples of the fundamental
octave interval between given tone and one with double or half its frequency
overtones sound waves of higher frequency than the fundamental, expressed in integral multiples only
pitch perceived tonal characteristic that is equivalent to frequency
resonance production of abnormally large vibration in response to external stimulus, occurring when stimulus frequency is at natural vibration frequency of system
sonic (*adj*) having to do with sound waves; equal to or being speed of sound in air
sonic boom shock wave associated with object moving through fluid or gas at speed greater than that of sound
sound wave longitudinal disturbance in matter that is audible to human ear; similar disturbance that exists above and below audible range
speed of sound approximately 741 miles per hour in air at sea level
subsonic (*adj*) less than speed of sound
supersonic (*adj*) greater than speed of sound
threshold frequency lowest sound intensity audible to average human ear
timbre quality of sound
ultrasound sound with frequency over 20,000 hertz, beyond upper limit of human hearing
white noise blend of all audible frequencies distributed equally over range of frequency band

ASTRONOMY AND SPACE SCIENCE

Celestial Bodies

Alpha Centauri trinary star containing Proxima Centauri
Andromeda Galaxy large, spiral galaxy relatively close to Milky Way, with similar size and shape
asteroid one of thousands of minor planets that revolve around sun, usu. between orbital paths of Mars and Jupiter; minor planet; planetoid
asteroid belt any group of asteroids that revolve around sun in orbital path between Mars and Jupiter
barred spiral spiral galaxy with barlike structure across its center
binary star two stars in orbit around one another; double star
black dwarf cold remains of white dwarf after thermal energy is exhausted
brown dwarf lump of celestial matter larger than a planet but not massive enough to be a star or produce thermonuclear reactions at its core
Canopus second brightest star in heavens, 650 light years distant
celestial body celestial object
celestial object any solid or gaseous entity moving through space; celestial body; heavenly body
Ceres first and largest minor planet to be discovered
comet diffuse cluster of gas, dust, and ice moving about sun in eccentric orbit, with dust tail trailing in its path and ion tail pointing away from sun
Crab Nebula supernova remnant in constellation Taurus
cynosure Polaris; northern constellation Ursa Minor
dark nebula nebula that obscures background starlight and does not reflect starlight toward Earth
diffuse nebula luminous formation of irregular cloud of interstellar matter within Milky Way
Dog Star Sirius
double star binary star
dwarf star with small size or mass and low luminosity
Earth fifth largest planet of solar system and third from sun: orbits sun in 365 days and rotates on its axis in twenty-four hours
elliptical galaxy galaxy having round or lenticular shape, without spiral arms as internal structure
fireball brilliant meteor that often trails bright sparks
galaxy vast system of about 100 billion stars, such as Milky Way, held together by gravity in spiral, elliptical, or irregular region about 100,000 light years across
gas giant large planet of low density, esp. one of major planets of our solar system; Jupiter, Saturn, Uranus, or Neptune
globular cluster large collection of closely grouped old and dead stars containing little or no gas between them
Great Wall huge chain of galaxies and superclusters stretching 500 million light years across universe
Halley's Comet famous comet visible from Earth every 76 years
heavenly body celestial object
Horsehead Nebula dark nebula in constellation Orion, silhouetted against bright nebula in shape of horse's head
irregular galaxy galaxy having neither spiral nor elliptical shape
Jupiter largest planet of solar system and fifth from sun, famous for its Great Red Spot: orbits sun in 11.9 years and rotates on its axis in 9 hours and 50 minutes
Large Magellanic Cloud larger of two irregular galaxies interacting with Milky Way as a satellite
lenticular galaxy elliptical galaxy in elongated form with nearly pointed ends
Local Group Milky Way, Magellanic clouds, Andromeda Galaxy, and other nearby galaxies

forming a local cluster in the universe two million light years across
Magellanic clouds two irregular galaxies near Milky Way, visible only from Earth's Southern Hemisphere
magnetic star star that emits strong magnetic field, detected by its effect on spectrum
major planets four largest planets of solar system: Jupiter, Saturn, Uranus, and Neptune; gas giants
Mars seventh largest planet of solar system and fourth from sun: orbits sun in 687 days and rotates on its axis in 24 hours and 24 minutes
Mercury eighth largest planet of solar system and nearest to sun: orbits sun in 88 days and rotates on its axis in 59 days
metagalaxy entire system of galaxies including the Milky Way
meteor very small particle of rock or metal orbiting sun, usu. in a swarm, that enters Earth's atmosphere and burns up; shooting star
meteorite portion of meteor that enters Earth's atmosphere and reaches ground without disintegrating
meteoroid small, solid chunk of iron, stone, or waxy material that flares to produce bright meteor
Milky Way twelve-billion-year-old spiral galaxy of which our sun is one of 150 billion stars
minor planet large asteroid in orbit around sun that is not large enough to be considered a planet
moon natural satellite of a planet, esp. the celestial body that revolves around Earth from west to east every 29 1/2 days
nebula diffuse cloud of interstellar matter
Neptune fourth largest planet in solar system, usu. eighth from sun, sometimes farther from sun than Pluto: orbits sun in 165 years and rotates on its axis in 15 hours and 48 minutes
neutron star collapsed star of extremely high density, such as a pulsar, that is composed primarily of neutrons
North Star Polaris
nova star that increases in brilliance by several magnitudes in a few hours due to explosive ejection of surface material
open cluster large collection of young, massive stars, loosely grouped with abundant gas between them
Orion Nebula bright, diffuse nebula formed around stars comprising sword region of Orion constellation
planet one of nine massive bodies in our solar system that revolve around sun and reflect its light; similar bodies that revolve around other stars
planetary nebula star in last stage of life, surrounded by expelled outer layers of gas, originally thought to be planets
planetoid asteroid; minor planet
Pluto smallest planet of solar system, usu. farthest from sun, with highly eccentric orbit that sometimes brings it closer to sun than Neptune: orbits sun in 248 years and rotates on its axis in 6 days and 7 hours
Polaris nearly stationary, bright, supergiant binary star located near north celestial pole; North Star; polestar
polestar conspicuous star that lies nearest to north celestial pole; Polaris
primary star or planet around which another celestial body revolves
Proxima Centauri closest star to sun
pulsar rotating, collapsed neutron star of high density, composed primarily of neutrons, whose radio emissions or light reach Earth in pulses, usu. at regular intervals
quasar quasi-stellar radio source; highly luminous galaxy at limits of known universe, probably undergoing violent explosion, being a powerful source of light and energy
radio galaxy galaxy that emits stronger-than-normal radio waves
radio source cosmic object or phenomenon that emits radio waves; radio star
radio star radio source
red dwarf small star of low spectrum-luminosity and surface temperature
red giant large star of low surface temperature in late stage of stellar evolution, with absolute magnitude near zero
red supergiant exceptionally luminous red giant having diameter 100 times that of sun
satellite one of many known moons of planets in solar system; artificial satellite set in orbit around planet
Saturn second largest planet of solar system and sixth from sun, famous for its rings: orbits sun in 29.5 years and rotates on its axis in 10 hours and 39 minutes
shooting star meteor
Sirius brightest star in heavens, only nine light years distant in constellation Canis Major; Dog Star
Small Magellanic Cloud smaller of two irregular galaxies interacting with Milky Way as a satellite
solar system group of planets that orbit around common star or stars, esp. portion of Milky Way subject to gravity of our sun, including nine planets
spiral galaxy galaxy with central nucleus and concentrations of matter that extend in curved arms to create its spiral or pinwheel appearance
star massive, very hot, luminous ball of highly ionized gases that derives its energy from continuous nuclear reactions
starburst galaxy galaxy undergoing rapid wave of stellar birth
sun any star that is center of a planetary system, esp. central star of Earth's solar system
supercluster clusters of galaxies and local groups up to fifty million light years across
supergiant star exceptionally luminous star of first magnitude, having diameter more than 100 times that of sun
supernova explosion of massive star near the end of its life, possibly due to gravitational collapse, causing greatly increased luminosity and loss of most of star's mass, sometimes leaving behind dense core; white dwarf star in close binary sys-

tem that produces explosions from mass taken from its companion star
supernova remnant portion of supernova blown outward to form nebula
terrestrial planets four inner planets of solar system: Mercury, Venus, Earth, and Mars
trinary star three stars bound to each other by gravitation
Uranus third largest planet of solar system and seventh from sun: orbits sun in 84 years and rotates on its axis in 23 hours
variable star star that varies in intrinsic brightness
Venus sixth largest and brightest planet of solar system and second from sun: orbits sun in 225 days and rotates on its axis in 244 days
Vesta one of first two minor planets discovered in solar system
Virgo cluster large collection of galaxies located visually in constellation Virgo
visual binary double star in which separate components may be distinguished through powerful telescope
white dwarf small, faint, cold star that has undergone gravitational collapse

Celestial Phenomena and Points

aberration apparent displacement of star due to Earth's orbit and bending of star's light rays
absorption lines dark gaps in spectrum of sun or star due to layers of cooler gases in its atmosphere
accretion disk rapidly spinning disk of gas, usu. found around neutron star or black hole
altitude angular distance of celestial object located vertically above plane of celestial equator
annular eclipse solar eclipse in which the moon's angular diameter is smaller than the sun's
apex point on celestial sphere toward which sun appears to move, relative to nearby stars
aphelion point in elliptical orbit of planet or comet that is farthest from sun
apocenter point on elliptical orbit that is farthest from body that is focus of orbit
apogee point in elliptical orbit of moon or artificial satellite that is farthest from Earth
arroyo channel formed by fluid erosion on Earth and sun
asterism pattern formed by stars on celestial sphere, esp. a constellation
atmosphere gaseous envelope surrounding star, planet, or other celestial body
atmospheric layers divisions of atmosphere that extend outward from surface of body: troposphere, stratosphere, mesosphere, thermosphere, and exosphere
aureole luminous area that surrounds sun as seen through thin cloud; corona
aurora display of changing colored light high in atmosphere at arctic and antarctic latitudes, caused by charged particles in Earth's magnetic field interacting with upper atmospheric gases
axis imaginary line through center of body about which it rotates
azimuth angle between celestial object and southern point of horizon, measured clockwise from horizon
Big Dipper asterism within constellation Ursa Major formed by seven stars in shape of dipper
biosphere ecosphere
black hole highly concentrated mass that has collapsed to such a degree that the escape velocity from its surface is greater than the speed of light, trapping light and all other energy and matter in an intense gravitational field
blue moon occurrence of two full moons within one month
blue shift shift of spectral lines toward shorter wavelengths at blue end of spectrum, observed in celestial objects approaching Earth
carbonaceous chondrites uncommon meteorite class believed to be most primitive form of matter in solar system
chondrite member of most abundant class of stony meteorites
chromosphere layer in sun's atmosphere between corona and photosphere
comet tail tail of dust that trails away from path of comet nucleus and points away from sun, appearing when comet is near sun
constellation pattern formed by stars on celestial sphere, used to describe positions of celestial objects; area of celestial sphere enclosing such stars
corona layer of ionized gases that surround and extend a great distance from sun, visible as halo in solar eclipse; aureole
cosmic noise radio frequency radiations that emanate from Milky Way; galactic noise
cosmic rays highly charged ions that move at enormous speed and strike Earth continuously from all sides
crater circular rocky formation located on surface of moon and some other celestial bodies, caused by meteoritic impact
crescent moon phase of moon halfway between quarter and new moon
declination angular distance of celestial object north or south of celestial equator
dust cloud of powdery matter floating in space
eclipse celestial event in which light from one celestial object is obscured by another object interposed between it and observer, esp. sun's light by moon on Earth or by Earth on moon
ecosphere zone of Earth or other celestial body in which living organisms could be supported
electromagnetic spectrum range of radiation wavelengths: gamma rays, X-rays, ultraviolet rays, visible light, infrared rays, microwaves, and radio waves
emission lines bright lines in spectrum of light emitted by glowing gas
equinox one of two points in which great circle of ecliptic intersects great circle of celestial equator on celestial sphere: vernal on March 21, autumnal on September 22
exosphere outermost portion of planet's atmosphere

extragalactic (*adj*) outside the Milky Way system
first point of Aries position of celestial bodies on first day of zodiacal calendar
flocculus one of the bright or dark patches on sun's surface, visible by spectroheliograph
force field space through which electric, gravitational, or magnetic force acts
full moon phase of moon when it is on side of Earth away from sun, so that its entire face reflects sunlight to Earth
galactic noise cosmic noise
geomagnetic axis single diameter of Earth that is axis of Earth's magnetic field in conventionalized symmetrical approximation
gibbous moon phase of moon halfway between quarter and full moon
gravitation force by which celestial objects attract and are attracted by other celestial objects
halo circle of definite size around sun or moon caused by ice particles in atmosphere
horizon great circle on celestial sphere perpendicular to hypothetical line that connects observer's zenith to nadir; distant line where sky seems to meet Earth
intergalactic (*adj*) existing or occurring between or among galaxies
interplanetary (*adj*) being or occurring within solar system but outside atmosphere of any planet or sun
interstellar cloud dense region of gas and dust from which stars are formed that lies between stars in galaxy
ionosphere very high layer in atmosphere of planets in which gases are largely ionized
lines of force field lines in force field: magnetic, electric, or gravitational
Little Dipper constellation Ursa Minor that contains Polaris and resembles a dipper
luminosity intrinsic brightness of any star when compared with sun
lunar (*adj*) of or relating to the moon
lunar eclipse passage of Earth between sun and moon that causes moon to be in Earth's shadow
lunar occultation disappearance of celestial body behind moon
magnetic field field arising from electric charge in motion that produces a force on another electric charge
magnetosphere region surrounding planet in which planet's magnetic field is stronger than interplanetary field
mare large, flat plain on moon, formerly called sea
meridian great circle on celestial sphere that passes through zenith, nadir, north, and south points on horizon
Messier object one of 109 objects numbered from M1 as cataloged by French astronomer Charles Messier to distinguish clusters, nebulae, and galaxies from comets
meteor shower apparent divergence from single point by luminous paths of members as meteor swarm encounters Earth's atmosphere
microwave background radiation redshifted radiation from glow of early universe that appears not as light but as microwaves
nadir point on celestial sphere opposite zenith and directly below observer
new moon first phase of moon when it is between Earth and sun with side toward Earth in shadow
Northern Lights aurora display in Northern Hemisphere
nutation slight, periodic oscillation in precession of Earth's axis in space
occultation passage of one celestial object in front of another, as in an eclipse
orbit elliptical path of one celestial sphere or satellite around another larger body, in accordance with Newton's laws of gravitation and motion
outer space space outside Earth's solar system
parhelic circle luminous circle or halo parallel to horizon at altitude of sun
penumbra partly lighted area that surrounds complete shadow of celestial body during eclipse
perigee point closest to Earth in orbit of moon or other object around Earth
perihelion point closest to sun in orbit of member of solar system
phase particular appearance of celestial body due to recurrent cycle in its illumination; recurrent stage in illumination and apparent shape of moon: new, quarter, full, and gibbous
photosphere visible surface of sun
plasma low-density, ionized gas with complex magnetic field that moves through space
polar cap large region of ice covering north or south polar region of planet, esp. Earth and Mars
precession slow shifting of celestial equator due to motion of Earth's axis from gravitational pull of sun and moon on Earth's equatorial bulge
proper motion apparent angular motion of star across observer's line of sight
quarter moon phase of moon halfway between new and full
radio wave electromagnetic wave that exists at radio frequency
ray beam of light from bright source; stream of particles emitted by radioactive substance
redshift shift, due to Doppler effect, in spectral lines of object toward longer wavelengths at red end of spectrum as it recedes from Earth, with amount of shift proportional to object's speed
regolith blanket of rubble on moon's surface from lunar impacts
rift valley elongated depression of planet's crust between two faults
ring system flat, thin, reflective band of dust and ice crystals that orbit and encircle a planet, esp. Jupiter, Saturn, Uranus, and Neptune
solar (*adj*) of or relating to the sun
solar corona outer atmosphere of sun
solar eclipse interposition of moon between Earth and sun
solar flare sudden, brief increase in intensity of sun's light, usu. near sunspots, accompanied by increase in radiations
solar nebula large cloud of hot gas and dust from

which sun and planets formed
solar wind stream of radiation and ionized gas that spirals outward from sun at high speed
solstice date on which sun reaches position farthest north or south of celestial equator; northern on June 21, southern on December 21
space three-dimensional continuous expanse in all directions that contains all matter; distance between and area not filled by celestial bodies
spectrum light emitted by star or other source, dispersed according to wavelength
spicule gas jet located in sun's chromosphere
spiral arm curved concentration of matter that extends from nucleus of spiral galaxy
star cloud large luminous patch of Milky Way that can be resolved with optical aid into dense concentration of stars
sunspot temporarily cooler region that appears as dark spot on sun's surface, accompanied by geomagnetic disturbances
tidal friction frictional effect of tides that very slowly retards rotational velocity of Earth
tides rising and falling of surface of bodies of water on Earth due to attraction of moon and sun as Earth rotates
transit passage of smaller body in front of larger one as seen from Earth
umbra dark central cone of shadow that projects from celestial body on side opposite sun; shadow of body in eclipse
Van Allen radiation belts doughnut-shaped regions around Earth in which high-speed, charged particles oscillate in Earth's magnetic field
visible spectrum portion of electromagnetic spectrum detectable by human eye
waning moon moon proceeding from full to new
waxing moon moon proceeding from new to full
zenith point on celestial sphere lying vertically above observer
zodiacal light faint glow above horizon, esp. at tropical latitudes, on clear moonless night after sunset in west and before sunrise in east
zone of avoidance region of sky where no galaxies can be seen due to light-absorbing clouds of dust

Branches, Laws, Theories, and Techniques

absolute magnitude astronomical measure of brightness of a star as it would appear at distance of 10 parsecs
absolute zero zero kelvins; temperature at which all molecular motion ceases
apparent magnitude brightness of star as seen from Earth
astrobiology study of living organisms beyond the atmosphere of Earth
astrolabe medieval instrument consisting of a graduated, vertical circle with movable arm, formerly used to find altitude of star
astrology study attempting to interpret the influence of celestial bodies on human events and individual personality, esp. at moment of birth
astrometeorology study of the theoretical effects of astronomical bodies and forces on Earth's atmosphere
astrometry branch of astronomy that deals with measurement of the positions of celestial objects
astronomer person trained in and expert at the practice of astronomy
astronomical unit AU; measurement based on mean distance of Earth from sun, approximately 93 million miles (149.6 million km)
astronomy observation and theoretical study of celestial bodies, space, and the universe
astrophotography photography of celestial objects
astrophysics branch of astronomy dealing with physical properties of celestial objects, space, and the universe
AU astronomical unit
big bang model theory that universe originated in explosion of hot, dense core that rapidly expanded to cooler, less dense states; expanding universe
big crunch singularity at end of universe in which universe contracts, opposite to big bang
Bode's law mathematical relationship which agrees with distances of planets from sun in astronomical units
celestial mechanics branch of astronomy concerned with motions and gravitational interactions of celestial objects
Chandrasekhar limit maximum possible mass of stable cold star, beyond which it will become a supernova or collapse to become a black hole
chaos disorderly and unpredictable universe
Copernican system first heliocentric theory of solar system, published by Nicolaus Copernicus in 1543
cosmogony study of possible origin and evolution of universe
cosmology study of structure of universe as a whole
cosmos orderly and harmonious universe
dispersion separation between different wavelengths in spectrum
Doppler shift change in wave frequency due to approach or recession of source relative to observer
eccentricity scale that expresses degree of flattening of elliptical orbit, with zero being circular and one being perfectly elliptical
ephemeris table giving computed position of celestial body for each day in given period
epicycle planetary motion described in Ptolemaic system as circle whose center moves along circumference of another larger circle
epoch time at which positions of celestial bodies are observed
expanding universe big bang model
Galilean telescope first refracting telescope with positive objective lens and negative eye lens, developed by Galileo Galilei in 17th c.
geocentric *(adj)* viewing universe as though Earth were its center
gnomon vertical plate of sundial, set parallel to Earth's axis; shaft perpendicular to horizon, used

to find sun's meridian altitude
harmonic law Kepler's third law, which states that the squares of periods of any two planets are in same proportion as cubes of their average distances from sun
heliocentric (*adj*) viewing universe as though sun were its center
Hertzsprung-Russell diagram graph that shows luminosities of stars plotted against their temperatures
horizon system system of celestial coordinates, such as altitude and azimuth, that are based on observer's horizon
horoscope positions of planets and stars relative to one another at time of person's birth, regarded in astrology as factor that determines one's character and destiny
Hubble classification scheme sequence of different types of galaxies: elliptical, spiral, and irregular
Kepler's laws Johann Kepler's three laws of planetary motion: *first law* orbit of each planet is ellipse with sun at one of its foci; *second law* each planet revolves so that imaginary line between it and sun sweeps over equal areas of space in equal intervals of time; *third law* harmonic law
light speed distance light travels in one second, equal to approximately 186,000 miles (299,792 km)
light year astronomical unit of measurement equal to distance light travels in one year, approximately 6 trillion miles (9.5 trillion km), used as measure of astronomical distances
magnitude brightness of star in sky measured on logarithmic scale from zero (brightest) to five (faintest), with fifth-magnitude stars being 100 times fainter than zero-magnitude stars
major axis maximum diameter across an ellipse
mass-luminosity law the greater the absolute magnitude of a star the greater its luminosity
mass spectrometry separation and measurement of molecules that have different masses by deflection of beam of ionized molecules
New General Catalogue NGC; listing of galaxies, clusters, and nebulae that includes all Messier objects, numbered from NGC1
Newton's first law of motion an object remains at rest or in motion with a constant velocity unless acted upon by an outside force
Newton's law of universal gravitation force of attraction between any two particles of matter is directly proportional to the product of their masses and inversely proportional to the square of the distance between their centers of mass
Newton's second law of motion the change in motion of an object acted upon by an outside force is directly proportional to the force and inversely proportional to the object's mass
Newton's third law of motion every action force has a reaction force equal in magnitude and opposite in direction
NGC New General Catalogue
objective lens in telescope nearest to object observed that focuses light to form image of object
observatory building equipped with large telescope and other devices used for astronomical studies
orrery mechanical model that shows positions, motion, and phases of bodies in solar system, as in a planetarium
parsec unit of astronomical measurement equal to 3.26 light years, distance required to produce parallax angle of one arc second
photometry process in which intensity of light or radiation emitted by celestial source is measured by electrical voltage or pulse counter
planetarium complex revolving projector used to simulate motion and position of celestial objects inside a dome; building that houses projector and dome used for this purpose
planetesimal any of numerous small bodies that moved in orbits through space and may have formed planets
plate tectonics theory that planets and some other celestial bodies consist of crustal slabs that are in constant motion against each other
Ptolemaic system geocentric model of universe, postulated by Claudius Ptolemaeus in second century A.D., in which planets, moon, and sun revolve around Earth
pulsating universe theory variation on expanding universe theory, in which cycle of expansion and contracting to and from primeval nucleus is endlessly repeated
quintessence substance other than fire, air, water, or earth believed to compose celestial bodies in ancient and medieval philosophy
radio astronomy study of radio energy sources in space by means of large, reflecting radio telescopes
radio telescope one or more radio antennas that receive and measure radio waves from celestial sources
reflector telescope with mirror as objective
refractor telescope with system of lenses as objective
right ascension angle in sky east of vernal equinox
Roche limit distance from planet's center below which a satellite cannot approach without suffering disruption
Schmidt telescope reflector telescope with spherical mirror as objective, used for wide-angle photography
seismometer instrument that measures seismic waves on Earth or moon
SETI search for extraterrestrial intelligence
sextant instrument used, esp. by navigators, to measure angular distance of celestial object from horizon
sidereal (*adj*) expressed or measured in reference to stars
sidereal period time in which planet or satellite completes one revolution around its primary relative to a star seen from the primary
sidereal time time measured by rotation of Earth with respect to stars, not sun
signal-to-noise ratio error inherent in measure-

ment of brightness of faint star based on background light or noise
singularity point in space-time at which space-time curvature becomes infinite, such as black hole
space-time four-dimensional order of universe specified by three spatial coordinates and one temporal coordinate
spectral type classification of star based on analysis of certain spectral lines and stated as letter (O, B, A, F, G, K, or M) in order of decreasing temperature and number within letter group, such as the sun, a G2 star
spectrograph combination of spectroscope and photographic equipment used in studying spectra of celestial objects
spectroscopy study of radiative output of celestial source
stargazing astronomy or astrology
steady state model theory of expanding universe stipulating continuous creation of matter, and stating that universe maintains uniform large-scale structure and constant average density at all times
telescope instrument used to collect light from celestial objects and resolve images of these objects: reflector, refractor, and Schmidt
universe sum total of potentially knowable objects, matter, and energy, believed to be infinite in space and time
uranography branch of astronomy that describes and maps the position of the heavens, esp. fixed stars
uranometry measurement of positions, magnitudes, and distances of celestial objects
X-ray burster source of intense X-ray flashes in Milky Way
zodiac band of twelve constellations on celestial sphere with ecliptic as its middle line that includes paths of every planet except Pluto, divided into twelve zones and used in astrology

Signs of the Zodiac

Aquarius the Water Bearer, a constellation between Capricorn and Pisces and eleventh sign of the zodiac; the fixed air sign and birth sign of persons born between January 20th and February 18th
Aries the Ram, a constellation between Pisces and Taurus and first sign of the zodiac; the cardinal fire sign and birth sign of persons born between March 21st and April 19th
Cancer the Crab, a constellation between Gemini and Leo and fourth sign of the zodiac; the cardinal water sign and birth sign of persons born between June 21st and July 22nd
Capricorn the Goat, a constellation between Sagittarius and Aquarius and tenth sign of the zodiac; the cardinal earth sign and birth sign of persons born between December 22nd and January 19th
Gemini the Twins, a constellation between Taurus and Cancer and third sign of the zodiac; the mutable air sign and birth sign of persons born between May 21st and June 20th
Leo the Lion, a constellation between Cancer and Virgo and fifth sign of the zodiac; the fixed fire sign and birth sign of persons born between July 23rd and August 22nd
Libra the Balance, a constellation between Virgo and Scorpius and seventh sign of the zodiac; the cardinal air sign and birth sign of persons born between September 23rd and October 22nd
Pisces the Fishes, a constellation between Aquarius and Aries and twelfth sign of the zodiac; the mutable water sign and birth sign of persons born between February 19th and March 20th
Sagittarius the Archer, a constellation between Scorpius and Capricorn and ninth sign of the zodiac; the mutable fire sign and birth sign of persons born between November 22nd and December 21st
Scorpio the Scorpion, the constellation Scorpius between Libra and Sagittarius and eighth sign of the zodiac; the fixed water sign and birth sign of persons born between October 23rd and November 21st
Taurus the Bull, a constellation between Aries and Gemini and second sign of the zodiac; the fixed earth sign and birth sign of persons born between April 20th and May 20th
Virgo the Virgin, a constellation between Leo and Libra and sixth sign of the zodiac; the mutable earth sign and birth sign of persons born between August 23rd and September 22nd

Space Exploration and Rocketry

abort (*vb*) cancel or terminate mission or procedure prematurely, esp. due to equipment failure
aerospace science study and exploration of Earth's atmosphere and space beyond; rocket science; space science
anti-G suit totally enclosed uniform that equalizes G-force on astronaut
A-OK (*adj*) *Informal.* all systems go; okay to proceed as planned
Apollo series of manned NASA missions to moon
artificial satellite man-made object set in orbit around Earth
astronaut person sent on space mission
astronautics science of spacecrafts and outer space travel; cosmonautics
Atlantis space shuttle orbiter vehicle
Atlas family of launch vehicles; first-stage booster rocket
backout reversal of launch countdown due to poor weather or mechanical failure
ballistic missile unmanned military rocket with warhead; rocket bomb
bearing horizontal direction of object or point measured clockwise from reference line
blastoff launch; liftoff
blowoff separation of portion or stage of rocket by explosive force
booster rocket first stage of multistage rocket that provides thrust for liftoff
burn firing of rocket engine

burnout moment of final oxidation or combustion of fuel in a rocket engine
burn rate rate at which solid propellant is consumed
capsule small, pressurized compartment for astronauts
cargo bay unpressurized part of fuselage in which cargo is carried
centrifuge apparatus with long arm in which individual is revolved to simulate effects of prolonged acceleration in space
Challenger NASA space shuttle which exploded in 1986
CM command module
Columbia first space shuttle orbiter, launched in 1981
command module CM; component of Apollo spacecraft attached to service module until reentry into Earth's atmosphere
communications satellite satellite designed to reflect or relay electromagnetic signals used in communications; comsat
cosmic particle cosmic ray
cosmic ray highly energized particle moving at near speed of light that strikes spacecraft; cosmic particle
cosmonaut Soviet astronaut
cosmonautics astronautics, esp. Soviet space program
Cosmos series of unmanned Soviet satellites
countdown backward counting off of seconds before launch; operations during such a count
cutoff termination of propellant flow in rocket; stoppage of combustion
decompression sickness disorder associated with reduced atmospheric pressure that causes gas bubbles in body and pain in chest and extremities
deep space region beyond Earth's solar system
descent drop from Earth orbit, reentry into atmosphere, and touchdown
Discovery space shuttle orbiter vehicle
docking maneuver in which two or more spacecraft or orbiting objects are joined together
docking maneuver change in spacecraft path or trajectory to facilitate docking
downlink radio or television transmission from spacecraft to Earth station
drift lateral divergence from prescribed flight path
drogue recovery system of spacecraft recovery after reentry that uses small and large parachutes to slow descent, stabilize vehicle, and decrease landing impact
escape velocity speed required to place spacecraft in orbit or break free of Earth's gravitational field
EVMU extravehicular mobility unit
exobiology study of extraterrestrial environments for living organisms
Explorer first series of NASA space probes
external tank liquid oxygen or hydrogen propellant tank on space shuttle
extraterrestrial (*adj*) not from Earth
extravehicular activity space walks and other experiments conducted outside confines of spacecraft
extravehicular mobility unit EVMU; space suit, including life support system and manned maneuvering unit; pressure suit; spacesuit
failsafe design that ensures ability to sustain malfunction yet successfully terminate or abort mission
flight movement of craft through space
flight deck area of orbiter module occupied by crew
flight path launch, orbit, and trajectory followed by spacecraft on mission
flyby mission in which spacecraft passes close to target planet but does not orbit or impact it
flying saucer unidentified flying object
footprint area taken up by spacecraft on ground
G acceleration due to gravity, equal to one G at sea level on Earth's surface
Gemini series of NASA Earth orbital missions manned by two astronauts
G-force force in excess of one G experienced by everything inside spacecraft during launch or reentry
go/no-go (*adj*) being the point at which decision to launch or not launch must be made
ground test procedure by which spacecraft, systems, or rockets are tested without launch
guidance system control system that selects flight path of spacecraft and directs its movements in space
gyro spinning wheel resistant to change of direction of its axis of rotation, used to steady orientation of spacecraft
hangfire faulty condition in rocket engine ignition system that causes delay in firing
heat shield structural overlay that protects reentry body of spacecraft from aerodynamic heating
heat sink material that absorbs heat, used for heat shield
Hubble Space Telescope powerful telescope operating outside Earth's atmosphere that has capability to see much deeper into universe than telescopes on Earth's surface
hydrogen gas used as fuel for space shuttle main engine when cryogenically cooled to liquid form
impact rocket or spacecraft striking surface of planet or any other object
inclination angle between orbital plane of satellite and plane of ecliptic
interplanetary travel hypothetical manned flights to other planets in solar system
Jet Propulsion Laboratory JPL; center for basic and applied research in space science, located in Pasadena, California
JPL Jet Propulsion Laboratory
Jupiter three-stage booster rocket used to place first U.S. satellite Explorer I in orbit in January, 1958
Kennedy Space Center KSC; primary launching base for U.S. spacecraft, located at Cape Canaveral, Florida
KREEP set of elements found in lunar rocks and soil: K, symbol for potassium; REE, rare Earth elements; P, phosphorus
KSC Kennedy Space Center
launch initiation of space flight with takeoff of rocket from Earth's surface; blastoff; liftoff

launcher structure with tubes and set of tracks from which rockets are launched
launch pad area from which spacecraft and booster rockets are sent forth, either tower, tube, or platform
launch window interval of time during which spacecraft can be launched to accomplish specific task or mission
LEM lunar excursion module
life-support system environmental control system that provides comfortable, shirtsleeve conditions for crew by control of temperature, pressure, humidity, and oxygen and nitrogen supply
liftoff moment in which rocket leaves launch pad on Earth; blastoff; launch
liquid propellant cryogenically cooled oxygen or hydrogen used in external fuel tanks of space shuttle
LM lunar module
LOX liquid oxygen, used as liquid propellant
lunar excursion module LEM; lunar module
lunar module LM; detachable vehicle on Apollo spacecraft used in manned moon landings; lunar excursion module
lunar orbiter command service module that remained in lunar orbit while lunar module landed on surface of moon
lunar rock rocks and soil returned to Earth by Apollo astronauts; moon rock
Mach number expressing ratio of speed of a body with respect to surrounding air or fluid; Mach 1 is speed of sound, supersonic being above Mach 1, subsonic below
Magellan unmanned spacecraft launched from shuttle to orbit and examine Venus during 1991
manned flight space mission with one or more humans on board
Manned Space Center MSC; NASA headquarters located in Houston, Texas, that serves as mission control for U.S. space flights
manned station orbiting space lab with crew on board
Mariner series of NASA spacecraft used for planet flyby missions
Mercury first series of NASA orbital and suborbital manned space missions
Mir small Soviet space station used primarily for scientific experiments
missile unmanned military rocket aimed at target, usu. with warhead
mission space flight with prescribed goals and operations
mission control ground center that provides manned space missions with total support and control over all phases of flight
module self-contained unit attached to launch vehicle or spacecraft; pressurized manned laboratory
moon rock lunar rock
MSC Manned Space Center
multistage rocket space vehicle that uses two or more firing stages to boost payload into orbit, each stage being jettisoned when fuel is exhausted
NASA National Aeronautics and Space Administration; U.S. government agency administering space program
NORAD North American Air Defense; U.S. defense radar network covering North America
orbit path followed by satellite or spacecraft around Earth or other celestial body
O-ring plastic sealing ring on propellant tanks
parking orbit orbit around Earth maintained for long duration
pass single orbit of Earth by spacecraft or satellite
payload passengers, cargo, instruments, equipment, supplies, and support hardware carried by rocket over and above what is necessary to operate vehicle in flight
photomosaic space photograph composed of many individual images of segments of photographed objects
Pioneer series of unmanned NASA probes that explore solar system as far as Jupiter and Saturn
pod detachable compartment of spacecraft
pressure hull main body of spacecraft comparable to aircraft fuselage
pressure suit extravehicular mobility unit
probe unmanned space mission on trajectory from Earth orbit to study another celestial object
propellant solid or liquid fuel used to provide thrust and launch rocket, place it in orbit, break it out of orbit, or slow its descent
propulsion system vehicle system of engines, fuel tanks, and lines providing thrust
proving ground testing ground
radar tracking station tracking station that maintains only radar contact with spacecraft
Ranger early series of NASA space probes
reentry return of space capsule into Earth's atmosphere
retroengine small engine used to produce retarding thrust and reduce velocity, esp. on reentry
retrofire ignition of retroengine
retrograde orbit of satellite in westerly direction, opposite easterly motion of earthbound observer
retrorocket rocket fired to reduce spacecraft motion, so that it descends from orbit or slows down in free fall
rocket portion of spacecraft in which combustible materials provide thrust for launch and orbit
rocket bomb ballistic missile
rocketry study and practice of aerospace science
rocket science aerospace science
Rover vehicle used on lunar surface by astronauts
satellite artificial object sent into Earth orbit
Saturn first-stage booster rocket on Apollo missions
scrub (*vb*) cancel flight or mission
sealing rings mechanical devices designed to prevent loss of cabin atmosphere
Sea of Tranquillity large lunar basin and landing point of Apollo 11, first manned lunar expedition
separation stage in which launch vehicle booster rockets are jettisoned once fuel is exhausted
service module section of spacecraft containing propulsion and electrical systems and supplies
shot space flight to specific celestial body, such as moonshot

shuttle reusable spacecraft that replaced expendable launch vehicles and can return payloads and land on Earth
silo large, underground facility for storage and launching of long-range ballistic missiles
Skylab large NASA space workshop operated in the 1970's
solid propellant chemical mixture or compound containing fuel and oxidizer that burn to produce very hot gases at high pressure
solid rocket boosters two solid fuel rockets that augment thrust of shuttle from launch through first two minutes of ascent and are then separated and retrieved for reuse
Soyuz series of Soviet manned spacecraft
Space Age era of space exploration that began with launch of first Sputnik on October 4, 1957
space colony hypothetical large, semipermanent community living on space station or on another planet
spacecraft manned or unmanned platform or object placed in Earth orbit or in trajectory to another celestial body
Spacelab laboratory payload on shuttle, product of joint effort between ESA and NASA
spaceman astronaut; extraterrestrial being
spaceport space station
space probe probe
space science aerospace science; astronomy
spaceship spacecraft or satellite
space station permanently orbiting, large spacecraft designed to accommodate long-term human habitation; spaceport
spacesuit extravehicular mobility unit
spacewalk extravehicular activity in which astronaut, often connected by support umbilical, leaves confines of spacecraft
splashdown spacecraft landing in ocean
Sputnik first Soviet artificial satellite series that began with October 4, 1957 launch
staging separation of spent stages of launch vehicle from capsule
starship interstellar spacecraft
suborbital flight one of early manned Mercury flights that did not enter Earth orbit
Surveyor class of unmanned NASA space probes undertaken in preparation for manned Apollo lunar flights
sustainer small rocket engine that maintains spacecraft's speed after booster is jettisoned
synodic period time between two consecutive orbital passes over one reference longitude on Earth
telemetry coding and measuring of data obtained on spacecraft in form comprehensible to digital computers and transmission to Earth stations for interpretation
terrestrial (*adj*) of the Earth
test flight flight for controlled observation of operations, rocket, and spacecraft
testing ground area and facilities designated for test flights; proving ground
test rocket rocket designed for test flight only
throttling varying thrust of rocket engine during flight by fuel line constriction or changes in nozzle expansion and thrust chamber pressure
thrust propulsive force developed by rocket engines during firing, used to launch spacecraft and place it in orbit or on trajectory out of Earth's atmosphere
Titan first-stage booster launch vehicle
touchdown landing of spacecraft on Earth or another celestial body
tracking station facility that observes, plots, and monitors path of spacecraft
trajectory nonorbital flight path from one point to another
t-time specific time, plus or minus, that refers to launch time or zero at end of countdown
UFO unidentified flying object; hypothetical spacecraft from another solar system; flying saucer
umbilical electrical or fluid servicing line between tower on launch pad and upright rocket prior to launch, or between spacecraft and astronaut on spacewalk
unidentified flying object UFO
unmanned flight space mission without humans on board
uplink transmission path for sending signals from earth station to communications satellite or airborne platform
upweight spacecraft weight at launch, including payloads, support items, and unburned fuel
Viking series of NASA spacecraft designed to land on Mars
visual tracking station facility from which visual sightings of spacecraft are possible
Vostok series of manned Soviet spacecraft, used to make world's first manned space flights in 1961
Voyager series of NASA probes that explored outer planets on flybys of Jupiter in 1979, Saturn in 1980, Uranus in 1986, and Neptune in 1989
V-2 German rocket bomb used in World War II
weather satellite unmanned spacecraft that returns meteorological data to Earth
weightlessness zero-G state
window gap in continuum; interval of time favorable to launch for specific mission
yaw angular motion of vehicle about vertical axis through center of gravity
zero-G condition of weightlessness and free fall experienced when no gravitational forces are acting on objects in spacecraft

MATHEMATICS

Branches and Computational Systems
Quantities, Relationships, and Operations
Geometric Shapes and Mathematically Defined Forms
Mathematical Tools

Branches and Computational Systems

algebra theory and practice of arithmetic operations that uses symbols, esp. letters, to represent unknown variables in equations
algorithm set of rules for solving problems through finite repetitions of basic given procedure
analysis approach to functions and limits, esp. by use of differential and integral calculus
analytic geometry use of coordinate graphing system to demonstrate numerical relationships of algebraic equations
applied mathematics study of physical phenomena using mathematical methods, as in mechanics, statistics, and physics
arithmetic study of usu. positive real numbers in addition, subtraction, multiplication, and division operations that yield sums, remainders, products, and quotients
Boolean algebra form of propositional calculus; algebra of elementary propositions in symbolic logic
calculus methods of calculation for continuously changing quantities, based on differentiation and integration of functions and related concepts
descriptive geometry theory of geometry treated by means of projections on two planes at right angles to each other
differential calculus branch of mathematics dealing with rate of change of functions with respect to variables on which they depend
elementary arithmetic simple arithmetic computations that involve one- and two-digit positive integers
Euclidean geometry study of geometry within limits of Euclidean space, i.e. ordinary one-, two-, and three-dimensional space
Fourier analysis expression of periodic function as sum of infinite series of trigonometric functions
game theory field of study concerned with decision-making problems in competitive situations governed by rules
geodesy measurement and theory of curvature, shape, and dimensions of Earth's surface
geometry branch of mathematics that deals with deduction of properties, measurement, and relationships of points, lines, angles, surfaces, and solid figures in space
group theory study of the properties and relationships of mathematical groups, with associated operations that obey specific set of rules
integral calculus branch of mathematics used to find indefinite integrals of functions, evaluate definite integrals, determine dimensions, and solve simple differential equations
linear algebra algebra of vectors and matrices as opposed to real numbers
mathematics science dealing through symbolic representation with the relationship of numbers, magnitudes, and forms, including quantitative operations and the solution of quantitative problems
matrix algebra generalized algebra that deals with operations and relationships among ordered sets of elements arranged in rows and columns
non-Euclidean geometry geometry not in accordance with all of the postulates of Euclidean space, esp. the single parallel postulate
number theory advanced arithmetic devoted to study of properties of integers
plane geometry elementary form of geometry that deals with two-dimensional figures
propositional calculus branch of symbolic logic dealing with analysis of relationships between statements that have been reduced into conjunctions, disjunctions, and negations of more elementary statements
quadratics form of algebra that treats quadratic polynomial equations
set theory branch of mathematics and symbolic logic dealing with nature and relations of aggregates or sets
solid geometry geometry that deals with solid, three-dimensional figures
statistics collection, analysis, interpretation, and presentation of masses of empirical, numerical data
symbolic logic science of developing and representing logical principles by means of symbols to provide rules of deduction for computations
systems analysis study of an activity by mathematical means to determine how most efficiently to attain desired ends
topology investigation of those properties of a geometric configuration that remain unaltered when subjected to one-to-one transformations that are continuous in both directions
trigonometry branch of mathematics that measures relations between sides and angles of triangles
vector analysis study of the properties of vectors

Quantities, Relationships, and Operations

abscissa horizontal coordinate of a point in a plane; distance from the y-axis
addend one of a group of numbers to be added together
addition arithmetic operation that combines numbers to generate sum
aggregate whole sum, total amount; set of mathematical elements with a common property

algebraic function sum, difference, product, quotient, or root of polynomial function
antilogarithm number of which a given number is the logarithm
Arabic numeral one of standard number symbols: 0,1,2,3,4,5,6,7,8,9; digit
area number of unit squares required to cover surface; measurement of surface
arithmetic mean average
associative law result of multiple operations does not depend on how they are grouped
asymptote straight line in relation to curve such that as point moves along infinite branch of curve the distance from point to line approaches zero
average result that occurs when sum of two or more quantities is divided by the number of quantities; arithmetic mean
axiom proposition assumed to be true without proof in order to study its applied consequences; self-evident truth
axis straight line for reference in graph, such as Cartesian coordinate; straight line through center of plane or solid around which it is symmetrically arranged
base number multiplied by itself in scientific notation; number that is raised to a power
binary (*adj*) designating system of numbers having two as its base
binomial expression that is a sum or difference of two unlike terms
binomial distribution probability function that indicates how often two outcomes with constant probability will occur in a succession of repetitive experiments
bisection division of angle or form into two equal parts
cancel (*vb*) remove either common divisor from numerator and denominator of fraction or equivalents from opposite sides of equation
cardinal number number used in simple counting to indicate an amount, such as how many of something are in a set
chi-square distribution widely used probability density function that shows distribution of sum of squares of several independent random variables
circular function trigonometric function
circumference distance measured around outside of circle
coefficient number that multiplies another quantity; factor of a product
combination a specific number of elements of a set, viewed without regard to the order in which they are arranged
common denominator common multiple of denominators of two or more fractions
commutative law rule of combination in which an operation on two terms is independent of the order of the terms
complement angle or arc that when added to another angle or arc equals a right angle
complex number real or imaginary number expressed as a + bi where a and b are real numbers and i is the square root of -1
composite function function obtained from two given functions by applying one function to an independent variable and applying the second function to the result
composite number integer divisible by a whole number other than itself or 1
compound number number expressed in more than one denomination or unit, such as 6 feet, 2 inches
computation act or method of determining an amount, esp. by arithmetic
concentric (*adj*) designating two or more figures having a common center
congruent (*adj*) having exactly the same size and shape
conjugate (*adj*) having the same or similar properties, such as two lines; (*n*) one of two adjacent angles that total 360°
constant quantity with fixed value, opposite of variable
conversion change in form but not value of quantity or unit
coordinates numbers associated with points on number line or graph
corollary theorem proved by application of a previously proved theorem
corresponding angles pair of nonadjacent angles on same side of line that crosses two other lines, one interior and one exterior
cosecant trigonometric ratio expressed as secant of the complement of an arc or angle
cosine trigonometric ratio expressed as sine of the complement of an arc or angle
cotangent trigonometric ratio expressed as tangent of the complement of an arc or angle
count (*vb*) recite numbers in standard order; add units in group one at a time
cross multiply determine two products by multiplying numerator of each of two fractions by denominator of other
cube third power of a number; number multiplied by itself two times
cube root number whose cube is given number
data numerical information
decimal (*adj*) designating system of numbers having ten as its base
decimal point mark indicating division between integers and fractions in mixed number
degree unit of angular measure; measure around fixed point, with total of 360 degrees in circle
denominator lower number of fraction, indicating number of parts into which the whole has been divided
dependent variable element in second set of a function associated with independent variable selected from first
derivative rate of change of mathematical function with respect to change in independent variable
deviation amount by which any single value differs from the mean
diameter straight line extending from edge to edge through center point of sphere or circle
difference amount of inequality between two quantities; result obtained when one quantity is subtracted from another

differential product of the derivative of a function of one variable times the small increment of an independent variable
digit one of Arabic numeral symbols: 0,1,2,3,4,5,6,7,8,9
distributive law rule of combination in which specified operation applied to combination of terms equals combination of that operation applied individually to each term
dividend number that is divided by divisor
division arithmetic operation that finds how many times one number is contained in another, producing a quotient
divisor number that divides dividend
domain set of elements by which a function is limited or defined
eccentricity number used to define form of a conic section as an ellipse, circle, parabola, or hyperbola
equation mathematical statement containing the equals (&equal;) sign between two different but equal algebraic formulations
exponent superscript symbol used to indicate how many times a number is to be used as factor or multiplied by itself
expression symbol or combination of symbols representing a value or relationship
extrapolation estimating value of a function beyond range of its known values
factor two or more numbers multiplied together, each number being a factor of the product
factor analysis statistical method that reduces large number of measures or tests to smaller number of factors that account for all results
factorial product of all positive integers from given positive integer down to 1
Fibonacci sequence unending sequence of numbers, each of which is the sum of its two predecessors
formula equation illustrating rule for mathematical relationship of quantities
fraction quantity expressed as the ratio of two integers that is not itself an integer
function exact association of one element from one set with element from another set
geodesic (*adj*) describing shortest line between two points on surface, esp. curved surface
geometric mean square root of product of two numbers
geometric progression sequence in which ratio of each succeeding term to preceding term is constant throughout
Gödel's incompleteness theorem theorem that within a given logical system there exists at least one mathematical formula that can be neither proved nor disproved
googol number that is equal to 1 followed by 100 zeros
googolplex number that is equal to 1 followed by a googol of zeros
hypotenuse side of right triangle opposite right angle
hypothesis provisionally true statement; supposition to be proved
imaginary number square root of negative number, esp. imaginary unit represented by square root of -1
independent variable element in function whose value is specified first and determines value of one or more other elements in expression of function
infinity boundlessly great number, amount, or geometric magnitude
integer whole number, whether positive, negative, or zero; any number in the infinite sequence ... -3,-2,-1,0,1,2,3 ...
integral the limit of the sum of a larger and larger number of smaller and smaller quantities, used to calculate the area of a curved figure; a function whose derivative is a given function
inverse proportion ratio of x to y when one unknown is multiplied by a number and its proportional unknown is divided by that number
irrational number any real number that cannot be expressed as the ratio of two integers
least common denominator smallest number that divides evenly into numerator of fraction; multiple of denominators of two or more specified fractions; lowest common denominator
limit value approached by function as its independent variable approaches some specific value
linear equation algebraic equation in which variables are in first power and whose graph is a straight line
locus set of all points satisfying given conditions
logarithm exponent of that power of a fixed base number that equals another given number
lowest common denominator least common denominator
magic square matrix in which each column, row, and both main diagonals produce same constant sum
mantissa decimal part of common logarithm
mathematical model set of formulae or equations that describe behavior of physical system in mathematical terms
matrix ordered set of elements arranged in rows and columns, esp. one that can be combined with similar arrays having comparable number of rows and columns
mean average
median middle item in array of data ranked from smallest to largest, used as statistical measure of primary tendency
minuend number from which another number is subtracted
mixed number number consisting of whole number and fraction
mode statistical measure of primary tendency made by determining item that occurs most frequently in a data set
multiplicand number to be multiplied by another
multiplication arithmetic operation in which additions of a number are repeated a specified number of times to produce a product
multiplier number by which multiplicand is multiplied

natural number positive integer
negative number real number less than zero
number abstract unit in numeral series that represents an arbitrarily determined quantity; arithmetic total, sum of units involved
numeral word, letter, symbol, or figure expressing or representing a number
numerator upper number of fraction, indicating number of parts taken of denominator
ordinal number number indicating position in a series, as *first* or *third*
ordinate vertical coördinate of a point in a plane; distance from the x-axis
origin point of intersection in coordinate system, esp. x-axis and y-axis system
parameter arbitrary constant whose values describe some member of a system of curves, expressions, or functions; independent variable used to express coordinates of variable point and their functions
percent percentage
percentage ratio with denominator of 100; rate or proportion per hundred; percent
percentile percentage of sample rated equal to or higher than given level in statistical study
perimeter distance measured around outer boundary of any two-dimensional figure
periodic function function of a real or complex variable that has graph that repeats after fixed interval of the independent variable
permutation a specific number of elements of a set, arranged in a particular order
pi ratio of circumference of circle to its diameter, with a value equal to 22/7 or approximately 3.14159265, designated &thgr;
polynomial expression containing sums or differences of monomials
positive number real number greater than zero
postulate unproved assumption
power product resulting from repeated multiplication of a number by itself, square being second power, cube third
prime number any integer other than one evenly divisible only by one and itself
probability ratio of number of outcomes in a given series of events to total number of possible outcomes in that series
product result of multiplication
proof sequence of axioms, postulates, and theorems used to conclude that a statement is true
proportion equality between ratios, esp. quotients of two fractions; ratio of x to y when both unknowns are multiplied or divided by the same number
Pythagorean theorem in a right triangle the square of the hypotenuse is equal to the sum of the squares of the other two sides
quadratic equation equation in which highest exponent of variable is two
quotient result of dividing one number by another
radian unit of angular measure equal to 57.296 degrees, being angle subtended at center of circle by arc of length equal to radius of that circle
radical root of number or quantity, esp. square root symbol
radicand expression under radical symbol; number whose square root is to be determined
radius line segment from center of circle or sphere to point on circle or sphere
radix base number
range complete set of values a function may assume
ratio comparison of two numbers, expressed as fractional quotient
rational number number that can be expressed as integer or ratio of two integers
real number part of complex number that is not imaginary, either rational or irrational
reciprocal multiplicative inverse; number which when multiplied by its reciprocal is one
recurring decimal decimal fraction ending in pattern of digits repeated indefinitely
remainder number left after subtraction; portion of the dividend, not evenly divisible, left after division
Roman numeral any of system of numerical notation based on values: I&equal;1, V&equal;5, X&equal;10, L&equal;50, C&equal;100, D&equal;500, M&equal;1,000
root quantity that when multiplied by itself a certain number of times produces a given quantity; square root or cube root
scientific notation method of expressing number as product of number between 1 and 10, with integral power of ten as exponent
secant trigonometric ratio of hypotenuse of right triangle to leg adjacent to its acute angle
series expression obtained by adding sequence of terms, finite or infinite
set collection of elements of same kind or class
significant digits all nonzero digits in a number and zeros either between them or at end, where they signify accuracy to a number of places
similar (*adj*) having the same shape but not necessarily the same size
simultaneous equations two or more equations having common solutions, when used in same problem
sine trigonometric ratio of side of right triangle opposite a given acute angle to hypotenuse
square product of number multiplied by itself
square root one of two equal factors of a number
standard deviation measure of variability in frequency distribution based on squares of deviations from mean
subset a set included within another set
subtraction arithmetic operation in which one number is reduced by another to produce a difference
subtrahend number to be subtracted from minuend
sum number resulting from addition of two or more numbers
supplement angle or arc that when added to another angle or arc totals 180 degrees
tangent trigonometric ratio between leg opposite acute angle in right triangle and leg adjacent to it

theorem statement that can be proved by mathematical deduction from given facts and justifiable assumptions
transcendental number number that cannot be root of algebraic equation with rational coefficients, such as pi
transpose (*vb*) transfer term from one side of algebraic equation to the other, reversing plus or minus sign in the process
trigonometric function function of arc or angle expressed as ratio of any pair of sides of right triangle; circular function
universe set of all objects that are admissible to that set based on its parameters
unknown variable whose value is to be found by solving equation
variable unknown placeholder in algebraic expression, opposite of constant, usu. indicated by a letter; (*adj*) having no fixed value
variance in statistics, the square of the standard deviation
variation manner in which two or more quantities change in relation to each other
vector quantity possessing both magnitude and direction, represented by line segment of specific length and direction
volume cubic magnitude of three-dimensional figure
whole number integer
x-axis the horizontal axis in a plane
y-axis the vertical axis in a plane

Geometric Shapes and Mathematically Defined Forms

acute angle angle of less than ninety degrees
angle open figure formed by two lines joined at common endpoint
arc portion of a curve
bi- prefix meaning two, as in *bisect*: divide into two parts
circle two-dimensional area defined by curved set of points all equidistant from a single, central point
complementary angle either of two angles that combine to form 90 degree angle
cone three-dimensional figure with circular base and single point as vertex
conic section curve formed by intersection of plane with right circular cone
cube three-dimensional figure with six congruent square faces
curve one-dimensional continuum of points in space of two or more dimensions
cusp tip of pointed curve
cylinder three-dimensional figure with two congruent, parallel, circular bases connected by a curved, lateral surface
deca- prefix meaning ten, as in *decagon*: ten-sided polygon
disk two-dimensional figure defined by all points enclosed by circle's circumference
dodeca- prefix meaning twelve, as in *dodecahedron*: twelve-faced figure
ellipse closed plane curve generated by point moving so that sum of point's distance from two fixed points is constant; plane section of right circular cone
ellipsoid solid figure, all plane sections of which are ellipses or circles
equi- prefix meaning equal, as in *equilateral* triangle: triangle with all sides of equal length
fractal geometrical structure having irregular or fragmented shape at all scales, such that certain phenomena behave as if the structure's dimensions are greater than they are in space
frustum conical solid with top cut off by plane parallel to base
helix three-dimensional curve whose spiral arms maintain constant angle relative to base
hemisphere half of sphere, formed by plane through sphere's center
hepta- prefix meaning seven, as in *heptagon*: seven-sided polygon
hexa- prefix meaning six, as in *hexagon*: six-sided polygon
hyper- prefix meaning beyond, extra, above the norm, as in *hyperspace*: space with more than three dimensions
hyperbola set of points in a plane whose distances to two fixed points in the plane have a constant difference
icosa- prefix meaning twenty, as in *icosahedron*: twenty-sided figure
iso- prefix meaning equal, as in *isosceles* triangle: triangle with two equal sides
line straight, infinitely long one-dimensional figure consisting of all points along path defined by two points
line segment the portion of a line that lies between two given points; segment
oblique (*adj*) neither perpendicular nor parallel; without a right angle
obtuse angle angle of more than 90 but less than 180 degrees
octa- prefix meaning eight, as in *octagon*: eight-sided polygon
parabola plane curve generated by movement of point at equal distance from fixed point and fixed line
parallel (*adj*) constantly equidistant and in the same plane
parallelogram four-sided, two-dimensional figure with both pairs of opposite sides parallel
penta- prefix meaning five, as in *pentagon*: five-sided polygon
perpendicular (*adj*) at right angle to plane or line
plane flat, unbounded, two-dimensional surface
point single, specific location with no extension in space; geometric element determined by ordered set of coordinates
poly- prefix meaning many, usu. three or more, as in *polygon*: multisided figure
polygon closed plane figure of three or more line segments
polyhedron closed, three-dimensional figure composed of faces, or polygonal areas, connected along edges
prism three-dimensional figure with two parallel, congruent, polygon-shaped bases

pyramid three-dimensional figure with polygonal base and three or more triangular faces that converge in single point at vertex
quadrant quarter of a circle; any of four parts into which plane is divided by rectangular coordinate axes
quadratic (*adj*) relating to or resembling a square
quadri- prefix meaning four, as in *quadrilateral*: four-sided polygon
rectangle two-dimensional figure with four sides at right angles
reflex angle angle greater than 180 degrees and less than 360 degrees
rhomboid oblique-angled parallelogram with only its opposite sides equal
rhombus equilateral parallelogram with oblique angles
right angle angle of 90 degrees
right triangle triangle with one right angle
scalene triangle triangle with sides of three different lengths
segment line segment
semicircle half of a circle, formed by arc from one end of diameter to the other
solid figure having length, breadth, and thickness
sphere three-dimensional figure formed by set of all points in space equidistant from central fixed point
square rectangle with all sides the same length
supplementary angle either of two angles that combine to form an angle of 180 degrees
tangent line touching a circle or other curve at only one point
tetra- prefix meaning four, as in *tetrahedron*: four-faced polyhedron
three-dimensional (*adj*) having length, breadth, and thickness
torus doughnut-shaped surface generated by rotation of a circle about an axis in its plane that does not intersect it
trapezium two-dimensional, irregular, four-sided figure with no two sides parallel
trapezoid two-dimensional, four-sided figure with two parallel sides
tri- prefix meaning three, as in *trisect*: divide into three parts
triangle three-sided, two-dimensional figure
two-dimensional (*adj*) having height and width only
vector line segment of specific length and direction, used to represent quantity that has both direction and magnitude
vertex point at which two lines or planes meet to form angle

Mathematical Tools

abacus counting and computational device consisting of beads mounted in groups of tens on wires in frame, esp. used in Asia
calculator machine that performs arithmetic functions
compass instrument used to draw arcs and circles
computer programmable electronic device for storage and retrieval of data that performs very rapid calculations
graph diagrammatic representation of numerical values and relationships, using coordinates
multiplication table graphlike arrangement used to memorize products of each number in series, usu. 1 through 12, multiplied by each number in same series
protractor instrument used to measure and lay down angles in drawing
quadrille (*adj*) marked or ruled with squares for making graphs
ruler straight-edged strip of hard material, used to measure distances and draw straight lines
slide rule instrument consisting of ruler and slide, each graduated with similar logarithmic scales used for calculations
Venn diagram diagram that uses overlapping circles to show relationship between sets

CHEMISTRY

Branches and Disciplines

alchemy medieval chemistry and speculative philosophy that attempted to transmute base metals into gold and to discover cures for disease
analytical chemistry branch of chemistry dealing with the qualitative and quantitative determination of the chemical composition of substances
astrochemistry study of chemical composition of universe beyond Earth
biochemistry study of chemical characteristics and processes occurring in living organisms or systems
chemical engineering industrial applications of chemistry
chemistry science dealing with the composition, structure, properties, and reactions of substances
chemosurgery chemical removal of diseased or unwanted tissue
chemotherapy use of chemical agents to treat and control disease, esp. cancer
chemurgy division of applied chemistry dealing with industrial utilization of organic materials, esp. farm products
crystallography study of crystal form and structure
cytochemistry study of the chemistry of cell

constituents, esp. by staining
electrochemistry study of the interaction of electric current, ions, atoms, and molecules
geochemistry study of chemical composition of Earth's crust, interior, and atmosphere
inorganic chemistry branch of chemistry dealing with compounds not containing carbon and certain simple carbon compounds
kinetics study of the rates of chemical reactions
magnetochemistry study of magnetic properties of compounds
microchemistry branch of chemistry dealing with microscopic and submicroscopic quantities
neurochemistry study of chemical composition and behavior of the nervous system
nuclear chemistry branch of chemistry dealing with radioactive materials; radiochemistry
organic chemistry branch of chemistry dealing with carbon-containing compounds, excepting certain simple carbon compounds
petrochemistry division of applied chemistry dealing with petroleum and natural gas products
physical chemistry study of effect of chemical structure on physical properties
piezochemistry study of effects of high pressure on chemical reactions
polymer chemistry study of structure and synthesis of polymer molecules
radiochemistry nuclear chemistry
spectroscopy investigation of matter by generation and study of spectra of light or radiation
stereochemistry study of structure of molecules and effects of molecular structure on chemical properties
stoichiometry study of quantitative relationships of elements in combination
thermochemistry study of relationship of heat to chemical change
zymurgy branch of applied chemistry dealing with fermentation

Substances, Particles, and Atomic Architecture

acceptor atom that receives pair of electrons from another atom to form covalent bond
acid substance that produces hydrogen ions (H+) in water solution, acts as proton donor, or acts as electron-pair acceptor
alcohol organic compound containing hydroxyl group (-OH)
alkali base that dissolves in water to give hydroxyl ions; soluble substance with pH over 7.0 that can neutralize acids
alkane series series of saturated hydrocarbons, including methane and ethane
allotrope one of two or more different molecular forms of an element in same physical state, with differences in physical and chemical properties
alloy combination of two or more metals or metal and nonmetal
anion negatively charged ion
atom smallest subdivision of an element that displays properties of that element and remains undivided in chemical reactions except for limited loss or exchange of electrons
atomic orbital region around atomic nucleus in which an electron may be found
atomic shell grouping of electrons in one or more atomic orbitals, grouped by average distance from nucleus
base substance that produces hydroxide ions (OH-) in water solution, acts as proton acceptor, or acts as electron-pair donor
benzene ring structural unit in molecules of aromatic organic compounds, based on ring of six carbon atoms with one hydrogen atom attached to each
bond force holding atoms together in molecule or crystal
buffer substance that minimizes changes in pH of a solution by neutralizing added amounts of acid or base
carbon nonmetallic element found in all organic compounds; diamond and graphite are its two main allotropes
catalyst substance that changes reaction rate without being consumed or affected itself
cation positively charged ion
chemical element or chemical compound obtained by a chemical process or producing a chemical effect
colloid mixture of fine particles in a continuous medium that do not settle out rapidly and are not readily filtered, being smaller than particles of a suspension but larger than those of a solution
complex compound in which molecules form coordinate bonds with a metal atom or ion
compound substance composed of atoms from two or more elements chemically united in fixed proportions
conductor substance that conducts electricity or heat
covalent bond chemical bond formed by sharing, rather than by transfer, of one or more electrons between atoms
crystal solid in which atoms, ions, or molecules are arranged in a regular, repeating pattern
dehydrating agent substance that absorbs water from other substances; desiccant
desiccant dehydrating agent
dipole molecule with oppositely charged ends; polar molecule
electrolyte liquid that conducts electricity due to presence of ions
electron subatomic particle of very low mass carrying single, negative electrical charge
element one of a class of substances composed of atoms having the same number of protons in each nucleus and incapable of being separated into simpler substances by chemical means; currently 107 such substances are listed on periodic table of elements
energy level definite, fixed energy that a molecule, atom, electron, or nucleus can possess
ester compound produced by reaction between an acid and an alcohol with the elimination of a water molecule

fluid material that flows; liquid or gas
free radical any neutral, usu. highly reactive fragment of a molecule with an unpaired valence electron
fuel any material used to produce energy, including combustible substances usu. derived from organic hydrocarbons or materials from which atomic energy can be liberated in a reactor
functional group group of atoms responsible for characteristic reactions of a compound
gas state of matter characterized by the nearly unrestricted, random motion of molecules that are far apart in relation to their diameters
ground state lowest stable energy level of a system
halogen any of the electronegative elements fluorine, chlorine, iodine, bromine, and astatine, that form binary salts by direct union with metals and comprise the group next to noble gases in periodic table
heterogeneous mixture combination of substances in which components remain physically separate and retain their individual chemical properties
homogeneous mixture combination of substances in which composition and concentrations of components are uniform throughout, the atoms or molecules of each substance being interspersed
hydrate substance formed by combining a compound with water
hydrocarbon organic compound containing only hydrogen and carbon
hydrogen bond exceptionally strong dipole-dipole attraction between hydrogen and a highly electronegative element such as oxygen or nitrogen
hydroxide chemical compound containing hydroxyl group
hydroxyl (*adj*) containing the negatively charged OH group
ideal gas hypothetical gas in which molecules are viewed as occupying no space, exerting no remote forces on each other, and whose collisions are completely elastic
indicator substance used to show the presence of a substance or ion by its color
inert gas noble gas
inhibitor catalyst used to slow or stop a reaction
intermolecular force force acting between molecules
intramolecular force force acting between atoms in the same molecule
ion charged particle formed by loss or addition of electrons in neutral atom or molecule
ionic bond strong electrostatic attraction holding ions of opposite charge together in molecule or crystal, often formed by transfer of electrons
ion pair cation and anion held together by ionic bond; smallest division of an ionic compound
isomer any of two or more compounds with the same molecular formulas but different structures
isomorph any of two or more substances that have the same crystal structure
isotope any of two or more forms of an element with same atomic number but different atomic mass
ligand ion or molecule that donates a pair of electrons during formation of a complex
liquid state of matter characterized by particles in proximity greater than that of a gas but less than that of a solid, restricting their random motions to vibrations around moving points
matter anything that occupies space and possesses mass
metal any of a class of elements that typically lose electrons in chemical reactions, conduct heat and electricity well, and form cations or coordinate covalent bonds
metallic bond electrostatic attraction holding atoms together in metal or alloy, with their valence electrons able to move almost freely
metalloid element with properties of both metals and nonmetals
mineral any naturally occurring, homogeneous substance having definite chemical composition and usu. crystalline structure
mixture aggregate of two or more substances in which each substance retains its identity and can be separated by physical means such as distillation or crystallization
molecular orbital region of molecule in which an electron, under the influence of two or more nuclei, can be found
molecule two or more atoms held together in a definite arrangement by electrical forces; smallest subdivision of a compound
monomer molecule that can join with others to form a polymer
multiple bond covalent bond in which two atoms share two or three electron pairs
neighbor atom to which another atom is bonded
neutron particle that occurs in all atomic nuclei except normal hydrogen, with neutral electrical charge and mass of about 1 amu
noble gas any of the class of stable gases, such as helium and neon, that do not easily react chemically due to electron-full outer atomic shells; inert gas
nonelectrolyte substance that does not conduct electricity when dissolved in water or another polar solvent
nonmetal any of a class of elements that typically gain electrons in chemical reactions, conduct heat and electricity poorly, and form anions or covalent bonds in compounds
nonorganic compound any compound not containing carbon
nucleus small, dense, positively charged central core of an atom, constituting a tiny fraction of the atom's volume but almost all of its mass, composed primarily of protons and neutrons
orbital atomic orbital, or molecular orbital
organic compound any compound containing carbon
oxide any compound in which oxygen is bonded to one or more electropositive atoms
oxidizing agent any substance that tends to gain electrons, oxidizing other substances while itself being reduced

particle any minute, distinguishable subdivision of matter
phase homogeneous part of a heterogeneous system that is separated by some distinguishable boundary, such as the solid, liquid, and gaseous phases of a system
physical state one of three states in which matter can exist: solid, liquid, and gas
plasma highly ionized gas, often at high temperature, in which free electrons and positive ions are present in approximately equal numbers
plastic any of various materials, generally made from synthetic resins, that can be shaped by applying heat or pressure and then hardened
polar molecule dipole
polymer large molecule made up of smaller monomers repeated many times
precipitate solid produced by reaction occurring in a solution
product new substance formed by chemical reaction
promoter substance added to catalyst to increase its activity
proton particle that occurs in all atomic nuclei, with a single positive charge and mass of about 1 amu
quantum minimum amount by which certain properties of a system, such as energy or angular momentum, can change
radical group of atoms, either in a compound or existing alone
reactant any substance that undergoes chemical change in a reaction
reagent any substance used to detect, measure, or examine another substance, or to transform it by causing a reaction
reducing agent substance that tends to donate electrons, reducing other substances while itself being oxidized
resin any of various semisolid, organic polymers formed synthetically or occurring naturally in plant secretions
salt compound formed by the positive ion of a base and the negative ion of an acid
solid state of matter characterized by particles in such close proximity that their random motions are restricted to vibration about fixed points
solute solid or gas dissolved in a liquid; substance present in lesser amount in a solution of two liquids; substance dissolved in a solvent
solution homogeneous mixture of two or more substances
solvent component of a solution that is present in the greatest amount or that undergoes no change of state; substance in which a solute is dissolved to form a solution
spectator ion ion present in a solution, but not taking part in a reaction
strong acid acid that dissociates completely in an aqueous solution
strong base base that dissociates completely in an aqueous solution
substance matter that has definite composition and distinct properties
superconductor substance that exhibits no measurable electrical resistance at low temperatures
suspension mixture in which relatively large particles are scattered throughout a continuous medium and can be filtered out or will settle out if left standing
synthetic (*adj*) man-made, not occurring in nature; (*n*) such a substance
valence electrons electrons in outermost atomic orbitals of an atom that take part in forming bonds with other atoms to form molecules
van der Waals' forces weak attractive forces between neutral atoms and molecules, including dipole-dipole, dipole-induced dipole, and dispersion forces; weak forces
weak acid acid that is only partially dissociated in an aqueous solution
weak base base that is only partially dissociated in an aqueous solution
weak forces van der Waals' forces

Elements

actinium Ac; atomic number 89, atomic weight 227
aluminum Al; atomic number 13, atomic weight 27
americium Am; atomic number 95, atomic weight 243
antimony Sb; atomic number 51, atomic weight 122
argon Ar or A; atomic number 18, atomic weight 40
arsenic As; atomic number 33, atomic weight 75
astatine At; atomic number 85, atomic weight 210
barium Ba; atomic number 56, atomic weight 137
berkelium Bk; atomic number 97, atomic weight 247
beryllium Be; atomic number 4, atomic weight 9
bismuth Bi; atomic number 83, atomic weight 209
boron B; atomic number 5, atomic weight 11
bromine Br; atomic number 35, atomic weight 80
cadmium Cd; atomic number 48, atomic weight 112
calcium Ca; atomic number 20, atomic weight 40
californium Cf; atomic number 98, atomic weight 249
carbon C; atomic number 6, atomic weight 12
cerium Ce; atomic number 58, atomic weight 140
cesium Cs; atomic number 55, atomic weight 133
chlorine Cl; atomic number 17, atomic weight 35
chromium Cr; atomic number 24, atomic weight 52
cobalt Co; atomic number 27, atomic weight 59
columbium niobium
copper Cu; atomic number 29, atomic weight 64
curium Cm; atomic number 96, atomic weight 247
dysprosium Dy; atomic number 66, atomic weight 163
einsteinium Es or E; atomic number 99, atomic weight 254
erbium Er; atomic number 68, atomic weight 167
europium Eu; atomic number 63, atomic weight 152
fermium Fm; atomic number 100, atomic weight 253
fluorine F; atomic number 9, atomic weight 19
francium Fr; atomic number 87, atomic weight 223

gadolinium Gd; atomic number 64, atomic weight 157
gallium Ga; atomic number 31, atomic weight 70
germanium Ge; atomic number 32, atomic weight 73
gold Au; atomic number 79, atomic weight 197
hafnium Hf; atomic number 72, atomic weight 178
hahnium Ha; atomic number 105, atomic weight 262; unnilpentium
helium He; atomic number 2, atomic weight 4
holmium Ho; atomic number 67, atomic weight 165
hydrogen H; atomic number 1, atomic weight 1
indium In; atomic number 49, atomic weight 115
iodine I; atomic number 53, atomic weight 127
iridium Ir; atomic number 77, atomic weight 192
iron Fe; atomic number 26, atomic weight 56
krypton Kr; atomic number 36, atomic weight 84
lanthanum La; atomic number 57, atomic weight 139
lawrencium Lw; atomic number 103, atomic weight 257
lead Pb; atomic number 82, atomic weight 207
lithium Li; atomic number 3, atomic weight 7
lutetium Lu; atomic number 71, atomic weight 175
magnesium Mg; atomic number 12, atomic weight 24
manganese Mn; atomic number 25, atomic weight 55
mendelevium Md or Mv; atomic number 101, atomic weight 256
mercury Hg; atomic number 80, atomic weight 201
molybdenum Mo; atomic number 42, atomic weight 96
neodymium Nd; atomic number 60, atomic weight 144
neon Ne; atomic number 10, atomic weight 20
neptunium Np; atomic number 93, atomic weight 237
nickel Ni; atomic number 28, atomic weight 59
niobium Nb; atomic number 41, atomic weight 93; formerly columbium
nitrogen N; atomic number 7, atomic weight 14
nobelium No; atomic number 102, atomic weight 254
osmium Os; atomic number 76, atomic weight 190
oxygen O; atomic number 8, atomic weight 16
palladium Pd; atomic number 46, atomic weight 106
phosphorus P; atomic number 15, atomic weight 31
platinum Pt; atomic number 78, atomic weight 195
plutonium Pu; atomic number 94, atomic weight 242
polonium Po; atomic number 84, atomic weight 210
potassium K; atomic number 19, atomic weight 39
praseodymium Pr; atomic number 59, atomic weight 141
promethium Pm; atomic number 61, atomic weight 147
protactinium Pa; atomic number 91, atomic weight 231
radium Ra; atomic number 88, atomic weight 226
radon Rn; atomic number 86, atomic weight 222
rhenium Re; atomic number 75, atomic weight 186
rhodium Rh; atomic number 45, atomic weight 103
rubidium Rb; atomic number 37, atomic weight 85
ruthenium Ru; atomic number 44, atomic weight 101
rutherfordium Rf; atomic number 104, atomic weight 261; unnilquadium
samarium Sm; atomic number 62, atomic weight 150
scandium Sc; atomic number 21, atomic weight 45
selenium Se; atomic number 34, atomic weight 79
silicon Si; atomic number 14, atomic weight 28
silver Ag; atomic number 47, atomic weight 108
sodium Na; atomic number 11, atomic weight 23
strontium Sr; atomic number 38, atomic weight 88
sulfur S; atomic number 16, atomic weight 32
tantalum Ta; atomic number 73, atomic weight 181
technetium Tc; atomic number 43, atomic weight 99
tellurium Te; atomic number 52, atomic weight 128
terbium Tb; atomic number 65, atomic weight 159
thallium Tl; atomic number 81, atomic weight 204
thorium Th; atomic number 90, atomic weight 232
thulium Tm; atomic number 69, atomic weight 169
tin Sn; atomic number 50, atomic weight 119
titanium Ti; atomic number 22, atomic weight 48
tungsten wolfram
unnilhexium provisional name for transuranic element with atomic number 106 and atomic weight 259
unnilpentium hahnium
unnilquadium rutherfordium
unnilseptium provisional name for transuranic element with atomic number 107 and atomic weight 262
uranium U; atomic number 92, atomic weight 238
vanadium V; atomic number 23, atomic weight 51
wolfram W; atomic number 74, atomic weight 184; formerly tungsten
xenon Xe; atomic number 54, atomic weight 131
ytterbium Yb; atomic number 70, atomic weight 173
yttrium Y; atomic number 39, atomic weight 89
zinc Zn; atomic number 30, atomic weight 65
zirconium Zr; atomic number 40, atomic weight 91

Physical Properties and Changes

absorbance measure of electromagnetic radiation absorbed by a substance, applied to total radiation or part of spectrum
absorption assimilation of one substance into another

adiabatic (*adj*) designating process in which no energy is transferred between a system and its surroundings
adsorption attachment of one substance to the surface of another
amorphous (*adj*) describing a solid without crystalline structure
Brownian motion random motion of colloidal particles due to bombardment of the particles by molecules of the surrounding medium
capillary attraction tendency of a liquid to rise in a narrow tube or move through absorbent material, due to greater adhesion of the liquid to the solid than the internal adhesion of the liquid itself
capillary repulsion tendency of a liquid to pull away from a solid surface, due to greater internal cohesion of the liquid than the adhesion of the liquid to a solid surface
cohesion physical force by which molecules of a substance are held together
concentration amount of solute per unit of solvent in a solution
condensation change from vapor phase to liquid phase
conductivity ability of a substance to transmit electricity or heat
crystallization formation of crystals or assumption of crystalline structure
density mass per unit of volume
diagonal relationship similarities observed among elements in the periodic table
diffusion mixture of one substance with another throughout a given volume as a result of random molecular motion
ductility ability of a substance to be drawn into a fine wire
effusion passage of gas molecules through a small opening
electron affinity attraction of an atom for an electron, expressed as the energy needed to restore neutrality by removing an electron from the atom's anion
electronegative (*adj*) having the ability to attract electrons in a molecule and form negative ions; nonmetallic
electropositive (*adj*) tending to migrate to the negative pole in electrolysis; basic, as an element or group
endothermic (*adj*) absorbing heat energy
energy capacity to do work, which diminishes in a system when work is done by an amount equal to work so done
enthalpy change measure of heat gained or lost by a system when it undergoes a chemical reaction or physical change at constant pressure
entropy thermodynamic quantity describing amount of disorder or randomness in system
equilibrium state in which forces acting on a system are balanced
evaporation change from liquid to gas at temperature below boiling point of liquid, occurring at surface of liquid as molecules with higher kinetic energies escape into their gas phase
excited state any of the energy levels of an atom, molecule, or other physical system that has higher energy than the lowest energy level
exothermic (*adj*) releasing heat energy
extensive properties additive properties such as mass or length that depend on the quantity of matter under consideration
ferromagnetic (*adj*) designating a metal strongly capable of modifying a magnetic field, and in which magnetization persists after removal of an applied field
fission nuclear reaction in which an atomic nucleus splits into fragments, usu. two nuclei of comparable size
fluorescence emission of light that does not persist significantly after the exciting cause is removed
fusion change from solid to liquid; nuclear reaction in which two or more smaller nuclei combine into one larger nucleus
hydration solution in which the solvent is water
immiscible (*adj*) designating two liquids that will not dissolve in each other
incandescence emission of light by a substance as a result of raising it to a high temperature
insoluble (*adj*) incapable of being dissolved in specific solvent
intensive properties nonadditive properties, such as temperature, that are independent of the quantity of matter present
ionization potential minimum energy required to remove an electron from the ground state in a specific atom
isobaric (*adj*) occurring at constant pressure
isoelectronic (*adj*) possessing same number of valence electrons
isomerism existence of chemical compounds with the same molecular formulas but different structures
isomorphism existence of two or more substances having the same crystalline structure
isothermic (*adj*) occurring at constant temperature
kinetic energy energy associated with motion
liquefaction change from gas phase to liquid phase
luminescence emission of light by a substance for any reason other than an increase in its temperature
malleability ability of a substance to be shaped or hammered into thin sheets
mass quantity of matter in an object, measured by its resistance to a change in its motion
miscible (*adj*) designating two liquids that are mutually soluble in all proportions
neutral (*adj*) having neither positive nor negative electric charge
optical activity ability of certain substances to rotate the plane of polarized light passed through the substance or a solution containing it
osmosis net movement of solvent molecules through a semipermeable membrane separating two solutions, the direction of movement tending to equalize concentrations of the solutions
phosphorescence emission of light that persists

significantly after the exciting cause is removed
physical property any trait that can be measured without changing the composition or identity of a substance, such as color, melting point, boiling point, density, or solubility
polar (*adj*) describing a covalent bond in which one atom has a stronger electron attraction than the other, or a molecule with oppositely charged ends
polarization separation of positive and negative charges
potential energy energy of an object due to its position in a force field
pressure force per unit area
radioactivity spontaneous disintegration of atomic nuclei accompanied by emission of alpha or beta particles or gamma radiation
solidification change from liquid phase to solid phase
solubility maximum amount of solute that will dissolve in a specific quantity of solvent at specific temperature
specific heat capacity thermal energy needed to raise temperature of one gram of specific substance one degree Celsius
sublimation process in which a substance changes state without becoming a liquid, usu. from solid to gas but also from gas to solid
superconductivity absence of electrical resistance in a substance at low temperature
supercooling cooling of a liquid below its freezing point without a change of state or solidification
surface tension property of a liquid that makes its surface behave like elastic skin due to unbalanced, molecular cohesive forces at or near surface
temperature property of a body or region of space that determines direction of net flow of heat with neighboring objects or regions
vapor equilibrium state in which evaporation and condensation take place at same rate
vaporization change from liquid phase to gas phase
viscosity resistance of a fluid to flow
volatility tendency of a substance to evaporate at normal temperatures and pressures
weight force that gravity exerts on an object

Chemical Properties and Reactions

acid-base reaction acid and base mixed together yielding water and salt
acidic (*adj*) describing a solution with pH less than 7
activation energy energy required to start a chemical reaction
addition reaction reaction in which a small molecule is added to the multiple bonds of an organic compound
amphoteric (*adj*) capable of acting as an acid or base
anhydrous (*adj*) having no water of crystallization
aqueous (*adj*) describing a solution in water
atomization decomposition into composite atoms
basic (*adj*) describing a solution with pH greater than 7
bioluminescence emission of light produced by a living organism
breakdown decomposition into composite elements or molecules
catalysis modification of the rate of a reaction by addition of an agent that does not undergo chemical change
chain reaction self-sustaining series of chemical reactions, as the products of one step initiate a subsequent step
chemical property manner and quality of substance's interaction with another substance in a reaction substance
chemiluminescence emission of light resulting from chemical reaction
combustion rapid oxidation accompanied by production of heat and light
common ion effect shift in ionic equilibrium upon addition of ion that takes part in the equilibrium
corrosion chemical or electrochemical deterioration of metal
covalence number of electron pairs an atom can share with its neighboring atom
decomposition breakdown of a substance into two or more simpler substances
diagonal relationship similarities observed between certain elements in the periodic table and elements appearing diagonally below and to their right
dissociation breakdown of molecule or other group of atoms into smaller groups of atoms or ions
double decomposition metathesis
dynamic equilibrium equilibrium in which both a reaction and its reverse are occurring at rates that are exactly balanced
electrolysis redox reaction produced by passing electric current through an electrolyte
endothermic (*adj*) absorbing heat energy
end point point at which an indicator changes color in a titration, showing that stoichiometric amounts of the reactants have been added; equivalence point
equilibrium state in which forces acting on a system are balanced
equivalence point end point
equivalent (*adj*) having the same capacity to combine or react chemically
exothermic (*adj*) releasing heat energy
free energy chemical potential energy of a substance or system, used to indicate condition under which reaction will occur
half reaction oxidation or reduction reaction only
hydrated (*adj*) formed by combination of water and another substance in definite molecular ratio
hydrolysis solvolysis in which the solvent is water
hydrophilic (*adj*) attracted to and interacting with water
hydrophobic (*adj*) not attracted to or interacting with water

hygroscopic (*adj*) capable of absorbing water from air
metathesis reaction involving an exchange of radicals; double decomposition
neutralization reaction between an acid and a base that produces water and a salt
oxidation reaction involving the loss of electrons or an increase of the oxidation number in a compound
oxidation number number equal to valence of an element or radical
precipitation reaction in which small, solid particles form in a liquid
reactivity tendency of a substance to interact chemically with other substances
redox reaction reaction involving transfer of electrons from one substance to another; simultaneous reduction and oxidation reactions
reduction reaction involving the gain of electrons or a decrease of the oxidation number in a compound
solvolysis reaction between a compound and its solvent
spontaneous (*adj*) occurring without outside influence
stability resistance of a substance to decomposition or disintegration
substitution reaction in which one atom or molecule is replaced by another atom or molecule
synthesis formation of a compound from two or more simpler compounds
valence measure of capacity of an element or radical to combine with another element or radical to form molecules

Constants, Theories, and Values

absolute zero lowest temperature theoretically attainable, at which substances will have minimal atomic and molecular kinetic energy; base of 0 degrees on Kelvin scale, equal to -273.2 degrees C or -459.7 degrees F
atomic theory theory of the structure, properties, and behavior of atoms
Avogadro's law equal volumes of different gases at the same temperature and pressure contain equal numbers of molecules
Avogadro's number number of molecules in a mole, approximately 6.023×10^{23}
boiling point temperature at which the vapor pressure of a liquid equals the pressure of a gas above the liquid
Boyle's law at constant temperature, the volume of a gas is inversely proportional to its pressure
Charles' law at constant pressure, the volume of a gas varies directly with its absolute temperature; Gay-Lussac's law
critical pressure pressure needed to liquefy a gas at its critical temperature
critical temperature temperature above which no amount of pressure will liquefy a gas
Curie point temperature at which magnetic properties of a substance change from ferromagnetic to paramagnetic
Dalton's law total pressure of a mixture of gases is sum of the partial pressures of its component gases
de Broglie's hypothesis theory asserting that material particles have wavelike characteristics that can give rise to interference effects
equilibrium constant ratio of the equilibrium concentrations of products to reactants, each raised to the power of its stoichiometric coefficient, the value of this ratio being constant for any reaction
equivalent weight measure of the combining power of a substance; mass of a substance that can combine with or displace one gram of hydrogen in a chemical reaction
exclusion principle Pauli exclusion principle
first law of thermodynamics energy can be neither created nor destroyed, merely converted from one form to another; law of conservation of energy
freezing point temperature at which liquid changes to solid
Gay-Lussac's law Charles' law
Graham's law rates at which gases diffuse are inversely proportional to the square roots of their densities
heat of combustion energy liberated by the combustion of one mole of a substance in excess oxygen
heat of formation energy liberated or absorbed when one mole of a compound is formed from its elements
heat of fusion energy absorbed in changing one mole of a substance from its solid to liquid state at the substance's melting temperature
heat of reaction energy liberated or absorbed by the complete reaction of molar amounts of reactants
heat of solution energy liberated or absorbed in dissolving one mole of a substance in a large volume of solvent
heat of sublimation energy absorbed in changing one mole of a solid to a gas without intervening phase as a liquid
heat of vaporization energy absorbed in changing one mole of a substance from its liquid to gaseous state at the substance's boiling temperature
Henry's law amount of a gas that will dissolve in a specific amount of liquid varies directly with the partial pressure of the gas
Hess's law enthalpy change of a reaction is equal to the sum of the enthalpy changes of individual steps of the reaction
heterogeneous equilibrium equilibrium between reactants and products that are in different phases
homogeneous equilibrium equilibrium between reactants and products in the same phase
Hund's rule the most stable arrangement of electrons in orbitals is that with the greatest number of parallel spins
ideal gas equation product of a gas's pressure and volume equals the product of its number of

moles, the universal gas constant, and Kelvin temperature

ionization constant equilibrium constant for ionization of a substance

Joule-Thomson effect cooling achieved when a gas expands through a small opening into a region of lower pressure

k rate constant, used in rate equation

kinetic theory theory explaining physical properties of matter in terms of the motion of its particles

law of conservation of energy first law of thermodynamics

law of conservation of mass and energy total amount of mass and energy in the universe is constant

law of conservation of matter in all changes, matter can be neither created nor destroyed; in a chemical reaction, the mass of the products equals the mass of the reactants

law of definite proportions elements composing a compound are always present in the same proportions by mass

law of multiple proportion for two elements that can combine to form more than one compound, the ratio by mass of one element to a given mass of the second is a small whole number

Le Châtelier principle when stress is placed on a system in equilibrium, the system's equilibrium will shift to offset the effect of the stress

melting point temperature at which a solid changes to a liquid

molal (*adj*) denoting a property of weight expressed per mole of a substance

molal boiling point constant value characteristic of a solvent, equal to the rise in the boiling point of one kilogram of the solvent when one mole of solute is added

molal freezing point constant value characteristic of a solvent, equal to the drop in the freezing point of one kilogram of the solvent when one mole of solute is added

molar (*adj*) denoting a property of volume expressed per mole of a substance

molecular orbital theory model of molecular structure, based on the formation of molecular orbitals from corresponding atomic orbitals

octet rule bonded atoms tend to be surrounded by eight valence electrons, except hydrogen, which has two valence electrons

Pauli exclusion principle no two electrons in a system can carry the same four quantum numbers

pH value on a logarithmic scale from zero to fourteen, used to express the acidity or alkalinity of a solution, with pH of seven being neutral

photoelectric effect emission of electrons from a substance when energized by exposure to electromagnetic radiation

Planck's constant h; fundamental constant of quantum theory, equal to the ratio of the energy of a quantum of radiation to its frequency, or 6.63×10^{-34} joule-seconds

quantum minimum amount by which certain properties of a system can change

quantum number one of a set of four numbers used to describe energy levels of an electron in an atom, the numbers representing orbital size, shape, orientation, and electron spin

quantum theory theory according to which energy is emitted in quanta, each with an energy proportional to the frequency of the radiation

R universal gas constant, used in the ideal gas equation

Raoult's law for dilute solutions and certain others, the partial pressure of the solvent is proportional to its mole fraction

rate constant k; the constant in a reaction's rate equation

rate equation expression for the rate of a chemical reaction in terms of concentrations, the form of which depends on the reaction mechanism

reaction mechanism step-by-step description of the interaction of atoms, ions, and molecules in a reaction

reaction rate rate of disappearance of reactant or appearance of product

second law of thermodynamics entropy or disorder of a closed system increases spontaneously and never decreases; in a reversible reaction, entropy remains unchanged

specific (*adj*) denoting a property of volume expressed per unit mass of a substance

standard atmospheric pressure average barometric pressure at sea level, equal to 760 mm of mercury or 101,325 pascal

standard state set of reference conditions for thermodynamic measurements, with temperature equal to 298.15 K, pressure equal to 101,325 pascal, and concentration equal to 1 mole

standard temperature and pressure STP; set of reference conditions for dealing with gases, with temperature equal to 273.15 K and pressure equal to 101,325 pascal

STP standard temperature and pressure

third law of thermodynamics temperature of a system cannot be reduced to absolute zero in a finite number of operations

universal gas constant constant value in ideal gas equation, equal to 8.31 joules per Kevin-moles

vapor pressure pressure generated by vapor in equilibrium with its liquid or solid phase

Tools, Tests, Units, and Scales

ampere A; SI unit of electrical current, equal to one coulomb of charge per second

amu atomic mass unit

anode positive electrode; electrode at which oxidation occurs in a cell

atmosphere unit of pressure equal to that exerted by a column of mercury 760 mm high, equal to 101,325 pascal, based on average atmospheric pressure at sea level

atomic mass mass of atom in atomic mass units, usu. referring to weighted average mass of naturally-occurring mixture of isotopes; atomic weight

atomic mass unit amu; unit of mass, based on 12 as mass of most common isotope of carbon, used to express mass of atomic and subatomic particles
atomic number number of protons in nucleus of each atom of an element
atomic weight atomic mass
barometer manometer that measures atmospheric pressure
beaker wide-topped, cylindrical glass container used in a laboratory
bell jar bell-shaped covering used to protect delicate instruments or maintain controlled environment in experiments
Brix scale graduated scale, used on hydrometer, that measures percentage by weight of sugar in aqueous sugar solutions
Buchner funnel funnel used with filter paper and suction device to separate solids from a liquid
Bunsen burner small gas burner for heating substances
burette glass tube with graduated volume markings and stopcock, used to deliver specific volumes of liquid accurately
calorie amount of heat necessary to raise the temperature of one gram of water from 14.5 to 15.5 degrees C, equal to 4.187 joules
calorimeter device for measuring change of enthalpy
candela SI unit of luminous intensity, based on monochromatic radiation of frequency 540 x 10^{12} hertz
capillary tube thin tube in which liquid rises by capillary action
cathode negative electrode; electrode at which reduction occurs in a cell
cathode ray beam of electrons emitted by cathode in gas discharge tube
Celsius C; temperature scale based on 0 degrees as freezing point and 100 degrees as boiling point of water at 1 atmosphere of pressure; formerly Centigrade
Centigrade former name for 100 point Celsius scale
centrifuge device with spinning chamber, used to separate substances of different densities by forcing those substances outward from center of rotation
chemical equation symbolic, shorthand representation of a chemical reaction, describing the nature and proportions of its reactants and products
chemical formula molecular formula
chromatography any of various techniques used for analyzing or separating a sample mixture of gases, liquids, or dissolved substances, based on the differential competition for molecules of the sample between a mobile phase sample and a stationary phase sample
coefficient number placed before a formula in a balanced chemical equation to indicate the relative amount of the substance involved in the reaction
colorimeter instrument used to determine the concentration of a solution by comparing it with the color of standard solutions
coulomb SI unit of electrical charge, equal to the charge transferred by a current of one ampere in one second
crucible container in which materials may be heated to high temperatures
desiccator drying chamber, esp. one that uses chemicals to absorb water or vapor
distillation process of evaporation and condensation, used to separate liquid mixture and purify liquids
electrophoresis technique for analysis and separation of colloids, based on differential migration of particles in an electric field
empirical formula expression showing simplest ratio between elements in compound
Erlenmeyer flask flat-bottomed, conical laboratory flask
evaporating dish flat dish, or watch glass, that allows liquids to evaporate
exponential notation scientific notation
Fahrenheit F; temperature scale based on 32 degrees as freezing point and 212 degrees as boiling point of water at one atmosphere of pressure
filtration process of separating solid particles from a liquid or gas by passing the mixture through a porous material
flask narrow-topped, wide-bottomed glass container used in laboratory
formula mass sum of atomic masses of atoms in a molecule, calculated from its molecular formula
fractional distillation method of separating a mixture of liquids, based on differences in their boiling points
fractionation separation of a mixture into its components, esp. by distillation
fuel cell cell in which chemical energy of a fuel is converted directly into electrical energy
funnel hollow cone with open tube extending from smaller end, used to catch and direct downward flow of a liquid
g symbol used in chemical equations to indicate that a substance is in its gaseous state
galvanometer device used to detect and measure small electric currents
glove box enclosed chamber with protective gloves sealed into its side, enabling someone to handle contents of box without incurring injury or causing contamination
graduated cylinder parallel-sided, closed-bottomed glass column with volume markings on its side, used for measuring
gravimetric analysis quantitative analysis involving measurements of weight
group any vertical column of the periodic table, containing elements with the same outer shell structure and hence similar properties
hydrometer floating device used to determine the specific gravity of a liquid
indicator any substance, such as litmus paper, used to show the presence of a substance or ion by its color

joule SI unit of energy, equal to the force of one newton acting through one meter, or 10^7 ergs

K symbol for Kelvin temperature scale

Kelvin K; temperature scale based on 0 degrees as absolute zero with units equal to Celsius scale, in which K &equal; degrees C + 273.16

l symbol used in chemical equations to indicate that a substance is in its liquid state

Leyden jar glass jar lined inside and outside with tin foil, used to store electric charge

liter SI unit of volume, equal to one cubic decimeter or 1.056 quarts

litmus paper paper impregnated with acid-base indicator litmus, used to determine pH by color

manometer device for measuring gas pressure

mass number sum of protons and neutrons in an atomic nucleus, esp. of an isotope

mass spectroscopy technique for determining the masses of atoms or radicals by measuring their deflections in electric or magnetic fields

molality unit of concentration by weight equal to number of moles of solute per kilogram of solvent

molarity unit of concentration by volume equal to number of moles of solute per liter of solution

molar mass mass of one mole of a substance; in grams, numerically equal to formula mass in atomic mass units

mole molecular weight of a substance expressed in grams, equal to its formula mass in atomic mass units, or 6.022×10^{23} molecules of a substance

molecular formula expression showing types and numbers of atoms present in a compound, using symbols for component elements and numerals for number of atoms of each element per molecule, such as H_2O for water; chemical formula

mortar round dish used with pestle for crushing and grinding solids

newton N; SI unit of force required to accelerate a one-kilogram mass at a rate of one meter per second

nuclear magnetic resonance spectroscopy technique for analyzing samples and determining structures based on the absorption of electromagnetic radiation by nuclei in a strong, external magnetic field

oxidation number number of electrons over which an element gains full or partial control when combined in a compound, a negative value indicating loss of control

pascal Pa; SI unit of pressure equal to one newton per square meter

percent yield actual yield of a chemical reaction, expressed as a percentage of the theoretical yield

period any horizontal row of the periodic table, containing elements with the same number of shells but increasing numbers of electrons in their outer shells as read from left to right

periodic table arrangement of the elements, in order of increasing atomic number, into horizontal periods determined by electron configurations, so that elements with the same outer shell structure and similar properties appear in vertical groups; currently consists of 107 elements

pestle club-shaped hand tool used with mortar for crushing and grinding solids

pipette narrow glass tube with volume markings, used to deliver specific small volumes of liquid accurately

qualitative analysis determination of the nature of a substance or the compounds present in a mixture

quantitative analysis determination of the proportions of substances contained in a mixture

rate equation expression relating the rate of a reaction to concentrations of the reactants

recrystallization purification of a solid by separating the crystals formed upon cooling a saturated solution

resonance structures two or more formulas for a single molecule that cannot be described by a single structure

retort enclosed vessel or chamber with long tube open at one end, in which substances are distilled, sublimed, or decomposed by heat

s symbol used in chemical equations to indicate that a substance is in its solid state

scientific notation method of expressing very large and small numbers as powers of ten; exponential notation

SI units Système Internationale units; internationally accepted system of units of scientific measurement, expressed in modified metric system based on meter, kilogram, second, ampere, kelvin, mole, and candela

standard solution solution whose concentration is known with precision, used for comparison with solutions of unknown concentration

still apparatus used in distillation, consisting of chamber in which vaporization is carried out and cooling device in which vapor is condensed

structural formula expression that shows how atoms are bonded to each other in a molecule

Syracuse watch glass round, flat-bottomed, shallow dish for staining and culturing

test tube plain or lipped tube of thin glass, closed at one end

thermochemical equation balanced chemical equation in which the value of change in enthalpy for molar amounts is specified

thermometer device for measuring temperature, esp. by the height of a column of mercury or by a thermocouple

titration technique for determining concentration of a reagent by adding measured amounts of another reagent of known concentration until their reaction is complete

tracer isotope used to trace path of a specific substance through a chemical or physiological system

ultraviolet spectroscopy optical technique used to determine electronic structure of atoms and molecules

valency measure of combining power of an atom or radical, equal to the number of hydrogen atoms that the atom could combine with or displace in a compound

voltaic cell cell in which reactions between electrodes and electrolytes produce potential difference between the electrodes

watt W; SI unit of power equal to one joule of work per second
Woulff bottle glass container with two or more necks, used for passing a gas through a liquid
X-ray crystallography technique for determining crystal structure, based on diffraction of X-rays projected through a crystal

MEDICINE

Disciplines and Specialties
Practitioners, Patients, and Facilities
Business and Practice of Medicine
Procedures
Tools and Equipment
Pharmacology
Dressings and Supports
Prefixes and Suffixes

Disciplines and Specialties

acupressure manual application of pressure at points where acupuncture needles would be inserted
acupuncture Chinese practice that involves insertion of needles into body at specific points along meridians to treat disease and reduce pain
aerospace medicine prevention and treatment of disorders related to flight in Earth's atmosphere
allergy study and treatment of allergies
allopathy treatment by remedies that produce effects opposite those of disease, as in general practice of contemporary medicine
anesthesiology specialty concerned with pharmacological, physiological, and clinical bases of anesthesia, including resuscitation of patients and relief of pain
audiology evaluation and treatment of hearing disorder
Ayurveda ancient Hindu medicine that uses herbs, purgatives, and rubbing oils
bacteriology study of bacteria
behavioral medicine study and prevention of disorders that combines behavior modification with medical techniques
biomedicine medical studies derived from biological studies
cardiology study and treatment of the heart and its diseases
chiropody podiatry
chiropractic treatment method using manipulation of muscular and skeletal system, esp. the spine
clinical medicine direct observation and treatment of patients, as opposed to laboratory study
community medicine assessing health needs and trends of regional populations rather than individuals
cosmetic surgery plastic surgery performed to improve appearance only
dental surgery oral surgery
dentistry care and treatment of diseases of teeth, gums, and jaw
dermatology study and treatment of skin disorders
ear, nose, and throat ENT; treatment of diseases of these parts; otorhinolaryngology
embryology study of embryo development
emergency medicine specialization in rapid treatment of patients in crisis
endocrinology study of endocrine glands and hormones
endodontics dental specialty concerned with diseases of soft dental pulp in center of tooth
ENT ear, nose, and throat
environmental medicine study of effect of environment on human organism
epidemiology study of causes and control of epidemics
etiology science of causes and origins of diseases
family medicine general practice for entire family
folk medicine traditional, often regional, medical practices employed by common people, esp. use of herbs
forensic pathology investigation of causes of death or injury in unexpected circumstances, esp. crimes
gastroenterology treatment of digestive system disorders
general medicine prevention and treatment of wide range of diseases and disorders that appear in broad spectrum of population
geriatrics care of aged and treatment of disorders of old age
gerontology study of aging process and problems of the aged
gynecology study and treatment of diseases of women and girls, esp. in reproductive system
hematology study of blood and blood diseases
histology microscopic study of tissue structure
holistic medicine system based on treatment of whole body rather than of parts
homeopathy treatment of disease through small doses of drugs that normally produce symptoms of that disease
hygiene science of preserving health by cleanliness, disinfection
immunology study of phenomena connected with body's defense mechanisms
industrial medicine treatment of injuries and diseases sustained in workplace
internal medicine diagnosis and nonsurgical treatment of diseases
laboratory medicine experimentation and research on diseases without direct treatment of patients
medical science general study of medicine
medicine science and practice of diagnosing, treating, curing, and preventing disease, relieving pain, and improving health
mental hygiene treatment of psychological and emotional disorders
naturopathy treatment of disease that employs

no surgery or synthetic drugs
neonatology study and treatment of children up to two months of age
nephrology study and treatment of kidney diseases
neurology study of functional processes and diseases of central nervous system and brain
neurosurgery surgical treatment of brain and spinal cord
nuclear medicine diagnosis and therapy using radioisotopes and radionuclides
nutrition study of proper diet to promote health
ob-gyn combined specialization in **ob**stetrics and **gyn**ecology
obstetrics care of women during pregnancy, childbirth, and first six weeks after birth; tocology
occupational medicine treatment of diseases associated with particular types of work
oncology study and treatment of tumors
ophthalmology study and treatment of eye diseases and disorders
optometry testing of eyes in order to prescribe corrective lenses
oral surgery surgery performed on mouth, esp. extraction of teeth and root canal; dental surgery
orthodontics treatment and correction of malocclusion of teeth
orthopedics correction of deformities or functional impairments of the skeletal system and associated structures
orthopedic surgery surgical correction of skeletal abnormalities or injury
osteopathy treatment of disease by manipulation and massage of musculoskeletal system
otolaryngology treatment of ear and throat diseases
otorhinolaryngology treatment of ear, nose, and throat diseases
parasitology study of parasites and treatment of diseases caused by parasites
pathology study of nature and causes of diseases, esp. through laboratory examination
pediatrics treatment and care of children
pedodontics care and treatment of children's teeth
perinatology practice concerned with phase surrounding birth, esp. obstetric care
periodontics branch of dentistry concerned with bones and tissue that support teeth
pharmacology study and practice of chemistry, preparation, use, and effect of drugs
physical medicine treatment of diseases and injuries by exercise, massage, heat, and light, but not drugs
plastic surgery reconstruction of damaged or deformed body parts after accident or burn or to improve appearance; reconstructive surgery
podiatry care of feet, esp. treatment of foot diseases; chiropody
preventive medicine study and practice of disease prevention, esp. through immunization and public health programs
proctology treatment of disorders of rectum, anus, and colon
prosthodontics dental surgery that replaces missing teeth with artificial teeth to maintain oral function
psychiatry diagnosis, management, and prevention of mental disorders, as by medication
psychoanalysis school of psychology and method of treating mental disorders based on teachings of Sigmund Freud
psychology study of behavior and related mental processes and disorders
psychopharmacology study of behavioral effects of drugs and medication
public health study and maintenance of health of an entire community
radiology use of X-rays and radioactive substances in diagnosis and treatment of disease and injury
reconstructive surgery plastic surgery
rehabilitation medicine use of massage, exercise, and physical therapy to restore normal health and function or to prevent worsening of condition
rheumatology diagnosis and treatment of joint, muscle, tendon, and ligament diseases and injuries
serology study of blood serum and its ability to protect body from disease
space medicine prevention and treatment of diseases associated with flight outside Earth's atmosphere
sports medicine treatment of injuries incurred in athletic activities
surgery treatment of diseases, injuries, and deformities by operation, manipulation of internal organs, removal of body parts, and sometimes by replacement of parts
symptomatology study of the aggregate symptoms of a disease
teratology study of developmental malformations and their causes
tocology obstetrics
toxicology study of poisons, esp. their effects and antidotes
tropical medicine treatment of tropical diseases
urology study and treatment of diseases of urinary tract
veterinary medicine science of prevention and treatment of diseases and injuries of animals, esp. domestic animals
virology study of viruses

Practitioners, Patients, and Facilities

Practitioners person trained in and practicing medicine or specialty; Christian Science healer
allergist, allopath, anesthesiologist, anesthetist, apothecary, attendant, attending physician
board certified physician
candy striper, charge nurse, chief resident, chiropractor, clinician, coroner
dental hygienist, dental technician, dentist, dietician, doctor, Dr., druggist
emergency medical service, emergency medical technician, EMS, EMT

faith healer, family doctor, family practitioner
general practitioner, G.P.
healer, homeopath
intern, internist
laboratory technician, licensed practical nurse, LPN
M.D., medic, medical examiner, medicine man, midwife
naturopathic doctor, nurse, nurse practitioner, nurse's aide, nutritionist
oculist, ophthalmologist, optician, optometrist, orderly, orthodontist, orthopedic surgeon, osteopath
paramedic, pharmacist, pharmacologist, physical therapist, physician, physiotherapist, practical nurse, practitioner, private duty nurse, provider, psychiatrist, psychotherapist
radiographer, radiologist, radiotherapist, registered nurse, resident, R.N.
school nurse, scrub nurse, shaman, specialist, Surgeon General
therapist
witch doctor
X-ray technician

Patients person examined by doctor for diagnosis or treatment of disease or injury.

ambulatory
bleeder, blood donor
cadaver, case, convalescent, corpse
donor
handicapped
inpatient, invalid
outpatient
patient
terminal

Facilities

asylum
backup hospital, base hospital, blood bank
CDC, Centers for Disease Control, children's hospital, clinic, community hospital, convalescent hospital, cooperative hospital, county hospital
day hospital, dispensary
emergency medical service, emergency room, EMS, ER, examining room
field hospital
health facility, hospice, hospital
ICU, infirmary, intensive care unit, isolation ward
maternity, maternity hospital, mental hospital
nursing home
operating room, OR
private hospital
recovery room, rest home
sick bay, sick bed, sick room, surgicenter
teaching hospital, trauma center
VA hospital, veteran's hospital
waiting room, ward

Business and Practice of Medicine

ABO system classification of human blood into four major groups, A, B, AB, and O, used in determining compatibility for transfusions
AMA American Medical Association
ambulatory care treatment provided patients not confined to hospital
American Medical Association AMA; professional organization of U.S. physicians
BAC blood alcohol concentration
bedside manner doctor's ability to put patient at ease during examination or treatment
bioethics concern for ethical implications in medical application of biological research
blood alcohol concentration BAC; measurement of amount of alcohol absorbed by body, used to determine intoxication
bloodmobile vehicle equipped and staffed to receive blood from donors
case history compilation of medical information about patient's illness for use in diagnosis and treatment
catastrophic coverage medical insurance that covers lengthy or expensive hospitalization and care
charity patient hospital patient who cannot pay for health care and is without medical insurance
closed panel practice medical practice with patients restricted to one prepayment group, usu. an HMO
code call call to resuscitate dying patient in hospital
cognitive service any medical service which is not a procedure, such as consultation or patient advocacy
coinsurance medical insurance plan in which patients pay portion of cost of treatment, often 20 percent
comprehensive medical insurance coverage that extends to all areas from doctor visits to hospitalization, surgery, medications, therapy, and nursing care
copayment portion of fee paid by patient, not by insurance company, in coinsurance plan
death certificate government document that states cause of person's death, time of death, and demographic information on deceased
DNR do not resuscitate; witnessed order and notation on chart of terminal patient who does not wish to be kept alive by extensive life-support efforts
fixed fee set prospective payment for care
follow-up return visit to health care provider to evaluate progress
for-profit (*adj*) designating any medical care facility or program owned by investors
group insurance health insurance available at special rates to company employees or organization members
group practice association of two or more doctors who share facilities and divide income
HCFA Health Care Financing Administration
health administrator person responsible for

supervising public health programs
Health Care Financing Administration HCFA; U.S. government umbrella organization that oversees Medicare and Medicaid
health insurance insured coverage for medical expenses
health maintenance organization HMO; prepaid group insurance plan that provides comprehensive care to defined portion of public in specific region
Hippocratic oath ethical code of medical profession traditionally sworn to by doctors
HMO health maintenance organization
hospitalization placement of patient into hospital for treatment and care; coverage of hospital stays by health insurance plan; insurance plan that covers only hospital stays
house call visit by doctor to patient's home for examination or treatment
independent practice association IPA; form of PPO in which each doctor receives standard fee per group member per year
IPA independent practice association
living will document instructing physicians and relatives not to prolong one's life artificially under certain circumstances, esp. by naming proxy to discontinue use of life-support systems
major medical medical insurance that covers regular doctor visits as well as hospitalization
malpractice harm caused to patient by negligent or unprofessional care and treatment
malpractice insurance expensive insurance that protects physician in malpractice suit
managed care health care under umbrella plan such as HMO
Medicaid health insurance for poor provided by U.S. government
medical insurance any of various forms of health insurance, including prepaid and group, hospitalization and major medical
Medicare health insurance for people over 65 provided by U.S. government
national health government sponsored, comprehensive health insurance, paid for by taxes
National Institutes of Health NIH; federally funded agencies for medical research
NIH National Institutes of Health
not-for-profit (*adj*) designating health facility or program owned by educational institution, foundation, or other nonprofit group
on-call (*adj*) available for consultation in person or by telephone during off-duty hours
patient advocacy advice and assistance given to patients in order that they may better handle costs and complexity of medical care
PCN primary care network
peer review organization PRO; doctors and hospital administrators who review quality of all admissions and medical practices for Medicare and Medicaid
physician liability medical malpractice
PPO preferred-provider organization
practice professional pursuit of career in medicine
preexisting condition patient condition that predates time insurance plan or HMO was joined
preferred-provider organization PPO; group insurance that covers care performed by specific list of doctors and hospitals
primary care care rendered by first physician contacted by patient before referral to specialist
primary care network PCN; variation on HMO in which each patient has private doctor as case manager who refers the patient to specialists or hospitals
private insurance health insurance program open to all individuals, usu. provided by profit-making company
private practice operation of medical practice that charges fee for services
PRO peer review organization
procedure any medical service that requires patient to be cut, jabbed, injected, or tested
Public Health Service U.S. federal agency that administers disease control, drug abuse, health, fitness, research, and public information programs
referral sending of patient to another physician, usu. a specialist
reimbursement amount of medical costs paid by insurance after patient has initially paid entire bill
rounds regular circuit taken by doctor among hospitalized patients
secondary care treatment by specialist or hospital staff after referral from primary care doctor making diagnosis
shift work hours, esp. at hospital or clinic
socialized medicine system that provides complete medical care to all persons in nation through public funds and has some control over physicians' decisions and actions
tertiary care treatment at special hospitals or clinics or by specialist doctors for disorders that cannot be treated by secondary care physicians and hospitals
WHO World Health Organization
World Health Organization WHO; United Nations agency for improvement of physical and mental health of world's people

Procedures

ablation removal of tissue, usu. by cutting
abortion expulsion or removal of fetus before it is capable of independent survival, usu. prior to twelfth week of pregnancy
abscission removal of tissue by cutting
AIDS test evaluation of blood sample for presence of antibodies to HIV virus; ELISA
alimentotherapy treatment of disease through diet and nutrition
amniocentesis analysis of amniotic fluid extracted by needle puncture from uterus early in second trimester of pregnancy, usu. to detect fetal abnormalities or sex
amputation surgical removal of limb or part of limb
analgesia any procedure that induces absence of pain in fully conscious patient
anesthesia introduction of local or general anesthetic into body, usu. preparatory to surgery

angiocardiography X-ray examination of heart chamber after radiopaque medium has been introduced into blood
angiography X-ray examination of blood vessels that contain radiopaque medium
Apgar score clinical measurement used to assess cardiopulmonary function in baby immediately after birth
appendectomy surgical removal of vermiform appendix
arthroscopy insertion of fiber optic device into space, esp. joint cavity, for diagnosis or treatment
artificial insemination mechanical introduction of semen into vagina
artificial respiration maintaining airflow in and out of lungs of patient who has stopped breathing, by mouth-to-mouth resuscitation or respirator
aspiration withdrawal of fluid by suction
auscultation act of listening through stethoscope to movement of liquid or gas inside body
autograft tissue or organ that is grafted into new position on body of individual from which it was removed
autopsy examination of corpse to determine cause of death
aversion therapy conditioning with unpleasant stimulus to reduce undesirable behavior
balloon angioplasty repair of damaged blood vessel by insertion of tiny inflatable balloon on catheter
ballottement technique that examines fluid-filled body part to detect floating object, esp. during pregnancy
barium meal ingestion of radiopaque barium sulfate as contrast medium for X-rays of digestive system
biopsy removal of small piece of tissue for microscopic examination and diagnosis, esp. for cancer
blood count determination of number of different blood cells in volume of blood
blood group classification of person's blood based on presence or absence of certain antigens in red blood cells
bloodletting phlebotomy
blood pressure measurement of pressure exerted by blood against walls of main arteries
blood typing determination of blood type and sorting of blood samples by type
bone graft transplant of piece of bone from one part of body to another, where it becomes permanently affixed
bridge dental cementation of immovable metal prosthesis as base for dentures in gap left by missing teeth
bypass surgical procedure in which artificial channel or channels allow blood to pass around arterial blockage
cap (*vb*) place artificial crown of gold or porcelain on top of damaged tooth
cardiopulmonary resuscitation CPR; revival of patient whose respiration and heartbeat have ceased by compressing sternum and blowing air into mouth
catharsis cleansing or purging of bowels by administration of laxative
CAT scan computerized axial tomography; soft tissue radiology in which cross-sectional images of body are generated by computer from series of X-ray scans of area examined
cautery destruction of tissue by direct application of heated instrument, esp. to remove small growth
Cesarean section surgical delivery of baby through abdominal wall; C-section
checkup regular basic physical examination by primary care practitioner
chemotherapy use of drugs and other chemicals to treat disease, esp. cancer
chest X-ray radiographic examination of chest
cholecystectomy surgical removal of gallbladder
circumcision surgical removal of foreskin of penis, usu. shortly after birth
cobalt therapy radiation cancer treatment using cobalt-60 radioisotope
colonic irrigation flushing of large bowel by repeated enemas
colostomy surgical drainage of large intestine in which part of colon is brought through abdominal wall
computerized axial tomography CAT scan
cordotomy surgical severing of nerve fibers of spinal cord to relieve chronic pain
corneal transplant replacement of diseased portions of cornea by clear corneal tissue grafted from donor; keratoplasty
coronary artery bypass bypass operation involving arteries of heart
cosmetic surgery plastic surgery, usu. of face, to improve appearance
CPR cardiopulmonary resuscitation
crown replacement of top of damaged tooth by porcelain, plastic, or gold crown
cryosurgery surgical use of extreme cold to destroy unwanted tissue, such as cataracts
C-section Cesarean section
culture examination made to identify population of microorganisms grown in laboratory from specimen taken from patient's body
decompression surgical reduction of pressure on body part or organ, usu. by incision
dermabrasion surgical scraping off of top layers of epidermis, usu. to repair scars
desensitization process of decreasing subject's allergy to certain substance by exposure to gradually increasing dosages of the offending allergen
detoxification removal of toxic substances, esp. addictive drugs, from body and neutralization of their effects
diagnosis evaluation of signs and symptoms to determine nature of disease or condition
dialysis use of semipermeable membrane to sift different-size particles from liquid mixture in artificial kidney
diathermy heating body part by exposure to high frequency current between two electrodes on skin, used to increase blood flow to relieve deep pain
dilation and curettage D and C; scraping tis-

sues of uterus walls by insertion of instrument through widened cervix for diagnosis or abortion
dilation and evacuation D and E; removal of contents of uterus by dilation and curettage
dosimetry calculation of required amount of radiation for cancer treatment
DPT immunization against diphtheria, pertussis, and tetanus, administered esp. to children
ECG electrocardiogram
echocardiography use of ultrasound waves to examine action of heart
echography use of ultrasound waves to display and analyze body's internal structure
EEG electroencephalogram
EKG electrocardiogram
electrocardiogram EKG; interpretation of tracing of electrical activity produced by contractions of heart recorded by electrocardiograph
electrocautery destruction of unwanted tissue, such as warts or polyps, by electrically heated needle
electroencephalogram EEG; interpretation of tracing of electrical activity in various parts of brain recorded by electroencephalograph
electrotherapy passing electric currents through tissue to treat disease or stimulate nerves and muscles
ELISA enzyme-linked immunosorbent assay; test used chiefly to safeguard blood supplies from contamination by virus that causes AIDS
enema infusion of fluid into rectum by tube passed through anus, usu. to evacuate and flush large intestine
enterostomy surgically constructed outlet from intestines to surface of abdominal wall
episiotomy incision of perineum to enlarge vaginal opening during childbirth
euthanasia act of causing or allowing painless death to end suffering of terminal patient, usu. when treatment is withheld or by active intervention; mercy killing
excision surgical removal of tissue or organ from body
exploratory surgery surgical investigation of patient to obtain correct diagnosis
extraction removal of broken or diseased tooth by dental surgery
face-lift cosmetic surgery in which facial folds are stretched taut
filling substance placed by dentist in hole drilled in carious tooth
first aid simple emergency procedures used to help patient until doctor arrives
gastrectomy surgical removal of part or all of stomach
gene therapy treatment of genetic disease by substitution of healthy genes for affected ones
graft transplantation of skin, bone, or other tissue from its original site to repair defect elsewhere, taken either from same individual or from donor
Heimlich maneuver emergency application of sudden sharp pressure to abdomen below rib cage to dislodge object stuck in trachea
hemodialysis removal of toxins from blood by dialysis
hepatectomy surgical removal of all or part of liver
hospitalization admission to hospital for treatment
hydrotherapy treatment of arthritis or partial paralysis by exercise and physiotherapy in swimming pool
hygiene sanitary practices used to maintain health and prevent disease
hyperbaric oxygenation therapy exposure to high pressure oxygen to treat carbon monoxide poisoning, severe burns, breathing difficulties, or gas gangrene
hypnosis artificially induced trance in which subject is susceptible to suggestion, used in psychotherapy and drug treatment
hysterectomy surgical removal of uterus
immune therapy administration of sera, vaccines, and other immune products to treat or prevent infectious diseases
immunization vaccination with treated antigens to stimulate antibody production that results in immunity
incision surgical cut into soft tissue with scalpel
injection introduction of drugs into body by hypodermic syringe and needle; shot
inoculation vaccination; introduction of vaccine into body
intravenous (*adj*) IV; designating blood transfusion, nutritional solution, or drugs fed directly into vein of patient
intubation insertion of tube into body part or cavity for diagnosis or treatment
irradiation use of electromagnetic radiation therapy
IV intravenous
keratoplasty corneal transplant
laparoscopy abdominal examination by illuminated tube inserted through small incision in abdominal wall
laparotomy surgical opening of abdominal wall
laser surgery use of very thin beams of focused light to operate on small areas without damage to neighboring tissue
laser therapy treatment with laser light, often to remove tattoos or birthmarks
lavage washing out of body cavity, such as colon or stomach
leeching use of sucking worm for bloodletting, no longer in practice
liposuction plastic surgery technique in which body fat is sucked out of tissues beneath epidermis
lobotomy cutting into skull to sever nerve fibers connecting thalamus with frontal lobes of brain, formerly used to treat mental disorders
magnetic resonance imaging MRI; use of high-powered magnetic field to scan body interior
major surgery surgical operation of significant scope, esp. on internal organ or system, usu. with general anesthesia
mammography X-ray or infrared photographic examination of breast
mastectomy surgical removal of all or part of breast

mercy killing euthanasia
microsurgery delicate operation performed under binocular microscope with miniature instruments
minor surgery brief or simple surgical operation on tissue or body part, usu. with local anesthesia
MRI magnetic resonance imaging
nephrectomy surgical removal of a kidney
noninvasive surgery surgical operation that does not require incision through soft tissue
open-heart surgery repair of exposed heart or coronary arteries while blood is circulated mechanically
operation any surgical procedure
oral surgery dental procedure that involves extraction of tooth, root canal, or other surgery of mouth
organ transplant surgical replacement of defective organ, such as heart or kidney, by implantation of healthy organ taken from donor
orthodontics dental procedures to correct malocclusion of teeth
palpation examination of body part by feeling and probing with hands and fingers
Pap test test that uses Papanicolaou stain to detect cancer of cervix or uterus by taking tissue specimen and studying it microscopically
patch test application of various allergens to scratches made on skin to determine patient's allergies
percussion striking or tapping of body part, either with fingers or plessor, during examination, thus producing sounds which are studied for diagnostic purposes
periodontics dental treatment of gum disease
PET scan positron emission tomography; measurement by tomography of emissions from injected radioactive molecules to evaluate tissue, esp. in brain
phlebotomy surgical opening of vein to remove blood; bloodletting
physical examination general medical examination of body
physical therapy exercise, massage, heat, and light treatments; physiotherapy
physiotherapy physical therapy
plastic surgery reconstruction and repair of damaged or defective external body parts
polishing mechanical cleaning and shining of tooth enamel
positron emission tomography PET scan
postmortem autopsy
pregnancy test any of various methods for determining presence of embryo or fetus in uterus, esp. by detecting the hormone human chorionic gonadotropin in urine
pressure point technique stoppage of bleeding by manual application of pressure to key arteries
prognosis forecast of likely course of disease
prophylaxis prevention of disease
prosthesis design, manufacture, and implantation of artificial body parts to replace missing or defective body parts
prosthodontics replacement of missing teeth and other oral fixtures with artificial parts
radial keratotomy incision into cornea of eye
radiation therapy treatment of disease, esp. cancer, with beams of X-rays, beta rays, or gamma rays, emitted by machine or radioactive isotopes, that penetrate body
reconstructive surgery surgical rebuilding of damaged or defective external body part
regimen systematic combination of treatments used over time
rehabilitation restoration of normal functions after disease or injury
relief treatment to eliminate symptoms and relieve distress
replacement therapy rapid replacement of lost substance, such as transfusion of blood and plasma into shock patient
resection surgical removal of portion of body part
rhinoplasty reparative or cosmetic surgery on nose
root canal dental surgery to repair infected base of tooth in gum
scan viewing inside of body without surgical incision, esp. by X-ray or CAT scan
scratch test test for allergies in which allergens are introduced into epidermis through scratches on it
section act of surgical cutting
sex change operation reconstructive creation of sex organs of opposite sex
shock therapy use of electric currents to stimulate nerves and muscles
shot injection
skin graft cutting piece of healthy skin from body and using it to replace damaged skin elsewhere
sonogram tracing that represents sound waves
stat (*adv*) short for Latin statim; designating procedure to be performed immediately
stress test comparison of heart's performance at maximum stress, at rest, and as it recovers
surgery treatment by operation, usu. by incision and removal or repair of internal part
test electronic, laboratory, or manual examination of body part or function for diagnosis or prognosis
therapy any procedure or combination of procedures that heal, induce health, relieve symptoms, or cure disease
tomography tracing produced by X-rays or ultrasound waves of image at specific depth inside body
tonsillectomy surgical removal of one or both palatine tonsils lying at base of tongue above pharynx
tracheotomy incision through skin of neck into trachea, or windpipe, to assist breathing
traction use of force that pulls on body parts, esp. to correct alignment of broken bone fragments or in physical therapy on spinal cord
transfusion injection of blood or blood products into circulation of patient
transplant organ transplant
treatment systematic course of medical care prescribed for specific condition
triage allocation of emergency treatment by priority of need

tubal ligation female sterilization procedure in which fallopian tubes are tied or surgically cut
tuberculin test injection beneath skin of protein extracted from culture of tubercle bacilli, which forms inflammation if patient has been exposed to tuberculosis
type and cross-match determine blood type and check its compatibility with blood of potential donor
ultrasonic therapy exposure of patient to concentrated sound at inaudibly high frequency over 20,000 Hz to treat deep tissue disorders
urinalysis physical, chemical, and microscopic tests to detect abnormalities in urine
vaccination injection of antigenic material to produce immunity to disease; inoculation
vasectomy male sterilization procedure in which vas deferens that carries sperm from testes to urethra is surgically cut
ventilation passage of air into and out of respiratory tract
workup evaluation of patient, esp. while hospitalized or in preparation for surgery
X-ray penetration of body by short-wavelength electromagnetic radiation to produce images used in diagnosis

Tools and Equipment

armamentarium all equipment used in practice of medicine
arthroscope instrument inserted into joint cavity to inspect contents
artificial heart prosthetic mechanical heart used as alternative to donor-organ transplant
artificial kidney portable dialysis machine
artificial limb man-made arm or leg or section thereof, used to replace limb lost by amputation or injury
artificial lung respirator
aspirator hollow instrument used to withdraw fluid, esp. from cysts or joints
audiometer apparatus that measures ability to hear sounds at different frequencies, used to diagnose deafness
autoclave device used to sterilize instruments by pressurized superheated steam
bedpan shallow receptacle used as toilet by bedridden patient
bitewing radiograph dental X-ray film in frame clamped between teeth
blood pressure cuff sphygmomanometer
braces metal bands attached to teeth to correct malocclusion
bridge mounting base for dentures, either fixed or removable, inserted in gap in teeth
bulb syringe syringe with pressure supplied by squeezing bulb rather than by plunger
catheter tube inserted into narrow opening for removal or introduction of fluids, esp. into urethra to drain urine and empty bladder
clamp surgical instrument used to compress blood vessel or close off end of intestine
clinical thermometer sealed glass tube with bulb ending that contains mercury, calibrated to register body temperatures between 95 and 110 degrees F
curette spoon-shaped instrument used to scrape tissue from body cavities
defibrillator agent or device for arresting cardiac fibrillation
dental floss thin, strong, waxed thread used to clean between teeth and on unexposed surfaces
dentures set of artificial teeth mounted on base that fits onto gums; false teeth
dialysis machine artificial blood filtration machine, used esp. for kidney malfunction
electrocardiograph machine used to record electrocardiogram
endoscope slender, tubular instrument used for viewing and examining interior part of body
false teeth dentures
fluoroscope fluorescent screen on which X-rays may be viewed, eliminating need to develop photographs
forceps any of various instruments used by surgeons and dentists to grasp and pull objects
gurney stretcher
heart-lung machine pumping apparatus that can temporarily assume functions of heart and lungs while heart surgery is performed
heating pad electric heating element encased in cloth pad, used to apply heat to external body parts
heat lamp focused heat source placed near body part, esp. in physical therapy
hemostat device used to stop or prevent hemorrhaging
hospital bed adjustable bed with criblike sides and optional positions for comfort and safety of patient
hyperbaric chamber sealed chamber in which high pressure is used to treat decompression sickness and infant heart defects and to retard bacterial growth
hypodermic needle and syringe used for subcutaneous injections
inhalator device used to administer medicinal vapors; inspirator
inspirator inhalator
iron lung respirator
Ishihara test sheet containing dots in various sizes and colors, used to detect color blindness
isolation chamber dark, silent container, free of stimuli, in which patient lies, used in physical therapy and psychotherapy
lancet wide, two-edged, pointed surgical knife
life-support system equipment that sustains life or substitutes for body functions in incapacitated patients
ligature nylon, wire, or catgut tied around structure to close or secure it to impede bleeding
manometer U-shaped tube with graduated scale, used to measure gas pressure, esp. sphygmomanometer
microscope combination of lenses used to greatly magnify image of examined object
needle slender pointed instrument used to make surgical sutures; hollow needle attached to syringe for injections

oral thermometer clinical thermometer inserted into mouth
otoscope apparatus with light source, magnifying lens, and speculum, used to examine eardrum and passage to ear
oxygen mask covering for mouth and nose connected by tube to oxygen supply
oxygen tank enclosed, pressurized container of oxygen that supplies mask or tent
oxygen tent transparent plastic enclosure around bed of patient into which oxygen is passed
pacemaker battery and insulated electrode used to stimulate normal heart rate
percussion hammer plessor
plessor small hammer used to check nervous reflexes; percussion hammer; plexor
plexor plessor
probe thin, flexible, metal rod with blunt end, used to explore cavities and wounds
rectal thermometer clinical thermometer inserted into anus
respirator device used to maintain respiration by inflation of lungs with mixture of oxygen and air; airtight container that encloses paralyzed patient except for head, in which pressure is increased and decreased; iron lung
resuscitator artificial respiration device that forces oxygen into lungs
retainer dental instrument used to correct minor malocclusion or maintain alignment of teeth
scalpel small, pointed surgical knife with convex blade edge, used to cut tissue
scope flexible fiber optic instrument for inspection of interior of body
scrub suit gown, often green, worn in surgery by doctors, surgical gown
Seeing Eye dog *Trademark.* dog trained to guide blind person in walking about
sigmoidoscope rigid or flexible tube for visual examination of rectum and sigmoid colon
sound rodlike surgical instrument with curved end, used to explore or dilate body structures
specimen bottle small glass container for collection of urine and other liquids
speculum instrument inserted into cavity, esp. vagina or ear, to hold it open during examination
sphygmomanometer device that measures blood pressure when sensor cuff connected to manometer and wrapped around upper arm is inflated and then deflated
spirometer device used to measure volume of air inhaled or exhaled
stethoscope diaphragm connected to earpieces, used to listen to sounds within body, esp. heart and lungs
stitches suture
straitjacket coat with arms that bind behind body, used to restrain violent persons
stretcher bedlike device on wheels, used to transport sick or injured person; gurney
surgical gloves sheer, hygienic plastic gloves worn by surgeons
surgical gown sterile cotton gown worn over clothes by surgeon and operating room personnel; scrub suit
surgical instruments various sterilized tools, such as forceps or scalpels, used in surgery
surgical mask cotton mask worn over mouth and nose by surgeons
surgical needle suture needle
surgical sponge soft, sterile material that absorbs blood and other body liquids during surgery
surgical staple device used to close surgical opening without sutures
suture sterile thread, often of silk or catgut, used to stitch closed a wound or surgical opening; stitches
suture needle needle used to make suture; surgical needle
syringe piston in tube attached to hollow needle, used to give injections or remove material, esp. blood, from body
thermometer clinical thermometer
tongue depressor flat piece of wood used to push tongue aside in throat examination
tracer often radioactive substance introduced into body whose circulation can be followed to assess body function
walker lightweight, four-legged framework on which old or disabled persons can lean while walking
wheelchair chair mounted on wheels, sometimes equipped with motor, for use by disabled, ill, injured, or elderly persons who cannot walk
whirlpool bath bath with swirling jets of warm water used in hydrotherapy
X-ray machine device that emits radiation and takes photographs for radiographic diagnosis

Pharmacology

abortifacient drug that induces abortion or miscarriage
acetaminophen mild analgesic without anticoagulant activity
acetylsalicylic acid active ingredient in aspirin
addiction dependence
addictive drug that causes physical or psychological dependence with habitual consumption
adrenalin epinephrine
amobarbital moderate hypnotic barbiturate
amoxicillin semisynthetic penicillin taken orally as broad-spectrum antibiotic
amphetamine central nervous system stimulant that alleviates fatigue and produces feeling of mental alertness
ampicillin broad-spectrum semisynthetic antibiotic
ampule sealed glass or plastic container that holds one dose of medicine
anabolic steroid steroid
analgesic drug that reduces or eliminates pain; painkiller
anesthetic agent that diminishes or abolishes sensation and can produce unconsciousness
anodyne substance that soothes or relieves pain
antacid substance that neutralizes acid, esp. intestinal
antagonism nullification of effect of one drug by another

anthelmintic vermifuge
antibiotic substance, derived from microorganism or fungus, that destroys or inhibits growth of another microorganism, used to treat bacterial infections
antibody protein manufactured by lymphocytes that reacts with specific antigen to fight invasion as principal component of human immunity
anticoagulant agent that prevents blood from clotting
anticonvulsant drug used to prevent or stop epileptic seizures
antidepressant drug that alleviates symptoms of depression
antidiuretic substance that inhibits discharge of urine by increasing water retention of kidneys
antidote agent that counteracts effects of poison
antiemetic drug that prevents vomiting
antihistamine drug that counters effects of histamines in body, esp. in allergies
antipruritic agent that relieves itching
antipyretic drug that reduces fever
antispasmodic drug that relieves smooth muscle spasms
antitoxin antibody, usu. obtained from animal, used to combat toxin, esp. from bacteria
antitussive substance that reduces coughing, esp. one that affects activity in the brain's cough center and depresses respiration
antivenin antiserum with antibodies against specific poison, esp. animal venom
aphrodisiac substance that increases sexual arousal
aspirin acetylsalicylic acid in tablet or pill form, used to relieve minor pain, reduce fever and inflammation, and reduce platelet aggregation in blood, available OTC
astringent substance that causes cell shrinkage, used to reduce secretions and slow or stop bleeding
AZT azidothymidine; drug that can eliminate symptoms of AIDS but may have deleterious side effects
bacitracin antibiotic for external use
bactericide substance that kills bacteria, esp. antibiotic or disinfectant
bacteriostat substance that retards growth of bacteria
baking soda sodium bicarbonate
barbiturate barbituric acid derivative that depresses central nervous system activity, induces sleep, and produces tolerance
barium sulfate opaque barium salt used as contrast medium in radiography
benzocaine topical anesthetic applied to skin or mucous membrane
beta blocker drug that decreases heart activity by affecting receptors of sympathetic nervous system
bicarbonate of soda sodium bicarbonate
birth-control pill oral contraceptive
bolus single, large mass of substance, esp. food or intravenous fluid, often injected into blood vessel as contrast medium or radioactive tracer
booster shot secondary inoculation that serves to maintain immunity
broad-spectrum (*adj*) describing a drug that is effective against wide variety of microorganisms
bronchodilator drug that relaxes bronchial muscle to open air passages to lungs
cachet flat capsule used to enclose unpleasant-tasting drug
camphor crystalline substance used in liniments and to treat flatulence
caplet tamper-resistant, solid tablet with capsule-like coating
capsule small, soluble gelatin container for single dose of medication
castor oil unpleasant-tasting, irritant laxative or cathartic
cathartic laxative
catholicon cure-all, panacea
chloramphenicol antibiotic used against various microorganisms
chloroform volatile liquid formerly used as general anesthetic
clove oil oil of clove, used to relieve toothache
cocaine alkaloid derived from coca leaves, used as local anesthetic, that causes dependence when ingested as stimulant
codeine drug derived from morphine, used as analgesic and cough suppressant
cod-liver oil oil rich in vitamins A and D, used for nutritional purposes, esp. for children
collyrium medicated solution used to bathe eyes
condom latex, rubber, plastic, or skin sheath for penis, used as contraceptive or to prevent disease
contraceptive medication or device to prevent conception
contraceptive foam frothy, spermicidal substance inserted in vagina to prevent conception
cortisone natural steroid hormone produced by adrenal cortex, used to treat various diseases
cough syrup cough suppressant in thick, sweetened solution
counterirritant agent that causes irritation when applied to skin in order to relieve more deep-seated pain
cresol strong antiseptic used in general disinfectants, occasionally applied to skin
curative any substance that tends to relieve symptoms and treat disease; sanative
cure medicine or remedy for disease
cure-all universal remedy; panacea
cytotoxin substance that has toxic effect on certain cells, used against some tumors
decongestant substance used to reduce nasal mucus production and swelling
dentifrice toothpaste or toothpowder
dependence physical and/or psychological compulsion to continue taking drug; addiction
depressant drug that lowers nervous or functional activity; sedative
DES diethylstilbestrol
dextran water-soluble polysaccharide used as blood plasma extender in treatment of shock
diaphragm hemispherical rubber disk fitted over cervix as contraceptive
diazepam tranquilizer, muscle-relaxer, and anticonvulsant used esp. to treat epilepsy and relieve tension; Valium

dicoumarin anticoagulant used to reduce and retard blood clots
diethylstilbestrol DES; synthetic compound that acts like estrogen, used in morning-after pill to prevent implantation of fertilized egg, dangerous during pregnancy
digitalis foxglove leaf extract used as heart stimulant
disinfectant cleansing agent that destroys bacteria and other microorganisms, used on surfaces and surgical tools
diuretic agent that promotes excretion of salt and water by kidneys
dose prescribed, measured quantity of drug to be administered at one time
DPT single vaccine that contains antigens for diphtheria, pertussis, and tetanus, administered esp. to children
dressing medicated and/or antiseptic substance applied to soothe and protect external wound
drug substance that affects structure or functional processes of an organism, esp. to prevent or treat diseases or relieve symptoms
electuary medication mixed with honey
elixir substance that contains alcohol or glycerin, used as solution for bitter or nauseating drugs
emetic substance that induces vomiting
ephedrine widely used drug similar to epinephrine
epinephrine hormone secreted by adrenal medulla that stimulates circulation, muscles, and sugar metabolism; adrenalin
erythromycin genetic antibiotic used to treat staphylococci, streptococci, and pneumococci infections
estrogen hormone produced by ovary that stimulates breast and uterine growth, used to treat amenorrhea and menopausal disorders and to inhibit lactation
ether volatile liquid formerly used as anesthetic by inhalation
expectorant drug that increases secretion of less viscous sputum by respiratory system, used in cough mixtures
febrifuge substance that relieves or reduces fever
fertility drug any hormonal substance used to induce ovulation and produce pregnancy
formaldehyde formic acid derivative, used to sterilize and disinfect
gargle antiseptic, often medicated, liquid used to rinse mouth and throat; mouthwash
general anesthetic agent that depresses central nervous system activity to induce unconsciousness, used in surgery
generic basic, nonproprietary form of medication without trade name, usu. priced lower than brand name drug
germicide any agent, such as an antibiotic or antiseptic,that destroys microorganisms
glycerin clear, viscous liquid used externally as emollient or internally as laxative
half-life time required for body to reduce initial peak concentration of drug in blood by one half
hallucinogen drug that produces hallucinations
heroin opiate produced when morphine is treated with acetic acid
hexachlorophene disinfectant used in soaps and skin treatments
hormone substance produced by endocrine gland that travels to another body site where it alters structure or function
hypnotic any sleep-inducing drug; sedative; sleeping pill; soporific
ibuprofen nonaspirin analgesic agent, esp. used to treat inflammation
immunosuppressant drug that reduces resistance to infection and foreign bodies by suppression of immune system, used in organ and tissue transplants
inhalant gas, vapor, or aerosol inhaled for treatment of respiratory conditions
insulin protein hormone secreted by pancreas that regulates blood sugar, injected to treat diabetes
interferon substance produced by infected cells that inhibits specific viral growth
intrauterine device IUD; small plastic contraceptive device inserted into uterus
isoniazid drug used in treatment of tuberculosis
IUD intrauterine device
killed-virus vaccine antigenic material composed of dead organisms, used to stimulate antibodies and create immunity to disease
laxative substance that stimulates bowel evacuation; cathartic; purgative
L-dopa synthetic substance used to control Parkinson's disease
lidocaine local or topical anesthetic, also injected into heart to correct abnormal rhythms, as after myocardial infarction
live-virus vaccine antigenic material composed of weakened organisms, used to stimulate antibodies and create immunity to disease
local anesthetic substance used to numb specific area without inducing loss of consciousness
lozenge medicated tablet with sugar that is dissolved in mouth to soothe throat
major tranquilizer antipsychotic drug such as Thorazine, used to treat serious mental illness
medication substance taken orally, by injection, or applied externally to body to treat disease or injury or relieve symptoms
medicinal (*adj*) having curative or symptom-relieving properties
medicine drug or preparation used for treatment or prevention of disease
megadose dosage many times that normally required or prescribed, esp. of vitamins
meprobamate substance used as tranquilizer for anxiety, tension, and muscle spasm
mercurous chloride powerful antiseptic, poisonous if ingested
methadone powerful, synthetic narcotic used as painkiller or as heroin substitute in detoxification therapy
microbicide substance that kills microorganisms
mineral oil colorless, tasteless petroleum derivative used as laxative
minor tranquilizer drug prescribed to relieve

minor tension and anxiety, such as Valium or Miltown
miracle drug substance supposed to cure all diseases or an incurable disease; panacea; wonder drug
MMR vaccine single vaccine that contains antigens for measles, mumps, and rubella, administered esp. to children
morphine potent narcotic used as analgesic, derived from opium
mouthwash gargle
muscle-relaxer depressant or tranquilizer that acts to relieve tension in muscles
narcotic sleep-inducing and painkilling drug, esp. opiate, usu. addictive
neomycin antibiotic, esp. for infections of eye or skin
nitroglycerin vasodilator used in crisis to prevent or treat angina
OD overdose
opiate derivative of opium that depresses central nervous system, relieves pain, and induces sleep
opium poppy extract that contains morphine and has a narcotic, analgesic effect
OPV oral polio vaccine; Sabin vaccine
oral contraceptive medication that contains synthetic female sex hormones and prevents conception when taken daily; birth-control pill
OTC over the counter; medication available without doctor's prescription
overdose OD; excessive amount of drug taken at one time, causing negative reaction and death in case of powerful hypnotics
painkiller agent that relieves or inhibits pain; analgesic
palliative medicine that relieves symptoms but does not cure disease
panacea cure-all believed to remedy all ailments
paregoric camphorated tincture of opium used to relieve diarrhea, formerly used as painkiller
patent medicine trademarked medication available without prescription
penicillin antibiotic, orig. derived from mold, used to treat bacterial infections
pentobarbital powerful barbiturate hypnotic and anticonvulsant; Nembutal
pharmaceutical drug or medication manufactured and sold by pharmacy
pharmacology study and practice of chemistry, preparation, use, and effect of drugs
pharmacopoeia official, authoritative reference book containing descriptions, formulas, uses, and tests for most drugs and medical preparations
pharmacy preparation and dispensing of drugs; place where this is done
phenacetin mild, nonaddictive painkiller and fever reducer, often combined with aspirin
phenelzine powerful inhibitor used to prevent certain kinds of depression
phenobarbital very slow-acting, barbiturate depressant
physic medicine or remedy, esp. laxative or cathartic
pill small ball or tablet of medicine to be swallowed whole; oral contraceptive
pitocin synthetic hormone administered to pregnant women to induce labor
placebo inactive substance taken by patient who believes that it is an effective drug, which often causes improvement in condition
polio vaccine Salk or Sabin vaccine against poliomyelitis
prednisone synthetic steroid, administered orally, used to treat leukemia and Hodgkin's disease
prescription medication that requires doctor's authorization for purchase and use; slip of paper with this authorization
preventive substance used to prevent disease
procaine synthetic local and spinal anesthetic
progesterone hormone that prepares uterus to receive and develop fertilized egg
prophylactic contraceptive device, esp. condom
psychedelic drug that induces altered consciousness, often hallucinogenic
psychoactive drug that affects central nervous system as depressant, stimulant, or hallucinogen
purgative laxative
purge purgative or cathartic medication
quinine alkaloid drug used to treat malaria
remedy medicine that cures, treats, or relieves symptoms of disease
reserpine derivative of the shrub rauwolfia, used to treat hypertension by acting as sedative, often also producing depressive side effect
reverse tolerance increased sensitivity to certain drugs the more they are taken, as with marijuana
Sabin vaccine polio vaccine that contains attenuated live viruses, administered orally; OPV
Salk vaccine polio vaccine that contains dead viruses, administered by injection
sanative curative
scopolamine belladonna derivative used to induce sleep or as sedative during labor in childbirth
secobarbital substance used as sedative and hypnotic
sedative drug that depresses central nervous system to induce calm or sleep; depressant; hypnotic
senna kind of laxative
sleeping pill drug that sedates or induces drowsiness; hypnotic; soporific
smelling salts preparation, as of ammonia, used as stimulant or restorative
sodium amobarbital sedative and hypnotic, sometimes called truth serum, used to facilitate interrogation
sodium bicarbonate salt of sodium that neutralizes acid, used for mild intestinal disorders; baking soda; bicarbonate of soda
sodium hypochlorite strong disinfectant
soporific hypnotic drug; sleeping pill
spermicidal jelly contraceptive substance that kills spermatozoa
spermicide agent that kills spermatozoa
sterile saline solution solution of 0.9 percent sodium chloride, used to dilute drugs for injection and as plasma substitute
steroid any of large family of chemical compounds including hormones produced by adrenal glands, ovaries, and testes; medication used for

immunosuppression and hormone replacement, often also used in physical therapy and to promote muscle building; anabolic steroid
stimulant substance that stimulates central nervous system, which prevents sleep and increases alertness and energy
streptomycin antibiotic used esp. to treat tuberculosis
sulfadiazine sulfa drug used to treat pneumococcal, streptococcal, and staphylococcal infections
sulfa drug sulfonamide
sulfonamide class of antibiotics, such as sulfadiazine and sulfapyridine, that stop bacterial growth and combat infection; sulfa drug
sympatholytic drug that affects sympathetic nervous system
synergism phenomenon in which each of two or more drugs is more active in combination than when used alone
syrup of ipecac solution prepared with dried root, used as emetic or purgative
tablet small disk, made from compressed powders of one or more drugs, that is swallowed whole
testosterone principal male sex hormone produced by testes, used in replacement therapy and as anabolic steroid
tetanus toxoid tetanus bacteria treated to eliminate toxic qualities, used as antigenic vaccine
tetracycline antibiotic compound effective against wide variety of bacterial infections
thalidomide tranquilizer known to cause birth defects in children born to women who used it during pregnancy
tolbutamide drug that stimulates release of insulin from pancreas, used to treat diabetes
tolerance decreased effectiveness of drug due to prolonged or repeated use, requiring larger dose for same effect
tolnaftate antifungal substance, used topically to treat superficial skin infections
tonic healing, soothing, or invigorating agent
toothpaste paste used to clean teeth, applied with brush; dentifrice
toothpowder powder used to clean teeth, applied with brush; dentifrice
topical (of a drug) applied directly to skin surface, not taken internally
toxin poisonous substance
toxoid vaccine made from poisonous waste products of disease-causing microorganisms
tranquilizer drug that produces calming effect and relieves anxiety and muscle tension without inducing sleep
troche small, medicinal lozenge that soothes mouth and throat
universal antidote mixture of activated charcoal, magnesium oxide, and tannic acid in water, used as antidote to unidentified poisons
vaccine antigenic preparation that stimulates antibodies and confers immunity against specific disease
valerian drug made from root of valerian plant, formerly used as sedative and antispasmodic
vasoconstrictor drug that narrows blood vessels and decreases blood flow, used to raise blood pressure during shock or severe bleeding
vasodilator drug that widens and opens blood vessels and increases blood flow, used to lower blood pressure
vermicide chemical agent that kills parasitic worms in intestine
vermifuge chemical agent used to expel parasites from intestine; anthelmintic
vitamin any of various organic compounds, natural or synthetic, required for normal metabolic functions
warfarin preparation of water-insoluble anticoagulant, used to manage potential or existing blood-clotting disorders; Coumadin
withdrawal cessation of use of drug to which one is addicted; symptoms associated with such withdrawal
wonder drug miracle drug, panacea

Dressings and Supports

Ace bandage *Trademark.* elastic bandage
adhesive tape plastic strips with sticky substance on one side, used to hold bandages in position
alcohol solution of ethyl alcohol used as preservative or antiseptic
ammonia pungent, colorless, gaseous solution, used as counterirritant and smelling salts
antiseptic slightly toxic chemical that destroys bacteria and other microorganisms, used on skin and mucous membrane to cleanse wounds and prevent infection or internally for intestinal and bladder infections
balm fragrant ointment or aromatic oil with medicinal value
bandage absorbent pad or strip of material applied to wound or injury
boric acid white, crystalline, mildly acidic compound used in mild antiseptic solution
brace device used to support weak, injured, or deformed body part
braces metal bands used by orthodontists to correct malocclusion of teeth
calamine lotion topical solution of pink zinc oxide powder used on skin irritations
camphor crystalline substance used in liniments to soothe irritations and relieve pain
carbolic acid phenol
cast rigid case made from bandage soaked in plaster of Paris, used to prevent movement of aligned bone ends in broken limb
compress moistened pad of folded cloth, often medicated, applied with heat, cold, or pressure to soothe body part
cotton ball fluffy clump of cotton for gentle application of medications or antiseptics
cotton swab small, flexible stick of cardboard or plastic with cotton tips, used for application in small or inaccessible places
counterirritant substance that impedes or reduces skin irritation
crutch tall support device with handgrip and padded crosspiece that fits under arm, used as walking aid

demulcent soothing, usu. oily substance used to relieve pain in irritated mucous surfaces
disinfectant cleaning agent that destroys bacteria and other microorganisms, esp. for use on tools and surfaces
dressing protective or healing material applied externally to wound or diseased body part
elastic bandage long strip of stretchable bandage wrapped tightly around injured extremity to hold it in position
emollient medical preparation that soothes and softens external tissue
Epsom salts white, crystalline magnesium salt used as cathartic in dilute solution, esp. bath
eyewash medicinal solution that soothes eyes
gauze thin, open material used in layers for dressing, swab, or bandage
glycerin glycerol
glycerol syrupy liquid prepared by hydrolysis of fats and oils for use as skin lotion; glycerin
hydrogen peroxide colorless liquid used in dilute solution as disinfectant
ice pack rubber or plastic container filled with ice and applied to relieve pain and prevent swelling
iodine nonmetallic chemical element used in tincture as antiseptic
lanolin fatty wool substance used as base for ointments
liniment soothing camphor and alcohol preparation rubbed into skin or applied on surgical dressing
lotion viscous liquid solution used to cleanse, soothe, or heal skin
lubricant greasy substance applied to reduce friction on body surface
menthol white, pungent, waxy alcohol crystal used in medications and emollients
merbromin water-soluble powder that forms red solution in water, used as antiseptic germicide
mercuric chloride poisonous white crystal used as powerful antiseptic or pesticide; mercurous chloride
mercurous chloride mercuric chloride
ointment fatty substance used to soothe or heal skin; salve; unguent
pack folded, moistened, often medicated pad of cotton or cloth applied to body or inserted in cavity
peroxide hydrogen peroxide
petrolatum colorless, greasy hydrocarbon mixture used as ointment base or salve; petroleum jelly
petroleum jelly petrolatum
phenol strong disinfectant used to clean wounds, treat mouth and throat irritations, and as preservative in injections; carbolic acid
plaster pasty medicinal dressing applied to body part on cloth as curative counterirritant
poultice thick, warm paste made from herbs and water, used in folk medicine
prosthesis artificial body part
rubefacient salve or plaster that causes skin to turn red
salve medicinal ointment used to soothe or heal skin irritations, burns, or wounds; ointment; unguent
sanitary napkin cotton pad worn to absorb menstrual discharge
sitz bath soothing bath, esp. with Epsom salts solution
sling loop of cloth that encircles neck, used to support injured arm
splint length of rigid material bandaged to injured limb to prevent movement
sponge soft pad of gauze or cotton used in surgery
support device used to relieve pressure on, or hold position of, injured part
surgical dressing medicated substance used as healing antiseptic during surgery
swab small cotton ball used to clear discharge or apply medicine; cotton swab
tampon plug of absorbent material used to absorb blood or secretions, esp. in vagina for menstrual discharge
tape strip of material, often adhesive, used to hold dressing, compress, or bandage in place
thimerosal water-soluble powder that forms red solution in water, used as antiseptic
tincture alcohol solution of medication
tincture of iodine alcohol solution of iodine used as antiseptic
tourniquet strip of cloth or bandage wrapped tightly around body part, esp. extremity or digit, to control bleeding temporarily through applied pressure
traction splint device that pulls limb to hold it in position, used to set fractured or dislocated bone
unguent fatty substance used to soothe and heal skin; ointment; salve
vapors mentholated salve applied to chest and nose to relieve congestion
witch hazel alcohol solution made with liquid extract from leaves and bark of this shrub, used as lotion
zinc oxide white powder that is active ingredient in calamine lotion and other ointments

Prefixes and Suffixes

Note: *When used before a word beginning with a vowel, most prefixes drop or change the final ""o", ""a", or ""i".*

adeno- gland
-agra seizure of pain
-aholic one having addiction to something
algo- pain
arterio- artery
arthro- joint
bacill- rodlike
bacteri- bacteria
blepharo- eyelid
brady- slow
broncho- windpipe, throat
carcino- cancer
cardio- heart
-cele tumor
cephalo- head
cerebro- brain, esp. cerebrum
chilo- lip
chiro- hand

cholo- bile
chondrio- cartilage
-coccus spherical bacterium
colo- lower intestine
coro- pupil of eye
cortico- cortex
costo- rib
cysto- bladder, cyst
cyto- cell
dacryo- tears
denti- tooth
dermato- skin
dextro- right side
dys- ill, impaired
-ectomy surgical removal
-emia blood condition
encephalo- brain
entero- intestine
erythro- red
febri- fever
fibro- fibrous
gastro- stomach
-genic producing or causing, produced or caused by
geronto- old age
glosso- tongue
-gram record or image made by a device
-graph recording or tracing device
gyneco- woman
hema- blood
hemo- blood
hepato- liver
histo- tissue
hydro- water
hyper- extreme, excessive, beyond
hypno- sleep
hypo- insufficient, below, under
hystero- uterus, womb
-ia name of disease or condition
-iasis disease
-iatrics medical treatment
-iatrist physician or healer
iatro- medicine
-iatry specific area of healing or medical practice
ilio- flank, upper hipbone
immuno- immune
-itis inflammation or abnormal condition
kerato- hornlike
labio- lip
laparo- flank, abdominal wall
laryngo- windpipe, larynx
leuko- white
lipo- fat
litho- stone, calcification
-logy science or body of knowledge
-lysis breaking down, decomposing
masto- breast
melano- black, dark
musculo- muscle
myco- fungus, mold
myelo- marrow, spinal cord
myo- muscle
narco- stupor, drugged state
nephro- kidney
neuro- nerve
-odont having or relating to teeth
odonto- tooth
-odynia pain
-oid resembling or referring to form
-oma tumor
ophthalmo- eye
-opia eye, sight
-opsy medical examination
opto- eye
orchido- testes
ortho- erect, straight, normal
-osis diseased or abnormal condition or state
ossi- bone
osteo- bone
oto- ear
ovi- egg
patho- disease, sickness, suffering
-pathy suffering, disease, or treatment
pedi- foot
pedo- child
pharmaco- drug or medication
pharyngo- pharynx
-phasia speech disorder
phlebo- vein
-phrenia lack, deficiency, disorder
-plasia growth
-plast cell, living substance
-plasty surgical repair or molding formation
pleuro- rib, side of body
pneumo- lung, air
podo- foot
polio- gray matter
procto- anus, rectum
psycho- mind
pulmo- lung
pyelo- pelvis
reni- kidney
-rrhagia rupture, profuse flow or discharge
-rrhaphy suture
-rrhea flow, discharge
-rrhexis rupture
sangui- blood
sarco- flesh
schizo- split
-scope instrument for viewing
-sect cut
sero- serum, blood
somato- body
somni- sleep
stomato- mouth
-stomy surgical operation involving creation of artificial opening
tachy- rapid
thanato- death
thrombo- blood clot, coagulation
-tome cutting instrument
tomo- cut, section
-tomy surgical incision or excision
-tonia muscle or nerve tension
toxico- poison
toxo- poison
tracheo- windpipe, trachea
tricho- hair

-trophic having nutritional requirements
tropho- nourishment
urino- urine
uro- urine
utero- womb, uterus
vaso- vessel
veno- vein
ventro- abdomen
vermi- worm
zymo- fermentation

MEASURES AND WEIGHTS

Systems and Units

angular measure units used to measure angles and sections of circles
apothecaries' measure units of weight used chiefly for dispensing liquid drugs
apothecaries' weight system of weights used chiefly in compounding and dispensing drugs
avoirdupois weight U.S. and British units of weight used for articles other than drugs, gemstones, and precious metals
circular measure units used to measure circles: quadrants, degrees, minutes, and seconds
cubage cubic measure
cubic measure units used to measure volume filled in three dimensions; cubage
dry measure units of capacity used to measure dry commodities
land measure units of linear and square measure, used to measure land
linear measure units used to measure length
liquid measure units of capacity used to measure liquids
mariners' measure units of linear measure used in navigation
measures units of standard systems, used to express dimension, extent, mass, and volume
metrication establishment of metric system as standard system of measurement
metric system decimal system of weights and measures, used in science and in most nations other than the United States, with basic units of meter, gram, and liter
metrology science of weights and measures
square measure units used to measure area covered in two dimensions
surveyors' measure units of linear measure used in surveying
time measure units used to measure the passage of time
troy weight system of weights used for precious metals and gemstones
U.S. units system of weights and measures, used primarily in the United States, with basic units of foot, ounce, and quart
weights units used to measure mass or heaviness
wood measure units of cubic measure used for wood

Measuring Devices

analytical balance precision balance having sensitivity of 0.1 milligram
balance weighing instrument that opposes a known weight to the object being weighed across a lever supported exactly in its middle
bathroom scale small platform scale on which one stands to measure body weight
caliper tool with adjustable, usu. curved jaws on pivot, used to measure thickness or diameter
compass instrument for drawing or measuring circles, consisting of two movable, rigid legs hinged at one end
conversion table tabular arrangement of equivalent values of units of measure of different systems
counterweight weight used to counterbalance an opposing object that is to be weighed
cyclometer instrument that records the revolutions of a wheel to measure distance or speed
extensometer instrument for measuring minute degrees of expansion, contraction, and deformation
folding rule rule made of hinged sections, usu. of light wood, that fold out to increase length; zigzag rule
measure instrument with graduated markings for measuring
measuring cup cup with graduated markings, used to measure dry and liquid volume
measuring spoons set of spoons in graduated sizes, used esp. in cooking
micrometer device for measuring minute distances and angles, esp. in connection with a telescope or microscope
platform scale scale with platform for holding object being weighed
rule rigid strip of material having straight edge marked off with units of measure; ruler
ruler rule
scale balance, platform scale, or other device for measuring weight
sonic depth finder device that uses sonar echolocation to measure underwater depths
tape measure length of flexible material with graduated markings that unreels to measure linear dimension
theodolite surveying instrument having telescopic sight for precise measurement of vertical and horizontal angles
weighbridge large platform scale standing flush

with roadway, used to weigh trucks or livestock
yardstick rule 36 inches in length
zigzag rule folding rule

Measures and Standards of Time

ab urbe condita *Latin.* lit. from the founding of the city; used in dating system based on founding of Rome in 753 B.C.; A.U.C
A.D. anno Domini; *Latin.* lit. in the year of the Lord; used to designate years of Christian era
age measure of one's time alive
alarm clock small clock that sounds alarm at set time to awaken sleeper
a.m. ante meridiem; *Latin.* lit. before noon; morning
analog clock timepiece with hands revolving on face to indicate time
ante meridiem *Latin.* lit. before noon; a.m.
atomic clock extremely accurate timepiece whose operation is based on vibrations of certain atoms
A.U.C ab urbe condita
B.C. before Christ; used to designate years before Christian era
B.C.E before Christian (or Common) era; equivalent of B.C.
bell device sounded on ship every half hour during each four-hour watch or segment of day
calendar system or device for marking time by days, weeks, months, and years
C.E. Christian (or Common) era; equivalent of A.D.
Central time time zone in U.S. Middle West, one hour earlier than Eastern time
century measure of time equal to 100 years
chrono- Greek prefix meaning time
chronograph instrument that measures and records time
chronology science of computing and measuring time and sequentially ordering events
chronometer instrument for measuring time; timepiece
chronoscope instrument for measuring time
clock mechanical timepiece marking passage of minutes, hours, and sometimes seconds
date designation by number of each day of each month
day basic unit of time equal to 24 hours
daylight-saving time time attained by moving timepieces one hour ahead of standard time from spring to fall
decade measure of time equal to 10 years
dial face of clock, watch or sundial showing time of day
digital clock timepiece indicating time by regularly changing display of numerical digits
Eastern time time zone in U.S. Atlantic coast region, three hours later than Pacific time
embolism insertion of time period to regulate calendar, esp. day added for leap year
gnomon raised part of sundial that casts shadow to indicate time
Greenwich mean time worldwide standard time relative to time at meridian running through Greenwich, England
Gregorian calendar corrected Julian calendar incorporating leap year every fourth year
horography art of making timepieces
horologe timepiece, esp. sundial
horology art or science of measuring time and making timepieces
hour unit of time equal to 60 minutes
hourglass necked glass vessel containing sand or mercury, used to measure time, esp. period of one hour
intercalary (*adj*) inserted into calendar, as with leap year's added day
International Date Line imaginary line at 180 degrees longitude, exactly opposite Greenwich meridian, at which one day is added when passing westward across it
Julian calendar standard twelve-month, 365-day calendar introduced in ancient Rome
minute basic unit of time equal to 60 seconds, or 1/60 of an hour
month unit of time equal to 1/12 of a year, usu. 30 or 31 days, except February, which has 28 or 29 days
Mountain time time zone in U.S. Rocky Mountain area, one hour later than Pacific time
o'clock (*adv*) of the clock, used in telling time, as in one o'clock
Pacific time time zone along U.S. western seaboard, three hours earlier than Eastern time
pendulum suspended, swinging mechanism used in clockworks or as timepiece
p.m. post meridiem; *Latin.* lit. after noon; afternoon and evening
post meridiem *Latin.* lit. after noon; p.m.
quartz clock timepiece whose mechanical operation is based on electrical frequencies and resulting regular vibrations of quartz crystal
real time actual elapsed time, as when editing film
second unit of time equal to 1/60 of a minute
sidereal time time measured by rotation of Earth relative to a star on celestial sphere other than the sun
solar time time determined by calculating time required for sun to cross same point in sky a second time
space-time four-dimensional continuum incorporating time with three physical dimensions as means of locating events
standard time worldwide time system based on Greenwich meridian; time attained when daylight-saving time is reversed and clocks are turned back one hour in fall; time officially adopted by a country or region
stopwatch watch with hand that can be stopped or started at any instant for precise timing
strike (*vb*) make known the time by sounding, esp. a bell
sundial instrument indicating time of day by casting shadow of sunlight on dial
tempo rate of movement, speed; time in which musical passage is written and/or played

time dimension of reality characterized by sequential flow of events and phenomena through irreversible procession of moments from past to present to future; systematized demarcation of the passage of such moments into units of seconds, minutes, hours, days, and years; period or point in time; fourth dimension in space-time continuum
time capsule container holding records or objects of current culture, deposited for discovery at future date
time machine hypothetical device permitting travel forward or backward through time
timepiece clock, watch, or other device for measuring and indicating time
timer device used to keep time or measure brief periods
timetable schedule of times for some event, esp. arrivals and departures of railroads, buses, or airplanes
time zone longitudinal region within which same standard time is used
watch small timepiece worn on wrist or carried in pocket
week measure of time equal to 7 days
year measure of time required for Earth to complete one revolution around the sun, equal to either 365 or 366 days, or 12 months

U.S. System

acre unit of square measure, usu. for land, equal to 43,560 square feet (4047 sq. m)
barrel unit of cubic measure equal to 5.8 cubic feet; unit of liquid measure equal to 31.5 U.S. gallons (119 l) or 42 U.S. gallons (159 l) for petroleum
board foot cubic measure used for lumber, equal to 144 cubic inches or 12 inches by 12 inches by 1 inch
bushel cubic measure equal to 2150 cubic inches
circle circular measure equal to 360 degrees
cloth yard unit of linear measure for cloth, formerly equal to 37 inches (0.93 m), now equal to 36 inches (0.91 m) or 1 standard yard
congius unit of liquid measure used in prescriptions, equal to 1 gallon (3.7853 l)
cord cubic measure of wood, equal to 128 cubic feet (3.6 cu. m)
cubic foot 1728 cubic inches; 1/27 cubic yard
cubic inch 1 inch by 1 inch by 1 inch
cubic yard 27 cubic feet
cup unit of liquid measure equal to 8 fluid ounces (237 ml) or 16 tablespoons
degree unit of angular or circular measure equal to 60 minutes or 1/360 of a circle
dram unit of apothecaries' weight equal to 60 minims or 1/8 fluid ounce (3.89 g); unit of avoirdupois weight equal to 1/16 ounce (1.77 g)
fathom unit of linear measure equal to 6 feet (1.8 m), used in nautical and mining measurements
fluid ounce unit of liquid measure equal to 2 tablespoons or 1/8 cup (29.573 ml)
foot basic unit of linear measure equal to 12 inches; equivalent to 30.48 centimeters
furlong unit of linear measure equal to 220 yards (201 m) or 1/8 mile (0.2 km)
gallon unit of liquid measure equal to 4 quarts (3.7853 l)
gill measure of liquid volume equal to 1/2 cup or 4 fluid ounces (118 ml); noggin
grain smallest measure of weight, being 437.5 grains per avoirdupois ounce
hogshead unit of liquid measure usu. equal to 63 gallons (238 l)
hundredweight unit of avoirdupois weight equal to 100 pounds (45.359 kg)
inch unit of linear measure equal to 1/12 foot; equivalent to 2.54 centimeters
lb. abbreviation for pound
mile unit of linear measure equal to 5280 feet (1.609 km); statute mile
minim smallest unit of liquid measure, equal to 1/60 of a fluid dram, or approximately one drop
minute sixty seconds in angular measure; 1/60 of a degree
nautical mile unit of linear measure equal to 6080.20 feet (1853.25 m), used in navigation
noggin gill
octant the eighth part of a circle, equal to 45 degrees
ounce unit of avoirdupois weight equal to 16 drams or 1/16 pound; equivalent to 28.35 grams
oz. abbreviation for ounce
peck unit of dry volume equal to 8 quarts or 1/4 bushel (8.81 l)
pennyweight unit of troy weight equal to 24 grains or 1/20 of an ounce (1.555 g)
pint unit of liquid measure equal to two cups (0.6 l); unit of dry measure equal to 35 cubic inches
pole unit of square measure equal to 1 square rod or 30 1/4 square yards (25.3 sq. m)
pound unit of avoirdupois weight equal to 16 ounces; equivalent to 0.45359 kilogram
quadrant unit of circular measure equal to 90 degrees, or one quarter of a circle
quart unit of liquid measure equal to 1/4 gallon, or 57.749 cubic inches (0.946 l); two pints; unit of dry measure equal to 1/8 peck, or 67.201 cubic inches (1.101 l)
road unit of square measure equal to 1/4 acre
rod unit of linear measure equal to 5.5 yards or 16.5 feet (5.029 m)
scruple unit of apothecaries' weight equal to 20 grains or 1/3 dram (1.295 g)
second unit of angular measure equal to 1/60 of a minute or 1/3600 of a degree
short ton measure of avoirdupois weight equal to 2000 pounds (0.907 metric ton)
square mile unit of square measure equal to 640 acres (2.59 sq. km)
statute mile mile
ton short ton; 2000 pounds
yard unit of linear measure equal to 3 feet or 36 inches (0.9144 m)

Metric System

are a; unit of land measure equal to 1/100 hectare or 100 square meters
centiare ca; one square meter
centigram cg; ten milligrams, 1/100 gram
centiliter cl; ten milliliters, 1/100 liter
centimeter cm; ten millimeters, 1/100 meter
centner fifty kilograms, or sometimes 100 kilograms
decigram dg; one hundred milligrams, 1/10 gram
deciliter dl; one hundred milliliters, 1/10 liter
decimeter dm; one hundred millimeters, 1/10 meter
dekagram dag; ten grams, 1/10 kilogram
dekaliter dal; ten liters, 1/10 kiloliter
dekameter dam; ten meters, 1/10 kilometer
gram g; basic metric measure of mass equivalent to 0.035 ounce or 15.432 grains
hectare ha; unit of surface or land measure equal to 100 ares, or 2.471 acres (10,000 sq. meters)
hectogram hg; one hundred grams, 1/10 kilogram
hectoliter hl; one hundred liters, 1/10 kiloliter
hectometer hm; one hundred meters, 1/10 kilometer
kilogram kg; one thousand grams; equivalent to 2.205 pounds
kiloliter kl; one thousand liters
kilometer km; one thousand meters; equivalent to 0.621 miles
liter l; basic metric unit of liquid volume equivalent to 1.057 quarts
long ton ton
meter m; basic metric unit of linear measure equivalent to 3.281 feet
metric hundredweight fifty kilograms
microgram ug; one-millionth part of gram, used primarily in chemistry
micrometer micron
micron u; one-millionth part of meter; micrometer
milligram mg; one-tenth centigram, one-thousandth gram
milliliter ml; one-tenth centiliter, one-thousandth liter
millimeter mm; one-tenth centimeter, one-thousandth meter
nanogram ng; one-billionth part of gram
nanometer nm; one-billionth part of meter
picogram pg; one-trillionth part of gram
quintal measure of weight equal to 100 kilograms or 1/10 ton
ton measure of weight equal to 1000 kilograms or 10 quintals; long ton

Special Measures

assay ton measure of weight used in assaying ore, equal to 29.167 grams
baker's dozen group of thirteen units or things; long dozen
bale large bundle of dry goods, approximately 500 pounds (U.S.)
bolt linear measure for cloth equal to 40 yards (36.576 m)
cable nautical unit of length equal to 720 feet (219 m) in U.S. Navy and 608 feet (185 m) in British navy
caliber diameter of a gun's bore measured in hundredths of an inch
carat measure of weight for gemstones, equal to 206 milligrams (3 grains); measure of amount of gold per twenty-four parts of gold alloy
case carton containing usu. four, twelve, or twenty-four units or things
chain unit of linear measure used in surveying, equal to 66 feet (20 m) and divided into 100 links
chiliad group of one thousand
cicero printer's measure approximately equivalent to one pica or 0.1776 inch (4.5 mm)
crate quantity, esp. of fruit, packed in crate, approximately 2 cu. ft. (0.05 cu. m)
dash a few drops or grains, used as cooking measure, esp. for liquids
double magnum jeroboam
dozen group of twelve units or things
em printer's measure designating square width of given type size
fifth unit of liquid measure equal to approximately one-fifth gallon (750 ml), esp. for spirits
freight ton unit of volume for shipping equal to 40 cubic feet
gauge diameter of a gun's bore measured in millimeters
gross group of twelve dozen, or 144, units or things
hand linear measure equal to 4 inches (10 cm), used esp. for horses
handbreadth unit of linear measure equal to 2.5 to 4 inches (6.4 to 10 cm)
jeroboam unit of liquid volume equal to two magnums or approximately 4/5 gallon (3 l), esp. for wine; double magnum
keel measure of coal equal to 21 long tons and 4 hundredweight (21.5 metric tons)
knot rate of speed equal to one nautical mile per hour
league any of various units of linear measure equal to 2.4 to 4.6 statute miles
light year unit of linear measure used in astronomy, equal to distance light travels in one year in a vacuum, or approximately 5.878 trillion miles (9.46 trillion km)
link unit of linear measure used in surveying, equal to one hundredth of a chain
long dozen baker's dozen
magnum unit of liquid volume equal to approximately two-fifths gallon (1.5 l), esp. for wine
megaton one million tons, esp. an explosive force equal to one million tons of TNT
military pace unit of linear measure equal to 2 1/2 feet
nail unit of cloth measure equal to 2 1/2 inches
nebuchadnezzar unit of liquid measure equal to 20 quarts (18.9 liter), used esp. for wine
pace unit of linear measure representing span covered by feet in taking one step, approximately 30 to 40 inches (75 cm to 1 m)
palm unit of linear measure equal to 3 inches (7.5 cm)

pica unit of measure in typography equal to one-sixth inch or 12 points
pinch a few grains, used as dry measure in cooking
pipe cask used as measure of liquid volume, equal to 4 barrels, 2 hogsheads, or half a tun, containing 126 gallons (477 l), esp. of wine
point unit of measure in typography equal to one seventy-second inch or one-twelfth pica
puncheon cask used as measure of liquid volume, equal to 80 gallons (304 l)
quire twenty-five sheets of paper
ream five hundred sheets of paper or 20 quires
rood unit of linear measure varying from 5 1/2 to 8 yards (5 to 7 m); unit of land measure equal to 40 square rods (0.101 ha); unit of 1 square rod (25.29 sq. m)
score group of 20 units or things
sextant unit of circular measure equal to 60 degrees or one sixth of a circle
span unit of linear measure representing distance between fully extended tips of thumb and little finger, usu. equal to 9 inches (23 cm)
tablespoon unit of measure equal to 3 teaspoons (14.8 ml)
teaspoon unit of measure equivalent to 4.9 milliliters
township unit of territory used in surveying, approximately six miles square (93.2 sq. km)
troy ounce unit of weight for precious metals and gemstones, equal to 31.103 g, with 12 troy ounces equal to 1 pound

Foreign and Historical Measures

amphora vase holding 10.3 gallons (38.99 l) (ancient Greece)
ardeb unit of dry measure equal to 5.62 U.S. bushels (Egypt)
arroba unit of avoirdupois weight varying between 25.37 pounds (9.5 kg) and 32.38 pounds (12 kg) in Spain, Portugal, and Latin America; unit of liquid measure equal to 4.26 gallons (16.1 liters) (Spain)
arshin unit of linear measure equal to 28 inches (71 cm) (Russia)
aune historical unit of measure for fabric equal to 47 inches (119 cm) (France)
barleycorn historical unit of length, equal to 1/3 inch (8.5 mm)
bath unit of liquid measure varying between 10 and 11 gallons (38 and 42 l) (Hebrew); 6.8 gallons (25.7 l) (ancient Rome)
bovate historical unit of land area varying between 7.5 and 20 acres, equal to one-eighth carucate (Britain)
braccio historical unit of length, usu. equal to 26 or 27 inches (66 or 68 cm) (Italy)
braza unit of length representing reach of outstretched arms, equal to 5.48 feet (1.67 m) (Spain, Latin America)
cab ancient liquid measure equal to 2 quarts (Hebrew)
carucate unit of land area varying between 60 and 160 acres (Britain)
catty measure of weight equal to about 1 1/2 pounds (680 g) (China, Southeast Asia)
chopin historical unit of liquid measure equal to one quart (Scotland)
congius unit of liquid measure equal to 0.8 gallons (3.2 liters) (ancient Rome)
crore total of ten million units, esp. rupees; 100 lacs (India)
cubit linear measure based on length of forearm, usu. equal to 17 or 18 inches (43 to 46 cm) (ancient Greece, ancient Rome)
denarius measure of weight equal to 4.6 grams (0.162 oz) (ancient Rome)
dessiatine unit of land measure equal to 2.7 acres (1.1 ha) (Russia)
drachma measure of weight equal to 4.36 grams (0.153 oz) (ancient Greece)
ell unit of linear measure for cloth equal to one thirty-second bolt or approximately 1 1/4 yards (114 cm) (Britain)
ephah unit of dry volume equal to 40 liters or approximately one bushel (Hebrew)
fanega unit of dry measure equal to 1.58 bushels (55.7 l) (Spain, Latin America)
fanegada unit of land measure equal to from 1.25 to 1.75 acres (0.5 to 0.7 ha) (Spain, Latin America)
feddan unit of area equal to 1.038 acres (0.42 ha) (Egypt)
firkin unit of liquid volume equal to 9 imperial gallons (41 l); one-half kilderkin (Britain)
haikwan tael customs unit equal to 1.20666 troy ounces of fine silver (China)
hekat unit of dry volume equal to 4.77 liters (4.33 qt) (Hebrew)
hide historical unit of land measure varying from 60 to 120 acres (24 to 49 ha) (Britain)
homer unit of volume equal to 10 baths liquid measure or 10 ephahs dry measure; kor (Hebrew)
imperial gallon 1.20095 U.S. gallons (Britain)
imperial quart 1.20095 U.S. quarts (Britain)
kantar measure of weight corresponding to hundredweight (Middle East)
kilderkin unit of liquid volume equal to 18 imperial gallons (82 liters), or 2 firkins (Britain)
koku unit of dry measure equal to 5.12 bushels (1.8 hl) (Japan)
kor homer
kos linear unit of land measure varying from 1 to 3 miles (1.6 to 4.8 km) (India)
lac total of 100,000 units, esp. rupees (India)
liang measure of weight equal to 1 1/3 ounce (37 g); tael (China)
livre measure of weight equal to 0.5 kilogram, equivalent to 1.1 pounds (France)
long hundredweight hundredweight equal to 112 pounds (50.8 kg) (Britain)
mark former measure of weight for precious metals equal to 8 ounces (249 g) (Europe)
maund measure of weight varying from 25 to 82.286 pounds (11 to 37.4 kg) (India)
mina ancient measure of weight and value equal to one-sixtieth part of talent

mite measure of weight equal to 1/20 grain (3.24 mg) (Britain)
momme measure of weight equal to 3.75 grams (0.13 oz) (Japan)
morgen old Dutch unit of land measure equal to 2 acres (0.8 ha) (South Africa)
mutchkin unit of liquid measure equal to slightly less than one pint (Scotland)
obolus measure of weight equal to 1/10 gram (Greece)
oka measure of weight equal to 2 3/4 pounds (1.25 kg) (Turkey)
perch measure of volume for stone equal to 24 cubic feet (0.7 cu. m) (Britain)
pfund measure of weight equal to 0.5 kilogram or 1.1 pounds (Germany)
picul measure of weight equal to 100 catties, or about 133 to 143 pounds (60 to 64 kg) (China, Southeast Asia)
pocket measure of weight, esp. for hops, equal to 168 pounds (76.4 kg) (Britain)
pood measure of weight equal to about 36 pounds (16 kg) (Russia)
pottle former liquid measure equal to two quarts
quart unit of liquid measure comparable to U.S. quart, equal to 69.355 cubic inches (1.136 l) (Britain)
quartern one-fourth part of certain weights and measures (Britain)
reed ancient unit of linear measure equal to 6 cubits
Roman mile unit of linear measure equal to 1620 yards (1480 m) (ancient Rome)
rotl measure of weight and dry measure varying widely, but approximately one pound (Islamic countries)
rundlet former measure of volume equal to 15 imperial gallons (68 liters) (Britain)
ser measure of weight usu. equal to one fortieth of a maund, varying in value but officially 33 ounces (950 gm) (India)
shekel measure of weight equal to 1/2 ounce (Hebrew)
stack unit of cubic measure, esp. for coal and wood, equal to 108 cubic feet (3 cu. m) (Britain)
stadion unit of linear measure equal to 622 feet (189.6 m) (ancient Greece)
stadium unit of linear measure equal to about 607 feet (185 m) (ancient Rome)
stone measure of weight equal to 14 pounds (6.4 kg) (Britain)
tael liang
talent ancient measure of weight equal to 3000 shekels or 6000 drachmas
tierce former unit of liquid volume equal to one-third pipe or 42 gallons (159 l), esp. for wine
tod measure of weight, esp. for wool, equal to 28 pounds (12.7 kg) (Britain)
toise former unit of linear measure equal to 6.395 feet (1.949 m) (France)
tola measure of weight equal to 180 grains (11.7 g) (India)
tower pound measure of weight equal variously to 12 ounces (350 grams), 15 ounces (437 grams), or 16 ounces (467 grams) (Britain)
tun unit of liquid volume equal to 252 gallons (953.9 l), esp. used for wine cask (Britain)
vara unit of linear measure varying from 32 to 43 inches (81 to 109 cm) (Spain, Portugal, Latin America)
verst unit of linear measure equal to 3500 feet (1.067 km) (Russia)
virgate former measure of land area equal to about 30 acres (12 ha) (Britain)

Combining Forms

atto- one-quintillionth part of given base unit
centi- one-hundredth part of given base unit
deci- one-tenth part of given base unit
deka- ten of given base unit
exa- one quintillion of given base unit
femto- one-quadrillionth part of given base unit
giga- one billion of given base unit
hecto- one hundred of given base unit
kilo- one thousand of given base unit
mega- one million of given base unit
micro- one-millionth part of given base unit
milli- one-thousandth part of given base unit
myria- ten thousand of given base unit
nano- one-billionth part of given base unit
peta- one quadrillion of given base unit
pico- one-trillionth part of given base unit
tera- one trillion of given base unit

Chapter Five
Technology

MACHINERY AND FABRICATION

Machinery and Mechanical Devices
Fabrication and Manufacturing Processes
Types of Construction
Builders and Construction Workers

Machinery and Mechanical Devices

agitator apparatus in machine that shakes and stirs objects
air pump machine that removes, compresses, or forces air into something
alternator alternating current generator or dynamo
apparatus complex device or machine that has a specific use
appliance device for specific purpose; machine for household task, usu. electric
arc lamp unit that produces light by maintaining arc between two electrodes, esp. carbon rods
automaton mechanical contrivance that appears to act by its own motive power; robot
backhoe hydraulic excavating tractor with hinged boom operating jawed bucket
baler device that compresses and wraps loose material into standardized bundles
ball bearing low-friction bearing in which moving parts revolve or slide on freely rolling metal balls
ball cock valve connected to hollow floating ball which rises and falls in tank to open and shut valve, controlling water supply to tank
battery device that generates electricity by chemical reaction
bearing machine part in or on which another part revolves or slides
bellows device that produces stream of air through narrow opening when sides are pressed together
belt endless, flexible band passing about two or more pulleys, used to transmit motion between pulleys or to convey materials
bevel gear gear having teeth cut into conical surface, usu. meshing with similar gear set at right angle
block and tackle combination of fixed and movable pulley blocks with rope or cable, used to hoist large weights
blower device for supplying air at moderate pressure
blowtorch small torch that produces hot flame from liquid fuel with pressurized air to melt metals
boiler closed tank in which water is heated and converted to steam in order to power engine or supply heat
brake device that connects moving part to frame, used to hold parts in position, control direction of motion, or absorb energy; any device that slows or halts motion, esp. by friction
burner part that produces flame or direct heat
business machine machine for doing office work, such as computer, photocopier, or calculator
butterfly valve disk-shaped valve on axis at its diameter, used esp. as damper in pipe or choke in carburetor
bypass engine turbine or jet engine in which compressed air is diverted to join exhaust gases to increase thrust
cam rotating wheel or projection on wheel that gives or receives uneven rotation or reciprocating motion to or from another wheel
camber slight arching, upward curvature or convexity of member, for specific purpose
capstan rotating drum with cable used to hoist heavy weights
carburetor device in which air and gasoline spray combine to form explosive mixture in internal combustion engine
caster swivel wheel that supports movable weight, esp. heavy furniture
centrifuge machine that rotates to generate centrifugal force, used to separate particles of varying density or shed moisture
cogwheel wheel with toothed rim that meshes with another wheel to transmit or receive motion
combine machine used to harvest crops
compactor device that crushes and compresses loose material into compact bundles
compressed air machine device operated by expansion of air under pressure in enclosed container
compressor pump that places air or gas under pressure
computer electronic device that stores information and performs complex calculations very rapidly
conveyor belt endless mechanical belt used to transport objects along its path
coupling linkage between machine shafts
crampon hooked device used to lift heavy weights
crane long-armed machine used to lift or lower objects at great height
crank arm bent at right angle and connected to shaft of machine, used to transmit or transfer circular motion to and from shaft
cylinder chamber in which piston moves in reciprocating engine
damper device that reduces shock, vibration, or air flow
deadbolt lock bolt that closes and opens by turning of knob or key
derrick hoisting beam with tackle rigged over it
device mechanical contrivance used for specific purpose
diaphragm dividing wall or partition between parts, usu. opening and closing to regulate entry or passage
die punch sheet metal cutter used to make exact duplicates of die shape in heavy machinery; permanent mold

diesel engine internal combustion engine that uses extremely high temperatures to burn fuel without spark
differential gear series of gears that permit two or more shafts to rotate at different speeds
differential motion movement in which speed of driven object equals difference in speeds of its connected parts
dredge apparatus used to scoop up mud and rocks from bottom of body of water
drill pointed instrument that makes holes in hard substances
drive belt endless loop that transmits power in engine
driver mechanism that imparts motion to another machine or part
dwell period in cycle of operation in which given machine part remains motionless
dynamo device that generates electric current by using coiled wire in magnetic field
electric motor motor that utilizes electric power to run machinery
electromechanical (*adj*) designating a device activated electrically, as by a solenoid, and also working mechanically
elevator platform or cage suspended on motor-operated cables to hoist or lower objects
engine machine or device that uses fuel or energy to develop mechanical power, often to transmit motion to another machine
floodgate gate designed to control and regulate flow of water
fluid coupling mechanism in which fluid, usu. oil, transmits torque from one shaft to another
flywheel heavy, notched wheel used to regulate machine's speed and uniformity of motion
four-stroke engine internal combustion engine with power stroke occurring once every four piston strokes
fulcrum support point on which lever turns
funicular device, esp. carriage, worked by overhead cable from which it hangs
gauge device used to measure dimensions or test degrees
gear device that transmits motion and power by contact between toothed wheels
generator machine that creates electrical power
gin machine used to hoist heavy objects
governor device for maintaining uniform speed of engine, as by regulating fuel supply
gyroscope wheel mounted in set of rings so that axis of rotation is free to turn in any direction
helical gear gear with teeth set at oblique angle to rotation of wheel
hoist device that lifts objects
hydraulic engine engine powered by liquid, esp. by pressure created when liquid is forced through an aperture
hypoid gear bevel gear designed to mesh with similar gear, with axes at right angle
idle gear gear placed between driving and driven gear to transmit motion between them
idle wheel wheel gear for transmitting motion between driving part and driven part
implement tool or other device required to perform given task
inclined plane simple machine: flat surface at angle to level ground
induction motor electric motor in which rotation is induced by interaction of magnetic fields
internal combustion engine fuel-burning reciprocating or rotary engine in which fuel/air mixture is converted into power in enclosed cylinder
jack support, brace; ratchet device used to lift heavy weight
jet engine engine that generates reaction force when compressed outside air and hot exhaust gases are forced through nozzle
laser beam cutting or welding tool that uses highly concentrated beam of light made up of particles in excited energy state
lathe machine that supports rotating object worked on by stationary cutting, boring, or drilling tool
lever simple machine: rigid bar that transmits or modifies lifting force applied at one point and is supported by fulcrum at a fixed point
linkage arrangement and coupling of simple machine elements into compound machines
loom frame for weaving horizontal and vertical elements
machine any device or instrument composed of interrelated functioning parts that aids in performing work by transmitting or modifying force or motion
machinery working parts of a machine; assemblage of mechanical devices or machines
machine tool heavy-duty power tool used to shape metal machine parts or wood, as on a lathe
mainspring principal spring in mechanism
mechanical advantage ratio of resistance or load to applied force of machine
mechanical device anything produced or operated by machinery or a mechanism, esp. used to produce, transmit, receive, or alter motion
mechanism any device for performing work or transmitting motion; piece of machinery; assembly of moving parts performing one function within larger machine
mill device or machine used to cut, grind, mix, shape, or process
mole powerful boring machine used in construction of tunnels through earth and rock
motor small engine; electric-driven machine that powers a mechanical device
pawl device with hinged tongue whose tip engages notches of cogwheel or ratchet to allow one-directional rotation
pendulum weight suspended from fixed point so as to swing freely back and forth due to gravity and momentum
permanent mold die punch
pile driver machine with heavy drop hammer used to sink large timbers into ground
plow device used to cut up, turn, and lift soil
plug electrical connection that fits into jack; device that closes off flow of liquid or gas

pneumatic engine engine powered by compressed air
power tool usu. electric device used to perform specific mechanical task
power train sequence of gears and shafting that transmits power from engine to driven mechanism
press device that uses pressure to form or manufacture
pulley simple machine: small wheel with rope or chain in grooved rim around its circumference, used to increase applied force, lift, or change direction of object at end of rope or chain
pump device that draws or moves liquids
rack and pinion large-toothed bar, or rack, that meshes with small gear, or pinion, to receive or transmit motion
ratchet device that converts continuous motion into intermittent motion, esp. toothed wheel on handle that imparts one-directional motion to tool
reciprocating engine engine in which back-and-forth movement of pistons causes rotary motion of crankshaft, either two-stroke or four-stroke
reduction gear combination of gears that reduces input speed to lower output speed
robot automaton
roller rotating cylinder used to press or shape some object
rotary engine engine in which rotary motion is produced directly by triangular rotor, not as reciprocating motion from pistons
rotor any mechanism that rotates, esp. in motor or dynamo
sander machine or device that smoothes and polishes with sandpaper or abrasive material
screw simple machine: inclined plane turned around a cylinder
screw conveyor device for moving loose material, consisting of shaft with broad, helically wound blade rotating in tube or trough; worm
self-regulating machine automated machine in which feedback input determines changes in future output
servomechanism automatic control system that compares input and output to regulate differential
shunt electrical switch or diverter
simple machine basic mechanical device, such as inclined plane, lever, pulley, screw, wedge, or wheel and axle
siphon tube bent into legs of unequal length with shorter leg placed in upper of two containers to draw liquid through and down into lower container by atmospheric pressure
spigot stopper plug, often with valve to regulate flow
spring elastic contrivance, esp. coiled length of wire, that regains its shape after being compressed, bent, or stretched, used to impart force
spring-loaded (*adj*) designating machine part held in specific position by spring
sprinkler device that disperses drops of liquid over wide area
spur gear gear having teeth cut on rim parallel to its axis of rotation
stator part of machine that remains fixed with respect to its rotating parts
steam engine engine that derives its power from steam under pressure in a cylinder
steam shovel excavating machine with bucket on arm, operated by boiler-driven engine
stopcock plug, spigot, or valve that controls fluid flow
subassembly structural or functional group of machine parts that forms part of larger assembly
sun gear central gear around whose axis other gears in epicyclic train revolve
switch device used to open, close, or divert, esp. electric current
synchronous motor electric motor whose speed is proportional to frequency of current driving it
tachometer instrument that measures rate of rotation
theodolite surveying instrument used to measure vertical and horizontal angles
thermometer device that registers temperature
thermostat instrument that regulates temperature
tool instrument, esp. handheld, that works, shapes, cuts, or joins
transformer device that converts one form of electricity into another
treadle lever or pedal that turns wheel
triple-expansion (*adj*) designating power source using same fluid to do work at three successive stages of expansion
turbine engine with curved blades or vanes on spindle that rotates to convert energy from fluid entering enclosed casing into rotary motion
two-stroke engine internal combustion engine having compression and power stages only, with power stroke occurring once every two piston strokes
universal joint flexible connection used to transmit rotary motion from one shaft to another shaft not in line with it
vacuum enclosed space out of which nearly all air or gas has been pumped
vacuum pump pump used to draw air or gas out of enclosure to form vacuum
valve device that regulates flow through pipe or tube, esp. one that permits flow in one direction only
vehicle means of conveyance or transport, sometimes motorized, that moves on wheels, runners, or tracks
ventilator device that regulates air flow, used to maintain fresh air
venturi tube with concave sides that controls flow of liquid by producing suction
waterwheel wheel on shaft moved by weight of water hitting floats or paddles, used to transmit motion
wedge simple machine: two inclined planes joined to form device with pointed end and thicker base
welding torch device used to fuse metal parts by heat

wheel solid disk or circular frame connected by spokes to central axis, used to transmit power or motion in machinery
wheel and axle simple machine: grooved wheel or pulley fixed to shaft or drum, used to increase mechanical advantage or speed
whorl flywheel on spindle, used to regulate its speed
winch device with crank on handle, used to transmit motion, esp. for hoisting
windlass rotating drum with cable wound around it, used for hoisting
windmill mill operated by large oblique vanes that radiate from shaft and rotate by force of wind
wind tunnel tunnellike chamber through which air is forced to test airplanes and motors
worm screw conveyor
worm gear mechanism consisting of rotating shaft cut with helical threads that engages with and drives toothed gear whose axis is at right angle to shaft

Fabrication and Manufacturing Processes

automate (*vb*) use only machine power in construction, assembly, production, or operation
bevel (*vb*) cut intersection of two faces to form third face at oblique angles to both
bond (*vb*) connect or fasten together two or more parts
bore (*vb*) drill out a hole or cavity to increase its size
braze (*vb*) solder with soft flux
broach (*vb*) remove metal from surface with toothed cutting edge
buff (*vb*) polish, shine, smooth
burnish (*vb*) polish, rub until shiny
cannibalize (*vb*) build or repair machine with parts salvaged from similar machines
cant (*vb*) tilt, pitch at an angle
cantilever (*vb*) construct as or support with projecting beam
caulk (*vb*) fill seam or joint with waterproof material
clarify (*vb*) separate suspended particles from liquid
cold-work (*vb*) work metal at temperature below level at which recrystallization occurs
collimate (*vb*) make parallel or level; adjust line of sight
countersink (*vb*) set below surface into fitted hole
couple (*vb*) join together, link, connect
crate (*vb*) box into large containers for shipping
crystallize (*vb*) form crystals by evaporation
cybernate (*vb*) use computers to control and carry out manufacturing or other operations
dam (*vb*) form barrier to flow of liquid
distill (*vb*) purify by vaporization into separate components
dredge (*vb*) enlarge or clear bottom of body of water
drop-forge (*vb*) hammer hot metal into shapes between two dies
elevate (*vb*) raise to higher position
extrude (*vb*) force fluid material through press to shape objects
fabricate (*vb*) construct, esp. from standardized parts
fire (*vb*) bake in oven to harden or glaze object, esp. pottery
fit (*vb*) join elements that conform in shape; insert; adjust elements to conform in shape
forge (*vb*) shape molten or heated metal
found (*vb*) lay the base for, begin to build
frame (*vb*) construct framework, support, or skeletal structure
glaze (*vb*) coat with smooth, impermeable finish
grade (*vb*) level, make smooth; sort by size or quality
hoist (*vb*) lift heavy weight mechanically
hone (*vb*) grind to smoothly finished surface
join (*vb*) fit; bond
knead (*vb*) work into pliable mass by folding over, squeezing, and pressing
knurl (*vb*) form beaded or ridged metal surface
lap (*vb*) machine to an extremely fine, smooth finish
lay (*vb*) establish and prepare groundwork for
manufacture (*vb*) produce items in quantity with standardized, technologically advanced equipment
mechanize (*vb*) make mechanical; operate or perform by machinery
mill (*vb*) grind, cut, or shape; process
mold (*vb*) form in frame, cavity, or matrix
plane (*vb*) cut away large, flat surface area
plaster (*vb*) coat with layer of plaster
press (*vb*) exert force upon, esp. form by stamping on die or template
pump (*vb*) move up and down, esp. move liquids by suction or pressure
quarry (*vb*) excavate stone by cutting or blasting at surface
ream (*vb*) widen a hole or opening
refine (*vb*) remove impurities
regulate (*vb*) systematically control operations
retrofit (*vb*) equip with parts not available at time of original construction
salvage (*vb*) repair and save from destruction
sand (*vb*) rub smooth with abrasive
shear (*vb*) stamp or cut into forms
solder (*vb*) join or cement with hot, liquefied metal
splice (*vb*) join by interweaving
stamp (*vb*) press and cut with a die
strip (*vb*) remove paint or finish, esp. from wood
thread (*vb*) apply ridges to smooth surface, usu. metal
toenail (*vb*) join with nail driven at oblique angle
tool (*vb*) work or shape with instruments or tools
turn (*vb*) form on rotating device, tool, or machine
water-cool (*vb*) cool engine or other machine part by water circulating around it in pipes
weld (*vb*) fuse metal components by application of heat

Types of Construction

bricklaying art of building structures with fired clay blocks cemented together into walls
bridge construction process of building structures that span waterways or other geographical features
cabinetmaking construction of finished woodwork and furniture
construction systematic devising, forming, and building of something with parts that fit together
dam building construction of barrier to water flow
fabrication making or constructing of something with parts that must be assembled
frame construction building a structural framework with wood, rather than masonry, steel, or concrete
framing process of using a wood frame for construction
general building construction of residential and commercial buildings without specialized features
heavy construction building of large-scale structures with complex and powerful tools and machinery
highway construction building of paved roadways
home building construction of residential buildings
HVAC heating, ventilation, and air conditioning installation
masonry building with stone, brick, or cemented elements: now also refers to plaster and concrete
modular construction design and building with units of standardized length and size
platform framing building process in which each story is framed and constructed independently
plumbing installation of water supply, drainage, and sewage system in buildings
post-and-beam construction wall construction of upright posts and crossbeams with planks laid crossways on beams
prefab building construction from standardized, prefabricated components
remodeling modification of existing structure to new needs or designs
roofing construction of protective top layer of building
steel-frame construction building a structure on a reinforced steel rod framework
tilt-up construction building method in which concrete walls are cast on site in horizontal frames, or wooden walls are preassembled, then lifted into final, vertical position
tunnel building excavation and surfacing of underground passageways
wattle and daub construction with upright rods or stakes interwoven with twigs or branches and plastered with clay and straw mixture
wiring installation of electrical facilities
wood-frame construction frame construction

Builders and Construction Workers

architect, asbestos worker
boilermaker, bricklayer, builder
cabinetmaker, carpenter, cement mason, construction worker, contractor
designer, drywaller
electrician, elevator constructor, engineer, equipment operator
floor covering installer
gardener, glazier
house painter
insulation worker, interior decorator, ironworker
laborer, lathe operator
machine operator, marble setter, mason, mechanical engineer, metalworker
operating engineer, operator
painter, paperhanger, pipe fitter, plasterer, plumber
rigger, roofer
sheet metal worker, stonemason, subcontractor
terrazzo worker, tilesetter
welder, woodworker

STRUCTURAL COMPONENTS

Building and Machine Parts
Carpentry

Building and Machine Parts

abutment plane or point designed to give support or withstand thrust, esp. on projecting part of structure
adapter connector that enables different parts or devices to fit or function together
angle iron metal brace used to reinforce corners or angles
aperture usu. narrow opening, slit, or crack
apron plate or covering for mechanical device that protects its operator; interior trim beneath window stool
arm small extension attached horizontally at angle to large base
axle shaft or spindle that supports rotating wheel
baffle obstructing member, esp. used to hold back or turn aside flow of gas or liquid
bail supporting half hoop; hinged bar that holds paper to platen in typewriter
ball-and-socket joint joint between rods or links in which ball-like termination fits into concave, spherical socket
baluster small vertical member connecting stair tread and handrail

baseboard finished interior trim where wall meets floor
batten narrow wood strip that covers seam between boards
beam horizontal structural member of wood or steel, used to support load
bearing sliding or turning machine part; point of support
bearing pile column sunk into ground or foundation to support vertical load
bed horizontal layer of masonry mortar that holds bricks
berm narrow dirt ledge that supports beams
block enclosure for pulley; mold; building unit
boom projecting beam, spar, or supporting arm
brace connecting or reinforcing element, usu. of wood
bridging rows of small diagonal braces nailed between ceiling joists to support floor weight
built-ins furniture and other nonstructural elements permanently incorporated in building
buttress projecting support structure
cantilever extension of structural member beyond point of support
casing trim or molding on doors or windows
caster small, swiveling wheel used to support or move furniture and heavy objects
chamfer beveled edge or channel on piece of wood
chase vertical groove in masonry wall for pipes, ducts, or conduits; frame that holds paper in printing press
chassis framework or support for working parts
chimney vertical flue that draws off gases and heat from furnace or fireplace
cleat wood brace
cog tooth or radial support on wheel or gear
coil spring wire spring coiled helically into conical or cylindrical shape
collar ring or flange, esp. on pipe, to connect parts or prevent sideward motion
column vertical structural support
conduit tube, pipe, or channel, esp. for fluids or electric wiring
cornice exterior trim at juncture of roof and wall, consisting of fascia, soffit, and molding
cotter split pin with spreadable ends
coupling machine part that connects two rotating shafts at their ends to transmit torque between them
cowling removable metal housing or cover for engine
crossbar connective bar placed in horizontal position
crossbeam transverse beam in structure, such as joist
crosstie beam or rod placed crosswise for support
curb enclosing framework or border; element that restrains or checks
curtain wall exterior wall that protects interior wall from weather but bears no structural load
deck horizontal structure extending from exterior wall
doorjamb door frame cut into wall
dovetail joint projecting, wedge-shaped tenon that fits into mortise
downspout vertical pipe that carries water from roof to ground
duct pipe or channel for passage of gas or liquid
elbow L-shaped fastener or connective piece, esp. for pipes
expansion joint joint in masonry or concrete that accommodates expansion and contraction of materials without damaging structure
facade exterior face on front of building
fastener hardware device that holds separate parts together: bolt, nail, plug, screw, pin, toggle, clasp, or clamp
fender guard, impact absorber
ferrule metal ring or cap at end of handle or tool
firestop fire-retardant element inside walls and floors, esp. horizontal wood member between studs to stop updrafts inside wall
fire wall partition made of fireproof material, used to prevent spread of fire within building
fitting small part or device, usu. of standardized size and shape
fixture plumbing or electrical unit
flange projecting rim or collar of wheel, pipe, rail, or beam, used to hold it in place or guide action
flashing sheet metal strip or wall for waterproofing or insulation, usu. by sealing joint
floorboard any of the strips of wood composing a floor
flue enclosed passageway used to direct current of gas; chimney, channel for smoke or air
foliated joint joint between overlapping, rabbeted edges of two boards, forming continuous surface
footing concrete pad that supports and distributes foundation weight
forelock cotter pin, split pin, or linchpin
forms panels joined as molds for concrete
foundation supporting part of structure beneath first floor joists, usu. concrete or masonry
frame open, supporting structure
furnishings usu. movable articles for use or decoration in structure
furring wood strips fastened to nonwood walls or ceiling to form straight surface for application of finished wall material
gasket flat sheet of material used to form gas-tight joint between engine parts
girder horizontal structural member that supports wall; floor joist between piers or columns; beam
grate metal grid or frame of parallel bars, used for support, ventilation, and filtration
gutter trough to siphon fluid, esp. rainwater from roof
guy reinforcing wire, chain
haft handle, esp. of knife or ax
hardware metal fittings and utensils for building construction
H-beam long iron or steel I-beam with wide flanges
hinge swiveling metal joint that fastens swinging

element to stable support: butt, spring, strap, T-hinge
housing frame or covering for part; recess in piece of wood for insertion of another piece
hub center part, esp. of wheel where it is fastened to axle
I-beam long iron or steel beam with cross section in form of I, used in heavy construction
insulation layer of material resistant to heat or sound conduction
jamb side frame of door or window in wall
jib projecting crane arm
joint point of contact between elements, usu. held by glue, nail, or screw
joist horizontal support beam for floor or ceiling
Lally column steel pipe with concrete-filled post used to support girders
landing floor area at top or bottom of stairs
lath narrow wood strips for lattice, trellis, and plastering base for wall; metal or gypsum panels nailed to studs on which plaster is applied
lattice wood strip framework
leader downspout connected to gutter
leaf sliding or hinged side or division, esp. of door or window
lever bar used to lift heavy object or pry open something
linchpin fastener that prevents slippage; linkage device
lintel horizontal, weight-bearing crosspiece above door or window
load-bearing wall wall that carries vertical load from above
lumber milled hardwood or softwood boards, used to build construction and cabinetry
molding wood strip with curved or decoratively cut surface
mortise notch or hole in wood that holds fitted tenon to form joint
mullion narrow bar that divides small windowpane glass or screen; vertical framing member that separates adjacent doors or windows
muntin wood member that separates glass panes in door or window
newel large post at foot of stairs
nonbearing wall wall that supports no weight other than its own
panel flat piece of wood fitted into larger surface area
pier vertical masonry column, usu. concrete, that supports beam or load from above
pilaster rectangular support or pier projecting from wall
pile concrete, steel, or wood column that supports building foundation
piloti column of iron, steel, or reinforced concrete that supports structure above open ground level
pinion small cogwheel, with teeth, that fits into large gearwheel or rack
plank long, flat, wood member 2-4 inches (5.1-10.2 cm) thick and 6 inches (15.2 cm) or more wide
platen flat plate in printing press, or roller in typewriter, on which paper rides
plenum box on furnace from which ducts run to outlets
pylon slender, towering structure flanking entrance or supporting wires
rack frame; toothed bar into which pinion fits
rafter horizontal wooden support member for roof
rampart barrier, bulwark
register heating duct unit that directs airflow
reinforcing rod round, steel bar used to strengthen concrete
revetment facing of stone or concrete to sustain embankment
rigging system of ropes or chains used to support, suspend, or position equipment
riser vertical part of stair
rung supporting piece or crossbar, esp. on ladder
sash movable frame that contains glass windowpanes
sconce cover, protective shell
shaft rotating cylinder; column that supports rotating machine elements
shell outer covering or framework
shim thin piece of material used to smooth, level, or finish area between two irregular surfaces
shoring wood or metal braces used for temporary support during building construction
siding surface covering for exterior building walls
sill horizontal member at base of window or door
skid plank or low platform on which load is supported
slab strip of concrete, poured as single piece, esp. reinforced concrete floor
sleeve tube that surrounds another part
sluice gated or valved water channel
soffit undersurface of cornice from fascia to wall; plancier
sound insulation section of insulating material that damps sound waves
spindle pin or shaft that holds rotating bit or wheel
spring flexible wire coil that provides resilience and absorbs shocks
sprocket one of series of teeth or points on wheel rim arranged to fit links of chain or another set of sprockets
stack vertical shelves, pipes, or flues
stanchion upright support bar or beam
standard upright support or support structure
stile vertical member, esp. of panel door
stilt pole that supports and elevates structure or load
stop wood strip used to hold window in place or against which door closes
strike plate metal plate set in door frame to receive lock plunger
stringer side of stair cut to receive threads; long, horizontal timber connecting upright posts
strut bar or piece that resists longitudinal pressure or stress along its length
stud vertical framing member for wall, usu. wood
subfloor boards nailed directly to floor joists,

used as base for finished floorboards or carpets
sump pit, trap, or reservoir that collects liquid
support element that bears weight of another part or parts
suspended ceiling ceiling hung from floor or roof above it
switch device used to open or close flow, esp. electric current
tackle rigging; ropes and pulleys used to hoist objects
tappet sliding rod struck by cam to move another part
T-bar iron or steel beam with flanges along one edge forming T-shaped cross section
template horizontal member of wall that receives and distributes pressure of beam or girder
tenon projecting part cut in wood to insert in corresponding mortise as joint
threshold beveled strip, usu. wood or stone, fastened to doorsill directly below door
tie structural member that joins stress pieces in frame
timber wood member, esp. one 5 inches (12.7 cm) or more in smallest dimension
tongue-and-groove joint joint between two boards, one of which is cut with a raised area on its edge that fits into corresponding groove in edge of other board to form flush surface
tooth regular projection on gear rim
trace bar hinged to two parts of machine, for transferring motion between them
track belt or tread that guides line of motion
transom crosspiece in structure, esp. above window or door
trave crossbeam; section between crossbeams
traverse rod horizontal rod on which curtains open and close
tread horizontal part of stair on which one steps
trellis lath lattice support
trestle reinforced supporting framework
trim wood molding, strips for finish and decoration
tripod three-legged support, usu. adjustable
trippet projection or cam that strikes another machine part at regular intervals
truckle small wheel or pulley
trundle small wheel or caster
truss rigid reinforcing framework; preassembled support unit used in roof construction, including rafters, joists, and bracing
tumbler single cog or cam on rotating shaft that transmits motion to the part it engages
underlayment materials on top of subfloor that form smoother surface for finished flooring
valve device that regulates flow of liquid or gas
vent opening, esp. in wall, serving as outlet for air, smoke, or fumes
wattle rod or stake interwoven with twigs or branches to form wall, fence, or roof
W-beam iron or steel beam with W-shaped cross section
weather stripping metal or fabric strips placed around edges of doors and windows to reduce heat loss
winding wire or thread coiled or wrapped around something, esp. single turn of such wire or thread
wing part extending laterally from main part
worm rotating shaft or cylinder cut with helical threads
yoke forklike end of rod or shaft within which another part is secured; viselike piece holding two parts firmly together

Carpentry

balloon framing building with continuous studs from sill to roof plate
benchmark reference mark on construction site for land measurements and elevations
bias angle between construction lines
blank piece of material to be cut or worked into finished item
blind nailing placing of nails where they will be hidden when unit is complete
blueprint architect's detailed drawings of construction plan in standardized form; working drawings
brick veneer construction in which wood-framed building has layer of bricks as exterior siding
building codes local regulations for design and construction of buildings
building permit document issued by local government that grants the right to build
built-up roof roof of alternate layers of building paper and asphalt with final gravel layer
carpenter worker who builds large structures, esp. of wood
carpentry work and trade of building structures with wood
catwalk narrow elevated bridge, esp. temporary walkway around building site
contractor person who agrees to supply materials and do construction work for set price and hires subcontractors and laborers
core central layer of plywood sheet
course continuous row of bricks or shingles
crossbands layers of veneer glued at right angles to form plywood
crosscutting cutting wood across the grain
cross section side view through construction, esp. on drawings
d symbol for penny, indicating nail size
dado groove cut perpendicular to wood grain
dead load permanent load, such as roof, on structure
elevation drawing that shows design of exterior walls; height of building part above established point
face nail nail driven through board so that it is visible
finish grade elevation of ground relative to building after landscaping
floor plan detailed drawing that shows layout and dimensions of building interior as viewed from above

foundation plan detailed drawing of foundation that includes its dimensions and location of footings, piers, and walls
framing joining of wooden structural members as skeletal structure for building
frostline depth frost penetrates into earth
grade line level at which ground intersects foundation of building
growth ring layer of wood developed during annual period of growth
half-timbered construction exterior walls in which exposed heavy wood members are separated by masonry
heartwood hard, older wood at core of tree
identification index stamp on plywood that indicates its quality
kerf slot in wood formed by saw blade
knocked-down (*adj*) something delivered to job with parts cut to size but not assembled
live load load on building structure, such as furniture, that may be moved or removed
lumbermill place in which logs are milled and dressed as lumber
lumberyard place with open areas and structures in which lumber is stored for sale
matched lumber lumber with edges shaped as tongue-and-groove
mil measure of thickness equal to one thousandth of an inch (.0254 mm)
millwork cutting, sizing, shaping, and planing of lumber and wood parts
miter (*vb*) cut piece of wood on 45-degree angle
on center measurement taken from center of one member to center of another
out-of-plumb (*adj*) not in proper vertical alignment
penny designation of nail length, shown as d
pitch ratio of rise to span of roof
platform framing framing in which studs extend for one floor only and rest upon subfloor of each story
plot plan drawing that shows size, slope, and location of structure on lot
plumb (*adj*) in true vertical position
quarter-sawed (*adj*) designating lumber cut at 90-degree angle to tree's growth rings
rabbet open groove cut into edge of board to form joint
ripping cutting wood in direction of grain
roughing-in installation of plumbing and electrical systems that will later be concealed by interior finishing
sapwood light-colored wood located between heartwood and bark in tree
sawhorse rack with two slanting legs at each end, used to support wood being sawed
scaffold movable platform supported by frame or suspended by ropes to support workers and materials above ground
scale proportion of drawings or blueprints to actual structure, represented by ratio
shear force producing opposite but parallel sliding motion in each of the contacting planes in a structural member
slope rise of roof in inches per foot of run
span distance between two supporting members, esp. between exterior walls
specifications architect's detailed instructions not shown on blueprints or working drawings
subcontractor person or company hired by contractor to do specialized tasks, such as plumbing or wiring
superstructure part of building above basement
toenail (*vb*) drive nails at slant
true (*adj*) precisely or accurately formed, fitted, placed, or calibrated, esp. to conform to pattern or form
warp variation in wood board from flat plane
weatherize (*vb*) secure structure against cold or wind by adding insulation, siding, strips, or storm windows
working drawings complete set of drawings that shows all details of structure to be built; blueprints

BUILDING AND CONSTRUCTION MATERIALS

Cuts, Sizes, Treatments, and Forms of Wood
Softwoods
Hardwoods
Paneling and Composite Boards
Stones, Bricks, Tiles, Glass, and Metals
Plastics, Paper, and Textiles
Adhesives and Binders
Surfaces and Finishing Materials

Cuts, Sizes, Treatments, and Forms of Wood

a/d air-dried
air-dried (*adj*) a/d; designating lumber stacked out of doors so that air circulates between boards to remove moisture
batten sawed strip of wood, esp. used as seam or fastener
beam long, thick piece of lumber, used esp. as support for roof
bevel siding siding cut with sloping surface at edge
board milled, sawed piece of wood up to 2 inches (5.1 cm) thick and 2 or more inches wide
board foot standard measure of lumber, equal to 1x12x12 inches or 144 cubic inches
caning slender, flexible wood stems split into narrow strands and woven together, esp. for chairs

ceiling board cut board used in ceilings
clapboard narrow board thicker at one edge, used for outside walls; weatherboard
close-grained (*adj*) designating wood having fine, compact grain
construction wood dimension lumber
cork light, thick, soft, elastic bark of cork oak tree
cut amount of wood; style in which wood is sawed
decking construction boards for exterior use
dimension lumber usu. softwood lumber used for framing or as sheathing
dowel solid, cylindrical rod of wood
dressed size dimensions of lumber after drying and planing
drop siding siding with tongue-and-groove, rabbeted, or shiplap joint; matched siding
edge-glued (*adj*) designating flat-edged lumber bonded by gluing
edge-matched (*adj*) designating lumber with tongue-and-groove edges
end-matched (*adj*) designating lumber with tongue-and-groove ends
excelsior fine, curled wood shavings that form resilient mass, used for packing
exterior plywood usu. rough-grade plywood sheets with exterior glue, used under finishing materials
fencing long, thin posts or rails used to make fences
finish lumber high-quality softwood lumber to be left natural or stained for appearance
flat-grained (*adj*) designating wood having smooth, consistent grain
flooring long strips of tongue-and-groove finishing lumber, used for flooring
framing softwood construction lumber used for skeletal frame of structure
furring strips narrow, unfinished wood strips attached to masonry or concrete as base for finishing material
grading standardized system of rating and marking wood to indicate quality
grape stakes thick, unfinished posts used to support vines
green lumber undried lumber
hardwood lumber made from the wood of deciduous trees, used primarily for trim, finishing, and built-ins
heartwood mature wood at center of tree
interior finish material used to cover interior walls and ceiling surfaces
jambs strips used as side frame of door or window
k/d kiln-dried
kiln-dried (*adj*) k/d; designating lumber dried in kiln using regulated steam and hot air
knotty (*adj*) designating lumber with cross-grained, rounded areas, or knots, formed by lump where branch grew out of tree trunk
lath thin, narrow strips nailed to two-by-fours and rafters as foundation for plaster, tiles, and finishing boards
log long section of tree trunk or thick branch of felled tree to be cut and milled into lumber
louver door door with overlapping, horizontal slats
lumber timber sawed and milled into standard size beams, planks, and boards
lumber sizing standard sizes of lumber, in inches: 1x2, 1x3, 1x4, 1x5, 1x6, 1x8, 1x10, 1x12, 2x2, 2x3, 2x4, 2x6, 2x8, 2x10, 2x12, 3x3, 4x4, 4x8, 4x12
matched siding drop siding
milling cutting, shaping, and shaving of lumber and wood products on large scale in manufacturing plant
mixed-grain (*adj*) designating wood with both closed and open grains
molding shaped strip of wood used to finish or decorate walls: astragal, base, batten, bead, casing saddle, chair rail, corner guard, cove, crown, full round, half round, handrail, lattice, mantel, nose and cove, ogee, oval, picture frame, pilaster, quarter round, round edge, scalloped, sprung cove, stop, threshold, and window stool
open-grained (*adj*) designating wood having irregularly patterned grain, usu. wide
paneling broad, flat sections of wood from which panels are cut
parquet flooring squares in which grains of adjacent squares run at right angles
partition large sheet of wood or other material used to divide interior areas
pinoleum fine wooden sticks, stitched together as blinds
plank long, broad, thick board
plywood thin sheet of wood made by gluing and pressing together layers, often with grains at right angles; grades: AB, ACX, AD
plywood circle round plywood sheet
plywood sizing standard sizes of plywood: 4x8 feet or 4x10 feet by 1/4, 3/8, 1/2, 5/8, 3/4, or 1 inch thick
pole long, slender piece of wood, usu. cylindrical
post thick square or cylindrical beam section used in upright position
pressure-treated (*adj*) designating wood with resin compressed under great heat to increase hardness and resistance to moisture and decay
puncheon short post, used upright in framing
rabbeted (*adj*) designating board or plank with groove cut in edge to accept another piece of wood to form joint
rattan slender, tough stem of palm tree, used in furniture
reed fencing thick grass stalks plaited into fence
roofing rafter beams or plywood sheets used in roof frame; exterior material, such as shingles or shake, used on roof
rush round, pliant stem of certain marsh grasses, used in thatch roofs, furniture, and baskets
sapwood light-colored, living wood layer between heartwood and bark
seasoning aging and drying process that matures lumber to improve its workability
shake long shingle split directly from log
sheathing layer of boards that covers roof rafters or outside wall studs

sheeting broad pieces of wood used to cover a surface
shelving thin, flat section of board to be fixed at right angles to wall
shingle thin, wedge-shaped piece of wood to be laid in overlapping rows over roof or wall sheathing
shiplap boards or siding rabbeted along edge to overlap and form joint
shutter louvered window covering
siding materials applied over wall sheathing as finished surface: hardboard, lap, metal, plastic, plywood
siding shingle shingle used over wall sheathing
slat thin, narrow wood strip
softwood lumber made from the wood of evergreen trees, used primarily for framing, construction, and some finishing
split flexible strip of wood or wood stem used in baskets or furniture
stake thin length of wood pointed at one end
stock tree trunk
stud boards, esp. 2x4s, used in upright position as framing to which sheathing, panels, or siding are nailed
thatch rushes or palm leaves used as roofing
timber heavy, dressed beam, usu. 5 inches (12.7 cm) or more in least dimension
tongue-and-groove (*adj*) designating lumber, esp. paneling and flooring, in which boards interlock along edges
treatment aging, drying, or seasoning done to improve quality of wood
trim finished interior and exterior moldings
two-by-four most common board used in framing, being 2 inches by 4 inches
veneer thin sheets of wood assembled in layers into plywood
vertical-grained (*adj*) designating lumber with grain running lengthwise
walling sheathing for walls
weatherboard clapboard
weatherizing treatment of exterior finish wood to conserve heat and resist water
wicker pliant twigs or rods plaited together into chairs or baskets
windows boards framed into windows
wood hard, fibrous substance beneath tree bark, cut and prepared as timber or lumber
woodwork interior moldings, doors, windows, and stairs

Softwoods

softwood lumber made from the wood of evergreen trees, used primarily for framing, construction, and some finishing
appearance pine
balsam fir
cedar, clear pine, cypress
Douglas fir
Englemann spruce
fir
hemlock
incense cedar
jack pine, juniper
knotty pine
larch, loblolly pine, lodgepole pine
mountain hemlock
Pacific yew, pine, ponderosa pine
red cedar, redwood
shortleaf pine, sound cedar, spruce, sugar pine
tamarack
white cedar, white fir, white pine
yellow pine, yew

Hardwoods

hardwood lumber made from the wood of deciduous trees, used primarily for trim, finishing, and built-ins
acacia, alder, American ash, American beech, American elm, apple, ash, aspen
balsa, bamboo, banyan, basswood, beech, birch, black cherry, black walnut, black willow, brasswood, briarwood, burl birch, buttonwood
calamander, cherry, chestnut, Circassian walnut, concept oak, cork, cottonwood, crystal elm, cypress
dogwood
ebony, elite walnut, elm, eucalyptus
frontier birch
Garry oak, golden oak, gum, gumwood
harewood, hazel, heirloom cherry, hickory
ironwood
lauan, lemonwood, linden, locust, logwood
magnolia, mahogany, maple
Niagara ash
oak, olive, orangewood, Oriental ash
peach, pecan, Philippine mahogany, plane, poplar
red oak, rock elm, rosewood
sandalwood, satinwood, Savannah hickory, sen, shagbark hickory, spartan oak, sugar maple, sumac, sweet gum, sycamore
teak, tulipwood, tupelo
walnut, white ash, white oak, wicker, willow
yellow birch, yellow poplar
zebrawood

Paneling and Composite Boards

ceiling tile usu. 2x4 foot acoustic tile sheet of composite board
chipboard compressed wood pulp, sawdust, and wood chips with resin binder
composite board class of high-strength, lightweight sheet materials made by combining various elements with a binder
compreg wood impregnated with resin, then compressed under great heat to increase hardness and resistance to moisture and decay; impreg
corkboard sheet of porous, elastic cork
drywall gypsum or hardboard panels joined as

interior wall finish; plasterboard
fiberboard compressed wood or vegetable fibers in sheets
gypsum board laminate with gypsum core and layers of fibrous paper; plasterboard
hardboard wood fibers placed under heat and pressure and pressed into sheets
impreg wood impregnated with resin, then compressed under great heat to increase hardness and resistance to moisture and decay; compreg
insulation board sheets of material that resist transfer of heat or sound
laminate very strong or stiff multilayered material, esp. of plastic
paperboard composite board of varying thickness and rigidity composed of layers of paper with binding
particle board panel of wood fibers, flakes, and shavings bonded together with synthetic resin
pasteboard layers of paper pressed together or pressed and dried paper pulp formed into sheets
pegboard composite or particle board pierced with holes into which pegs are placed for hanging objects
perfboard hardboard with holes into which hooks or pegs can be inserted for hanging objects
pinboard cork or soft board that can be pierced with pins to hold papers
plasterboard plaster of Paris core covered with heavy sheets of paper, used for walls or partitions; drywall; gypsum board
plastic laminated wood plastic coating bonded to plywood or particle board, used as countertop
wallboard fibrous material made with gypsum in sheets for covering walls or ceilings or for displays
weatherboard laminate clapboard for exterior use

Stones, Bricks, Tiles, Glass, and Metals

acoustical tile sound-absorbent ceiling tiles made with slotted insulation board, polystyrene, or fiberglass
adobe mixture of reddish clay, straw, and water, used for building walls
aggregate cement formulation made from sand, gravel, and rock fragments, used esp. for tiles and shingles
alloy metal that is a mixture of two or more metals or a metal and nonmetal
aluminum lightweight, noncorrosive metal used in various forms
aluminum siding aluminum panels for exterior walls
asbestos tile insulating tiles made from fireproof fibrous mineral
ashlar thin, square-cut, dressed stone used for facing masonry walls
asphalt brown or black bituminous coal tar residue used for paving and to make roofing tiles
barbed wire strands of twisted wire with sharp barbs projecting at regular intervals, used for fencing
bead small, round piece of glass, metal, or wood, usu. strung with others like it
bitumen natural asphalt; hard or semisolid, tarlike residue from distilled coal, wood tar, or petroleum
blacktop bituminous asphalt mixture, used for road surfaces
brass yellowish alloy of copper and zinc
brick molded clay baked into hard oblong blocks, esp. of reddish-brown color, used as building blocks
brownstone reddish-brown sandstone used in large blocks for building
castiron hard, molded iron alloy
ceiling tile tile made from acoustical material or fiberboard, used in ceiling
ceramic clay pottery, earthenware
chain link galvanized steel links interwoven into fencing
chicken wire thin, flexible wire fencing with large, hexagonal mesh
chrome chromium alloy used in plating
cinderblock concrete and cinder aggregate building block in any of various shapes, typically having a lateral hole through its center
cobblestone rounded stone used in paving
common brick standard size, oblong, reddish-brown brick; red brick
concrete mixture of cement, sand, gravel, and water that dries to form hard surface
corrugated steel thin sheet of galvanized steel shaped into parallel grooves and ridges for added strength
cut glass ornamental flint glass with patterns cut into its surface by abrasive wheel
damask steel with wavy damascene markings
ferroconcrete high-strength, reinforced concrete, usu. layered in thin sheets
flag flat slab of stone; flagstone
flagstone flat piece split from hard stone, used for paving
freestone stone, such as limestone or sandstone, that may be cut freely without splitting
glass hard, brittle, usu. transparent substance composed of fused and rapidly cooled silicates mixed with potash or soda and lime
glass block square or oblong, hollow glass structure, used as decorative building block; glass brick
glass brick glass block
glass wool fine glass fibers woven into dense mass, used for insulation
glazing panes or sheets of glass to be set in frames such as windows or mirrors
gravel mixture of pebbles and rock fragments graded by size from coarse to fine, used for outdoor surfaces
linoleum hard, smooth floor covering made of solidified linseed oil mixed with gum, cork dust, or wood flour set on a backing of burlap or canvas, often cut into kitchen tiles
macadam rock fragments mixed with tar or asphalt to form roadway
marble hard, crystalline limestone with white, streaked, or mottled surface that takes high polish

marl brick composed of loose, crumbling earth
masonry brick, cinderblock, stone, or tile bonded with mortar or concrete
mirror glass coated on one side with reflective substance
pane glass transparent glass sheets cut to size for windows
paving gravel, stone, concrete, or asphalt, used to surface outdoor area or roadway
plate glass clear ground glass in large sheets, used for windows; sheet glass
prestressed concrete concrete reinforced with embedded cables or wires under tension to increase strength
quarry tiles durable fired tiles of unrefined clay, used as flooring
red brick common brick
reinforced concrete concrete masonry embedded with steel bars or mesh for greater tensile strength
rough-cut stone rubble; irregular, rough-dressed rock fragments
safety glass shatterproof glass made by placing layer of resin or transparent plastic between two panes of glass
scrap discarded fragment, esp. of metal, that can be reused, often in altered form
screening fine, close mesh composed of metal wires, used esp. to allow ventilation through doors or windows while excluding insects
sheet glass plate glass
sheet metal metal cut into large, thin, flat pieces
slate hard, bluish-gray, fine-grained rock used for roof tiles
smoked glass glass colored or darkened by smoke
spun glass fine threads of liquid glass
stained glass glass colored by fusing of metallic oxides, enameling, or burning pigments into its surface, used for decorative windows
steel hard, tough, rust-resistant iron alloy, used extensively for many purposes
stone hard, solid, nonmetallic mineral substance of which rocks consist
terra cotta hard, reddish-brown clay earthenware, used for ornamental facing
tile thin, usu. square or rectangular piece of stone, concrete, or fired clay, used for roofing or flooring
tinfoil paper-thin sheet of tin, or alloy of tin and lead, used for insulation
wrought iron tough, malleable, soft commercial iron with 1 or 2 percent slag content, used for furniture and fixtures

Plastics, Paper, and Textiles

asbestos fibrous material of fireproof mineral, used for insulation and tiling
batting cotton, wool, or synthetic fiber wadded and quilted into sheets
batt insulation insulation made of batting
buckram stiffened linen cloth
bunting thin, translucent cloth used for decorations
burlap coarse sacking; hessian
canvas coarse, dense hemp or cotton cloth
cardboard thick, stiff material made from paper pulp; paperboard
carpeting thick, heavy wool, cotton, or synthetic fiber woven with pile, used for floor covering
cellophane thin, transparent, moisture-proof material made from cellulose
cellulose chief substance in fibers of all plant tissue, used in making paper and textiles
chamois soft leather made from skin of goatlike, European antelope or sheep, used as polishing cloth
cheesecloth very loosely woven thin cotton cloth
crepe paper thin, stiff, crinkled paper
fiberglass finespun glass filaments woven into sheets, used with backing as thermal or acoustical insulation or pressed and molded with resin as plastic
flax fibers of flax plant spun into thread
foam rubber rubber treated to form firm, spongy mass
grass cloth soft fabric made from plant bark fibers
grass paper fine grass fibers plaited into paper
hessian coarsely woven cloth; burlap
jute strong fiber used for rope, burlap, and mats
kraft paper strong, brown paper made from wood pulp prepared with sodium sulfate solution, used for wrapping
leather animal skin prepared by removing hair and tanning
millboard strong, heavy cardboard used for book covers or furniture panels
muslin cotton with plain weave, often heavyweight with coarse finish
paper very thin, flexible sheets made from wood pulp or other fibrous material
paperboard stiff, heavy material made from wood pulp, thicker than paper; cardboard
papier-mâché shredded paper mixed with glue to form highly plastic molding material
pasteboard stiff material made from pasted layers of paper or pressed and dried paper pulp
plastic laminate plastic glued to plywood or particle board, used for countertops
plastics various nonmetallic organic compounds produced synthetically by polymerization, which can be molded, hardened, or formed into pliable sheets, fibers, or foams
polyester polymeric synthetic resin used in making plastics and synthetic fibers
polypropylene polymerized propylene, a very light, highly resistant thermoplastic resin, used for packaging and coating
polystyrene tough, clear, colorless plastic polymer of styrene, used esp. for containers and apparatus
polyurethane various synthetic polymers, used in elastic fibers, foam, insulation, molded products, and coatings
raffia fiber obtained from Mediterranean palm, used for baskets or ropes
rice paper thin, translucent paper made from straw of rice grass
rubber hard, elastic substance obtained by coagu-

lating and drying sap or latex of various tropical plants, or made synthetically
strawboard coarse straw cardboard, used esp. for boxes
styrene easily polymerized aromatic liquid, used to make synthetic rubber and plastics
tagboard strong cardboard
tarpaper heavy paper impregnated with tar, used as base for roofing
textiles woven fabrics made of natural or synthetic fibers
vinyl compound derived from ethylene and polymerized into various resins and plastics
wallpaper decorative strips of paper used to cover walls, usu. applied with glue

Adhesives and Binders

acrylic resin transparent, thermoplastic, polymeric resin, used in making molded plastics, paints, and textile fibers
adhesive any substance that binds or adheres
adhesive tape long, narrow, wound strip of tape with sticky substance on one side
astringent substance that causes binding by contraction
binder substance that holds things together
birdlime extremely sticky substance made from holly bark
caulking whitish tar or oakum putty used to stop crack or fill joint
cement soft substance that binds objects together when it hardens between them
compo composite mortar or plaster
creosote brownish, oily liquid distilled from coal tar, used as wood preservative
daubing soft, sticky plaster or grease smeared on surface
double-stick tape tape with adhesive substance on both sides
duct tape wide, silver-gray, strong adhesive tape, used for Sheetrock work, household repairs, etc.
electrical tape strong, highly elastic, black adhesive tape
epoxy thermosetting, quick-drying chemical resin blended with other chemicals to form strong, hard, adhesive bond
glue sticky, viscous liquid made by boiling animal skins, bones, and hoofs to a jelly
grout thin mortar or plaster, used to fill joints in masonry, tiles, or brick
gum adhesive substance made from sticky colloidal carbohydrate found in certain trees and plants
gutta-percha rubberlike gum latex, used for insulation and binding
gypsum naturally occurring hydrated sulfate of calcium, used in making plaster of Paris for binding plasterboard
lute clayey cement used as sealing agent
masking tape thin, weak, usu. beige adhesive tape
mortar mixture of lime or cement with sand and water, used to bind bricks or stones in building or as plaster
mucilage thick, sticky plant substance; watery gum or glue solution
oakum loose, stringy hemp fiber treated with tar, used for caulking
paste mixture of flour or starch with water and alum or resin, used as adhesive on light materials
pitch dark, sticky substance distilled from coal, wood tar, or petroleum, used for waterproofing, roofing, or paving
plaster of Paris calcined gypsum in heavy, white powder form, mixed with water to form quick-setting paste
Portland cement cement that hardens underwater, made by burning mixture of lime and clay, used to bind aggregate
putty mixture of powdered chalk and linseed oil, used to secure glass panes and fill cracks; cement composed of quicklime, water, and plaster of Paris or sand, used as plastering coat
resin any of various viscous, usu. clear or translucent, substances exuded from trees or plants, used in varnish, lacquer, and in making synthetic plastics
rubber cement unvulcanized rubber in solvent, used to bind light materials
sealant wax, plastic, or silicone substance used for making a joint airtight or watertight
sizing thin, pasty substance used as glaze or filler on porous paper, plaster, or cloth prior to finishing
solder metal alloy melted and used to join or patch metal parts when it hardens
spackling compound gypsum plaster mixed with glue, silica flour, and water, used as putty or filler
stucco plaster applied as finish to interior walls and exterior surfaces
tar thick, sticky, dark brown to black, viscous, liquid hydrocarbon obtained from distillation of wood, coal, or peat, used esp. in roofing and paving
tarmac bituminous binder used for surfacing roadways
wax plastic, dull-yellow substance, insoluble in water, used as sealant or to protect surfaces
weather stripping thin length of metal, fabric, wood, or composite, used to cover joint and keep out wind or water

Surfaces and Finishing Materials

acrylic paint pigments in solution of acrylic resin, quick-drying and brilliant
alabaster translucent, whitish, fine-grained gypsum
brecciation process of giving surface the appearance of sharp rock fragments cemented together
carnauba wax hard brittle wax obtained from palm leaves, used in polishes
cladding process of covering one material, esp. metal, with another by bonding

clinquant imitation gold leaf
cottage cheese lumping plaster, used esp. for finishing ceilings
damascene wavy patterns like watered silk on metal; inlays of precious metals on iron or steel
dye natural or synthetic substance, esp. in solution, used to produce color
enamel opaque, usu. glossy, vitreous coating for metal, glass, and earthenware; paint drying to such a glossy finish
finish manner in which surface is painted, varnished, coated, smoothed, or polished; material applied to complete or perfect surface
gild (*vb*) overlay with very thin layer of gold
gold leaf very thin layer of gold overlaid on surface
high-gloss (*adj*) designating very bright, lustrous surface finish, esp. of enamel paint
lacquer durable, nonoily varnish, esp. of sumac, applied in layers to wood and polished to mirrorlike finish; comparable synthetic organic solution
lamina thin flake or scale of metal or animal tissue
latex waterbase paint made by suspending particles of synthetic rubber or plastic in water; milky, resinous liquid present in rubber trees
leaf very thin sheet of metal; lamina
marbling painting technique that gives veined, mottled, marblelike appearance to objects
matte flat finish without shine or luster, esp. in paints
moire watery, wavy design, as on silk
oil any of various greasy substances obtained from animal, vegetable, or mineral sources, used to treat absorbent surfaces
oil-base paint paint made by grinding pigment in drying oil, esp. linseed oil, not soluble in water
paint mixture of pigment with water, oil, or latex in liquid or paste form, applied to surfaces for protection and coloring
parging application of mortar to masonry surface to smooth and waterproof it
patina surface coating due to aging, esp. green coloration on copper
planish (*vb*) toughen, smooth, or polish metal by hammering or rolling
plaster pasty mixture, made from lime or gypsum, sand, and water, that hardens on drying, used to coat walls and ceilings
polish wax, oil, or liquid plastic rubbed onto surface to provide bright, glossy finish
primer paint or sizing applied to raw surface prior to finishing coat
roughcast coarse stucco used on exterior walls
semigloss (*adj*) designating paint that dries to a finish more lustrous than matte and less lustrous than high-gloss
shellac thin, clear solution of refined lac resin in alcohol, used as wood filler and finish
stain liquid coating to darken or color wood and bring out grain
stencil design cut out of waxed paper or acetate and reproduced on surface below paper with paint or ink
swirling allowing undercoat of paint to show through top coat
thinner turpentine or other substance added to dilute paint or varnish
turpentine colorless, volatile hydrocarbon used in paint and varnish
varnish resin dissolved in oil or thinner that dries to hard, lustrous, usu. transparent finish on wood
veneer thin overlay of finishing material, esp. wood, on base of another material
verdigris greenish-blue coating that forms naturally on brass, bronze, or copper
waterbase paint pigment mixed with water or latex, soluble in water
wax soft, resinous, water-resistant substance rubbed on surfaces, esp. wood and leather, to protect and shine

TOOLS AND HARDWARE

Common Tools and Tool Types

bit detachable, usu. interchangeable cutting, drilling, or boring part of a drill or other tool, available in various sizes suited to hole desired or specific need
blade broad, thin, flat, sharpened edge of cutting tool
chisel any of various wedgelike tools with cutting edge at end of blade, used for shaping solid materials, esp. wood or stone
clamp device that holds two or more objects tightly together between parts that draw together
digging tool any shovel, hoe, spade, or rake used for moving earth or rocks
drill shafted device, usu. affixed to handle, with point and two or more cutting edges for piercing hard surfaces, usu. by rapid rotations
edged tool tool with cutting edge or blade
fastening tool any screwdriver, clamp, vise, or

cord used to hold parts together
file steel hand tool with abrasive surface for shaping and smoothing objects
gauge any device for measuring, testing, or registering measurements
gripping tool tool with jaws or pincers, such as pliers
hammer any of various handheld or power tools with hard, metal head at end of handle, used for pounding and nailing
hardware metalware usu. forming functional or decorative component part
hook curved, pointed, often barbed device for clasping or moving objects
knife blade, either attached to a handle or part of a machine, used for cutting, slicing, or shaping
marking tool device for scratching surface or applying mark at specific spot
measuring tool any device such as scale, rule, level, or square, used to determine magnitude, dimension, precision, or trueness
plane tool with horizontally mounted, adjustable blade in handle, used for smoothing or paring wood surfaces and for forming moldings, chamfers, and grooves
pliers small pincer tool with long, grasping jaws and two handles
pointed tool tool tapering to sharp point at one end
power tool any tool driven by more than human energy, esp. electrical power
rule length of straight hard material marked in units for measuring
sander power tool for smoothing surfaces with abrasive material, usu. on belt or disk
saw toothed blade attached to handle or in machine, used for cutting wood and other hard materials
scraping tool file or rasp for roughly removing surface material, esp. from wood
screwdriver handle with long, narrow, metal extension that tapers and flattens so as to fit into screwheads to turn and drive them
shaping tool any plane, sander, router, or lathe that precisely trims surface material to predetermined design
sharpener device for honing blade of edged tool
shaving tool device for removing excess material from surface
shovel broad, slightly hollowed, blade-edged scoop on handle for digging, scooping, or lifting heavy, often loose material
smoothing tool sandpaper, hone, or plane for finishing surface of shaped object
square instrument with straight edges and at least one ninety-degree angle, used to plot right angles
tightening tool screwdriver, clamp, or vise for forcing parts together
tool any implement, instrument, or device held in hand or driven by machine power and used to facilitate some physical or mechanical task
trowel small hand tool with flat blade attached to handle, used to spread or smooth loose material
wrench any of various hand or power tools for holding or turning a bolt or nut in a set or adjustable mouth at end of handle

Edged, Pointed, Carving, and Turning Tools

adz thin, curved blade mounted at right angles to handle, used for trimming and shaping wood
awl small, pointed instrument for marking and piercing holes, esp. in leather
ax heavy blade head attached to handle, used esp. for chopping and splitting wood
barb sharp point projecting in opposite direction from main point of tool
bill curved blade set on handle, used for pruning or cutting
blade broad, thin, flat, sharpened edge of cutting tool
bodkin slender, pointed instrument for piercing cloth or leather
bradawl awl for making small holes in wood for brads
burin engraving tool with steel blade and sharp point
chisel any of various wedgelike tools with cutting edge at end of blade, used to shape solid materials, esp. wood or stone
church key small, flat implement with pointed triangular head for penetrating beverage can tops
cleaver heavy cutting tool with broad blade, usu. used by butcher
clipper tool for cutting or shearing, often with multiple blades
colter sharp blade or wheel attached at front of plow, used for cutting earth
crampon spiked plate attached to boot for use in climbing; device for lifting or grasping loads, usu. consisting of two hooks suspended from a cable or chain
dibble small, handheld, pointed device for poking holes in earth for plants or seeds
frow cleaving tool with wedge-shaped blade at right angle to handle
gouge grooving chisel with concave blade, used esp. in turning
grapnel small anchor with several flukes or claws
grappling iron hook for anchoring boat to dock or to another boat
graver any of various bladed tools, such as burin or scauper, used for engraving
hatchet short-handled ax, often with a hammerhead
knife blade, either attached to a handle or part of a machine, used for cutting, slicing, and shaping
machete large heavy knife, often with blade widening at end away from handle
nibbler edged device for cutting sheet metal
pick tool with heavy metal head, pointed at one or both ends, attached to wooden handle
pickax head having ax blade and pick point attached to long handle

pinking shears shears with serrated edges for cutting fabric
pipe cutter hand tool with three wheels, one for cutting and two for guiding, that are pressed inward to cut through pipe as tool is rotated
piton spike pounded into rock fissure or ice for support in climbing
punch small, metal spike, used for perforating and stamping materials, marking layout lines, and driving nails
puncheon pointed stamping tool for goldsmith work
razor very fine-edged cutting blade, usu. of steel
scissors two hinged blades that cut when edges move past each other as handles are squeezed together
scraper edged tool used in turning on lathe
scythe long, curving blade on handle, esp. for cutting grass
shears large, powerful scissors for gardening or metalwork
sickle curved, hooklike blade on short handle, used for cutting grain
spring shears scissorslike cutting tool with nonpivoting jaws that spring open when released
spur pointed, sometimes barbed hook or metal device
square-end chisel chisel with blade ending square to its length
stylus hard-pointed needle for cutting or marking
tang projecting point or prong on chisel, file, or knife
utility knife razor blade held in small handle
wedge metal rod tapering to blade end, used for raising weights or splitting hard objects
wire cutter plierslike tool with edged jaws, used to cut through wire

Other edged and pointed tools

alpenstock
belt punch, bistoury, bob punch, bolster chisel, bread knife, bricklayer's chisel, brick set, broadax, bushwhacker, butcher knife, butt chisel
cant hook, carpet knife, carving chisel, carving knife, carving set, case knife, celt, chaser, chopping knife, clasp knife, claw hatchet, cold chisel, cold cutter, croze, cutting pliers
dogleg chisel, drawshave, drove chisel
eaves hook, electric razor
firmer chisel, fluted gouge, framing chisel, frowglass cutter
garnish awl, glazier's chisel, goosewing ax, groover, grub ax, grub hoe
hack, half hatchet, hedge trimmer, hook blade, hot cutter, hunting knife
iron
jackknife, jeweler's chisel
kranging hook
lance, lancet, letter-opener, linoleum knife
masonry chisel, mason's chisel, mat knife, mill knife, mortise chisel
nippers, nooker knife
palette knife, panga, paper cutter, paper knife, paring chisel, paring knife, penknife, plowshare, pocketknife, pole tree pruner, prick punch, pruner, pruning hook, pruning shears, putty knife
reed knife, rigger's knife, ripping chisel, roofing knife, roughing-out gouge
safety razor, saw knife, sax, scalpel, scauper, scoop, scorper, scraper, scuffle hoe, share, shearing hook, sheath knife, sheet metal punch, shingling hatchet, sidecutters, slotter, snips, spear, spindle gouge, surgical knife, swan neck chisel
table knife, taping knife, tin snips, turning chisel
wood chisel
Xacto knife

Saws

backsaw short saw with reinforced back
band saw saw consisting of endless, toothed steel band passing around two wheels
bayonet handsaw with long, deep-toothed, bayonetlike blade on small handle
bench saw circular saw mounted on workbench
bucksaw saw with blade mounted across upright frame, held in both hands for cutting wood on sawhorse
buzz saw stationary, power-operated, circular saw with teeth on large disk attached to shaft
chain saw usu. portable power saw with teeth set on endless, revolving chain
circular saw handheld electric saw with disk-shaped blade
compass saw small handsaw with narrow, tapering blade for cutting curves; keyhole saw
coping saw saw with thin, light blade in U-shaped frame with handle, used to cut small curves or do ornamental work in thin wood; fret saw
crosscut saw saw for cutting wood perpendicular to grain
crown saw rotary saw consisting of hollow cylinder with teeth at one end or edge; cylinder saw; hole saw
dial saw small blades mounted on circular plate whose diameter can be adjusted, used to cut holes
flush cut saw single-edged saw with extremely flexible, thin, unbacked blade that will bend to cut off pegs without marking adjacent surface
frame saw saw, often with multiple detachable blades that are attached to handle at both ends, used esp. for precision work
friction saw high-speed, usu. toothless, circular saw that cuts metals by melting them with frictional heat
hacksaw narrow, fine-toothed blade fixed in frame, used to cut metal

handsaw common saw with handle at one end for manual operation
jigsaw usu. stationary electric saw with narrow blade mounted vertically in frame, used to cut curves and other irregular lines
keyhole saw compass saw
log saw sturdy blade with large, deep teeth for cutting logs or timber
miter saw portable, electric, circular saw with adjustable guide for cutting miters
panel saw stationary power tool, either horizontal or vertical, used to cut large sheets of material accurately
power saw any of various electrical, gas-powered, pneumatic, or battery-driven saws
radial arm saw stationary, electrically powered saw with blade on overhead arm that moves across width of wood
ripsaw saw used for cutting wood with the grain
saber saw portable, handheld electric jigsaw
saw toothed blade attached to handle or in machine, used for cutting wood and other hard materials
scroll saw narrow saw mounted vertically in frame and moved up and down in cutting curved ornamentation, usu. benchtop power saw
stationary circular saw power saw with disk-shaped blade, affixed to bench or in standing unit
table saw small, stationary power saw with bench-like table on which wood is placed for cutting
veneer saw small saw with a handle that is flat on one side and has a blade along its length, this blade having teeth facing in both directions, used for cutting veneer sheets
whipsaw saw operated between two persons, used to divide timbers lengthwise

OTHER SAWS

azibiki
belt saw, board saw, bow saw, builder's saw, butcher's saw
contractor's saw, cordwood saw, cutoff saw, cylinder saw
diamond saw, double-cut saw, dovetail saw, dry-wall saw
electric saw
flooring saw, fret saw
helicoidal saw, hikimawashi, hole saw
jeweler's saw
kerf saw, kitchen saw
lightning saw, logging saw, lumberman's saw
marquetry saw, meat saw, mill saw, mortise saw
pad saw, panther-head saw, pitsaw, plumber's saw, plywood saw, pocket saw, portable saw, portable sawmill, pruning saw
reciprocating saw
saw knife, saw machine, Sawzall, scribe saw, skewback saw, Skilsaw, splitsaw, surgeon's saw, sweepback saw
tenon saw, trim saw, trock saw, two-handed saw
utility saw
vertical saw
wallboard saw, wire saw, wood saw

Shaving, Shaping, Sharpening, and Smoothing Tools

abrader handheld scraping tool
anvil heavy iron block on which metals are placed for shaping by pounding
belt sander electric sander with abrasive surface on continuous belt
block plane small plane for cutting across grain
buffer any of various polishing devices, usu. with smoothing surface attached to handle or other mechanism
bullnose plane small, blunt-ended planing tool
circular file file with cylindrical abrasive surface, often tapering toward end away from handle
die any of various tools for forming material into a specific shape, esp. by pressure of cutting
disk sander electric sander with abrasive surface attached to rotating disk head
drum sander usu. stationary power tool with rotating cylinder, used to smooth curved surfaces
electric sander electrically powered, orbital or straight-line hand tool for smoothing surfaces
file steel hand tool with abrasive surface for shaping and smoothing objects
flatiron device with flat metal bottom that is heated and used to smooth materials, esp. cloth
float trowellike tool with thick rubber face attached at each end to handle, used for smoothing grout or similar material
grinding wheel circular head of abrasive material for sanding and grinding
grindstone revolving wheel of abrasive material, usu. Carborundum, for grinding and shaping
hone abrasive whetstone for sharpening bladed cutting tools
jointer large plane for smoothing wood surfaces; stationary power tool used to achieve smooth, flat surface on wood
lathe stationary power tool with fixed tool mechanism and machine that rotates work around axis, used for shaping cylindrical objects
machine tool power-driven device used to shape or trim objects
multiplane versatile plane, with up to forty interchangeable cutting blades, for large variety of uses
oilstone block of fine-grained stone, usu. oiled, for sharpening certain cutting tools by abrasion
plane tool with horizontally mounted, adjustable blade in handle, used for smoothing or paring wood surfaces and for forming moldings, chamfers, and grooves
planer power tool for surfacing rough wood
power sander high-speed electrical sander, either rotary, orbital, or straight belt, with attachments from fine to coarse grain
punch press power tool used to cut and shape metal sheets with dies under pressure

putty knife broad, flexible blade on short handle for spreading putty
rasp metal file with coarse raised nubs
router machine with rotating, milling, or cutting bits mounted on vertical spindle, used for gouging wood surfaces
sander power tool for smoothing surfaces with abrasive material, usu. on belt or disk
sandpaper paper with sand or other abrasive glued to one side, used for smoothing surfaces, esp. wood
scraper any of various hand tools with blades that are usu. pulled, rather than pushed, to shape wood surface
shaper any of various tools or machines for shaping and pressing sheet metal; stationary power tool with cutters, used to contour edge of wood
slipstone sharpening stone with rounded and tapering edges, used on gouges and other carving tools
spokeshave blade set between two winglike handles, used for forming and dressing curved edges of wood
steel wool matted mass of steel shavings used by hand for shaving and smoothing surfaces
stone grindstone or whetstone
stroke sander stationary power tool with continuous overhead belt, used to sand large panels or surfaces
strop strip of leather for sharpening razors
tamper wide blade set perpendicular to handle, used for flattening and evening out soft or loose materials
thickness planer plane with strong blade and wide cut, used for shaving deeply into wood surfaces
trowel small hand tool with flat blade attached to handle, used for spreading or smoothing loose material

OTHER SHAVING, SHAPING, SHARPENING, AND SMOOTHING TOOLS

auger bit file
bastard file, beading plane, bench plane, bench stone, bending fork, brick trowel, buffing-and-polishing bonnet
cabinet scraper, cabinet rasp, capping plane, chuck, circle trowel, circular plane, combination plane, compass plane, contour sander, core box plane, corner trowel, cove trowel, curbing trowel
dado plane, dovetail plane
edge plane, electric plane
faceplate lathe, fillister plane, finger plane, finishing sander, flat file, fore plane
grinder, grooving plane, guttering trowel
hand plane, hand sander, hand scraper
jeweler's lathe
lute
match plane, mill file, molding plane, multiplane
needle rasp
orbital sander
pad sander, palm plane, perimeter sander, plasterer's float, plastering trowel, plough plane, plunge router, pointing trowel, portable handheld shaper, portable router, power plane
radius trowel, reed plane, rotary rasp, roughing plane, round bastard file
sanding belt, sash plane, scraper plane, scrub plane, seaming router, shoe rasp, shoulder plane, slick, smoothing plane, surform plane
tamping bar, tamping pick, tamping stick, tape file, thumb plane, tonguing plane, toothing plane, trenching plane, trimmer, trimming block
violin plane
warding file, wood plane, wood rasp

Shovels and Digging and Lifting Tools

bail scoop for removing accumulated water, esp. from boat
bull tongue wide plow blade for cultivating or marking soil
crowbar metal bar with flattened wedge at one end, used as a lever
cultivator implement with flat blade, drawn between rows of plants to loosen earth and remove weeds
fork pronged tool for lifting, throwing, or piercing
hoe flat blade at end of long handle, used for working earth around plants
lever rigid bar on axis or fulcrum, used to lift weight or exert pressure to dislodge something
loy long narrow spade, esp. one with broad chisel point for digging post holes
mattock pickaxlike tool with one broad end, used for loosening soil by digging
pitchfork large, two- or three-tined fork on long handle, used for lifting and tossing
plow implement with blade for cutting or lifting soil or clearing away debris
rake head with multiple, sometimes splayed prongs on long handle, used for gathering loose material or leveling ground
scoop deeply concave shovel or hollowed spoon for digging and carrying earth
scooper shovel, scoop, or ladle
shovel broad, slightly hollowed, blade-edged scoop on handle, used for digging, scooping, or lifting heavy, often loose material
spade small, flat blade at end of long handle, pushed into ground with foot for digging
spatula spreading or scooping tool with flat, thin blade on handle
spud spadelike tool with narrow blade, used esp. for digging up weeds
tire iron crowbar used to remove hubcaps and lug nuts
trowel small, scooplike hand shovel

OTHER SHOVELS AND DIGGING AND LIFTING TOOLS

air shovel, air spade
bar spade
coal shovel
ditch spade, drain spade, draw hoe
entrenching tool
fire shovel
garden spade, garden trowel, gasoline shovel, grub hoe, gumming spade
irrigating shovel
peat spade, posthole digger, power shovel
salt shovel, scuffle hoe, split shovel, stump spud
trenching spade
wedge bar, Wonder bar

Drills and Bits

auger boring tool consisting of bit rotated by transverse handle
auger bit long bit with square tang at upper end, rotated by brace to bore through wood
bench drill large, stationary power drill
bit detachable, usu. interchangeable cutting, drilling, or boring part of drill or other tool, available in various sizes suited to hole desired or specific need
bore tool with bit, such as an auger, used for boring out holes
bow drill antique drill operated by cord wrapped around shank with ends attached to bowlike device
brace device for holding and turning a bit for boring or drilling
breast drill portable drill with plate at end of handle that is pressed against the chest to force drill against work
center bit bit with sharp, projecting point, easily centered in hole to be drilled
chamfer bit bit used to bevel edge of hole
chaser tool with multiple teeth for cutting screw threads
chuck threaded portion of drill that holds bit
corkscrew pointed, metal spiral on handle, inserted in corks to pull them from bottles
countersink drill bit or funnel-shaped metal piece used to enlarge upper part of hole, allowing a cone-shaped screwhead to lie flush with surface
drill shafted device, usu. affixed to handle, with point and two or more cutting edges for piercing hard surfaces, usu. by rapid rotations
drill press powerful, stationary drill with single vertical spindle and hand lever used to apply pressure in drilling accurate holes
eggbeater drill antique drill operated by rotary motion of handle similar to an eggbeater
electric drill any electrically powered hand tool for drilling holes
gimlet small boring tool with spiral point and cross handle
hand drill any small, hand-cranked drill
jackhammer powerful, portable drill operated by compressed air, used to break up rock or concrete
nail set short steel rod used to drive nail below or flush with surface
plug cutter special bit that routs a circular groove
push drill hand drill operated by pressure of handle along line of shank
reamer rotary tool with helical or straight flutes, used for finishing or enlarging holes drilled in metal
screw starter threads on tapering point of short shank with bulb handle, used to make threaded holes for screws
snake device with head at end of flexible metal band, fed into curved pipes to remove obstruction
tap pluglike device with sharp ridges, inserted in opening and twisted to cut screw threads in it

OTHER DRILLS AND BITS

accretion borer, air drill, angle drill, automatic drill
beading bit, bench grinder, bevel trim bit, bitstock, bore bit, brad point bit, breast auger, broach, burr
carbide bit, circle cutter, compressed-air bit, core box bit, cross bit
diamond drill, disk drill, dovetail bit, dowling jig, drill set, drill stand
expansive bit, extensive bit
flat drill, Forstner bit
gimlet bit, glass bit
hinge bit
keyway drill
lockset bit
masonry bit, mortising bit, multispur bit
ogee fillet bit
panel pilot bit
parallel hand reamer, portable drill, post drill, posthole auger, Powerbore bit, power drill, pump drill, punch drill
raised panel bit, ratchet drill, roman ogee bit, rose reamer, rotary drill, round over bit, router bit
shell drill, shell reamer, spade bit, spade-handle drill, spike bit, star drill, strap drill
taper drill, tapping drill, tile bit, trepan, trephine, twist bit, twist drill
vix bit

Hammers

ball-peen hammer machinist's hammer with one cylindrical and one hemispherical head
battering ram heavy beam or bar used to knock down walls and doors
beetle heavy, usu. wooden instrument for hammering, ramming, or driving wedges
brad pusher tool with long, narrow head on small bulb handle, used to drive brads while avoiding hammer marks on surface
brick hammer hammer having one broad flat

head and one long, axlike head
claw hammer hammer with one head curved and forked into claw for pulling nails
club heavy, wooden rod, often narrowing at one end
double-claw hammer hammer with claws on both heads and no pounding surface
hammer any of various handheld or power tools with hard, metal head at end of handle, used for pounding and nailing
mallet hammer of wood, plastic, rubber, or metal, usu. with a barrel-shaped head, used esp. for driving a chisel
maul sledgehammer for driving piles, sometimes with wooden head, sometimes with one ax edge for splitting wood
peen hammer hammer with hemispherical or wedge-shaped head, used esp. for shaping material
ram battering ram or other device for driving something by impact
sledgehammer large, heavy hammerhead on long handle, swung with both hands
tack hammer light hammer, often with magnetized head that holds tack
tamp tool for driving down an object or firmly patting down a filling
triphammer heavy hammer raised and released by means of tripping device to fall on object being hammered

OTHER HAMMERS

adz-eye hammer, air hammer
blacksmith's hammer, boilermaker's hammer, bushhammer
chipping hammer, cooper's hammer, cross peen hammer
demolition hammer, die hammer, drilling hammer, drop hammer, drywall hammer
electric hammer, engineer's hammer
framing hammer, goathead hammer
hand drilling hammer, hardie, high nailer
joiner's mallet
long-handled hammer
machinist's hammer
nail claw hammer
pile hammer
pneumatic hammer
raising hammer, ripping claw hammer, riveting hammer, rubber mallet
set hammer, shingler's hammer, shoemaker's hammer, soft-faced hammer, spalling hammer, steam hammer, stone hammer, stonemason's ax, stonemason's hammer, stud driver
tiler's hammer
upholsterer's hammer
veneer hammer
wooden mallet

Wrenches

adjustable wrench any wrench with adjustable jaws
Allen wrench hexagonal bar bent at right angle, used to turn Allen screw having axial hexagonal hole in its head
alligator wrench wrench with V-shaped, serrated jaws set at right angles to shank, used for turning cylindrical or irregularly shaped parts
box-end wrench wrench having closed ends that completely surround nut or bolthead
box/open-end wrench wrench having one closed box end and one open end
Crescent Wrench *Trademark.* hand wrench with parallel, adjustable jaws that have smooth surfaces
crowfoot wrench box or open-end wrench with opening set at right angle to shank
lug wrench wrench with hollow end, used to loosen or tighten lug nuts
monkey wrench wrench with adjustable jaws, used to grasp nuts or boltheads of different sizes
obstruction wrench wrench with bent shank for use in confined areas
open-end wrench wrench having partially open end that slips over nut or bolthead
pipe-gripping wrench any of various wrenches with differing jaw shapes, used to grip pipes
pipe wrench tool with two toothed jaws, one fixed and one free to grip pipes when wrench is turned in one direction only
ratcheting box-end wrench box-end wrench with teeth mounted in round openings and ratchet lever
socket set series of different-sized socket attachments for ratchet-style socket wrench
socket wrench wrench with hollow end, or socket, that fits nut or bolt, often ratchet-operated and equipped with socket set
spanner wrench having curved head with hook or pin at one end for engaging notches or holes in collars and certain nuts
speeder wrench socket wrench with long offset handle
torque wrench wrench having register that shows amount of torque, or rotational force, being applied
wrench any of various hand or power tools for holding or turning a bolt or nut in a set or adjustable mouth at end of handle

OTHER WRENCHES

adjustable spanner
bicycle wrench
carriage wrench, chain wrench
end wrench
flare-nut wrench
gooseneck wrench
hexagonal wrench
lever wrench
Mack truck wrench
pin wrench,
ratcheting box
screw key, S-wrench
tappet wrench, tap wrench, tuning wrench
valve wrench

Gripping, Tightening, and Fastening Tools

anchor device that firmly binds one part of a structure to another, usu. by being implanted in one part
bar clamp clamp with two jaws attached to bar, one jaw fixed and one adjustable by means of a screw mechanism
bench dog device that fits in hole on workbench top and in moving face of bench vise, used to hold work in place
bench vise vise that clamps to bench or table
brace device that clasps or connects two pieces
C-clamp C-shaped clamp with a screw threaded through one end in the direction of other end
chuck device for centering and clamping work in a lathe
clamp device that holds two or more objects tightly together between parts that draw together
claw device with forked end for removing nails
clip gripping device using pinching action of two hinged arms
diagonal-cutting pliers pliers with clipping blades set at an angle in jaws
electric riveter power tool for fastening rivets
forceps hinged device for gripping small objects
grip pinching or grasping tool
hand screw clamp with two wooden jaws, tightened by two long screws passing through both jaws
impact driver screwdriver that turns when downward pressure is exerted on handle
lineman's pliers pliers with reinforced jaws and insulated handles, used with electrical cable and wire
locking pliers pliers whose jaws connect at sliding pivot that may be temporarily locked to aid in grasping and turning
nail puller plierslike device with strong, wide, curved jaws for removing nails from wood
needlenose pliers pliers with jaws tapering to point, used for grasping small objects
Phillips screwdriver screwdriver with cross-shaped, pointed tip
pincers two-handled gripping device with pivoting jaws
pinchcock clamp for compressing flexible pipe or tube to regulate flow of liquid
plate joiner electric doweling machine that fastens wooden members together using oval biscuits
pliers small pincer tool with long, grasping jaws and two handles
pneumatic stapler compressed-air powered staple gun
power nailer automatic nailer driven by compressed-air chamber
pucellas pointed gripping jaws on spring pivot, used for handling molten glass
puller device for gripping and removing spikes or nails
riveter device for pressing rivets together in order to fasten pieces of material together
screw clamp any clamp tightened by a screw mechanism
screwdriver handle with long, narrow, metal extension that tapers and flattens so as to fit into screwheads to turn and drive them
screw gun power screwdriver
slip-joint pliers pliers having sliding joint that permits adjustment of jaw span
snap ring pliers tool with short jaws for removing and replacing snap rings on power tools
spring clamp any clamp tightened by an elastic spring mechanism, rather than by a screw mechanism
staple gun pneumatic or electrically powered stapler
stapler small hand implement for affixing objects with thin wire staples
stubby screwdriver screwdriver with very short shank and thick handle
tongs two hinged arms used for grasping objects
tweezers small device with two jointed arms held between thumb and forefinger, used to grasp small objects
veneer press press frame for small veneering and assembly jobs
vise tool with two clamping jaws that are brought together or separated by means of a screw or lever, used to hold objects and work tight and steady
vise grip handheld vise that screws tight to hold work

Other gripping, tightening, and fastening tools

adjustable bar clamp, auger screwdriver
band clamp, bent-nose pliers
cabinet-pattern screwdriver, channel-lock pliers, clamp-on vise, clutch-head tip screwdriver, corner clamp, cutting pliers
edging clamp, electric screwdriver, electric staple gun
flat-head screwdriver
glue gun
hammer staple, handspike, hand vise, hold-down clamp
joint fastener
long-nose pliers
machinist's vise, magnetic screwdriver, miter clamp
nippers
offset screwdriver
patternmaker's vise, piling clamp, pin vise, pipe clamp, plastic tape, punch pliers
ratcheting screwdriver, ring pliers
saw vise, slab-handle screwdriver, spiral ratchet screwdriver
tacker, toggle clamp, tongue-and-groove pliers
utility tweezers
web clamp, welding clamp, wood bar clamp, wood hand screw
Z-bar, Z-clip

Measuring and Marking Tools

bevel rule with adjustable arm that opens to form measured angles, used for drawing or shaping sloped edges

butt gauge gauge with three cutters for marking mortise outlines, as for door butts
caliper adjustable, often curved jaws on pivot, used for measuring thickness or diameter
center punch small device with conical point for marking shallow impressions, used to center drill bits for making holes
combination square adjustable device used as level, miter square, and try square
compass instrument consisting of two movable legs hinged at one end, used to draw arcs and circles
dividers pair of compasses used to measure lines or divide a large space into sections
folding rule measuring device with multiple, pivoting lengths for compact storage
level any of various devices for determining true horizontal lines, esp. one that has a bubble suspended in liquid in a glass tube set in a long straight board
marking gauge any device for marking measurements with a sharp point, usu. having graduated scale on sliding arm
micrometer precision instrument with spindle moved by finely threaded screw, used for measuring thicknesses and, by machinists, for turning shafts and boring holes
miter box fixed or adjustable guide for saw angle, used in making a miter joint or crosscut
miter square two straightedges joined at a 45-degree angle
plumb bob weight hung on line, used to determine true vertical line; plummet
plumb rule narrow board with plumb line and bob suspended from upper edge, used to determine verticality
plummet plumb bob
protractor device for measuring and marking off angles, esp. on drawings and plans
rafter square roofer's square with premarked rafter tables for cutting hips and joists
rule length of straight, hard material marked in units for measuring; straightedge
ruler rule
scale any of various devices for determining weight of objects
scratch awl long blade tapering to sharp point for making fine marks
screed wooden strip that serves as guide for making a true level surface, esp. by dragging it across freshly poured concrete
scriber pointed tool for marking wood as guide for cutting or assembly
slide caliper pocket caliper with ruler along which one arm slides
square any instrument with straight edges and at least one ninety degree angle, used to plot right angles
straightedge length of straight, rigid material for measuring or marking; rule
tape measure narrow strip of flexible material, often in coil, marked off in measuring units
try square pair of straightedges fixed at right angles to one another, used to lay out right angles or test squareness
T square rule with perpendicular crosspiece at one end, used for marking parallel lines
turning caliper caliper into which a cutting or parting tool fits, used to make repetitive sizing cuts in turning
vernier caliper caliper in which two pieces slide across one another, one piece having a movable, graduated scale running parallel to the scale on the other piece

Other measuring and marking tools

adjustable bevel, adjustable square, automatic center punch
bevel square
carpenter's level, carpenter's square, chalk, chalk line, charcoal
depth gauge, dial caliper, diameter gauge, dovetail square
feeler gauge, flex, flex tape, framing square
grease pencil, guide
height gauge
machinist's rule, machinist's square, mortise gauge
pencil, power miter box
right angle
sizing caliper, sliding bevel, spirit level, steel rule, studfinder
T-bevel, trammel
wing divider
zigzag rule

Miscellaneous Tools, Objects, and Supplies

blowtorch small, portable device blasting out intense gasoline flame, used in metalworking
carpenter's apron heavy, often canvas, protective covering for trunk and upper legs, having pouches, pockets, and loops to hold tools and supplies
carpenter's belt heavy leather belt with loops and other attachments for carrying tools
dolly wheeled platform, sometimes with handles, for moving heavy objects
dust mask small filter in frame that fits over mouth and nose, providing protection from dust and nontoxic fumes
earplug plug placed in ear to block out job noise
extension ladder adjustable ladder with two or more levels which may be extended and locked in place for greater height
face guard face shield
face shield protective visor covering entire face with transparent section for eyes; face guard
funnel hollow cone narrowing to long tube for focusing downward flow of liquids
glue gun device that holds and fires stream of melted glue
grease gun handheld device for directing pressurized flow of thick lubricant

hard hat sturdy, framed, protective helmet made of metal or fiberglass
hearing protectors earplugs or coverings for ears designed to reduce damage from exposure to noise of power tools
jack any of various portable devices for lifting or supporting weight
jackscrew jack operated by a screw that is steadied by a threaded support, having a plate to bear load
ladder two long, rigid strips connected at intervals by crosspieces on which one steps to climb
nail pouch bag for carrying nails, as on carpenter's belt
plumber's helper plunger
plunger rubber suction cup on handle, used to unblock obstructed pipes and traps by suction; plumber's helper
respirator protective mask used when spraying toxic finishes
safety goggles protective eyeglasses, sometimes tinted and ventilated at sides, encased in frames that rest on cheeks and brow
sawbuck sawhorse
sawhorse movable frame or trestle for supporting wood being sawed; sawbuck
scaffold elevated platform for supporting workers during building construction or repair
soldering iron often electrically powered device for melting and applying metal alloys used to fuse metal objects together
squeegee rubber blade on handle for spreading or wiping liquids over a surface
stepladder small, freestanding, portable ladder with hinged support stand
straight ladder usu. tall, single length of ladder that is leaned against a stationary surface for support
toolbox receptacle or case, often of metal, in which tools are stored
tool cabinet shelf with multiple compartments and hooks for storage and display of tools
tool kit small, portable tool container
welder gas-powered or electrical machine tool, used for cutting and joining metal parts by heating them to molten state
wood-burning kit electrical hand tool with multiple attachments, used to burn ornamental details and designs into woodwork
workbench sturdy table with broad surface at which work is performed

Hardware and Supplies

Allen screw screw turned by insertion of Allen wrench into hexagonal hole cut into axis of screwhead
alligator clip clip with long, narrow, toothed jaws, used esp. for electrical connections
anchor bolt bolt inserted and fixed in masonry to hold timbers or shelves
ball bearing bearing composed of several hard balls running in grooves of two concentric rings, one of which is mounted on a rotating or oscillating shaft
bit detachable, usu. interchangeable cutting, drilling, or boring part of tool, available in various sizes suited to hole desired or specific need; drill bit
blade broad, thin, flat, sharpened edge of cutting tool
boat nail nail having convex head and chisel point
bolt metal fastening rod, threaded at one end, held in place by nut
box nail long nail with flat head
box nut nut with blind hole closed off at one end; cap nut
brace device that clasps or connects two pieces
bracket projecting support element, esp. for attaching a horizontally set piece to a vertical surface
brad thin wire nail with barrel head; thin nail, tapering in width, with lip at top of one side of head
bushing removable lining or sleeve inserted in an opening to resist wear or serve as guide
butt hinge hinge secured to the butting surfaces of a door or the like
cap nut box nut
caster small, swiveling wheel used to support and move heavy objects, esp. furniture
catch latch or other device for checking motion
chain length of connected metal links used for support or transmission of power
chuck clamplike device by which work to be turned is held; threaded portion of drill bit
clamp device holding two or more objects firmly together
collar protective or controlling ring or band at one end of a rod or shaft
common nail any of various size nails, distinguished from finishing nail by having wider head
cotter pin, wedge, or key fitted or driven into opening to hold parts together
cotter pin split metal strip, whose arms are separated after insertion in hole to hold position
cut nail tapering, rectangular-shaped nail with blunt point
drill bit bit
eyelet grommet
female adapter recessed element of connection that receives male adapter
finishing nail thin nail with very small, globular head, driven to point just beneath wood surface and concealed by filler or sawdust
flange strip along length or around end of object, such as pipe, for directing or strengthening it
gasket ring, esp. of rubber or tallowed rope, placed or packed around piston or joint to make it fluid-tight
grommet metal ring for lining small opening in soft material to protect or strengthen it; eyelet
hanger bolt bolt with tapered lag-screw thread on one end and machine-bolt thread on the other, used in timber construction

hardware metalware usu. forming functional or decorative component part
hasp fastening device consisting of hinged, metal strap held in place over staple by pin
hinge jointed device on which a movable part turns or swings freely
hook bent piece of inflexible material for restricting movement of attached object
hook and eye latching device consisting of hook and loop or screw eye through which the hook slips
jam nut thin, supplementary nut screwed down on regular nut to prevent it from loosening
joint connection, often reinforced, between two pieces of similar material, esp. between two sections of pipe
lag screw wood screw with flat, boltlike head, used esp. with expandable metal anchor in concrete or stone
latch bar sliding into a catch, groove, or hole, used to hold movable part in place
lock nut nut with extra friction between itself and screw to prevent it from loosening
lug nut capped nut used esp. to attach automobile tires
machine bolt large bolt with square or hexagonal head and threads on lower portion for use with nut; machine screw
machine screw machine bolt
male adapter extending element of connection that enters female adapter
nail thin, tapering, pointed fastening device, usu. of metal, with head that is pounded to drive point into object that is to be held in place, made in various lengths designated by penny number, usu. up to sixty penny or 6 inches (15 cm) long
nut any open ring-shaped, hexagonal, or square piece of metal with internal threads for tightening over end of bolt
O-ring ring made of rubber or other flexible material, used as gasket
Phillips head screw screw with cross-shaped notches in its head
pipe length of hollow, cylindrical tubing for conducting gas or liquid
pipe fitting coupling, such as elbow or tee, for connecting pipe sections
plug small stopper that fits securely into opening to prevent passage of gas or liquid; wooden filler produced by plug cutter
pull handle, knob, or other piece of hardware that is pulled
rivet metal pin or bolt passed through two or more pieces and pressed down at both ends to fasten them
roofing nail short nail with broad head, used for nailing down asphalt roofing shingles
screw thin fastening device with spiral groove threaded around its length, secured by rotating it into object that is to be held: lag, machine, set, or wood
screw nail fastener with helical thread and point that can be driven into wood with hammer and removed with screwdriver; drive screw
setscrew machine screw that passes through threaded hole in one part and into another to prevent movement
shackle U-shaped fastening or coupling piece, esp. bar of a padlock
snap ring ring that must be forced open for use and snaps shut to make snug fit
spike long, heavy, naillike fastener for heavy timbers or railroad ties
spring spiral elastic device for exerting pressure by compression or contraction, recovering original shape when released
square nut nut with square sides
staple U-shaped loop of metal attached to something and through which a hasp, bolt, wire, or rope is secured fast
strap-hinge hinge having one long flap attached to face of movable object such as door
stud projecting rivet or infixed rod used for fastening or as a support
tack short, sharp nail with broad head
thumbscrew screw with head shaped so that it can be turned with thumb and forefinger
thumbtack tack with wide flat head that can be pushed into material with thumb
toggle bolt bolt consisting of screw and two hinged arms which open when inserted, used to hold heavy objects in soft material
treenail wooden pin that swells when moist, used to fasten timbers together
turnbuckle sleeve with swivel at one end and internal screw thread at other, or thread at each end, used for coupling or tightening two parts
U bolt U-shaped bolt with screw thread and nut on each arm
upholstery tack small tack used to attach material in upholstering furniture
washer flat, thin ring used, esp. with bolt and nut, to increase tightness, prevent leakage, or distribute pressure
waste nut internally threaded floor flange for pipe
wing bolt bolt having flared head like wing nut
wing nut nut with two flat, flared sides for turning between thumb and forefinger
wire nail thin nail made of wire, designed for specific use such as finishing
wood screw screw tapering to sharp point for use in wood

Other Hardware and Supplies

angle brace, angle bracket, astragal
backflap hinge, ball catch, bar bracket, barrel bolt, bell, bend, B nut, brad nail, brass screw, bullet catch, bullet latch, bumper, butterfly hook, buttonhook
cabinet knob, cabinet pull, cad cut washer, castellated nut, chain bolt, channel, climbing iron, coated nail, coil spring, concealed hinge, Condulet, continuous pull, corrugated nail, coupler, coupling, cover plate, crook, cross, cutoff riser
deadlock, deep thread screw, door slide, dowel screw, drawer slide, driftpin, drive

screw, drop-leaf hinge, drop ring pull, drywall screw
edge pull, ell, extension bolt
fence bracket, finger pull, finish washer, flat head screw, flat washer, flex connector, flipper slide, flush mount, flush pull
galvanized nail, gate, glide
hexagonal nut
jet rail bracket, joist hanger
kep nut, kick plate, knife bracket
lazy Susan, lead shield, leg bracket, leveler, lock washer
magnetic catch, masonry nail, mending plate, metal screw, Molly fastener
nut-driver, nut-runner
outlet, oval head screw
panhead screw, piano hinge, pipe strap, pivot hinge, plastic shield, plate strap, plug clip, P-trap, pushpin
Rawl plug, riser extension, rod coupling, rope clip, round head screw
safety plate, sash lock, screw shield, sheave, shelf rest, socket head screw, Soss hinge, speed nut, spiral spring, spud washer, square U bolt, stanchion, standard, stay, strip, studfinder
tapping screw, tee, T hinge, threaded insert, threaded rod, Tite-joint, T nut, Toggler, touch bar, touch latch, track
union
wall box, wet post anchor, wire nut

KNOTS

anchor knot fisherman's bend
barrel knot fisherman's knot used esp. to fasten together two strands of leader; blood knot
becket bend sheet bend
bend any loop or knot for joining end of one rope to another rope or to some other object, esp. nautical
bight middle portion of rope, esp. when looped or bent, as distinct from ends
bitter end inboard end of nautical line
Blackwall hitch hitch for temporarily securing line to hook
blood knot barrel knot
bow knot comprised of two or more loops and two ends, used esp. to tie together ends of ribbon or string; bowknot
bowknot bow
bowline knot used to make nonslipping loop at end of rope
builder's knot clove hitch
carrick bend knot or bend for joining ends of two ropes
cat's-paw nautical hitch in middle of rope forming two eyes to hold hook
clinch knot in which eye is made by looping the rope and seizing one end to a standing part
clove hitch knot for fastening rope to spar or larger rope, consisting of two half hitches made in opposite directions; builder's knot
crown knot made by interweaving the strands at the end of a rope, usu. as first stage in tying knot
cuckold's neck nautical hitch for holding spar, consisting of single loop with overlapping parts of rope held together; ring seizing; throat seizing
diamond hitch knot for tying pack to an animal, in which interlacing ropes form a diamond atop the load
diamond knot diamond-shaped knot tied in strands of rope
double knot any knot formed by repeating the tying process
eye loop formed at end of rope
figure of eight knot resembling the numeral 8, formed by looping rope around itself twice, the second loop above the first
fisherman's bend knot for attaching rope to an object, made by passing end of rope around object and the standing part and then under the round turn; anchor knot
flat knot reef knot
flat seizing seizing in which lines are parallel and a single binding layer is used
granny knot faulty square knot in which bights cross each other in the wrong direction; lubber's knot
half hitch knot made by forming loop and passing end of rope around the standing part and through the loop
half-knot common knot joining the ends of two ropes, used to make square and other knots
harness hitch hitch forming loop around rope, esp. at end of bowline
hawser bend nautical knot joining the ends of two lines
heaving-line bend nautical knot for attaching the end of a weighted heaving line to a hawser
hitch any of various knots used to attach rope to something so as to be easily loosened
inside clinch clinch knot with the seized end of line inside the noose
knot interlacing, looping, bending, hitching, or folding together of pliant, slender length of cord or rope so as to fasten, bind, or connect two such lengths together or one length to something else
lanyard knot stopper knot
lash binding or fastening with rope or cord
loop section of rope folded or doubled upon itself, leaving an opening between parts
loop knot knot made by doubling over line at its end and tying both parts into square knot so as to leave a loop; open hand knot
lubber's knot granny knot
Magnus hitch knot for fastening rope to spar or larger rope, consisting of clove hitch with one more turn around object to which rope is bent
manrope knot double wall knot with double

crown, used to attach a manrope railing to its gangway or ladder
marlinespike hitch hitch into which pointed metal implement is inserted in order to draw the seizing taut
marling hitch one of a series of knots used to lash long rolls or bundles
Matthew Walker knot formed at end of rope by retying loosened strands
mesh knot sheet bend
midshipman's hitch nautical hitch made by tying a rolling hitch with end of line to the standing part
nail knot nooselike fisherman's knot that tightens when pulled and does not slip
netting knot sheet bend
noose loop with running knot that tightens as rope is pulled
open hand knot loop knot
outside clinch clinch knot with seized end of line outside noose
overhand knot simple, small knot that slips easily, used as part of another knot or to prevent ends from fraying; single knot; thumb knot
prolonge knot knot made up of three overlapping loops formed by passing a single rope over and under itself at crossings; sailor's breastplate
reef knot nautical square knot used in tying down sails; flat knot
reeving-line bend nautical bend for joining two lines so that they will pass easily through a hole or ring
ring seizing cuckold's neck
rolling hitch nautical hitch on a spar, composed of two round turns and a half hitch, that tightens under stress applied parallel to the spar
rope-yarn knot knot made by splitting rope yarns apart and joining their ends in half-knots
round turn complete turn of rope around object
running bowline slipnoose made by tying end of bowline around its own standing part
running knot knot made around and sliding along the standing part of the same rope, thus forming a noose
running part part of rope or tackle that is hauled upon, separate from the standing part
sailor's breastplate prolonge knot
seizing method of binding or fastening together two ropes or parts of same rope by a number of longitudinal and transverse turns
sheepshank knot, bend, or turn used to shorten rope, often temporarily
sheet bend bend or hitch used to fasten rope temporarily to the bight of another rope or to an eye; becket bend; mesh knot; netting knot; weaver's knot
single knot overhand knot
slide knot knot formed by two half hitches on the standing part, the second hitch being next to the loop, which can be tightened
slipknot any knot that rides easily along rope or cord around which it is made, esp. an overhand knot on the standing part
slipnoose noose whose knot slides along the rope, tightening as the rope is pulled
splice joining together of two ropes or rope strands by interweaving of strands
square knot common knot formed of two half-knots, used to join two rope ends that emerge alongside standing part
standing part length of rope that is in use and terminates in a knot or around which a knot is formed
stevedore's knot stopper knot
stopper knot knot forming a lump to prevent rope from passing through a hole or opening; lanyard knot; stevedore's knot
surgeon's knot knot similar to reef knot, used by surgeons to tie ligatures
tack bend bend or loop used for temporary fastening
throat seizing cuckold's neck
thumb knot overhand knot
timber hitch nautical knot or hitch formed by taking a turn on the spar, wrapping the end around the standing part, then several times around itself
truelove knot elaborate, ornamental double knot formed by two interlacing bows
Turk's-head turbanlike knot of small cords, formed around rope or spar
turle knot fisherman's knot used to attach artificial fly or eyed hook to leader
turn passing or twisting of rope or cord around itself, another rope or cord, or some object
wall knot overhand or double knot made by interweaving strands at end of rope, terminating in crown or double crown
weaver's knot sheet bend
Windsor knot wide, triangular knot used for tying four-in-hand necktie

CONTAINERS

Receptacles and Casks
Basins, Ladles, Cups, and Pots
Bottles
Cases, Boxes, and Bags
Baskets

Receptacles and Casks

ashtray small receptacle for tobacco ashes, cigarette and cigar butts
barrel bulging cylindrical vessel made of staves held together with hoops and having flat parallel ends the same size
breaker small water container in lifeboat
butt large cask for wine, beer, or water
caddy small box, can, or chest, used to store frequently used items

cage enclosure with wire or bars, used to confine people or animals
can cylindrical receptacle, usu. of metal, open at one end or closed off to seal in contents
canister cylindrical metal receptacle with removable, close-fitting top
cannikin wooden bucket; small can
cask barrel-shaped container for liquids
cistern large, underground reservoir for storing rainwater or other liquid
coal scuttle deep metal bucket with handle and lip, used to hold coal
container anything that holds other objects within itself
drum large, cylindrical receptacle, usu. for liquids
firkin small, lidded, wood or metal cask
garbage can usu. metal container in variety of sizes, used to hold trash
harness cask tub on ship, used to soak and store salt meat prior to use
hogshead large barrel or cask holding 63 to 140 gallons (238 to 530 l)
hopper funnel-shaped receptacle with opening at bottom, used for temporary storage and delivery of material; tank for liquids with mechanism that allows release of contents through pipe
jemcan container for liquids holding 5 gallons (18.9 l)
keg small cask or barrel holding 30 gallons (113.6 l) or less
kilderkin cask equal in size to half a barrel
mess kit portable container used to cook and hold food, usu. by soldiers
mortar small, bowllike porcelain vessel used to pound substances with pestle
pail cylindrical vessel, usu. with handle, used to carry liquids or solids
palette thin oval or oblong board on which artist saves and mixes pigments
piggin wooden, pail-shaped vessel with one stave reaching above rim as handle
pipe cask, esp. for wine, holding two hogsheads, or 126 gallons (476 l)
pitcher container that holds and dispenses liquids, made of glass, earthenware, or plastic, with wide mouth having lip on one side and handle on other
plate shallow, usu. round vessel of earthenware, glass, plastic, or metal that holds food
powder horn container for gunpowder made from horn of ox or cow
puncheon large cask in variety of sizes, usu. 80 gallons (304 l)
receptacle any open storage container
salver tray used to serve food or drinks
saucer small plate, esp. with indentation at center for holding cup
spittoon low, round receptacle used for disposal of tobacco juice; cuspidor
trough long, shallow receptacle that holds animal's water or feed
tank large enclosed container, often cylindrical, used for storing or carrying gas or liquid
trash can large metal container, esp. for dry refuse
tray flat receptacle with low rim, used to carry, hold, or exhibit objects
tub wide, low receptacle with flat bottom
tun large cask that holds wine or beer
vat large tub or barrel, usu. for liquids
waiter tray on which tea service is carried
wastepaper basket small trash can, used for discarded papers
watering can metal can with long spout and narrow mouth, used to water plants by hand

Basins, Ladles, Cups, and Pots

basin shallow, round vessel with sloping sides, used to hold water, esp. for washing
beaker large, widemouthed drinking cup without handles
bowl deep, round dish with wide opening at top
caldron large kettle
cannikin small can or cup
cistern large, silver vessel used to cool wine at dinner table
cup small, bowl-shaped drinking vessel with handle and base
cuspidor spittoon
dipper cup or ladle with handle, used to scoop up liquids
flowerpot usu. round container with small hole in bottom, used for growing plants
gourd hard rind from any of various fruits, used as dipper or kettle
jardiniere large, round, decorative flowerpot
kettle container for boiling liquids, cooking foods, etc.
ladle long-handled, cuplike spoon used for dipping or conveying liquids
mug cylindrical drinking cup, usu. with handle
pan broad, shallow, open household container, usu. round
pipkin small metal or earthenware pot with horizontal handle
porringer small, shallow, one-handled bowl used to feed children; pottinger
pot deep, metal or earthenware container with handle, usu. round, used esp. for cooking
pottinger porringer
scoop any of various open, hemispherical utensils used to remove liquid or loose materials
shovel large hand tool with broad scoop and handle, used for lifting or scooping
spade heavy digging tool with flat blade and long handle
urn vase on pedestal
vase tall, hollow vessel of porcelain, glass, metal, or earthenware, used to hold flowers or decoration
vessel hollow or deep container that holds objects, esp. liquid
washbasin bowl used for washing hands or face
washtub usu. round metal tub used to wash clothes

Bottles

amphora tall jar with narrow neck and base and two handles (ancient Greece)
beaker deep, thin, glass laboratory vessel with lip, used for pouring
bottle usu. glass or plastic rigid container for liquids with narrow neck and no handle, sometimes with cap
canteen hip flask used by soldiers or campers to carry water
carafe ornamental glass vessel with narrow neck and wider mouth, used for holding water or wine
carboy large bottle encased in protective wooden crate, used to hold corrosive liquids
caster small glass container used to serve condiments; cruet
cruet caster
cruse small earthenware container for oil, honey, or water
decanter ornamental glass bottle used to serve wine
demijohn glass bottle with capacity of 1 to 10 gallons (3.79 to 37.9 l), encased in wicker, with one or two handles
ewer wide-mouthed jug or pitcher made of brass or ceramics
fifth bottle that holds 1/5 gallon (0.76 l) of liquid
flacon small flask with tight cap, used to hold perfume
flagon large vessel with handle, spout, and lid, used to hold wine or liquor
flask flat container with neck and stopper, used for holding liquid, usu. carried in jacket or pants pocket
jar usu. cylindrical glass or earthenware container with no spout and large opening on top, capable of being sealed at top
jeroboam oversize wine bottle that holds 3 liters (3.17 quarts)
jug large, deep glass or earthenware container for liquids, with handle and small opening at top
hip flask flask worn attached to belt
hot-water bottle soft rubber container with stopper, used to hold hot water
krater jar with broad body, wide neck, and two handles (ancient Greece)
magnum wine bottle that holds 2/5 gallon (1.52 l)
phial small, sealed glass container, used esp. to hold medicine; vial
potiche vase or jar made of porcelain with rounded body that narrows at top
rehoboam oversize champagne bottle holding 5 quarts (4.73 l)
tankard tall, one-handled vessel, esp. of pewter, often with hinged cover, used for drinking
thermos vacuum bottle
vacuum bottle tall, cylindrical container, usu. of metal or plastic, with glass or stainless steel vacuum liner and tightfitting lid, used for maintaining liquids at original temperature for several hours; thermos
vial phial

Cases, Boxes, and Bags

ammunition box container used to store firearm ammunition
ark orig. covered basket or small chest
backpack lightweight canvas or nylon sack, often on frame, used to carry objects on back while walking
bag flexible, pouchlike container that may be closed, used to hold, store, or carry objects
bin box, frame, or enclosure used for storage
bindle bundle that contains clothes and cooking utensils
box rigid, usu. rectangular container used to store or carry nonliquid articles
caisson ammunition box; watertight enclosure used for underwater construction
carton cardboard box
case usu. flat box or receptacle that closes, used to store, ship, or carry objects
casket small ornamental chest; coffin
cedar chest large box made of cedar, used for protective storage of woolen items
chest storage box with lid, often with lock
coffer strongbox
coffin long, heavy box used for burial of corpse; casket
crate large, wood-framed container used for shipping wares
diplomatic pouch sealed mail pouch, used to carry communications between diplomatic offices
dispatch box oblong box or case with lock, used to carry written dispatches
envelope flat paper container with gummed sealing flap
file metal or wooden cabinet used to organize stored papers for easy reference
file folder light, cardboard, folded cover or large envelope, used to hold loose papers stored in a file
folio case or folder that holds loose papers, often tied with ribbon
footlocker small, flat trunk with lock, esp. one that stands at foot of bunk in army barracks
golf bag bag used to carry golf clubs and balls
gunny sack loose burlap bag
holster leather pistol case, open at the top, worn on belt or under one arm
hope chest box used to store young woman's collection of clothing and linen in anticipation of marriage
kit bag rectangular leather traveling bag with straps and sides that open
locker usu. metal storage case, often built into wall
mail pouch large reinforced envelope in which objects are sent through mails
matchbox small wood or cardboard box that holds matches
monstrance receptacle holding consecrated host for veneration by Catholics; ostensorium
nesting box one of a series of boxes in graduated sizes that may be stored within one another
net mesh of interwoven threads or ropes, used esp. to catch birds, fish, or insects

nose bag canvas bag that covers horse's muzzle and ties at top of head, used for feeding
ostensorium monstrance
packing case wooden shipping crate used for bulk goods
packsack leather or canvas backpack
pillbox small case that holds pills, usu. carried on person
pod protective pouch or removable housing
portfolio large flat case with handle, used to carry papers or drawings without folding them
pouch sack or satchel of moderate size, used to store or transport goods
powder box heavy case, usu. metal, used to store gunpowder
quiver long, thin, cylindrical case, open at one end, used to carry arrows
reliquary casket or container used to exhibit relics
sack soft, large, usu. oblong bag
sarcophagus stone coffin with sculpture, placed in a church, tomb, or vault
satchel small bag, often with shoulder strap
scabbard leather or metal sheath that encloses blade of sword or dagger when not in use
scrip small bag or wallet carried by pilgrim or shepherd
sheath tightfitting rigid case for sword or dagger
skippet small box that covers and preserves seal for documents
sleeping bag large, warmly padded bag in which to sleep outdoors
strongbox solid chest or case used to store money or valuables; coffer
tea chest square wooden case lined with lead or tin, used for shipping tea
till money drawer behind counter in store or bank
tinderbox metal box that holds tinder, flint, and steel used in striking spark
trunk luggage with rigid frame, usu. too large to carry by hand, used for transporting clothes and personal items; enclosed storage compartment of car
vanity bag small case or handbag used to hold or transport toilet articles
vanity case rigid vanity bag
wallet flat, folding leather case, used esp. for holding paper money
wineskin bag of animal skin, used to hold wine

Baskets

basket container made of interwoven cane, rushes, or strips of wood, open at top
bassinet small basketlike crib for infant, hooded at one end
bushelbasket round receptacle with capacity of 32 dry quarts (35.24 l)
clothes hamper wooden or plastic receptacle with lid, used to hold soiled laundry
corbeil sculptured basket of fruit or flowers, used as architectural ornament
creel wickerwork basket used to carry fish and fishing tackle
dosser pannier
flower basket wickerwork basket that holds or displays cut flowers
frail basket made of rushes, used for shipping figs or raisins
hamper basket with lid, used for storage or to send food or other items; clothes hamper
pannier wicker basket used to carry loads on back, often used in pairs when carried by pack animal or over rear wheel of bicycle; dosser
scuttle shallow wood or wicker basket, used to carry or move loose substances
skep rough farm basket of twisted straw
splint basket rectangular basket of woven splints, with handle
stave basket basket formed of wood strips
trug coarse basket of wood strips, used to carry vegetables or flowers
wastebasket small, open basket for discarded papers

WEAPONS AND ARMAMENTS

Blades, Clubs, and Projectiles
Guns and Firearms
Firearm Parts, Accessories, and Processes
Bombs, Mines, and Explosives

Blades, Clubs, and Projectiles

arrow pointed shaft, shot from bow
atlatl spear or throwing stick (ancient Mexico)
ax short, heavy blade affixed to long handle
backsword single-edged sword
barlow sturdy inexpensive jackknife
bastinado cudgel
baton cudgel, truncheon
battering ram heavy beam used to beat down fortifications
battle-ax ax with heavy curved blade
bayonet short dagger; blade fitted on end of rifle
billy club bludgeon
blackjack leather-covered club with flexible handle; cosh
blade flat, pointed, usu. sharp-edged piercing or slashing part of sword or knife
bludgeon club with thick, heavy striking end
bola two or more stones or iron balls at ends of cord, hurled at target (Latin America)
bolo knife long heavy single-edged knife, used for hacking
bolt missile or shaft shot from catapult; crossbow arrow, shorter than longbow arrow
boomerang club bent at angle, thrown in arc; throwing stick (Australia)
bow and arrow curved, flexible frame fitted with arrow that is launched by spring tension

bowie knife foot-long straight blade with slightly curved point
brass knuckles metal piece fitted over fingers at knuckles
catapult ancient tension-powered device that hurled stones or other missiles
clasp knife pocketknife with one large, folding blade held open by catch
cleaver butcher's heavy chopping knife, often with wood handle
crossbow bow set horizontally on rigid stock or brace, used to fire arrows or bolts
cudgel heavy short stick or club
cutlass short curved sword
dagger weapon with short, straight, pointed blade attached to handle
epee sharppointed sword with three-sided blade; fencing sword
foil blunt or button-pointed fencing sword with four-sided blade
halberd long-handled, broad-bladed sword; pikestaff with axlike blade and spike
harpoon large spear with barbed head
hatchet ax with heavy hammer-shaped head
hunting knife large knife with stout blade, used for skinning and cutting up game
jackknife small knife with folding blade
javelin light spear thrown long distances
knife any small sharp-edged blade attached to handle
lance long, spearlike, sharp-headed weapon
longbow large wooden bow, drawn by hand
mace spiked heavy club, usu. metal
machete large, broad-bladed knife
maul heavy club with metal-studded head
nunchaku two hardwood sticks joined at ends by short length of cord or chain (Japan)
pocketknife small knife with folding blade
point sharpened forepart of arrow, sword, knife, or spear
poleax battle ax, esp. one with hook opposite blade
poniard dagger with slender blade of triangular or square cross-section
projectile object fired or thrown through air, often long and pointed
rapier straight double-edged sword
saber long curved sword
scimitar saber with sharply curved single-edged blade
scythe long curved blade fastened at angle to long handle
shillelagh cudgel
sling device for hurling stones, consisting of short strap with long cords at each end, operated by placing stone in strap, which is then whirled until one cord is released to project the stone
slingshot forked handheld bow used to launch stones or other projectiles
spear sharply bladed head mounted on long shaft
spike sharp-pointed piece of metal set with its point outward or upward
stave club, cudgel, or staff
stiletto short dagger with thick blade
switchblade knife with folding blade that springs open; flick-knife
sword any long, bladed, pointed weapon
tomahawk lightweight ax; combination pipe and ax (American Indian)
trident three-pronged spear, used for fishing
truncheon club, cudgel; spontoon

Guns and Firearms

air gun air rifle
air rifle firearm powered by compressed air; air gun; toy rifle
AK-47 automatic rifle
antiaircraft gun firearm used against attack by airplanes
arms weapons, esp. firearms
assault rifle usu. automatic rifle firing high-powered ammunition, often having pistol grip and long, detachable magazine
autoloader semiautomatic weapon, either gas-operated or recoil-operated
automatic rifle firearm that loads, fires, and ejects cartridges automatically while user depresses trigger
bazooka shoulder-fired rocket launcher
BB gun firearm that shoots small-sized shot, designated BB
blunderbuss short, old-fashioned, highly inaccurate firearm
bolt-action rifle firearm with hand-operated bolt as breechblock that unlocks to eject empty case and seals new cartridge in bolt assembly
breechloader firearm loaded with cartridges at its rear or breech
Browning automatic rifle .30 caliber, gas-operated, magazine-fed automatic rifle (World War II)
Browning machine gun .30 or .50 caliber, recoil-operated machine gun, fed by cartridge belt (World War II)
cannon gun; large firearm mounted in place, firing explosive charges
cap gun toy pistol with paper holding very small explosive
carbine lightweight rifle of short overall length
derringer large caliber, very short-barreled pocket pistol
double-barreled shotgun double-action shotgun with two barrels, either side-by-side or over-and-under, often with two triggers
elephant gun very large caliber gun, .410 caliber or greater, used for hunting heavy, often dangerous game such as elephant, rhinoceros, lion, or Cape buffalo
Enfield rifle muzzle-loading .577 caliber rifle used by British in Crimean War; .30 caliber rifle used by U.S. troops (World War I)
firearm weapon that uses explosive charge to fire projectile at high speed
firelock gun having lock in which priming is ignited by sparks struck from flint and steel

flamethrower mounted or portable device that sprays ignited incendiary fuel at some distance
flintlock gun with old-fashioned firearm lock, esp. musket
forty-five .45 caliber pistol
forty-four .44 caliber pistol
Gatling gun early, mounted machine gun with revolving cluster of barrels
gun any weapon consisting of metal tube (barrel) from which projectile (bullet or shell) is discharged by force of explosive
handgun small, handheld firearm; pistol; revolver
Henry .44 caliber, lever-action repeating rifle holding 16 rounds (U.S., 1860's)
howitzer lightweight, short cannon that fires charges with curved trajectory
lever-action rifle early repeating firearm in which ejection of shell case and recocking are accomplished by hand-operated lever arm near trigger
M-1 .30 caliber, gas-operated, clip-fed semiautomatic rifle (World War II)
M-14 7.62 mm gas-operated, magazine-fed automatic rifle
M-16 5.56 mm gas-operated, magazine-fed automatic rifle (1960's)
machine gun firearm that automatically loads and discharges cartridges for sustained periods
machine pistol fully automatic pistol; submachine gun
magazine gun repeater
magnum firearm using cartridges equipped with extra-large charge
matchlock firearm with old-fashioned slow-match mechanism as gunlock, esp. musket or handgun
mortar short cannon
musket old-fashioned firearm with long barrel and smooth bore
muzzleloader firearm loaded through front end or muzzle by pouring powder in and stuffing rag patch down barrel
over-and-under double-action shotgun with barrels placed one above the other
piece gun
pistol small handheld firearm; handgun
pump-action (*adj*) designating manually-operated repeating shotgun or rifle; slide-action
pump gun firearm operated by pumping action that advances new cartridges
recoil-operated rifle firearm that utilizes kickback movement of parts to operate action
repeater rapid-firing, small firearm; magazine gun
revolver small firearm with revolving chamber for cartridges; handgun; pistol
rifle firearm having long bore cut with spiral interior grooves that spin and thus stabilize bullet's flight, usu. fired from shoulder
rocket launcher tube used to fire rocket shells; bazooka
Saturday night special *Informal.* cheap, easily obtained handgun
sawed-off shotgun smoothbore firearm with barrel cut off to scatter shot more widely
scattergun shotgun
semiautomatic weapon firearm that automatically ejects cartridges and reloads after each firing, activated by successive squeezing of trigger; autoloader
shotgun smoothbore firearm, often double-barreled
side arm handgun; pistol; revolver; weapon worn at side in holster or in belt
single-action (*adj*) designating firearm that requires cocking of hammer before firing each shot
six-gun six-shooter
six-shooter six-chambered revolver; six-gun
slide-action (*adj*) designating rifle or shotgun with mechanism that ejects shell case and cocks and reloads firearm when slid back and forth quickly; pump-action
small arm handheld firearm
Springfield rifle .30 caliber, bolt-action repeating rifle (World War I)
stun gun battery-powered, handheld firearm that discharges nonlethal cartridges, darts, or electric charges to immobilize its target
submachine gun portable automatic firearm, fired from shoulder or hip; machine pistol
10-gauge shotgun using shells of 2 cm diameter
thirty-eight .38 caliber handgun
thirty-thirty .30 caliber rifle that fires cartridge with thirty-grain powder charge
thirty-two .32 caliber handgun
Thompson submachine gun .45 caliber submachine gun with magazine, pistol grip, and detachable buttstock; Tommy gun
Tommy gun Thompson submachine gun
trench gun portable cannon or mortar fired from trenches in warfare
twenty-two .22 caliber firearm
Uzi short, 9 mm submachine gun
Winchester rifle *Trademark.* any rifle made by Winchester Arms Company, esp. magazine rifle of 19th c.
zip gun crude, homemade gun that fires real bullets

Firearm Parts, Accessories, and Processes

action mechanism by which firearm is operated
ammo *Informal.* ammunition
ammunition bullets, grenades, or bombs; explosive projectile fired from weapon; munitions
armaments weapons, military equipment
armory repository of arms
arsenal place of manufacture and storage of arms
artillery mounted missile-launching or projectile-firing weapons, esp. larger cannon, guns, and catapults
ballistics science and study of projectile motion; study and development of missile weapons
barrel tube of gun, through which bullet fires

bead careful aim
blank cartridge without projectile
bolt breech closure of gun that controls opening of bore
bore cylindrical, hollow part of gun barrel, usu. longer than it is wide; caliber measure
breech part of firearm at rear of bore
buckshot large-sized lead shot of .24 to .33 inches diameter, used in shotgun shells carrying nine to fifteen of such pellets
bullet small projectile discharged from firearm at great speed
buttstock shoulder end of firearm at rear of breech mechanism
caliber diameter of firearm bore; diameter of bullet
cannonball round, solid missile fired from cannon
cap explosive paper or metallic cap, used to ignite larger charge
cartridge cylindrical casing, usu. of brass, that holds primer, powder charge, and bullet
chamber firearm compartment that holds cartridge
charge (*vb*) load a weapon; (*n*) amount of powder or shot used to load weapon; load
clip clasp that holds bullets to be fed into firearm chamber
cock hammer; (*vb*) pull back and set hammer prior to firing
conventional weapons nonnuclear weapons
cradle part of gun carriage on which recoiling gun slides
detonator device, esp. small amount of explosive, used to set off larger explosive
firing pin plunger in firing mechanism that strikes cartridge primer, thus igniting charge
flintlock old-fashioned firearm lock that ignites powder charge when hammer holding a flint strikes spark from metal
gauge unit of measure of internal diameter, or bore, of shotgun barrel, 12 gauge being equal to approximately 3/4 inch (19 mm)
grapeshot cast iron balls formerly used as cannon charge
gunflint small flint that produces spark, formerly used in firearm ignition
gunpowder explosive chemical mixture used to propel firearm projectile
hair trigger sensitive firearm trigger
hammer firearm part that strikes firing mechanism of gunlock; cock
holster leather case for pistol, opening at top, usu. worn on belt
home (*vb*) proceed toward specified target, esp. under control of automatic guidance mechanism
jacket metal outer casing of bullet
load charge; single cartridge with bullet and powder; (*vb*) fill weapon with cartridges
loaded (*adj*) containing ammunition or explosive charge
magazine sometimes removable or reloadable storage receptacle that holds extra cartridges in repeating rifles and shotguns; military storehouse for arms and ammunition
magnum (*adj*) designating a cartridge equipped with larger charge than other cartridges of comparable size; (*n*) firearm thus equipped
matchlock old form of gunlock in which priming is ignited by slow match
munitions ammunition; military equipment
mustard gas oily liquid used as chemical weapon
muzzle fore end of firearm barrel, point of departure for bullet
open sight rear sight of firearm, consisting of notch in which gunner aligns front sight on target
ordnance large firearms; military supplies, esp. weapons, ammunition, and artillery
payload size of weapon's explosive charge
peep sight plate with small hole through which gunner makes sighting
pistol grip handle, esp. of rifle, shaped like butt of pistol
propellant explosive substance used to force projectile out of firearm barrel
range finder instrument used to determine distance to target
rear sight sight nearest breech of firearm
recoil distance through which a weapon moves backward after discharging
round unit of ammunition equal to one shot
safety device on gun that prevents inadvertent firing
scope telescopic sight
shell cylindrical casing that holds firearm charge; bullet, cartridge, or torpedo shell
shot lead pellets discharged from firearm: bird shot, buckshot, grapeshot
shrapnel cartridge filled with bursting charge; fragments from exploding charge
side lock method of discharging rifle in which hammer and percussion mechanism are on side of firearm rather than in line with barrel
sight mechanical or optical device used to guide aim of firearm; (*vb*) visually direct or aim firearm
silencer attachment to muzzle of firearm that muffles noise
slug bullet
target practice shooting at targets to test or improve accuracy in one's use of firearms
telescopic sight firearm aiming device equipped with magnifying lens; scope
tracer bullet that emits trail of smoke or luminous gas
trigger mechanism pulled by finger to fire gun
wheel lock obsolete gunlock in which revolving wheel strikes flint to make spark

Bombs, Mines, and Explosives

ABM antiballisticmissile
A-bomb atomic bomb
antiballistic missile ABM; missile designed to intercept and destroy ballistic missiles
antimissile missile ballistic missile designed to detect and destroy missiles in flight
antipersonnel bomb bomb that produces

shrapnel designed to damage persons more than property
atomic bomb immensely powerful bomb that utilizes nuclear fission reaction; A-bomb
ballistic missile unmanned military rocket with warhead
bomb highly explosive charge thrown at or dropped on target
buzz bomb V-1 rocket
cherry bomb powerful, globular firecracker
depth charge explosive charge detonated underwater against submarines
dynamite safe-handling, solid explosive that contains nitroglycerin, used esp. in mining, quarrying, and engineering
explosive substance that can blow up or detonate; weapon containing such a substance
fireball grenade, bomb
firebomb explosive device with incendiary effects
firecracker paper cylinder holding weak, noisy explosive and fuse, used in displays and celebrations, not as weapon
fission bomb bomb detonated by atomic fission reaction; atomic bomb
fuel-air explosive explosive that achieves powerful, concussive blast effect by releasing and detonating highly volatile fuels in the air, used on troops in bunkers or tunnels and to clear mine fields
fusion bomb bomb detonated by atomic fusion reaction; hydrogen bomb
gas bomb bomb that contains poison or chemical gas
grenade missile or container with charge of explosive or chemical gas, launched or hand-thrown
ground mine land mine
H-bomb hydrogen bomb
hydrogen bomb immensely powerful bomb that utilizes atomic fusion reaction; H-bomb
ICBM intercontinental ballistic missile; supersonic missile with range of at least 3500 nautical miles (6500 km), usu. with thermonuclear warhead
incendiary bomb bomb that sets target on fire
intercontinental ballistic missile ICBM
land mine explosive charge shallowly buried underground, detonated by pressure from person or vehicle; ground mine
mine explosive charge in container buried underground or placed in sea, detonated by contact
MIRV multiple independently targetable reentry vehicle; missile with two or more warheads aimed at separate targets
missile projectile with explosive charge, launched through air toward target
Molotov cocktail homemade bomb consisting of gasoline-filled bottle ignited by rag in bottle neck
napalm incendiary bomb consisting of aluminum soaps in jelling gas
neutron bomb nuclear bomb that kills by radiation, with detonation that is destructive to persons but not property
nitroglycerin oily, highly explosive liquid
nuclear bomb violently explosive bomb with power derived from splitting nuclei of heavy chemical elements such as uranium or plutonium
nuke *Informal.* nuclear or thermonuclear bomb
Patriot U.S. antiaircraft missile with range of 37 miles (60 km), launched from a tracked vehicle with computer guidance, also effective against low-flying missiles
pipe bomb homemade or primitive bomb made with explosive charge inserted into lead pipe
plastic explosive puttylike substance holding and concealing explosive charge, detonated by fuse or remote control
plutonium bomb atomic fission bomb in which plutonium is bombarded by neutrons to produce explosive chain reaction
report loud noise of explosion
rocket explosive charge inside missile
SAM surface-to-air missile
Scud medium-range Soviet tactical missile with 200 pound (90 kg) warhead for surface-to-surface attacks
Sidewinder short-range, air-to-air missile that homes in on heat of target aircraft's engine exhaust
smart bomb *Slang.* steerable air-to-surface bomb guided to its target by television or laser beam
smoke bomb explosive charge yielding large amount of smoke
stink bomb chemical charge that detonates to produce foul odor
submarine mine underwater mine that floats at predetermined depth
surface-to-air missile SAM; rocket launched from ground or water surface, aimed at aerial target
tear gas bomb grenade filled with chemical that causes extreme eye irritation
thermonuclear bomb bomb that utilizes nuclear fusion reaction; hydrogen bomb
time bomb explosive charge set to detonate at prearranged moment
TNT trinitrotoluene; highly explosive chemical used as charge in bombs
torpedo explosive underwater projectile
TOW tube-launched optically-guided wire-tracked missile; short-range antitank missile that trails thin wire
V-1 rocket pilotless, jet-powered plane with explosive warhead, used by Germans in World War II; buzz bomb
V-2 rocket early rocket with explosive charge, used by Germans in World War II
warhead front section of torpedo, missile, shell, or bomb, containing explosive charge

ELECTRICITY AND ELECTRONICS

AC alternating current
accumulator storage cell or battery of storage cells

alternating current AC; current that periodically changes direction at certain levels, measured in volts; current from wall socket
alternator electrical generator that produces alternating current
ammeter instrument that measures electric current in amps
amp ampere; *Informal.* amplifier
ampere unit of electric current produced by one volt acting through one ohm, equal to one coulomb per second; amp
Ampere's law electric current and changing electric field create a magnetic field
amplifier device or circuit that increases voltage or current of an input signal
amplitude maximum deviation of AC current from its average value during its cycle; peak value of waveform
analog (*adj*) designating electronic process in which data is represented by physical quantities that correspond to the variables involved
anion negative ion drawn to anode in electrolyzed solution
anode positive terminal of electrolytic cell; negative terminal of storage battery
arc luminous bridge formed between electrodes or across gap in circuit
arc lamp light in which current passes between electrodes through pressurized gas
armature wound rotor in generator that transforms electric current in coil into mechanical motion
attenuator device that reduces amplitude of signal with minimal distortion
ballast device used to maintain current in circuit by varying resistance in response to changes in voltage
band specific range of wavelengths or frequencies
band-pass filter filter that amplifies frequencies in specific range and reduces all others
battery number of primary or secondary cells that work together to produce flow of electric charge
blackout period of darkness due to electric power failure
bombardment stream of particles against surface, such as electrons against TV screen
boost (*vb*) raise voltage through circuit
bridge network configuration in which no two elements are in series or parallel; two-branch instrument that measures unknown impedance by balancing ratio of voltages in each branch to a known ratio
brownout enforced reduction of electric power usage
bulb rounded glass housing for filament of incandescent lamp
bus common path for multiple connections
cable strands of electrical conductor insulated from each other and laid together, often twisted around central core
capacitance measure of capacitor's ability to store a charge
capacitor device that accumulates and holds a charge of electricity; condenser
cathode negative electrode that emits stream of electrons and attracts positive ions in electrolytic cell; positive terminal of storage battery
cathode-ray tube CRT; heated filament that emits electron beam that can be controlled by externally applied potentials to produce luminous effect when electrons hit screen, as in a television or computer
cation positively charged ion drawn to cathode in electrolysis
cell housing for electrodes and electrolyte, used to generate electricity or in electrolysis
cesium alkali metal used in photoelectric cells; most electropositive element known
charge basis of electric energy, manifested in current, voltage, and electric field as positive or negative element that attracts unlike and repels like charged bodies
chip tiny electronic integrated circuit; microchip
circuit continuous path along which current flows: generator, resistors, conductors, other elements
circuit breaker switch that automatically interrupts electric circuit under abnormal conditions to prevent harmful, excessive current
coaxial cable insulated cable with two conductors, central signal line, and outer shield, used to transmit telephone, telegraph, and television signals
coil copper wire wound around solid object, used to produce electromagnetic effect and conduct current; inductor
commutator device for changing frequency or direction of a current
condenser capacitor that accumulates and holds a charge
conductance reciprocal of resistance, measured in mho units
conductivity capacity of a substance to conduct electric current
conductor material, esp. metal, through which electrons can flow as electric current
contact connection of touching but not soldered electric conductors, usu. metal
converter mechanical device that changes the form of electric energy or converts the frequency of radio signals
core middle part of coil or solenoid, often a metal rod
coulomb quantity of charge transferred by one ampere in one second between two points in circuit
coupling connection of two electric circuits by part common to both; interaction of circuit elements
CRT cathode-ray tube
current rate of flow of electric charge through solid or liquid, measured in amperes
DC direct current
digital (*adj*) designating an electronic process that defines frequencies and other data as discrete, binary bits of information

diode solid-state device or tube with anode and cathode that rectifies AC and allows current to pass freely in one direction only
dipole two equal but opposite charges held a small distance apart
direct current DC; current that flows in one direction only and has virtually invariable magnitude; current produced by a battery
dry cell battery one or more cells that work together in an ammonium chloride paste instead of a solution
electric (*adj*) describing any device that uses or produces a charge of electricity
electrician specialist in the installation, maintenance, and repair of electrical equipment
electricity physical agency caused by movement of electrons and other charged particles, manifested as attraction, repulsion, light, and heat
electrode wire, rod, or plate that conducts electric current into or out of any device
electrolysis passage of current through electrolyte with migration of charged ions to like-charged electrodes
electrolyte conducting medium in which flow of current leads to movement of charged ions
electromagnet coil with soft iron core that acts as magnet when current flows through it
electromagnetism interaction of electricity and magnetism, esp. magnetic effects produced by currents
electromotive force EMF; potential difference, expressed in volts, between terminals of a source of electric energy
electron negatively charged particle in all atoms that is basis of electricity
electronics branch of physics dealing with the emission and flow of electrons and the application of the energy produced to various devices
electron tube vacuum tube that controls passage of current through it by variations in grid potential; thermionic valve
electrostatic (*adj*) describing effects caused by charges at rest, such as electric charge on object
EMF electromotive force
extension cord long electric cord fitted with plug at one end and receptacle at other
farad unit of capacitance equal to one coulomb per volt
faraday quantity of electricity transferred in electrolysis and electric flux
ferromagnetic (*adj*) designating materials that retain magnetism
field region of space containing lines of force with direction and strength
filament thin, conductive heating element, usu. wire in vacuum tube, that produces light in light bulb
flux field lines of direction and strength
flux density number of field lines per unit area
frequency number of complete oscillations per unit time of an electromagnetic wave or alternating current
fuse safety device that breaks circuit if current is too great, usu. a piece of wire that melts
galvanometer instrument used for comparative measurement of small currents in units other than amperes
gamma ray shortest wavelength of electromagnetic radiation
gauss basic unit of flux density; magnetic induction equal to magnetic flux density necessary to move electromotive force along wire at specific speed
generator machine used to transform mechanical energy into electric energy through electromagnetism
gilbert unit of magnetomotive force equal to 0.7958 ampere-turns
grid element that controls electron flow between anode and cathode in tube
ground large conductor connected to electric circuit as general return point; connection to such a body; circuit reference point at which potential is zero
henry unit of inductance in which a variation of one ampere per second produces an induced electromotive force of one volt
IC integrated circuit
impedance total resistance to AC flow in circuit, combining resistance, inductance, and capacitance
induced current current that flows in coil moved in magnetic field
inductance flux in magnetic field caused by changing current in electric circuit or device, inducing voltage in that circuit or a nearby circuit
induction process by which electrification, magnetization, or electromotive force is produced in bodies and circuits through proximity to charge or field
inductor loop or loops of conducting material that produces oriented magnetic field when current is passed through it; coil
infrared rays electromagnetic waves with wavelengths longer than those of red light in visible spectrum
input impedance total opposition to AC by circuit, measured in ohms
insulation material that prevents current from escaping or entering where it is not wanted, used esp. to separate conductors
insulator material that prevents flow of current, including most nonmetals and gases
integrated circuit IC; electronic circuit conducted on single semiconductor wafer or microchip
inverter device that converts direct current into alternating current
ion electrically charged atom or group of atoms that results from loss or gain of one or more electrons by neutral atom
ionization conversion of atoms into positively or negatively charged particles
jack connecting device in circuit into which plug is inserted
laser light amplification by stimulated emission of radiation; device that excites atoms to higher energy levels in order to generate intense, coher-

ent beam of light from electromagnetic radiation
loop continuous current path
magnetic field condition of space in vicinity of magnetic substance or current-carrying body, in which forces can be found
maser microwave amplification by stimulated emission of radiation; laser that functions only in microwave region of spectrum
maxwell unit of magnetic flux per square centimeter in which magnetic induction is one gauss
microchip chip
microphone device that transforms sound waves into current by use of vibrating diaphragm
microwave electromagnetic radiation with wavelength between infrared and radio waves
modulation alteration in waveform frequency or amplitude due to superimposition of another wave or signal
motor device that transforms electric energy into mechanical energy, esp. one that produces motion by means of coil of wire around armature turning between poles of a magnet
ohm unit of resistance in circuit when potential difference of one volt produces current of one amp between two points
Ohm's law the ratio of voltage to current in a circuit is equal to the resistance
open circuit discontinuous circuit in which current cannot flow
oscillator wave generator
oscilloscope instrument that uses cathode-ray tube to display waveform images of periodic changes in voltage or current
outlet electric receptacle that leads to power source, into which electric devices are plugged
parallel circuit circuit in which positive and negative terminals connect to two distinct points, with voltage applied equally throughout
patchboard central jackfield that connects all elements in circuit configuration; patchbay
period time required for one waveform cycle to be completed; inverse of frequency
phasor diagram that illustrates phase and amplitude relations in AC circuits
photoelectric cell cell whose electrical properties are modified by illumination by light waves
piezoelectricity production of electric current in certain crystals through deformation by mechanical stress
pile several disks of two dissimilar metals stacked in alternating series and separated by pads of cloth or paper moistened with an electrolyte, used to produce current
plug fitting inserted into receptacle to establish contact connection in circuit
polarization effect produced when simple primary cell produces current; deposits of gas on plate that increase cell resistance during electrolysis
potential work needed to bring unit of positive charge from distance to given point
potentiometer variable resistor directly controlled by dial, knob, or lever
power time rate of electric energy in device or circuit, measured in watts
power cord insulated electric cord with specific current and material ratings, used as power supply line
power supply source of current and voltage
primary cell nonrechargeable device that produces flow of electric charge by means of chemical reaction of two different metals in acid
raceway tube used to protect electric wiring
radio use of electromagnetic waves to send message from microphone to receiver
radio wave longest wavelength of electromagnetic radiation
reactance impedance of AC circuit due to capacitance or inductance, expressed in ohms
receiver device that transforms electromagnetic radiation signals into electric current and voltage
rectifier device used to change AC to DC
regulator automatic device used to maintain current or voltage in circuit
relay device that uses small current to control greater current in another circuit by electromagnetic switching
resistance force that opposes flow of current through a conductor, measured in ohms; reciprocal of conductance
resistor passive circuit component that exhibits relatively constant resistance to current flow at all frequencies at same temperature
resonance peak frequency response characteristic of AC-driven circuit
resonator hollow enclosure of conductor resonated by certain frequencies of electromagnetic radiation
rheostat device that regulates current by means of adjustable resistors
schematic standardized diagram of circuit
secondary cell device that produces current by chemical reaction, rechargeable by passing current in opposite direction from discharge; storage cell
semiconductor any of class of materials with conductivity near that of conductor at high temperatures and nearly absent at low
short circuit abnormal condition caused by direct connection between points of low resistance on circuit, usu. resulting in bypass or break due to excess flow of current
socket receptacle for plug or screw-in devices
solenoid coil with length very much greater than its diameter that acts as magnet when current passes through it; simple polar magnet equally magnetized along its full length
solid-state (*adj*) designating electronic device that utilizes properties of semiconductor materials, not electron tubes
spark instantaneous appearance of light and sound in electrostatic discharge of very short duration
speaker transducer that changes electric energy into sound waves
static disturbance of radio or television reception by natural, atmospheric, or electrical phenomena
steady state long-term continuous circuit condition
storage cell secondary cell

superconductivity ability of certain metals to conduct current without resistance at very low temperatures
surge control multiple outlet plug that provides transient protection from sudden increases in current in electronic devices
switch device used to join or break parts of circuit, thus permitting or preventing flow of current
terminal point of current entry or departure from circuit; metal nut on screw or other mechanical device that connects wire to another apparatus
thermistor semiconductor device that exhibits negative coefficient of resistance with temperature
thermocouple electric circuit composed of two dissimilar metals joined at different temperatures
thermoelectric (*adj*) describing production of electric current directly from heat
tracer device that follows current through circuit to locate trouble
transducer device that receives power from one system and supplies power in a different form to another system, usu. by converting physical quantity into electrical quantity
transformer two coils of wire on same core that induce AC transfer from one circuit to another at same frequency
transistor small block of semiconductor with three terminals that acts like a vacuum tube in solid-state electronic devices
transmission emission of electromagnetic waves and their passage from one location to another
transmitter device that sends electromagnetic waves
triode three-electrode tube with negative grid between anode and cathode, used to increase voltage
tube device that controls passage of current through it by variation in grid potential, named for number of its electrodes: diode, triode, or tetrode
tuner device for receiving AM, FM, and shortwave radio signals
turn ratio ratio of number of turns of wire in primary and secondary windings of transformer
turns number of loops of wire in coil
tweeter small speaker that operates most efficiently at high frequencies
ultraviolet rays electromagnetic waves with wavelengths shorter than those of violet in visible spectrum
vacuum tube sealed glass bulb used to amplify, detect, or rectify AC to generate electrical oscillations, composed of plate, grid, and triode; electron tube
volt unit of potential difference between two points of conductor with constant one ampere current when one watt of power is dissipated between them
voltage measure of volts in a circuit, or energy per unit charge
voltaic cell two electrodes made from different metals in solution, used to produce electromotive force by chemical action
voltmeter instrument used to measure electromotive force or potential difference in volts
watt unit of power equal to one joule per second or one ampere flowing across potential difference of one volt
wave progressive disturbance or variation that propagates energy from point to point in a medium; undulating or jagged representation of this action
waveform repeating pattern of wave shape
wavelength distance along wave between points of same phase
weber practical unit of magnetic flux, equal to one volt second or 10^8 maxwells
winding wire wound around armature to act as coil
woofer large speaker that operates most efficiently at low frequencies
X-ray electromagnetic radiation of extremely short wavelength that penetrates solid bodies, acts like light on photographic film and plates, and ionizes gases

TELECOMMUNICATIONS

TeleData Transmission
Voice Transmission and Telephony

TeleData Transmission

AT command set the standard commands for controlling modems
bandwidth smallest range of frequencies within which certain signal can be transmitted
baud unit of measure of speed at which information is transmitted in number of signal impulses or bits per second
broadband type of data transmission in which a single medium carries several separate signals at once
bulletin board service accessed by modem, permitting users to leave, store, and retrieve messages
bus topology network architecture in which all devices are connected to a central cable
cable telegram; (*vb*) send a telegram
cablegram message transmitted by underwater cable
channel hardware device or path that transfers data between two elements of system
coaxial cable high-frequency telecommunications transmission line made up of insulated central conductor surrounded by conductive material that protects central conductor from interference
communications satellite artificial satellite used in radio, telephone, and television transmission by means of reflection or amplification and retransmission of signals between Earth stations
continental code international Morse code
converter device for changing electric energy or data from one form to another
cybernetics science of communication and information theory, esp. automatic control and regula-

tion of communication between humans and machines; information theory
dash telegraph signal of longer duration than dot, used in combination to represent letters in Morse code
data transfer rate speed at which information moves between two devices, measured in bits per second or bauds
day letter low-priority telegram to be delivered on following day
dedicated line phone or other communication line devoted to one device, such as a fax machine
demodulation conversion of alternating carrier wave or current into direct, pulsating current equivalent to transmitted data signal, esp. by modem; detection
detection demodulation
dish satellite dish
dot telegraph signal of shorter duration than dash, used in combination to represent letters in Morse code
download transmit data from one computer to another computer or device
duplex (*adj*) designating a telecommunications system capable of simultaneous transmission of messages in opposite directions on one channel
electronic mail message system using telecommunications network lines between computers; E-mail
E-mail electronic mail
Ethernet standard protocol for local area networks, using bus topology
facsimile method or device for reproducing graphic material in permanent form and transmitting it over telephone line; fax; phototelegraphy
fax facsimile
fax modem device combining the functions of a fax and modem on one board or unit
fiber optics branch of optics that deals with thin, transparent, flexible glass or plastic fibers used for high-speed, clear transmission of signals carrying masses of data along their length
full duplex communication mode in which data can be transmitted and received simultaneously
half duplex communication mode in which data can be sent in only one direction at a time
hardware electronic systems and devices used in telecommunications
hub central connection base for distribution of data to networked computers
Kermit file-transfer protocol for data transmission over phone lines via modem
information theory mathematical theory concerned with statistical analysis of information and communications between humans and machines; cybernetics
Intelsat International Telecommunications Satellite organization; global communications satellite network
interface meeting place of systems and means by which communication occurs there
interference imperfect or distorted signal reception, esp. due to stray or unwanted signals
international Morse code form of Morse code used in international telegraphy; continental code
Internet large computer network linking other networks worldwide
ISDN integrated services digital network; digital transmission of voice and data simultaneously over several channels on one line
kilobaud one thousand bits per second
link one element of telecommunications system or network
log on (*vb*) enter code or password to access telecommunications network
modem modulator/demodulator; device for converting and transmitting or receiving digital computer signals over telephone lines linking computer to network or to another computer
modulate (*vb*) vary amplitude, frequency, phase, or intensity of carrier wave in accordance with signal wave of much lower frequency
Morse code code system of long and short sounds or dots and dashes used in transmitting telegraph signals
multiplex telecommunications system capable of simultaneous transmission of multiple signals over single channel
network service for electronic distribution of data to subscribers
night letter reduced-rate telegram sent in evening and delivered on following day
packet switching efficient data transmission system in which initial message is broken into relatively small units that are sent independently and subsequently reassembled
phototelegraphy facsimile
plug electrical device that fits into jack to make connection
radiotelegraph telegraph in which messages or signals are sent by radio waves rather than through wires or cables
remote device that controls communications system without direct wire connection
satellite dish transmitter or receiving antenna in wide, concave, often round shape
signal sound or data conveyed over telephone or telegraph line, radio link, or optical fiber
stock ticker device for electronic transmission of stock prices from stock exchange receivers in brokerages and banks
switch device for establishing, breaking, or altering electrical connections in circuit
telecommunications all forms of electromagnetic transmission and reception of data, sounds, and images
telecommuting working at home at computer terminal linked to another site, as by modem
telefacsimile facsimile
telegram message sent by telegraph
telegraph device that transmits messages by sending signals by electronic impulses through wire or by conversion to radio waves
telegraphy construction and operation of telegraph systems
Telephoto *Trademark.* apparatus for electronic transmittal of photographs

teleprinter device that types out material received as electrical impulses over communications system
teletypewriter TTY; form of telegraph in which typewriter keys produce electrical impulses conveyed to receiving unit
telex teleprinter exchange; service using teletypewriter to send and receive information
terminal originating or receiving point for signals in telecommunications system
ticker telegraphic receiver that prints messages on paper tape
time-out (*vb*) disconnect automatically from a remote connection because of lack of input
topology the basic shape or architecture of a local-area network
TTY teletypewriter
twisted-pair cable type of network cable using two insulated copper wires, as in a phone cable
uplink transmission path from Earth station to communications satellite
upload transmit data from a computer to a network, bulletin board, etc.
videotex system for transmission of data over telephone lines for display on video terminals
WAN wide-area network, linking computers that are geographically distant from each other
Western Union *Trademark.* national telegraph service company
wire telegram; (*vb*) send a telegram
wireless telegraphy without use of wires
wire service press association news wire that transmits news dispatches via Teletype to radio, TV, and newspapers, esp. Associated Press, United Press International, and Reuters

Voice Transmission and Telephony

access ability to connect to line, circuit, or exchange, usu. denoting long-distance company's connection to local telephone company
answering machine electronic device that answers unattended phone and tapes incoming message
answering service service in which calls are picked up and messages taken by attendant when called party is unable to answer phone
area code prefix to phone number, specifying region in U.S. or Canada to which call is being made
auto-dial service feature whereby call is made automatically in response to pressing of single, preprogrammed button
bad connection telephone transmission with distortion or interference
beeper device carried to alert bearer that phone call has been received at home or office; pager
busy signal standard, repeating tone indicating that telephone line is engaged
caller ID telephone service that allows subscriber to identify caller, whose telephone number is displayed on a small screen, before answering call
call forwarding automatic transfer of incoming calls to another telephone line on which called party can be reached
calling card credit card with individualized customer number for billing calls to home or business phone when call is placed from another location
call waiting system in which a tone alerts user that another incoming call is on line and allows user to switch from one call to another on a single line
car phone cellular or other radiotelephone installed in automobile
cellular phone mobile radiotelephone connected to computer-controlled communications system divided into small cells, each with its own transmitter; cell phone
channel frequency bandwidth suitable for two-way telephone communication
circuit two-way communications path
coin-operated (*adj*) describing public telephone requiring insertion of coin to place call
collect call operator-assisted call in which charges are paid by receiving party
conference call multiparty call requiring simultaneous connection of three or more telephone lines; teleconference
cordless phone mobile phone connected without wiring to base station that is connected by wire to standard telephone outlet
cradle part of telephone instrument in which handset rests when not in use
dead (*adj*) having no dial tone on the line; nonfunctioning
dial-a- designation used as prefix by businesses offering service or product over the phone (as: dial-a-prayer)
dial tone buzz heard when functioning phone receiver is lifted
direct dialing placing call without operator assistance, esp. long distance call
directory book listing all residential and business telephone numbers in region or district
directory assistance assistance obtained by contacting special operator, usu. by dialing 411, to provide number that cannot be found in directory
disconnect breaking off of call due to electronic problem or intentional action to halt telephone service, usu. for nonpayment of bill
800 number special area code for numbers that permit calls without charge to calling party
emergency number special, often three-digit, number for use in emergency or to summon help
exchange central telephone office where local lines are connected and area served by it
extension one of several extra telephones connected to a single incoming line, often with its own number
foreign exchange central receiving station for all international calls to specific foreign country or region; any exchange outside local calling area
411 standard three-digit code for local directory assistance
handset telephone mouthpiece transmitter and earpiece receiver mounted on handle

headset earphone receiver and microphone transmitter for telephone mounted on attachment fitting onto head, used instead of handset
hold status on multiline phone in which call is removed from auditory circuit and caller waits without being disconnected
hot line direct line between two phones always kept open for instant access without dialing
information former term for directory assistance
intercom simple, two-way, short-range communication system with microphone and loudspeaker at each end
international call telephone call to location outside nation of origin
international country code routing code that directs call to correct nation without operator assistance
international dialing prefix three-digit code, usu. 011, giving caller access to international connection
LATA local access and transport area; one of 161 local telephone calling areas established after breakup of AT&T: calls from one LATA to another are long distance
line telephone wiring that connects individual, local, and national systems; single telephone connection
lineman telephone repairman responsible for maintenance of aboveground lines strung between telephone poles
listing single entry of name, address, and telephone number in directory
local access and transport area LATA
local call call placed to phone within immediate area, usu. at no additional cost
long distance telephone service beyond local area, billed for timed toll
memory phone telephone instrument equipped with programmable memory that holds frequently dialed numbers accessed by punching a single key
modular equipment standardized, interchangeable instruments, wiring, and jacks for easy removal and connection
network large, interconnected system of communications lines, central exchanges, and processing computers
900 number special area code for numbers that charge a fee to the caller, used in marketing, public opinion surveys, and sales
911 emergency number for police, fire, or ambulance
nonpublished listing telephone number not printed in directory at customer's request, also not revealed by directory assistance; unlisted number
not in service designating telephone line that has been disconnected or is not functioning properly
operator person who controls routing, connection, and disconnection of calls through telephone switchboard
pager beeper
party line shared telephone circuit that connects two or more customers to exchange
pay phone telephone in public place requiring coin deposit or credit card number for use
PBX private branch exchange; telephone system that functions within one business or building
person-to-person (*adj*) designating operator-assisted call connected only to person designated by calling party
phone telephone instrument; (*vb*) place a telephone call
PIN personal identification number; computerized code used in placing credit card calls
prefix first three digits of seven-digit telephone number, often indicating location of line and exchange
private line telephone line intended for exclusive use of one person, family, or organization
public telephone telephone located in public place, operated by coin or credit card
push-button phone phone on which push-button keys bear numbers and letters used in placing a call
radiotelephone telephone in which communication is carried on through radio waves only
receiver portion of telephone equipment that converts incoming electrical signals into auditory sound waves
signal sound conveyed over telephone or telegraph line
speakerphone telephone equipped with loudspeaker and microphone so that it can be operated without using handset or headset
speed calling service permitting memory storage of frequently called numbers and quick dialing with one or two digits
station-to-station (*adj*) designating operator-assisted call to anyone answering number dialed or any direct dial call
subscriber customer paying for use of telephone service
switchboard device for connecting, controlling, and disconnecting multiple phone lines, as in office
tap (*vb*) make secret connection into telephone circuit to eavesdrop on private conversations; wiretap
teleconference conference call
telephone instrument for converting sound into electrical impulses to be transmitted over distances by wire; (*vb*) communicate by telephone
telephone tag repeated unsuccessful attempts by two persons to reach each other by telephone
telephonics science of conveying sound over distances, as by telephone
telephony construction and operation of telephone systems; telecommunications system based on telephone equipment that transmits speech or other sounds between two points, with or without wires
three-way calling service that allows customer to call two other parties and speak to them simultaneously
tie line direct line connecting extensions in two or more PBX systems
toll call call requiring payment of fee beyond basic service charge

toll-free (*adj*) requiring no additional fee beyond basic service charge
touch-tone tone-dialing system equipped with push-button keys for indicating number called by transmission of electronic beeps
transmitter device, esp. mouthpiece, for converting sound waves into electrical impulses to be sent by telephone wire
trunk line circuit between two central telephone exchanges for making multiple connections; line from central office to PBX
unlisted number nonpublished listing
videoconference teleconference conducted via television equipment
videophone telephone with both audio and video capabilities
voice mail electronic system for recording and storage of voice messages, often in digitized form, for later retrieval by intended recipient
WATS Wide Area Telecommunications Service; special fixed-rate, long-distance service for companies making many toll calls, with cost unrelated to number of calls made
white pages alphabetical directory listing names and addresses with residential and business phone numbers in specific area
wiretap act or instance of tapping a telephone so as to eavesdrop on calls made or received; (*vb*) tap
wrong number undesired telephone connection due to dialing of incorrect digits
yellow pages directory listing business names, addresses, and telephone numbers in specific area, organized by category of business

COMPUTERS

General Technology
Hardware and Peripherals
Software, Languages, and Programming
Memory and Data Storage
Internet and World Wide Web

General Technology

abort termination of program that returns control to operating system
access code password that allows entry into computer
access time interval required to retrieve information from memory or a disk
ADP automated data processing
AI artificial intelligence
algorithm predetermined instructions for step-by-step solution to specific problem
alphanumeric (*adj*) consisting of both alphabetic and numeric characters
Alt key used alone or in conjunction with control and/or shift key to change meaning of another key with which it is used
analog signal with continuous range of values, opp. of digital
applications areas or operations of business, art, and technology in which computers are useful
artificial intelligence AI; capacity of machines to perform operations similar to learning and decision making
automated data processing ADP; processing data using computer program or system that reduces human intervention to a minimum
automation science and technology concerned with making self-regulating machines in which electronic devices replace or enhance human control
backup duplicate copy of program or file made as insurance against loss or damage
bar code thin and thick lines alternating in a coded pattern readable by scanner, typically printed on packaging to represent price and other data
batch group of records or transactions that can be processed together
batch processing noninteractive computing mode in which input is gathered into groups or batches and additional input cannot be made once program is being executed
baud unit of measure of speed at which information is transmitted in number of signal impulses or bits per second
BBS bulletin board system
bells and whistles *Informal.* unessential, but often attractive, features
binary system in which numbers are represented as sequences of zeros and ones, which is basis of digital computing
Boolean (*adj*) describing systems in which variable values are restricted to true and false
boot (*vb*) start up computer by loading operating system
bootstrap set of instructions that begin operation of operating system
bug error, esp. in program
bulletin board service, accessed by modem, that permits users to leave, store, and retrieve messages, shareware, and public-domain software
bundling selling hardware and software or several software programs together at set price
bus series of communications channels in which signals are passed, usu. sockets into which components are plugged
CAD computer-aided design; system that uses graphics display to design products
CAI computer-aided instruction; interactive teaching software system
channel hardware device or path that transfers data between two elements
chip very small piece of silicon processed or burned to form integrated circuit; microchip
cold boot loading sequence in which entire operating system is loaded into computer at start-up or after reset

command coded instruction to computer
compatible (*adj*) able to use same programs or hardware, esp. matched to major brand but manufactured by smaller company
computer-aided design CAD
computer-aided instruction CAI
computerese argot of computers, their users, and their designers
computer graphics conversion of digital information into visual format for display on terminal or output on printer
computerize (*vb*) equip with or automate by computers
computer literacy nontechnical study and understanding of computers and basic familiarity with their uses in society
computer science study of design and use of computers and software
configuration computer and all devices connected to it; collection of set-up choices for software program
control Ctrl, command key that changes meaning of another key with which it is used
crash system failure and shutdown due to software or hardware malfunction
crunch (*vb*) perform many numerical calculations and manipulations of data
cursor special character used to denote position on video display, usu. an underline, solid block, or highlight arrow
cyber- combining form connoting computers or virtual reality (cyberspace, cyberart)
D/A conversion from digital data into analog signal such as voltage or sound
data entry inputting of information for processing by computer
data management system series of commands used to search and retrieve data and update or reference portions of database
data processing basic computer operations in general
debug (*vb*) locate and correct malfunction or error in program code
dedicated (*adj*) designed for specific application or function
delimiter blank space, comma, character, or symbol that indicates beginning or end of character string, word, or data item
desktop publishing DTP; use of personal computer with graphics and typographic layout programs to design and create publications
digital signal with two discrete values, zero and one, represented by presence or absence of electric pulse
digital imaging scanning and recording of visual images in digital form
digitizer device that converts images into numeric form comprehensible to computer
directory table of contents that lists files
documentation written and graphic material describing and explaining use, operation, maintenance, or design of piece of hardware or software
down (*adj*) not operational; said of a computer, network, or system
download (*vb*) transfer programs or files from one computer to another device or computer
downtime interval when computer is inoperable due to malfunction
drag (*vb*) move cursor across screen by sliding mouse or other pointing device
DTP desktop publishing
dump (*vb*) print or display contents of internal storage on output medium, esp. during program failure
electronic mail message system that uses telecommunications network links between computers; E-mail
E-mail electronic mail
end user person who uses specific hardware or software product
enter key command to perform operation
escape ESC; ASCII control key used in combination with others to provide added functionality, esp. to interrupt command or return to previous level of program
execute (*vb*) perform command or series of commands
exit (*vb*) leave specific context, often to return to system
expert system basis of artificial intelligence that captures information in particular domain through hierarchy of if/then questions
field unit of data forming part of a record in structured database
FIFO first in, first out; processing of information in order received
fifth generation computer systems that use artificial intelligence and parallel processing by multiple CPUs capable of handling billions of calculations per second
flow chart symbolic, logical representation of program control
footprint area of desk or floor space occupied by piece of hardware
format (*vb*) prepare disk to receive information; (*n*) organization of data on disk into tracks and sectors
fractal geometrical structure that has regular or uneven shape repeated over all scales of measurement and a dimension that is greater than the spatial dimension of the structure
function key key designated to send specific command code
fuzzy (*adj*) approximate, not precise: used to describe search or operation that generates a set whose members lie across a spectrum of values approximating a central value
generation hardware developed at one period based on previous level of technology
GIGO garbage in, garbage out; output quality is dependent on input quality
glitch *Slang.* sudden, inexplicable malfunction
graphics use of computer to generate and display images on screen
hacker *Slang.* person extremely knowledgeable about computers, frequently an amateur programmer

hang (*vb*) cause (a computer or application) to lock up
high resolution video display system or printer that depicts images in great detail with high degree of accuracy
hit useful or informative response to a query or online search
hypermedia combination of computer and hypertext system with CD audio, VCR, or laser disc capabilities
IC integrated circuit
icon graphic representation, esp. of option on computer menu accessed by mouse
inheritance network hierarchical organization of data for artificial intelligence in which elements in each descending level have characteristics of those in levels above them
input data received by computer from external source
instruction command; single operation to be executed
integrated circuit IC; electronic circuit on single chip of material, usu. silicon; microchip
interactive (*adj*) designating any program or system that has a dialogue with human user and responds to input
interface hardware and/or software required to connect peripheral to computer system, one computer system to another, or for user's access to system; point at which any two parts of system connect
interrupt signal from I/O device or peripheral to CPU to stop current processing and start new operation
job program and data submitted to computer for execution
joystick mechanical lever used to control cursor movement on video display; esp. for games
jump programming instruction that stops sequential processing and transfers control to another point in program
jumper nonmechanical switch that provides options on circuit board
keystroke single depression of one key on keyboard
kilobaud one thousand bits per second
LAN local area network; system for linking terminals, PCs, or work stations with each other or with mainframe to share data, peripherals, and programs, usu. in one building
LED light-emitting diode; feedback device permitting current to flow in one direction only
light pen photoelectric stylus that sends signals to computer by movement against CRT screen
line feed control key used as return or to advance to next line
load (*vb*) move data or program instructions from storage medium into computer memory for execution
local area network LAN
lock up (*vb*) cease functioning or responding to input
log on (*vb*) enter personal identification data, such as name and/or password, into multiuser system so as to access it
loop set of instructions designed to be repeated
management information system MIS
manual book containing operating instructions and sometimes design specifications for particular piece of hardware or software
microchip integrated circuit; chip
MIPS millions of instructions per second; measure of processing speed
MIS management information system; software or department in corporation that supports management in keeping track of and running organizations or departments under it
mnemonic programming code or other shortened form that is easy to remember
mouse small handheld device that is rolled across a surface to point at objects and control cursor movement on video display
multimedia combination of text, graphics, video, animation, voice, and music in computer system
multitasking ability of user to have multiple activities or programs in progress simultaneously
nesting programming technique that employs hierarchical levels of instruction
network set of communications channels that connect computers
neural network basis for advanced artificial intelligence by which computer forms and recognizes patterns, enabling it to reach conclusions not laid out for it by binary architecture
noise random signals, interference, or nonmanaged data
OCR optical character recognition
off-line (*adj*) designating equipment not directly linked to central computer or CPU
on-line (*adj*) designating equipment directly linked to central computer or CPU
operand data unit or equipment item operated upon
operator user of computer system
optical character recognition OCR; process that optically scans printed text and converts it into machine-readable code
optical reader wand mechanical device that reads bar codes
output result of computer operation, usu. in form of hard copy or video display
override instruction that stops execution of previous command
parallel processing data processing by multiple CPUs acting simultaneously
parameter definable characteristic or limit of system or program
parity error-detecting technique using eighth bit; odd parity or even parity
parity bit eighth bit in ASCII code that becomes zero or one to make sum of all eight bits even or odd as a data check
password code or sequence of characters used to protect system or specific file from unauthorized use
patch piece of program code inserted to debug or modify existing program
pico one thousandth of a billionth; one trillionth

pixel single dot and smallest element in visual display; square picture unit that is basis of computer graphics
plotter device used to make drawing on video display
power down orderly shutdown of computer and peripherals
power surge sudden, dangerous fluctuation in AC voltage
power-up orderly start-up of computer and peripherals
procedure logical set of program commands called by single name
prompt character displayed on terminal that indicates that computer is awaiting further instructions from user, often also identifying logged drive
protocol set of rules governing information exchange
queue FIFO-organized sequence of items awaiting processing or action by peripheral
QWERTY designation for traditional typewriter keyboard layout, named after six letters at upper left
readout manner in which computer presents processed information, such as visual display or line printer
real time actual time required for computer operations involving rapid analysis of data, esp. as it affects a physical process
reboot (*vb*) restart (a computer) by resetting or powering down and back up
record group of related fields forming unit of information in structured database
refresh (*vb*) update a screen display to show current status
relational (*adj*) describing development of database as large matrix
response time interval between input of data and computer output or response
RISC reduced instruction set computer; computer designed with chip that eliminates all but minimum number of instructions needed to perform most common tasks, providing increased processing speed
robotics control by computer of machine programmed to perform industrial or other tasks
rollover keyboard ability that allows rapid typing yet codes characters in order struck
semiconductor material that can be manipulated to improve its conductivity for the passage of electrons, esp. silicon used for integrated circuits
serial processing computer operations in which programs are run sequentially, not simultaneously
Silicon Valley area in northern California, south of San Francisco in the Santa Clara valley region, with concentration of semiconductor and computer companies
solenoid device that converts electric current into linear motion by magnetizing hollow coil
SPOOL simultaneous peripheral operations online; technique that allows I/O operation of peripheral device such as printer while simultaneously executing another program
string ordered sequence of data elements, usu. characters, treated as a unit
stylus light pen; scanning device used for input on graphics tablet
support personnel, documentation, or programs that complement hardware or software technology
surge control device that protects system from AC power surges
sysop *Informal.* systemsoperator; operator of bulletin board
systems analysis examination of operations in order to improve them or determine how to accomplish specific goals
tag indicator of beginning or end of unit of information
technical support assistance offered by vendor of hardware or software to end user, usu. by telephone or through bulletin board
telecommuting working at home at computer terminal linked to another site, as by modem
throughput measure of system's execution efficiency in instructions per second
timesharing sharing of CPU by several users at once for different purposes through buffers and switching
toggle on/off switch with two positions that initiates or halts function
turnaround time interval needed to provide answer to question or execute task
tweak (*vb*) *Slang.* make fine adjustments to
unbundling pricing of system's hardware and software separately
universal product code UPC; machine-readable bar code used for labeling merchandise
up (*adj*) functioning properly
UPC universal product code
user-friendly (*adj*) easy for user to understand and execute without extensive training
variable named program entity capable of representing different values during program execution
very large scale integration VLSI; placement of from one hundred thousand to one million circuits on single chip
virtual reality creation of imaginary, animated, three-dimensional landscape that one may explore and change by means of sensors attached to one's body and connected to computer that generates scenes; cyberspace
VLSI very large scale integration
voice recognition ability of system to accept spoken words as input
voice synthesis system capable of generating audio output responses in simulated voice using specific vocabulary of electronic phonemes
warm boot function that reads directories and reloads portions of operating system into RAM
window individually controlled portion of screen on which information can be shown, esp. without exiting document file or program
work station powerful, single-user computer, esp. one used for CAD, often networked
WYSIWYG what you see is what you get; term

designating video display that shows text as it will appear in printout

Hardware and Peripherals

bidirectional printing operation of printer from left to right and right to left for added speed
buffer intermediate, temporary storage device for holding data until computer or peripheral such as printer is ready to process it
cathode-ray tube CRT; common computer display screen
CD drive disk drive that accepts compact disk storage medium
central processing unit CPU; main part of computer system
clock speed measurement, in megahertz, of the processing speed of a CPU
computer general purpose, digital, information processing device composed of a central processing unit, memory, input and output facilities, power supply, and housing
configure (*vb*) adjust printer, modem, or other peripheral to follow central processor; set up software with user-designated parameters
console part of computer, such as keyboard and monitor, that enables operator to communicate with system
CPS characters per second; designation of dot-matrix or daisy wheel printer speed
CPU central processing unit; key component of computer that processes and executes program instructions
CRT cathode-ray tube used as monitor to display characters or designs
digitizer device that converts information into numeric form comprehensible to digital computer
disk drive electromechanical device that spins magnetic disk and allows data to be written to or read from disk through read/write head
display video monitor, such as CRT or LCD, that temporarily shows information
dot pitch measurement, in millimeters, of the vertical distance between pixels on a display screen
drive disk drive
dual-processor (*adj*) designating computer system with two CPUs performing different operations simultaneously
execute (*vb*) run (a program)
expansion slot connection to which new board can be added
external slot point at which additional peripherals and modules can be connected to motherboard
file server computer acting as file storage for other networked computers, allowing multiple users access to individual file
first generation earliest model of hardware in specific upgrade path
front end processor small computer interfacing large host computer and peripherals that reduces I/O interruptions to host
graphics tablet wire grid embedded in screen, activated by stylus to record points traced by stylus
hard copy computer output printed on paper; printout
hard drive device, either external or internal, that spins and reads high-capacity storage hard disk
hardware physical components of system: computer, external memory system, terminal, printer, modem
hard-wired (*adj*) built into hardware, as through electronic circuits, rather than functioning through software
impact printer printer that generates characters by character striking ribbon against paper
ink-jet printer printer that generates characters by squirting ink droplets against paper, controlled by deflection magnets
input/output I/O; devices or communications channels that move information into and out of computer
I/O input/output
IRQ interrupt request line, a setting that controls communication of peripheral devices with the CPU
keyboard device for inputting data by depressing keys that generate all standard characters (letters, digits, punctuation marks) and other keys that have special functions, such as cursor arrow keys or programmable function keys
keypad special purpose numeric keyboard to which other commands or characters may be assigned; numeric pad
laptop computer very small personal computer, designed to fit on lap
laser printer high-quality printer that forms images by focusing laser beam on photosensitive drum
LCD liquid crystal display
line printer impact printer capable of producing full line of 80 to 132 characters at one time
liquid crystal display LCD; flat-panel video screen that uses solution of liquid crystal subjected to voltage to block rear light transmission and generate display
local area network computers in close proximity sharing peripherals
logic board motherboard for Apple and Macintosh computers
mainframe giant institutional computer that requires conditioned environment and allows for multiple users at work stations
microcomputer small home or office desktop computer that uses a CPU on a single chip, with power supply and I/O interfaces
microprocessor complete CPU in integrated circuit on single chip
minicomputer intermediate size, usu. multiuser computer frequently used as work station or connected to work stations
modem modulator/demodulator; device linking two computers by telephone lines
module computer circuit board with specific function, used as building block in system

monitor high-resolution display screen
motherboard circuit board with series of parallel bus sockets into which computer modules and circuitry are plugged
notebook computer small laptop or portable computer, usu. under seven pounds in weight
numeric pad keypad
open architecture system design that permits easy replacement and upgrading of circuit boards, even the use of those made by third parties
optical scanner device that scans light from surface of printed matter and converts analog signals into machine-readable input for storage in computer
page printer printer that determines character pattern for entire page at once, rather than printing line by line
palmtop very small portable computer that can be held in one hand
parallel configuration interface between computer and peripheral that transfers entire byte or word of data at once, with separate line for each bit
parallel port actual connection in parallel configuration
parallel printer printer designed for parallel interface with computer
PC personal computer
peripheral device such as printer, modem, or hard drive, connected to and dependent on computer
personal computer PC; small, relatively low-cost microcomputer designed for home or business use
plug-and-play (*adj*) designating a peripheral device, etc., designed for easy, non-technical installation and use
port channel connecting I/O device to computer
printout hard copy; printed version of document file
reconfiguring resetting instructions that connect computer to peripheral such as printer
retrofit (*vb*) upgrade hardware, esp. with components that were not available at time of original manufacture
scanner device that digitally records images and text from paper
screen video display terminal; contents of what appears on monitor
SCSI small computer system interface; pronounced ""scuzzy"; cable or other method of connecting peripheral to computer
serial configuration interface between computer and peripheral that passes information one bit or character at a time
serial port actual connection in serial configuration
serial printer printer designed for serial interface with computer
server file server
sheet feeder tray or other device that feeds paper into printer one sheet at a time
smart terminal terminal with buffer to store certain amount of information and with microprocessor that allows for some processing capabilities
split screen screen divided into two or more windows that display independent or connected data
supercomputer very fast, powerful mainframe, esp. for military and scientific research
supermini fastest and most powerful minicomputer, with capabilities nearly equal to those of a mainframe
surge protector device installed on a power supply line to protect against irregularities in electrical current
SVGA Super VGA, an improvement on the VGA graphics standard, allowing higher resolution and more colors
system computer and all its related components
terminal peripheral device through which user communicates with computer, including keyboard for input and video display for output
thermal printer low-speed, moderate quality, small format, nonimpact printer that forms characters by applying heat to specially sensitized paper
VDT video display terminal; CRT monitor or other screen used to display computer output and communicate with computer; VDU
VDU video display unit; VDT
VGA video graphics array, a widespread graphics standard for PCs
video card control device that runs color monitor
word processor dedicated computer used to write and process text documents
workstation computer with more processing power and graphics capabilities than a standard PC

Software, Languages, and Programming

ALGOL algorithmic language; early, high-level mainframe language, esp. used for teaching; forerunner of Pascal
app particular software application, as a word processor or spreadsheet
applet applications program that can be executed within another application
application software programs designed to handle particular types of information to achieve specific results, such as word processing or spreadsheet
ASCII American Standard Code for Information Interchange; code most commonly used to represent characters, using seven bits to represent each of 128 characters, including control codes
assembler program that converts assembly language into binary machine language
assembly language machine-specific, low-level, mnemonic language used to write efficient programs
authoring system group of programming tools used to develop usu. multimedia product
background program multitask program executed when CPU is not busy with priority task
backslash oblique stroke slanted to left, used as delimiter in some computer operating systems
BASIC Beginner's All-purpose Symbolic

Instruction Code; simplified language for programmers on microcomputers
beta introductory version of new software program still being tested by outside users
beta test test of new or upgraded software conducted at select user sites just prior to release of product
BIOS communications medium between DOS and machine language
block operation task involving manipulation of information block
bridgeware software that serves as bridge between one kind of system or platform and another
bundled software several software programs sold together or sold with piece of hardware
C high-level programming language
C++ widely used high-level programming language, incorporating object-oriented features
chaining breaking up of program that exceeds memory capacity into smaller units that are executed sequentially
click single, quick tap and release of a mouse button
COBOL common business oriented language; high-level business language used on mainframes
code programming language that tells machine what to do
command line line on a display where a command is expected to be entered
compatibility ability of software to run on specific computers
compiler program that translates high-level language into machine code that computer can execute
compression programming technique that compacts large amounts of data for storage on disks or inclusion in program
control character non-printing ASCII character used to control device functions
conversion translation of data from one operating system or program to another
courseware educational software designed esp. for classroom use
CP/M *Trademark.* Control Program for Microcomputers; early operating system for eight-bit microprocessors
data bank database or number of databases
database systematically structured collection of information organized for easy input, access, retrieval, storage, and update
DBMS database management system; program that creates, maintains, and accesses database
DDT dynamic debugging tool; program used to analyze and correct software problems
default option or value built into program or system in lieu of user input, but able to be overriden; default setting or parameter
delete word processing command to remove one or more characters
delimiter marker of the end of a tag, field, record, etc., in a data string
diagnostic program used to find source of errors or malfunctions
directory in DOS, a top-level storage area for files and collections of files
disk operating system DOS; program managing operation of entire disk drive-based system
DOS disk operating system
drag-and-drop (*adj*) allowing movement of icons, etc., to another area on the screen via mouse control
driver software that controls the basic operation of a device, as a printer, mouse, video display, etc.
EBCDIC extended binary-coded decimal interchangecode; eight-bit character code for 256 characters, used by IBM mainframes instead of ASCII
edit (*vb*) make changes in document file
emulation real-time simulation program that allows one computer to mimic operations of another
EOF end of file
.exe suffix in DOS designating an executable file, one that will launch an application
executable code machine-readable version of code that machine can actually run, all in bits
expert system application that can perform operations formerly done only by human experts, as diagnosing an illness
export (*vb*) format data for use in another application
extension secondary part of a file name; in DOS, the three characters following the dot, often specifying a file type
file management system program or programs that facilitate creation and management of files
firmware program stored in ROM and built into computer, usu. to implement function previously provided in software
folder in Macintosh operating systems, a storage area for individual file and other folders
FORTRAN formula translator; early general-purpose, high-level compiled language, used primarily for mainframes and minis
front-end (*adj*) designating software that provides a user interface for access to an application
GIF graphics interchange format, a bit-mapped graphics file format for storing and compressing images
global search program or command that searches for and acts upon every occurrence of a character, word, or phrase within file
graphical user interface GUI; video-display environment based on icons, WYSIWYG screen, and mouse operations, used orig. on Macintosh computers
groupware business or office software designed for use by network of users at connected work stations
GUI graphical user interface
high-level language programming language, such as C, COBOL, or Pascal, with form similar to English or mathematics
hit a successful result from a query or search of a database
hot key keyboard sequence to perform a command or open another application
hyperlink a built-in link from one word, icon, etc

to another related item, as a cross-reference, image, audio or video clip, etc.
hypertext file or database system with built-in links from text to other related texts, images, sounds, or video clips
icon small graphic representation of a file, folder, application, etc., ready for use
import (*vb*) read and display data from another application
intermediate compiler program that translates high-level computer language into object code and saves it, prior to conversion into executable machine language
interpreter program that translates high-level language into machine language to allow immediate execution of program
kluge makeshift or inelegant remedy or fix that circumvents a software or device problem
language arbitrarily designed and coded syntax and vocabulary that allows user to communicate with computer
LISP list processing language; high-level interpretive or compiled language used in artificial intelligence
LOGO powerful programming language for use by children
low-level language coding specification that is close to language understood by computer and therefore more difficult for people
machine language binary code language that can be directly executed by CPU; basic language understood by computer
machine-readable (*adj*) encoded in or translated into form suitable for processing, such as ASCII
macro single command that expands into series of instructions temporarily or permanently saved as that command
memory resident designating program that remains in internal memory while other programs are being executed
menu list of program options displayed for user
menu driven (*adj*) run by choosing from presented options rather than by entering commands
merge (*vb*) combine two files of ordered information into single file
multitasking ability of a computer to perform more than one task or run more than one application at a time
object code intermediate stage between source code and executable code
operating system OS; software that organizes and manages resources of system, communicates with peripherals, interacts with users, handles files, and accesses software
OS operating system
output information computer produces by executing program; means of displaying or extracting information from computer
parent directory the directory containing another directory
Pascal popular, high-level structured programming language
platform major piece of software, such as an operating system, operating environment, or database, under which various smaller applications are designed to run
pop-up window window that can appear from background, remains hidden until needed, and goes away after use
PostScript *Trademark.* an object-oriented page description language developed by Adobe Systems, widely used in the printing and publishing industries
presentation software graphics program designed for use in live presentation to audience
print command to send file to printer to produce hard copy of file
productivity software business applications that directly aid work of an organization, such as word-processing, spreadsheet, database, or desktop-publishing programs
program sequence of instructions to computer to perform specific work
programmer individual trained to design, write, and implement programs in any of various computer languages
programming study and practice of designing and building computer software programs; translation of problem from physical environment to a language computer can understand
radio button selection among two or more options in a window or menu, only one of which may be selected at any time
readme file file supplied with an application that notes improvements, cautions, etc., not found in the product manual
relational database collection of data arranged logically into tables rather than hierarchically
reprogram (*vb*) rewrite or revise computer program
restore (*vb*) recover a file that has been lost, deleted, or corrupted
retrofit correction of one facet of program while program is in effect
return key that instructs computer to perform command just entered; key that produces hard-carriage return in word processing
root directory highest-level directory in a file system
save command to write data or an update to a hard disk, floppy, etc.
screen saver application that automatically changes the screen display when there has been no input for a set time, to prevent burn-in of an unchanging image
scrolling using screen as window on a file while moving vertically or horizontally through the file
search and replace capacity of editing program to find any appearance of specified character, word, or phrase in file and replace it with another specified character, word, or phrase
SGML Standard Generalized Markup Language, a standard for marking and defining data descriptively to enable use on differing systems and platforms
shareware often simple programs available at no charge, but for which a token donation is requested

shell user inferface program enabling access to applications; large macro of saved keystrokes used as special commands
slash character slanting downward from right to left (/; also called virgule, or solidus)
SNOBOL string-oriented symbolic language; high-level programming language used to manipulate character strings
software instructions and programs that tell hardware what to do
software package computer program and documentation designed and marketed to fill a specific need, such as word processing
source code program in commonly understood, high-level language that must pass through compiler or interpreter to execute
speech synthesis recognition of text characters and conversion of these to audible speech
spell check program designed to find and/or correct spelling errors in document
spreadsheet program that simulates business or scientific worksheet and performs calculations when data is changed
SQL structured query language, a standard language used in database management software
stand-alone (*adj*) designating self-contained software program or computer system that operates independently
structured language high-level computer language such as Pascal or ALGOL that stresses logical flow of control and extensive self-documentation
subscript usu. small character printed below normal line of type
superscript usu. small character printed above normal line of type
systems software collection of essential utilities programs for use with particular computer system
text editor program for revising stored documents and moving text
toolbar onscreen area with selection of most-used options
Unicode standard for representing characters digitally, using 16 bits for each character
unzip (*vb*) decompress a file that has been zipped
upgrade new, improved version of previously released software program
user interface part of program that provides interaction between person and rest of software through video display and input devices
utility operating system-specific software used to perform routine tasks such as sorting, debugging, formatting, and copying
vaporware software that is promoted or marketed while still in development and may never be produced
virus self-replicating program intentionally designed to disrupt operations of one computer or computer network
wild card character that stands for any other possible keystroke, usually represented by an asterisk or question mark
word processing computer creation and manipulation of text by editing, formatting, storing, and printing
word wrap word-processing program's capacity to automatically place word on next line if it extends beyond margin
worm computer virus that spreads from one computer to another over a network, etc.
zip (*vb*) compress a file to save storage space

Memory and Data Storage

access time time required for a device, as a hard drive, to find requested data
address label designating numerical position of storage location in memory
bad sector area on a hard disk or floppy disk that cannot be used for storage
bank logical unit of memory
batch group of records or programs considered as single unit for processing
bit one binary digit, whose value is either zero or one; basic unit of computer memory
block logical unit of stored data
bubble memory high-capacity semiconductor memory technology that stores information in tiny magnetic bubbles
buffer temporary storage area for input, as data to be printed
byte eight bits of information, usu. represents one character of data in memory
cache memory very high-speed, not addressable semiconductor storage device for executing instructions
cartridge removable module holding secondary storage medium, esp. magnetic tape; similar module holding program stored in ROM, such as computer game
cassette cartridgelike tape storage device using 1/8 inch (3.2 mm) tape
CD-ROM compact disc read-only memory; compact disc used for permanent storage of massive amounts of data
close operation in which file is stored on external memory device and rendered unreadable until reopened
copying duplicating files or programs from one magnetic storage medium to another
corrupted (*adj*) designating a file, etc., in which data is jumbled or has been lost
DAT digital audio tape, a storage medium using magnetic tape on removable cartridges
data information that may be organized and processed by programs
data file information stored in external memory and recalled under unique file name
direct access random access
diskette floppy disk
double density storage density of some disk media, greater than single density and less than high density
double-sided disk disk able to store data on both sides
DRAM dynamic random-access memory; fast-

access, rewriteable, volatile memory chip
drum cylinder coated with magnetic material, used as high-speed external memory device in mainframe computers
dump (*vb*) copy or transfer contents of memory, esp. from one level to another
dupe (*vb*) duplicate information, esp. from one disk to another
EPROM erasable programmableread-only memory; read-only memory that can be erased under high intensity ultraviolet light and reprogrammed
external memory disk drive, cassette, or other storage device not directly addressed by CPU and not part of main memory
fetch (*vb*) read contents of specific memory location
field sector of memory designated for specific kind of information
file organized collection of data stored under single name
flash memory type of ROM memory that can be updated within a PC
floppy disk mylar disk storage medium in cardboard jacket
fragmentation condition in which files are stored in fragments on separate areas of a disk, lengthening access time
GB gigabyte
gigabyte GB; 1,024 x 1,024 x 1,024 bytes or approximately one billion bytes
hard disk high-speed, large capacity disk made of rigid substratum covered with magnetic oxide
head device that reads or writes information on magnetic media
high density storage density of some disk media, greater than double density
index hole hole in floppy disk indicating beginning of first sector of track, used to trigger drive
K kilobyte
KB kilobyte
kilobyte K or KB; 1,024 bytes
laser disc optical disc
load (*vb*) move data or program instructions from storage medium into computer memory for execution; move disk drive read/write head into operation
logged disk drive engaged drive in dual drive system
magnetic card flexible, plastic 3x7 inch card with magnetic surface used for data storage
magnetic disk flat, round, magnetic-mechanical data storage medium coated with oxide that is selectively magnetized to record data and rotates on drive past read/write head which records data on concentric circles called tracks
magnetic media material used to store information on cards, tapes, floppy disks, hard disks, or drums by magnetizing particles
magneto-optical drive type of removable-disk drive using both magnetic and optical storage technologies
mailbox file for storing electronic mail
main memory internal memory of computer, generally RAM
mass storage external memory device such as a disk or cassette
MB megabyte
mechanical memory external memory device such as disk or drum
megabyte MB; 1,024 x 1,024 bytes or approximately one million bytes
memory internal or external storage area and capacity to store and retrieve binary data and programs; storage
memory management use of hardware and software to control and allocate memory resources
microfiche 4x6 inch film used to store miniaturized photographic images of data
microfloppy newer floppy disk, actually rigid, with 31/2-inch (8.9-cm) diameter
minifloppy original 51/84-inch (13.3-cm) diameter floppy disk
mirror (*vb*) copy on an ongoing basis for security
nibble four bits or half a byte
nonvolatile memory memory that retains contents on storage medium when power is shut off
optical disc grooveless disk on which digital data are stored as tiny pits in the surface and read by laser beam scanning the surface
punch card standardized, stiff paper card that stores information via punched holes denoting numerical values
RAM random-access memory; volatile read/write memory that allows direct access to data and loses its data contents when power is turned off
random access technique for storing or retrieving data in location where access does not require sequential search; direct access
random access memory RAM
read-only memory ROM
register high-speed storage location in CPU that operates on small amounts of data
reset key button or key that clears computer's volatile memory back to cold boot
retrieval accessing of data in storage
ROM read-only memory; memory storage device that can be written to once and not changed, used for nonvolatile, machine-specific instructions
ROM chip integrated circuit with read-only memory implanted on it
save place data on nonvolatile magnetic media for storage
scratchpad small, fast, volatile storage in certain computers
sector one of contiguous portions of disk track, so divided for rapid and efficient data storage
sequential access storage method, such as on magnetic tape, that allows access to elements only in fixed order
single density storage density of some disk media, less than double density
single-sided disk disk that stores data on one side only
SRAM static random-access memory; volatile memory technology using RAM chip that holds contents without being constantly refreshed fro

CPU, faster and more expensive than DRAM
storage memory
storage capacity amount of data that can be stored in computer memory
streaming mode magnetic tape system for copying data from hard disk as backup
swapping technique for transfer of program and data code from one storage medium to main memory and back, or between levels of main memory
TB terabyte
terabyte TB; 1,024 x 1,024 x 1,024 x 1,024 bytes or approximately one trillion bytes
TPI tracks per inch; measure of disk storage density
track concentric circle on disk or drum surface for storage of data at designated address
virtual storage extension of addressable memory through secondary storage controlled by systems software that treats it as addressable main storage
volatile memory memory that does not retain data when power is turned off
WORM write-once, read many, a type of optical-storage disk that may be written to once only
write (*vb*) record data in memory
write-protect (*adj*) designating notch on 5 1/4-inch disk that, when covered, prevents inadvertent writing-over of stored information; designating similarly functioning mechanical switch on 3 1/2-inch disk

Internet and World Wide Web

address string of identifying characters for directing e-mail, accessing a Web site, etc.
anonymous FTP most common use of FTP, allowing data transfer without need of a password
archie software tool giving access to archives of the indexed contents of anonymous FTP sites
ARPA Advanced Research Projects Agency (later DARPA), the agency of the US Department of Defense that in the late 1960s developed ARPAnet, the precursor of the Internet
avatar Web graphic representing a person, as a portrait or facial image on that person's home page
backbone large network enabling connection to other subordinate networks
BITNET Because It's Time Network, university-based computer network later connected to the Internet
chat real-time communication between sites, as in a telephone conversation
.com domain designator (at the end of an Internet address) for a commercial enterprise
connect time time connected to an online service, often the basis for a fee charged by the service
cyberspace term (from William Gibson's novels) for the non-physical reality and culture of the Internet and the Web
DARPA Defense Advanced Research Projects Agency, later name for ARPA
dial-up (*adj*) pertaining to a service, account, etc., accessed via modem
domain final portion of an Internet address, following the final dot
dot character (in other contexts known as a period) used as a separator in addresses
.edu domain designator (at the end of an Internet address) for an educational institution
e-zine an electronically published, online magazine
emoticon combination of keyboard characters to express emotion, attitude, etc., such as a smiley
FAQ frequently asked question, usually collected into a list for newcomers to a newsgroup, FTP site, etc.
firewall security software limiting access to data at a particular site or local network
flame (*vb*) insulting, critical, or demeaning comment in E-mail or a posting to a newsgroup, etc.
forum discussion group on a BBS or online service
freenet a service providing free Internet access to members of a community
FTP file transfer protocol, the standard for file transfers on the Internet
gate computer enabling connection and communication between networks or systems with differing formats; gateway
gopher software tool enabling browsing of data available on the Internet or Web
.gov domain designator (at the end of an Internet address) for a government institution
home page starting point for a Web site, with links to other graphics, documents, data, sites, etc.
host name leftmost portion of an Internet address, designating a specific computer
HTML hypertext markup language; a variety of SGML specifying how to tag text for use on the Web
HTTP hypertext transfer protocol, controlling how Web sites request data
Internet global network for communication of data among computers and smaller networks using the TCP/IP protocols
intranet local network utilizing Internet protocols for sharing of data, graphics, etc., as within a company's offices
IRC Internet relay chat, a protocol enabling real time communication on the Internet
listserv type of automated mailing list software developed for mainframe computers
mailbox file or storage area used to hold transmissions until pickup
mailing list discussion group in which each address on the list receives a copy of all postings by any member of the group
.mil domain designator (at the end of an Internet address) for a military facility
Net the Internet
.net domain designator (at the end of an Internet address) for a network
netiquette unofficial code of acceptable behavior on the Internet
newbie someone new to Internet or Web use
newsgroup discussion group on Usenet

.org domain designator (at the end of an Internet address) for a nonprofit organization
post message sent to a mailing list or newsgroup; (*vb*) send such a message
protocol agreed set of rules enabling communication between otherwise incompatible software, networks, etc.
put (*vb*) copy a file to a remote site
session single, continuous period of connection to the Internet, Web, or an online service
shouting typing E-mail in ALL CAPS, done for emphasis
sig block information appended to the end of E-mail messages, etc., identifying a particular user (name, address, favorite quote, etc.)
site Internet or Web location allowing remote access
smiley :-) emoticon made by typing colon, hyphen, and close parenthesis; viewed with head tilted left, looks like a smiling face
snail mail surface mail, delivered by postal or courier service
spam (*vb*) post huge amounts of data, or post a message to many users
spoiler part of a message that reveals an identity, solution to a puzzle, etc.
surf (*vb*) browse serendipitously from one Internet or Web site to another
TCP/IP Transmission Control Protocol/Internet Protocol, the standard protocols for Internet data exchange, developed by DARPA in the late 1970s
telnet protocol for terminal emulation, enabling remote login
thread related theme or topic running through a series of messages or posts
tunneling encapsulating data that uses one protocol within that of a different protocol to allow transport across a backbone that does not support the original protocol
URL uniform resource locator; an address on the Web (begins ""http://")
Usenet User Network, that part of the Internet devoted to newsgroups
Veronica searchable index of gopher menus
WAIS wide-area information server, a program for finding information on the Internet
Web, the World Wide Web
Web browser software enabling use of hypertext documents on the Web, such as Mosaic or Netscape Navigator
Web page home page
Web site computer or server accessible via a Web address
World Wide Web global computer network for communication of documents that include graphics, sound, etc., and hypertext links
WWW World Wide Web

Chapter Six

Transportation

AIRCRAFT

Types of Aircraft
Aviation and Aerodynamics
Airframe and Engines
Avionics and Instrumentation
Commercial Airlines, Airports, and Air Force

Types of Aircraft

ACV air cushion vehicle
aerostat balloon or other lighter-than-air craft lifted by container of gas
aircraft structure designed to travel through the air; aerodyne or aerostat
air cushion vehicle ACV; Hovercraft
airplane fixed-wing, heavier-than-air craft kept aloft by aerodynamic forces and powered by screw propeller or jet propulsion, also, *esp. Brit.* aeroplane
airship steered lighter-than-air craft with engine, esp. dirigible or blimp
air taxi small commercial airliner carrying passengers and mail to places not regularly served
amphibian aircraft capable of takeoff and landing on water and land
autogiro aircraft with freely rotating rotor in place of fixed wing and propeller for propulsion, cannot take off vertically or hover
balloon lighter-than-air, engineless aircraft propelled by airflow and lifted by enclosed bag of gas
biplane airplane with two sets of wings mounted one above the other
blimp nonrigid or semirigid airship
bomber air force plane designed to drop bombs
chopper *Informal.* helicopter
crop duster small aircraft that flies low over crops to spray pesticide
dirigible airship with lifting cells, as zeppelin
dive bomber aircraft that releases bombs while diving at target
fighter small, fast, highly maneuverable craft used in aerial combat
glider heavier-than-air craft supported in flight by action of air against lifting surfaces, not dependent on engine and usu. not having one; sailplane
gyroplane rotorcraft with rotors started by engine but rotated by action of air, with independent propellers for propulsion
heavier-than-air craft aircraft that is heavier than air it displaces and is lifted by application of propulsion to aerodynamic forces
heavy aircraft class of aircraft capable of takeoff weights over 325,000 pounds
helicopter rotary-winged aircraft having one or more power-driven rotors on vertical axes, dependent for horizontal motion on rotors
high-altitude reconnaissance plane military surveillance craft capable of flying at altitudes over 50,000 feet (15,240 m)
hot-air balloon aerostat lifted by enclosure filled with heated air; gas balloon
Hovercraft vehicle that travels across land or water on cushion of air formed by downward thrust of jet engines; air cushion vehicle
hydroplane seaplane
interceptor fast-climbing fighter jet used defensively against attack
jet aircraft powered by jet propulsion
jetliner jet-powered commercial airliner
jumbo jet very large commercial jet airliner, such as the Boeing 747, DC-10, or Tristar L-1011, that holds over 300 passengers
lighter-than-air craft aircraft that rises and remains suspended by use of contained gas weighing less than the air it displaces, esp. balloon
monoplane aircraft or glider with one pair of wings
pursuit plane pre-World War II air force fighter plane
rotorcraft heavier-than-air craft principally dependent for flight on lift generated by one or more rotors
sailplane glider
seaplane aircraft designed to land on and take off from water; hydroplane
short takeoff and landing STOL; aircraft capable of operating from short runway
spy plane high-altitude military reconnaissance plane
SST supersonic transport
STOL short takeoff and landing aircraft
supersonic transport SST; commercial airliner that flies faster than speed of sound
tandem airplane craft with two or more sets of wings with similar dimensions, placed one in front of the other on same level
tanker aircraft carrying fuel for in-air refueling of other aircraft
tilt-rotor amphibious military aircraft with rotors that stand vertically during takeoff and tilt to horizontal position to act as propellers in flight
transport large military aircraft used to convey troops or cargo
ultralight class of extremely low-weight, single-seat aircraft not requiring pilot's license for operation
vertical takeoff and landing VTOL; term applied to aircraft capable of taking off and landing vertically and flying horizontally, such as helicopter
VTOL vertical takeoff and landing aircraft
warplane military fighter or bomber
widebody jumbo jet with two aisles in passenger cabin, usu. able to carry over 300 passengers
zeppelin any rigid airship

Aviation and Aerodynamics

abort (*vb*) terminate preplanned maneuver, esp. takeoff
absolute altitude vertical distance between aircraft and Earth's surface

absolute ceiling altitude beyond which aircraft cannot climb in standard atmospheric conditions
aero- prefix meaning aircraft or flying
aerobatics intentional, abrupt maneuvers that alter normal flight pattern, esp. done in performance
aerodonetics science of flying gliders
aerodynamics science of the motion of air and other gases and the forces they produce on bodies in relative motion
aeronautics science, art, and business of designing, building, and flying aircraft
aerophotography long-range photography from aircraft
airborne (*adj*) carried through air by aerodynamic forces
airflow stream of air in motion relative to a body
airframe icing formation of ice on parts, esp. airfoil, due to certain moisture and temperature conditions, causing instability and control problems
air lane route regularly used by aircraft: jet route, victor airway
airman aviator
airsickness nausea, dizziness, headache, and cold sweat due to motion and altitude of air flight
air space space extending vertically above area of Earth's surface
airspeed speed of aircraft relative to air through which it is moving rather than Earth's surface
airstream airflow around aircraft in flight
airway specific route for air travel
airworthy (*adj*) safe and fit for flying
altitude height above Earth's surface or sea level
angle of attack angle between airfoil and relative flow of wind
angle of incidence angle between chord line of airfoil and thrust of aircraft
approach final period of descent prior to landing
asymmetric landing emergency landing in which engine on one side has failed
attitude position of aircraft expressed as inclination of its three axes (pitch, roll, and yaw) to frame of reference
autorotation condition of flight achieved when lift is derived solely by effect of aerodynamic forces on unpowered rotor of autogyro or helicopter, or when power is lost
aviation art and science of flying aircraft; development of heavier-than-air aircraft
aviatrix female aviator
bank (*vb*) roll to attitude in which one wing tip is higher than the other; (*n*) condition of flight in which aircraft slopes laterally during turn
barnstorm (*vb*) tour country to give short demonstration airplane rides and stunt flying exhibitions
barrel roll complete roll by aircraft around longitudinal axis while simultaneously completing one spiral revolution in air
bearing horizontal direction to or from any point, measured in degrees clockwise from true north
belly landing emergency landing directly onto bottom of fuselage with landing gear retracted
blind landing instrument landing in zero visibility
buffeting vibration of aircraft part caused by a burble
buzz (*vb*) fly aircraft very low, esp. over structure
calibrated airspeed indicated airspeed corrected for installation error of cockpit gauge
CAT clear air turbulence
ceiling height above Earth's surface of lowest significant cloud layer; altitude at which rate of climb of given aircraft falls to 100 feet (30 m) per minute
center of gravity point in body toward which every external particle of matter is attracted by gravity
chandelle abrupt, steep climb caused by aircraft's momentum
chord line imaginary line from leading to trailing edge of airfoil
circling flight pattern adopted by pilot while awaiting landing clearance or to position aircraft for landing
clear air turbulence CAT; unpredictable high-altitude turbulence with no clouds present, esp. wind shear due to jetstream
climb ascent, esp. to cruising altitude
climbout portion of flight between takeoff and initial cruising altitude
close formation flying in which several aircraft maintain relative positions near one another, often as exhibition
contrail white trail of condensed water vapor behind aircraft in flight; vapor trail
corridor flight route designated by international agreement
crabbing sideways motion of aircraft with respect to ground due to crosswind
crash landing forced landing in which aircraft is brought down without landing gear away from airport runway surface
critical altitude maximum altitude at which it is possible to maintain specified power and manifold pressure in standard atmosphere
crosswind wind not parallel to path of aircraft or runway
cruise (*vb*) maintain constant speed and altitude for period of time
cruising altitude constant altitude maintained for portion of flight
decision height point in ILS at which pilot sees runway and begins visual landing
decompression formation of nitrogen bubbles in blood or body tissues due to rapid ascent, causing pain in joints and convulsions
density altitude altitude corresponding to given air density in standard atmosphere; pressure altitude corrected for temperature
depressurization loss of cabin pressurization
direct stability propensity of aircraft to remain in stable flight attitude
ditch (*vb*) make crash landing in water and abandon aircraft
dive steep, sudden descent
drag sum of air resistance encountered in flight plus induced drag created by airfoil

drag ratio ratio of lift to drag as characteristic of wing; lift ratio
drift deviation from course, esp. due to crosswinds
feather (*vb*) change pitch of propeller blades to reduce drag as engine is stopped
final approach period of final instrument approach from fixed point to landing, usu. last five to seven miles
flame-out failure of jet engine combustion in flight
flight distance covered by aircraft between takeoff and landing
flutter abnormal vibration in control surface due to aerodynamic force
flying blind flying by instruments only in low visibility
forced landing emergency landing on surface other than airport runway prior to completion of flight
formation flying flying in which several aircraft maintain positions relative to each other in simultaneous flight
goaround abandoning of approach just prior to landing in order to circle around airport
ground speed aircraft speed relative to ground it is passing over; airspeed corrected for headwind or tailwind
guidance direction of course of craft
gust sudden, brief change of wind speed or direction
heading compass reading expressing horizontal direction in which aircraft is facing
headwind wind blowing in direction opposite to course flown by aircraft
hedgehop (*vb*) fly very close to ground, esp. for crop-dusting
hypersonic (*adj*) designating supersonic speeds of Mach 5 and above
icing accumulation of ice on exterior of aircraft during flight; airframe icing
IFR instrument flight rules
ILS instrument landing system
indicated airspeed speed as shown on cockpit gauge
induced drag portion of wing drag resulting from generation of lift
in-flight (*adj*) done or occurring while aircraft is airborne
instrument flight rules IFR; type of flight plan and rules governing procedures for instrument flight
instrument landing avionic approach and landing in which ILS, PAR, or VOR is used
instrument landing system ILS; precision instrument approach based on beams transmitted from glide slope on ground that give vertical and lateral guidance by localizer up to decision height for visual landing
jet propulsion momentum derived from ejection of exhaust stream or rapid flow of gas from within propelled body by mechanical, thermal, or chemical process: turbojet, fanjet, ramjet, pulsejet, rocket
jet stream migrating stream of high-speed winds at high altitudes
jettison (*vb*) lighten load by dropping objects from aircraft in flight, esp. fuel in emergency
jet wash slipstream
lateral axis axis from side to side of aircraft, perpendicular to direction of flight; pitch axis
lateral stability minimal pitch rotation; tendency of aircraft to return to equilibrium following forces applied to pitch
lift upward aerodynamic force exerted on wing
liftoff vertical takeoff, esp. of helicopter or rocket
lift ratio drag ratio
limit load factor maximum pull of gravity to which airframe may be subjected in flight without structural damage
load in-flight weight carried by aircraft, including cargo, fuel, passengers, crew, and weight of aircraft when empty
load factor pull of gravity in absence of acceleration (load factor of 4 equals 4G); amount of load an aircraft can carry
longitudinal axis axis from nose to tail of aircraft, parallel to direction of flight; roll axis
loop circular figure performed as flight maneuver, beginning with aerobatic pull-up through vertical plane and ending with return to horizontal flight in same direction
mach number ratio of airspeed of an object to the speed of sound at given altitude and atmosphere, being 762 mph at sea level
manifold pressure factor used to determine grade of fuel required by aircraft engine
mass ratio ratio between mass of aircraft with fuel and after fuel has been used up
Mayday international radiotelephone distress signal, repeated three times to indicate imminent, grave danger
missed approach approach aborted by pilot at decision height when instrument approach cannot be completed safely
nose dive swift, steep downward plunge of aircraft with nose toward ground
parachute umbrellalike cloth contrivance used to retard falling speed of person or object dropped from aircraft
payload commercial revenue-producing load; expendable or deliverable load, such as bombs, used in military operations
pitch distance advanced by propeller in one revolution; movement of aircraft about lateral axis
polar (*adj*) having directional setting at north magnetic pole
power loading ratio of gross weight of airplane to its power
precision approach standard instrument approach in which electronic glide slope is provided by precision approach radar or instrument landing system
pressure altitude altitude relative to given pressure in standard atmosphere, uncorrected for temperature
pressurization regulation of cabin pressure for comfort of crew and passengers at high altitudes with low atmospheric pressure
propulsion driving force in engine that moves aircraft

prop wash slipstream
pull out (*vb*) exit from dive
pull-up maneuver in which nose of plane is lifted from level flight through vertical plane
quadrant quarter of circle centered on navigational aid, oriented clockwise from magnetic north
range distance aircraft is capable of flying without refueling or landing
roll rotation of aircraft about longitudinal axis
skyway air lane, flight route
skywriting tracing words or figures in sky by trail of smoke released from small aircraft
slipstream current of air thrust backward by spinning propeller or jet; jet wash; prop wash
sonic (*adj*) designating speed of sound at given altitude
sonic barrier critical speed at which shock waves cause increased drag by exceeding speed of sound; sound barrier
sonic boom loud shock wave formed when speed of body exceeds speed of sound in same medium
sound barrier sonic barrier
spin nose-first descent along spiral path of large pitch and small radius; tailspin
spiral circling around longitudinal axis
stall loss of lift, sudden drop, and possible loss of control due to exceeding critical angle of attack and disruption of airflow around airfoil
straight-in landing landing on runway aligned within 30 degrees of final approach course
supersonic (*adj*) greater than speed of sound at given altitude
tailspin nose-first spiraling descent with tail up
tailwind wind blowing in same direction as course flown by aircraft
takeoff act or moment of lifting off from ground to begin flight
thrust force in direction of motion of aircraft produced by jet exhaust
torque force that tends to produce rotation
touchdown point at which aircraft makes contact with landing surface
transonic (*adj*) just below or just above speed of sound
true airspeed indicated airspeed on cockpit gauge corrected for installation error, compressibility of air, pressure, and temperature; equivalent airspeed corrected for pressure and temperature
turbulence irregular motion of air that disrupts smooth flight
vapor trail contrail
vector compass heading; course followed by aircraft, provided by air-traffic control
velocity rate of motion in particular direction
VFR visual flight rules
visibility distance at which unlighted objects can be seen under existing atmospheric conditions on ground or in flight
visual flight rules VFR; flight plan or maneuvering and rules governing conduct of flight based on pilot's visual observations in acceptable weather conditions
volplane downward glide with engine turned off
wake turbulence turbulence caused by passage of aircraft through atmosphere
wind shear change of wind speed or direction over short distance, esp. due to thunderstorm
wing loading gross weight of aircraft expressed as weight per unit area of wing surface
yaw rotation of aircraft about vertical axis; deviation from line of flight, controlled by rudder
zero visibility weather condition in which pilot can see nothing and must rely on instrument flight and air-traffic control
zoom (*vb*) climb suddenly and sharply at greater than normal angle

Airframe and Engines

actuator motor that moves elevators
aft (*adj*) toward the tail
aileron hinged or movable control surface, usu. on trailing edge of wing near tip, that regulates banking by causing movement about longitudinal axis
air brake airfoil that can be extended to produce additional drag for slowing aircraft
airfoil any surface, esp. wing, designed to produce a useful reaction when properly positioned in airstream
airframe any part of aircraft other than engine: fuselage, booms, nacelle, cowlings, fairings, airfoils, landing gear
airscrew propeller
antitorque rotor tail rotor on helicopter
articulated blade helicopter rotor blade hinged at hub
baffle device for deflecting airflow
bay compartment in fuselage
belly bottom of fuselage, esp. with landing gear retracted
bulkhead upright partition separating compartments and providing structural strength
cabin enclosed portion of aircraft for passengers and crew
camber curvature of airfoil surface from leading to trailing edge
canard airframe with stabilizing and control surface ahead of main supporting surfaces and wings
canopy transparent, hinged cockpit cover
cantilever beam or member supported at one end only
cockpit compartment with controls for pilot and crew
control surface movable surface used to control attitude or motion and guide aircraft: airfoil, aileron, elevator, or flap
control tab device that provides aerodynamic actuation of control surface
control yoke steering wheel with two arms used to operate elevator and ailerons in transports, bombers, and airliners
cowling metal cover, usu. faired, enclosing aircraft engine and portions of fuselage
deceleron aileron used to slow aircraft in flight
ejection seat emergency escape device by which both pilot and seat are catapulted from plane

elevator movable airfoil in tail assembly, usu. hinged to stabilizer, that controls vertical movements and rotation of aircraft about lateral axis
fanjet engine turbofan
fin fixed, vertical stabilizing surface on tail assembly; tail fin
flap hinged or pivoted airfoil on trailing edge of wing that increases lift by reshaping or fattening wing on takeoff and landing
flight deck front compartment of aircraft housing crew; runway portion of aircraft carrier
fuselage elongated main body of airplane housing engines, crew, cargo, passengers, and equipment
gas turbine propulsion engine using hot, compressed gas as working fluid, consisting of compressor, combustion chamber, and turbine through which expanded gases are discharged to drive compressor and propel aircraft
hatch doorway in side or bottom of fuselage
hold cargo storage area in belly of fuselage
horizontal stabilizer stabilizer mounted horizontally in tail assembly, to which elevators are attached for lateral stability
hull main body of airship
hydroplane attachment to bottom of fuselage of seaplane that allows it to glide across water
inboard (*adj*) close or closest to fuselage or body of aircraft
inlet throat
jet engine any aircraft engine based on jet propulsion, always incorporating a gas turbine: turbojet, fanjet, ramjet, pulsejet, rocket
joy stick *Informal.* control stick, esp. one located between pilot's legs
landing gear understructure, such as wheels and shock absorbers, capable of supporting weight of aircraft on ground; undercarriage
lap joint point at which sections of skin are connected
leading edge foremost edge of airfoil or propeller blade
mixture control control over fuel/air mixture in piston engine of light or older aircraft
nacelle wing housing for engine; enclosure other than fuselage for people, cargo, and engine; basket under balloon
nose foremost section of fuselage enclosing cockpit
nose cone foremost portion of nose, usu. tapering to point and made of heat-resistant material
onboard (*adj*) inside aircraft cabin, cockpit, or cargo hold
outboard (*adj*) far or farthest from fuselage or body of aircraft
plating heavy metal skin, esp. covering wings of large aircraft
propeller assembly with airfoil blades on hub of engine-driven shaft, used to propel aircraft; airscrew
propjet turboprop
pulsejet jet engine that burns fuel intermittently with air from outside that is compressed by ram effect due to forward motion
pylon structure used to attach engine and fuel tank to aircraft, usu. under wing
ramjet jet engine having no compressor and depending for operation on ram compression of air due to high forward velocity of aircraft
RATO rocket-assisted takeoff
retrofire (*vb*) reverse direction of thrust on engine or rocket
rib structural crosspiece attached to spar to strengthen wing
rocket jet engine carrying its own oxidizer along with fuel; missile propelled by rocket engine
rocket-assisted takeoff RATO; takeoff aided by auxiliary rocket device that provides extra thrust
rotor one of rotating set of bladelike wings that provides lift for helicopter
rudder vertically hinged airfoil for yawing aircraft about vertical axis in flight
sandwich structural material with two skins stiffened by thick core; honeycomb
shock absorber device built into landing gear to absorb impact of landing
skin panels of metal riveted in place to cover fuselage
span maximum distance from tip to tip of any airfoil
spar main lengthwise support member of wing or airfoil
spoiler surface designed to be extended from wing under certain conditions to spoil airflow over it, decrease lift, or increase drag
stabilator horizontal structure serving as both stabilizer and elevator
stabilizer fixed or adjustable airfoil designed to give stability; vertical or horizontal stabilizer
stick control movement of elevator and ailerons by control stick
stressed skin covering that contributes to strength of structure
strut supporting brace bearing compression and/or tension loads
supercharger engine-driven compressor that increases flow of air and fuel into cylinders to improve power in nonjet engines and maintains pressure in cabin and engine
sweepback wing with leading edge at sharp angle to fuselage; swept-back wing
swept-back wing sweepback
tab small hinged surface on trailing edge of control surface, used to assist movement or to trim control surface
tail rear part of aircraft, providing stability
tail fin fin; vertical stabilizer
tail rotor small rotor mounted on shaft at tail of helicopter to counteract torque of main rotor and provide directional control; antitorque rotor
tail wheel small wheel that supports tail of aircraft with conventional landing gear on ground
throttle hand-operated lever connected to valve that controls amount of fuel delivered to engine cylinders; fuel control for gas turbines in jet engines
thrust chamber chamber of jet engine, in which combustion of fuel and air, or oxidizer, takes place
trailing edge rearmost edge of airfoil or propeller blade

trim tab attached to trailing edge of airfoil
truss assembly of structural members forming rigid framework for fuselage
turbine rotary engine with drive shaft powered by action of liquid or gas against curved vanes of wheel or escaping through nozzles located around wheel
turbofan turbojet engine that creates additional thrust by diverting secondary airflow around combustion chamber; fanjet engine
turbojet jet engine supplied with air from compressor driven by turbine that is activated by energy of jet exhaust gases
turboprop variation of turbojet in which gas turbine also drives conventional propeller to produce major portion of thrust; propjet
turret transparent dome for gunner on bomber or fighter
undercarriage landing gear
variable-sweep wing sweepback whose angle can be changed during flight
vertical axis axis from top to bottom of aircraft, perpendicular to direction of level flight
vertical stabilizer section of airfoil on tail forward of rudder, providing longitudinal stability; fin
wing part of airplane that provides lift, esp. main lateral airfoil, usu. in pairs
wing flap flap
wing rib chordwise member that gives wing its shape and transmits load from skin to spars
wingspan lateral distance between tips of wings
yaw control equipment designed to reduce and control yaw: ailerons, elevators, rudder
yoke pilot's steering wheel with two upward-pointing arms

Avionics and Instrumentation

absolute altimeter radar altimeter
accelerometer instrument that measures acceleration or deceleration
ADF automatic direction finder
ADI attitude direction indicator
air log instrument that records distance traveled by aircraft relative to air through which it moves, used to calculate true airspeed
airspeed indicator dial or gauge showing airspeed
altimeter device for measuring altitude, usu. above sea level
anemometer gauge for determining wind speed
attitude direction indicator ADI; instrument showing attitude of aircraft in space
automatic direction finder ADF; aircraft navigation radio
automatic pilot self-regulating control mechanism for keeping aircraft in level flight and on set course, or for executing maneuvers; autopilot
autopilot automatic pilot
avionics development and use of electronic equipment and control systems for aircraft
bank indicator instrument that tells pilot rate at which airplane is turning
black box flight data recorder and cockpit voice recorder encased in fire- and shock-resistant container, used in accident investigations; any replaceable unit that plugs into avionics rack
bombsight instrument on bomber that determines when to drop bomb in order to strike target
Bourdon-tube gauge crescent-shaped tube with one closed end, used to measure pressure in high-pressure fluid systems
chronometer device for precise measurement of time
cockpit voice recorder device in black box that records radio and direct conversations of crew
compass card circular card on pivot to which magnetic compass is attached, marked in increments of 5 degrees
console cockpit instrument panel with controls, gauges, and meters
deviation deflection of magnetic compass due to installation error
directional gyro gyro rotor mounted on pair of gimbals with horizontal spin axis, set to magnetic compass and used for directional reference
direction finder radio receiver with direction-sensing antenna, used in navigation and to take bearings
distance measuring equipment DME; instrument that measures nautical miles between aircraft and VOR station
drift meter instrument that shows drift of aircraft from left to right over ground
Earth inductor inclinometer
emergency locator transmitter ELT; automatic radio transmitter attached to aircraft structure and operating at set frequency on its own power source, used for locating downed aircraft
flight data recorder device in black box that monitors flight data, used esp. in accident investigations
galvanometer device for detecting and measuring very small electric current
glide slope device that emits electronic signals to provide vertical guidance during approach or takeoff during ILS
gyrocompass motor-operated gyroscope whose rotating axis is kept parallel to axis of Earth's rotation and points to geographic, not magnetic, North Pole
gyroscope wheel mounted on spinning axis that is free to rotate around one or both of two axes perpendicular to each other and to the spinning axis, used as directional reference for keeping aircraft level in flight
hygrometer device for measuring absolute or relative humidity in air
inclinometer instrument that shows inclination of longitudinal axis of aircraft to horizontal plane of flight; Earth inductor
inertial guidance self-contained, automatic guidance system composed of gyroscopes, accelerometers, and computers used to maintain course in automatic pilot; inertial navigation system; INS

inertial navigation system INS; inertial guidance
INS inertial navigation system; inertial guidance
instrument panel cockpit console
localizer landing instrument that provides course guidance to runway, esp. in ILS
LORAN long range navigation; electronic navigational system that measures difference in time of reception of synchronized pulse signals from two transmitters
magnetic compass instrument with needle that indicates direction of North Pole due to action of Earth's magnetic field
manometer gauge for measuring pressure of gases or vapors
NAVAID navigational aid; visual or electronic device, airborne or on Earth's surface, that provides guidance or position data
PAR precision approach radar
pelorus device for taking bearings that fits over compass card or gyrocompass
Pitot-static system method of providing or measuring pressure to operate altimeter, airspeed indicator, or other instrumentation
position indicator navigational instrument that displays horizontal situation of aircraft
precision approach radar PAR; radar equipment used in final approach course to airport to provide precision instrument approach
pressure altimeter aneroid instrument that measures differences in atmospheric pressure to determine altitude
pressure head Pitot-static tube used to actuate air-speed indicator
radar radio detecting and ranging; system for determining direction, distance, height, and speed of aircraft by reflection of radio waves, also used as weather sensor on aircraft
radar altimeter instrument that uses reflection time of radio waves to and from ground to determine altitude of aircraft; absolute altimeter
radio direction finder little-used direction finder employing radio waves
rate-of-climb indicator instrument that indicates rate at which aircraft is ascending or descending in feet per minute
sextant simple navigational instrument for measuring angular distance of celestial body from horizon, rarely used on aircraft
slip indicator instrument for measuring longitudinal deviation about vertical axis; yawmeter
static tube Pitot-static tube carrying static pressure of outside air
synchroscope instrument for determining difference in phase between two engines
TACAN tactical air navigation; ultra-high frequency electronic navigation aid used primarily on military aircraft
tachometer instrument that measures rate of rotation of revolving engine shaft
telemetry electronic tracking system, esp. for missile or experimental aircraft
thermostat device for automatically regulating temperature
transponder electronic device that receives radio signals and generates distinctive reply pattern on radar
turn-and-bank indicator instrument for showing rate of turn of aircraft
turnmeter instrument for measuring angular velocity of aircraft about predetermined axis
venturi tube suction gauge in slipstream that indicates reduction in pressure
vertical-speed indicator instrument that registers rate of climb
very high frequency VHF; band for radio communication and navigation
very high frequency omni range VOR; basic radio navigation system that relies on communications between aircraft and transmitting stations on ground, used esp. by military aircraft
viscometer instrument for measuring viscosity, esp. of fuel
VOR very high frequency omni range

Commercial Airlines, Airports, and Air Force

air base military facility for operation and maintenance of aircraft
air carrier person or company that undertakes transportation of cargo by air
aircraft carrier large warship that serves as floating air base
air force aviation branch of armed forces
Air Force One jet aircraft used by U.S. president
air freight shipping of goods and cargo by air
airline company that moves freight and passengers on aircraft
airliner large passenger aircraft, usu. jet, operated by airline
airmail mail transported by air
airman enlisted person in Air Force or Naval Air Corps
air piracy skyjacking
airport area of land with control tower and runways for landing and takeoff of aircraft, facilities for storage and maintenance, and terminal for passengers
airstrip hard-surfaced area used as runway
air-to-air (*adj*) designating weapon launched from aircraft and directed at airborne object
air-traffic control ATC; radar facility with tower from which approaches and departures of air traffic in and around airports and along air routes are monitored and directed
approach lights lights that indicate direction and termination of runway to approaching aircraft
apron area of land at airport used for loading and unloading of passengers and cargo, refueling, parking, and maintenance; ramp
ATC air-traffic control
boarding pass ticket distributed at gate that permits passengers to enter aircraft
bombardier member of bomber crew who operates bombsight and releases bombs

bumped (*adj*) refused seating on flight for which one has reservation
CAB Civil Aeronautics Board
captain commanding officer of aircraft, esp. commercial airliner; air force commanding officer
carousel circular baggage conveyor from which passengers retrieve luggage at airport
carrier airliner; commercial airline
carry-on luggage small items of luggage taken on board by passenger and placed in overhead rack or under seat
centerline line marked down center of runway, imagined to extend beyond it onto clearway or stopway
charter flight flight on aircraft hired by group or organization for special trip not regularly scheduled
chock block or wedge set against wheel to keep it from turning
Civil Aeronautics Board CAB; federal agency that regulated airline industry activities until deregulation in 1978
clearance permission from air traffic control, esp. for approach, landing, takeoff, or routing
commuter flight frequently scheduled short flight between two nearby metropolitan areas; shuttle
computer reservation system CRS; computer linkup between all commercial airlines and travel agents for booking flight reservations
controlled airspace airspace within which aircraft may be subject to air-traffic control
copilot assistant pilot who relieves pilot; first officer
deregulation federal removal of certain restrictions on commercial airline practices, esp. ticket pricing and routes, in 1978
direct flight journey without change of aircraft but with one or more intermediate landings
ETA estimated time of arrival; scheduled or anticipated time for completion of flight
evacuation slide inflatable chute used as emergency escape device
FAA Federal Aviation Administration
Federal Aviation Administration FAA; federal government agency responsible for administering air-traffic control and investigating accidents
first officer copilot and second in command of commercial airliner
flight scheduled trip on airplane to fly specific route at certain time; such a scheduled route
flight attendant person on commercial airliner responsible for passengers' comfort and safety; stewardess or steward
flight plan information filed with air-traffic control that describes intended flight
flight simulator pilot training device that simulates flight conditions on ground
forward cabin first-class passenger compartment nearest cockpit
frequent-flyer program marketing incentive that rewards passengers with free flights for accumulated mileage
gate location where passengers board or disembark from airliner
gate hold air-traffic control instruction that requires loaded aircraft to remain at gate due to departure delay of over five minutes
ground crew maintenance and repair workers
hangar large enclosure for storage, repair, and maintenance of aircraft
helipad landing and takeoff area used by helicopters
heliport small land or water area or structure used by helicopters for landing and takeoff
hijacking skyjacking
hop very short flight
hub and spoke system system of air transportation in which local flights are made to central hub airport from which connections are made to final local or long-distance destinations
jetway tube-shaped bridge from terminal to aircraft for boarding passengers
layover break partway through journey, esp. overnight away from home base
Mae West inflatable life jacket vest designed for use in water
marker beacon aural and visual signal transmitter that provides aircraft with its position on landing
milk run routine military mission, unlikely to be dangerous
mission flight by military aircraft, esp. bomber
navigator flight officer responsible for plotting course
nonstop service flight directly to final destination with no intermediate stops
no-show passenger with confirmed reservation who fails to arrive for flight
off-line (*adj*) designating travel on carrier other than one that sold ticket
offset parallel runways staggered runways with parallel centerlines
overbooking airline practice of selling more seats than are available based on statistical likelihood that some passengers will not show up
overhead rack compartment above seat for stowing carry-on luggage on airliner
overshoot (*vb*) fail to come to complete stop on runway; fly through final approach course
paratrooper military parachutist
radar contact appearance of aircraft on radar display at air-traffic control
radar service services provided by air-traffic control to aircraft in radar contact
ramp apron
red-eye *Informal.* all-night, transcontinental flight arriving near dawn
run regularly scheduled flight between two points
runway defined rectangular area marked off on airport or aerodrome surface and prepared for landing and takeoff, usu. with centerline and marker lights on sides
second officer member of flight crew with least seniority who monitors instruments and observes flight
shuttle frequently scheduled flight between two nearby metropolitan centers; commuter flight
skycap airport employee who helps passengers with luggage or assists disabled passengers
skyjacking taking control of aircraft by force and making it alter destination by holding crew and

passengers hostage; air piracy; hijacking
standby status of passenger waiting for open place on flight for which he or she does not have confirmed reservation
stopover brief landing at intermediate airport en route to termination point of flight
stopway area beyond takeoff runway and centered on its extended centerline, used in aborted takeoff
stow (*vb*) pack away in safe, orderly manner, esp. luggage
taxi (*vb*) move slowly on ground, esp. on airport ramps and aprons to and from runways (said of aircraft)
terminal airport structure used by arriving and departing passengers and for cargo handling; connection point on flight
test flight monitored flight on which new aircraft or equipment is tested
test pilot specially trained operator of experimental or new aircraft and equipment
tower tall airport structure from which air-traffic control services are provided
traffic routes and positions of aircraft in specific area
turnaround flight on which crew returns to home base on day of departure from it
undershoot (*vb*) miscalculate approach so that touchdown occurs before reaching runway
upgrade (*vb*) move to business or first class seat from tourist or business class
Valsalva maneuver technique for relieving pressure in head due to imbalance of air pressure in ascending or descending aircraft by blowing hard with nose and mouth closed
widebody jumbo jet, usu. able to carry over 300 passengers
wind tunnel tunnellike structure used for testing aircraft parts or models by forcing wind past them at known velocity

AUTOMOBILES

Types of Automobiles
Trucks and Buses
Internal Combustion Engine
Working Parts
Body Parts and Accessories
Driving and Repair

Types of Automobiles

automobile four-wheel passenger vehicle, usu. having internal combustion engine; car
beach buggy dune buggy
compact small car
convertible automobile with retractable canvas roof
coupe small, enclosed, two-door, two-passenger automobile
dragster customized car modified for rapid acceleration racing
dune buggy roofless recreational car with oversize tires for sand traction; beach buggy
fastback car with slanting aerodynamic roof that sometimes opens at rear
go-kart miniature self-propelled chassis without body, esp. for racing
grand touring car sporty two-passenger coupe; orig. large, vintage, open sedan with side rails
gypsy cab cab licensed to pick up passengers on call, but that often illegally cruises in search of passengers
hatchback usu. two-door car with roof lifting open at rear in lieu of trunk
hearse long station wagon for carrying corpse at funeral
hot rod modified or souped-up, customized car
jalopy dilapidated automobile
Land Rover *Trademark.* jeeplike vehicle designed for rough terrain
lemon *Informal.* bad car, esp. one that is new but has mechanical problems
limo limousine
limousine long, luxurious chauffeur-driven sedan; limo
lowrider customized car fitted with specialized suspension that allows the chassis to ride just a few inches above pavement
midget racer tiny, open racing car
minivan small van
motorcar motorized automobile
off-road vehicle vehicle, such as a four-wheel drive Jeep, beach buggy, or snowmobile, designed for travel off public roads
patrol car squad car
race car specially-designed, high-speed car for racing
ragtop *Slang.* convertible
roadster open two-seater automobile with folding top and rear luggage compartment or rumble seat
sedan enclosed car seating four to seven persons, often four-door
snowmobile small motorized vehicle equipped with ski-like runners and revolving tread
sports car low, small, high-powered, agile two-seater automobile
squad car police vehicle; patrol car
station wagon passenger car with roof extended to rear to increase cargo and passenger space, seating up to ten persons
stock car factory-built passenger car modified for racing
stretch extra-long limousine with bar, TV, and other amenities
subcompact smallest automobile used in U.S.
touring car vintage auto with two seats, four doors, and folding top
town car four-door car with rear passenger compartment separated from driver by sliding glass partition
utility vehicle vehicle designed chiefly for use or service

Trucks and Buses

amphibian flat-bottomed vehicle that moves over land or water on tracks with fins

armored car vehicle with bullet-resistant panels and doors, used by military or police
big rig *Slang.* multiunit or eighteen-wheeler truck
bulldozer tractor with broad, blunt blade for moving earth and debris, used in road building and construction
bus motorized, box-shaped vehicle used to transport numerous paying passengers, usu. on a fixed schedule
camper van with bed and kitchen
caravan large vehicle with living quarters
Caterpillar *Trademark.* tractor or construction vehicle propelled by two endless belts
club cab pickup truck with expanded cab that includes rear seat and/or storage area
diesel large truck with diesel fuel engine
dray small truck for hauling goods
dump truck heavy, open truck used to transport loose freight
eighteen-wheeler large tractor and semitrailer truck with eighteen wheels
fire engine heavy truck or tractor and trailer with firefighting equipment
flatbed truck with open platform or shallow box body
float trailer with platform for parade exhibit
forklift small work vehicle that hoists heavy loads on steel prongs
grader truck equipped with earth-leveling device
haulaway truck with two-level trailer, used to transport new automobiles
hook and ladder fire engine with ladders and other apparatus
jitney small passenger bus or van with flexible schedule over regular route
light truck a pickup, utility vehicle, minivan, and the like
mobile home large van or trailer with living quarters; motor home
motor home mobile home
omnibus public carrier for at least twelve passengers, usu. with door in rear
paddy wagon panel truck used to transport prisoners
panel truck enclosed, windowless van
pickup small truck with cab, shallow box body, and tailgate
recreational vehicle RV; large van with living facilities
RV recreational vehicle
semitrailer freight trailer designed so that most of its weight rests on another vehicle, attached to tractor by fifth wheel or pivot
skidder four-wheel tractor equipped with grapple, used to haul logs or timber over rough terrain
steamroller steam-powered tractor with heavy roller for roadwork
tank military armored tractor propelled by two endless metal belts
tow truck pickup equipped with winch for hauling other vehicles; wrecker
tractor powerful vehicle with large rear wheels or endless belt treads, used to haul equipment or do work; cab and engine section that hauls semitrailer
trailer engineless container drawn by tractor or other vehicle; auto-drawn highway vehicle with living facilities
truck self-propelled motor vehicle designed for transportation of goods or special-purpose equipment, often with swivel for hauling trailer
van multipurpose, enclosed, box-shaped vehicle having side panels, with or without windows in panels

Internal Combustion Engine

afterburner auxiliary device that burns exhaust fumes from combustion
automatic choke temperature- or time-controlled device that enriches air/fuel mixture for cold starts
block aluminum or iron casting housing cylinders and crankshaft
cam one of rotating pieces along camshaft
camshaft shaft that changes rotary motion into linear motion to operate valves
carburetor device that controls and monitors air/fuel mixture fed to cylinders
choke plate near top of carburetor that can be partially closed to restrict air entering carburetor and enrich fuel mixture
combustion chamber area within cylinder above piston where fuel/air mixture ignites
crankcase lower part of engine that contains lubricating oil
crankshaft main engine shaft that converts linear motion of pistons into rotary motion
cylinder hollow tube in engine block, containing piston
diesel engine compression-ignition engine in which air is heated by compression and diesel fuel is injected directly into the combustion chamber, where it then self-ignites
exhaust manifold metal casting that routes exhaust from each combustion chamber to common exhaust pipe
exhaust valve device that opens to allow burned gases to be expelled from combustion chamber
four-stroke cycle engine internal combustion engine working in four stages: intake, compression, power, and exhaust
fuel injection fuel delivery system in which a high-pressure pump meters and atomizes fuel directly into diesel engine cylinder or into intake manifold of spark ignition engine
head gasket packing element that seals cylinder head from engine block
intake manifold tube or casting with combination of passages that routes fuel/air mixture from carburetor to combustion chamber in spark ignition engine
intake valve device in four-stroke cycle engine that opens to allow air or fuel/air mixture to be drawn into combustion chamber
internal combustion engine reciprocating or rotary engine in which combustion of fuel is in direct contact with pistons or rotor

piston component moving up and down in cylinder, linked by connecting rod to crankshaft, and converting pressure of combustion into work
piston ring circular device fitted into groove in piston to keep oil out and seal gases in
reciprocating engine two-stroke or four-stroke cycle engine
rocker arm pivoting lever that pushes valve open
rotary engine internal combustion engine without pistons, in which triangular rotor moves orbitally and rotationally; Wankel engine
slant six six-cylinder engine with row of cylinders mounted at an angle
stroke one phase in piston cycle
supercharger engine-driven compressor that increases density of fuel/air mixture
throttle device that controls volume of mixture delivered to spark ignition engine or quantity of fuel injected into diesel engine
torque measure of twisting force generated by crankshaft
turbocharger compressor driven by exhaust heat to increase density of fuel/air mixture
two-stroke cycle engine internal combustion engine that works in two stages, compression and power, with blower or other means of delivering fresh air and fuel with piston at bottom dead center prior to compression stroke
V-6 six-cylinder engine with three cylinders in each of two banks set at ninety degree angle forming a V
V-8 eight-cylinder engine with four cylinders in each of two banks set at ninety degree angle forming a V
valve device used to close off and meter flow of intake and exhaust into and out of combustion chamber
Wankel engine rotary engine

Working Parts

accelerator pedal operated by driver's right foot that varies amount of fuel fed to engine, thus controlling speed
air conditioner refrigeration and ventilation system for lowering temperature of passenger compartment
air filter device that keeps solid particles out of fuel/air mixture
alternator alternating current (AC) generator that supplies power to run car's electrical system
automatic transmission gearbox that changes gear ratios independently of driver based on speed and load
axle full shaft on which wheels revolve
battery electrochemical storage unit of 6 or 12 volts
bearing part, such as wheel bearing, on which another part revolves
brake drum metal arc mounted on hub against which shoes rub to stop car
brake lining replaceable friction material attached to brake shoes and pressed by shoes against brake drums to stop car
brake shoes arc-shaped pieces that fit inside and press against drums
breaker points electrical switch in distributor used to control high voltage needed by spark plugs; points
capacitor device for storage of electrical energy
catalytic converter emission control device for converting pollutants to benign substances
clutch coupling mechanism by which rotating shafts of engine and transmission may be engaged and disengaged; pedal operated by driver's left foot in manual transmission cars
clutch plate flat coupling disc in clutch mechanism
coil pulse transformer that increases voltage to fire spark plug
condenser electrical device that prevents arcing
cruise control automatic setting for continuous, high-speed driving
differential gear system that allows outer wheel to travel greater distance than inner wheel during turn
disc brakes brakes whose friction is generated by pads rubbing rotor mounted on wheel assembly
distributor device for directing high voltage from coil to appropriate spark plugs in turn
distributor cap top of distributor with wires to each spark plug
drive shaft shaft connecting transmission to rear axle in rear-wheel drive car
drive train universal joint and drive shaft connecting transmission to axles
drum brakes brakes with lined shoes that rub against inner circumference of metal, hub-mounted drums for friction
electronic ignition spark ignition system without breaker points
fan belt engine-driven belt that operates fan
flywheel heavy disk at rear of crankshaft that smooths separate power pulses from each cylinder
four-wheel drive system in which differential conveys power to all four wheels
front-wheel drive system in which differential conveys power only to front wheels, which steer and propel car
fuel pump device that supplies fuel from gas tank to carburetor or fuel injection system
fuse safety device that controls current flow to elements in electrical system
gear one of toothed wheels in transmission that determine direction and relative speed of travel and mechanical advantage of engine
gearbox transmission
gear ratio ratio of speeds between input and output shafts of transmission in each gear
generator direct current (DC) generating device
ignition switch key switch in dashboard that sets ignition system in operation
ignition system electrical system designed to produce spark in cylinders and ignite fuel, consisting of battery, coil, condenser, breaker points, distributor, spark plugs, and wires
linkage series of metal rods or levers that transmit motion from one unit to another
manifold exhaust manifold and/or intake manifold

manual transmission gearbox in which selection of gear is controlled by driver through clutch and gearshift
muffler baffle exhaust device used to lessen noise of combustion
oil filter engine-mounted device that removes contaminants from engine oil
oil pump device that forces lubricating oil through engine
overdrive device used to lower overall gear ratio and hence reduce rpms necessary to achieve given road speed, thus decreasing fuel consumption
PCV valve positive crankcase ventilation valve; device that prevents crankcase vapors from discharging directly into atmosphere
plug spark plug
points breaker points
power brakes hydraulically actuated brakes with vacuum assist mechanism that reduces brake pedal pressure needed
power steering hydraulically assisted steering linkage that reduces turning effort
rack-and-pinion steering system in which rotation of steering wheel is translated into linear motion by pinion gear mounted in toothed rack
radiator unit of pipes that dissipates heat in engine coolant
rear-wheel drive conventional system in which differential conveys drive power to rear wheels only
reduction gear combination of gears that reduce input speed so as to lower output speed
regulator device that controls voltage sent by alternator to battery
seals permanently installed rubber or leather components that keep lubrication from leaking
shift driver-operated lever that controls transmission
shock absorber device fitted to each corner of suspension to damp spring oscillations and smoothen ride
solenoid magnetic device that exerts force when current flows through coil
spark plug electrical component threaded into cylinder head whose spark initiates combustion; plug
springs main suspension units that absorb force of road shocks by twisting or flexing
starter high-torque electric motor used to start engine
steering column central pivoting unit of steering system
steering wheel wheel connected to steering column by which driver steers car
stick shift device by which driver controls gears in manual transmission
suspension springs, shock absorbers, and other components that connect wheels to car body
sway bar torsion coupling between right and left front-wheel suspensions to reduce roll and sway
thermostat device that regulates engine temperature by controlling flow of coolant through system
timing setting that initiates spark at appropriate point in piston's compression stroke
torsion bar flexible steel bar that twists to provide spring in suspension
transmission assembly of gears and selector linkage that connects engine output shaft to rest of drive train by matching engine speed with desired road speed; gearbox; tranny
universal joint multidirectional joint in drive shaft that permits changes in angle while shaft is rotating
water pump device that circulates water coolant through engine

Body Parts and Accessories

aerial metal rod mounted on body for receiving radio signals
air bag bag that inflates during collision to prevent driver or passenger from being thrown forward
antifreeze glycol and water mixture used in water-cooled engine to lower freezing point of coolant
bias-ply tire tire with supporting cords embedded at angle to rotational direction
body external housing and structure of vehicle
brake fluid viscous liquid used in hydraulic brake cylinders
brake pedal foot control by which driver operates brakes
bucket seat low, individual, front seat for one passenger
bulb electric lamp
bumper protective member fitted over front and rear wheels; fender
cab enclosed passenger portion of truck
camber angle of wheel when viewed head-on
chains chain-link units attached to tires to increase traction on snow, ice, or mud
chassis substructure on which components of car are mounted
chrome shiny chromium alloy used to coat parts of body trim
coolant alcohol or glycol mixed with water to increase efficiency of cooling system
dashboard instrument panel facing driver in compartment
defroster heating/ventilation system that directs air onto windshield to clear ice or condensation
diesel fuel fuel oil burned in diesel engine
directional signal turn signal
emergency light hazard light
fairing custom part added to smooth contour of body and reduce drag
fender bumper
fuel gasoline or oil burned to supply power for engine
gas gasoline
gasket packing that seals joint, as between cylinder head and engine block
gasohol combination of gasoline and up to ten per cent alcohol, used as fuel
gasoline complex hydrocarbon blend used as fuel by internal combustion engines; gas

gas tank storage container for gasoline attached to chassis
gearshift mechanism by which gears are engaged and disengaged
glove compartment small storage area with door in dashboard
grill gridlike chrome covering placed over front of engine compartment to permit air to flow freely through engine
hatchback vehicle with rear hatch opening into passenger compartment
hazard light blinking front or rear light used when vehicle is stopped for mechanical trouble or in dangerous place; emergency light
headlights high-powered lamps that illuminate area in front of car for night driving
headrest unit attached to seat top as head support
heater unit using engine heat to warm passenger compartment
high beam second headlight for added illumination at distance
hood hinged cover over engine compartment
horn audible electric warning device controlled by driver
housing protective metal covering for engine part
hub wheel mounting on end of axle
hub cap often decorative chrome covering for lug nuts that attach wheel to axle
inner tube replaceable rubber lining that held air in old-fashioned tires
instrument panel dashboard with gauges and meters
jack device for lifting side of car to change tires
jumper cable insulated electrical cable for recharging battery or starting car with dead battery
jump seat removable or folding seat for extra passenger, esp. in limousine or taxicab
license plate metal plate issued by state bearing car's identifying number
loaded (*adj*) having many optional features
lubricant engine oil or grease that reduces friction and heat on operating parts
lug nuts bolts that hold wheel on axle
mag wheel shiny magnesium wheel rim
mud flap splash guard
odometer accumulated mileage gauge mounted on dashboard
oil gauge meter that indicates engine oil pressure
parking light small front or rear light
pedal foot control by which driver operates accelerator, brake, or clutch
premium high-octane gasoline used in high-compression engines
radial tire tire with supporting cords embedded in line with direction of rotation
rearview mirror small mirror affixed above windshield that allows driver to see what lies behind car
retread used tire with new tread applied
rim outer metal band on wheel to which tire is attached
roll bar protective bar over open driving compartment, esp. in racing cars
rumble seat uncovered folding seat in back of car
running board footboard at base of door on side of car
seat belt safety device strapped across passenger to secure position in case of accident
shift knob end of gear shift handled by driver
side mirror rearview mirror mounted on side of car
snow tire special tire with deep tread or rubber cleats to provide traction on snow or ice
spare tire extra tire, usu. stored in trunk
speedometer road speed gauge mounted on dashboard
splash guard flap suspended behind rear wheel to prevent tire splash from muddying windows of following vehicles; mud flap
stick shift upright gearshift protruding from floor, used to operate manual transmission
stud metal cleat inserted in snow tire to increase traction
sump part of oil pan containing oil
sunroof retractable section of roof
sun visor flap that may be lowered to shield passenger's eyes from sun
tachometer gauge mounted on dashboard that measures engine speed in revolutions per minute (rpms)
tailgate small gate at rear of vehicle that can be lowered to form horizontal surface
taillight rear light
tailpipe pipe that routes exhaust fumes from muffler to rear of car
tire pneumatic casing mounted on wheel forming interface between car and road: tubeless, tube, bias-ply, or radial
tow bar unit attached to rear bumper, used to haul another vehicle or trailer
transmission fluid viscous liquid used in hydraulic transmission
tread grooved portion of tire that touches road
trim decorations, chrome, and insignia attached to auto body
trunk enclosed storage compartment, usu. at rear
tubeless tire tire without inner tube
turn signal external, front and rear, driver-controlled lights used to indicate direction of turn; directional signal
unleaded fuel gasoline with low lead content, less polluting and forming fewer deposits than leaded fuel
vanity plate license plate customized with owner's initials, nickname, or other chosen letters or word
wheel circular frame at hub of axle to which tire attaches
whitewall tire with circular white strip on black
windshield front window of passenger compartment; windscreen
windshield wiper motor-driven device with rubber blade for clearing water from windshield
wiper blade rubber attachment to windshield wiper

Driving and Repair

backfire improperly timed explosion of fuel mixture, esp. occurring outside cylinder in exhaust system

balance (*vb*) adjust new tires for even rotation
bleed (*vb*) drain brake fluid to clear hydraulic brake lines of air
blindside (*vb*) strike another car without warning from rear or side
blow-by leakage of combustion gases between piston and cylinder wall into crankcase
blowout sudden, severe flat tire while driving
body shop garage for repairs to body and repainting
bodywork nonmechanical repairs
bottleneck narrowing roadway that causes traffic congestion
Botts dots raised, reflective markers on roadway that alert driver when car drifts out of its lane
broadside (*vb*) strike another car full on side
bumper-to-bumper (*adj.*) describing long line of slow-moving traffic
center divider barrier down center of two-way road
chicken game in which two drivers drive toward each other or toward obstacle, with first driver to turn away losing contest
cornering ability of driver or car to negotiate curves and turns
crank (*vb*) start engine
crosswalk lane marked off for pedestrian use while crossing street
cruising driving slowly back and forth along particular roadway in city
curb low bump at edge of roadway that separates it from sidewalk; also, *esp. Brit.*, kerb
customizing additions or alterations made by owner to standard body and engine
Denver boot device locked in place on wheel of illegally-parked car to prevent it from moving
double parking illegal parking on street side of another parked car
downshift (*vb*) change to lower gear when decelerating
driver's license permit to operate car issued by state; license
driveway narrow private roadway leading to garage or residence from public roadway
drop the engine remove entire engine for repairs; pull the engine
drunk driving driving recklessly while intoxicated; DUI
DUI driving under the influence; drunk driving
emission control smog control
EPA Environmental Protection Agency; government agency that sets smog standards and tests cars for gasoline mileage
freeway divided highway with several lanes in each direction for fast driving
grade steep hill
gun the engine increase rpms
hit-and-run (*adj.*) describing accident in which driver flees the scene
hitchhike (*vb*) stand by roadside with thumb extended seeking a ride
horsepower unit measuring power of engine, equal to 550 foot-pounds per second
hot-wire (*vb*) *Slang.* contact wiring around ignition switch to start car without key
hydroplane (*vb*) skid over very shallow water
idle running speed of engine with no load and closed throttle
jackknife accident in which tractor-trailer truck folds in half like knife blade closing
jump-start (*vb*) start car by using jumper cables to connect dead battery to good battery in another vehicle
knock noise from poorly controlled combustion in cylinder
learner's permit state-issued permit to operate car only in presence of licensed driver
lube addition of lubricant and transaxle grease
mileage miles traveled for each gallon of gasoline consumed
moving violation violation of driving laws cited by police; traffic violation
no-fault insurance insurance system in which liability is not dependent upon who is at fault in accident
octane measure of gasoline's ability to resist knock and detonation
oil change replacement of dirty crankcase oil
parallel parking parking in space parallel to direction of street
passing lane lane nearest center of roadway on two-way street, designed for cars traveling fastest
ping mild knock in detonation
pit stop *Informal.* stop for fuel and servicing, esp. on long drive or in race
pop the clutch *Informal.* disengage clutch abruptly, not smoothly
pull the engine drop the engine
rear-end (*vb*) strike another vehicle from behind
rebuild (*vb*) do complete engine overhaul
registration annual record of auto ownership filed with state
rev (*vb*) increase engine rpms suddenly
ride shotgun *Informal.* ride in passenger seat located to driver's right
roadway usu. paved strip of land designated for use by automobiles
roll start roll standard-transmission car and pop clutch to achieve ignition when electrical system fails
rpm revolutions per minute; measure of engine speed
rubberneck (*vb*) strain to see accident scene from passing vehicle, causing slowing of traffic and danger
rush hour period of heavy traffic at beginning and end of workday
servicing tune-up, oil change, lube, and other basic maintenance
shunpiking driving on back roads to avoid highways
sideswipe (*vb*) graze another car's side in minor accident
skid loss of control due to ice, water, or sudden stop
slipstreaming driving closely behind another vehicle to take advantage of reduced air resistance
souped-up (*adj*) *Slang.* customized for increased power and speed; stroked

specifications precise measurements of proper settings for engine operations
speed limit maximum driving speed allowed by law on given roadway
spin-out rotating skid made by automobile, causing it to leave roadway
stall come to a halt though failure of enough fuel to pass through carburetor to engine, causing engine to cease operating
sticker price undiscounted price for car, usu. affixed to window as itemized list on sheet of paper
stock (*adj*) designating standard design, parts, and color of factory-manufactured automobile
stroked (*adj*) *Slang.* souped-up, esp. by lengthening piston stroke for greater power
test drive trial run to evaluate new car
toe-in slight forward convergence given to front wheels to improve steering alignment
tool (*vb*) drive, esp. down highway
total (*vb*) damage one's car beyond repair in accident
towaway zone no-parking area from which cars are removed to city or police garage, esp. at rush hour
towing pulling another vehicle or trailer with one's vehicle
traffic court local court with jurisdiction over violators of traffic laws
tune-up periodic adjustment of ignition, valve clearance, and fuel delivery system and replacement of electrical parts
upshift (*vb*) change to higher gear when accelerating
U-turn reversal of driving direction on same roadway
vapor lock boiling or vaporizing of fuel in lines due to excess heat, often causing stoppage of fuel flow
vehicle ID identification number stamped on engine block or dashboard
wheel alignment proper adjustment of wheel's caster, camber, and toe-in
whiplash neck strain due to sudden, violent accident involving rear-end impact
winterize (*vb*) prepare auto for cold weather by adding antifreeze, thinner oil, and insulation
wrecker one who hauls away and disposes of cars after accidents

RAILROADS

Types of Trains, Cars, and Lines
Railroad Personnel
Parts, Practices, and Argot

Types of Trains, Cars, and Lines

baggage train train that carries freight and passenger baggage
bar car passenger train car in which refreshments are served
booster extra engine used to assist on steep grade
boxcar roofed freight car with sliding doors on its sides; crate
bullet train very fast express train
bunk car sleeping car for loggers or track workers
cable car car powered by loop of underground cable
caboose last car on freight train, occupied by conductor, rear brakeman, and crew, in which their meals are taken
cannonball express *Slang.* fast express train
car individual railway vehicle, carrying passengers or freight, coupled to other cars to form train
chair car passenger car with pairs of adjustable seats down each side of aisle
coach car with seats for passengers
cog railway rail line on steep mountain with locomotive that uses a cogwheel to engage cogs on tracks to gain traction
diesel locomotive engine powered by internal combustion engine that uses diesel fuel fired by compressed air in cylinders
dining car car in which meals are served to passengers; diner
doubleheader train hauled by two locomotives
drawing room car sleeping car with lounge areas
drill switch engine
el elevated
electric railway railroad car or cars powered by electricity from cables or generator
elevated railway raised above ground on trestle
express train fast train that makes few or no stops
feeder line secondary rail line connecting to main line
flatcar platform freight car without roof or sides; platform car
freight car any of various cars designed to haul freight, usu. enclosed with sliding doors on sides
freight train nonpassenger train
funicular cable railroad that travels up and down a slope, often suspended from cable
gondola freight car with sides but no roof
gravity car unpowered car that runs downhill only
handcar small, flat, four-wheeled railway car propelled by two-handled pump, used to carry section gangs to work
hand truck hand car built like flat truck
helper auxiliary engine in doubleheader to aid on grade
hopper car steel-sided freight car with chutes that discharge freight such as gravel or coal
house track section of track at station, used for loading or unloading
idler unloaded flatcar placed ahead of or behind oversize load projecting from next car
jitney four-wheel electric baggage car in terminal
limited top-service train with few cars making selected stops
line track and roadbed following specific route
local passenger train that stops at every depot along line
local express passenger train that stops at most depots

locomotive steam-, electric-, or diesel-powered railroad engine that pulls or pushes other cars; engine
lounge car passenger car with seats at windows, bar, and refreshment facilities
metro metropolitan underground railway (France)
milk train *Informal.* train that makes frequent stops
model railroad miniature-scale railroad built and run as hobby
monorail train running along single track
observation car passenger car with large sight-seeing windows or elevated split-level section
parlor car first-class lounge or day car with plush seats
passenger train train that carries only passengers and their baggage
platform car flatcar
Prairie locomotive with 2-6-2 wheel arrangement
puller switch engine that hauls cars around yard
Pullman car comfortable, well-appointed passenger car that converts into sleeping car or is divided into roomettes
rack-and-pinion railway railway with rack between rails that meshes with gear wheel or pinion on locomotive to assist on steep grades
railhead farthest point from terminus to which rails have been laid
railroad roadway of parallel steel rails that serve as track for passenger or freight cars drawn by locomotive; system of such tracks; company operating trains on railroad
railway railroad, esp. lightweight line operating locally
refrigerator car freight car with refrigerated compartment for perishables; reefer
rolling stock railroad cars of all types, esp. those owned by one company
shuttle train that makes short, frequent, round-trip runs over same track; scoot
sleeper sleeping car
sleeping car car outfitted with sleeping berths, esp. Pullman car; sleeper
smoker smoking car
smoking car passenger car in which tobacco smoking is allowed; smoker
special train running on irregular schedule or carrying unique cargo or passengers
steam shovel large mechanical shovel connected to motor in small enclosure on flatcar (snow plow and pile driver can also be thus connected)
stemwinder brakeless trolley; locomotive with special gear system
stock car ventilated or slatted car for livestock, esp. cattle, often with feeding mangers on sides
streetcar passenger car on municipal railway
streetcar line system of rails that provides public transportation on city streets
street railway rail system on city streets
string line of coupled cars
subway underground municipal railway, usu. electric; underground
supply train train that gathers scraps and delivers supplies to all points along division
switch engine engine used solely to switch cars in yard; drill
tank car freight car for hauling fluids or gases in large, enclosed tank; tanker
tanker tank car
tap line short feeder line, owned by industrial concern, leading from regular tracks to factory or warehouse
tender car fuel and water supply car coupled directly behind engine
trailer flatcar pushed ahead of engine to couple to other cars on section unfit for locomotive
train several railroad cars coupled together
tram *Chiefly Brit.* streetcar; open railway car used in mines
tramway *Chiefly Brit.* streetcar line; system in which cars are supported by overhead cables
trolley street railway car
truck carriage with one or more pairs of wheels that guide one end of car or locomotive on sharp curves
trunk line main line of railroad system
underground subway
wagon-lit sleeping car (Europe)
wrecking crane flatcar with enclosure at one end holding steam boiler, engine, and hoisting mechanism
wreck train train equipped to clear tracks of debris or damaged equipment following storm or accident
yard engine engine used to switch and move trains in yard

Railroad Personnel

air jammer worker who connects air hoses and air signals between coupled cars
baggage master person who supervises baggage room at terminal
brakeman person who operates train brakes; roughneck
brotherhood railroad workers' union, esp. one of Big Four: engineers, firemen, conductors, trainmen
conductor person who supervises train crew and collects passenger fares; person in charge of street railway
crew track workers and trainmen
dispatcher person who manages train movements, schedules, and track assignments
end man rear brakeman
engineer person trained to operate locomotive and drive train
field man yard brakeman
fireman person who shovels coal into firebox and puts water in boiler to maintain steam level; apprentice to engineer who works with him in cab
flagman person who gives signals at designated sites
gripman porter
head brakeman brakeman at front of train who

opens and closes switches, takes on water, and acts as flagman
hostler roundhouse or terminal engine maintenance worker
lineman track inspector who reports damage to section gang
parlor brakeman rear brakeman in caboose on freight train
paymaster railroad employee who travels about paying salaries
porter passenger baggage carrier at terminal; sleeping car attendant; gripman; hop; redcap
railroader one who works on railroad
redcap porter
section gang group of section men who weed right of way, replace ties, reballast, and repair tracks
section man worker who maintains certain section of track
spiker worker who drives spikes when laying rails
stationmaster operations supervisor at depot or terminal
steward passenger train crewman who manages provisioning of food and serves passengers
stoker fireman
switchman operator of switches that run cars from one track to another, either manually or electrically
ticket agent person in station or railroad office who sells passenger tickets
trainman member of train crew supervised by conductor
trainmaster person who maintains schedules and operates switch yards
watchman safety inspector, esp. in shack at junction of two tracks
yardmaster supervisor of operations in railroad yard

Parts, Practices, and Argot

adverse uphill road grade
air brake system of continuous brakes worked by compressed air and pistons
air pump machine that compresses air in cylinders to drive air brake
alleyway passage beside compartments in sleeping and parlor cars
apron flat, metal platform separating locomotive and tender
baggage room terminal area in which incoming and outgoing luggage is held for pickup or shipment
ballast gravel or slag bed for railroad ties
berth bed or bunk built into sleeping car
blizzard lights two emergency lights flanking locomotive headlight
block signal signal at block entrance that controls trains entering and leaving
block system organization of railroad line into three- or four-mile sections governed by signals which assure that one train leaves block before another enters
blue flag warning that workers are repairing crippled car
board conductor's cry of "all aboard" as passenger train prepares to leave station
boiler metal tank in which water is heated and converted to steam to drive locomotive
broad gauge road with rails wider than 4 feet 8 1/2 inches (1.43 m) apart
bunk elevated bed built into wall of sleeper compartment
cab enclosed area of locomotive in which engineer and fireman operate controls
cattle guard device with projecting triangular spikes or widely spaced bars placed at road crossings to prevent cattle from passing
catwalk rungs or plank running board on boxcar or locomotive platform, used by brakeman to clamber between cars
clinker fused mass of hot coals
commutation ticket reduced fare, multitrip, time-limited ticket good on one line only
consist conductor's report by which yardmaster at next stop plans switchings
couchette fold-out, shelflike bed in low-fare compartment of European passenger train
coupler device used to fasten together individual cars; drawbar; pin
cowcatcher outthrusting metal bumper on front of locomotive that pushes aside obstructions, esp. cattle
crossing intersection of railroad tracks and public roadway
crosstie tie
crown (*vb*) couple caboose to line of freight cars
cupola observation area atop caboose
dead freight bulky, nonperishable freight
deck front part of cab, catwalk atop boxcar
depot train station or terminal for loading passengers and freight
derailing accident in which one or more cars slip off tracks; intentional forcing of car off tracks
division section of line between terminals, approx. one hundred miles
drawbar coupler
drop bottom door and chute at base of hopper car or gondola for emptying cargo such as coal or gravel
em one thousand pounds of tonnage
engine cab enclosed cab on locomotive
extra train not listed on timetable
ferrophiliac amateur lover of railroading
flag colored cloth signal used in daylight
flange inside projecting rim on wheel that guides it down track
frog implement used to derail car wheels or permit them to cross intersecting tracks
full stroke at top speed
full throttle at top speed
gangway space between rear of steam locomotive cab and tender
gantlet section of track through narrow passage in which two track lines overlap, one rail of each line lying between rails of the other
gantry bridgelike framework over tracks that supports signals or is used for loading

gate switch that may be opened or closed to control movement of trains on tracks
gauge recognized standard measure of distance between two rails: narrow 3' 6" (1.07 m), standard 4' 8 1/2" (1.43 m), broad 5' 6" (1.68 m)
grade tracks running up steep hill
green flag signal indicating permission to proceed, displayed at front of train
highball signal in which hand or lantern sweeps in high, wide semicircle to indicate full speed ahead
hump rise built at end of freight yard from which cars roll to separate tracks for coupling
hump yard yard built on incline to allow switching by natural, gravitational momentum
ingersoll trainman's open-faced watch
Johnson bar reverse lever on locomotive
joint length of rail, usu. 33 to 39 feet (10 to 12 m)
junction intersection of two tracks or lines
ladder central track in yard, from which other tracks lead off
layover time lost in delay connecting with another train
marker signal on rear of train, flag by day, lantern by night; signal on main line
Morse code standard telegraphic code by which most railroad messages were sent prior to electronic telecommunications
mule cable-operated device used to lift coal cars up incline for dumping
narrow gauge road with rails less than 4 feet 8 1/2 inches (1.43 m) apart
off-peak (*adj*) designating noncommuting hours with reduced passenger fare
pass free entry to car for passenger
pin coupler
pod intentional derailing to prevent cars on siding from entering main line
point intersection of gauge lines in switch or frog
rack rail third rail used for traction when engaged by gear on locomotive
rail long metal bar laid upon ground parallel to another such bar and connected to it by crossties, serving as track for railroad cars; railroad as means of transport
railroading construction and operation of railroads; travel by railroad
railway bridge trestle or covered bridge supporting tracks across land depression or water
right of way land occupied by and immediately surrounding railroad main line
roadbed base upon which rails, ties, and ballast of railroad track rests
roadway railroad right of way with tracks, stations, and signals
roomette individual compartment in Pullman car
roundhouse circular structure in yard housing idle locomotives for storage and repair
round trip journey to specific destination and back to starting point over same route
run regular route of train line
runaway train that is out of control and unstoppable by normal means, usu. due to mechanical failure
semaphore apparatus giving signals to trains by position of movable arms
sidetrack siding
siding short track connected by switch to main line and used for bypassing or unloading; sidetrack
signal marker, either flag or lantern
span bridge or trestle
spar pole for clearing cars when switching; stake
spot (*vb*) place car in designated location, esp. for loading or unloading
spur short sidetrack connecting to main line, often dead end
stake pole used to move cars in manual switching operation; spar
standard gauge railroad track and carwheel width of 4 feet 8 1/2 inches (1.43 m)
stateroom lavish, first-class suite of connected passenger compartments with separate sitting and sleeping areas
station regular stopping place for train line, with loading platform and usu. shelter for passengers
steam brake emergency braking procedure in which valve gear is reversed to slow engine
steam stop halting train by steam braking cars but not engine
stroke single movement of piston rod; measure of engine speed or drive
switch device consisting of two movable rails that connect to tracks, used to direct cars from one siding to another or onto main line
switchback zigzag line over hill too steep for direct ascent
switching moving of cars or trains from one track to another
switch tower elevated lookout point in switch yard
switch yard yard in which cars are moved from one track to another to make up trains
tack coupling pin
temporary track tracks laid for use while regular tracks are being repaired
terminal city or town at endpoint of line with station or depot; station at junction of lines; yard at end of division
terminus endpoint of line
third rail extra rail added on curves to prevent derailing
throat fan-shaped convergence of tracks at tunnel entrance
throttle equipment that determines amount of steam entering cylinders and thus controls speed of engine
ticket punch handheld device used by conductor to cancel tickets by perforation
tie wood plank supporting and connecting rails; crosstie
tonnage weight carried by entire train or individual car; amount of weight locomotive can pull
trackage lines of railroad tracks
tracks pair of parallel metal rails, usu. with crossties, that guide car or engine wheels
transfer table flat, movable or rotating surface

with single track that is turned to align with other tracks to transfer locomotive to new track
trestle framework support on piles for tracks across river or depression; rudimentary railroad bridge
turntable platform with track used to rotate locomotives in yard at end of track and outside roundhouse
undercarriage frame and running gear of locomotive
walkway area for walking along side of locomotive
washout emergency stop signal, in which arms or lamp are swung in wide, downward arc across track
way bill document prepared by carrier with details of shipment, routing, and charges
way station small, often remote station at which train stops only on signal
whistle railroad sound used to signal departure, arrival, approach to station, or crossing, also used to send message or warning by coded series of blasts
whistle stop small town at which passenger train does not normally stop
Whyte classification system that classifies locomotives by wheel arrangement, such as 4-8-2, 4-4-2, 2-8-8-4, etc.
wye tracks off main line arranged in Y-formation, used to reverse cars and engines without turntable
X designation for empty car
yard open area at terminus of line with network of tracks for storage of cars and assembly of trains

SHIPS AND BOATS

Types of Ships and Boats

airboat light, flat-bottomed, aluminum vessel driven by propeller revolving in air
aircraft carrier very large, flat-decked seagoing airbase; carrier
argosy large, richly laden merchant ship; fleet of ships
ark large, flat-bottomed riverboat
barge flat-bottomed cargo vessel without power
bark three- or four-masted square-rigger
bathyscaphe submarine-shaped float filled with fluid lighter than water, used for deep-sea diving
bathysphere enclosed globe for deep-sea observations
battleship large, armored naval ship heavily outfitted for war
bireme galley with two banks of oars
boat small vessel used at sea or on inland waterway
brigantine two-masted ship with square-rigged topsail on mainmast
bumboat small boat used in port or at anchor to sell goods to ships' crews
cabin cruiser motorboat with enclosed cabin and living facilities
canal boat flat boat that operates on inland canals
canoe light, narrow boat with sharp or pointed ends, powered by one or more paddles
caravel small, fast sailing ship with narrow, high poop and lateen sails (Portugal and Spain, 15th-16th c.)
carrack galleon or merchant vessel used in Mediterranean (15th-16th c.)
carrier aircraft carrier
catamaran twin-hulled sailing vessel
clipper speedy, fully rigged sailing vessel with sharp bow (19th c.)
container ship freighter outfitted to carry large cargo containers
coracle small, round or very broad boat made of interwoven laths or wicker covered with skin or tarred or oiled cloth (Ireland, Wales)
corsair pirate ship
corvette small, fast warship, esp. for convoy; formerly a sailing warship larger than a sloop, smaller than a frigate
craft boat or vessel, esp. small one
cruiser speedy, armored warship with six to eight guns; cabin cruiser
cutter single-masted vessel with fore-and-aft rigged sails; sloop
destroyer speedy warship armed with guns, torpedoes, and depth charges
dhow coastal ship with lateen sail and raised deck at stern (Indian Ocean)
dinghy small rowboat; small boat carried on ship or used as tender
dink small boat, esp. for duck hunting
dory small, flat-bottomed boat with sharp bow and tapering stern
dreadnought large armored battleship armed with heavy-caliber guns in turrets
dredge low workboat that scrapes bottom of waterway to make it navigable
dromond large, fast medieval galley or cutter
dugout boat or canoe hollowed out of large log
felucca small, narrow ship propelled by oars or lateen sails (Mediterranean)
ferry vessel used to convey passengers and cargo back and forth across bay or stream
fishing smack fore-and-aft rigged vessel equipped with well for holding live catch
flatboat boat with flat bottom, esp. for use in shallow waterway
fore-and-after sailing vessel with fore-and-aft rigging
freighter large cargo vessel
frigate light boat orig. propelled by oars, later by

sails; intermediate, square-rigged war vessel (18th-19th c.); heavy, missile-firing warship (20th c.)
full-rigged (*adj*) designating sailing vessel with three or more square-rigged masts
galiot small, swift ship propelled by sails and oars, formerly used in Mediterranean
galleon heavy square-rigger with several decks and elaborate poopdeck; Spanish treasure ship (15th-18th c.); carrack
galley large, low, ancient or medieval ship propelled by sails and oars
gig captain's boat; long lifeboat rowed with four to eight oars
gondola small, flat canal boat sculled with single oar or hand-propelled by pole
houseboat boat outfitted with living quarters, usu. moored permanently in one place
hydrofoil small, high-speed racing boat equipped with hydrofoils
hydroplane light, high-speed motorboat that skims along water on hydrofoils or flat bottom rising toward stern
iceboat triangular frame with sail mounted on runners, used on frozen waterways
icebreaker sturdy, powerful vessel for cutting channels through heavy ice
ironclad wooden warship armored with steel plate (19th c.)
johnboat flat-bottomed, square-ended fishing boat, used on inland waterways
jolly boat small boat carried at stern of sailing vessel
junk flat-bottomed boat with high stern and lateen sails (China, Japan)
kayak canoe made of skins that entirely cover frame except for paddler's seat in middle (Eskimo); small boat resembling this
ketch small, two-masted vessel rigged fore-and-aft
knockabout small, single-masted sailboat with no bowsprit
launch largest off-boat on warship; open motorboat
lifeboat small boat carried on ship or kept ready ashore for emergency use
life raft small, inflatable or balsa raft carried on ship for emergency use
liner large, elaborately-outfitted passenger ship
longboat largest boat carried on merchant sailing ship
lugger small ship rigged with lugsails on two or three masts
man-of-war warship
merchant ship commercial oceangoing vessel
minesweeper military vessel equipped to detect underwater explosive mines
motorboat usu. small, open boat powered by internal combustion or electric engine
New Orleans lugger broad-hulled fishing boat with single mast and large, dipping lugsail
ocean liner large, elaborately-outfitted passenger ship for ocean crossings
off-boat small boat carried on ship, esp. for emergency use as lifeboat
paddle steamer river-going steamboat propelled by wheels with paddles set at right angles about their circumference; paddle wheeler
paddle wheeler paddle steamer
pinnace small sailing ship, esp. tender to larger ship
pirogue dugout canoe or canoe-shaped boat having two masts
pontoon wooden, flat-bottomed boat or float used in building bridges; type of barge
pram small, flat-bottomed sailboat with square bow
proa swift sailing boat with flat lee side and balancing outrigger (Indonesia)
PT boat patrol torpedo boat; small, speedy torpedo boat
punt small, flat-bottomed riverboat with square ends
raft flat structure of logs or boards fastened together; small, flat-bottomed, inflatable rubber boat
riverboat steam-powered passenger boat used on inland waterways, esp. paddle wheeler
rowboat small, oar-powered boat
runabout light, open motorboat
sailboat boat with at least one mast, propelled by wind in sails secured to mast
sampan small boat with sail, steered with stern oar, often with small cabin of mats (China, Japan)
schooner fore-and-aft rigged vessel with two or more masts, mainmast at aft, and square sails
scow large, flat-bottomed boat with square ends, used to carry coal or sand, often towed by tug
scull light, narrow racing boat for four or fewer rowers
shell long, narrow, thin-hulled racing boat rowed by team of up to eight
ship large vessel navigating sea or other deep waterway, powered by sails or engine
side-wheeler vessel with paddle wheels on sides
skeeter small iceboat
skiff small boat, usu. rowed
skipjack small sailboat with flat, V-shaped hull and vertical sides
sloop fore-and-aft rigged, one-mast vessel; cutter
smack small sailboat, usu. rigged as sloop; fishing boat, esp. trawler, with well for keeping fish alive
speedboat very fast motorboat
sportfisherman inboard motorboat, usu. 36 to 42 feet (12 m) long, used for offshore fishing
square-rigger sailing ship rigged with square sails
steamer steam-powered vessel
steamship ship driven by steam-powered engine
sternwheeler vessel with paddle wheel at rear
sub *Informal.* submarine
submarine warship carrying torpedoes and missiles that can function underwater; sub
supertanker extremely large tanker, usu. for oil
tanker cargo ship with large tanks in hull for carrying oil or other liquid
tender auxiliary vessel used in the supply and repair of other ships
tern three-masted schooner
torpedo boat small, fast, maneuverable warship that fires torpedoes
towboat tugboat; boat for pushing barges on inland waterway

tramp vessel that will go anywhere for profitable cargo
transport ship used to carry soldiers or freight over long distance
trawler fishing boat that uses net to drag bottom of sea or lake
trimaran catamaran with three parallel hulls
trireme galley outfitted with three rows of oars
tug small, powerful vessel that aids in docking or towing larger ships
twelve-meter internationally recognized racing yacht
U-boat German submarine
umiak large, open rowboat of skins stretched on wooden frame (Eskimo)
vaporetto large motorboat for public transport on Venetian canals
vessel ship or boat
warship ship armed for combat, esp. battleship; man-of-war
whaleboat small, oar-powered boat used in whaling industry; whaler
whaler craft used in whaling
wherry light rowboat for rivers; one-person racing scull
windjammer large sailing ship
yacht pleasure boat, esp. narrow-hulled sailboat
yawl ship's small boat; two-masted vessel with small aftermast behind wheel

Parts of Ships, Sails, and Equipment

abeam (*adj*) directly outward from or at right angle to fore-and-aft line of ship
aft rear of ship; stern; (*adj*) toward the stern, behind
aftermast mast closest to stern
alleyway narrow passageway below decks
anchor large hook that grips bottom and holds ship in place
athwartships (*adv*) running across ship from side to side
backstay line or cable running aft from masthead to side or stern
ballast heavy object used to maintain ship at proper draft
batten strip used to fasten canvas over hatchways or to stiffen sails
beam ship's breadth at widest point; side of ship; direction outward from fore-and-aft line
becket looped rope or grommet for securing lines, oars, and spars
belowdecks (*adv*) in area within hull beneath deck surface
berth bed or bunk mounted in wall of cabin belowdecks; dock space at wharf
bibb wooden support bracket fastened to ship's mast
bight any part within ends of line, esp. a bend
bilge low point of ship's hull
binnacle case, box, or stand for ship's compass and lamp
block heavy pulley used for rigging
bobstay rope, chain, or rod from outer end of bowsprit to cutwater
boiler room location of power-generating boilers belowdecks on steamship
booby hatch covering over small hatchway
boom long pole or spar that extends and holds bottom of sail
bow most forward part of ship
bowsprit large spar projecting forward, used to carry headsail
brace any of various support pieces, esp. rope to sway yards on sailing vessels
bridge uppermost front cabin; platform for captain
brig place of confinement, ship's prison
broadside side of ship above waterline; volley fired simultaneously by all guns on one side of warship
bulkhead upright wall or partition separating compartments
bulwark rail around ship's deck
buttock convex, aftmost part of ship above waterline
cabin room used for passengers or officers
camel float between ship and pier that prevents chafing
capstan cylindrical spool revolving on shaft, used to wind cable
chock metal casting on deck through which lines and hawsers pass
companionway narrow stairway
compass navigational instrument with magnetized needle indicating north, used to determine heading
conning tower heavily armored pilothouse on warship
crossjack lowermost square sail set on mizzenmast of ship with four or more masts
crosstrees two short bars across masthead, used to spread rigging that supports mast
crow's nest lookout station atop mast on sailing vessel
cuddy small deck cabin; galley or pantry; platform on which fishing net is stored
cutwater forward edge of stem at and below waterline
davit crane projecting over side for hoisting lifeboats, anchors, or cargo on board
deadlight heavy plate glass window in portholes
deck flat, open surface of ship; floor
deck chair lightweight folding chair with arms, used on deck
depth charge underwater explosive directed against subs
depth sounder device for determining depth of water by measuring time required for sound wave to reach and return from bottom
derrick pivoting mast with tackle used to raise and lower boom
fantail aft overhang of ship shaped like duck's bill
fore (*adj*) ahead, toward the bow
fore-and-aft sails rigged lengthwise from bow to stern; (*adj*) having no square sails; running lengthwise

foredeck deck area toward bow
foremast mast nearest bow
foresail sail rigged on mast toward bow
gaff iron hook; spar rising aft from mast for sails
galley ship's kitchen
gangplank movable bridge used to board and leave ship; gangway
gangway gangplank
genoa large jib overlapping mainsail on yacht
gimbal suspended setting for ship's compass that allows it to remain stable in rough seas
gooseneck curved member at foot of boom that pivots so that boom can be pointed in wide angle vertically or horizontally
grapnel light anchor with many hooks or prongs
grappling iron hooked iron used to pull another vessel alongside or for anchoring
gunwale side rail where topsides and deck meet
halyard line or tackle for raising sails and flags
hatch door in deck or floor; covering over such a door
hatchway covered opening in deck with stairs that lead belowdecks
hawser heavy line, esp. for towing or mooring ship to dock
head ship's toilet
headsail small sail rigged forward of mast
heaving line light line with weight on free end and other end attached to hawser, used to draw heavier line into position
helm lever or wheel for controlling rudder to steer ship; wheel
hold cargo area within hull belowdecks
hull frame or main body of ship that sits in water
hydrofoil winglike structure attached to hull that lifts boat to skim along water at high speed
Jacob's ladder portable ladder with wooden rungs and flexible rope or wire sides
jib triangular sail forward of foremast, fastened to foredeck
jigger small hoisting tackle; small, aftmost sail of yawl
kedge light anchor used for getting off shoal
keel longitudinal structural member along center of ship's bottom, running from stem to stern
keelson beam or plates fastened longitudinally inside hull along keel to add structural strength
lanyard line for fastening shrouds and stays or raising flags; cord around sailor's neck with knife hung on it
lateen triangular, fore-and-aft rigged sail on long yard suspended obliquely from short mast
lee side of ship facing away from wind
mainmast principal mast of sailing vessel
mainsail primary sail rigged on mast
mainstay line extending forward from and stabilizing mainmast
marlinespike iron tool that tapers to point, used to separate strands of rope
mast long pole or spar rising from deck to support yards, booms, and rigging
masthead top part of mast
midship (*adj*) in or at middle of vessel
mine explosive charge in container placed in sea
mizzenmast mast nearest stern, esp. third mast from bow in ship with three or more masts
moonraker light, square sail rigged high on clipper ship mast in light winds
orlop deck lowest deck of ship with four or more decks
outboard (*adv*) in lateral direction from hull
outboard motor engine hung off stern of small, open boat
outrigger support, brace, or float extending from side of boat
paddle wheel wheel with paddles set at right angles about its circumference, used to propel steamboat
pelorus compasslike navigational instrument with two sighting vanes instead of magnetic needle
pennant small, triangular signal flag
periscope upright tube fitted with prisms and mirrors, extended upward from submarine for observation above sea level
pole long slender piece of wood used to hand-propel raft, small boat, or gondola
poop raised deck at stern, usu. roofed
port left side of vessel when facing bow
porthole round window in ship's hull
propeller slanted blades turning on shaft extending from hull, used to propel ship
prow bow above the waterline
quarterdeck ceremonial open space on after deck
rigging cables, chains, lines, blocks, and tackle
rudder pivoting vertical blade at vessel's stern, used for steering
sail large canvas or synthetic fiber sheet hung from mast to catch wind and propel ship forward: flying jib, foresail, gaff, gennaker, headsail, jib, lateen, mainsail, mizzen, moonraker, reefed sail, royal sail, skysail, spinnaker, square sail, staysail, studding sail, topsail
scull long oar mounted at stern and worked from side to side; one of a pair of light oars used on each side of boat
scupper drainage opening at deck level through ship's side
seabag sailor's large cylindrical bag for personal items
sextant optical instrument used to measure angular distances at sea to determine latitude
sheer upward curve of deck toward bow and stern
shrouds heavy lines bracing mast athwartships; stays
sick bay ship's infirmary
skeg after part of keel to which rudder is secured
skin outer surface of hull
spanker fore-and-aft sail on aftermost lower mast of ship with three or more masts
spar mast, gaff, or boom that supports sails
spinnaker baggy, triangular headsail on yacht, used to run before wind
sprit pole or spar reaching diagonally from mast to topmost corner of fore-and-aft sail to extend it

square-rigged (*adj*) having square sails as principal sails
square sail four-sided sail rigged on yard set athwart keel and horizontal to mast
staff post that supports flag or banner at stern or bow
stanchion upright bar or post that supports life line
starboard right side of vessel when facing bow
stateroom private cabin
stay heavy line or cable bracing mast
staysail fore-and-aft sail rigged on stay
stem front or bow of vessel, esp. upright piece at prow to which side timbers are attached
stern back or rear of vessel
stringer longitudinal plank or plate for strengthening deck
strut outboard support piece between stern and propeller
tackle blocks and rope lines used in rigging
taffrail upper, flat part of ship's stern with panels; rail around ship's stern
thole pin set vertically in gunwale as fulcrum for oar
tiller handle for turning rudder
topgallant mast mast fixed to head of topmast on square-rigged vessel
topgallant sail sail set on yard of topgallant mast
topmast mast usu. formed as a separate spar above lower mast and used to support yards or rigging of topsails
topsail sail next above lowermost sail on mast of square-rigger
topsides deck and outer surface of hull above water
transom transverse part of squared stern
truss iron band around mast with gooseneck for securing yard
turret armored revolving platform for heavy guns on naval vessel
water line one of several lines painted on side of hull that indicates submergence due to load
wheel helm
winch deck engine with drum for hoisting heavy objects
windlass crank-driven spindle for hoisting lines or hauling
yard long, slender rod fastened horizontally across mast to support sail
yardarm either half of yard supporting square sail

Nautical Occupations

able-bodied seaman able seaman
able seaman experienced seaman qualified to perform routine duties, rating below boatswain's mate; able-bodied seaman
admiral top-ranking naval officer
boatswain foreman; warrant officer in charge of deck crew's work; bo's'n
bo's'n boatswain
bowman deck hand on yacht who sets spinnaker and works at bow
buccaneer pirate
cabin boy boy who serves officers and passengers on ship
captain officer who is master or commander of ship; skipper
CB construction battalion crewman in navy; Seabee
chief petty officer CPO; highest ranking naval enlisted man
commander captain of vessel
commodore naval captain commanding two or more vessels
coxswain naval petty officer in charge of steering small boat; person who steers racing shell and calls rhythm to rowers
CPO chief petty officer
crew personnel working on ship, usu. excluding officers
deck hand ship's lowest-ranking worker
dockhand longshoreman
ensign lowest-ranking naval commissioned officer
first mate ranking crew member below captain
gondolier operator of gondola
gunner naval warrant officer specializing in guns and torpedoes
helmsman person who holds helm and steers ship; pilot
longshoreman laborer who loads cargo from docks; dockhand; stevedore
marine member of military unit associated with navy, esp. Marine Corps
mariner person involved in navigation of ship; seaman or sailor
mate deck officer on merchant ship ranking below captain
merchant seaman crewman of merchant ship
middy *Informal* midshipman
midshipman naval recruit, esp. student at Naval Academy
navigator person responsible for guiding ship's course
oarsman crew member who works oars to propel vessel
pilot harbor officer who boards and steers ship's entry into harbor; person who steers a ship into port; helmsman
pirate person who commits robbery on high seas; buccaneer; rapparee
privateer crewman, esp, commander, of armed private ship or pirate ship cruising against commercial ships or warships of enemy
purser agent handling passengers' money and valuables
quartermaster steersman or signal and weather expert
sailor seaman; member of ship's crew; member of navy
Seabee CB; young sailor
sea dog seasoned sailor, mariner
seaman person who sails the seas; mariner
ship chandler person dealing in ship's supplies
shipfitter welder who fits together structural parts of ships
shipmaster commander of vessel other than warship

shipmate fellow member of ship's crew
shipwright carpenter skilled at shipbuilding and repair
skipper *Informal.* captain
stevedore longshoreman
steward waiter, porter, or kitchen help in crew
warrant officer noncommissioned naval officer, usu. specialist such as electrician, pay clerk, machinist, or gunner
watch person responsible for observation duty on ship
yachtsman yacht owner; recreational sailor on yacht
yeoman naval petty officer with duties of clerk

Seamanship and Port

aboard (*adv*) on board a vessel
aground (*adv*) snagged on shore or bottom of waterway
ahoy (*interj*) call of attention; hello
all hands entire ship's personnel
amphibious (*adj*) used on both land and sea
armada fleet of warships
avast (*vb*) command to stop, cease, or give attention
aweigh (*adj*) designating anchor coming up
backwater reverse rowing stroke employed to halt vessel or propel it in reverse
barnacles hard-shelled sea growth on pier or ship bottom
bear down (*vb*) approach from windward
bearing navigational term indicating direction of one point with reference to another
bear off (*vb*) prevent vessel from touching or rubbing against dock or another vessel
belay (*vb*) fasten or secure with lines; stop
bells indication of time on ship
berth mooring place or slip in docks
bitter end inboard end of ship's line
bollard post on pier, used to secure hawsers
breakwater offshore barrier that protects shore or docks from waves
buoy floating marker anchored to bottom, used to indicate channel or underwater object
cabin class accommodations better than tourist class, inferior to first class
cant (*vb*) pitch to one side
capsize (*vb*) overturn at sea
cat's-paw hitch in middle of rope, forming two eyes to hold hook
chart navigational map
circumnavigate (*vb*) sail around, esp. the Earth
clear the decks send all idle crew belowdecks
clove hitch knot for fastening rope to spar or large rope
colors flag or flags
come to (*vb*) bring ship's prow nearer the wind; stop moving, drop anchor
conn (*vb*) direct ship's steering
convoy merchant vessels under protection of warships
course direction taken, stated in degrees from north
crank (*adj*) unstable, liable to capsize
current horizontal flow of water
dead ahead located directly before bow
dead reckoning calculation of position from course and distance sailed
displacement weight of water displaced by ship
dock long, often wood structure, extending into water, to which ships are moored; pier
dockyard storage and repair facility for ships
downwind (*adv*) in same direction as wind
draft depth to which ship is submerged, measured from keel
draw (*vb*) require specific depth of water to float
dry dock artificial, drainable basin in which ships are repaired
even keel condition of floating properly upright in water
fag end frayed or untwisted end of line
fast (*adj*) secured, tied, fastened, or arranged, esp. of lines
fathom unit of nautical measurement equal to six feet (1.8 m)
fleet large group of ships of various sorts
flotsam floating wreckage
following sea waves running in same direction as course
founder (*vb*) take on water to point of capsizing and sinking; struggle in storm, going nowhere
free port port where goods may be unloaded, stored, and reshipped without paying customs or duty
furl (*vb*) roll up or take in sails
gale strong wind of 30-55 knots (32-63 mph)
harbor protected body of water deep enough for anchoring, usu. with docks constructed along shore; port
hawser bend knot joining ends of two lines
heading compass direction of vessel
heave (*vb*) throw; (*n*) vertical oscillation of vessel
heel (*vb*) list to one side
high seas open ocean outside national territorial waters; international waters; open sea
hitch knot used to secure line to spar
hoist (*vb*) pull on line or halyard to raise something
horse latitudes area on each side of equator where westerlies change to trade winds and reverse direction
international waters high seas
jetsam cargo and equipment, cast overboard to lighten load in storm, that sinks or is washed ashore
jettison (*vb*) abandon or discard cargo overboard
knot unit of speed equal to 6076 feet (1851 m) per hour or one nautical mph
landfall sighting of land
landlubber land-bound person not familiar with sea
latitude distance measured in degrees north or south of equator
leeward (*adj*) at side of vessel away from wind
lie to (*vb*) remain stationary with bow to wind
list (*vb*) tip to one side in water

lock section of canal filled with water to carry vessels through
log record of all events during voyage
longitude distance measured in degrees east or west of Greenwich, England
lubber's knot faulty square knot
luff (*vb*) turn bow toward wind; sail close or closer to wind, causing sails to flap
make sail (*vb*) raise or set sails or additional sail; set out on voyage
manifest itemized list of ship's cargo, esp. for customs
Mayday international radiotelephone distress signal
merchant marine personnel and ships of one nation used in commerce
mole breakwater or stone barrier in harbor
moor (*vb*) attach lines or cables, usu. to dock, to hold vessel in place
mooring place where vessel is secured by lines or cables, esp. dock or slip; such securing lines or cables
mothball (*adj*) designating vessel not in current use or held in reserve, often older vessel
nautical (*adj*) of or pertaining to ships, sailors, or navigation
nautical mile international unit of measurement for sea navigation equal to 6076 feet (1851 m) or 1.15 statute miles (1.85 km)
navigable (*adj*) passable to vessels
navigation plan and direct course of ship at sea
open sea high seas
overboard (*adv*) over ship's side and into the water
pay out (*vb*) let out line
pile upright post driven into bottom that shows above water
pitch rocking, fore and aft motion at sea
plot (*vb*) plan course on map or chart
port harbor
put about (*vb*) reverse direction
put out to sea begin voyage; join ship's crew
quay stone dock, often parallel to roadway along edge of water
reach tack in which wind crosses side of boat
reefed sail sail partly lowered and secured
registry certificate showing nationality of merchant ship
ride at anchor float in position with anchor dropped
rolling hitch hitch on spar that tightens under stress parallel to spar
run tack in which wind crosses stern of boat
run aground (*vb*) encounter waters too shallow for depth of keel
sail (*vb*) travel by water, esp. on vessel propelled by wind in sails
sea legs ability to walk on board ship, esp. in rough seas
seamanship skill in sailing, navigation, and handling ships
seaworthy (*adj*) fit to travel on the open sea
seizing means of binding together two objects or lengths of rope by number of longitudinal and transverse turns of thin line or wire
set manner and position in which sails are rigged
set sail begin voyage, depart from mooring
shakedown initial test cruise for ship
shipboard (*adj*) aboard ship
ship's papers legally required papers carried on board, showing ship's registration and nature of cargo; registry
shipyard facility in which ships are built and repaired
slip mooring place or berth in dockyard
SOS save our ship; Morse code distress signal
soundings depth measurements
squall sudden, intense, localized storm at sea
steamer rug heavy woolen blanket used to cover lap and legs of passenger in deck chair
steerage space below forward deck, allotted to passengers paying lower fare
stem-to-stern (*adv*) from front to back of vessel
stowaway person concealed on board to secure free passage
strike (*vb*) shorten or take down sails
swab (*vb*) mop the deck
sway horizontal oscillation of ship's hull; (*vb*) heave object aloft
swell long, heavy undulation in sea's surface caused by distant disturbance
tack (*vb*) make course back and forth through wind by reversing after corner of sail; (*n*) direction of movement in relation to position of sails
take bearings determine one's position at sea relative to other objects
take in sail lower or remove sail from mast or yard
tender (*adj*) riding too high in water, therefore unstable; tending to heel excessively under sail
territorial waters area within three-mile (4.8-km) limit over which nation has jurisdiction
three-mile limit extent of territorial jurisdiction of any nation outward from its coastline
tides rise and fall of ocean level due to gravitational force of sun and moon
trade winds easterly winds prevailing at low latitudes and blowing toward equator
trim way in which boat floats in water; (*vb*) rig and put sails in order for sailing
turn turtle capsize
upwind (*adj*) sailing toward direction of wind; (*adv*) to windward
wake water disturbance pluming up behind moving vessel
watch observation of surrounding sea for storms, danger, or enemies, esp. four-hour period of such duty
water line line to which surface of water comes on hull
weigh (*vb*) hoist anchor
westerlies prevalent westerly winds of Temperate Zone
wigwag act of signaling by movement of two flags waved according to code
windward (*adj*) at side of vessel facing wind
yachting sport or recreation of sailing yachts
yaw (*vb*) deviate back and forth from course

OTHER VEHICLES

Trolleys
Carriages
Wagons, Carts, and Sleds
Cycles
Litters

Trolleys

autobus omnibus
cable car trolley operated by underground or overhead cable loop
el elevated trolley or railway
elevated railway urban passenger trolley suspended from overhead rail
funicular overhead cable railway up hill or mountain
monorail trolley suspended from or balanced on single rail
omnibus public carrier for at least twelve passengers, usu. with door in rear
streetcar vehicle usu. on rails, esp. for city passengers
subway underground trolley or municipal railway, usu. electric
tram streetcar on overhead rail or cable
trolley wheeled carriage, usu. with overhead cable, often electric
trolley bus trackless electric bus with overhead cable
trolley car trackless electric streetcar with overhead cable

Carriages

barouche four-wheel carriage with facing double seats and folding top
brougham low, closed, four-wheel carriage for two passengers with driver's seat outside
buckboard four-wheel carriage with seat mounted on springlike board
buggy light, four-wheel, one-horse, two-passenger carriage
cab orig. cabriolet; light closed carriage for hire
cabriolet light, two-wheel, one-horse carriage with folding hood
carriage any horse-drawn vehicle, esp. for private use
chaise small, usu. two-wheel carriage suspended on leather straps
chariot ancient, two-wheel, seatless, horse-drawn battle car
chuckwagon large, closed supply wagon (U.S. West, 19th c.)
coach large, four-wheel, enclosed carriage with driver's seat outside
Conestoga broad-wheeled covered wagon drawn by six horses
covered wagon large, canvas-topped, four-wheel vehicle for moving families west (U.S., 19th c.)
dray low, sturdy cargo cart with detachable sides
droshky low, open, four-wheel carriage with narrow bench (Russia)
fiacre small, four-wheel hackney coach
four-in-hand carriage drawn by four horses
gig light, two-wheel, one-horse carriage
hack hackney
hackney four-wheel, two-horse, six-seat carriage kept for hire; hack
hansom two-wheel, two-horse, two-passenger, covered carriage with driver's seat elevated at rear; hansom cab
hansom cab hansom
landau large, four-wheel carriage with top that folds into two parts (Germany)
phaeton light, four-wheel carriage with seats front and rear, folding cover, and no coachman's seat
prairie schooner broad-wheeled covered wagon used in cross-country travel (U.S. West)
rig general term for carriage and horse
stagecoach public passenger and mail coach that ran on regular schedule (U.S. West, 19th c.)
stanhope light, open, one-seat, two-wheel carriage
sulky light, one-passenger, two-wheel carriage used in trotting races
surrey modest, four-wheel, two-seat carriage used for pleasure or to carry family, with or without top
troika sleigh or carriage drawn by three horses abreast (Russia)
victoria large, luxurious, four-wheel, two-horse carriage

Wagons, Carts, and Sleds

barrow two-wheel cart with shallow body and shaft handles
bobsled large, metal racing sled on runners
caisson two-wheel wagon used to carry artillery ammunition
camion strongly built cart or wagon for transporting heavy loads; dray
cariole light covered cart; dog-drawn toboggan
cart heavy, horse-drawn, two-wheel vehicle used to carry freight
dogsled small sled hauled by dogs
dolly platform on rollers for moving heavy loads
dray strong, low, sideless cart for hauling goods; camion
go-cart lightweight handcart; small framework on wheels for children
gurney flat, wheeled cot for transporting disabled or injured person
handcart hand truck
hand truck small, hand-propelled, two-wheel carrier; handcart
jinrikisha small, two-wheel passenger cab drawn by one or two persons (Japan, China)
luge small racing sled driven in supine position down chute
ricksha jinrikisha
skid low platform on wheels for moving heavy objects
sled vehicle made of flat body on runners for use over snow and ice
sledge any of various carts on runners for carry-

ing goods over ice, often drawn by draft animals
sleigh large passenger sled on runners, usu. open and horse-drawn, for use over snow and ice
stroller seat on wheels for baby
toboggan long, flat-bottomed sled with one end curved up and handrails
trundle low hauling cart on wheels
tumbrel farm tipcart, used to carry prisoners to execution (France, 18th c.)
wagon any of various four-wheel vehicles, motorized, animal-drawn, or human-propelled, ranging in use from child's toy to transportation of bulky goods
wheelbarrow single-wheel cart with shallow body, held and pushed by handles, used to transport small loads

Cycles

ATV all terrain vehicle; sturdy three-wheel motorcycle for cross-country driving
bicycle two-wheel cycle operated by foot pedals; bike
bicycle-built-for-two two-wheel, two-seat, pedal-driven cycle; tandem
cycle open, pedaled or engine-powered, single-passenger vehicle, usu. having two wheels in tandem
dirt bike small, motor-driven cycle with extra-heavy tires
minibike small motorcycle with raised handlebars
monocycle unicycle
moped pedal-started motor scooter with small engine
motorbike low-power, lightweight motorcycle
motorcycle two-wheel, motor-driven cycle; chopper
motor scooter small, lightweight motorcycle; bicycle propelled by attached motor
mountain bike rugged, fat-wheeled bicycle with deep tread for traction and stability on dirt trails
ordinary early bicycle with a very large front wheel and a very small rear wheel
pedicab tricycle with separate two-seat passenger compartment; trishaw
penny-farthing *Chiefly Brit.* bicycle with large front wheel and small rear wheel
scooter small motorbike; child's two-wheel, self-propelled vehicle with long, narrow footboard
skateboard short board with pair of wheels at each end, powered by free foot while standing on board
tandem bicycle-built-for-two
ten-speed powerful, lightweight bicycle with ten gears
trail bike small motorcycle designed for use on unpaved roads
tricycle small, three-wheel, pedal-driven bicycle, esp. for young children
trishaw pedicab
unicycle one-wheel bicycle with very tall seat, often used in circus; monocycle
velocipede early, lightweight wheeled vehicle, self-propelled by rider

Litters

brancard stretcher
handbarrow light, flat, rectangular frame with handles at both ends
howdah covered seat carried by elephant or camel (India)
jampan sedan chair borne on two poles (India)
jinrikisha two-wheel passenger cab with fold-down top, pulled by one or two persons (Japan, China); ricksha
litter covered, often curtained couch on long shafts or poles, borne by animals or people
palanquin enclosed litter (Asia)
ricksha jinrikisha
sedan chair portable, covered, single chair borne on poles
stokes litter wire basket for transporting ill or injured person
stretcher flat, open litter for carrying ill or injured person; brancard
travois platform or net on two trailing poles drawn by animal (American Indian)

Chapter Seven
The Home

BUILDINGS

Living Places
Types of Buildings

Living Places

abode place where one lives
accommodations lodgings, sometimes including food
apartment single unit within multiunit residential building, rented by person who usu. occupies the space
camp group of tents or cabins used as temporary shelter
caravan wagon or vehicle equipped with living quarters
cave underground chamber opening at earth's surface, used as dwelling by prehistoric man
cliff dwelling cavelike dwelling built into rock face of cliff
condominium single unit within multiple-unit structure, owned by its individual deed holder, usu. its occupant
co-op unit within multiunit structure jointly owned by residents of all units
den shabby dwelling or cave, esp. used as hiding place
dive *Informal.* disreputable establishment, esp. commercial
domicile customary, fixed, permanent dwelling; legal residence
dwelling abode, living place
edifice usu. large, elaborate building
estate privately owned land with substantial residence on it
hacienda primary dwelling on large ranch or estate (Spain, Latin America)
haunt place regularly visited or inhabited
homestead land and buildings in which a family dwells
lair hidden lodging place
lodging place for dwelling, often temporary
nest safe, often secluded living place
quarters lodging, dwelling place
ranch rural house and surrounding land used for raising stock animals
rancho ranch, hut for ranch workers (Spain, Latin America)
residence place in which one regularly lives
retreat hidden or secluded dwelling
roost place for resting or lodging, often temporarily
squat public or unoccupied dwelling used without permission
unit portion of structure partitioned for occupation by single person or group of persons

Types of Buildings

A-frame building constructed of a three-piece frame shaped like capital A
amphitheater roofless oval or circle with rising tiers of seats
apartment building with several separate dwelling units
arena large, open or enclosed building for contests, entertainments
auditorium large room or hall for public gathering
barn large, open building for storing farm equipment, housing animals
barracks set of buildings, often resembling sheds or barns, housing soldiers in garrison
basilica oblong building with broad nave flanked by colonnaded aisles, ending in semicircular apse
bathhouse structure containing baths, often also pools, steam rooms, and whirlpools; structure housing changing rooms for bathers, as at beach
boardinghouse home converted to rooms for rent, with food sometimes included for tenants
booth small enclosure isolating occupant
bungalow one-story residence with low, sweeping lines, often with veranda
cabana tentlike structure with projecting canopy
cabin small, simple, one-story, low-roofed dwelling
campanile tall, freestanding bell tower
caravansary hotel or inn, orig. where caravans rested
castle large, fortified building or group of buildings, usu. stone, housing ruler or nobleman
chalet dwelling with unconcealed structural members emphasized by decorative carvings
chateau large country house, esp. in French wine regions
church Christian house of worship, often with spire, finial cross
condominium multiple-unit residence jointly owned by deed holders, who are usu. its occupants
conservatory glass-roofed house for plants
coop roofed cage or small enclosure for poultry
cottage small, detached dwelling, often rural
crib small, narrow dwelling; framework stall
dormitory large residence hall with many bedrooms
duplex single residence divided into two units
flat apartment built on one floor of building
garage small, enclosed building for storing cars and equipment
gazebo freestanding, roofed summerhouse open on sides
greenhouse glassed enclosure for growing plants
hangar high-roofed, enclosed shed for repairing and storing aircraft
high-rise multistory apartment house or office building
hippodrome oval arena for equestrian events
hogan rough log and mud dwelling (Navajo)
hostel housing maintained by institution for specific group
hotel building of many rooms licensed to provide lodging
hovel small, miserable shed or open-roofed structure
hut small, rudimentary structure for temporary habitation
hutch animal pen or coop; shack, shanty
igloo dome-shaped dwelling of ice blocks (Eskimo)

inn public house for lodging, usu. in countryside
kiosk small structure with one or more open sides; open summerhouse or pavilion
lean-to rough shed, its roof having one slope
lighthouse tower with powerful light as signal of coastline to ships
lodge inn or resort hotel; house set aside from main house for hunting or other special use
loft upper floor of warehouse building converted to living area
log cabin rustic dwelling built of logs laid horizontally
long house long wooden communal dwelling (Iroquois)
maisonette *French.* small house or apartment
mall very large building housing stores, with adjacent parking lots
manor large hall on estate property
manse large, elegant residence
mansion grand, elaborate dwelling
market public building for wholesale trade
mobile home movable trailer with living facilities
mosque Islamic place of worship with rounded spires and minaret
motel hotel for automobile travelers, usu. long and low
outbuilding small structure, such as stable or woodshed, separate from main residence
outhouse small enclosed toilet set apart from main house, usu. without plumbing
pagoda structure resembling tower of several stories with projecting, concavely curved roofs (Asia)
palace large, stately house, usu. ruler's official residence
palazzo palace or large residence (Italy)
pavilion large, often sumptuous tent or canopy
pen small, open enclosure for animals
penthouse dwelling unit built on roof of building
pied-à-terre temporary or second lodging; townhouse
prefab structure built of interchangeable, prefabricated parts
pueblo communal dwelling, esp. contiguous flat-roofed adobe houses several stories high or arranged in terraces (Southwest American Indian)
pyramid massive stone structure, having square base with four triangular walls that meet in point at top (ancient Egypt)
Quonset hut prefabricated structure with semicircular arched corrugated steel roof on bolted steel truss foundation
ranch house low, sprawling, one-story suburban residence
resort complex of structures for recreational use
roadhouse inn or hotel, usu. beyond city limits
rotunda round, domed building
saltbox frame dwelling, two stories in front, one in rear, with double-sloping roof extending farther in back
semidetached (*adj*) designating pair of residences joined by common wall
shack small, roughly built, crudely furnished house
shanty small, crudely built, shabby dwelling, usu. of wood
shed small structure, usu. for storage
skyscraper very tall urban office or apartment building
split-level residence with rooms built on floor levels differing by about half a story
stable shelter for horses or stock animals
stadium very large, unroofed structure with tiered seats, used for sporting events
stall small booth or stand for retail sales, open at one side
synagogue Jewish house of worship
tabernacle usu. large meeting house or assembly hall, used esp. as place of worship
tavern building used as bar or saloon
temple edifice for non-Christian religious observance
tenement multiunit apartment building, usu. a cheap dwelling for urban poor
tent small shelter of canvas supported or suspended on poles
tepee conical tent of skin drawn on poles, used as dwelling (American Plains Indian)
terminal central transport station serving multiple lines
theater edifice that is site of various kinds of performances on stage
town house often luxurious house in the city, esp. distinguished from house in country owned by same person; one of group of two- or three-story houses of uniform design joined by common sidewalls
tract home one of many identical, prefab residences in suburban cluster
triplex single residence divided into three units
trailer movable structure with living facilities
villa large country estate; *Chiefly Brit.* small suburban house
warehouse large storage or manufacturing structure, often windowless
wickiup elliptical hut used as residence by nomads (American Indian)
wigwam domed structure of poles overlaid with bark, used as residence (Great Lakes American Indian)
woodshed crude shed for storing wood
yurt circular, domed tent of skin on collapsible lattice frame, used by Mongol nomads (Mongolia, Siberia)
ziggurat temple pyramid built in successive stepped-back stages with shrine at top (ancient Mesopotamia)

EXTERIOR STRUCTURE

Windows, Walls, and Facades
Roofs and Towers
Entryways and Lateral Extensions
Ornamental and Structural Parts
Outbuildings, Gardens, and Fences

Windows, Walls, and Facades

bailey outer wall or space between two outer walls of castle
bay window large window set in bay or recess in room and projecting from outside wall, often three-sided
bow window rounded bay window; compass window
bulkhead retaining wall
casement hinged window frame with two windows opening outward from middle
Catherine wheel window small, round window with spokes extending outward from its center
clapboard narrow board, thicker at one side, used in covering outside of house, usu. painted white
clerestory outside wall carried above adjoining roof, pierced with windows
compass window bow window
cornerstone first stone laid where walls meet
curtain wall nonbearing exterior wall in framed building
dormer vertical window set in projection beneath sloping roof; entire projecting structure with such a window
double-hung window window with top and bottom sashes that move vertically
embrasure opening in wall for door or window, sloped or beveled to enlarge interior outline
facade outer surface of building, esp. front wall; face
face facade
fanlight semicircular window with radiating bars like ribs of fan, often above door or rectangular window
French window pair of casement windows reaching to floor and opening in middle
front building facade facing street
frontispiece highly ornamental, principle feature of a facade
grille grating forming barrier or screen over opening
horizontal sliding window window that opens sideways on tracks
Judas hole small window with sliding panel set in door, used as peephole
lancet window high, narrow, sharply pointed window set in lancet arch
louver opening in wall with overlapping slats that allow ventilation, prevent entry of rain, and provide privacy
mullioned window window with multiple panes divided by slender vertical strips
oriel large projecting bay window supported by corbel or bracket
Palladian window central arched window with two small flanking compartments, usu. mullioned
perpend wall wall built of bricks or large stones passing through entire thickness of wall and acting as binders
picture window large, undivided window usu. opening onto scenic view
porthole small, round window, esp. on ship
quarrel small, quadrangular or diamond-shaped glass set diagonally in latticed window
retaining wall wall that resists lateral pressure, esp. from earth
revetment stone or concrete facing used to protect embankment
scarp vertical side of ditch below parapet of fortification
siding weatherproof boards or facings that form outer wall or facade
skylight opening in roof and ceiling covered with transparent material, usu. overhead window of glass
storm window protective window set in jamb outside permanent window in winter to conserve heat
transom window above door or other window, usu. hinged to horizontal crosspiece; such a crosspiece separating windows or door and window
Trombe wall glass-fronted, exterior masonry wall that absorbs solar heat for radiation into building
wall continuous upright surface connecting floor and ceiling or foundation and roof, subdividing interior space, or supporting other parts of structure
window opening in wall for admission of air and light, set with frame holding transparent substance, usu. glass

Roofs and Towers

barbican fortified tower at gate or bridge
barrack roof movable roof sliding on four posts, used to cover hay or straw brick
bartizan small, overhanging turret on wall or tower, esp. of castle
bastion projecting part of fortification
battlement parapet atop wall with alternating open spaces and merlons, used for defense or decoration
belfry tower, cupola, or turret in which bell is housed
buttress projecting support structure providing stability for wall or building
campanile tall, straight, freestanding bell tower
castellated (*adj*) designating upward projection with battlements, like a castle
chimney vertical structure usu. of brick or stone, with flue for carrying off smoke from fireplace
crenel opening in battlement between projecting merlons
crenelation series of open spaces and notches atop battlement
cupola small dome on roof; rounded roof or ceiling

dome hemispherical roof, usu. large
donjon massive central tower or stronghold in castle
dormer gabled extension off attic room, with sloping roof and vertical window
eave edge of roof projecting beyond side of building
gable extending, ridged roof section of triangular wall enclosed by sloping sides, usu. with window
gambrel roof roof having two slopes on each side, with lower slope steeper than upper
geodesic dome domed roof made of light, straight, structural elements forming polygons in tension
gutter metal drainage trough under roof eaves
helm roof four-faced, steeply pitched roof, rising to point from base of four gables
hipped roof roof with sloping ends and sloping sides
lean-to roof having one slope, often projecting from wall
louver roof turret with slatted aperture for vent; slanted fins opening off attic to exclude rain and sun and admit light and air
mansard roof having two slopes on each of four sides, with lower slope steeper than upper
merlon solid interval between battlement crenels
minaret tall, slender mosque tower with projecting balconies from which Moslems are called to prayer
obelisk tapering, four-sided monolithic tower with pyramid at top
pagoda tower with projecting, encircling roofs at each of several levels (Asia)
pitched roof roof with sloping sides
pyramid roof four triangular slopes rising to point from square base
rainspout pipe or duct that drains roof gutter
roof top covering of building
sawtooth roof two or more parallel roofs like teeth of a saw, with one slope steeper than the other
spire tower or steeple tapering to point
steeple pointed tower, esp. atop church
stupa domed-shaped tower, esp. on Buddhist shrine
thatched roof roof made of thick layer of interwoven straw or reeds
tower tall, standing structure attached to larger structure or freestanding
turret short, projecting tower, usu. at corner of building
widow's walk railed lookout platform or walkway on roof
ziggurat pyramidal temple tower in successive stories with winding outside staircase and shrine at top (ancient Mesopotamia)

Entryways and Lateral Extensions

ambulatory sheltered place for walking in cloister
archway entry or passageway beneath series of arches
areaway sunken space leading to cellar or basement entrance or window
atrium open court leading into building, often with a glassed side and roof
balcony railed platform attached to upper story of building
bay three-sided projection from side of building
belvedere open, roofed, upstairs gallery, esp. overlooking pleasant scene
breezeway roofed passage between two buildings or sections of one building
bulkhead inclined door over stairway leading to cellar or shaft
cloister covered walkway along wall of monastery, usu. opening through columns onto inner court
doorway entryway to building in which door is set
drawbridge bridge which may be raised or lowered to prevent or allow passage
entryway passage for or point of entry
extension added portion of building attached to main structure
fire escape structure of metal platforms and ladders or stairways down outer wall of structure, used for escape in case of fire
French doors adjoining doors that open in middle, with rectangular glass panes
frontispiece highly ornamented portico or principle entryway
gallery outdoor balcony; roofed promenade or colonnade
gate swinging, grated doorway in fence or exterior wall, usu. opening onto drive or grounds
gateway entrance that may be closed by gate
hatch small door or opening, esp. in airplane or ship; opening in ship's deck or in floor or roof of building
lanai porch, veranda (Hawaii)
passageway opening or hallway allowing entry to room
porch covered approach or appendage to building
portal doorway or opening, esp. elaborate or imposing one
portcullis grating of iron bars or timbers suspended over gateway, lowered to prevent passage
porte-cochere arched entryway for carriages, leading from street to inner courtyard
portico roof supported by columns and attached to building as porch
revolving door two or more doors turning on common axis within cylindrical vestibule
scaffolding elevated platform, esp. movable one for workers
skywalk enclosed elevated walkway connecting two buildings
storm door additional protective door placed outside regular door
torii post and lintel gateway of Shinto temple (Japan)
trapdoor lifting or sliding door flush with surface of roof, ceiling, or floor
turnstile four revolving arms pivoted atop post to permit single-file passage of people, usu. in one direction only
veranda large balcony or open porch along side of building, often roofed and railed
walkway open or covered passageway from area to area within or between structures

wing section or room projecting from main structure

Ornamental and Structural Parts

arch curved masonry support structure spanning an opening: basket-handle, flat, horseshoe, lancet, ogee, parabolic, round, shouldered, trefoil, Tudor
capital upper end of column atop shaft, bearing weight of entablature
caryatid sculptured, robed female figure used as column (ancient Greece)
cheval-de-frises row of projecting spikes atop wall for defense
colonnade series of columns at regular intervals
column tall, round support member on pedestal in one of three basic types: Corinthian, Doric, or Ionic; other styles include Byzantine, Gothic, Moorish, Romanesque, and Tuscan
corbel bracketlike member that supports weight, esp. one projecting upward and outward from wall surface
Corinthian column column of late classical period characterized by high base, slender fluted shaft with fillets, and ornate capital with acanthus leaves
cornerstone quoin
cornice prominent, projecting horizontal member surmounting a wall or dividing it horizontally
courtyard interior walled area surrounded by building
crawlspace shallow, unfinished area beneath first floor or under roof, usu. for plumbing and wiring
Doric column undecorated column of early classical period characterized by short fluted shaft and convex circular molding as capital, with no distinct base
engaged column column attached to wall, not freestanding
finial ornament atop spire or gable
gargoyle elaborately carved creature, often functioning as a waterspout, projecting from a building
gingerbread showy, elaborate trim on house
Ionic column column of middle classical period characterized by slender fluted shaft with molded base and volute or spiral capital
jamb upright structural member at side of door or window
lintel horizontal member carrying weight above opening or doorway
miter covering on top of chimney to keep rain out
mudsill lowest lip of structure, often embedded in mud
parapet low wall or railing on balcony, bridge, or roof to prevent falls and provide cover from below
pediment low, triangular gable with horizontal cornice set above colonnade or section of facade
peristyle row of columns around outside of temple (ancient Greece)
pier vertical, structural support
pilaster upright, rectangular pier projecting less than half its width from wall
pillar firm, upright support column or shaft
pylon massive structure flanking entry or towers by gate; tower or support post for bridge
quoin one of several large stones forming corner of masonry wall; cornerstone
sash frame in door or window in which panes of glass are set
shaft column, esp. main cylindrical central portion of column
stilt pile or post supporting raised structure
story any entire level or floor of a building
telamon sculptured male figure, similar to female caryatid, used as column or pilaster
trestle support brace with crossbar on two pairs of legs
trough gutter under eaves of building for rain drainage
vane movable device atop spire or tower that indicates wind direction; weather vane

Outbuildings, Gardens, and Fences

apiary collection of beehives; shed where bees are kept
aqueduct elevated structure that supports water pipe or conduit
arbor plot of grass, lawn, or garden; lattice trellis or vine bower for shade
arboretum place where trees, shrubs, and herbs are grown for study or display
artesian well deep-bored well in which water rises under pressure like a fountain
backyard outdoor area at rear of house, often fenced
bed plot of soil where plants are cultivated
belvedere small summerhouse
botanical garden outdoor garden and greenhouses for growth, study, and display of unusual plants
bower arbor or leafy shelter of twined boughs or vines
cabana small cabin or tent opening onto beach or pool
carport open-sided automobile shelter with roof, often extending from main building
cesspool underground cistern or pit for household sewage
chain-link fence fence of thin wire mesh
conservatory glass-enclosed greenhouse for growing or displaying plants
corral pen or enclosure for livestock
court open space surrounded wholly or partly by building
curtilage enclosed area of land occupied by structure, gardens, and outbuildings
espalier trellis or lattice on which shrubs are trained to grow
flagstone large, flat slab of stone for paving garden or walk
fountain mechanical water spout, usu. in decorative, raised structure containing a pool
garage enclosed area for storage of automobiles and other equipment, usu. adjoining main building
garden plot of cultivated, manicured lawns, plants, and flowers
gazebo open or screened pavilion or summerhouse set on lawn
greenhouse glass-enclosed building for growing plants

grotto cavelike summer structure or shrine
grounds land surrounding house, esp. lawns and garden
guesthouse small building separate from main structure, often with bathroom and kitchen, used to accommodate visitors
hedge dense shrubbery forming boundary or enclosure; hedgerow
hothouse artificially heated greenhouse for tropical plants
kennel series of cages or living quarters for dogs
kiosk small pavilion, open on one or more sides, used as newsstand, bandstand, or covered entryway
latrine outdoor pit used as toilet, often enclosed; outhouse
manger open food trough in stable, for horses or cattle
moat wide trench around building or fortified place, usu. filled with water
nursery building in which plants are grown, esp. for transplanting
orchard field of cultivated fruit trees
outhouse latrine
paddock enclosed field for pasturing or exercising animals
palisade stake or paling fence used for defense
parterre ornamental flower beds set among paths
patio usu. paved area adjoining house, used esp. for outdoor dining and recreation
pavilion open tent, building, or shelter adjoining main body of building or separate from it
pergola openwork arch or covering for walkway with plants trained on it; arbor or trellis
picket fence fence of thin, white, vertical boards pointed at tops
privy outhouse, latrine
promenade public walk; gallery or balcony for walking
quad *Informal.* courtyard surrounded by buildings on four sides
rail fence barrier of crossed stakes connected by bars
rock garden ornamental garden laid out among rocks
septic tank sunken container in which solid organic sewage is decomposed by bacteria
snake fence zigzag fence of rails lying across one another at an angle; Virginia fence; worm fence
snow fence barrier on windward side of structure, serving as protection from drifting snow
stable building for housing livestock
stall compartment for domestic animal in barn; small booth or freestanding display stand
stile series of steps for passing over fence or wall
stockyard large holding area for livestock being transported, often to slaughter
swimming pool large water-filled tank for swimming, usu. made of concrete, set above or sunk into ground adjacent to house
tack room stable room for storage of riding gear and display of trophies
tennis court measured area with net for playing tennis, adjacent to house and yard
terrace unroofed, paved area adjacent to building
topiary hedge of trees or shrubs trimmed into ornamental, often fantastic shapes
trellis open structure of thin crossed strips used to support vines or plants
viaduct bridge of several short spans, supported on towers, that carries road or railroad across valley
vineyard field of cultivated grapevines
Virginia fence snake fence
walkway open or covered passageway through garden
weir stake fence or net enclosure in waterway for catching fish
well hole sunk into earth to tap water supply
worm fence snake fence
yard open area adjacent to house, often walled and paved; lawns and unpaved grounds of building

INTERIOR STRUCTURE

Rooms
Parts of Rooms
Doors, Partitions, and Walls
Structural and Decorative Elements
Plumbing, Heating, and the Bathroom

Rooms

antechamber outer room leading to another room, often used as waiting room
atelier artist's studio or workshop
atrium central hall, often with open roof, off which other rooms open (ancient Rome)
attic room immediately below roof; cockloft; garret
auditorium large, open room used for public gatherings
ballroom large, open room for dancing
banquet room large room, esp. in hotel or restaurant, used to serve elaborate meals to numerous persons
basement room wholly or partly beneath ground level; cellar
bathroom room containing bathtub or shower, wash basin, and toilet
bedchamber bedroom
bedroom room containing bed, used for sleeping
boudoir *French.* bedroom
catacomb burial vault beneath ground level
cave cellar; underground storage room, esp. for wine
cavern large underground chamber
cell small, single room for one person, esp. in prison or monastery
cellar storage room beneath ground level; basement; cave
chancellery office of chancellor or secretary to high personage
chapel room for meditation, prayer, or religious services

checkroom place where baggage or clothing is left for safekeeping
closet small, private room
cockloft small garret; attic
conservatory glass-enclosed room for growing and displaying plants or flowers; greenhouse
corridor hall
cubiculum small family burial chamber in catacombs (ancient Rome)
den small room for solitary work; study
drawing room formal reception room; living room; sitting room
dressing room small room adjoining bedroom, with mirror, dressing table, wardrobe; backstage area in theater where actors put on costumes
entertainment center TV room
exhibition hall salon
family room informal living room for leisure activities, often with television; playroom
foyer vestibule
garret room just below roof, esp. with sloping roof; attic; cockloft
greenhouse conservatory
guest room bedroom reserved for use by guests
keep strongest, most secure part of castle
kitchen room where food is prepared, usu. equipped with oven, range, refrigerator, sink, and counters
landing level area at end of flight of stairs
larder small room or closet for food storage
living room room for common social usage, often largest room in house; drawing room; sitting room
lobby corridor or hall serving as passageway or waiting room adjoining larger rooms; hotel or theater foyer
loft attic; room above floor level within larger room
master bedroom large bedroom used by primary adult occupants of house
nursery baby's room
pantry small room for storage, esp. of kitchen supplies; serving room between kitchen and dining room
parlor room for entertaining guests
pavilion detached or semidetached division of building, often for display of objects
playroom family room; children's rumpus room
porch roofed or enclosed projection from main portion of structure, serving as entrance or sunroom
powder room women's rest room, esp. in restaurant or nightclub
refectory dining hall, esp. in monastery or convent
repository storage room
rest room bathroom, esp. in public building
room partitioned section of inside of building, usu. for some specific purpose
rumpus room room for parties, games, or recreation, often in basement
salon elegant apartment or living room; exhibition hall
sitting room drawing room; living room
solarium glass-enclosed sunroom
stoop small porch at entrance of house, often enclosed
storm cellar basement room or excavation secured for protection against windstorms
studio artist's workroom; place in which audio or video recordings are made
study office, library, or room for studying
sunroom solarium
throne room formal audience room containing sovereign's throne
tomb subterranean chamber or vault, esp. for burial of the dead
veranda roofed, screened porch or gallery
vestibule small entrance hall or room; enclosed passageway leading into building; foyer
ward section of prison; hospital room for several patients
wing portion of building that projects from main part
workshop room for performing manual labor or making handicrafts

Parts of Rooms

aisle passage for walking between sections of seating or tall shelves
alcove recessed portion of room, open at one end; niche
altar raised structure for religious rituals
ambry recess in church wall for storage of sacramental vessels
apse recessed, usu. vaulted, semicircular portion of room, esp. at end of choir in church
archway passage beneath arch; arch over passage
balcony railed platform extending from wall of second or higher story
bay angular, recessed section of room projecting outward from exterior wall, often with windows on several walls
bema part of Eastern church containing altar
cabinet case with doors and shelves, sometimes attached to wall
chancel enclosed space around altar of church, designed for use by clergy and officials
china closet closet for storing dining supplies
coffer recessed panel in ceiling or vault
cubbyhole small space open on one side
cubicle small space partitioned off from main room
cupboard attached cabinet with shelves for storing kitchenwares and supplies; *Chiefly Brit.* any small closet
dais platform raised above floor level in hall or large room
dumbwaiter small elevator for conveying food, dishes, etc. from one floor to another
gallery balcony or covered walk along wall at second story
hearth fireplace
ledge narrow flat surface projecting from wall
loft raised section of room with floor, often reached by ladder
loggia roofed or open gallery, esp. facing inner court, often extending several stories
mantel facing of stone, marble, wood, or brick above and around fireplace; shelf above fireplace

mezzanine mid level of room between floor and ceiling, extending partway over ground floor
niche alcove
panel flat, rectangular, distinct section of wall
paneling wall area composed of panels
riser series of long, narrow platforms that are combined like steps for group of spectators or performers
rostrum raised platform, esp. for public speaker
split-level section of room raised above floor level, reached by stairs
stage large platform, usu. at end of room, for performances
staircase structure containing stairs; flight of stairs
stairway one or more flights of stairs with connective landings
stairwell vertical shaft in building containing stairway
wardrobe large closet for clothing

Doors, Partitions, and Walls

baffle screen or partition used to control passage of light or sound
bulkhead upright partition
door swinging or sliding barrier across entryway
double leaves two doors, hinged at sides, opening in middle
Dutch door door divided horizontally so that upper or lower half may be opened independently
folding door door with hinged sections that can be folded back, accordion style; one of pair of sliding doors between rooms
French doors two adjoining doors, hinged at sides, opening in middle, with glass panes throughout all or most of their length
jalousie window shade or door made of adjustable slats to regulate flow of air or light
partition interior dividing wall, sometimes movable and not reaching to ceiling
pier wall between two openings; vertical structural support; section of wall between windows
pocket door usu. one of a pair of communicating doors that slides into and out of recess in wall
screen movable partition used to conceal or protect area of room
sliding door unhinged door, frequently of glass, that slides open and shut, esp. between rooms
standing wall wall providing support to ceiling and floor above
transom small, hinged window directly over door
trapdoor lifting or sliding door covering opening in and flush with ceiling or floor
wall one side of room connecting floor and ceiling

Structural and Decorative Elements

arch curved structural support member spanning an opening: basket-handle, flat, horseshoe, lancet, ogee, parabolic, round, shouldered, trefoil, Tudor
architrave molded, decorated band of wood forming panel or opening for door or window; lowest part of entablature
archivolt ornamental molding around arch
backsplash strip of water-resistant tile or formica above sink or beside bathtub
baluster upright, vase-shaped support for railing
balustrade row of balusters topped by railing
banister handrail or balustrade
baseboard molding covering juncture of wall and adjoining floor
bas relief raised ornamental molding, plasterwork, or sculpted stone on flat wall surface
brace structural element that transmits or supports weight
bracket projecting shelf support, often decorative
canopy rooflike covering of fabric on poles
casement hinged frame opening outward for French doors or double windows
casing enclosing frame around door or window
colonnade series of columns at regular intervals
column vertical supporting pillar; post
console member projecting from wall to form bracket
coving carved molding that connects ceiling and wall
dado lower part of wall separated from upper part by rail, molding, or border
embrasure side of window between frame and outer surface of wall; opening in wall sloped to large interior outline; reveal
frieze richly ornamented band; entablature between architrave and cornice
girder primary horizontal structural member supporting vertical load
handrail railing on staircase or gallery; banister
jamb side post of doorway, window frame, or other opening
lacunar coffered vault, ceiling, or soffit
machicolation opening between corbels or in gallery floor for discharging missiles onto assailants below
molding ornamental strip of wood separating sections of wall or at juncture of wall and ceiling: bird's beak, cavetto, congé, cyma recta, cyma reversa, fillet and fascia, ovolo, plate rail, quarter round, reeding, scotia, torus
mullion slender, vertical dividing bar in window or screen
newel central upright pillar of winding staircase
parapet protective low wall or railing
pargeting ornamental plasterwork on walls or ceiling
parquetry inlaid woodwork in geometric forms of different colors, esp. in floor
pillar firm, upright support or post; ornamental column or shaft
plate rail narrow shelf on upper wall for holding plates and ornaments
rafters angled crossbeams in roof, sometimes exposed
railing barrier, fence, or baluster of rails and supports; handgrip on baluster or gallery
reveal embrasure

scalloping continuous series of circle segments or angular projections forming border
scrolling spiral or convoluted ornamentation, esp. in wood
soffit underside of structural member or part of building, such as overhang of staircase
squinch support at corner of room for superimposed mass such as arch, lintel, or corbel
tracery branching, interlacing ornamental work, esp. stonework in upper part of Gothic window or vault
trave division or bay in ceiling made by traverse beams
valance strip of fabric on frame that covers sides of bed or top of window frame
vault arched, domed, usu. masonry structure forming ceiling
wainscoting lower section of wall or story when distinct from top section, esp. when wood-paneled

Plumbing, Heating, and the Bathroom

basin circular vessel with sloping sides and drain, used to hold water for washing
bathroom room containing bathtub and/or shower, plus wash basin and toilet; sometimes used to denote room with toilet and wash basin only
bidet chairlike fixture for bathing genitals and anus
commode movable washstand with cupboard underneath; box holding chamber pot under open seat
Franklin stove iron fireplace connected to chimney by funnel
furnace enclosed chamber, usu. in basement, where heat is produced to warm building
half bath bathroom with basin and toilet only
head toilet, esp. on ship
lavatory toilet; bathroom
radiator nest of pipes for heating room by steam
sauna hot, dry-air bath in enclosed wooden room, used to induce perspiration
steam room tiled room designed to expose user to steam in order to induce sweating
tank enclosed vessel holding water, esp. for toilet
toilet bathroom fixture with seats over bowl through which water is flushed to dispose of human waste material; bathroom
wash basin sink with running water used in bathing, esp. washing face and hands
water closet WC; toilet
WC water closet
wet bar counter for mixing drinks, with built-in sink and running water
whirlpool soothing bath in which jets agitate very hot water
wood-burning stove enclosed metal unit that burns wood for heat, with vent to dispense smoke out of house

FURNISHINGS

Chairs and Sofas
Beds
Tables and Desks
Cases, Cupboards, and Chests
Stools and Stands
Curtains, Draperies, and Screens
Carpets and Rugs
Lamps and Mirrors
Accessories and Appliances

Chairs and Sofas

Adirondack chair wooden outdoor chair with sloping back and seat declining to rear
armchair chair, often hardback, with sidepieces to support person's forearms or elbows
banquette long, upholstered bench, often built into wall; sofa with one rollover arm
barber chair heavy-duty, adjustable, swiveling chair with headrest and footrest
Barcelona chair armless, leather-covered chair with cushioned seat on X-shaped stainless steel frame
basket chair deep wicker chair with rounded back and adjoining arms
Bath chair hooded, often glassed invalid's wheelchair
bench long, backless seat for several persons
Brewster chair heavy colonial chair with upright spindles in two tiers on the back and below the seat
butterfly chair canvas or leather sling chair, with sling suspended from metal frame
camp chair light, folding chair, often with canvas seat and back
captain's chair chair with rounded back in which vertical spindles support rail that forms arms
chair seat for one person, usu. four-legged, with backrest and sometimes armrests
chaise couchlike lounging seat with leg and back supports
chaise longue couchlike seat lengthened to form leg rest and with raised back support at one end
chesterfield large, heavily stuffed sofa with upholstered upright arms
Chippendale chair graceful, ornately ornamented chair in English style (18th c.)
club chair deep, low, heavily upholstered easy chair with low back, solid sides and arms
couch long, upholstered, stuffed seat for two or more persons, with back and armrests at one or both ends; sofa
courting chair love seat
davenport large, upholstered sofa that converts to bed
daybed armless couch with long seat and sloping back, for reclining or sleeping (18th c.)
deck chair folding chair of metal or other durable material for outdoor use

director's chair folding armchair with canvas seat and back panel on wood frame
divan large couch or sofa, usu. without back or arms
dos-à-dos seat or sofa built so occupants sit back to back
Eames chair armless chair with seat and back of molded plywood attached to tubular steel frame
easy chair stuffed, upholstered, comfortable chair
ergonomic chair work chair specially designed for comfort and support of back and neck
fanback chair Windsor chair having spindle back spread like fan from seat to upper rail
Glastonbury chair small, light, folding chair, with two crossed straight legs at each side and arms connected to front seat rail
highchair infant's chair on tall legs with attached shelf for food
inglenook bench in nook by open fireplace
lawn chair reclining chair, usu. of durable material, for outdoor use
lounge chair long seat with headrest, used for reclining
love seat small sofa with arms, suitable for two persons; courting chair
morris chair easy chair with adjustable back and removable cushions
ottoman stuffed, long, low cushioned seat without back or arms, sometimes circular, able to accommodate several people
pew long wooden bench with back for seating in church
platform rocker rocking chair with base set on curved rockers
potty-chair infant's low seat with removable bowl, used for toilet training
pouf plumply cushioned, usu. circular, backless couch
prie-dieu low bench fitted with shelf, used for kneeling during prayer
recliner chair with adjustable reclining back
rocking chair chair on two curved members that connect its front and back feet, allowing it to rock back and forth
seat any chair, bench, or stool on which people sit
sectional sofa composed of modular sections that can be arranged in various combinations
settee medium or small seat or bench with back and usu. arms
settle wooden bench with arms and straight back
sling chair canvas or leather back and seat loosely fitted onto wood or metal frame
slipper chair low, armless bedroom chair with skirt covering short legs
sociable S-shaped sofa with two seats partially facing each other
sofa upholstered seat for three or more persons with fixed back and arms at each end; couch
sofa bed sofa with removable cushions and foldout mattress
spindle-back chair chair with woven seat and carved rods from seat to top rail
stool low seat without back or arms on three or four legs
studio couch small, armless, backless, upholstered couch, convertible to double bed
swivel chair chair that revolves on its base
tablet chair seat with one arm widened for use as writing surface, esp. in schools
tête-à-tête S-shaped sofa that allows two people to face each other when seated
throne royal chair of state, usu. large and ornate
triclinium couch or set of couches surrounding three sides of table
tuxedo sofa overstuffed sofa with slightly curved arms at same height as back
wicker chair chair of plaited or woven twigs, often with high, fan-shaped back
Windsor chair wooden chair with curved spindle back, legs slanting outward, and saddle seat (18th c.)
wing chair large, upholstered armchair having high, solid back and winged sides

Beds

bassinet infant's portable bed with hood over one end
bed usu. stuffed mattress with springs, in various sizes, for sleeping upon, often with frame of wood or metal
bedstead frame and headboard for bed that supports springs and mattress
berth sleeping accommodation on ship or vehicle, often folding out from wall
box spring mattress base of spiral springs enclosed in cloth-covered frame
bunk bed two beds on frame set one above the other
canopy ornamental rooflike structure over bed, esp. cloth
car bed portable bed for infant, used in automobile
cot flat, folding bed without padding, often of canvas
cradle infant's bed on legs with rockers
crib infant's bed, usu. having slatted sides
davenport large, upholstered sofa that converts to bed
double bed mattress and box spring for two persons, smaller than queen-size bed, 54 inches (137 cm) wide; full-size bed
foldaway bed bed designed to double over and slide aside or out of view when not in use
folding bed foldaway bed
fourposter traditional bed with upright post at each corner to support canopy or curtains
French bed postless bedstead with head and foot rolled outward in scroll form
full-size bed double bed
futon folding, Japanese-style sleeping pad stuffed with cotton batting
gurney rolling cot or stretcher for carrying sick or injured persons
hammock hanging bed of netting or canvas suspended from supports by cords attached at each end
king-size bed extra large mattress and box spring, at least 76 inches (193 cm) wide
mattress fabric case filled with resilient material, used as bed or on bedstead or box spring
Murphy bed bed on metal frame that folds into wall or closet when not in use

pallet straw bed or hard mattress of poor quality
poster bed bed with upright posts at two or four corners
queen-size bed mattress and box spring larger than double bed, smaller than king-size bed, 60 inches (152 cm) wide
rollaway bed on folding frame with wheels for easy storage
single bed narrow mattress and box spring for one person, 39 inches (102 cm) wide
sofa bed sofa with removable cushions and foldout mattress
tatami mat thick, woven, straw floor mat, usu. grouped together in sections, on which futon rests (Japan)
tester bed with frame for canopy
truckle bed low bed on casters, rolled under higher bed when not in use; trundle bed
trundle bed truckle bed
twin bed one of pair of single beds, 39 inches (102 cm) wide
waterbed bed having large rubber or plastic sack filled with water and set in rigid frame, able to conform to sleeper's body position for comfort

Tables and Desks

banquet table large dining table; long, flat serving table
bench long, flat worktable
billiard table rectangular, felt-covered slate table of standardized dimensions for playing billiards
buffet counter or table for serving food
butterfly table small drop-leaf table with round or oval top, leaves supported by brackets shaped like butterfly wings
card table small, flat, square table with folding legs; folding table
carrel table or desk with three sides raised above surface to serve as partitions for private study, esp. in library
coffee table long, low table usu. set before sofa
computer table multilevel desk adapted to hold computer and printer
console table small table supported by ornamental brackets fixed to wall
counter level surface over which transactions are conducted or food served, usu. long and narrow
credence small sideboard or table for valuables, esp. bread and wine used in Eucharist; credenza
credenza credence
desk table with flat surface for writing, often with drawers or compartments
dinette small table for informal dining, usu. in kitchen
dining table large round, rectangular, or oblong table, often with leaves, at which meals are eaten
drawing table flat surface adjustable to various heights and angles
drop-leaf table table with hinged ends or leaves that may be lowered and insertible sections to increase length, esp. for dining
end table small table, usu. with one drawer, that stands at end of couch or beside chair
escritoire writing desk
extension table table with insertible leaf or leaves to increase length
folding table usu. small, flat table with legs that flatten against the underside of the top surface when stored; card table
gate-leg table table with movable paired legs on hinges that swing out to support drop leaves
kneehole desk flat-topped desk with space for knees between drawers
leaf hinged or removable section of table that changes table's length
lectern chest-high, stand-up reading desk for school or church
nesting tables set of usu. three or four tables graduated in size so that they may be stacked together
nightstand small, low table standing at bedside, often with single drawer
Parsons table square, contemporary table whose straight legs are flush with the edges of the top so as to appear jointless
refectory table long, heavy, narrow table with trestlelike legs connected by a single strip
roll-top desk writing desk with sliding, flexible cover that rolls up beneath top
secretary upright writing desk with bookshelves on top and foldout writing space
sideboard dining room table with compartments and shelves for table service articles
side table small table without drawers, usu. placed beside dining table or against wall
table smooth, flat surface supported usu. by four legs
tray table small folding table with low rim around surface, often with crossed pairs of legs
tripod stool, table, or altar with three legs
trolley cart or stand on wheels used for conveying things
workbench large, flat, sturdy table at which craftsman works
writing desk flat-topped table with drawers or pigeonholes; escritoire
writing table desk with retractable drawer used as writing surface and pigeonhole cupboard above, sometimes roll top

Cases, Cupboards, and Chests

armoire tall, movable cupboard or wardrobe
bin enclosed box, frame, or crib for storage
bookcase set of bookshelves in freestanding unit
breakfront large cabinet with center section standing out from flanks
buffet drawers and cupboards for storage of dishes and linen; sideboard
bunker storage bin or compartment, esp. on ship
bureau chest of drawers for storage, often with mirror standing on top
cabinet standing storage unit with shelves and drawers
caddy container or rack for storing objects when not in use
case box or receptacle for enclosing objects

chest large, solid wood piece with lid and often interior drawers for storage; chest of drawers
chest of drawers upright set of enclosed storage receptacles on frame with short legs; dresser
chiffonier ornamental cabinet with shelves, drawers, and sometimes with mirror; tall, narrow chest of drawers
chifforobe combination wardrobe and chest of drawers
china cabinet standing storage shelves for china that requires protection or deserves display
coffer chest or strongbox for valuables
commode low, ornate chest of drawers; movable washstand with cupboard underneath
console large cabinet that rests on floor, esp. housing radio and/or television
credenza large buffet or sideboard, often without legs; closed cabinet for papers and office supplies, often of desk height
crib rack or framework storage enclosure
cupboard small closet with storage shelves
dresser chest of drawers for clothing with flat top, often with mirror
étagère cabinet of tiered shelves open on all sides
filing cabinet vertical storage unit for papers, with two or more sliding drawers, usu. metal
hamper large, covered basket for storage or transport
highboy tall chest of drawers with legs; tallboy
hope chest trunk in which young woman collects linens and clothing in anticipation of marriage
hutch bin or chest for storage
kitchen cabinet enclosed unit containing storage shelves, usu. mounted on kitchen wall
locker small drawer or compartment for secure storage when closed with lock
lowboy three-foot-high dressing table with drawers on short legs
mantel shelf above fireplace
playpen small, often collapsible enclosure in which young child may play without close supervision
rack framework of open shelves on which articles may be placed
sarcophagus wooden, coffinlike wine cooler under sideboard
sideboard buffet or dining-room piece, used for storage of linen, silver, and china, or for serving food
strongbox sturdy receptacle with lock for storage of valuables
tallboy chest with seven or more drawers in two stacks and two small drawers on top; highboy
tea caddy small box, can, or chest for storing tea
trunk large storage box of wood or metal
vanity lady's dressing table with small case for cosmetics; wide shelf around wash basin, often with shelves or drawers
wardrobe freestanding closet fitted with hooks and bars for hanging clothes
wet bar small bar with sink and compartments, used for mixing and serving drinks

Stools and Stands

bar stool tall stool, sometimes with low back, for sitting at bar
campstool small, portable folding stool with crossed legs and canvas seat
catafalque elaborate stand for coffin
coatrack tall wood or metal stand with hooks for hanging coats
easel upright support frame, often with three legs joined at top, esp. for artist's canvas
foldstool small stool that folds into compact unit for storage
footrest low stool set before chair for feet
footstool surface on short legs, used for resting feet while seated
hall stand small, flat table in hall
hassock firmly stuffed mat or cushion used as footstool
hatrack tall spindle with hooks for hanging hats
music stool round stool with adjustable seat that swivels up or down
pedestal flat-topped base or stand for display of ornamental object
sawhorse rack for holding wood with crosspiece linking two sets of legs that form inverted V's
stand support frame on or in which articles may be placed
step stool stool with one or two steps which fold away beneath seat
stool low seat without back or arms on three or four legs
tripod three-legged stand
work stand small, metal stand with several movable leaves, covered with loops and hooks for holding supplies

Curtains, Draperies, and Screens

blind roll-up or retractable window shutter or shade
café curtains pair of curtains that cover only lower half of window
curtain fabric hung on hooks or rod to cover window or adorn wall
draperies heavy decorative material hung in long, loose folds on wall or opening and closing over window; drapes
drapes draperies
fire screen standing metal screen that keeps sparks from fireplace off rugs or floor
jalousie blind with adjustable horizontal slats that admit light and air while excluding rain and sun's rays
panel flat wall section used as partition to divide room
partition interior wall or barrier that divides room into sections
priscilla curtains pair of ruffled, tieback curtains
screen freestanding partition, often hinged, that shields or separates an area of a room
shade flexible screen or fabric mounted over window
shoji screen rice paper mounted on wood frame, used as sliding door or partition (Japan)
shutter solid, movable cover or screen for window or door
tapestry heavy woven cloth with designs, hung on wall or used as furniture covering

valance drapery hung at top of window or along edge of bed, altar, table, or shelf to conceal another member
venetian blind window shutter with overlapping, horizontal slats that may be opened, closed, raised, or lowered by pulling a cord

Carpets and Rugs

area rug small rug covering only part of floor; scatter rug
Aubusson ornate rug woven to resemble figured scenic Aubusson tapestry, often in pastel colors
Axminster carpet machine-woven carpet with pile tufts in variety of textures and many colors
bearskin fur of bear used as rug
Bokhara rich Persian rug
broadloom carpet woven on wide loom, esp. in solid color
Brussels carpet carpet of colored worsted yarns drawn up in uncut loops to form pattern
carpet heavy woven or felted fabric used as floor covering, usu. attached to entire floor and nonmovable
chenille deep pile fabric used for rugs
dhurrie type of Indian rug
flokati handwoven, woolen Greek rug with thick, shaggy pile
hooked (*adj*) designating rug made by drawing loops through coarse fabric with a hook
kilim pileless woven rug from Turkey, the Caucasus, or Iran
Kirman Persian rug with ornate, flowing designs in soft colors
mat coarse woven fabric or plaited reeds used as floor covering
Oriental rug rug or carpet from Far East or Asia
Persian carpet distinctive rug or carpet in rich colors and intricate designs, made in area of Iran: Afshar, Ardabil, Aubusson, Bijar, Belouch, Farahan, Hamedan, Heriz, Indo-Heriz, Indo-Tabriz, Isfahan, Joshegan, Kashan, Kirman, Ladik, Mashad, Moud, Nain, Pak Persian, Sarough, Serapi, Taba, Yalameh
pile velvety surface of rug made by cutting off upright loops of yarn; rug with such a surface
rag American folk art rug of cotton or garment scraps in cheerful colors, usu. with rounded ends
rug thick, heavy fabric, usu. with nap or pile, used as movable floor covering
runner long, rectangular hall rug
rya handwoven Scandinavian rug with deep, resilient, flat pile
scatter rug small rug that covers only part of floor; area rug
shag rug with long, coarse, loose pile
Tabriz Persian rug with cotton warp and wool pile, in medallion design
tapestry rug rug woven in intricate pattern, designed to hang on wall
throw rug small rug
wall-to-wall carpeting that covers entire floor of room

Lamps and Mirrors

arc light electric light in which current passes in arc between two incandescent electrodes surrounded by gas
chandelier branched, ornate, multibulb lighting fixture suspended from ceiling
cheval glass full-length mirror that can be tilted in hinged frame
Chinese lantern light enclosed in translucent paper globe or shade
fluorescent lamp tubular electric lamp coated on inner surface by fluorescent material and containing mercury vapor
gaslight light fixture that burns illuminating gas
glass mirror
gooseneck lamp desk lamp with long, thin shaft, usu. curved or flexible
halogen lamp high-incandescent lamp containing the chemical halogen
incandescent electric light lamp in which filament heated by electric current gives off light
lamp device holding electric bulb, gas, or burning wick, used for illumination
lantern light enclosed in portable, protective case with transparent openings
mirror reflecting glass surface set in frame, usu. mounted on dresser, door, or wall; glass
neon lamp discharge bulb containing neon gas that glows when voltage is applied across two electrodes
night-light small light fixture that faces wall, providing dim light in dark room
reading light small light placed above bed or beside chair
searchlight light and reflector on rotating base, used to project beam to great distance
speculum optical reflector; ancient mirror of polished bronze or silver
spot spotlight
spotlight lamp that produces powerful, focused beam of light; spot
sunlamp electric lamp that emits ultraviolet radiations, used to tan skin indoors
task lighting lamp mounted to illuminate specific work area, such as kitchen counter or portion of desk
Tiffany lamp lamp with shade of Tiffany stained glass
toilet glass dressing table mirror, often with attached drawer
torchiere tall floor lamp that emits indirect light from source within reflecting bowl that is open at top
track lighting series of small, adjustable spotlights arranged along track, usu. mounted on ceiling
trumeau mirror with carved panel above or below glass set in same frame
uplight lamp that projects illumination upward
Venetian lamp delicate lamp with shade of Venetian glass

Accessories and Appliances

AC air conditioner
air conditioner AC; electrical device that reduces interior temperature and humidity of building or room
appliance any of various service units, usu. operated electrically, found in contemporary homes, esp. in the kitchen: refrigerator, freezer, stove, washing machine, dryer, dishwasher, vacuum cleaner, air conditioner, toaster, blender, food processor, can opener
bidet chairlike fixture for bathing genitals and anus
ceiling fan large fan with circular blade motion, suspended from ceiling
dishwasher enclosed electrical appliance for automatically washing and rinsing dishes
dryer enclosed heater for drying washed clothing
Franklin stove iron, wood-burning stove with exhaust funnel running to chimney
freezer section of refrigerator or separate appliance with temperature low enough to freeze and preserve foods
furnace enclosed structure in which heat is produced by gas, oil, coal, or electricity to warm home
icebox insulated container with section for ice, used to cool foods
meat locker very large freezer, esp. for meat
oven fixed or freestanding chamber for baking, heating, roasting, or drying, using heat produced by gas or electricity
potbelly stove stove with rounded, bulging body, esp. wood-burning stove shaped thus
range cooking stove with oven and flat top equipped with gas burners or electrical heating elements
refrigerator large, airtight cabinet or box for chilling foods by means of ice or electrical condensation
stove fixed or portable fuel-burning or electrical device for cooking food or heating room
toilet bathroom fixture with seat over bowl through which water is flushed to dispose of human waste material
washing machine electrical apparatus with enclosed tub for cleaning clothing and linens
water heater apparatus with large storage tank where water is heated by gas or electricity for use in bathroom and kitchen
wood stove heavy metal heating and cooking apparatus, with heat supplied by wood burned in large chamber

ORNAMENTAL AND FUNCTIONAL ARTICLES

Decorations, Ornaments, and Symbolic Objects
Functional Household Articles and Appliances
Linens and Fabrics
Glass and Ceramics

Decorations, Ornaments, and Symbolic Objects

aigrette heron's plume, sometimes placed in vase
bas relief sculptural relief in slight projection from surrounding surface
bibelot small household ornament or trinket; elegant miniature book
bijou small, dainty ornament of delicate workmanship, usu. jewelry
birdbath small, ornamental basin set outside for birds to bathe in
bric-a-brac small objects placed about room for ornamentation; curios; knickknacks
calabash large, hard-shell gourd, used as utensil
candelabrum large, branched candlestick
candlestick holder with socket for candle or candles
cartouche ornate frame; oval or oblong figure enclosing sovereign's name (ancient Egypt)
centerpiece decorative display at center of table
chalice large cup or goblet, often of gold or silver, esp. for Eucharist wine
chandelier branched, ornate, multibulb lighting fixture suspended from ceiling
Chinese lantern light with large paper shade, often globular
cornucopia curved goat's horn overflowing with fruit and grain, representing abundance
crucifix symbolic representation of Christ on cross, or cross itself
cuckoo clock clock equipped with mechanical birds that appear and emit sounds to announce hours
curio knickknack, bric-a-brac, or objet d'art
decoration any object used for its ornamental value
diptych two-leaved hinged tablet with pictures painted or carved on it
figurine small carved, molded figure; statuette
filigree precious metal ornamentation of fine wire, applied to surfaces or in openwork setting
globe spherical model of Earth on stand
girandole ornamental, branched candlestick or mirror frame
grandfather clock tall pendulum clock standing on floor
jardiniere ornamental stand for plants, often a large ceramic flowerpot

knickknack small, often trivial, ornamental object; curio; objet d'art
menorah candelabrum, esp. one holding nine candles for use during Jewish festival of Hanukkah
objet d'art decorative object of artistic value; curio; knickknack
ornament any object used to adorn or embellish
salver serving tray for food and drink; tray on which letters or calling cards are presented
samovar elaborate urn with spigot, used for heating water to brew tea
sconce bracket candlestick hung from wall; similar electric fixture
statuary collection of statues
statue sculpted, modeled, or cast three-dimensional representation, usu. of person or animal
statuette small statue; figurine
swag suspended wreath or garland
taper squat, round candle used for religious observance
torchère tall, ornamental candlestick on tripod base (18th c.)
trappings largely ornamental household articles
trefoil ornament in form of stylized trifoliate leaf
trim material used for decoration or embellishment along borders of larger piece
trinket small, inexpensive ornament
triptych picture or panel in three panels side by side
urn ornamental vase on pedestal, used for storage; closed vessel on stand with spigot for serving beverages
vermiculation decorative markings in irregular fine lines
wind chimes cluster of small pieces of glass or metal that tinkle in wind
wreath ornamental circle of flowers and greenery

Functional Household Articles and Appliances

alarm clock small bedside clock equipped with bell or buzzer set to sound at particular time
andirons metal supports with horizontal bar on legs, used to hold firewood on hearth
appliance any of various service units, usu. operated electrically, found in contemporary homes, esp. in the kitchen
aquarium enclosed, glass-sided container filled with water, serving as home to fish and other underwater life
bed tray stand with short, retractable legs, used for holding dishes and other objects while person is sitting up in bed
bellows blower that draws air through valve and expels it through tube, esp. to fan open fire
bibcock faucet having bent-down nozzle
billet chunky piece of firewood
birdcage grated enclosure that houses birds
bookends heavy supports that hold books in place on shelf
broom bundle of firm, stiff fibers or twigs bound together on long handle, used for sweeping floor
brush bristles set into handle, used for scrubbing, sweeping, or smoothing
bucket round vessel for catching, holding, or carrying liquids
bulletin board soft board attached to wall for posting notices; pegboard
caddy small box, can, or chest for storage
candlesnuffer long device having hollow cone at end of handle, used for extinguishing ceremonial candles
cantilever bracket-shaped support for balcony or cornice; projecting beam supported at one end only
carboy protective rectangular container housing bottle with capacity of 5 to 15 gallons (18.9 to 56.8 l)
censer cup-shaped vessel with holes, suspended on chains and used for burning incense
coaster shallow container, small mat, or plate used to hold glasses and protect surfaces, esp. from moisture
cresset iron vessel or basket for holding illuminant, mounted as torch or suspended as lantern
cuspidor spittoon
fixture item of movable property incorporated into structure, both ornamental and functional
frog small metal, glass, or plastic holder with spikes or perforations for holding flowers in place in vase
grate frame of parallel or crossed bars, esp. of iron, used to contain stove or furnace fire
iron usu. electrical device with flat, long, metal base, heated to press clothes
ironing board flat, padded, cloth-covered surface on which clothes are pressed with an iron
lantern portable, protective light case with transparent openings or covering, usu. with handle
mop absorbent material fastened to long handle, used to clean floors
nesting box one of a series of boxes in graduated sizes that may be stored within one another
pail bucket, usu. with handle, for carrying liquids
pegboard flat section of porous material attached to wall for posting notices; bulletin board
planter wood, ceramic, or glass receptacle used to hold live plant and earth
plunger rubber suction cup on handle for clearing plumbing traps
scuttle shallow, open basket for carrying something, esp. metal pail for carrying coal
shoe rack hanging or floor device for storing shoes
silent butler receptacle with hinged lid for collecting table crumbs or emptying ashtrays
sleeveboard small ironing board for pressing garment sleeves
spice rack narrow storage shelves with front strips, usu. attached to wall
spittoon receptacle for expectorate; cuspidor
terrarium small glass enclosure for keeping, raising, and observing plants or animals
tie rack hanging device with slots or bars for storing ties
tray open, flat-bottomed receptacle with rim for carrying or holding objects
vacuum cleaner electrical device that sucks dirt and dust through hose into chamber
valet rack or tray for holding clothing and personal effects

whisk broom small broom with short handle
window box box holding soil for growing plants on windowsill
wine rack wood frame with slots for storing bottles of wine on their sides
wringer device for pressing liquid out of washed clothes, usu. between two rollers, operated with crank handle

Linens and Fabrics

antimacassar, arras
backrest, banderole, banner, bath mat, bath towel, beach towel, bedding, bed pillow, bedsheet, bedspread, blanket, bolster, bunting
comforter, cover, coverlet, crazy quilt, cushion
dish towel, doily, doormat, duvet
eiderdown
facecloth, fitted sheet, flag
hand towel, hanging
lap robe, linens
mattress pad
napkin
pennant, pillow, pillowcase, place mat
quilt
sampler, sham, sheet, slipcover, spread, standard, streamer
tablecloth, tapestry, throw pillow, towel
upholstery
washcloth, white goods

Glass and Ceramics

bell jar bell-shaped glass vessel for covering objects
carafe liter or half-liter glass bottle, esp. for holding wine
caster small glass bottle for serving condiments; cruet
china plates, cups, and serving platters of delicate, translucent ceramic porcelain
cistern large, usu. earthenware vessel for storing water
crock thick earthenware pot or jar
crockery earthenware plates, cups, and serving utensils
cruet caster
crystal objects, esp. bottles and drinking glasses, made of fine, cut glass
cut glass glass with ornamental patterns cut into its surface
decanter ornamental bottle for wine, port, or sherry, often made of cut glass
etched glass decorative cut-glass objects
faience decorative, enameled French Renaissance earthenware
jeroboam oversized wine bottle with capacity of 3 liters (3.3 quarts)
Limoges enamelware or porcelain made at Limoges, France
majolica glazed, richly colored, ornamental Italian earthenware
porcelain hard, fine-grained, nonporous ceramicware, usu. translucent and white
stoneware decorative white earthenware crocks, jugs, plates, and cups
vase ornamental glass or earthenware vessel of greater depth than width, often used to hold flowers

Chapter Eight

The Family

KINSHIP AND FAMILY RELATIONS

Kinship and Ancestry
Relationships by Blood and Marriage
Family Affairs

Kinship and Ancestry

affinity kinship relationship by marriage
agnate paternal kinsman, esp. male relative on father's side
ancestor person from whom one is descended, usu. more remote than grandparent; forefather
antecedents ancestors
bloodline sequence of direct ancestors
blood relation family member by birth
branch division of family descended from common ancestor
breed persons of the same stock
clan extended family; tribe
collateral kin descended by different line from same stock, such as uncle and nephew
common descent blood relationship of two or more people with common ancestor; consanguinity
congenital (*adj*) existing at birth
consanguinity relationship by descent from common ancestor
crossbreed (*vb*) interbreed
descendant person born of same blood as ancestor in later generation; progeny
distaff female side or branch of family; spindle side
extended family ancestors and descendants by birth and marriage over several generations
extraction ancestry; descent or lineage
family tree generational chart of ancestry
female line descent through mother
forefather ancestor
full-blooded (*adj*) of pure, unmixed ancestry
genealogy account of person or family's descent from first known ancestor
generation persons constituting single step in line of descent
gens clan, esp. one tracing patrilineal descent
heir one receiving endowment from parent or predecessor
heredity sum of qualities transmitted from ancestor to descendant
heritage property or trait descending to heir, transmitted by immediate ancestor
hybrid one born of mixed breeds, races, or diverse cultural traditions
inbred (*adj*) born of closely related individuals; from the same stock
incest sexual relations or interbreeding between two closely related persons, esp. between siblings or parent and child
interbreed (*vb*) breed within closed population; crossbreed
kin one's relatives; persons of common ancestry
kindred group of one's relatives; kinship
kinship group individuals composing one's kin
kith close friends, neighbors, or relatives
kith and kin close friends and relations
line lineage; bloodline
lineage descent in direct line from common progenitor; ancestry or extraction
matriarch female, esp. mother, who rules or dominates family
matrilineal (*adj*) tracing descent through mother's line
moiety one of two basic tribal or clan subdivisions based on unilineal descent
next of kin one's closest relative
nuclear family family unit composed of parents and children only
offspring children
parentage descent from parents or ancestors; lineage
patriarch male, esp. father, who rules or dominates a family
patrilineal (*adj*) tracing descent through father's line
patrimony anything derived from one's father, esp. an estate; heritage
pedigree ancestral line, esp. of distinguished lineage
philoprogenitive (*adj*) tending to produce offspring
posterity all future generations descended from one progenitor; descendants
progenitor forefather; ancestor in direct line
progeny descendants; children
pure blood one of unmixed ancestry, bred from members of recognized strain, group, or class
race family, tribe, or people of same stock
relative person connected to another by blood; relation
sire father; male ancestor or progenitor
spear side male side or branch of family
spindle side female side or branch of family; distaff
stirp line descending from common ancestor; stock
stock descendants of one individual; family, lineage
strain group with common ancestry producing physiological distinctions
tribe people of common stock; clan
unilineal (*adj*) tracing descent through maternal or paternal line only

Relationships by Blood and Marriage

aunt sister of one's father or mother; uncle's wife
brother-in-law brother of one's spouse; husband of one's sister; husband of one's spouse's sister
cater-cousin intimate friend; one not related
cousin child of one's uncle or aunt; relative descended from one's grandparents or ancestors in different line
cousin-german first cousin
cousin once removed cousin by marriage or by descent from grandparents, not through parents' line
cousin twice removed relative descended from grandparents' line through marriage or from more remote ancestors

daughter-in-law wife of one's son
father-in-law father of one's spouse
first cousin child of one's uncle or aunt; cousin-german
grandaunt great-aunt
grandchild child of one's child
grandnephew male child of one's sibling's child; great-nephew
grandniece female child of one's sibling's child; great-niece
grandparents grandmother and grandfather; parents of one's parents
granduncle great-uncle
great-aunt sister of one's grandparent; grandaunt
great-nephew grandnephew
great-niece grandniece
great-uncle brother of one's grandparent; granduncle
half brother brother related through one parent only
half sister sister related through one parent only
in-law any relation by marriage
maternal grandfather mother's father
maternal grandmother mother's mother
mother-in-law mother of one's spouse
nephew son of one's sibling or sibling-in-law
niece daughter of one's sibling or sibling-in-law
novercal (*adj*) relating to one's stepmother
parent mother or father; progenitor
paternal grandfather father's father
paternal grandmother father's mother
second cousin cousin descended from grandparent, not through parent's line
sibling brother or sister
sister-in-law sister of one's spouse; wife of one's brother; wife of one's spouse's brother
son-in-law husband of one's daughter
spouse husband or wife; person to whom one is married
stepbrother son of one's stepparent by former marriage
stepchild child of one's spouse by former marriage
stepdaughter daughter of one's spouse by former marriage
stepfather husband of one's mother by subsequent marriage
stepmother wife of one's father by subsequent marriage
stepparent spouse of one's parent by subsequent marriage
stepsister daughter of one's stepparent by former marriage
stepson son of one's spouse by former marriage
uncle brother of one's father or mother; aunt's husband

Family Affairs

adult one who has reached specified age of majority
baptism Christian sacrament of naming and admission to Christian community
bar mitzvah celebration of Jewish boy's coming of age
bat mitzvah celebration of Jewish girl's coming of age
birthday date of one's birth; annual celebration of date of birth
blood feud multigenerational dispute between families
bonding formation of close personal relationship through constant association, esp. between mother and child
change of life climacteric; menopause
charge person, esp. child, committed to one's care
climacteric period in male of declining sexual activity; change of life
cognomen surname; last name
dowager widow holding property or title of deceased husband
elder respected, senior member of family or tribe
family planning use of contraception to control number of children
fraternal (*adj*) brotherly
given name first name, chosen by parents
guardian adult who is legally responsible for another's child
household those living together as a family in same dwelling
junior child bearing same given name as parent
kissing cousin friend or relative known well enough to kiss upon meeting
last name surname
majority age at which child is legally an adult
matron mature or distinguished married woman
menopause time of natural cessation of female menstruation and associated changes, usu. occurring between ages forty-five and fifty; change of life
middle age period of life from about ages forty to sixty
midlife period of emotional turmoil associated with aging; middle age
minor individual beneath age of legal majority, usu. eighteen to twenty-one years old
name day feast of saint for whom one is named
noblesse oblige obligation of honorable behavior associated with noble birth
parricide act of killing a member of one's family
patronymic name derived from father or paternal ancestor, usu. by addition of suffix or prefix
propagate (*vb*) breed or produce offspring
retirement age at which one ceases working, usu. around sixty-five years old
reunion reconciliation or gathering of separated family members
rite of passage ceremony marking major transition in life, such as birth, puberty, marriage, or death
senior citizen elderly member of clan or society
surname name borne in common by family members; cognomen; last name

MARRIAGE AND DIVORCE

Marriage and Divorce

adultery sexual intercourse by married person with someone other than spouse
affair temporary, often secret romance outside marriage
affiance promise of marriage; betrothal
alimony legally required financial support paid to one marriage partner by the other as term of divorce
anniversary annual celebration on wedding date
annulment legal invalidation of marriage
bachelor unmarried man
banns public announcement of proposed marriage, esp. in church
benedict newly married man formerly a longtime bachelor
best man principal groomsman at wedding; paranymph
betrothal engagement to be married
bigamy illegal marriage to more than one person at a time
bride woman just married or about to be married
bridegroom man just married or about to be married
bridesmaid woman or girl attending bride at wedding; paranymph
broken home single-parent family in which child of divorced parents is raised
celestial marriage Mormon marriage held to be binding in present and future life
celibacy state of being unmarried
child support payments made by one party following divorce for care and upbringing of children
chuppah *Hebrew.* canopy beneath which bride and groom stand during Jewish wedding ceremony
civil marriage marriage performed by magistrate
cohabitation living together, esp. while unmarried
common-law marriage marriage based on declaration, intent, or length of time living together without benefit of wedding
community property property acquired after marriage that is jointly owned by both partners and that by law must be divided equally upon divorce
concubinage cohabitation of persons not legally married
conjugal (*adj*) pertaining to marriage or the relationship between husband and wife; connubial; marital; nuptial
conjugal rights rights of husband and wife to union and affection
connubial (*adj*) conjugal; marital; nuptial
consanguineous marriage marriage between blood relatives
consort spouse of monarch
consummate (*vb*) complete or fulfill marriage bond by sexual intercourse
courtship social activities of potential mates culminating in engagement and marriage
cuckold man with sexually unfaithful wife
custody immediate charge and care of children, usu. given to one partner in divorce
Darby and Joan very devoted elderly married couple
desertion abandonment of one's spouse and family
deuterogamy digamy
digamy second marriage after divorce or death of first spouse; deuterogamy
dissolution divorce
divorce legal termination of marriage; dissolution
divorcé divorced man
divorcée divorced woman
dowager widow with title or property derived from dead husband
dower dowry; property woman brings to her marriage; right of widow to interest in husband's property
dowry money and real or personal property brought to marriage by woman
dual-career marriage marriage in which both spouses have full-time jobs or careers outside of household responsibilities
eligible (*adj*) single; available for marriage
elope (*vb*) run away to be married, esp. without parental consent
endogamy marriage traditionally within one's social, kinship, religious, or ethnic group
engaged (*adj*) describing one who has announced an intent to marry
Enoch Arden divorce divorce based on disappearance of one partner for specified length of time
espousal wedding; marriage ceremony
estrangement physical separation of married couple
exogamy marriage traditionally outside one's social, kinship, religious, or ethnic group
extramarital (*adj*) describing that which occurs outside the bonds of marriage
family man married man who is deeply involved in family life
father-in-law father of one's spouse
fiancé man to whom one is engaged to marry
fiancée woman to whom one is engaged to marry
flower girl young girl who carries flowers before bride at wedding
gay marriage formalized, monogamous union between two persons of the same sex
golden anniversary fiftieth wedding anniversary
groom bridegroom
groomsman man attending groom at wedding
group marriage marriage between more than two persons, illegal in U.S.
hausfrau housewife; married woman (Germany)
helpmate spouse
holy matrimony state of being married
homemaker housewife
homogamy marriage among persons of similar age, social class, race, education, and religion

honeymoon vacation taken by newlyweds to begin their marriage
honeymoon period transitional time between single and married life; early, romantic period in marriage
househusband man who stays home to manage the household while his wife goes out to work
housewife woman whose work is caring for home and children
hypergamy marriage into caste at least as high as one's own, esp. by Hindu woman
hypogamy marriage to person of lower socioeconomic status
incompatibility grounds for divorce based on mutual inability to live together with shared values, goals, and lifestyles
inconstancy fickleness in affections; infidelity
infidelity sexual unfaithfulness in marriage
in-laws relatives by marriage, esp. spouse's parents
intended one's future husband or wife
interlocutory preliminary divorce decree prior to final settlement
intermarry (*vb*) marry outside one's racial, religious, or ethnic group
legal separation legal arrangement to live apart made by estranged marriage partners
levirate ancient Hebrew marriage custom requiring brother of deceased man to marry his widow
maiden name woman's surname prior to marriage
maid of honor principal unmarried woman attending bride at wedding ceremony
marital (*adj*) pertaining to marriage; conjugal; connubial; nuptial
marriage social and legal institution of formalized union between man and woman, typically foundation of family unit; matrimony, wedlock
marriage counseling therapy for partners in troubled marriage
marriage license document required for completion of legal establishment of marriage
marriage of convenience legal union based on circumstances other than love or affection, such as financial gain or naturalization
marry (*vb*) join in wedlock; unite man and woman in marriage; take another as one's spouse
matrimony marriage; rite, ceremony, or sacrament of marriage
matron long-married woman; wife; widow
matron of honor principal married woman attending bride at wedding ceremony
mental cruelty nonphysical abuse used as grounds for divorce
miscegenation marriage between persons of different races
mixed marriage marriage between persons of different races, religions, or ethnic groups
monandry practice and custom of having one husband at a time
monogamy practice of having only one spouse at a time
morganatic marriage union between person of high rank and person of lower rank in which children do not inherit higher-ranking parent's title or property
mother-in-law mother of one's spouse
nest (*vb*) settle into cozy, safe living place as couple or family; (*n*) family home
no-fault divorce legal dissolution of marriage in which neither partner is blamed for its failure
nonsupport failure of one mate to provide financial support for spouse and family, as contracted in marriage agreement
nubile (*adj*) marriageable, esp. in reference to young girls
nuptial (*adj*) pertaining to marriage and the wedding ceremony
nuptials marriage ceremony
open marriage arrangement whereby partners are free to have sexual relations outside marriage
palimony financial compensation paid to person previously lived with, but not married to, by more financially able partner
philander (*vb*) have sexual relations with no possibility of marriage
plight one's troth become engaged; take wedding vows
polyandry practice and custom of having more than one husband at a time
polygamy marriage to two or more spouses simultaneously
proposal offer of marriage
prothalamion song or poem that celebrates a marriage
proxy marriage ceremony conducted with another person substituting for one of partners to be wed
reception party following wedding ceremony
reconciliation resolution of differences between estranged or separated couple
sannup married man; husband (American Indian)
scarlet letter badge of an adulterer, esp. letter "A" worn as symbol of adultery
separation move to independent living quarters by couple with marriage problems, often prior to divorce action
serial monogamy series of monogamous relationships, none of which leads to marriage
seven-year itch supposed temptation to have affair in seventh year of marriage
shivaree noisy mock serenade to newly married couple
shotgun wedding marriage compelled by bride's pregnancy
shower celebration with gifts for bride-to-be, given by her female friends
significant other mate or spouse
spinster unmarried woman past common age for marrying; old maid
spouse one's husband or wife
support payments money paid by one parent under terms of divorce settlement to care for children in custody of other parent
suttee custom in which widow is cremated on funeral pyre of her husband (India)
trial separation temporary break in cohabitation by married couple to determine whether they should separate permanently and initiate divorce proceedings

troth pledge of fidelity at engagement or wedding
trousseau bride's gown and accessories
uncontested divorce dissolution of marriage without legal dispute between partners
union joining in marriage; physical consummation of marriage
uxorious (*adj*) inordinately submissive to one's wife
visiting privilege right of divorced person to visit children living in custody of other parent
vows promise of fidelity; formal marriage pledge
war bride woman marrying in wartime, esp. one whose husband leaves for military service immediately after wedding
wedlock marriage; matrimony
widow woman whose husband is dead
widower man whose wife is dead
widowhood state of being widowed
woo (*vb*) court

PARENTS AND CHILDREN

Pregnancy and Birth
Infancy
Upbringing and Development
Names and Relationships

Pregnancy and Birth

afterbirth placenta and fetal membranes expelled from uterus in parturition
artificial insemination introduction of semen into uterus by other than sexual means
barren (*adj*) unable to conceive or produce offspring
bar sinister proof, condition, or stigma of illegitimacy
bastard illegitimate child
biological clock woman's natural life cycle that controls ability to conceive and bear children
biological parent parent who has conceived or sired child, though not always legal parent or guardian
birth act or process of bringing forth child from mother's womb; parturition
birth certificate official hospital record of birth
birth control devices and methods used to prevent conception and reduce number of children born by woman
birth defect physical defect present at birth that may be inherited or environmentally induced during pregnancy
Cesarean section delivery of child by surgical incision through walls of abdomen into uterus; C-section
conception act of becoming pregnant, in which sperm fertilizes ovum and embryo begins growth in woman's uterus
confinement period of lying-in immediately preceding birth of child
congenital (*adj*) describing trait derived or inherited from parents through genes
contraceptive device used to prevent pregnancy; (*adj*) tending to prevent conception
couvade practice among some peoples in which husband enacts birth experience in his bed immediately preceding birth of his child
C-section Cesarean section
embryo unborn child developing in mother's womb
false pregnancy signs of pregnancy, esp. absence of menstruation, without presence of embryo, due to psychological or glandular disturbance or tumor
family planning use of birth control to limit number of children in family
fertile (*adj*) able to conceive children
fertility capability of reproducing; ability to conceive
fertility drug medication used to enhance ability to conceive
fetus embryo from three months after conception to birth
fraternal twins twins of either sex, developed from separately fertilized ova, therefore not identical
full term pregnancy lasting nine months
gestation period of embryonic growth from conception to birth
gravid (*adj*) heavy with child; pregnant
identical twins twins of same sex, developed from single fertilized ovum, very similar in appearance
illegitimate (*adj*) born out of wedlock; misbegotten
inbreeding conception of children among closely related individuals
in utero conception in uterus of woman; unborn
in vitro fertilization and conception outside living body, in artificial environment
labor painful physical activities and sensations involved in giving birth
Lamaze method system of special exercises and breathing used in childbirth
legitimate (*adj*) lawfully begotten and born in wedlock
love child illegitimate child
lying-in confinement; period immediately preceding childbirth
maternity motherhood; hospital ward for childbirth and care of newborn infants
midwife woman who assists mother during childbirth
midwifery practice of being a midwife
miscarriage expulsion of underdeveloped fetus, usu. between twelfth and twenty-eighth weeks of pregnancy
morning sickness nausea associated with first months of pregnancy
natal (*adj*) relating to or associated with birth
natural childbirth birth in which mother does not use anaesthesia

ovum female germ cell that, when fertilized, develops into embryo
parturition process of giving birth
paternity fatherhood
paternity test test to determine biological father of child by comparison of genetic traits
placenta structure within uterus connected to umbilical cord through which fetus receives nourishment and eliminates feces
pregnant (*adj*) having unborn child in one's body; expecting; gravid; with child
premature birth birth occurring after a gestation period of less than thirty-seven weeks
prenatal (*adj*) before birth
primipara woman bearing a first child
pro-choice (*adj*) advocating legalized abortion
procreation reproduction; act of begetting and bringing forth young
pro-life (*adj*) opposing legalized abortion
quadruplets birth of four children from one pregnancy
quintuplets birth of five children from one pregnancy
sextuplets birth of six children from one pregnancy
spermatozoon male germ cell in semen that fertilizes ovum to produce embryo
sperm bank supply of spermatozoon used for artificial insemination
stillborn (*adj*) describing infant dead at birth
term nine months of normal pregnancy
test-tube baby embryo produced by laboratory fertilization and surgical implantation in uterus
trimester one of three three-month periods during pregnancy
triplets birth of three children from one pregnancy
twins birth of two children from one pregnancy
umbilical cord structure connecting navel of fetus with mother's placenta; emotional connection of mother and child
uterus womb
womb female organ where embryo develops; uterus

Infancy

baby food purée of easily digested food for toothless infant
baptism Christian sacrament involving ritual use of water and naming of child, who is thus received into faith; christening
bassinet infant's basketlike, hooded bed
bris Jewish circumcision ceremony performed on eighth day following birth as rite of inclusion into religious community
carriage light-wheeled seat, often with hooded cover, for transporting infant
chrisom child infant that dies in first month of life
christening baptism, esp. naming of child in Christian faith
circumcision removal of prepuce from tip of male infant's penis
cradle infant's bed, often with spoke walls; infancy
crib baby's small bed with high sides
crib death inexplicable sudden infant death syndrome
dandle (*vb*) bounce baby playfully on one's knee
diaper folded cloth or absorbent material worn between legs and around waist by infant to collect urine and feces
diaper rash irritation that develops under wet diapers
formula milklike mixture used for bottle-feeding infants
foundling infant discovered when abandoned by unknown parents
infancy period of early childhood
infant child in first year or two of life
lullaby song sung to lull child to sleep
mewling (*adj*) crying weakly, whimpering; (*n*) an infant
neonatal (*adj*) relating to infant in first month of life
newborn child in first month of life
nurse (*vb*) suckle or breast-feed an infant
nursery infant's room in house
pacifier rubber nipple or teething ring for infant
postnatal (*adj*) referring to period after birth
postpartum (*adj*) referring to period following birth, esp. mother's depression during this time
preemie *Informal.* prematurely born infant
puling (*adj*) whining, whimpering, mewling
suckle (*vb*) breast-feed an infant
suckling infant still feeding on mother's milk; act of breast-feeding
swaddling clothes strips of cloth wrapped around infant to restrict movements
teether object for baby to bite while teething, esp. ring
teething painful first growth of teeth through infant's gums
toddler child who is beginning to walk, usu. aged one or two; tot
toilet training process of teaching child to control bladder and bowel functions and use toilet
wean (*vb*) accustom child to take nourishment other than by nursing
wet nurse woman who suckles infant not her own

Upbringing and Development

adolescence period of growing up, from puberty to maturity
adoption legal taking of a child born to someone else as one's own
age of consent age at which child is legally allowed to give consent to sex or marriage, usu. eighteen years old
allowance weekly stipend given by parent to child as spending money, often earned by doing chores
apron strings state of being under dominance or control of one's parents at an advanced age
au pair foreign person, usu. young girl, living with family and serving as domestic and baby-sitter
baby-sitter person hired to care for children; sitter
bedwetting inability of toilet-trained child to control urination in sleep
changeling child secretly substituted for another, usu. at birth

chaperone older person accompanying youngsters at social function to ensure proper behavior
child abuse physical mistreatment of children
chores household tasks performed by child, often rewarded by payment
Christian name first name; name given by parents
coming of age reaching majority or age of consent
corporal punishment physical punishment, such as spanking
curfew time, set by parents, at which child must return home, esp. in evening
custody immediate charge and care of child; right to be child's guardian as determined in divorce or separation
day care supervision of preschool children, esp. while parents work
development stages of growth and maturation of child
domestic household help during day; maid
familial (*adj*) of or relating to the family
filial (*adj*) befitting relationship of child to its parent
foster home place in which child lives with foster parents
foster parents individuals caring for a child not theirs legally or by birth
gifted child child with superior intelligence or talents
godparents individuals who sponsor a child at baptism, thereby assuming certain responsibilities
growing pains emotional adjustments encountered during stages of development
guardian individual other than biological parents taking responsibility for child's upbringing
infancy first year or two of childhood
JD juvenile delinquent
juvenile teenager
juvenile delinquent JD; incorrigibly ill-behaved adolescent
latchkey child young child of working parents who spends part of day at home unsupervised
majority age at which full civil rights are accorded, usu. twenty-one years
maturity final stage of development in which child is fully grown and able to care for itself
minor child under age of consent, which is usu. eighteen or twenty-one years of age
nanny child's nursemaid
nest security of the family group; home
nonage period of youth before majority; immaturity
nubile (*adj*) of marriageable age, esp. young girl
nursemaid person employed regularly to care for children
only child child with no siblings
orphan child whose parents are both dead or unknown
parent person who has begotten a child or is legally responsible for its upbringing; mother or father
phase behavior and problems associated with particular period in child's development
philoprogenitive (*adj*) producing offspring; having deep affection for one's children
preadolescent child just below age of puberty, approximately ages nine to twelve; preteen
prepubescent (*adj*) designating child just before age of puberty, about twelve years old
preteen preadolescent
puberty period marked by sexual development, when child is first capable of reproducing, usu. age fourteen in boys, age twelve in girls
rite of passage ritual associated with development stage, such as puberty
sibling rivalry natural hostility and competition between siblings
single parent individual raising child without spouse
stripling youth
subadult adolescent youth
subdeb adolescent girl
subteen preadolescent child
teenager child between ages of twelve and twenty; juvenile
terrible two's difficult phase in child's life that occurs around age two, when child is first able to interact with environment and must learn limits
tomboy boyish preadolescent or adolescent girl
transitional object familiar object, esp. blanket or doll, carried by child in stage of early socialization
unfilial (*adj*) not befitting child's relations with parents
upbringing manner in which parents supervise child's development
waif orphan; lost child
ward child under supervision of court or court-appointed guardian
working parent parent who is unavailable to care for child while at job
youth young person, esp. child or adolescent but not infant

Chapter Nine
Eating

EATING VERBS

bolt swallow food or drink hurriedly
break bread eat, esp. with another or others
consume eat or drink, esp. in large amounts
devour eat voraciously, often to excess
diet eat sparingly; restrict one's intake of food
digest alter food by action of body chemicals into form that can be absorbed by body
dine eat dinner or any substantial meal
dispatch eat up quickly
drain drink everything in (container)
eat out have meal in a restaurant
engorge eat greedily; gorge
fall to begin eating
feast eat rich, elaborate meal
feast on enjoy eating (some specific, usu. lavish, food)
feed eat, esp. out of hunger only, usu. said of animals
gobble eat hurriedly and sloppily
gorge stuff oneself with food
graze snack continuously or nibble small portions and samples of food
gulp swallow hastily and greedily in large amounts
guzzle drink greedily in large amounts
imbibe drink, esp. alcoholic beverage
ingest take food into body, usu. by swallowing
ingurgitate consume greedily in large amounts
inhale *Informal.* eat or drink very rapidly
lap consume liquid food by licking it up with the tongue like an animal
lap up eat or drink greedily with the tongue
masticate chew
munch chew steadily and slowly; eat with pleasure
nibble eat small amounts of something, esp. in quick bites
nosh *Informal.* munch or eat a snack
partake eat or drink one portion of a meal, esp. with others
peck at eat in small amounts
quaff drink deeply and thirstily
refect refresh with food or drink (archaic)
sample eat small portions of (several different foods), esp. to taste quality
savor enjoy the taste of one's food
set to begin eating
slurp drink or eat noisily
snack eat small portions of food, esp. between regular meals
stuff oneself eat until one can eat no more
sup dine; eat supper or evening meal
swig drink in large mouthfuls or quantities
swill drink greedily in large quantities
taste sense flavor of one's food; test flavor of by placing a little in one's mouth; eat or drink a small amount of
toss down gulp or eat rapidly, almost without chewing
wash down ease the swallowing of (food) by drinking liquid
wine and dine entertain (guests) with food and drink
wolf down eat ravenously and quickly

FOODS

Food in General

aliment food as nourishment
board daily meals, esp. at table or provided for pay or with lodging
bread food in general
comestibles food; edibles
cuisine prepared food; specific style of food
daily bread basic sustenance
delicacy very rare, costly, or fine food
diet foods or cuisine one eats regularly, esp. when low in calories
edibles anything that may be eaten
fare food, esp. specific kind of diet or cuisine
fodder food given to animals; feed

food anything eaten as nourishment for sustenance; solid food as distinguished from liquid
foodstuffs edible substances
goodies *Informal.* foods one especially likes; treats
leftovers food remaining after completion of meal, often saved
mess food eaten by a group together, esp. soldiers
morsel small portion of food
nourishment food eaten for sustenance
nutriment food taken as nourishment
provisions supply of food
rations supply of food, esp. for soldiers
refection food eaten esp. after interval of hunger
refreshment food and drink, esp. taken to restore energy
scraps bits of food remaining after completion of meal, often discarded
slop unappealing food, esp. leftovers
sustenance any substance consumed to keep one alive
swill unappealing food, often table scraps
tidbit small morsel of food
viand food, esp. choice dish
victuals food; provisions
vittles victuals (colloq. spelling)

Types of Food

additive often chemical substance added to improve some aspect of food, esp. as preservative or flavor enhancer
aromatic any of certain herbs, spices, or vegetables, such as onions, garlic, or shallots, that give off a distinctive flavor and aroma
confection any sweet, esp. one prepared with fruit
cut part of an animal's flesh cut as one piece
dressing sauce or stuffing
pulse edible seeds of certain legumes, such as peas, beans, or lentils
salad combination of usu. raw, chopped vegetables
seafood fish or shellfish and their parts
seasoning herb or spice, used to enhance flavor of food
shortening butter, lard, or fat, used to make pastry or bread flaky and crumbly
syrup thick, sweet liquid prepared from sugar, molasses, or glucose

Common Foods

beverage, bread
cake, candy, cereal, cheese, condiment, cookie, cracker
dairy, dessert
fat, fish, flour, fruit, fungus
game, grain
herb
leavening, legume
meat
noodle, nut
oil
pasta, pastry, pâté, poultry
roll
sauce, sausage, seed, shellfish, soup, spice, stew, sweetener
vegetable

Meats and Cuts of Meat

meat flesh of mammals raised to be eaten, esp. cattle, pigs, and sheep
bacon, beef, beefburger, braciola, brains, breast, brisket, burger, butt, butterfly
Canadian bacon, center loin chop, charqui, Châteaubriand, chitterlings, chops, cold cuts, corned beef, cutlet
filet mignon, flanken, flitch
gizzards, goat
ham (Danish, picnic, prosciutto, Serrano, Smithfield, Virginia, Westphalian), hamburger, hock
jerky, joint
kid, kidney, knuckles
lamb, liver, loin chop
marrow, medallion, mountain oysters, mutton
noisette, numbles
oxtail
pastrami, pig's feet, pork, prairie oysters
rack, red meat, ribs, roast (blade, chuck, crown, eye of round, pot, rack, rib, rolled, round, rump, shoulder, sirloin tip, standing rib)
saddle, salt pork, short ribs, shoulder chop, slab bacon, spare ribs, steak (blade, club, cube, Delmonico, fillet, flank, hamburger, New York, porterhouse, rib, rib eye, round, rump, saddle, Salisbury, shank, shell, shoulder, sirloin, skirt, Spencer, strip, T-bone, tenderloin, top loin, top round), sweetbreads
tongue, tournedos, tripe
umbles
veal

Sausage and Pâté

pâté paste of meat, animal organs, and seasonings
sausage chopped, seasoned meat, usu. stuffed into thin casing
andouillettes
bangers, blood sausage, bologna, boudin blanc, boudin noir, Bratwurst, Braunschweiger
chicken liver pâté, chorizo
duck sausage
fish sausage, foie gras, forcemeat, frank, frankfurter
galantine, Genoa salami
head cheese, hot dog, hot link
Italian sausage
kielbasa, knockwurst, kosher salami
linguiça, liver pâté, liverwurst
merguez, mortadella, mulliatelle
pâté de foie gras, pâté de campagne, pâté en croûte, pork sausage
salami, saucisse, saucisson, sausage, scrapple
terrine

Vienna sausage
weenie, wiener, wurst
zampone

Poultry and Game

game flesh of wild birds or animals
poultry flesh of fowl raised to be eaten
bear, boar
capon, chicken (broiler, free range, fryer, roaster, stewer), Cornish hen
deer, duck
fowl, frog legs
game, goose, grouse, guinea fowl
hare
partridge, pheasant, pigeon, pullet
quail
rabbit
squab
turkey
venison
wild turkey

Fish and Shellfish

fish flesh of cold-blooded vertebrate animals living in water
shellfish flesh of invertebrate, aquatic animals covered by hard shells
abalone, anchovy, angelfish
bacalao, bass, blackfish, bluefish, bonito, brisling, butterfish
calamari, catfish, caviar, clam, cod, codfish, conch, coral, crab, crawdad, crawfish, crayfish
eel, escargot
finnan haddie, flounder
gravlax, grunion
haddock, halibut, herring
John Dory
kipper
langoustine, lobster, lotte, lox
mackerel, mahimahi, milt, monk, mussel
octopus, orange roughy, oyster
perch, pompano, prawn
red snapper, roe
salmon, sand dab, sardine, scallop, scampi, scrod, scungilli, sea bass, sea urchin, shark, shrimp, skate, smelt, smoked salmon, snail, snapper, softshell crab, sole, sprat, squid, striped bass, sturgeon, surimi, swordfish
teal, terrapin, tile, tomalley, trout, tuna, turbot
weak, whitefish
yellowtail

Dairy Foods

dairy food food derived from milk, esp. cow's milk
bonnyclabber, butter
cheese, clabber, cream, crème fraîche, curds
eggs
goat's milk
half-and-half, heavy cream
ice cream
kefir
leben, light cream
milk (buttermilk, condensed, dry, evaporated, homogenized, lowfat, nonfat, pasteurized, raw, skim, whole)
sour cream, sweet butter
ultrapasteurized heavy cream
whey, whipping cream
yogurt

Cheese

cheese solidified form of ripened curds of soured milk
American
Banon, Bel Paese, blue, Boursin, brick, Brie
Caciocavallo, Caerphilly, Camembert, cheddar, Cheshire, chèvre, Chevret, clabber, coeur à la crème, colby, comte, coon cheese, cottage cheese, cream cheese, crema Danica
Danish blue, Derby, Dunlop
Edam, Edelpilzkäse, Emmenthaler, Epoisses
farmer's cheese, feta, fontina, fromage blanc
Gammelost, Gjetost, Gloucester, goat cheese, Gorgonzola, Gouda, Gruyère
Havarti, hoop cheese
jack cheese, Jarlsberg
Kumminost
Lancashire, Leicester, Liederkranz, Limburger, Liptauer, Livarot, long horn
Maroilles, Mimolette, Monterey Jack, Montrachet, mozzarella, muenster
Neufchâtel
Parmesan, Pecorino, Pont L'E&vacute;êque, Port-Salut, pot cheese, processed cheese, provolone
Quargel
rat cheese, red Windsor, ricotta, Romano, Roquefort
sapsago, smoked cheese, Stilton, St. Marcellin, string cheese, Swiss
Teleme, Tillamook, Tilsit
Vacherin, Velveeta
Wensleydale, white cheddar

Vegetables, Legumes, and Fungi

fungus edible, growing, parasitic organism
legume pod or seed of certain herbs or shrubs
vegetable edible plant, eaten raw or cooked
alfalfa sprout, artichoke, arugula, asparagus, aubergine
bamboo shoot, bean (aduki, black, broad, butter, chickpea, fava, garbanzo, green, haricot, kidney, lentil, lima, mung, navy, northern, pink, pinto, red, soya, string, wax, white), bean sprout, beet, Bermuda onion, black-eyed pea, bok choy, broccoli, Brussels sprout
cabbage, cactus, cardoon, carrot, cassava, cauliflower, celeriac, celery, chard, chayote,

chicory, Chinese cabbage, chive, collard greens, corn, courgette, cowpea, cress, cucumber
daikon, dandelion greens
eggplant, endive, escarole
finocchio
green bean, green onion
Japanese eggplant, Jerusalem artichoke
kale, kohlrabi
leek, lettuce (Bibb, Boston, butter, corn salad, cos, curly, green leaf, iceberg, mache, red leaf, romaine), lovage
maize, manioc, mung sprout, mushroom (black, button, champignon, chanterelle, enoki, fungi, morel, oyster, porcini, shiitake, tree ear), mustard greens
nopal, nori
okra, onion, oyster plant
parsnip, pea (black-eyed, green, snow, split, sugar), pearl onion, pepper (bell, capsicum, chile, green, Italian, jalapeìo, pimiento, red, serrano, wax, yellow), potato, pumpkin
radiccio, radish, rampion, ramson, red cabbage, red onion, rhubarb, rutabaga
salsify, scallion, seaweed, shallot, snap bean, sorrel, soybean, spinach, sprout, squash (acorn, butternut, crookneck, cymling, spaghetti, summer, winter, yellow, zucchini), string bean, succory, sugar pea, sweet potato, Swiss chard
taro root, tomatillo, tomato, truffle, turnip
water chestnut, watercress, wax bean
yam
zucchini

Fruits

fruit edible portion of mature flowering plant
ananas, apple (Baldwin, delicious, empire, golden, Granny Smith, gravenstein, Jonathan, Macintosh, macoun, pippin, Rome, winesap), apricot, atemoya, avocado
banana, berry (bilberry, bearberry, blackberry, black raspberry, blueberry, boysenberry, candleberry, checkerberry, cloudberry, cranberry, dewberry, elderberry, gooseberry, huckleberry, lingonberry, loganberry, mulberry, raspberry, strawberry, whortleberry), black currant, blood orange, breadfruit, bullace
calmyrna, canistel, carambola, cherimoya, cherry, citron, clementine, coconut, copra, crabapple, currant, custard apple
damson plum, date, durian
fig
granadilla, grape (Cabernet Sauvignon, cardinal Chardonnay, Chenin Blanc, Concord, Delaware, Italia, Merlot, Muscadet, muscat, Pinot Blanc, Pinot Noir, Riesling, seedless, Thompson seedless, Tokay, zinfandel), grapefruit, greengage, guava
jackfruit, jujube
kiwi, kumquat
lemon, lime, loquat
mandarin orange, mango, medlar, melon (cantaloupe, casaba, Crenshaw, honeydew, muskmelon, Persian, watermelon, winter melon)
naartje, navel orange, nectarine
olive, orange, ortanique
papaya, passion fruit, pawpaw, peach, pear (Anjou, Bosc, Bartlett, Comice, winter nellis), pepino, persimmon, pineapple, pitahaya, plantain, plum, pomegranate, pomelo, prickly pear, prune, pummelo
quince, quinoa
raisin, rambutan
sapodilla, sapote, satsuma, soursop, spanspek
tamarillo, tamarind, tangelo, tangerine
ugli fruit
Valencia orange

Nuts and Seeds

nut edible kernel of certain one-seeded fruits
seed fertilized, matured ovule of certain flowering plants, usu. eaten dried
acorn, almond
beechnut, ben, betel, black walnut, Brazil, butternut
candlenut, cashew, chestnut, chinquapin, cobnut, corozo
dika
filbert
grugru
hazelnut, hickory, horse chestnut
kola
litchi
macadamia
palm, peanut, pecan, physic nut, pignola, pine, pistachio, pumpkinseed
quinoa
sassafras, sesame seed, souari nut, sunflower seed
walnut

Herbs and Spices

herb seed plant used esp. as seasoning
spice portion of plant, esp. seed or leaf, used to season food
achiote, allspice, angelica, anise, asafetida
basil, bay leaf, benne seed, berbere, black pepper, borage, bouquet garni
cacao, calamint, capers, caraway seed, cardamom, carob, cayenne, celery seed, chervil, chicory, chili pepper, chili powder, Chinese parsley, chives, cilantro, cinnamon, cloves, coriander, cubeb, cumin, curly parsley, curry
dill
elephant garlic
fennel, fenugreek, fines herbes, finochio, flaxseed
garam masala, garlic, ginger, green peppercorn
iodized salt, Italian parsley
juniper berry

kosher salt
lemon basil, lemon grass, licorice, lovage
mace, marjoram, mint, mustard
nutmeg
oregano
paprika, parsley, pepper, pepper flakes, peppermint, pickling spice, poppy seed, pumpkin seed
red pepper, rock salt, rosemary
saffron, sage, salt, sea salt, sesame seed, shallots, sorrel, St. John's-bread, summer savory, sunflower seed, sweet basil
table salt, tarragon, thyme, turmeric
vanilla
white pepper

Grains and Flours

flour fine powder of ground grain, used esp. in baking
grain small, hard seed of certain cereal grasses
barley, blue cornmeal, bran, buckwheat, bulghur
corn, cornmeal, couscous
farina, flour (bleached, enriched, gluten, pastry, rice, rye, semolina, unbleached, wheat, white)
grits, groats
hominy
kasha
masa, millet
oat bran, oats
polenta
rice (basmati, brown, enriched, long-grain, minute, quick-cooking, short-grain, white), rye
semolina
wheat, wheat germ, wild rice

Pasta and Noodles

noodle flat strip of dough
pasta flour or semolina dough dried in various shapes
angel hair
bucatini
cannelloni, cappelletti, chow fun noodles, chow mein noodles, conchiglie
dumpling
egg noodles
farfel, fettuccine, fettucelle, fusilli
gelatin noodles, glass noodles, gnocchi
knodel, kreplach
lasagne, linguine, lo mein noodles
macaroni, mafalde, manicotti, mostaccioli
noodles
penne
quenelle
ravioli, rice, rigatoni, rotelli, rotini
soba, spaetzle, spaghetti, spaghettini
tagliatelle, tortellini
vermicelli
won ton
ziti

Cereals

cereal grain produced from grass, used esp. as breakfast food
Cheerios, Chex, corn flakes, Cream of Wheat
Frosted Flakes
granola, Grape Nuts, grits, gruel
mush
oatmeal, porridge, puffed rice
Raisin Bran, Rice Krispies, rolled oats
Shredded Wheat
Wheaties

Breads, Rolls, and Crackers

bread baked food, usu. made from flour or meal mixed with water and yeast
cracker thin, crisp, often unleavened bread
roll small bread
anadama bread
bagel, baguette, bialy, biscuit, black bread, bran muffin, breadcrumbs, breadstick, brioche, brown bread, bun
challah, chapati, cheese bread, cornbread, corn dodger, cracknel, crisp, croissant, crouton
egg bread, English muffin
French bread
garlic bread, graham cracker
hardtack, hush puppy
johnny cake
matzo, melba toast, muffin
nan, nut bread
oatcake
papadam, pita, poori, popover, pretzel, pumpernickel bread
raisin bread, roll (cinnamon, dinner, hard, Kaiser, onion, Parker House, sourdough), rusk, rye bread
saltine, seeded rye bread, semolina bread, ship biscuit, sippet, soda biscuit, soda bread, sourdough bread
toast, tortilla
unleavened bread
wafer, water biscuit, whole-grain bread, whole-wheat bread
yeast cake
zwieback

Cakes

cake baked or pan-cooked, sweetened dough, often frosted
angel food cake
Banbury tart, Battenberg cake
cheesecake, chocolate cake, coffeecake, cupcake
devil's food cake
fruitcake
gâteau, genoise, gingerbread
honey cake
jelly roll
kuchen
layer cake, loaf cake
marble cake

pancake (battercake, blini, blintz, buckwheat, crêpe, flapjack, griddle cake, hotcake, johnnycake, latke, potato, waffle), pound cake
Sacher torte, sally lunn, savarin, shortcake, simnel cake, spice cake, sponge cake, stollen
tart, tartlet, teacake, torte
upside-down cake
waffle, wedding cake, white cake
yellow cake

Pastry

pastry fancy, sweetened baked good, often with filling
baba au rum, baklava, beignet, berry pie, Boston cream pie
cake, cornet, cream pie, cream puff, crescent, cruller, crumpet
Danish, doughnut
Eccles cake, éclair
feuilletée, frangipane, fritter, fruit pie
jelly doughnut
madeleine, meringue pie, mille-feullles
napoleon
pain au chocolat, pâté à choux, petit four, phyllo, pie, profiterole, puff
quiche
schnecken, scone, shoo-fly pie, sopaipilla, strudel, sweet roll
tart, timbale, turnover
Washington pie

Cookies

cookie small, sweet cake
animal cracker
bar, biscuit, brandy snap, brownie, butter
chocolate chip cookie
fig bar, florentine, fortune cookie
garibaldi, gingersnap
hermit
jumble
lady finger
macaroon
oatmeal cookie, Oreo
palm leaf, panettone, peanut butter cookie
ratafia
shortbread, sugar cookie
tollhouse
wafer

Candy

candy flavored food sweetened with sugar or syrup, usu. in small chunks
bark, bonbon, brittle, butterscotch
candy bar, candy cane, caramel, chocolate, chocolate bar, confection, cotton candy
fondant, frosting, fudge
halvah
icing
jawbreaker, jellybean, jimmies, jujube
kiss
lemon drop, licorice, Lifesaver, lollipop
marchpane, marshmallow, marzipan, mint, M'n'M
nonpareil, nougat
peanut brittle, penuche, peppermint, praline
rock candy
saltwater taffy, sweets
taffy, toffee, Turkish delight, tutti-frutti

Desserts

dessert usu. sweet substance eaten at end of meal, often frozen or baked
apple pandowdy
baked Alaska, banana split, Bavarian cream, blacking pudding, blancmange, bombe, Boston cream pie, brown betty
cannoli, cassata, charlotte russe, clafoutis, cobbler, compote, coupe, crème brûlée, crème caramel, crêpe suzette, custard
deep dish pie, duff
Edinburgh fog, flan
floating island, flummery, frappé, frozen custard, frozen dessert, frozen yogurt, fruit cup, frumenty
gelato, glacé, granita
ice cream, ice cream bar, ice cream sandwich, Indian pudding, Italian ice
Jell-O
marrons glacés, meringue, moor-in-a-shirt, mousse, mud pie
parfait, pashka, peach Melba, pie, poached pear, pudding
rice pudding
Sacher torte, sherbet, snow cone, snow pudding, sorbet, soufflé, strawberry shortcake, streusel, sundae, syllabub
tiramisu, tortoni, trifle
vacherin
zabaglione, zuppa inglese

Dessert Sauces

dessert sauce sweet liquid used as flavoring or dressing over dessert
butterscotch
charlotte russe, chocolate, crème Anglais, crème Chantilly, crème pâtissière
frangipane
hard sauce, hot fudge
marshmallow
Nesselrode
pineapple
topping

Sweeteners

sweetener sugar or syrup used to make food sweet
corn syrup
fructose
honey
Karo syrup

maple sugar, maple syrup, molasses
sorghum, sugar (barley, brown, cane, caramel, castor, confectioner's, cube, granulated, icing, light brown, powdered, raw, spun, superfine), syrup
treacle

Cooking Fats and Oils

fat greasy substance forming most of adipose tissue of animals
oil greasy liquid obtained from animal, mineral, or vegetable source, used in cooking
almond oil, avocado oil
bacon fat, butter
canola, chicken fat, cocoa butter, coconut oil, corn oil, cottonseed oil, Crisco
drippings
extra virgin olive oil
fat
ghee, goose grease, grapeseed oil
hazelnut oil
lard
margarine
oleomargarine, olive oil
partially hydrogenated vegetable oil, peanut oil
rapeseed, rendered chicken fat
safflower oil, schmaltz, sesame oil, shortening, solid vegetable shortening, soya oil, soybean oil, suet, sunflower oil
vegetable oil, virgin olive oil
walnut oil, wheat germ oil

Additives and Thickening and Leavening Agents

additive often chemical substance added to improve some aspect of food, esp. as preservative or to enhance flavor
leavening substance that causes baked goods to rise
agar, alum, arrowroot
baking powder, baking soda, brewer's yeast
cornstarch, cream of tartar
food coloring, flour
gelatin
hydrolyzed vegetable protein
isinglass
lecithin
monosodium glutamate, MSG
neat's-foot jelly
potato flour
rennet, roux
sago, sodium benzoate, starter
tapioca, tomato paste
yeast

Salad Dressings

salad dressing usu. sharply flavored liquid mixture poured over raw vegetable salad
aioli
blue cheese
creamy garlic, creamy Italian
French
honey Dijon
Italian
oil and vinegar
ranch, Russian
Thousand Island
vinaigrette

Sauces

sauce liquid flavoring or dressing of mixed ingredients added to other foods
aioli, allemande, A-1 sauce, applesauce
barbecue, Béarnaise, béchamel, Bercy, Bordelaise, brown
chasseur, chili, cranberry, cream, curry
diable, duck
espagnole
giblet gravy, gravy
hoisin, hollandaise sauce, hot sauce
marinara, mayonnaise, mole, Mornay, mousseline, mushroom
nantua
oyster
pan gravy, pesto, pistou
ravigote, red-eye gravy, rémoulade
satay, soubise, soy sauce, suprême, sweet-and-sour sauce
Tabasco, tahini, tamari, tartar, tomato sauce
velouté
white, Worcestershire sauce

Condiments

condiment substance eaten with another food to add flavor
anchovy, angostura bitters, aspic
bread and butter pickle, brine
caper, catsup, chutney, confiture, conserves, cornichon
dill pickle
gherkin
horseradish
jalapeìo relish
ketchup
jam, jelly
lemon curd, lemon peel
marmalade, mustard
picante sauce, piccalilli, pickle, pimiento, preserves
relish, rosewater
salsa, sambal, sweet pickle
tahini
vinegar (balsamic, cider, malt, red wine, rice wine, white wine)
wasabi
zest

Soups and Stews

soup liquid food, usu. with bits of solid food, made by cooking meat, fish, vegetables, and seasonings in water or milk

stew mixture, esp. of meat and vegetables, cooked in liquid
alphabet soup, avgolemono
beef broth, beef stew, bird's-nest soup, bisque, blanquette, borscht, bouillabaise, bouillon, broth, Brunswick stew, burgoo
callaloo, caldo verde, chicken broth, chicken noodle soup, chicken soup, cholent, chowder, cioppino, civet, cock-a-leekie, consommé, cream soup, cullis
daube
egg drop soup
fumet
gazpacho, goulash, gumbo
hasenpfeffer, hot and sour soup
lobscouse
madrilène, matelote, matzo ball soup, menudo, minestrone, miso soup, mulligan, mulligatawny, mushroom, navarin
olla podrida, onion soup, oxtail soup
pepper pot, potage
ragout, ramen, rassolnik
Scotch broth, shark's fin soup, slumgullion, split pea soup, stock
tomato soup, turtle soup, tzimmes
vegetable soup, vichyssoise
won ton soup

Beverages

beverage liquid food
ambrosia, apple juice
barley water, beef tea, beer, birch beer, black tea, bouillon, buttermilk
café au lait, café filtre, café noir, caffé latte, cappuccino, chocolate milk, cider, club soda, cocoa, coconut milk, coffee, cola, cordial, cranberry juice, cream soda
Darjeeling tea, decaf(feinated coffee)
Earl Grey tea, egg cream, eggnog, espresso
float, frappe, fruit juice
ginger ale, ginger beer, ginseng tea, grapefruit juice, grape juice, green tea
herb tea, hot chocolate
ice cream soda
kava, kefir, kumiss
lemonade, limeade, lime rickey, liqueur
malted, maté, milk, milk shake, mineral water, mixer, mocha, mulled cider
nectar
orangeade, orange juice, orange pekoe tea
phosphate, pineapple juice, punch
root beer
Sanka, sarsaparilla, seltzer, shrub, soda water, soybean milk, spice tea, spirits, syllabub
tea, tisane, tomato juice, tonic water, Turkish coffee
vegetable juice
water (branch, distilled, mineral, seltzer, soda, sparkling, spring, tap, Vichy) whiskey, wine

COOKING AND CUISINE

Preparations and Presentations
Cooking Techniques
Cuisines, Meals, and Restaurants
Cooks and Servers
Prepared Dishes

Preparations and Presentations

à la king (*adj*) served with cream sauce
à la mode (*adj*) in the style of; served with ice cream
al burro (*adj*) served with butter
al dente (*adj*) firm to the bite
amandine (*adj*) served with almonds
anglaise (*adj*) boiled
aspic jellied stock or juice
au fromage (*adj*) with cheese
au gratin (*adj*) covered with sauce and crumbs; toasted
au jus (*adj*) served with natural juices
beurre blanc butter, shallots, and wine
beurre manie flour kneaded with fat for sauce base
bouquet garni herb mixture in cheesecloth, removed after cooking
broth liquid in which meat, fish, grains, or vegetables have been cooked; stock
cacciatore (*adj*) hunter's style; containing tomatoes, mushrooms, herbs, and other seasonings
calzone folded pizza
canapé small, savory sandwich appetizer on toast, cracker, or crustless bread
chasseur (*adj*) brown sauce usu. containing tomatoes, mushrooms, shallots, and white wine
chiffonade mixture of minced herbs and vegetables, used in soups
clotted cream cream thickened by cooking; Devonshire cream
consommé clear soup made from stock
cracklings crisp residue left after rendering hog or chicken fat
creole (*adj*) spicy sauce or dish, usu. with rice
crêpes thin pancakes rolled with filling or jam
croustade baked or fried pastry shell, sometimes made of noodles, rice, or mashed potatoes, filled with ragout
Devonshire cream clotted cream
dough flour or meal combined with water or milk and shortening, to be shaped and baked
drawn butter melted, clarified butter, often seasoned
dress (*vb*) prepare for cooking or serving
drizzle (*vb*) sprinkle drops of liquid lightly over food
en brochette (*adj*) cut into chunks and broiled on a skewer
en croûte (*adj*) encased in pastry and baked
entremets vegetables or savories served with main course
farci (*adj*) stuffed

flambé (*adj*) served aflame after dousing with potable alcohol
florentine (*adj*) with spinach
fondue melted cheese with flavorings
garnish (*vb*) decorate with edible ornaments, such as parsley
hash fried, chopped meat and vegetables
hull (*vb*) remove leaves and stem of soft fruit
jardiniere (*adj*) with variety of fresh vegetables
julienne (*vb*) cut into matchstick-shaped pieces
kabob skewered, grilled cubes of meat and vegetables
lyonnaise (*adj*) with onions
meunière (*adj*) with browned butter, lemon, and parsley
nesselrode (*adj*) with chestnuts
Newburg (*adj*) with cream, egg yolk, butter, and paprika sauce
niçoise (*adj*) with tomatoes, garlic, and olive oil
omelette sautéed eggs mixed with or folded around other ingredients
over easy (*adj*) describing fried egg that is flipped over and cooked briefly before serving
pancake egg and flour batter fried into circular cakes on griddle
patty thin, round, molded piece of ground or minced food; piece of food covered with batter and fried or baked
peel (*vb*) remove outer skin or layer of food, esp. of vegetable or fruit
piccata (*adj*) with lemon and parsley, also sometimes with capers
pizza circular, flat bread baked with cheese and tomato topping
Provençale (*adj*) with tomatoes, garlic, onions, and herbs
quiche savory egg custard tart with filling
rare (*adj*) cooked briefly, esp. meat
roast meat, game, or poultry cooked over fire or in oven
roulade rolled, stuffed slice of meat or pastry
roux mixture of melted fat and flour, used as sauce base
salad fresh greens and other ingredients served cold and usu. raw: Caesar, chef's, coleslaw, composed, green, niçoise, pasta, potato, salmagundi, slaw, tabbouleh, tossed, Waldorf
sandwich assorted cold meats and fillings between bread slices: BLT, club, cold cuts, Cuban, Dagwood, double-decker, grinder, hero, hoagie, Italian sandwich, poor boy, Reuben, Sloppy Joe, submarine, torpedo, triple-decker, wedge
sashimi raw fish cut into very thin slices, arranged with ginger and wasabi horseradish
scallopine thinly sliced, flour-dredged, sautéed meat
stock meat, fish, or poultry broth, esp. when stored for use at later time
stroganoff (*adj*) with sour cream and mushrooms
subgum (*adj*) prepared with mixed vegetables in Chinese style
sunnyside up (*adj*) describing egg fried on one side only
tandoori (*adj*) baked in a clay tandoor oven
vacuum-packed (*adj*) sealed in a jar or can with nearly all air evacuated before sealing to preserve freshness
vol-au-vent flaky pastry shell for filling with meat or vegetables and sauce
well done (*adj*) thoroughly cooked until all redness is gone, esp. meat
zest outer peel of citrus fruit, used for flavoring

Cooking Techniques

bake (*vb*) cook with dry oven heat
barbecue (*vb*) cook over hot coals on grill or spit; grill
baste (*vb*) spoon liquid over food to moisten it while cooking
batter (*vb*) coat with flour, eggs, and breadcrumbs before frying
beat (*vb*) blend ingredients with rapid, rotary motion
blacken (*vb*) cook meat or fish over high, direct heat
blanch (*vb*) rinse or cook briefly in boiling water
blend (*vb*) stir ingredients together
boil down (*vb*) boil until reduced in volume
braise (*vb*) brown in fat, then cover and cook in liquid
bread (*vb*) coat with breadcrumbs
broil (*vb*) cook with hot coals or direct flame
brown (*vb*) sear surface of meat in pan, broiler, or oven to seal juices
bruise (*vb*) crush partially to release flavor
butterfly (*vb*) cut open and flatten
can (*vb*) preserve by sealing in airtight can or jar
candy (*vb*) cook in heavy syrup until glazed; coat with sugar
caramelize (*vb*) cook sugar until it forms brown syrup
carbonado (*vb*) score and broil, usu. meat
charbroil (*vb*) broil or grill until blackened on outside
chop (*vb*) cut loosely and rapidly into small pieces
churn (*vb*) agitate milk in a container to make butter
clarify (*vb*) purify solid matter from fats or stock
coddle (*vb*) cook in water just below boiling point
concentrate (*vb*) make less dilute
cream (*vb*) blend until creamy and soft
crisp (*vb*) make brittle, usu. by frying
crystallize (*vb*) coat with sugar
cube (*vb*) cut into cube-shaped pieces
curdle (*vb*) coagulate, esp. milk; turn sour
cure (*vb*) prepare meat or fish for preservation by smoking, drying, or salting
cut in (*vb*) incorporate shortening into flour using two knives, so that mixture resembles uneven, coarse crumbs
deep fry (*vb*) cook by entirely submerging in hot fat
deglaze (*vb*) dissolve browned particles with liquid in sauté pan
degrease (*vb*) remove accumulated fat from surface of hot liquid

dehydrate (*vb*) remove moisture from, esp. to preserve
desiccate (*vb*) preserve by drying or dehydrating
devein (*vb*) remove dark dorsal vein from shrimp
devil (*vb*) season with mustard, cayenne, and other hot spices
dice (*vb*) cut into small cubes
draw (*vb*) remove entrails
dredge (*vb*) coat with flour, sugar, or crumbs
dry (*vb*) remove moisture from
dry-roast (*vb*) roast without oil, esp. nuts
enrich (*vb*) restore nutrients that have been lost in processing
eviscerate (*vb*) remove entrails from
fillet (*vb*) remove bones, esp. backbone from fish
flash-freeze (*vb*) quick-freeze
fold (*vb*) blend ingredients lightly and gently so as to retain air
freeze-dry (*vb*) dry a heat-sensitive food by freezing it and converting the ice to vapor in a high vacuum
fricassee (*vb*) cut up, brown, then cook in liquid
fry (*vb*) cook in hot fat, either in deep fat or by pan-frying
glaze (*vb*) cover with glossy coating of juices, aspic, syrup, or egg
grate (*vb*) shred into particles or strips
gratiné (*vb*) bake or broil with sauce and crumbs in au gratin style
grill (*vb*) cook on open grid over hot coals; barbecue
hard-boil (*vb*) boil an egg until white and yolk solidify
homogenize (*vb*) prepare emulsion of milk by reducing size of fat globules to distribute them equally throughout
knead (*vb*) mix and work dough with one's hands
lard (*vb*) stuff meat with slices of fat
macerate (*vb*) steep in liquid, esp. liqueur
marinate (*vb*) soak in seasoned broth, juices, or wine
mash (*vb*) reduce food, usu. boiled, to soft, pulpy mass by pressure
microwave (*vb*) cook in a microwave oven
mince (*vb*) chop finely
nap (*vb*) cover with sauce that adheres to outline of food
pan-broil (*vb*) cook in uncovered frying pan over direct heat, using little or no fat
pan-fry (*vb*) fry in small amount of fat in skillet or shallow pan; sauté
parboil (*vb*) partially cook by boiling
pare (*vb*) remove skin or peel
pickle (*vb*) preserve in spiced brine
poach (*vb*) cook in liquid at or near boiling
preserve (*vb*) prepare fruit or vegetable by cooking with sugar, pickling, or canning, so as to resist spoilage
purée (*vb*) put solid food through sieve or blender or mash in mortar
quick-freeze (*vb*) freeze cooked or uncooked food very rapidly to facilitate lengthy storage; flash-freeze
raise (*vb*) make light by using yeast but not baking powder or soda
refresh (*vb*) plunge hot food into cold water to halt cooking
render (*vb*) remove animal fat
ripen (*vb*) advance or bring to maturity or best condition for use, esp. cheese
roast (*vb*) cook with dry oven heat, esp. meats
salt (*vb*) cure or preserve meat or fish by coating with salt
sauté (*vb*) brown quickly in small quantity of hot fat; pan-fry
scald (*vb*) heat food just to boiling point
scallop (*vb*) bake in layers topped with breadcrumbs
scramble (*vb*) stir vigorously and then cook in pan while stirring
sear (*vb*) brown surface quickly with high heat
shirr (*vb*) bake in shallow dish, esp. eggs
shred (*vb*) cut or grate into thin, irregular strips
sift (*vb*) remove lumps from dry ingredient by passing it through strainer or sieve
simmer (*vb*) cook in gently boiling water
smother (*vb*) steam slowly in heavy, closed vessel with minimal liquid
soft-boil (*vb*) boil an egg until white and yolk partially solidify, usu. for three to four minutes
souse (*vb*) pickle in vinegar or brine
steam (*vb*) cook over boiling water without allowing food to touch the water
steep (*vb*) pour boiling water over food and allow it to sit
stew (*vb*) simmer for a long time
stir (*vb*) mix with rotary motion
stir-fry (*vb*) cook quickly over high heat in wok or large fry pan
stuff (*vb*) fill cavity with seasonings, grains, or chopped vegetables; force
sweat (*vb*) cook vegetables or fruits slowly to release their juices
thread (*vb*) form a fine stream when poured boiling from a spoon
toast (*vb*) brown surface on grill, oven, or toaster, esp. bread
toss (*vb*) mix by flipping ingredients together
truss (*vb*) tie or sew legs and wings of poultry while roasting
whip (*vb*) beat lightly to incorporate air and increase volume
whisk (*vb*) beat vigorously until mixed or blended

Cuisines, Meals, and Restaurants

à la carte (*adj*) designating foods priced and chosen separately by dish
alfresco (*adj*) eaten outdoors
antipasto assorted Italian appetizers, esp. marinated vegetables and sliced meats
appetizers snacks; small items eaten before main course: antipasto, canapés, cold cuts, crudités, dim sum, dips, finger foods, hors d'oeuvres, kickshaw, rollmop, rumaki, spreads, starters, tapas, vorspeise
banquet large, sumptuous spread of many dishes
barbecue outdoor meal consisting of meats cooked over charcoal; cookout

bistro small, unpretentious restaurant or tavern serving simple fare
blue plate special restaurant main course at special low price
box lunch prepared lunch packaged in box
brasserie informal restaurant serving hearty food
brown bag lunch carried in brown paper sack, esp. to office
brunch late morning meal, combining breakfast and lunch
buffet foods arranged for self-service
carryout establishment that sells food to be eaten away from premises
carte du jour *French.* menu for the day
carvery roasted meats and poultry carved to diner's request in restaurant; restaurant providing such meats
catering food and service supplied at banquet
charcuterie delicatessen
chophouse restaurant that specializes in steaks and chops
chuck wagon provisions and cooking wagon used in American old west
clambake shellfish baked in sand on beach
cocktail party early evening gathering at which appetizers are served
coffee shop simple, low-priced restaurant serving plain fare
cookoff contest in which competitors prepare their specialties
continental breakfast breakfast of breads and coffee or tea
course one element of a meal, served at one time
C ration prepared, packaged soldier's meal
crudités sliced raw vegetables
cuisine manner of preparing food; style of cooking
cuisine minceur *French.* light foods prepared with minimal fat
déjeuner *French.* lunch
delicatessen shop serving prepared cooked meats, salads, and cheeses at counter; deli
doggie bag bag supplied by restaurant in which leftovers are taken home
drive-in restaurant in which patrons are served or place orders while sitting in their cars
early-bird special reduced-price meal at restaurant for those seated early
entrée dish served as main course of meal
fast food cheap, mass-produced dishes served quickly at walk-in or drive-in outlets
finger foods appetizers that can be eaten with one's fingers, usu. in bite-size chunks
haute cuisine classic French cooking with rich sauces
health food natural or organic food with high nutritive value and low sodium or fat content, believed to promote good health
high tea *Chiefly Brit.* substantial late-afternoon snack with tea
home cooking simple, hearty fare
hors d'oeuvres appetizers
junk food low-quality, low-nutrition, starchy, sugary food
kosher (*adj*) prepared according to Jewish dietary laws
luau outdoor Hawaiian feast with entertainment
macrobiotics dietary philosophy based on yin and yang principles of balancing foods
meal customary time for eating, such as breakfast, lunch, or dinner; foods eaten at such a time
mess military self-service dining
nouvelle cuisine modern style of cooking emphasizing fresh, local ingredients and imaginative presentation
petit déjeuner *French.* breakfast
plat du jour *French.* featured entrée of the day at restaurant
pot luck meal to which each guest contributes one dish
power breakfast breakfast meeting for usu. high-level business discussions
prix fixe *French.* meal served at restaurant at set price
repast meal; food consumed at one time
restaurant establishment serving and selling meals
salad bar self-service selection of ingredients for salad in restaurant or takeout establishment
smorgasbord Swedish cold buffet
soup du jour featured soup of the day at restaurant
square meal substantial, full-course meal
surf'n'turf meat and seafood, esp. steak and lobster, served on same plate
table d'hôte *French.* complete meal served at stated time and set price
takeout food bought at restaurant to eat at home
tea *Chiefly Brit.* late-afternoon snack with tea
trattoria small, inexpensive Italian restaurant
vegetarian (*adj*) describing meals or cuisine without meat, chicken, or fish

Cooks and Servers

busboy person who clears dishes and resets tables in restaurant
carhop waiter or waitress at drive-in restaurant
caterer person who supplies, prepares, or serves food at large or private gatherings
chef chief cook, esp. one who plans menus and supervises others in preparation of food
confectioner person who makes or sells candy and sweets
headwaiter person who supervises waiters and busboys in restaurant
host person who receives and assists patrons at restaurant
maître d' maître d'hôtel
maître d'hôtel headwaiter; maître d'
pastry chef person who prepares pastries; pastry cook
prep cook kitchen assistant responsible for preparing ingredients to be used by chef
short-order cook cook who prepares foods quickly, esp. at lunch counter
soda jerk *Informal.* person who prepares and serves ice cream dishes at soda fountain

sommelier wine steward
sous-chef person ranking next after chef in kitchen
steward person who supervises tables, wine, and waiters in restaurant or club
waiter person, esp. male, who serves food to others at tables
waitperson waiter, either male or female
waitron waitperson
wine steward waiter responsible for serving wine in restaurant; sommelier

Prepared Dishes

adobo Philippine dish of marinated chicken or pork that is simmered and fried
angels on horseback appetizer of oysters wrapped in bacon
arroz con pollo Latin American dish of chicken and rice cooked with saffron
baba ghanouj Middle Eastern mashed eggplant salad with olive oil, garlic, and tahini
baked Alaska dessert of ice cream encased in sponge cake and meringue, lightly browned in an oven
beef Bourguignonne French beef dish with red wine, onions, and mushrooms
beef stroganoff beef dish with sour cream, onions, and mushrooms
beef Wellington beef fillet with pâté de foie gras, covered with pastry
bird's nest soup Chinese soup made from swallows' nests simmered in a rich stock
blini Russian buckwheat pancake, often served with caviar and sour cream
blintze crêpe filled with cheese or fruit and sauteed
boiled dinner meal of boiled meat, potatoes, and vegetables
borscht Eastern European beet soup
Boston baked beans navy beans cooked with molasses and salt pork
bouillabaisse French stew of variety of fish and shellfish in seasoned vegetable broth
bubble and squeak British dish of fried cabbage and potato, sometimes with meat
buffalo wings spicy fried chicken wings, usu. served with hot sauce
burrito Mexican dish consisting of flour tortilla stuffed with meat, rice, beans, and cheese
cabbage rolls cabbage leaves stuffed with a filling of rice and ground meat and simmered in sauce
Caesar salad salad of romaine lettuce, grated Parmesan cheese, and croutons in dressing of raw egg, lemon juice, and oil, sometimes with anchovies
cannelloni stuffed tubular pasta baked with sauce
carbonara pasta sauce of minced pancetta, egg yolks, and grated cheese
cassoulet French casserole of beans baked with meat
Charlotte russe dessert mold of ladyfingers and a cream filling
chateaubriand thick slice of rare beef tenderloin, served with bearnaise or other sauce
chicken Kiev boneless chicken breast stuffed with butter and chives, breaded and deep-fried
cheese soufflé light, puffed, baked dish made with cheese, white sauce, and beaten egg whites
chicken à la king diced cooked chicken and vegetables in a creamy sauce, usually served on toast or rice
chicken cacciatore Italian chicken dish with herbs, tomatoes, and white wine
chicken cordon bleu breaded, sautéed chicken stuffed with ham and cheese
chicken divan chicken and broccoli baked in a creamy wine sauce
chicken Kiev boneless chicken breast stuffed with butter and chives, breaded and deep-fried
chicken Marengo chicken casserole with tomatoes, wine, onions, and mushrooms
chicken Tetrazzini baked dish of diced chicken, noodles, mushrooms, and cream sauce
chili con carne highly spiced Texas dish of beef, chilies, and usu. beans
chili dog hot dog covered with chili con carne
chilies rellèos Mexican dish of stuffed jalapèo peppers
chimichanga crisp tortilla filled with meat and covered with salsa and sour cream
chipped beef dried, smoked beef sliced very thin
cholent Jewish stew of beef, beans, and potatoes, traditionally eaten on the Sabbath and cooked slowly for twenty-four hours
chop suey Chinese-American dish of bean sprouts, meat, mushrooms, and bamboo shoots, served with rice
chow-chow pickled mixture of cucumbers, onions, tomatoes, green beans, cauliflower, celery, and red pepper
chowder soup usu. with milk, salt pork, vegetables, and often seafood
chow mein Chinese-American stew of meat and vegetables, served with fried noodles
clams casino broiled clams on the half shell, topped with bacon, breadcrumbs, and butter
cobb salad salad of chopped greens and tomatoes, topped with diced chicken, bacon, avocado, and hard-boiled egg
coleslaw salad of shredded cabbage, carrots, etc., in a mayonnaise or sour cream dressing
compote dessert of fruit stewed in syrup
confit duck or goose cooked in its own fat and preserved
coq au vin French dish of chicken cooked in red wine with mushrooms and onions
coquilles St. Jacques scallops cooked in cream sauce with mushrooms, white wine, and Parmesan cheese
corn dog hot dog impaled on a stick and baked or deep fried in corn bread coating
corned beef hash mixture of diced corned or salted beef, potatoes, white sauce, and seasoning
Cornish pasty British dish of meat and vegetables wrapped in pastry and baked

couscous North African dish of steamed, cracked wheat, usu. served with lamb or chicken and sauce with vegetables
creamed chipped beef chipped beef simmered in milk and seasoned
crème bruleé dessert of egg custard topped with carmelized brown sugar
crêpe very thin French pancake, usually with a savory or sweet filling
crêpes Suzette dessert dish of crêpes in a butter and orange sauce, served flambe
croquettes small, rounded masses of cooked meat and vegetables coated with breadcrumbs and egg and deep-fried
curry Indian stew seasoned with combination of ground spices
deviled eggs hard-boiled eggs with yolk mixed with mayonnaise or sour cream and paprika
deviled ham chopped, highly seasoned ham
dim sum Chinese-style steamed dumplings and other savory dishes, served in small portions
duck à l'orange roast duck served with an orange sauce and sliced oranges
egg foo yong Chinese-American dish of beaten egg fried with meat and onions
eggplant parmigiana casserole of eggplant slices, tomato sauce, and cheese
egg roll Chinese appetizer of thin pastry with a filling of chopped meat and vegetables, deep-fried
eggs Benedict poached eggs and ham served on an English muffin and covered with hollandaise sauce
empaìadas Central American sweet or savory turnovers
enchilada Mexican dish of rolled tortilla with meat or cheese filling, baked with chili-flavored tomato sauce
fajitas Mexican marinated beef or chicken cooked with variety of sauces and rolled in a tortilla
falafel Middle Eastern spicy, deep-fried patty of ground chickpeas or other vegetables
fettuccine Italian-style egg noodles in the form of flat, narrow strips
fettuccine alfredo fettuccine served with a rich cream and cheese sauce
fish and chips British dish of fried, batter-coated fish with French-fried potatoes
flambé (*adj*) designating a dish served in flaming brandy or other liquor
fondue dish consisting of small pieces of meat, fruit, or bread dipped into a hot liquid such as melted cheese or chocolate
French onion soup onion soup topped with toast and cheese, then baked
French toast bread dipped in egg-and-milk batter, then fried
fricassee chicken or turkey simmered with onions, carrots, celery, and rice
fried rice Oriental dish of rice fried with meat and vegetables
frijoles Mexican-style beans
frittata chopped vegetables or meat cooked in egg mixture
fritter battered, deep-fried food mixture
gazpacho Spanish soup with tomatoes, cucumbers, peppers, and onions
gefilte fish Jewish dish consisting of cakes of seasoned, chopped fish, eggs, and matzo meal cooked in fish broth
German potato salad hot salad of potato chunks, bacon, and a vinegar dressing
gorp trail mix
goulash Hungarian stew with meat, vegetables, and paprika
guacamole Mexican dip or salad of mashed avocado, lemon juice, salsa, garlic, and sometimes cilantro
gumbo Creole soup with okra, including seafood, vegetables, and meat
haggis Scottish dish of lungs, heart, and liver of a sheep or calf, with suet, oatmeal, and seasoning, boiled in the animal's stomach
hash dish of chopped potatoes and meat, often corned beef, usually fried and served with eggs
hot pot British dish of mutton or beef cooked in a pot with potatoes
hummus Middle Eastern dish of mashed chickpeas with olive oil, garlic, lemon juice, and tahini
hush puppy deep-fried cornmeal fritter
Irish stew stew of lamb or beef, vegetables, and spices
jambalaya Creole stew of rice, meat, vegetables, and spices
kedgeree Indian dish of rice, lentils, fish, seasonings, and sometimes egg
kidney pie British meat pie of kidney stew wrapped in dough
kishke animal intestine stuffed with flour, fat, onion, and seasoning; stuffed derma
knish dough stuffed with a filling, such as chopped meat and mashed potatoes, and baked
kugel baked pudding of potatoes or noodles
lasagne Italian baked dish consisting of layers of wide, flat pasta, tomato sauce, cheese, and usu. meat
linguine pasta in the form of very thin ribbons
lobster Newburg dish of diced lobster cooked in cream sauce
lobster thermidor dish of lobster in cream sauce that is stuffed into lobster shell and browned
London broil flank or other steak marinated and broiled, sliced thin
macaroni and cheese usu. tubular pasta baked with cheese sauce
manicotti Italian pasta tubes usu. stuffed with a meat or cheese mixture and baked with a tomato sauce
marinara tomato sauce with garlic and spices served over pasta or seafood
meatballs small clumps of ground, seasoned meat, often served with gravy or sauce
meat loaf baked loaf of ground meat, egg, breadcrumbs, and seasoning
minestrone Italian vegetable and macaroni soup
mole Mexican sauce made with chili peppers and unsweetened chocolate
Mornay (*adj*) designating a dish served with a white cheese sauce

moussaka Greek dish with layers of ground meat and sliced eggplant, baked with seasoned sauce and cheese
mulligatawny soup East Indian curried chicken or turkey soup
ossobuco Italian dish of veal shanks stewed in white wine and tomatoes
oysters Rockefeller oysters topped with mixture of spinach, bacon, and seasonings and broiled on the half shell
paella Spanish dish of saffron-seasoned rice baked in stock with meat, seafood, and vegetables
pâté appetizer of seasoned liver, etc., chopped very fine into a paste, often molded
peach Melba chilled poached peaches served with vanilla ice cream and raspberry puree
Peking duck Chinese dish of roasted duck with crisp skin, served in thin crêpes
pemmican American Indian dish of powered dried meat mixed with hot fat and dried fruits and pressed into a loaf
pepper steak strips of beef cooked with green peppers
pig in a blanket hot dog or sausage wrapped in dough and cooked; also, *esp. Brit.*, toad-in-the-hole
pilaf dish of seasoned rice or wheat
piroshki small pastry turnovers stuffed with meat, cheese, or vegetables
pizza thinly rolled dough covered with spiced mixture of tomatoes, cheese, and meat or vegetables and baked
poi Hawaiian dish of taro root that is baked, pounded, moistened, and fermented
pork pie pork stew covered with dough and baked
potage thick French soup, esp. made with cream
potatoes O'Brien potato cubes fried with green peppers and onions
pot-au-feu French dish of boiled meat and vegetables
potpie meat and vegetables covered with pastry and baked in a deep dish
pot roast cut of beef stewed in a pot, usu. with vegetables
profiterole pastry puff, served with savory or sweet filling
quennelle poached dumpling of minced fish or meat
quiche open egg-custard pie made with various fillings
ragout Eastern European stew of meat, potatoes, and spices
ratatouille seasoned vegetable stew of eggplant, tomatoes, zucchini, and peppers
ravioli square pockets of pasta stuffed with meat or cheese
rigatoni pasta in the form of small, ribbed tubes
risotto Italian dish of rice cooked in broth and seasonings
rumaki chicken liver or water chestnut wrapped in bacon and broiled as appetizer
salsa Mexican-style seasoning dip made with tomatoes, onions, and jalapeòo peppers
Salisbury steak seasoned ground beef formed into patties, broiled or fried
sauerbraten beef marinated in vinegar, onions, and spices before cooking
sauerkraut cut cabbage fermented in brine of its own juice with salt
scallopine thin slices of meat, esp. veal, sautéed in herbs and wine
scampi large shrimp broiled in garlic flavored sauce
schnitzel fried, breaded cutlet of veal or chicken
Scotch egg British dish of hard-boiled egg encased in sausage, breaded and deep-fried
scrapple seasoned chopped pork and cornmeal mush, formed into loaves that are sliced and fried
shepherd's pie British meat pie baked with mashed potato crust
shish kabob Middle Eastern dish of meat marinated, skewered, and broiled
souvlaki Greek shish kabob consisting of small pieces of marinated meat and vegetables on a skewer
spaghetti pasta in the form of thin, long strings
Spanish rice rice cooked with tomatoes, green peppers, and onions
spoon bread baked side dish of cornmeal, milk, eggs, and shortening
steak tartare raw ground steak mixed with onions and seasonings
stuffed cabbage cabbage leaves wrapped around seasoned meat and rice mixture
succotash lima beans and corn kernels cooked together
sukiyaki Japanese dish of thinly sliced meat, vegetables, and bean curd, cooked with soy sauce, sugar, and sake
sushi Japanese dish consisting of cold cakes of rice flavored with vinegar and garnished with raw fish or vegetables
sweet-and-sour (*adj*) designating a Chinese-style dish of meat, seafood, etc., cooked in a sugar and vinegar sauce
Swiss steak steak pounded with flour and browned with vegetables and seasonings
tabbouleh Middle Eastern salad of cracked wheat, parsley, and tomatoes in olive oil and lemon juice
taco Mexican dish of fried tortilla that is folded and filled with mixture of meat, cheese, and salad
tahini Middle Eastern sauce of sesame-seed paste
tamale Mexican dish of ground meat and peppers rolled in cornmeal, wrapped in cornhusks, and steamed
tempeh fermented soybean cake
tempura Japanese dish of seafood or vegetables dipped in egg batter and deep-fried
teriyaki Japanese dish of meat or fish marinated in spicy soy sauce and grilled or broiled
terrine chopped meat or vegetable mixture cooked in earthenware dish
tofu curdled, thickened soybean milk
torte layered, filled cake usu. made with ground nuts instead of flour
tostada Mexican dish consisting of deep-fried, flat tortilla covered with meat, cheese, and salad
trail mix mixture of nuts, grains, seeds, and dried fruits, eaten as snack for energy; gorp

veal parmigiana veal cutlets coated with breadcrumbs and fried, served with tomato sauce and Parmesan cheese
veal scallopine veal cutlet dredged in flour and sautéed in butter and wine sauce
vichyssoise French potato soup, usually served cold
vol-au-vent French puff pastry shells
Waldorf salad salad of chopped apple, celery, and walnut in mayonnaise
Welsh rabbit melted, seasoned cheese, often mixed with beer, served on toast
western omelette containing ham, green pepper, and onion
Wiener schnitzel breaded veal cutlet that is fried and sometimes garnished with lemon slice and anchovy
wonton Chinese fried dumpling, usu. filled with a meat mixture
yakitori Japanese dish of small cubes of marinated chicken skewered and grilled
Yorkshire pudding unsweetened batter of flour, salt, eggs, and milk, baked under roasting meat to catch drippings or baked alone with drippings from roast
zabaglione Italian dessert made with beaten egg yolks, sugar, and Marsala wine
ziti pasta in the form of small tubes

THE KITCHEN

Cookers
Pots and Pans
Utensils and Appliances
Dishes and Serving Containers
Glassware
Cutlery and Flatware
Linens and Accessories

Cookers

autoclave pressure cooker
barbecue grill or rack over hot coals, often on movable stand
brazier simple cooker containing live coals covered by a grill
broiler oven compartment with overhead flame or heated coil
camp stove portable stove for outdoor cooking, usu. by gas
convection oven oven unit with fan that circulates and intensifies heat, decreasing normal heating time
cooktop cooking surface consisting of a flat sheet of glass and ceramic material over a heating element, usu. electric
griddle flat, wide, rimless cooking surface
grill metal grid rack over coals
hibachi small barbecue grid over hot coals (Japan)
immersion heater electric heating coil dipped in liquids
microwave oven electronic cooker in which short microwave penetrations of food produce heat to cook food rapidly
oven dry-heat cooker: electric, gas, pizza, tandoori
pressure cooker airtight, steam-pressure cooking pot, usu. of reinforced steel or aluminum; autoclave
range appliance with oven, broiler, and burners
roaster oven or open fire for cooking with little liquid
rotisserie small oven with attached spit, operated electrically
salamander small browning or glazing broiler
smoker enclosure for flavoring or curing foods with smoke
spit pointed skewer to hold meat over fire or coals
steam table warming table on which food is held over boiling water
stove cooking appliance with oven, broiler, and top burners; range
tandoor cylindrical clay oven (India)
toaster browning oven with electric heating coils, positioned vertically esp. for browning and crisping bread
toaster oven electric appliance that toasts, broils, or bakes on heating coils positioned horizontally
waffle iron two hinged metal griddles that close to cook batter

Pots and Pans

baba small mold
bean pot deep, round earthenware pot with narrow opening at top
bread pan usu. rectangular pan for baking bread
casserole deep, heavy pot with lid, used for baking
cauldron very large pot or kettle
chafing dish dish for cooking and keeping dishes warm on stand over low flame
coquille shell-shaped ovenproof dish
double boiler pot fitted snugly atop another pot filled with boiling water
Dutch oven cast-iron pot with lid
jelly-roll pan cookie sheet with one-inch-high lip around edge
kettle metal pot for boiling water, often with narrow opening or spout at top
marmite large, steep-sided, metal or ceramic pot
mold pan used to form food into shapes: butter, charlotte, chocolate, pâté, ring
paella pan very wide, shallow pan, often with two handles, used for baking
pan broad, shallow, open, metal cooking container with handle
percolator coffeepot in which boiling water bubbles up through tube and filters down through ground coffee held in perforated container near top
poacher poaching pan
poaching pan long, narrow pan with removable, porous tray; poacher
pot usu. round, deep, covered cooking container with handle

ramekin small, shallow, ovenproof baking dish
ring mold circular form used to set food into ring shape
samovar urn with spigot and heating element for boiling water to make tea
saucepan medium-deep pot with handle
sauté pan thick-bottomed, straight-sided skillet
savarin ring mold
spider cast-iron frying pan, orig. with legs to stand on hearth or over coals
springform pan baking pan with detachable bottom
steamer pot fitted with perforated insert that sits above water
stockpot large, tall, heavyweight pot
terrine earthenware baking dish, often rectangular
timbale small, cylindrical mold
tube pan deep, doughnut-shaped cake pan
wok large, bowl-shaped frying pan (China)

Utensils and Appliances

appliance usu. electrical device used in food preparation
blender electric appliance with rotary blades that chop, purée, or liquefy foods
brochette spit or skewer
bulb baster rubber tube and bulb for siphoning fats and liquids
butcher block slab of wood up to three inches thick for cutting food, esp. meat; chopping block
cake break wide-tined fork for slicing cake
cake rack low grid for cooling baked items
calabash large, hard-shell gourd used as scoop or ladle
canister wide-mouthed container with tight-fitting lid, used for storing dry goods
china cap cone-shaped sieve; chinois
chinois china cap
chopping block butcher block
chopping board wooden cutting surface
chopsticks two small sticks for lifting food, operated in one hand
church key device for opening cans by punching V-shaped hole in top
churn container with paddle or agitating mechanism in which cream or milk is stirred to make butter
cleaver heavy knife with broad blade, used esp. to cut meat through bones or joints or into large chunks
colander perforated bowl for rinsing and draining
cookie press tube and plunger used to form cookie dough
corkscrew spiral, lever, or pincer used to extract cork from wine bottle
dasher plunger with paddles at one end for mixing liquids in churn or ice cream freezer
drum sieve round frame with screen in bottom through which food is forced with a pestle
egg beater rotary beater also used for whipping cream and smoothing batter
food mill perforated pot with crank for puréeing
food processor electric appliance with set of blades revolving inside container, used for cutting, blending, grating, and puréeing solid foods
funnel cone open at top and leading into thin tube opening at bottom
garlic press small perforated masher with handle
grapefruit spoon teaspoon with serrated tip
grater punched metal surface for shredding foods, sometimes rotated by handle or freestanding with different size holes on each side
ice cream maker electric or hand-cranked device packed with ice around container that holds ice cream ingredients
ice pick pointed metal stick for breaking ice cubes
juicer electric appliance for extracting juice from fruit and vegetables
ladle deep, large spoon for serving soups
mandolin grater and slicer with wooden frame and adjustable blade
masher stiff wire instrument for puréeing, esp. potatoes
meat grinder blades that rotate on handle to reduce meat to pulp
meat pounder wooden mallet with smooth and rough surfaces, used for thinning or tenderizing meat
meat thermometer gauge on pointed stem that is inserted in meat to register internal temperature and determine when it is properly cooked
melon baller bowl-shaped spoon for scooping melon
mixer manual or electric beating instrument for blending ingredients
mortar and pestle heavy bowl and grinding stick for pulverizing
nutcracker pliers for breaking nutshells
nutpick slender, pointed implement for removing meat from nut shells
oyster knife short, rigid knife with hand guard at base of handle
pastry bag cloth bag with nozzled tube for shaping dough
pastry scraper flat blade on handle, used for manipulating pastry dough
pastry tube conical tube with patterned opening at one end, fitted on cloth bag for shaping icings and soft foods as they are squeezed through the bag
pepper mill peppercorn grinder
peeler rotating blade used to skin fruits and vegetables
pitter clamping device with small punch for removing fruit or olive pits
pizza cutter circular blade that rotates on handle, used for cutting pastry or pizza
reamer ridged cone for juicing citrus fruits
ricer utensil with small holes through which soft food is forced to produce rice-size particles
rolling pin long, narrow cylinder for flattening dough
salad spinner enclosed salad basket operated by handle
scoop small shovel, esp. used to take up dry materials
sharpening steel solid block or long tube of steel on handle, used for sharpening knives
sieve dome-shaped strainer with mesh bottom, esp. for separating coarse from fine parts of loose matter
sifter strainer for flour or sugar

skewer long, slender, pointed utensil of metal or wood, inserted through meat or other food while cooking
skimmer flat, very fine mesh strainer on handle, used for removing scum or particles from surface of liquid
slotted spoon large spoon with perforations, for removing solid pieces from liquid
spatula flat, usu. flexible-bladed device of metal, wood, or rubber, used for scraping or turning
spork combination spoon and fork, esp. for removing spaghetti from water
strainer device for retaining solid bits and passing liquids
tea ball perforated enclosure on chain for brewing tea
tongs pincers for lifting and holding food
trivet metal support or rack, decorative or protective
trussing needle metal pin used to fasten meats while roasting
utensil implement, instrument, or vessel used in cooking
vegetable parer pair of parallel blades on handle, joined at tip, used to peel fruits and vegetables
whip whisk
whisk beater consisting of several wire loops held together in handle; whip
zester small knife with serrated lateral blade, used for cutting citrus rind

Dishes and Serving Containers

boat small, deep, usu. oblong serving dish
bowl deep, rounded, hemispherical container that is open at the top: cereal, chopping, compote, cream, finger, fruit, porringer, punch, revere, salad, soup
charger large, shallow dish or platter
compote long-stemmed dish for serving fruit or sweets
creamer small pitcher with spout for serving cream or milk with coffee or tea
cruet small glass bottle with stopper, used esp. for holding oil and vinegar
cup small, open beverage container, often round and with handle: breakfast, coffee, custard, demitasse, egg, kylix, mug, noggin, tea
decanter decorative, quart-size, glass bottle with stopper for serving wine
demitasse small, delicate cup for serving strong black coffee
dessert plate plate smaller than salad plate
dish shallow, slightly concave, usu. round container made of glass or ceramics, on which food is served
eggcup small, deep-bowled cup for serving boiled egg
finger bowl small, low bowl that holds water in which to rinse fingers at table
gratin dish low, round baking and serving dish with two handles
gravy boat medium serving pitcher with handle, often on saucer
kylix shallow bowl with two handles, used as drinking cup (ancient Greece and Rome)
lazy Susan revolving serving platter, usu. placed in center of table
noggin small mug or cup
plate shallow dish, usu. round, from which food is eaten: bread and butter, dessert, dinner, luncheon, salad, saucer, service
platter large, flat serving dish, usu. with lip: charger, chop, fish, nappy, well-and-tree
porringer low dish with handle, from which soup or porridge is eaten
punch bowl large bowl from which punch is served, usu. with ladle
salad plate medium-sized plate intermediate between dessert plate and dinner plate, holding one serving of salad
salt cellar small container with perforated top for storing and shaking out salt
salver tray on which food is served
saucer small, round, shallow dish used under another container, esp. with indentation to hold cup
tea service complete set of china or silver pots, pitchers, bowls, cups, and saucers for serving tea
thermos bottle with inner and outer walls enclosing vacuum to keep liquids at or near original temperature
tureen large, deep serving dish with lid, esp. for soups

Glassware

balloon large, round, stemmed red-wine glass
brandy snifter balloon-shaped, stemmed glass
champagne coupe glass with shallow bowl, flared lip, and stem
champagne flute narrow, conical, stemmed glass
champagne saucer very wide, flat, stemmed glass
champagne tulip gently curved, stemmed glass
cocktail tall, narrow glass for mixed and iced drinks
collins tall, narrow, iced drink glass
cooler tall, narrow, iced drink glass
copita stemmed sherry glass
cordial small, stemmed glass
flagon large metal or pottery vessel with handle
footed pilsener tall, conical beer glass with wide base on stem
glass any drinking vessel made of hard, brittle, transparent, crystallized material
goblet large, round, stemmed wineglass
highball tall, straight-sided cocktail glass
hock glass thick or knobby-stemmed wineglass
hourglass glass that narrows in middle to stemmed bottom
jigger small glass used to measure 1 1/2 fluid ounces
juice glass plain, cylindrical glass for fruit juice
old-fashioned short, squat tumbler
parfait small, narrow, stemmed glass
Paris goblet glass with large, round bowl and tall stem
pilsner tall, conical beer glass with short stem

pony small beer glass; small liqueur glass
port glass small, narrow, conical, stemmed glass
punch cup small, bowl-shaped cup with handle
red-wine glass large, stemmed wineglass
rock glass short glass for liquor over ice
schooner large beer mug
seidel large beer mug, often with hinged lid
sham pilsner short, conical beer glass
sherbet small, slant-sided glass
sherry glass flared-lipped, wide, conical glass with short stem
shot very small, heavy-bottomed, narrow glass
snifter balloon-shaped, stemmed glass
sour glass small, slant-sided glass, often with stem
stein large, usu. earthenware beer mug
tankard tall, one-handled, lidded mug, often pewter or silver
tulip goblet round bowl glass with flared rim and stem
tumbler medium-tall, cylindrical glass
whiskey sour glass tall, narrow, stemmed cocktail glass
white-wine glass medium-size, stemmed wineglass
wineglass tall, rounded glass on stem, often of crystal
zombie very tall cocktail glass

Cutlery and Flatware

chopsticks two small sticks of wood or ivory held in one hand and used to lift food to mouth, esp. in Asia
cutlery knives
flatware eating tools, esp. forks, spoons, and knives
fork instrument with two or more prongs at end of handle, used to lift food to mouth: carving, cake break, cocktail, cold meat, dessert, dinner, fish, lemon, olive, oyster, pickle, salad
knife small blade on handle, used for spreading and cutting: butter, carving, cheese, fish, jelly, oyster, pie, steak
runcible spoon combination fork and spoon with concave body and pronglike tines
silverware cutlery and utensils of silver
spoon device with small, shallow, concave bowl on handle, used for stirring or eating liquids: coffee, cream, dessertspoon, five o'clock, fruit, grapefruit, iced tea, nut, pierced, runcible, salt, serving, soupspoon, tablespoon, teaspoon, tomato
tablespoon spoon larger than teaspoon or dessertspoon, used in serving food and as standard measure
teaspoon small spoon, used esp. to stir coffee and tea or eat desserts

Linens and Accessories

aluminum foil paper-thin sheet of aluminum on roll, used to wrap foods, line cookers, and serve as lid
cheesecloth fine mesh cloth for straining broth or binding herbs
cozy padded covering used to retain warmth of liquid in container, esp. in teapot
hot pad potholder
linens objects made of cloth, esp. napkins
napkin paper or cloth square for wiping hands and lips; serviette
paper towels thin sheets of absorbent paper, usu. on roll, for drying and cleaning surfaces
parchment thick parchment paper used to wrap certain baked items
place mat decorative cloth, reed, or plastic sheet for place setting, used to protect table
plastic wrap very thin sheet of clear plastic on roll, used to wrap foods and seal moisture or flavor
potholder heavy, insulated, usu. square piece of material for lifting very hot objects; hot pad
silent butler receptacle with hinged lid, used for collecting table crumbs and emptying ashtrays
tablecloth large, decorative cloth covering entire table
tidy porous plastic container for collecting garbage in sink
trivet support or rack used to protect surfaces from hot serving dishes
wax paper thin sheet of waxed paper on roll, used to cover surfaces or placed on standing sauces to prevent formation of skin

Chapter Ten
Clothing

OUTER GARMENTS

Overcoats and Cloaks
Coats and Jackets
Suits and Uniforms
Sweaters and Vests
Shirts and Tops
Dresses and Skirts
Trousers, Shorts, and Leggings
Sporting and Exercise Wear
Liturgical Vestments
Armor

Overcoats and Cloaks

academic gown long, flowing robe worn during college ceremonies, esp. graduation
anorak parka, often hooded (Eskimo)
caftan cotton, ankle-length, long-sleeved cloak (Middle East)
cape sleeveless garment with fitted neck that hangs loose over shoulders
capote long, hooded overcoat
capuchin woman's hooded cloak
car coat hip-length overcoat or jacket
chesterfield topcoat with fly front and velvet collar, often double-breasted
cloak long, sleeveless, capelike concealing robe
cowl monk's hooded cloak
domino loose, hooded cloak worn as costume with half-mask
duffle hooded coat of heavy wool with toggle fasteners
duster lightweight protective driving coat
frock tunic, mantle, long coat, smock, or monk's robe
gaberdine long, coarse coat or smock worn esp. by medieval Jews
greatcoat *Chiefly Brit.* heavy, full-length overcoat; long coat
Inverness overcoat with detachable cape (Scotland)
kimono long, wide-sleeved, sashed robe (Japan)
loden coat of short-piled, waterproof, loden fabric
long coat greatcoat
macfarlane heavy, caped overcoat with sides slit open for arms
mackintosh *Chiefly Brit.* lightweight raincoat
manteau loose coat, cloak, robe
mantle loose, sleeveless cloak
mantua woman's loose-fitting cloak (17th-18th c.)
monk's robe long, usu. dark cloak worn in religious orders
oilskin raincoat of oiled, waterproof cloth; slicker
parka fur, down, or nylon cold-weather jacket; hooded jacket
peacoat sailor's hip-length coat of dark blue wool; pea jacket
poncho wool blanket with slit opening for head; similarly cut nylon or rubber raincoat
raglan topcoat with sleeves extending to collar, esp. for improved water resistance
rebozo colorful wool shawl (Mexico)
robe long, loose outer garment, often ceremonial
serape man's wool shoulder shawl (Mexico)
shador garment that covers all of body and head, worn by Muslim women
shawl heavy oblong, triangular, or square cloth worn over head and shoulders, esp. by women
shearling coat of sheepskin from recently shorn sheep
shroud burial garment
slicker oilskin
smock loose, protective, often yoked outer shirt garment
sou'wester sailor's long oilskin coat with buckles
stole long scarf or shoulder wrap with hanging ends in front
tabard knight's short, loose, and sleeveless tunic; herald's cape emblazoned with lord's arms (medieval Europe)
toga crescent-shaped fabric that is wrapped and draped around the body (ancient Rome)
topcoat lightweight overcoat
trench coat double-breasted raincoat with deep pockets, wide belt, and epaulets
tunic loose, draped gown, gathered at hips (ancient Greece and Rome)
ulster long, loose, belted, heavy coat, esp. with hood or cape (Ireland)
wrap outer garment worn wrapped and overlapping around body

Coats and Jackets

blazer single-breasted, informal coat with three patch pockets and metal buttons, in solid color or stripes
bolero very short, open jacket without lapels, often sleeveless
bomber jacket fitted leather jacket, orig. for bomber pilot
box coat short, square cut coat
bush jacket safari jacket
car coat protective coat for driving; coach coat
cardigan close-fitting, knitted jacket that opens down front
combat jacket adaptation of close-fitting, waist-length woolen jacket with tight cuffs and waist, formerly worn by military personnel
cutaway single-breasted coat with knee-length skirts in back
dinner jacket short, dark coat with silk rolled collar and no tails; tuxedo jacket
dolman woman's coat with wide dolman sleeves tapering at the wrists
double-breasted jacket jacket having deep, overlapping front closure and two rows of buttons
doublet man's close-fitting jacket, sometimes sleeveless (16th c.)
Eton jacket short, black jacket with wide lapels and long sleeves
formal man's evening jacket
frock coat close-fitting dress coat with no waist seam and long skirts front and back
hacking jacket riding jacket with tight waist and flared skirt having slit sides or back

lounge coat single- or double-breasted informal coat with no waist seam; smoking jacket
mackinaw short, belted coat of heavy, nappy mackinaw wool, often in plaid
Mao jacket jacket with long, close-fitting cut and narrow, tight, stand-up mandarin collar, popular in China
maxicoat full-length coat
morning coat coat with front cut away to tails at center-vented back
Nehru jacket lightweight, fitted jacket with band collar (India)
Prince Albert long, double-breasted frock coat
reefer short, double-breasted jacket
safari jacket long, belted cotton jacket with pairs of pleated pockets above and below belt; bush jacket
shell jacket short, tight, front-buttoning military jacket
shrug woman's tight-fitting, one-button, waist-length jacket
ski jacket lightweight, waterproof jacket, insulated for protection from cold, usu. worn in snow
smoking jacket lounge coat
sport coat man's casual coat
sport jacket sport coat
swallow-tailed coat tails
tails man's fitted dress jacket cut short in front, with two long, tapering skirts at back; swallow-tailed coat
tuxedo jacket dinner jacket without tails

Suits and Uniforms

bib and tucker *Brit. slang.* entire outfit of clothing, esp. formal
black tie man's semiformal evening wear, usu. tuxedo jacket worn with black bow tie
blues formal blue U.S. military uniform; dress blues
bodysuit close-fitting, one-piece torso garment, often with sleeves and snap crotch opening
business suit traditionally tailored, two- or three-piece suit
cap and gown ceremonial, full-length gown with sleeves and mortarboard cap, worn at commencement and other academic ceremonies
civvies *Informal.* civilian clothes, as opposed to military uniform
coverall one-piece protective garment reaching from neck to ankles
dress blues blues
dress whites whites
fatigues heavy-duty military work uniform, often colored khaki or in camouflage design
full dress most formal military uniform
gray flannel suit conservative gray wool business suit
jumpsuit one-piece garment consisting of shirt with attached trousers
leisure suit man's casual trousers and matching jacket styled like a shirt, often in pastel polyster (1970's)
livery identifying uniform of servants or workers
olive drab sturdy military field uniform
pantsuit woman's suit with slacks instead of skirt matching jacket
pinstripe suit dark suit with thin, white, vertical stripes
regimentals military uniform of particular regiment
riding habit fitted jacket and breeches worn while riding horseback
sailor suit traditional white or blue cotton naval uniform with wide collar and bell-bottomed trousers
scrub suit gown worn in surgery by doctors and assisting personnel
snow suit child's one- or two-piece cold-weather garment consisting of heavily lined pants and jacket
sport suit outfit of casual cut and cloth
suit jacket and trousers or skirt in matching material, sometimes including vest
three-piece suit jacket, trousers, and vest
tuxedo man's semiformal outfit consisting of single- or double-breasted jacket with satin lapels and trousers with stripe down their sides
two-piece suit suit consisting of jacket and trousers only, without vest
undress informal military uniform, as opposed to full dress
whites formal white U.S. military uniform; dress whites
white tie man's formal evening jacket with tails, usu. worn with white vest and white bow tie
zoot suit flashy suit with extremely baggy trousers, padded shoulders, and high waist

Sweaters and Vests

bodice woman's laced vest worn over blouse or dress
bulky thickly knit, voluminous sweater
bulletproof vest protective vest of bulletproof mesh worn under shirt or jacket
cardigan close-fitting, casual sweater buttoning down front
crew neck pullover with round, collarless neck
fisherman sweater heavy wool sweater knit in traditional patterns
pullover sweater with no fastenings, slipped on over head; slipover; *Chiefly Brit.* sweater
ski sweater heavy wool sweater for cold weather
slipover pullover
Sloppy Joe girl's loose, baggy sweater
sweater knitted or crocheted jacket, usu. of wool, silk, acrylic, or cotton, in pullover or cardigan style
turtleneck close-fitting sweater with high, folded band collar
vest short, tight-fitting, sleeveless garment worn under jacket or coat, esp. by men
V-neck sweater with neck forming V open to sternum
waistcoat *Chiefly Brit.* vest

Shirts and Tops

blouse woman's loose shirt extending from neck to waistline, with or without collar and sleeves

blouson voluminous shirt with close-fitted waistband
bush shirt loose-fitting, cotton shirt with patch pockets
bustier woman's tight-fitting, sleeveless, strapless, waist-length top
button-down shirt shirt on which collar points button to shirt body
camp shirt short-sleeved shirt or blouse with notched collar, usu. having two breast pockets
dashiki voluminous, collarless pullover shirt, often in bright colors (Africa)
dickey detachable insert worn to fill neckline and simulate shirt front
dress shirt man's shirt to be worn in evening or with necktie
flannel shirt durable work shirt of flannel cotton
hair shirt rough shirt of animal hair, worn over skin as penance
halter woman's top that covers breasts and leaves shoulders bare, often with straps around neck
Hawaiian shirt loose-fitting, short-sleeved shirt of lightweight fabric printed in colorful, bold designs, usu. of nature scenes
jersey casual, close-fitting, stretchy-knit cotton or wool shirt
middy blouse woman's or child's loose-fitting, hip-length, pullover blouse with sailor collar
muscle shirt *Informal* shirt with sleeves cut off at shoulders; tank top
polo shirt close-fitting casual knit pullover with short sleeves and turned collar or banded neck
rugby shirt knitted pullover sport shirt, usu. in broad, horizontal stripes with white collar
shell woman's simple sleeveless blouse
shirt cloth garment for upper part of body, usu. with collar, sleeves, and open front
shirtwaist woman's blouse tailored like man's dress shirt
tank top sleeveless, scoop-necked shirt of thin fabric
top garment worn over chest and shoulders, sometimes with sleeves
T-shirt collarless, short-sleeved, cotton-knit casual shirt
tunic blouse extending to hips or knees and gathered at waist
turtleneck long-sleeved jersey with high, turned down, tubelike collar

Dresses and Skirts

apron protective cloth panel tied around waist at back
bridal gown elaborate white wedding dress
bustle framework that supported full skirt (19th c.)
cheongsam dress with slit skirt and high mandarin collar (Asia)
coat dress dress with buttons in front, from neck to hem
cocktail dress short-skirted party dress
crinoline petticoat of stiff netting and/or taffeta, worn under hoop skirt
culottes full skirt divided into knee-length pants
dirndl full skirt gathered at waist or dress with close-fitting bodice and full skirt
dress woman's garment with top and skirt in one piece
evening gown formal, full-length dress of high-quality fabric such as silk or satin
flounce wide ruffle attached to skirt
formal full-length evening gown
gown loose-flowing, usu. full-length, often formal dress
grass skirt skirt of grass reeds hung from waistband; hula skirt (Oceania)
harem skirt skirt divided into two parts and gathered at ankles
hoop skirt full skirt stiffened with hoops
housedress loose, casual cotton dress
hula skirt grass skirt
johnny hospital patient's gown that is open at back, collarless, and short-sleeved, usu. in white or green
jumper sleeveless, one-piece dress
kilt man's plaid, wool, wraparound skirt, hanging to knees
maxiskirt ankle-length skirt
microminiskirt skirt ending at top of thighs
midiskirt midcalf-length skirt
miniskirt midthigh-length skirt
muumuu loose, full-length dress, usu. of bright print fabric (Hawaii)
pant dress dress with culotte-style skirt
peplum short, flared skirt with overskirt hanging in points
petticoat fancy underskirt, often with ruffled or lace hem
pinafore sleeveless dress with biblike bodice over blouse
pleated skirt girl's skirt with multiple pleats from waist to knees
sari long, wrapped silk or cotton dress, worn with one end draped over head or shoulders (India)
sarong full-length, wrapped or draped skirt (Oceania and Malaysia)
sheath woman's close-fitting, unbelted dress
shift woman's loose-fitting dress that hangs straight and has no waistline
shirtdress dress tailored like shirt, with button-down front closure
skirt free-hanging outer garment that extends downward from waist
slit dress usu. close-fitting dress, cut open along one thigh at side
sundress sometimes strapless dress with bodice that exposes arms, shoulders, and back
tent dress loose-fitting dress without waistline that flares outward from shoulders to great fullness at hem
trousseau bridal gown and accessories
tutu ballerina's very short, stiff, projecting skirt
wraparound skirt or dress that encircles body and overlaps at full-length opening

Trousers, Shorts, and Leggings

baggies *Slang.* loose, knee-length swim trunks
bell-bottoms trousers widely flared at hem
Bermuda shorts knee-length shorts, often in bright plaids

bloomers woman's or child's full trousers, gathered at knee
blue jeans denims
breeches trousers, esp. knee-length
britches breeches; trousers
buckskins heavy leather trousers
Capri pants fitted casual pants to midcalf, with slit at bottom of sides
chaps cowboy's protective leather leggings, worn over pants and joined by belt or lacing
chinos casual trousers of polished chino cotton
clam diggers midcalf casual pants
cords corduroys
corduroys trousers of corduroy cotton with vertical wales; cords
culottes knee-length shorts, cut wide to resemble skirt
cutoffs full-length trousers cut off above knee to form shorts
denims pants of durable blue denim cotton; blue jeans; dungarees; jeans
ducks trousers of durable duck cotton
dungarees denims
gabardines dress trousers of gabardine wool
gaiters cloth or leather leggings buttoned over shoe tops and ankles
hiphuggers woman's trousers that fit tight over hips and flare below knee
hot pants short shorts
jodhpurs riding breeches cut full at thigh, with stirrup foot strap; riding breeches
knee breeches pants fitted at knees like knickers
knickers short, loose pants, banded at knee, usu. for women and children
lederhosen leather shorts with suspenders (Bavaria)
leggings protective covering for leg below knee, esp. of leather or canvas
loincloth simple cloth wrapped around waist and groin
matador pants toreador pants
moleskins pants of durable cotton with thick nap on one side
overalls loose protective trousers with bib front and shoulder straps
pantaloons short, loose-fitting trousers
pants outer garment covering each leg separately from waist to ankle; trousers
pedal pushers woman's tight-fitting, calf-length pants
pegleg trousers trousers cut full at hips and narrow at ankles
plus fours voluminous breeches hemmed four inches below knees
puttees cloth wrapped around lower leg; buckled leather leggings with straps
riding breeches jodhpurs
rompers child's one-piece playsuit with bloomer pants
shorts casual trousers hemmed above knee
short shorts very brief shorts, barely covering buttocks; hot pants
spandex pants skintight pants of spandex stretch fabric
tights skintight, often sheer, knitted leggings extending from waist to toes or neck to toes
toreador pants fitted trousers banded at knee, patterned after bullfighter's trousers; matador pants
trousers pants
waders waterproof trousers reaching from armpits to attached rubber boots, worn over regular trousers

Sporting and Exercise Wear

bathing suit man's or woman's swimming outfit: trunks, two-piece bikini, or one-piece leotard; swimsuit; swimwear
bikini woman's scanty two-piece bathing suit comprised of panties and brassiere
body stocking sometimes sheer, tight-fitting torso garment, often with sleeves and legs
gym suit track suit or jogging suit
jams *Trademark.* long, baggy, brightly colored men's swim trunks
jogging suit usu. matching, loose-fitting top and pants, worn during athletic workout
leotard close-fitting torso garment, with or without sleeves, worn by dancers and acrobats
muscle shirt sleeveless T-shirt, usu. tight-fitting, worn typically by body builders
ski suit stretch pants and parka, worn for skiing and outdoor winter activities
string bikini skimpy two-piece bathing suit that barely covers crotch and nipples
sweatpants loose, fleece-lined, cotton athletic pants, gathered at waist with drawstring or elastic
sweatshirt loose, long-sleeved, cotton-knit, fleece-lined shirt for athletic wear
sweat suit loose, cotton-knit exercise pants and pullover
swimsuit bathing suit
track suit loose-fitting sweat worn by athletes, esp. runners, before and after competition and during workouts
trunks shorts, esp. for swimming or boxing
two-piece bathing suit woman's bathing suit comprised of brassiere and panties; bikini
unitard close-fitting, clingy, full-body garment reaching from ankles to neck and wrists
wetsuit close-fitting rubber suit, sometimes worn in parts, that covers body from ankles to wrists and neck and retains body heat in cold water

Liturgical Vestments

alb priest's long, white, linen robe for Mass
amice priest's square cloth worn over shoulders
cassock priest's full-length garment with tight-fitting sleeves; soutane
chasuble priest's ornamented, knee-length outer garment without sleeves
cincture cord looped twice around waist to hold alb in place
clerical collar priest's narrow, stiff collar that buttons at back
cope bishop's long, open cloak
dalmatic deacon's tunic with wide sleeves and stripes descending from shoulders
maniple priest's long, silk band, worn looped over left arm

miter tall, pointed bishop's hat
mozzetta short shoulder cape with hood, worn by pope, cardinals, and bishops
pallium thin, ringlike band of wool across shoulders, with lappets in front and back, worn by pope and archbishops
soutane priest's cassock or tunic
surplice loose, white, knee-length outer garment with wide sleeves
vestment any garment worn by clergy or their assistants during religious service

Armor

ailette protective shoulder plate of forged steel worn over coat of mail
armor protective body covering of metal, leather, or chain mail (medieval Europe)
backplate piece of armor covering back from shoulders to waist
brassard upper arm covering of armor
breastplate cuirass
brigandine medieval body armor of scales or plates
chain mail lightweight, flexible armor of interlinked metal rings
coat of mail upper body chain mail
cubitiere rounded elbow covering of armor; elbow piece
cuirass fitted leather or cloth bodice armor that protects breast and back; breastplate
cuisse plate armor for thigh front
elbow piece cubitiere
epaulière shoulder covering of armor; pauldron
fauld armor piece below breastplate, comprised of thin, overlapping plates
footpiece attached covering of armor for top of foot; solleret
gauntlet reinforced protective glove
gorget neck-encircling collar of armor on which helmet sits
greave lower leg protector of armor; jambeau
hauberk knee-length tunic of chain mail
heaume armor helmet outside mail hood that rests on shoulders
helmet rigid covering for head and neck with visor front
jambeau greave
kneepiece circular armor joint at knee; poleyn
pallette round armor plate above heart, upper chest, and shoulder
pauldron epaulière
placate piece of armor that reinforces breastplate over lower torso
plastron plate armor for front of upper torso
poleyn kneepiece
skirt of tasses armor plates hung around hips to which tasses and sword attach
solleret footpiece
surcoat garment worn over medieval armor, often embroidered with heraldic arms
tasses overlapping armor plates forming skirt at hips
tuille hinged armor plate above thigh
vambrace piece of plate armor for forearm
visor protective helmet plate that lowers over face

UNDERGARMENTS

Lingerie and Support Garments
Men's Underwear
Nightclothes and Dishabille
Hosiery

Lingerie and Support Garments

bandeau strapless, band-shaped brassiere
bikini very brief, high-cut underpants
bloomers full, loose underpants, gathered at knee
body stocking close-fitting, one-piece torso garment with sleeves and legs
bodywear leotard, tights, or body stocking
bra brassiere
brassiere garment supporting breasts in two cups; bra
bustle framework used to support full skirt
camisole light, loose bodice worn over corset or brassiere; sheer blouse with shoulder straps and low neck
chastity belt belt of leather or forged metal that covered crotch to prevent sexual intercourse (medieval Europe)
chemise loose, short slip
corselet combination brassiere and girdle
corset boned, laced, elasticized foundation garment, used to firm waist and hips, often including garter belt and brassiere
crinoline coarse, stiff petticoat worn under hoop skirt
drawers woman's knee-length undershorts
falsies *Informal.* shaped pads worn inside a brassiere; padded bra
foundation garment woman's support garment, such as corset
garter belt belt with straps attached, used to hold up stockings; suspender belt
girdle light corset extending from waist to thighs
G-string backless panties covering crotch only, held up by cord at waist
knickers loose underpants, banded at knee; *Chiefly Brit.* panties
leotard close-fitting, skintight torso garment consisting of briefs and often sleeveless top
lingerie woman's underwear, often lacy or decorative
padded bra brassiere with foam padding in each cup to make breasts appear larger
pannier hoop worn to extend skirts (19th c.)
pantalets long drawers with attached ruffle visible below knee (19th c.)
panties underpants
panty girdle girdle with sewn-in crotch, often with garters
pasties small, round coverings for woman's nipples, chiefly worn by striptease dancers

peek-a-boo brassiere with openings at each nipple
petticoat underskirt with ruffled or lace hem
pettipants thigh or knee-length underpants, banded in lace
slip dress-length undergarment with shoulder straps
smock yoked undershirt; chemise
support garment usu. elastic device that binds or bears up part of body
suspender belt garter belt
tap pants loose-fitting underpants, similar to pants worn for tap dancing
teddy loose-fitting, one piece underslip with crotch; combination chemise and panties
truss extremely binding girdle, used esp. for treatment of hernias
underpants woman's or child's underwear that covers groin, buttocks and crotch

Men's Underwear

athletic supporter tight-fitting support garment for genitals, esp. worn by dancer or athlete; cup; jockstrap
boxer shorts loose-cut underpants reaching to midthigh
breechcloth loincloth
briefs abbreviated, jockey style underpants
cup athletic supporter
drawers underpants, esp. boxer style
jockey shorts brief, close-fitting underpants that end at top of thigh
jockstrap athletic supporter
loincloth cloth wrapped around waist and loins that covers genitals; breechcloth
long johns *Informal.* long underwear
long underwear full-length, usu. cotton-knit underwear that covers limbs, worn esp. in cold weather
shorts underpants
skivvies *Informal.* man's underwear
tank top sleeveless, low-necked undershirt
thermals knitted cotton or wool long underwear, designed to retain body heat
T-shirt collarless, short-sleeved, cotton-knit undershirt
underpants undershorts
undershorts underwear for groin, crotch, and buttocks; underdrawers; underpants
underwear undergarments, shirt or shorts; underclothes
union suit *Chiefly Brit.* one-piece undergarment

Nightclothes and Dishabille

baby doll woman's sheer, two-piece nightgown
bathrobe loose, absorbent robe worn before or after bath or as dressing gown
bed jacket upper body sleepwear
camisole woman's short negligee
dishabille casual, informal dress worn inside one's home
dressing gown robe, esp. of silk, worn while dressing or resting
dressing jacket coat worn while dressing or resting
housecoat woman's long-skirted, informal coat
kimono long, sashed, wide-sleeved traditional robe (Japan)
negligee woman's loose, diaphanous, often lacy nightdress
nightclothes sleeping garments
nightgown loose, dresslike garment worn in bed
pajamas loose, lightweight sleeping shirt and trousers; also, *esp. Brit.,* pyjamas
peignoir negligee or dressing gown, esp. with fur cuffs, lace, or other decoration
p.j.'s *Informal.* pajamas
robe loose, informal garment for dressing, bathing, or resting
sleeper child's pajamas with attached foot coverings
smoking jacket man's loose-fitting lounging jacket

Hosiery

anklet woman's short sock that reaches just above ankle
argyles socks knitted in varicolored diamond pattern
athletic sock thick cotton sock, usu. white
bobbysocks girl's socks that fold above ankle
crew sock short, bulky, ribbed sock
fishnet stocking full-length stocking woven in coarse mesh
footlet woman's thin, very low sock, worn as protective shoeliner instead of hosiery and not meant to be seen
garter stocking stocking extending to midthigh, held up by garter
halfhose elasticized stocking extending to just above knee
hose knitted coverings for foot and leg; hosiery
hosiery garments for foot and leg, esp. socks and stockings; hose
knee-high sock or stocking that reaches to knee
knee-sock hose that reaches to knee
leg warmer footless knit legging for dancers or athletes
nylons woman's stockings of synthetic material, esp. nylon
pantyhose woman's one-piece undergarment, combining panties and skintight, full-length hose
seamless stocking sheer stocking without seams
sheer stockings finely knit thin hose
silk stockings finely knit silk hose
slouch sock sock with long top that is bunched around ankle
sock knitted foot covering that extends above ankle
stocking close-fitting knitted covering for foot and leg
support hose elasticized stocking that provides support for leg
sweat sock heavy wool or cotton sock
tights skintight sheer garment that extends from waist to toes
tube sock sock with unformed heel, knitted in cylindrical shape

ORNAMENTS AND ACCESSORIES

Ornaments

armlet band around upper arm
bodkin ornamental pin-shaped clasp for hair
bouquet bunch of flowers fastened together
boutonniere single flower worn in lapel buttonhole
bow ribbon doubled into two or more loops, usu. worn in hair
comb strip of hard material with teethlike projections, used to hold hair in place
corsage arrangement of flowers worn pinned to clothing, esp. by women
crest plume on helmet; heraldic emblem
epaulette often fringed shoulder ornament on military jacket
netsuke small, finely carved toggle on kimono sash (Japan)
nosegay small bunch of flowers; bouquet; posy
pompom tuft or ball of fabric and fringe
posy bouquet of flowers; nosegay
sporran fur pouch hung off belt in front of kilt (Scotland)
wreath braided, circular band of flowers worn in hair

Jewelry

aigrette spray of gemstones depicting plume of feathers, worn in hair or on hat
anklet band around ankle
band narrow ring encircling finger, usu. of precious metal
bangle rigid, ring-shaped, slip-on or clasped anklet or bracelet
bauble decorative trinket
beads rounded, pierced pieces of glass, metal, wood, or stone strung together in strands
bezel groove and flange holding gem in setting; slanting facets of exposed portion of cut gem in setting
bibelot small trinket of curiosity, beauty, or rarity
bijou small piece of delicate jewelry; trinket
brooch large pin with clasp, worn at breast
cameo gem carved in relief, esp. portrait
carat unit of weight for gemstones equal to 200 milligrams
charm representational item worn as protection from evil, token of luck, or to invoke magic powers
costume jewelry inexpensive jewelry made from nonprecious substances
crown jewels crown, scepter, and other royal regalia
cuff links ornamental buttons joined by chain or shank for fastening French cuff
diadem royal headdress; crown
earring ornamental object hung from earlobe either by clasp or through hole pierced in lobe
fob chain for pocket watch
gem precious stone or pearl cut and mounted as ornament
gemstone precious or semiprecious stone used as a gem
girandole earring or brooch with large gemstone surrounded by smaller ones
intaglio ornament with engraving beneath surface of material
labret gemstone or other small ornament worn in hole pierced in lip
locket small, lidded case of precious metal on chain necklace, inside of which a memento or photograph can be placed
necklace ornamental string or chain worn around neck
nose ring ring worn through hole pierced in one nostril of nose
parure set of jewelry worn together, such as earrings, bracelet, and necklace
pearl smooth, hard, rounded, white nacreous growth found within shell of some oysters, mounted or strung and used as jewelry
pendant decorative object hanging on chain or from earring
pin ornamental fastener attached to clothing with pointed wire or shaft
pinkie ring ring worn on little finger, esp. by men
post straight bar that pierces ear, often with attached setting that holds single pearl or stone as earring
precious stone class of gemstones of great value, esp. diamond, emerald, ruby, sapphire
rhinestone colorless synthetic gem, often of glass
ring band of precious metal worn on finger, often set with gem
rivière necklace of precious stones, usu. in several strands
rondelle small round bead used as spacer in necklace
scrimshaw carved, engraved object of whalebone
semiprecious stone any of a class of gemstones of moderate value, such as amethyst, garnet, opal, or topaz
setting decorated metal base in which stone or stones are placed, esp. on ring
signet ring ring bearing seal or initials
solitaire single gem set alone, esp. on ring
stickpin ornamental pin, esp. worn on necktie
stud solid button mounted on metal post and inserted in garment as ornamental fastener
tiara small, crownlike, jeweled headdress, often in semicircular shape
tie clip tiepin

tiepin tie clasp or stud with ornamental head, used to attach tie to shirt; tie clip
wampum polished shells strung as beads (American Indian)

Eyeglasses

aviator glasses contoured, metal-framed goggles worn by fliers
bifocals eyeglasses with lenses that have separate sections, one for seeing close up and one for distance
contact lens thin lens that fits directly on cornea
eyeglasses glass lenses that correct impaired vision, set in a frame with earpieces; spectacles
goggles protective glasses in flexible frame fitting snugly against face
granny glasses round lenses in thin metal frames
horn rims glasses with frames of variegated animal horn or similarly colored plastic
lens glass portion of eyeglasses that is ground to correct vision
lorgnette eyeglasses with attached handle; opera glasses
lorgnon monocle, pince-nez
monocle eyeglass for one eye, attached to cord; lorgnon
opera glasses lorgnette
pince-nez eyeglasses attached by spring or clamp to bridge of nose; lorgnon
reading glasses glasses used exclusively to aid in reading or close work
spectacles eyeglasses
sunglasses glasses with dark lenses that protect eyes from sunshine

Neckwear

ascot necktie or scarf knotted under chin, with broad ends hanging loose
bandanna large, colorful, patterned handkerchief tied around neck
boa long stole or scarf of fur or feathers
bolo tie thin cord with ornamental clasp; long string tie
bow tie small tie formed into bow at neck
choker necklace that fits snugly around neck, often of velvet
clerical collar priest's narrow, stiff collar, buttoned at back; priest's collar; Roman collar
clip-on tie necktie that clips onto shirt collar instead of tying around neck
cravat necktie or scarf worn around neck
dickey detachable collar and shirt front
dog collar chain with military identification tag
fichu woman's light, triangular scarf worn over shoulders and fastened in front, esp. to fill low neckline
foulard necktie or scarf of light foulard silk in small print design
four-in-hand long necktie or scarf tied in slipknot or Windsor knot with ends hanging
Geneva bands two narrow strips of white cloth hanging from front collar of some Protestant clergy
jabot lace cravat or frill on bodice front, often attached to neckband
kerchief square of cloth worn around neck or shoulders
lei necklace of flowers (Hawaii)
muffler wool or fur scarf
necktie narrow band of fabric looped around neck and fastened or tied in front
priest's collar clerical collar
Roman collar clerical collar
ruff stiff, wide neckpiece gathered in deep folds and radiating from neck
scapular band of cloth slitted for head opening and draped over shoulders by monks
scarf broad cloth or woven band worn over head or shoulders or around neck
school tie necktie with school colors or emblem
shawl rectangular or triangular piece of fabric worn over head and shoulders
stock clergyman's wide-banded scarf; long neckerchief worn with formal riding dress
stole woman's long, wide cloth worn around shoulders; priest's narrow scarf with ends crossed over chest
string tie narrow cord or cloth tie with ornamental clasp
tallith fringed prayer shawl worn by Jewish men
Windsor tie broad necktie knotted in loose bow or wide triangular knot

Handwear and Gloves

brass knuckles set of connected metal rings worn as weapon on fist
cesta long, curved wicker basket worn on hand for jai alai
gauntlet high-cuffed glove; armored glove
glove hand covering with separate sheath for each finger and thumb
kid gloves soft kid leather gloves
mitt fingerless glove; athletic glove, esp. baseball glove
mittens gloves with thumb sheath and single wide section for all fingers
muff fur or wool cylinder open at both ends to insert hands for warmth
weight gloves tight-fitting leather gloves that terminate at knuckles, used for weightlifting

Waistbands and Belts

baldric ornamented belt worn over one shoulder, used to hold sword or bugle
bandolier ammunition belt worn over shoulder and across chest
belt waistband used esp. for holding up trousers or for decoration
cartridge belt belt holding ammunition, usu. worn around waist
ceinture belt or sash
cestus woman's symbolic belt, esp. for bride
cincture cord that holds priest's alb in place
cummerbund man's broad, tight-fitting waist sash, worn with formal attire

fascia broad, distinctly colored band worn at waist
garter belt undergarment belt with clips to hold up stockings
girdle close-fitting, elasticized support garment worn around waist and hips, usu. by women
hamaki wide, often elasticized belt worn for warmth (Japan)
obi broad sash for kimono (Japan)
sash ornamental band, ribbon, or scarf draped over shoulder and around waist
surcingle beltlike fastening for cassock or other garment
suspender belt garter belt with elastic straps for stockings
waistband strip of fabric attached to waistline of trousers or skirt, sometimes elasticized

Functional Attire and Accessories

accessory article or set of articles added to basic clothing for decoration, convenience, or completeness
apron protective, skirtlike piece of material tied around waist
barrette clip or comb with toothlike projections for holding hair
blindfold covering for eyes, tied at back of head
fan folded, collapsible silk or paper semicircle on rods splayed from pivot, moved back and forth to create cooling air current
handkerchief soft square of linen, cotton, or silk for grooming face or wiping nose
hatpin long stickpin with ornamental top, used to fasten hat
holster leather case for pistol, open at top, worn on belt or under one arm
money belt waistband with pouch to conceal money
pomander aromatic mixture in bag used to scent stored clothes
sachet small bag or pad holding potpourri or perfumed powder, usu. placed in drawer or closet to scent clothes
scabbard leather or metal sheath for tool or sword
shield broad piece of protective material, esp. armor, carried on arm as defense against blows and projectiles
suspenders straps attached to trousers in front and back and slung over shoulders; braces
sweatband strip of absorbent material worn around head and across forehead, esp. when exercising

Symbolic and Emblematic Attire

amulet good-luck charm, often a necklace
ankh cross with looped upper arm, viewed as symbol of life (ancient Egypt)
badge emblem, often metal, denoting membership or rank of wearer
crepe black band of crinkled silk fabric, worn as token of mourning
fourragère braided, decorative, military cord worn on shoulder
prayer shawl cloth worn around neck during prayer
rosette fabric gathered to resemble rose, worn as badge of office
tallith fringed prayer shawl worn by Jewish men
zizith fringe of tassels on Jewish man's ceremonial garments

Luggage and Cases

attaché case briefcase
backpack lightweight canvas or nylon sack, often on lightweight frame, carried on back while hiking
baggage luggage
bandbox cylindrical cardboard or wood box for lightweight items
barracks bag sturdy military cotton bag for personal items
belt bag small bag worn attached to belt
billfold leather case that folds flat, used to hold paper money
briefcase flat, rectangular, usu. leather container for business papers and documents
caddie bag golf bag
carpetbag small traveling bag made of carpeting
carry-on bag small luggage taken on airplane
case small box or receptacle for storing items
cedar chest chest made of or lined with cedar, used for storage of clothing for protection against moths
clutch woman's small, strapless handbag
ditty bag sailor's bag for small articles
duffel bag large, oblong, frameless, often canvas bag
fanny pack small zippered pouch suspended from belt around waist
flight bag small, lightweight travel bag, usu. with zippered outside pockets
footlocker small trunk, usu. placed at foot of bed
garment bag long, soft, folding bag with hangers for clothing
Gladstone bag leather bag on rigid hinged frame that opens flat into two compartments
golf bag upright bag on frame, used for carrying golf clubs; caddie bag
grip hand luggage
gripsack traveling bag with handles
gym bag small, usu. nylon bag for athletic wear and equipment
handbag woman's small, leather bag for holding personal effects
hatbox cylindrical, rigid box for storing a hat
haversack knapsack with single strap worn over one shoulder
impedimenta baggage and other encumbrances
kit bag rectangular leather traveling bag with straps and sides that open
knapsack canvas or nylon bag strapped on back; rucksack
locker storage chest with lock
luggage suitcases or traveling bags; baggage
musette bag small knapsack with one shoulder strap
pocketbook woman's handbag; wallet or billfold
portfolio large, flat leather case for holding photographs or drawings

portmanteau large leather trunk or suitcase that opens into two compartments
pouch small drawstring bag; lockable case for diplomatic papers
purse woman's handbag; small bag or case for coins
reticule woman's small handbag of beaded silk, brocade, or netting
rucksack knapsack
saddlebag two bags on straps slung over horse
satchel small bag, often with shoulder strap
snuffbox small, ornamental, lidded case for snuff
suitcase rectangular or oblong traveling bag with rigid frame
tote bag large handbag, esp. canvas
trunk large, sturdy, boxlike luggage or storage container
valise traveling bag or suitcase that can be carried by hand
vanity bag small case or handbag for toilet articles
wallet small, flat, folding pocketbook with compartments for personal papers, currency, and credit cards
wardrobe standing box or chest for clothes on hangers
wardrobe trunk upright trunk with clothes hangers and storage compartments

CLOTHING MATERIALS

Fabrics and Cloth
Synthetic Fibers and Textiles
Laces
Furs, Leathers, and Pelts

Fabrics and Cloth

alpaca long, soft, silky fleece of Peruvian llama wool
Angora soft hair of Angora goat or rabbit, esp. for sweaters
astrakhan lustrous, closely curled wool of young Russian lamb
batik fabric that is hand-dyed, using wax to repel dye in a marblelike pattern
batiste fine, sheer linen or muslin in plain or figured weave
bombazine twilled silk or rayon dyed black, having worsted filling
bouclé tufted, nubby cloth with loose yarn loops
broadcloth densely woven fabric with soft finish in plain or twill weave
brocade heavyweight silk cloth with elaborate raised design, often in gold or silver
buckram stiff, sized cotton or linen, esp. for linings or bookbinding
bunting coarse, open-weave worsted or cotton fabric, esp. for flags
burlap coarse cloth of jute, flax, or hemp, esp. for sacking or wallpaper
calico plain-woven cotton cloth with figured pattern
cambric fine white linen, esp. for linings or handkerchiefs
camel's hair soft, silky, felted camel wool or fabric resembling it, esp. for coats
canvas stiff, closely woven, heavy fabric of hemp or cotton, esp. for shoes, sails, and tents
cashmere very soft, downy wool from hair roots of Kashmir goat
challis soft, lightweight cotton or wool in plain weave, esp. for neckties
chambray lightweight cotton, silk, or linen with colored warp and white weft
charmeuse lightweight, drapable silk with semilustrous satin face and dull back
cheesecloth lightweight cotton gauze in open mesh
chenille tufted, velvety cord of silk or worsted, esp. for trim, embroidery, spreads, and nightgowns
chiffon sheer, fluffy silk or synthetic fabric, esp. for blouses and dresses
chiné fabric with variegated Chinese designs dyed or printed on warp threads before weaving
chino durable, twilled khaki cotton
chintz often glazed, printed cotton, esp. for draperies and upholstery
cloth woven, knitted, felted, or pressed fabric of fibrous material, such as cotton, wool, silk, hair, or synthetic fibers
corduroy sturdy cotton with piled surface in lengthwise ridges
cotton soft, white, absorbent fabric woven from fibrous hairs of cotton plant
covert durable cotton or woolen twill of mixed color yarns, sometimes waterproofed
crepe lightweight, crinkled fabric of silk, cotton, or rayon
crepe de Chine soft, silky fabric with minute irregularities of surface
crinoline coarse, stiffened horsehair or cotton, esp. for linings
damask fine, twilled, reversible silk, linen, or cotton in figured weave
denim heavyweight, durable twill cotton, esp. for blue jeans
dimity sheer, plain weave, usu. checked or striped cotton, esp. for curtains and bedspreads
Donegal tweed heavyweight, plain wool with colorful weft (Ireland)
drill durable twilled cotton
duck heavy, closely woven cotton, esp. for bags and outer garments
duffel rough, woolen, thickly napped cloth, esp. for coats and luggage
dungaree denim
ecru satin, unbleached linen, or raw silk of very pale brown color
fabric material made from fibers or threads by means of weaving, knitting, or felting
faille semilustrous ribbed fabric of silk, cotton, rayon, or lightweight taffeta
felt nonwoven fabric of wool, cotton, or hair pressed together with heat

fiber slender, filamentous substance formed into threads for making fabric
flannel soft, loosely woven, napped wool or wool blend
flannelette lightweight cotton flannel, napped on one side
fleece soft knit or woven fabric with silky pile
foulard lightweight silk or rayon with printed design, esp. for ties and scarves
fustian stout cotton or linen in twill weave with short pile
gabardine firm woolen cloth in twill weave
galatea durable cotton, usu. striped, esp. for children's clothing
gauze thin, transparent cotton or silk
Georgette sheer silk or rayon crepe with pebbly surface
gingham striped or checked cotton in plain weave, esp. for housedresses
gossamer very thin, delicate cloth, esp. gauze for veils
grenadine thin silk or synthetic in leno weave
grogram coarse, loosely woven fabric of silk, silk and mohair, or wool
grosgrain heavy, closely woven, corded silk or rayon, esp. for ribbons
gunny coarse, heavy jute or hemp, esp. for sacks
herringbone twilled fabric in pattern resembling fish skeleton, with series of V's in vertical row
homespun plain-weave wool or linen made from homespun yarn
hopsack coarse, loosely woven cotton or wool
horsehair sturdy, glossy fabric woven from horse's mane
jacquard intricate, variegated woven fabric
jardiniere multicolored material in floral or fruit print
jean denim
jersey soft, often elastic knit cotton, esp. for shirts
khaki durable, twilled, dull yellow-brown cotton, esp. for military uniforms
knit any fabric made with interlocking loops of yarn
lace delicate, netlike, figured fabric of thread or yarn, esp. for trim
lamé fabric in which silver or gold threads are interwoven with silk, cotton, or rayon
linen cloth woven from flax yarns
loden heavy, waterproof wool, esp. for coats
mackinaw heavy, napped wool in plaid design, esp. for coats
mackintosh lightweight, waterproof, rubberized cotton, esp. for raincoats
madras fine, hard cotton or durable silk, in colorful plaid or stripes
melton heavy twilled wool with smooth face in solid colors
merino fine, soft wool of Spanish merino sheep, esp. for stockings
mesh woven, knit, or knotted material of open texture with evenly spaced strands
mohair long, silky wool made from fleece of Angora goat
moiré silky fabric with watered or wavy pattern; watered fabric
muslin plain-weave cotton with sheer to coarse finish, often printed or embroidered; mousseline
nainsook fine, lightweight cotton, often striped
nankeen durable, brownish-yellow Chinese cotton, esp. for trousers
net open-mesh fabric twisted or knotted at uniform intervals
oilcloth cotton cloth waterproofed with oil and pigment, esp. for table or shelf covering
organdy very sheer, stiff, lightweight cotton with crisp finish, esp. for blouses
organza sheer silk, nylon, or rayon with crisp finish, stiffer than organdy, used for gowns and trim
oxford cotton in plain, twill, or basket weave, esp. for shirts
paisley soft woolen fabric or silk printed with colorful, swirled designs
panne velvet or satin with lustrous, flattened pile
percale fine, closely woven cotton, esp. for bed sheets
Pima fine broadcloth cotton, esp. for shirts
pique durable, ribbed cotton, rayon, or silk
plaid fabric in checkerboard, crossbarred pattern, esp. twilled wool
plush fabric with pile higher than 1/8 inch (3 mm), less dense than velvet
pointelle lacy, openwork fabric
pongee thin, soft, tan raw silk (China); similar cotton or rayon fabric in uneven weave
poplin sturdy, plain-weave cotton with fine ribs
ragg sturdy wool fiber blended with nylon to make flecked, grayish yarn
raw silk woven fabric of spun silk without sericin, a natural binder, removed
sackcloth coarse, rough cloth, orig. of goat's hair, now of hemp or jute, esp. for mourning clothes
sailcloth lightweight canvas, esp. for curtains and outer garments
sateen smooth, durable, lustrous cotton in satin weave
satin rich silk with glossy face and dull back; similar acetate, nylon, or rayon
seersucker lightweight, crinkled linen or cotton, usu. striped
serge twilled worsted or wool, esp. for suits
sharkskin smooth wool or worsted with small woven design; similar fabric of acetate or rayon with dull appearance
Shetland wool soft, fine wool from undercoat of Shetland sheep
shirting cotton or other fabric, such as broadcloth or oxford, esp. for shirts
silk soft, fine fabric of thread woven from fibers of silkworm cocoons
stockinette soft elastic cotton, esp. for bandages or infant wear
taffeta finely woven, stiff silk, cotton, or rayon, with high sheen and fine crosswise ribs
tartan emblematic plaid-patterned, multicolored, twilled wool (Scotland)
tattersall fabric with colored crossbars on solid background
terry absorbent cotton fabric with uncut pile loops on both sides
textile fabric woven or knitted from natural or synthetic fiber

ticking durable linen or cotton, esp. for upholstery and covers
toweling narrow fabric of cotton or linen, in plain, twill, or huck weave, for towels
tricot plain, warp-knit fabric of wool, silk, or nylon, with fine ribs
tulle thin, fine netting of silk, acetate, nylon, or rayon, esp. for veils and gowns
tussah tan, medium-coarse Oriental silk
tweed coarse woolen fabric in plain or herringbone weave
twill any fabric woven in parallel diagonal lines or ribs
velour cloth with velvetlike nap, esp. for upholstery and draperies
velvet richly woven fabric of silk, acetate, nylon, or rayon, with soft, thick pile
velveteen twilled, plain-weave cotton with short, velvety pile
vicuna very soft, light brown wool made from undercoat of South American llama
voile sheer cotton, wool, silk, or rayon in plain weave, esp. for dresses or curtains
wool fabric woven from the soft, curly undercoat or fleece of mammals such as sheep, goats, and camels
worsted woolen fabric with smooth, hard surface and no nap

Synthetic Fibers and Textiles

acetate acetic ester of cellulose with satiny appearance
acrylic quick-drying synthetic fiber made by polymerization of acrylonitrile
double-knit polyester material
durable press permanent press
fiberfill resilient, lightweight, fluffy synthetic fiber, used esp. as filling for quilts or sleeping bags
leatherette synthetic leather of paper and vinyl
nylon strong, elastic, thermoplastic polyamide textile
permanent press textile treated with resin and heat to resist wrinkling; durable press
polyester synthetic, woollike knit material made from fibers formed by polymerization
polypropylene lightweight fiber that is a polymer of propylene, used in bonded fabrics
polyvinyl textile of polymerized vinyl compounds
rayon synthetic textile fiber of woven or knit cellulose that resembles wool, silk, or cotton fabric
ripstop nylon durable, tear-resistant nylon, esp. for parkas and tents
spandex highly elastic, long-chain polymer fiber
synthetic fiber slender, threadlike structure derived from mineral or chemical components and used to make synthetic textile
vinyl polymer textile derived from vinyl
vinyon strong, easily molded, long-chain polymer vinyl textile fiber
wash-and-wear fabric permanent press fabric that can be washed and dries quickly

Laces

Alençon delicate, fine mesh needlepoint in solid floral pattern
bobbin lace handmade lace formed by intertwisting threads on bobbins over patterns marked by pins in pillow; pillow lace
bobbinet machine-made net in hexagonal mesh
Brussels lace needlepoint or bobbin lace with floral design, orig. made near Brussels
Chantilly delicate silk or linen bobbin lace in hexagonal mesh with scrolled or floral design, usu. black, handmade in France
duchesse fine Flemish bobbin lace in delicate floral designs
gros point Venetian point lace with large, raised designs
guipure heavy, large-patterned lace of linen or silk
illusion delicate, gauzy tulle, esp. for veils
lace delicate, netlike, figured fabric of thread or yarn
mignonette narrow bobbin lace with scattered small designs, of French and Flemish origin
needlepoint lace handmade lace worked entirely with needle over paper pattern in buttonhole stitch; point lace
pillow lace bobbin lace
point lace needlepoint lace
raised point needlepoint lace with padded floral design in high relief, orig. from Venice, Italy
reticella old-fashioned needlepoint lace in geometric pattern
rose point needlepoint lace in rose designs, orig. from Venice, Italy
tambour lace made on a frame of two interlocking hoops with designs embroidered or darned onto machinemade net
tatting lace made by hand looping and knotting a single, heavy thread
torchon durable bobbin lace of coarse linen or cotton in simple, open, geometric patterns with scalloped edges
Venetian point needlepoint lace from Venice, Italy, esp. raised and rose point laces

Furs, Leathers, and Pelts

alligator skin of alligator with distinctive block pattern
broadtail fur of very young karakul lamb
buckskin pliable, suede-finished skin of deer
buff supple, oil-tanned cowhide
cabretta light, soft leather from skin of hairy sheep
calfskin young, domestic cowhide
capeskin flexible sheepskin with natural grain, esp. for gloves
chamois soft, pliant antelope or sheepskin
chevrette leather made from skin of young goat
chinchilla soft, pearly gray fur of chinchilla
cony rabbit fur
coonskin raccoon fur, esp. for hats
Cordovan fine-grained, dense, nonporous skin of horse, pig, or goat
cowhide sturdy hide of domestic cow
doeskin skin of female deer or sheep

deerskin skin of wild deer
ermine soft, white weasel fur, esp. for coats and trim
frosted mink fur of mink with chemically lightened strands, giving it a streaked appearance
fur soft, thick mammal hair; skin bearing such hair, stripped and processed
kid leather made from skin of young goat, esp. for gloves
krimmer dressed lambskin with loose soft curls of pale wool, from Crimea
lambskin soft skin of young sheep
leather animal skin prepared for use by removing all hair and tanning
maribou thick fur of northern deer, esp. for capes
mink brown, black, or white fur of cultivated mink
mocha pliable, suede-finished African sheepskin, esp. for gloves
morocco fine, firm, flexible goatskin tanned with sumac, having pebbly grain and reddish color
muskrat glossy, dark brown fur of muskrat
nappa soft leather from sheepskin or lambskin, used for gloves and shoes
nutria beaverlike fur of coypu, used for coats, hats, and trim
patent leather stiff, shiny, varnished or lacquered leather, esp. for shoes
pelt skin of fur-bearing animal stripped from carcass, with hair removed
pigskin tough leather of swine skin, esp. for footballs
rabbit soft, light rabbit fur
raccoon long, coarse raccoon fur, esp. for coats
ranch mink fur of commercially raised, semiaquatic mink
rawhide untanned hide
Russia leather fine, smooth leather, esp. dyed dark red
sable rich, dark brown sable fur
shagreen untanned horsehide or sharkskin with granular surface
shearling tanned skin from recently shorn sheep or lamb
sheepskin hide of sheep, used esp. for parchment
suede tanned leather with flesh side buffed to a slight nap
swakara fur of karakul sheep, from Namibia
vair bluish-gray or white squirrel fur
white leather animal hide bleached of natural color
wild mink brown fur of noncultivated mink

FOOTWEAR

Parts of Shoes and Accessories
Shoes and Footwear

Parts of Shoes and Accessories

aglet tag that covers end of shoelace
arch midsection of shoe that supports arch of foot
breasting inside forepart of heel
bootjack yokelike instrument for removing boot by catching its heel
bootstrap strip of material, esp. leather, sewn at top rear or sides of boot and grasped to help pull boot on
buckle latch fastening for two loose straps
captoe forepart of shoe, set off by line of stitching from one side of foot to other
collar top of shoe that encircles foot, ankle, or leg
counter stiffener inserted between liner and outside leather to shape shoe around heel
creeper attachment with iron points that is strapped to shoe to prevent person from slipping on ice
cuff trimming or finishing strip sewed around outside top of shoe
eyelet small hole through which shoelace passes
French heel high, curved heel used on women's shoes, characterized by heel breast that curves into shank
heel rigid attachment to sole beneath rear of foot
hook curved piece of metal through which shoelace passes
insole thin support strip inside shoe
lace stay part of oxford into which eyelets and laces are inserted
lift special arch support built into or inserted in footwear; one of the layers of leather forming heel
outsole sole
platform insert that adds height to heel
seam stitching where sections of shoe are attached
shank portion of sole of shoe beneath instep that provides support for arch section; metal or fiber piece that gives this part shape
shoehorn stiff, troughlike blade on handle, held at back of shoe to aid in inserting heel
shoelace cloth or leather string for binding shoe closed
shoetree form of wood or metal inserted in shoe to preserve its shape when not in use
sole thick bottom of shoe that rests on ground; outsole
tassel ornamental knob of loose, knotted strands of leather hanging over upper
thong upright piece between toes on certain sandals
toe box piece of stiffened material placed between lining and toecap of shoe
toecap piece of leather or other material covering toe of shoe, sometimes of different color than upper
tongue attached piece across top of foot, esp. under laces
upper main part of shoe above sole
vamp upper covering forepart of foot, extending back
wedge heel heel on woman's shoe formed by triangular wedge that extends from front or middle to back of sole
welt strip of leather between insole and outsole through which they are stitched or stapled together
wingtip toecap perforated in wing-shaped design

Shoes and Footwear

athletic shoe canvas or leather shoe with rubber sole
blucher shoe with one-piece tongue and front vamp, overlapped by quarters that lace together
boot fitted leather upper reaching above ankle; waterproof rubber or plastic covering for shoe and ankle
bootee ankle-length boot; infant's knitted or crocheted sock worn as indoor shoe
bootie soft, sometimes disposable sock or bootlike covering for foot or shoe, for protection or informal wear
brogan heavy leather, ankle-high work shoe; stogy
brogue heavy shoe with punched design on uppers, such as wingtips or oxfords
buck light brown buckskin shoe
chukka ankle-high, laced, leather boot with two eyelets
cleat athletic shoe with metal or hard rubber grips on sole
clodhopper large, heavy, rustic shoe
clog shoe with thick wooden sole; klomp; wooden shoe (Holland and Scandinavia)
combat boot sturdy, high-laced military boot
cowboy boot midcalf boot with high heels, pointed toe, and fancy stitching, traditionally for horseback riding
decker flat, rubber-soled sandal; flip-flop; zori
docksider casual, rubber-soled leather moccasin
duck casual slip-on, water-resistant shoe with canvas upper and rubber sole
espadrille shoe with hemp or crepe sole, canvas upper, and flat or wedge heel; rope-sole shoe
flats woman's casual, low-heeled shoes
flip-flop flat, loose, backless, rubber sandal held on with thong between first two toes; decker; zori
flippers broad, flat, usu. rubber attachments to feet, with toe end expanded into paddle for swimming, diving, or body surfing
footwear shoes, sandals, and slippers intended as outer covering for feet
gaiter ankle-high shoe of cloth or leather with elastic inserts in sides
galoshes high rubber overshoes for protection from snow and rain; overshoes
geta wooden clog elevated by transverse supports on bottom of sole (Japan)
gillie low-cut shoe with decorative lacing through loops and around ankle
gumshoe rubber overshoe or boot
gym shoe comfortable, rubber-soled athletic shoe, often with canvas upper
half-boot boot ending just above ankle
heels woman's high-heeled dress shoes
high heels woman's dress shoes with elongated heels and low-cut upper
high-topped sneakers athletic shoe extending over ankle for extra support
hiking boot sturdy, lightweight boot with nonslip sole
hip boot tall boot extending above knee to top of thigh
huarache woven leather sandal with rubber sole (Mexico)
jazz shoe close-fitting, low-heeled oxford of soft leather or fabric, having thin, flexible sole, worn for jazz dancing
kiltie shoe with long tongue in tassels or fringe folding over instep
klomp wooden shoe; clog
lace shoe shoe with lace and eyelet closure
loafer low-cut, slip-on shoe
moccasin soft leather, heelless shoe with sole stitched to upper
mukluk heavy sealskin or reindeer boot (Eskimo)
mule woman's low-heeled house shoe or lounging slipper, with upper across open toes
overshoes galoshes
oxford shoe laced over instep, with facings sewn on front of vamp for laces
paratrooper boot sturdy boot that laces to knee
patent leather shoe dress shoe of shiny patent leather
penny loafer casual slip-on shoe with flap in vamp, sometimes used to hold coin
platform shoe shoe with very thick, elevated sole
plimsoll light, rubber-soled shoe with mudguard and canvas top
pump woman's low-cut, low-heeled, thin-soled, casual shoe
puttee leather legging secured by strap or catch
riding boot high, close-fitting boot for horseback riding
Roman sandal flat-soled shoe with long straps tied around foot, ankle, and calf
rope-sole shoe shoe with thatched rope sole; espadrille
rubber low rubber shoe worn over regular shoes for protection from rain
running shoe athletic shoe with sole and support designed for running
sabot wooden shoe with strap across instep
saddle oxford saddle shoe
saddle shoe oxford-style, two-tone shoe, esp. in brown and white; saddle oxford
sandal usu. leather sole attached to foot by straps
scuff flat-soled slipper with no quarter or heel strap
seaboot high, waterproof wading boot for fishing and sailing
shoe outer covering for foot, usu. with sturdy sole and attached rigid heel
ski boot heavy boot that clamps to ski
slipper soft, low-cut, slip-on shoe, esp. for indoor wear
sneaker canvas or leather sport shoe with pliable rubber sole
snowshoe oval, light, wooden frame strung with thongs that attaches to shoe for walking over deep snow
soft-sole shoe infant's shoe with moccasin seam and soft leather bottom
spectator pump woman's medium-heeled shoe with contrasting colors at heel and toe of upper
spike athletic shoe with metal spikes in sole
spike heel woman's very tall, narrow-heeled shoe; stiletto heel

stiletto heel spike heel
tennis shoe canvas athletic shoe with rubber sole
thigh boot boot extending to midthigh, flexible at knee
thong sandal with strip of material fitted between toes, strapped across foot
toe shoe woman's ballet slipper with wood block inside toe for en pointe dancing
track shoe light, heelless shoe with steel spikes for running outdoors or rubber sole for running on indoor track
wafflestomper ankle boot with ridged sole, esp. for hiking
wader knee-high or chest-high waterproof boot for fishing and hunting
Wellington boot leather boot loosely fitted above knee
white buck casual oxford of white buckskin
wingtip man's dress shoe with toecap perforated in wing- shaped design
wooden shoe clog or other wood-soled shoe
zori lightweight, usu. rubber, thong sandal (Japan)

HATS, HEADGEAR, AND HAIRPIECES

Hats
Helmets, Headdresses, and Hairpieces

Hats

astrakhan hat of curly astrakhan wool (Russia)
baseball cap hat with close-fitted crown, front brim, and insignia
beanie small, close-fitting skullcap, formerly worn by college freshmen
beret soft, round, flat, visorless, wool cap, banded to fit head
bicorne hat with brim turned up in two places
biretta square cap with three corner points and tassel on top, worn by Catholic clergy
boater flat-topped, stiff straw hat with round, flat brim
bonnet woman's brimless hat with chin ribbon
bowler felt hat with low, round crown and narrow brim
busby tall, military dress hat of fur, with bag hanging on one side
cap usu. close-fitting hat, esp. with visor and no brim
chapeau *French.* hat
cloche woman's bell-shaped, close-fitting hat worn well down on head
cocked hat tricorne with brim turned up in three places
coolie hat conical, straw sunhat (Asia)
coonskin cap of raccoon skin, often with tail at back
cowboy hat wide-brimmed hat with large, soft crown
crusher soft, felt, crushable hat
deerstalker close-fitting woolen cap with visor in front and back and earflaps that are tied across top of crown when raised, orig. worn for hunting
derby man's stiff, felt hat with narrow brim and domed crown; billycock; pot hat
dink beanie with button on top
dunce cap tall, conical, brimless hat, formerly worn as punishment by poor students
Dutch cap woman's cap of triangular cloth rolled back at each side
fedora low, soft, felt hat with crown creased lengthwise
felt hat soft fedora or other hat made of felt
fez brimless, cone-shaped felt hat with tassel (Turkey)
fool's cap three-crowned or conical cap or hood with bells, worn by jesters; jester's cap
garrison cap overseas cap
glengarry woolen cap with straight sides, crease along top, and sometimes ribbon streamers at back (Scotland)
hard hat protective rigid hat of metal or fiberglass worn by construction workers
hat shaped head covering, usu. with brim (projecting edge) and crown (rounded or peaked top)
havelock cloth cap with flap hanging down back of neck as sun shield
homburg hard felt hat with indented crown and rolled-up brim with ribbon edge
jester's cap fool's cap
juliet cap close-fitting beaded or jewel-embroidered cap
kepi military cap with close-fitting band, round, flat top sloping toward front, and visor
leghorn hat or bonnet of fine leghorn straw
liberty cap limp, close-fitting, conical cap worn as symbol of freedom in French Revolution
lid *Slang.* hat
millinery women's hats in general
mobcap woman's indoor cap with full, high crown, tied with strap under chin
monkey cap small pillbox hat with chin strap
montero round hunter's cap with earflaps
mortarboard close-fitting academic cap with flat, square top and tassel
mutch *Scot.* woman's or child's close-fitting linen cap
nightcap soft, brimless cap worn in bed
opera hat silk top hat, often collapsible
overseas cap visorless wool or cotton cap without stiffening; garrison cap
Panama hat high-crowned, brimmed hat of pale, plaited jipijapa leaf fibers
picture hat woman's dressy, broad-brimmed day hat
pillbox woman's small, stiff, brimless, cylindrical cap
porkpie low-crowned felt hat with creased top and brim turned up in back, down in front
sailor stiff straw hat with low, flat crown and circular brim; soft cotton sailor's hat with brim folded up
shako stiff, high-crowned, plumed military hat with metal plate in front
silk hat top hat

skimmer flat-crowned straw hat with wide, straight brim
skullcap close-fitting, brimless cap that fits high on head
slouch hat soft felt hat with wide flexible brim
snap brim soft felt hat with brim pulled down in front
sombrero large, high-crowned, felt or straw hat with very wide, turned-up brim (Mexico)
sou'wester waterproof hat with brim that is wide and slanted at back
stocking cap knitted conical cap with tassel or pompon on top, for winter wear
stovepipe hat *Slang.* man's tall, silk top hat
straw hat hat of woven straw, usu. flat and stiff, with straight brim
sunbonnet ruffled cloth poke bonnet with protective neck cover
sun hat broad-brimmed hat with high crown for sun protection
tam *Informal.* tam-o'-shanter
tam-o'-shanter soft, flat, knitted wool hat with pompon on top; tam
ten-gallon hat large cowboy hat
three-cornered hat tricorne
top hat tall, formal hat, often collapsible, esp. of silk; silk hat; topper
topper top hat
toque woman's small, close-fitting, brimless hat (16th c.)
tricorne hat with brim turned up in three places; three-cornered hat
Tyrolean hat wide-brimmed felt or straw hat with feather on side
watch cap knitted, close-fitting, navy blue, cold weather cap worn by sailors
Watteau hat straw hat with feather and ribbon trim
yarmulke skullcap worn by Jewish men
zucchetto skullcap worn by Catholic ecclesiastics, with color indicating rank

Helmets, Headdresses, and Hairpieces

aigrette long white heron's plume headdress
babushka kerchief or scarf worn as woman's headdress (Russia)
balaclava hoodlike, close-fitting, knitted pullover mask that reaches to shoulders
bandanna large, colored kerchief tied around head
bandeau band or ribbon worn around head to hold hair
cowl monk's hood
crash helmet usu. round, rigid, protective helmet for drivers and fliers
crest feather plume worn on helmet
crown jeweled headdress for royalty
diadem bejeweled cloth headband for royalty; type of crown
earmuffs soft, warm ear coverings connected by band across skull
eyeshade visor attached to head to shield eyes from sun
fall long, false hairpiece
fanchon kerchief folded into triangle and worn as cap
hair net mesh cap of fine material that holds hair in place
hairpiece section of false hair
headband fabric, leather, or flower headpiece that encircles head across forehead
headcloth kerchief, bandanna, or other cloth worn on head
headdress any decorative covering for head
headgear head covering of any kind
helmet protective head covering of hard material
hood soft fabric covering for head and neck
kerchief small square of cloth used as head covering
mantilla woman's veil covering head and shoulders
miter bishop's tall, peaked headdress
panache feather plume, esp. on helmet
penna headdress of feathers
periwig long, formal wig, often white (17th c.)
pith helmet round, broad-brimmed, protective jungle helmet
plumage plumes and feathers worn as headdress
postiche artificial hairpiece
ribbon strip of often colorful material tied around hair for decoration or to hold hair in place
scarf cloth worn over head
ski mask pullover woolen hood with openings for eyes and mouth
snood fine material or net, pinned at back to contain hair
switch long, thick strand of usu. real hair, fastened together at one end and added to one's own, esp. by women
tiara crownlike headdress of jewels or flowers
topee jungle helmet with cloth covering and cork insulation for protection from sun
toupee false hairpiece worn to cover baldness, usu. by men
turban long cloth wrapped around head or over cap by Muslims (Asia and Middle East)
veil length of cloth worn as woman's head covering, often covering face as well
war bonnet Native American headdress consisting of headband and tail of ornamental feathers
wig synthetic hairpiece for entire skull
wiglet small wig used to supplement existing hair
wimple nun's headcovering of cloth that extends in folds over cheeks, chin, and neck
wreath braided foliage encircling head
yashmak Muslim woman's veil wrapped around upper and lower parts of face so that only eyes show

FASHION AND GARMENT PARTS

Clothing in General
Garment Parts
Fashion, Trim, and Sewing
Fasteners

Clothing in General

accouterments personal clothes and effects
activewear sportswear designed for exercise, hiking, bicycling, and other sports activities
apparel clothing; garments; robes
array finery, fancy dress
attire clothing, esp. finery
beachwear bathing suits and other garments designed for use at beach or swimming pool
caparison richly ornamental outfit of clothing
clothing usu. cloth articles worn on body for covering and decoration; garments
costume complete outfit in specific style, esp. worn in some type of performance
disguise outfit designed to conceal identity
dress clothing, esp. when suited to specific occasion
ensemble complete outfit, esp. when well-coordinated
evening dress complete outfit of formal clothing
fashion specific, esp. current, style of clothing
finery fancy, decorative apparel
formals clothing suitable for ceremonies and elegant parties
garb attire, esp. in characteristic style
garments clothing, esp. outerwear
glad rags *Informal.* showy or fancy clothing
habiliment clothing, esp. for specific work or event
habit characteristic garb
hand-me-downs used clothing received from another
fashion current or specific style of dress
mufti ordinary clothes worn by person normally in uniform
outfit complete set of clothing
playclothes casual or functional clothing worn for leisure and recreational activities
raiment clothing, general attire
regalia fancy or ceremonial attire
sportswear activewear designed for exercise, hiking, bicycling, and sports; casually styled pieces of clothing that can be worn singly or in combination
Sunday best one's finest outfit of clothing
togs clothing in general, esp. specific outfit; toggery
uniform outfit of clothing characteristic of position or occupation
vestments official, esp. ecclesiastical, garments
wardrobe one's complete supply of clothing

Garment Parts

accessory article or set of articles of dress that adds completeness, convenience, or decoration to basic outfit
arm tube of material from shoulder to wrist
armhole opening at shoulder for arm attachment
barrel cuff cuff formed from single band of material, usu. fastened by button
batwing collar man's high, flaring collar
batwing sleeve loose, long sleeve that fits into shoulder, ending at fitted wristband or cuff
bell-bottom leg trouser leg that widens at bottom
bishop sleeve full sleeve gathered to fitted wristband
bodice blouse or upper part of dress
bosom front section across chest
bustline portion of garment covering woman's breasts
button-down collar collar with points that button to shirt front
button stand strip of cloth on front edge of coat for buttons or buttonholes
cap sleeve short sleeve extending from bodice and covering top of shoulder
caul network at back of woman's cap
coattail rear skirts of dress, cutaway, or frock coat
collar piece of fabric surrounding neck opening of shirt or coat
cowl neckline loose, draped neckline
crew neck round neckline without collar
crotch point at which two pant legs meet
cuff wristband on shirtsleeve; turned-back hem of trouser leg
décolletage neckline, esp. woman's low-cut neckline
dolman sleeve sleeve as an extension of bodice, with deep armhole tapering to fitted wrist
dropped waist waistline set below natural waist
drop seat rear section, as on children's pajamas, that may be opened and lowered independently
empire waist high, fitted waistline (France, 19th c.); Directoire
epaulette decorative tab across shoulder, often fringed, esp. on uniform
Eton collar broad, stiff collar worn folded outside of Eton jacket
fastener device for joining or attaching garments or garment parts, such as zipper, button, or hook
fly front cloth overlap concealing buttons or zipper, esp. from waist to crotch at front of pants
French cuff folded double shirt cuff fastened by cuff links
gigot sleeve sleeve with full shoulder and fitted wrist
gore tapering wedge of material that adds fullness to skirt or shoe
gusset triangular expansion insert in seam
kimono sleeves large, square sleeves with underarm seam open, cut in one piece with garment
lapel turned-back fold on front of coat, jacket, or blouse, joined to collar
leg tube of material from hip to ankle

magyar sleeve very full sleeve cut in one piece with bodice
mandarin collar narrow collar that stands up from neckline, often open at front
neck opening at top of garment, across upper chest
neckline style of opening at top of garment
notched collar collar forming notch with lapels of garment at seam where collar and lapels meet
patch pocket pocket made by sewing piece of material to outside of garment
peg leg trouser leg that tapers to tight hem at ankle
peplum short, flared flounce attached at waist of dress, blouse, or coat and extending over hips
Peter Pan collar flat, attached, close-fitting collar with rounded ends meeting at round neckline
placket faced slit at top of garment, esp. skirt, that facilitates putting it on and taking it off
Prussian collar high collar with ends almost meeting in front
raglan sleeve sleeve cut in one piece with shoulder; set-in sleeve
revers usu. wide lapels on jacket, coat, or dress
roll-neck collar collar that turns back on itself
sailor collar collar with neckline that is square at back, narrowing to point at front closure
set-in sleeve sleeve joined to body of garment at shoulder by seam at that juncture; raglan sleeve
shawl collar attached collar and lapels in one piece, rolled back continuously along neckline to closure
shirttail part of shirt below waist, usu. worn inside trousers; tail
shoulder pad cushion in shoulder providing protection or shape
skirt free-hanging material from waist down, either in single strip or encircling body
slash pocket pocket set into garment, esp. below waistline, opening with exterior vertical or diagonal slit
sleeve part of garment covering all or portion of arm between shoulder and wrist
spaghetti strap very narrow shoulder strap on dress or blouse, sometimes decorative
stay strip of stiffening material in corset or shirt collar
stiff collar starched or stiffened upright shirt collar
tab collar shirt collar with small flap on one point that fastens to opposite point to hold both points in place
tail shirttail
tails divided skirts of man's formal jacket
train length of material attached to and trailing behind gown
turtleneck tall, close-fitting collar that rolls over on itself
Vandyke collar wide lace or linen collar with scalloped edge or deep points
vent small opening or section of permeable material allowing passage of air through garment
V neck neckline cut in deep V shape
waist torso covering that extends from neck to waistline
waistband belt or band of trousers or dress fitted around waist
watch pocket small pocket just below front waistband of man's trousers or at front of vest
welt pocket pocket with reinforcing cord sewn to open edges
wing collar standing collar with high, stiff, turned-back corners
yoke fitted top of bodice, shirt, coat, or skirt to which lower part is sewn

Fashion, Trim, and Sewing

accordion pleats narrow pleats resembling accordion folds
acid washed (*adj*) describing denim processed with bleach to fade color
A-line shape of woman's skirt, dress, or coat that is narrow at top and flaring to bottom, like letter A
appliqué flat, decorative material or trim sewn on garment
argyle fabric with diamond-shaped designs, esp. in socks
backstitch hand stitching, one backward on garment front, two forward on reverse, to form solid line of stitching
bargello straight stitch used to form variety of zigzag and oblique designs in high and low relief; Florentine stitch
basket weave checkered weave resembling plaited basket
baste (*vb*) make long, loose, temporary stitches for fitting
batting layers of cotton or synthetic fiber for stuffing or lining
bias line at forty-five-degree angle to border in cutting for fit
blanket stitch embroidery or sewing stitch of variable size and width, often used to finish fabric edges decoratively
bobbin spool of thread or yarn on sewing machine
bolt measured roll of fabric of standard length
bonded (*adj*) made of two layers of the same fabric, or of a fabric and lining material, attached to each other by a chemical process or adhesive
braiding strips of interwoven yarn, fabric, or leather for binding or decoration
burl small knot of wool, thread, or yarn for imparting nubby texture
buttonhole stitch closely worked loop stitch making firm, finished edge; close stitch
cable-stitch series of knitting stitches used to produce cable appearance
caddis worsted ribbon or binding for garters and girdles
candlewicking series of knot stitches made in fabric with cotton embroidery thread
casing tunnel of stitched fabric holding elastic or drawstring
chain stitch looped, ornamental stitch resembling chain links
ciré highly glazed finish made by applying wax to fabric
clew ball of thread or yarn
close stitch buttonhole stitch

colorfast (*adj*) describing fabric with permanent color dyed into its yarn, so that it will not fade or run
color scheme selection of colors in outfit or garment to form some type of pattern
coordinate (*vb*) combine complementary elements and colors into outfit
couching stitching with two threads, one of which stitches the other to the fabric
crewel embroidery loosely twisted wool yarn decoration
crimping act of pressing fabric into narrow, regular folds like pleats
crocheting needlework done with single strand of yarn or thread interlocked in loops to form fabric or garment
cross-stitch series of needlework stitches forming Xs
cutwork openwork embroidery on linen, with pattern outlined in buttonhole stitch and ground fabric cut away
damassé (*adj*) woven in reversible, figured pattern like damask
darn (*vb*) mend with crossed or interwoven stitches; embroider with rows of running stitches
dart tapering tuck of fabric stitched down to improve fit
designer (*adj*) created by or carrying label of specific fashion designer, but often mass-produced
diaphanous (*adj*) transparent or translucent and gauzy
double-knit fabric made with double set of knitting needles that produce double-thick, ribbed fabric joined by interlocking stitches
double stitch two loops of single thread fastened in center of fold
dry cleaning cleaning of garments with chemical rather than water
dye colorfast coloring agent for textiles
embroidery various types of decorative stitching with a needle
facing plain or decorative lining at garment edge
fagoting openwork fabric decoration in which thread is drawn in crisscross stitches across open seam
featherstitch embroidered ornament in which succession of branches extends alternately on each side of central stem
fell seam with one raw edge folded under other, sewn flat on underside
felting nonwoven fabric of wool or hair, matted together by heat, moisture, and pressure
fiber slender, threadlike structure from which either natural or synthetic yarn is made
filling yarn that interlaces the warp in fabric; yarn carried by shuttle
Florentine stitch bargello
flounce wide strip of material attached by one edge as trim, usu. at the bottom of skirt
fluting long, round, ornamental grooves
frayed (*adj*) worn or ragged from use or age, esp. collars and cuffs
French seam seam in which raw edges of cloth are completely covered by sewing them together on both sides
fringe border or trim of loose or bunched threads
frog ornamental braided loop fastener with button
froufrou frilly ornamentation usu. on women's clothing
furbelow flounce on woman's clothing
garter stitch knitting stitch that produces evenly pebbled texture on both sides of work
gathers soft folds in cloth formed by drawing fabric along a thread
gros point large embroidery stitch
hand tactile quality of fabric
hangtag tag attached to garment providing information about its size, manufacturer, fabric, care, and sometimes price
haute couture high fashion (France)
hem bottom of dress or pants folded back and stitched down
hemline height of skirt relative to leg and knee, changing with fashion
herringbone twilled wool weave in pattern resembling fish skeleton, with series of Vs in vertical rows
high fashion most up-to-date international styles
hound's tooth small, broken checks in cloth
inseam inner seam of trouser leg from crotch to bottom of leg
interfacing layer of fabric between facing and outer fabric
inverted pleat reverse of box pleat, with folds meeting on face
jetted pockets pockets piped and bound with same material
kick pleat inverted pleat extending as much as 10 inches (25 cm) upward from hemline at back of narrow skirt, to allow freedom in walking
knife pleat one-directional pleat folded so only one crease shows
knit (*vb*) make cloth by looping yarn or thread together with special needles
lining inner garment, constructed separately and joined to outer garment at major seams
locker loop loop at back of garment near neck, orig. for hanging up garment
long-waisted (*adj*) having greater than average length between shoulders and waistline
macramé decorative knots tied in geometrical patterns
mannequin model of human body used to design and display clothes; person who models clothes
mercerizing treatment of cotton fiber with caustic alkali under tension to increase strength and luster
nap soft, hairy surface of fabric
needlepoint embroidery worked on a gridlike formation of canvas
needlework process or result of stitching with a needle, esp. embroidery, needlepoint, and appliqué
nonwoven fabric material with fibers interlocked by heat, moisture, or adhesives, as in synthetics or felting
notions sundries or small articles, esp. trim, ribbon, and buttons
nubby (*adj*) having rough, knotted weave
off-the-rack (*adj*) readymade; not made to individual specifications

overcasting sewing along edges of material with long, spaced stitches to prevent raveling
overlock seam special stitch connecting fabric and finishing edge in one operation
pattern instructional plan of design for sewing garment
permanent press process in which fabric is treated with resin and heat to hold shape and resist wrinkling
petit point small embroidery stitch
pile upright yarn loops that produce velvety surface when cut
piping narrow, bias-cut cloth strip folded as edging or seam
plaid checkerboard or crossbarred pattern
plain weave most common and tightest weave, in which filling threads pass over and under successive warp threads
pleat fold of material doubled over on itself and stitched or pressed in place
plissé puckered finish on fabric produced by caustic soda solution treatment that causes shrinkage
preshrunk (*adj*) designating a cotton garment shrunk to fit before sale
prewashed (*adj*) designating garments washed before sale, usu. to produce faded or worn look or soft texture
primary color red, blue, or yellow
pucker crimp, wrinkle, or furrow in fabric finish
purl (*vb*) embroider or edge with twisted gold or silver thread; invert stitches in knitting for ribbed effect; finish a garment with looped edge
quilting two layers of fabric stitched together over soft filling material
raveled (*adj*) unwoven, untwisted, or unwound
readymade any garment made in advance for sale, not custom tailored
ready-to-wear (*adj*) designating mass-produced apparel, esp. synthetics
reversible (*adj*) being a garment that may be worn with lining side out
ribbing vertical ridge on cloth, esp. on knit material
rickrack flat, zigzag braid or ribbon used for trim
ruffle trim with ornamental pleats or gathers along one edge
run ravel in knit fabric, esp. hosiery
running stitch small, consistent stitching made by passing needle in and out of fabric
saddle stitch decorative running stitch near edge of fabric
sartorial (*adj*) relating to tailoring and tailored clothes
satin weave weave in which filling threads are interlaced with warp at wide intervals, giving effect of smooth surface
seam stitched line where two pieces of fabric are joined
seconds manufactured garments with small imperfections, sold at discount
selvage narrow, woven border of heavy material finished so as to prevent raveling
sequin small, shiny disk or spangle
sewing act of forming and fastening by thread stitches
shirring decorative gathering of fabric in parallel rows of short stitches to control fullness
short-waisted (*adj*) having less than average length between shoulders and waistline
shuttle device that holds thread in place or passes woof through warp
silkscreen printing dyeing method in which pattern is made by letting dye seep through unsealed areas of silkscreen
sizing glutinous solution used for covering or stiffening fabric
slip stitch concealed stitch for sewing hems; unworked knitting stitch
smocking honeycomb stitches dividing and holding together tiny pleats
spangles small, shiny, metal disks sewn on fabric
static cling tendency of clothing to adhere to surfaces due to accumulation of static electricity, esp. in synthetic fibers
stitching small loops of thread or yarn used to fasten garment parts
stonewashed (*adj*) washed prior to sale with pebbles or stones to give worn appearance
strapless (*adj*) designating dress or woman's top made without shoulder straps
swatch fabric sample
tack (*vb*) fasten together with temporary stitches
tailor (*vb*) make, style, fit, trim, mend, or adapt garments; (*n*) person who does this work
tambour round embroidery frame consisting of two hoops, one fitting within the other; embroidery done on such a frame
tassel tuft of ornamental thread hanging from knot
tatting cotton lace made by looping and knotting single heavy thread on hand shuttle
tent stitch short, slanting embroidery stitch
terry loop forming uncut pile
thimble small, protective cap worn on fingertip, used for pushing needle through cloth
thread single strand of fibers used in making cloth or in sewing pieces of cloth together
tie-dyeing process of hand-tying portions of fabric or yarn to prevent absorption of dye and to produce pattern
tinsel glittery, sparkling thread or strip in fabric
topstitch line of stitches sewn on face side of garment along seam
tram double, twisted silk thread used as weft in silk and velvet
tuck fold of material stitched down partway or completely
tuft cluster of closely drawn threads fastened at base
twill fabric woven in parallel diagonal lines or ribs
two-ply (*adj*) designating fabric woven with two sets of warp thread and two of filling
underlining fabric layer stitched to back of each piece of outer fabric
understitching row of stitches that prevents facing from rolling to outside of garment

wale even, lengthwise ridge in woven fabrics, esp. in corduroy
warp yarns woven lengthwise in fabric and crossed by weft
warp knit knit made with several yarns
water repellent (*adj*) designating fabric treated to resist water absorption
water resistant (*adj*) designating fabric sometimes slightly more absorbent than that which is water repellent
weave any pattern of interlinking threads to form cloth; (*vb*) make cloth by interlacing strands of yarn or thread
webbing sturdy, narrow, closely woven tape for straps and upholstery
weft yarns carried horizontally by weaving shuttle, crossing and interlaced with warp
welted pocket slit pocket with reinforcing cord sewn on open edge
welting reinforcing strip or double edge at garment seam
whipstitch stitch that passes over an edge for joining, finishing, or gathering
woof yarn carried by shuttle and crossing warp in weaving; texture of woven fabric
worsted smooth, hard, twisted thread used to make wool with smooth, hard surface

Fasteners

bobby pin flat, metal or plastic hairpin with pinching arms
buckle fastener for two loose ends, attached to one end and grasping the other by catch or prong
catch fastener that holds something in place, usu. by clamping or hooking
cinch tightly gripping belt or girth
clasp hook and loop that holds objects together
drawstring cord or thin rope that tightens to close an opening when its ends are pulled
D-ring D-shaped metal ring through which belt or strap passes to close or secure something
frog ornamental braided button and loop through which it passes
safety pin pin bent back on itself to form spring, with guard covering point when pin is fastened
stud small, buttonlike device with smaller button or shank on back, inserted through shirt front to fasten two sides together
suspenders thin bands worn over shoulders, with clasps at end to hold up trousers or skirt
tack temporary stitch holding materials together while they are being sewn
toggle ornamental, rod-shaped button passed through loop or frog
zipper two parallel rows of interlocking teeth, metal or plastic, on strips of material drawn together by sliding pull piece

Chapter Eleven
Social Order

THE CITY

Cities, Towns, Villages, and Districts
Roadways and Driving
Urban Structures and Phenomena

Cities, Towns, Villages, and Districts

bedroom community suburb
boom town town experiencing rapid unplanned growth due to economic activity
borough one of five political divisions of New York City; *Chiefly Brit.* incorporated, self-governing urban area, comparable to municipality
burbs *Informal.* suburbs
burg city or town
capital city serving as seat of government; city renowned for some activity
city densely inhabited place larger and more important than town or village, usu. incorporated as an administrative and judicial unit
community group of individuals living together as a unit within larger population; area occupied by such people
conurbation connected series of urban communities
county seat city where county administrative offices are located
cow town small, unsophisticated town, esp. within cattle-raising area
crossroad town located at juncture of two or more roads
district quarter, ward, or section of city
dynapolis planned city consisting of several communities along central roadway
exurb area outside city and beyond suburbs, often inhabited by wealthy families
exurbia region of exurbs
ghetto district occupied primarily by one religious or ethnic group, usu. poor
ghost town once active town that is now deserted, usu. due to depletion of a natural resource
greater (*adj*) designating metropolitan area surrounding city
hamlet small village
hick town small, often isolated, unsophisticated town
hometown city or town of one's birth or principal residence
inner city older, densely populated, often rundown central district
market town city to which farmers and artisans from surrounding countryside bring goods to sell at market
megalopolis very large city; heavily populated region encompassing several cities
metropolis large or important city, often a capital or center of business or cultural activity
metropolitan area large city and its immediate suburbs
midtown central section of city or town, esp. main shopping district
municipality incorporated, self-governing, urban political unit
one-horse town small, rural town
outskirts districts far from center of city
Podunk small, insignificant, or remote town
polis city-state (ancient Greece)
precinct electoral subdivision of town, city, or ward; section of city for police control
purlieu outlying district
quarter division or district of town or city
red-light district area with houses of prostitution
residential area nonbusiness district of private homes
satellite suburban community
settlement place newly settled; small village
shtetl *Yiddish.* formerly a small Jewish village in Eastern Europe
suburb residential community lying just outside or within commuting distance of city; bedroom community
suburbia outlying part of city or town
town any group of structures considered a distinct place with a distinguishing placename; closely populated area larger than a village but smaller than a city, having fixed boundaries that distinguish it from surrounding rural territory
township small incorporated city
uptown fancier residential or commercial district of city or town
village often rural community larger than a hamlet and smaller than a town; small incorporated municipality
ward administrative or electoral district of city
zone division of city designated for specific purpose, esp. numbered postal delivery

Roadways and Driving

alley narrow street, often providing access to rear of buildings
alleyway narrow street or passageway
artery principal roadway in branching system of roads
autobahn high-speed multilane expressway (Germany and Austria)
autoroute high-speed multilane expressway (France and Canada)
autostrada divided expressway connecting major cities (Italy)
avenue moderate-sized roadway wider than a lane and narrower than a boulevard; *Chiefly Brit.* driveway to house off main road
back street small, remote, obscure, or inaccessible roadway
beltway highway encircling an urban area; ring road
bottleneck narrowing point of traffic congestion
boulevard broad landscaped thoroughfare
bumper-to-bumper (*adj*) marked by heavy traffic with long rows of slow-moving cars
bypass route around town
byway rarely traveled roadway
carpool arrangement among automobile owners to take turns driving a group to some common activity

causeway highway
checkpoint designated inspection place for vehicles
chuckhole rough hole or rut in road
circle rotary
cloverleaf intersection of two highways where traffic is routed from one highway onto branches leading in a circle to another highway
cobblestone road paved with rounded stones larger than pebbles and smaller than boulders
concourse open space where roads or paths meet; junction
congestion excess traffic clogged or concentrated in too small a space
court broad alley with single opening onto main street
crossroads intersection of two or more roads
crosswalk lane designated for pedestrians to cross road in safety
cul-de-sac street closed at one end; dead end
dead end street without exit at one end
deck roadway across multilevel bridge
detour roundabout route temporarily replacing section of roadway that is damaged or being repaired
double-park (*vb*) park vehicle on street side of vehicle already parked along curb
drive-in place of business laid out so that patrons can be served while remaining in vehicles
driveway road leading from public roadway to private building
expressway high-speed, divided, multilane highway for through traffic with limited access at intersections with other roadways; thruway
freeway toll-free highway
frontage road local road alongside expressway that provides access to property along it; service road
gas station service station
grade sloping road; degree of inclination of sloping road
grade crossing crossing of rail or roadway or pedestrian walkway on one level
gridlock traffic jam, esp. at intersection, in which all vehicles are blocked from moving
gutter recessed area at side of street to carry off surface water
hairpin turn extremely sharp U-shaped bend in road
highway main direct roadway, usu. high speed and multilane
interchange multilevel junction of two or more highways that makes it possible for traffic to change roadway without obstructing cross traffic
interstate multilane divided highway connecting major cities in several states
jaywalk (*vb*) cross roadway heedlessly or illegally so as to be endangered by traffic
jersey barrier strip of concrete at center of highway that divides oncoming traffic
junction intersection of roads, often where one terminates
lane narrow roadway, esp. between barriers or trees; strip of roadway designated for single row of vehicles
macadam roadway constructed by compacting a layer of small broken stone using bituminous binder
manhole opening in street that provides access to underground utilities
main drag *Slang.* principal roadway in town or city
main street principal business street, esp. in small town
median strip paved or planted area that divides highway into sections for traffic moving in opposite directions
mew back street, alley
one-way (*adj*) designating roadway for movement in one direction only
overpass crossing of highways, or of highway and pedestrian crossing, at different levels, allowing traffic to pass on lower level; upper level of such a crossing
parkway broad, usu. landscaped, thoroughfare
pike turnpike
pileup serious collision involving several vehicles
plaza point in toll road at which tollbooths are located
post road road used for mail conveyance
pothole large hole in road surface
ring road road encircling city; beltway
road long, open way with paved surface for traveling, esp. by vehicle
road hog aggressive driver of vehicle who invades others' traffic lanes
road test check of vehicle under normal operating conditions; test of driving ability required for obtaining license
roadway land over which road is built and on which vehicles travel
rotary circular roadway at multiple intersection around which all traffic moves counterclockwise; circle; traffic circle
route course for travel from one point to another; highway
rumble strip one of a series of rough or raised strips of highway pavement, used to make drivers slow down speed of their vehicles
rush hour period at beginning or end of business day when traffic is at its peak
safety island portion of roadway from which vehicles are excluded
secondary road feeder or artery to main roadway
service road frontage road
service station retail outlet for care of vehicles, esp. sale of gasoline; filling station; gas station
shoulder edge of roadway alongside driving area
side street small roadway; roadway leading off main street
sidewalk paved strip for pedestrians at side of street
signpost post with information or directions for drivers
skyway elevated highway
speed limit maximum legal driving speed permitted on given roadway

speed trap roadway patrolled by concealed police officers to catch drivers exceeding speed limit, esp. by radar
speedway public roadway for high-speed driving; expressway
square open area where two or more streets converge, usu. surrounded on all sides by buildings
stop-and-go slow driving in heavy traffic involving frequent stops
stop sign octagonal sign, usu. red, that requires drivers to come to full stop
street roadway that is wider than alley or lane and usu. includes sidewalks; thoroughfare with abutting property
subway underpass beneath street
superhighway wide highway designed for high-speed travel between major points
tailgate (*vb*) drive too closely behind another vehicle
tarmac roadway of tarmacadam
thoroughfare main roadway
through street street that provides for continuous passage of traffic, with outlets at both ends
thruway expressway
ticket summons issued for traffic violation
tie-up stoppage of traffic due to congestion, construction, or accident
toll tax or fee paid for use of roadway
tollgate barrier at which driver of vehicle must pay toll to pass
towaway zone no-parking area from which vehicles are removed by authorities
traffic vehicles or pedestrians moving between points or along roadway
traffic circle rotary
traffic island paved or planted area in roadway that controls flow of traffic in opposite directions
traffic jam congestion and slow movement of traffic due to excess of cars on roadway, construction, or accident
traffic signal electrically-operated visual device for controlling traffic by use of colored signals; traffic light
turnpike toll road or road that previously charged toll; pike
two-way street roadway that allows passage in both directions
underpass lower level of overpass roadway interchange
U-turn 180-degree change in direction
zebra crossing pedestrian crosswalk marked by series of thick white stripes

Urban Structures and Phenomena

agora city marketplace (ancient Greece)
alameda public walkway lined by trees
aqueduct channel for large volume of flowing water
arcade long, arched gallery or passageway between shops
arch bridge span supported by series of arches and towers
asphalt jungle large, crowded urban area, esp. dangerous part where people must struggle to survive
Bailey bridge bridge constructed from interchangeable latticed steel panels joined by steel pins
barrio Spanish-speaking quarter in U.S. city
bascule bridge movable bridge in which rising section is counterbalanced by a weight
block rectangular unit in city grid, enclosed by intersecting streets and occupied by buildings; length of one side of such a unit; row of houses between two streets
boardwalk raised promenade along beach
bridge structure carrying roadway for vehicles and/or pedestrians over depression, obstacle, or body of water: arch, bascule, cantilever, draw, flyover, foot, lift, pontoon, suspension, swing, toll, truss
canal man-made waterway for transportation or for draining and irrigating land
cantilever bridge span consisting of rigid construction elements that extend horizontally well beyond its vertical support members
city planning rational organization of urban growth
commute (*vb*) travel back and forth regularly between home in suburbs and work in city
commuter person who commutes regularly, esp. to work
complex large group of buildings or apartments
courthouse building that houses law courts
covered bridge bridge with roofed or enclosed roadway
crosstown (*adj*) located at opposite points of town; (*adv*) from one side of town to the other
dike bank of earth constructed to control or hold back water; ditch
drawbridge bridge built in sections that may be raised or lowered to permit or obstruct passage
elevated railroad urban or interurban railroad that runs along tracks raised above ground level
embankment raised area along waterway or roadway
emporium commercial center; large retail establishment
esplanade flat expanse of paved or grassy land along shore, esp. for driving or walking
footbridge bridge for use by pedestrians only
forum marketplace and central public area of city (ancient Rome)
greenbelt area of parkways or farmland encircling city
high rise multistory building with elevators
housing development cluster of individual residences or apartment buildings of similar design under one ownership
housing project publicly financed and administered housing development for low-income families
kiosk small, open, circular building used as newsstand or telephone booth
landfill low area of land that is built up from trash and garbage wastes embedded between layers of earth

lift bridge bridge having section that can be raised vertically to permit passage beneath it
mall large complex of shops and restaurants with attached passageways and parking space; public promenade lined with trees and closed off to motor vehicles; paved or planted divider in roadway; pedestrian passageway providing access to rows of stores
marina basin providing dockage for motorboats and yachts, with supply and repair facilities
metro subway system
metropolitan (*adj*) relating to or characteristic of a city
municipal (*adj*) restricted to one self-governing locality
noise pollution environmental pollution consisting of bothersome or harmful noise
off-hour period of time other than rush hour or outside regular business hours
off-peak off-hour period with reduced public transportation fares
pedestrian one who moves by foot
people mover movable sidewalk
piazza open square (Italy)
playground outdoor area equipped with children's recreational facilities
plaza public square
pontoon bridge bridge supported by series of floats
promenade public walkway
quay paved bank or landing beside navigable waterway
rapid transit fast, modern, public transportation system
rialto exchange or marketplace; theater district
right of way strip of land over which a public road is built; land used by a public utility
shopping center group of retail stores and service establishments with parking facilities, serving community or neighborhood
shopping mall shopping area with stores facing enclosed area restricted to pedestrians
skid row downtown district of cheap bars and hotels for transients
skyscraper very tall building
skywalk enclosed, elevated walkway that connects two buildings
slum densely-populated urban area marked by crowding, poor housing, poverty, and social disorder
span bridge or overpass
straphanger person who commutes on public transportation, esp. while standing up holding a strap for support
strip long stretch of land, often used as highway divider; commercially-developed roadway
subway underground electric railway
suspension bridge bridge with roadway suspended from two or more cables that pass over towers and are anchored at ends
swing bridge bridge that opens by pivoting on central pier to permit passage
terrace row of houses or apartments on raised ground; strip of park in middle of street; small avenue or lane
transit local transportation of passengers by public conveyance
truss bridge bridge supported by bracketlike framework
urban (*adj*) of, relating to, characteristic of, or constituting a city
urban blight decay and poverty of old inner city
urban planning systematic development of new urban areas or renovation of existing areas to improve conditions there
urban renewal planned renovation of older city districts
urban sprawl spreading of urban phenomena onto undeveloped land near city
utility service such as water, gas, or electricity provided by public or private company
viaduct bridge made up of several short spans supported by reinforced concrete arches and towers, carrying road or railroad over obstruction or valley
walk-up multistory building without elevator
walkway pedestrian passage
waterfront land or district adjacent to body of water
wharf structure built along shore of navigable waters at which ships may lie to receive and discharge cargo or passengers
zoning partitioning by ordinance of city, borough, or township into sections reserved for specific purposes

GOVERNMENT

Forms, Systems, and Philosophies
Governmental Bodies and Institutions
Government Officials and Citizens
Acts, Powers, Conditions, and Procedures
Postal Service

Forms, Systems, and Philosophies

absolute monarchy kingdom in which monarch has complete power
absolutism theory and practice of government by single absolute ruler
anarchy absence of government; advocacy of this state
aristocracy government by wealthy, privileged minority or hereditary ruling class
autarchy absolute sovereignty; autocracy
autarky economic self-sufficiency of a state
authoritarianism principle of submission to authority; concentration of power in hands of autocratic leader or powerful elite not constitutionally bound or responsible to the people
autocracy government power placed in hands of one ruler; autarchy

autonomy self-government, esp. state and local
benevolent dictatorship nonrepressive absolute rule that works for good of citizens
bicameral (*adj*) having two legislative houses in government
caliphate government ruled by Islamic civil and religious leader
caretaker government temporary regime during lapse in normal government functions
centralization organization under single authority; shift of political authority from local to state government
checks and balances principle of interdependency of governmental branches through power of limitation
city-state self-governing state composed of independent city and adjacent territory controlled by it, esp. in ancient Greece and medieval Europe; polis
civil government government established by laws made by citizens or their representatives; nonmilitary, nonreligious authority
civil liberty freedom from arbitrary governmental interference, esp as prescribed in U.S. Bill of Rights
coalition government temporary alliance of members of two or more parties to form governing majority
collective group or institution organized and run by all members equally
colonialism control by one state over dependent state or people
common law unwritten law developed over time and based on accepted notion of right and wrong
commonwealth government in which ultimate authority lies with people
concurrent powers rights exercised by both national and state governments
constitutionalism government based on written constitutional principles
constitutional monarchy government headed by monarch and regulated by constitution
council-manager plan form of city government in which strong elected council hires city manager to administer laws
crown monarch; government in constitutional monarchy
decentralization distribution of power among several groups
democracy government by the people, with majority rule exercised in periodic free election of representatives
despotism system of government in which ruler exercises absolute power
dictatorship government in which absolute power rests with one person or a few
divine right of kings authority of sovereign considered to be granted by God, not people (16th-17th c.)
dominion sovereignty, authority over; self-governing member of British Commonwealth giving allegiance to British monarch
duarchy government by two equally powerful rulers; duumvirate
duumvirate government in which two persons rule jointly; duarchy
dyarchy dual responsibility shared by colonial government and native ministers
empire several territories, nations, or peoples governed by single sovereign authority
fascism government based on establishing oppressive, one-party, centralized national regime
federal government system in which political units surrender individual sovereignty to central authority but retain designated powers; such central authority
federalism principle of shared power between national and state governments
feudalism political system in Europe from 9th to 15th century in which lord owned all property worked by vassals
governance a method or system of government; exercise of government authority
government organized political institutions, laws, and customs by which state fulfills its authorized functions
home rule provision allowing local self-government while under state control
kingdom monarchy ruled by a king
local government authority over town, city, county, or other small locale by citizens rather than state or federal government
martial law temporary suspension of law and use of military to maintain order during emergency
matriarchy government or monarchy in which power rests with females or descends through female line
mayor-council plan system of municipal government with elected mayor as executive and elected council as legislature
meritocracy government in which criterion for leadership is skill or intellectual achievement
militarism belief that war and its preparation are most important functions of state
monarchy government with absolute hereditary ruler who serves for life
municipal (*adj*) pertaining to local self-government
nationalism loyalty to interests of one's own nation
neocolonialism economic domination of one nation by a more powerful nation without imposition of colonial government
oligarchy government by small group of privileged individuals
parliamentary government system in which executive (prime minister) is chosen by elected legislature (parliament) from among its members
participatory democracy democratic system permitting direct involvement of individuals
paternalism benevolent, fatherly control by authority of individuals' interactions with each other as well as with government
patriarchy government or monarchy in which power rests with males or descends through male line
pluralism governmental system that embraces cultural diversity and advocates general participation in decision making
plutocracy government by the wealthy
police state repressive system dominated by all-powerful police, esp. secret police, instead of elected officials

polis city-state (ancient Greece)
principality state ruled by prince, often part of larger state or empire
regency reign of nonmonarch during youth or indisposition of monarch
regime system of administration and its practitioners
representative democracy indirect democracy in which people's will is expressed through elected representatives
republic government in which power is vested in elected representatives of citizenry
self-government political power lying in hands of inhabitants of state or territory rather than outside authority; self-rule
self-rule self-government
separation of powers doctrine that division of responsibility among legislative, executive, and judicial branches is conducive to equitable government
social contract understanding between citizens and government on which government is based
sovereignty political autonomy and freedom of state from outside authority
state government authority over single state
statism highly centralized government control of economy
stratocracy government by the military
technocracy government run by experts and technicians
theocracy government by church officials, who believe they have divine authority
totalitarianism authoritarian political system in which citizen is totally subject to will of state
triarchy government ruled jointly by three persons; triumvirate
tricameral (*adj*) having three legislative houses or chambers in government
triumvirate triarchy
tyranny government by single absolute authority, esp. one exercising oppressive power
unicameral (*adj*) having a single legislative chamber in government
unitary government system in which power is held by single central source and local governments are merely administrative agents, the opposite of federalism
welfare state system in which ultimate responsibility of government is well-being of all citizens

Governmental Bodies and Institutions

administration activity and actions of all branches of government; collective body managing government affairs
agency unit of executive branch that administers programs, sets rules, and settles disputes in specific policy area
assembly lower legislative house
board group of elected or appointed functionaries
brain trust informal group of advisers
branches of government tripartite division of U.S. government: executive, legislative, judicial
bureau independent government office
bureaucracy large body of appointive government officials; complex structure of executive branch
cabal secret group seeking to exercise authority over government
cabinet chief advisory body to chief executive, president, or prime minister
camarilla secret group of advisers, often engaged in intrigue; cabal
canton small territorial division (France and Switzerland)
capital seat of government
capitol building where congress or state legislature meets
Capitol building in Washington D.C., in which Congress meets
Capitol Hill small hill on which U.S. Capitol stands; U.S. Congress, the Hill
chamber legislative house
civil service nonmilitary governmental employees selected through merit system
commission government agency with authority in one area; individuals appointed to investigate specific issues
committee body delegated to consider specific legislative matters
commonwealth federation of nations; official designation of four U.S. states: Kentucky, Massachusetts, Pennsylvania, and Virginia
commune smallest administrative district of some European nations; rural community based on collectivism
confederacy alliance for some specific purpose; eleven Southern states that seceded from United States in 1860; confederation
confederation confederacy
conference committee committee composed of members of both legislative houses
congress national legislative branch of government, esp. in republic; national or international representative assembly
Congress national legislative body of United States, consisting of Senate and House of Representatives
Congressional committee group of legislators chosen to consider details of legislation in one area and advise on Congressional action
council small governmental body, esp. for city
county political subdivision of state
court judicial body; reigning sovereign with his or her family, retinue, and officers
department large administrative division of executive branch headed by cabinet member; regional division within nation comparable to state
diet national or provincial legislative body; assembly of princes
emirate state or territory ruled by an Islamic emir or prince
exchequer national treasury and revenue department, as in Great Britain
executive branch law-enforcing and administrative branch of government, in United States headed by President

federation alliance of autonomous states
floor working area occupied by members of U.S. House or Senate
Hill *Informal.* short for Capitol Hill, where U.S. Congress is located
house one division of bicameral legislature
House of Commons elective lower house of British Parliament
House of Lords upper house of British Parliament, in which peers and church officials sit for lifetime appointments
House of Representatives lower house of U.S. Congress, with two-year elective term
interest group private organization attempting to influence government policy; lobby on specific issue
joint committee legislative committee composed of members from both houses
judicial branch section of government that administers justice and tries cases involving governmental or constitutional issues, composed primarily of judges
judiciary combined system of federal and state courts
kitchen cabinet unofficial, sometimes secret, advisers to head of state
legislative branch lawmaking branch of government, usu. composed of elected representatives
legislature body charged with enacting laws
lobby interest group
lower house one branch of a bicameral legislature, usu. containing more members than upper house; U.S. House of Representatives; British House of Commons
nation independent, politically organized territory and its citizens
national assembly legislative body of nation
office public position or job
parish political subdivision of Louisiana
parliament usu. bicameral elected legislature, as in Britain
possession territory ruled by government of another state
privy council board of personal advisers to monarch
province administrative division of a nation
puppet government government whose policies are orchestrated by another state
regulatory commission small board within executive chosen to manage particular government function
Rules Committee House committee that sets procedures for debate on bills
secretariat administrative department of government organization
Secret Service unit responsible for protecting U.S. President and Vice President
select committee legislative committee established for specific task and limited time
senate lawmaking assembly; state council
Senate upper house of U.S. Congress, with two senators from each state elected to six-year terms
shadow cabinet leaders of minority or opposition party in parliamentary system
sinecure public office requiring little or no work
sovereignty self-governing territory or state
standing committee permanent committee intended to consider specific subject
state politically organized community independent of other states; sovereign nation; major subdivision of United States
statehouse building housing offices of state government
steering committee committee of legislative or deliberative body that prepares agenda for session
subcommittee division of committee with limited purpose or authority
supreme court highest court in political unit with ultimate authority in judicial and constitutional matters
Supreme Court highest federal court in United States, consisting of nine judges
synod governing council or assembly of church
town municipal settlement larger than a village, smaller than a city
town hall location of mayoral and council offices; city hall
town meeting assembly of local citizens acting as legislative body
triumvirate group or association of three
troika administrative body of three
upper house one branch of bicameral legislature; U.S. Senate; British House of Lords
watchdog agency commission responsible for protecting public by regulating an industry

Government Officials and Citizens

alderman city council member in some U.S. cities
appointee nonelective official, usu. chosen by executive branch
assemblyman member of legislative assembly
assemblywoman female member of legislative assembly
attorney general chief law officer of nation or state; chief of U.S. Department of Justice
backbencher any member of British Parliament other than leaders of the party
bureaucrat member of bureaucracy
chair chairperson
chairman official in seat of authority
chairwoman female official in seat of authority
chairperson chairman or chairwoman
chancellor chief minister of state in certain parliamentary governments; prime minister; premier
chief executive principal administrative officer of government
chief justice ranking justice of court, esp. supreme court
chief of staff person responsible for supervising top executive's assistants and advisers
citizen native or naturalized person owing allegiance to specific government
civilian person not in military or government service
civil servant member of civil service; elected or appointed government official serving the people
commander in chief supreme commander of armed forces; U.S. President

congressman member of House of Representatives
congresswoman female member of House of Representatives
constituent resident of legislator's district
coroner county official responsible for investigating circumstances of deaths
councilman member of city council
councilor member of city council
councilwoman female member of city council
crown office or person of monarch
czar absolute hereditary monarch of Russia until 1917; one having authority over major program
deputy member of lower legislative house; chief assistant to department head
designate (*adj*) used following title it modifies to indicate that person has been selected for office but not yet installed, as in ambassador-designate
despot absolute ruler
dictator absolute ruler, esp. oppressive tyrant
disenfranchised citizens denied right to vote
duce Italian fascist leader, esp. Mussolini
dynasty sequence of rulers from same family or group
emperor monarch governing an empire
fed *Informal.* employee of federal government, esp. law enforcement officer
freshman newly elected member serving first term in U.S. Congress
Führer *German.* leader, esp. Hitler
governor chief executive of U.S. state or imperial possession
head of state sovereign or chief executive, sometimes in ceremonial capacity only
lawmaker legislator
legislator member of legislature, usu. elected
lieutenant governor official next in line to state governor
magistrate public official entrusted with administration of law, often with judicial function
manager one who directs or supervises others
mayor highest executive official of city or town
minister high official managing government department or serving as diplomatic representative in foreign state
minister without portfolio government official with responsibilities in various areas
monarch hereditary ruler of kingdom, empire, or constitutional monarchy
MP Member of Parliament (Britain)
official middle- or high-level government employee
ombudsman government official who serves as intermediary between public and government and investigates complaints of misconduct by public officials
page person who carries messages and runs errands for members of legislature
Pharaoh absolute hereditary sovereign in ancient Egypt
philosopher king one who rules based on wisdom, proposed in Plato's *Republic*
premier prime minister
president head of executive branch
president pro tempore presiding officer of Senate when vice president is absent, usu. senior member of majority party
prime minister first minister; head of cabinet in parliamentary government; chancellor; premier
public servant government employee owing first allegiance to citizens of nation he or she serves
regent one who rules monarchy when sovereign is disabled or too young
representative one elected to legislative body to serve interests of specific constituency
secretary executive official supervising operations of one department
secretary-general primary administrative official of organization
selectman municipal official in New England
senator member of senate
sergeant at arms officer of legislative or judicial body charged with preserving order
sovereign one exercising absolute power; monarch
Speaker of the House presiding officer in U.S. House of Representatives
statesman one exercising leadership and conducting governmental business at a high level
subject citizen governed by sovereign authority
treasurer officer responsible for public funds
tyrant single absolute ruler, often oppressive or cruel and violent
under secretary second in command in executive department
vice- prefix indicating official first in line to take place of immediate superior, as in vice-chancellor
vice president official next in line to president
viceroy governor of territory who represents monarch
warlord supreme military leader, often holding civil power by force

Acts, Powers, Conditions, and Procedures

abdicate (*vb*) give up throne or office
abstain (*vb*) withhold one's vote or participation
acclamation vote of legislature by voice only
act law passed by legislative body
ad hoc with specific or particular purpose
adjourn (*vb*) end legislative session
advice and consent constitutional power of Senate to approve all presidential appointments and treaties
affirmative action plan to rectify discrimination against minorities and women
amendment formal alteration of bill, law, or constitution
amnesty pardon by government authority, usu. head of state, to violators of federal law
annexation addition of territory into existing domain
apportionment distribution and assignment of legislative seats
appropriations funds set aside by law for specific purpose
arbitration hearing or judgment of controversy by statutorily appointed body

articles divisions of U.S. Constitution containing procedures for organization and implementation of government
assessment listing and evaluation of property for tax purposes
bill proposed piece of legislation
bill of attainder legislative act finding a person guilty of treason or felony without court trial
Bill of Rights first ten amendments to U.S. Constitution
bloc voting united voting of legislators or delegates to advance or obstruct action
bond certificate indicating government has borrowed money from individual or organization and will pay interest until bond is sold
briefing act of providing information or instructions
budget financial plan for funding operations of government
carry (*vb*) secure passage or adoption; win majority of votes
casting vote deciding vote cast by presiding officer when other votes are equally divided
caucus closed meeting of legislative party members to decide status of forthcoming issues or select leaders
censure condemnation by vote of legislature
census official population count and informational survey taken every ten years
charter fundamental law or constitution granted cities by state legislature
civil disobedience refusal to obey government demands and laws, usu. passive resistance as matter of conscience
civil law laws pertaining to disputes between private parties or between private parties and government
classified (*adj*) secret
clause separate article of law or other formal document
clearance official authorization to know of or participate in classified activities
cloture procedure by which legislative body, esp. U.S. Senate, limits debate
commonweal general welfare
concurrent powers powers held by both states and federal government
concurrent resolution congressional opinion requiring approval of both houses, but not a law
confirmation legislative approval of executive appointment
conflict of interest incompatibility between private interests and public responsibilities
Congressional Record official transcript of proceedings of both houses of Congress
constitution fundamental written law of state or nation
Constitution fundamental written law of United States
constitutionality accordance with constitution of a nation
convene (*vb*) come together as legislative body to commence session
coronation act or ceremony of crowning a monarch
debriefing questioning and instruction of one privy to classified information
debt ceiling upper limit set for national debt
Declaration of Independence proclamation of liberty by American colonies in 1776
decree executive proclamation having force of law
deregulation removal of established controls over business or industry
devolution transfer of power from central government to local government
dissenting opinion written view on case by minority of U.S. Supreme Court
domestic (*adj*) pertaining to internal affairs of state
draft compulsory selection of persons for military duty
edict official order or proclamation with force of law
eminent domain constitutional power of government to take private property for public use
enactment passage of bill into law
enumerated powers powers of federal government stated in U.S. Constitution
exclusive powers powers exclusive to federal or state government
executive order rule issued by President, governor, or administrative authority that has force of law
executive privilege right of President to withhold certain information, usu. to protect national security
executive session hearing held by legislative body or committee that is closed to public
extradition return of criminal from one state or nation to another for trial
fiat authoritative government order or decree
filibuster delaying tactic to prevent legislative action
first reading initial submission of bill before legislature, often by number or name only
fiscal policy governmental use and manipulation of public revenues
foreign policy principles and goals determining one nation's relations with other nations
franking privilege right to mail official papers without charge, enjoyed by members of Congress, President, and cabinet
gag rule any rule restricting open discussion or debate on a given issue in a deliberative body
gavel-to-gavel (*adj*) designating entire period from opening of legislative session to adjournment
grant-in-aid federal money given to state or local government for use in health, education, or public works
impeachment formal accusation brought to remove civil official from office; charges articulated in U.S. House of Representatives and tried in the Senate
implied powers authority of federal government based on indirect expression in U.S. Constitution
inauguration installation of President or other official into office
inherent powers authority of all national governments based on sovereignty as nation-states
initiative petition to place legislation or constitutional amendment on ballot for voters' direct approval

internal revenue money collected by government from citizens in form of taxes
interregnum temporary lapse in government functions, esp. during transition between two regimes or administrations
item veto executive veto of part of bill without rejection of entire measure
joint resolution formal expression of congressional opinion with force of law, esp. on unusual or temporary matter
judicial review power of courts to decide constitutionality of act of government
jurisdiction authority over people or territory
kill (*vb*) prevent enactment of bill into legislation or veto enacted bill
law binding legislative act
legislative power constitutional authority allowing Congress to make laws
lobby (*vb*) attempt to influence government policy on specific issue, esp. by swaying legislative votes
measure legislative bill or enactment
minutes written notes and record of meeting
motion formal proposal
move (*vb*) introduce a motion
national supremacy constitutional doctrine that national laws supersede state or local laws
ordinance law, statute, or government regulation
override legislative vote to annul executive veto of legislative act
pardon legal forgiveness for crime granted by executive without judicial action
parliamentary procedure any of the rules and precedents governing proceedings of legislatures or meetings of other legislative bodies
passage legislative enactment of bill into law
patronage awarding of government positions in return for support or other favors
petition formal written request, often signed by many citizens and submitted to government, esp. as means of placing referendum on ballot
pocket (*vb*) retain legislative bill without action to prevent it from becoming law
pocket veto process by which President prevents bill from becoming law by leaving it unsigned past end of legislative session
portfolio office and duties of minister of state
position paper detailed report on an issue, usu. advising specific action
proclamation official public executive announcement
progressive tax tax rate that increases as taxable income increases
proportional representation allocation of legislative seats by party based on percent of popular or electoral vote received
proviso clause stating conditions of bill or document
public assistance government funds used to satisfy basic needs of poor citizens
public lands territory owned by federal government
public policy government programs approved by legislature or initiated by executive departments and agencies
public service actions that supply essential commodity or service for benefit or welfare of people
public works roads, dams, and other structures for public use that are paid for by government funds
quorum number of members of body required to transact official business, usu. a majority
railroad (*vb*) rush legislation through without considering opposition
ratify (*vb*) vote approval; sanction formally
reapportionment reorganization of electoral districts by new formula
recall procedure by which public official is removed from office by popular vote
recess suspension of legislative session or procedure
redistricting revision of legislative district boundaries
red tape excessive bureaucratic procedure that causes delay
repeal (*vb*) cancel or revoke legislative enactment
reserved powers powers not delegated to federal government by U.S. Constitution and not denied to states
resolution formal expression of opinion or intent by governmental body
revenue government income, primarily from taxation
revenue sharing system by which state and local governments receive fixed amounts of federal tax revenues
rider provision that might not pass on its own but that is likely to pass when attached to important bill
secession formal separation from organized body or government
second (*vb*) endorse another's parliamentary motion
second reading legislative proceeding in which a bill is reported back from committee for full debate before vote
sedition verbal incitement of resistance to lawful authority
sittings sessions of U.S. Supreme Court
special session legislative assembly at abnormal time
states' rights governmental authority exercised by states, not to be infringed upon by federal government
statute law; act of legislature
statutory law law enacted by legislative body such as congress, state legislature, or city council
strict construction interpretation of U.S. Constitution to mean that federal government has no powers or rights not expressly granted by Constitution, esp. limiting use of presidential power
succession order in which officials move up to vacated higher position, esp. procedure for filling presidential vacancy
table (*vb*) remove bill from consideration, usu. indefinitely; *Chiefly Brit.* place bill or motion on agenda
tax monies collected by government from citizens to support government

treason betrayal of one's government by making war on it or giving aid and comfort to its enemies
unwritten constitution informal constitution based on series of laws over time
veto power of executive to reject legislation passed by Congress; (*vb*) exercise such power
voice vote vote by acclamation
vote exercise of political franchise in election of officials or expression of views on issues
vote of confidence formal expression of political support for governing ministry by legislative majority in parliamentary system
war powers extended presidential powers of commander in chief in time of war
ways and means manner of raising and allocating revenues for conduct of government business
white paper detailed government report on specific subject
yield (*vb*) allow another member of body to express views in debate

Postal Service

air express system for overnight delivery of letters and packages by air
air freight shipment of packages by air
airmail postal transportation by aircraft, formerly at higher rate than first-class mail, now at standard rate
bulk mail low-cost, slowest class of postal service, esp. for large quantities of printed matter
certified mail first-class mail for which proof of delivery is obtained and often returned to sender
express mail guaranteed overnight delivery
first-class mail regular priority mail service, sent by air over long distances; priority mail
forwarding address new address given to post office when moving to guarantee mail forwarding
general delivery department at post office where mail is held for pickup at window
indicia postal markings or labels affixed to mail
mail nation's postal system; letters and other matter sent by mail; bags of postal matter; (*vb*) send a letter or package by post
mail drop receptacle for deposit of outgoing mail
mail carrier one who delivers mail, esp. door-to-door on foot or by vehicle
mail forwarding postal service by which mail sent to person's old address is forwarded to new address
mail order business of selling of goods by mail; order for goods sent through mail
parcel post postal service and fees for handling packages
PO box post-office box
post national postal delivery system; single delivery of mail; (*vb*) send a letter or package
postage fee required for postal service; stamps
postage due additional fee required for delivery of letter with insufficient postage
postage meter device that prints postage on mail, records amount, and subtracts it from amount prepaid to postal service
postage stamp government-issued, adhesive-backed design on paper indicative of prepayment of specified postage fee; stamp
postal service nation's institutions, regulations, and personnel for delivery of mail
postcard small card on which message is written and to which stamp is affixed for mailing without envelope
postcode *Brit.* code of numbers and letters for routing mail
postmark official mark showing date and place of mailing, printed over stamp as cancellation symbol
postmaster supervisor of post office
postmaster general director of national postal system
post office government department handling mail service; local branch of this department through which mail is processed; building housing local branch
post office box PO box; numbered box at post office used as address for receipt of mail
postpaid (*adj*) having postage prepaid by sender
priority mail first-class mail
registered mail mail recorded in originating post office and at successive points of transmission for guarantee of special handling and safe delivery
return to sender postal designation indicating recipient is no longer at address and no forwarding address is known
RFD rural free delivery
RR rural route
rural free delivery RFD; designation for postal service to rural location
rural route RR; postal delivery route in rural area
special delivery mail delivery for extra fee by messenger immediately upon arrival at destination post office
star route route in rural area serviced by private carrier under contract with postal service
stationery writing paper and envelopes used for letters and other mail
zip code five- or nine-digit postal code that indicates local post office through which mail should be routed to recipient

POLITICS

Philosophies, Principles, and Parties
Party Functions and Political Practices
Politicians and Activists
Elections and Campaigns
Revolution and Antigovernment Activity

Philosophies, Principles, and Parties

anarchism belief that all government authority is harmful; advocacy of government by voluntary personal cooperation

Bill of Rights basic human rights and privileges guaranteed in first ten amendments to U.S. Constitution
Bolshevism doctrine of wing of Russian Communist party advocating violent revolution, which seized power in 1917
capitalism political and economic system in which capital goods are privately or corporately owned and managed
center principles midway between liberal and conservative views
centrist (*adj*) being party of moderate views; positioned at middle of one's own party
civics study of government, politics, and the duties and rights of citizenship
civil rights fundamental protections and nonpolitical rights, esp. individual freedoms, enjoyed by all citizens under Constitution
collectivism socialist system in which centralized group controls production and distribution of goods and services
commons third estate
communism political system based on elimination of private property and state ownership and control of means of production and distribution of goods and services
Communist party political party advocating principles of communism, esp. Marxism-Leninism
conservatism political posture based on preservation of traditional, established values and systems
Democratic party more liberal of two major U.S. parties
egalitarianism advocacy of removal of inequalities among people based on belief in human equality
evolutionary socialism belief that transition from capitalism to socialism can be made through voting, without revolution
extremism political views of far right or far left
fourth estate the press, esp. as it wields political power and influence
freedom of speech right of citizens to express their opinions publicly without government interference, subject to laws against libel and incitement to violence
freedom of the press right to publish information or opinions without government restriction, subject only to laws of libel, obscenity, and sedition
free enterprise freedom of business activity from government interference or control
geopolitics influence of and concern with geography and demographics in nation's politics and foreign policy
GOP Grand Old Party; U.S. Republican Party
Green party liberal political party focusing on environmental issues, esp. in Germany
hard line uncompromising or unyielding position or policy
ideology systematic body of sociopolitical theories and programs based on particular vision
iron hand often cruel authoritarian rule, esp. by military
John Birch Society ultraconservative, white supremacist, anticommunist political group
laissez faire opposition to government interference with personal freedom, esp. in economic affairs
left wing those supporting progressive reform and greater welfare of common man
liberalism belief in personal liberty and autonomy, progress, and government aid to those in need
libertarian advocate of absolute free will and freedom of thought
loyal opposition minority party in legislature that maintains allegiance to government
Maoism theory and practice of communism developed in China by Mao Zedong (mid-20th c.)
Marxism system of socioeconomic and political thought developed by Karl Marx that is basis of communism, esp. doctrine that class struggle will be main agency of change from exploitative capitalist system to classless society under socialist order
middle-of-the-road (*adj*) moderate
national socialism Nazism
Nazism totalitarian system of Third German Reich, based on racial supremacy
neofascism fascist movement or principles promoted after defeat of fascist states in World War II
New Left movement advocating radical political and social change, begun by U.S. students in 1960's
New Right movement advocating conservative social values and nationalistic foreign policy, orig. 1960's United States
nihilism belief in nothing; advocacy of destruction of government without creation of something new
nonpartisan (*adj*) holding views and policies without regard to party
partisan (*adj*) advocating or based on views of one party
party group of like-minded individuals organized to direct and control government policy by winning elections
party line official, often standardized, policies and principles of one political party
patriotism love for one's country and loyalty to its government
politics art or science of guiding and controlling government, esp. in conjunction with attaining political office; principles and doctrines on which such activity is based
populism egalitarian political philosophy or movement that promotes interests of common people
radicalism advocacy of doctrines and policies for extreme change in political system
reactionary (*adj*) holding ultraconservative political views that firmly support status quo and advocate suppression of those favoring change
realpolitik politics based on practical considerations, not theoretical objectives
reign of terror maintenance of power through violence and terrorism

Republican party GOP; more conservative of two major U.S. parties
right wing those supporting conservative positions, established order, and traditional values
social democracy socialist state marked by gradual, peaceful, nonrevolutionary transition from capitalism to socialism
socialism various political and economic theories based on government ownership of all or most of means of production and distribution of goods, with control over aspects of social welfare and planning
soft line moderate or flexible position or policy
splinter party minor party that has split from major party
state socialism partial socialism introduced by moderate political action
suffrage right to vote
syndicalism communism based on direct seizure of government control by workers; anarcho-syndicalism
Tammany Hall organized group exercising political control of a city through corruption, orig. 19th-century New York
third estate third class in threefold political division of kingdom; commons
Tory political conservative, esp. 17th-19th c. British supporters of royal authority
Trotskyism branch of communism advocating worldwide revolution
ultraconservative (*adj*) reactionary, right wing, extremely conservative
ultraliberal (*adj*) radical, left wing, extremely liberal
utopian socialism belief in transition to socialism by voluntary transfer of property from owners to state
Whig parliamentarian, esp. advocate of limited royal authority (Britain, 17th-19th c.)

Party Functions and Political Practices

affiliation association of like-minded individuals, esp. with specific party
apparat political organization or existing power structure
appointment nonelective office
back room meeting place for small inner circle to plan and manipulate political moves, often in secret
bipartisan (*adj*) pertaining to both major parties
clout political influence
coalition alliance among members of different parties for specific vote or cause
cronyism practice of granting political favors to friends
doctrine basic political policy of party
gerrymandering arranging legislative voting districts to favor one party
graft use of political influence or position to acquire personal gain
jawboning use of influence and office to affect behavior
jobbery corruption in public office
junket personal trip financed by public funds
logrolling trading of legislator's vote for reciprocal support on future votes
machine disciplined influential political organization, esp. under control of boss or clique
nepotism granting of political favors to relatives
party line official, established policies of one party
patronage system executive appointments reflecting partisan bias
pork barrel legislation manipulated for political advantage to one's constituency or district, usu. public works projects
power base source of political power, usu. support of organized bloc of voters or ethnic minority
pressure group individuals with specific common interest organized to influence public policy
propaganda techniques used to influence or control the opinions of groups or individuals, esp. to promote one's views or damage an opponent's by dissemination of rumors and allegations
prorogue (*vb*) suspend or terminate legislative session, esp. of British Parliament, by royal prerogative
public interest group individuals organized to influence government policy for benefit of general citizenry
public opinion poll questions asked of random sampling of potential voters to determine views and preferences
seniority legislative system by which members with longest continuous service achieve positions of privilege and power
smoke-filled room private gathering place where inner circle of politicians plan and scheme
smoking gun evidence of indisputable guilt
special interest group political group organized to further its specific common concerns; lobby
spoils system practice of appointing party loyalists to public office
vested interest special interest in existing economic or political system for personal advantage
war chest campaign funds held in reserve by incumbent to defeat future challengers
watchdog function role of political party out of power in monitoring conduct of party in power

Politicians and Activists

activist individual engaged in direct action for political change or to influence specific issue; party worker
agent provocateur one who infiltrates suspect organization and incites its members into incriminating actions
alternate one who acts as substitute, esp. for convention delegate
apparatchik member of political organization, esp. Communist
bedfellow close political ally
boss powerful politician who controls votes or party, often by corrupt practices
cabal secret union of conspirators or advisers
cadre inner group of dedicated leaders who advocate particular views

candidate one who aspires to public elected office
conservative adherent to political conservatism
dark horse relative unknown; underdog in election
delegate representative
demagogue one who appeals to and manipulates mass prejudice
Democrat member of more liberal of two major U.S. political parties
dove opponent of military action as political solution
elector one entitled to vote in election
éminence grise individual with unofficial, secret powers
extremist advocate of extreme political positions
favorite son state's candidate for presidential nomination and leader of delegation to party convention
floor leader party member in charge of strategy during legislative sessions
handler one who manages political campaign, esp. media exposure
hatchet man one employed to engage secretly in unscrupulous activities that would tarnish elected official
hawk supporter of military action as political solution
henchman political supporter seeking personal gain or performing unsavory tasks
holdover one continuing in same office
ideologue political theorist rather than practitioner; zealous advocate of an ideology
incumbent officeholder
kingmaker person wielding sufficient political power to influence choice of candidates for office
lame duck officeholder who has been defeated in bid for reelection, during interval before inauguration of successor
liberal advocate of progressive reform
lobbyist person who works for special interest group
majority leader ranking member of party holding majority in legislature
minority leader ranking member of party in minority in legislature
moderate one supporting views midway between right and left
mouthpiece spokesperson, esp. for political leader
mugwump political independent, orig. one who left Republican party in 1884
nominee one selected by party to oppose other party's candidates in election
old guard veteran political figures, usu. resistant to new ideas
old-line (*adj*) conservative, established, having seniority
politician person engaged in party politics or government, esp. one seeking or holding elected office; politico
politico politician
pollster one who polls public to determine preferences and advises candidates based on findings
president-elect one who has been elected president but not yet inaugurated into office
progressive one supporting political change and social improvement by moderate government policies
radical advocate of extreme, sometimes violent, measures to improve society or alter established form of government
reactionary advocate of ultraconservative political views, esp. suppression of those favoring change
reformer one seeking to change and improve political institutions and government policies
Republican member of more conservative of two major U.S. political parties
running mate candidate for lower office linked with candidate for higher office, usu. of same party, esp. vice president
stalking-horse candidate put forth to draw votes from rival or to conceal candidacy of another person
standard-bearer head of party's slate in election
suffragette female activist advocating voting rights for women
superdelegate party leader or official chosen as uncommitted delegate to national political convention
troubleshooter one skilled at mediating political disputes
ward heeler worker in local political machine
whip party leader in legislature appointed to enforce party discipline and voting solidarity
Young Turk insurgent within group

Elections and Campaigns

absentee ballot vote cast by mail when voter is not at designated polling place on election day
absolute majority more than half of eligible voters
at large designating legislator, esp. member of British Parliament, elected by all voters rather than by voters of single district
backlash negative reaction to events among voters that causes swing to opposite view
ballot printed list of candidates and measures; voting
ballot box receptacle where ballots are placed after voting
bandwagon party, cause, or movement that readily attracts followers or supporters because of its mass appeal or apparent strength
barnstorm (*vb*) conduct campaign by making brief stops in many small towns
body politic people who compose a politically organized unit under a single government authority
by-election special parliamentary election between general elections (Britain)
campaign process undertaken to secure public office; (*vb*) actively run for office
canvass count or sample of public opinion; soliciting of votes
carry (*vb*) win majority of votes or gain passage
caucus party meeting to choose candidates and plan strategy
closed primary election to select party candidates limited to registered party members
coattail effect tendency of strong candidate for higher office to increase votes for weaker candidates of same party

convention assembly of delegates to nominate candidates for office and draft platform, usu. for one party
crossover vote vote of person registered in one party cast for another party's candidate
delegation representatives at convention from one state
direct primary preliminary election in which voters of one party select candidates for final bipartisan election
district electoral unit composed of precincts
election selection of public officials or expression of views on issue by poll of voters
electioneer (*vb*) work for candidate or party; (*n*) one who does so
electoral college pledged presidential electors from each U.S. state, determined by popular vote in that state, assembled to elect president and vice president
electorate total number of people qualified to vote
fund-raiser event held to raise money for candidate or cause
general election regularly scheduled election for state, local, or national officials
grass roots local organization or opinion, esp. as symbolized by constituents at district level
hustings any place from which campaign speeches are made; campaign trail in general
initiative procedure whereby voters sign petition to place issue or proposed law on ballot before electorate
keynote address opening speech that sets tone and outlines primary issues for convention
landslide overwhelming majority of votes
mandate desires of constituents as expressed through votes and interpreted by politicians
national convention assembly every four years of major party's representatives to select presidential candidate and articulate a party platform
nomination selection of candidate to run in election
nonpartisan election election in which candidates are not identified by party
off year year without major, esp. presidential, election
open primary election to select party candidates in which any qualified voter may participate, regardless of party
PAC political action committee
plank party policy on specific issue stated in platform
platform principles and policies supported by party or candidate in election
plebiscite vote in which district or nation expresses yes or no opinion, esp. choice of government or ruler
plurality largest number of votes, esp. when no one candidate receives a majority
political action committee PAC; organization that collects contributions and distributes funds to candidates and causes
poll survey of a scientifically selected sample of voters prior to election to determine preferences; expression of opinion by voting; (*vb*) process or count votes
poll tax tax levied on every voter for right to vote
precinct smallest voting subdivision of city or ward
preferential voting system of voting in which voter indicates order of preference for candidates listed on ballot
primary preliminary election to determine party candidates in general election
projected winner election night estimate of eventual winner based on early returns and projection of trends
proposition statement of issue or suggested plan placed on ballot for direct popular vote on whether it will become law
proxy authority, esp. of deputy, to act for another
public opinion views on issues and candidates held by enough of electorate to be politically significant
rally meeting to arouse group enthusiasm or support for candidate
recall removal of unpopular elected official by special election
recount counting of votes a second time in case of possible mistakes or illegalities
referendum popular vote on measure proposed by legislature or by popular initiative
run (*vb*) place oneself before voters as candidate for office
runoff election held when primary is not conclusive
safe seat incumbency that faces only token opposition in election
secret ballot process by which voters' privacy is ensured
slate list of candidates, usu. all from one party; ticket
slush fund party campaign fund, the size and purposes of which are not necessarily legal
smear campaign crude, unsubstantiated attacks against opposing candidate
special election preliminary election held when issue must be decided by voters before primary or general election is held
split ticket votes cast for candidates of more than one party on same ballot
straight ticket vote for all candidates of single party
straw poll unofficial, random sample vote taken as measure of public opinion
stump (*vb*) move from town to town making speeches on behalf of issues or candidates
swing vote determining vote in close election, often one that changes at last moment
ticket list of candidates; slate
turnout percentage or number of eligible voters who cast ballots
voting booth place where voter marks ballot
ward political subdivision of city, esp. as basis for election of city council members
whistle stop political stop in small community
winner-take-all system electoral college system in which candidate receiving majority of popular vote in state receives all of its electoral votes
write-in handwritten vote for candidate not listed on ballot

Revolution and Antigovernment Activity

activism direct, often intense, engagement in actions for political change
anarchist one who opposes all forms of authority and advocates violence to overthrow existing order
antiestablishment (*adj*) working against existing power structure
assassination murder of political officeholder
blacklist list of people or organizations considered undesirable, used to exclude them from jobs or organizations
card-carrying (*adj*) firmly identified with one party or group, esp. Communist party
cell smallest group within party organization, esp. Communist party
civil disobedience nonviolent refusal to obey authorities as means of political pressure
civil disorder riot or disruption of normal activities as means to political change
counterrevolution movement to overthrow government created by earlier revolution
coup coup d'état
coup d'état sudden exercise of political force, esp. violent overthrow of government by small group; coup
direct action action such as strike or boycott that seeks an immediate response from established authority
fifth column group undermining a cause from within
guerrilla one conducting irregular warfare, sabotage, and terrorism to foment revolution
insurgency minor, often disorganized revolt against government
insurrection organized revolt against established government authority
junta small group controlling government after seizing power
popular front coalition of leftist and sometimes centrist political factions to oppose common opponent, usu. reactionary government
proletariat workers who will control government after Communist revolution
putsch sudden surprise revolt against government
resistance underground organization opposing government, esp. occupying force, through sabotage
revolution activities intended to overthrow and replace existing government with preferred system
sabotage destruction or obstruction aimed at disrupting government authority
safe house refuge for political fugitive
sit-in obstruction of public place through refusal to leave as nonviolent protest of government policy
terrorism systematic use of terror as political tool
underground secret, usu. antigovernment, terrorist group

LAW

Courts, Legal Bodies, and the Law
Judges, Lawyers, and Others in the Court System
Laws, Procedures, and Court Proceedings
Decisions, Judgments, and Conditions
Customs, Formalities, and Practices
Crimes, Criminals, and Civil Offenders

Courts, Legal Bodies, and the Law

administrative law statutes governing procedures before government agencies
admiralty law maritime law
appellate court higher court that reviews decision of lower court
bar entire body of lawyers and counselors-at-law
bar association local or state organization of lawyers voluntarily or mandatorily registered in that jurisdiction
bench entire body of judges; where judge sits in court
canon law codified law governing church
case law precedent-setting judicial opinions
chambers judge's private office in courthouse
chancery separate judicial system that administers natural right or golden rule in courts of equity without jury, used esp. for obtaining relief other than financial
circuit court court sitting at two or more places
civil law codes, statutes, and case law governing civil actions; Roman law set forth in Justinian Code
code systematic statement of body of law
commercial law body of laws governing all business transactions not covered by maritime law
common law precedents set by court decisions, distinguished from statute law; body of English law forming foundation of legal system
constitutional law body of decisions and precedents that results from interpreting a constitution
court official assembly for transaction of judicial business; session of such an assembly; chamber for such an assembly
court of appeals court hearing appeals of lower court decisions
court of claims court with jurisdiction over claims, esp. against government
court of inquiry military court that investigates military matters
court of law court hearing and deciding cases based on statutes and common law
criminal law statutes and common law of crimes and their punishment
customs court federal court having jurisdiction over tariff law cases

district court trial court with jurisdiction in specific judicial district
divorce court court handling dissolution of marriages
equity natural right or justice; flexible body of law and nonjury court system, esp. for gaining relief other than financial
federal court court established under U.S. Constitution, esp. to deal with violations of federal statutes
grand jury body of usu. twelve to twenty-three citizens who investigate facts to determine whether a crime has been committed and return indictment
Hammurabi Code ancient Babylonian code of criminal and civil law written in cuneiform characters (18th c. B.C.)
international law body of rules recognized as binding between national states, based on treaties, agreements, and customs; jus gentium
judiciary court system; governmental branch charged with administration of justice
jurisdiction scope of authority of specific court to hear particular cases
jurisprudence system, body, or philosophy of law
jury body of citizens sworn to weigh evidence and decide facts of case; petit jury as opposed to grand jury
justice establishment and administration of rights based on rules of law and equity
Justinian Code Byzantine revision and codification of Roman law with addition of Corpus of Civil Law (6th c.)
juvenile court court with jurisdiction over children under age of legal responsibility regarding matters of delinquency or dependency
kangaroo court unauthorized, irregular court operating with disregard for normal legal procedures
law body of recognized rules of conduct and order established and enforced by government
legal aid legal assistance to those who cannot afford lawyers' fees
lex talionis *Latin.* law of retaliation; principle of correspondence between punishment and crime, as an eye for an eye
maritime law branch of commercial law relating to commerce and navigation; admiralty law
military law system of rules governing military personnel, including establishment of tribunals
moot court pretend student trial
municipal court city or town court with jurisdiction over local criminal and civil cases
Napoleonic Code civil code of France and basis of civil law (early 19th c.)
patent law legal system for issuance and court jurisdiction over patents that protect rights of invention
petit jury trial jury made up usu. of twelve citizens, as distinct from grand jury
probate court surrogate court
pro bono lit. for the good (Latin); legal work undertaken on behalf of public for little or no fee
procedural law prescribed steps and methods of enforcing one's rights in court, opposite of substantive law
Roman law legal system of ancient Rome that is basis of modern civil law and English common law
small-claims court special court handling disputes over minor debts
substantive law law that describes what one's legal rights are, opposite of procedural law
superior court court of general jurisdiction in many states
Supreme Court usu. highest judicial tribunal of a political entity
surrogate court court with jurisdiction to prove wills and administer estates and guardianships; probate court
tax court court that decides tax cases
tort law form of law settling rights of monetary damages for injuries in civil and private cases
tribunal court of justice; seat of particular judge
unwritten law law based on custom rather than legislative statute
venue court's geographic jurisdiction; place where significant elements of cause of action took place or where case is tried

Judges, Lawyers, and Others in the Court System

accused one charged with an offense; defendant in criminal case
adversary opposite party in litigation
advocate lawyer, esp. one pleading client's cause in court
agent person authorized to act for principal in case
alleged one accused of crime before proven guilty
alternate juror jury member chosen to fill in should regular juror be unable to continue
amicus curiae *Latin.* lit. friend of the court; counselor assisting and seeking to persuade court on case to which he or she is not a party
arbitrator private, disinterested person chosen to conduct arbitration
associate subordinate member of law firm
attorney one who acts for another, esp. in legal proceedings
attorney-at-law lawyer admitted to bar and qualified to litigate in court
attorney general chief law officer of state or nation
attorney-in-fact one given power of attorney to act for another but not necessarily an attorney-at-law
bailiff court attendant charged with keeping order and escorting prisoners in court
barrister counsel admitted to plead at bar and in public superior court trials (Britain)
bondsman one who assumes responsibility of paying bond if defendant fails to appear in court
character witness one who verifies another's reputation as honest and law-abiding
chief justice presiding judge of court, esp. Supreme Court
circuit judge judge presiding over circuit court
claimant one asserting claim, esp. in civil case

clerk one who keeps records, has power to issue specific writs, and files documents
competent party individual who is legally able to enter into binding contracts
conservator person designated to protect interests of an incompetent
convict one found guilty of a crime
counsel lawyer managing court trial; lawyer advising and representing an individual, corporation, or public body on legal matters
counselor lawyer; counsel
counselor-at-law lawyer
court judge as embodiment of a particular court
DA district attorney
defendant party sued by plaintiff or accused by state
defense attorney lawyer representing a defendant
district attorney DA; public officer acting as lawyer for government in prosecuting criminal cases; prosecutor
executor one responsible for administration of decedent's estate and for carrying out terms of a will
executrix female executor
eyewitness person who actually saw crime committed
fiduciary one entrusted to care for another's property
garnishee one in possession of another's property pending settlement of debts
guardian one legally empowered to manage affairs of a minor or incompetent person
heir one who would be entitled to inherit property of deceased by intestate succession under terms of will
hostile witness witness unfriendly to side calling him, subject to cross-examination by that side
judge presiding court officer, elected or appointed
jurist judge or lawyer
juror member of jury
justice judge; member of Supreme Court
justice of the peace local magistrate empowered to administer oaths, perform marriages, and handle minor cases
law clerk law student working for lawyer or judge, usu. at low pay to learn from experience
lawyer one licensed to represent people in court and advise on legal matters; attorney or counselor-at-law
legal secretary specially trained secretary for lawyer
litigant party to a lawsuit
litigator lawyer who participates in court trials; trial lawyer
magistrate public officer, esp. judge of lower criminal court
maker party executing a promissory note
marshal officer of judicial district who executes court processes, performing duties similar to those of sheriff
material witness witness whose testimony is essential to case
mediator person who settles disputes and serves as intermediary between parties
notary officer of state authorized to administer oaths and acknowledge signing of documents; notary public
ombudsman government official who investigates complaints against public officials
paralegal specially trained aid to lawyer
partner member of law firm who shares ownership of firm
party one who sues or is sued in court
petitioner one seeking court remedies or making formal complaint or statement of cause of action in civil suit
pettifogger unethical lawyer who engages in petty arguments and obstruction of justice
plaintiff one who complains of another by bringing court action to obtain remedy
presiding (*adj*) designating judge who directs court proceedings, including assigning cases to be heard by other judges
principal one on whose behalf an agent acts; party to contract
process server person who hands over process to person sought by court
prosecutor lawyer hired by government to conduct criminal proceeding; district attorney
public defender lawyer hired by government to defend accused who cannot afford lawyer's fees
receiver person appointed to hold property to be disposed of by court order; one who receives goods knowing they are stolen
referee court officer appointed to hear argument on matter whose decision is final or is reported back to court
respondent defendant in certain proceedings; one required to answer appeal from judgment; party replying to petition
sheriff elected chief law enforcement officer of county
solicitor personal lawyer; lower court trial lawyer who prepares cases for barristers in higher courts (Britain)
surety person promising to make good another's obligation
surrogate judge in court that administers estates and guardianships
trial lawyer lawyer who participates in trials; litigator
trustee one who holds property in trust for another as a fiduciary
ward minor child or incompetent person in care of guardian or conservator
witness one who testifies under oath in judicial proceeding as to what he or she has seen or observed; one present at some event, such as the signing of a document

Laws, Procedures, and Court Proceedings

accusation charge of wrongdoing
acknowledgment formal declaration that one has executed a particular legal document
action lawsuit or court proceeding
adjourn (*vb*) suspend court proceedings until later stated time

admission voluntary declaration of facts made by one party in suit, esp. acknowledgment of guilt
affidavit written statement sworn under oath before authorized officer or notary
allegation contention or accusation; statement by party to legal action as to what will be proved
appeal procedure by which case is brought from lower to higher court for revised ruling or rehearing
arbitration investigation and resolution of dispute by persons named by involved parties, usu. agreed on in contract as way to settle dispute without formal court trial
argument attorney's statements in support of client's case
arraignment calling of accused before court to hear charges and enter plea
arrest restraint or detention of person by legal authority
bail payment of bond that is forfeited if one fails to appear in court
bench warrant arrest order issued by judge, usu. for failure to appear in court
binding arbitration arbitration stipulated in contract as obligatory to all parties
bind over (*vb*) put under bond to appear in court for trial; shift case to grand jury or superior court from lower court
case court action, cause, suit, or controversy
cause case, claim, or lawsuit seeking recovery from another
certiorari *Latin.* lit. to be made more certain; higher court's review procedure on actions of lower court or government agency
challenge objection to prospective juror during pretrial jury selection
charge judge's instructions to jury at close of trial regarding what to consider in reaching verdict
citation writ issued by court commanding person to appear in court and perform some duty or show cause why not
citizen's arrest arrest made by private citizen rather than law officer
civil action lawsuit between private parties, usu. to recover money, property, or remedies, or to enforce rights
civil case lawsuit between private parties, as distinguished from criminal case
claim demand for something rightfully due but possessed by another
class action suit brought on behalf of many persons with similar interest in alleged wrong
closing final exchange of title and monies in real estate transaction
codicil amendment or addition to will
community property property recognized in some states as owned in common by spouses
contest (*vb*) dispute or challenge by litigation
continuance deferral of court proceedings to future date
contract voluntary, lawful, mutual agreement to do or not do something in return for consideration
cop a plea *Informal.* plead guilty to lesser offense to avoid standing trial for more serious one
court hearing preliminary examination of arguments by judge
court-martial judicial court proceeding in armed forces
cross-complaint complaint arising from original complaint, made by defendant against codefendant or third party
cross-examination questioning of witness by lawyer for other party in case
deed document transferring ownership of real property
defense reasons of law put forth as to why adversary or claim should be denied
depose (*vb*) elicit testimony outside court under oath or by affidavit; take witness's deposition
deposition sworn testimony of witness taken outside court proceedings
discovery pretrial fact-finding through interrogatories, depositions, and other investigative procedures
double jeopardy repeat prosecution for same criminal offense, prohibited by U.S. Constitution
ex post facto *Latin.* lit. after the fact; fixing or changing punishment for act after it was committed, now forbidden by U.S. Constitution
file (*vb*) perform first act of lawsuit, place among official records, return to office of court clerk
gag rule court order banning all parties involved in case from publicly disclosing anything about it or reporting on it in the media
habeas corpus *Latin.* lit. have the body; court order requiring that detained prisoner be produced in court to inquire into legality of detention
impanel (*vb*) select jury from official list of names
impeachment of witness providing evidence or engaging in questioning that attacks credibility of witness
in camera *Latin.* lit. in chambers; judicial proceeding from which public is excluded
indictment criminal charge made by grand jury
inquest official inquiry or examination before jury; coroner's investigation of cause of death
instructions judge's explanation of applicable law to jury
interrogatories written questions answered under oath by witness before trial
intervention third-party protection of alleged interest in legal proceeding begun by others
jury trial consideration of case by jury as opposed to by judge or arbitrator
law rule of conduct or action formally recognized as binding and enforced by controlling authority
lawsuit case in court instituted by one party to achieve justice from another
legal age minimum age at which person has capacity to enforce legal rights and fulfill obligations
litigation legal case contested in court before judge
majority age at which person is legally responsible for his or her actions
motion formal oral or written request to court, seeking judge's ruling
nolle prosequi *Latin.* lit. not wishing to prosecute; choice by district attorney or plaintiff not to proceed with action

nolo contendere *Latin.* lit. I do not wish to contest; essential admission of guilt by defendant, appealing to mercy of court
objection lawyer's protest to judge over statement or question by opposition
open court proceedings that are accessible to public
own recognizance condition of release of accused person without payment of bail
patent government grant of exclusive intellectual property rights for an invention
peremptory challenge veto challenge by lawyer to prospective juror that precludes any debate
personal injury physical damage to body, usu. as a result of accident or negligence, forming grounds for suit
plea legal suit or action; defendant's answer to plaintiff's declaration; accused's answer to criminal charge
plea bargaining agreement whereby defendant pleads guilty to reduced charge
plead (*vb*) argue case in court of law; make allegation or answer previous pleading
post bail pay bond to guarantee appearance in court
power of attorney written authority allowing one person to act for another in specific situations
preliminary hearing hearing before magistrate to determine whether sufficient evidence exists to justify trial
pretrial hearing meeting in which lawyers and judge plan procedures for upcoming trial
prior restraint court order prohibiting publication or broadcast of certain material, generally not used in society committed to free speech and freedom of the press
probate proof that will is valid and genuine
proceeding legal action, esp. in court
process summons, subpoena, or warrant used to compel witness or party to appear in court
prosecution government proceeding in court against person accused of crime
rebuttal reply; evidence counter to that of opponent
reconvene (*vb*) continue court proceedings after recess
replevin action to recover actual item of personal property rather than its value in damages
restraining order court order barring one party in suit from contacting, harassing, or acting against another
search warrant court order authorizing search of certain premises or persons for stolen or illegal property
sequester (*vb*) isolate jury in private place for purposes of discussion and reaching a verdict
stand trial defend oneself in court of law, usu. against criminal charges
statute legislative act with power of law
statute of limitations legislative act limiting time in which plaintiff may bring civil suit or state may bring criminal action and also limiting period of liability
statutory (*adj*) designating crime or law enacted by legislature
subpoena (*vb*) *Latin.* lit. under penalty; command to appear in court and testify
sue (*vb*) bring suit against another, usu. to collect damages
suit court action or proceeding to recover rights or make claim
summons court paper announcing suit and stating time for court appearance
testimony oral evidence given by witness under oath
tort civil wrong or injury, other than breach of contract, that is grounds for suit
transcript written record of court proceedings; copy of document
trial court examination of facts to decide issue in dispute
true bill grand jury endorsement of indictment as warranting trial
voir dire *French.* lit. to speak truly; preliminary examination of qualifications of juror or witness
waiver intentional abandonment of right
warrant court order authorizing action by public officer, usu. arrest or search and seizure
writ written court order issued to serve administration of justice, usu. stipulating that something be done or not be done

Decisions, Judgments, and Conditions

accountable (*adj*) answerable, responsible for some action
acquittal not-guilty verdict absolving accused party from guilt
advisory opinion nonbinding court opinion on legal question submitted by government official but not on specific case
alimony court-ordered payment to be made by one spouse to former spouse in divorce case
annul (*vb*) cancel or make void, esp. marriage deemed void from beginning
assessment determination of amount of damages, fine, or tax
attachment taking another's property by legal process, esp. as payment of debt
award final judgment; decision of arbitrators on case; document containing arbitrators' decision
bankruptcy procedure used when person's total assets are insufficient to cover debts
bequest gift by will of personal property
binder preliminary real estate or insurance agreement
capital punishment execution as criminal sentence
cease and desist order prohibiting a specific activity; mandatory injunction
clemency reduction of sentence, usu. by executive branch
community service punishment requiring convicted person to perform unpaid work for community instead of serving term of imprisonment
commutation reduction of sentence after conviction
compensatory damages damages measured by harm suffered or loss incurred

consent decree consent judgment
consent judgment judicial decree sanctioning voluntary agreement between parties in dispute to cease activity and drop action; consent decree
conveyance transfer of ownership title in real property
conviction guilty verdict in criminal trial
costs expenses other than attorney's fees incurred in litigation, sometimes awarded to prevailing party to be paid by losing party
countermand (*vb*) revoke an order or decree
court order decree issued by court, usu. requiring party to do or not do something
custody care and keeping of something, esp. parent's right to raise child in divorce case
damages compensation sought by or awarded to litigant for loss or injury
decision verdict or determination in case
decree final decision and judgment of court
default judgment judicial decision rendered without trial proceedings, usu. due to default by one party, esp. failure to appear in court
dictum portion of opinion contained in court decision that is not essential for deciding narrowest construction of the facts
directed verdict judge's decision in civil case so one-sided that reasonable minds could not conclude otherwise and jury need not hear it
disbarment expulsion of attorney from legal profession; revocation of right to practice law
disclaimer act of declining to accept gift by will or trust, thereby allowing it to pass to next beneficiary entitled to it
dismiss (*vb*) throw case out of court, drop charges; relieve hung jury of duties
dissent minority opposition to majority judgment
divorce legal dissolution of valid marriage
extradition transfer of accused fugitive from state where arrested to state where charged
finding basis in fact or law for judgement
fine money payment required by decision
foreclosure procedure forcing sale of property to meet unpaid obligation
garnishment collection of judgment debt by interception of money owed to debtor
grant transfer of real property or interest therein
guilty (*adj*) found justly responsible for offense and liable to punishment
hung jury trial jury unable to reach minimum consensus needed for verdict
immunity protection of potentially incriminated witness or informer from prosecution based on information given
indemnify (*vb*) secure against loss or damage
indemnity exemption from penalties or liabilities; reimbursement for loss sustained
injunction court order directing someone to do or not do something
instrument formal legal document, such as deed, bond, or contract
interdict prohibitory act or decree of court
interlocutory decree temporary court decision that becomes final after certain time period
intestate (*adj*) having died without a will
joint custody sharing of child's upbringing by divorced parents
judgment court's final decision on matter in favor of plaintiff or defendant
lease agreement by which tenant rents property from landlord
legacy gift of property or bequest by will
levy seizure of property to satisfy judgment
liability legal obligation, duty, or accountability
license permissive right to do something granted by authority or by owner
lien claim on property for debt
living trust trust that takes effect during life of its creator
mandamus *Latin.* lit. we command; superior court writ ordering specific act or duty
mandatory injunction cease and desist order
martial law suspension of judicial procedures and imposition of military rule by executive branch of government in emergency circumstance
mistrial trial without legal effect due to error or prejudicial misconduct in proceedings
moratorium legally authorized period of delay for performance of some obligation
naturalization granting of citizenship to one born in another country
obligation duty or payment owed to another
opinion formal court decision with factual determinations and legal reasons supporting it
order judgment or formal direction of court to do or not do something; request for silence in courtroom
out-of-court settlement agreement reached between parties in civil suit before or outside court proceedings
pardon executive act releasing convict from court sentence of punishment
parole release of prisoner after serving sentence, with assurance that he or she will abide by law
precedent former decision based on same or similar facts used as guide for judicial reasoning in current action
probation relief from all or part of prison sentence on promise of proper conduct
promissory note written promise to pay money to another
proprietary (*adj*) having exclusive legal right to use, make, or market
punitive damages damages in excess of actual loss awarded to wronged plaintiff to punish defendant
quit claim deed releasing all claims against real property
recovery gaining by legal process
remand (*vb*) return to custody pending further trial or detention; return case from appellate to lower court for further proceedings
remedy legal means to recover right or obtain redress for wrong; relief given by court for wrong
reprieve delay in execution of sentence
rescission cancellation, annulment, or vacating of law, judgment, or contract, as by restoration to opposite party of what one has received from that party

restitution restoration to rightful owner; making good or providing equivalent for some harm
reversal judicial decision to overturn lower court ruling
reversion return of title to real estate to former owner or owner's heirs at termination of temporary grant
review judicial reexamination, esp. of lower court proceedings
satisfaction discharge of legal obligation, esp. compensation for loss or injury
sentence court judgment stating punishment in criminal case
settlement resolution of civil case, usu. without trial
stay delay or suspension of legal proceedings, esp. execution of sentence
sub judice *Latin.* lit. under a judge; awaiting judicial determination, therefore not open to public discussion
summary judgment judicial decision in civil case, usu. pretrial, deciding particular issues or entire matter
suspended sentence deferment of punishment, usu. over period of probation
temporary restraining order court order barring one party from action that might harm another, esp. through physical contact, until hearing on specific date
trust arrangement in which person or institution holds legal title to property with obligation to care for it for the benefit of another
verdict decision of jury
void (*adj*) having no effect; without legal force to bind
will declaration on disposition of property and guardianship of minor children, taking effect upon death

Customs, Formalities, and Practices

abstract of title compiled history of land ownership
admissible (*adj*) allowable in court, being pertinent to case, esp. with regard to evidence
alibi proof that accused was not physically present at scene of crime; excuse
amicus brief statement or report by friend of court
bail bond obligation to pay bail if defendant fails to appear in court
bar exam lengthy test prospective lawyer must pass before being authorized to practice law in specific jurisdiction
bond written, sealed obligation to pay sum of money
brief lawyer's written presentation of statutory and case law to support client's case
burden of proof duty to produce evidence to prove disputed facts, which lies with prosecutor in criminal case and with plaintiff in civil case
calendar schedule of cases coming to trial
caseload number of cases handled by court or lawyer in particular period
caveat *Latin.* lit. let him beware; warning
charge judge's instructions to jury; criminal accusation
chattel item of personal property other than real property and land
circumstantial evidence indirect evidence not based on direct observation that tends to prove other facts
civil rights personal liberties guaranteed by U.S. Constitution, its amendments, and acts of Congress
closing statement lawyer's summation of case to judge or jury
collateral (*adj*) incidental or additional to matter being discussed
competency minimum requirements to qualify as witness or party to contract or to serve in some capacity
consensual (*adj*) existing or made by mutual consent but usu. unwritten
consideration thing or act of value that one party provides another when entering into contract
corpus delicti *Latin.* lit. body of the crime; proof that crime has been committed and that charges should be brought
corroboration evidence from two or more witnesses that is identical or supports the other's word
covenant written promise, esp. owner's obligations in deed on property
cui bono *Latin.* lit. to whose advantage; principle that probable responsibility for an act lies with one having something to gain by it
de facto *Latin.* lit. actual, in reality; how matters are by custom, though not required by law to be thus
de jure *Latin.* lit. by right, by law; how the law requires that matters be
disclosure descriptive information and revelations, esp. in patent application
docket court's official record of proceedings and calendar of upcoming cases
due process orderly administration of justice by proper court according to established rules and laws, entitling one to proper notice and fair opportunity to be heard
earnest money deposit or token sum paid as binder or to indicate intention to consummate deal
eminent domain government right to take private property for public use with just compensation
encumbrance right in real property held by third party that diminishes its value
estate grouping of all property of person, esp. deceased, in legal category
estoppel doctrine precluding change of one's previous position to detriment of others
evidence everything considered by court or jury to settle question of what truly is fact
exclusionary rule prohibition from use at criminal trial of evidence obtained by unreasonable search and seizure
exhibit physical object or paper used as evidence

extraterritoriality immunity and exemption from arrest enjoyed by diplomats
fair use conditions under which copyright material may be used by another
fiduciary position of high trust and confidence required of one entrusted with care of another's property
flagrante delicto *Latin.* lit. while the crime is burning; caught in the act of committing a crime
forensics relation of principles and facts from another profession, such as medicine, to legal proceedings
freedom of the seas principle of international law that holds that no state has sovereignty beyond its territorial waters
gavel wooden mallet used by judge to call court to order
grandfather clause legal provision that exempts a business or class of persons from new regulations that would affect prior rights and privileges
gravamen most significant part of grievance or complaint
hearsay evidence inadmissible secondhand evidence, usu. told to witness by another
holograph will or document in handwriting of its maker
insanity plea not-guilty plea based on accused's inability to comprehend wrongful conduct
intellectual property individual's creative or artistic work, protectable under copyright or patent law
intent design or resolve with which one acts; external manifestation of an inward will
J.D. *Latin.* Juris Doctor; Doctor of Laws degree; Doctor of Jurisprudence
J.D.S. Doctor of Juridical Science degree
jeopardy defendant's risk of conviction and punishment when brought to trial
jury duty obligation of citizen to serve on jury
law review law school publication with authoritative articles on legal trends or developments, written and edited by top students
leading question question by lawyer that suggests answer desired from person being questioned
legalese jargon and argot of lawyers and court system
litigious (*adj*) prone to engage in lawsuits
LL.B. *Latin.* Legum Baccalaureus; Bachelor of Laws degree
LL.D. *Latin.* Legum Doctor; Doctor of Laws degree
LL.M. *Latin.* Legum Magister; Master of Laws degree
malice aforethought premeditated evil or antisocial intent
material evidence facts with significant bearing on case
mens rea *Latin.* lit. guilty mind; criminal intent required for conviction of particular crime
mitigating circumstances conditions under which crime was committed that reduce punishment due
motive implied reason for action, as distinct from intent
non compos mentis *Latin.* lit. of unsound mind; used to indicate insanity, temporary or permanent, and lesser forms of mental incompetence that make person unfit to stand trial
oath affirmation or solemn pledge binding one to tell the truth according to the law, after which false statements are punishable as perjury
opening statement outline of position and proposed proof by lawyer near start of trial
overrule (*vb*) refuse to honor lawyer's objection, esp. judicial refusal to do so
personal property all tangibles and intangibles in which one may hold interests of ownership other than real property
polling the jury asking each juror in open court to confirm concurrence with verdict
premeditation prior intent or design to commit crime
prima facie *Latin.* lit. at first sight; sufficient evidence to prove case unless contradicted
privileged communications statements and confidences that cannot be inquired into by others or made basis for suit, esp. between lawyer and client, husband and wife, or doctor and patient
probable cause having good reason to believe a crime has occurred and sufficient basis for arrest and accusation but not conviction
pro forma *Latin.* lit. as a matter of form; carried out with proper formality
proxy authority to act for another; document granting such authority
public domain unprotected status of intellectual property whose copyright has expired or that never had copyright
read rights state legal rights to person at time of arrest, required of arresting officer
real property real estate; land or buildings on it
reasonable doubt principle of law establishing criteria jury must apply to prosecution's case in order to return guilty verdict
res judicata *Latin.* lit. the matter has been decided; rule that case decided in court may not be pressed again by same parties and that decision is therefore final
retainer advance fee paid on hiring lawyer's services
rights proprietary interest in intangible thing; something one may claim as justly due; protections guaranteed by law and constitution
security pledge of money or property as means of assuring payment of debt or performance of some act
self-defense act of repelling physical assault by force, used as plea to justify otherwise criminal act
self-incrimination statement that implicates oneself in a crime
show cause provide good reason why something should or should not be done in case, usu. ordered of litigant
stare decisis *Latin.* lit. to stand by decided matters; doctrine of following rules and principles from previous judicial decisions unless they contravene general principles of justice
strike (*vb*) eliminate from official record of court proceedings

summation lawyer's final argument and closing statement to jury
suppress (*vb*) keep secret by failure to disclose, esp. evidence
sustain (*vb*) grant lawyer's objection, esp. judicial decision to do so
tangible property physical objects taken as property, as distinguished from real and intellectual properties
title evidence or right of property ownership
trademark distinguishing design, symbol, or words used by manufacturer or dealer to identify product or service from competitors, registered by its owner and designated TM
under advisement with careful deliberation or consultation, esp. by judge
warranty promise related to contract
witness stand space in courtroom occupied by witness while testifying
wrongful death condition giving survivors right to sue for damages in death caused by some person or persons
your honor proper form of address to judge

Crimes, Criminals, and Civil Offenders

abduction kidnapping, esp. of underage female for sex or prostitution
accessory one who unlawfully aids a criminal
accessory after the fact one who helps criminal elude arrest
accessory before the fact one who induces or counsels another to commit a crime
accessory during the fact one who witnesses a crime but does nothing to prevent it
accomplice criminal's active partner in crime
adultery voluntary sexual intercourse between married person and nonspouse
aggravated assault common assault combined with intent to commit another crime or with use of deadly weapon
arson willful and malicious burning of another's property
assault threat or attempt to inflict physical harm on another
battery unlawful act of touching, beating, or inflicting physical violence on another person; assault
bigamy state of having two or more living spouses
blackmail extortion by threat
breach violation of law, failure to meet obligation
breaking and entering entry into another's property, forcibly or with criminal intent
bribery payment offered for favors, esp. to public officer
brutality unlawful ruthlessness or harshness, esp. by legal authorities
burglary unlawful presence in a building to commit crime, esp. theft
capital crime offense punishable by death
civil offense violation of civil statutes
coercion force or compulsion used to make person act against his or her will
collusion cooperation between persons to commit crime
conspiracy agreement between two or more persons to commit illegal act or use unlawful means to carry out legal act
contempt of court willful disobedience or disdain for court rules
convict one found guilty of a crime
crime violation of public law punishable by state
criminal one found guilty of violating the law
defamation harm to another's reputation by libel or slander
default failure to fulfill legal obligation, esp. failure to appear in court when case is called
disorderly conduct any of various activities that disturb public peace
duress force, compulsion, threat, or pressure that deprives another person of free will
embezzlement appropriation of property by one to whom it has been entrusted
extortion act of taking another's money or property by threat or duress, esp. under pretext of authority
false pretense taking another's property by trickery or fraud
felony serious crime, punishable by imprisonment in penitentiary and loss of some rights
forgery act of making, altering, or counterfeiting a document or signature with intent to deceive
frame (*vb*) *Informal.* contrive false evidence to make innocent party appear guilty
fraud perversion of truth with intent to deceive
graft bribery, esp. of public official
grand larceny theft of personal property exceeding specified value
homicide unlawful taking of human life
infringement unauthorized use of patented or copyrighted invention or intellectual property
injury violation of person's rights so as to cause damage
involuntary manslaughter taking of human life through criminal negligence
kidnapping willful abduction or detention of another against his or her will
larceny wrongful possession or use of another's property
libel written statement defaming another's reputation
malfeasance act wrongful in itself or which perpetrator had no right to do, esp. performed by public official
malicious mischief willful or reckless damage to another person's property
malpractice wrongful conduct by a professional, through neglect or lack of ethics
manslaughter taking of human life without malicious intent
mayhem willful damage or violence to another person
misdemeanor lesser offense than felony, punishable by fine or imprisonment in jail but not penitentiary
misfeasance wrongful performance of lawful act
moral turpitude depraved, immoral, antisocial behavior
murder taking of another's life, esp. by deliberate and premeditated design

negligence failure to act in a reasonably prudent manner to protect interests of others, often encompassing recklessness
nonfeasance failure to do something one is duty-bound to do
nuisance wrongful use of one's property, causing damage or inconvenience to another
obscenity purveying of something having indecent, offensive content without redeeming value
obstruction of justice hindrance to or prevention of completion of the legal process
peculation embezzlement of public funds
perjury false statement made under oath
petty larceny theft of personal property of less than legally specified value
racketeering operation of business characterized by systematically dishonest practices
rape sexual intercourse forced on another person, usu. a woman
receiver one who accepts goods knowing they are stolen
reckless endangerment action that could result in injury to another though it may not have
resisting arrest attempting to evade or physically prevent one's arrest
robbery theft aggravated by force or threat of assault
slander defamation of another's reputation by spoken falsehoods
smuggling import or export of goods that are outlawed or in avoidance of customs duty
sodomy unnatural sexual intercourse, esp. anal or oral
statutory rape sexual activity with person under the age of consent
subornation inducement to commit illegal act, esp. perjury
trespass illegal entry of another's property or injurious encroachment on another's rights
undue influence threat or improper persuasion that overcomes one's free will to govern actions
usury practice of charging higher interest rate than allowed by law
vandalism wanton and malicious damage to another's property
voluntary manslaughter taking of human life with mitigating circumstances

PUBLISHING AND THE PRESS

Publishing

abridge (*vb*) shorten or condense a text
academic press publishing house usu. specializing in scholarly works, often owned by university; university press
acknowledgments author's credit and thanks to family, colleagues, assistants, contributors, editors, and researchers, usu. in front matter
acquisitions editor publishing house editor who reviews and secures new writers and projects
addendum supplementary information published after book's initial publication
advance publisher's payment to author that is earned back from a percentage of book's income from sales and subsidiary rights
advance copy copy of book available before publication date
appendix supplementary information or material at back of book
author writer, esp. of books
backlist list of publisher's previous publications still in print
back matter information following main body of book text, including appendix, index, bibliography, and/or glossary
bestseller book that sells extremely well, usu. for a short period of time
bibliography list of source materials and related readings
binding spine, cover, and end papers of bound volume
blockbuster enormous bestseller
blueline contact print from offset negative that is final proof before press run; blues
blue-pencil (*vb*) make editor's corrections, usu. in blue pencil
blues *Informal.* blueline
blurb comment, usu. from well-known person or authority, praising book, used in promotion and advertising; puff
boards rigid covers for book, attached at spine
bodice ripper *Informal.* cheap, sensationalist, often hackneyed romantic or thriller novel
book club membership organization offering books for sale through mail
book jacket often decorative, removable paper cover that protects book binding and usu. gives information about book and author
bookplate label identifying book's owner
bound galleys uncorrected galleys cut and bound in booklike form for final corrections and revisions

caption description under illustration or photograph
caret proofreader's mark indicating place where material is to be inserted
cast off (*vb*) estimate number of pages a manuscript will make in book form
censorship practice of removing or restricting material published
clothbound (*adj*) designating hardbound book with cloth-covered boards
colophon publisher's logo or identifying mark
contents list of book parts, including chapters, bibliography, index, and illustrations
copyediting correction and revision of grammatical, stylistic, and factual elements of book
copyreader person who checks proofs or copy for errors
copyright exclusive legal right to publish and sell a written work, designated ©
dedication inscription of book to person or cause
desktop publishing publication of materials using personal computers and printers with graphic capabilities and various type fonts
dime novel melodramatic or sensational novel of late 19th and early 20th century, sold in paperback for ten cents
dust cover protective paper jacket around hardbound book; dust jacket; jacket
dust jacket dust cover
edition particular imprint or publishing run of book
editor person who works with writers and prepares written material for publication
editorial director supervisor of editorial staff and policies of publishing house; editor in chief
editor in chief policymaking executive and principal editor, esp. of magazine or journal; editorial director
end papers decorative binding papers inside book cover
epilogue additional commentary at end of book
errata slip list of errors in a publication with their corrections, inserted on a separate sheet of paper slipped into book
excerpt passage of book reproduced, esp. for review
ex libris *Latin.* lit. from the library; owner's bookplate
f and g's printed, folded, gathered sheets ready for binding into book form
fascicle one section of book published in separate parts
fiction imaginative work involving invented prose narrative
first edition book printed in first print run of publication
flyleaf blank leaf in front or back of book
folio book page size; one-half sheet of foolscap
footnote note at page bottom with additional information or commentary on text
foreword introductory statement
frontispiece illustrated page preceding title page of book
front matter material preceding book's main text, esp. acknowledgments, dedication, foreword, and introduction
galley proof first printed correction proof, orig. pulled from type in galley tray
genre distinct literary category such as poetry, thriller, detective novel, or gothic novel
ghost writer person who writes for another person, under that person's name, without receiving credit as author
glossary list of defined vocabulary terms used in text
gothic novel fiction genre using melodramatic, dark, romantic, and often frightening elements
half title title set on first page of book and before beginning of text
hard copy printout of text stored on computer
hardcover book bound in stiff boards rather than paper
house style editorial style of particular publishing company
imprint publisher's name printed on book's title page; division within publishing house
index list of names, terms, ideas, and facts in book arranged alphabetically with page numbers for location in text
in-print (*adj*) designating book currently available for sale
International Standard Book Number ISBN; unique number code imprinted on book
introduction formal statement of intention or scope of book
ISBN International Standard Book Number
jacket dust cover
juvenile books books of fiction or nonfiction for children, often illustrated
leaf single sheet or page
line editing working line by line through manuscript to improve and clarify tone, text, sequence, phrasing, and style
list publisher's catalog of new titles to be published in particular season, esp. spring or fall
literary agent author's representative, esp. in sale and contract negotiations with publisher
long discount forty or fifty percent discount given by publisher when selling books in multiple quantities, usu. to wholesalers and retailers
mail-order publishing book publication or distribution by mail, esp. through book clubs
manuscript book in author's original form, usu. typewritten or word-processed
mass market (*adj*) designating small, rack-size paperback book, esp. for distribution on newsstands
ms manuscript
nonfiction writing based on fact, not invention
option right to develop published literary work for other media; publisher's right of first refusal on author's next work
oral history oral recollections of people representative of certain historic period, usu. tape-recorded
out-of-print (*adj*) designating book no longer available from publisher

overrun copies of book printed beyond actual orders received
overstock excess copies of specific book that publisher cannot sell
packager independent contractor who conceives idea for book, finds authors, illustrators, and designers, and makes business arrangement with publisher for publication and, sometimes, production
page proofs printed sheets in page form
paperback book bound in flexible, paper cover
piracy illegal publishing of copyrighted material
plagiarism appropriation and publication of another's writing without consent
preface introductory matter at front of book
presentation copy book copy to be formally presented by author as gift, often with special binding
printer's error error introduced into typeset copy by compositor, who cannot charge to correct it
printing mass production of printed material into book or periodical form
proof trial impression of type, for correction and revision
proofreader person who checks printed copy for errors
proofreading marks standardized symbols used to indicate corrections and revisions in text sent to printer
pub date *Informal.* publication date
publication printing and distribution of book or periodical; something that is published
publication date date on which published book is first available for sale; pub date
public domain material that is not copyrighted and can be published without permission or payment
publicist person responsible for informing media and public of book's publication
publicity exposure and promotion of new book in media
publisher person or company engaged in publication of books and periodicals; chief executive of publishing house
publishing business and practice of reproducing and issuing for sale books or periodicals
publishing house company engaged in soliciting, editing, publishing, and selling of books
puff piece uncritical article written to publicize book
pulp cheap, hackneyed fiction
recto right-hand page of book
reissue newly printed edition of previously published book; reprint
rejection slip notice of publisher's rejection of manuscript
release date or act of publication; sheet sent out to media to publicize book, author, or event
remainder (*vb*) sell book at lowered price, usu. from overstock; (*n*) book that has been remaindered
reprint reissue
reserves royalty payments withheld from author until it is certain that bookstores will not return distributed copies of book
returns unsold books returned by bookseller for credit from publisher
review published critical assessment of new book
review copy advance complimentary copy of book for reviewer
revision change in manuscript or edition
rights and permissions right to reprint, excerpt, condense, or otherwise exploit published matter in some form, negotiated by department of publishing company; permissions
romance fiction genre that presents melodramatic love story
royalty author's percentage of profits from book sale
running foot material printed at bottom of each page, usu. title, author's name, chapter title, or subject of page or section
running head material printed at top of each page, usu. title, author's name, chapter title, or subject of page or section
sales conference marketing meeting where new books are presented to publisher's salespeople, who then solicit orders
sales force publishing house employees involved with selling books to bookstores, wholesalers, and others
science fiction fiction genre focusing on speculation about future, other worlds, or highly advanced alien technologies
self publishing books financed and published by author
serial rights commercial rights to publication of parts of work in magazine or newspaper, either before or after book publication
shelf life duration for which books are stocked by bookstores before being returned to publisher
short discount discount given by publishers to libraries, colleges, and other institutions who will not resell the books
signature folded, printed sheets to be bound into book pages
slush pile *Informal.* unsolicited manuscripts submitted to publishing company, rarely published
small press publishing house with limited output, sometimes in specialized field
special sales sales of book other than through normal wholesale and retail channels, as in special outlets or to particular market
spine binding that connects book's covers along one edge
submission manuscript offered to publisher, usu. by agent
subsidiary rights allied rights related to a book, including paperback, serialization, television and motion picture, electronic, and foreign publication rights
synopsis abstract of written work, as by reader in publishing house
title name of publication; published book
title page book page with title, author's name, and publisher's imprint
trade book book for general market, distributed largely through bookstores and libraries
trade paperback large-size paperbound book

for general market, distributed largely through bookstores
trim size page size after final cutting; dimensions of cover
typescript typewritten manuscript copy
unabridged (*adj*) designating complete text of book, story, or article; uncut
university press academic press
vanity press company that charges authors a fee to publish their work
verso left-hand page of book
vetting legal and expert checking of book's contents, esp. facts

Publications

almanac book published annually, with seasonal information; yearly reference book with general information about countries of the world
annals written account of year's events in chronological order
annual yearbook, esp. of school or organization
anthology selection of poems, stories, or essays published together; compilation; treasury
article report, story, or essay complete in itself and forming part of a publication
atlas book of maps and charts
audio book audio recording of reading of a book; book on an audio cassette
autobiography story of one's own life
biography story of another person's life
book large number of sheets of printed material bound together along one edge between protective covers and published; text and graphic material printed on such pages
booklet small book, esp. paperbound
boxed set multivolume book packaged and sold as one unit
brochure pamphlet, usu. promotional or descriptive
bulletin regular publication for members of organization or community group
catalog comprehensive descriptive listing, esp. of articles for sale or college courses
circular letter or advertisement printed for mass distribution
codex manuscript volume, esp. of classic text or scripture
comic book paperbound booklet of extended cartoons in series, usu. humorous or adventurous
communiqué official bulletin or correspondence
compendium brief treatment or account, usu. of extensive subject
compilation anthology
concordance alphabetical listing of significant words used in text or by particular writer, citing where they occur, used esp. with Bible
cookbook book of recipes
dictionary alphabetical listing of words with definitions and etymological information
digest condensation or abridgment of material
directory listing of names, addresses, and other information about a specific group of people
encyclopedia book or set of books with information on many branches of knowledge, usu. arranged alphabetically
gazette newspaper; official publication with announcements
gazetteer dictionary of geographical terms
guidebook listing of directions and information for particular place, esp. for tourists
handbook manual of information on particular subject
hornbook book or primer providing basic information on particular subject
house organ in-house publication
how-to book manual or instruction book on particular subject
incunabula extant copies of earliest printed books, pre-1500
index extensive alphabetical listing of items, esp. in collection, with information on each
journal any periodical or newspaper, esp. daily newspaper; regular publication of specific profession
lexicon dictionary or other vocabulary book
magazine periodic publication, usu. bound in paper, containing articles by various writers, often with photographs and illustrations, frequently focusing on some unifying theme or subject
manual book of facts and instruction on particular subject
monograph scholarly book or long article on specific subject
newsletter regular informational bulletin for subscribers, employees, or organization members
newspaper regular publication, esp. daily, containing news, opinion, general interest features, photographs, illustrations, and advertisements
pamphlet thin, simply bound or stapled collection of sheets, usu. on topic of current interest
periodical any publication appearing at regular intervals
position paper formal, detailed statement of policy
primer elementary handbook on particular subject or used to teach reading
reference book authoritative book used for research and information gathering on one or many subjects
serial something published in series of continuous segments at regular intervals
textbook book giving detailed instruction in principles of some subject for students
thesaurus extensive listing of words and their synonyms, arranged alphabetically or topically
tome large, scholarly book
tract treatise, esp. proselytizing on politics or religion
treasury anthology
volume one of two or more separate books constituting a complete set; any single book
who's who listing of well-known people, in one specific field or many, with biographical information
yearbook periodical published once a year, esp. with information on previous year; annual publication of graduating class of school or college
yellow pages telephone directory of businesses, arranged topically

Journalism

add new copy added to already written article
advance copy story prepared before event it describes has occurred and held until release date
advertorial copy that is paid for by advertisers but laid out and written in style of regular copy
agony column newspaper advice column
alternative press journalism devoted to counterculture or antiestablishment interests
angle point of view taken in news story or feature
attribution credit given to source of news story
banner large, front-page headline extending width of page
beat reporter's regular, assigned geographical or topical territory
bio *Informal.* background material, often prepared by publicist, used in profile or feature on an individual
blackout absence of news coverage due to power failure, labor dispute, or strike, or at news subject's insistence
blind lead beginning of news story that does not identify its subject directly or by name
boilerplate syndicated, standardized periodical material
break division of word onto two lines
broadcast journalism news programming on radio and television
bulldog edition earliest daily edition of a newspaper
bulletin brief announcement of latest news, usu. coming directly from news source
bureau news department covering geographical or topical area
byline author's printed name appearing with story
canned copy copy supplied by news agency, public relations firm, or other outside source
caption description under illustration or photograph
cartoon illustration, esp. for political commentary, amusement, or as space filler, in newspaper or periodical
censorship deletion of material deemed objectionable from publication
centerfold foldout double page at center of magazine, usu. containing illustration, sometimes featuring nude photographs
circulation publication's readership and subscribers
city editor newspaper editor in charge of local news and distribution of assignments
city room office of city editor and staff, where assembly of local news takes place
classified advertisement newspaper advertisement listed according to type of goods or services offered or desired; want ad
clipping article cut from journal
clips collection of journalist's published writings, used as résumé or portfolio in soliciting future work
clipsheet newspaper sheet reissued by another organization
cold type type set by a method that does not use the casting of molten lead
column feature in newspaper by regular writer, often including personal views; printed block of type, usu. justified between vertical lines
column inch one vertical inch of copy in one column
columnist writer of regularly featured article in periodical
comic strip humorous series of illustrations with text, regularly featured in newspaper or magazine
contributor writer whose name is not listed on masthead but who has article appearing in periodical
copy written text of article
copyboy errand person at newspaper, esp. one who carries copy for processing
copyediting correction, revision, and refinement of copy before publication
correspondent reporter covering stories in location distant from newspaper offices
critic person who reviews artistic and literary works for newspaper or magazine
cub reporter beginning reporter
dateline line at beginning of news story indicating place and time of origin of story
deadline time at which prepared story must be submitted for editing and publication
dispatch news item filed by correspondent
edition updated version of daily newspaper published at certain hour, such as morning, early, late, or final edition
editorial column by editor expressing newspaper policy or view on current issue
editor in chief supervisor of editorial policy of publication
essay often first-person column expressing writer's point of view on one subject
exposé news story revealing scandal or hidden corruption
extra special edition of newspaper, published between regular editions to cover news of unusual importance
fanzine usu. nonprofessional magazine produced by and for enthusiasts of specific field or person, esp. in pop music
feature general interest story, often of human interest or providing background on news, as distinguished from hard news
filler general-interest material plugged into empty newspaper space
First Amendment amendment to U.S. Constitution that guarantees freedom of the press
first-time rights sale of publication rights based on assumption that article or photograph has not been previously published
flag masthead
follow-up continuing coverage of ongoing news story
fourth estate the press
freelancer worker, esp. writer, not on staff of periodical
free press uncensored publication of newspapers and periodicals
gossip columnist writer who reports on real and rumored activities of celebrities
graveyard shift lobster shift

hard news current-events stories of importance
headline large-type descriptive heading over printed news story
investigative journalism in-depth coverage of news story and related background material, often requiring extensive interviewing and research
journal any periodical or newspaper, esp. daily newspaper
journalism factual writing, esp. news coverage, and photographs in support of such writing
journalist person who researches, photographs, or writes news, current events, or feature stories
jump continuation of article on another page or column
kicker brief head in small type above headline to indicate subject or draw reader's interest
kill (*vb*) abandon intention to publish story or article
kill fee reduced payment to writer or photographer for work that has been assigned but will not be used
layout page design
lead introduction of news story, esp. its first sentence; most important news story of day; information or clue that draws reporter to story
lead-in introductory or transitional sentence in article
leading spacing inserted between lines by printer
libel publication of false or defamatory statements
lobster shift *Informal.* night shift in newspaper office; graveyard shift
makeup layout of pages
managing editor person below editor in chief who oversees output of senior editors and regular production of periodical
mass media newspaper, radio, television, and movie media capable of reaching general public
masthead statement of staff, address, and other vital statistics of publication; flag
media all means of communication providing information to public
muckraking search for and exposure of scandal, corruption, hidden crime, or abuse
news agency organization for gathering and distributing news, features, and photos to subscribers
newsmagazine periodical, esp. weekly, covering major news stories and features
obit *Informal.* obituary
obituary announcement of person's death with information on his or her life; obit
Op-Ed page special features and commentary page *op*posite *ed*itorial page in newspaper
pan (*vb*) give highly negative review of event; (*n*) such a review
paparazzi photographers who pursue celebrities without regard for their willingness to be photographed
personals classified advertisements for those seeking personal relationships
photo essay group of photographs, often with supplementary text, that conveys a unified story
photojournalism news coverage emphasizing photographic images that depict current-events stories; pictorial journalism
pictorial journalism photojournalism
pipeline channel for passing information to journalist
plug *Informal.* favorable publicity in news media
press newspaper publishing; news media; newspaper
press agent person who writes and circulates news items about organization or important person; publicist
press association organization of journalists and newspaper publishers
press box area set aside for members of press, esp. at sports events
press card newspaper reporter's credentials, used to cross police or security lines
press conference prearranged interview with reporters to provide requested information or generate publicity
press corps group of journalists from various publications and media who regularly cover the same beat
press release information on event, organization, or person written by publicist and circulated for use by news media
press secretary person responsible for handling press and public relations for prominent figure or organization
profile in-depth article focusing on one individual
propaganda persuasive, esp. biased, dissemination of information
publicist press agent
puff piece *Informal.* coverage of subject that is exaggerated in praise and totally uncritical
put to bed complete all editorial work on newspaper and send it to printer
reportage stories based on research or detailed coverage of documented observation of news events, including photo essays
reporter person who investigates news event and writes story for media
retraction printed statement reversing previously held position or relinquishing previously made claim
review critique of current event, esp. in arts
rewrite editorial revision of copy; (*vb*) revise copy
running head headline repeated on continuous pages
runover story material exceeding allotted publication space and carried over to an extra line, column, or page
scandal sheet cheap newspaper featuring tawdry stories about celebrities
scoop *Informal.* major news story published ahead of one's competitors
screamer newspaper headline with extremely sensational slant
section part of newspaper covering sports, news, features, advertisements, or finance
senior editor magazine or newspaper editor responsible for specific region, beat, or field
sensationalism extreme reportorial style intended to arouse readership interest based on emotional appeal, often with questionable accuracy
service piece article offering consumer information for specific industry

sidebar additional material presented alongside major story
silly season late summer news slump that inspires far-fetched news stories
slant angle or approach to coverage of news story
slipsheet paper fitted between freshly printed pages to prevent offsetting
slug one- or two-word label for news story
soft news background or feature stories of general interest
spread article or illustration covering large amount of space, esp. two facing pages
squib filler or short news item
stet *Latin.* lit. let it stand; proofreader's mark indicating that material marked for deletion should remain
stringer part-time reporter for newspaper, often paid by the column-inch
syndication service company selling newspaper columns and features to many newspapers
tabloid newspaper characterized by sensationalism; newspaper or journal with small page size, usu. half of regular size
tag attention-grabbing item at end of story
tear sheet sheet of newsprint or magazine copy retained for reference
teaser headline that arouses curiosity
thumbnail *Informal.* capsule news story or summary
trade journal magazine catering to specific business, industry, or field
underground press journalism devoted to counterculture and/or radical interests
update follow-up article that brings news story up to date
volume year's issues of periodical, esp. bound into single volume
want ad classified advertisement
wire service news agency supplying news stories to newspapers
yellow journalism newspaper coverage in sensationalized, often irresponsible, style

Newspaper Names (*usu. capitalized*)

banner bulletin
call, capital, chronicle, clarion, courier
daily, diario, diary, dispatch
enquirer, examiner, exponent
free press
gazette, globe
herald
independent, inquirer, intelligencer
journal
leader, ledger, light,
mail, mercury, messenger, mirror, monitor
news
patriot, post, press
review
sentinel, star, sun
telegraph, times, tribune
union
weekly, world

WAR AND MILITARY

Types and Techniques of Warfare
Soldiers and Military Life
War Machinery and War Zones
Military Ranks
Army, Air Force, and Marines
Navy and Coast Guard

Types and Techniques of Warfare

abort (*vb*) cancel mission before completion
action military encounter or battle
act of war provocation by one nation of sufficient seriousness to start war
advance attack; forward movement of troops
aggression use of armed force to accomplish goals
air cover use of aircraft to protect ground or naval operations
air raid air strike
air strike attack using airplanes, esp. bombers; air raid
air support bombing used esp. to support ground forces
alert warning of impending attack; readiness for attack
ally army of another nation fighting one's common enemy
amphibious operation military maneuver using troops and vehicles able to travel on land and water
armistice general truce; cessation of war
array battle order; deployment of troops for battle
assault attack
attack sudden, violent armed aggression; assault
barrage wave of continuous artillery fire, often protective
barricade obstacle across roadway to prevent enemy advance
battle armed conflict between armies or forces
besiege (*vb*) surround with forces and attack continuously
biological warfare use of toxic organisms to kill and incapacitate enemy; germ warfare
blitzkrieg *German.* lit. lightning war; intense infantry attack spearheaded by tanks and supported by aircraft
bloc group of nations acting together for military and political purposes
blockade action aimed at restricting movement of enemy troops and supplies
bombardment attacks by artillery, bombs, or missiles
brush-fire war local, quickly escalating war
camouflage colors and materials such as nets, foliage, and special clothing used to make equipment or personnel blend in with natural setting
campaign specific stage or area of war

cannonade bombardment, heavy artillery fire
capitulation surrender
carpet bombing massive bombing of specific area
cease-fire truce; temporary stoppage of attacks
charge sudden, rapid advance on enemy
chemical warfare use of weapons composed of toxic chemicals, generally recognized as illegal
civil defense organized system for protection of lives of noncombatants during wartime
civil war war between factions within one nation
cold war state of international tension with conflict expressed not in armed hostilities but in economic, ideological, and political measures
collateral damage civilian casualties and damage to nonmilitiary targets, esp. due to bombing raids
conflict armed hostilities, including undeclared war
containment policy and actions to prevent expansion of hostile forces or ideology
controlled war warfare conducted according to continuous flow of information to commanders of troops
conventional war war using no nuclear, chemical, or biological weapons
convoy ships or vehicles traveling together for mutual protection
counterintelligence information gathering and processing to thwart or distort enemy's intelligence efforts
cryptanalysis translation of enemy's secret encoded communications by breaking codes and ciphers
deployment positioning of troops into place in readiness for battle or maneuvers
deterrence steps taken to prevent armed actions
disarmament reduction, by mutual agreement, of armed forces and weapons
dogfight engagement between two or more airplanes
electronic warfare use of electronic technology to thwart enemy weapons and disrupt communications
engagement battle or encounter with enemy
escalation increase in violence, arsenal, or area of conflict
fail-safe safety plan aimed at deterrence of accidental nuclear attack whereby bomber pilot must receive confirmation of attack plan at preordained stations before proceeding with attack orders
firefight intense, usu. brief, encounter with heavy gunfire between small tactical units
first strike use of one's nuclear weapons before enemy, esp. surprise attack
formation position of troops for battle or maneuvers
friendly fire artillery or other fire that causes damage or casualties to one's own forces
general warfare large-scale armed conflict between major powers, with national survival at stake
germ warfare biological warfare
give ground retreat
ground war attack or operation by infantry and artillery only
guerrilla warfare small-scale military operations conducted inside hostile territory by irregular units
gunboat diplomacy policy employing threat of armed aggression
infiltration passage of troops through gaps in enemy lines
insurgency insurrection
insurrection revolt against existing political structure and power; insurgency
intelligence collection and evaluation of military information regarding enemy
interdiction preventive action that blocks enemy's access to routes, areas, or supplies
intervention interference in affairs of another state, esp. insertion of military presence
invasion large-scale assault to take over enemy territory
launch-on-warning policy of firing ballistic missiles immediately on detection of enemy missile attack without waiting for missiles to reach targets before retaliating
limited conventional warfare general warfare without use of nuclear or biological weapons and with observance of voluntary restrictions on both sides; limited strategic warfare
limited strategic warfare limited conventional warfare
logistics science of planning and executing troop movements, procurement and supply, provision, and related support services
low-intensity conflict isolated acts of violence, esp. hostage taking, terrorism, and counterinsurgency
MAD Mutually Assured Destruction
maneuver movement to place military supplies or personnel in advantageous position
military posture strength, capability, and readiness of armed forces
military science study of causative factors and tactical principles or warfare
mobilization preparations for war
mutually assured destruction MAD; deterrence based on capacity for total reciprocal annihilation
national security protection of state from external aggression and subversion
neutrality attitude of impartiality during period of tension or armed conflict
nonalignment policy of neutrality in situations of international armed conflict, esp. with respect to United States and other world powers
nuclear nonproliferation policy aimed at control and restriction of acquisition of nuclear weapons by nations that do not have them
nuclear proliferation process of additional nations acquiring nuclear weapons
nuclear winter global darkness and extreme cold over prolonged period due to dust cloud blocking sunlight following nuclear holocaust
offensive aggressive action

operation military action; combat, attack, defense, or maneuver
order of battle orderly disposition of military force in response to identification and assessment of enemy strength
orders military commands
overkill excessive destructive capability beyond what could be required for victory; use of such capability
peaceful coexistence avoidance of armed conflict by adversaries
penetration aggressive advance into enemy territory
phalanx body of troops in close ranks and files
pincers movement maneuver using two-sided attack formation to enclose enemy
pitched battle intense conflict
privateering use of armed vessel by private person against hostile nation
preemptive strike nuclear attack in anticipation of enemy's nuclear attack; preventive strike
preventive strike preemptive strike
proxy war limited war between allies of actual enemies
psychological warfare use of propaganda and pressure to weaken and confuse enemy
Pyrrhic victory military supremacy won at debilitating cost
raid sudden attack on enemy by air on small land force
rear guard unit protecting rear of larger force
reconnaissance movement to gather information about enemy
red alert final stage of readiness when enemy attack appears imminent
regroup (*vb*) change military formation, esp. reorganize after defeat or retreat
retreat forced withdrawal of troops in face of enemy attack
revolutionary war military action aimed at seizing political power, esp. from existing government
rout decisive, overwhelming victory
saber-rattling show or threat of military force, used to intimidate other nations
sabotage destruction or injury to national defense, security, or resources through covert operations
sally rushing forward of troops from defensive position to attack enemy
salvo volley
scorched-earth policy devastation of property and agriculture in a region before abandoning it to enemy
second strike retaliatory nuclear attack in wake of first strike
show of force intentional display of military strength to deter enemy action
siege blockade of enemy city or fort to force depletion of resources and ultimate surrender
skirmish brief, inconclusive battle
sortie sudden attack from defensive position; combat air mission
strafe (*vb*) attack from the air with gunfire
stratagem tactical maneuver to surprise or deceive enemy
strategic (*adj*) pertaining to overall military power and goals
strategy long-term deployment and use of military forces and national resources with intent to achieve position of advantage
strike attack, esp. preemptive, preventive, first, or second thermonuclear attack; aircraft attack on surface target
subversion action from within to undermine military strength and national security
surgical strike precisely planned and executed military attack on specific target area
surrender formal declaration and acceptance of defeat; capitulation
surveillance observation for intelligence purposes, esp. from air or concealed position
sweep rapid movement of forces through area to assume control and eliminate enemy
tactical (*adj*) pertaining to battlefield operations or any immediate military objective
tactical maneuver purposeful operation involving deployment of forces and weapons in combat
tactics detailed plans and methods used to accomplish specific military objectives
terrorism employment of unethical tactics and violence in civilian settings, esp. hostage taking and assassination, for political or military advantage
tooth-to-tail ratio proportion of combat forces to administrative or logistical support
treason betrayal of one's country, esp. in wartime
trench warfare fighting from makeshift battlefield defenses over prolonged period
triage process of dividing war wounded into groups requiring immediate treatment, delayed treatment, and those beyond treatment
truce temporary cessation of hostilities
unconventional warfare military operations in enemy-held territory; clandestine hostilities and espionage; undeclared warfare; chemical, biological, or nuclear warfare
underground organized resistance to occupying army
vanguard troops at forefront of advancing army, sent to prepare main attack or maneuver
volley simultaneous discharge of numerous weapons; salvo
war sustained, often widespread, armed conflict, esp. between nations
war crimes unethical, criminal behavior and actions contrary to laws of war
warfare armed conflict between nations
war games simulations of battle or military operations that depict possible actual situations, used to test strategy and tactics
war of independence insurrection against colonial or oppressive powers; revolution
wedge troops arrayed in formation that tapers to a point at the front
withdrawal retreat; backward movement of troops
wolf pack group of submarines or fighter planes making coordinated attack
world war extensive combat involving many nations around the world

Soldiers and Military Life

active duty full-time military service
adjutant administrative assistant to commanding officer
admiral highest ranking naval officer
aide-de-camp assistant to commanding officer
airborne (*adj*) designating ground forces carried in aircraft
air force military branch of airborne forces
Air Force air force of the United States
airman enlisted member of Air Force or aircrew member in another service branch
armada fleet of warships
armed forces military personnel and resources used in protection of national interests against enemies and aggressive action against foreign powers
armored division military unit with tanks and other armored vehicles
army major national defense force; military branch of land forces; largest military unit, commanded by general
Army army of the United States
attention erect soldier's posture with heels together, arms at sides, eyes to front
AWOL absent without leave; unauthorized desertion of post or duty
barracks building used to lodge soldiers
basic training initial period of military training for molding recruits into soldiers
battalion tactical unit larger than company and smaller than regiment, commanded by lieutenant colonel
battle fatigue combat fatigue
bombardier member of bomber crew who releases bombs; noncommissioned officer in British artillery
boot camp training facility for recruits
break ranks move out of formation
brig jail on warship or naval base
brigade tactical unit larger than regiment and smaller than division, commanded by colonel
buck private lowest grade of private
cadet student at military academy
cavalry troops mounted on horseback
chevron one of one or more inverted V-shaped stripes, worn on arm by noncommissioned officers
chief petty officer top-ranking naval noncommissioned officer
chief warrant officer top-ranking noncommissioned officer, below second lieutenant or ensign
coast guard military forces that guard coastal waters and maritime traffic
colonel highest field grade rank in army
color guard honor guard that carries flags
combat fatigue posttraumatic stress disorder among soldiers engaged in combat; battle fatigue; shell shock
command and control centralized decision-making, intelligence-gathering, and communications system of a military force
commandant senior officer and head of U.S. Marine Corps
commander ranking officer; commissioned naval officer below captain
commander in chief top-ranking leader of armed forces
commanding officer officer in charge of tactical unit
commando soldier specially trained for close combat, raids, and dangerous missions
commissary military supermarket and provisions store
commissioned officer military officer holding by commission a rank of second lieutenant or higher
commodore naval rank equivalent to that of brigadier general
company basic army unit, larger than a platoon and smaller than a battalion, commanded by captain and first sergeant
conscientious objector person who refuses to serve in armed forces on religious or moral grounds
conscription compulsory registration of selected individuals for military service; draft
corps any unit of soldiers; esp. tactical unit larger than a division and smaller than an army, commanded by lieutenant general
court-martial trial for military crimes presided over by military personnel; (*vb*) try by court-martial
C ration combat ration, usu. canned or powdered food
deferment temporary exemption from induction into military service
Delta force U.S. Army elite force trained in antiterrorist tactics
deserter soldier who intentionally abandons his or her post, disappearing from military authority without intention of returning
detail specific assigned task
division tactical unit larger than a brigade and smaller than a corps, commanded by major general
dogtag identification piece worn on chain around neck
doughboy *Informal.* U.S. infantryman, esp. in World War I
draft conscription
drill sergeant noncom who trains recruits in basic soldiering
echelon level of military command; military formation in parallel lines
enlist (*vb*) join military of one's own free will
ensign lowest-ranking commissioned officer in U.S. Navy
fall in (*vb*) form up and come to attention as unit
fall out (*vb*) break ranks
fatigues drab uniform worn on fatigue duty, while laboring in camp, or in training
field marshal highest-ranking military officer (Britain); officer of second-highest rank (France)
five-star general highest-ranking general of the U.S. Army
flak bursting shells fired from antiaircraft guns
flank extreme left or right side of array of troops
fleet group of ships under single command
frogman underwater operative equipped with air

tanks and wet suit, esp. for salvage, demolition, and reconnaissance
garrison permanent military post or installation
general top-ranking army or air force officer
GI government issue; common soldier
Green Berets Special Forces
ground forces infantry and artillery, excluding naval and air forces
guerrilla member of unofficial or independent fighting unit operating in hostile territory
gunner occupational title in artillery; Marine warrant officer
honor guard ceremonial escort for important person or casket
induction act of drafting someone into military service
infantry armed foot soldiers
insubordination disrespect and disobedience toward any person of higher rank
Joint Chiefs of Staff principal military advisory board of U.S. president, including Chiefs of Staff of Army and Air Force, Marine Corps Commandant, and Chief of Naval Operations
kamikaze Japanese pilot who suicidally crashed airplane into target during World War II
kitchen police KP; soldiers assigned to assist cooks
KP kitchen police
lance corporal U.S. Marine enlisted rank between private first class and corporal; *Chiefly Brit.* corporal
lieutenant lowest-ranking commissioned officer in U.S. Army or Air Force
Marine Corps branch of U.S. armed forces specially trained for land, sea, and air combat in conjunction with troops of other branches
master sergeant next-to-highest noncommissioned officer in Army, Air Force, and Marine Corps
medic *Informal.* medical officer or member of military medical unit
mercenary soldier for hire, not fighting for his or her own nation; soldier of fortune
mess place where meals are prepared and eaten by military personnel; mess hall
mess hall mess
mess kit soldier's personal plate and utensils
MIA missing in action; military person lost in action whose fate is unknown
midshipman cadet at U.S. Naval Academy; middie
military entire armed forces, its personnel and resources
military police MP; Army unit that fulfills police functions
militia military troops liable for call only during emergency, usu. civilians on nonactive duty
mission operational task ordered by command to be completed before reporting back to headquarters
MP military police
muster (*vb*) assemble troops, esp. for inspection or discharge
national guard peacetime military force commanded by governor of each U.S. state, used for police work
navy military branch consisting of sea forces
NCO noncommissioned officer
noncommissioned officer NCO; enlisted person above rank of private, esp. corporal or sergeant; noncom
officer commissioned military person
parade rest position with feet one foot apart, hands clasped behind back, and head forward
paratrooper soldier trained to parachute from airplane
patrol small group of soldiers on reconnaissance
petty officer noncommissioned naval officer
platoon tactical unit larger than a squad and smaller than a company, commanded by lieutenant and sergeants
plebe freshman at military or naval academy
point man soldier who leads a patrol
post exchange PX; department store on base for sales to military personnel and families only
POW prisoner of war
present arms salute position in which rifle in held vertically before chest with muzzle upward
presidio garrison; military post
prisoner of war POW; military person captured and held by enemy forces during war
private soldier of the lowest rank
Purple Heart medal awarded by United States for wounds received in action
PX post exchange
quartermaster officer who provides clothes and provisions for troops; petty officer who attends to ship's helm and signals
R and R rest and recreation
recruit person who recently joined armed forces
recruitment campaign to generate enlistment in armed forces
regiment tactical unit larger than a battalion and smaller than a brigade, commanded by colonel
regular member of standing army
Reserve Officers Training Corps ROTC; body of students being trained at college or university to become officers in armed forces
reserves soldiers not on active duty but subject to call in emergency
reveille wake-up call, esp. played on bugle or drum
ROTC Reserve Officers Training Corps
salute formal gesture of respect, esp. by raising right hand to side of headgear
sapper soldier who builds trenches or tunnels to undermine enemy positions
SEALS sea-air-land forces; special forces of U.S. Navy
section eight dishonorable discharge for physical or emotional incapacity
selective service compulsory military service
sentry soldier standing guard and preventing passage of unauthorized persons
sergeant noncommissioned officer in U.S. Army, Air Force, or Marines
serial number identification number given to all military personnel
service period as member of armed forces; military forces, collectively
service stripe stripe worn on left sleeve indicating period of time on active duty

shell shock combat fatigue
shore leave permission to leave ship and go ashore in port
shore patrol U.S. Navy personnel having police duties similar to those of military police
situation room area at headquarters through which latest reports are channeled
soldier military fighting person; member of armed forces, esp. army
soldier of fortune mercenary
Special Forces U.S. Army personnel trained to work with indigenous forces engaged in guerrilla warfare and counterinsurgency operations and to conduct unconventional warfare; Green Berets
specialist enlisted person with technical or administrative duties but no command, ranked in four grades comparable to corporal through sergeant first class
squad smallest tactical unit, consisting of ten or more people, commanded by staff sergeant
squadron naval or airborne unit, esp. subdivision of fleet; armored cavalry unit; Air Force unit smaller than group, composed of two or more flights
standard any of various military or naval flags
standard-bearer soldier who carries flag
stockade fortification; military jail
stripes chevron or strip of cloth on sleeve indicating rank
tactical units subdivision of military; for U.S. Army, from smallest to largest, with commanding officer: squad (staff sergeant), platoon (lieutenant), company or battery (captain), battalion (lieutenant colonel), regiment (colonel), brigade (colonel), division (major general), corps (lieutenant general), army (general)
taps bugle sounded at end of day or at funeral
top-secret (*adj*) pertaining to security classification for information vital to national defense
tour of duty period of time on active military duty; period enlisted for
troops soldiers
unit any of various subdivisions of military; tactical unit
Unknown Soldier unidentified soldier killed in combat whose tomb is a memorial to all unidentified dead service personnel
veteran former member of armed forces
warison bugle call to attack
warrant officer officer ranking above noncommissioned and below commissioned officer, holding rank by certificate
wing administrative and tactical unit of U.S. Air Force consisting of two or more groups, headquarters, and support services
yeoman naval petty officer who performs clerical duties

War Machinery and War Zones

AAM air-to-air missile
ABM antiballistic missile
aircraft carrier large, flat-topped ship used as mobile airstrip
ammo *Informal.* ammunition
ammunition projectiles fired from guns, including fuse, charge, and cartridge; any military explosive; ammo
antiaircraft artillery fired from ground or ships against enemy planes
antiballistic missile ABM; missile for interception and destruction of incoming ballistic missiles
antimissile missile ballistic missile used to detect and destroy enemy missiles in flight
antipersonnel (*adj*) designating weapons intended to maim or kill human beings rather than to damage property and equipment
antitank (*adj*) designating missile or artillery designed for use against armored vehicles
armada fleet of warships
armaments military equipment, esp. weapons
armored personnel carrier tracked vehicle with armored hull and light armament, for transporting troops in combat
armory place for storage of arms and equipment, esp. for training of reserves
artillery projectile-firing weapons
ASM air-to-surface missile
assault boat portable boat for landing troops on beaches
AWACS Airborne Warning And Control System; sophisticated aircraft with powerful radar and computer, used to track other aircraft
ballistic missile self-propelled missile guided in trajectory ascent and falling freely in descent
base permanent center of military operations
battery tactical unit of artillery composed of six guns; two or more artillery pieces; guns on battleship
battleship heavily armed and armored ship designed to shell other ships and shore targets
beachhead shore area in occupied territory seized as landing point for invading troops
bivouac temporary encampment, often with little or no shelter
bomber airplane designed principally to drop bombs
bunker fortified underground chamber of reinforced concrete with slant-sided openings
cannon large-caliber mounted gun
clean weapon nuclear bomb producing relatively little fallout
combat zone area in which battle is occurring
conventional weapons traditional weapons and warheads, excluding nuclear, biological, and chemical weapons
cross fire gunfire from two or more points located so that lines of fire transect
cruise missile winged, jet-powered guided missile designed to fly low and carry a warhead
D-day day of pl'anned military operation; June 6, 1944, day of Allied invasion of western Europe in World War II
decoy device that misleads soldier or weapon as to its target
defensive weapons armaments used for protection from attack
defoliating agent chemical that causes foliage to die, thus exposing hidden enemy

demilitarized zone DMZ; area forbidden to military installations and operations, often between opposing lines
depth charge powerful explosive dropped from ship or airplane that explodes underwater
destroyer speedy warship with guns, torpedoes, and depth charges
dirty bomb nuclear weapon producing large amount of fallout
DMZ demilitarized zone
field area of active operations or combat, usu. away from command headquarters
field artillery mobile artillery that accompanies troops in combat
fighter plane small, maneuverable military plane equipped with automatic guns to attack other planes
firepower amount of gunfire or explosives deliverable by weapon or armed forces unit
fleet organized unit of ships, aircraft, and marine troops under one administrative command
fort fortified structure occupied by troops, often surrounded by ditch, moat, rampart, or parapet
foxhole hastily dug pit for protection from enemy gunfire
front point of contact between two enemy forces; battlefront; battle line
ground zero area directly beneath a nuclear explosion
gunnery design, construction, and firing of heavy guns
ICBM intercontinental ballistic missile
interceptor fighter plane utilized to divert or shoot down attacking enemy planes; missile used to explode incoming enemy missiles
intercontinental ballistic missile ICBM; rocket-propelled missile carrying warhead at long ranges
jump jet jet aircraft capable of nearly vertical takeoff that requires little or no airstrip
land-based missile missile fired from site on land rather than air or sea
matériel arms, ammunition, and other equipment
minefield area filled with hidden explosive charges
Minuteman ICBM with nuclear warhead
missile pilot, jet- or rocket-powered vehicle for delivering nuclear or conventional warhead
mobile missile launcher large truck and trailer used to launch missiles, allowing launch site to change rapidly
MRV multiple reentry vehicle
multiple reentry vehicle MRV; ballistic missile with two or more warheads
mustard gas oily liquid used as chemical weapon that causes blisters, blindness, and often death
MX ICBM with multiple nuclear warheads, capable of attack against bases, often concealed in underground silo
nerve gas often odorless and colorless, poisonous, easily absorbed liquid that interferes with nervous system and inhibits respiration
nuclear weapons bombs using atomic fission or fusion to create massive radiation doses and often irrecoverable damage to environment and property
occupied territory area under control of hostile armed forces
ordnance explosives, bombs, and ammunition
paravane toothed, torpedo-shaped, protective device used by ship to cut moorings of underwater mines
payload warhead
poison gas nerve gas or other chemical weapon
SAM surface-to-air missile
silo underground installation of concrete and steel that houses ballistic missile and mechanism for launching it
SLBM submarine-launched ballistic missile
smart weapons steerable bombs and missiles electronically programmed to find target, esp. by heat detection
stealth technology use of special design and materials to enable aircraft to evade detection, esp. by radar
stinkpot jar of combustibles that generate noxious odors, formerly used as weapon
strategic weapons weapons intended to attack enemy's military and industrial facilities
stronghold fortified position secure from enemy attack
tactical aircraft planes providing air attack in support of ground forces
tactical weapons armaments designed for limited or specific purposes, usu. nonnuclear weapons
tank heavily armed, turreted, armored vehicle that moves on two continuous steel belts
theater geographical area of warfare
turret low, armored, revolving structure for guns on fortress, warship, airplane, or tank
warhead part of missile or rocket that contains explosive charge of nuclear, toxic, or detonating substance; payload
war machine military hierarchy, infrastructure, weapons, technology, equipment, and personnel working together to wage war
war zone combat area
yield force of nuclear explosion, measured in equivalent tons of TNT

MILITARY RANKS (*IN DESCENDING ORDER*)

Army, Air Force, and Marines

general of the army (5-star)
marshal (Europe)
general (4-star)
lieutenant general (3-star)
major general (2-star)
brigadier general (1-star)
colonel
lieutenant colonel
major
captain
first lieutenant
second lieutenant
chief warrant officer (W-4)
chief warrant officer (W-3)
chief warrant officer (W-2)
warrant officer (W-1)

sergeant major
first sergeant
chief master sergeant
master sergeant
sergeant first class
specialist 7
gunnery sergeant
technical sergeant
staff sergeant
specialist 6
sergeant
specialist 5
corporal
specialist 4
lance corporal
private first class (PFC)
airman first class
private
airman
recruit
cadet

NAVY AND COAST GUARD

fleet admiral
admiral
vice admiral
rear admiral
commodore
captain
commander
lieutenant commander
lieutenant
lieutenant junior grade
ensign
chief warrant officer (W-4)
chief warrant officer (W-3)
chief warrant officer (W-2)
master chief petty officer
senior chief petty officer
chief petty officer
petty officer 1st class
petty officer 2nd class
petty officer 3rd class
seaman
seaman apprentice
seaman recruit
midshipman

INTERNATIONAL RELATIONS

Diplomacy and Diplomats
World Relations and Conditions
Security and Defense
Espionage and Intelligence

Diplomacy and Diplomats

accord formal agreement; treaty
alliance agreement of mutual support between independent states
ally state or ruler associated with another by treaty
ambassador highest-ranking diplomatic officer
ambassador-at-large high-ranking diplomat not assigned to one particular foreign state
amnesty pardon granted to individual or group by government
annexation acquisition of another state or territory by a sovereign state
asylum protection, esp. from extradition, given political refugees by state or agency with diplomatic immunity
attaché official of nondiplomatic government department attached to diplomatic post
bilateralism agreement between two nations to pursue common interests of mutual benefit
bloc group of aligned nations
cartel international group joined together for common political or economic purpose; agreement between belligerents
chancellery office and personnel of embassy or consulate
chargé d'affaires envoy sent to state to which higher level diplomat is not sent; diplomat of lowest class who takes charge of business during temporary absence of ambassador or minister
communiqué official statement issued by parties at meeting
concession yielding on some point so as to reach agreement
concordat official agreement or compact; agreement to which pope is one party
consul official sent by one state to another to protect and assist its nationals in commercial relations
consular agent consular officer of lowest rank
consulate office or position of consul; premises occupied by consul
consul general top-ranking consul in key station or having authority over several consulates
convention general agreement among states regarding matters of common concern, less binding than treaty
courier diplomat bearing confidential documents
covenant formal, binding agreement between two or more nations
delegate representative of nation at conference or meeting
deputy substitute or assistant who assumes authority in absence of diplomatic superior
détente lessening of world tension
diplomacy art and practice of conducting international relations
diplomat political representative of one national government to another, appointed to conduct official negotiations and maintain relations between the two governments
diplomatic corps diplomatic personnel in residence in another state
diplomatic immunity special exemption from foreign laws afforded to diplomatic corps
diplomatic pouch case or package in which messages and information are transported
diplomatic privilege diplomatic mission's exemption from local jurisdiction
diplomatic service body of professional diplomats

dollar diplomacy diplomatic activities to increase economic power of nation in foreign states
embassy ambassador's mission, entourage, and official residence in foreign nation
emissary representative, sometimes secret agent
entente international agreement of friendship or alliance, usu. stipulating common course of action; parties to such an agreement
envoy diplomatic agent of any rank
exequatur written recognition and empowerment of consul by government of nation in which he or she is stationed
extradition return of criminal to officers of state in which crime was committed
foreign policy system of methods and objectives for maintaining relations with other states
General Assembly highest deliberative body of United Nations, with representatives from all member nations
Geneva Convention internationally recognized rules for treatment of dead, wounded, and prisoners of war
high seas oceans and connecting waters not within territorial jurisdiction of any state
International Court of Justice judicial agency of United Nations that arbitrates disputes between nations; World Court
international relations branch of political science concerned with military, economic, and diplomatic affairs between states
League of Nations post-World War I organization of nations dedicated to promoting peace
legate emissary from one nation to another
legation diplomatic mission sent to foreign state; offices of diplomatic staff
minister diplomatic agent of second rank
minister plenipotentiary diplomat ranking below ambassador but wielding full powers
nuncio top-ranking papal legate to civil government
pact international agreement or treaty
protocol preliminary diplomatic agreement or records of diplomatic conference that form basis for final treaty
secretary-general principal officer of United Nations; principal officer of a secretariat
secretary of state appointed official who supervises department conducting U.S. foreign affairs
Security Council permanent peacekeeping council of United Nations, composed of five permanent and ten rotating two-year members
shuttle diplomacy negotiations between two hostile states conducted by intermediary traveling back-and-forth between them
sovereignty independence from external control by another nation
State Department U.S. executive department responsible for conduct of foreign affairs
statesman national leader with international respect
statesmanship exercise of astute national leadership based on world vision
summit conference of highest level officials from two or more states
three-mile limit ocean waters within three miles of coast considered part of national territory
trade mission delegates to foreign state seeking economic cooperation
treaty international agreement
trust territory nonself-governing region under authority of United Nations prior to becoming independent
United Nations post-World War II organization of nearly all nations dedicated to peace, economic development, and social welfare
vice-consul diplomatic officer subordinate to consul
vice-legate diplomatic officer subordinate to legate
World Court International Court of Justice

World Relations and Conditions

alien resident of a state who is not a citizen or national of that state
Balkanize (*vb*) divide a territorial entity into smaller, often hostile, units
banana republic small Latin American state, dependent on foreign investment, often governed by despot
carnet customs document allowing automobile to be driven across international border at no cost
client state nation that is dependent on richer, more powerful nation for its political, economic, or military welfare
colonialism control of one state over other dependent territories or states
colonization acquisition and maintenance of dependent colonies
colony territory and citizens of state dependent on another state
Common Market European Economic Community
compatriot fellow countryman
crown colony British colony without constitution or representative government, controlled directly by crown
customs duty tax on goods imported into country
dependency subject territory that is not an integral part of ruling country
developed nation industrialized state with well-developed economy and high standard of living
developing nation poor state in process of industrializing, with low standard of living
dominion territory over which single government rules; sovereign authority over such territory
domino theory belief that unsuccessful containment, esp. of communism, in one state will be repeated in neighboring states
dual citizenship status of person who is legal citizen of two or more countries
EEC European Economic Community
embargo governmental prohibition on export of goods to specific foreign state
emigrant one who emigrates from native state
emigration departure of citizen of one state so as to become citizen of another
enclave territory completely enclosed by another state

European Economic Community EEC; cooperative economic partnership among states of western Europe, esp. for trade and finance; Common Market
exile compulsory or voluntary departure from homeland due to differences with government; banishment
expatriation citizen's voluntary renunciation of national allegiance
extraterritoriality right of state to extend its jurisdiction over its nationals into territory of another state
fatherland one's native country or that of one's ancestors; motherland
foreign affairs relations of one nation with others
foreign aid assistance, esp. economic, given to poorer nation by richer one
free trade international commerce without restrictive tariffs
geopolitics study of connections between geography and relations among nations
glasnost *Russian.* Soviet policy of openness about internal affairs and receptivity to Western influence during 1980's
global economy interrelated trade and development factors that affect all nations
globalism involvement of a country in international affairs and alliances, opposite of isolationism
hegemony influence or authority of one nation over others
human rights basic freedoms and welfare of all world citizens, with which governments have no rights to interfere
IMF International Monetary Fund
immigrant one who immigrates into foreign state
immigration movement into country by noncitizens with intent to settle
imperialism policy of extending rule over other states
incident seemingly minor occurrence between nations that can lead to serious consequences
international (*adj*) that which involves two or more sovereign states
internationalism principle of cooperation among nations to promote the common good
International Monetary Fund IMF; agency that promotes trade and development through contributions from member nations
iron curtain symbol of Soviet ideological and political isolation from West after World War II
irredenta territory historically or culturally related to one state but presently subjected to another
isolationism policy that peace and economic growth are best achieved by abstaining from alliances with and commitments to other nations
Manifest Destiny doctrine that it is U.S. destiny to expand territory in North America (19th c.)
ministate small, independent nation
Monroe Doctrine early 19th-century U.S. policy that opposed outside interference in Americas
most-favored-nation (*adj*) pertaining to treaty signatory that is accorded most favorable commercial benefits by another nation
nation people who share specific territory, have common customs, history, language, and culture, and are organized under a single government; sovereign state
national noncitizen who owes allegiance to a nation and enjoys its protection
nationalism allegiance to one's sovereign state
nationality status of citizenship in particular nation by birth or naturalization; people sharing common culture, organized to constitute sovereign state
nation-state sovereign state inhabited by fairly homogeneous group of people who share feeling of common nationality
naturalization process, other than by birth, through which citizenship is attained
nonaligned nation country not siding with one of the Great Powers
OAS Organization of American States
OPEC Organization of Petroleum Exporting Countries
open door policy of equal and impartial trade opportunities for all foreign nations
Organization of American States OAS; group that promotes cooperation and trade among nations of Latin America
Organization of Petroleum Exporting Countries OPEC; policy and price-setting cartel of oil-producing nations
patriotism love for or devotion to one's country
realm sphere of dominance, esp. royal domain over which monarch rules
reciprocity trade policy based on mutual benefit to both nations through exchange of special privileges
refugee one who has fled or been driven from his or her country to avoid persecution or danger
sanction coercive economic or military action taken by one or several nations against another
sphere of influence influence exerted by a Great Power over nearby states
state independent, sovereign nation
superpower extremely powerful nation with worldwide influence
suzerain nation controlling another state's foreign affairs
tariff government duty on imported goods
territorial waters waters, traditionally within 3 miles (4.8 km) of its shore, that are regarded as under jurisdiction of a state
territory geographical area under authority of single national government; area under U.S. authority that is not actually a state
Third World underdeveloped nations of Asia, Africa, and South America
trade balance equilibrium of imports and exports between nations
World Bank international bank that makes loans to developing nations

Security and Defense

Allies nations united against central European powers in World War I, or against Axis powers in World War II

Arab League confederation of Arab states formed in 1945 to promote unity and cooperation
armistice suspension of military operations between belligerents
arms control international agreements and diplomacy designed to regulate or stabilize use of weapons and armed forces
arms race competition between nations in building and stockpiling weapons to attain military superiority
atomic power status of any nation that possesses nuclear weapons
Axis Germany, Italy, and Japan, opponents of Allies in World War II
belligerent nation at war that has been granted status in international law subjecting it to obligations and laws of war
brinkmanship tactic of maneuvering a dangerous situation to the limits of safety
buffer state small, neutral state separating two belligerents
capitulation act or terms of surrender
Cold War post-World War II ideological conflict between the United States and Soviet Union, conducted without direct military action
containment policy that seeks to restrict influence of nation by confining it geographically
détente lessening of world tension
deterrence maintenance of large military arsenal to discourage belligerents from attacking
disarmament abolition, reduction, or limitation of arms
insurgency status in international law given to revolutionaries who possess insufficient organization to be granted the status of belligerency
irenic (*adj*) conducive to peaceful relations
jingoism aggressive, militaristic national policy
massive retaliation use of nation's nuclear arsenal in response to attack
militarism belligerent international posture of intervention and intimidation
mutual defense treaty agreement among nations to provide military assistance to any member coming under attack
national security nation's system of protection from foreign infiltration or attack
National Security Council NSC; U.S. executive agency that deals with defense, intelligence, and foreign affairs
NATO North Atlantic Treaty Organization; post-World War II organization formed among Western nations for mutual defense against Soviet aggression
neutrality state of impartiality and abstention from hostility in time of war
nonaggression pact pledge to refrain from acts of war
North Atlantic Treaty Organization NATO
NSC National Security Council
peaceful coexistence willingness or intention of belligerent nations to avoid armed conflict
peace offensive intensive diplomatic effort to achieve peace
police action localized military action undertaken without formal declaration of war, esp. against violators of international law
reprisal retaliatory force short of war
revanche policy of regaining areas that have been lost to other states as result of war
sabotage action intended to disrupt or destroy nation's military or economic capabilities
SEATO Southeast Asia Treaty Organization; post-World War II alliance between United States and small Asian nations to protect those nations from Communist influence or attack
security measures taken to ensure national freedom from espionage, sabotage, and military attack
Southeast Asia Treaty Organization SEATO
state of war condition or period marked by armed conflict between nations, which are subject to international laws of war
strategic nuclear weapons long-range nuclear weapons capable of destroying enemy's civilian and military targets
tactical nuclear weapons nuclear weapons intended for specific, limited purpose
treason acts intended to overthrow government of one's own nation
truce temporary suspension of hostilities
Warsaw Pact post-World War II organization formed by Soviet Union and eastern European nations for mutual protection from the United States and NATO states

Espionage and Intelligence

agent one engaged in intelligence operations
Central Intelligence Agency CIA; covert intelligence gathering agency of U.S. government since World War II
CIA Central Intelligence Agency
cipher secret code used in diplomatic communications
collaborator traitor who works with enemy state
counterespionage spying intended to offset enemy espionage
counterintelligence actions intended to deceive or misinform enemy intelligence service and halt sabotage
counterspy one engaged in counterespionage
courier spy bearing secret documents
covert (*adj*) secret, hidden
disinformation deliberately false information, esp. about one's military strength or plans, released to confuse enemy government
double agent spy working for two opposed states
espionage spying to obtain information about plans and activities of foreign government
infiltration subtle or covert subversive involvement in another nation's affairs
intelligence political, military, economic, or other information about another state
Interpol International Criminal Police Organization; international criminal investigative organization
laundered money illicit funds given the appearance of legitimacy by passing through hands of third party

mole undercover agent, esp. one who infiltrates another nation's intelligence agency
quisling traitor, collaborator with enemy
reconnaissance covert intelligence gathering, esp. regarding enemy military capabilities
safe house secret location where individuals may hide or plot sabotage and terrorism
secret agent spy, undercover operative
spying secret intelligence-gathering activities against another nation
traitor person disloyal to his or her own nation

TITLES OF RANK

archbishop bishop at head of ecclesiastical province
archduchess wife or widow of archduke; woman holding rank of archduke in her own right
archduke sovereign prince of imperial family in Austria
ayatollah religious leader among Shiite Muslims, esp. one who is not an imam
baron lowest grade of peerage in Great Britain; continental European nobleman; lowest order of nobility in Japan
baroness wife or widow of baron; woman holding rank of baron in her own right
baronet peerage rank below baron and above knight
beefeater yeoman of the guard of English monarch
bishop high-ranking Anglican, Eastern Orthodox, or Roman Catholic clergyman having authority over other clergy and usu. governing a diocese
brother male member of religious organization having a priesthood
cacique native Indian chief in areas dominated primarily by Spanish culture; local political boss in Spain and Latin America
caliph spiritual head of Islam
capo chief of branch of Mafia family
cardinal highest official of Roman Catholic Church below pope
caudillo head of state in Spanish-speaking country, esp. military dictator
centurion commanding officer of century unit in ancient Rome
chamberlain chief officer in household of king or nobleman
chancellor secretary of nobleman, prince, or king; chief secretary of embassy
chaplain clergyman in charge of chapel or attached to branch of military, institution such as a college, important family, or royal court
chevalier lowest rank of French nobility, comparable to knight
commissar Communist party official assigned to military unit to teach and ensure party loyalty
constable warden or governor of royal castle or fortified town; police officer
consul either of two annually elected chief magistrates in ancient Rome
count European nobleman corresponding to British earl; former name for British earl
countess wife or widow of earl or count; woman holding title of earl or count in her own right
crown prince heir apparent to crown or throne
crown princess wife of crown prince; female heir apparent or presumptive to crown or throne
czar emperor of Russia until 1917 revolution; tsar
czarevitch son and heir of czar
czarevna daughter of czar or wife of czar's son
czarina empress of Russia, wife of czar
Dalai Lama former ruler and chief monk of Tibet, believed to be reincarnation of Buddhist saint
dame wife or daughter of lord; female member of order of knighthood
dauphin eldest son of king of France
dean Roman Catholic priest supervising one district or diocese
doge chief magistrate in republics of Venice and Genoa
Don Spanish title equivalent to Mr. or Sir, prefixed to man's given name; Spanish nobleman or gentleman
Doìa Spanish title equivalent to Madam or Lady, prefixed to woman's given name
dowager widow holding property and title from deceased husband
duce *Italian.* leader; title of Benito Mussolini
duchess wife or widow of duke; woman holding ducal title in her own right
duke European nobleman of highest hereditary rank; member of highest rank of British peerage, ranking above marquis
earl British peer ranking below marquis and above viscount, formerly called count
emeritus (*adj*) honorary title held after retirement and corresponding to that held during active service
eminence person of high rank or attainment, esp. Roman Catholic cardinal
emir native ruler in parts of Asia and Africa
emperor sovereign or supreme monarch of an empire
empress wife or widow of emperor; woman who holds imperial title in her own right
esquire member of English gentry ranking below knight
excellency title for certain high dignitaries of state and church
Führer *German.* leader; used chiefly in reference to Adolf Hitler
grand duchess wife or widow of grand duke; woman who holds rank of grand duke in her own right
grand duke sovereign duke of certain European states
headmaster man heading staff of private school
headmistress woman heading staff of private school
heir apparent next in line to title whose right to inheritance is indefeasible in law if he survives legal ancestor

heir presumptive next in line to title whose right to inheritance may be eliminated by birth of nearer relative
hidalgo member of Spanish lower nobility
highness title of address for person of exalted rank
imam Islamic ruler claiming descent from Muhammad and exercising spiritual and temporal leadership over region
infanta daughter of Spanish or Portuguese monarch
kaiser emperor; ruler of Germany from 1871 to 1918
khan local chieftain or man of rank in countries of central Asia
khedive title of ruler of Egypt from 1867 to 1914, governing as viceroy of Turkish sultan
knight man honored by sovereign for merit, ranking in Great Britain below baronet
lady woman having proprietary rights or authority as feudal superior
ladyship title of address for woman having rank of lady
lama Tibetan Buddist priest or monk
legate deputy or emissary
lord ruler by hereditary right or preeminence to whom service and obedience are due; holder of feudal tenure
madame title for woman of rank or office; French prefix for married woman
mademoiselle French prefix for unmarried woman
magistrate official entrusted with administration of laws; principal official exercising governmental powers over major political unit
maharajah Hindu prince ranking above raja; also maharaja
maharani wife of maharajah; Hindu princess ranking above rani; also maharanee
maître d' maître d'hotel; majordomo; headwaiter
majesty form of address for reigning sovereign power, authority, or dignitary
majordomo man having charge of a large household; head steward; maître d'
mandarin public official of Chinese Empire
marchesa Italian woman holding rank of marchese
marchese Italian nobleman next in rank above count
marchioness wife or widow of marquis or marchese; woman holding title of marchesa in her own right; marquise
marquess marquis
marquis British peer ranking below duke and above earl; hereditary European or Japanese nobleman; marquess
marquise marchioness
mikado emperor of Japan
milady term of address for Englishwoman of noble or gentle birth
milord term of address for Englishman of noble or gentle birth
minister Christian Protestant clergyman; diplomatic representative below ambassador; cabinet-level officer administering specific ministry in government
miss conventional title for young unmarried woman
mister Mr.; conventional title for man not entitled to rank, honorific, or professional title
monarch hereditary sovereign or constitutional ruler of kingdom or empire
monseigneur French dignitary
monsieur French term of address for man, equivalent to mister; Frenchman of high rank or station
monsignor Roman Catholic prelate having dignity or titular distinction conferred by pope
Most Reverend term of address for archbishop or Roman Catholic bishop
Mr. conventional title before name of man not holding title of rank, honorific, or professional title; mister
Mrs. conventional title before name of married woman not holding title of rank, honorific, or professional title
Ms. title used instead of Miss or Mrs. when marital status of woman is unknown or irrelevant
mullah Muslim religious teacher of quasi-clerical class
nobleman man of noble rank or birth
noblewoman woman of noble rank or birth
nuncio papal legate of highest rank, permanently accredited to civil government
overlord lord over other lords; lord paramount; absolute or supreme ruler
padre Christian clergyman; military chaplain
parson Protestant pastor
pasha Turkish or North African man of high rank or office
pastor clergyman of local church or parish
patriarch Roman Catholic bishop ranking immediately below pope; bishop of Eastern Orthodox sees of Alexandria, Antioch, Constantinople, or Jerusalem, or of Western see of Rome; jurisdictional head of various Eastern churches
patrician person of high birth; orig. member of one of citizen families of ancient Rome
peer member of one of five ranks of British peerage: duke, marquis, earl, viscount, baron
pharaoh sovereign ruler of ancient Egypt
pontiff Roman Catholic pope
pope prelate who, as bishop of Rome, is head of Roman Catholic Church
potentate individual wielding great power; sovereign
prelate high-ranking ecclesiastic, such as bishop
priest Anglican, Eastern Orthodox, or Roman Catholic clergyman ranking below bishop and authorized to perform certain rites
priestess female priest
prince male member of royal family, esp. sovereign's son or grandson; monarch or ruler of principality or state
prince consort husband of reigning female sovereign
princeling young, subordinate, or minor prince
princess female member of royal family, esp. daughter or granddaughter of sovereign; consort of prince; woman holding sovereign power
principal chief administrator of educational institution

prior officer ranking below abbot in monastery

proctor person appointed to supervise students, esp. during examinations

professor faculty member of highest academic rank at college or university

provost chief dignitary of collegiate or cathedral chapter; chief magistrate of Scottish burgh; keeper of prison; high-ranking university administrative officer

purser official on ship or aircraft responsible for papers, accounts, and comfort and welfare of passengers

queen wife or widow of king or tribal chief; female monarch

queen consort wife of reigning monarch

queen mother queen dowager who is mother of reigning monarch

rabbi Jewish master or teacher; Jew trained and ordained for professional religious leadership; leader of Jewish congregation; reb

rajah Indian or Malay prince or chief; Hindu title of nobility; also raja

rani Hindu queen; rajah's wife; also ranee

reb rabbi

rector Episcopal clergyman in charge of parish; Roman Catholic priest directing seminary or college

regent one who governs kingdom in minority, absence, or disability of sovereign; member of governing board of state university

registrar officer of educational institution responsible for registering students and keeping academic records; admitting officer of hospital, university, or other institution

reverend member of clergy; clergyman's title preceded by "the" and followed by name

sachem North American Indian chief, esp. Algonquian; Tammany Hall political boss

sagamore subordinate chief of Algonquian Indians

samurai military retainer of Japanese daimyo practicing chivalric code of Bushido; aristocratic warrior of Japan

scoutmaster adult leader of band of boy or girl scouts

secretary officer of business or organization who keeps records of meetings; cabinet-level officer of state directing government administrative department

seigneur seignior

seignior man of rank or authority; feudal lord of manor; seigneur

seìor Spanish equivalent of Mr.

seìora Spanish equivalent of Mrs.

seìorita Spanish equivalent of Miss

signor Italian equivalent of Mr.

signora Italian equivalent of Mrs.

signorina Italian equivalent of Miss

sexton church officer who cares for church property, rings bell, and digs graves

shah sovereign of Iran

shammes sexton of Jewish synagogue

sheik Arab chief or ruler

sheriff important official of shire or county charged primarily with judicial duties; police officer for county

shogun military governor ruling Japan until revolution of 1867-1868

sir man of rank or position, esp. title before given name of knight or baronet

sire man of rank or authority; lord; sovereign

sister female member of religious community that observes vows

sovereign one exercising supreme power in specific sphere; monarch, ruler, or king

squire shield- or armor-bearer of knight; male attendant; member of British gentry ranking below knight and above gentleman

sri conventional title of respect for distinguished Hindu Indian

stadtholder viceroy in a province of the Netherlands; chief executive officer of the Netherlands

steward one employed on estate to manage domestic affairs; employee on ship, aircraft, or train who buys and obtains provisions and is responsible for comfort of passengers

stewardess woman performing duties of steward

subaltern person holding subordinate position

subdeacon cleric ranking below deacon; person ranked lowest in major orders of Roman Catholic and Eastern Orthodox churches

suffragan Anglican or Episcopal bishop assisting diocesan bishop but not having right of succession

sultan king or sovereign of Muslim state

sultana female member of sultan's family, esp. wife

superintendent top executive for jurisdiction or organization

suzerain superior feudal lord to whom fealty is due

swami Hindu ascetic or religious teacher

trustee one of a body of persons appointed to administer affairs of a company or institution

tsar czar

verger church official who keeps order during services and serves as usher

vicar Episcopal clergyman having charge of mission or chapel; clergyman exercising broad responsibility as representative of prelate

vicereine wife of viceroy

viceroy governor of country or province ruling as representative of king or sovereign

viscount member of British peerage ranking below earl and above baron

viscountess wife or widow of viscount; woman holding rank of viscount in her own right

vizier high executive officer of various Muslim countries, esp. Ottoman Empire

warden chief operating officer of prison; British governor or officer in charge of administrative department; chief administrator of college or governing officer of certain guilds in Britain

warlord supreme military leader; military commander exercising civil power by force in limited area

worship respectful term of address to British person of importance

Chapter Twelve

The Economy

BUSINESS AND ECONOMICS

Economics and Economic Theory
Commerce and Trade
Corporations and Business Practices
Labor
Employers, Employees, and Business People

Economics and Economic Theory

aggregate total of some measured element of economy
aggregate demand total spending on goods and services by all sectors, including consumers, business, government, and foreign
aggregate equilibrium macroeconomic situation in which national demand for goods and services equals national supply of goods and services
agribusiness growing, processing, and marketing of crops by large corporations instead of individual farmers
agriculture growing crops and raising livestock, esp. as basis of economic structure
antitrust (*adj*) pertaining to policies or laws designed to curb monopolies
assumed debt others' liabilities taken on, as in a merger
autarky national policy of self-sufficiency, including elimination of imports
balanced budget spending equal to revenue, esp. in government
balance of payments periodic summary of difference between a nation's total payments to foreign countries and its receipts from them
balance of trade difference in value between nation's imports and its exports
bankruptcy inability to pay one's debts; legal insolvency
boom high level of economic activity; period of business expansion
bourgeoisie middle class or class of owners
break even achieve minimum sales needed to cover expenses and costs of production
budget plan of expenditures based on anticipated revenues, as for a nation or company
budget deficit state in which government expenditures exceed revenues
business cycle periodic rise and fall in economic activity
buyer's market market in which supply exceeds demand, giving buyers leverage
cap upper limit to spending
capital money, assets, or property used as means of production or for investment
capitalism economic system based on private ownership and profit incentive
cartel group of producers acting cooperatively to control production and prices
circular flow diagram schematic representation of relationship between major economic sectors
class social rank or caste as determined by income or economic status
clean up (*vb*) *Informal.* reap large profits
collectivism political/economic system based on public ownership of production
command economy system, such as communism, in which government controls factors of production and policy
commercialism practice and spirit of commerce or business, esp. high regard for profits
common market association of countries seeking economic cooperation, esp. through tariff concessions
Common Market European Economic Community
communism economic system based on collective ownership of means of production and control of distribution of goods and services
compensation payment for services or labor, esp. wages
conspicuous consumption acquisition and use of goods and services beyond one's needs as a display of wealth
consumerism consumption of goods and services; protection of consumers from poor products or misleading claims
consumer price index measure of fluctuation in prices of common consumer goods and services over fixed time period
convergence theory theory that capitalist and socialist societies are becoming more alike
cost-benefit analysis ratio of dollar cost of project to dollar benefit it will produce, used to compare worthiness of various proposed projects
cost of living average cost for basic necessities of life
deficit budget imbalance in which expenditures exceed revenues
deficit financing financing of budget deficit by borrowing
deficit spending government spending in excess of revenues, esp. to stimulate national economy
deflation decrease in money supply, causing sharp fall in prices
demand capability and desire of consumer to purchase goods and services
demand-side economics Keynesian economic theory emphasizing stimulation of aggregate demand
democratic socialism economic system based on socialist government regulated by democratic electoral process
depression severe, prolonged decline in business activity
deregulation planned, usu. gradual, removal of governmental control over business
devaluation official lessening of value of currency relative to other currencies
diminishing returns any additional unit of one factor of production that yields a smaller increase in production while other factors remain constant

discomfort index statistic combining rate of inflation with unemployment rate
discretionary income money available for luxuries after basic needs have been met
disposable income income remaining after paying all taxes
diversify (*vb*) expand business or economy by increasing number of goods produced or operations undertaken
downside downward trend, esp. loss on investment such as securities
earning power potential for earning wages, income, or profits, esp. over a lifetime
econometrics statistically oriented economic theory and models used in forecasting changes
economic model simplified representation of a real-world phenomena based on likely reactions to economic changes
economics study of wealth and its creation, dissemination, and consumption
economic system manner in which a nation uses its resources and manages production and distribution
economy organization of social and political institutions and businesses for production, distribution, and use of goods and services; frugality or careful spending
embargo ban on import or export of specific item to or from particular nation
European Economic Community economic association established to abolish barriers to free trade among member nations
expansion period of recovery and growth in business cycle
false economy seemingly effective but misguided efforts to save or cut back on costs
farm economy national economy based on agriculture
food stamps coupons for food at reduced prices, issued monthly by government to qualifying poor persons
free enterprise system economic system based on private individual ownership of production with decision making based on profit motive in competitive market; capitalism
freehold land held for life with right to pass it on through inheritance
free trade area nations that have agreed to reduce or eliminate trade barriers and tariffs among themselves while external tariffs vary
freeze fixing of some economic factor, such as prices, employment, expenditures, or taxes, at a given level
full employment economic condition in which unemployment is deemed minimal and acceptable, usu. under six percent
gainful employment work for which one is paid wages
GNP gross nationalproduct
goods things produced and purchased
goods and services end results of production: things people buy and activities performed for others
gross national product GNP; combined annual monetary value of all goods, services, and products sold on markets of national economy
heir person who will inherit or does inherit another's property upon his or her death
index number showing percentage variation over time of economic factors from an arbitrary standard, usu. 100
index of leading indicators statistical measure capable of predicting economic conditions in near future, based on several factors
industrialization replacement of hand tools by machine and power tools and development of large-scale production, beginning in late 18th c.
inflation sustained rise in price of goods and services
inflationary spiral continuous increase in prices, costs, and wages
insolvency inability to pay bills and debts
Keynesian economics theory emphasizing stimulation of aggregate demand over supply
labor-intensive (*adj*) designating production using more labor than capital
laissez faire economic system with minimal government regulation of business, trade, and competition
loose money policy stimulation of economy by making credit inexpensive and abundantly available
Lorenz curve graph showing variance between equal and actual distribution of income
lottery game of chance in which people buy numbered tickets and prizes are awarded by lot, used to raise funds by some states
lower class people occupying bottom rung of socioeconomic ladder
macroeconomics economic branch dealing with broad aspects of the economy, esp. aggregates on national level
Malthusian (*adj*) pertaining to the theories of T.R. Malthus regarding dichotomy between geometric population growth and arithmetic increase in means of subsistence, causing shortages unless war or famine intervenes to eliminate the imbalance
manufacturing production of commodities for sale
market activity of buying and selling; trade; potential customers for a product
market economy economic system ruled by opportunity of consumers to buy and producers to sell
market equilibrium condition of equal supply and demand with stable prices
market share percentage of total sales in specific market accounted for by one company
market socialism public ownership of means of production and use of market mechanism for distribution
mass production manufacture of large quantities of goods using standardized parts and assembly lines
material assets wealth, property, or businesses owned

measure of value function of money as standard unit measure for value of commodities
mercantilism preindustrial economic system emphasizing controlled balance of exports and imports (16th-18th c.)
microeconomics branch of economics dealing with single units of production and consumption
middle class heterogeneous socioeconomic group with common values, comprised of business and professional people, bureaucrats, farmers, and skilled laborers
mixed economy system combining elements of market and command economies
monetarism theory that level of economic activity depends primarily on quantity and growth rate of money supply
money supply amount of money in circulation at a given time
monopoly domination of market by single company
national debt total amount owed by federal government at given time to other nations, businesses, and individuals
nationalization government assumption of control over privately owned industry
natural resources industrial materials and capacities found in nature
oligopoly market condition in which there are few sellers, enabling them to influence price and other factors
open market competitive market free from price control and not restricted to any individual or group
panic public fear that economic entity, market, or system is failing, and consequent rush to liquidate assets
peak highest point in business cycle; boom
per capita income total national income or GNP divided by total population
petite bourgeoisie lower middle class, such as small shopkeepers and artisans
planned economy socialist or other economic system with centralized government control of production and distribution
political economy social science that deals with economics in connection with politics and society
poverty lack of socially acceptable amount of money and material possessions
poverty line government standard for personal or family income used for measuring portion of population living in poverty; poverty level
PPI producer price index
price controls government ceiling set on prices of basic goods and services to fight inflation
price index measure of fluctuation in prices from arbitrary standard over period of time
price supports government payments, esp. to farmers, to maintain minimum prices by buying up surpluses
prime cost that part of cost of commodity derived from labor and materials directly used in its manufacture
private enterprise capitalist economic system with minimal government interference, allowing individual ownership of property and encouraging competition and profit incentive
private sector part of economy that is composed of individuals and privately owned businesses
producer price index PPI; scale that compares cost of producing goods now with cost in past year
productivity measure of ability to produce more output from given input
profit net amount earned after deducting costs in business enterprise
proletariat working class
proprietary rights right to ownership of a tangible or intangible thing or idea
proprietorship ownership, esp. of one's own business
public sector part of economy composed of federal, state, and local governments
public utility industry providing essential public service, such as electrical, water, or telephone service, in which single firm is granted local monopoly
purchasing power value of currency in terms of what it can buy compared with buying power at time established as base period; ability to purchase goods and services
quotation current price of commodity or security
rationing limited distribution of a product so that everyone receives a fixed amount
raw goods materials gathered in original state from nature for use in production
real wages amount that can be purchased at given time with one's income, computed by dividing money wages by consumer price index
recession period of no growth in national economy for at least six months; stage in business cycle with decreased demand for goods, increased unemployment, and decline in GNP
recovery increase in business activity following recession or depression; upturn in business cycle
regulation government control and supervision of certain economic activities
renewable resources natural resources that are not exhausted by use
restrictive practices trade agreements deemed to be unfair to competitors or against public interest
revaluation government increase in exchange rate to increase value of currency relative to other currencies
revenue total income of business, government, or individual before expenses
sanctions coercive economic restrictions placed on one nation by another
service work performed for another for payment
service economy economy emphasizing services over industrial production, esp. automated, cybernetic services
shakeout drop in economic activity that eliminates marginal or unprofitable businesses and products
shortage situation in which demand for goods exceeds supply, esp. at given price
shortfall shortage or deficiency
sliding scale variable scale, as for wages or prices charged, based on changes in other factors or ability to pay

socialism state ownership of all or most of means of production and distribution, with control over aspects of social welfare and planning
social security federal government payments to elderly, unemployed, and disabled persons, financed by contributions from employers and employees
socioeconomic (*adj*) involving interrelation of social and economic factors
stagflation inflation and stagnation or high unemployment occurring together
standard of living quality of life measured by general level of consumption of material goods
stipend regular payment
subsidy government payment to business or individual to improve economic condition
subsistence level level of production and consumption barely adequate for survival
supply quantity of goods or services available
supply and demand basic economic law stating that as price of a good increases, suppliers will be willing to produce more but consumers will demand less, so that price and quantity are both directly and inversely related
supply-side economics macroeconomic theory emphasizing stimulation of production as basic factor in growth
surplus situation in which supply of goods exceeds demand, esp. at given price
title right of ownership, esp. document stating such right
trade barriers tariffs, quotas, and customs regulations used by one country to discourage importation of certain goods
trade deficit imbalance in which nation's imports exceed its exports
transfer payment disbursement, such as social security or unemployment payment, for which no goods or services are received
trickle-down theory theory that government financial incentives to big business will eventually benefit smaller businesses and general public
trust several companies acting together to control production, pricing, and distribution of a product
upper class social class at top of society, possessing wealth and owning means of production
urban economy economy in which most wealth and economic activity is centered in cities
value market price; worth of something in money at specific time; purchasing power of unit of currency; Marxist expression of labor embodied in commodity
wage-price controls laws intended to stabilize economy by limiting increase in wages or prices
ways and means methods of raising money and obtaining resources for use by company or nation
wealth money, real property, or human resources; assets
welfare government assistance to poor; state or degree of well-being
welfare capitalism modified capitalism that incorporates government-funded social welfare programs
welfare state social system based on political responsibility for improvement in condition of all citizens
wholesale price index measure of changes in commodity prices at all stages of production; producer price index
work ethic belief system emphasizing social and personal value of work
working class those who work for a living with little control over working conditions, esp. unskilled manual and factory laborers; proletariat
worth material value expressed in terms of money

Commerce and Trade

asking price amount initially sought for goods or services
auction public sale at which items are sold one by one to highest bidder
bar code set of vertical bars printed on consumer product with coded information to be read by computerized scanner
bargain basement basement floor of department store, where goods are sold at reduced prices
barter (*vb*) exchange commodities, goods, or services without use of money
bill of lading document issued to shipper by carrier describing goods shipped and terms of carriage
bill of sale written certification of transfer of ownership
black market illegal trade to avoid government regulation or taxation
boycott organized effort to deter customers from patronizing a business or industry
buyer's market market in which supply is plentiful and prices are favorable to consumers
cabotage trade in coastal waters or air space between two points within one country
cartage act or cost of delivering goods, esp. by truck
cash-and-carry (*adj*) sold for cash payment with no delivery included
cash on delivery COD; payment due when shipped goods are received
cash register business machine with money drawer and tapes that display and tabulate amount of each sale
catalog sales distribution of merchandise by mail with orders placed from catalogs
caveat emptor *Latin.* lit. let the buyer beware; principle that one buys at one's own risk
chain store individual outlet of retail chain
chamber of commerce organization of business people promoting economic development in particular area
charge account credit account in which merchant allows customer to pay for purchases over time
CIF cost, insurance, and freight; seller's designation that quoted price includes packing, shipping, and insurance charges
clearance sale to get rid of old goods and make room for new ones
clientele all of one's customers

closeout sale to dispose of all goods, esp. when ending business venture
COD cash on delivery
cold call telephone sales call to stranger who is unfamiliar with product or service
commerce organized exchange of commodities on large scale, usu. involving transport from place to place; trade
commissary food and supply store, esp. in army camp
commission percentage of sales price paid to broker by owner of merchandise sold
commodity good traded in marketplace, esp. one that is transportable
common carrier company in business of transporting goods at uniform rates
comp *Informal.* free service or good, esp. admission ticket to event; (*adj*) complimentary
consumer goods products made for and sold directly to individuals to be used as sold
consumerism movement to educate consumers to obtain better, safer products from manufacturers
contraband unlawful or prohibited goods; trade in such goods
convenience store store open very long hours, carrying limited selection of goods, usu. at inflated prices
co-op cooperative store owned by and operated for benefit of members
cost amount paid for goods or services, esp. wholesale price paid by retailers
cross sell (*vb*) attract customer by offering one product or service while selling another
customer person who buys, esp. regularly at same place
department store large retail store with departments selling many kinds of goods
door-to-door (*adj*) selling by calling at each house or apartment in an area; shipped directly from point of pickup to point of delivery
drive-in service establishment in which customers remain in cars
dry goods cloth or clothing products
durable goods consumer items with long-term market life, esp. cars or furniture; hard goods
emporium marketplace, trading center; large store selling variety of products
exchange place of trade; barter, trade; (*vb*) return one purchased item and replace it with another
excise tax tax on manufacture, sale, or consumption of goods and services
export product sold outside country of origin; (*vb*) sell goods outside one's own country
factory outlet warehouse serving as point of sale for discount goods
fair market value price something can be expected to bring on open market at given time
fire sale sale of commodities actually or supposedly damaged in fire at greatly reduced prices
five-and-dime low-priced general merchandise store
flagship central or largest store in chain
flea market usu. outdoor market with numerous stalls selling used or handmade new articles
fly-by-night *Slang.* unreliable business
FOB free on board; assumption of responsibility by shipper for all costs until goods are placed on carrier
franchise contract or license permitting regional distributor to use name and sell products of another company or manufacturer
full-service (*adj*) offering broad range of services in one basic line of business
futures purchases or sales of commodities at speculative prices for future delivery or receipt
garage sale sale of used household and personal articles held at seller's home, usu. in yard or garage
general store usu. small store selling different kinds of goods
generic product lower-priced version of brand name product with plain label indicating kind of product only
glut large oversupply of goods
gouge (*vb*) grossly overcharge
gratis (*adj*) at no cost, free
gray market discount market that operates somewhere between legitimacy and the black market
handout *Informal.* something given at no cost
hard goods durable goods
hard sell high-pressure salesmanship
hawk (*vb*) sell goods in public, esp. by shouting advertisements
import product bought from another country; (*vb*) buy products made in other countries
impulse buying sudden purchase of goods without prior intent, usu. stimulated by display or advertising
installment purchase purchase made on credit and paid off in series of payments over time
in stock (*adj*) available for sale at the present time
interstate commerce trade among and between states, regulated by federal government
inventory all items of merchandise in stock at given time
invoice itemized list of goods or services to be paid for
IOU informal written memorandum of indebtedness
lading load of freight, shipment of goods
license legal right to use or sell another's patented or copyrighted material
liquidation disposal of all remaining merchandise at reduced prices
list price official retail price; nondiscounted price
loss leader popular item sold at a loss or negligible profit to attract customers to retail outlet
mail order technique of selling items and taking orders through the mail
mall large, usu. completely enclosed shopping complex comprised of many different shops and restaurants
markdown reduction in price to promote sales
market place where people gather to sell and trade goods; store or shop for sale of provisions; (*vb*) offer for sale

market research collection and analysis of information to determine goods and services preferred by certain groups
markup amount added to cost by retailer to set price for customer
merchandise consumer goods for sale
mom-and-pop (*adj*) designating small, family-owned business, usu. retail
nondurable goods items that will be consumed in a relatively short time, such as clothing or food
notions small, useful items sold in store, esp. for sewing
OEM outside equipment manufacturer; company that exploits or develops another company's product as part of its own
on time (*adj*) purchased on credit with payments to be made over fixed period of time
outlet store selling goods for specific manufacturer or distributor
packaging container or wrapping in which product is sold; design of such wrapping, often intended to attract customers
patron person who is customer or client, esp. regular one, of store or other establishment
penetration pricing pricing of new product at low level to lure customers away from established product
pitch salesperson's discourse intended to persuade customers to buy
planned obsolescence design of consumer goods for limited use, necessitating frequent replacement or repair
point-of-purchase (*adj*) relating to place where sales are made or purchases paid for
premium something offered free or at low price as inducement to buy something else
price discrimination selling of same product to two different buyers at different prices
price fixing setting of prices by government or among competing businesses contrary to free market dictates
price war business competitors' repeated lowering of prices
profit amount of sales revenues left for business after paying cost, overhead, taxes, and operating expenses
promotion something devised to advance a product or service in order to persuade consumers to buy or use it
protectionism policy of strict trade regulations to support domestic industry
quality control maintenance of standards in production by checking product at stages during manufacture
rebate discount made by refunding percentage of purchase price
recall removal of defective product from market for correction
receipt written acknowledgment that payment has been received
repossession taking back of commodity from buyer who has failed to make payments when due
retail sale of goods directly to consumers
rollback action that returns prices to earlier, lower level, as by government order
sales force employees engaged in selling
salesman person engaged in selling, esp. male; salesperson
sales tax tax levied by city or state on retail sales of merchandise
self-service practice of serving oneself without assistance of salesperson
seller's market market in which demand exceeds supply, with prices rising
service center authorized establishment for repair and purchase of replacement parts, esp. for cars and appliances
service mark trademark applied to service offered, designated SM
shopping center outdoor complex of stores, restaurants, and movie theaters usu. grouped around common parking lot
shrink wrap clear, flexible, plastic film that shrinks when exposed to heat, used to wrap and seal products
soft goods items lasting a relatively short time, esp. clothing
staple chief commodity of region; item regularly stocked due to constant demand
stock finished goods on hand or in storage and available for sale
sublicensing granting of licenses to other companies to exploit, develop, or market one's product
supermarket large, self-service retail food store, often part of a chain
surcharge additional amount added to price
surplus store retail outlet selling extra or leftover goods at discount prices
territory area in which traveling salesman solicits orders
test marketing offering new product for limited time in small area to assess national sales potential
tie-in sale at which two or more items, only one of which is in demand, must be bought together as a unit
trade commerce; exchange of goods for money
trademark symbol, design, or name used to distinguish product from its competitors, designated TM
trade show convention at which related companies in single industry show and compare new products and ideas
traffic exchange of goods
traveling salesman business representative soliciting orders in assigned territory
undersell (*vb*) set price for a product that is lower that one's competition
unit pricing standard measurement for pricing different brands of same product
Universal Product Code UPC; computer code of bars and numerals printed on merchandise to identify it and confirm price
UPC Universal Product Code
variety store retail outlet selling many different commodities, esp. small, nondurable goods
vendor one who sells
voucher written document showing expenditure or receipt of money
warehouse building where merchandise is stored before shipment to retailers

warranty guarantee on product for limited time after purchase
wholesale sale of goods in large quantity to retail businesses at cost substantially below retail price
will-call department in a store where merchandise is held for payment and pickup by customer
window shopping looking at merchandise without purchasing

Corporations and Business Practices

advance partial payment of amount due on signing of contract
amalgamation combining of corporations into a new business entity
annual report corporate management's financial report to shareholders at end of fiscal year
annual review supervisor's regular assessment of job performance of subordinates
articles of incorporation formal document establishing corporation, describing its business, directors, finances, and stock issued
assembly line manufacturing process in which each worker performs specialized task in assembling product that passes by on moving belt or track
bailout instance of government coming to assistance of failing business
bankroll (*vb*) finance, supply with money
bankruptcy legal insolvency; inability to pay debts; procedure to dissolve company and be released from certain debts
big business major corporations with political interests
board of directors group of top managers setting corporate policies and direction
bonus payment over and above salary given to employee, esp. executive, as incentive or reward
bottom line last line of financial statement, indicating net profit
budget schedule of expenses adjusted to estimated revenue for set period
business commercial, mercantile, or industrial enterprise conducted to make a profit
buyout outright purchase of business, esp. by management or employees with borrowed money
capital-intensive (*adj*) requiring large capital investment or expenditure relative to need for labor
capitalization total funds of corporation, including stocks, bonds, undivided profits, and surplus
cash cow *Informal.* business with dependable source of income
cash flow measure of liquidity equal to excess or deficiency of net income relative to cash expenses
ceiling upper limit set for spending
Chapter 11 bankruptcy code section that applies to a corporation going out of business which may require restructuring
charter legal form establishing corporation and defining its purpose
close (*vb*) officially conclude business transaction
closed corporation company whose stock is held by a small group, usu. persons also involved in management
commission fee paid to broker or agent for services in business transaction
company organization formed for doing business
concern company, business firm
concession entitlement to operate business granted by government or other business
conglomerate corporation composed of smaller corporations in diverse business fields
consideration something of value given or done in return for comparable action by another as part of contract
consolidation organization combining two or more companies, each of which retains partial autonomy
consortium business alliance of companies
contract legally binding agreement between parties
controlling interest ownership of enough stock in company to set policies and make decisions
corner monopoly ownership of commodity, stock, or security
corporate veil protection of corporate owners from personal liability
corporation business organization existing and treated as legal entity independent of its individual owners
cost-effective (*adj*) producing good results for amount invested; efficient in use of funds
cost overrun amount by which project exceeds estimated cost
cottage industry small or home-based business
dba doing business as; fictitious business name
diminishing returns additional investments resulting in smaller proportion of profits
dissolution dismantling of business, contract, or partnership
divestiture sale or dissolution of subsidiary business or investment
dividend portion of corporation profits distributed regularly to stockholders
endowment money placed in tax-exempt foundation by corporation
enterprise quality of risk-taking or initiative in business; company, venture, or firm
escalator clause contract provision requiring increases in payments based on economic fluctuations
Fortune 500 list of 500 largest American corporations published annually by *Fortune* magazine
foundation tax-exempt institution, funded by corporate profits, that contributes to charities, arts, and education as means of avoiding corporate tax and generating goodwill
franchise government permission for company to carry on particular business in certain place, often involving partial monopoly
golden parachute substantial compensation given to top executive as severance bonus when dismissed due to corporate merger or takeover
go public (*vb*) offer stock of privately owned company for sale to public
headhunting search by professional recruiters for executives to fill high-level positions
holding company corporation whose business is buying and selling stock in other companies

home office headquarters of business with branches
honorarium payment in lieu of professional fee, usu. token amount
horizontal merger merger involving competitive companies that perform or produce the same or similar functions or products
incentives financial or other benefits offered for labor or services
industry large-scale business activity; particular branch of manufacturing
institution established corporation, esp. one serving public needs
investment business expenditure made for eventual profit
license government permission to operate business
liquidation sale of business in which all assets are converted to cash
management organizational and administrative aspect and personnel of business
merger assimilation of one business or corporation into another
multinational corporation large company based in one country with interests, investments, and operations in others
nonprofit corporation business operating for reasons other than profit making, and paying no taxes
operating expenses ongoing, recurring costs of conducting business, not including costs of production
operations research systematic analysis, usu. mathematical, of problems in business operations
overhead total direct expenses in operating a business
Parkinson's law statement that work expands so as to fill the time available for its completion
partnership association of two or more individuals or business entities joined as part owners in business
pension fund fund created and maintained by corporation or government to provide benefits under pension plan, with assets usu. invested in securities
perk *Informal.* perquisite
perquisite nonmonetary benefit for employee, such as free trip or company car
personnel employees; department responsible for hiring new employees
Peter Principle statement that every employee in a hierarchy tends to rise to the level of his or her incompetence
petty cash cash fund on hand for small daily expenses
plant machinery, buildings, and grounds of factory or business
privately held corporation corporation not offering stock for sale to public
prospectus description of company, its property, and its operations, circulated to prospective investors
proxy fight contest between factions of stockholders for control of company, in which each group solicits signed proxy statements for votes needed to gain control
public corporation corporation whose stock is traded on stock exchange
public relations activities intended to create favorable public opinion about company or product
public-service corporation private corporation chartered to provide essential commodity or service to the public
quality control maintenance of production standards by checking product at stages during manufacturing process
retainer fee paid to lawyer or other professional adviser as advance on services
royalty payment for rights to property based on percentage of revenue generated by it
sole proprietorship unincorporated business with one owner
speculation engagement in transaction or venture involving risk in hopes of large gains
spin-off new company created by distribution to stockholders of stock of another company
staff regular, full-time, permanent employees
start-up company newly established company
start-up expenses costs involved in establishing a business
stock equipment, materials, and supplies of a business; shares of a company sold to public with value based on company assets and income
subcontract (*vb*) hire secondary company or individual to do part of contracted job
subsidiary business owned by parent company
sunrise industry industry with high growth potential, such as electronics industry
sunset industry industry, such as heavy manufacturing, with declining market due to social or technological changes
syndicate association of corporations formed to carry out costly financial project
syndication sale or licensing of commodity to network of similar businesses
takeover merger forced on one business by another
tender offer of money made to satisfy obligation
underwrite (*vb*) guarantee financial support for business
venture business enterprise, esp. one with high degree of risk but potential for large profits
venture capitalism financing of new businesses for eventual share in profits
vertical merger purchase by one company of a supplier or distributor
windfall profit unexpected return on investment
working capital portion of company's capital readily convertible into cash for paying expenses and wages

Labor

affirmative action government-regulated program ensuring that employers hire women and minorities
AFL-CIO American Federation of Labor and Congress of Industrial Organizations
agency shop work situation in which worker need not be union member but must pay union an amount equal to its dues

American Federation of Labor and Congress of Industrial Organizations AFL-CIO; umbrella organization for most American labor unions
arbitration negotiation between management and labor mediated and decided by neutral third party
base pay basic rate of pay before overtime, bonuses, or raises
benefits payments under annuity, pension plan, insurance, unemployment, or disability
blacklist roster of workers excluded or persecuted by management for pro-union views
blue-collar (*adj*) pertaining to factory or manual labor
bonus amount above regular salary given as reward or for motivation
casual labor temporary or part-time work, often unskilled
closed shop business prohibited from employing nonunion members, outlawed by right-to-work laws
codetermination mutual setting of policy by labor and management
collective bargaining negotiations between employer and union representatives, esp. over wages or benefits
common situs picketing picketing of entire construction site by union in dispute with only one subcontractor
company union workers in union in single company, not affiliated with group of unions, often under employer's control
compulsory arbitration negotiations requiring union and management to accept binding decision of outside mediator
contract labor-management agreement renegotiated regularly to determine wages, benefits, and working conditions
cost-of-living allowance guaranteed annual pay raise based on increase in cost of living
craft occupation requiring special training or skill
day job temporary or part-time position, esp. in field other than one's primary vocation
day shift regular hours of employment, usu. 8 or 9 A.M. to 5 or 6 P.M.
disability insurance guarantee of continued income for worker seriously or permanently disabled on the job
double time pay scale at twice the normal rate for work done on holidays, weekends, or after hours
earning power lifetime potential for earning wages, income, and profits
farm labor unskilled agricultural work
fringe benefit benefit in addition to wages, esp. health insurance, profit sharing, or paid vacation
general strike work stoppage by entire labor force of city or nation
giveback union agreement to relinquish benefits previously granted as part of new contract
graveyard shift hours of night employment, usu. midnight to 8 A.M.; lobster shift; night shift
guild union of people in same craft or trade
injunction court or executive order, usu. requiring strikers to return to work
labor work force; work performed by laborers
labor force total number of persons over age sixteen who hold or are looking for jobs
labor union organization of workers for protection, representation, and benefits in dealings with employers
layoff dismissal of workers, esp. temporarily
lobster shift graveyard shift
lockout shutdown of business by management to pressure workers and union into agreement
malingering pretending to be ill to avoid work
manual labor unskilled, physical work
mechanization use of machines in combination with semiskilled workers to replace unskilled workers
mediation arbitration of union-management dispute by neutral third party
minimum wage legally fixed lowest hourly rate payable to certain types of workers
moonlighting working at a second job, often at night
National Labor Relations Board NLRB; federal agency regulating and investigating unfair labor practices
night shift graveyard shift
NLRB National Labor Relations Board
occupational hazard danger inherent in particular job, esp. unsafe working conditions
on spec (*adj*) performed or made without guarantee of payment for work or service
overtime payments at higher than normal rate for extra hours worked during day or week
paycheck regular payment of wages or salary
payday day on which paycheck is received
pay period regular interval between paydays
payroll roster of employees and record of their wages
pension regular payments made to employee upon retirement
pension plan systematic plan by which corporation or government makes regular payments to retired or disabled employees, sometimes partially funded by employee contributions
picket (*vb*) stand or march with signs in front of workplace as display of dissatisfaction during strike; (*n*) striking worker who does this
piecework work done and paid for by unit produced instead of at hourly rate
pink slip notice of dismissal from one's job
preferential shop shop in which management hires only union members as long as they are available
premium additional wages paid for overtime or dangerous work
profit sharing division of portion of company profits among employees
rank and file all regular union members
retirement permanent termination of employment; pension benefits paid to former employee
right-to-work law state law allowing workers to work whether or not they join a union and outlawing a closed shop

salary money earned for regular work, paid periodically
scab strikebreaker who works for company being struck
seasonal unemployment annual, temporary loss of jobs due to seasonal conditions, esp. absence of farm work in winter
semiskilled labor usu. manual work requiring some training
seniority status obtained from length of time worker has been on job, usu. rewarded with higher pay and other benefits
severance pay payment made to employee at time of termination of employment
sit-down strike strike in which workers remain idle in workplace until settlement is reached
skilled labor work, such as craft or trade, that requires training
slowdown intentional reduction in output by workers to force employer concessions without a strike
specialty skill or specific job performed by worker
split shift workday divided into two periods, with intervening break longer than meal or rest period
straight time standard work hours without overtime
strike organized and deliberate work stoppage used to attain benefits, esp. changes in working conditions or wages
strikebreaker worker hired to replace striking employee
sweatshop exploitative workplace characterized by long hours, low pay, and substandard conditions, esp. employing immigrants
sweetheart agreement agreement between employer and union on terms favorable to employer, often without approval of union members
swing shift work period between day and graveyard shifts, usu. 3 or 4 P.M. to midnight
sympathy strike work stoppage by laborers in support of striking workers elsewhere
syndicalism worker ownership and management of industries achieved by revolutionary movement and general strike
Taft-Hartley Act federal law protecting public welfare during labor disputes by allowing president power of injunction to halt certain strikes
take-home pay gross wages less deductions for taxes, insurance, union dues, retirement, or savings
time and a half pay scale at one and half times normal rate, for hours worked beyond normal workday; overtime
trade union organization of workers within craft, trade, or industry
turnover number of employees leaving jobs in given time period
underemployed overqualified or part-time workers
unemployable (*adj*) designating person unable to find work because of age, lack of skills, or disability
unemployment lack of work; number or percent of persons not holding jobs
unemployment compensation regular payments, usu. from state funds into which employers have paid, to qualified unemployed persons
unfair labor practices union and employer activities banned by legislation to promote peaceful industrial relations
union workers' mutual benefit and protection organization
union scale minimum wage for particular category of worker as fixed by union contract
union shop business employing union members and requiring nonmembers to join within stated time, often three months
unskilled labor manual or factory work requiring little or no training
vocation trade, profession, or occupation, esp. one for which one feels a calling
wage payment for labor on hourly or piecework basis
walkout spontaneous strike
white-collar (*adj*) pertaining to office, sales, or professional work, usu. involving people, information, and ideas
wildcat strike work stoppage not authorized by labor union
workers' compensation protection provided by state governments for workers injured on job
work stoppage cessation of work by employees to protest working conditions; strike
yellow-dog contract illegal requirement that worker not join union

Employers, Employees, and Business People

administrator, agent, apprentice, arbitrator, artisan, assistant, associate, auctioneer
backer, bagman, baron, blue-collar worker, boss, breadwinner, broker, bureaucrat, businessman, businessperson, businesswoman
CAO, capitalist, captain of industry, CEO, CFO, chairman of the board, chief, chief administrative officer, chief executive officer, chief financial officer, clerk, common laborer, comprador, comptroller, controller, counsel, craftsman
dealer, director, distributor, domestic
employee, employer, entrepreneur, executive, exporter
fat cat, field rep, financier, foreman, freelancer, fund-raiser
hand, headhunter, help, high roller, hired help, hireling
importer, industrialist, intrapreneur
Jaycee, jobber, journeyman
laborer, lackey
magnate, management, manager, mediator, mercenary, merchant, middleman, middle management, migrant worker, mogul, moneychanger, monger, movers and shakers
nabob
officer, office worker, official, operator,

organization man, overseer, owner
part-time worker, patron, paymaster, peddler, player, plutocrat, president, professional, profiteer, prole, proletarian, proprietor
rainmaker, rep, representative, retailer, retainer, robber baron
salesman, salesperson, sales rep, sales representative, saleswoman, secretary, self-employed, servant, service worker, shopkeeper, silent partner, slave, small businessman, sponsor, staff, subordinate, superintendent, superior, supervisor
taskmaster, team player, temp, trader, tradesman, traveling salesman, treasurer, tycoon
underling, unskilled laborer
vassal, vendor, venture capitalist
wage earner, wage slave, white-collar worker, wholesaler, wildcatter, workaholic, worker, working girl, workingman, working mother, working stiff, workingwoman

FINANCE

Banking and Financial Services

account record of all financial transactions for specific person or entity
accrued interest interest owed but not yet paid
adjustable rate interest rate, esp. on mortgage, that varies with predetermined factors
amortization paying off of debt in installments over time, with each payment covering current interest and part of principal
annuity investment plan providing guaranteed retirement income
appraisal estimate of property's true value, esp. by expert
arrears overdue debts
ATM automated-teller machine
automated-teller machine ATM; computerized electronic device for depositing and withdrawing funds from account; cash machine
balance amount standing as credit in checking or savings account
balance due amount standing as debit on charge account
balloon payment large final loan payment after many smaller payments
bank institution receiving money on deposit, lending money on interest, and simplifying fund exchanges by use of checks and notes
bankbook small booklet in which account transactions are recorded
bank card personalized, magnetically imprinted plastic card used in combination with secret code for ATM transactions
bank check check drawn by bank on itself and signed by authorized bank officer; cashier's check
bank draft check drawn by bank against funds deposited to its account in another bank
banking business and practice of operating a bank
bank note paper note issued by bank for use as money; currency
bearer holder of note or other financial instrument
blind trust trust in which public official, to avoid conflict of interest, places assets under control of independent trustee who manages them without owner's oversight
borrow (*vb*) take out a loan with understanding that it will be repaid in specified time, usu. with interest
bounced check check returned by bank due to insufficient funds
building and loan association savings and loan association
bursar treasurer, esp. of college
call loan loan repayable on demand
call money funds loaned by bank to stockbrokers that may be demanded at any time
capital money, assets, and property used as means of production; owner's equity in business plus creditors' advances
capital funds total capital accounts of bank, including par value of capital stock, surpluses, undivided profits, and capital reserves
cashier's check bank check
cash machine automated-teller machine
CD certificate of deposit
central bank banker's bank, such as Federal Reserve
certificate of deposit CD; receipt for funds deposited, usu. for specified amount of time at fixed interest rate
certified check check with bank guarantee that sufficient funds are on deposit to cover it, usu. indicated by special stamp
charge purchase made on credit to be paid in cash over specified time, often with interest
charge account account, usu. with retail store, that allows customer to buy merchandise on credit
check written order for bank to pay funds held for depositor; also, *esp. Brit.*, cheque
checkbook book containing detachable forms for writing checks on bank account
checking account account at bank against which checks may be drawn
Christmas club savings account from which funds are withdrawn at Christmas to pay for shopping

clearinghouse central bank in which representatives of local banks meet daily to exchange checks and settle balances
collateral assets pledged by borrower to guarantee repayment of loan
co-maker person signing another's note to strengthen credit
commercial bank bank primarily involved in taking demand deposits for checking accounts and offering short-term loans
commercial paper short-term negotiable debt instrument arising out of corporate commercial transactions
compound interest interest calculated on total of principal plus accrued interest
correspondent bank bank that carries deposit balance for bank in another locality and exchanges services with that bank
cosigner person signing loan contract and promising to repay loan if borrower defaults
counter check check available at counter for use of depositors in making withdrawals
countersign (*vb*) sign another person's document in order to verify authenticity
courtesy card personalized card entitling bearer to special banking privileges
credit arrangement for future payment, usu. with interest, on goods or money obtained immediately; funds available to borrower
credit bureau agency providing information to lenders on credit rating of individuals or companies
credit card plastic card certifying bearer's entitlement to charge purchases to credit account
credit line line of credit
creditor person or business to whom amount is owed
credit rating measure of past credit reliability, used to gauge degree of risk involved in loan or extension of credit to individual or business
credit union cooperative association for pooling savings of members or employees and making loans to them at low interest
debt amount owed to lender by borrower
debt service total interest on loan over full term of payments
default failure to make timely loan payments
deferred payment money withheld until certain date
delinquency failure to meet agreed-upon time for debt repayment
demand deposit bank deposit that may be withdrawn without notice
deposit money stored in bank or financial institution; partial payment for goods, services, or property
depreciation gradual devaluation or drop in price
deregulation elimination of government regulatory controls on deposits and loans, allowing freer banking activities
discount interest paid at beginning of loan period, deducted from principal in advance
discount rate interest charged by Federal Reserve Bank on loans to member banks
down payment initial payment required on credit purchase
dunning harassment of debtor for payment
early withdrawal withdrawal of funds from timed deposit before maturity, usu. involving interest forfeiture
earnest money funds given as partial payment and binding pledge in agreement
EFT electronic funds transfer
electronic funds transfer EFT; banking transaction via telecommunications network
embezzlement illegal appropriation of property or funds entrusted to one's care
endorsement signature on back of item, usu. check, authorizing payment or transferring rights to someone else
equity money invested in property or business entity with mortgages, debts, and liens deducted
escrow written agreement deposited with third party, usu. bank, as custodian, to be delivered upon fulfillment of some condition
extortion obtaining money illegally, esp. by misuse of authority
FDIC Federal Deposit Insurance Corporation
Federal Deposit Insurance Corporation FDIC; government agency guaranteeing funds placed in banks
Federal Reserve System federal banking system that regulates flow of money and acts as central clearinghouse for banks
fiduciary trustee administering estate, executing will, or serving as guardian of minor's assets
finance dealings concerning money in the business world, including circulation of currency, granting of credit, banking, and investment
finance charge monthly interest on revolving credit account
financial services services provided by banking and investment banking institutions, savings and loan associations, mortgage companies, and brokerage houses
financial statement report summarizing impact of business transactions during fiscal period
financier person trained and engaged in large-scale financial operations
float uncollected amount of check cashed by one bank on another bank's account; brief interim before collection when bank on which check is drawn has use of depositor's money for free
floating debt short-term debt arising from current operations and having no specific time of repayment
foreclose (*vb*) deprive mortgagor of right to redeem property mortgaged for failure to fulfill conditions
frozen assets funds made unavailable to their owner
guaranty written promise to creditor by guarantor to be liable for debt should principal debtor fail in his or her obligations
high finance practices and institutions involved in banking and investment
honor (*vb*) accept and pay an obligation when called for
IMF International Monetary Fund
insolvency lack of resources to pay one's debts

installment loan note repaid in equal periodic payments, each including interest and part of principal
instrument formal legal document, such as deed, bond, note, or draft
insufficient funds deposits that are inadequate to cover check or withdrawal
interest fee charged for use of capital or extension of credit; sum paid as percentage of money on deposit
internal revenue taxes collected on wages and business profits by government
international banking large-scale financial operations, esp. involving debt and credit to nations
International Monetary Fund IMF; international agency established to promote trade and economic cooperation and to stabilize balance of payments by making loans to member nations
investment outlay of money for income or profit
investment banking activities of financial institutions whose primary business is issuing and trading securities of other companies
IOU informal promissory note; written acknowledgment of indebtedness
kiting writing check against insufficient funds or moving funds from bank to bank to create temporarily expanded credit
laundering concealing source of large sums of money, usu. by moving it through several accounts
layaway plan method of making installment purchase on revolving credit account
letter of credit document from one bank to correspondent bank requesting that letter bearer be given credit
line of credit credit limit set by lending institution; credit line
liquidity ease with which asset can be converted to cash
loan amount of money borrowed or lent on interest
loan officer bank employee responsible for interviewing loan applicants and approving and setting terms of loans
loan shark *Informal.* lender charging excessive interest
M-1 money held by public for use in current spending, including coins, paper currency, demand deposits, and traveler's checks
M-2 M-1 plus savings and time deposits, money market funds, overnight repurchases, and Eurodollars
M-3 M-2 plus large time deposits, institutional money market funds, and term repurchases
magnetic ink character recognition number MICR number; electronically coded number printed at bottom of check
maker person who signs and executes note or promise to pay
maturity due date of mortgage, note, draft, acceptance, or bond
MICR number magnetic ink character recognition number
moneychanger person who exchanges national currencies at established rates
money market high-interest, unregulated, nonbanking investment entity that originated in 1970's
money market mutual fund entity that pools assets of investors and puts funds into short-term, high-interest bank CDs, treasury bills, and commercial paper
money order order for payment or draft sold by bank for fee
mortgage method of pledging property as guaranty of payment of debt with interest
national bank federally chartered bank
near money assets with high degree of liquidity, such as savings deposits
negotiable instrument note or other instrument legally transferable to another by proper endorsement
negotiable order of withdrawal account NOW account; checking account in which unused money earns interest
note promissory note issued to creditor (note payable) or accepted from customer owing money (note receivable)
noteholder one to whom loan payments and interest are due
NOW account negotiable order of withdrawal account
numbered account bank account identified by number only, to conceal identity of depositor, esp. in Swiss bank
obligation debt security, such as mortgage or corporate bond
on-demand (*adj*) pertaining to note payable immediately upon receipt
outstanding check check that has been written but not yet paid by bank on which it was drawn
overdraft bank withdrawal in excess of funds available
overdraw (*vb*) draw on an account in excess of available funds
passbook bankbook recording deposits, withdrawals, interest, and service charges on account
pawnbroker person licensed to lend money at specified rates on items of personal property deposited as collateral
PIN personal identification number; secret code used to access ATM
points small percentage of loan, esp. mortgage, prepaid as origination fee and deemed interest
postdated check check dated in future and not payable until that date
premium amount paid for loan in addition to interest
prepayment penalty additional fee charged for paying off loan before it is due
prime rate rate of interest charged by banks on loans to major borrowers, esp. businesses
principal face amount of loan, excluding interest
promissory note written contract to pay specified amount at set future date
recoup (*vb*) recover original investment
redlining discriminatory refusal or limitation of loans based on geography, esp. within inner-city neighborhoods

regulation control of U.S. banking operations by government
reimburse (*vb*) pay back, esp. for money already spent
remit (*vb*) make payment
remittance money paid, esp. sent as payment
repossession taking back of article by creditor when debtor fails to make payments
repurchase agreement contract between bank and investor in which bank agrees to buy back security it has sold to investor at fixed price on designated date
reserve bank bank holding money reserves of other banks
return on capital profit or yield achieved on investments
revolving credit charge account in which portion of total is due each month and interest is added monthly
safe-deposit box rented space in bank vaults to which only renter has access, used for secure storage of valuable property
S and L savings and loan association
savings assets set aside for future use
savings account interest-bearing bank account
savings and loan association S and L; institution owned by depositors and making long-term real estate and other loans; building and loan association
savings bank institution specializing in small, timed deposits
secondary reserves bank assets, such as government securities or commercial paper, that can quickly be converted into cash
secured loan cash loan based on collateral that ensures repayment of borrowed money
security item standing as means of assuring payment of debt; person bound to pay debt if another fails
service charge fee charged by bank on depositor's account statements for services rendered, usu. in connection with checking account
share draft interest-bearing checking account in a credit union
short-term loan loan with maturity date usu. under one year
simple interest interest computed by multiplying principal by rate and by number of years
smart card plastic credit card with memory chip for financial transactions
stale check check invalidated by lapse of time between writing and cashing
state bank bank chartered by nation or state, regulated by its laws
statement regular, usu. monthly, description of all transactions, deposits, and running balance in account
stop payment request by depositor that his or her bank refuse payment of check written on account
surety person liable for another's debts
surety company institution that insures against various types of losses and executes bonds
survivorship account account in name of two persons that belongs to either survivor on death of other
Swiss account numbered account, esp. in Swiss bank
teller bank clerk who pays out and receives money directly from public
term length of time over which promissory note must be paid
terms conditions of promissory note, obligation, or contract
thrifts thrift institutions, savings and loan banks, or credit unions
till place for keeping cash; ready cash
time deposit savings account deposit that may not be withdrawn without penalty until specified time
transit number number printed on check identifying bank, its location, and proper routing
traveler's check replaceable check sold by banks, to be countersigned and used as money by those traveling away from home bank
treasurer person in charge of funds or finances of business or institution
trust obligation on person (trustee) to hold and use property according to terms of special grant, esp. for benefit of others
trust company bank that handles trusts and all banking operations except issuance of notes
trustee person legally empowered to administer on behalf of beneficiary
trust fund trust account, esp. held for use by children after depositor's death
unsecured (*adj*) not guaranteed by collateral
usury charging of excessive interest on loans
variable-rate mortgage mortgage with adjustable rate, often linked to prime rate
venture capital funds used for investment in high-risk enterprises, usu. for start-up companies
void (*vb*) invalidate check, as by writing ""void" across it
voucher written statement attesting to expenditure or receipt of money and accuracy of account
withdrawal removal of funds from account
World Bank U.N. agency established to make loans to underdeveloped member nations
yield percentage of money returned on investment

Securities

acquisition purchase of one company by another, including gaining control of its stock
arbitrage selling of assets in one market after purchase in another to profit by price differential; purchase and sale of large block of securities in company in expectation of profit, esp. when engaged in discussions of merger or takeover
baby bond bond with value of less than $1,000
bearish (*adj*) pessimistic about security prices; causing or describing a fall in stock prices
bear market market in which stocks are declining
bid-and-asked price highest price offered and lowest price accepted for security at specific time
bid price amount initially offered for block of stock
block very large number of shares in one company sold as unit to one buyer

blue chip high-quality, generally nonspeculative stock or security
blue-sky law law designed to prevent sale and promotion of fraudulent securities
bond security certificate of loan, with principal to be repaid by issuing body, usu. government or corporation, at specified maturity date, with interest usu. paid at intervals
bond issue offering of bonds for sale with set interest rates and maturity dates
book value theoretical value of security based on company balance sheet
broker one who buys and sells stocks as agent for others, receiving a commission for this service
brokerage business that buys and sells stocks as agent for others
bullish (*adj*) optimistic about security prices; causing or expecting a rise in stock prices
bull market upward trend indicating stock market vigor
buy back purchase by corporate management of stock in its own company to reduce number of outstanding shares
buy-out purchase and retirement of outstanding securities of a company, which is thus taken private
call option to buy given quantity of stock at stated price within a specified time, purchased in anticipation of increase in price
capital gain profit on sale of a security: sales price less commissions less cost or basis
capital stock total value of corporate capital divided into negotiable shares of stock
closely held describing securities not available for trading
commission broker's fee on stock sale or purchase
commodities exchange place where trading in contracts on staple products is conducted
common stock share of ownership in company, providing eligibility for dividends and vote on company decisions
correction brief movement of market in opposite direction from general trend, esp. to offset sharp advance or decline
coupon detachable printed statement specifying interest due on bond at given time
crash abrupt, sharp decrease in asset prices, esp. stocks
cross trade simultaneous, offsetting buy and sell orders taken by single broker without recording trade, often depriving investor of chance to trade at more favorable rate
curb market dealing in securities not listed on exchange
debenture unsecured bond
discount difference between issuing price and selling price of security
discretionary account account that empowers broker to make transactions on own discretion, without consulting client
diversify (*vb*) place investments in several different companies and forms to guard against collapse of one
dividend regular return on investment paid to stockholders from business profits
Dow Jones Average *Trademark.* index of relative price of securities based on daily price of selected industrial, transportation, and utility stocks traded on New York Stock Exchange
employee stock ownership plan ESOP; system by which employees acquire stock in company for which they work and receive distribution at retirement
ESOP employee stock ownership plan
exchange place where trading of securities or commodities is conducted by brokers; commodities exchange; mercantile exchange; stock exchange
ex dividend recently declared dividend that is not paid to recent purchaser of security
Fannie Mae FNMA; any of various publicly traded securities backed by a pool of mortgages held by federal agency
financial district area where banks, investment houses, brokerages, and exchange are located, esp. Wall Street in New York City
float (*vb*) place securities, esp. bond issue, on market; (*n*) amount of common stock not closely held and available for trading
floor area of stock exchange occupied by brokers and traders
FNMA Federal National Mortgage Association; Fannie Mae
futures contracts to buy specific commodity at set price, to be delivered at future date
futures exchange exchange that sells futures contracts on indexes for future value
gilt-edged (*adj*) designating highest quality securities and bonds
Ginnie Mae GNMA; bond or certificate issued by federal agency based on mortgages purchased from lenders
GNMA Government National Mortgage Association; Ginnie Mae
go private (*vb*) take company private by buying back all public-issue securities
go public (*vb*) offer stock of privately owned company on market
government bond bond issued by municipal, state, or federal government as means of obtaining capital
greenmail practice of purchasing large block of company's stock at special rate, either to force rise in stock prices or as offer to buy back stock at premium, often to thwart possible takeover
growth stock common stock in company with significant sales and earnings, having some degree of instability but opportunity for substantial increase in price
high yield strong return on investment, usu. anything over ten percent
high-yield security security that pays interest at significantly higher rate than government or corporate bonds, often carrying lower credit rating
hostile takeover assumption of control of company against wishes of management by appealing directly to shareholders, often for purpose of reselling stock at significant gain

income fund mutual fund providing current income
income stock stock in relatively stable company that produces regular return on investment with small chance of rapid price increase
indenture document detailing terms of bond issue
index arbitrage form of program trading based on manipulation of fleeting differentials between share price and futures price contracts
industrials stocks of industrial corporations, esp. those listed on New York Stock Exchange
insider information information that is not publicly available, used to obtain large, often illegal, profits on stock transactions
institutional trading buying and selling of large blocks of securities by banks, pension and mutual funds, and other financial intermediaries
investment outlay of money for income or profit
issue circulation or offering of securities for sale
junk bond high-yield, speculative bond often issued by lower credit-rated company, sometimes to finance corporate takeover
LBO leveraged buyout
leverage use of credit in business activity, esp. to enhance speculative capacity; borrowed capital used in business
leveraged buyout LBO; change of company ownership through purchase of large block of stock financed by debt to be paid off out of future revenue
listed (*adj*) designating a security traded on one of the exchanges
margin cash or collateral required to be deposited with broker to protect broker and allow client to purchase securities on credit
margin account brokerage account in which trading on margin can occur
market institution of and place where trading of securities occurs; stock market
market index number showing percentage variation from arbitrary standard, used to measure rise and fall of market
market price prevailing price for security or commodity in given market
mercantile exchange place where trading in securities occurs, as distinguished from commodities exchange
merger combining of two or more companies by issuing stock of controlling corporation to replace most of stock of other companies
mergers and acquisitions department of investment banking firm or brokerage handling corporate mergers and acquisitions
municipal bond bond sold by local or state government
mutual fund investment company owned by shareholders and using funds to purchase stocks and bonds of other corporations
NASDAQ National Association of Securities Dealers Automated Quotations; system for quoting and trading over-the-counter securities
New York Stock Exchange primary security trading exchange, located on Wall Street in New York City
odd lot quantity of stock purchased in units other than 10 or 100 shares
offering security made available for purchase at specific price for set period of time
option right to buy or sell security at fixed price within specified time
OTC (*adj*) over-the-counter
outstanding (*adj*) of securities, publicly issued and in circulation
over-the-counter (*adj*) OTC; designating stocks not listed on any exchange, sold directly to buyers
panic sudden, widespread fear of financial collapse that results in attempts to sell off securities at any price
par issue security offered at face value
par value face value of share of stock or bond
penny stock highly speculative common stock, usu. selling for less than one dollar per share
PIK security paid-in-kind security; usu. high-yield security on which interest accrues as additional securities, not as interest, dividends, or cash
point unit of variation in security market prices
portfolio investor's sum total of stocks, bonds, and securities
preferred stock share of ownership in business that provides first claim on assets after creditors, priority in receipt of dividends, but not necessarily a voice in company management
premium amount over par value for which preferred stock is sold
price-earnings ratio current price of a share of common stock divided by earnings per share over one-year period
proceeds earnings from security sale less commissions
profit taking selling of securities to take advantage of temporarily inflated price
program trading large, computerized security transactions, usu. made by institutional investors, that occur automatically at predetermined prices
public issue offer of securities for sale to public on exchange
publicly traded designating stock available for sale on exchange or over-the-counter
put option to sell given quantity of securities at specific price and within specified time, purchased in anticipation of decline in price
quotation current price of stock or commodity; record of opening and closing prices and number of shares traded on particular day
raider financier who uses greenmail, leveraged buyout, and arbitrage in attempt to purchase publicly owned entity against the wishes of its management
rally period of rising stock market prices
risk arbitrage investment in securities or commodities subject to takeover or other speculation
Sallie Mae SLMA; student loans issued by federal agency based on mortgages purchased from lenders
SEC Securities and Exchange Commission
securities government-regulated class of investments, including bonds, notes, stock certificates, and mortgages

Securities and Exchange Commission SEC; federal agency that regulates stock and commodity market transactions and conduct of market participants
sell-off decline in prices of certain securities due to pressure to sell
sell short (*vb*) sell securities that seller does not yet own but expects to cover later at lower price
Series E bond widely held bond issue of U.S. Treasury
Series H bond widely held bond issue of U.S. Treasury
shakeout rapid decrease in value of certain securities, often forcing speculators to sell holdings
share single unit of stock or other security
shareholder owner of share or shares in company
SLMA Student Loan Marketing Association; Sallie Mae
slump general decrease in stock prices over period of time
soft market weak, declining market
speculation buying or selling of securities at high risk in anticipation of rise or fall in price
speculator one who speculates in securities
split dividing of securities by substituting multiple of original shares with equal par value but proportionately lower value per share
spot market market in which cash is exchanged for actual delivery of commodities
stock unit of ownership of corporation; outstanding capital of a company
stock bonus payment in company stock in addition to wages, esp. to corporate executive
stockbroker agent buying and selling shares of ownership in corporations for clients who pay sales commission
stock certificate written evidence of ownership of shares of stock
stock exchange market for trading in stocks; association of brokers who meet daily to buy and sell securities; stock market
stockholder owner of share or shares in capital of corporation
stockjobbing sales and promotion of often worthless securities
stock market market for stocks throughout a nation; stock exchange
stock option put or call
stocks and bonds securities in general
straddle option in which a put and a call are combined at same market price for same set period
street name broker's as opposed to owner's name on security, usu. for convenience
subscription agreement to pay certain amount for fixed number of securities
surety company company that insures against various types of losses and executes bonds
takeover assumption of management or ownership of company through acquisition of its stock
tax-exempt bond government obligation on which interest is exempt from federal and/or state income tax
T-bill U.S. Treasury bill or note
technical correction brief movement of market counter to general trend due to mechanics of pricing
tender offer offer at stated price for stock purchase from shareholders in takeover, often with promise of better management
ticker computer recording and displaying current stock prices
trader person whose business is buying and selling of commodities or securities
trading exchange, purchase, and sale of stocks and bonds
trading pit area of intense activity where trading occurs at exchange
Treasury bill short-term, interest-bearing obligation of U.S. Treasury, maturing in one year or less; T-bill
Treasury bond any of various series of bonds issued by U.S. Treasury, maturing over long periods of time
Treasury note interest-bearing obligation of U.S. Treasury, maturing in one to ten years
triple witching hour last hour of trading on any of four Fridays each year when options and futures expire, regarded as highly volatile time
underwrite (*vb*) agree to buy or guarantee purchase of securities issue on given date at fixed price
utilities stocks issued by corporations that provide power, water, or telephone services, forming a separate market index
voting stock shares of stock that give owner right to vote on certain corporate decisions
Wall Street street at center of New York City financial district serving as location of New York Stock Exchange; U.S. financial interests and business in general
war bond government bond issued to obtain revenue to support war effort
warrant call option with much longer maturity period than option, usu. up to two years or more
wash sale sale of stock at a loss and repurchase within thirty days for tax purposes; simultaneous purchase and sale of same stock or commodity to give impression of activity
watered stock stock illegally issued at above face value without corresponding increase in corporate assets
yield ratio of annual dividends or earnings per share to market price
zero-coupon bond bond sold at discount from face value and paying no regular interest, which is paid in full at time of maturity

Taxation, Types of Taxes

ad valorem tax tax applied to value of what is being taxed, esp. imports
alcohol tax tax on sale of alcoholic beverages
amusement tax tax on movies, plays, and other performances, included in admission price
capital gains tax tax on disposition of securities, business assets, or real property
customs duty tax on goods imported from another country

death tax inheritance or estate tax
direct tax tax levied directly on person by whom it is to be paid, as income or estate tax
duty tax on imported, exported, or manufactured goods
estate tax tax on assets of deceased person
estimated tax income tax paid quarterly by persons not subject to withholding, esp. self-employed people
excise tax tax on the manufacture, use, or sale of certain goods, esp. alcohol, tobacco, or firearms
federal tax tax levied by national government
franchise tax tax levied on corporations for right to do business in state or locality
gas tax tax on sale of gasoline as fuel
gift tax tax on very large gifts, paid by giver
graduated tax income tax with rates increasing at higher levels of income
hidden tax tax paid by manufacturer, supplier, or seller and passed on to consumer in market price; indirect tax
income tax federal, state, and local government tax on individual and business earnings, providing most of government revenues
indirect tax hidden tax
inheritance tax state tax on assets of deceased person, usu. paid by beneficiary
levy imposition and collection of tax; amount of tax
local tax tax levied by city or county government
luxury tax excise tax on certain luxury items, such as boats
municipal tax tax levied by city government
personal property tax tax paid on movable items such as automobiles, furniture, or machinery used in business
poll tax tax sometimes levied for right to vote; capitation tax
progressive tax variable income tax rate that increases as amount to be taxed increases
property tax tax paid by owner of real property based on assessed value; real estate tax
proportional tax income tax that takes same percentage of income at all income levels
protective tariff tax on imports, intended to give domestic producers advantage in competitive pricing
real estate tax property tax
regressive tax tax rates that tax lower incomes at higher rates than higher incomes; tax rates equal at all levels of income, effectively taxing lower incomes more heavily
revenue stamp government stamp indicating payment of tax on commodity such as alcohol or tobacco
revenue tax tax usu. imposed on alcohol or tobacco
sales tax tax levied by city, county, or state on retail sales of merchandise
school tax local tax, usu. on property, with revenues used for support of schools
self-employment tax Social Security tax paid as percent of net income by usu. self-employed persons not subject to FICA withholding by employers
severance tax tax on lump-sum distribution at termination of employment
sin tax *Informal.* tax on alcohol, tobacco, gambling, or other activities considered to be neither luxuries nor necessities
Social Security tax tax withheld from wages by FICA or paid as self-employment tax by sole proprietors
state tax tax levied by state government
surtax extra tax or charge; tax levied on income exceeding specified amount
tariff schedule of taxes on imports
tax compulsory federal, state, or local charge levied on income, imports, or retail purchases and used to finance government expenditures
taxation act of taxing; revenues derived from tax
toll tax or fee paid for privilege such as crossing bridge or driving on highway
unemployment tax amount paid by employer, and sometimes by employee, to be used as unemployment compensation to workers who lose their jobs
value-added tax sales tax on producer based on value of contribution to final product
windfall profits tax federal excise tax on profits from domestically produced crude oil
withholding tax tax deducted by employer from wages as income and Social Security tax

Income Tax

ability to pay basis of principle that highest tax burden should fall on those with greatest ability to pay
accelerated cost recovery system ACRS; method of calculating depreciation, giving larger deductions in earlier years and smaller ones in later years
ACRS accelerated cost recovery system
adjusted gross income AGI; total taxable income before deductions and exemptions but after certain adjustments
adjustments reductions to gross income in determining AGI
AGI adjusted gross income
amended return corrected version of return previously filed based on new or corrected information
amortization method of deducting intangible expenses by prorating them over fixed period, similar to depreciation
assessment amount of tax liability as determined by taxing authority
at-risk loss net loss on business for which taxpayer is ultimately liable
audit examination of books and records by taxing authority to determine validity of return
backup withholding federal tax withheld at source on nonwage income such as interest, dividends, or pensions
capital gain profit on sale of business assets, securities, real property, personal property, or intangible property
capitalization transferring cost of certain assets to balance sheet rather than taking full expense in year of purchase

capital loss loss on sale of business assets, securities, real property, personal property, or intangible property
carryback application of tax benefit or credit to previous year's tax return
carryforward application of unused tax benefit, credit, or capital loss to following year's tax return; carryover
carryover carryforward
casualty loss loss not reimbursed by insurance due to act of God or criminal act, partially accepted as an itemized deduction
charitable contribution itemized deduction allowed for cash or goods donated to nonprofit organization
contract labor business expense for payments to individuals subcontracting on job but not regular employees of taxpayer
corporation business entity that is organized under incorporation laws of one state and usu. pays taxes on net profits
cost of goods sold initial amount, either cost of merchandise and warehousing or direct labor and materials, by which gross income is reduced in determining gross profit before expenses
credit any of various amounts by which tax liability is reduced
decedent for tax purposes, a person who died in previous tax year
declare (*vb*) report received income on return
declining balance depreciation depreciation figured as percent of remaining undepreciated basis, which declines each year
deductible (*adj*) designating an amount or type of expense that may be used to reduce adjusted gross income before calculating tax
deduction standardized or itemized amount by which adjusted gross income is reduced in determining taxable income
dependent person half of whose support is paid by taxpayer, who claims an exemption for this person
depletion depreciation of certain intangible assets, esp. oil and natural gas
depreciation allowance made for decrease in value of capital assets over time; various means of prorating the cost of such assets as an expense over fixed number of years
dividend annual taxable payment to shareholders on earnings of securities
earned income credit amount added to withholding and estimated payments in determining overpayment or tax due, for low-income persons with dependents
EID employer identification number
employee business expense unreimbursed expenses incurred in course of work by salaried employee, an itemized deduction; such expenses reimbursed in W-2 as an adjustment
employer identification number EID; government-issued number that identifies corporation, partnership, trust, or individual who employs others
estimated tax quarterly payment of income tax in lieu of withholding, made esp. by self-employed persons
exemption set amount allowed as deduction from income or credit on taxes for taxpayer, spouse, dependents, and those over sixty-five or blind
expense any of various costs associated with income production or a business, deductible from income
extension application for or permission granted to file return after due date
Federal Insurance Contributions Act FICA; legislation under which taxes are levied for support of Social Security
FICA Federal Insurance Contributions Act
fiduciary return tax return filed by trustee of an estate or trust
filing act of filling out and submitting tax return to taxing authority
foreign earned income exclusion amount of foreign earned income not liable to U.S. tax but subject to foreign tax
foreign tax credit reduction of U.S. tax liability based on taxes paid to foreign country on income from that country
gain profit on sale or exchange of asset
garnishment deduction of person's unpaid taxes or other debts directly from paycheck or bank account by order of court
gross income total income received before deductions
head of household unmarried person who pays over half the cost of maintaining home for child or other dependent
holding period period of time between acquisition and disposition of capital asset, used to determine whether asset is short or long term
income various forms of taxable and nontaxable revenue received by taxpayer
income property commercial or residential real property on which rent is paid to taxpayer
individual retirement account IRA; tax-free savings account into which annual contributions are made that allows deferment of tax payments until retirement
informational return tax return showing income and expenses but no tax liability, such as partnership or fiduciary return
in-kind contribution value and cost of services rendered to charitable organization, an itemized deduction
interest income income derived as percentage of return on bank or savings deposits, bonds, or mortgages
internal revenue money collected by government from sources within country
Internal Revenue Service IRS; tax-collecting agency of U.S. government
investment expense deductible amount, such as margin interest, incurred in production of investment income
involuntary exchange/conversion casualty, theft, or condemnation resulting in loss or decreased value of capital asset
IRA individual retirement account

IRS Internal Revenue Service
itemized deduction personal expense, such as medical or charitable outlay or mortgage interest paid, allowed as deduction from adjusted gross income in determining taxable income
joint return tax return reporting income for both members of married couple
Keogh plan personal retirement plan for self-employed individual, with contribution based on net income
K-1 form issued by partnership, trust, fiduciary, or subchapter S corporation showing individual's share of net profit or loss and certain other income, distributions, and deductions
limitation standardized amount or amount based on individual return that credit or deduction may not exceed
limited partnership partnership with at least one general partner who has unlimited liability and at least one limited partner who is liable only for his or her investment
long-term capital gain profit on sale of assets held over one year
loophole means of reducing taxes by careful use of laws; law written to benefit one class or group of taxpayers
lump-sum distribution single payment from pension or profit-sharing program to which employee contributed, usu. received at time of separation from job
moving expense expense allowed as itemized deduction for cost of moving personal belongings and family when employee moves over 35 miles to take new job
net operating loss NOL; condition in which business expenses exceed total income for year, resulting in loss applicable to previous or later year's tax return
net profit gross income less all expenses
NOL net operating loss
nonemployee compensation amounts paid to self-employed person, subject to self-employment tax
nonprofit organization tax-exempt corporation filing informational return
nonresident taxpayer who is part-year resident or not a resident of taxing authority
nontaxable (*adj*) not liable to taxation
office-in-home portion of residence used for business, with percentage of housing costs taken as expense
ordinary income noncapital gains income that is taxable in full
passive activity any source of income, esp. a limited partnership with real estate investment or a trust, in which taxpayer has no active involvement
points percent of face value of mortgage paid at closing and fully deductible as itemized deduction when paid on principal residence
portfolio income income derived from investments and securities, considered unearned income
preenactment (*adj*) designating property acquired or activities begun prior to tax reform act of October 23, 1986
premature distribution taxable distribution from retirement plan or IRA prior to designated age of collection
recapture adding back of investment tax credit or depreciation taken on asset that has been disposed of before end of useful life
refund amount of overpayment returned to taxpayer after filing of return
reimbursement payment received for out-of-pocket expense that reduces deduction
rental income income derived from rental of business or residential real property
retirement credit credit for low-income, elderly, retired and totally disabled persons
return forms, schedules, and statements used to report income and expenses and determine tax liability
rollover reinvestment of distribution, esp. from pension or IRA, to postpone payment of tax
salvage value estimated remaining value of asset once it is fully depreciated
schedule tax form listing itemized expenses or showing income from various sources
self-employment tax Social Security tax paid as percentage of net income by those not subject to FICA withholding by employers
SEP simplified employee pension
short form simplified tax form for those with wages and unearned income but no enumerated deductions or credits
short-term capital gain profit on sale of securities, business assets, or real property held less than one year
standard deduction specified amount allowed to all taxpayers as deduction from AGI when not itemizing
straight-line depreciation traditional depreciation in which basis is divided equally by number of years over life of asset
taxable income income subject to taxation after subtracting deductions, adjustments, and exemptions
tax bracket income range with set tax rate
tax break legal means of reducing one's tax liability by taking advantage of specific regulation
tax-exempt status condition or requirement by which entity, usu. nonprofit organization, makes its income not liable to taxation
tax-free exchange usu. like-kind exchange of business assets or real property in which transaction is nontaxable
tax haven nation or state with very low or no income tax
tax liability amount of tax due
tax lien claim on or confiscation of wages, bank deposits, or other property by taxing authority for payment of overdue tax
tax rate specified percentage of commodity, income, or service that is taxed
tax rate schedule list of variable taxes at different levels of income or assessed value
tax return annual report on earnings and calculation of tax due federal and state governments
tax shelter investment designed to postpone or

avoid payment of taxes rather than generate taxable income

TIN taxpayer identification number; either social security number or employer identification number

trust taxable entity controlling assets for benefit of individual beneficiaries, with trust distributions being deductions to trust and usu. taxable to beneficiaries

unemployment compensation payment received by individual from unemployment insurance, often taxable in full or part

useful life period over which capital asset may be depreciated

wages salary paid to employee by employer, subject to withholding tax

W-4 form filed by employee indicating number of exemptions, used by employer to determine withholding

windfall profit profit on domestically produced crude oil, subject to special tax

withholding payroll deduction for taxes and other items made by employer for direct payment to government

write-off expense allowable as tax deduction

W-2 form prepared at year's end by employer, and filed with government, showing employee's compensation and taxes withheld

Accounting

account subdivision of basic accounting system used to record assets, liabilities, equity, sales, or expenses

accounting system of recording and summarizing business and financial transactions

accounts payable amounts owed to creditors

accounts receivable amounts to be received from customers for credit purchases

accrual entering in books items of income or expense that have been earned or incurred but not yet received or paid; such an item of income or expense

adjustment amount added to or subtracted from account to bring balance up to date

allowance amount set aside for specific purpose, actual or budgeted

annualize (*vb*) project income or expenses for full year based on results for part of year

appreciation increase in value of asset over time

assessment determination of income or value of property for purpose of fixing tax

assets articles or property of value; property, materials, and economic resources owned by business or individual

at risk (*adj*) denoting the amount an owner or investor stands to lose should business go bankrupt

audit examination of business financial accounts

balance amount standing as debit or credit on account

balance sheet report of total assets, liabilities, and owner's equity accounts at specific time

black (*adj*) showing a profit; in the black

bookkeeping systematic recording of financial business transactions and records

books general accounts or records of business transactions

book value value of asset at specific point in time, equal to initial cost less accumulated depreciation

bottom line net profit or loss after expenses, shown at bottom of profit and loss statement

capital account total amount of investment in business entity by each owner or all owners

capital contribution investment of capital or value of goods invested in business entity

certified public accountant CPA; accountant who has passed state licensing examination

close the books balance out all income and expense accounts at end of period

compound entry journal entry having two or more debits and/or two or more credits

comptroller controller

continuous budget rolling budget

controller chief accounting officer of business or government, esp. responsible for internal auditing of books; comptroller

cost accounting system of recording, analyzing, and allocating production and distribution costs for internal use by business; managerial accounting

CPA certified public accountant

credit amount of liability, equity, or revenue recorded as entry into account books on right side of T account

current assets liquid and semiliquid assets, such as cash, accounts receivable, and inventory

current liabilities business debts coming due for payment within next accounting period

debit amount of asset or expense recorded as entry into account books on left side of T account

double-entry accounting financial recordkeeping in which there must be an equal credit for each debit

entry recording of single item in account book or ledger

equity owner's financial claim to or investment in assets or property of business

financial accounting system of accounting used for reporting to investors, banks, and taxing authorities

financial statement report summarizing changes due to transactions during accounting period

fiscal year annual accounting period for business, either calendar year or sometimes July 1 to June 30 or October 1 to September 30

fixed costs expenses that are not variable during an accounting period, many of which are paid regularly

general ledger journal in which all business transactions are recorded and accounts balanced

gross total revenue before deduction of costs and expenses

gross profit difference between total sales revenue and cost of merchandise sold before deduction of other expenses

horizontal analysis comparison of changes in accounting statements from one period to next
income money received in sales, wages, or profits
independent contractor one who does work for another without being a regular employee, usu. setting own hours and conditions and hiring own workers
intangible asset property, such as patent, that represents value but has no physical form
in the black (*adj*) operating at a profit; black
in the red (*adj*) operating at a loss; red
journal entry orderly, usu. chronological, record of business transactions
ledger book containing each business account on separate page, to which all journal entries are transferred
liabilities amounts owed to creditors; accounts payable
limited liability risk of loss fixed at some maximum amount, such as total investment
liquidation closing of business by collecting assets and settling debts
liquidity ease with which assets can be converted to cash
managerial accounting cost accounting
negative amortization increase of principal of loan by amount by which periodic loan payments fall short of interest due, usu. because of interest rate increase
negative cash flow excess of expenses over income
net money free from all charges, costs, and expenses
net income total revenue less costs and expenses
net loss amount by which expenses exceed revenue; deficit
net profit amount by which revenues exceed expenses
net sales total sales for period less returns, allowances, and discounts
net worth total assets minus liabilities of individual or business
number cruncher *Informal.* accountant or clerk involved in bookkeeping and computer or statistical operations, but not management or decision making
P and L profit and loss statement showing gross income, expenses, and net profit
positive cash flow excess of income over expenses
posting transference of transactions from journal entry to ledger account
proceeds amount of cash received from transaction after commissions, costs of sale, and interest deductions
public accounting accounting services provided to clients for fee by licensed practitioners
realize (*vb*) convert into money; gain as net result of transaction
reconciling process of determining and accounting for discrepancies between accounts, balances, or statements
red (*adj*) showing a loss; in the red
revenue money earned from sales of goods, services, or other business transactions
rolling budget budget prepared month by month instead of annually; continuous budget
spreadsheet worksheet on which financial information is presented in two-dimensional matrix; computer program for maintaining such a record
stockholders' equity value of stockholders' claims to corporate assets
T account account record shaped like a T, used in analyzing transactions, with left side showing debits and right side showing credits
tangible assets items having material form and intrinsic value
trial balance statement of debit and credit balance on all open accounts, used to check their equality and make adjustments in double-entry accounting
value worth in financial terms
vertical analysis restating of dollar amounts on financial statement as percentage of base amount
worth value of assets and securities
write-off uncollectable debt; worthless asset
zero base accounting method in which each item is justified on basis of cost and need

Spending, Receiving, and Possessing Wealth

acquisition accumulation and retention of wealth
advance payment made or received before due
aid financial help, esp. institutional assistance to poor
alimony regular payments made by one spouse to the other as required by divorce decree
annuity payment of fixed sum at regular intervals, usu. yearly
appropriation money given over or set aside for specific use; amount taken for one's own use, often improperly
assets all that one owns, all wealth possessed
assignee person to whom rights have been transferred and payments are due
avarice excessive desire for wealth; greed
award amount given by court decision, as result of judgment in competition, or for merit
barter direct exchange of goods and services without use of currency
beneficiary person named to receive income, inheritance, or proceeds of trust or insurance policy
benefit public event or performance held to raise funds for specific group, person, or cause
blackmail extortion of payment by threat, esp. to reveal embarrassing information
charity money given voluntarily to help those in need
deep pockets abundance of wealth
disinherit (*vb*) exclude from inheritance
donation contribution or gift, esp. to charity
double-dipping practice of receiving more than one form of compensation from same employer or organization
dowry wealth and property brought by bride to husband at time of marriage
endowment gift or bequest used to provide income for institution or person
estate one's fortune or property, esp. when deceased

fixed income uniform rate or amount of income received over period of time
frugality thrift, economy, and care in spending
generosity willingness to give to others; giving in abundance
gift something freely handed over to another
graft illicit profits gained by taking advantage of privileged position
grant formal gift, usu. by institution or government
gratuity money given for service provided in excess of regular price; tip
honorarium payment for acts or services for which custom or propriety forbids a price to be set
inheritance wealth and property received upon another's death
investment use of one's existing capital to generate income or profit and thus increase wealth
kickback reimbursement of funds based on secret collusion, often illegal or unethical
legacy money or property left to another by will; bequest
net worth total value of one's possessions, property, and wealth
patron wealthy person who provides financial support for an activity, person, or institution
philanthropy charitable donations or gifts to needy individuals or nonprofit institutions
plutocracy group of wealthy, politically influential persons; rule by the wealthy
prodigality free spending
ransom money paid for release of confiscated property or kidnap victim
savings funds set aside for future use
scholarship gift of money to assist needy student in paying for education
sponsor person responsible for providing financial support for an individual, activity, or institution
stipend regular payment for service; allowance
tribute regular, often forced, payment as show of subjugation
underwrite (*vb*) agree to pay costs and cover losses of undertaking or institution
usance income and other benefits derived from ownership of wealth
wealth large amount of money and property
worth value of one's assets, property, and money

Money, Currency, and Denominations

agio fee paid to exchange one currency for another
bank note promissory note issued by bank, used as form of paper money
bankroll conspicuous wad of bills
bill of exchange written order to pay specific sum of money to particular person
bullion gold or silver ingots or bars, held as standard for currency
capital accumulated wealth, esp. used to increase wealth
cash paper currency and metal coins; actual money
cash in hand money available at given moment
circulation paper currency and coins passed from person to person
C-note *Slang.* hundred-dollar bill
coinage metal currency; making of coins
counterfeit forged money not printed and issued by government
currency money circulated as medium of exchange in any country, esp. paper money
demonetization stoppage of use of gold or silver as currency standard
devaluation reduction of currency's value relative to international monetary values
doubloon obsolete gold coin of Spain and Spanish America
ducats *Slang.* money, esp. cash; gold or silver coins formerly used in Europe
Eurodollar U.S. dollar deposited in or credited to European bank
exchange rate value of one nation's currency in relation to that of another; cost of exchanging one currency for another
fiat money currency without gold or silver backing, issued by government decree
G-note *Slang.* thousand-dollar bill
gold yellow precious metal formerly used for coins, often held by nation as standard for issued currency
gold standard monetary system in which value of nation's currency is based on and backed by gold
greenback U.S. legal-tender note, printed in green on the back
K one thousand U.S. dollars
kitty small, informal savings fund; money pooled for specific purpose
legal tender official form of money, recognized as national medium of exchange in payment for purchases or debts; coin of the realm
lucre monetary gain or riches, often used in derogatory sense
mad money *Informal.* extra spending money for emergencies or impulse buying
medium of exchange currency used as measure of value in exchange for goods and services
mint manufacturing site, depository, and government agency responsible for authorized coinage from metal
monetary system coinage and circulation of currency
money medium of commerce, exchange, and banking that serves as recognized measure of value; paper currency and coins
money order order for payment of specified sum issued by bank or post office, serving as cash in exchange
nest egg savings
note single piece of paper currency issued by bank or government
numismatics science and study of coins and coinage
pecuniary (*adj*) pertaining to money
petrodollars accumulation of surplus dollars by petroleum-exporting nations
petty cash small fund of money kept on hand for incidental expenses

pin money extra money; small savings
revaluation increase in currency's value relative to international monetary values
roll *Informal.* large number of paper bills, esp. rolled into bundle
silver white precious metal used in manufacture of coins and as monetary standard
silver certificate former U.S. paper currency redeemable for silver
small change coins of low denomination
specie coined money, as opposed to paper notes
sterling standard of British coinage in silver; British money
wampum *Informal.* money; beads used as medium of exchange by American Indians

World Currencies

afghani currency of Afghanistan
austral currency of Argentina
baht currency of Thailand
balboa currency of Panama
birr currency of Ethiopia
bolivar currency of Venezuela
cedi currency of Ghana
colon currency of Costa Rica, El Salvador
cordoba currency of Nicaragua
cruzeiro real currency of Brazil
dalasi currency of Gambia
denar currency of Macedonia
deutsche mark currency of Germany
dinar currency of Algeria, Bahrain, Bosnia and Herzegovina, Iraq, Jordan, Kuwait, Libya, Serbia and Montenegro, Tunisia
dirham currency of Morocco, United Arab Emirates
dobra currency of São Tomé and Principe
dollar currency of Antigua and Barbuda, Australia, Bahamas, Barbados, Belize, Bermuda, Brunei, Canada, Dominica, Fiji, Grenada, Guyana, Hong Kong, Jamaica, Kiribati, Liberia, Micronesia, Nauru, New Zealand, Singapore, Solomon Islands, St. Kitts-Nevis, St. Lucia, St. Vincent and the Grenadines, Taiwan, Trinidad and Tobago, Tuvalu, United States, Zimbabwe
dong currency of Vietnam
drachma currency of Greece
dram currency of Armenia
emu proposed common currency of the European Union
escudo currency of Cape Verde, Portugal
forint currency of Hungary
franc currency of Andorra, Belgium, Benin, Burkina Faso, Burundi, Cameroon, Central African Republic, Chad, Comoros, Congo, Djibouti, Equatorial Guinea, France, Gabon, Guinea, Ivory Coast, Lichtenstein, Luxembourg, Madagascar, Mali, Martinique, Monaco, Niger, Rwanda, Senegal, Switzerland, Togo
gourde currency of Haiti
guarani currency of Paraguay
guilder currency of the Netherlands, Netherlands Antilles, Suriname
inti currency of Peru
karbovanets currency of Ukraine
kina currency of Papua New Guinea
kip currency of Laos
koruna currency of Czech Republic, Slovakia
krona currency of Iceland, Sweden
krone currency of Denmark, Greenland, Norway
kuna currency of Croatia
kwacha currency of Malawi, Zambia
kwanza currency of Angola
kyat currency of Burma (Myanmar)
lat currency of Latvia
lek currency of Albania
lempira currency of Honduras
leone currency of Sierra Leone
leu currency of Moldova, Romania
lev currency of Bulgaria
lilangeni currency of Swaziland
lira currency of Italy, Malta, San Marino, Turkey, Vatican City
lit currency of Lithuania
loti currency of Lesotho
manat currency of Azerbaijan, Turkmenistan
mark currency of Germany (also deutsche mark)
markka currency of Finland
metical currency of Mozambique
naira currency of Nigeria
ngultrum currency of Bhutan
ouguiya currency of Mauritania
pa'anga currency of Tonga
pataca currency of Macao
peseta currency of Andorra, Spain
peso currency of Bolivia, Chile, Colombia, Cuba, Dominican Republic, Guinea-Bissau, Mexico, the Philippines, Uruguay
pound currency of Cyprus, Egypt, Ireland, Lebanon, Sudan, Syria, United Kingdom

pula currency of Botswana
quetzal currency of Guatemala
rand currency of South Africa
rial currency of Iran, Oman, Yemen
riel currency of Cambodia
ringgit currency of Malaysia
riyal currency of Qatar, Saudi Arabia
ruble currency of Belarus, Russian Republic, and former Soviet Union
rufiyaa currency of the Maldives
rupee currency of India, Mauritius, Nepal, Pakistan, Seychelles, Sri Lanka
rupiah currency of Indonesia
schilling currency of Austria
shekel currency of Israel
shilling currency of Kenya, Somalia, Tanzania, Uganda
som currency of Kyrgyzstan, Uzbekistan
sucre currency of Ecuador
taka currency of Bangladesh
tala currency of Western Samoa
tenge currency of Kazakhstan
tolar currency of Slovenia
tugrik currency of Mongolia
vatu currency of Vanuatu
won currency of North Korea, South Korea
yen currency of Japan
yuan currency of China
zaire currency of Zaire
zloty currency of Poland

AGRICULTURE

Farming and Crops
Ranching and Animal Husbandry
Soils and Soil Management
Tools, Machinery, and Structures
Business and Science of Agriculture

Farming and Crops

agrarian (*adj*) pertaining to the land or farmers
agrichemical fertilizer, pesticide, or feeding supplement
alfalfa deep-rooted perennial of pea family used for fodder and as cover crop
annual plant that lives for only one year or one season
barley cultivated cereal grass, one of man's first grains
bone meal fertilizer made of fine bone, a natural source of phosphorus
cereal any grain produced from grass and used as food
chaff useless husks of wheat or other grains, separated in threshing
citrus thorny trees and shrubs that grow in warm climates and produce pulpy edible fruit
clear-cutting removing all trees in a stand of timber
cocoa beans of small evergreen cacao tree, used primarily in making chocolate
coffee beans of coffee tree, grown in tropical highland regions, used to make beverage
complete fertilizer fertilizer containing three primary plant nutrients: nitrogen, phosphorus, and potassium
corn tall cereal plant whose kernels are used extensively for fodder and human food; maize
cotton most important textile fiber, produced from seed pods of shrubby tropical plant
cover crop grass or legume that improves soil by adding organic matter and discouraging erosion
crop plant or agricultural product grown and harvested for profit or subsistence; yield in a single season or place
cultivation growing of plants or crops from seeds, bulbs, or shoots
cutover land cleared of vegetation, esp. trees
cutting plant section from leaf, stem, or root capable of developing into new plant
DDT dichlorodiphenyltrichloroethane; hazardous pesticide in widespread use on crops
dirt farmer owner of small farm who works his or her own land
dry farming agriculture without irrigation, relying on drought-resistant crops and moisture-conserving soil cultivation techniques
dust (*vb*) sprinkle crops with insecticides, esp. from a low-flying airplane

everbearing (*adj*) continuously producing or bringing forth fruit
extensive cultivation farming system in which limited work is put into relatively large area of land
fallow (*adj*) designating cultivated land left unsown for one season or more
farm tract of land devoted to any agricultural purpose; (*vb*) engage in raising crops or animals
farmer person who cultivates land or raises crops or livestock, esp. one who owns farmland; grower
farm hand hired farm worker
farming business of agriculture and farm operation
fertile (*adj*) rich in resources, fruitful; able to reproduce by seeds or spores
fertilizer organic or chemical soil additive that increases or accelerates growth
field cleared area of land used for pasture or growing
field crops crops grown on large tracts of land
flax annual plant grown for its fiber and seed
force (*vb*) cause plants to grow faster by artificial means
furrow narrow groove in ground made by plow
garden plot of land where vegetables, fruits, flowers, or herbs are grown, esp. small plot for personal use
germination sprouting of spore, seed, or bud as growth begins
glean (*vb*) collect grain after reaping
grain seed or fruit of some plants, including cereal grasses
granary repository for grain storage
harvest crop gathering season; process of reaping and gathering crops; season's yield of crops
headland strip of unplowed land at ends of furrows
herbage nonwoody vegetation, esp. grasses upon which animals graze
hull outer covering of seed or fruit; (*vb*) remove this covering
husk dry outer covering of various crops, such as corn; (*vb*) remove this covering
intensive cultivation farming system in which significant and continuous work is lavished on relatively small area to maximize yield
intercrop (*vb*) grow one crop between rows of another
irrigation any of various systems of bringing water to plants, including flood, border, furrow, sprinkler, drip, or surface irrigation systems
legumes plants with fruits or seeds in dry pods with two sutures, such as beans or peas, used for food or forage
lumbering work and business of tree farming or felling trees to make lumber
maize corn
manure fertilizer of livestock excrement
migrant worker seasonal farm laborer who moves from place to place to get work
monoculture growing only one type of crop on a piece of land
nitrogen one of three essential plant nutrients
no-tillage direct seeding without plowing of soil
nut dry fruit or seed with kernel inside separable rind, shell, or hull
open-field cultivation system in which farmer owns and cultivates strips of land, unfenced and scattered over several large fields
orchard area planted with trees that bear fruit or nuts
organic farming farming that relies on natural materials to control pests and for use as fertilizers
paddy plot of continuous wetland, esp. where rice is grown
pest insect, small animal, fungus, or weed that damages or kills crops
pesticide any of various pest killers, including fungicides (kill fungi), insecticides (kill insects), miticides (kill mites), molluskicides (kill snails and slugs), and ovicides (kill eggs), esp. chlorinated hydrocarbons (organochlorines), organic phosphates (organophosphates), and carbamate compounds
phosphate any substance containing salt and phosphoric acid, used as fertilizer
plantation large farm or estate on which cultivated crops are grown by resident workers, usu. in tropical or semitropical region
produce fresh agricultural products, esp. fruits and vegetables
pruning pinching, heading, thinning, or shearing plants to direct growth or improve health or appearance
rice starchy seeds or grain of marsh grass, requiring much moisture and warm temperatures, used to feed more people than any other cereal
rotation of crops cultivation system in which crops are systematically changed on each plot to prevent nutrient loss in soil and to discourage weeds, pests, and diseases; crop rotation
rye main bread grain in parts of northern Europe, where wheat cannot be cultivated due to cold weather
seed (*vb*) sow; plant with seeds from which plants grow
sharecropper farmer who exchanges works for share of crop's value less credited expenses
shifting cultivation primitive system in which crops are grown in one area until it is exhausted and growers move on
slash-and-burn (*adj*) of a cultivation technique in which land is made usable by burning trees and undergrowth, thereby clearing as well as nourishing the land
slit planting tillage method in which seeds are dropped into narrow openings cut into soil
smudge smoky fire used to protect fruit trees from frost
spring wheat wheat grain sown in spring to avoid harsh winter weather
stand group of trees growing together
stone fruit any fruit, such as a plum, having a hard, stonelike seed
strip farming planting of strips of closely growing plants, such as grasses or clover, between crops to hold up rainwater, thereby reducing erosion
subsistence crops crops grown for farmer's own food needs

sugar product of crystallization of juice of crops, esp. sugar beets and sugarcane
swath strip of space from which grain plants have been cut down
swidden tract of land cleared for planting by burning vegetation on it
tea white-flowered evergreen plant, grown throughout Asia, whose dried leaves are used to make a beverage
terrace cultivation system of cultivating mountains and hills by carving out and reinforcing small fields with low embankments
thin (*vb*) remove weaker plants to maximize growth of remaining crop
threshing separating grains or cereals into usable and nonusable parts
till (*vb*) plow, cultivate, and fertilize land for the purpose of raising crops
timber forest trees used for lumber
top dressing plant nutrients applied to surface of land
tract large area of land used for cultivation
transplant (*vb*) dig up growing plant or tree and place it in ground elsewhere
tree farming business and practice of growing trees, esp. for lumber
vegetable any herbaceous edible plant
vernalize (*vb*) shorten plant's growth period, usu. by chilling it or its seeds or bulbs
vineyard land used for cultivating grapevines, esp. for winemaking
weed undesirable plant that harms or inhibits growth of crop plants; (*vb*) remove such plants from soil
wheat cereal grass with dense, erect spikes that produces grain used as staple food throughout temperate regions
windrow row of hay or sheaves of grain raked together to dry
winnow (*vb*) blow off undesirable chaff from grain by current of air
winter wheat wheat grain sown in fall in regions where it can survive winter weather

Ranching and Animal Husbandry

animal husbandry care and raising of domesticated animals, esp. cattle, horses, and sheep
barn raising gathering of local people to help their neighbor build a barn
beekeeper one who raises bees and gathers honey
branding iron long-handled metal rod with distinctive design at one end, used for marking livestock
break (*vb*) tame and train a horse
breed (*vb*) supervise the sexual propagation of animals; (*n*) group of animals of one species differentiated by common characteristics and descent
corral enclosure for domesticated animals, esp. horses
cote pen or enclosure for livestock
cud mouthful of swallowed food regurgitated by cattle for second chewing
dairy farm or ranch for raising dairy cattle, producing milk and milk products; creamery
domestic animal animal tamed or bred for human purposes
ensilage green fodder preserved in a silo
fodder domestic animal food
forage food eaten by browsing or grazing animal; fodder
free-range (*adj*) designating livestock and poultry permitted to graze or forage freely outside a small confinement
grazing feeding of animals on growing grass or herbage
hatchery place for hatching eggs
hay grass, alfalfa, or clover cut and dried for fodder
haystack large heap of hay piled outdoors; hayrick
herd group of cattle, sheep, or other animals living together under human supervision; (*vb*) control movement of livestock, esp. from horseback
hutch animal pen, esp. for rabbits
incubation sitting on or keeping eggs in warm environment favorable for hatching
livestock domestic animals kept for work, by-products, or sale, esp. cattle, sheep, hogs, and horses
pack animal animal bred for strength and used to carry loads, esp. mule, donkey, or horse; sumpter
pasturage practice of grazing livestock on a pasture
ranch large farm, esp. in U.S. West, for raising cattle, horses, or sheep; (*vb*) operate or work on a ranch, esp. raise livestock
range large open area over which livestock can roam and graze
ruminant (*adj*) cud-chewing, esp. cattle and sheep
shearing cutting or clipping of animal hair, esp. for use as wool
shepherd herdsman, esp. for grazing sheep
silage succulent feed made from fermented fodder in silo
silo usu. cylindrical, airtight tower for making and storing silage
sire male parent of four-legged animal, esp. horse; (*vb*) father a horse
slaughterhouse structure in which livestock are butchered
stock strain or related group of animals; livestock
stock horse horse used in herding cattle
stockyard enclosure for livestock, esp. where cattle, sheep, hogs, or horses are held before slaughter or shipment
straw mass of grain stalks, dried and used as fodder
stud male animal, esp. horse, used for breeding
swine domesticated pig or hog
transhumance seasonal movement of livestock from valley to mountain pastures and back again
winterfeed feed given to livestock in winter when pasturage is impossible

Soils and Soil Management

adobe soil heavy clay soil
aeration supplying abundant oxygen to soil through cultivation
alluvial soil sand or clay deposited at shore of waterway
amendment soil-conditioning substance that promotes plant growth by addition of vitamins, fertilizer, or other additive
arable (*adj*) fit for cultivation
backfill soil soil, sometimes amended, used to refill planting hole
bog wet, spongy soil with decaying mosses and peat
bole easily pulverized, reddish clay
chernozem fertile soil, rich in humus, covering large areas of temperate regions
clay firm, fine-grained soil, plastic when wet
contour plowing erosion-prevention technique in which land is plowed around rather than up and down a slope, creating rain-catching furrows
decalcified soil soil deprived of lime or calcium compounds
deflocculated soil soil lacking well-aggregated structure, caused by soft water
desertification spread of desertlike conditions on previously arable land
diatomaceous earth soil amendment formed by skeletal remains of microscopic organisms
drought prolonged period without rain that causes soil failure and crop death
dust bowl region that endures long droughts and intense dust storms
erosion gradual eating or wearing away of soil by water, wind, snow, or ice
fertile soil earth capable of sustaining growth
friable (*adj*) describing easily crumbled soil
ground water water stored within porous rock in earth, esp. near surface
horizon layer of soil with distinct characteristics
humus organic matter in soil resulting from decomposition of plants and animals
illuviation accumulation in one layer of soil of materials leached from another layer
laterite red, residual soil in well-drained tropical rain forest
leaching washing away of soluble plant foods from topsoil by rain
leaf mold rich soil composed largely of decayed leaves
loam fertile soil consisting of humus, clay, and sand
loess particles of soft, porous rock, carried by wind, that mix with humus to form loam
marl soft, friable mixture of clay and limestone, used as fertilizer in lime-deficient soil
mold loose, soft, easily worked soil rich with decayed animal or vegetable matter
mulch leaves, straw, or peat moss spread on ground around plants to prevent evaporation of water from soil and to protect roots
peat brownish, fibrous substance resulting from vegetative decay
pedology soil science
plow sole compressed layer at bottom of furrow resulting from repeated plowing
podsol grayish, relatively infertile soil in coniferous forest
reclamation making dry or useless land capable of cultivation
regosol soil composed of unconsolidated material without stones and without distinct horizons
rill erosion formation of numerous small channels that occurs on recently cultivated soil
sand soil composed of loose, gritty particles of worn or disintegrated rock
scarify (*vb*) loosen soil with a cultivator
sheet erosion type of soil erosion, esp. on sloping farmland, in which rain washes away thin layer of topsoil
silt soil composed largely of sediment carried by moving water, with particles larger than clay but smaller than sand
soil source of food and moisture for plants, consisting of small particles of rock together with humus
soil management organized soil conservation and care programs
spodosol acidic forest soil of low fertility, found in cool, humid areas of Northern Hemisphere
subsoil layer of harder soil beneath topsoil
terracing forming of hillside into series of flat, raised mounds to reduce erosion in growing areas
topsoil upper layer of soil, usu. darker and richer than subsoil
wind erosion type of soil erosion in which powdered topsoil, due to cultivation, is carried away by wind

Tools, Machinery, and Structures

backhoe excavating vehicle with hinged bucket on arm for digging
baler machine for compressing, binding, and wrapping grasses and hay in standardized bundles
billhook curved blade set on handle, used for pruning or cutting
binder attachment to harvester or reaper that binds cut grain
chisel plow plow that exposes minimal soil, aiding moisture retention and reducing soil runoff and wind erosion
colter sharp blade or wheel used to cut ground ahead of plowshare
combine multiprocess, in-field grain harvesting machine
crop duster device for spreading chemical dust over crops, often from low-flying airplane
cultivator tool drawn between rows of plants to loosen earth and uproot weeds
dibble pointed tool for making holes in soil for seeds, bulbs, or small plants
flail short, thick wooden stick loosely attached to handle, used for threshing
grader machine that levels a slope, roadway, or plot of ground
grain elevator tall, cylindrical warehouse for grain

grange farmhouse and its outbuildings
greenhouse glass building with controlled temperature and humidity for cultivating plants out of season, sprouting seeds, or forcing plants
grub hoe heavy hoe used for digging up roots and stumps
harness assemblage of leather straps and metal pieces by which horse or mule is fastened to plow or other vehicle
harrow horse or tractor-drawn frame with spikes or sharp-edged disks for breaking up and leveling plowed ground
harvester machine for cutting and gathering crops or grain
hayfork mechanical device for moving hay; pitchfork
hayloft elevated area in barn for storage of hay
hay rake tool used to rake hay from swath into windrow
hoe thin, flat-bladed, long-handled cultivation tool
hovel open shed, esp. for cattle or tools
incubator enclosed, warm environment for keeping and hatching eggs
lathhouse structure of thin narrow wood strips for support or protection of plants
manger trough in stable holding feed for livestock
mattock pickaxlike tool with one broad end, used for loosening soil by digging
mill building and machinery for grinding grain into flour or meal
moldboard curved metal plate attached to plow for turning soil
pick heavy tool with pointed iron or steel head on long handle, used to loosen and break up soil
pitchfork long-handled tool with sharp prongs for lifting and tossing hay or straw; hayfork
plow implement used to cut, turn up, and break soil
plowshare furrow-cutting blade of moldboard plow
reaper machine for cutting standing grain, often with mechanism for bundling and tossing out bundles of cut grain
rotary plow implement with spinning blades set on power-driven shaft, used to break up unplowed soil prior to planting
rototiller electrically powered device with spinning blades for cultivating soil
scuffle hoe spadelike hoe that is pushed instead of pulled
scythe long, single-edged blade set at right angle to long curved handle, for hand-cutting grass or grain
shears device with multiple sharp edges for cutting wool, esp. from sheep
sickle crescent-shaped blade on short handle for cutting tall grass or weeds
spade flat blade on long handle for digging or turning soil by pressing blade into ground with foot
spike-tooth harrow harrow with straight teeth set horizontally, used to smooth soil for planting or sowing
thresher machine for beating out grain from husks
tiller machine used to plow and cultivate soil
tractor vehicle with powerful engine and large rear wheels or endless treads, for pulling farm machinery
trough low, narrow receptacle for food for animals
windbreak hedge, row of trees, or fence for protection from wind
windmill machine for grinding grain powered by wind's rotation of large oblique vanes radiating from shaft

Business and Science of Agriculture

aeroculture practice of growing plants without soil by suspending them above spraying outlets that constantly moisten their roots; aeroponics
aeroponics aeroculture
aggie *Informal.* agricultural school or college; student at such a school
agribusiness business associated with processing, manufacturing, producing, and distributing of agricultural products
agricultural engineering design of farm machinery, mechanization of farming, and soil management
agricultural extension service government organization providing information and consultation services, often at state's land-grant university
agricultural sciences disciplines related to agricultural production, including mineralogy, virology, plant physiology, animal nutrition, microclimatology, and watershed management
agriculture science and practice of cultivating soil, raising crops, and raising livestock; farming
agrobiology science of plant growth and nutrition as applied to improvement of crops and soil management
agrology study of agricultural production
agronomy science and economics of soil management and crop production
agrostology branch of botany dealing with grasses and grains
aquaculture cultivation and regulation of water plants and water animals for human consumption
arboriculture cultivation of trees and shrubs, esp. for ornamentation
asexual propagation reproduction without union with another member of species
botany science of plant life, structure, growth, and classification
citriculture cultivation of citrus fruits
collective farm cooperative
commodity agricultural product seen as economic unit
conservation management of natural resources for their protection and preservation
conservation tillage erosion-reducing techniques, including plowless farming, reduced-tillage, no-till, eco-till, and slit planting
cooperative farm with several owners or group of farms organized by and operated for benefit of owners or members; collective farm

cross-pollination exchange of pollen between two plants, naturally or artificially
deforestation clearing of trees from tract of land
demesne land legally held in one's possession
ecology science concerned with the interrelationship of organisms and their environment
environmental protection programs and techniques of assuring continued balance and abundance of Earth's resources
forestry science of planting and caring for trees, esp. systematic management of timber production with regard for conservation
genetic engineering technique of producing new, improved hybrid species by cutting and splicing of genetic units of DNA from different organisms
geoponic (*adj*) having to do with agriculture
grange farmers' association
horticulture cultivation of fruits, vegetables, shrubs, and herbaceous and ornamental trees and plants
husbandry cultivation of plants and animals
hydrology science dealing with properties, distribution, and circulation of water on Earth's surface
hydroponics growing of plants in nutrient-rich solutions without soil
logging cutting trees for lumber
microclimatology study of weather and its impact on a small region
milling grinding of grain into flour; cutting of timber into lumber
mineralogy science of minerals found in soil and rocks
mixed farming farming of both crops and livestock
nursery place where young plants are raised
olericulture production, storage, and marketing of vegetables for home market
pisciculture artificial breeding and transplantation of fish
plant physiology study and experimentation on functions and growth of plants
pomology fruit-growing science
reforestation planting of forests on denuded land
sharecropper tenant farmer paying rent in form of crops
silviculture cultivation of forest trees
subsidy government payment to farmers to support prices, esp. on surplus products
target prices income supplements, set higher than loan rates, calculated to reflect national average cost of producing crop
tenant farmer person farming land owned by another and paying rent in cash or share of crops
truck farming growing of vegetables or fruit to be marketed locally
vermiculture raising and production of earthworms and their by-products
viniculture cultivation of wine grapes
virology study of viral diseases, esp. as they affect livestock
viticulture science and cultivation of grapes
watershed ridge dividing areas drained by different river systems; area drained by river system

ADVERTISING

A-board display in which two sloping boards are joined at top, used for outdoor signs
account executive advertising agency employee who oversees marketing and administrative efforts for one or more clients' campaigns and deals directly with client
action cards mail-order device in which set of postcards with order forms and return addresses for a variety of products and companies is sent to potential customers
AD art director
advertisement paid public announcement describing something for sale
advertising calling public attention to a particular product by paid announcements so as to arouse desire to buy it; any public notice
advertorial advertisement that resembles newspaper editorial but promotes advertiser's product, service, or point of view
art director AD; person responsible for creative positioning and graphic design of advertisement
audiovisual (*adj*) A/V; pertaining to simultaneous use of tape recordings, slides, and video to support pitch, presentation, or display
billboard very large outdoor printed sign
billings gross income to agency from one account or several accounts
blister pack display package in which clear plastic seals product against cardboard sheet
book talent agency listing, with pictures, of actors and models
booking scheduling of talent and staff offered work on shoot or photo session
broadside sheet printed on one or both sides with advertising message
brochure folded leaflet with advertising message, usu. illustrated
bumper sticker advertising strip attached to automobilebumper
bus card advertising poster attached to side or back of bus, esp. in city public bus system
buzzword word or phrase that takes on added significance or new meaning through repetition or special usage
campaign total planned sales effort on behalf of specific client, usu. multimedia and over period of time
catalog illustrated booklet listing available products
classified ad brief listing in periodical of items for sale and services offered, arranged by category; want ad
Clio annual award given for excellence in radio and television advertising
color separation photographic process using separate plates for each color
commercial advertising announcement on television or radio or in movie theater; (*adj*) designating product or service suitable for wide, popular market

concept general idea behind slogan, pitch, or campaign
cooperative advertising sharing of cost of advertisement between manufacturer and retailer
copywriter person responsible for writing advertising copy and creating concept with art director
cost per thousand CPM; cost of advertising per thousand potential customers reached through publication, broadcast, or outdoor advertisement
CPM cost per thousand (roman numeral M)
creative director person responsible in agency for developing concepts, coordinating production of art and copy, and executing campaign
dealer spot spot advertisement placed by retail dealer of product rather than manufacturer
decal specially prepared paper from which graphics can be transferred to another surface
direct mail direct marketing exclusively by mail
direct marketing marketing via leaflets, brochures, letters, catalogs, or print ads mailed or distributed directly to potential consumers; any medium used to elicit responses directly from consumers
display ad illustrated advertisement in newspaper or magazine
drive time *Slang.* ads directed at commuters in cars, esp. during morning and late afternoon
dummy rough layout of assembled work for print advertisement
dump-bin floor display holding an assortment of loose items
exclusivity prohibition on performing in commercial for product that is competitive with one for which actor has commercial currently on hold or running; right to use specific talent, art, music, etc., in advertising
exposure number of potential consumers reached through specific medium
flack press agent or publicist, sometimes considered disparaging
flier fly sheet
flip chart chart with series of illustrated pages bound at top so that pages can be lifted vertically and dropped behind other pages, used in presentation
fly sheet handbill, loose sheet with printed advertisement; flier
focus group group of potential consumers used in market research to determine likely effectiveness of advertising
giveaway promotion involving free novelties or gifts
graphic design any form of visual artistic representation of product or layout of advertisement
grinder *Slang.* actor impersonating doctor or other professional authority on television commercial
halftone printed image formed by close-set dots of varying sizes
handbill small, printed advertising sheet distributed by hand
hard sell aggressive advertising technique
head shot glossy 8 x 10-inch picture of actor's or model's face
hidden persuaders subtle or subliminal advertising messages and techniques
hook clever phrase or melody used to capture consumer's attention; peg; slant
hype *Informal.* extravagant promotion of person, idea, or product
ink *Slang.* print publicity; press coverage
insert printed sheet or sheets inserted into publication or enclosed with mailing
jingle catchy, repetitious musical refrain used in radio or TV advertising
junk mail unsolicited advertising material sent by post
knockdown display or exhibit that can be disassembled easily for shipping
launch introduction of new product or service
layout design for graphic advertising production, roughly depicting look of advertisement
linage total lines of advertising placed in publication in one issue over period of time
live tag voice-over at end of prerecorded commercial that provides current or local information
logo recognizable trademarked design and lettering for trade, product, or organization
Madison Avenue advertising in general; New York City street that is location of many large agencies
mailer advertisement sent by mail
mail order retail sales conducted by mail
mall-fixture advertisement poster advertisement mounted in glassed frame in kiosk or other public place in mall or transportation depot
marketing strategy and specific techniques used in reaching consumers
market research study of consumer groups and business competition used to define projected market
market share percentage of specific market reached or sold by given product, advertisement, or agency
marquee billboard advertising theater performance
media forms of mass communication that carry advertising, esp. newspapers, magazines, television, and radio
media buying service company that specializes in buying print and television or radio time for advertisements
mention brief item in press or on broadcast referring to person, product, or service
mockup scale-dimensional display model used in planning
multimedia (*adj*) involving use of several media simultaneously in single advertisement or campaign
novelties free items, such as matches, calendars, or buttons, bearing advertiser's logo
paste-up formation of graphic design or layout by pasting objects to stiff board; mechanical
peg *Informal.* strong, appealing, notable element of press release or campaign; hook; slant
photo opportunity sometimes staged event having visual appeal or interest to photographers, used to generate publicity and free advertising
piggyback (*vb*) run group of commercials back to back, usu. for same client, in time frame such as four fifteen-second spots for price of one sixty-second spot

pitch presentation of advertising message
plug *Informal.* favorable mention or picture of product in nonadvertising portion of media presentation
point-of-purchase advertising signs, displays, and other techniques of attracting attention and promoting products at their point of sale, such as at the counter of a retail store
point-of-purchase display arrangement of goods in retail store with conspicuous advertising copy
POP point-of-purchase
portfolio large, bound volume containing pictures from ads, used by agency or talent to generate new jobs
poster graphic advertisement attached to flat surface or standing up with clip backing
PR public relations
press kit collection of editorial and promotional materials distributed to press
principal performer in commercial who can be recognized or identified, including but not limited to speaking parts
print advertising in newspapers, magazines, catalogs, or mailers, usu. photographs or other graphic material
promotion method of increasing sales of merchandise through advertising; any activity aimed at increasing sales
propaganda promotion of specific ideas or views, esp. political
publicity dissemination of promotional material to draw interest or generate sales
public relations PR; business of inducing goodwill and acceptance in public toward individual, cause, company, or product
rating measure of audience for television show, used to establish rates
release signed permission given by person to use his or her photo, voice, name, or testimonial statement commercially
remnant space unsold print advertising space sold at a discount
residual payment to model, actor, or singer each time advertisement is played, shown, or run
rollout *Informal.* geographic expansion of campaign from test market, as to regional or national market
sandwich board two hinged boards with advertising messages on them, worn hung over shoulders
SAU standard advertising unit
scatter package arrangement to air television commercials at various times or intervals
shill person planted in audience to lure onlookers into buying product or participating in activity
shoot taping or filming of commercial in studio or on location
skywriting writing across sky with chemically produced smoke emitted from airplane, usu. for purposes of advertising
slant emphasis of a campaign or advertisement; hook; peg
slice-of-life (*adj*) denoting advertisement that depicts naturalistic, everyday activities
slogan short, memorable advertising phrase
sniping pasting up outdoor posters over billboards or on empty structures, walls, and traffic poles, often without permission
soft sell subtle advertising technique
space page or section of page bought for advertisement in newspaper, magazine, or catalog
spokesperson well-known person serving as regular advocate of specific product or cause
spot spot announcement
spot announcement radio or television commercial of fifteen, thirty, or sixty seconds; spot
stabile display that is suspended or that rises from pedestal at different levels and on different planes, none of which move
standard advertising unit SAU; system of standard dimensions for print advertising based on six columns, each 2 1/16 inches wide
static ad photographic or print advertisement
storyboard series of panels roughly depicting scenes, copy, and shots in television commercial
streamer long, narrow sign with message in bold type hung across open area, window, or doorway
subliminal advertising concealed appeal to consumers' unconscious to buy product
subway card advertising poster attached to interior or exterior side of subway car
sweepstakes lottery in which winners are randomly selected, often used to induce purchase of product as means of entering contest
talent actors, models, and singers employed in advertisements
target audience consumer group most likely to buy product, identified by region, age, demographics, or economic status; target market
teaser advertisement or publicity that arouses interest or curiosity about forthcoming product or event, sometimes without naming it
telemarketing selling, advertising, or market research done by telephone
tent display card folded and set up with two sloping sides, like inverted V, esp. for small displays on tables
testimonial statement, often by celebrity or prominent person, affirming truth, fact, character, or value of a product, event, or service
test market consumer group interviewed to determine target audience
throwaway handbill or other printed matter that is distributed free to residences and contains local advertising; novelty item used to entice consumers into buying more costly item
tie-in campaign to link products, media, or markets
trade name name used by company to describe and distinguish its brand of a generic product, usu. trademarked
trade-out barter arrangement for exchange of commercial time, advertising space, products, or services
triptych three-sided display with central element and two wings
VO voice-over
voice-over VO; recorded offscreen voice heard on television or radio commercial
volume dollar amount of billings or revenue
want ad classified ad

INSURANCE

accident unplanned event causing injury, death, or damage
act of God usu. catastrophic event arising from natural causes
actuarial tables tables showing life expectancies
actuary statistical specialist who computes insurance rates
adjustment estimate of loss; settlement of claim
adjustor insurance company representative trained to make accurate estimates of loss or liability
agent representative selling policies for insurance company
annuity periodic payments of specific amount made by insurer, often for life
assigned risk high-risk client assigned to insurance company by lottery-style method
beneficiary person eligible to receive insurance payments
benefits payments to insured person or his or her beneficiary
bond guarantee against financial loss caused by default of third party or by circumstance over which guarantor has no control
carrier insurance company, insurer
catastrophe sudden, violent loss
claim insured's application to receive benefits
cleanup fund life insurance policy covering expenses after insured's death
coinsurance jointly held insurance policy; policy in which insured pays portion of costs or losses
comprehensive auto or health insurance policy covering all risk contingencies
coverage inclusion within scope of policy; insurance
damages amount paid to cover loss
deductible that part of loss to be paid by insured party, deductible from insurer's payment
disability insurance government payments to cover loss of employment due to injury or sickness
disaster insurance coverage for damage due to act of nature, such as flood, hailstorm, or earthquake
double indemnity clause in policy providing for payment of twice the basic benefit
dramshop law liquor liability law making server of alcohol liable for possible loss caused by intoxicated person
endowment insurance life insurance policy that matures on set date or at death of insured, whichever occurs first
errors and omissions coverage for mistakes made in documents, esp. instances of libel and copyright infringement
estimate appraisal of loss for claim
excess carrier company that insures insurance company for losses in excess of policy liability limit
exclusion contingency not covered by policy
exposure maximum amount company may have to pay on claim
fair market value estimated value of lost property at time of loss, used for determining cost of replacement
fault liability under coverage
fine print often overlooked small type on policy outlining exclusions or limitations
gravamen essential part of claim
group insurance coverage for all members of organization or employees of company
hazard situation that increases possibility of loss
health maintenance organization HMO; health coverage in specific region in which doctors hired by HMO provide services for prepaid subscribers
HMO health maintenance organization
homeowner's policy coverage for fire, theft, or other damage to one's home
indemnification protection from loss or damage and promise to pay for what has been lost or damaged, usu. seen as basic premise of insurance
indemnity payment, repair, or replacement of insured loss
inland marine insurance coverage for freight on inland waterways
insurance system or business of insuring property or persons against loss or harm due to specific contingencies; contract providing for indemnification against loss
insured person paying premiums and receiving guarantee of indemnities
insurer insurance company or entity providing indemnities
liability insurance coverage for loss arising from insured's actions; insured's responsibility for damage or loss
lien charge or claim on policy by third party
life insurance coverage guaranteeing payment of specified sum to beneficiary on death of insured
limitations areas excluded from or not covered by policy
line particular type of insurance offered by company
loading extra charge above premium to cover special risks
major medical coverage of all medical and hospital expenses resulting from illness or injury
malpractice insurance coverage for professionals, esp. doctors, for damage caused by neglect or poor treatment, usu. at very high premium
maturity date at which policy becomes payable
Medicaid government-subsidized medical insurance
Medicare government-subsidized medical insurance for aged
mortality table graph of selected population's death to age ratio, used to calculate risk
mortgage insurance government coverage for institutions making loans for purchase of property
natural death death other than from accident, homicide, or suicide
no-fault insurance covering loss regardless of responsibility for accident
nuisance value amount paid by insurer to dispose of claim

overage excess coverage
payable indemnity due on claim
peril cause of possible loss, such as fire or flood
personal injury condition that is basis for claim against carrier for damages or suffering resulting from accident
policy contract stipulating terms of insurance coverage
premium periodic payment made by insured to maintain coverage
primary insurer company issuing policy to insured
redlining discriminating in issuing property insurance based on location
reinsurance insurance taken by insurance company with another insurer to deflect excess costs in case of catastrophic loss
reparation compensation paid on claim
rider attachment or amendment to policy
risk uncertainty of outcome of situation; likelihood of loss
schedule list in claim of losses; items covered by policy with corresponding values
self-insurance insurance of one's property or interest by creating special fund instead of seeking coverage with underwriter
settlement payment by insurer on claim for loss
spendthrift clause clause preventing beneficiary's creditors from attaching life insurance benefits paid to beneficiary
subrogation assumption by third party of insured's right to seek reimbursement on policy
surety guarantor, usu. insurance company
term time during which policy is in effect
term insurance policy that provides coverage for limited period
term life insurance policy with premiums paid until death of insured
tontine life insurance in which chief beneficiaries are those whose policies are in force at end of specified term
underwriter expert in evaluating risks and assigning rates and coverage
unemployment insurance periodic payments, usu. by state government from payroll contributions, to qualified unemployed person
uninsured motorist coverage automobile insurance protection against losses incurred in accident caused by driver without insurance
workman's compensation government disability insurance for workers

REAL ESTATE

Real Estate Practice
Deeds, Leases, and Real Property Law
Mortgages and Financing

Real Estate Practice

absentee owner owner living away from site of property
abutment bordering of two pieces of property
acreage land measured in units equal to 43,560 square feet
acreage zoning zoning that permits development at low-density locations only
addition expansion of building to include new rooms or outbuildings
agent person legally empowered to represent owner, buyer, or landlord in sale or rental of real estate
appraisal authorized valuation of property based on market value, cost of replacement, or multiplying income derived from it by chosen constant
appreciation increase in property value over time
as is (*adj*) designating property to be purchased in its present condition with no guarantee of its future state
assessed value value placed on property by government for purpose of taxation
board of realty local agency or council supervising real estate transactions
broker agent licensed to sell, rent, or manage property on commission
building codes local ordinances regulating standards of building construction
building inspector licensed official who checks construction sites to guarantee compliance with building codes
chartulary register of estate titles and deeds
commission fee paid to agent or broker on sale or rental
conversion change of building's use and status, as from rental to condominium
co-op cooperative
cooperative multiple-unit property collectively owned by owners of individual units, who hold proprietary leases on their apartments; co-op
depreciation decrease in value of property over time
develop (*vb*) purchase real property with intention of increasing its value, usu. by subdivision, improvement, and construction
duplex single building divided into two residences
exclusive listing listing given to one broker only while reserving right to sell property oneself
exclusive right to sell listing in which broker receives commission no matter who sells property
fair market value highest attainable asking price for property at a given time
finder's fee reward paid to third party for locating buyer or seller of property

first-and-last payment of two month's rent on commencement of rental
fixer-upper *Informal.* run-down property in need of substantial remodeling and repair, purchased at bargain price; handyman's special
fixture any article permanently attached to building or property
flip immediate resale of property, usu. at a profit, sometimes before closing
frontage property line abutting public street or waterway
garden apartment apartment on ground floor of multiple-unit dwelling with private landscaped area; low-level apartment building surrounded by landscaped areas
habitable (*adj*) capable of being inhabited, usu. according to law
handyman's special fixer-upper
homestead tract of federally owned land awarded to claimant meeting statutory requirements
housekeeping care and management of property
improved land property offered with necessities such as lights, sewers, sidewalks, and water lines
improvements facilities or amenities added to property to increase its value
income property property held primarily or exclusively for production of revenue
listing property offered for sale by one or more real estate brokers
loft floor of warehouse transformed into residence, usu. above ground level
market value amount a piece of property is likely to bring when offered for sale on open market
model home decorated, vacant residential structure shown to prospective buyers of similar units
occupancy use to which property is put; possession of land taken to acquire ownership
open house house or apartment open during specified hours for inspection by prospective buyers or tenants
open listing listing given to brokers on nonexclusive basis
option right but not obligation to purchase or lease property
outbuilding independent structure considered part of real property along with primary building
parcel tract or plot of land with set boundaries
property tax tax levied on real property
railroad flat long, narrow apartment in which one room follows another
real estate property in form of land and buildings; practice and business of selling, renting, and developing real property
Realtor *Trademark.* person who works in real estate and is a member of the National Association of Real Estate Boards
realty real estate; practice and procedures involved in disposition of real estate
record of title title to piece of real estate shown in public record
rental property property occupied by tenant for regular payment of set amount to landlord
rent control government regulation of rental charges
rent stabilization rent increases regulated by law
row house one of a series of uniformly built homes connected by common sidewalls
security deposit or pledge made to guarantee contractual obligation
snob zoning exclusionary residential zoning requiring large lots or prohibitively costly design standards
starter home relatively inexpensive, low-end home that is buyer's first owned property, purchased with the intent to sell it for a profit and acquire a better property in future
steering illegal direction of potential buyers toward or away from minority neighborhoods
studio one-room apartment with kitchen and no separate bedroom
subdivision tract of land divided into several lots for construction of individual residences
tax shelter property that generates negative income, held for purpose of obtaining tax deduction
time-share unit single property, esp. vacation home, with multiple owners, each allocated specific amount of time for occupancy
title search examination of public records for liens prior to granting title to new owner
townhouse single-family, multistory urban dwelling, usu. attached to adjacent dwelling by common wall
tract house dwelling on defined area of land, usu. in development, built on similar model to that of adjacent dwellings
vacation property dwelling used only for vacation, often rented as income property
valuation assessment of value of land and buildings
variance exception permitting noncompliance with normal building codes
walk-up apartment above ground floor in building without elevator
zoning dividing city or town into areas by specifying uses, such as commercial or residential, to be made of property in each zone

Deeds, Leases, and Real Property Law

abstract of title official records giving history of title to piece of property
access right to enter and leave property
adverse possession legal acquisition of someone else's real property through prolonged, open, exclusive, unauthorized occupation
air rights legal right to use air space above building
alienation transfer of title of ownership to property from one person to another
attorn (*vb*) agree to remain as tenant under new owner at same property
boilerplate *Informal.* standard legal language for deeds, contracts, or leases
certificate of occupancy municipal issuance stating that property meets minimum requirements for intended use

chain of title documentary history of ownerships of real estate parcel
clear title ownership free of all limits or conditions
cloud on title outside encumbrance or condition that impairs title of ownership
common element area or element of condominium in which each owner has an undivided interest
condemnation legal process by which government purchases private property for public use
conveyance instrument by which property title is transferred
cotenancy ownership or rights to property shared by two or more persons
deed legal document transferring or establishing ownership of property
devise (*vb*) assign or transfer real property by will
easement privilege allowing use of or access to another's property for specific purpose
encroachment unauthorized occupancy or trespass upon another's property, esp. by structure or improvement
encumbrance hindrance that delays clearing of title
escalator clause provision in lease that increases or decreases rent under stated conditions
escheat reversion of property to state when no heir or legal claimant can be found
estate all property, real and personal, owned by a person
estate at will leasehold that can be terminated at will by either party
eviction legal dispossession of tenant by landlord
fee simple estate real estate with absolute ownership and no binding restrictions
foreclosure legal procedure depriving mortgagor of right to sell mortgaged property other than to pay debt
free and clear title property ownership with no claims against it
freehold estate in land, inherited or held for life
future estate right to property contingent on some future event
grant transfer of property
holdover tenant tenant whose lease has expired and against whom eviction action may be brought
index lease lease with rate escalation provision
lease terminating agreement covering possession, use, or occupancy of property
leasehold property acquired under a lease; rights in such property
lessee tenant to whom lease is granted
lessor landlord, grantor of rights to property through lease
lien claim on property to satisfy outstanding debt or duty
lot legally identified parcel of land
marketable title title to property that is free of encumbrances and can be readily sold or mortgaged
mechanic's lien lien secured on property by contractor who has repaired or built it in order to ensure payment for labor and materials
property single piece of real estate owned or possessed
proprietary lease lease granted to shareholders of a cooperative for use and occupancy of their individual space
quiet enjoyment covenant in lease stating that tenant will peaceably enjoy possession of property
quitclaim transfer of all one's interests in property without warranty of title
real property land and permanent structures on it
recording act of entering a document into abstract of title of property
reversion return of property to original owner or heirs at expiration of temporary grant
right of survivorship right of one joint tenant to inherit real estate interest of a deceased joint tenant
riparian rights rights of owners of land adjoining a body of water
squatter person occupying public or private land or residence without benefit of legal title
sublease lease by tenant to third party on already leased premises
survey legal description of land based on observations of licensed professional surveyor
tenant person with temporary, conditional use of property owned by another
title all elements and written documents constituting legal ownership of property
title deed document constituting evidence of legal ownership
trust property interest held by one party for benefit of another
trust deed document that conveys interest to a trust as security for loan

Mortgages and Financing

acceleration clause provision of mortgage that advances date for payment of balance under certain circumstances
adjustable-rate mortgage variable-rate mortgage
assumable mortgage mortgage taken over from seller by buyer
balloon payment single, large, final payment on loan
binder preliminary, temporary agreement to make down payment and purchase property pending formal contract
buy-down arrangement in which mortgage carries below-market interest rate for first few years
chattel mortgage loan secured by personal property
clear escrow receive approval of application for mortgage loan, required to gain title to property
closing final approval of escrow in property purchase; gathering of all parties to consummate real estate transaction; settlement
earnest money good-faith sum of cash used as binder
equity value of property in excess of claims and loans against it
escrow deed held by neutral party, such as bank,

for delivery upon fulfillment of certain conditions, usu. making of payments
financing arranging purchase of property through down payment and mortgage loan
first mortgage mortgage having priority over other mortgages on property
Freddie Mac Federal Home Loan Mortgage Corporation, which buys mortgages from lenders
Ginnie Mae GNMA; Government National Mortgage Association; agency of federal government that buys pools of mortgages from lender institutions and sells interest in them to the public
interest charge made at set rate on money borrowed to purchase property, added to principal amount borrowed
loan-to-value ratio fraction of appraised value that lender will loan on property
mortgage transfer or conveyance of real property as security for debt; written instrument for such transfer
mortgagee person to whom property is mortgaged
mortgage insurance guarantee of mortgage payment to mortgagor by third party
mortgagor person who mortgages property
origination fee points charged on face value of mortgage at time of purchase
points percentage of loan principal added to cost of purchase, one point equaling one percent
principal amount of money borrowed from mortgagor, on which interest is computed; authorized party to sale, lease, or rental agreement
refinance (*vb*) borrow additional funds against equity in property
satisfaction of mortgage recordable document stating that loan has been repaid
second mortgage mortgage taken by third party on property already mortgaged
settlement closing
variable-rate mortgage loan on which interest rate changes with predetermined factors, such as prime rate; adjustable-rate mortgage
wraparound mortgage mortgage that contains obligation to repay a smaller, previously existing mortgage; second mortgage

OCCUPATIONS

Trades and Crafts
Occupations and Job Titles

Trades and Crafts

armorer maker and repairer of armor and arms
artisan skilled craftsman
barber beardcutter and hairdresser
blacksmith maker of forged iron objects
boatwright maker of seagoing vessels
bookwright maker of books
brazier brass worker
brewer maker of malt liquors
butler house servant in charge of wines and table service
candlewright maker of candles
carpenter cutter and framer of wooden structures
cartwright maker of carts and wagons
carver cutter of meat at table
chandler candle maker; dealer in provisions and small wares
cobbler shoemaker
collier coal miner
cooper maker of barrels and casks
die maker maker of dies or cutting and shaping tools
draper maker and seller of cloth
fletcher maker of arrows
founder caster of metal objects
fuller maker of gathers in cloth garments
gatewright maker of gates
glassblower maker of glass vessels or sheet glass through blowing process
glazier maker and installer of glass
goldsmith gold worker
haberdasher retail dealer in men's furnishings
joiner one who does finishing woodwork, esp. construction by joining pieces of wood
lather worker on a lathe
luthier maker of stringed instruments
mason builder using stone or brick
mercer dealer in expensive fabrics
miller keeper or operator of mill or processing plant for grain, wood, coffee, or cotton
millwright builder of mills; one tending workshop fixtures
monger trader or dealer
pitwright carpenter working in or about a mine
playwright writer of dramatic pieces
plowright maker and repairer of plows
potter maker of fired earthenware vessels
puttier cementer; glazier
rigger scaffolder; person tending to rigging, esp. of ships or aircraft
saddler maker of horse saddles
shipwright builder of ships
silversmith forger or shaper of silver objects
smith worker who shapes or forges, esp. in metals, including: anvilsmith, blacksmith, bladesmith, boilersmith, clocksmith, coppersmith, goldsmith, gunsmith, hammersmith, ironsmith, jobsmith, knifesmith, locksmith, sawsmith, scissors smith, silversmith, stonesmith, swordsmith, tinsmith, toolsmith
steeplejack repairer of steeples and chimneys
stonecutter cutter, carver, and dresser of stone
stonemason cutter of stone or builder in stone
tanner maker of prepared animal hides
tilewright maker of tiles
tinker mender of metal objects
turner maker of articles turned on a lathe
vintner maker and seller of wines
wainwright maker of carts and wagons
weaver maker of textiles by loom or by mechanical or manual interlacing of threads

welder joiner of metals by use of heat
wheelwright maker and repairer of wheels
wright workman in construction; mechanic

Occupations and Job Titles

accountant, account executive, acrobat, actor, actress, actuary, adjustor, adman, administrator, adviser, aeronautical engineer, aerospace engineer, agent, agricultural engineer, agronomist, air traffic controller, amateur, ambassador, analyst, anthropologist, apartment manager, apparel salesperson, appraiser, apprentice, archaeologist, architect, architectural engineer, archivist, arc welder, army engineer, arrowsmith, artisan, artist, asbestos worker, assembler, assistant, associate, astrologer, astronaut, astronomer, astrophysicist, athlete, attendant attorney, auctioneer, auditor, au pair, author, automotive engineer, auto repairman, auto worker

babysitter, baggage handler, bailiff, baker, ballerina, banker, bank teller, barber, bartender, bath attendant, beautician, beekeeper, bellboy, bellhop, bench carpenter, billing clerk, biochemist, biologist, biophysicist, blacksmith, blue-collar worker, boarding housekeeper, body worker, boilermaker, boniface, bookbinder, bookie, bookkeeper, bootblack, boss, botanist, bouncer, bounty hunter, brakeman, braze welder, brewer, bricklayer, brickmaker, bridge operator, broadcaster, broker, budget analyst, builder, bus driver, businessman, businesswoman, butcher, butler

cabdriver, cabinetmaker, calligrapher, candy maker, carny worker, carpenter, cartographer, carver, cashier, caster, caterer, cement mixer, ceramic engineer, ceramicist, chairman, chairwoman, chauffeur, checkout clerk, chef, chemical engineer, chemical worker, chemist, chief administrative officer, chief executive officer, chief operating officer, chimney sweep, chiropractor, choreographer, cinematographer, city manager, civil engineer, civil service employee, cleaner, clergyman, clerk, clockmaker, clothier, clown, coach, cobbler, commercial artist, commodities broker, common laborer, communications engineer, communications specialist, composer, comptroller, computer programmer, computer technician, concessionaire, conductor, confectioner, con man, construction engineer, construction worker, consul, contractor, cook, cooper, coppersmith, copyeditor, copywriter, coremaker, coroner, correctional officer, cosmetologist, costermonger, counselor, courier, couturier, cowboy, craftsman crier, critic, cryptographer, curator, custodian

dancer, data processor, dealer, decorator, defender, dental hygienist, dental supply salesman, dental technician, dentist, designer, detective, die maker, dietitian, diplomat, director, disc jockey, dishwasher, distiller, distributor, docent, doctor, doll maker, domestic, doorman, door-to-door salesman, drafter, drainage worker, dramatist, dramaturge, driver, dustman

ecologist, economist, editor, educator, electrical engineer, electrician, electronics engineer, electroplater, elevator operator, embalmer, embroiderer, employee, employer, employment agent, engine driver, engineer, engraver, ensign, entertainer, entrepreneur, etcher, evangelist, excavator, executive, extra

fabricator, farmer, farm hand, farrier, fashion designer, federal employee,

field hand, fieldworker, file clerk, filmmaker, filtration worker, financier, firefighter, fireman, fire-protection engineer, firer, fisherman, fishery worker, fitter, flier, floor layer, food processor, foreman, forester, forest ranger, forger, forklift operator, founder, foundryman, freelancer, freight operator, fuel engineer, functionary, furnace engineer, furniture maker

gamekeeper, game maker, garbageman, gardener, garment worker, gas fitter, gas welder, gate clerk, gem cutter, gem dealer, geneticist, geographer, geological engineer, geologist, glassblower, glazier, goldsmith, governess, government worker, grammarian, graphic artist, gravedigger, groundskeeper, guard, guide, guru, gynecologist

haircutter, hairdresser, hand, hand sewer, handyman, hardware salesman, harvester, hatcheck person, hat maker, heat-treater, helper, high school teacher, highway engineer, highwayman, historian, hod carrier, home economist, homemaker, horologist, hostess, hostler, houseboy, housecleaner, housekeeper, housewife, hunter, hydraulic engineer

illuminating engineer, illustrator, indexer, industrial engineer, industrialist, information clerk, inspector, installer, instructor, instrumentalist, insulation worker, insurance salesman, interior designer, intern, interpreter, interview clerk, investigator, investor, irrigation engineer

jack, jailor, janitor, jester, jeweler, jewelry maker, journalist, journeyman, judge, juggler, jurist, juror, justice

keypunch operator, kitchen worker, knitter

laborer, labor leader, lab technician, laundress, lawyer, layman, layout artist, leatherworker, legal secretary, legislator, lexicographer, librarian, lighting technician, linguist, liquor salesman, lithographer, locker room attendant, locksmith, logger, logician, longshoreman, lumberjack

machine operator, machinist, magician maid, mailroom worker, maintenance man, maître d'hôtel, maker, manager, manicurist, manufacturer, marine, marine biologist, marine engineer, marine mechanic, marshal, mason, masseur, master, mate, mathematician, meat cutter, mechanic, mechanical engineer, melter, mental health worker, mercer, mercerizer, merchandise displayer, messenger, metallurgical engineer, metallurgist, metal processor, metalworker, meteorologist, meter maid, midwife, migrant worker, military engineer, miller, miner, mining engineer, minister, model, model maker, molder, mold maker, mortician, mover, municipal employee, municipal engineer, musician

nanny, naval engineer, navigator, net fisherman, newscaster, night watchman, novelist, nuclear engineer, nuclear physicist, nurse, nursemaid, nutritionist

obstetrician, occupational therapist, oceanographer, office worker, official, ombudsman, opera singer operator, ophthalmologist, optician, optometrist, orderly, ordnance engineer, ore refiner, orthopedist, osteopath, overseer

page, painter, paleontologist, paperhanger, park ranger, partner, patternmaker, paver, payroll clerk, performer, personnel officer, pest control worker, petroleum engineer, petroleum worker, pharmacist, philosopher, photoengraver, photographer, physical therapist, physician, physicist, physiologist, pickler, pilot, pimp, plasterer, plastics worker, playwright, plumber, poet, policeman, political scientist, politician, pornographer, porter, potter, power engineer, power plant operator, power supply engineer, practical nurse, practitioner, president, press agent, press secretary, priest, printer, private investigator, producer, product engineer, production clerk, professional, professor, projectionist, proofreader, proprietor, prosecutor, prostitute, psychiatrist, psychoanalyst, psychologist, public administrator, publicist, public relations man, public servant, publisher, puddler, purchasing agent

quality control officer

rabbi, rack jobber, radar engineer, radio commentator, radio engineer, radio operator, railroad conductor, railroad engineer, rancher, real estate broker, receptionist, refrigerator engineer, registered nurse, rehab counselor, repairman, representative, research assistant, research engineer, researcher, retail clerk, rigger, riveter, road worker, rocket engineer, rocket scientist, roofer, rubber worker

sailor, salesperson, sanitary engineer, screenwriter, scribe, sculptor, seamstress, seaweed gatherer, secretary, securities analyst, security guard, semanticist, semiotician, serf, servant, service station attendant, sheet metal worker, shipper, ship's captain, ship's mate, shoemaker, shopkeeper, silversmith, skilled laborer, slave, smith, smuggler, social worker, sociologist, solderer, soldier, sole proprietor, solicitor, sound engineer, sound man, speech pathologist, spinner, sponge gatherer, sporting goods salesman, spotter, stainer, stand-in, state employee, statistician, steam engineer, steam fitter, steeplejack, stenographer, stevedore, steward, stewardess, stockbroker, stock clerk, stonecutter, stonemason, stoneworker, street sweeper, structural engineer, stunt man, stylist, subcontractor, superintendent, supervisor surgeon, surveyor, swami, systems analyst

tactician, tailor, talent agent, talent scout, tax collector, tax preparer, teacher, teamster, technician, telegraph operator, telephone engineer, telephone operator, telephone repairman, teller, tender, tester, textile engineer, textile worker, therapist, thermal cutter, thief, ticket agent, ticket taker, tile setter, tinner, tinsmith, tobacconist, tobacco worker, toll taker, tool engineer, tour guide, tractor driver, trader, tradesman, trade unionist, traffic officer, trainer, translator, transportation engineer, transport worker, trapper, travel agent, traveling salesman, treasurer, tree farmer, truck driver, trucker, tutor, type-caster, type composer, typesetter, typist

undertaker, unskilled worker, upholsterer, urban planner, usher, utility worker

valet, vending machine operator, vendor, ventilation engineer, venture capitalist, veterinarian, vice president, videotape engineer, vintner, vocalist, vocational therapist

waiter, waitress, wallpaperer, warden, warder, wardrobe attendant, warehouseman, waterproofer, water-supply engineer, waxer, weatherman, weaver, welder, welding engineer, wet nurse, white-collar worker, wholesaler, winemaker, woodcutter, woodworker, worker, wrecker, wright, writer

yeoman

zookeeper, zoologist

Chapter Thirteen

Social Sciences

ANTHROPOLOGY

Branches and Disciplines
Ages, Species, and Races of Humankind
Kinship, Marriage, and Other Customs
Practice, Techniques, Artifacts, and Tools

Branches and Disciplines

anthropogeography study of geographical distribution of humankind and relationship of peoples to their environment
anthropological linguistics study of relationship between language and culture, esp. in preliterate societies
anthropology study of physical and sociocultural aspects of humankind, including human origins, evolution, biological characteristics, customs, and belief systems
applied anthropology purposive study of specific, often primitive society, esp. by authorities making practical decisions about it
archaeology scientific study of early historic and prehistoric cultures by excavation and analysis of their artifacts, monuments, and other remains
business anthropology study of group behavior, workplace design, and other human problems derived from corporate environments
cultural anthropology study of characteristics, similarities, and differences among various human cultures, based esp. on fieldwork and empirical data
dendrochronology method of dating past events by analysis of annual rings of trees
epigraphy study of ancient inscriptions
ethnoarchaeology study of contemporary primitive cultures, esp. as means of understanding prehistoric cultures
ethnobiology study of how different human cultures use plants and animals
ethnobotany study of agricultural customs and plant lore of a culture
ethnography systematic description of individual cultures
ethnohistory study of development of cultures, esp. through analysis of archaeological findings
ethnolinguistics study of interplay between language and culture
ethnology analysis of cultures, esp. with regard to their historical development, similarities, and dissimilarities
ethnomethodology study of rules and rituals on which most social interactions are based
ethnomusicology study of relationship between primitive or folk music and culture to which it belongs
ethnoscience study of systems and concepts of knowledge and classification of objects and concepts among primitive peoples
paleontology study of life forms existing in earlier geologic periods, based on their fossil remains
philosophical anthropology study of basic nature and essence of humankind
physical anthropology branch of anthropology concerned with fossil origins of man, evolution, and human behavior
praxeology study of human conduct
social anthropology branch of anthropology concerned with social relationships, esp. those institutionalized into fixed behavior patterns such as ritual, religion, kinship, marriage, and political and economic structures
structural anthropology branch of anthropology based on principles of structural linguistics

Ages, Species, and Races of Humankind

anthropoid member of primate suborder Anthropoidea, including monkeys, apes, and human beings
Australopithecus extinct genus of small-brained, large-toothed, bipedal hominid near-men whose fossil remains date back to four million years in Africa and who had the ability to stand fully erect
Australopithecus afarensis earliest species of *Australopithecus* that lived four million years ago in East Africa
Australopithecus africanus species of *Australopithecus*, characterized by small stature and use of simple weapons, that lived three million years ago
Australopithecus boisei species of rugged *Australopithecus*, characterized by large teeth, that lived one to two million years ago
Australopithecus robustus species of *Australopithecus*, larger in stature but probably less intelligent than *Australopithecus africanus*, that lived two million years ago
bipedalism locomotion on two feet, characteristic of hominids
Bronze Age period beginning around 4000 B.C. characterized by use of bronze tools, the wheel, and ox-drawn plows, and by growth of first civilizations in Egypt and Sumeria
Caucasian race one of three traditional human racial groupings, characterized by light skin pigmentation, straight to curly hair, and light to dark eyes, inhabiting Northern Hemisphere, esp. Europe
cave man cave dweller, esp. of Stone Age
Copper Age cultural period between Neolithic and Bronze ages, characterized by ability to extract copper for use in making tools
Cro-Magnon man tall, erect Upper Paleolithic prototype of modern *Homo sapiens* in Europe between 40,000 and 30,000 years ago, that used stone tools and produced cave paintings
Eolithic Age Dawn Stone Age, between 2.5 and two million years ago, in which hominoid near-men used primitive, fractured stone tools

Folsom culture early North American hunting-gathering culture that flourished about 9000 B.C., characterized by use of fluted stone spearheads
Heidelberg man species of primitive hominid contemporary with *Pithecanthropus* around 500,000 years ago, having massive teeth but undeveloped chin
hominid any of modern or extinct bipedal primates of family Hominidae, including genera *Homo* and *Australopithecus*
hominoid member of superfamily Hominoidea, including modern great apes, humans, and their extinct ancestors
Homo genus of bipedal primates in family Hominidae, including modern *Homo sapiens* and several extinct species
Homo erectus extinct species of hominid, formerly known as *Pithecanthropus erectus*, known from Peking and Java man discoveries, having erect stature and postcranial skull but smallish brain, low forehead, and protruding face, characterized by use of crude stone tools and possibly simple speech, that lived from 500,000 to 250,000 years ago
Homo habilis extinct species of upright hominid in East Africa that existed two to 1.5 million years ago
Homo sapiens species of bipedal primate to which modern human beings belong, beginning 250,000 years ago during Stone Age with *Homo sapiens neanderthalensis*, characterized by use of tools and language
humankind all members of human race
Iron Age period following Bronze Age, in which humankind learned to smelt iron for tools and weapons, beginning around 2000 B.C. in Near East
Java man extinct race of early hominid, *Pithecanthropus erectus*, with apelike skull and human limb structure, whose skeletal remains were found in Java
Lower Paleolithic period earliest portion of Old Stone Age, between two million and 200,000 years ago
Mesolithic period Middle Stone Age following Paleolithic age, from 10,000 to 8000 B.C. in Europe, characterized by first food-producers, development of boats and sleds, and use of microliths
Middle Paleolithic period middle portion of Old Stone Age, between 200,000 and 40,000 years ago
missing link hypothetical species assumed to bridge evolutionary gap between anthropoid apes and human beings, sometimes identified as *Australopithecus*
Mongoloid race one of three traditional human racial groupings, characterized by yellowish complexion, straight black hair, and epicanthic folds about eyes, esp. inhabiting Asia
Neanderthal man extinct race of Middle Paleolithic man, powerful and physically robust with brain capacity comparable to modern man, that inhabited Europe and western Asia between 100,000 and 40,000 years ago
Negroid race one of three traditional human racial groupings, characterized by dark skin pigmentations, curly hair, and wide features, primarily inhabiting Southern Hemisphere, esp. Africa
Neolithic period New Stone Age preceding Bronze Age, between 8000 and 4000 B.C. in Near East, characterized by settlement into villages, domestication of animals, grain cultivation, pottery, textile weaving, cave painting, and flint-mining
Olmec (*adj*) of or pertaining to an early prehistoric New World civilization, from 1500 to 500 B.C. in Mexico, characterized by extensive agriculture, dating system, pyramids, trade, and fine artwork
Paleolithic period Old Stone Age period from two million years ago through 10,000 B.C., characterized by hunting-gathering society and use of increasingly sophisticated stone tools, divided into Lower, Middle, and Upper Paleolithic periods
Peking man extinct, early *Homo erectus* whose fossil remains were discovered in China, characterized by hunting and use of fire and stone tools
Piltdown man hypothetical early modern human being whose existence was based on skull fragments found in England, believed to be missing link between apes and man but later exposed as fake
Pithecanthropus former genus of extinct hominids now assigned to proposed species *Homo erectus*
prehistoric man certain hominid species of genus *Homo* that lived before recorded history
prehistory period of human development prior to recorded events, known through archaeological discoveries
Proconsul extinct hominoid subgenus that lived 17 to 20 million years ago and may have been ancestral to modern chimpanzees and apes
protohistory period of transition between prehistory and earliest recorded history
pygmy term denoting groups whose typical male averages less than 59 inches (150 cm) in height, generally hunter-gatherers with few crafts, found esp. in central Africa and Philippines
race one of the three major human groupings whose members tend to breed among themselves and share inherited physical characteristics: Caucasian, Mongoloid, Negroid
Ramapithecus extinct genus of late Miocene hominoid, formerly believed to have been ancestral to hominids, that lived about twelve million years ago
recorded history written record of history made by culture having formal language
Stone Age period beginning around two million years ago, characterized by use of increasingly sophisticated stone tools and weapons and, in latter ages, by development of food cultivation, villages, and crafts, usu. divided into Paleolithic, Mesolithic, and Neolithic periods and ending with dawn of civilization in Bronze Age around 4000 B.C.
Sumer ancient region in Near East in which city-states and written language first developed in late Neolithic period, after 4000 B.C.

troglodyte prehistoric cave dweller
Upper Paleolithic period latter portion of Old Stone Age, between 40,000 and 10,000 B.C.

Kinship, Marriage, and Other Customs

affinity kinship relationship based on marriage
ancestor worship veneration of spirits of dead ancestors believed to influence affairs of the living
animism belief in spiritual beings and esp. that natural objects and phenomena possess souls
anthropophagy cannibalism
bigamy accepted practice of marriage to more than one person at a time among certain cultures
cannibal person who eats human flesh, esp. as part of tribal religious or magical ceremony
cargo cult any messianic native religious system found in southwestern Pacific islands, formed in response to white civilization, and characterized by belief that ancestors will return with cargoes of modern goods
caste system any endogamous, hereditary social grouping based on status, economic position, and mores
clan unilineal kinship descent group, either through male (patrilineal) or female (matrilineal) line
conventionalized art art based on accepted manner of depicting subject matter; stylized art
death rites ceremonies, burial, and mourning that accompany passage of person from world of the living to the dead
dietary laws secular or religious rules for what foods may be consumed under certain conditions, used to maintain group's unique social identity
dowry money or goods given by bride's family to bridegroom at marriage
endogamy rules defining boundaries of marriage within specific tribe or social group; marriage within such tribe or group
exogamy rules defining social unit within which marriage is forbidden; marriage outside specific tribe or social group
extended family kinship group including nuclear family and relatives, esp. when living in one household
family group of persons related by blood, esp. parents and children, forming basic biosocial unit
kinship family relationships and system of social rules governing descent, inheritance, marriage, residence, and sexual relations within kinship groups
marriage state in which two persons are bonded together under socially prescribed rules, esp. for procreation and child-rearing
matriarchy social organization in which mother is head of family and descent is traced through female line
matrilocal (*adj*) designating extended family in which husband joins household of wife's parents; uxorilocal
moiety one of two divisions of tribe based on unilineal descent through either mother's or father's line
monogamy social practice of marriage with only one person at a time
naturalistic art realistic art
neolocal (*adj*) living away from both husband's and wife's relatives
nuclear family basic family unit restricted to parents and their offspring
patriarchy social organization in which father is head of family and descent is traced through male line
patrilocal (*adj*) designating extended family in which wife joins household of husband's parents; virilocal
polyandry practice of having more than one husband at a time
polygamy socially approved practice of having more than one spouse at a time
polygyny practice of having more than one wife at a time
realistic art art that strives to represent objects with exact likenesses; naturalistic art
representative art art that portrays nature and life in recognizable manner
rite formal or ceremonial act or procedure prescribed in solemn and religious occasions
rites of passage ceremonies or rituals that accompany individual's passage from one social status to another, such as puberty, initiation, marriage, and burial
ritual established procedure or ceremony prescribed by custom for solemn occasions, such as rite of passage
stylized art conventionalized art
symbolic art art that employs symbols to signify objects and convey meaning
taboo culture-specific prohibition of certain behavior, word, or object
totem animal, plant, or object with which clan, tribe, or people identifies in its rituals, often believing it to be an ancestor
tribe group of persons, usu. of common descent, occupying one community and sharing common language, customs, and traditions
unilineal (*adj*) having descent traced through either male or female line
uxorilocal (*adj*) matrilocal
virilocal (*adj*) patrilocal

Practice, Techniques, Artifacts, and Tools

anthropometry measurement of size and proportions of human body using calibrated instrument
artifact object made or used by human beings, esp. one found at archaeological excavation, providing evidence of an earlier culture's existence
barrow tumulus
bladelet small, blade-shaped, sometimes reworked piece of stone used as cutting edge of tool or weapon in late Stone Age
cave paintings art form characteristic of Upper Paleolithic period, practiced in European caves from around 30,000 B.C.
cephalic index measurement of head used in

physical anthropology, consisting of ratio of maximum width to maximum length, with results classified as dolichocephalic (long-headed), mesocephalic, or brachycephalic (short-headed)
cist prehistoric tomb or casket with stone walls
civilization stage of cultural development marked by written records, development of cities, and advanced levels of science, government, and art; one culture or people of a specific place and time
cliff dwellings shelters in caves or on cliff ledges built by members of prehistoric people in southwestern United States
convergent evolution tendency of different lines of descent to develop similar characteristics in adapting to specific environmental conditions
core tool stone tool made by chipping flakes from stone core until it has assumed desired size and shape
crannog lake dwelling built on artificial island
cromlech megalithic chamber tomb
cross dating method of determining age for archaeological site of unknown age by comparing its distinguishing traits to those of another site of known age
culture shared knowledge, beliefs, and ways of living built up by members of group and transmitted from one generation to next; specific group sharing such knowledge, beliefs, and ways of living over defined period of time
cuneiform triangular or wedge-shaped pictographic writing system characteristic of cultures of ancient Near East from around 3500 B.C.
Darwinism theory of origin and evolution of species which postulates survival of the fittest individuals or species through natural selection, based on works of Charles Darwin
dig excavation
dolmen megalithic tomb consisting of stone slab laid across two or more large, upright stones
ethnic group people distinguished by common racial or cultural background
ethnocentrism belief in inherent superiority of one's own ethnic group or culture; tendency to view alien groups or cultures through prism of one's culture
evolution theory of development of species from simpler forms, based on work of Charles Darwin
excavation archaeological site at which layers of earth have been systematically exposed by digging to uncover human artifacts or remains of earlier cultures; dig
flint piece of hard stone used as primitive tool or to strike spark for making fire
folklore traditional beliefs, customs, and legends of a people, esp. those expressed orally through memory and practice
folkways patterns of behavior and belief common to particular group of people, learned from other members of group
genealogy study and record of family origins and history of descent
graffito drawing or writing scratched on wall or other surface
hand ax large, bifacial stone tool of Lower Paleolithic period
henge Neolithic monument consisting of circular area enclosed by ditch and containing circles of upright stone or wood pillars, used for ritual purposes or astronomical observations
hieroglyphics pictographic script of ancient Egyptians, in which the symbols used are conventionalized, recognizable pictures of the things represented
indigenous native to or characteristic of a particular region
kitchen midden shell mound
kiva large, underground chamber used in Pueblo Indian religious ceremonies
megalithic monuments large stone tombs and dolmens of undressed stone, such as Stonehenge, built in Europe during Neolithic period and early Bronze Age
menhir upright monumental stone standing alone or in arrangement with others
microlith tiny flint scraping tool for dressing skins, characteristic of Mesolithic cultures
monolith monument such as obelisk constructed of a single, huge stone block, typical of Neolithic period
nomadism pastoral lifestyle in which group with no fixed residence moves from place to place on seasonal circuit
pastoralism often nomadic mode of subsistence, usu. among small groups, based on herding of domesticated livestock
petroglyph prehistoric drawing or carving on stone
potsherd pottery fragment used in dating excavation sites or tracing cultural contacts, esp. in Neolithic period
preliterate (*adj*) designating culture or people who lack any writing system; nonliterate
primitive (*adj*) pertaining to preliterate or tribal people with strong cultural and physical similarities to their early ancestors
Rosetta stone stone slab, discovered in Egypt, bearing parallel inscriptions in Greek, Egyptian hieroglyphs, and demotic characters, facilitating decipherment of hieroglyphs
shell mound prehistoric refuse heap containing remains of shellfish and human artifacts; kitchen midden
site exact location of single unit of territory studied by archaeologists
society autonomous community of persons sharing common customs, beliefs, goals, and attitudes, organized together under accepted rules
stele monumental, upright stone slab or pillar bearing an inscription or design
Stonehenge prehistoric, megalithic monument erected by a Bronze Age culture in England around 1500 B.C.
tablets flat rock slabs bearing hieroglyphs or cuneiform characters, used to reconstruct Bronze Age and Iron Age history
trilithon prehistoric structure consisting of two upright stones supporting a horizontal stone

tumulus artificial mound, esp. over grave; barrow
village small, settled community of several hundred people living together

SOCIOLOGY

Attitudes and Behavior

adaptation ability to learn behavior that helps in adjusting to individuals, groups, and technology
ageism discrimination based on age
agnosticism belief that human beings cannot know whether there is a God or understand things beyond the material world
anthropocentric (*adj*) regarding human beings as center of the universe
anthropomorphism attribution of human shape and character to animals, deities, or inanimate objects
anti-Semitism prejudice against and persecution of Jews
apartheid policy of strict racial segregation and discrimination in South Africa
apolitical (*adj*) having no interest in politics
atheism conviction that there is no God
bigotry intolerance of those different than oneself
chauvinism unreasoning devotion to one's race, sex, or country
class consciousness awareness of belonging to one class in the social order
conformity living according to social expectations and norms
convention customary social practice or rule
crime against humanity crime or crimes, such as genocide, directed against particular group that has committed no criminal act
crusade actions pursued zealously and vigorously to further some cause
custom traditional social convention enforced by general disapproval of its violation
decorum propriety and good taste; polite behavior
deviance marked divergence from society's accepted norms
discrimination different treatment for certain racial, ethnic, religious, or sexual groups
double standard moral code applying more stringent standards to one group than to another, esp. between sexes
doxy accepted belief, esp. religious
ethnocentrism belief that one's nation, culture, or ethnic group is superior
ethos characteristic and distinguishing attitudes and habits of group
etiquette established conventions of polite social intercourse
fellowship companionship, generosity toward others
flag-waving display of zealous patriotism
folkways beliefs, preferences, and customs of social unit or group
groupthink conformity to group values and ethics
hero worship idolizing of an individual, esp. a sports star or entertainer
honor system system that trusts people, esp. students or prisoners, to work honestly, without supervision
iconoclasm opposition to accepted ideas and beliefs
ideology body of beliefs and ideas of one person, group, or culture
indoctrination training others in one's beliefs
internalization incorporation of cultural values and attitudes within oneself, consciously or unconsciously
isolationism opposition to involvement in affairs external to one's community or nation
Jim Crow discrimination against blacks
jingoism excessive, often warlike, national chauvinism
lifestyle consistent pattern of one's life, attitudes, customs, values, and economic standing
manners prevailing customs of polite, conventional behavior
martyrdom willingness to die rather than renounce one's beliefs or principles
mass hysteria irrational behavior on a wide scale caused by unfounded belief or fear
master race race that is supposedly biologically equipped to rule all others
middle-of-the-road (*adj*) favoring a point of view midway between extremes
mores essential folkways and binding customs of a society
nationalism patriotism, belief in one's country
nihilism belief that there is no purpose to existence; rejection of established laws and institutions
nonviolence abstention from use of violence on moral grounds
passive resistance opposition to established government by nonviolent acts of noncooperation
politically correct (*adj*) marked by or conforming to typically progressive, orthodox views such as environmentalism, pacifism, and social equality for those outside the white male power structure and Western, Judeo-Christian tradition
prejudice predisposition toward baseless intolerance and hatred for particular group
propriety socially acceptable conduct
provincialism narrow concern with one's own locale or people
racism segregation and persecution based on doctrine of superiority of one race over others
religious tolerance acceptance of those practicing faith different from one's own

reverse discrimination bias against majority as a result of efforts to improve lot of minority
ritualistic (*adj*) performed according to a rigidly prescribed order
role pattern of expected behavior for individual in given situation in relation to social status
role conflict problems that occur when a person's roles conflict with each other or with his or her values
scapegoating blaming members of minority group for social or economic problems
segregation social separation, esp. of races
sexism discrimination and denial of opportunity on basis of sex, esp. against women
sexual harassment unwanted advances and persistent pestering for sexual favors, esp. by person in position of authority such as employer
taboo prohibition or superstition established through accepted social custom
tokenism practice of making a token gesture by hiring or admitting a small number of minority group members
tolerance liberal attitude toward differing lifestyles, cultures, and beliefs
tradition long-established custom or practice of a society
upward mobility ascension of the socioeconomic ladder
values principles, standards, and goals given high intrinsic worth by society

Cultural Movements, Events, and Institutions

affirmative action program to increase presence of women and minorities in public and private sectors
asphalt jungle the city, esp. crowded, urban neighborhoods regarded as dangerous
baby boom burst of population in generation born just after World War II
backlash reaction opposite to that intended by a particular social movement
Big Brother officials of authoritarian state that erodes privacy of the individual to exercise control
blacklist privately circulated list of those to be denied employment because of allegedly subversive views
black nationalism advocacy of establishment of separate black nation in United States
black power political and economic power sought by black Americans
busing transferring schoolchildren out of their neighborhoods to achieve racial balance in schools
cause principle or movement vigorously upheld and supported
consciousness-raising increasing awareness, esp. among women, of their secondary status and particular group needs and goals through interaction with other women
cooptation winning over of an adversary to one's own belief
counterculture culture and lifestyle of late 1960's, esp. among young, characterized by opposition to war and society's prevailing values
crisis intervention intervention by group offering immediate help to potential suicides, addicts, and other troubled persons
Cultural Revolution radical sociopolitical movement in China during 1960's in which Mao Zedong attempted to restructure society and reinvigorate his revolution
culture shock trauma resulting from movement from one culture or society to another
current affairs events, movements, institutions, and trends in political and social life at present time
environmentalism active concern for state of Earth's natural resources
equal opportunity employment hiring of employees without regard to race, sex, or national origin
establishment society's ruling class, representing all vested interests
feminism doctrine and programs promoting rights and interests of women, esp. in male-dominated society
future shock disorientation and anxiety due to inability to cope with continual, rapid, technological change and breakdown of old values
gay liberation sociopolitical movement to combat legal and social discrimination against homosexuals
genetic engineering biological creation of improved species through recombining of spliced DNA from different species
gentrification restoration of run-down urban neighborhoods by upper- or middle-income families
global village the world as one single community, esp. owing to mass media, communications, and rapid transportation
green revolution increased food production for underdeveloped nations through improved agricultural methods
groundswell rapidly growing wave of popular sentiment or opinion, often lacking overt leadership
halfway house place for societal readjustment after institutional confinement
holocaust large-scale destruction of human life
Holocaust systematic murder of European Jews by the Nazis during World War II
hotline direct telephone line to assistance, for use in personal crisis
hunger strike refusal to eat, usu. by prisoners or demonstrators, until certain demands are met
inner city blighted, poor section of metropolitan area
life-care (*adj*) designed to provide for basic needs of elderly residents, usu. in return for a regular fee
lunatic fringe extreme minority on periphery of any larger movement
movement organized actions taken by group working together to achieve specific goal
old-world (*adj*) pertaining to traditional European customs and values
peaceful coexistence policy of cooperation and

noninterference between United States and Soviet Union
pop culture contemporary style, art, and media
radical chic patronage of extremists and left-wing radicals by the rich and famous, sometimes without genuine conviction
rally mass demonstration in support of specific cause
riot violent, large-scale public disturbance, often for purposes of protest
sit-in occupation of an institution to protest its policies
soup kitchen place set up in run-down neighborhood to feed poor and homeless
special interest group group seeking to advance specific cause by gaining government favors
storefront group self-help community action group housed in storefront
teach-in lectures and debates at university or college to protest school's policy
test ban multinational agreement to stop nuclear testing
Third World underdeveloped countries of world
underground secret resistance organization, esp. in totalitarian country
urban renewal redevelopment of run-down parts of city
women's liberation movement to combat sexual discrimination and achieve full rights and opportunities for women equal to men, orig. late 1960's

Social Types, Norms, and Symbols

baby boomer person born just after World War II
bag lady poor, homeless, usu. old woman living in streets and carrying belongings in shopping bag; shopping bag lady
beatnik member of Beat Generation of 1950's, who were nonconformist in dress, attitude, and artistic expression
beautiful people wealthy or famous trendsetters
blue blood member of aristocratic or socially prominent family
blue book directory of socially prominent persons
bohemian person living unconventionally, esp. an artist
café society fashionable high society
canaille riffraff
DINK dual income, no kids; married couple without children, both of whom work
empty nester parent whose child or children have moved away from home
everyman typical or common man
expatriate person who has rejected allegiance to native land and lives elsewhere
flower child hippie
gaybasher heterosexual, often homophobic person, who physically assaults or defames gays
glitterati chic, wealthy, famous people
good old boy *Informal.* stereotypical white male of U.S. South who drinks beer, hunts, jokes, and socializes with his friends
gray eminence one who exercises great power unofficially
hard-hat *Informal.* working-class person, often holding politically conservative ideas
high society those who are fashionable, wealthy, and famous
hillbilly person from backwoods or remote rural area, esp. in U.S. South
hippie member of 1960's youth culture, alienated from society and interested in mysticism, pacifism, nature, psychedelic drugs, and sexual freedom; flower child
hoi polloi common people
indigenous (*adj*) native
intelligentsia intellectual and academic leaders
jet set rich, fashionable group frequently traveling in pursuit of pleasure
John Doe anonymous average man
John Q. Public average person
literati persons of letters
lonely-hearts (*adj*) pertaining to persons seeking companionship or love
loose cannon person whose reckless behavior endangers efforts or welfare of others
lumpenproletariat segment of underclass degraded by nonproductivity and shiftlessness, including tramps, beggars, and criminals
man about town worldly man who is a member of fashionable society
man in the street average person
minority group group within larger society with different language, culture, or religion, often subject to discrimination
moral majority largely fundamentalist, conservative Christians of Middle America
power elite those in control of nation's government, economy, and resources
rank and file ordinary people constituting major part of an organization, esp. a labor union
refugee person who flees his or her home or country to seek safety from war or persecution
refusenik *Informal.* Soviet citizen, esp. a Jew, who was denied permission to emigrate
role model person whom others copy when developing attitudes, values, and behavior patterns
sacred cow individual or institution deemed exempt from criticism or questioning
senior citizen person who is elderly or aged, esp. one living on a pension
silk-stocking member of wealthy or aristocratic class
stereotype oversimplified, often unfavorable, commonly held picture of all members of certain group
street person homeless person living on city streets
Tom, Dick, and Harry common man; people generally
transient homeless person looking for work or place to live
troglodyte individual with reclusive habits or outmoded behavior; outcast from society
Uncle Sam personification of U.S. government as bearded man in red, white, and blue top hat
Uncle Tom black whose behavior is regarded as servile

underdog victim of social injustice; one attempting to overcome adversity
underprivileged (*adj*) socially and economically deprived
untouchable person outside and below the Hindu caste system
upper crust aristocratic, wealthy high society
urban guerrilla member of violent, terrorist, underground political group in urban area, esp. in 1970's
vanguard leaders or advance position of political or artistic movement
wannabe person who idealizes successful individuals and imagines being like them
WASP white anglo-saxon protestant; member of dominant group setting standards and values of American society
working poor employed persons living at subsistence level
Yuppie young urban professional characterized as ambitious, materialistic, and faddish

Social Structure and Conditions

anomie condition in which social norms have weakened or disappeared
assimilation integration of customs and values from previously distinct cultures into dominant culture
atomism society composed of clearly distinct elements and factions
biculturalism presence of two distinct cultures in one society
bureaucracy authority concentrated in complicated structure of administrative bodies
caste station in life defined by birth, more rigid than class and allowing no chance for change
clan group with interest in common, often related persons
class social rank according to status, economic interest, and way of life
clique small, exclusive circle of people; coterie
commonweal general welfare
community any group with shared interests, feelings, values, or geographic location
counterculture segment of society with values and lifestyle opposed to those of prevailing culture
dynamic culture society undergoing rapid change
environment social conditions and surroundings as they affect behavior and attitudes
ghetto section of city to which minority group is confined or lives by choice
heterogeneous (*adj*) composed of varied elements
homeostasis tendency of society to maintain social stability
homogeneous (*adj*) composed of similar elements
indigenous (*adj*) native to a specific society or region
infrastructure basic facilities and systems serving country, region, or city, including transportation, communications, power, and schools
institutionalized racism racial discrimination not based on individual attitudes but inherent in social structures and institutions
interaction coming together of individuals with mutual influence
lower class working class, characterized by low standard of living
macrocosm model that is a large-scale and complex representation, often of one of its components
melting pot society that incorporates diverse social and cultural groups
microcosm group believed to be representative of a much larger entity
middle class socioeconomic group with comfortable standard of living and conventional beliefs and lifestyle
mythos underlying and enduring attitudes and beliefs characteristic of a society, esp. in connection with supernatural forces
neighborhood community of people living near one another
peer group those of same age and social position
power structure those established in ruling positions in government or other institutions
Procrustean bed pattern into which one is arbitrarily forced
psychosocial (*adj*) relating psychological development to social environment
reservation public land on which American Indians are resettled
rite traditional, customary, often ceremonial or formal observance or procedure
royalty hereditary social class that rules certain countries
shantytown section of city with substandard housing, esp. rickety little huts
skid row area of city frequented by alcoholics and vagrants
slum densely populated urban area marked by crowding, poverty, poor housing, and social disorder
social contract theoretical agreement between people to establish government and abide by its laws
social convention norm of behavior or belief
socialization process by which a child acquires and internalizes society's beliefs, values, and habits, so as to become functioning member of group
Social Register *Trademark.* book that lists members of high society
social structure framework of society's institutions governing interpersonal and group relations
social welfare system of services for improving condition of the disadvantaged
society institutions and value systems of people with similar traditions and customs who inhabit same geographical area over several generations; autonomous structure based on such institutions and value systems that provides group identity and basis for community living
strata specific socioeconomic level of society
subculture group within society whose social status, ethnic background, religion, or shared values and interests distinguish it from others in that society or culture

suburbia social and cultural aspects of life in residential communities lying just outside a city
trend prevailing direction in which society is moving at a given time
underclass lowest level of society, consisting of impoverished persons with low social status, often self-perpetuating from generation to generation
upper class highest level of society, made up of those with wealth, power, and prestige
urban (*adj*) relating to cities
zero population growth condition in which birthrate and death rate are equal and population remains constant, esp. due to family planning

Schools and Doctrines

behavioral science study of human activity in attempt to discover recurrent patterns and postulate rules
behaviorism theory that all human behavior is learned or based on conditioning and that observed behavior forms only valid data
biosociology study of interactions between human biological characteristics and social behavior
conflict theory view of society as groups in conflict
criminology scientific study of crime, criminal nature, and its impact on society
cultural diffusion spread of cultural characteristics from one society to another
determinism theory that choice of action is determined by causes other than human will
ekistics scientific study of human settlements and communities
environmental determinism theory that social environment rather than hereditary factors determines personality
ergonomics study of adjustment to environment, esp. in workplace
eugenics science dealing with improvement of hereditary factors through social control of reproduction
euthenics science dealing with improvement of hereditary factors for human welfare through environmental control
evolutionary theory belief in gradual, sequential development of society
functionalism social theory of Émile Durkheim emphasizing integration of institutions, their interaction with society, and consensus of values that is external to individual and influences his or her actions
human ecology study of how human beings relate to their political, economic, and social environment
humanism nontheistic, rationalist belief that people are capable of self-fulfillment and ethical conduct without recourse to the supernatural
industrial sociology study of social relationships and institutions as influenced by industry
interactionist doctrine belief that social processes and institutions derive from one person reacting to action of another
labeling theory view that society creates deviance by prematurely labeling a person as inadequate or undesirable
linguistics study of structure, development, social impact, and interrelationship of languages
looking-glass theory theory that people develop their sense of self in response to how they think others see them
metalinguistics study of relationship of language to other culturally determined behavior
mutualism social dependence for general welfare
occupational sociology study of working roles on a broader scale than in industrial sociology
penology branch of criminology that evaluates programs and institutions dealing with criminals
Protestant ethic theory of Max Weber that the hard work and frugal life conducive to capitalism developed from the Calvinist doctrine of predestination
rising expectations theory that revolutions are more likely to occur as social and economic conditions begin to improve, causing increased expectations and frustration
Social Darwinism view that individuals will advance in society based on their ability to adapt to living conditions
social pathology study of social factors, such as poverty or crime, that tend to increase social disorganization and inhibit personal adjustment
social science scientific study of different aspects of society, including disciplines of political science, anthropology, sociology, criminology, and economics
sociocultural approach propaganda theory based on defining cultural norms that guide people's social behavior
sociology application of specific doctrines and techniques to systematic study of social institutions, collective behavior, and human relationships
sociology of knowledge study of relationships between social and political structures and intellectual life
sociology of leisure study of social impact of increased leisure as by-product of technology and modernization
structural functionalism analysis of social phenomena within narrowly defined concepts of observable structures and functional consequences
structuralism theory based on study of social status systems and interdisciplinary analysis of social behavior, used to define the patterns of interaction between diverse modes of behavior that form society's underlying structure
urban sociology study of the relationship between urban environment and social structures within it

Tools and Techniques

case study study and research that analyzes a single group, person, or institution
casework social work that deals directly with individuals' specific needs and problems
census official population count and collection of demographic information on general population

cohort group having one demographic factor in common
content analysis study of document to learn about culture, esp. to determine number of times one term or value appears in given context
control group group of participants used as basis of comparison in controlled experiment
cultural base total number of cultural traits in given culture at one time
cultural relativity evaluation of culture's customs and their functions in context of entire culture
culture trait specific tool, act, or belief related to particular situation or need in one culture
demography study of relationship between human populations and vital and social statistics, esp. marital status, age, sex, and employment, usu. by statistical and quantitative methods
historical analysis study of historical records and writings to support or disprove a cultural hypothesis
random sample portion of population chosen at random to ensure impartiality in a study
real-life laboratory observation of people in arranged settings or natural environments without their awareness of being observed
scientific method application of empirical, objective, and systematic data collection and analysis to study of culture and society
secondary document document written by someone not actually present at described event
social engineering application of findings of social science to solution of social problems
social service actions by professionals to improve social circumstances of people and communities
sociogram sociometric diagram representing pattern of relationships between group members
sociography use of statistical data to describe social phenomena
sociometry measurement of attitudes of social acceptance or rejection as expressed by group preferences
statistical analysis research technique using statistical data to formulate and test hypotheses
stratified random sampling method of selecting sample for survey that reflects proportions of different groups in population being studied

PSYCHOLOGY

Schools and Doctrines
Syndromes, Disorders, and Conditions
Phobias
Manias
Tools, Techniques, Principles, and Practitioners
Mental States, Processes, and Behavior

Schools and Doctrines

abnormal psychology branch of psychology concerned with basic theory, but not treatment, of psychotic and personality disorders
Adlerian psychotherapy theory of psychotherapy developed by Alfred Adler emphasizing overcompensation in denial of feelings of personal weakness or inferiority
analytic psychology school of psychoanalysis developed by Carl Jung
applied psychology use of psychological knowledge and skills to solve problems
associationism theory that holds that development proceeds from association of simple ideas gained from sensory data
behaviorism doctrine that emphasizes observable data, esp. from stimulus and response studies, as foundation for theories of behavior
bioenergetics school of therapy that employs breathing exercises, physical movement, and free expression to relieve stress and muscle tension
blank-slate hypothesis theory that human thought and behavior are based on experience, not innate components
child development child psychology focusing on weaning, feeding, and toilet training and acknowledging both environmental and hereditary factors
client-centered psychotherapy treatment in which client talks without direction or interpretation from therapist, whose attitude is characterized by unconditional empathy
clinical psychology branch of psychology that focuses on human development and interaction and supports therapeutic intervention to aid the problem solving of individuals, couples, families, and groups
cognitive psychology branch of psychology that bases research and treatment on analysis of mental processes in all aspects of human thought or cognition
community psychology subdivision of clinical psychology concerned with individuals' adaptation to their community
comparative psychology study of comparative behavior of different animal species to enhance understanding of human behavior

constitutional psychology psychological doctrine that attributes behavior patterns to body type
consulting psychology study and relief of individual problems in business, school, and government settings
cultural relativism belief that no absolutely correct standards of behavior exist against which varying cultural and personal behavior patterns can be measured
demonology superstitious belief in demons and evil spirits as cause of abnormal behavior
depth psychology study of unconscious mental processes
developmental psychology specialty that focuses on the course of social, emotional, moral, and intellectual growth over a lifetime
eclectic psychology branch of psychology drawing information, theories, and intervention techniques from different schools of thought
engineering psychology design of man-machine systems to fit human physiological and psychological needs
ethology scientific study of animal behavior
existential psychotherapy therapy emphasizing patient's subjective experience of existence, based on philosophical systems associated with Sartre, Heidegger, Jaspers, and Kierkegaard
experimental psychology research aimed at better knowledge of learning, memory, perception, and other basic mental processes
Freudian psychoanalysis psychoanalytic theories developed by Sigmund Freud, emphasizing importance of early stages of development, the dynamic unconscious, and the interplay of id, ego, and superego
functionalism psychological approach stressing mental functioning rather than mental structure
gestalt school of psychology that asserts that perceptual experience is a configuration or pattern in which the whole is more than the sum of its parts
hedonism theory that pleasure is the primary principle motivating human behavior
holistic approach approach emphasizing person as a whole, not isolated functions or disorders
humanistic psychology branch of psychology emphasizing individual and collective human behavior and its improvement
individual psychology branch of psychology emphasizing uniqueness of human personality and psychological struggle
industrial psychology specialty that focuses on issues and problems specific to organizations and deals with questions of management and power distribution within such groups
Jungian psychology psychological doctrines of Carl Jung regarding mythological, cultural, and racial inheritance and the collective unconscious
metapsychology high-level speculation on the origin, structure, and function of the mind
nativism theory that personality and behavior are primarily inherited, not learned
neoanalytic psychology psychoanalytic theory based on Freud and incorporating modern science
parapsychology study of phenomena beyond range of normally observable psychological events
personality theory integrated set of principles that explains the development of those characteristics that make each person unique
phenomenological approach psychological approach that focuses on individual's way of perceiving and interpreting the world
phrenology method of studying personality by measurement of skull shape and its irregularities (19th c.)
physiognomy outmoded theory of personality based on belief that outward appearance indicates inner character
psychoanalysis study and long-term treatment of personality disorders using free association, interpretation of dreams, transference, and empathic neutrality; Freudian psychoanalysis
psychobiology study of anatomy and biochemical processes as they affect behavior
psychodrama psychotherapy using role-playing
psychology scientific study of the mind, mental states and processes, and human behavior
psychopathology science of causes and development of mental disorders
psychophysics study and measurement of relationship between intensity of stimuli and of sensations they produce
psychophysiology study of interaction between physiological and psychological processes
psychotherapy treatment of mental disorders and difficulties by psychological methods
sleep and dreams psychological discipline concerned with interrelated phenomena of sleep and dreams
social psychology study of effects of social interaction on group behavior, individuals, and mental processes
somatopsychology study of effects of physical problems and disfigurement on behavior and methods of treating related adjustment problems
structuralism psychological school that emphasizes definition and structure of consciousness in formation of human behavior
theoretical psychology branch of psychology that emphasizes formulation of a general integrated set of principles rather than treatment of patients
transactional analysis psychotherapy emphasizing interpersonal exchanges, psychological games, and roles played over a lifetime

Syndromes, Disorders, and Conditions

abnormal behavior unhealthy, disturbed, or disintegrated behavior that interferes with normal, positive functioning
abulia loss of will or ability to act
acting out unconscious expression of previously repressed feelings through specific behavior
addiction physical dependence on chemical substance
affective disorder neurotic disorder involving disturbances in mood
aggression hostile, destructive behavior toward others

agita condition of general anxiety or agitation
alienation psychological isolation from interaction or identification with society and its values; withdrawal
amentia mental deficiency, esp. low intellectual capacity
amnesia partial or complete memory loss
animality expression of animal instincts in human behavior
anomie feeling of isolation or disconnectedness from social norms; cultural alienation
anorexia nervosa pathological fear of obesity, esp. in young women, leading to inability to retain food, loss of appetite, malnutrition, and sometimes death
antisocial personality disorder characterized by chronic violation of rules and customs of social group
anxiety state of general fear or dread, not necessarily connected to particular object or idea
asthenic reaction fatigue as response to anxiety
autism condition marked by infantile onset of pervasive lack of responsiveness to others, with gross deficiency in language development
battle fatigue posttraumatic stress disorder affecting soldiers engaged in combat
bedwetting urination in bed at night by children who have been toilet trained, usu. due to repressed anxiety or resentment
bestiality act or fantasy of engaging in sexual relations with animals
bipolar disorder disorder involving alternation or intermixture of manic and depressive episodes
borderline personality disorder characterized by impulsiveness, intense and unstable relations with others, identity disturbance, marked mood shifts, and chronic feelings of emptiness or boredom
bruxism unconscious grinding and gnashing of teeth, usu. during sleep
bulimia bouts of excessive eating followed by self-induced vomiting, accompanied by preoccupation with weight
catatonia syndrome, usu. in schizophrenia, marked by stupor with musculature rigidity or agitated overactivity
combat fatigue trauma following acutely stressful conditions of warfare
compensation defense mechanism in which sense of weakness or lack is offset by emphasizing positive traits
complex specific constellation of psychological symptoms arising from powerful emotions buried in unconscious mind and affecting behavior
compulsion repetitive behavior serving no rational purpose; need to act without understanding motives
compulsive personality disorder marked by rigid, inhibited, excessively orderly, and often unemotional character and inability to relax
condition state of one's mental health, esp. abnormal or unhealthy state
conversion disorder neurosis characterized by the conversion of psychological disturbances into physical symptoms
cretinism mental deficiency caused by thyroid disorder
cultural alienation anomie
cyclothymic personality disorder in which normally extroverted person suffers fluctuations in mood between sadness and elation
defense mechanism any of various mental processes, including compensation, denial, displacement, negation, procrastination, projection, rationalization, reaction formation, regression, repression, and substitution, used by the ego for protection against instinctual demands and to reduce anxiety
delusion false or distorted belief firmly maintained though contradicted by reality
dementia praecox schizophrenia
denial defense mechanism in which one refuses to acknowledge the existence of an unpleasant reality, esp. the significance of one's behavior
depression depressive neurosis or psychosis
depressive neurosis disorder involving chronic feelings of sadness, lethargy, and hopelessness; depression
depressive psychosis major depressive episode involving feelings of self-hate and negativity, sometimes marked by hallucinations, delusions, or mutism; depression
disorder abnormality, unhealthy condition, or dysfunction of mental health
disorientation disturbance in understanding one's position in time or place or one's identity
displaced aggression transference of hostility from true object to another object
displacement defense mechanism in which repressed emotion or idea is transferred to more acceptable object
dissociative disorder separation or disunity among aspects of single personality
dysfunction abnormality or failure of mental process
Electra complex psychological consequences of girl's sexual attraction to her father and feelings of competition with mother
escapism behavior and fanciful thought processes induced to escape from reality
euphoria unstable feeling of well-being; in manic depression, elevated end of cycle
exhibitionism need to shock others, esp. those of opposite sex, by exposing one's genitals or engaging in overt sexual behavior when inappropriate
fetishism sexual dysfunction in which object or body part is essential to sexual arousal
fixation extreme attachment to objects or ideas associated with earlier stage of psychic development; halting of stage of personality development
flattened affect general impoverishment of emotional reaction in which victim appears distant and removed
flight of ideas disorder involving inability to keep to point of narrative; constant digression and lack of continuity
frigidity inability of woman to achieve orgasm through coitus

fugue combination of temporary amnesia with apparent rational behavior
guilt recurrent feeling of self-reproach or self-blame for something wrong, often something beyond one's control
hallucination sense impression for which there is no real external stimuli, either visual, auditory, or olfactory
hyperactive child syndrome syndrome involving inability of child to pay attention, sit still, or be calm or quiet
hypochondria neurotic preoccupation with one's own health; formation of imaginary symptoms and exaggeration of minor discomforts
hysteria anxiety reaction involving dissociation and conversion, characterized by excitability, high anxiety, and sensory and motor disturbances
infantilism abnormal regression to childish behavior in adulthood
inferiority complex feelings of inadequacy, negative self-perception
insanity legal definition of personality disturbance that causes an inability to bear responsibility for one's actions
insomnia chronic or extreme sleeplessness
involutional psychosis severe disturbance, often of middle age, involving depression, guilt, and insomnia
learning disability any condition that interferes with the learning process or ability to learn specific skills
malaise persistent, vague feelings of unease and listlessness
mania extreme, chronic obsession with something, excessive excitability, manic or excited phase of manic depression
manic depression psychosis affecting moods, alternating between extremes of elation and dejection
martyrdom tendency to take blame or burdens upon oneself, esp. to elicit sympathy or guilt in others
masochism condition in which pleasure, esp. sexual, is derived from pain inflicted by another on oneself
melancholia deep sadness
minimal brain dysfunction nervous system impairment that may cause hyperactivity in children
multiple personality extreme dissociation resulting in belief that two or more distinct personalities reside within oneself, each taking conscious control at different times; split personality
narcissism immature self-love manifested by grandiose sense of importance, need for constant attention and admiration, hidden sense of shame, and difficulty in relating to or having true feelings for others
narcolepsy frequent, uncontrollable desire for sleep
nervous breakdown lay term for temporary, abrupt impairment of normal functioning due to psychotic or neurotic disorder
neurosis emotional disorder involving basic repression of primary instinctual urge and reliance on defense mechanisms that results in symptoms or personality disturbance
neurotic depression common disorder involving inability to recover speedily from depression
noctambulism somnambulism
nymphomania compulsive desire for sex in females
obsession persistent, pervasive, disturbing fixation on an emotion, idea, object, or person
obsessive-compulsive neurosis disorder involving fixation on disturbing ideas and impulsive repetition of certain acts
Oedipus complex psychological consequences of boy's sexual attraction to his mother and feelings of competition with father
overcompensation extreme, unbalanced effort to overcome feelings of inadequacy or guilt
paranoia persistent delusions of persecution or suspicion of others
paranoid schizophrenia disintegration of perception of reality combined with delusions of grandeur or persecution
passive aggressive personality personality marked by extreme passivity combined with hostility, stubbornness, lack of cooperation, and uncommunicativeness
pathology any abnormal condition or mental disease
pedophilia desire for sexual activity with children
persecution complex tendency to feel that one is being unfairly and constantly harassed
phobia unfounded, persistent fear of something based on externalization of anxiety
postpartum depression depressive symptoms in mothers associated with period immediately following childbirth; similar feelings experienced after completing some task
posttraumatic stress syndrome pattern of reactions and disorders that appears some time after a traumatic experience, esp. in soldiers after combat; battle fatigue
procrastination defense mechanism involving postponement or avoidance of stressful task or situation
projection defense mechanism involving attribution of one's own unacceptable or unwanted qualities and motives to others
psychopathic personality individual with personality disorder involving stunted or nonexistent moral values, antisocial or violent behavior, and inability to identify with others
psychosexual disorder sexual disorder in which psychological rather than organic factors are of major importance
psychosis severe mental illness, such as manic depression, paranoia, or schizophrenia, involving loss of contact with reality and breakdown of comprehensible behavior, speech, and thought
psychosomatic disorder physical illness or perception of illness arising from psychological disturbances
rationalization defense mechanism involving substitution of rational motive for genuine, but irrational, motive as excuse for one's behavior
regression defense mechanism involving return to behavior expressive of earlier developmental stage, usu. due to trauma, fixation, anxiety, or frustration

repression defense mechanism in which threatening or unacceptable ideas or urges are forgotten
resentment feeling of displeasure toward source of supposed injury or offense
retardation congenital subnormality of intelligence or lack of normal mental capacity or development
reversion return to former or regressed condition
SAD seasonal affective disorder
sadism condition in which pleasure, esp. sexual, is derived from inflicting pain on others
sadomasochism condition in which pleasure, esp. sexual, is derived from inflicting pain on others and from pain inflicted on oneself
satyriasis compulsive desire for sex in males
schizophrenia psychosis involving break with reality and disintegration of rational thought and communication; dementia praecox
seasonal affective disorder SAD; phenomenon in which mood changes are alleged to correspond to the seasons, esp. depression in winter
senile psychosis disorder in elderly involving memory loss, irritation, and regressive behavior
sleepwalking somnambulism
sociopath psychopathic personality who exhibits extreme asocial and antisocial behavior
somnambulism walking in one's sleep; noctambulism; sleepwalking
split personality multiple personality
sublimation defense mechanism involving substitution of socialized behavior for unacceptable acting out of primary urge
substitution defense mechanism involving replacement of unacceptable behavior with acceptable behavior
suicidal (*adj*) having intense, uncontrollable, self-destructive impulses, often due to depression
superiority complex condition in which one considers oneself better than others, often due to lack of genuine self-esteem
syndrome group of symptoms characterizing ongoing disease or disorder
tic involuntary muscle twitch, esp. of face, usu. indicating unreleased tension
vertigo dizziness and loss of balance
victimization tendency to view oneself as victim of unfair treatment; martyrdom
voyeurism practice of deriving sexual gratification from watching others naked or engaged in sexual acts
withdrawal detachment from meaningful relationships with others and retreat into inner world; cessation of consumption of addictive substance and attendant unpleasant symptoms

Phobias

acrophobia fear of heights
aerophobia fear of drafts of fresh air
agoraphobia fear of crowds or open places
agyrophobia fear of crossing the street
ailurophobia fear of cats
algophobia fear of pain
amathophobia fear of dust
androphobia fear of men
Anglophobia fear or dislike of England or anything English
anthophobia fear of flowers
apiphobia fear of bees
arachnaphobia fear of spiders
astraphobia fear of lightning and thunder
autophobia fear of loneliness
bathophobia fear of deep places
brontophobia fear of thunder
chrometophobia fear of money
claustrophobia fear of enclosed places
clinophobia fear of going to bed
coitophobia fear of coitus
coprophobia fear of feces
cremnophobia fear of precipices
cryophobia fear of cold
cynophobia fear of dogs
dipsophobia fear of drunkenness
doraphobia fear of fur
dromophobia fear of crossing streets
eisoptrophobia fear of mirrors
eleutherophobia fear of freedom
emetophobia fear of vomiting
entomophobia fear of insects
eremiophobia fear of being alone
ergophobia fear of work
erythrophobia fear of blushing and the color red
galeophobia fear of sharks
gametophobia fear of marriage
gephyrophobia fear of crossing bridges
gerascophobia fear of old age
gymnophobia fear of nudity
gynephobia fear of women
hedonophobia fear of pleasure
helminthophobia fear of worms
hematophobia fear of blood
hippophobia fear of horses
hodophobia fear of travel
homophobia fear or dislike of homosexuals
hydrophobia fear of water
hypegiaphobia fear of responsibility
hypnophobia fear of sleep
ichthyophobia fear of fish
ideophobia fear of ideas or reason
lalophobia fear of speaking, esp. in public
logophobia fear of words
lyssophobia fear of madness
maieusiophobia fear of pregnancy
microphobia fear of germs
musophobia fear of mice
mysophobia fear of dirt or contamination
necrophobia fear of death
neophobia fear of novelty
nyctophobia fear of night or darkness
ochlophobia fear of crowds
onomatophobia fear of a name or particular word
ophiciophobia fear of snakes
ornithophobia fear of birds
pathophobia fear of disease
pedophobia fear of children

peniaphobia fear of poverty
phasmophobia fear of ghosts
phobophobia fear of fear
phonophobia fear of noise
photophobia fear of light
pneumatophobia fear of spirits
pnigophobia fear of choking
pyrophobia fear of fire
scotophobia fear of dark
siderodromophobia fear of trains
tachophobia fear of speed
tapephobia fear of being buried alive
teratophobia fear of monsters
thalassophobia fear of the sea
thanatophobia fear of death
thermophobia fear of heat
tocophobia fear of childbirth
tomophobia fear of surgery
topophobia fear of a particular place
toxiphobia fear of being poisoned
traumatophobia fear of injury
triskaidekaphobia fear of the number thirteen
xenophobia fear or dislike of foreigners
xerophobia fear of dry places, esp. deserts
zoophobia fear of animals

Manias

ablutomania chronic obsession with bathing
ailuromania intense enthusiasm for cats
anthomania inordinate interest in flowers
arithmomania craze for counting and numbers
automania compulsion toward solitude
bibliomania inordinate interest in acquiring books
cacodemonomania inordinate obsession with demonic possession
cheromania compulsion toward gaiety
choreomania craze for dancing
chrematomania obsessive desire for money
coprolalomania obsession with foul speech
cynomania intense enthusiasm for dogs
dipsomania irresistible craving for alcoholic beverages
dromomania intense enthusiasm for traveling
egomania inordinate obsession with oneself
eleutheromania irresistible craving for freedom
entheomania obsessive zeal for religion
entomomania inordinate fascination with insects
eremiomania irresistible craving for stillness
ergomania obsessive zeal for work
erotomania uncontrollable obsession with sexual desire
florimania intense interest in plants
gephyromania irresistible fascination with bridges
glazomania inordinate fascination with listmaking
gymnomania compulsion toward nakedness
gynecomania obsessive and uncontrollable desire for sex in males; satyromania
hedonomania irresistible craving for pleasure
heliomania uncontrollable craving for the sun
hippomania fascination with and enthusiasm for horses
homicidomania irresistible impulse to commit murder
hydromania uncontrollable fascination with water
hypnomania uncontrollable desire for sleep
ichthyomania excessive fascination with fish
kathisomania uncontrollable compulsion to sit
kleptomania irresistible impulse to steal
letheomania obsessive fascination with narcotics
logomania obsession with talking
megalomania uncontrollable obsession with grandiose self-importance and extravagant acts
melomania excessive fascination with music
monomania obsessive zeal for one topic or interest in one idea
mythomania irresistible impulse toward exaggeration and lying
necromania excessive interest in the dead
nesomania intense obsession with islands
noctimania intense fascination with night
nymphomania obsessive and uncontrollable desire for sex in females
ochlomania intense obsession with crowds
oikomania irresistible craving for home
oinomania inordinate fascination with wine
oniomania uncontrollable compulsion to buy
ophidiomania excessive interest in reptiles
ornithomania inordinate fascination with birds
paramania irresistible impulse to derive joy from complaints
parousiamania obsessive zeal for the second coming of Christ
phagomania irresistible craving for food and interest in eating
phaneromania uncontrollable impulse to pick at a spot or growth on one's body
pharmacomania chronic fascination with medicines
phonomania obsession with noise or sound
photomania irresistible craving for light
plutomania uncontrollable craving for great wealth
pyromania compulsion to set things on fire
satyromania obsessive and uncontrollable desire for sex in males
scribomania obsessive zeal for writing
siderodromomania intense fascination with railroad travel
sitomania abnormal craving for food
sophomania inordinate estimation of one's own wisdom
thalassomania intense fascination with the sea
thanatomania inordinate obsession with death
timbromania inordinate enthusiasm for postage stamps
tomomania inordinate interest in surgery
trichomania intense fascination with hair
xenomania obsessive interest in foreigners
zoomania craze for animals

Tools, Techniques, Principles, and Practitioners

analysis method in which therapist treats subject through long-term series of regular psychoanalytic sessions
anima in Jungian theory, female aspect of a male's personality

animus in Jungian theory, male aspect of a female's personality
archetype in Jungian theory, primal character and predisposition to behavior within collective unconscious of individuals
aromatherapy use of scented oil to influence mood and treat stress
atomism theory that reduces all psychological phenomena to simple elements
autosuggestion idea arising within oneself and affecting one's thinking and behavior
aversion therapy technique of linking deeply felt revulsion with a behavior to be reduced or eliminated
behavior modification altering of behavior through conditioning and behavior therapy
behavior therapy treatment aimed at eliminating unacceptable symptoms or behavior rather than exposing underlying causes
Bender-Gestalt test test for neurological disorders in which subject must copy nine geometrical designs
biofeedback behavior therapy technique involving control of health and personality problems by sensitization of individual to internal body mechanisms to reduce stress
brainwashing extreme psychological conditioning used to change ideological attitudes
case study detailed psychoanalytic history of an individual used for teaching or reporting purposes
catharsis therapy that allows pent-up, socially unacceptable emotions to be expressed
classical conditioning process linking a conditioned stimulus with a conditioned response; Pavlovian conditioning
client-centered therapy therapy that emphasizes nonjudgmental support of client's point of view and encouragement of expression of feelings and growth needs
clinical psychologist professional in field of counseling individuals with psychological problems
conditioned response acquired response to stimulus not originally capable of causing it; Pavlovian conditioning
conditioning form of learning that produces automatic response to stimulus
control group experimental group equal in all respects to other groups being tested but not subjected to experimental conditions
counseling therapeutic psychological treatment program involving professional testing, interviews, and guidance
desensitization therapy therapy emphasizing reduction of unwanted behavior by gradual pairing of another response with original stimulus
diagnosis clinical identification of disorder affecting patient
dream interpretation psychoanalytical technique involving symbolic explanation of dream content
electric shock therapy therapy that uses passage of electric current through patient's brain; electroconvulsive therapy
electroconvulsive therapy ECT; electric shock therapy
encounter group small group that meets, usu. with professional leader, for collective therapy through open exchange of intimate thoughts and feelings
feedback information on results of behavior used to influence future behavior
free association technique requiring patient to speak freely about anything coming to mind so as to explore the unconscious
group therapy treatment of several patients at one time by therapist, with emphasis on group interaction
halfway house residence offering supportive environment and counseling in which patients live following release from mental institution to ease reentry into society
Holtzman technique projective technique for personality evaluation based on interpretation of ninety ambiguous inkblots
horizontal study study of individual's current status, not history
hypnotherapy therapy employing hypnosis to treat symptoms and make suggestions for improvement of future behavior
idiographic (*adj*) involving study or explication of individual cases or events
implosion therapy technique of reliving frightening event in therapeutic setting until original trauma has lessened or disappeared
inkblot test Rorschach test; Holtzman technique
intelligence quotient IQ; ratio of mental age to chronological age, multiplied by 100
IQ intelligence quotient
mental age average level of mental ability for specific age group
mental hygiene development and maintenance of a wholesome, integrated personality
negative reinforcement reinforcement obtained by stopping of punishment after a response, thus increasing appearance of that response
norm average performance or score on psychological test
occupational therapy treatment using crafts, sports, and skills development to restore confidence and build social skills
organismic theory belief that all behavior stems from a whole, integrated personality guided by the drive for self-actualization
paradoxical effect effect opposite the normal effect, as with certain stimulant drugs given to calm hyperactive children
Pavlovian conditioning conditioning that creates reflex in which response is occasioned by secondary stimulus that has been repeatedly associated with primary stimulus
placebo treatment that has no effect except in patient's own mind
positive reinforcement rewarding stimulus that strengthens learned behavior
posthypnotic suggestion instruction given during hypnosis in regard to behavior or experience to take place after hypnosis has terminated

prefrontal lobotomy surgical severing of neural connections in brain to control extremely violent patients
primal scream therapy treatment in which patient reenacts disturbing past experiences, esp. of infancy, and expresses repressed anger through screams, hysteria, or violence
psychiatrist medical doctor specializing in treatment of mental disturbances, including by prescription of medications
psychoanalyst professional therapist practicing psychoanalysis as originated by Freud and later developed and modified by others
psychologist professional who has completed graduate training in any branch of psychology and fulfilled state requirements for licensing
psychotherapist professional therapist who treats psychological disorders through verbal methods; therapist
rehabilitation restoration of normal health and functioning following period of impairment due to mental or physical disorder
reinforcement reward that increases likelihood of appearance of a particular response
role-playing assumption and acting out of role to resolve conflicts and practice appropriate behavior, usu. in group therapy
Rorschach test personality evaluation involving patient interpretation of inkblot images; inkblot test
security blanket child's blanket used as transitional object
sensitivity training group therapy in which patients seek deeper understanding of themselves and others by exchange of intimate thoughts and feelings, sometimes through physical contact
sensory deprivation experimental technique in which subject is confined in soundproof chamber and deprived of variation in sensory stimuli
shock therapy use of electric shock in cases of severe disorder, catatonia, or depression; electric shock therapy
Skinner box laboratory device for study of operant conditioning in which animal learns to press lever for reinforcement such as food
speech therapist person who specializes in treatment of speech dysfunctions
standardized test psychological measure whose administration, scoring, and interpretation are identical for all who take it, providing a reliable and valid norm for comparison
stress psychological or physiological pressures that threaten health, stability, or functioning of personality
subliminal (*adj*) involving stimuli intended to take effect below level of consciousness
suggestion induction of an idea that is accepted and readily acted on, esp. under hypnosis; idea so induced
support group group of people who meet regularly to discuss problems affecting them in common, such as alcoholism or bereavement
systematic desensitization technique for reduction or elimination of oversensitivity, esp. fear
therapist psychotherapist
therapy treatment intended to improve psychological condition and assist in understanding and resolving emotional problems
transference patient's identification of therapist with pivotal person in his or her life and subsequent transferral of feelings about that person to therapist
transitional object familiar object to which child clings during early socialization and that substitutes for mother's care
twelve-step program method of recovery from addictive and obsessive-compulsive conditions through group reinforcement and spiritual awareness
unconditioned response response occurring naturally, without training or reinforcement
visualization technique of encouraging subject to imagine or picture self in altered and improved condition, having achieved desired goal
word association technique involving subject's pairing of given word with whatever word comes to mind

Mental States, Processes, and Behavior

abandonment feeling of having been forsaken or neglected, esp. by one's parents
abreaction release of repressed feeling by mentally reliving experience causing that feeling
addictive personality person who has a tendency toward compulsive behavior associated with one specific activity or object
aggression drive characterized by anger, hostility, or territoriality
angst anxiety
anticipatory grief experience of grief or mourning in period leading up to expected tragic event, which is often experienced as a relief when it occurs
archetype Jungian characterization of fundamental personality trait held in collective unconscious
avoidance behavior characterized by evasion and/or withdrawal
behavior actions and activities of humans and animals
body language body movements, positions, and gestures that communicate an attitude
bonding development of close and powerful relationships with family or friends based on initial attachment of infant and mother
castration complex unconscious male fear of castration or emasculation, esp. as punishment for oedipal feelings
codependency any of various problems or disorders based on one person's close association with another's habits or addictions, resulting in blurred individuation
cognition perception
cognitive development stages of growth in thinking and perception from childhood concern with objects to adult use of symbols and logic
cognitive learning learning by understanding rather than by conditioning

collective unconscious Jungian characterization of major part of unconscious mind, containing ancestral memories and images from humanity's history
compensation effort to replace feelings of inadequacy with feelings of adequacy
concept learning ability to form an abstraction from some aspect of a group of objects or common events, which increases from childhood to maturity
conscience moral sense of right and wrong and accompanying desire to do right
coping ability to function in society despite any of various conditions or disorders
defense ego mechanism used to channel energy to middle area between id's wishes and ego's reality
dysfunctional family family in which emotional and physical support needed for individuation and healthy development are missing and family members are sacrificed to the family group itself
ego reality-oriented, structured component of personality that enables individual to function autonomously in the world; one of three divisions of psyche in psychoanalytic theory
eidetic imagery photographic memory in which vivid mental images can be described in detail
emasculation deprivation or reduction of male's sense of power, esp. by mate
emotion strong psychophysical response of individual
externalization perception of one's own difficulties as being caused by external forces, not innate characteristics
extrasensory perception phenomenon of perception or communication occurring independent of powers of sense organs
extroversion tendency to direct one's interest toward things outside the self
Freudian slip statement or action that inadvertently reveals unconscious motive or desire
frustration disturbed state occurring when individual cannot attain goal or relieve tension
functional fixedness inability to perceive and use objects in innovative ways or engage in alternative thinking processes
gestalt unified whole, esp. the psyche, having properties that cannot be derived from the sum of its parts
group dynamics ways in which group members interact, esp. to achieve group goals
hyperactive (*adj*) abnormally animated or active, esp. in relation to children
id unconscious, unsocialized component of personality, containing unexpressed desires and motivations and driven by pleasure principle; one of three divisions of psyche in psychoanalytic theory
identity crisis period or episode of psychological distress during which questions of self-definition become paramount
imago idealized mental picture of another, esp. one's parent
imprinting early learning that occurs quickly and thoroughly
impulse wave of psychic energy that is either discharged, inhibited, directed, or sublimated
individuation development of a distinct personality, separate from one's mother's, and a sense of boundary between self and others
inhibition process of stopping an impulse
inner child part of a person's self that remains as it was in childhood and influences the way that person sees and relates to the world as an adult
internalization adoption of values through identification
introjection replacement of relationship with external object with relationship with internal, imagined object
introversion tendency to withdraw from others and turn inward upon the self
kinesthesis sensory ability to feel body positioning
leveling forgetting; failing to perceive adequate detail
libido in Freudian terms, sexual energy; in Jungian terms, psychic energy
looking-glass self self-image based on perceived view of other's, esp. child's perception of parent
midlife crisis feelings of anxiety and uncertainty about one's identity, relationships, and values, usu. experienced between ages 35 and 55
mind-set fixed point of view, attitude, or mood
mneme retentive basis in the mind accounting for memory
nesting forming strong relationships and creating secure home environment, esp. for rearing family
nocturnal emission ejaculation, esp. among boys undergoing puberty, usu. after erotic dream; wet dream
nurturing care and warmth that promote healthy development
onychophagia habitual nail-biting, usu. as sign of anxiety neurosis or other suppressed feeling
paramnesia distortion of memory in which fact and fantasy are confused
penis envy in Freudian theory, female feelings of inadequacy and jealousy because of repressed wish to have a penis
perception process of conscious sensory input
persona in Jungian view, individual's facade or mask of socialized behavior
personal unconscious in Jungian view, unconscious mental contents unique to individual and not part of collective unconscious
primal (*adj*) having to do with basic, primitive urges and emotions
process course of action or form of behavior
psyche mental or psychological structure of an individual, esp. in connection with motivation
psychic energy in Jungian theory, general life force
psychodynamics in Freudian view, interplay of unconscious mental processes that determine human thought, feelings, and behavior
REM sleep rapid eye movement sleep; cyclical sleep state characterized by increased brain activity, dreams, and rapid eye movements
self-actualization fulfillment of individual's potential as independent, functioning, healthy, adjusted person

self-denial sacrifice of one's own desires or needs
self-fulfilling prophecy unconscious tendency to make behavior and events conform to anticipated outcomes
sentiment positive or negative feeling about idea, object, or person
shadow in Jungian theory, unsocialized, primitive, idlike aspect of self
sibling rivalry competition among brothers or sisters within family structure
sleep deprivation reduced sleep over prolonged period, causing personality disorganization, diminished cognitive abilities, and sometimes psychotic delusions and hallucinations
slough of despond hopeless dejection and depression
somatotype body type, classified as endomorphic (heavy), ectomorphic (frail), or mesomorphic (muscular), each associated with a type of temperament or personality
state specific mental or emotional condition
stream of consciousness personal conscious experience regarded as an uninterrupted series of events
stress bodily reaction to danger, difficulty, or threat
subconscious mental activity and impulses occurring below threshold of active awareness; (*adj*) existing in mind beyond conscious level
superego aspect of personality involving conscience, guilt, imposition of moral standards, and introjected authoritative and ethical images; one of three divisions of psyche in psychoanalytic theory
suppression conscious attempt to forget unpleasant idea or object or inhibit an impulse
tantrum violent, uncontrollable outburst of rage, esp. in children
temperament characteristic mental, physical, and emotional aspects of an individual
trance state of altered and diminished consciousness, esp. under hypnosis, in which voluntary movement is lost
unconscious aspect of mind and personality that holds thoughts, desires, images, and urges of which individual is not aware; (*adj*) not actively aware of oneself
verbal intelligence grasp of ideas, language, information, and numbers
wet dream nocturnal emission

PHILOSOPHY

Schools, Doctrines, and Movements
Notions, Ideas, and Methods
Logic

Schools, Doctrines, and Movements

aesthetics branch of philosophy concerned with beauty and values in the judging of beauty, esp. in art; esthetics
Age of Reason Enlightenment
analytic philosophy highly structured approach to philosophical problems through modern logic, developed by Ludwig Wittgenstein (20th c.)
animism belief in the conscious life, or soul, of inanimate objects as well as living beings
anthroposophy doctrine that cultivating spiritual development is humankind's most important task
antinomianism doctrine that rejects conventional moral law and maintains that salvation derives from faith and grace alone
Aristotelianism practical, empirical philosophy of Aristotle, highly influential throughout course of Western history (Greece, 4th c. B.C.)
atomism theory that reality consists of minute, independent material units or atoms (Greece, 5th c. B.C.)
axiology science of and inquiry into values, as in aesthetics and ethics
bioethics study of ethical issues arising from medical and biological research (late 20th c.)
Cartesianism doctrine of René Descartes that all knowledge can be firmly established based on certain truths (France, 17th c.)
conceptualism theory that universal ideas exist as mental objects available to all minds
Confucianism quasireligious ethical system of China, based on sayings of Confucius (6th c. B.C.)
cosmology study of origin and totality of universal realities as basis for metaphysical speculation
critical philosophy doctrine of Immanuel Kant that the world is understood only insofar as it conforms to the mind's structure
Cynicism school originating with Diogenes, professing moderation and virtue as sole good, later based on protest and opposition to prevailing philosophical ideas (Greece, 5th c. B.C.)
Cyrenaics hedonistic philosophy of bodily pleasure, precursor to Epicureanism (Greece, 4th c. B.C.)
determinism theory that reality and events unfold according to a predetermined, inevitable course
dialectical materialism Marxist form of materialism based on Hegelian dialectic applied to philosophy of social history
dualism theory that two basic, irreducible opposites, such as light and dark, good and evil, or mind and matter, constitute reality
Eleaticism Presocratic doctrine of Parmenides that absolute reality is undifferentiated and immutable while change is merely apparent (Greece, 6th c. B.C.)
empiricism view that sense perception and experience are sole foundations of knowledge, esp. held by John Locke (Britain, 17th c.)
Encyclopedism rationalist, humanistic movement to compile an encyclopedic compendium of knowledge, edited by Denis Diderot (France, 18th c.)
Enlightenment Age of Reason; intellectual movement toward tolerance, positive social action, and humanism, based on belief in perfectibility of people through reason (18th c.)
Epicureanism ethical doctrine of Epicurus, holding pleasure to be highest good, with pleasure deriving from moral conduct (Greece, 3rd c. B.C.)
epistemology theory of knowledge; critical study of nature, limits, and validity of knowledge

esthetics aesthetics
ethics science and study of morality and human conduct
eudaemonism ethical system defining moral behavior in terms of happiness and well-being
existentialism philosophy emphasizing free will in coming to terms with subjective meaning and meaninglessness in one's existence, based on teachings of Sören Kierkegaard (20th c.)
fatalism doctrine that all events and occurrences are predetermined and inevitable
formal logic branch of logic that emphasizes form and principles of deductive reasoning rather than content of propositions
hedonism ethical doctrine of pleasure as highest or only good
historicism deterministic explanation of phenomena in terms of their origins and development, associated with Hegel and Marx (19th c.); historical materialism
humanism any philosophical doctrine emphasizing human concerns, motives, and aspirations rather than other natural or spiritual forces, holding human reason to be the source of its authority
idealism theory that reality is a creation of mind, and that mental and spiritual values, rather than matter, constitute reality; immaterialism
ideology scope of ideas within a particular theory or belief system
immaterialism idealism
instrumentalism school of pragmatism that maintains that the value of ideas lies in their practical application to human problems
logic philosophical inquiry into principles and methods of validity and proof
logical empiricism logical positivism
logical positivism school rejecting metaphysics and emphasizing methods of criticism and analysis of science, with reliance on principle of verifiability in experience or language (20th c.); logical empiricism
materialism theory that reality consists solely of matter, without separate reality of mind or spirit
metaphysics branch of philosophy concerned with ultimate nature and categories of reality; study of being, existence, and essence; ontology and cosmology
monism doctrine that reality of mind and body are fundamentally one and undifferentiated and can be reduced to one fundamental force, advocated by Spinoza in 17th c.
mysticism doctrine of direct, inexplicable knowledge and experience of truth and reality without rational processes or reliance on creed, orthodoxy, or belief system
naturalism theory that reality consists solely of the natural, observable world, with no supernatural or spiritual realm
Neoplatonism school synthesizing Platonic, Aristotelian, Christian, Jewish, and mystical traditions (3rd-5th c. A.D.)
nihilism doctrine that social and economic order is inherently corrupt and morality cannot be justified (Russia, 19th c.)
nominalism theory emphasizing that ideas and objects exist only in particular, not in abstract or general forms, influenced by William of Occam (14th c.)
objectivism theory emphasizing external, objective, rather than internal, subjective, aspect of reality; ethical theory that good is of value independent of human feelings but based on universally valid moral truths
perspectivism doctrine that reality and truth are known only from perspective of individual or group viewing them at particular moment
pessimism doctrine holding that reality is fundamentally evil and the world is governed by malevolent forces
phenomenalism empirical theory that knowledge exists solely in the appearance of phenomena, or sense data, rather than in the ultimate reality of objects themselves
phenomenology science of describing and analyzing classes of phenomena and consciousness (20th c.)
philosophy study and pursuit of fundamental principles underlying knowledge, conduct, and universal reality, esp. disciplines of aesthetics, epistemology, ethics, logic, and metaphysics
Platonism idealistic philosophy of Plato, derived from teaching of Socrates; classic idealism and belief that the human mind can attain absolute truth (Greece, 4th c. B.C.)
pluralism theory that reality consists of several distinct, fundamental realities
political philosophy study of people as political animals and relationship between government and citizens
positivism theory that truth or knowledge is based solely on what is scientifically verifiable by direct experience, based on teachings of Auguste Comte (19th c.)
pragmatics branch of semiotics concerned with causal relationships between symbols and words and their users
pragmatism philosophical view emphasizing consequences and practical results of one's conduct rather than principles and categories of reality (19th c.)
pre-Socratics those Greek philosophers of nature who lived before Socrates, esp. the Pythagoreans
Pythagoreanism doctrines of Pythagoras, esp. that universe is manifestation of various combinations of mathematical ratios (Greece, 6th c. B.C.)
rationalism theory emphasizing reasoned, not empirical, foundations of knowledge; truth apprehended by deductive reasoning independent of experience or observation (17th c.)
realism theory that universal concepts and reality exist independently of perception
relativism theory that truth and ethical values are relative, not absolute and independent, and are contingent on nature of mind
scholasticism medieval, Christian philosophical school based on empiricism of Aristotle and teachings of Thomas Aquinas (11th-13th c.)
semantics branch of semiotics concerned with signs and things they signify

semiotics theory of signs and symbols used in communication
Sophists wandering teachers who emphasized rhetoric over truth and taught whatever their students wanted to learn (Greece, 5th-4th c. B.C.)
Stoicism pantheistic philosophy founded by Zeno of Citium encompassing doctrine of submission to divine will and freedom from passions (Greece, 3rd c. B.C.)
subjectivism doctrine limiting knowledge of reality to that which is consciously apprehended, with moral values dependent on personal and subjective tastes; truth seen as relative to human nature and ability to comprehend
syntactics branch of semiotics concerned with formal properties of language or symbolic systems
Thomism theological philosophy of Thomas Aquinas; rational system teaching that at some point reason fails and faith provides revelation (13th c.)
transcendentalism philosophy emphasizing thought processes in discovery of reality; philosophy emphasizing intuitive and spiritual rather than empirical basis of knowledge, developed by Ralph Waldo Emerson and Henry David Thoreau (U.S., 19th c.)
utilitarianism theory of moral conduct based on attainment of maximum good for greatest number of people (19th c.)

Notions, Ideas, and Methods

abstraction that which is theoretical, dissociated from specific instances or phenomena
academicism purely speculative thoughts and opinions
agnosticism belief that we cannot know whether God exists
altruism principle or practice of unselfish concern for the good of others, esp. as a moral act
antithesis second stage of dialectical process, being a proposition directly opposite and apparently contradictory to the thesis
a priori (*adj*) *Latin.* lit. from what precedes; independent of and prior to experience; based on reason or inherent logic, independent of empirical data; from a general law to a particular instance
archetype original model from which all others follow, esp. perfect example of type
association of ideas basic principle explaining all mental activity in terms of combining and recombining of certain component elements
automatism view of body as a machine and consciousness as noncontrolling element of body
casuistry skill in science and application of moral decisions and judgments; employment of specious reasoning in moral questions
categorical imperative unconditional moral rule of conduct, not dependent on personal preferences
cogito ergo sum *Latin.* lit. I think, therefore I am; fundamental argument for idealism, attributed to René Descartes
concretion that which is founded in fact; hard evidence, specific instances, or phenomena
connotation implication of a term, as distinguished from its denotation
deduction mode of reasoning leading from general observation to particular conclusion
denotation specific meaning of a term, as distinguished from its connotation
dialectic orig. Socratic philosophic discourse or style of inquiry based on critical examination, later developed by Hegel as dynamic process of thesis, antithesis, and synthesis
discourse orderly, systematic communication, esp. in philosophic discussion
empirical (*adj*) pertaining to the senses; dependent on experience and direct observation
essence inherent nature of an object, inseparable from its identity and contingent on nothing
evil moral wrongdoing; malevolence or ethical perversion
Forms absolute, eternal, immutable, and perfected Platonic models of which all earthly things are imperfect copies
four elements basic constituents of physical world: earth, air, fire, and water
free will option and power of moral choice in determining one's behavior
golden mean Aristotelian ethical doctrine of moderation as way to virtuous action
Gordian knot intricate and difficult problem or circumstance best resolved by cutting through it boldly and imaginatively
hermeneutics science of interpretation and explanation
heuristic (*adj*) characterized by ability to persuade or reveal rather than to convince logically
Hobson's choice choice between unacceptable alternatives; absence of real alternatives
holism notion that fundamental entities have existence beyond sum of their parts
hypothesis assumption, theory, or proposition made to account for some phenomena
idea something present in consciousness; in Platonic terms, an archetype or essential concept
immanent (*adj*) existing within the mind only
induction mode of reasoning leading from particular observations to general conclusions
inference mode of reasoning in which conclusion is derived from premises accepted as true
innate ideas inborn ideas not based on experience
maieutic (*adj*) pertaining to the Socratic method for clarifying ideas
monad *Greek.* lit. unit; ultimate, indivisible force center that is unit of all existence
natural law naturally occurring moral rules that form universal law higher than man-made law
noetics science of the intellect or of pure thought
noncontradiction principle that statement cannot be both true and false and object cannot both have and not have some quality
noumenon *Greek.* lit. that which is conceived; reality that cannot be experienced, as opposed to appearance or phenomena

nous *Greek.* lit. mind; universal principle of reason, embodied in God
Occam's razor principle that simplest explanation or theory is correct and should not be needlessly multiplied
ontological argument attempt to prove existence of God by analysis of definition of God
ontology metaphysical study of the essence of being and reality
Peripatetic follower of Aristotle, so called from practice of walking while teaching
phenomena objects and events known through sensory experience
quintessence essence of a substance; substance other than four elements believed to compose celestial bodies
reality that which exists independently of ideas about it and independently of all other things, but from which all else derives
reason intellectual faculty, ability to comprehend by rational powers; systematic thinking, judgment of truth of propositions
sentience ability to sense or feel
situation ethics moral evaluation of any action in relation to specific circumstance
social contract concept that society is based on agreement among people to be governed
Socratic method dialectic technique of inquiry developed by Plato's teacher Socrates (Greece, 5th c. B.C.)
solipsism theory that one can be aware of nothing outside the self and one's personal perceptions and feelings
sophistry use of persuasive but misleading or unsound argument
sufficient reason principle that there is a reason for every phenomenon being as it is and not otherwise
summum bonum *Latin.* lit. highest good; moral principle of action based on effecting the greatest good
synthesis dialectical combining of thesis and antithesis into higher stage of truth
tabula rasa *Latin.* lit. blank tablet; empiricist description of human mind at birth, with no innate ideas, awaiting experience to develop ideas
teleology belief in purpose and design in nature and phenomena
theorem principle, rule
theory hypothesis or speculation rather than action
thesis proposition held for proof by argument
universal general concept having unrestricted application; proposition true for all members of its class
values moral standards and social goals held worthy for their own sake
vice moral corruption or evil
virtue moral integrity or excellence
will ability to make choices

Logic

ambiguity possibility of having more than one meaning
amphiboly argument in which statement's meaning can be interpreted in more than one way
analogy relation based on similarity; inference based on shared qualities
antecedent conditional element in proposition
antinomy contradiction or opposition of one law to another
argument set of reasoned statements leading from assumptions and premises to conclusion
assumption statement taken to be true without proof
axiom assumption accepted as basis for deductive reasoning
biconditional (*adj*) designating a proposition that asserts the mutual interdependence of two things or events
circular (*adj*) describing reasoning in which apparently proved conclusion has been assumed as premise
compound proposition combination of at least two simple propositions using conditional word such as "if," "or," or "then"
conclusion reasoned deduction drawn from argument's premises
conditional "if-then" proposition in which existence or occurrence of one phenomenon or event depends on existence or occurrence of another phenomenon or event
constant term with invariable meaning
contradiction logically false statement
converse statement with elements expressed in reverse order of original proposition; reverse
counterexample fact that refutes a generalization
deductive logic formal logic; study of relationship between premises and conclusions of arguments; reasoning in which premises necessarily lead to particular conclusions
demonstration proof of an argument
dilemma syllogism in which major premise contains two or more conditional propositions and minor premise is a disjunction
disjunction compound proposition, either inclusive or exclusive, produced by joining two simple propositions by the word "or"
fallacy incorrect reasoning; invalid argument; instance of false conclusion drawn from premises
generalization proposition applying to all members of certain class of things or indefinite portion of that class
implication relation between two propositions whereby one may be logically deduced from the other
inductive logic study of relationship between premises and conclusions of inconclusive arguments
inverse statement reversed in order, directly opposite form of original
lemma subsidiary proposition that helps prove another proposition
logic study and use of formal reasoning process for analyzing relationship between premises and conclusions of arguments
major premise premise in syllogism containing predicate of conclusion
metamathematics study of general properties of logical systems

minor premise premise in syllogism containing subject of conclusion
modal logic logic that classifies propositions according to their necessity and probability
obverse proposition inferred from another by denying the opposite of that which given proposition affirms
paradox self-contradictory statement
postulate statement or proposition assumed to be true without proof
predicate that which is affirmed or denied concerning subject of proposition
premise general statement used as basis for argument and to support conclusion
proof series of statements used to show validity of argument
proposition point to be discussed, proved, disproved, or maintained in argument
QED quod erat demonstrandum; *Latin.* lit. that which was to be demonstrated; designation for conclusion, equivalent to "therefore" or "thus"
quantifier term, such as "all" or "some," that establishes or restricts the quantity of a proposition
rational (*adj*) having reason; capable of reasoning
rationale explanation of principles or opinion
relationship connection by means of conditionals and/or quantifiers between two or more propositions
sorites series of related syllogisms forming closed circle of premises leading to conclusion that connects back to original premise
statement true or false sentence existing as part of argument
subject term of proposition concerning which predicate is affirmed or denied
syllogism form of deductive argument based on two premises or assumptions and conclusion drawn from them
symbolic logic mathematical logic using symbols to express propositions, quantifiers, and relationships; propositional calculus and functional calculus
tautology proposition necessarily true by virtue of its components; redundant proposition adding no new knowledge
truth-functional logic form of logic using connective terms "and" and "or"
truth-value truth or falsity of a statement
universe of discourse all objects possibly referred to in establishing and proving argument
valid (*adj*) correctly argued as a conclusion based on premises
variable term with different meanings depending on context
vice versa (*adj*) expressed as contrary of original statement
vicious circle two propositions that establish each other or two terms that define each other

EDUCATION

Colleges and Universities
Schools and Classes
Teachers and Students
Curricula, Studies, Learning, and Tests
Extracurricular Activities and Concerns

Colleges and Universities

A and M Agricultural and Mechanical college
academia community life or environment of a university; academe
academic (*adj*) relating to an institution of higher education
accredited (*adj*) issuing degrees recognized as valid
advanced degree degree beyond baccalaureate
alma mater college or school from which one received a degree
B.A. Bachelor of Arts degree
baccalaureate bachelor's degree
bachelor's degree degree given at completion of studies at four-year college; baccalaureate; undergraduate degree
B.S. Bachelor of Science degree
bursar financial officer at college
certificate special degree, lower than bachelor's, awarded by junior college or training institution
chancellor university president; chief executive of state educational system
college institution of higher education that provides general course of studies leading to bachelor's degree; part of university offering specific course of study
colloquium conference or informal meeting at which specialists speak and answer questions on designated topic
commencement ceremonies surrounding awarding of degrees and graduation
community college junior college serving local residents
credential degree awarded in professional field, such as teaching, after or separate from bachelor's degree
cum laude (*adv*) *Latin.* lit. with praise; designation on diploma indicating graduation with honors
dean official in charge of division, faculty, or school within a college
diploma official document bearing seal and recording receipt of degree
divinity school division within college providing training for ministerial candidates
D. Litt. *Latin.* Doctor Litterarum; Doctor of Letters degree
doctorate highest university degree, esp. Ph.D.; doctor's degree
D.Th. Doctor of Theology degree
fellowship stipend given to support advanced study

graduate school university division in specific field attended after receipt of bachelor's degree
honorary degree degree awarded in recognition of achievement, not for completion of studies
institute educational establishment usu. devoted to technical field
interdisciplinary major course of study involving two or more academic disciplines
intersession period between academic terms
ivory tower place remote from worldly things, esp. institution of higher education
junior college two-year community college issuing certificates or associate degrees, often a vocational or technical school
land-grant college government financed college providing low-cost higher educations, esp. in agriculture and mechanical arts
liberal arts college studies emphasizing general knowledge rather than professional or vocational training
LL.D. *Latin.* Legum Doctor; Doctor of Laws degree
M.A. Master of Arts degree, achieved after B.A.
magna cum laude (*adv*) *Latin.* lit. with great praise; designation on diploma indicating graduation with great honors
major student's primary field of study; (*vb*) select one's primary field of study
master's degree university graduate degree received after bachelor's and before doctorate
matriculation enrollment as student in college or university as degree candidate
M.D. Doctor of Medicine; doctoral degree awarded at completion of medical school
minor student's secondary field of study; (*vb*) select secondary field of study
M.S. Master of Science degree, received after B.S.
multiversity large university composed of many schools, colleges, or divisions
Ph.D. Doctor of Philosophy; highest university postgraduate degree
Phi Beta Kappa national university honor society for scholars
postdoctoral (*adj*) designating work and study undertaken after receipt of doctorate
postgraduate student who takes advanced work after graduation; (*adj*) designating study leading to postgraduate degree
predoctoral (*adj*) designating student or course of study leading toward doctoral degree
premed program of undergraduate studies preparatory to medical school admission; student enrolled in such a program
provost high-ranking university administrator
regent member of governing board of some state universities
registration enrollment in specific classes at beginning of term
sabbatical leave of absence for professor, originally granted every seventh year
Sc.D. *Latin.* Scientiae Doctor; Doctor of Science degree
scholarship funding granted to student, esp. on basis of need or merit
semester either of two, usu. eighteen-week, divisions of academic year, September to January or February to June
seminary institution that trains candidates for ministry or priesthood; theological seminary
S.J.D. *Latin.* Scientiae Juridicae Doctor; Doctor of Juridical Science degree
state college government-funded college, esp. for students of one state
summa cum laude (*adv*) *Latin.* lit. with highest praise; designation on diploma indicating graduation with highest honor
teachers college college for training elementary and secondary school teachers, usu. in two-year program
tenure permanent employment granted to college or university professor after trial period
term division of academic year during which courses begin and end
theological seminary seminary
trimester segment of academic year divided into three quarters or semesters, usu. September to December, January to March, and April to June
tuition fee required for registration at educational institution
undergraduate degree bachelor's degree
university public or private educational institution operating at highest level, with facilities for teaching and research, undergraduate colleges granting bachelor's degrees, and graduate programs and professional schools granting master's degrees and doctorates
war college institution that provides training in military theory and practice

Schools and Classes

academic year period of school sessions, usu. September through June
academy high school or college emphasizing specific subjects; private high school
adult school institution providing education for adults, usu. without college credit
alternative school nontraditional elementary or secondary school
Bible school parochial school, esp. one run by fundamentalist religious order
boarding school school at which students reside during school year
class specific course of study, group of students, or period of instruction
conservatory school or academy offering training in one of the fine arts, esp. music
convent girls' school run by community of nuns
country day school private, nonboarding elementary or secondary school outside city limits
course lectures, assignments, class meetings, and tests on particular subject over set period of time
day care daytime supervision of preschool children
day nursery day school
day school place where day care is provided; nursery school; nonboarding private school; day nursery

elementary school grades one through six or eight, often including kindergarten; grade school; grammar school; primary school
finishing school exclusive girls' private school emphasizing social and cultural activities, not academics
grade school elementary school
grammar school elementary school, grades one to six
gymnasium secondary school for students planning to go to university (Germany)
Hebrew school school for instruction in Jewish traditions and Hebrew language, usu. holding weekly sessions for Jewish children
high school secondary school, usu. grades nine through twelve, sometimes grades ten through twelve
homeroom classroom where students begin and sometimes end day
intermediate school elementary school, grades four through six; junior high school
junior high school seventh and eighth grades
kindergarten first year of school, for five-year olds, before first grade
magnet school public school with specialized curriculum that draws students from broad region
middle school school between elementary and high school, usu. grades six through eight
military academy institution providing training in war and soldiering as well as academic disciplines
Montessori school institution following system of training young children developed by Maria Montessori, stressing free-form physical activity, individual instruction, and early literacy
night school school offering evening classes in continuing education, generally for older students employed during day
nursery school prekindergarten facility providing day care and some training for children from about three to five years of age
parochial school private elementary or secondary school supported and administered by religious body, esp. Catholic Church
preparatory school usu. private secondary school aimed at preparing students for college; prep school
prep school preparatory school
preschool day-care or nursery school instruction for children prior to entering kindergarten
primary school elementary school
private school school maintained by nongovernment funds, including students' tuition fees
public school government-supported, usu. tuition-free, school (U.S.); privately-endowed secondary school offering classical curriculum (Britain)
school institution providing instruction, esp. for children in grades one to twelve and kindergarten
secondary school institution after elementary school and before college, particularly grades nine to twelve, public or private
seminary parochial, usu. Roman Catholic, secondary school, esp. for girls
senior high school four-year secondary school, grades nine through twelve
summer school classes held between June and August, when school is normally not in session
Sunday school class held on Sunday for religious instruction, esp. Christian
trade school secondary school teaching vocational skills
vocational school school providing instruction in industrial or commercial skills needed for particular trade or profession
yeshiva school for Talmudic study; Orthodox Jewish school for religious and secular studies

Teachers and Students

adviser teacher or school administrator who counsels students on academic or personal difficulties
alumna female graduate of institution; *pl.* alumnae
alumni collective term for all graduates of institution
alumnus male graduate of institution; *pl.* alumni
apprentice individual receiving training in specific profession through work experience
assistant professor lowest level of university professor
associate professor intermediate level of professor, below full professor
autodidact self-taught person
cadet undergraduate at military academy
chairperson head of university department, formerly and sometimes still chairman
coach tutor or trainer providing special instruction to individual student or help with specific problem
coed female college student
docent college or university teacher or lecturer
educator teacher or school administrator
emeritus (*adj*) designating retired college professor holding honorary title
exchange student high-school or college student studying at foreign institution, usu. for one year, as part of reciprocal program between two schools or countries
faculty teaching staff of educational institution
fellow individual appointed to position and receiving allowance to pursue research or advanced study
freshman first-year student at high school or college; frosh
full professor tenured professor of highest rank
headmaster man heading staff of private school
headmistress woman heading staff of private school
intern advanced or graduate student in professional field, esp. medicine, receiving supervised work experience in addition to academic training
junior third-year student at high school or college
lector college lecturer
lecturer teacher who instructs class through long, formal discourses; university teacher below rank of assistant professor
licentiate person who has received license to practice an art or profession; holder of intermediate degree between baccalaureate and doctorate

mentor teacher or older student who provides guidance and support for less experienced student
monitor student appointed to assist teacher
pedagogue teacher
philomath lover of learning
plebe freshman at military academy
preceptor headmaster or principal of school; teacher
principal chief executive officer of school
proctor individual chosen to monitor or supervise students, esp. at examination
prodigy extraordinarily talented child; wunderkind
professor highest-ranking university faculty member
protégé student receiving special attention and encouragement from teacher or elder
pundit teacher; learned individual
rector chief administrator of school or university, esp. parochial school
salutatorian student ranking second in graduating class behind valedictorian
scholar student, esp. one doing advanced study in some subject; learned, erudite person
schoolmaster man who teaches school
schoolmistress woman who teaches school
seminarian student in seminary, esp. Roman Catholic
senior final-year student at high school or college
sophomore second-year student at high school or college
student individual who attends school; one who studies so as to learn; pupil
student body all students at school or college
student teacher assistant teacher still studying to receive teaching credential or degree; practice teacher
substitute teacher elementary or secondary school teacher hired as interim replacement for absent teacher
TA teaching assistant
teacher one trained to be and employed as an instructor of students; instructor; pedagogue
teacher's aide noncredentialed assistant to teacher
teaching assistant TA; graduate student aiding professor in instruction of undergraduate class
teaching fellow graduate student granted free tuition in return for assisting professors in class or laboratory
tenured (*adj*) designating college professor holding permanent employment
truant student inexcusably or habitually late or absent from school
tutor private teacher for one individual; individual providing personalized instruction in British university
tyro novice or beginner in some field
underclassman first- or second-year college student
undergraduate student in four-year college program
upperclassman third- or fourth-year college student
valedictorian student with highest grade ranking in class, selected to present valedictory address
wunderkind precociously bright child or prodigy

Curricula, Studies, Learning, and Tests

ABC's the alphabet; basic primary education
achievement test test that measures learning in a specific area
adult education courses offered to adults who have completed or discontinued formal education; continuing education
A level second of two standardized secondary school examinations required for university admission (Britain)
aptitude test measure of various abilities, esp. verbal and mathematical
audiovisual aids educational materials and teaching devices, such as films and recordings, that appeal to both sense of hearing and sense of sight
audit (*vb*) attend class as an observer, without receiving credit
basal (*adj*) fundamental, esp. of a reading book
bilingual education classes given in two languages
black studies college curriculum on history and culture of African-Americans
blue book small notebook with blue cover, often used for taking college examinations
CAI computer-assisted instruction
CEEB College Entrance Examination Board
civics study of government and politics, esp. in high school
classical education traditional academic course of study, sometimes including study of Greek and Latin; classicism
College Entrance Examination Board CEEB; organization that administers SAT and achievement tests used to judge applicants for college admission
computer-assisted instruction CAI; instruction in which computer leads student through programmed lesson
continuing education adult education
correspondence course class conducted by mail
course series of lectures, assignments, class meetings, and tests on particular subject over set period of time
cram (*vb*) *Informal.* prepare for test at last minute
crash program intensive course for rapid learning of material
credit acknowledgment that student has completed a class requirement leading to a degree; unit of such acknowledgment, accumulated toward graduation requirement
crib (*vb*) *Informal.* plagiarize, copy, or cheat
curriculum all courses offered by an institution; set of courses in area of specialization; course of study
curve grading system based on relative position of student within class, not raw score

dean's list honor roll of students with high grades
didactic (*adj*) designed to instruct
dissertation extended written treatment on subject, usu. involving research, esp. by degree candidate
Education Testing Service division of CEEB that administers SAT and achievement tests
elective course outside student's major field of study
ESL English as a second language; course of study in English for nonnative speakers
extension program that makes courses available to those without normal access to them, as by correspondence
fescue long stick for pointing to letters to aid children learning to read
final exam examination given at conclusion of course, covering all material studied
flashcard small card with words, numbers, or pictures on it, used in learning drills
4.0 perfect, straight-A grade point average
functional illiterate person with reading ability less than that needed to function in modern society
grade-equivalent score measurement of test score by decimal representation of year and month of student's grade level, such as 7.3 for third month of seventh grade
grade point average average of total earned grade points on scale from zero to four divided by total class credits
honor roll list of students with high grades
humanities branch of learning concerned with human activities and institutions
independent study course of study designed by student outside normal curricula or requirements of major
industrial arts training in use of tools and machinery
intelligence testing tests designed to identify exceptional children, measure intelligence levels, and diagnose disturbed children
language arts reading, writing, spelling, and speech skills
language laboratory facility in which taped, question-and-answer material is used to aid learning of foreign language
learning acquisition of knowledge and understanding, esp. by study
learning disability physiological or emotional impairment of capacity for learning
lesson plan teacher's outline of class session and assigned work
lexicon book containing alphabetical arrangement of words and definitions
midterm exam given halfway through course
mnemonic device trick or technique used to assist memory
multiple-choice test examination offering several possible answers to each question, one of which is correct
new math theory of mathematics instruction based on set and number theory leading to principles of arithmetic
O level first of two standardized secondary school examinations required to continue education (Britain)
orals oral examination by panel of professors as final test in doctoral program
phonics rote memorization of syllable and letter sounds to learn reading
placement test entrance examination used to assign students to appropriate class level
polytechnic (*adj*) relating to instruction in technical arts and applied sciences
practicum curriculum that includes supervised practical experience and training, esp. for teachers
précis brief written summary
programmed learning instruction in which student proceeds through a series of highly structured materials at his or her own pace, receiving immediate feedback and testing from materials
progressive education instruction that rejects rote learning and strict discipline in favor of individual stimulation, group discussion, and more diverse curriculum
quadrivium upper division studies in medieval university, comprising arithmetic, music, geometry, and astronomy
raw score actual score on test unadjusted for student's relative position in group tested; number of correct answers on test
reading disability learning problem that impairs person's reading skill
refresher brief course in subject previously studied
remedial (*adj*) designating courses intended to correct poor study habits or improve skills in specific field
report card periodic record of student's grades issued by school to parents
rote learning mechanically by memory without really understanding
SAT Scholastic Aptitude Test
Scholastic Aptitude Test *Trademark.* SAT; standardized test used by colleges in evaluating reading and mathematics skills of applicants for admission
seminar small group of students pursuing advanced studies with professor
shop high school class providing vocational training, esp. in automobile mechanics, metalwork, or carpentry
social studies study of government, history, and culture; civics
special education course of study aimed at group of students with particular needs, problems, or goals
spoon-feed (*vb*) present information so thoroughly that independent thought is curbed and initiative destroyed
standardized test achievement test that measures knowledge in specific skill or subject without taking into account other factors
study use of one's mind for the gaining of knowledge; such activity in a particular field
syllabus outline or summary of course of study
team teaching program in which two teachers incorporate their subjects into one course which they teach together

term paper lengthy written assignment in high school or college that displays student's progress and knowledge at end of course
test examination, measurement, and evaluation of student's knowledge and progress in course
theme written assignment, essay
thesis lengthy essay based on original research written by candidate for degree, esp. doctorate
Three R's reading, writing, and arithmetic; basic primary education
tracking assignment of students to specific curriculum based on aptitude level
trivium lower division studies in medieval university, comprising grammar, rhetoric, and logic
tutorial class conducted for one student or small number of students
viva oral examination at university in Britain or Europe
vocational education vocational training; career education
vocational training instruction in industrial or commercial skills needed for particular trade or profession; vocational education
whole language basis for method of teaching reading, used as alternative to phonics, in which students read interesting books, write stories before they can spell, and learn correct usage through correction of their work

Extracurricular Activities and Concerns

academic freedom education without government or other external interference
busing transportation of students from one area to another to achieve racial balance in schools
common room lounge for use by faculty or residents of dormitory
commons plot of land on campus for general use by students
corporal punishment physical punishment of students
detention keeping students at school after school hours as punishment
dormitory residence building for students at college, university, or boarding school; dorm
extracurricular (*adj*) designating student activities not receiving academic credit or engaged in outside classroom
extramural (*adj*) relating to extension courses (Britain)
fraternity selective men's social organization, usu. with its own residence, at college
hazing cruel pranks and harassment, esp. as fraternity initiation rite
homecoming annual weekend during which alumni return to college, usu. highlighted by athletic contest
hooky nonattendance at school
intercollegiate (*adj*) designating contests or activities conducted among or between colleges
interscholastic (*adj*) designating contests or activities conducted among or between schools
intramural (*adj*) designating contests or activities conducted within a single university or school
jayvee junior varsity athletic team
open enrollment voluntary enrollment in public school other than one indicated by residence; college acceptance of students regardless of qualifications
Parent-Teacher Association PTA; national society that brings parents in contact with their children's teachers
Pledge of Allegiance oath of loyalty to U.S. flag, repeated by class at beginning of day in some elementary and secondary schools
PTA Parent-Teacher Association
recess brief suspension of studies for exercise and recreation
reunion gathering of alumni to commemorate graduation
rush recruiting drive by fraternity or sorority
school prayer brief prayer recited at beginning of day in some schools, but banned in others
show and tell period in elementary school during which students describe or display things of interest to class
sorority selective women's social organization at college, usu. with its own residence
student union college building devoted to extracurricular student activities; center of student affairs; union
varsity athletic team representing school or college in contests against other schools
work-study program program that offers high school or college students work experience and income in addition to schooling
yearbook annual publication that reviews year's activities and lists all students or all graduating students in high school or college

Chapter Fourteen

Fine Arts and Literature

PAINTING

Schools and Styles of Fine Art
Painting Tools and Techniques
Kinds of Paintings
Display of Art

Schools and Styles of Fine Art

abstract art nonrepresentational and nonfigurative style emphasizing formal values over representation of subject matter

abstract expressionism nonrepresentational style emphasizing emotion, strong color, and giving primacy to the act of painting (mid-20th c.)

action painting active, aggressive methods of applying paint (U.S., mid-20th c.)

aestheticism movement characterized by eclectic search for beauty and interest in Japanese and classical art (U.S. and Britain, late 19th c.)

art deco style characterized by repetitive, ornamental, and highly finished curvilinear and geometric designs, esp. in synthetic materials such as plastics (1920's-1930's)

art nouveau decorative style emphasizing fluid, biomorphic lines and swirling motifs (late 19th c.)

ashcan school antiacademic, realistic depiction of the grimmer aspects of everyday life (U.S., early 20th c.)

avant-garde innovative art in advance of popular ideas and images, characterized by unorthodox and experimental methods

Barbizon School style emphasizing idyllic landscapes and nature (France, 19th c.)

baroque emotional, dramatic style, anticlassical in form and spirit (late 16th-18th c.)

Bauhaus school emphasizing the functional and geometric by incorporating craft elements in design (early 20th c.)

Blaue Reiter *German.* expressionist group; Blue Rider School (early 20th c.)

Byzantine (*adj*) designating a style with Oriental and Occidental elements and strong religious content (2nd-13th c.)

cave art prehistoric paintings and engravings on Paleolithic-era cave walls

classical style with emphasis on symmetry, proportion, and harmony of line and form (ancient Greece and Rome)

computer art electronically produced images displayed on video screens (late 20th c.)

conceptual art avant-garde, idea-oriented style with emphasis on performance, theory and criticism, and attitude (late 20th c.)

concrete art realism, opposed to abstract art (early 20th c.)

constructivism style with geometric abstraction and emphasis on three-dimensionality (Russia, early 20th c.)

cubism departure from traditional, naturalistic view of reality, emphasizing multifaccted, simultaneous views of subject and distorted perspectives (early 20th c.)

dada style with antirational approach and nihilistic, absurdist, and incongruous themes (1915-1925)

de Stijl school of art characterized by minimalism, geometric abstraction, and use of primary colors; neoplasticism (Netherlands, early 20th c.)

expressionism style emphasizing emotional expression, strong color and composition, and a distorted, theatrical treatment of image (early 20th c.)

Fauvism style with brilliant, unrestrained color and offhand approach to composition (France, early 20th c.)

fin de siècle *French.* sophisticated stylization (late 19th c.)

folk art any untrained, nonacademic, or unschooled style

Fontainebleau School style emphasizing the elegant and decorative (France, 16th c.)

Gothic style emphasizing Christian imagery, brilliant color, and strong verticality in composition (12th-16th c.)

Hellenic (*adj*) of the classical style of Greek antiquity (8th-4th c. B.C.)

Hellenistic (*adj*) of the post-classical Greek style before the Roman conquest (4th-2nd c. B.C.)

Hudson River school group of American painters whose style was characterized by idyllic landscapes, esp. of the Hudson River area (19th c.)

Impressionism style emphasizing the depiction of light and its effects, with the act of seeing as its primary subject (France, 19th c.)

international style style with detailed depiction of Christian subjects and Gothic verticality in composition (14th c.)

Italianate (*adj*) conforming to the style of the Italian Renaissance masters

kinetic art art marked by incorporation of painted and sculpted mechanical parts into art piece that moves or creates the impression of movement (mid-20th c.)

Mannerism anticlassical style characterized by dramatic gestures and poses of figures, intense color, and complex perspective (16th c.)

Ming (*adj*) characteristic of a highly academic classicism, esp. in porcelains (China, 14th-17th c.)

minimal art abstract, simple, reductionist style with absence of all but basic formal elements and primary colors (U.S., mid-20th c.)

modernism style that breaks with traditional art forms and searches for new modes of expression (early 20th c.)

naturalism style emphasizing the depiction of the actual appearance of nature and the visible world

neoclassicism style modeled after proportion and restraint of Greek and Roman classical antiquity (late 18th-early 19th c.)

neo-expressionism style using expressionistic emotionalism in post-expressionist era (mid-20th c.)

neo-impressionism style with emphasis on the scientific application of the optical effects of light and color (France, late 19th c.)
neoplasticism de Stijl
new wave combination of cartoon, graffiti, and performance art in a minimalist, unsophisticated style (late 20th c.)
New York school abstract expressionism practiced by artists in New York City that emphasized the emotional, dramatic, and heroic in scale and theme (mid-20th c.)
op art style with graphic abstraction and pattern-oriented optical effects (mid-20th c.)
performance art use of paintings, sculpture, and video in live theatrical performance by artist (late 20th c.)
photorealism style emphasizing the meticulously realistic depiction of banal contemporary subjects, esp. suburban, snapshotlike scenes (mid-20th c.)
pointillism neo-impressionism employing tiny, closely spaced points of color that blend to pro duce a luminous quality (France late 19th c.)
pop art style-making use of images from popular culture and commerce, often reproduced exactly (mid-20th c.)
Post-Impressionism emotionally expressive, formally modern style with nontraditional approach to color and composition (late 19th-early 20th c.)
postmodernism style reflecting the exhaustion of modernist experimentation and a partial return to more traditional forms (late 20th c.)
pre-Columbian (*adj*) of or pertaining to native American art before the arrival of Columbus (pre-16th c.)
prehistoric (*adj*) pertaining to cave painting and other forms of Paleolithic art
pre-Raphaelite (*adj*) designating a style modeled on romanticized vision of medieval, pre-Renaissance styles (19th c.)
primitivism style with unsophisticated, pretechnological, simple approach to form and content
Quattrocento art of Indian Renaissance (15th c.)
realism depiction of reality as it appears, without idealization or stylistic, imaginative distortion
Renaissance (*adj*) pertaining to humanistic art that is classical in form and content; (*n*) revival of aesthetics of classical antiquity (14th-17th c.)
representational (*adj*) designating art concerned with accurate, naturalistic depictions of reality
rococo style with ornamental, poetic, curvilinear forms and lyrical themes (18th c.)
Romanticism style characterized by an emotional, intuitive exaltation of nature over culture and imagination over realism (late 18th-early 19th c.)
social realism depiction of ordinary life as emblematic of social and political truths (20th c.)
surrealism style using subconscious mental activity as its subject matter, characterized by dreamlike, hallucinatory imagery (early 20th c.)
Symbolism movement that rejected realism and expressed subjective visions through evocative images (France, late 19th c.)
T'ang classical period (China, 7th-9th c.)
Tantra art mystical, diagrammatic, and symbolic art (Buddhist, Hindu)

Painting Tools and Techniques

acrylic paint synthetic, fast-drying pigment
aerial perspective type of perspective involving subject perceived from above by viewer
airbrush nozzled tube used to apply paint in spray form
appliqué application of foreign material to surface of painting for ornamentation
aquatint etching of spaces rather than lines, producing tonal effect like wash or watercolor
architectonic (*adj*) controlled, linear, geometric in rendering
atelier artist's studio
base inert pigment used in manufacture of lakes
batik painting on wax-treated cloth
binder substance combining pigment particles into pliable, fluid medium
brilliance radiance or intensity of color
brush bristles fixed on handle for applying paint or varnish: angular liner, bamboo, blender, bright, bulletin cutter, camel's hair, cutter, dabber, dagger striper, easel, fan blender, filbert, fitch, flat, highliner, lettering, limp, liner, mop, oval, poster, quill, red sable, round, script, shader, varnish, wash
brushwork artist's distinctive way of applying paint with brush
canvas woven fabric of linen, cotton, or hemp stretched on frame and used as painting surface; completed painting
cartoon full-size, preliminary painting or sketch for completed work
chalk soft, white limestone, sometimes with color added, used in drawing
charcoal pencil made from chunk of soft, porous, black carbon
chiaroscuro technique of depicting light and dark tones to create an illusion of depth and modeling
chinoiserie work patterned after Chinese art
chroma strength or purity of a color, measured by its departure from neutral color
chromolithograph colored picture printed from impressions made by a series of stone or metal plates, each in a different color
coat single application of paint on surface
collage pasting together bits of found objects, newspaper, and cloth over other materials on a single surface
color paint, pigment, or dye that reflects light waves of a particular length
complementary colors two colors at opposite points on color scale, such as red and green
composition aesthetically pleasing, harmonious, and effective arrangement of parts to form whole
construction paper heavy colored paper, esp. for cutouts

contrast use of striking differences, esp. in color or tone, between adjacent parts of painting
cool colors blue-green portion of spectrum
crayon small stick of chalk, colored wax, or charcoal used for drawing
crepe paper thin, crinkled paper
crosshatching shading technique that uses many parallel strokes
decoupage cutting out designs from paper or other material, mounting them on surface, and applying varnish or lacquer
distemper water-base paint with glue binder; mix of powdered pigment and size
drawing picture, design, or sketch done with lines in pen or pencil; skill at using lines to depict something
easel vertical frame for supporting painting in progress
enamel pigment mixed with varnish that dries to a hard, glossy finish
encaustic (*adj*) designating painting done with pigment mixed with beeswax and blended with heat
finger paint water-soluble, nontoxic, creamy paint applied with fingers, esp. for children and crafts
foreshortening technique of creating the illusion of a painted object projecting through the picture plane; use of linear perspective to depict three-dimensionality
framing designing and fashioning borders for paintings, usu. of wood, often ornamental
fresco technique of painting directly on a wet, plaster surface
gesso plaster of Paris used as white primer for painting surface, esp. canvas
gilding application of gold leaf to picture surface
glaze thin, translucent layer of color
gouache opaque watercolor bound with gum
graphic art art and technique by which copies of an original design are printed, as from a plate or block
grisaille monochrome in primarily gray tints, esp. on glass, having appearance of relief
hachure hatching
hatching shading technique that uses parallel lines; hachure
highlight bright, light area emphasizing modeling
hue distinct qualities of a color that position it in the spectrum
iconography representation by images; study of such images
illumination decorative, esp. miniature, painting in books
impasto thick application of paint that forms an opaque relief surface
imprimatura painting surface prepared with a thin glaze of color
japan varnish mixed with pigment
lacquer protective, transparent, resinous liquid that dries to a glossy surface
limn (*vb*) represent in painting or drawing
linear perspective type of perspective involving view perceived from in front of subject by viewer in arbitrarily fixed position
line drawing drawing done in lines only, showing gradations of tone through variations in width and density of lines
mandorla halo of light on holy figure (Buddhist, Christian)
medium liquid in which pigment is mixed to form paint; type of paint or coloring matter used in painting
model person who poses for a drawing, painting, or sculpture
modeling technique of depicting three-dimensional objects on two-dimensional surface
monochromatic (*adj*) having a one-hued color scheme
oeuvre *French.* entire body of an artist's work
oil paint pigment mixed with drying oil, esp. linseed oil
paint pigment ground to a powder, then mixed with a liquid binding medium
painting art and technique of applying colored pigments and other materials to a flat surface, esp. stretched canvas, to depict an image or represent a feeling with consideration for composition, form, and color
palette handheld board for mixing paints
palette knife thin, flexible blade for mixing and applying paint
pastel crayon made of color ground with chalk and compounded with gum water into paste, often of pale color
pastiche jumble of different styles
perspective system of realistically depicting three-dimensional objects or views onto two-dimensional, flat surfaces through convergent lines and planes; portrayal of objects in space
pigment coloring matter mixed with binder to form paint
planes successive stages of depth within a painted image, foreground to background
polychromatic (*adj*) painted in many colors
poster paint opaque, water-base paint with gum or glue-size binder, sold in large jars, typically in bright colors
primary colors red, yellow, and blue, from which all other colors in spectrum can be mixed
proportion aesthetic relation of parts to whole
representational (*adj*) depicting recognizable objects, figures, or scenes
restoration repair of damaged or worn painting
sand painting painting composed of colored sands spread on the ground
saturation degree of purity of a color; intensity of hue
secco painting on dry plaster on wall or ceiling
secondary colors orange, green, and purple, being those colors produced by mixing two of the primary colors
shellac thin, clear varnish made from lac resin and alcohol
size glue and water preparation for canvas
sizing process of applying a surface with size
sketch quick, preliminary drawing used as basis for painting

solvent liquid component of paint that evaporates to leave dried pigment on surface painted
spectrum series of colored bands arranged in order of respective wavelength from infrared to ultraviolet
stretcher backing frame for canvas
study detailed drawing or painting of a section of the planned work
taboret artist's chest with shelves and tabletop palette
tempera pigment mixed with water and an albuminous or gelatinous material, esp. egg yolk
texture characteristic visual and tactile quality of surface of work of art, resulting from manner in which materials are used
thinner solvent used to dilute paint
tint gradation of a color relative to the amount of white mixed into it
tone general coloration or balance of dark and light in a painting, creating harmony
tracing copy made by following lines as seen through transparent paper superimposed on original
trompe l'oeil extremely deft illusion in which a painted object appears real through depiction in fine detail
turpentine colorless, volatile oil used in paints and for cleaning brushes
value degree of lightness or darkness in a color
varnish protective film composed of resin dissolved in drying oil
wash thin coat of water-base paint
water-base paint pigment soluble in water; watercolor
watercolor pigment in binder of gum arabic, water, and glycerin; translucent stain of color on paper

Kinds of Paintings

altarpiece devotional image or shrine in church or temple
cherub representation of a winged angel, or chubby child clothed in red, who supports the heavenly throne
cityscape depiction of an urban scene
contrapposto depiction of a strongly twisted human torso
diablerie depiction of hell and its inhabitants
diptych two-paneled altarpiece
dreamscape depiction of a fantasy world or figments of dreams
easel painting canvas painted at an easel, then framed and hung
figure drawing of a human body and face
genre realistic depiction of scenes from everyday domestic life
grotesque work combining animal, human, plant, and fantastical forms
hieratic (*adj*) designating a style characterized by prescribed religious content
history painting usu. academic depiction of scenes from mythology, history, or the Bible
icon image, esp. portrait
illuminated manuscript miniature painting used as decoration in a handwritten text; psalter
kakemono vertical scroll painting (Japan)
landscape depiction of natural landforms, sometimes allegorical
life drawing drawing of human figure, often nude
makemono horizontal scroll painting (Japan)
mandala schematized representation of the cosmos, usu. in form of concentric geometric shapes, in Oriental art
miniature very small painting
mosaic illustration composed of small, colored stones or tiles set into cement
mural large-scale painting, usu. on a wall or ceiling
nude undraped human figure, sometimes allegorical
panel painting painting supported on freestanding framework, as distinct from a mural or fresco
pastoral (*adj*) designating painting that depicts rural life, often in idealized manner
pictograph picture symbolizing an idea or object, used as early form of writing
Pietà depiction of the Virgin Mary mourning over the dead Christ
polyptych altarpiece with more than three panels
portrait depiction of a person, esp. the face
psalter illuminated manuscript
rotulus illuminated manuscript in scroll form
seascape depiction of scene at sea
self-portrait depiction of artist's own face
silhouette side view of subject, esp. figure or head, filled in with black
stick figure depiction of human figure as single lines with circle for head
still life realistic depiction of inanimate objects, esp. flowers, fruit, or domestic items; nature morte
tanka scroll painting of a deity (Tibetan Buddhism)
triptych three-paneled altarpiece
vignette small, decorative painting used at intervals in a book
wall painting mural painted directly on wall

Display of Art

auction showing of valuable artwork offered for sale to highest bidder
collector person who owns and displays artwork in his or her home
cooperative gallery noncommercial gallery run by artists
curator person in charge of a museum and the objects in it
docent tour guide at museum
gallery building devoted to exhibition and sale of artworks
group show showing of works by more than one artist
hanging aesthetic placement of paintings on wall, using considerations of light, shadow, and height
juried show show for which works are selected by panel of judges

opening first day of show
patron individual who supports the arts and artists
portfolio large, flat case for carrying drawings or paintings
private collection large number of valuable artworks owned by individual, sometimes lent out for public showing
retrospective show covering several phases in artist's career
show display of artworks in gallery or museum for specific length of time
studio artist's workroom, also used for casual display of works

SCULPTURE

Types of Sculpture
Sculpture Tools and Techniques

Types of Sculpture

akrolith statue made of two materials, esp. with wooden body and stone head
anaglyph ornament sculptured or embossed in low relief
assemblage sculptural collage of unrelated parts, materials, or objects
bas-relief sculpture projecting less than half its depth from matrix; low relief
bust sculpture of upper part of body, esp. head and shoulders
colossal extremely large-scale sculpture, larger than heroic
discobolus statue of athlete about to toss discus (ancient Greece)
heroic sculptural scale larger than life-size
high relief sculpture projecting more than halfway out from matrix
ice sculpture carving made from ice block in freezing environment
installation placing of sculptures and other objects in physical environment or room, which becomes part of piece
low relief bas-relief
mezzo-relievo sculpture projecting half its depth from matrix
mobile freely moving, three-dimensional sculpture made of several counterbalanced objects suspended at different levels and moving in the air
relief sculpture attached to a matrix or flat background, not freestanding
sculpture in the round freestanding piece with no supporting backing or matrix
stabile abstract sculpture constructed of stationary parts attached to fixed supports
statuary groups of statues; art of making statues
statue three-dimensional sculpture of human or animal form
totem carved emblem, esp. animal or plant form

Sculpture Tools and Techniques

alabaster translucent, marblelike stone for carving
annealing softening of hammer-hardened metal by heating and gradual cooling
anodize (*vb*) coat metal with protective oxide film by electrolysis
armature framework used to support sculpture in modeling process
banker sculptor's workbench for dressing stones
base lowest part of sculpture, often separate part on which it rests
boss projecting volume to be carved or cut
boucharde toothed, metal, stone-carving hammer
brazing method of joining metals; coating with brass or giving brasslike appearance
bronzing process of coloring a plaster cast to make it appear like bronze
bush chisel toothed, stone-carving hand tool
carving cutting away of wood or stone to create three-dimensional forms, as opposed to modeling
casing plaster reinforcing shell used to hold flexible, negative mass
casting reproduction technique using a mold
casting plaster white plaster of Paris
cavo-relievo relief carving within recessed surface, in which highest point is flush with background stone
charge (*vb*) fill negative mold with positive material
chase (*vb*) finish metal surface
chisel sharp, metal carving tool: bush, claw, oval, pointed, or T-shape
chryselephantine (*adj*) covered with ivory and gold, esp. antique Greek statuary
cire perdue lost-wax process
coil method technique of construction with clay coils
core solid, internal portion of mold in metal casting
damascene decorative inlay of one metal on another
drill tool for boring holes in wood, metal, or stone
electrum alloy of gold and silver for fine sculptural details
emboss (*vb*) decorate with low relief design
fabricate (*vb*) assemble parts into sculptural whole
file abrasive metal tool for smoothing and shaping
filler inert ingredients used to add bulk to mixture
foundry process of melting, casting, or molding metals
galvanize (*vb*) add zinc plating to metal
ganosis application of colored wax to stone sculpture to dull glare during carving
goggles transparent, protective eye coverings, esp. used when welding metal
gouge curved chisel
gradine toothed chisel
grounding finely polished marble
hammer malletlike tool for applying force to chisel
lathe device for shaping a piece by holding it against an abrading or cutting tool

lost-wax process technique for casting metal, in which modeled wax form is melted away and space between core and outer mold is filled with molten metal such as bronze
mallet cylindrical wooden block on handle
mantle clay mold around a wax model
maquette small, preliminary model of finished work
marble very hard limestone rock used as classic carving material
matrix base material to be carved
modeling building up of three-dimensional form, as opposed to carving
mold form for making cast of sculptural form
moulage process of making a mold, esp. with plaster of Paris
negative shell-like mold or impression into which casting material is poured or pressed
origami art of folding paper to depict objects (Japan)
papier-mâché shredded paper soaked in water and glue to form pulpy medium
paraffin colorless, odorless, waxy hydrocarbon used for casting
patina usu. green film on surface of old bronze, caused by exposure to atmosphere or chemicals
pedestal base or stand for sculpture, esp. bust
peen wedgelike or spherical striking surface of hammerhead, used to shape material
pick pointed, metal hammer for removing large areas of stone
plaster of Paris mixture of calcined gypsum with water to form quick-setting paste used for casts, moldings, and statuary
pointing system of copying from three-dimensional model by drilling holes to required depths
pointing device apparatus that marks or drills into a sculpture to set proportionate volumes in order to make copies on any scale
polychromy use of many colors, esp. on statuary
positive cast formed by filling negative mold with casting material
quarry excavation site for marble or stone
quenching quick-cooling of heated metal by immersion in brine, oil, or water
rasp sharply toothed carving and finishing tool
repoussé process of hammering metal into decorative forms in relief
sandblasting etching glass, or cleaning and grinding metal or stone surface, by application of sand carried at high speed by air or steam
sander hand or power tool for smoothing surfaces
sand molding coating the inside of a mold with sand to prevent material from sticking
sculpture art and technique of carving, molding, or welding plastic or hard materials into three-dimensional works of art
site-specific (*adj*) designating a sculpture which is created, designed, or selected for a specific location
slush casting casting of hollow, metal shape by pouring metal into mold and immediately pouring it out, leaving thin layer that hardens on walls of mold
soapstone soft, easily carved stone
spall chip or splinter broken from stone in carving
stone carving cutting away of stone from a block to form three-dimensional shape
temper (*vb*) achieve desired consistency or hardness by mixing or treating, esp. by suddenly cooling heated metal
term pedestal supporting a bust or merging into a biomorphic shape
torch welding and heating tool
turn (*vb*) work on a lathe
vent passage in mold through which gases escape during casting
waste mold negative mold that must be destroyed to free positive cast
welding process of uniting metals by fusing them when molten or pressing them together when soft

LITERATURE

Schools, Styles, and Forms

abstract poetry poetry emphasizing use of sound rather than the meaning of words to convey emotional tone
accentual verse poetry based on number of accents rather than duration of sounds or syllabic recurrence
aestheticism literary movement emphasizing aesthetic values over social and moral values (19th c.)
angry young man one of a group of writers whose works were characterized by an iconoclastic style reflecting bitter dissatisfaction with traditional society (Britain, mid-20th c.)
apologue allegorical fable typically containing a moral
autobiography account of author's own life; memoirs
avant-garde innovative style that challenges traditional and established forms
ballad poem that tells a story, often meant to be performed out loud
ballad stanza four-line stanza of iambic tetrameter with second and fourth lines rhymed
baroque style emphasizing dramatic or distorted elements presented in classical ordered form (17th-18th c.)
Beat Generation rebellious style emphasizing colloquial language and nonconformist values (U.S., 1950's)
belles-lettres literature, esp. with creative and artistic style and content; letters
Bildungsroman novel narrating story of young person's coming of age and development

biography narrative of another person's life
Bloomsbury group group of writers and intellectuals, including Virginia Woolf and John Maynard Keynes, associated with Bloomsbury district in London (1920's)
Byronic (*adj*) characterized by romantic melancholy and melodrama, as in the works of Lord Byron
Celtic Renaissance revival of Gaelic language and literature (late 19th-early 20th c.)
chanson song; poem to be sung
chanson de geste song of great deeds; epic poem
chronicle medieval and Renaissance historical writing
classical (*adj*) pertaining to a style with great scope, depth, clarity, and elegance; pertaining to Greek and Roman classics
classicism adherence to classical principles, esp. in contrast with Romanticism (19th c.)
comedy literary and dramatic form emphasizing humor, treating events lightly or satirically, and having a happy ending
comedy of manners comic style emphasizing use of manners and conventions of sophisticated society
comic relief humorous episode or scene intended as contrast in serious drama or literary work, often to emphasize primary action
concrete poetry unconventional, graphic arrangement of letters, words, and symbols to convey meaning
confession autobiography addressing very private topics
criticism analysis and evaluation of literary works
cyberpunk science fiction characterized by violence, computer technology, and nihilism (1980's)
cycle collection of poems or narratives related by common subject matter, usu. a central character
dada literary and dramatic artistic movement emphasizing nihilism, irrationality, absurdism, and sometimes violent opposition to conventional values (Europe, 1915-25)
deconstruction literary analysis based on rejection of notion of hierarchy and belief that nature of language and usage prevents any text from having a fixed, coherent meaning that represents reality (mid-20th c.)
detective story literary form with crime and the apprehension of criminals as its subject
diary daily journal of personal activities and reflections
dime novel cheap paperback fiction, esp. detective story or melodrama; penny dreadful
drama composition in verse or prose, usu. for theatrical performance, that portrays character through story involving conflicts in which emotions are expressed through dialogue and action
eclogue pastoral poem
elegy song, poem, or speech lamenting one who is dead; poem in elegiac couplets
Elizabethan (*adj*) of or pertaining to drama and literature of the reign of Elizabeth I of England, including the works of Shakespeare (late 16th c.)
epic literary work recounting deeds of legendary hero
epic poem traditional form of long narrative poem recounting deeds of legendary hero
epigram terse, witty, often paradoxical saying, often in form of concise poem with ingenious ending
epistle letter, esp. formal or elegant one
erotica literary works devoted to sexual themes
essay brief, analytic, interpretive prose composition dealing, often formally, with a single subject from a subjective viewpoint
exemplum anecdote or short narrative with moral point, esp. used to sustain argument
Expressionism depiction by nonnaturalistic means of subconscious thoughts, subjective realities of characters, and the struggle of abstract forces (20th c.)
fable narration demonstrating a useful truth, esp. in which animals speak as humans; legendary, supernatural tale
faction *Informal.* novel or other writing that treats real events and people as if fictional; roman à clef
fairy tale story about fairies or other magical creatures, usu. for children
fantasy fiction with strange or otherworldly settings or grotesque characters
farce light, dramatic composition with improbable plot, broad satirical comedy
festschrift collection of learned essays by students and colleagues honoring a scholar on a special occasion
fiction invented or imagined story
fin de siècle *French.* style characteristic of the end of the 19th century, esp. fashionably sophisticated despair
Gothic fiction with emphasis on horror and macabre, mysterious, or violent events, often in desolate, remote settings
graveyard school melancholy, romantically gloomy style (18th c.)
grotesque fanciful, fantastic, and bizarre representations of human life and events (19th-20th c.)
haiku unrhymed verse form with 17 syllables, usu. in three lines (Japan)
heroic (*adj*) dealing with or describing the deeds and attributes of heroes
high comedy comedy that employs subtle characterizations and witty language, often to satirize upper class lifestyles
historical novel fictional account of historical events or story of fictional characters and events in historical setting
idyll short lyrical poem or prose composition describing pastoral scenes or any charming episode of everyday life
Jacobean (*adj*) of or pertaining to the literary style characteristic of the age of James I of England (early 17th c.)
journal daily record of experiences and reflections, esp. for private use
lampoon harsh satire usu. directed against an individual

letter personal, written message directed to a person or organization
letters literature; belles-lettres
limerick humorous verse rhymed aabba, usu. with a's of three anapestic feet and b's of two anapestic feet
literature writings in which ideas of permanent or universal interest are expressed through artistic use of forms such as novels, poetry, plays, histories, biographies, or essays
Lost Generation American writers living in post-World War I Europe
low comedy often farcical comedy of action with simple characters, burlesque, and horseplay
lyric poetry poems expressing intense personal emotion
masque short, allegorical drama performed by masked actors (16th-17th c.)
melodrama work of extravagant theatricality, unlikely plot, and overwrought and simplistic characterizations
memoir record of events written by person having intimate knowledge of them; biography or biographical sketch
minimalism style characterized by spare, simple, often impersonal and repetitive tone (mid-20th c.)
miracle play medieval drama based on the life of a saint or martyr
missive letter, usu. formal or official
mock-heroic (*adj*) of or pertaining to a form of satire in which trivial subjects, characters, and events are treated in the heroic style
modernism self-conscious break with past and search for new forms of expression (early 20th c.)
monograph scholarly work on some specific subject
mystery fiction dealing with the solution of a crime or the unraveling of secrets
mystery play medieval drama based on Scriptural incidents
myth legend or traditional narrative, often based in part on historical events, that reveals human behavior and natural phenomena by its symbolism
naturalism literature based on scientific observation of life, without idealization
New Criticism style of literary criticism emphasizing close textual analysis (mid-20th c.)
New Humanism works that reflect a belief in moderation, dignity, permanent values, and dualistic existence (20th c.)
nonfiction prose composition dealing with noninvented, nonimagined subject
novel extended fictional prose narrative, usu. involving a central character: novel of character, of incident, of manners, of sensibility, of the soil, or psychological novel
novelette brief novel or long short story
novella brief novel with compact plot
nursery rhyme short, simple, traditional rhymed poem or song for very young children
occasional verse poetry created for particular occasion
ode lyric poem marked by exalted feeling, varying line length, and complexity of form
parody composition that imitates the style of another author or work for comic effect
pasquinade publicly posted lampoon or satire
pastiche literary work that borrows from or mimics the style of one or more sources
Petrarchan sonnet sonnet consisting of an octave with the rhymed scheme abbaabba and a sestet in one of several rhyme schemes, such as cdecde or cdcdcd
picaresque novel episodic adventures of usu. roguish protagonist
poem verse composition
poetry sometimes rhymed, usu. rhythmic writing with concentrated imagery in language selected to create an emotional response to its sound and sense; metrical writing; verse
polemic art of disputation; an argument
postmodernism any of various reactions to modernist explorations and austere forms, often entailing some return to past forms, minimalism, fantasy, complexity, and pessimism
poststructuralism any of various theories of literary criticism, such as deconstruction, that hold that there is no single true reading of a text
potboiler usu. inferior work written for profit, esp. fiction
prose unrhymed, nonmetrical writing
prosody system or style of versification and metrical structure; science and art of versification
psychobiography biography that stresses childhood trauma or other bases for the unconscious motives of its subject
psychological novel novel delving deeply into characters' feelings and motivations
quantitative verse poetry based on temporal quantity or duration of sounds
Rabelaisian (*adj*) characterized by coarse, broad humor, suggestive of the work of François Rabelais
realism nonidealized fidelity to accurate literary representation of real or everyday life
Renaissance (*adj*) designating literature marked by the humanistic revival of classical influence in Europe (14th-17th c.)
rhyme verse composition that rhymes
roman *French.* novel
roman à clef *French.* novel depicting real persons and actual events under fictional names
Romanticism period and style emphasizing emotional and imaginative intensity (19th c.)
rondeau verse based on two rhyme sounds, composed of ten or thirteen lines in three stanzas, in which the opening words of the first stanza are used as a refrain after the second and third stanzas
rondel short poem, usu. of fourteen lines on two rhymes, of which four are made up of the initial couplet repeated in the middle and at the end
saga heroic narrative about historic or legendary figures; lengthy, multigenerational, fictional narrative; roman-fleuve
satire work holding up human vices and follies to

ridicule; ironic, witty work exposing or discrediting vice or folly
science fiction stories based on impact of actual, imagined, or potential science, usu. set in future or on other planets
serial work appearing in installments
Shakespearean sonnet sonnet having the rhyme scheme abab, cdcd, efef, gg, and consisting of three quatrains and one couplet
short story compact, fictional narrative with few characters, unified effect, and often more mood than plot
sirvente medieval poem or song, either heroic or satirical, composed by a troubadour
sketch short, usu. descriptive composition, intentionally slight, discursive in style, and familiar in tone
soap opera serialized melodrama for TV or radio
song short musical composition with lyrics
sonnet fixed verse form of fourteen lines, usu. in iambic pentameter with set rhyming pattern, often ending in rhymed couplet
speech public address or discourse
Sturm und Drang German literature characterized by rousing action and high emotionalism, often featuring individual revolt against society (18th c.)
surrealism style emphasizing production of fantastic, incongruous imagery through unnatural juxtapositions (1920's)
Symbolism French reaction to realism, exalting symbolic representation over actuality (late 19th c.)
tanka five-line poem consisting of 31 syllables (Japan)
technothriller action-suspense novel featuring use of sophisticated technology, esp. weapons systems
textual criticism close analysis of a literary work, often aiming to determine author's original text
thriller gripping work with intrigue, adventure, and suspense
tragedy serious narrative or drama having a sad or disastrous ending; in ancient drama, downfall of a great person due to a tragic flaw or fate
tragicomedy drama blending tragedy and comedy
trilogy literary work in three connected parts
true life realistic narrative or drama, esp. of everyday life
verse poetry; metrical writing in general
versification act of composing verses; particular metrical structure or style; prosody
Victorian (*adj*) denoting writing often associated with strict moral standards and conduct in Britain during reign of Queen Victoria (late 19th c.)
western simple, action-packed narrative set in old American West, usu. involving cowboys
whodunit *Informal.* mystery story

Devices, Techniques, and Elements

agon dispute or debate between chorus and characters in classic Greek tragedy
Alexandrine verse with six iambic feet; iambic hexameter
allegory extended metaphor using objects, characters, and events to represent larger meanings
alliteration repetition of initial sound in two or more consecutive words
allusion figure of speech employing reference to famous or identifiable person, place, event, or literary passage
ambiguity expression of an idea in words that may be interpreted in more than one way
amphigory nonsense verse or composition
amplification figure of speech using restatement for emphasis
analects literary fragments or passages
analogy comparison of apparently or largely dissimilar objects to reveal similarities
anapest metrical verse foot with two short or unstressed syllables followed by one long or stressed syllable
anecdote brief narrative describing a particular interesting event or person
anticlimax narrative moment involving a small or trivial resolution in place of the expected larger and more significant resolution
antiphrasis irony; use of word or description to convey the opposite of its normal or literal meaning
antithesis figure of speech using emphatically contrasting images or words
assonance juxtaposition of similar sounds without actually rhyming, esp. vowels
atmosphere dominant mood or tone of a work
bathos unsuccessful attempt at profundity, resulting in ridiculous or humorous effect
blank verse unrhymed verse; unrhymed iambic pentameter, often with each second line accented
bowdlerize (*vb*) censor or abridge by cutting offensive sections
cacophony harsh, discordant sounds in recited poetry
cadence measured, rhythmic emphasis of language
caesura break in poetic rhythm
canto one of the main divisions of a long poem
caricature description employing extreme and comic exaggeration
characterization creation, presentation, and exposition of personalities in literature
character sketch brief essay or story that describes a person
clerihew light verse quatrain rhyming aabb, usu. dealing with person named in first line
cliche timeworn and commonplace expression; trite description
climax culmination of dramatic narrative, often turning point in story
coda concluding or summary part of literary wo
cognomen distinguishing name or epithet
colloquialism informal usage of word or phras usu. not acceptable in formal use
common meter four-line stanza with lines one and three in iambic tetrameter, lines two and fou in iambic trimeter

conceit dramatic, witty, ingenious metaphor or analogy
conflict struggle or contrast of opposing forces in plot
couplet two rhyming lines of verse
dactyl metrical foot with one long or stressed syllable followed by two short or unstressed syllables
dead metaphor overused figure of speech drained of its original power to evoke analogy
denouement final unfolding of plot; resolution or outcome
device word pattern, figure of speech, or dramatic convention used to evoke desired effect in literary work
diatribe bitter argument, accusation, or harangue
digression insertion of material unrelated to main body of work
dithyramb short poem or chant in wild, irregular strain
ditty short, simple, or whimsical lyric
doggerel trivial or bad poetry
double rhyme rhyme consisting of two syllables of which the second is unstressed
elegiac couplet of dactylic hexameters with second lacking arsis in third and sixth feet
elision omission of unstressed vowel or syllable to achieve metrical uniformity
epilogue concluding section after main body of work
epithet characterizing word or phrase used with or in place of name, esp. a disparaging or abusive term
euphony pleasantness of sounds in recited poetry
euphuism elegant Elizabethan style characterized by the frequent use of antithesis, alliteration, and mythological simile
exegesis critical interpretation of text
exposition dialogue or descriptive material intended to convey information or background or to explain something
eye dialect use of misspellings to convey character's poor education or humorous dialectal pronunciations
falling rhythm stress occurring on first syllable of each foot
fantasy fanciful design or imaginative creation
feminine rhyme rhyme of two or three syllables of which only the first syllable is stressed
figurative language metaphorical expression abounding in figures of speech
flashback narrative device by which an event that takes place outside the narrative framework is brought into the chronology of the story
flash-forward narrative device by which a future event or scene is inserted into the chronology of a story
foil one character serving as contrast to another
foot basic unit of verse meter, consisting of any of various fixed combinations of stressed and unstressed, long and short syllables
footnote explanatory comment or reference to documentation at bottom of page
free verse unrhymed verse of irregular meter and nonmetrical rhythm
fustian pretentious or banal writing
genre category of composition with particular style, form, and content
georgic poem with agricultural theme
gloss brief marginal explanation of difficult or obscure passage; continuous commentary accompanying text; interlinear translation
hamartia tragic flaw that causes hero's misfortune in Greek tragedy
hapax legomenon word or phrase occurring one time only in a text or works of an author
heroic couplet rhyming couplet in iambic pentameter
hexameter line of verse with six metrical feet
hiatus two vowel sounds that come together without pause or intervening consonantal sound
Hudibrastic verse mock-heroic verse in humorous octosyllabic couplets
hyperbole extravagant exaggeration for effect
iamb metrical foot of one short or unstressed syllable followed by one long or stressed syllable
iambic pentameter poetry consisting of five metrical feet per line, each foot having one short or unstressed syllable followed by one long or stressed syllable
imagery figurative language used to evoke mental picture or create atmosphere
interactive fiction adventure or mystery story in which reader is given choices as to how story line will develop
interior monologue extended representation in monologue form of a fictional character's thoughts and feelings; stream of consciousness
internal rhyme correspondence of sounds within units of composition
irony literary form in which words express something other than, or opposite to, their literal meaning
lampoon harsh satire directed against an individual
leitmotif dominant recurring theme
macaronic (*adj*) composed of Latin words mixed with vernacular words or non-Latin words given Latin endings
metaphor word or phrase used in place of another to suggest likeness or analogy between them
meter rhythm in verse with continuously repeating basic pattern
metonymy figure of speech in which the name of one thing is used in place of something else with which it is associated
metrics study or theory of verse meter
mimesis imitation or mimicry of another's style or language
monologue long speech by one individual; dramatic soliloquy
motif recurring thematic element, esp. one dominant idea
narrative story or account of events, either fictional or true, usu. in chronological or linear order
octave verse stanza of eight lines
octet first eight lines of Petrarchan sonnet
onomatopoeia formation of a word that names a thing or action by imitation of a sound associated

with it; use of words whose sounds suggest or imitate their meaning
pandect treatise on an entire subject
parable short story illustrating moral attitude or principle
passim (*adv*) *Latin.* lit. here and there; used to indicate repetition of phrase or idea throughout book or article
passus section or division of story or poem
pathetic fallacy ascription of human traits and feelings to inanimate objects or nature
pathos evocation of sympathetic pity
pentameter verse line with five metrical feet
personification representation of an object or abstraction in human form or as an imaginary being
plagiarism literary theft; stealing another's work without giving credit, passing it off as one's own
plot plan or main story of work; story line
poetic license deviation from fact, rule, or convention for effect
point of view perspective of character from whose standpoint narrative events are seen
polymythy inclusion of many diverse subplots in literary work
proem preface or introduction
prolegomenon formal essay or critique introducing extended work
prologue preface or introduction; speech addressed to audience at beginning of play
purple prose excessively affected or sentimental writing intended to manipulate reader's feelings
pyrrhic metrical foot of two short or unstressed syllables
quatrain four lines of verse
refrain regularly recurring phrase or verse, esp. at end of each stanza in poem
rhyme correspondence in sounds of units of composition, esp. terminal sounds
rhythm ordered, recurrent alternation of strong and weak elements in flow of language
roundelay poem with regularly repeated refrain
sarcasm caustic, ironic language directed esp. against an individual as a taunt
satire wit and irony used to expose and discredit a vice or folly
scansion metrical analysis of verse
simile figure of speech comparing two unlike things
soliloquy dramatic monologue expressing unspoken thoughts
spondee metrical foot of two long or stressed syllables
sprung rhythm poetic rhythm approximating natural speech
stanza division of poem; series of lines arranged together in recurring pattern
stream of consciousness continuous, unedited flow of conscious experience and thoughts; interior monologue
strophe two or more lines of verse constituting rhythmic unit; stanza; movement of the classical Greek chorus, characterized by turning from side to side of orchestra
style distinctive manner of expression, tone, or use of language, esp. characteristic of one author or genre
stylized (*adj*) conforming to established, conventional pattern or style rather than natural style
subplot subordinate story line in fiction or drama
subtext implicit, unstated, metaphorical meaning behind literary text, esp. dialogue
suspense use of uncertainty and anxiety as to outcome to heighten excitement
symbol something that stands for or suggests something else by association or convention
tetrameter verse line of four dipodies or metrical feet
text original words of written composition; main body of written work
theme unifying subject or topic of composition
tragic flaw defect in tragic hero's character that causes downfall
trimeter verse line of three dipodies or metrical feet
triple rhyme rhyme consisting of three syllables of which the second and third are unstressed; feminine rhyme
trochee metrical foot of one long or stressed syllable followed by one short or unstressed syllable
verisimilitude depiction of characters and setting, giving them the appearance of truth; realism
vignette brief incident, scene, or story
villanelle short poem of fixed form, usu. five groups of three rhyming lines followed by a quatrain
voice author's distinguishing style, tone, point of view, and use of language
wordplay use of rhetorical figures of speech and verbal wit to enhance literary work
writer's block psychological inhibition that prevents writer from continuing or completing work

Books and Pages

abridgment shortened version of work
adaptation rewriting an original work to fit another form
almanac book with calendar, tables, information, and forecasts on various fields
anthology collection of writings by different authors
atlas book of maps and geographical charts
bestiary medieval collection of moralized fables about real and mythical animals
bibelot miniature book of elegant design
bible publication accepted as the preeminent authority in any given field
bibliography list of resources used in compiling a text, or works relating to a subject
canon works ascribed to author and accepted as genuine
classic work of universally recognized and enduring excellence, great authority, and importance
codex manuscript book, esp. Biblical writing or other classic text
compendium concise but comprehensive treati[se] or abstract

concordance alphabetical index of principal words in book, esp. the Bible; alphabetical index of subjects or topics
dictionary alphabetical list of words in one language with their definitions; list of defined terms in a given field
draft unfinished, preliminary version of manuscript
edition particular form or version in which text is published; redaction
encyclopedia book or set of books containing information on many branches of knowledge in alphabetically arranged articles
fascicle one section of a book being published in separate parts
folio book page size, equal to one-half sheet of foolscap
foolscap large sheet of paper folded to form book pages
glossary alphabetical list of difficult, technical, or occupational terms with definitions, esp. for one field
hornbook rudimentary treatise on some subject; child's primer
incunabula copies of work of early art or industry, esp. book printed before 1501
lexicon any wordbook or dictionary, esp. of an ancient language; the vocabulary of a particular field, subject, social class, or person
little magazine usu. noncommercial literary magazine featuring works of little-known authors
magnum opus one author's classic masterpiece
manuscript written or typewritten work, as distinguished from printed copy
marginalia marginal notes in book
omnibus volume containing collection of previously published works by single author or on single theme
opus literary work
palimpsest parchment or tablet used more than once, from which the earlier writing has been erased
passage paragraph, verse, or brief section of written work
primer small introductory book on one subject, esp. for children
quarto book page size, equal to one-quarter sheet of foolscap; book printed on quarto pages
redaction something put in writing; edition
reference authorative work containing many useful facts of organized information
reprint reissue of book previously published
signature sheet of foolscap folded into leaves of book pages
thesaurus extensive listing of words and their synonyms
tome very large or scholarly work
tour de force work of great skill, ingenuity, and brilliance
treatise systematic exposition of arguments, principles involved, and conclusions reached
trilogy three connected works

Literary Characters and Practitioners

amanuensis one employed to take dictation or copy manuscripts
antagonist character opposed to protagonist; rival
antihero modern protagonist without traditional heroic qualities
archetype character embodying basic, universal human qualities
bard composer, singer, or declaimer of epic verse
belletrist author of amusing, sophisticated works
bibliognost person with comprehensive knowledge of books
bibliophile lover of books and literature
bouquiniste person who buys and sells used books
character literary depiction of a fictional person, esp. one having some recognizable human trait or symbolizing an archetype or universal personality
chorus character or group of characters commenting on the action of a drama
copywriter writer of advertising or magazine copy
critic person who assesses the value or merit of literary works
dramatis personae list of characters in a literary or dramatic work
dramatist playwright
editor person who revises and corrects manuscripts and advises authors on their work
fabulist person who writes or relates fables
farceur writer of broad, satirical comedy
fictioneer prolific writer of generally mediocre works of fiction
ghost writer one who writes for another without receiving credit
hack writer working for hire, usu. producing material of little merit
hero usu. male protagonist, esp. of epic, tragedy, or adventure
heroine female protagonist, esp. of epic, tragedy, or adventure
literati persons concerned with, and knowledgeable about, literature
man of letters author, often in more than one form or genre; literary scholar
metaphrast person who translates or changes a literary work from one form to another, as prose into verse
nom de guerre *French.* lit. war name; pseudonym
nom de plume *French.* lit. pen name; pseudonym
pen name pseudonym
persona character in a play, novel, or poem
playwright writer of dramas for theatrical performance; dramatist
poetaster inferior poet
poet laureate most eminent poet of one nation during a specific time, often having official standing
protagonist main character in narrative; hero or heroine

pseudonym fictitious name used for writing; nom de guerre; nom de plume; pen name

screenwriter author of scripts for movies or television

scribe official clerk and copier of manuscripts before invention of printing; author, esp. journalist; scrivener

scrivener professional or public copyist or writer; scribe

speechwriter author of public speeches for another

stock character standard character in many literary works, easily recognized and classified by the reader or audience, who requires little or no development by the author

troubadour lyric poet and musician who told of courtly love in France and Italy (11th-13th c.)

wordsmith author, esp. one skilled at the use of language; writer

Chapter Fifteen

Performing Arts

CLASSICAL MUSIC

Types of Music and Composition
Harmony, Melody, and Structure
Time and Tempo
Opera and Vocal Music
Musicians and Performance

Types of Music and Composition

accompaniment vocal or instrumental part that complements melody
adaptation piece based on existing melody or composition
air simple tune, melody, or song
allemande composition in moderate duple or quadruple time, basis for German court dance (17th-18th c.)
arabesque short, highly ornamented composition, esp. for piano
aubade sunrise music, esp. love song
bagatelle short, simple piece, usu. for piano
ballade piano composition in romantic mood suggesting epic ballad
ballet music written to accompany balletic dance
baroque (*adj*) designating music of period 1600-1750
bourrée composition in quick duple time, basis of French dance (17th c.)
cantata vocal work in several movements, based on religious or dramatic subject
chamber music instrumental music for small group in which each performer has a different part
classical (*adj*) denoting music of the European tradition marked by sophistication of structural elements and embracing vocal, symphonic, chamber, and solo music, esp. as distinguished from popular and folk music and jazz; designating typically homophonic music of the period 1750-1830
composition any written piece of music, esp. one of scope and complexity
concertino short concerto
concerto composition for one or more solo instruments with orchestral accompaniment, usu. in three movements
dirge slow, mournful piece, esp. accompanying funeral
divertimento instrumental form similar to suite and symphony, containing dances and short movements
divertissement short ballet used as interlude between acts of opera
duet composition for two instruments or voices; duo
duo duet
étude piece intended to aid student in learning instrument
evensong evening prayer, vespers music
fantasia composition in fanciful improvisational form
fugue contrapuntal composition with melodic themes announced or imitated by each voice entering in succession
gavotte French dance music used in suites (18th c.)
gigue early Italian dance in various triple times
incidental music music performed during play to project mood or accompany action
interlude brief musical passage played between parts of longer piece, drama, or religious service
intermezzo movement between main sections of longer work, such as an opera
march music for marching, usu. in 4/4 time
minuet early French dance in 3/4 time
music art and science of combining tones or sounds in single line (melody), in combination (harmony), and in time relationships (rhythm) to express ideas and emotions in a structurally complete and unified work having an appealing sound when produced by one or more voices or instruments, or both
nocturne dreamy, romantic piece, esp. for piano (19th c.)
opus composition, usu. numbered to indicate order in which composer's work was published
overture musical introduction to ballet, opera, or oratorio that foreshadows themes that appear later
pastorale piece of music, esp. opera or cantata, suggestive of simple, rural life
polonaise music for stately Polish dance in triple time
prelude orig. a musical introduction, later an independent piece
quartet composition for four instruments, usu. two violins, viola, and cello, or voices
raga music following traditional formula for melody, rhythm, and ornamentation (Indian)
requiem composition written for funeral mass
rhapsody composition in free, irregular form
romantic (*adj*) designating music of the late 19th century marked by free expression of imagination and emotion, virtuosic display, and some experimentation with form
rondo piece that alternates main and contrasting themes, usu. gay, playful, and fast
roundelay song in which phrase or line is continually repeated
sacred music compositions for religious services
saraband stately dance music in triple time (17th-18th c.)
scherzo playful piece in rapid triple time
serenade romantic song; instrumental piece for small group of string and wind instruments
sextet composition for six instruments or voices
sonata composition for one or two instruments, esp. piano, usu. in three or four movements in contrasting forms and keys
sonatina short, simplified sonata
string quartet composition for two violins, viola and cello
suite instrumental music in several movements, each in a different dance form, all in the same key
symphonic poem large narrative orchestral work in one movement; tone poem
symphony composition for orchestra, usu. in four movements in contrasting tempos, moods, and keys

toccata keyboard piece with bold, rapid passages in contrapuntal style
tone poem composition for symphony orchestra, usu. in one movement, based on literary or historical subject; symphonic poem
transcription arrangement of composition for voice or instrument other than that for which it was written
trio composition for three instruments or voices
twelve-tone (*adj*) pertaining to serial composition using all twelve chromatic tones (early 20th c.)
waltz music for German dance in triple time (19th c.)

Harmony, Melody, and Structure

accent recurring stress or emphasis
accidental sharp or flat not found in key signature
alto clef clef placing middle C on third line of staff
arpeggio playing notes of chord in succession rather than simultaneously
arrangement orchestration and structure of composition
atonal (*adj*) without reference to key or mode, using all twelve tones of chromatic scale at random
augmentation modification of theme by increasing time value of all its notes
bar measure of set number of beats
bass clef clef placing F below middle C on fourth line of staff
cadence chords at end of phrase or piece that suggest harmonic resolution
cadenza brilliant virtuoso passage at end of solo
canto melody in choral or instrumental music
chord two or more notes sounded together
chromatic (*adj*) containing all twelve half steps in octave
clef sign at beginning of musical staff that indicates pitch of notes
coda passage added to final section of piece
coloratura florid ornamentation in vocal music, esp. runs, trills, and arpeggios
composition art and practice of writing pieces of music
consonance interval or chord that provides a feeling of satisfaction and resolution: third, fourth, fifth, sixth, octave
continuo figured bass part for keyboard or strings, esp. in baroque ensemble; basso continuo
contrapuntal (*adj*) based on counterpoint
counterpoint several independent but related melodies played simultaneously
crescendo gradual, steady increase in volume; (*adj*) gradually increasing in volume
decrescendo gradual decrease in volume; (*adj*) growing softer
degree tone or step of the scale
development elaboration of theme through counterpoint, modulation, rhythm, and tempo changes
diatonic (*adj*) designating major and minor scales; designating eight-tone scale without chromatic deviation
dissonance interval or chord that is restless and discordant
dolce (*adj*) soft and sweet
double flat lowering of note's pitch two chromatic half-steps from natural
double sharp raising of note's pitch two chromatic half-steps from natural
downbeat first beat of measure
fanfare trumpet flourish, esp. at dramatic entrance
final bar heavy, vertical double line indicating end of piece
finale closing part or movement of composition
flat lowering of note's pitch one chromatic half step from natural
forte (*adj*) loud, forceful
fortissimo (*adj*) very loud
glissando gliding effect, esp. series of adjacent tones sounded in rapid succession on keyboard
grace note brief, ornamental tone sounded before another
homophony music in which one melody and set of chords predominates
interval difference in pitch between two tones
intonation production of a tone with a voice or instrument
inversion chord with tones in other than standard order
key major or minor scale with set flats and sharps, used as basis for composition
key signature flats and sharps on staff that indicate key of composition
measure notes and rests contained between two bar lines
melody tune, air, or theme composed of tones arranged in a pleasing succession
middle C C note nearest middle of standard piano keyboard
modal (*adj*) of or relating to a diatonic eight-tone scale other than major or minor; pertaining to mode, as distinguished from key
mode any of various arrangements of the diatonic tones of an octave, differing from one another in the order of whole and half steps; one of the Greek modes; scale
modulation change from one key to another within a single composition
monophony music consisting of unaccompanied melody
motif recurring subject, theme, or idea; motive
motive motif
movement section of sonata, symphony, suite, or concerto
musicology scholarly study of music history, theory, and acoustics
natural return of a sharp or flat tone to its original pitch; original or normal pitch of note
notation standardized system of characters and symbols used to represent musical composition
note written character indicating duration and pitch of tone with value that is relative and dependent on time signature of piece; a single tone
octave interval of eight diatonic tones

orchestration arrangement of composition for instrumental ensemble, esp. full orchestra
overtone acoustical frequency higher in frequency than the fundamental; harmonic
part notes performed by one instrument or voice as solo or in combination with other parts
pedal prolonged or continuously repeated tone
phrase complete musical figure
pianissimo (*adj*) very soft
piano (*adj*) soft, subdued
pitch frequency of tonal vibrations per second
pizzicato (*adj*) played with plucked strings
polyphony music consisting of two or more independent melodic lines sounding together
portamento continuous gliding from note to note, sounding all intervening tones, usu. by voice or stringed instrument
progression series of chords
range limits of pitch encompassed by a melody; full extent of tones falling within capacity of a voice or instrument
refrain regularly recurring musical figure
register different parts in the range of a voice or instrument
repeat vertical arrangement of two dots on staff, indicating that preceding passage is to be repeated
reprise repetition of musical phrase
resolution progression from dissonance to consonance, esp. to the tonic note
rest interval of silence between tones; sign indicating duration of such silence, with value relative and dependent on time signature of piece
rhythm temporal relationship of successive notes; regular tempo, grouping, and accenting of tones that impel music forward
roulade series of rapid notes inserted in composition as ornamentation, esp. vocal coloratura
scale series of notes arranged in steps at fixed intervals; mode
segue seamless transition between sounds, themes, or pieces
semitone interval equal to one half of major second; half of a whole tone
sharp raising of note's pitch one chromatic half step from natural
signature arrangement of sharps and flats on staff to indicate key; numerical indication of beats per measure
slur curved line indicating that notes be sounded without pause; ligature
staccato (*adj*) with abrupt, distinct breaks between notes
staff five horizontal lines and four spaces on which music is written; stave
stanza division in a vocal composition, formed by a recurring pattern of words
stave staff
step one degree of a scale; interval between two adjacent scale degrees, as a second
strain passage of composition; melody
syncopation accenting of normally unaccented beats to create rhythmic displacement
tablature notation indicating string, fret, key, or finger to be used rather than note to be played
timbre characteristic quality of sound produced by an instrument; degree of resonance
tone cluster group of notes played simultaneously on keyboard with forearm, elbow, or fist
tonic first note of a scale
transition modulation; passage that connects one part of a piece to the next
transpose (*vb*) write or perform a piece in a key other than the original
treble upper register of vocal or instrumental range; highest part in harmonic music
treble clef clef with G above middle C on second line of staff
tremolo rapid reiteration of tone or alternating tones to produce a tremulous effect
trill ornament consisting of rapid alternation between note and another note one half step above
triplet three notes played in amount of time normally required for two notes of same duration
turn melodic embellishment or grace note consisting of principal tone with auxiliary tones above and below it
tutti (*adj*) all; performed by all voices or instruments together
unison simultaneous performance of identical parts by several instruments or voices
upbeat unaccented beat, often last beat of measure, sometimes beginning phrase or composition
variation change in key, meter, rhythm, harmony, speed, or mood of basic theme
vibrato slight, rapid alternation in pitch that produces a pulsating effect less pronounced than tremolo
voicing arrangement of notes in chord or parts in composition

Time and Tempo

accelerando (*adj*) gradually faster
adagio (*adv*) slowly, in a leisurely manner, (*adj*) slow; slower than andante, faster than lento
alla breve 2/2 time with one breve per measure
allegretto (*adj*) light and moderately fast; faster than moderato, slower than allegro
allegro (*adj*) brisk or rapid; faster than allegretto, slower than presto
andante (*adj*) moderately slow and flowing; faster than adagio, slower than moderato
andantino (*adj*) slightly faster than andante
breve note equal to two whole notes
common time 4/4 time
compound time time in which each beat of bar is divisible into three
courante music in quick triple time; mixture of 3/2 and 6/4 time
dotted note note with dot after it, indicating it is to be prolonged by one-half its length
duple time two, or multiple of two, beats per measure, such as 2/4 or 4/4
eighth note note having duration equal to one eighth of whole note; quaver

eighth rest rest equal in duration to eighth note
4/4 time time signature indicating four beats per measure with quarter note lasting one beat; common time
grave (*adj*) serious; slower than lento, faster than largo
half note note having duration equal to one half of whole note; minim
half rest rest equal in duration to half note
larghetto (*adj*) slow; faster than largo, slower than grave
largo (*adj*) very slow; slower than grave
lento (*adj*) somewhat slow; faster than larghetto, slower than adagio
meter regular, recurrent grouping of beats and accents, indicated by time signatures such as 4/4 and 6/8
minim half note
moderato (*adj*) at moderate speed; faster than andante, slower than allegretto
presto (*adj*) very fast; faster than allegro
quarter note note having duration equal to one quarter of whole note; one quarter of entire measure in common time; crotchet
quarter rest rest equal in duration to quarter note
sixteenth note note having duration equal to one sixteenth of whole note; demiquaver; semiquaver
sixteenth rest rest equal in duration to sixteenth note
sixty-fourth note note having duration equal to one sixty-fourth of whole note; hemidemisemiquaver
sixty-fourth rest rest equal in duration to sixty-fourth note
tempo pace or rate of speed of piece, from slowest to fastest: largo, larghetto, grave, lento, adagio, andante, andantino, moderato, allegretto, allegro, presto
thirty-second note note having duration equal to one thirty-second of whole note; demisemiquaver
thirty-second rest rest equal in duration to thirty-second note
time time signature or rhythm of piece
time signature numerical fraction, such as 3/4 or 9/8, that shows number of beats per measure and kind of note that lasts one beat
triple time three, or multiple of three, beats per measure, such as 3/4 or 6/8
whole note note equal in duration to four quarter notes, lasting entire measure in common time; semibreve
whole rest rest equal in duration to whole note, lasting entire measure in common time

Opera and Vocal Music

a cappella (*adj*) without instrumental accompaniment
alto female voice or voice part lower than soprano; male countertenor voice or voice part
anthem sacred vocal composition with words from the Scriptures; song of praise
antiphony alternate or responsive singing or chanting of psalm or verse by two sections of choir
aria solo song in opera, cantata, or oratorio
art song song usu. set to poem and performed in recital with interdependent vocal and piano parts
ballad vocal song telling story, usu. of love
barcarole song of Venetian gondoliers
baritone male voice or voice part lower than tenor and higher than bass
bass lowest normal male voice or voice part; basso
basso bass
basso profundo exceptionally deep bass voice
bel canto agile, operatic vocal technique that stresses even tone
bravura florid, virtuoso composition or performance
buffo male opera singer who specializes in comic parts
canon strict form of composition in which each voice has same melody starting at different times
cantata vocal composition with instrumental accompaniment in several movements, based on religious or dramatic subject
canticle liturgical song based on Biblical text
canto part of choral work that carries melody
carol traditional song of faith, esp. heard at Christmas
chanson song (France)
chant sacred song and oldest form of choral music
chanteuse singer, vocalist (France)
choir group of singers, esp. one employed in church service; chorale
choral vocal music performed by chorus or choir; (*adj*) relating to or composed for a chorus or choir
chorale hymn or psalm sung to traditional melody in religious service; choir
chorister member of choir, esp. its leader
chorus organized group of singers, esp. singing in unison; such a group singing in connection with soloists in opera or oratorio; piece of music to be sung in unison
coloratura florid ornamentation, esp. runs, trills, and arpeggios, in vocal music; one who sings such music
comic opera light, humorous, often sentimental opera
contralto lowest female voice or voice part
countertenor adult male able to sing in alto range
descant counterpoint sung above main melody
falsetto artificial method of singing used by males to obtain notes above their normal vocal range
glee club choral group, usu. large
Gregorian chant unharmonized liturgical chant with free rhythm, used in ritual of Roman Catholic Church
hymn religious or sacred song
leitmotif short, recurring phrase associated with single character or situation in opera
libretto words and text of opera or oratorio
lieder stylized German song
light opera operetta
madrigal unaccompanied choral music in coun-

terpoint, based on nonsacred text
Mass music for solemn Roman Catholic service in sequence of established parts
mezzo-soprano female voice between alto and soprano
monody elegy or dirge sung by one person
opera drama in which the text is entirely sung and acted to orchestral accompaniment, usu. with elaborate scenery and costumes
opera buffa farcical comic opera (Italy, 18th c.)
opera seria dramatic, classical opera (Italy, 18th c.)
operetta light, romantic, comic opera with songs and spoken dialogue
oratorio fairly long, usu. religious work for solo voices, chorus, and orchestra, performed without action, costume, or scenery
part song contrapuntal composition for three or more unaccompanied voices
plainsong liturgical chant, esp. Gregorian
processional hymn or organ solo performed in church during entry procession of choir and clergy
recessional hymn sung at conclusion of religious service
recitative speechlike vocal composition without fixed rhythm, used for dialogue in opera
requiem funeral mass
round canon in which voices enter at regular intervals repeating the same melody
sol-fa syllables tones of scale sung as syllables: do, re, mi, fa, sol, la, ti
solfeggio vocal exercise using the sol-fa syllables
soprano highest female vocal range or voice part
tenor male voice or voice part above baritone and below alto or countertenor
threnody dirge, song of lamentation at funeral
tremolo prominent vocal vibrato
vocal portion of composition written for voice
vocalist person who has received formal voice training to perform lieder, opera, or choral music

Musicians and Performance

absolute pitch ability to sing or name a single isolated note out of context
accompanist single instrumentalist, usu. pianist, who plays for dancer or singer
baton conductor's light rod, used to keep time
chamber orchestra small ensemble for performing chamber music
coloration subtle variation in intensity or tone by performers
composer person who creates and writes down musical compositions
concert live performance of music before audience
conductor leader of orchestra
consort ensemble of singers and instrumentalists
ensemble several musicians who perform together
improvisation composition of music while performing
instrumentalist performer on specific instrument
maestro respected conductor, orchestra leader, or composer
musician composer, conductor, or instrumental performer
orchestra large group of musicians performing on many instruments of all sorts, usu. over 100 members
philharmonic symphony orchestra
pit sunken area in front of stage in which orchestra sits during opera or ballet performance
pitch pipe small reed pipe used to tune instruments or establish pitch for singer
recital concert given by individual performer
score written copy of composition with all parts arranged on staves, used during performance
sheet music printed copy of composition
sight-read (*vb*) play or sing written music on sight without rehearsal
sinfonietta small orchestra, often composed solely of stringed instruments
string quartet ensemble of two violins, viola, and cello
symphony full orchestra
virtuoso performer with great technical skill and artistry

POPULAR MUSIC

Styles and Genres
Performance, Airplay, and the Recording Industry
Sound Reproduction Technology
Rock Era Dances

Styles and Genres

a cappella singing without instrumental backing
acid rock free-form, psychedelic music of 1960's
acoustic rock rock-'n'-roll played on nonelectric instruments, esp. acoustic guitar
alternative rock style of hard rock music popular in the 1990's, characterized by angst-filled lyrics, raw vocalization, and use of distortion
anthem highly emotional and dramatic song, often patriotic or devotional
ballad slow, sentimental, romantic song; song that tells a narrative story in short, repetitive verses
barrelhouse jazz piano style with lively beat, orig. 1920's
bebop jazz style emphasizing aggressive, energetic playing, esp. rapid and difficult chord changes, orig. 1940's; bop
big band style associated with large jazz orchestras, orig. popular in 1920's and 1930's
bluegrass traditional acoustic country style
blues spiritual and melancholy folk music song form originated by blacks in rural southern United States, derived in part from field hollers; major source of jazz, urban blues
boogie blues rock style popular in 1960's
boogie-woogie frenetic blues style, usu. on piano
bop bebop
bossa nova Brazilian jazz interpolations on samba dance music

bubblegum *Slang.* light, trendy, innocuous pop music
cabaret song style typical of nightclub entertainment
Cajun country music style of Cajun or French-Canadian residents of southern Louisiana
calypso popular Caribbean dance music, sometimes with improvised lyrics
chantey sailor's work song; shantey
country popular style derived from traditional English folk music, blues, and rock-'n'-roll, orig. a regional style
country-and-western recording industry designation for country music
cradlesong lullaby
disco dance-oriented pop music emphasizing heavy backbeat, simplistic lyrics, and polished production techniques, orig. late 1970's
ditty brief, simple, often humorous, song
Dixieland upbeat, brass-oriented jazz, orig. 1920's
doo-wop a capella, harmony-oriented rock-'n'-roll vocal style, orig. 1950's
electronic music music performed on electronic instruments such as synthesizers, orig. 1970's
elevator music Muzak
folk music traditional and ethnic songs usu. performed on acoustic instruments
folk rock modern or traditional folk songs played on electrified instruments
funk dance-oriented, predominantly black soul music, usu. with horns and irregularly accented beat
fusion combination of jazz and electric rock, orig. 1970's
gangsta rap rap music featuring themes of violence and criminal behavior
glitter rock highly theatrical rock with showy costumes, spectacular staging, and decadent themes, orig. early 1970's (U.S. and Britain)
gospel popular Christian church music, esp. influenced by black spirituals from American rural south
hard rock rock with a simple, driving, repetitive dance beat and usu. accessible lyric themes
heavy metal highly dramatic, guitar-based rock noted for lyrics about adolescence and rebellion
hip-hop rock and dance style emphasizing spoken lyrics, contemporary urban themes, and acrobatic steps; rap
honky-tonk white, country-inflected rhythm-and-blues
jazz major modern popular music form originating in New Orleans around 1900, derived from blues, ragtime, and gospel roots, characterized by free improvisation, virtuoso solo performances, syncopated rhythm, and a variety of original vocal and instrumental styles of varying complexity: bebop, big band, cool, Dixieland, fusion, hot, modern, New Orleans, progressive, ragtime, and swing
jug band blues and jazz style using primitive instruments such as washboards or jugs, orig. 1920's
jungle British hip-hop music
klezmer Yiddish folk music of Ashkenazi Jews performed by small band featuring clarinet and accordion
lullaby song sung to lull a child to sleep; cradlesong
Motown upbeat, pop-influenced rhythm-and-blues originally produced by group of black artists recording in Detroit, esp. in 1960's-70's
Muzak *Trademark.* string-based adaptation of classical, show, and pop tunes, recorded as unobtrusive, environmental background music; elevator music
New Age repetitive, ambient acoustic jazz and serene background music, orig. 1980's
new wave punk-derived, dance-oriented pop, emphasizing uninhibited performance and anti-authority lyrics, orig. late 1970's
polka Bohemian dance and folk music in distinctive duple rhythm
pop music popular music; contemporary music aimed at a mass audience and receiving wide exposure while evolving rapidly
psychedelic music hallucinogenic, drug-influenced 1960's rock
punk rock fast, loud, anarchic rock popular in late 1970's and early 1980's
ragtime syncopated jazz piano style of 1890's to 1920's
R&B rhythm-and-blues
rap dance-oriented pop style with insistent beat and rhyming, spoken lyrics, often couplets, that treat modern urban themes, esp. social protest and commentary, orig. 1980's among young blacks in inner cities; hip-hop
rave electronic dance music with a strong beat, often accompanied by lighting effects
reggae liltingly syncopated, Rastafarian-influenced popular music of Jamaica
rhythm-and-blues R&B: urban, dance-oriented form derived from blues and rock-'n'-roll, orig. late 1940's
rock rock-'n'-roll
rockabilly country-influenced, white rhythm-and-blues style of rock, orig. 1950's
rock-and-roll rock-'n'-roll
rock-'n'-roll blues-influenced, popular, youth-oriented, usu. electric dance music emphasizing strong beat and repetitive phrasing, orig. 1950's; rock; rock-and-roll
salsa modern Latin-American dance music
scat jazz vocal style in which singer imitates the sound and style of a horn playing without using words
scratch urban, black dance music similar to rap but using rhythmic sound made by manually moving a record back-and-forth under a turntable needle, orig. 1980's
shantey chantey
show tunes popular songs from Broadway musical shows
ska Jamaican dance pop of 1950's, precursor of reggae
skiffle unsophisticated, acoustic folk music using washboard, jug, and other homemade instruments
soft rock melodic pop rock without driving beat,

not emphasizing electric guitars, and often having soothing or romantic lyrics
soul pop music derived from rhythm-and-blues, orig. 1960's
soundtrack musical score for film
spirituals gospel music
steel band rhythmic Caribbean music played on tuned steel drums
surf music rock-'n'-roll, esp. from California during 1960's, featuring close treble harmonies and exuberant lyrics about beach life
swing big band jazz of 1930's-1940's, esp. for dancing
Tejano Mexican-American popular music that features the accordion
torch song steamy love song or ballad
urban contemporary slick, blues-based, romantic pop of 1980's
washboard lively blues style using primitive instruments; jug band music
work song folk song sung by workers to the rhythm of their work
world beat indigenous, usu. third-world musical forms, such as reggae and African popular music, sometimes influenced by another culture's music, esp. Western rock and pop styles
zydeco blues-influenced Cajun dance music popular with French-speaking black people in Louisiana and Texas

Performance, Airplay, and the Recording Industry

air guitar imaginary guitar played by singer or dancer, usu. with wild, highly expressive mannerisms
airplay exposure of record on radio program
album group of six to fifteen songs released together on compact disc, cassette, and/or a 33-rpm, long-playing record in a cardboard jacket
AM radio amplitude modulation radio broadcasting, generally associated with popular music programming
AOR album oriented rock; easy listening, light pop or soft rock radio programming
arranger person responsible for orchestrating a song for performance or recording
A-side primary hit side of 45-rpm single record
backbeat danceable beat characteristic of rock-'n'-roll
backup singer harmony or background singer who complements featured vocalist
bootleg recording pirated recording
bridge segment of pop song that connects verses and chorus
B-side secondary song released with a single, not the hit; flip side
cassingle prerecorded cassette sold to promote a single song
charts written musical arrangements; record industry tabulations on sales of popular records
chorus recurring segment of song, usu. after each verse, often containing the song's title or hook
concept album long-playing record with songs united by theme, narrative, and style
crossover hit song belonging to a particular genre that achieves commercial success in another genre
cut individual song on an album; (*vb*) record a song
DAT digital audio tape
deejay disc jockey
demo demonstration recording submitted by musicians seeking recording contract; rough version of a song, to be polished for finished recording
disc jockey DJ; announcer who hosts a radio music program or dance; deejay
discography descriptive listing of recordings by category, artist, composer, label, or date
discotheque dance club with recorded music
DJ disc jockey
dub technique of mixing record or performance for very heavy bass line; mix without lead vocals; copy tape to tape
ear candy *Slang.* light, syrupy, easy-listening music
eight-track tape former enclosed-cartridge medium for prerecorded tape with four stereo channels
EP extended play
extended play EP; four-song, 45-rpm single
fanzine rock or pop music fan magazine
flip side B-side
format radio programming style and content
45 seven-inch, 45-rpm record, usu. with one song on each side; single
golden oldie *Informal.* hit pop song from earlier years, esp. rock-'n'-roll; oldie
groupie *Informal.* pop music fan, esp. female, who follows the fortunes of a particular band, hoping to become intimate with its members
headbanger *Slang.* fan or performer of heavy metal; metalhead
hit song achieving large commercial success
hook immediately memorable and appealing musical catch phrase
hootenanny folk song festival or sing-along
jam jam session; (*vb*) improvise with other musicians
jam session impromptu musical performance; jam
jewel box hinged plastic case for a compact disc
jingle brief, catchy song advertising a product
jukebox mechanical record-playing machine, esp. in bars and dance halls
juke joint roadhouse, esp. in rural South, in which blues and rhythm-and-blues music is performed
karaoke equipment that provides recorded instrumental music so that a person can sing lyrics to the music, either for a recording or broadcast by speakers as entertainment
label company producing recordings, identified by a distinctive label or logo featuring its trade name on its releases

liner notes text sold with a recording offering background on musical content of record
lip-sync (*vb*) mouth lyrics in sync with recording during performance
live recording recording made at live performance
LP long-playing record, usu. 33 1/3 rpm with a 12-inch diameter
lyricist person who writes words that are set to another person's music to form song
metalhead headbanger
MOR middle-of-the-road; radio programming style, precursor of soft rock or AOR
music video commercial or promotional videotape featuring a performance of a song, often incorporating dancing, a narrative line, action, or animation, orig. 1980's; video
novelty record humorous pop song, often capitalizing on a topical subject
oldie pop song from earlier years; golden oldie
payola *Informal.* bribe taken by disc jockey from record company to promote a recording on radio
pirate (*vb*) illegally record, manufacture, or sell records and tapes
platter *Slang.* a phonograph record
playlist specified songs to be aired on radio show
record grooved disc on which music has been imprinted; (*vb*) register music on a medium from which copies can be made
record club mail order membership club for the purchase of compact discs, cassettes, and records
release distribution of a recording; date such distribution begins
riff short melodic passage played on an instrument
rim shot *Informal.* comic punctuation played by drummer after punch line of joke
roadie *Slang.* equipment handler for touring band
set complete performance for audience, including selection of songs played
sideman musician employed on recordings or performances, usu. not member of band
single featured song promoted from an album to boost sales or performance tour
sleeve envelope covering record inside album jacket
solo single instrument lead played over rhythm section, usu. in absence of vocals
standard familiar, often-played popular song with widely known lyrics
top 40 AM radio format emphasizing the forty most-popular pop songs; list of these songs calculated and distributed weekly
track one song on album; single recording; each element of instrumental music behind vocals
unplugged *(adj)* performed without electronic amplification or effects
video music video
video jockey VJ; host on music video program
VJ video jockey
wall of sound full, lush sound quality in pop record production, originated by Phil Spector in 1960's

Sound Reproduction Technology

amplifier device that increases voltage of sound waves
analog recording storage of sound waves directly on tape in form of electromagnetic energy; recording made this way
cartridge small, closed container for cassette tape; case on phonograph holding needle and apparatus for converting stylus motion into electrical voltage
cassette small, enclosed tape cartridge
CD compact disc
compact disc CD; means of sound reproduction that uses laser to read digitally encoded disc
console mixing console
deck tape recorder
digital delay conversion of analog signal into digital information, which is stored briefly on a memory chip then released in analog form
digital recording sound recording in which a frequency or waveform is sampled at regular intervals, then assigned numerical value, usu. a binary notation; record or tape made this way
dub (*vb*) copy mix onto cassette; (*n*) such a copy
echo chamber empty chamber in recording studio for live creation of echo effects
emulator digital computer synthesizing sounds from voice or other source
EQ equalizer
equalizer EQ; tone control that divides the audio range into intervals and accentuates its parts
fade (*v*) decrease volume; control varying volume between two set of speakers
feedback electronic sound made by reflux of speaker output to a microphone
filter device for suppressing or minimizing certain frequencies
flanging slight slowing of tape machine produced by touching flange of reel with thumb; phase shifter
half-track tape recorder with two tracks, both in same direction, covering entire width of tape, used for final mix to stereo
headphones small speakers in frame that fits over ears
hi-fi *Informal.* high fidelity
high fidelity reproduction of sound with high degree of faithfulness to original; system doing this; hi-fi
isolation booth chamber in studio for recording vocals or single instruments
loop endlessly repeating section of tape
master (*vb*) transfer taped recordings onto lacquer mold, disk, or tape from which other copies will be pressed or duplicated; (*n*) such a disk or tape; matrix
matrix master
microphone transducer that changes sound waves into electric current measured in voltage: condenser, crystal, dynamic, or ribbon; mike
MIDI musical instrument digital interface; language used by keyboard instruments to talk to each other and to computers or sequencers

mike *Informal.* microphone
mix blending of tracks to produce completed recording; (*vb*) execute such a blending
mixing console master board that controls the mixing of all specialized functions on all recording tracks; console
overdub track added in sync with already existing tracks
PA public-address system
patchbay central field of jacks connecting all elements of recording system
playback act of reproducing a newly made recording to check it
preamplifier device that increases signal strength for detection and further amplification
public-address system PA; combination of microphones and speakers that makes sound audible to many people
quadraphonic (*adj*) designating sound reproduction system using four speakers, usu. set in four corners of room
receiver radio tuner with built-in amp and preamplifier
reel-to-reel (*adj*) of or pertaining to a system using large, open spools of tape: quarter-inch, half-inch, or three-quarter inch
reverb electronically produced echo effect
sampler device that allows digital encoding of any signal picked up with microphone or direct recording box
sequencer digital keyboard computer that records sequences of notes and tells other keyboards when to play them
speaker transducer that changes voltage into sound waves
stereophonic (*adj*) designating sound recording having two transmission paths
tape magnetic tape impregnated with metal oxide, used to record sound waves in form of voltage
tape recorder means of storing sound in form of voltage on magnetic tape; deck
track one channel on multitrack recorder
transducer device, such as microphone or speaker, that is activated by power from one system to supply power in either the same or a different form to another system
tuner device that receives AM and FM radio signals
turntable revolving platform carrying phonograph record
tweeter speaker that is most efficient at high frequencies
vibrato device that electronically produces slight, rapid variations in pitch to impart a tremulous effect to sound
woofer speaker that is most efficient at low frequencies

Rock Era Dances

1950's (birdland, continental walk, handjive, hucklebuck, hully gully, Madison, shake, slop, stroll)
1960's (alligator, bird, boogaloo, Boston monkey, camel walk, dear lady twist, dog, fly, frug, freddie, funky chicken, funky pigeon, hitchhike, jerk, locomotion, mashed potato, monkey, Philly dog, pony, skate, slauson, swim, temptation walk, twine, twist, Watusi)
1970's (bump, disco, hustle, L.A. hustle, Latin hustle, line dance, New York hustle, night fever, popcorn, rocking chair, roller coaster, roller disco, shuffle, special K, sway)
1980's (acid house, bedrock, break dancing, dirty dancing, Egyptian, ET, file dance, guess, le freak, moonwalk, nasty, neutron dance, pogo, salsa, slam dance, snake, vogue, walk)
1990's (achy-breaky, boot scoot and boogie, cabbage patch, dive, electric slide, happy hitchhiker, hop, macarena, moshing, NY slide, running man, smurf, tush push, watermelon crawl)

MUSICAL INSTRUMENTS

Instrument Types and Groupings

big band brass, winds, piano, and drums
brass any wind instrument made of metal with a metal mouthpiece
chamber orchestra small orchestra of less than twenty-five players, largely strings and woodwinds
drum membranes stretched on a frame, esp. a hollow cylinder, that are struck with hand or stick
electronic any instrument producing sounds by electronic synthesis
instrument any contrivance or apparatus that produces musical sounds
jazz band horns, drums, woodwinds, guitars, and keyboards
jug band band with strings, rudimentary percussion, and jug, playing folk music
keyboard any instrument composed of strings of varying lengths held taut and struck or plucked mechanically
marching band horns, drums, woodwinds, and percussion instruments played while marching before crowd or in parade
mariachi guitars, percussion, and brass (Mexico)
mirliton any instrument composed of membranes stretched and vibrated by air, not struck
orchestra large musical ensemble, with woodwind, brass, percussion, and string instruments, that performs symphonic music
palm court orchestra small string group and piano

percussion any instrument that is a solid or hollow object struck, shaken, or scraped
piano trio piano and violin with either viola or cello; piano, drums, and bass
rock band electric guitars, bass, drums, and keyboards
string any instrument composed of strings, usu. of uniform length, stretched on a frame and bowed or plucked by hand
string quartet two violins, viola, and cello
wind any instrument composed of a hollow tube made of wood or metal, with small holes and a mouthpiece that is blown into while fingers cover the holes
wind quintet flute, oboe, clarinet, bassoon, and horn
woodwind any wind instrument made of wood with a reed mouthpiece

Drums

banana drum long, narrow, tubular drum (Congo)
barrel drum drum with convex sides
bass drum large, double-headed, cylindrical drum used in modern orchestra
bongo one of a set of small, cylindrical, single-headed drums played with the hands (South America)
conga long conical drum played with the hands
conical drum drum that tapers to a point or small head
cylindrical drum hollow frame drum with same diameter top to bottom
double drum two drums bound together
footed drum drum that stands on legs, often with carved bases in form of human feet
frame drum any drum with membrane stretched on a rigid frame
friction drum drum in which cord or stick pierces drum membrane and vibrates to form sound
gong drum single-headed cylindrical drum used in modern orchestra
kettledrum single membrane stretched over large pot or container
kit set of drums and percussion instruments used by pop or jazz bands: snare drum, tom-toms, side drum, bass drum, suspended cymbals, and hi-hat cymbals
peyote drum iron pot drum, filled with water (Native American)
side drum small cylindrical drum equipped with snares, used in modern orchestra
snare drum small, double-headed drum with wires across bottom for amplified reverberation
steel drum metal barrel cut to form drum: ping-pong, guitar pan, bass pan, rhythm pan, cello pan
tabor small cylindrical drum hung around neck (Europe)
tambour circular drum
tambourine shallow frame drum with metal disks attached for added percussion (Spain and Portugal)
tenor drum high-toned cylindrical drum used in modern orchestra
timbale one of a set of single-headed cylindrical drums mounted on stand (South America)
timpanum tuned, orchestral kettledrum, mounted on footed base; *pl.* timpani
tom-tom hand-beaten drum (Native American); medium-pitched drum in trap set
trap set pop or jazz drum and percussion kit: snare drum, tom-toms, side drum, bass drum, cymbals, high-hat

Percussion

bell metal, cup-shaped resonator with clapper or pellet inside that strikes wall to produce tone: cowbell, camel bell, temple bell, handbell, windbell, church bell
bell-lyra portable glockenspiel mounted on lyre-shaped frame, used by marching bands
carillon set of tuned bells
castanets hand-held wood or bone clappers, clicked together
chimes set of bells on pole or frame
clappers pair of sticks or blocks, held and struck together
clave one of a pair of wood sticks or blocks, struck together
cowbell large, metal bell struck with stick
cymbals conical or dished metal disks, struck together or with stick
electric xylophone vibraharp
glass harmonica water-filled wineglasses in box or set, resonated by rubbing rims
glockenspiel metallophone on stand, carried in marching band
gong metal disk struck by stick
high-hat two cymbals on stand, crashed together by foot pedal
Jew's harp small frame with flexible metal tongue, plucked by finger while instrument is held to mouth
jingle small bell or rattle, often worn as ornament
lithophone set of graduated stones in box frame
maraca gourd filled with beans or seeds that rattle when shaken (South America)
marimba xylophone with wood resonators under bars (Latin America)
metallophone set of graduated metal bars over resonating box, struck with mallet
rattle hollow form with seeds or stones inside, shaken to produce raspy sound
rhythm stick small wood stick struck against any surface; child's rudimentary percussion instrument
suspended cymbal single cymbal loosely attached to stand
tam-tam large bronze gong
thumb piano hollow resonating box with tongues of various lengths to be plucked; sansa
triangle metal rod bent into triangle, struck with stick
vibraharp percussion instrument that resembles a marimba, played with mallets and having metal

rather than wooden bars and electrically powered resonators that create vibrato effect; electric xylophone; vibraphone
vibraphone vibraharp
washboard washing board scraped with rod or stick
woodblock resonant, hollow block of wood, struck with wooden sticks
xylophone set of tuned bars in box frame, struck with sticks or mallet

Mirlitons

comb and paper hair comb with paper folded around it
kazoo toy horn with membrane-covered blowhole
zobo kazoo-like toy horn in shape of conventional horn

Keyboards

accordion keyboard that controls vibrating reeds set in motion by bellows-forced air; piano accordion
baby grand small grand piano
barrel organ mechanical organ with revolving cylinder turned by hand
calliope steam-powered organ
cembalo harpsichord or keyed dulcimer
chord organ simplified organ on which each key sounds a full chord
clavichord early keyboard, smaller than piano, having strings struck by brass pins attached to key ends
clavier any of various keyboard instruments, including piano and harpsichord
concert grand largest, highest-quality grand piano with richest tone
concertina small accordion
grand piano large piano with horizontal frame and strings, supported on three legs
harmonium small reed organ powered by bellows
harpsichord early wire-stringed double keyboard with seven stops, having strings plucked by quills; cembalo (17th-18th c.)
hurdy-gurdy mechanical violin with strings activated by keyboard
melodeon small reed organ; accordion
organ set of pipes resonated by air: barrel, electric, mouth, pipe, portative, reed
piano steel strings struck by felt hammers operated from keyboard: grand, baby grand, upright, spinet, player, table, electric; pianoforte
piano accordion accordion
pianoforte piano
pipe organ large organ in which tones are produced by passage of air through sets of variable-length pipes operated by keyboard
player piano upright piano operated by moving scroll perforated with notations
reed organ organ in which tones are produced by set of free metal reeds
spinet compactly built, upright piano; early harpsichord with one keyboard
square piano piano with rectangular, horizontal body
synthesizer electronic console that produces sounds using keyboard-controlled oscillators, filters, mixers, and amplifiers, and sometimes by digital computer
upright piano with vertical frame and strings
vocoder electronic instrument that resolves human voice signals and transmits tones of same pitch by keyboard

Stringed Instruments

aeolian harp rectangular zither on which strings are not plucked but rather sounded by air currents
archlute lute with two pegboxes, one for bass strings
balalaika flat, triangularly shaped lute with two to four strings (Russia)
bandore ancient lute, cittern, or pandora
banjo shallow, circular body with parchment belly, long neck, and one short and four long strings
baryton bass viol
bass fiddle double bass
bass viol double bass
bouzouki lute with strings in double courses (Greece)
bow string attached to flexible stick
bull fiddle double bass
bumbass long, single string that is bowed or plucked (Europe, 17th c.)
cello large, bass violin with floor stand; violoncello
cittern flat-bodied, long-necked, pear-shaped instrument, similar to guitar (Europe, 15th-18th c.)
contrabass double bass
crowd crwth
crwth ancient lyre with shallow body, either plucked or bowed; crowd (Ireland)
double bass largest, deepest-pitched member of violin family; bass fiddle; bass viol; bull fiddle; contrabass; string bass
dulcimer zither struck with mallets or sticks
fiddle any stringed instrument bowed rather than plucked, esp. violin
guitar flat-backed, long-necked, stringed instrument, usu. with waisted shape to soundbox that produces sounds when plucked: acoustic, electric, double-neck, electric bass, pedal steel, Hawaiian
gutbucket crude bass made of gut string attached to bucket, used in folk and some jazz music
hammer dulcimer set of tuned strings in frame, struck with hammer
harp angled strings set in frame attached to soundbox: bow, angle, frame, double, orchestral
lira three-stringed, pear-shaped folk fiddle (Greece)
lute pear-shaped resonating box with long, often bent neck holding strings stretched over bridge, plucked to produce sound
lyre resonating box with attached strings on two curved arms joined by a yoke, struck with plectrum (ancient Greece and Egypt); solid wooden box with strings stretched over bridge (Europe)

mandolin classical lute with usu. four pairs of strings (Italy)
pedal steel guitar box-shaped guitar on legs, having ten strings altered in pitch by foot pedal and plucked while being pressed by movable steel bar
psaltery medieval board zither that was plucked (Europe)
samisen long-necked, shallow-bodied, three-stringed lute (Japan)
sitar large lute made from a gourd, having arched metal frets on a long neck (India)
string bass double bass
ukulele very small, four-stringed guitar (Hawaii)
viol predecessor to violin with flat back, broader bow, and fretted fingerboard (Europe, 17th c.)
viola four-stringed member of violin family, slightly larger than violin and with deeper pitch
violin small, finely shaped, curved, resonating body with four strings that are bowed or occasionally plucked
violoncello cello
zither long resonator body with many strings attached over its entire length: raft, stick-shaped, trough, tube

Wind Instruments

alpenhorn long, powerful horn of wood with curved bell that produces single notes
bagpipe air-filled bag with reeded mouth pipe, drone pipe, and melody pipe
bassoon double-tubed bass horn with double reed mouthpiece
bombardon E-flat bass tuba
bosun's pipe whistle with variable pitch
bugle simple metal horn with reedless mouthpiece
clarinet horn or tube with reed inserted in mouthpiece that vibrates when blown
clarion ancient, curved trumpet
contrabass largest orchestral clarinet
contrabassoon double bassoon that reaches very low octaves
cornet trumpet-shaped, flared metal horn played with valves
didgeridoo large, aboriginal bamboo pipe (Australia)
English horn large, deep-pitched oboe having pear-shaped bell; cor anglais
euphonium large, valved tenor tuba
fife small, side-blown flute
fipple flute any instrument with tubular body, finger holes, and whistle mouthpiece
flügelhorn valved, flared brass horn, esp. for military bands
flute tube producing tones by air blown through or across mouthpiece hole, with or without keys
French horn valved brass horn with coiled tube ending in flared bell
glass flute tube made of glass
harmonica set of reeded tubes in box-shaped, metal shell; mouth organ
helicon coiled tuba carried over shoulder in marching bands
horn curved, conical animal horn with reedless mouthpiece; any flared metal tube with reedless mouthpiece
hornpipe folk clarinet, often of animal horn
hunting horn earliest form of modern horn, consisting of coiled conical tube with flaring bell
jug large, deep, glass container with small opening at top, across which player blows
lyricon wind synthesizer fingered like clarinet that controls analog synthesizer
megaphone cone-shaped device for intensifying or directing voice
mouth organ harmonica
musette early bagpipe with air supplied by bellows (France, 17th-18th c.)
nose flute tube played with breath from nostril instead of mouth
oboe keyed wood pipe with double-reed mouthpiece and conical tube
ocarina simple, oval-shaped flute with finger holes and mouthpiece
panpipe set of small flutes of graduated sizes joined together in one unit; syrinx
piccolo small flute that reaches high octaves
post horn straight or coiled metal horn with no valves or slide
recorder wood whistle flute in one of various pitches (Europe)
saxhorn any of a family of brass instruments similar to cornet and tuba
saxophone metal horn with reed mouthpiece: sopranino, soprano, alto, tenor, baritone, bass, contrabass, subcontrabass
saxtuba large, bass saxhorn
shofar curved ram's horn that produces tones one-fifth apart, used to signal Jewish High Holidays
sousaphone large bass tuba
syrinx panpipe
trombone brass tube with a reedless mouthpiece and a slide for varying tube length
trumpet flared brass tube with reedless mouthpiece, usu. with three valves
tuba large, valved, deep-pitched brass horn with flared bell

Accessories

bell large end of tube of wind instrument, usu. with edge turned out and enlarged
bottleneck glass tube slid along guitar strings for glissando effect
bow horsehairs stretched on wood rod for playing stringed instrument
capo movable bar attached to fingerboard of fretted, stringed instrument to raise pitch
chanter melody pipe of bagpipe
damper device that deadens sound, esp. by halting vibration of string
drumstick wood stick for striking drumheads
fret lateral ridge on fingerboard of stringed instrument, used to regulate pitch and finger placement
key elements depressed by fingers and connected to strings in keyboard

ligature metal binding that holds reed on wind instrument
metronome device for exactly measuring tempo through regular, repeated clicking sounds
mute device used to muffle tone, esp. inserted in bell of brass instrument
pick plectrum
pitch pipe small reed pipe used to tune instruments or establish pitch for singer by producing specific tone; tuning pipe
plectrum thin piece of ivory, wood, metal, horn, quill, or plastic, used to pluck strings of stringed instrument; pick
reed thin, elastic tongue of wood fastened over mouthpiece in wind instrument and set vibrating by air current
string thin cord of nylon, gut, or metal stretched and plucked or bowed
tuning fork two-pronged metal device that produces specific tone when struck, usu. 440 frequency A
tuning pipe pitch pipe

DANCE

Dances of the World
Ballet
Events, Steps, and Dancers

Dances of the World

allemande court dance performed with interwound arms, developed from German folk dance (17th-18th c.)
ballet classical dance form based on conventional steps and positions with precise, graceful movements; a theatrical entertainment that conveys story or atmosphere through such dance and music
barn dance rural American social dance, variation on schottische in triple time, sometimes held in barn
belly dance solo dance performed by woman that emphasizes undulations of stomach (Middle East)
bolero lively dance in triple time, performed with sharp turns, stamping feet, and sudden stops (Spain)
bop shufflelike dance to modern bebop jazz
bossa nova dance similar to samba, with jazz influence (Brazil)
bunny hug ragtime dance that is variation on Charleston
cakewalk African-American stage dance with eccentric strutting followed by solemn processional walk (19th c.)
cancan high-kicking stage dance performed by women while holding up skirt front (France, 19th c.)
carioca variation on samba (Brazil)
cha-cha fast, rhythmic, ballroom dance, based on three quick steps and a shuffle (Latin America)
Charleston vigorous 1920's ballroom dance in which knees are swung in and out and heels turned outward on each step
clog dance in which performer beats out rhythm on floor with heavy wood shoes
conga ballroom dance for group in single line doing three steps forward and a kick (Cuba)
cotillion lively social dance similar to quadrille with frequent changing of partners under leadership of one couple (France, 18th c.)
country dance traditional dance in which dancers form facing lines (Britian)
erotic dance striptease
fan dance solo dance performed by nude or seminude woman using one or more large fans to cover her body
fandango dance in lively triple time performed by one couple with castanets to guitar accompaniment (Spain, Latin America)
flamenco vigorous, rhythmic gypsy dance performed with stamping of feet and clapping of hands (Spanish Andalusia)
foxtrot two-step ballroom dance in quadruple time
galliard spirited, five-step dance for two dancers, performed in triple time (Europe, 16th-17th c.)
gavotte dance of peasant origin performed in quick quadruple time (France, 18th c.)
Highland fling lively folk dance characterized by tossing of arms and legs; fling (Scotland)
hoedown square dance
hootchy-kootchy pseudo-Oriental carnival dance that involves suggestive torso movements performed by woman dancer
hora traditional round dance (Israel and Romania)
hula dance with sinuous hip movements and mimetic hand gestures that tell story to drumming and chanting accompaniment (Hawaii)
interpretive dance highly personal form of modern dance
jazz dance modern dance form performed to jazz music, esp. in quadruple time, based on standardized movements
jig lively, springy folk dance in triple time
jitterbug American jazz two-step, performed by couples in the 1940's, consisting of standardized patterns with acrobatic swings, twirls, splits, and somersaults
juba American southern plantation slave dance, accompanied by rhythmic clapping and slapping of knees and thighs
lambada ballroom dance that combines elements of merengue, samba, and salsa, in which partners' bodies interlock closely to strong, sensual rhythm (Brazil)
limbo competitive, acrobatic dance in which dancer bends backward from knees and moves under horizontal pole at progressively lower heights (West Indies)
lindy energetic jitterbug (1930's)
mambo ballroom dance similar to rumba and

cha-cha with more complex steps (Cuba)
mazurka lively folk dance in triple time (Poland)
merengue ballroom dance performed with one stiff leg dragged on every step (Haiti)
Mexican hat dance lively courtship dance for solo male performed around brim of sombrero placed on ground (Mexico)
minuet slow, stately dance in triple time, performed with bowing and toe pointing (18th c.)
modern dance expressionistic, theatrical dance, developed after 1915 as alternative to ballet, with no formal conventions and unorthodox movements, done to eclectic music and based on one of various specialized techniques for using the entire body
morris dance vigorous rural dance for men wearing Robin Hood costumes, performed esp. on May Day (Britain, 16th c.)
one-step ballroom round dance in duple time, performed to ragtime with quick walking steps backward and forward
pas de deux ballet dance for couple
polka lively dance for couples, performed in duple time using hop-step-close-step pattern (Bohemia)
polonaise stately promenade or march in slow triple time (Poland, 19th c.)
quadrille square dance with five complete parts, performed by four couples in duple and sextuple time
rain dance ritual native dance invoking rain
reel lively traditional Highland folk dance (Scotland)
round dance folk or ballroom dance in which couples move in circular motion around room
rumba ballroom dance performed in duple or quadruple time with step-close-step pattern and complex shifting of weight (Cuba)
salsa popular dance performed to rhythmic, big-band jazz (Latin America)
samba dance of African origin, consisting of a step-close-step-close pattern with dips and leaps on the beat, performed to relaxed jazz music (Brazil)
shag dance performed with vigorous hopping on each foot in turn (1930's-1940's)
shimmy ragtime dance characterized by shaking of shoulders and hips (1920's)
shuffle dance characterized by scraping feet across floor
slow dance contemporary popular dance in which couples embrace and sway gently to slow ballads
snake dance ritual dance performed with snakes, or in which their images are invoked or imitated by sinuous movements
soft-shoe tap dance steps in soft-soled shoes without metal taps
square dance set folk dance for four couples arranged in a square; hoedown
stomp dance to jazz music with driving rhythm, usu. marked by stamping of feet
striptease burlesque dance in which performer suggestively removes clothing piece by piece; erotic dance
swing jazz dance performed in moderate, lilting syncopation to big band music
sword dance native male ceremonial dance performed around swords or in circle with flourished swords
tango ballroom dance performed by couple in quadruple time with long pauses, varied steps, and stylized poses (Latin America)
tap dance rhythmic variations tapped out audibly by dancer usu. wearing shoes with metal taps or special hard soles
tarantella rapid, whirling folk dance in sextuple time (Italy, 18th c.)
Texas two-step variation on two-step done to country-and-western swing music
toe dance women's ballet executed on tips of toes while wearing pointe shoes with reinforced toes
turkey trot ragtime round dance having springy steps with straightened knees, body swings, and up-and-down shoulder movements
two-step ballroom dance performed in duple time with sliding step-close-step pattern
Virginia reel dance in which two facing lines of couples execute a series of figures in turn (19th c.)
waltz classical ballroom dance performed in moderate triple time with accent on first beat of step-step-close pattern and dancers revolving in circles (19th c.)

Ballet

adagio slow, sustained movement stressing grace, balance; ballerina's lyrical performance in second part of grand pas de deux
allegro rapid movements accompanied by jumps, turns, and batteries
allongé extension of arms in arabesque
arabesque standing on one leg with raised leg extended in straight line to rear and foot pointed
assemblé rising off floor, straightening both legs in air, and returning to fifth position
attitude standing on one leg with raised leg behind body and knee bent; same position with raised leg in front of body
balance light, rocking waltz step in which weight is shifted from side to side
ballet d'action ballet that tells a story, often tragic
ballet master ballet company's principal instructor, often also choreographer
balletomane enthusiastic and knowledgeable follower of ballet
ballon dancer's spring and lightness in leaps
ballonné broad leap with battement kick
barre horizontal bar opposite mirrors and along wall in studio for class exercises
battement high or low kick: grand battement or petit battement
batterie beating together of feet or legs, esp. in midair
bourrée traveling movement with feet moving in tiny steps from tight fifth position
brisé jump in which one leg beats against the other in midair

cabriole man's batterie with one leg kicked high and the other leg rising to beat against it one or more times
cambré bending back or to one side
chaîné series of short, usu. rapid turns made while moving across the floor
changement de pied jump begun in fifth position, ending in fifth position with opposite foot forward
chassé traveling movement in which one foot follows and displaces the other
choreography art of devising form, sequence, and purpose of ballet movements
ciseaux scissorslike leap with legs wide apart in midair
closed positions first, third, and fifth positions, in which feet are in contact with each other
coda final section of classical grand pas de deux
contretemps step taken in counter time
corps de ballet ensemble or chorus of company dancers who perform together, not solo, usu. the junior members of a company
coupé linking movement between steps, in which one foot replaces the other on a spot
croisé movement with body at oblique angle to audience and working leg crossing behind or in front of body
danseur male ballet dancer
danseur noble principal male dancer, equal to prima ballerina
dégagé freeing of foot prior to taking step, with working leg brushed out so that toes rise a few inches off the floor
demi-plié movement in which knee or knees are half-bent with heels on floor
demi-pointe dancing with weight of body on toes and ball of foot
developpé slowly bending and then straightening knee as leg is raised in extension from floor
divertissement dance or series of short dances without plot
écarté separated body position; position with perfectly square head and body leaning away from raised leg turned out to extreme
échappé jump with feet moving from a closed fifth to an open second position
effacé position with torso and hips at oblique angle to audience, working leg extended to front or back, and opposite arm raised above head
emboîtés little hopping steps from leg to leg with working leg lifted in low front attitude
enchaînement linking together of two or more movements to fit phrase of music; combination
entrechat directly upward jump with body straight and feet reversing position several times in midair, named by number of reversals, as in entrechat quatre or entrechat six
épaulement bringing one shoulder forward in presenting step to audience with head turned over forward shoulder
extension dancer's ability to lift leg above head in nearly straight line from hip
fifth position closed position with feet fully turned out and crossed one in front of the other, so that the heel of each touches the big toe of the other
first position closed position in which feet form straight line perpendicular to body with heels touching
fish dive forward dive in which ballerina is caught by partner with her head and shoulders just above the floor
fondu lowering of body by slowly bending the knee of supporting leg with working foot pointing frontward
fouetté spin on one leg in which body is propelled by whipping motion of raised leg, performed by ballerina, usu. in series
fourth position open position with feet turned out from hip and placed horizontally, one in front of the other, a foot apart
frappé movement beginning with small beat with foot extended out strongly from knee
glissade gliding step from fifth to second to fifth position, performed on floor in low leap or prior to leap
grand battement high kick in any direction
grand jeté high leap covering a long distance in air
grand pas de deux formal, five-part pas de deux: entrée, ballerina's partnered adagio, male solo, female solo, coda
grand plié knees bending as deeply as possible with heels rising off floor
jeté leap made by pushing off on one leg and landing on the other
open positions second and fourth positions, in which feet are placed apart
pas formalized step; designation for type of dance
pas de basque linking movement between steps
pas de bourrée traveling step in any direction on pointe or demi-pointe
pas de chat leap from plié in fifth position
pas de cheval movement from fourth position that resembles a horse pawing the ground
pas de deux dance for two dancers, esp. grand pas de deux
passé movement with working leg raised to side and knee bent, in which foot is pointed downward and brushed against standing leg
petits battements small, quick movements with foot beating from front to back of ankle
petit tours short, fast turns made while progressing in straight line or circle
piqué stepping out onto pointe; little hop preparatory to traveling movement
pirouette turn of body while standing on one leg with raised leg held in position, performed on pointe for female, demi-pointe for male
plié bending of knees while back is held straight with hips, legs, and feet turned out
pointe dancing on tips of toes; ballerina's dancing while maintaining continuous straight line from tips of toes to hip
pointe shoes ballerina's slippers with hard block in toes, used for standing on pointe
posé tours series of turns executed diagonally,

around, or straight across floor
premier danseur principal male dancer
première danseuse principal ballerina
prima ballerina ballet company's principal ballerina
principals prima ballerinas and premier danseurs of ballet company
promenade slow turn of body on planted foot in adagio
relevé rising onto pointe or demi-pointe
révérence deep bow or curtsy
rond de jamb rotary movement of leg on floor or in air
royale changement de pied in which calves are beaten together before feet change position
saut de basque jump straight up, made with one leg bent at knee
saut de chat jump similar to grande jeté but with front leg passing through attitude
second position open position in which feet form straight line perpendicular to body while a foot apart
sissonne jump with legs straight and one leg extended to side
soubresant leap from both feet to landing on both feet in fifth position
sous-sous rising from fifth position on flat feet to fifth position on pointe
soutenu (*adj*) sustained, esp. of battement rising into fifth position demi-pointe with equal weight on both legs
stulchak move in which male dancer holds ballerina above his head on one straight arm
sur le coup de pied position of pointed foot lightly wrapped around front of ankle or touching back of calf near floor
temps step in which weight is not transferred from foot to foot
temps de flèche sharp, hitch-kick jump in which legs pass in the air
temps levé hop taken from one foot starting in any of various positions
temps lié connected movement that combines leg and arm movements on second, fourth, and fifth positions of feet
tendu (*adj*) stretched and extended straight, esp. a leg
third position closed position with feet placed horizontally, one in front of the other, each heel at midpoint of the other foot
tour à la seconde turn in second position
tour en l'air complete turn or turns executed in the air, begun and ended in fifth position
tour jeté high jump combining fast turn in the air and whiplike change of leg positions, ending in arabesque demi-plié
turnout outward rotation of legs at as close to 180-degree angle from hips as possible
tutu ballerina's short, flaring, fluffy skirt
variation solo dance, esp. third and fourth solo parts of classical grand pas de deux
vole traveling movements

Events, Steps, and Dancers

ballroom dance any social or recreational dance, such as the foxtrot, tango, or waltz, performed by couples often in a ballroom
bunny hop short leap forward to toe of one foot, followed by quick step onto other foot
chorus line group of background dancers who perform in unison in musical theater
do-si-do square dance figure in which woman passes around her partner and then the man on her right
folk dance indigenous dance common to one region or people
formal ball; large social gathering with ballroom dancing
go-go dancer dancer who performs on platform raised above patrons of disco or nightclub
heel-and-toe (*adj*) pertaining to locked knee step in which heel of one foot touches ground before toe of other foot leaves it
hop informal dance, esp. 1950's teenage rock-'n'-roll dance held to live or recorded music
masked ball ball at which participants wear disguises, esp. face masks
mixer informal dance and social gathering
prom formal dance or ball for high school students
sashay square dance figure in which partners sidestep in circle around each other, man moving behind woman
stag dance gathering to which men and women come separately, not as couples
taxi dancer woman employed to dance with patrons, as of cabaret or club, who pay her a fee
tea dance dance held in late afternoon
terpsichorean dancer; (*adj*) pertaining to dance

THEATER

Theatrical Forms and Venues
Stagecraft, Production, and Dramatic Structure
Actors, Characters, and Theater People

Theatrical Forms and Venues

agitprop informal drama supporting radical leftist ideology
amphitheater large, esp. round, outdoor space with raised tiers of seats around a stage; originally a natural dip
arena theater central stage surrounded by seats without proscenium; performed in the round
avant-garde experimental or new drama
ballet theatrical form that uses dance and music to convey a story without words
black comedy comedy emphasizing morbid, gloomy, grotesque, or calamitous themes and events
Broadway professional, legitimate, mainstream theater; the street in New York City where such theater occurs
burlesque satire; variety entertainment featuring comic skits, striptease, and magic
cabaret dancing, singing, and skits performed in a bar or café
circus traveling troupe of acrobats, clowns, and trained animals, usu. performing in oval arena
classical theater Greek tragedies, Shakes-pearean plays, or other long-established dramas or comedies
closet drama play intended to be read, not performed
comedy dramatic form using wit, humor, and satire; narrative with happy ending
comedy of manners dramatic form depicting and satirizing fashionable society
commedia dell'arte popular, folk-based comedic tradition of masked carnival mimes and acrobats, based on stock characters and situations (Italy, 16th-18th c.)
community theater little theater
dinner theater theater in which production is performed for audience that has been served dinner
drama theatrical form based on exposition of conflict through dialogue and actions of performers
experimental theater avant-garde; new and nontraditional dramatic form and narrative
farce low comedy, based on horseplay and absurd situations
floor show cabaret or nightclub theater; entertainment staged in conjunction with drinking and revelry in audience
guerrilla theater performance, sometimes in streets, used esp. for social protest or propaganda; street theater
high comedy dramatic form characterized by witty, satiric depictions of upper class life
improv *Informal.* improvisation
improvisation unrehearsed, impromptu performance, usu. within larger dramatic structure or in rehearsal; type of entertainment featuring spontaneous, unrehearsed skits by a troupe of actors; improv
Kabuki highly choreographed, stylized, all-male theater (Japan)
legitimate stage professionally produced, traditional theater, as opposed to burlesque, vaudeville, and nonprofessional stagings
little theater amateur, neighborhood theater; community theater
low comedy dramatic form that employs burlesque, farce, and slapstick, usu. involving common folk, without clever or witty dialogue
masque elaborate costume play, orig. traditional folk theater and dance spectacles
melodrama dramatic form that exaggerates emotions and emphasizes plot over characterization
minstrel show theatrical entertainment featuring white performers in blackface who sing, dance, and tell stories, based on stereotypes of African-American culture (U.S., late 19th c.)
miracle play medieval drama based on the Bible or the life of a saint or martyr
morality play medieval, allegorical dramatic form that provided instruction in Christian orthodoxy
musical light dramatic entertainment featuring musical interludes, story told largely through song and dance
musical comedy comic musical play
mystery play medieval drama based on Scriptural events, often illustrating points of religious doctrine and faith
Nō classical, all-male theater, elegant and serious in tone and form (Japan)
odeum small theater or concert hall
off Broadway low-budget, theatrical productions performed in modest venues, esp. in New York, sometimes as a pre-Broadway venture
off off Broadway highly experimental, sometimes nonprofessional theatrical productions performed in small venues far outside realms of legitimate theater
open-air theater performance in unenclosed auditorium or amphitheater, esp. Globe-type theater
opera musical drama composed of vocal pieces sung to orchestral accompaniment, esp. with tragic themes on grand scale
operetta romantic, light opera with songs and dance
pageant elaborately staged, open-air dramatic production, often with historical theme
pantomime performance without spoken words
passion play medieval religious drama dealing with Christ's passion
performance art often experimental, dramatic form combining theatrical performance, visual art, music, dance, cinema, or video in non-narra-

tive, multimedia piece, originated in 1970's
repertory company company that presents several works regularly or alternately using same performers
revue series of unrelated, often comic, skits, songs, dances, and monologues; olio
road show theatrical performance that travels from city to city
send-up mocking parody or spoof of another work
shadow play theater in which the shadows of puppets are cast on a screen between puppets and audience
showboat floating riverboat used as theater (U.S., 19th c.)
showcase small production used to expose actors to talent agents, producers, and directors; equity waiver
slapstick low comedy dependent on physical humor or horseplay
stand-up (*adj*) designating comedy in form of monologue delivered while standing alone before audience
strawhat (*adj*) pertaining to summer theater
street theater theatrical form using public areas or streets as a stage, often politically radical in theme; guerrilla theater
summer stock acting company that produces plays during summer
theater building in which plays are performed, usu. having stage and audience seating area
theater-in-the-round theatrical presentation in which the audience sits on all sides of an open stage; arena theater
theater of the absurd theatrical form that dispenses with linear narrative and realistic dialogue and explores existential dimensions of life, esp. popular since 1950's
tragedy dramatic form dealing with a flaw, moral weakness, or maladjustment of the central character, resulting in downfall or catastrophe
tragicomedy dramatic form mixing elements of tragedy and comedy
variety show entertainment consisting of a series of different acts, orig. performed in music halls
vaudeville theatrical entertainment that featured a variety of performances by different singers, dancers, comedians, and other specialty acts (early 20th c.)

Stagecraft, Production, and Dramatic Structure

act major division of play; (*vb*) perform in dramatic stage production
ad lib spontaneous line or lines not part of script
apron section of stage floor closest to audience, usu. in front of proscenium; forestage
aside actor's lines spoken to audience, not other actors
audition brief trial performance held to appraise actor's talent and suitability for role
backdrop curtain painted as scenery, hung at rear of stage
backlight lighting of stage from upstage area behind actors used to create visual depth
backstage wings, dressing rooms, and other areas behind proscenium out of audience view
balcony elevated seating area in auditorium, usu. jutting out over orchestra floor
barnstorm (*vb*) travel about country performing plays
bill performance or piece being shown in theater
blackface black facial makeup, orig. burnt cork, worn by performers esp. in minstrel shows
blackout abrupt switching off of all stage lights at end of scene
blocking director's charting of actor's stage movements
boards stage floor; the theater in general
border narrow curtain or strip of canvas hung above stage to mask flies
box private seating compartment in theater, esp. an elevated one
box office small room near theater entrance in which tickets are sold; number and value of tickets sold for show
bravo audience shout of approval
break a leg actor's traditional expression of good luck
callback actor's second audition for same part
cast actors chosen to perform parts in a play; (*vb*) select actors to play parts
cattle call *Slang.* publicly announced audition open to all comers
cold reading audition or rehearsal of previously unseen script
counterweight system a vertically tracked weight arbor corresponding to pulleys and pipe (baton) for hoisting scenery
cue word, phrase, or action signaling actor's line, entrance, or exit, or change in lighting or sound
curtain call return of actors to stage to take bows in response to applause at play's end
cyclorama curved backdrop used to create the illusion of sky, space, or distance
dark (*adj*) description of theater on night without performance
decor scenery, sets, or backdrops
denouement resolution of plot; outcome or dramatic unraveling of story complications and conflicts
deus ex machina *Latin.* lit. god from a machine; character or device introduced from outside the story to resolve plot
downstage area of stage nearest audience
dramatic structure traditional, formal composition of dramatic piece, based on resolution of conflict
dress circle first balcony seating area above boxes
dress rehearsal rehearsal in full costume just prior to opening night
engagement run of scheduled performances
ensemble piece play or performance in which all actors share equal billing and size of part
entr'acte short performance, as music or dance, between acts of a play; interval between acts of a play or other production

epilogue brief section at conclusion of play
finale final scene or musical number of performance
flat theatrical unit covered in muslin or lawn used as walls
flies area above stage with weights and ropes for manipulating scenery down and up
footlights row of lights set along front edge of stage floor; acting profession in general
forestage apron
fright wig wig with spikey hair standing out in all directions, worn for comic effect
gallery top balcony, usu. containing the cheapest seats
grease paint theatrical makeup
green room backstage room in which performers relax before, between, or after appearances on stage
hit one's mark stop movement in precisely designated spot marked on stage
houselights theater lights in auditorium, not those on stage
instrument Method term for actor's body or theatrical light
intermezzo short, light interlude between acts
intermission interval between acts
jack stage brace for scenery
light bridge platform or elevated room from which lights are positioned
limelight brilliant stage light that illuminates major characters; center of attention
lobsterscope punched metal disk rotating in front of spotlight for lighting effects
loge balcony seating area of theater
marks tape or chalk marks on stage indicating actor positioning
marquee canopy on front of outside theater advertising play
matinée afternoon performance
Method naturalistic acting technique, developed by Konstantin Stanislavski, that emphasizes actor's personal exploration of and identification with character
mezzanine lowest balcony in theater, esp. first few rows in this balcony
mise en scène *French.* props and scenery used in a performance; setting of play
monologue speech delivered at length by one actor
Muse mythological spirit believed to inspire poetry and drama (ancient Greece)
number song performed in theatrical production
orchestra audience seats on ground floor of theater
parados passageway between sets and wings
parterre seats on main floor of theater behind orchestra
patch manual or computer assignment of dimmers to channels on control board
peanut gallery *Informal.* rear balcony seating in theater; cheaper seats, from which rabble traditionally threw peanuts
performance any entertainment presented before an audience; act of performing a theatrical piece; particular instance of presenting a theatrical piece
pit sunken area directly in front of stage in which orchestra musicians sit
playbill theatrical program; handbill identifying cast and production members for audience
premiere first performance of play
preview performance of play given before official opening
production all elements involved in one particular staging of a play
program brochure or sheet describing play and listing performers and production staff, handed out before performance begins
prompt (*vb*) supply (an actor) with forgotten line or missed cue from offstage
prop property
property any article used to dress the stage for scenes, or any object carried by an actor; prop
proscenium arched part of stage, located in front of curtain, that separates stage from auditorium
rake slope of stage floor from apron to rear wall
rave extremely favorable review
repertoire stock of plays performed by actor or company
repertory presentation of a stock of plays by a theater company over a regular season; company or troupe that presents plays this way
ring down the curtain lower the curtain
ring up the curtain raise the curtain
riser stairlike theater seating or stage area
routine theatrical skit; dance combination; comedian's material
run total number of consecutive performances of a play at one theater or on tour
run-through rehearsal of entire piece
scene uninterrupted action within play; division of an act
scenery backdrops or structures on stage that represent the play's locale
sensory technique used by actors in Method training in which specific sensory input is re-created by imagination
set scenery, flats, and properties composing play's environment
show-stopper dramatic or musical moment during performance that draws prolonged applause, halting action
sides pages of a script with lines and cues for one role only, commonly used at auditions
sight gag funny bit without dialogue
sightline line of vision from audience to extreme corners of stage
slapstick comedy stressing farce, horseplay, or sight gags
soliloquy monologue expressing character's inner thoughts, addressed to no one
spike marks taped marks for furniture, prop, or set placement
spotlight powerful light used to illuminate individual actor, manually operated on a rotating axis
SRO standing room only; designating a sold-out performance
stage area on which plays are performed before an audience

stagecraft skill in theatrical performance; art and practice of staging plays; art of set construction
stage direction instruction in script of play indicating production requirements or performer's action or appearance
stage left stage area on actor's left when facing audience
stage right stage area on actor's right when facing audience
stage whisper loud, easily overheard, mock whisper
standing room area at rear of orchestra in which audience may stand during sold-out performance; SRO
strike (*vb*) take apart and remove (scenery or set) from stage
striplights encased set of lights on 3 or 4 separate circuits, used for color washes of cyclorama
swan song actor's final performance
tableau stage picture created by actors posing motionless
teaser drapery or flat member across top of proscenium arch that frames stage opening and conceals flies
thrust stage stage extending beyond the proscenium, usu. surrounded by audience on three sides
touring company group of performers moving from city to city to present a play or musical, esp. one already successful on Broadway
trap removable section of stage floor through which actors can enter or exit or scenery be brought in or removed
typecasting assigning role to actor based on actor's appearance, personal style, or previous experience
upstage rear portion of stage; (*vb*) to move upstage from another actor, forcing him or her to turn away from audience; to draw audience's attention from another actor by distracting behavior
vehicle theatrical work with role designed or well-suited to display or exploit the talents of particular performer
venue type of performance space
walk-through early or casual rehearsal
whiteface white pancake makeup, used esp. by mimes
wings sides of stage beyond view of audience

Actors, Characters, and Theater People

actor stage performer, esp. male, but may also apply to female; player; Thespian
actress female stage performer
angel *Informal.* financial backer, as of play production
backer investor in production
bard epic poet, national minstrel
barker person who stands at entrance to show, esp. carnival, attracting passersby
barnstormer traveling actor; actor in road production
bit player actor who performs a small role, usu. with few lines of dialogue
busker street performer
cameo small role played by a famous actor; brief appearance in play
cast actors who portray all the roles in play
character actor player who specializes in roles depicting strong or memorable personalities, but not hero
company group of actors, esp. stock company
contortionist circus acrobat capable of assuming unnatural positions
costume designer person responsible for costuming the actors
crew all nonperformers; stagehands and technicians involved in a production
director person responsible for blocking stage movements, motivating actors, and providing unity to production
dramatis personae cast of characters in a dramatic work
dramaturge composer of dramas; company's script analyst
dresser personal assistant responsible for helping actor into costume at time of performance
emcee master of ceremonies
ensemble group of actors performing together; full company
extra actor in minor, nonspeaking role
harlequin masked, comic character, usu. dressed in multicolored, diamond-patterned tights and carrying a sword or magic wand, in commedia dell'arte
heavy villain
impresario manager, director, or fund-raiser for theater company
ingénue role of innocent, naive young woman in drama
lead principal character in drama
librettist writer of song lyrics for a musical
master of ceremonies MC; person who presides over revue or variety show, esp. introducing acts and filling breaks with patter; comprere; emcee
matinée idol handsome actor popular with female audiences
mime actor who uses gestures and bodily movements to silently portray a character or communicate moods and ideas
minstrel medieval entertainer who traveled from place to place singing and reciting stories
pantomime actor in dumb show or silent performance
producer person responsible for financial and administrative aspects of production, esp. fund-raising
prompter person hidden from audience who supplies next line of dialogue or other cue when actor forgets
protagonist main character in drama; hero or heroine
repertory company in which actors share leading roles in several different plays performed in rotation; stock company
saltimbanque street performer, esp. juggler or contortionist
Scaramouch cowardly braggart who is easily

vanquished in farce and commedia dell'arte
set designer person responsible for design and creation of stage sets and scenery
song-and-dance man entertainer who specializes in musicals
stagehand person who sets up and changes scenery before and during performance
stage manager theater staff person responsible for functional details of production during rehearsal and performance
stand-by actor prepared to substitute for regular performer in part as needed but usually not a member of cast
stock company troupe of actors, each specializing in certain types of roles and sharing others, who perform a series of plays, usu. at one theater; repertory company
straight man actor whose lines set up jokes for comedian
supernumerary actor in walk-on part; extra
Thespian actor
troupe company of actors
understudy actor versed in another's part, ready to step in if needed, usu. a member of the cast
usher theater attendant who guides audience members to their seats
villain character who opposes hero; bad guy; heavy
walk-on small, nonspeaking part; actor playing such a part

CINEMA

Genres and Types of Pictures
Cinematography Tools and Techniques
Movie People and Show Business

Genres and Types of Pictures

action adventure fast-paced, exciting narrative of some dangerous or bold undertaking
animation series of drawings that depict action by means of slightly progressive changes, each photographed separately to create movie; cartoon
A picture high-budget, high-quality feature film, usu. with stars
art film low-budget, nonstudio, often nonnarrative film utilizing experimental techniques
biographical film film based on life story of actual person
biopic biographical film
blue movie pornographic film
B picture low-budget studio film, often in genre and without major stars, formerly shown as added feature on bill with A picture
buddy picture narrative about adventures shared by two friends, usu. male
cartoon animated film
chiller *Informal.* horror film
cinéma vérité documentary filmed with hand-held camera without added effects, authentic and candid in action and style
cowboy picture western
detective picture story involving criminal investigation
disaster picture narrative about effects on characters of natural or man-made catastrophe
documentary nonfiction narrative about actual event or characters in journalistic vein
epic long, episodic, large-scale story with heroic characters
experimental film avant-garde, unconventional, or abstract film
exploitation film film with highly commercial appeal to specific audience, esp. particular sex, race, or age group
fantasy fanciful departure from known realities
film noir 1940's American black-and-white style of film, esp. with a private detective as hero, that emphasized dark, sinister moods and bleak viewpoints
gangster film melodramatic narrative film about a violent, criminal antihero, esp. popular in the Depression era
genre film using a specific technique, style, story, or setting, such as western or gangster
hard-core (*adj*) pruriently explicit, as in pornography that vividly depicts sex acts
horror films with strange, frightening events that threaten characters, esp. those emphasizing bloodshed or supernatural forces
horse opera western
independent film usu. low-budget film not produced by major studio
industrial promotional film for product or company
melodrama sensational story emphasizing emotional content over characterization
musical story told in large part through musical productions, esp. song-and-dance numbers
newsreel short documentary account of current events
period piece narrative occurring in another era, with appropriate historical sets and costumes
pornographic film low-budget picture designed for sexual titillation; blue movie; skin flick
prequel sequel that depicts events preceding those of the original work
romantic comedy light comedy involving love interest
science fiction film depicting effect of science on society, esp. future society or other planets
sci-fi *Informal.* science fiction
screwball comedy light, imaginative, fast-paced film with witty dialogue and improbable plot line
sequel continuation of story or characters depicted in an earlier film
shoot-'em up *Informal.* film that emphasizes gunplay and violent action
short subject short motion picture, usu. of less than 3000 feet of 35 mm film (or half an hour), often a documentary
silent film motion picture without sound, either from pre-1930 era or for effect
skin flick *Slang.* pornographic film

slapstick comedy humorous film that features boisterous, physical jokes and mugging
slasher movie film depicting violent killer who runs amok maiming or dismembering other characters, esp. young females
snuff film *Slang.* pornographic film that shows actual murder of performers
soft-core (*adj*) sexually stimulating, as in pornography that features nudity but not explicit sex acts
spaghetti western *Informal.* Italian-made, low-budget cowboy film
stag movie pornographic film intended for male audience
talkie early film produced with sound (1920's-1930's)
tearjerker *Informal.* sentimental melodrama
thriller suspense drama
travelogue documentary motion picture showing and describing travels
western narrative set in lawless, 19th century American frontier; cowboy picture; horse opera
whodunit *Informal.* detective or thriller film

Cinematography Tools and Techniques

academy leader countdown from 9 to 2 that appears on screen before film begins
animation process of creating moving graphic images on film by small progressive changes between each drawing cel
animatronics use of electronics to animate puppets or other figures for motion pictures
answer print first acceptable, color-balanced print made from original negative
arc light high-powered light for set illumination
assembly editing and splicing for rough cut
backlighting illumination from behind subject
back projection projection from rear of previously photographed material on translucent screen, used as background for shot
beep tone beep lasting 1/24 of a second that occurs at number 2 in academy leader countdown
big closeup BCU; shot of face filling screen
blackout abrupt fade to black at end of scene
boom mic overhead microphone on extendible crane
bridging shot film shot connecting discontinuous images
camera mount any of various bases for a camera: crane, dolly, specialty mount, sticks
cel transparent celluloid sheet used for animation drawing, constituting one frame of an animated film
celluloid film; plastic formerly used for photographic film
changeover marks white circles that appear twice for a split second in upper right corner of frame just before reel ends
cinematography art and science of motion-picture photography
cinema verité technique in which camera records actual persons and events without directorial intervention
Claymation *Trademark* animated film made by taking series of photographs of clay figures set in different positions
closeup CU; full screen shot of subject, esp. a person's head
composite print married print
continuity editing technique yielding smooth, coherent narrative from scenes shot out of sequence
crane mobile, counterweighted camera mount allowing camera great height and vertical movement
creeping titles titles or credits scrolled over film image
crosscutting jumping back and forth between two scenes happening simultaneously
cross-fade merging of images from end of one scene into beginning of next
cut quick transition from one shot to another
cut director's command to actors to cease playing scene
cutaway quick movement of camera away from shot; shot focusing on something other than main action
cut-in still shot inserted in film and interrupting the action or continuity; insert
cyclorama studio or stage background creating illusion of open scenery
dailies hastily printed footage from previous day's shooting, assembled for daily viewing by director and producer before editing or sound synchronization; rushes
dissolve one shot gradually fading into another
dolly movable camera mount, usu. a small wheeled platform
edge code code imprinted after filming at one-foot intervals on picture and sound to facilitate editing in sync
editing arrangement, splicing, and assemblage of film footage into desired sequences and synchronization of film with soundtrack
emulsion sensitive chemical solution that forms coating on film
establishing shot shot setting time and place of scene; master shot
fade-in gradual emergence of image from black ground
fade-out gradual disappearance of image into black ground
file footage stock film footage, such as scenes of crowds and natural backgrounds, kept on file for use
film strip of cellulose acetate coated with sensitive emulsion for recording images when exposed to light, usu. 35 mm wide
film clip brief section extracted from film; clip
final cut edited version of film that is approved and nearly ready for distribution
Foley *Trademark.* technique for adding special effects to soundtrack
footage section of film
frame single picture on strip of film, usu. 16 frames per foot of film; (*vb*) compose a single shot
freeze frame optical effect in which single frame is

held as persistent, still image in film; stop motion
FX *Slang.* special effects
gauge width of film in millimeters
head shot closeup of person's face and head
insert close shot of an object, such as a newspaper headline or clock; cut-in
iris-in gradual appearance of on-screen image through an expanding circle, esp. in silent films
iris-out gradual disappearance of on-screen image through a contracting circle, esp. in silent films
klieg light carbon arc lamp producing intense light
locked cut final edited version of film, ready for postproduction work
long shot scene filmed from considerable distance, usu. wide angle
looping editing process in which speech and sound effects are synchronized to film already shot
married print image, sound, and dialogue tracks synchronized for projection or reproduction; composite print
master shot establishing shot
montage fast-moving sequence of superimposed images
moving shot shot in which camera focus moves, as in dolly or pan shots
optical effect special visual effect: dissolve, fade, freeze
outtake footage deleted from final edit of film
pan panoramic shot of wide, horizontal view; movement of camera eye across wide area as camera moves horizontally on mount
print reproduction of original film
process cinematography special effects illusion in which foreground action or scene is superimposed on separately shot background
reaction shot shot showing subject reacting to action of preceding shot
rear projection special effect using prefilmed background against which scene is set and photographed; rear-screen projection
rear-screen projection rear projection
reel flanged spool for film; one section of feature film consisting of more than one reel
retake shot or scene that needs to be taken more than once; reshoot
rolling (*adj*) indication that cameras are shooting scene
rough cut preliminary edit; first version of motion picture following initial cutting and editing
rushes dailies, esp. East Coast usage
70 mm film size twice as large as standard 35 mm
shot continuous shooting of scene without stopping camera
skypan big, bowl-shaped light used to illuminate wide area
slo-mo *Informal.* slow motion
slow motion effect of very slow action achieved by overcranking camera, then replaying film at normal speed; slo-mo
special effects visual and sound effects added to film by various laboratory techniques; FX
splice joining of two film sections; an edit
split screen process shot showing two different scenes at same time
stereoscope optical instrument used to create a three-dimensional projection effect
stock shot prefilmed shot taken from newsreels or travelogues to insert into film as establishing shot
stop-action photography special effect technique in which performers stop moving and camera is stopped while something or someone is added to or removed from set, creating illusion of sudden appearance or disappearance
stop motion freeze frame
sweetening enhancing soundtrack quality electronically after filming and recording are complete
take shot filmed without stopping camera or action
3-D processing of film to give illusion of three-dimensional action when viewed through special lenses
time code series of marks along edge of film used to synchronize sound and other effects
time-lapse photography technique in which slow, continuous process is photographed by exposing one frame at a time, creating speeded-up effect when projected at normal speed
titles written text on screen often superimposed over filmed images, usu. stating time and place of action or credits
tracking shot shot in which camera and action both move in parallel direction; dolly shot
wide-screen (*adj*) denoting panoramic dimension in film projection
workprint first, unmarried print made from original negative that editor splices together
zoom effect created by camera action or use of lens with variable focal length, not by moving camera or camera mount

Movie People and Show Business

above-the-line designating those on film budget not considered part of crew, such as the director, producer, and actors
AD assistant director
adaptation screenplay with story taken from another medium
agent actor's, writer's, or director's representative for finding work, making deals, and creating packages
art direction direction that results in overall look of a film
art house theater that shows primarily art films, foreign films, and classics
assistant director AD; person on set responsible for implementing the director's orders and overseeing the actors; first or second assistant director
associate producer person attached to project but not functioning as producer; line producer
auteur film director with strong personal style
back-end deal arrangement by which all or some of one's compensation for work on a film comes from final profits after all expenses have been met
backlot outdoor area, usu. adjoining studio, for

shooting exterior scenes that depict locations
bankable star actor whose presence in film guarantees production and likely financial success
below-the-line designating crew, equipment, and production costs of film
best boy *Slang.* gaffer's assistant
billing order in which actors' names appear in credits, on marquee, and in advertising for film
boom operator technician who controls crane equipped with boom mike
buzz *Slang.* advance word on film in industry
cameo small part played by actor who is usu. featured
casting director person responsible for preauditioning and selecting right actor for each role
cineaste devotee of films; person professionally involved in making films
cinematheque small movie house showing avant-garde films
cinematographer person responsible for photographing film; director of photography
clapboard boards hinged at one end and banged together to mark filmed sequences with scene numbers for synching
closing credits long list of all actors and technicians involved in production, shown at end of film
colorization addition of color to films originally shot in black and white
coming attractions trailers previewing upcoming films
commissary dining room or cafeteria on motion-picture studio lot
credits lists of actors, artists, and technicians involved in making film, shown at beginning and/or end of movie
director creative overseer of motion picture who guides actors, determines narrative style, and selects camera angles
distribution placement of released film in theaters, usu. by studio acting as distributor
dolly grip crew member who helps move dolly
double feature two films shown in theater for the price of one; double bill
dresser actor's wardrobe assistant on set
drive-in outdoor theater where audience remains inside cars
dubbing replacing part or all of an existing soundtrack, esp. with a translation into another language, or adding background music or special effects
executive producer person responsible for raising money and initiating project, but not for daily administrative tasks
feature film motion picture at least 3000 feet long in 35 mm film
film motion picture
filmmaker individual who creates movies, esp. director
focus puller second assistant cameraman, who adjusts camera focus
Foley artist person who integrates special sound effects into soundtrack
front-end deal arrangement by which one's compensation for work on a film comes out of money that is available before or during production
gaffer electrician who operates and rigs lights
greensman crew member who tends trees and plants
grip member of film crew who moves equipment, esp. lighting
in-between assistant artist responsible for animation frames inserted between main frames drawn by chief animator
indie *Informal.* independent motion picture production company outside major studio system; film made by such a company
in the can (of a film) completed but not yet ready for distribution
key grip head of grip crew
line producer studio executive responsible for day-to-day coordination of production and staying within budget
lot motion-picture studio and its surrounding property
majors large Hollywood studios
method actor student or practitioner of the naturalistic Stanislavski method of acting, which emphasizes a personal exploration of the character being played
motion picture series of photographic images projected in rapid succession on a screen to give the illusion of continuous action
movie motion picture
movie theater building in which films are displayed for public viewing
multiplex movie theater with several screens in different rooms showing different films
nickelodeon early movie theater, in which films were viewed individually through a small machine operated by a nickel
option purchase by individual, company, or studio of exclusive right to develop film project during designated time
PA production assistant
postproduction editing, dubbing, and addition of special effects after conclusion of filming
post punch supervisor person who supervises photocopying of cels and drawings used in animation
producer executive and financial overseer of film production; packager of film idea for sale and distribution
production assistant PA; person responsible for carrying out day-to-day assignments given by line producer
projection booth room in movie theater from which film reels are projected onto screen
property story idea, concept, novel, or script, the rights to which are owned by potential producer or studio
ratings system of motion picture grading based on age of admissible audience: G (general); PG (parental guidance suggested); PG-13 (no one under 13); R (restricted admission if under 17); NC-17 (no one under 17)

release distribution of completed film to theaters
revival house movie theater showing old films only
rigger crew member who hangs suspended equipment, esp. lights
scale minimum pay approved by union for a specific job
score musical background for film; (*vb*) compose background music for film
screening showing of a film before an audience
screenplay written form of film containing dialogue, description of scenes, characters, and action; script
screen test audition in which actor is filmed to check appearance on film and suitability for role
screenwriter person who conceives, writes, and rewrites screenplays
script screenplay
script doctor writer who makes usu. minor revisions of someone else's script
script girl director's assistant who holds shooting script
script reader person hired to read and synopsize new scripts submitted to producer, studio, or agent
script supervisor person who takes notes on arrangement of set for continuity and editing
second-assistant cameraman person who pulls focus while camera is operating
second unit crew filming minor scenes or extras, often without director present
set sound stage or location where filming takes place
show business *Informal.* art, practice, and business of making films; entertainment industry in general
sides pages of scene given to actor at casting audition
sound editor person who builds reels of sound effects and dialogue for mixing
sound stage cavernous, soundproof building or room on studio lot for shooting films
spin-off project developing as adjunct to existing film
stage manager second assistant director for video production
stand-in actor who substitutes for another during setup of scene for camera and lighting
storyboard graphic representation of each scene in film sequence, serving as guide for production
story editor person responsible for development of story from initial concept to shooting script
stunt dangerous or difficult feat required by scene; *Informal.* person who performs such feats
stylist hairdresser and wardrobe assistant on set
subtitles text at bottom of screen providing continuous translation of foreign language film
third-assistant cameraman person who loads film in magazine, operates clapper, and cleans filter; clapper loader
tie-in project related to existing film
Titan crane large, movable crane with seat for director
toon *Informal.* character in animated cartoon
trades movie industry journals, esp. *Variety* and *Hollywood Reporter*
trailer film clip used as in-theater advertisement; preview of upcoming release
unit publicist press and media liaison responsible for publicizing specific film during production and release
VO voice-over
voice-over VO; narration heard over film sequence, not spoken as dialogue by actors on screen
wrap conclusion of filming day and esp. of entire production

TELEVISION AND RADIO

Television Programming and Institutions
Broadcast Journalism
Television Technology
Radio Programming
Radios and Radio Technology

Television Programming and Institutions

across-the-board scheduled daily at same time
action line phone-in service for television viewers with consumer problems
affiliates local stations across nation associated with a major network and receiving its feed
blackout mandated interruption or restriction on broadcast, esp. local sporting event
bleep sound covering censored material on soundtrack or tape
blooper *Informal.* embarrassing gaffe made on the air
broadcast journalism news reporting by television or radio
cable television station or network broadcasting programs receivable only by paying subscription fee for hookup
candid camera program showing unwitting or unrehearsed subjects reacting to situations, filmed with small, hidden camera
canned laughter prerecorded laugh soundtrack for comedy program
clip specific section of film or tape
commercial television station or network in business for profit by selling advertising time to sponsors
couch potato *Slang.* chronic television viewer
counterprogramming offering a different type of program from others in given time slot in order to attract specific audience
daytime drama soap opera
dead air unintentional period of silence or a blank screen
dedicated channel cable channel for local government, educational, or public use
docudrama narrative, fictionalized treatment of actual event, person, or topic

documentary nonfiction program covering current events, issues, or personalities
docutainment documentaries that sacrifice information for sensationalism and entertainment values
dramatic series noncomic, recurring weekly program
dramedy dramatic comedy, as opposed to situation comedy
educational access channel small, local, noncommercial channel offering the public an opportunity to transmit educational programs
episode regular installment of ongoing program
fairness doctrine policy mandated by FCC, requiring that stations grant equal time to political views and candidates in opposition to these already aired
FCC Federal Communications Commission; government agency that licenses and regulates operations of radio and television stations
format specific type of programming provided by station or shown at particular time of day or week
game show program in which contestants compete for prizes by playing a game
guest star well-known actor playing episodic role
infomercial program-length commercial cast in standard format, as a documentary or talk show, to disguise that it is an advertisement
infotainment programming that is both informative or educational and entertaining
instant replay immediate video rerun of section of broadcast event, esp. live sport
in-the-can (*adj*) designating a completed program or material that has been shot
kidvid *Slang.* television programs intended for children
laugh track canned laughter, esp. for sitcom
live (*adj*) broadcast as event or performance occurs, as opposed to prerecorded
local station affiliate of network in specific region, or small, independent broadcasting entity
magazine documentary show covering several topics in single broadcast; newsmagazine
mass media means of communication, such as television and radio, that reach and influence large numbers of people
media means of public communication, such as television and radio, providing public with news, entertainment, and advertisements
medium television or radio as media
miniseries specially programmed, serialized drama or documentary broadcast over two or more days
narration voice-over description of events on screen or gaps in visual story
narrowcast (*vb*) aim a program at specific, limited audience or market
network association of stations affiliated with one of the major broadcasting companies; ABC, CBS, CNN, Fox, or NBC
newsmagazine magazine show
Nielsen rating widely accepted estimate of relative audience share for particular program, based on monitoring of preselected sample of viewers by A.C. Nielsen Company
paid political announcement advertisement for political candidate or cause
pay-per-view ppv; special cable hookup requiring single payment for one broadcast
pay television commercial service that broadcasts programs to viewers who pay monthly charge or per-program fee; subscription television
people meter device for recording in-home response to programming
pilot introductory test episode of proposed new program
plug *Informal.* advertisement, esp. mention of product within context of program, not in paid commercial spot
ppv *pay-per-view*
preempt (*vb*) replace with another program
prerecorded (*adj*) taped or filmed prior to broadcast
prime time midevening hours of broadcast time, when largest audience is watching; 8 p.m. to 11 p.m.
programming determination or nature of broadcast content and balance of news, talk shows, sitcoms, dramas, documentaries, variety shows, movies, or sports programs
public access television local cable television station providing free time for low-budget, often nonprofessional programs; system of such stations
public service announcement advertisement or announcement done for public good with time donated by station
public television nonprofit television station or broadcast network emphasizing educational and cultural programming
quiz show program in which contestants compete for prizes by answering questions
rating measure of relative audience size for competing programs at same hour, used esp. to set price for commercials
repeat reshowing of program in same season
rerun repeat broadcast of program, usu. in later year
segue seamless transition from program to program or segment to segment
serial program appearing in regular installments
share percentage of viewers watching particular show
sign off (*vb*) make closing announcement and show station identification at end of broadcast day
simulcast program broadcast over cooperating radio and television stations at same time to provide improved audio, esp. for televised music program
sitcom *Informal.* situation comedy
situation comedy usu. half-hour, comedic show with recurring characters in simplistic situations
soap opera melodrama series, usu. showing five days a week during daytime hours; daytime drama; soap
sound bite brief segment of audio and video transmission, esp. on talking-head show
special program that appears one time only or is not part of regular schedule

spin-off series or program derived from a previously popular show or its characters
spokesperson popular or compelling individual who speaks on behalf of product or cause
sponsor advertiser buying time on particular show to promote product
sportscast broadcast of sporting event
spot announcement brief advertisement or promotional blurb on upcoming program, newsbrief, or station break; spot
standards and practices network department responsible for insuring that program content meets specific moral standards
stand by instruction to hold for further information or continuation of broadcast
station identification brief spot giving call letters and channel number of station or name of network, usu. before and after program or on the hour and half-hour
STV subscription television
subscription television STV; pay television
superstation independent, local television station that is distributed and broadcast nationally via satellite to cable systems
sweeps thrice-yearly rating surveys that coincide with highly competitive programming weeks for networks
syndication reissue of series for broadcast after show has ceased production of new episodes; marketing of show on station-by-station basis and not to networks
tag identification of producer or syndicator at end of program
talking head *Slang.* closeup shot of someone talking or being interviewed; programming based on such shots
talk show program with host interviewing unusual guests and celebrities
telecast single television broadcast or program
teleplay script for a television program
telethon lengthy, uninterrupted program raising money for charitable cause
televangelist religious minister preaching over television and frequently soliciting donations for a church
viewing public those who watch television and are potential consumers for advertised products

Broadcast Journalism

advance news story circulated ahead of scheduled release date
air personality engaging announcer who attracts viewers to newscast
all-news station exclusively airing news programs
anchor principal journalist on news program
A roll interviews and stand-up portion of news broadcast
blind interview interview with unnamed source
blurb brief news release
bridge transition within story, esp. use of stand-up or walk and talk to relate portion of report
broadcast journalism reporting of news events on radio or television
B roll footage used to illustrate reports during news broadcast
bulletin report of news development important enough to warrant interruption of regular programming
color commentary interpretation and background during sports play-by-play
commentary editorial analysis and interpretation of news
correspondent person supplying news and broadcasting from remote location
electronic news gathering ENG; use of video equipment instead of film to expedite news gathering and eliminate delays in processing
ENG electronic news gathering
equal access broadcasters' desire for equality with newspapers in access to courtrooms and other news sources
equal time legal requirement that stations grant equal airtime to qualified political candidates and others with opposing viewpoints
eyewitness news news format stressing casual responses by news anchors
flash brief news report on something extraordinary that has just occurred; bulletin
follow-up news story providing additional or new information on previously broadcast item
hard news serious events of immediate, general interest and value
hold for release agree not to air news story until specified date
human-interest story report designed to engage attention and sympathy of audience members who identify readily with people and situations described
kicker cheery final story on newscast
kill (*vb*) decide not to air story
lead newscast's opening and most important or attention-grabbing story
lead-in introduction to news story
local news news broadcast based at local station, covering regional news and human-interest stories
media event public appearance or event staged deliberately to gain attention from media
national news news of national and international significance broadcast by network from central studio
newscast regularly scheduled news broadcast
nonevent media-induced or -conceived news story
panel show news show in which several journalists interview knowledgeable person on given issue
parachute journalism practice in which reporter arrives on location after producer has prepared story, tapes segment for on-screen appearance, and departs immediately
play-by-play live description of sporting event
press conference appearance of person, esp. government official, for questioning by group of reporters
public affairs program news or news analysis

broadcast, esp. dealing with timely subjects related to general public welfare
recap news summary, esp. at end of broadcast
release copy advance copy or announcement of impending news story
rip and read tear news item from wire service teletypewriter and broadcast it immediately
segment relatively brief but complete treatment of specific news story, comprising portion of news broadcast
sidebar brief item dealing with secondary aspect of news story
slant (*vb*) distort information to express a particular bias or viewpoint
soft news local human-interest stories of passing interest
spin control *Slang.* attempt to give bias to coverage of political candidate, esp. by casting potentially damaging information in a more favorable light
straight news serious stories relating esp. to politics, business, and international affairs
tag newscaster's final on-screen words added to taped news story
update news story rewritten to include latest developments
wrap-up summary of day's news, esp. in final few minutes of broadcast

Television Technology

airwaves pathways of broadcast frequencies
antenna metallic rod or wire for receiving radio or television waves, often placed on top of building; aerial
audio electronically reproduced sound
band group of communication frequencies, such as VHF or UHF
beam stream of radio waves sent continuously in one direction
big-screen television television with screen over 23 inches across
blip interruption of sound reception; spot of light on the screen
cable alternate way of transmitting television signals by cable lines rather than through air, requiring hookup to cable for reception
cathode-ray tube CRT; electronic tube used as television screen
CC (*adj*) closed-captioned
channel band of broadcasting frequencies used by station
character generator small computer producing letters and graphic images directly on screen, without use of camera
closed-captioned (*adj*) CC; designating programs having subtitles for hearing-impaired viewers, with captions appearing only on specially equipped television sets
closed circuit broadcasting signal sent only to televisions connected by cable to transmitter
coaxial cable electronic cable used to transmit television signals to cable subscribers
contrast degree of difference between black and white or colors of picture
CRT cathode-ray tube
cue card large card with dialogue held near camera to prompt performers
definition clearness with which televised images are reproduced
feed program transmitted by network to affiliates for broadcast, usu. sent out before airtime; recording of event or live report transmitted to studio
frequency number of oscillations of wave per second
ghost secondary image that repeats main picture image, caused by signal interference
HDTV high-definition television
headphones device worn over head with tiny speakers positioned over ears to receive audio transmission
headset device with headphones and attached microphone
high-definition television HDTV; receiver with high number of scanning lines per frame, producing extremely sharp image and resolution
horizontal hold control that regulates back-and-forth image
interference static or unwanted signals that distort image or audio
lapel mike tiny microphone attached to clothing on chest; lavaliere microphone
lavaliere microphone small microphone clipped to person's clothing or placed around neck; lapel mike
line recording recording both picture and sound at the same time
minicam small, portable videotape camera
mobile unit truck equipped with videotape recording and transmission equipment for on-the-spot coverage of events
monitor television set with no audio output, used on stage to show performers and technicians what is being shot and/or broadcast
off-camera (*adj*) designating activity unseen by viewers
on the air designation that studio is in taping or broadcast mode
outtake section of tape not used on broadcast
pickup reception of network transmissions by individual station or affiliate
picture tube electronic device that transforms broadcast signals into patterns of light on screen; cathode-ray tube
rabbit ears dipole receiving antenna on television set
receiver television set with cathode-ray tube
reception process by which radio or television waves are transformed into images on screen; clarity of these images
relay links devices activated by signal and operating other devices that connect elements in transmission path
remote control device for tuning television set from short distance away
resolution measurement of picture sharpness

satellite artificial station orbiting Earth and relaying television signals from one point on Earth to another
satellite dish large, shallow hemisphere used to receive transmissions relayed by satellite
scramble (*vb*) encode audio or visual signal so that only certain subscribers can receive it
small screen television in general, as distinguished from cinema, which is big screen
snow fluctuating white spots that partially obscure image on screen due to weak signal
splice (*vb*) join together two pieces of film or tape
steadycam portable video or film camera attached to operator by harness and frame to eliminate wavering of tracked image
telecine device that converts film or slides into television signal
telecommunications electromagnetic transmission and reception of data to produce sound and images
teletext broadcast information services, esp. for news, stock market, and consumer goods; videotext
television TV; electronic system for transmitting images and sound over wires or through space by conversion of light and sound into electrical waves and reconversion at receiving set into visible light projected by CRT and audible sound; receiving set in such a system
test pattern fixed picture, often color bars, broadcast by station to assist viewers in adjusting reception
transmitter tower sending wave transmissions from source to viewers
UHF ultra high frequency; frequency range between 300 and 3000 megahertz
VCR videocassette recorder; device that plays and records cartridge tapes
vertical hold control of up-and-down image
VHF very high frequency; frequency range between 30 and 300 kilohertz
video television production in general, outside major commercial and subscription systems; film process used in television production
videodisk flat disk storing and playing back recorded image and sound
videotape (*vb*) record visual images and sound as electronic impulses on magnetic tape for television broadcasting; (*n*) magnetic tape used for such recordings
videotext teletext

Radio Programming

all-news radio format airing news programs only
all-talk talk radio
alternative radio avant-garde, noncommercial programming
AOR radio format emphasizing album-oriented rock music
call in show in which listeners telephone host to discuss issues live on the air
call letters initials identifying radio station
countdown playing of top pop hits in reverse order up to number one
country-and-western station broadcasting country-and-western and bluegrass music
disc jockey DJ; radio announcer for music program
DJ disc jockey
drive time periods in morning or evening when commuters typically are in their cars and listening to radio broadcasts
easy listening programming consisting of relaxing, bland music; middle-of-the-road
Emergency Broadcast System radio frequencies reserved for use by government and police agencies in an emergency
format emphasis and content of broadcasting, such as all-news, country music, talk show, Top 40 call-in, AOR, or classical
middle-of-the-road MOR; easy listening
MOR middle-of-the-road
National Public Radio NPR; noncommercial, publicly funded, educational and cultural radio network
pirate radio unlicensed radio station
program director person responsible for establishing format and determining programming of station
radio drama dramatic show broadcast over radio
shock radio broadcasting format featuring ethnic jokes and other tasteless humor
sigalert traffic advisory warning broadcast
signature station identification, jingle, or slogan
talk radio broadcasting format featuring phone-in audience participation and guest interviews by radio personality; all-talk
top 40 programming format featuring current popular-music hits and issuing weekly list of forty most popular songs

Radios and Radio Technology

AM amplitude modulation broadcasting band
amplifier radio component that strengthens signal received
band group of broadcasting frequencies, such as AM or FM
beacon radio transmitter; signal transmitted by radio transmitter
boom box *Informal.* very large but portable radio/cassette player
bug *Informal.* hidden radio transmitter
CB Citizens Band
channel radio wave frequency of sufficient width for one- or two-way communication, used by broadcasting station
Citizens Band CB; short-range, two-way radio frequency
clear channel strong signal on frequency with no interference; frequency cleared for long-distance transmission
clock radio alarm clock that turns on radio at designated hour
crystal radio nonelectric receiver sensitive to radio waves

descrambler device that makes radio signals intelligible by systematically tuning receiver to transmitted frequencies
FM frequency modulation broadcasting band
frequency number of oscillations of wave per second
ham amateur two-way radio operator
hertz measurement of frequency in vibrations per second
hi-fi high fidelity
high fidelity radio with excellent sound reproduction; hi-fi
kilohertz one thousand hertz
link radio relay station serving as connection in communications system
megahertz one million hertz
radio conversion of sound signals into electromagnetic waves and transmission of these waves through space to receiving set, which then converts them back into sound; such a receiving set
radiophone equipment, such as a walky-talky or CB, for carrying on two-way communication by radio waves
radiotelegraphy transmission of messages by radio waves rather than through wires or cables
radio wave electromagnetic wave moving at radio frequency, between 10 kilohertz and one million megahertz
receiver device for transforming radio waves into sound
shortwave radio radio that transmits or receives radio waves shorter than used in AM broadcasting, corresponding to frequencies over 1600 kilohertz
signal power of sound transmitted by station
speaker device for changing electrical signals into sound waves
stereophonic (*adj*) designating transmission of FM radio signals using two channels
tower very tall structure transmitting station's programs as radio waves
transceiver combination radio transmitter and receiver
transistor tiny electronic device that controls flow of electricity in radio equipment
transmitter radio wave broadcasting device
tuner device sensitive to different radio wave frequencies, which permits selection of specific radio station by receiver

Chapter Sixteen
Applied Arts

ARCHITECTURE

Schools and Styles
Classical Elements and Design
Building Construction and Design

Schools and Styles

architecture art and science of designing and building habitable structures, esp. with aesthetically pleasing, coherent forms
art deco architectural style using stylized, repetitive geometric designs, esp. zigzags and lozenges, with emphasis on facades in tile and relief (early 20th c.)
art nouveau architectural style using decorative, biomorphic forms with curved, irregular lines (late 19th c.)
baroque architectural style using strong, dramatic design with imaginative use of theatrical, chiaroscuro effects (Europe, 17th-18th c.)
Bauhaus architectural school characterized by clean geometry and functionalism (Germany, 1920's)
Byzantine synthesis of Oriental and Occidental architectural styles, marked by domes and minarets (eastern Europe, 4th-13th c.)
classical (*adj*) of the architectural style of ancient Hellenic Greece and imperial Rome, emphasizing columniation
Colonial variation of Georgian architectural style prevalent in colonial America (18th c.)
Directoire (*adj*) noting or pertaining to a style of architecture and decoration in France similar to Regency style in Britain (late 18th c.)
Egyptian (*adj*) of an architectural style prevalent from the third millennium B.C. through the Roman era, characterized by the use of massive, pillared stonework with emphasis on religious monuments
Egyptian Revival architectural style using monolithic, columnar forms, flat roofs, and ancient Egyptian decorative motifs (19th-early 20th c.)
Georgian (*adj*) of a style incorporating classical, Renaissance, and baroque elements of architecture, emphasizing formal, symmetrical design (U.S. and Britain, 18th c.)
Gothic architectural style with emphasis on verticality and intricate, decorative, pointed arches (Europe, 12th-16th c.)
Gothic Revival architectural style marked by a resurgence of Gothic verticality and sharply pitched roof forms (U.S. and Britain, late 18th-19th c.)
Greek Revival architectural style marked by a resurgence of classical Greek and Roman forms, with columns supporting pedimented roofs (U.S. and Britain, early 19th c.)
Hellenic (*adj*) of a monumental style of religious architecture, characterized by columnar supports of pediment-roofed temples (Greece, 8th-4th c. B.C.)
Hellenistic (*adj*) of a classical style that influenced imperial Roman architecture (Greece, 4th-2nd c. B.C.)
International Style modern architectural style and construction, emphasizing horizontal bands of windows, undecorated glass, curtain-wall facades, and skyscrapers (20th c.)
Moorish (*adj*) of an architectural style emphasizing overall decoration, carving, arabesque design, and intricate stuccowork (Spain, 11th-14th c.)
neoclassical (*adj*) marked by a return to classical architecture in response to romantic themes (Europe, 18th-19th c.)
Norman (*adj*) of an architectural style using massive stonework and rounded arches (Britain, 11th c.)
Palladian (*adj*) of an architectural style patterned after northern Italian Renaissance (Britain, 18th c.)
postmodern (*adj*) of an architectural style with eclectic, sometimes whimsical use of a variety of styles, esp. classical elements, often large-scale for corporate or institutional use (late 20th c.)
Queen Anne (*adj*) of a style of architecture and furnishing characterized by simplicity and restraint, esp. using red brick (Britain, 18th c.)
Regency (*adj*) of a style of architecture, furnishing, and decoration characterized by simple lines and increasing use of Greco-Roman forms (Britain, early 19th c.)
Renaissance resurgence and reinterpretation of classic forms of architecture with focus on symmetry, balance, and elegance (Europe, 15th-16th c.)
rococo architectural style using fanciful, carved spatial forms and excessively elaborate ornamentation (Europe, 18th c.)
Romanesque architectural style using massive forms and geometrical patterns (Europe, 11th-12th c.)
Tudor (*adj*) characteristic of a transitional style between Gothic and Palladian, with emphasis on privacy and interior design (Britain, 16th c.)
Victorian (*adj*) characteristic of a highly decorative architectural style with Gothic elements (U.S. and Britain, late 19th c.)

Classical Elements and Design

abacus flat slab forming uppermost member of capital of column
acanthus decorative scrolled leaf form
apse vaulted, semidomed end of aisle or building
arabesque abstract, curled, or plantlike decorative forms
arcade series of arches bounded by columns
arch curved structural member spanning an opening and serving as support, esp. of stone blocks: barrel, basket-handle, bell, blunt, cinquefoil, cusped, elliptical, equal, flat, horseshoe, inflected, keel, lancet, ogee, parabolic, pointed, primitive, rampant, relieving, round, rowlock, scalloped, segmental, shouldered, trefoil, Tudor
architrave beam across tops of columns, forming base of the entablature
atrium open courtyard bordered by walkways

attic part of the entablature above cornice that hides the roof
barrel vault continuous, semicircular, arched vault
base bottom of column taken as architectural unit, consisting of torus, scotia, plinth, and fillets
basilica church with aisles and elevated nave
bas-relief sculptured relief on wall or pediment
bay area between columns; deeply recessed window
buttress masonry supporting arch or vault
campanile freestanding bell tower
canopy decorative, rooflike covering over altar, tomb, or doorway
cantilever extension of beam, floor, or roof beyond its vertical support
capital decorative cap atop column, supporting entablature
capstone keystone of arch
caryatid column sculpted in form of standing female figure
cloister courtyard bounded by walkways
colonnade series of columns at regular intervals
column round, vertical, supporting pillar with pedestal, shaft, and capital: Byzantine, Composite, Corinthian, Doric, Gothic, Ionic, Moorish, Romanesque, Tuscan
Composite column Roman order combining Corinthian acanthus with Ionic volutes
corbel short, decorative cantilever projecting from wall
Corinthian column late-style column having high base, slender, fluted shaft with fillets, ornate capital, and acanthus
cornice projecting top level of building or entablature
crown uppermost part of column
cupola small, rounded structure atop roof
cusp pointed projection at intersection of two arcs or foils
Doric column earliest known style of column, undecorated, without base, and having short, fluted shaft
engaged column column attached to wall, not freestanding
entablature horizontal element above columns, including architrave, frieze, and cornice
entasis slightly convex curve in column, giving it the appearance of perfect verticality
facade exterior face of building
filigree ornamental work of delicate, intricate design
finial ornament atop spire or gable
fluting vertical grooves in column shaft
flying buttress arch or arch segment projecting from wall and transmitting the thrust of a roof or vault outward and downward to a solid buttress or pier
frieze horizontal band in entablature between architrave and cornice, usu. ornamented
gable triangular area of wall at end of pitched roof
gargoyle waterspout in form of elaborately carved creature projecting from gutter
Ionic column middle period column with an elegant base, tall, slender, fluted shaft, and a volute or spiral capital
keystone center stone of arch
lintel horizontal beam over door or window
loggia gallery or balcony open on at least one side
masonry construction with stones or bricks
metope Doric frieze panel between triglyphs
minaret tall tower attached to mosque
molding decorative recessed or contoured strip used for finishing, usu. at juncture of wall and ceiling: beak, cavetto, congé, cyma recta, cyma reversa, echinus, facia, fillet, ovolo, plate rail, quarter round, reeding, scotia, torus
narthex porch at church main entrance of church
nave main axis of church or cathedral
niche recessed area in wall
order one of the classical styles of base, column, and entablature: Corinthian, Doric, or Ionic
pantheon classic domed temple form in ancient Greece and Rome
parquetry geometrically patterned, inlaid wood, esp. for floors
pedestal support at foot of column
pediment triangular shape at end of pitched roof
peristyle colonnaded courtyard behind entrance
pilaster flat, columnar form against wall
pillar upright support column or shaft
plinth projecting block at base of building or column
portico covered entryway or porch with columns
pylon monumental temple gateway (ancient Egypt)
quoin corner of building; stone forming building corner
relief moldings and ornamentation that stand out from a surface
sarcophagus ornamental stone coffin
soffit undersurface of arch
spandrel wall area above curved sides of arch
spire tall, tapering Gothic tower
steeple tall, narrow, conical tower
stereobate foundation or base upon which building, esp. classical temple, is erected
stupa domed, Buddhist shrine
telamon male figure, similar to caryatid, used as column or pilaster
tholos circular building (ancient Greece)
transept transverse arms of cross-shaped church, usu. perpendicular to nave
triglyph grooved projecting panels in Doric frieze
triumphal arch monumental gateway
tumulus earth or stone mound over grave
Tuscan column Roman order of column, similar to Doric with fluted shaft
vault arched, domed, usu. masonry ceiling or roof: barrel, dome, fan, groin, ribbed
ziggurat mound built with stepped sides

Building Construction and Design

attic space between ceiling joists and roof rafters
balloon frame one-piece studs extending from foundation to roof of two-story structure

baseboard wooden finish strip where interior wall meets floor
bearing wall wall that supports a vertical load, esp. the floors and walls above; load-bearing wall
blocking placement of wooden framing members between other members to add strength and provide nailing surface
blueprint detailed architectural design diagram
board measure system for measuring lumber, in which each board foot is equal to one inch by twelve inches by twelve inches
breast wall retaining wall
building codes ordinances regulating construction standards
casement window window hinged on one side, swinging outward
contractor builder responsible for implementing architectural designs and drawings, purchasing materials, and hiring labor
crawlspace area between floor joists and earth beneath building
curtain wall exterior wall that protects an interior wall from weather, but bears no structural load
deflection vertical distance that beam moves under load stress
double glazing door or window made of two panes of glass sealed together with a dead air space between them to provide insulation
double-hung window window with two sashes that move vertically
dry wall interior wall composed of gypsum board panels
elevation building face; front drawing of structure projected geometrically on vertical plane parallel to one of its sides
ell wing of building at right angle to main structure
excavation pit dug in earth for foundation
fascia vertical boards at end of rafter forming face of cornice and attached to overhanging outer edge of roof
fixture plumbing or electrical equipment
floor plan drawing that shows the top view of one floor of a house
foundation masonry or concrete substructure of building beneath first-floor joists
grade elevation above sea level of building site; slope of ground for building site
half-timbered (*adj*) relating to exterior walls with exposed, heavy, wooden members separated by masonry
interior trim molding, casing, and bargeboard used to finish walls, doors, or windows
load-bearing wall bearing wall
mechanical drawing stylized, precise drawing of plans and blueprints done with aid of rulers, scales, and compasses; drafting
modular unit factory-built finished section of building, room-size or larger, for modular construction
monolithic (*adj*) constructed of concrete, with all members cast at the same time as a single unit
nonbearing wall wall that bears only its own weight
orientation positioning of building with regard to sun, wind, or view
platform frame building in which each story is built on the story below but framed independently
prefabricated (*adj*) assembled into complete, standardized, structural units at factory
retaining wall wall built to resist lateral pressure, esp. to hold back soil; breast wall
scale use of proportional measurements in drawings
setback zoning regulation that limits how near to a street a building can be
specifications record of design and construction details not shown on drawings
subfloor floor material nailed directly to floor joists and covered by finished wood or carpet
sump pit in basement that collects water
water table level of underground water beneath structure
weather stripping metal or fabric strips placed at edges of doors and windows to reduce heat loss
zoning (*adj*) of or pertaining to ordinances regulating type, size, and uses of buildings which may be constructed in specific area

GRAPHIC DESIGN AND PRINTING

Graphic Design
Graphic Arts
Printing and Typefaces

Graphic Design

acetate flexible plastic film used to protect artwork
airbrush handheld tool for spraying paint and touching up artwork
artwork any graphic image prepared for reproduction
asymmetry dynamic compositional principle that states that design not be identical on both sides of central line
bleed extension of image up to or beyond edge of page
burnishing transfer of color overlay or dry transfer letters by rubbing with hard, smooth edge
calendered paper paper glazed and pressed to glossy finish
calligraphy beautiful, stylized, highly decorative handwriting, often with many flourishes
camera lucida prismatic device used to project image for tracing; lucie
camera-ready (*adj*) designating project that is ready to be photographed for reproduction
caricature exaggerated drawing, esp. of human subject, portraying humorous or grotesque qualities
cartoon preliminary drawing; humorous sketch or drawing, as in comic strip
chart any organizational or quantitative diagram containing information and revealing relation-

ships in visual arrangement of elements
collage compositional technique using various materials not normally associated with one another
color overlay transparent sheet of color film transferred by burnishing
color separation composite negative used to reproduce separate plates or layers for primary colors and black
comp comprehensive; detailed mock-up of a layout for presentation purposes
compass instrument for drawing arcs and circles
comprehensive comp
crop (*vb*) trim edges of illustration or photograph
crop marks indicators used to establish parameters of area to be reproduced
desktop publishing creation and printing of graphic presentations and designs using a computer
diagram graphic visualization of abstract data designed to reveal relationships
die steel rule with edge for cutting out paper or cardboard shapes very precisely; metal stamp for impressing or embossing a design
drafting mechanical drawing
drop cap bold or stylized initial letter of chapter or paragraph set into body of text
dry-transfer letters sheet imprinted with letters of alphabet in various styles for transfer to surface by rubbing
dummy prototype layout of assembled graphic work
duotone reproduction of image in two colors, one for darker shade with greater detail, one for lighter flat tint
electrostatic printing process such as xerography in which images are produced by attraction between electrostatic charge and particles of toner
emboss (*vb*) raise printed design in relief by pressure of plate on which image is engraved below surface
felt-tip pen pen with absorbent cloth nib, filled with ink that dries instantly
final art camera-ready version of project
fixative aerosol varnish
foundry establishment in which typefaces originate through casting or technical encryption prior to distribution
four-color process reproduction of a wide range of colors by printing superimposed sequence of cyan, magenta, yellow, and black in varying intensities
French curve drafting instrument for tracing curved lines
graphic design art, discipline, and profession of visual communication that combines images, words, and ideas to purposefully convey information to an audience, esp. to produce specific effect or achieve desired goal
hairline thinnest of printing rules
halftone simulation of solid or continuous tone image by breaking it into pattern of dots of varying sizes
ichnography drawing with compass and rule
illumination detailed hand-decoration of manuscript books
ink viscous fluid or powdered substance used for writing, printing, and graphic reproductions
justification spacing of letters and words within text lines so that all full lines in type column have even margins on both right and left sides
kerning fine adjustment of spacing between letter forms to attain uniform appearance
layout design of text and images for reproduction
lead thin strip of graphite used as marking part of pencil
light box display unit for viewing color transparency, consisting of frosted glass with diffuse light from incandescent bulb beneath it
line art high-contrast rendering for reproduction without screening, consisting of lines or areas of solid black and solid white
logo distinctive design, emblem, and trademark of product or organization; logotype
logotype logo, esp. one made of letter forms
loupe small, freestanding magnifying lens used to inspect transparent and reflective surfaces
lucie camera lucida
markup instructions for typesetting or color treatment
mat stiff cardboard frame for photo or artwork
mat knife blade on handle for cutting paper or art boards
mechanical artwork and type pasted into position on boards, ready for photo-transfer to printing plate or silkscreen; paste-up
mechanical drawing precise drawing done with aid of rulers, scales, and compasses; drafting
mechanical pencil tube holding thin pencil lead
moiré interference pattern of dots arising from overlaying regular patterns while printing four-color process
montage image made of composite graphic elements that are overlaid and superimposed
pantograph device for enlarging or reducing drawing size
parallel rule hinged straightedges for drawing parallel lines at varying widths
paste-up mechanical
pixel picture element; single dot, or smallest element in visual display; square picture unit that is basis of computer graphics
positive film or paper print made from photographic negative; stat
printing reproduction of image using inked surface to make copies: intaglio, lithography, offset, planography, relief
proof printing impression made for examination, correction, or approval
protractor instrument for measuring and drawing exact angles
repro image or type proof ready for paste-up
reproduction exact copy of visual image
retouch (*vb*) change details of negative or photographic print with pencil, brush, airbrush, or computer
screen creation of tonal value in artwork by regu-

lar pattern, usu. measured as dots per square inch
set square flat, triangular tool used to ensure correct alignment of paste-up
silhouette (*vb*) outline an image so that it is separated from its background; close crop
specifications specs
specs *Informal.* complete description of job, esp. for printing; specifications
stencil waxed cardboard or thin metal or plastic with letters or designs cut out, so that ink may be applied to surface through cut-out area
stipple gradation of light and shade produced by separate touches of small points, larger dots, and longer strokes
stock specified quality or kind of paper for printing
straightedge blade guide for drawing or cutting very straight lines
surprint overprinting of one image on top of another
symmetry classical principle that states that design be identical on both sides of center line
template drawing guide for shapes, symbols, or lettering
tracing paper thin, semitransparent paper laid over earlier artwork to compare or relate parts of design
transparency image recorded on color film, viewed by projection of light shining through it, as on light box
T square drawing guide for parallel and perpendicular lines
vellum translucent paper used for tracing; thin, treated calfskin used for writing or printing
wax (*vb*) apply heated beeswax as adhesive to repro for paste-up
white space empty space or white area that gives contrast to layout
xerography electrostatic printing technique in which areas on paper are sensitized with static electrical charge so that they attract oppositely charged dry-ink particles from toner, which are then fused onto the copy paper

Graphic Arts

block print design printed by means of one or more wood or metal blocks
brayer small rubber roller for inking printing blocks or plates by hand, usu. for making proofs
cartouche oval or rounded decorative border around frame
cerography process of engraving design or text by incision into wax surface
chalcography art of copper engraving
chamois soft leather cloth used to blend charcoal lines
crayon powdered pigment in waxy binder molded into drawing stick
decal design or picture printed on special paper for transfer to another surface
drypoint engraving technique using a sharply scratched, inked copperplate
enchase (*vb*) decorate with inlay, embossing, or engraving
engraving graphic reproduction technique in which lines are cut into a metal or wooden surface, which is then inked and printed; design so produced
etching process of making graphic design on a metal plate or glass by corrosive action of acid instead of with a pointed tool as in engraving; design so produced; impression made from such an etched plate
fitch lettering brush, made of bristle, with straight chiseled edges
frottage technique of obtaining textural effects or images by rubbing pigment on paper stretched over an irregular surface
glyptography art and process of engraving on gems
graphic arts arts and techniques by which copies of an original are printed, as from blocks or plates; printmaking
gravure intaglio process of photomechanical printing
hachure series of parallel lines for shading or modeling; hatching
hyalography technique of etching or engraving on glass
inlay design or decoration made by inserting or applying fine materials in surface of object
intaglio engraving process in which ink-retaining lines are cut into metal surface
lithography printing and reproduction process using stone slab marked with greasy ink; similar process using another substance, such as aluminum or zinc
mezzotint engraving process using coarse, random-dot screen burred by chisel on a metal plate, which is then inked and printed
monotype single print made from engraving process
overlay decoration or layer of some material applied onto another surface
pastel chalk or crayon stick of ground pigment and nonoily binder
photogravure process by which intaglio engraving is formed on metal plate, from which ink reproductions are made
printmaking art and technique of making prints, esp. by engraving, etching, drypoint, woodcut, or serigraphy
rag paper high-quality paper made from cotton and linen mixed with wood pulp
repoussé relief design on paper
resist protective layer applied to parts of printing plate
restrike new print made from old engraving, woodcut, or lithographic stone
serigraphy printing technique using silkscreen process
silkscreen printing technique that uses inked silk cloth, mounted on frame, to which stencil film is affixed; serigraphy
stump rolled chamois for blending chalk or pencil on paper
sumi *Japanese.* black ink used by calligraphers

tooth abrasive quality of paper that helps it to hold pigment, charcoal, or chalk
woodblock image carved into surface of wood, then inked and printed
woodcut technique of printmaking from woodblock; print or impression formed this way
zincography process of producing printing surface using zinc plate etched by acid

Printing and Typefaces

ascender part of lowercase letter that rises above x-height, as in b, d, f, or h
beard sloping part of type that connects face with shoulder of body
bleed (*vb*) print so that material runs off edge of page after trimming
blueline (*vb*) check for and mark typos on first run of laid-out page with blue pencil; (*n*) proof of final negatives made on light-sensitive paper, used for checking specifications before making plates
boldface thick, heavy typeface, used for emphasis
bond paper superior quality paper, usu. with high cotton fiber content
card out (*vb*) add extra space between lines of text to fill out column or page exactly
cold type type set by any method other than casting of molten lead, esp. handset composition
composition typesetting
computer typesetting high-speed phototypesetting, eliminating need for mechanical setting of type
condensed (*adj*) designating type that is narrow and elongate in proportion to its height
cursive style of typeface simulating handwriting
descender part of lowercase letter that goes below main body of letter, as in g, j, p, or y
dingbat typographic symbol or ornament such as fist, arrow, or heart
dummy prototype layout that shows length and placement of items indicated for sizing
elite letter size measuring twelve characters per inch, widely used in typewriters
em unit of measure of column width in terms of type size
en unit of measure equal to one half the width of an em
engraving graphic reproduction technique in which lines are cut into a hard surface such as metal or stone, which is then inked and printed
expanded (*adj*) designating type that is wider in proportion to its height, having a flattened, oblong appearance
f and g's folded and gathered, unbound printed sheets in proper sequence for binding
font full assortment of letters and symbols in one size and family of type
four-color process reproduction of range of colors by printing a superimposed sequence of cyan, magenta, black, and yellow in varying intensities
galley sheets of final type proofs; with hot type, shallow tray holding typeset pages
gatefold spread that opens from center to reveal additional pages
grain direction of long fibers in sheet of paper
graphics photographs or illustrations to be printed
gravure process of intaglio printing, in which plate is inked only beneath its surface
hot metal type cast from molten lead; hot type
hot type hot metal
impression all copies of publication printed in one operation
italics scriptlike style of letters or type
kern portion of typeface projecting beyond body or shank; (*vb*) adjust space between specified letter pairs for printing
laser printing high-speed computer printing technique using laser to form dot-matrix patterns and electrostatic process to fuse metallic particles to paper
leading insertion of thin strips of type metal for spacing between lines of text; space so created
letterpress method of printing from raised type
ligature character or type combining two or more letters, such as æ
majuscule uppercase letter
mimeograph printing machine using waxed stencil wrapped around rotating, ink-fed drum, past which sheets of paper are fed; mimeo
minuscule lowercase letter
newsprint cheaply produced, disposable wood pulp paper, used chiefly for printing newspapers
offset lithography printing process in which stone or metal or paper plate makes inked impression on a rubber blanket, that in turn transfers it to the paper being printed, instead of taking direct impression of plate on paper; photo-offset
offset printing printing method in which image is photographically engraved on metal sheet and then offset onto paper
orphan poor line break that dangles first line of new paragraph at end of column or bottom of page
overrun copies in excess of specified pressrun
pallet typeholder
photocomposition method of composition in which type is set photographically
photoengraving reproduction technique using light-sensitive, emulsion-coated metal plates
photo-offset offset lithography
phototypography any of various techniques for making printing surfaces by light or photography
pica letter size measuring ten characters per inch; unit of measure equal to twelve points or 1/6 of an inch
plate cast to be printed from, made from mold of set type or photo-offset negative
point standard unit of type measurement, approximately equal to 1/72 of an inch
press printing press
pressrun operation of printing press for specific job; number of copies so printed
printer's mark individual printer's identifying mark, usu. on copyright page
printing technique, process, and business of reproducing written or graphic material, esp. by

impression from movable types or plates
printing press any of various machines for printing in mass form from inked type, plates, or rollers; press
proof sheet inked page made from galley or plate, used to check for errors before printing
reprography duplication of documents or designs by any process using light rays and photography, such as offset printing or xerography
roman (*adj*) designating common, upright style of typeface
rotary press printing press with plates mounted on cylinders that pass over paper fed from continuous roll
rotogravure intaglio printing process using rotary presses
sans serif style of letters or type without serifs, or typefaces without serifs, such as Helvetica and Franklin Gothic
score (*vb*) make furrows in paper to facilitate folding
serif fine cross-stroke that terminates main stroke at top and bottom of letters; style of typefaces having serifs, such as Bodoni, Garamond, and Times Roman
signature letter or symbol placed at foot of first page of every sheet to guide binder in folding and gathering; printed sheet folded to page size for binding
slug line of type cast in single piece by Linotype machine
small capitals capital letters that are smaller than standard size for that font, designed to align visually with ordinary type line
swash extending ornamental flourish on letters of certain fonts of italic or cursive type
thermography technique for imitating embossed appearance by dusting printed areas with powder that adheres to wet ink, then fusing ink and powder to paper by heat
toner cartridge containing dry ink particles, used in xerography and laser printing
type piece of metal with raised letter or symbol in reverse on one end and used collectively, inked, and pressed against paper to leave impressions
typeface any of various distinctive styles of letters to be reproduced by printing or photography; alphabet designed with specific attributes that unify the character set
typefaces common text and display faces include:
Baskerville, Bembo, Bodoni
Caledonia, Caslon, Century, Cheltenham, Clarendon
Electra, English
Fraktur, Franklin Gothic, Futura
Garamond, Goudy
Helvetica
Janson
Melior
Old English, Optima
Palatino, Plantin
Renaissance
Times Roman
Univers
type family grouping of printing types with common design but different weights and styles, such as roman, italic, bold, condensed, or expanded
typesetting arrangement of type for printing, usu. by computer or machine; composition
typography art and process of setting and arranging type for printing; creation of typefaces
underlay sheets of paper placed under type to bring it to required height for printing
watermark paper mark indicating maker or trademark of stock
web press printing press using continuous roll of paper
widow poor line break in which a single word or short line ends a paragraph; last line of paragraph when it is carried over to next column or page

PHOTOGRAPHY

Types of Photography

aerial photography pictures taken from airplane or satellite
animation graphic images sequenced for motion effect
black and white pictures using monochrome black-and-white film, without color
cinematography motion-picture photography
daguerreotype silver-plate photography, now obsolete
electron micrography image seen and photographed through electron microscope
ferrotype iron-plate photography, now obsolete; tintype
holography three-dimensional photography, using split laser beam
infrared photography exposures using infrared light, often at night
laser photography holography and other photography using lightwave amplification by stimulated emission of radiation
photocopy photographic reproduction of graphic material or document
photogram silhouette produced by direct exposure of paper, without lens or negative
photography reproduction of images of objects on sensitized film by exposure to light and chemical processing
photojournalism form of journalism in which pictures associated with news events, specific editorial content, or documentary features dominate the written material
portraiture photographs of posed individuals, done in selected environment or studio
print photography fashion and commercial

photography for publications
product photography stylized, precise photographs of an object for advertising
radiography x-ray photography
reportage photojournalism, esp. photo essays based on research or detailed coverage of documented observation
still photography still shots taken on the set of a movie or television show, or a single frame of film used like a still shot; unit photography
stroboscopic photography photography of moving subjects, using pulsing light source to apparently freeze movements
tintype ferrotype
unit photography still photography
xerography photocopying directly onto paper

Cameras

aerial-reconnaissance camera long-range camera designed for military and defense use
animation camera camera designed to expose one frame at a time, used for animated sequences
autofocus camera camera that automatically sets aperture and shutter speed for operator, sometimes also equipped with automatic flash
box camera simple, low-cost camera
flash camera using high-powered burst of illumination
folding camera camera in which bellows collapses into fold when camera is not in use
minicam portable, handheld video camera
panoramic camera camera equipped with motor that swivels it to take panoramic view in one exposure on 35 mm negative
pinhole camera rudimentary camera having tiny aperture and no lens
portrait camera camera fitted with portrait lens
single-lens reflex camera camera in which image appears on ground-glass viewer after being reflected by mirror or passing through prism or semitransparent glass
stop-action camera that stops at intervals to allow for manipulation of photographed subject
35 mm camera any camera that uses standard 35 mm film
twin-lens reflex camera camera with two lenses in single focusing mount, using 2 1/4-inch format
video camera camera for electronically processed videotape that requires no developing

Lenses

achromatic lens finely made, expensive lens with no chromatic aberration
anamorphic lens lens for wide screen effects
fisheye lens short focal-length, wide-angle lens of over 180 degrees, used to create distorted image
fixed-focus lens usu. wide-angle lens with nonvariable focus
long-focus lens lens with narrow angle of view for greater magnification
normal lens lens with angle of view approximately equal to human vision, or 50 to 55 degrees
portrait lens moderately soft-definition, medium-long focal- length lens
process lens lens with precise color-separation capacity for reproduction and engraving work
standard lens normal lens usu. provided with camera at time of purchase, such as 50 mm lens with 35 mm camera
telephoto lens lens that reduces depth of field for distant objects: with 35 mm camera, telephotos are 80 mm, 105 mm, 135 mm, 180 mm, 200 mm, and 300 mm
wide-angle lens lens with wide field of view
zoom lens lens with focal length continuously variable to close in on small or distant objects or open up for wide view

Tools and Techniques

actinic light part of light spectrum that exposes photographic film and paper
aperture opening that controls amount of light admitted into camera through lens
camera lightproof box that records the image of an object viewed through the aperture of a lens onto light-sensitive film
circle of confusion area outside focal point that is not in focus
color separation separate negative containing portion of picture to be printed in one color
color transparency color positive on transparent film or glass, viewed by projected light
contact sheet print consisting of all frames of a developed roll of film on one sheet of paper, with prints the same size as actual negatives; proof sheet
coppertoning (*adj*) designating chemical additives that give warm brownish tinge to black-and-white photo
crop (*vb*) remove outer portion of print
darkroom lightproof processing laboratory for film and prints
definition clarity of detail, image sharpness
depth of field zone between focal point and unfocused area in which image is reasonably sharp
developer chemical solution producing images on exposed film or paper
diaphragm variable opening that allows light onto film in camera
dip and dunk method used in most color and some black-and-white film processing in which film is draped or dipped into chemical and rinsing baths
emulsion light-sensitive chemical coating on film and paper
exposure opening of shutter to allow light onto film, producing latent image; allowing light onto paper, producing print
exposure meter light meter
film light-sensitive chemical coating on flexible, plastic ribbon: black and white, color, microfilm, negative, nonchromatic, panchromatic, sheet, sound

filter glass or plastic gel or disc that screens certain light frequencies or colors from film exposure, also used in printing to alter contrast
finder camera indicator of focus or light
fixative chemical solution that makes negative or print exposure permanent by removing light-sensitive silver halides; fixer
flash any device providing high-powered bursts of illumination
focus point at which image is seen distinctly
format negative size, such as 35 mm
f-stop ratio of aperture opening to lens focal length
glossy shiny photographic print
grain size of silver particles in photographic film or paper, determines fineness of image
grease pencil marker for contact sheets, prints, and negatives
head shot close-up of face, esp. for actors or models; mug shot
leader black or transparent strip at end of film roll
lens curved-glass device that directs light rays from object onto camera plate to create image
light box container for color-corrected lights with one translucent side, used to view negatives or slides
light meter device that indicates light intensity; exposure meter
loupe small magnifying lens worn directly on eye to inspect photos
magazine unit loaded with film that can be removed from camera and replaced by another unit in order to change film in use in middle of roll
matte photographic print lacking gloss and luster
microfilm film containing miniaturized copy of graphic material, esp. newspapers for archives
negative exposed film image with light and shade tones opposite original image
overexposure film or photographic paper exposed to too much light or radiation
paparazzo freelance photographer who pursues celebrities for candid photos
parallax slight difference in fields of view between lens and viewfinder
plate glass or plastic sheet coated with light-sensitive emulsion to be exposed, developed, and printed as photograph
platinum process contact printing process that gives photograph a very beautiful, silver hue with long tonal ranges, used for long-lasting archival pictures for museums
positive film that records light and shade tones similar to original image
projection display of slides or transparencies on screen by shining light through them
proof sheet contact sheet
range finder focusing system that measures distance from camera to subject, sometimes coupled to camera lens so that both work together
resolution sharpness of photographic image; ability of camera to record distinct detail
semigloss (*adj*) designating most common surface of paper for color prints
sepia print or photograph made in a brownish hue that resembles sepia
shutter mechanical system that controls the length of time that light acts on sensitive emulsion by opening and closing aperture
slide developed, mounted color-film exposure
soft focus photograph with indistinct outlines of images
speed length of time shutter remains open to record image; sensitivity of film, expressed numerically as ASA rating
still photographic print of motion picture scene
stock house photo agency that sells photographer's stock photos to periodicals but does not make assignments
stop bath chemical solution that halts development of film or print
strobe electronic flash, balanced like blue daylight at 5200° K
tear sheet proof sheet of single or multiple images torn from printed matter
time exposure exposure of film for more than one-half second, usu. to take photograph without sufficient light
toner solution used to impart color or hue to silver photographic image, such as in cyanotype, gold tone, palladium, platinum, or selenium process
transparency film negative viewed by projection of light shining through it
tripod three-legged support used to hold camera steady
tungsten light orange, halogen-quartz light source at 3200° K, used esp. for motion pictures and portraits
umbrella color-corrected white, silver, or gold concave material used to bounce light onto subject
underexposure film exposed to insufficient light or radiation
viewfinder finder indicating focus
vignette photograph gradually lightened or darkened at its edges to leave no definite line at border

CRAFTS

Ceramics and Glassmaking
Other Crafts

Ceramics and Glassmaking

argil potter's clay
batch raw materials mixed in proper proportions for making glass
biscuit once-fired clay object, before glazing; bisque
bisque biscuit
blister glaze fault caused by impurities
bloat ceramic fault caused by impurities in clay
blow (*vb*) shape glass with steady current of air
blowpipe long metal tube used to gather and blow molten glass

bone china fine, naturally white china made with bone ash
celadon greenish, iron-containing glaze used in Oriental porcelain and stoneware
ceramics manufacture of works of art by firing of earthenware, porcelain, or brick at high temperature; works so produced
china delicate porcelain ceramic ware
clay potter's clay
crackle cracking of glaze after firing; craze
crackleware ceramic ware with finely cracked glaze
craze crackle
crockery earthenware
dead clay overly wet clay
delft glazed earthenware, usu. blue and white
Dresden china porcelain ware produced near Dresden, Germany, characterized by dainty design
earthenware coarse wares of kiln-baked clay; crockery
enamelware metalware or pottery covered with a glassy, opaque enamel surface
faience glazed earthenware for blocks or tiles
fettling knife sharp, pointed blade for finishing surfaces
fictile (*adj*) made of earth or clay by a potter
firing baking ceramic objects in hot oven
flux material used to lower melting point of glaze
frit flux and silica compound for strengthening porcelain
gaffer master glassblower who shapes glassware
glacure thin glaze for fine pottery
glass hard, transparent substance formed by melting silica and soda ash
glassblowing art and practice of shaping a mass of molten glass by blowing air into it through a tube
glassmaking art and technique of making glass, usu. by fusing silicates containing soda and lime
glaze glossy, vitreous, waterproof coating fused by heat to pottery; glost; (*vb*) apply such a surface to a ceramic
graffito technique of scratching design through glaze
greenware unfired ceramics
grog fired and crushed clay, added to fresh clay to reduce plasticity and shrinkage or give texture
hollowware deep ceramic dishes
impasto enamel or slip forming low-relief decoration on ceramic object
ironstone hard, white ceramic ware
jasperware fine, hard Wedgwood stoneware, stained in various colors by metallic oxides, with raised designs in white
kaolin pure, fine-grained white clay
kiln oven for firing pottery
lead glass glass containing lead oxide
luster metallic, iridescent sheen of glaze
majolica enameled, richly colored Italian pottery
Ming (*adj*) designating fine porcelains in brilliant colors made during Ming dynasty (China, 15th-17th c.)
mishima decoration of pottery by carving raw clay and filling the cuts with different-colored clay
nankeen Chinese porcelain having blue ornament on white background
overglaze additional glaze or color applied to an existing glaze
oxidation firing with oxygen-rich flame
paddling beating clay with stick to shape or decorate it
Parian (*adj*) denoting fine, unglazed, marblelike porcelain
porcelain hard, white, nonporous ceramic ware composed of kaolin, feldspar, and quartz
pot usu. round earthenware vessel of any size
potsherd broken pottery fragment
potter's clay finely textured, pliable earth that is free of impurities and suitable for making ceramic objects: argil, ball, china, fire clay, kaolin, petuntse, porcelain, refractory, terra cotta
potter's wheel revolving disk for throwing pottery forms, usu. foot-operated; wheel
pottery clay objects, either glazed or unglazed, shaped and hardened by heat: Albin ware, basalt, biscuit, blackware, bone china, china, crackleware, delft, Dresden china, earthenware, eggshell porcelain, faience, Imari ware, ironstone, Leeds pottery, Limoges, lusterware, majolica, Meissen, porcelain, saltglaze, Satsuma ware, Sèvres ware, Spode, spongeware, stoneware, terra cotta, Wedgwood
pressed glass molded glass shaped while molten by thrusting plunger into mold
prunt small lump of glass fused to larger glass piece
pug mill machine used to mix clay
punty iron rod used in handling hot glass in glassmaking
pyrometer device used to measure kiln temperature
reduction high-temperature firing
refractory (*adj*) having high heat resistance
relief decoration raised above surface of piece
resist decoration by treating selected areas so that they reject slip or glaze
sagger box of clay for packing ceramic ware in kiln
salt glaze process in which salt is vaporized in kiln to leave pebbly texture on piece
semiporcelain vitreous ceramic ware similar to but less hard and translucent than true porcelain
sieve sifter for removing clay lumps
slip watery, liquid clay for decorating and cementing biscuit
slip glaze glaze containing plastic clay, applied to raw earthenware
slurry watery clay
soft (*adj*) fired at low temperature
spun glass blown glass in which fine threads form surface texture
stoneware high-fired clay pottery, often glazed with salt
terra cotta hard, brown-red, unglazed earthenware
terre verte glazing clay
throw (*vb*) form pottery on wheel
underglaze color or decoration applied to piece before glazing
vitreous (*adj*) resembling glass in transparency, brittleness, hardness, or glossiness

vitrification fusing of clay body to state of glasslike imperviousness
ware ceramic objects
wash thin coating of glaze
wedge (*vb*) pound clay to remove air bubbles and improve workability
wheel potter's wheel
willowware china using decorative design of willow tree, bridge, and two birds (Britain, 18th c.)

Other Crafts

appliqué decoration, as a cutout design, sewn on to a piece of material
bargello needlepoint done in straight stitches, esp. in a zigzag pattern
basketry crafting of functional or decorative containers by interweaving strips of grass, reed, or other flexible material
batik technique of hand-dyeing patterns on fabric by using wax to resist dyes
beadworking decorative working or weaving of beads onto surface of clothing, accessories, or household objects; stringing of beads, as to produce a necklace
block printing printing with ink from engraved blocks of wood or other hard material
bookcraft making of books with particular attention to paper, printing techniques, folding of pages, and binding
calligraphy art of highly decorative handwriting, as with many flourishes
caning making of articles by interweaving slender, flexible stems of certain plants
carving making of articles by cutting, shaping, or chipping a hard substance, as a block of wood
casting process or craft of making forms in plaster or resin from a mold
ceramics craft of making fired earthenware, porcelain, or brick pottery; pottery
chenille work making of small figures from a wire core covered with soft chenille fabric
cloissoné enamelwork in which the enamel surface is set in hollows between wires soldered on metal
copper enameling process in which heat is used to fuse enamel powder colored with copper oxide to surface of articles; etui
craft any art, trade, or occupation requiring the skilled working of materials to form decorative or useful objects, often practiced as a recreational activity; handicraft
crewelwork decorative embroidery done with crewel yarn on cotton or linen, employing simple stitches worked in floral patterns
crocheting knitting with a hooked needle that draws thread or yarn through intertwined loops
cut-paper collage decoupage
damascening craft of making gold inlays
decalcomania process of transferring designs from specially prepared paper to wood, metal, or glass
decoupage technique of decorating a surface with paper cutouts; cut-paper collage
discharge printing bleaching designs onto dyed fabric
doll making making of small figures shaped like humans, usu. as toys, esp. out of paper, fabric, rag, or wood
dyeing process of tinting fabric or other absorbent material with colorants derived from plant extracts or synthetic chemicals
embossing decorating surfaces with raised ornamentation
embroidery working of raised and ornamental designs with a needle on woven fabric using contrasting or brightly colored thread
enameling fusing of clear, glassy flux of silica and potash, colored with metal oxides, to surface of metal or pottery as ornamentation
engraving cutting or corroding of designs into hard surfaces, such as metal or wood, which are usually inked for making impressions
etching technique of making designs on a metal plate or glass by the corrosive action of acid
etui copper enameling
fabric painting process of painting designs on fabric
featherwork making of decorative objects out of feathers
fiber arts design and crafting of objects from natural fibers or fibrous materials
flower making art or technique of making artificial flowers out of cut, folded, and mounted crêpe, tissue paper, or other stiff fabric
fraktur stylized and highly decorative watercolor painting, often bearing elaborate calligraphy
frottage technique in which textural effects or images are obtained by rubbing lead, chalk, crayon, or charcoal over paper laid on a granular or relief surface; rubbing
gem cutting craft of cutting and engraving gemstones; lapidary
glassblowing shaping of molten glass by blowing air into it through a tube
handicraft craft
ikebana Japanese art of arranging flowers in highly aesthetic designs, based on one of four traditional styles: Moribana, Nageire, Rikka, or Seika
inlay design or decoration made by inserting or applying layers of fine materials, such as gold or silver, in surface of object
intaglio process by which a design is incised or engraved into surface of plate or other object
jetworking craft of making beads, jewelry, buttons, or other items from polished, dense, black coal
jewelsmithing making of jewelry, esp. with cut stones
knitting interlacing loops of yarn to form decorative or functional garments and accessories
lacquerwork process of coating wood with resinous varnish obtained as sap from Japanese tree
lapidary gem cutting
lithography printing process using stone slab, or zinc or aluminum plate, marked with greasy ink
macramé technique of making elaborately patterned knotwork with hand-knotted twine or

rope, used esp. for wall decorations and hangings
marbling process of coloring or staining in imitation of marble by swirling ink or oil colors on water, then lowering paper onto its surface to pick up the design
mosaic making of designs by inlaying small pieces of colored stone, tile, or glass in mortar
needlecrafts handicrafts involving sewing with cloth or threads: crocheting, knitting, embroidery, crewel, needlepoint, quilting, rug hooking, trapunto
needlepoint embroidery using woolen yarn, esp. on canvas, usu. with uniform spacing of stitches
needlework art and process of working with a needle, esp. in embroidery, needlepoint, tapestry, quilting, and appliqué
niello ornamental work produced by inlaying metal with a black metallic substance consisting of silver, copper, lead, and sulfur
origami Japanese decorative art of folding paper to form recognizable shapes, esp. animals
paper sculpture making of decorative objects by cutting and folding paper into shapes
papier-mâché forming decorative objects from substance made of pulped paper or of rags or paper soaked in glue, formed into shapes when moist and becoming hard when dried
patchwork sewing together of pieces of cloth of various colors and shapes
perfumery art of blending natural and synthetic scents to make perfume
plaiting and braiding interlacing of three or more lengths of yarn to create strong, decorative strips
pokerwork pyrography
poonah work painting or stenciling on velvet; theorem painting
potato printing cutting of relief designs in raw potato and using it to make prints
pottery making or collecting of decorative and functional vessels of fired clay; ceramics
printmaking art or technique of impressing designs on cloth or other material
pyrography process of burning designs on leather, wood, acrylics, or foam with heated tool such as electric pen; pokerwork
quillwork craft in which stiff paper is cut in strips, rolled tightly, and glued on surface such as small box to form patterns
quilting creation and collection of needlework or patchwork bedcovers, often antique
raffia fiber obtained from raffia palm, used to make baskets, hats, and mats
repoussage embossing by hammering designs on metal
resist printing process of printing designs on cloth with paste of flour and water that acts like wax in batik to resist dyes
rubbing frottage
rug hooking creating patterned rugs with a hooked tool
rushwork weaving of rush stems into chair bottoms or mats
scrimshaw carving or engraving of ivory, bone, or shell
serigraphy silkscreening
sewing process of creating or repairing garments by stitches
silhouetting making of cutout profiles of figures in black paper
silkscreen printing process using inked silk cloth, mounted on frame, to which stencil film is affixed, esp. used for posters and clothing; serigraphy
spinning making of yarn or threads from fibers or filaments
stained glass work design and creation of objects, esp. windows and lampshades, from colored glass pieces, usu. joined by leaded strips
stenciling printing process in which ink or paint is applied to sheets perforated with designs or letters
stitchery decorative needlework, including embroidery or crewelwork
string pictures technique of gluing various types of string, thread, and yarn on surface to form design
textiles making cloth by weaving or knitting
theorem painting poonah work
tie-dyeing creating of designs on textiles by tying parts of the cloth so they will not absorb dye or forming barrier to dye with a clip or rubber band
trapunto quilting done in high relief through two or more layers of cloth, produced by padding a stitched pattern with yarn or cotton
tritik form of tie-dying in which strong thread is stitched along line through fabric and pulled tight to exclude dye
weaving design and creation of fabrics, rugs, or textiles on a loom by interlacing threads or yarns
whittling carving of decorative or functional objects by trimming and shaping a stick of wood

Chapter Seventeen
Leisure and Recreation

HOLIDAYS, CELEBRATIONS, AND VACATIONS

Annual National and Religious Holidays
Celebrations, Observances, Rites, and Gatherings
Parties and Partying
Vacations and Interludes
Travel and Tourism

Annual National and Religious Holidays

Advent Christian: beginning fourth Sunday before Christmas, period of fasting and prayer through Christmas celebrating Jesus' birth and anticipating his second coming

All Saints' Day Christian: November 1, feast day to honor martyrs and saints

All Souls' Day Christian: November 2, day to pray for and honor departed souls

April Fools' Day April 1, traditional day for playing jokes

Arbor Day U.S.: last Friday in April, set aside for preserving trees, often by planting, and encouraging environmental awareness

Armed Forces Day U.S.: third Saturday in May, honoring the members of armed forces

Armistice Day Veterans Day

Ascension Day Christian: tenth day before Pentecost, forty days after Easter, feast day commemorating Christ's departure from Earth to heaven

Ash Wednesday Christian: first day of Lent, forty days before Easter

Assumption Day Christian: August 15, feast day commemorating Virgin Mary's ascension to heaven

autumnal equinox U.S.: September 22, first day of fall

Bastille Day France: July 14, celebrating beginning of French Revolution

Boxing Day Great Britain: December 26, day after Christmas, originally celebrated by giving Christmas boxes or gifts to service workers and domestics

Canada Day Canada: July 1, commemorating union of provinces into a nation; Dominion Day

Candlemas Christian: February 2, celebrating presentation of Christ child and purification of Virgin Mary

Carnival Mardi Gras

Chinese New Year first new moon after sun enters Aquarius, in late January or early February, festive celebration of new year in Chinese calendar

Christmas Christian: December 25, holiday honoring the birth of Christ; Noel

Christmas Christian: January 6 on Eastern Orthodox Julian calendar

Christmas Eve Christian: December 24, day or evening before Christmas

Cinco de Mayo Mexico: May 5, holiday commemorating the defeat of Napoleon III's forces in 1867

Columbus Day U.S.: second Monday in October, orig. October 12, commemorating Columbus's landing in America in 1492

Commonwealth Day British Commonwealth: May 24, anniversary of Queen Victoria's birthday

Corpus Christi Christian: eleventh day after Pentecost, festival celebrated by Catholics honoring the Eucharist

Decoration Day Memorial Day

Dominion Day Canada Day

Easter Christian: first Sunday after full moon, occurring on or after March 21, celebrating resurrection of Christ

Election Day U.S.: first Tuesday after first Monday in November, reserved for electing public officials

Epiphany Christian: January 6, twelfth day after Christmas, celebrating the Magi's visit to Jesus

Father's Day U.S.: third Sunday in June, honoring fathers

Flag Day U.S.: June 14, anniversary of adoption of American flag in 1777

Fourth of July U.S. Independence Day

Good Friday Christian: Friday before Easter, commemorating Christ's crucifixion

Groundhog Day U.S.: February 2, traditional day for predicting spring's arrival by observing a groundhog's shadow, indicating six more weeks of winter, or lack of shadow, indicating spring is imminent

Halloween U.S. and Canada: October 31, festive tradition including dressing in costume, trick-or-treating, and playing pranks

Hanukkah Jewish: eight days beginning twenty-fifth day of Kislev (December), festival of lights marking rededication of Temple of Jerusalem and miracle of oil lamp that burned for eight days on a one-day supply of oil

High Holy Day Jewish: Rosh Hashanah or Yom Kippur

Human Rights Day December 10, observed by member states of United Nations

Immaculate Conception Roman Catholic: December 8, honoring Virgin Mary's freedom from original sin in conception

Inauguration Day U.S.: January 20 following presidential election, day of inauguration of newly elected president

Independence Day U.S.: July 4, honoring adoption of Declaration of Independence by American colonies in 1776; Fourth of July

Kwanza African: December 26 to January 1, harvest festival

Labor Day U.S. and Canada: first Monday in September, honoring workers

Lent Christian: forty days from Ash Wednesday to Easter Sunday, period of penitence and fasting in preparation for Easter

Lincoln's birthday U.S.: February 12, celebrating birth in 1809 of U.S. President Abraham Lincoln, now celebrated on Presidents' Day

Mardi Gras Christian: Tuesday immediately before beginning of Lent, celebrated by feasting, carnivals, and parades; Carnival
Martin Luther King Day U.S.: third Monday in January, orig. January 15, celebrating birth of civil rights leader Dr. Martin Luther King, Jr.
Maundy Thursday Christian: Thursday before Easter, commemorating Christ's Last Supper
May Day May 1, traditional spring festival, also international holiday honoring workers
Memorial Day U.S.: May 30, honoring soldiers who died in battle; Decoration Day
Michaelmas Christian: September 29, feast of the archangel St. Michael
Midsummer Day Great Britain: June 24, feast of St. John the Baptist; traditional night when spirits are believed to wander
Mother's Day U.S.: second Sunday in May, honoring mothers
New Year's Day January 1, first day of new year on Gregorian calendar
New Year's Eve December 31, celebrating last day and night of year on Gregorian calendar
Palm Sunday Christian: Sunday before Easter, commemorating Christ's triumphal entry into Jerusalem
Pan American Day U.S. and Latin America: April 14, honoring understanding and cooperation among the Americas
Passover Jewish: eight days beginning fourteenth day of Nisan (March or April), commemorating Hebrews' deliverance by Moses from slavery in Egypt; Pesach
Pentecost Christian: seventh Sunday after Easter, commemorating arrival of Holy Spirit to the apostles; Whitsunday
Pesach Passover
Presidents' Day U.S.: third Monday in February, interim date celebrating birthdays of Washington (February 22) and Lincoln (February 12)
Purim Jewish: fourteenth day of Adar (March), celebrating Persian Jews' deliverance by Esther from massacre by Haman
Ramadan Islamic: ninth month of Islamic calendar, period of fasting commemorating revelation of the Koran to Mohammed
Rosh Hashanah Jewish: New Year, first two days of Tishri (September or October)
Sadie Hawkins Day U.S.: first Saturday after November 11, when women invite men to dance or celebrate
Saint Patrick's Day March 17, honoring Saint Patrick, patron saint of Ireland
Saint Valentine's Day Valentine Day
Shavuot Jewish: sixth and seventh days of Sivan (June), commemorating revelation of Ten Commandments to Moses at Mount Sinai
Shrovetide Christian: three days before Ash Wednesday, time of feasting in preparation for Lent
Shrove Tuesday Christian: last day of Shrovetide
Sukkot Jewish: beginning fifteenth day of Tishri (October or November), Feast of Tabernacles, celebrating fall harvest and commemorating period when Hebrews wandered in wilderness after Exodus, marked by building of shelters
summer solstice June 21 in Northern Hemisphere, first day of summer
Tet Vietnam: New Year, ocurring first new moon after sun enters Aquarius, late January or early February
Thanksgiving Day U.S.: fourth Thursday in November, day of giving thanks, commemorating Pilgrims' harvest festival
Trinity Sunday Christian: seventh day after Pentecost, honoring the Holy Trinity
Twelfth Night Christian: January 5 or 6, eve of Epiphany
United Nation's Day October 24, celebrating ratification of U.N. Charter in 1945
Valentine Day February 14, day for sending messages or gifts of love; Saint Valentine's Day
V-E Day May 8, anniversary of Allied victory in Europe at end of World War II
vernal equinox March 21 or 22, first day of spring
Veterans Day U.S.: November 11, honoring veterans of armed forces and commemorating end of World War I; Armistice Day
V-J Day August 14, anniversary of Allied victory in Japan at end of World War II
Walpurgis Night eve of May Day, April 30, believed in medieval times to be night when witches celebrate their sabbath
Washington's birthday U.S.: February 22, celebrating birth in 1732 of George Washington, first U.S. president, now celebrated on Presidents' Day
Whitsunday Pentecost
winter solstice December 21 in Northern Hemisphere, first day of winter
Women's Day March 8, honoring work of women, esp. in socialist states
World Health Day April 7, observed by member states of the United Nations
Xmas Christmas
Yom Kippur Jewish: tenth day of Tishri (September or October), day of atonement marked by fasting and prayer

Celebrations, Observances, Rites, and Gatherings

baptism sacrament of admission into Christian church, enacted by sprinkling of water on child
bar mitzvah initiation ceremony marking coming of age of thirteen-year-old Jewish boy
bas mitzvah bat mitzvah
bat mitzvah initiation ceremony marking coming of age of thirteen-year-old Jewish girl; bas mitzvah
bee gathering for specific purpose, often for a competition; such as a spelling bee
benefit public performance, dinner, or gathering, proceeds of which go to certain person, group, or cause
black-tie (*adj*) designating formal affair to which tuxedo is worn

bris Jewish rite of circumcision
carnival period, usu. several days, of feasting and merrymaking, esp. before Lent
celebration instance or observation of holiday, religious ceremony, or festivity
church feast festive observance of religious holiday, esp. saint's day
clambake outdoor social gathering, esp. at beach with food baked on hot rocks
cocktail party informal gathering, usu. in early evening, where refreshments are served but not a complete meal
coffee klatsch informal gathering for conversation at which coffee is served; kaffee klatsch
coming out debut in formal society
commencement ceremony at which school or college degrees are conferred
communion Christian sacrament commem-orating Christ's death by taking bread and wine
confirmation generally nonsacramental Christian rite of admission to full church membership
cotillion formal dance, esp. honoring debut
debut party and dance honoring young woman's entrance into formal society; coming out
-fest suffix added to indicate festival or celebration, as in sunfest or lovefest
fête *French.* festival; elaborate party or outdoor gathering, often commemorative
fiesta processions, festivities, and dances on saint's day (Spain, Latin America)
funeral ceremony of burial or cremation of the dead; procession accompanying corpse to final resting place
gathering any assemblage of several persons for a specific, often social or ceremonial, purpose
harvest home feast at end of harvest season
high tea substantial late afternoon snack at which tea is served, esp. in Britain
holiday season last two months of the year in United States, including Thanksgiving, Christmas and Hanukkah, and New Year's Eve
homecoming occasion marking return of group of people to their home, esp. annual celebration of university alumni
honeymoon vacation taken by newlyweds immediately after wedding
hootenanny informal folk or country song performance, often with audience sing-along
housewarming party celebrating one's move to a new home
jamboree large, festive gathering, often with mixed entertainment
jubilee special anniversary, esp. twenty-fifth, fiftieth, or sixtieth
klatch small, informal gathering, esp. for idle chitchat
last rites Roman Catholic sacrament administered to person near death
legal holiday nationally established holiday on which banks and government offices are closed
luau feast or banquet (Hawaii)
masquerade social gathering, esp. dance, at which guests wear masks and costumes
Mass celebration of Catholic church service and the Eucharist
mixer friendly, informal get-together
movable feast religious feast that occurs on a different date in different years
name day church feast honoring saint after whom one is named
observance standardized ceremony or rite honoring something
Oktoberfest fall beer-drinking festival (Germany)
open house informal, daylong hospitality offered at one's home to invited and uninvited guests
opening night celebration of first performance of public entertainment
pageant extravagant display, esp. procession with floats
powwow Native American ceremony with feasting and dancing, usu. in expectation of some beneficial result
prom formal dance at school or college
reception social gathering of welcome, esp. for guests after formal event such as wedding
reunion gathering of persons after period of separation
rite standardized, ceremonial act or occasion
roast gathering to humorously honor or kiddingly defame someone
Sabbath day of rest and religious observance; Saturday for Jews, Sunday for Christians
Sadie Hawkins party or dance to which females invite males
saturnalia wild, orgiastic, excessive celebration
séance gathering to communicate with spirits
seder Jewish dinner service on first evening of Passover
Shabbat *Hebrew.* Jewish Sabbath, observed from sunset Friday to sunset Saturday
shindig *Informal.* lavish social gathering, usu. with dancing; shindy
shower party at which gifts are given to guest of honor, esp. bride-to-be or mother-to-be
sit-down dinner formal dinner at which one is served while seated at table
soiree social gathering in evening
tea light, late afternoon meal at which tea is served, esp. in Britain
tea ceremony traditional, formal, highly stylized Japanese green tea service for guests
tribute formal expression or show of support and respect
vacation period of rest from normal activities, often spent away from home
wake often festive vigil over corpse prior to burial; *Chiefly Brit.* annual holiday or vacation
wedding ceremony and festivities marking marriage
white-tie (*adj*) designating extremely formal affair to which men wear swallow-tailed coats and white bow ties
yuletide feast of Christmas

Parties and Partying

after-hours (*adj*) occurring or operating in early morning hours after regular bars close, when only a few, sometimes private, social clubs are open
bacchanalia drunken feast, orig. honoring Roman god Bacchus
bachelor party gathering of men honoring friend about to be married
bridge party gathering at which groups of four people play bridge
BYOB bring your own bottle/booze/beer; designation that host will not supply drinks at party
catering act or business of supplying and serving food and drink at parties
cut in (*vb*) take another's place, esp. as a dance partner
debauch orgy
fast lane *Informal.* social life marked by attendance at many parties and social functions, esp. the trendiest and most boisterous affairs
frat party *Informal.* party at college fraternity house
garden party outdoor gathering in garden or backyard
gate-crasher *Informal.* person attending party uninvited, often forcing way into gathering
high jinks *Informal.* boisterous fun, esp. lively pranks
key club private club where each member has key to premises
la dolce vita *Italian.* the sweet life; hedonism, good times, and dissipation
lark playful merrymaking, sometimes involving pranks
lawn party outdoor gathering on grass field, often under tents
life of the party gregarious, charming, entertaining individual at social affairs
man about town worldly man who frequents fashionable clubs and parties
orgy unrestrained merrymaking and dissipation in group, esp. with free sexual activity; debauch
pajama party slumber party
party informal social gathering for amusement or celebration; (*vb*) *Informal.* engage in social activities in boisterous, unrestrained manner
partying *Informal.* indulging in and enjoying parties
regale (*vb*) entertain others with splendid feast or amusing stories
revelry noisy party or merrymaking
roister (*vb*) engage in noisy revelry and carousing
Roman holiday time of debauchery and licentiousness
RSVP *French.* répondez s'il vous plaît; request on invitation that one indicate whether he or she will attend
salon regular gathering of distinguished guests in private drawing room, esp. in celebrity's home
slumber party overnight house party, esp. for teenage girls; pajama party
smoker informal social gathering for men only
social informal gathering, esp. for group or organization
stag party party for men only; bachelor party for bridegroom, often with pornographic movies
taxi dancer girl employed by dance hall to dance with patrons for a fee
vanity fair place or group characterized by pursuit of idle pleasures, decadence, and ostentation
wallflower shy or unpopular person who remains at periphery of social gathering
work the room *Informal.* move from person to person at party, esp. seeking advantage or influence

Vacations and Interludes

absenteeism deliberate or habitual absence from work or school
AWOL absent without leave; unauthorized absence from military service
breather pause for rest, esp. from difficult task
busman's holiday vacation spent pursuing one's regular activities
cocktail hour early evening, at end of workday
coffee break brief pause in workday for rest and refreshment
downtime period of worker inactivity or equipment repair, esp. on machinery such as computer or communications system
escape getaway from regular activities, esp. to exotic place for relaxation
excursion brief, often one-day pleasure trip, esp. at bargain rates
field trip excursion, esp. to place under study for observation
furlough leave of absence from duty, esp. for soldier
getaway departure from home for vacation
halftime midpoint intermission during sports event
happy hour early evening, at end of workday, when bars reduce price of drinks
hiatus interruption or break in normal activities
hooky unexcused absence from school
idyll romantic or bucolic interlude
interim period of time between two events
interlude brief respite from normal activities
intermission brief, scheduled interval between two events, esp. between acts of a performance; entr'acte
jaunt usu. short pleasure trip
junket trip or journey, esp. one taken by politician at public expense
knock off (*vb*) *Informal.* leave work at end of day
leave authorized absence from work or military duty, esp. for extended period; leave of absence
Lord's day for Christians, Sunday, traditionally a day off from work
paid vacation scheduled, authorized absence from work without loss of salary
R and R rest and recreation
respite temporary interval of relief from duties
rest and recreation R and R; regular vacation period from military duty
retreat act of withdrawing into seclusion or retirement; place of refuge or seclusion

sabbatical leave from regular work, esp. for extended period with pay
safari journey or hunting expedition, esp. in eastern Africa
shore leave authorized permission for sailor to go ashore briefly
sick leave authorized absence from work, with full or partial pay, due to illness or injury
sojourn temporary stay away from home
truancy unexcused absence, esp. from school
vacation period of rest from normal activities, often spent traveling away from home

Travel and Tourism

accommodations lodgings, sometimes including meals
Baedeker guidebook to foreign country, orig. published by Karl Baedeker in Germany during 19th century
bed-and-breakfast overnight accommodation, esp. in private home, that includes breakfast
bellboy man or boy employed to carry luggage and run errands at hotel; bellhop
bellhop bellboy
bon voyage *French.* lit. pleasant journey; expression of farewell to traveler
booking advance reservation for lodging or travel
business class travel at level between first class and coach class
cabin class accommodations on passenger ship superior to tourist class but inferior to first class
caravan company of persons traveling together, esp. in series of vehicles following one another
charter hire or lease of ship, bus, or airplane to transport large group at reduced fare
coach class standard travel facilities
Cook's tour guided, often cursory sightseeing tour
double occupancy travel accommodation designed for two persons
excursion fare low fare with special requirements
expedition journey or voyage for some definite purpose
exploration traveling in unknown region for educational purposes
first class finest accommodations in hotel or on public conveyance
globetrotter person who travels widely and frequently
grand tour journey through continental Europe, usu. at completion of education
guide person hired to lead tourists or travelers through unknown area, usu. providing information about it
hostel inexpensive, supervised lodging place for young travelers
hotel commercial establishment providing lodging and often meals for travelers
inn establishment providing lodging and often food and drink for travelers, usu. smaller than hotel
itinerary detailed plan or record of journey
motel hotel for automobile travelers at which car can be parked close to one's room
open return round-trip ticket with unspecified return date
overbook (*vb*) accept more reservations than places available in expectation of no-shows
package tour group travel in which all accommodations and activities are organized and paid for in advance
pension modest European hotel or boardinghouse, esp. one serving meals
pilgrimage long journey to religious shrine or place of historical interest
porter person employed to carry one's baggage, esp. at hotel or depot
resort place where people go for vacations, esp. to rest and relax
safe passage successful journey through dangerous region
spa resort with mineral spring or health facilities and sauna, esp. fashionable spot
tourism travel of foreign visitors to another nation and income derived therefrom; similar travel within one's own country
tourist class lowest-priced accommodations on ship or train
travel agency company that arranges itineraries, lodging, and transportation for tourists and other travelers
traveler's check replaceable bank draft issued to traveler, signed at issuance and again at time of cashing
travelogue lecture, accompanied by slides or film, about travel to foreign or out-of-the-way place
trek slow, laborious travel, often by foot over long distance

ENTERTAINMENTS AND SPECTACLES

acrobatics art and performance of gymnastics and tumbling
aerialism performance of feats in the air, esp. on a trapeze
aerobatics spectacular flying stunts and maneuvers such as rolls and dives by an airplane
amateur night entertainment featuring nonprofessional performers, often in competition for prizes
amusement park outdoor facility providing rides, shows, exhibitions, and other amusements
aquarium building in which live aquatic organisms are exhibited
arm wrestling contest in which opponents face each other gripping hands and attempt to force each other's arm down
beauty contest staged show, usu. made up of women, in which panel selects most beautiful contestant

belly dancing solo performance, usu. given by woman, involving gyrations of abdomen and hips
botanical garden outdoor garden and greenhouses for study and exhibition of plants
bullfight public spectacle in which men excite, fight with, and ceremonially kill bulls
bumper cars amusement park ride in which padded electric cars purposely collide with each other
burlesque broadly comic theatrical entertainment of short skits and sometimes striptease acts
carousel merry-go-round
casino facility for gambling, sometimes featuring floor show
cavalcade parade; procession of riders or carriages
circus public performance, often in tent, of feats of skill, acrobatics, animal acts, and clown shows
contortionism acrobatics in which performer twists body into unusual postures
county fair annual exhibition at county fairgrounds featuring displays of livestock, stage shows, and rides
crafts fair gathering for display and sale of handmade crafts
demolition derby exhibition in which old automobiles are intentionally rammed until just one is left running
drum corps marching band, esp. of drummers, under direction of drum major and majorettes, who often twirl batons
entertainment diverting, amusing, and engaging public performance
equestrian show exhibition of horsemanship, esp. jumping
escape artist person who breaks free of seemingly impossible confinement
exposition public exhibition or show, esp. of commodities; expo
fair exhibition designed to acquaint buyers or public with products; gathering for exchange and display of articles
Ferris wheel amusement park ride consisting of a tall, rotating, upright wheel with attached cars for riders
figure skating dance performance on ice skates
fireworks pyrotechnics; explosive devices with loud discharge and spectacular appearance
float low, flat, decorated vehicle that carries exhibits or tableaux in a parade
freak show public exhibition of oddities or freaks of nature
funambulism tightrope walking
fun house building in amusement park containing devices designed to startle, amuse, or frighten visitors
gymkhana automotive meet with several events that test driving skills
high-diving diving from very high platform into small pool
high-wire act tightrope walking and acrobatics
jamboree noisy, festive gathering; assembly of Boy Scouts or Girl Scouts
juggling keeping several objects in motion in the air by alternately catching and tossing them
light show kaleidoscopic display of colored lights and film loops
magic producing illusions by sleight of hand or conjuring
marching band band composed of brass, woodwind, and percussion that performs while marching before crowd in parade or at athletic event
marine park public display of marine animals and fish in outdoor tanks
merry-go-round amusement park ride with seats, often in form of animals, on revolving platform; carousel
mime show pantomime
pantomime act conveying a story or idea without words through facial gestures, hand movements, and dance; mime show
planetarium facility housing a large model of the solar system, which is projected onto its ceiling or dome for view from seats below
prestidigitation sleight of hand
pyrotechnics spectacular display, esp. of fireworks
regatta series of rowing, sailing, or speedboat races
revue stage performance consisting of a series of skits, songs, and dances; variety show
rodeo public performance by cowboys, featuring broncobusting, Brahma bull riding, calf roping, and steer wrestling
roller coaster elevated railway constructed in curves and inclines as frightening amusement park ride
roller derby staged contest between two roller-skating teams on oval track
scavenger hunt party contest with time limit for locating several difficult-to-obtain articles
scenic railway brief, elevated railway for viewing scenery
shadow play show in which shadows of puppets or performers are cast on screen
sleight of hand magic and conjuring tricks requiring deception through manual dexterity and skill; prestidigitation
snake charming entertainment involving professed power to charm and control venomous snakes
son et lumière *French.* sound-and-light show
sound-and-light show outdoor spectacle at historic sight using recorded narration with sound and light effects
spectacle public exhibit or performance of something unusual, striking, notable, or entertaining, often on a large scale
synchronized swimming water ballet
theme park amusement park in which structures and displays focus on central theme or motif
three-ring circus large circus with three acts performing simultaneously
tightrope walking balancing act performed on wire or rope suspended at some height; funambulism

tournament medieval contest between mounted knights armed with lances; series of contests leading to a championship in various sports and competitive fields
tumbling acrobatics involving somersaulting, rolling on floor, and handsprings
ventriloquism performance in which voice seems to come not from speaker but from dummy or other source
water ballet synchronized movement to music by performers in a pool of water; synchronized swimming
water park amusement park in which most or all of rides involve passing through water
wax museum exhibit of life-size wax effigies of famous people; waxworks
waxworks wax museum
Wild West show performance depicting scenes of U.S. Old West and displaying feats such as horsemanship, marksmanship, and rope twirling
zoo parklike facility for public display of living animals; zoological garden
zoological garden zoo

SPORTS

Team Sports

Australian Rules football
bandy, baseball, basketball, beach volleyball, bobsledding
Canadian football, crew, cricket, curling
doubles tennis
field hockey, flag football, football
handball, hardball, hockey, hooverball, hurling
ice hockey
kickball
lacrosse
polo, pushball
relay race, Roller Derby, rounders, rugby
shinny, slow pitch softball, soccer, softball, speedball, stickball, stoolball, stoop ball
tag football, team handball, touch football
volleyball
water polo, whiffleball
yachting

Individual Sports and Competitive Events

acrobatics, Alpine skiing, archery, arm wrestling
balance beam, bareknuckle boxing, barrel racing, baton twirling, biathlon, biathlon relay, bicycling, bobsledding, boloball, bowling, boxing, Brahma bull riding, broad jump, broncobusting, bullfighting, bull riding
calf roping, candlepins, canoeing, court tennis, cross-country, cross-country skiing, cycling
decathlon, deck tennis, discus, distance running, diving, downhill skiing, draw, dressage, duckpins
enduro biking, equestrian
fencing, field events, figure skating, fives, foot racing, freestyle wrestling
giant stride, golf, Greco-Roman wrestling, gymnastics
hammer throw, handball, high jump, hurdling
ice dancing, ice skating, Indian wrestling
jai alai, javelin, judo
kayaking, korfball
lawn bowling, lawn tennis, long jump, luge
marathon, martial arts, medley relay, miniature golf, modern pentathlon, motocross
ninepins, Nordic skiing
paddle tennis, pancratium, parallel bars, pelota, pentathlon, ping-pong, platform diving, platform tennis, pole bending, pole vault, pugilism
racquetball, relay race, rings, road racing, rowing, running
sambo wrestling, shooting, shot put, side horse, skiing, ski jumping, slalom, sled-dog racing, speed skating, springboard diving, sprint, squash, stall bar, steeplechase, steer-wrestling, sumo wrestling, surfing, swimming
table tennis, tennis, tenpins, track, track and field, triathlon, triple jump
ultramarathon
vaulting

walking, water skiing, weightlifting, wrestling, wrist wrestling

General Sports Terminology

AAU, all-American, All-Pro, all-star, all-star team, amateur, Amateur Athletic Union, America's Cup, anchorman, arena, athlete, athletic scholarship, at large, attackman (lacrosse, rugby), average
backup, ball, ballpark, barnburner, batsman (cricket), bench, bench press (weightlifting), bench warmer, best-of-five series, best-of-seven series, big game, bird cage, black belt (karate), blackout, blank, bleachers, bluff, body English, bonus, boo, boobirds, book, booster, box seat, breeze, Bronx cheer, brown belt, bulk up, bull's-eye (archery), burn, bush, bye
call, cape work (bullfighting), captain, carom, cash in, cellar, champion, championship, chaw, cheap shot, cheat, cheerleader, chukker (polo), chula (jai alai), circuit, clean and jerk (weightlifting), cleats, clock, club, clubhouse, clutch, clutch play, coach, cocaptain, colors, comeback, competition, conference, consolation prize, coxswain (crew), crosse (lacrosse), cuadrilla (bullfighting), cup
dark horse, deadlock, defender, dog it
eligibility, epée (fencing)
fan, field, field house, finesse, first division, first string, fix, forfeit, formation, free agent, fronton (jai alai), front runner
game ball, gamer, goal, good hands, go the distance, grandstanding, groundskeeper, guile, gym, gymkhana, gymnasium
halftime, Hall of Fame, homecoming, home field, home stand, host, hot dog
innings (cricket), in play, instant replay, iron man
jackpot, jam (roller derby), jammer (roller derby), jayvee, jib (yachting), jock, juice, junior varsity
keel (yachting), kill shot, kill the clock
laugher, light tower, lock, locker room, longshot
mainsail (yachting), manager, matador (bullfighting), match, match play, miscue, misplay, muff
NAIA, National Association of Intercollegiate Athletics, National Collegiate Athletic Association, NCAA
odds, odds-on favorite, official, officiate, off-season, Olympics, on a roll, out-of-play, overmatched, overtime
Pan American Games, parry (fencing), pase (bullfighting), phenom, phys ed, physical education, picador (bullfighting), pickup game, play, play-by-play, play catch-up, playing field, play-off, point, position, prelims, press box, pro, professional, promoter, prospect, psyched, psych-out, psych-up, push
quarter, quarterfinal, quickness
razzle-dazzle, recruiting, redshirt, ref, referee, regatta (yachting), rematch, repechage (crew, cycling), replay, reserve, ringer, roll, rookie, roster, round robin, rover (archery), rugger (rugby), runner-up, run out the clock
saber (fencing), score, scoreboard, scorecard, scrub, scrum (rugby), scull (crew), season, season ticket, second division, second effort, second string, second wind, seed, seesaw, semifinal, semipro, semiprofessional, series, set a record, shave points, shirts'n'skins, shoo-in, shuttlecock (badminton), side, sleeper, slump, snatch (weightlifting), spark plug, spectator, spoiler, spot points, spotter, spread, squad, stadium, standings, standoff, stiff, streak, stroke (crew), sub, substitution, sudden death, suit up, Summer Games, Summer Olympics, sweep
tailgate party, tally, taw (marbles), team, team play, teamwork, television time-out, test match (cricket), the wave, throw (rodeo), throw-in, thrust (rodeo), tie, timekeeper, time-out, to play, tossup, tote board, touché (fencing), tournament, tourney, trade, trading deadline, trainer, training, try (rugby), tryout, tune-up
underbird, underdog, upset
varsity, versus, vigorish
wager, waivers, walk-on, warmup, water boy, white belt, wicket (cricket), wild card, wind sprint, Winter Olympics, world champion, world championship, world class
yell leader
zip

Auto Racing

auto racing racing of stock or specialized automobiles by drivers competing over racing course or on closed public roadways
apron, autocross
black flag
checkered flag, cyclocross
demolition derby, draft, drag race, dragster
formula one, funny car
go-carting, Grand Prix, green flag, groove
Indianapolis 500, infield
kick
lap, lap money, LeMans
midget racer, motocross
NASCAR, nitro-fueled
off-road race
pace car, pace lap, pit, pit crew, pit stop, pole position
qualifying
rally
spin-out, stock car racing
winner's circle
yellow flag

Baseball

baseball game of ball between two nine-player teams played for nine innings on field built around a diamond, with home plate and three other bases at its points, around which a runner must pass after successfully hitting a pitched ball with a wooden or metal bat in order to score one run, the object being to score more runs in nine innings than one's opponent

ace, AL, alley, all-star, All-Star Game, American League, apple, artificial turf, assist, Astroturf, at bat, average, away

Babe Ruth league, backstop, backup, balk, ball, ball boy, ball club, ball game, ball girl, ball hawk, ballpark, ballplayer, Baltimore chop, barehanded, base, baseball, baseball bat, baseball cap, baseball card, baseballer, baseball game, baseball glove, baseball player, base hit, baseline, base on balls, base path, baserunner, basket catch, bat, bat boy, batter, batter's box, batter up, battery, batting average, batting cage, bean, bean ball, beat out, big league, blank, bleachers, bloop, blooper, bobble, book, boot, bottom, bottom of the ninth, box, boxscore, box seat, broken bat, brush, brushback, bull pen, bunt, bush league, bushleaguer

cage, called strike, catch, catcher, catcher's mask, caught looking, center field, center fielder, chance, change-of-pace, change-up, chase, check swing, chin music, choke up, chopper, classic, cleanup, cleanup hitter, clear the bases, closed stance, closer, clothesline, clout, club, clutch hit, coach, comebacker, commissioner, complete game, concessions, connect, control, Cooperstown, count, cover a base, curve, curve ball, cut, cut fastball, cutoff, cutoff man, Cy Young Award

day game, dead ball, deck, deep, designated hitter, DH, diamond, dinger, dish, doctor the ball, double, doubleheader, double play, double play depth, double steal, double switch, drag bunt, drive, ducks on the pond, dugout, dying quail

earned run, earned run average, ERA, error, extra-base hit

fadeaway, fadeaway slide, fair ball, fall classic, fan, farm, farm club, farm system, farm team, fastball, field, fielder, fielder's choice, fielding average, fireman, first base, first base coach, first baseman, fly, fly ball, fly out, follow through, force, force out, force play, forkball, foul, foul ball, foul line, foul out, foul pole, foul territory, foul tip, fourbagger, frame, free agent, free pass, free trip, fungo

game-winning hit, gapper, glove, glove man, go-ahead run, gold glove, good eyes, gopher ball, grand slam, ground ball, grounder, groundout, ground rule double, ground rules, gun

Hall of Fame, handle, hang, hardball, head-first slide, heat, heater, heavy hitter, hickory, hidden-ball trick, high, high-and-inside, high-and-tight, high hard one, high heat, hill, hit, hit-and-run, hit batsman, hit by pitch, hit for the cycle, hitter, hit the corner, hold, hold the runner, home plate, homer, home run, home stand, hook, horsehide, hot corner, hot-stove league, hummer, hurler

infield, infield back, infielder, infield fly rule, infield hit, infield in, infield out, inning, inside, inside pitch, inside-the-park home run, insurance run, intentional walk, in the hole

junior circuit, junk, junkball pitcher

K, keystone, knock, knuckle ball, knuckle-baller, knuckler

LCS, lead, lead off, leadoff hitter, league, league lead, League Championship Series, leather, leatherman, left field, left fielder, left-handed batter, left-hander, leg out a hit, line drive, line out, liner, line score, lineup, little league, load the bases, long relief, low, low-and-away, low-and-outside

major league, major leaguer, manager, middle relief, minor league, minor leaguer, mitt, most valuable player, mound, move, MVP

nail the runner, National League, night game, nine, NL, no hits, no runs, no errors, no-hitter

official at bat, on, on base, on base percentage, on deck, one-bagger, one-base hit, one-hitter, open stance, opposite field, out, outfield, outfielder, outside, outside pitch, overthrow

pass, passed ball, payoff pitch, peg, pennant, pennant race, pepper, perfect game, pick-off, pick-off move, pill, pinch-hit, pinch hitter, pine tar, pitch, pitcher, pitcher's mound, pitchout, pivot, plate, play ball, pocket, Pony League, pop, pop fly, pop-up, power hitter, prospect, pull, pull hitter, pull the string, punch, put-out

rain check, rain delay, rainout, rally, rbi, reached on error, relay, relief pitcher, reliever, retire the batter, rhubarb, ribby, rifle, right field, right fielder, right-handed batter, righthander, rip, road trip, rocket, rookie, Rookie-of-the-Year, rosin bag, rotation, Rotisserie League, rounders, round-tripper, rubber, rube, run, run batted in, rundown, runless, runner, runners at the corners, running catch, run through the sign

sack, sacrifice, sacrifice bunt, sacrifice fly, safe, safety squeeze, sandlot, save, score, scorecard, scorekeeper, scoring position, scout, scratch hit, screwball, scuff, season, second base, second baseman, senior circuit, series, shag, shell the pitcher, shift, shinguard, shoestring catch, short relief, shortstop, show, shutout, side, sidearm, single, sinker, slam, slice, slide, slider, slow pitch softball, slug, slugfest, slugger, slugging percentage, slurve, smash, smoke, softball, southpaw, speed gun, spitball, spitter, split-fingered fastball, spring training, squeeze bunt, squeeze play, stadium, stand, starter, steal, stickball, stolen base, stoopball, stopper, straightaway, stretch, stretch drive, strike, strikeout, strike zone, stroke, stuff, suicide squeeze, swat, swing, swinging strike, swipe, switch hit, switch-hitter

tag, tag up, take, take an extra base, take the pitch, tee off, Texas leaguer, third base, third base coach, third baseman, three-bagger, three-base hit, three up, three down, throw, throw behind the runner, throw out, tip, top, top of the inning, toss, total bases, trap, trip, trip to the mound, trip to the plate, triple, triple-A, Triple Crown, triple-header, triple play, turn a double play, tweener, twin bill, twi-night, twirler, two-bagger, two-base hit

ump, umpire, uncork, underarm, underhand, unearned run, up, up-and-in, uppercut, upper deck, upswing, utilityman

waivers, walk, warmup, warning track, webbing, wheel, wheels, whiff, wide, wild pitch, win, windup, winning percentage, World Series

yield

Basketball

basketball game played between two teams of five players each on a rectangular court with a raised basket at each end, points being scored by shooting a round, inflated ball through the opponent's basket

air ball, alley-oop, assist, at the buzzer

backboard, backcourt, backcourt foul, backcourt violation, bank, bank shot, baseline, basket, basketball, bench, block, blocked shot, blocking, boards, bonus situation, bounce pass, boxing out, break, breakaway foul, brick, bucket

carom, carrying-over, center, charge, charging, charity stripe, cherry pick, chest pass, coast-to-coast, cold, continuation, conversion, cords, court, courtside, crosscourt pass

dead ball foul, defensive rebound, delay of game, deliberate foul, dish, disqualification, double dribble, double pump, double-team, downtown, draw iron, dribble, drive, dunk, dunk shot

ejection, elbow, endline

fadeaway, fadeaway jumper, fast break, field, field goal, field goal percentage, fill the lanes, Final Four, finger roll, five second violation, flagrant foul, follow shot, forty-five second clock, forward, foul, foul line, foul out, foul shot, free throw, free throw attempt, free throw lane, free throw line, front, front court, full-court press

give-and-go, glass, goaltending, guard, gun

hack, half-court game, hand check, hanging on the rim, hang time, high post, hit, holding, home court, home court advantage, hook shot, hoop

illegal defense, in and out, inbounds, inbounds pass, inside, in your face, iron

jam, jump ball, jump circle, jumper, jump shot

key

lane, lane violation, lay-up, line, loose ball foul, low post

man-to-man defense

National Basketball Association, National Invitation Tournament, NBA, net, NIT, no-look pass

offensive foul, offensive rebound, off guard, off the dribble, one-on-one, outlet pass, outside, over the limit, over the top

paint, palming, pass, penetration, perimeter, perimeter shooting, personal foul, pick, pick-and-roll, pivot, platoon, playmaker, point, point guard, post, post position, post up, power forward, press

quarter

reaching in, rebound, rejection, reverse dunk, rim, rotation, run-and-gun

screen, set a pick, set a screen, set shot, shoot, shooter, shot, shot clock, shot selection, sixth man, skyhook, slam dunk, small forward, spot up, steal, stuff, swingman, swish, switch

tap-in, team foul, team rebound, technical foul, ten-second rule, three-point line, three-point play, three-point shot, three-second violation, tip-in, tipoff, top of the key, touch, transition, transition game, trap, trap defense, traveling, triple double, turnaround jumper, turnover, twenty-four second clock, twenty second timeout

uptempo game

walking

yo-yo

zone defense

Bowling

bowling game in which a heavy ball is rolled down an alley toward ten pins standing in a triangular pattern, the object being to knock down all the pins at once

alley

bedposts, boccie, break

candlepins

duckpins

foul line, frame

guide marks, gutter

hook

kingpin

lane, lawn bowling, league bowling

open
perfect game, pin, pinsetter, pocket, poodle
scratch, seven-ten split, skip, spare, split, strike
tenpin, triple, turkey

Boxing and Wrestling

boxing contest between two fighters who punch each other with gloved fists over the designated number of rounds or until one has been knocked out
wrestling contest between two opponents who struggle hand to hand in order to pin each other's shoulders to a mat, held under varying styles and rules
airplane spin, apron, arm wrestling
back-pedal, bantamweight, bareknuckle, bicycle, body slam, bout, boxer, break, bum, butt
canvas, card, cauliflower ear, clinch, club fighter, combination, contender, corner, count, counterpunch, cross, crown, cut man
dance, decision, dive, draw, duck
fall, featherweight, fight, fighter, fisticuffs, flyweight, footwork, freestyle wrestling, full nelson
glass chin, glass jaw, glove, Golden Gloves, gouge, Greco-Roman wrestling, guard
half nelson, hammerlock, handler, hand lock, haymaker, headlock, heavyweight, hook
Indian wrestling
jab, judge, junior weight
kayo, kick boxing, kidney punch, knockdown, knockout, KO
lace finger, left, light heavyweight, lightweight, lock, low blow
Marquis of Queensberry rules, mat, match, middleweight
nelson, neutral corner
one-two, on the ropes
pin, point, prefight instructions, preliminary, press, prizefight, prizefighter, promoter, pug, pugilism, pugilist, puncher, punching bag, punchy
rabbit punch, rassling, referee, reversal, right, ring, ringside, roadwork, rope-a-dope, ropes, round, roundhouse
scissors, scissors hold, second, semifinal, shadowbox, sleeper hold, slugfest, spar, sparring partner, speed bag, speed work, split decision, stop, stranglehold, sumo wrestling
tag team, takedown, tandem, technical knockout, ten point must system, throw, thumb, title fight, titleholder, titlist, TKO, toehold, trainer, trunks
undercard, unranked, uppercut
weigh-in, welterweight, white hope, windmill, wrestler, wristlock

Football

football game in which two opposing teams of eleven players each defend goals at opposite ends of a 100-yard rectangular field, points being scored by carrying an inflated oval ball across the opponent's goal line or by kicking this ball over the crossbar between the posts of the opponent's goal
AFC, American Football Conference, armchair quarterback, audible, automatic
back, backfield, backfield in motion, back judge, ball-carrier, batting the ball, blindside, blitz, block, blocker, blocking back, bomb, bootleg, bowl, bowl game, breakaway, bring a load, broken field, bump and run, buttonhook
Canadian Football League, carry, catch, center, CFL, chair pattern, cheap shot, chip shot, clip, clipping, clothesline tackle, coffin corner, completion, conversion, convert, cornerback, corner pattern, Cotton Bowl, counterplay, coverage, crackback, crawling, crossbar, cut, cutback, cutoff block
deep, defense, defensive back, defensive coordinator, defensive end, defensive tackle, delay, dive play, double-team, down, down-and-out, downfield, down lineman, draft, draft pick, draw, draw play, drive, drive block, drop back, drop kick
eat the ball, encroachment, end, end around, end line, end run, end zone
face mask, fade, fair catch, fake, field goal, field judge, first-and-goal, first down, flanker, flanker back, flare pass, flare pattern, flat pass, flats, fleaflicker, flex, flex defense, flow, fly pattern, football, footballer, football player, formation, forward pass, fourth down, free kick, free safety, fullback, fumble
gain, game plan, gap, goal line, goal line stand, goalpost, goal-to-go, grass drills, Grey Cup, gridder, gridiron, guard
Hail Mary pass, halfback, halftime, handoff, hash mark, head linesman, Heisman Trophy, helmet, hit, holding, hook pattern, huddle
I formation, illegal procedure, inbounds, ineligible receiver, in motion, in play, inside, inside linebacker, instant replay, intentional grounding, interception, interference
juke, jump pass
keeper, kick, kicker, kickoff, kickoff return, kick return specialist
lateral, left side, line, linebacker, line judge, lineman, line of scrimmage, linesman, look-in pass
man-to-man defense, middle linebacker, misdirection, Monday morning quarterback, motion, muff
National Football Conference, National

Football League, neutral zone, NFC, NFL, nickel defense, no-huddle offense, nose guard, nose tackle
offensive coordinator, offensive lineman, official, offside, off tackle, onside kick, open field, option, Orange Bowl, outlet pass, out-of-bounds, out-of-play, outside linebacker
pass, PAT, pay dirt, penalty, personal foul, physical, pigskin, pileup, pitchout, pits, place kick, placekicker, placement, platoon, play-action pass, playbook, pluggers, pocket, point after touchdown, post pattern, power play, power sweep, prevent defense, Pro Bowl, pulling guard, punt, punter, punt formation, punt return
quarter, quarterback, quarterback sneak, quick kick, quick read, quick release
read, receiver, reception, red-dog, red zone, ref, referee, release, replay official, return, reverse, right side, ring his bell, roll, rollout, Rose Bowl, run, run and shoot, runback, runner, running back, running play, rush, rushing
sack, safety, safety blitz, sandwich, scatback, scramble, screen pass, scrimmage, seam, secondary, second down, set position, shift, short, short yardage, shotgun, shovel pass, side judge, sideline, single wing, slant, snap, sneak, soccer-style kicker, special teams, spike, spiral, split backs, split end, spread formation, sprint-out, squib kick, Statue of Liberty play, stickum, stiff-arm, straight-arm, strong left, strong right, strong safety, strong side, stunt, stutter step, sudden death, Sugar Bowl, suicide squad, Super Bowl, sweep, swing pass, swivel hips
tackle, tailback, taxi squad, TD, T formation, third down, throw, tight end, touchback, touchdown, touch football, touchtackle, trap, trap block, trenches, triple option, triple threat, try for point, turf, turnover, two-minute warning
umpire, unnecessary roughness, unsportsmanlike conduct, upfield, upright, up the middle
veer offense
weak safety, weak side, wedge, wide receiver, wig-wag, wind field, wingback, wishbone
yardage, yard line, yards gained, yards per carry
zebra, zone, zone defense

Golf

golf game in which a small, white ball is struck with wooden or metal-headed clubs over a course of usu. eighteen holes placed at some distance from one another around natural or artificial obstacles, the object being to sink the ball into each successive hole in as few strokes as possible

address the ball, approach shot, apron
back nine, backspin, backswing, bag, best-ball foursome, best-ball match, birdie, bisque, bogey, brassie, bunker
caddie, carry, chip, chip shot, club, clubhouse, country club, course, cup, cut shot
divot, dogleg, dormie, double bogey, double eagle, downswing, drive, driver, driving range, drop, dub, duffer
eagle, eighteen holes
fade, fairway, fairway trap, fairway wood, flag, flagstick, follow-through, foozle, fore, foursome, fringe, front nine
gallery, gimme, golden ferret, golf ball, golf club, golf course, golf widow, Grand Slam, green, greens fee, grip
hacker, handicap, hazard, heel, hit up, hole, hole in one, hole out, hook
iron
leader board, lie, links, lip, loft
mashie, Masters, match play, medal play, mulligan
nassau, niblick, nineteenth hole
out-of-bounds, overplay, overshoot
par, pass-through, penalty stroke, pill, pin, pin high, pitch shot, play through, plus fours, press, pro-am, pull, putt, putter, putting green, putt out
rim, rough, round, run
sand trap, sclaff, shaft, shag, shank, shoot, skull shot, slice, slope, snap hook, spoon, stableford, stance, stroke, stroke play, stymie, swipe
tee, tee off, tee shot, three-ball match, threesome, toe, top, topspin, trap, triple bogey, twosome
unplayable lie
waggle, water hazard, wave up, wedge, wiff, wood
yips

Gymnastics and Calisthenics

calisthenics conditioning exercises usu. performed with little or no special apparatus
gymnastics performance of physical exercises that require strength, balance, and agility, esp. on special apparatus, usu. in judged competition
ariel
backflip, balance beam
chin-up, crossbar, crunch
dismount
flip, floor exercise, freestyle
gymnast
handspring, handstand, high bar, horizontal bar, horse
Indian club, iron cross
jumping jack
parallel bars, pommel horse, pull-up, push-up
rings, roadwork
scissors, setting-up exercises, sit-up, somersault, springboard, straddle
tilt board, trapeze, tuck, twist

uneven bars
vault, vaulting horse
walkover

Hockey

hockey game played on round-ended rectangle of ice between two teams of six skaters each, object being to shoot a hard rubber puck past defenders and goalkeeper into opponent's net using bent wooden stick
assist
back-check, blades, blue line, board check, boards, body check, break, breakaway goal
Campbell Conference, center, change-on-the-fly, charging, check, chippy, crease, cross-check, cross-ice
defenseman, draw, dribble, drop pass
empty net goal, end
face, face mask, face-off, fore-check, forward
glove save, goal, goalie, goalkeeper, goaltender, goon
hat trick, high-sticking, hip-check, holding, hooking
icing, interference
left wing, line, line change, linesman
major penalty, minor penalty
National Hockey League, net, neutral zone, NHL
offside
pass, penalty, penalty box, penalty killer, penalty shot, period, playmaker, point, power play, puck
rebound shot, red light, red line, right wing, rink, roughing
save, shorthanded, shot on goal, skate, slap shot, slashing, spearing, Stanley Cup, stick, sticked, stickhandler, stickhandling, stick save
tripping, T-stop
Wales Conference, white line, wing
Zamboni machine, zone

Horse and Dog Racing

dog racing contest of speed over track between dogs, usu. chasing a mechanical rabbit
horse racing contest of speed over oval track between horses either ridden by jockeys or pulling sulkies and their drivers
allowance race, also-ran
backstretch, Belmont Stakes, blind bet, blinders, blinkers, box bet, boxed-out, break, break away, break-from-the-gate, break stride, Breeder's Cup, buggy
chicane, claiming race, closer, colors, course
daily double, derby, distance, double play
exacta
fast track, favorite, feature race, filly, finish line, furlong, futurity
gelding, grandstand, grass, greyhound
handicapping, handle, head
jock, jockey, juvenile
Kentucky Derby
length, long shot
maiden race, mudder
neck, neck and neck, nose
odds-on favorite, off and running, offtrack betting, OTB
pacer, paddock, parimutuel, parlay, perfecta, photo finish, place, post, post race, post time, Preakness, prohibitive favorite
quarter horse, quinella
rabbit, race, racecourse, racehorse, racetrack, racing form, railbird
saddle, saddling barn, scramble, short odds, show, silks, simulcast, sire, speed horse, stable, stake horse, stake race, starting gate, starting price, steeplechase, steward, stretch, stretch run, stretch runner, string, stud, sulky
thoroughbred, tote, trainer, trial horse, trifecta, Triple Crown, trotter, turf, turfman, turn, twin double
walking ring, walkover, water jump, weigh-in, wheel bet, whip, win, winner's circle, wire, wire-to-wire
yearling

Ice Skating

artistic impression aesthetics of a skating program, especially the judges' opinion of a skater's ability to keep time with the music, interpret the music, etc.
axel jump made from the front outer edge of one skate, followed by 1 1/2 turns, landing on the back outer edge of the other skate [for Axel Paulsen, Norwegian skater who popularlized it]
broken leg spin sit spin in which the skater's extended leg is bent at the knee and held off to the side
butterfly movement in which the skater jumps into the air and arches the back while extending both the arms and legs and throwing back the head
camel spin spin made with the skater's body bent forward at the waist so that the upper body, with one leg extended behind the skater, is parallel to the ice
choctaw turn in which the skater changes from the outside edge of one skate to the inside edge of the other, or from the inside edge of one skate to the outside edge of the other
crossing straight straightaway area opposite the starting line in speed skating, where skaters must change lanes
compulsory (school) figures patterns made on the ice by the skate blade, as circles, figure eights, etc., required of competitive skaters
death spiral pair-skating movement in which the man pivots while holding the hand of the woman, who lowers her body to a horizontal position while skating a circle around her partner
double jump jump in which the skater makes

two complete revolutions in the air
free dance ice dancing program that combines elements of set dances with free skating movements and usually features intricate footwork
free skating (program) skating that includes a variety of figures, movements, steps, and jumps, choreographed to express the mood of the accompanying music
freestyle informal name for free skating
Hamill camel spin that starts as a back camel spin and finishes as a back sit spin [for US skater Dorothy Hamill]
ice dancing skating by a man and woman together who execute certain steps in tempo with the music, usually traditional ballroom dance music
layback spin spin in which the skater bends backward at the waist
lift pair skating movement in which the woman is held above the ice by her partner
long program informal name for the free skating program
Lutz jump made from the back outer edge of one skate with an assist from the toe pick of the other skate, followed by one full rotation in the air and a landing on the back outer edge of the opposite skate [for Austrian skater Alois Lutz]
mohawk turn in which the skater goes from one skate's inside edge to the inside edge of the other skate, or from the outside edge of one skate to the outside edge of the other
pair skating skating by a man and woman together with the partners assisting one another in lifts and spins
precision skating skating performed by a group of skaters who interweave complex patterns
quadruple jump jump in which a skater completes four rotations in the air
Salchow jump in which the skater takes off from a back inside edge, swinging the other leg in front to assist the rotation [for Swedish skater Ulrich Salchow]
school figures compulsory figures
score (marks) in competitive skating, skaters are given two sets of marks—one for technical merit and one for artistic impression—with 6.0 as the highest possible mark
scratch spin fast upright spin in which the toe pick slightly scratches the ice
shadow skating skating by a pair who perform the same movements but do not touch
short program skating program of seven skating movements chosen by the officials, lasting no more than two minutes, in which the skater chooses the order of the movements and the music
sit spin spin in which the skater spins on one skate while in a squatting position, usually with the other leg extended straight in front of the body; also called the Haines spin [for US skater Jackson Haines]
spiral skating movement in which one leg is held extended behind the skater higher than the hip level
spread eagle skating position in which the skater's feet are turned outward, with the toes pointing in opposite directions
technical merit composition of a skating program, especially the judges' opinion on the difficulty and execution of the program
three jump jump in which the skater takes off on the right skate, makes half a turn in the air, and lands on the left skate; also called a waltz jump
three turn semicircular turn with a slight dip in the middle done on one skate, resembling a figure three
(toe) loop jump made from the back outer edge of the skate with a jab of the other toe pick into the ice, after which the skater makes one or more complete turns in the air before landing on the back outer edge of the same skate
triple jump jump in which the skater's body turns three revolutions while in the air
Walley jump in which the skater takes off from one skate's back inside edge, makes one turn in the air, and lands on the same skate's back outside edge; also called the low [for US skater Nate Walley]

Skiing

skiing racing over snow on a pair of long, narrow runners of wood, plastic, or steel; maneuvering between obstacles or jumping for distance on such runners over snow
Alpine skiing, au alement
bathtub, bunny
cement, chairlift, christie, cover, cross-country skiing
downhill
fall line
gate, giant slalom
hot dog
jumping
kick turn
langlauf
mogul
Nordic skiing
off-piste
piste, powder
rope tow
schuss, ski, ski bob, ski boots, skijoring, ski jump, ski lift, ski mask, ski pants, ski pole, ski run, ski suit, ski tow, slalom, snowplow, stem, stem turn, super giant slalom, swing
telemark, traverse, tuck
unweight
Vorlage
wedeln, wedge

Soccer

soccer game played between two teams of eleven players each on a long rectangular field in which a round inflated ball is advanced by kicking or bouncing it off any part of the anatomy except the hands and arms, the object being to put the ball in

the opponent's net, which is defended by a goalkeeper who may use his hands to stop shots
association football
center, corner kick, crossbar
defenseman, dribble
football, footballer, forward, free kick, fullback
goal, goalie, goalkeeper, goal kick, goal kicker, goalmouth, goaltender
halfback, hat trick, header
kickoff
left wing, linesman
midfield, midfielder
NASL, North American Soccer League, nutmeg
offside
pass, penalty, penalty kick
red card, right wing, roughing
tiebreaker, touchline
volley
winger, World Cup
yellow card
zone

Surfing

surfing riding shoreline ocean waves while standing on a long, shaped board of wood or foam and fiberglass coated with resin, sometimes in judged competition
aggro
baggies, barney, beach break, bellyboard, board, body surf, body whomping, boogie board
choppy, close out, come up, crank a turn, crash and burn, curl
ding, drop, drop in
flat
glass-off, glassy, gnarly, goofy-foot, gremmie, gun
hang five, hang ten, ho-dad, hot curl, hot dog
jams
kick-out
leash, left, lineup, locked in, long board
noseride, noserider
offshore wind, onshore wind, outside, overhead
paddleboard, pearl
quasimodo
radical turn, rail, reef break, right, rip
set, shaper, shoot the curl, shoot the pier, shoot the tube, shore break, short board, stoked, surfboard, surfer, surfriding, swell
thruster, tube, tubed, turn
wahine, walk the nose, wall, wet suit, wipeout

Swimming and Diving

diving judged competition in which contestants plunge headfirst into water after leaping from an elevated platform and performing specified maneuvers in the air
swimming racing contest in which swimmers propel themselves across surface of water over designated distance, usu. in one of four strokes
back dive, backstroke, bathing cap, belly flop, breaststroke, butterfly
cannonball, crawl
diver, diving board, dolphin kick
flip turn, flutterboard, flutter kick, freestyle, frog kick, full gainer
gainer
half gainer, heat
individual medley
jackknife
kick lap, kick turn
medley relay
overarm
paddleboard, pike position, platform diving, pool, poolside
scissors kick, scull stroke, sidestroke, splits, springboard diving, starting block, stroke, swan dive, swimming pool, synchronized swimming
triathlon, tuck, twist
whip kick

Tennis

tennis game played on a rectangular court between two players or pairs of players who use strung rackets to bat a small, hollow ball back and forth across a low net that divides the court in half, the object being to place an unreturnable shot within the opponent's half of court
ace, advantage, approach
backcourt, backhand, backspin, backstroke, ball boy, baseline, bisque, break, break point, break service
charge the net, clay court, country club, courtside, crosscourt
deuce, dink, double fault, doubles, drop shot
fault, fifteen, follow-through, footwork, forecourt, forehand, forty
game point, good, Grand Slam, grass court, ground stroke
hack, hard court
lawn tennis, let, line judge, linesman, lob, long, love
match, match point, mishit, mixed doubles
net, netball, net judge, netman
on serve, overhand, overhead smash
paddle, passing shot, placement, placement shot
racket, racquet, rally, retrieve, return
seed, serve, server, service, service break, service court, set, set point, sideline, singles, skein, slice, stop volley, stroke
tennis ball, tennis elbow, tennis shoe, thirty, tiebreaker, topspin
undercut, unforced error
volley
webbing, Wimbledon

Track and Field

track and field indoor or outdoor contest made up of several competitive events, including running races, hurdling, vaulting, jumping, and tossing objects
anchor, anchor lap
baton, break, broad jump
cinder track, cross-country
dash, decathlon, discus, distance medley, distance runner, distance work
fast start, field event, finish line, flying start, Fosbury flop
get set, go, gun lap
hammer throw, heat, heptathlon, high hurdles, high jump, homestretch, hop, step, and jump, hurdles
individual medley, infield, intermediate hurdles
javelin
kick
lap, long jump, low hurdles
marathon, medley relay, metric mile, middle distance, miler
neck and neck
on your mark
pacesetter, pentathlon, pole vault, prelim, pull up, put
qualifying race
relay, run, running start
shakedowns, shot put, speed work, splits, sprint, start, starter, starting block, steeplechase, stopwatch, straddle, straightaway
thin clads, time trial, track meet, track shoe, track suit, triple jump
walk, water jump, weightman, wind sprint

HUNTING AND FISHING

Hunting Practice and Techniques
Fox Hunting
Hunting Equipment
Fishing Practice and Techniques
Fishing Equipment and Tackle

Hunting Practice and Techniques

archery hunting with bow and arrow
bag (*vb*) *Informal.* kill or capture game; (*n*) amount of game taken during one hunting trip
bay position of stag or any cornered animal that has turned to face pursuers
beater person who flushes game birds or hoofed game to guns
big game any large game that is hunted, esp. deer, elk, bear, moose, bison, caribou, antelope, sheep, mountain goat, mountain lion, jaguar, peccary, or wild hog
blood sport any sport in which animals are killed, esp. hunting
closed season time of year when hunting for particular game is prohibited
cold scent scent left by quarry some length of time before hounds pick it up
competition shooting skeet, trap, or target shooting as competitive event
covert hiding place of fox or upland game, esp. shrubs or thicket
dead set stiff posture of hunting dog indicating presence and location of game
drag scent left by fox or other animal
falconry hunting with falcons, hawks, or eagles; training hawks to hunt
fault loss of scent; break in line of scent
ferreting using ferrets to drive rabbits and other rodents from underground
flush (*vb*) cause game, esp. birds, to break cover or take flight
game wild animals and birds that are hunted and killed for sport and/or meat
game birds hunted land birds, esp. blackcock, capercaillie, dove, grouse, partridge, pheasant, pigeon, ptarmigan, quail, snipe, turkey, wild turkey, and woodcock
gamekeeper person employed to maintain game preserve, prevent poaching, and nurture animal life
hunting practice and techniques associated with the pursuit and search for game for purpose of killing them
open season time of year when hunting for certain game is permitted
plinking shooting at tin cans or other stationary targets with handgun
poach (*vb*) hunt or kill game illegally on another's property or preserve
point (*vb*) of hunting dog, stand rigid, facing in direction of located game to indicate its position; (*n*) *Chiefly Brit.* distance between two extreme ends of hunt in straight line
predator any animal that exists by hunting other animals for food, esp. bobcat, coyote, crow, fox, lynx, skunk, or wolf
preserve area designated for maintenance of game for hunting
prey hunted animal
quarry game hunted, esp. by hounds or falconry
safari hunting expedition for big game in Africa
scent distinctive odor left by animal that has passed, used by dogs in tracking prey
season legally designated time of year when specific game may be hunted in given region
shorebirds hunted birds that live by water, esp. curlew, plover, snipe, rail, gallinule, and yellowlegs
skeet shooting trapshooting in which clay targets are propelled singly or in pairs from several different positions at varying heights and speeds to simulate flight of game birds
small game any small, wild animal that is hunted, such as hare, rabbit, racoon, squirrel, woodchuck, groundhog, opossum, or prairie dog
stander hunter with gun over whom beater

drives birds or toward whom deer hunter pushes deer
still-hunt (*vb*) hunt game alone, usu. in heavy, wooded cover and as silently as possible, esp. without a dog
tracking pursuing prey by following readable track or physical markings, or by using hounds to follow scent
trapping capturing game and wildfowl by setting mechanical contrivance that springs shut when triggered
trapshooting shooting at clay pigeons hurled into air from mechanical trap
upland game birds hunted game birds such as grouse, pheasant, pigeon, quail, and wild turkey
venatic (*adj*) of or pertaining to hunting
waders hunted wildfowl, such as coots, curlews, and plovers, found in shallow waters
warrantable (*adj*) of legal age for being hunted, esp. deer
waterfowl hunted birds that live on water, such as brant, bufflehead, canvasback, coot, duck, eider, gadwall, goose, mallard, scoter, shoveler, teal
wildfowl hunted game birds such as wild ducks, geese, swans, or waders
winged predators birds that live by feeding on other animals, such as crow, eagle, hawk, jaeger, or owl
woodsman person skilled at hunting and trapping

Fox Hunting

all on cry of whipper-in indicating that all hounds are accounted for
bait (*vb*) set dogs on prey
bolt (*vb*) force fox out of hiding place into open
challenge cry of hound on picking up scent
chop (*vb*) attack and kill fox that has not begun to run; mob
course (*vb*) run fox into full view
crop whip
gone away huntsman's cry indicating hounds are in pursuit and hunt is on
hound breed of dog trained to pursue game by scent, used esp. in fox hunting; foxhound
line trail of scent left by fox
mort note played on hunting horn signifying that hunted animal has been killed
pink coat usu. scarlet coat worn by members of fox hunt
tally ho cry of huntsman indicating that fox or other prey has been sighted
tantivy cry of huntsman when chase is at full tilt
thruster rider who remains at front of field in fox hunt
view halloa cry of huntsman on seeing fox break cover
whip whipper-in
whipper-in member of hunt responsible for hounds; whip
yoicks huntsman's cry used to encourage hounds

Hunting Equipment

block *Slang.* set of decoys
bow and arrow curved, flexible frame bent by string stretched between its ends to fire pointed shafts
buckshot lead shot, larger than BB, used in shotgun shells for hunting deer, boar, and similar game
camouflage clothing or other gear made of material with mottled design in brown and green that simulates forest environment
coursing hound hound used to run game into view, such as greyhound, whippet, or Afghan
deadfall trap in which disturbance of bait triggers fall of heavy weight onto prey
decoy lifelike dummy or model of hunted species, esp. game bird or wildfowl, set out to attract others of species; trained bird or animal used for same purpose, now illegal
float flat-bottomed, wide boat such as johnboat, used for hunting shorebirds and waterfowl
floating blind boatlike concealment used for hunting ducks or geese
gamebag bag with shoulder strap, usu. of canvas or leather, used to carry dead game birds
goose block set of decoys used to attract geese
hip boots waterproof boots reaching to midthigh or hips, used for wading through water
hound breed of dog trained to pursue game by scent, used esp. in fox hunting
hunting dogs any dog used for hunting game, such as pointers, retrievers, setters, hounds, spaniels, beagles, bassets, and weimaraners
license formal permission authorizing bearer to hunt in specified place or time or for specific game
lure feathered decoy swung at end of line, sometimes baited with raw meat, used in falconry
natural blind natural growth or formation used as concealment while hunting ducks and geese
pointing dog any of various breeds of dog, including setters and Brittany spaniels, used for pointing game
profile decoy depicting bird in profile
purse net net with drawstring that fits over rabbit hole
rail boat low, flat-bottomed boat with protective rails, used in hunting waterfowl
recurve bow bow that is bent backward from its primary curvature at the tips
retriever dog used for retrieving game
rifle firearm with spiral grooves cut inside long bore, imparting more precise trajectory to bullet, usu. fired from shoulder
setter dog used to set game, including breeds such as longhaired pointing bird dogs
shotgun smoothbore firearm, often double-barreled, firing either single slug or multiple-pellet loads
silhouette two-dimensional representation of game animal or bird, used as target
snare nooselike trap used esp. for rabbits
spring trap trap that springs shut on prey when triggered

straight bow bow that curves in one direction only
trap mechanical contrivance that springs shut or open when triggered by prey
waders waterproof boots reaching to mid-chest, used esp. by duck hunters for wading through water

Fishing Practice and Techniques

angling art and practice of fishing with hook and line
backcast in fly casting, action of lifting line off the water through an upward and backward flip of fly rod's tip prior to forward cast of line that presents fly to quarry
backhand cast fly-fisherman's cast made across own body
backing between 100 and 250 yards of lighter, usu. braided line tied in behind heavier fly line as margin of safety against long run by big fish
backlash overrun of reel spool resulting in snarled line
bait casting casting of artificial lure or plug, as well as bait, with revolving-spool reel on fiberglass rod 4 to 7 feet long
bottom-fishing fishing with live or dead bait for fish that are bottom feeders, such as ocean fish like flounder and sole or freshwater fish like catfish and carp
bowfishing shooting fish in shallow water with bow and arrow, esp. freshwater carp or bottom fish such as stingrays, skates, and sharks
casting act of projecting and placing artificial lure, fly, or bait within intended area and distance
closed season time of year when fishing for particular species is prohibited
dap (*vb*) allow fly to bounce lightly over surface of water using long rod up to 17 feet (5 m) in length
deep-sea fishing fishing from boat in ocean waters at some distance from shore
double haul fly casting technique used to achieve distance
dress (*vb*) prepare a fly or bait a hook for use
drift-fishing fishing in which the fly's action is due entirely to current; still fishing with bait from a moving boat
electric fishing catching fish by submerging positive and negative electrodes, causing fish to swim toward positive electrode and become unconscious, illegal for sportfishing but used to move fish to other waters
false cast cast in which line and fly are prevented from hitting water by switching line forcefully back and forth
fish culture artificial breeding and propagation of fish to provide stock for angling or commercial sale
fishing technique, practice, and diversion of catching fish for sport, usu. with line, hook, and rod
float-fishing river fishing in which boat continuously drifts while angler casts
fly-fishing method of fishing with artificial flies, in which weight of line, not lure, is propelled through air by switching it back and forth from a long rod to achieve velocity, with reel mounted below rod grip and used primarily to store line
freshwater fish most popular fish for freshwater fishing: esp. trout (brook, brown, golden, rainbow) also bass, bluegill, bullhead, carp, catfish, char, crappie, gar, grayling, perch, pike, salmon, sauger, shad, walleye, whitefish
game fish any species of fish that may legally be taken for sport and tends to resist capture
greased-line method fishing for salmon in stream with fly that sinks just beneath surface and plastic-coated line that floats with no drag; formerly, this line was greased to make it float
hand line line that is pulled in by hand rather than reeled in, used esp. to extricate fish from weeds
horizontal cast method of casting line beneath overhanging branch or rock by swinging rod parallel to surface of water
ice fishing tecnique of fishing through a hole cut in ice, usu. in frozen lake in winter
jigging imparting up and down motion to lure or bait, esp. in ice fishing
keeper fish that is legally big enough to keep
kite fishing method of offshore fishing in which airborne kite trolls skipping bait or holds live bait at surface of water
lake fishing fishing in freshwater lake, from shore or by trolling from boat
margin fishing technique of fishing under bank on side of lake toward which wind is blowing food by placing rod on rests and floating bait, which is blown back under bank
permit official license granting an individual permission to fish
piscatory (*adj*) relating to fishing or fishermen
play amount of slack in a line, allowing it to move freely in response to fish
playing fish maintaining proper tension on line to tire out and bring in fish without breaking line
plug casting bait casting using plug as lure
reef-fishing fishing on or from shallow ridge of rocks or sand in ocean
rise act of fish coming to fly; circular ripples on water's surface indicating fish coming up to feed
roll cast fly-casting technique in which line does not go behind angler, used on streams with close overhangs
saltwater fish most popular fish, for saltwater fishing: esp. tuna, cod, salmon, and striped bass; also albacore, barracuda, blackfish, bluefish, croaker, dolphin, flounder, mackerel, marlin, pollock, pompano, red snapper, sailfish, shark, whiting
shoot line in fly casting, act of allowing forward cast of fly line to pull out extra loops of line held by noncasting hand, used to lengthen cast
sidearm cast cast performed by swinging rod parallel to ground at side of body, esp. to avoid overhang
sink-and-draw fishing with dead bait that is alternately allowed to sink, then drawn up to surface

spin casting fishing with lure or bait and closed-face reel with fixed spool from which line peels off at end of long spinning rod, different from spinning
spinning method of casting light lure with fixed-spool reel, mounted on underside of rod, in which line uncoils but spool remains stationary; spin fishing; thread-line fishing
sportfishing fishing for sport with rod and reel, usu. from motorboat for saltwater fish
still fishing fishing with stationary bait from shore or boat
stock supply (stream or lake) with fish for fishing
stream fishing fishing in fresh waterway, either from shore or by standing in boots in water
surf casting technique and practice of using 8- to 12-foot spinning or bait-casting rod to cast heavy-duty line into sea while standing at shoreline
trawl (*vb*) fish by dragging net along bottom of sea, or with buoyed trawl line having numerous baited hooks spaced at intervals along it
trolling fishing from slow-moving boat with lure or bait trailing behind at varying depths and speeds in lakes or saltwater
trotting angling in fast-moving water, using float and line that holds bait near bottom
tying art and practice of designing and making flies
underhand lob casting technique in which rod tip is raised vertically to propel bait or lure outward from fisherman

Fishing Equipment and Tackle

angleworm earthworm commonly used as live bait
antenna float float with long tip on top that shows above water surface
artificial bait object made to resemble fly, worm, fish, or animal and placed on hook
artificial fly imitation of fly, insect, or larva made from feathers, fur, silk, thread, and/or tinsel, with hook attached; fly
bait living creatures such as minnows, earthworms, grubs, or grasshoppers attached to hook and used to entice fish into striking
bait-casting rod fiberglass rod for bait casting, usu. 5 to 6 feet (1.5 to 1.8 m) long
balanced tackle tackle used esp. in fly-fishing, in which relationship between rod action and reel-and-line weight is essential to effective casting
barb point projecting off hook in opposite direction from point, used to prevent fish from spitting out hook
bass bug large fly-rod lure with cork or deer-hair body that imitates bass food such as frog, bee, dragonfly, or mouse
bend crook in fishhook, often ending at barb
boat rod rod for casting or trolling with lure or bait from boat, usu. 5 to 6 1/2 feet (1.5 to 2 meters) long
bobber float usu. made of cork and quills, used in still fishing to suspend bait at set depth and indicate strike; bob
boulter long, heavyweight line with several hooks attached
bubble float transparent, spherical float partly weighted with water
bucktail artificial fly with long wing, often of hair from deer's tail, that imitates minnow or other small baitfish
bucktail jig lure with weighted head and bucktail wings
casting rod fishing rod, usu. 4 to 8 feet (1.2 to 2.4 m) long, for casting bait or spinning lure, usu. fitted with revolving reel that allows angler to control line with thumb during cast
chum ground bits of bait or food discarded into water to attract game fish
close-faced reel reel enclosed in housing with hole at center or edge of cover through which line passes
cloudbait finely minced bait discarded into water to attract fish
corkball float float made of ball of cork
cork bug fly with solid cork body that floats and imitates action of frog, mouse, or grasshopper, used in bass fishing
crawlers rubber cleats that attach to boots to prevent slipping on rocks
creel basket, esp. of wicker, for holding fish, often carried by strap over shoulder
disgorger rodlike device with forked end, used to remove hook from fish's throat
dobber float or bob
drift net fishing net held upright in water by floats at upper edge and sinkers at bottom edge, so as to be carried by current or tide
drop net circular net lowered by weighted cords at four points into water to catch fish and small crustaceans for bait
dry fly fly that imitates appearance and action of floating insect, with hackles projecting at right angles from hook to keep fly on surface
eye loop at end of fishhook shank through which line or leader passes
ferrule any of several fitted, usu. metal joints, composed of socket and plug, that are spaced along length of rod so that it can be dismantled and reassembled
fiberglass rod basic material used for fishing rods, replacing bamboo after 1948
fighting chair seat attached to deck at stern of fishing boat, used by angler in landing very large fish
fishfinder surf fishing device with pyramid sinker and barrel swivel that allows bait to cover broad area
fishhook slender, recurved, usu. barbed piece of metal wire at end of lure or on which fly is tied or bait placed for catching fish; hook
fishing line line of braided or twisted silk, cotton, or monofilament, used to connect hook to rod and reel; fishline
fishing pole rudimentary gear consisting of long, thin rod with line and hook fastened to one end for catching fish

fishing rod long, thin, flexible rod of bamboo, fiberglass, or graphite with reel attached, used with line and hooks for catching fish; rod
fishing smack large, usu. commercial fishing vessel containing well to keep catch alive
fishline fishing line
fixed-reel seat frame by which fixed spinning reel is attached to rod
fixed-spool reel spinning reel with open top
float cork, hollow plastic, or bobber used to buoy up baited line in water
fly artificial fly
gill net mesh wall held vertically in water by corks on top and lead weights on bottom, capturing anything too large to slip through it
harpoon barbed, spearlike missile attached to rope, fired or thrown at whales or large fish
hip boots waterproof boots reaching to hips
ice auger device used to cut hole in ice for ice fishing
ice skimmer slotted, ladlelike device used to clear ice chips from hole and surrounding area in ice fishing
ice spud device with chisel-like blade on heavy handle, used to punch hole in ice for ice fishing
ice sounder device consisting of lead weight with spring clip on line, used to determine depth of water beneath ice in ice fishing
jig lure with weighted head, fixed hook, and tail made of feathers or nylon, often attached by wire leader
keep net long, cylindrical net used to keep catch alive
landing net any baglike net on handle large enough to lift exhausted fish from water and land or boat it
leader length of wire or monofilament that protects line from fish or forms invisible link between main line and lure, bait, or fly
line part of tackle that connects cast lure or baited hook to rod in fisherman's hand, usu. monofilament, also: braided nylon, copper, cotton, Dacron, linen, nylon, silk, or wire
live bait any natural organism placed on a hook and used to catch fish: angleworm, caterpillar, crayfish, cricket, darter, dragonfly, fish egg, frog, grasshopper, grub, hellgrammite, mayfly, minnow, night crawler, worm
lobster pot baited box trap dropped to seafloor for catching lobsters
lure any artificial bait used to attract fish, usu. distinguished from artificial flies
monofilament single strand of extruded nylon used for fishing line
multiplier very free-running reel used for bait casting and spinning
net any of various mesh devices with handles, used to snare fish in water for landing or boating
plug lure made of wood, plastic, or metal that darts through water imitating a small fish, fitted with one of more gang hooks
point last section of tapered leader in fly fishing; tippet
purse seine large seine drawn by two boats around school of fish and closed at the bottom by means of a line passing through rings
reel device with rotating or fixed spool attached to butt of fishing rod, used to let out or bring in line
saltwater bait live bait used for deep-sea fishing and surf casting: baitfish, crab, cut bait, herring, mullet, shrimp, squid
seaboot tall, waterproof wading boot
seine vertical fishing net suspended in water between floats at surface and submerged sinkers
single-action fly reel fly reel whose spool makes one turn with each turn of the reel handle
sinker metal weight, usu. made of lead, molded in various shapes and sizes, used to lower, troll, or anchor bait or lure at desired depth
spear long staff with sharply pointed metal head, used for stabbing fish
spinner lure with oval metal blade mounted on shaft that revolves when drawn through water
spinning reel fixed-spool reel with adjustable drag and antireverse lock, mounted on underside of rod
spinning rod lightweight bamboo, fiberglass, or graphite rod for spinning with small lure, lure-fly combination, or bait
spool revolving apparatus in reel, around which line winds and unwinds
tackle equipment and apparatus used in fishing; gear; rig
tackle box sturdy, waterproof, metal or plastic box in which fishing tackle is stored, usu. having several compartments
tilt ice-fishing device with crosspieces that span hole in ice, used to hold baited line leading from underwater revolving-spool reel and attached to cocked arm that releases when fish strikes; tip-up
tippet finest end of tapered leader; tail or wing of artificial fly made from shaft of certain cock feather; point
trammel net three-layered net with a fine-meshed middle layer between two coarser outer layers, so that fish become entangled in one or more of the nets
trawl net net dragged along sea bottom to catch fish
trident fishing spear having three-pronged point
waders thigh-high rubber boots, often with studded soles to provide traction over rocks; chest-high, waterproof boot trousers with suspenders
wading staff rod used to test bottom firmness while wading through water
waist boots waterproof boots reaching to waist
wet fly sparsely dressed, usu. flat fly that imitates action and appearance of submerged insect

GARDENING

Gardens and Gardening Systems
Practice, Tools, and Techniques
Plants and Plant Parts

Gardens and Gardening Systems

alpine garden garden of plants native to high altitudes
arboretum garden in which trees and shrubs are grown and displayed
bonsai garden of dwarf trees artfully cultivated in pots (Japan)
botanical garden collection of plants and trees kept for exhibition and scientific study
conservatory elaborate greenhouse where plants are grown and displayed
dry garden garden of cactus and other plants requiring little water for cultivation
formal garden elaborate, manicured, and carefully pruned decorative garden
garden plot of ground where plants are cultivated
greenhouse translucent structure in which environment is controlled to allow delicate plants to develop and thrive
hanging garden garden with plants suspended in pots rather than growing from ground
hedge dense row of shrubs used to form boundary
herbarium collection of dried plants, esp. for botanical study
hortorium museum for collection, preservation, and study of plant specimens
Japanese garden manicured garden with bonsai, teahouse, and still water
kitchen garden small vegetable garden for personal use
orchard cultivated fruit or nut trees
ornamental garden garden of flowers and decorative shrubs
rock garden artificial landscape containing natural-looking rock outcrops and soil surfaces
roof garden potted plants growing on roof of building, esp. in urban area with no open land surrounding buildings
rose garden ornamental garden of carefully pruned rose bushes
tea garden Japanese garden with teahouse
terrarium miniature garden enclosed in glass container
truck garden garden in which vegetables are grown to be marketed
vegetable garden garden of cultivated, edible plants
victory garden home vegetable garden grown during wartime to supplement crop production
vineyard plantation of cultivated grapevines
xeriscape garden for drought-tolerant plants

Practice, Tools, and Techniques

agronomy science and management of crop production
air layering propagation method by which roots develop on stems while attached to mother plant
arbor latticework bower on which vines are trained
arboriculture cultivation of trees and shrubs for ornament
backfill soil returned after being dug up to cover positioned roots, often mixed with additives to improve its condition
balled and burlapped designating soil-covered roots bundled and wrapped for protection until planting
blanch (*vb*) shield plant, esp. vegetable, from sunlight to promote paler color in stems or leaves
botany science of plant life, including structure, growth, and classification; characteristics of a plant or plant group
budding putting forth of buds; asexual propagation technique
cloche transparent protective covering for delicate plants
cold frame low, transparent, unheated greenhouse box
compost nutrient-rich decomposed organic matter
cutting portion of plant removed and induced to propagate
deadhead (*vb*) pinch off dead flower heads from stems to promote blooming
dibber dibble
dibble pointed tool used to make holes in soil for insertion of plants or seeds; dibber
edger revolving blade on long handle, used for trimming lawn or flower bed
espalier lattice or trellis on which tree or shrub branches are trained to grow in flat pattern
evapotranspiration process of transferring moisture from earth to atmosphere by evaporation of water and transpiration from plants
fertilizer material containing one or more plant nutrients
flat rooting box for cuttings or seeds
floriculture cultivation of ornamental and flowering plants
floristry growing and selling of flowers and ornamentals
force (*vb*) artificially induce rapid growth or blooming of plant
friable soil easily crumbled soil
furrow planting trench made by plow
gardening process of making, caring for, and working in gardens
germination sprouting of seeds for planting
graft union of one plant to another so that two will grow as one
greenhouse hothouse
green thumb exceptional facility for gardening and growing plants successfully
ground cover low, dense-growing plants used to

cover ground where grass will not grow
groundskeeping care of gardens, playing fields, and lawns
harrow tool with spikes or sharp-edged disks for cultivating soil
herbaceous (*adj*) designating nonwoody plant
hoe hand tool with thin, flat blade on handle for loosening soil and weeding
horticulture science and art of growing plants
hotbed plot of earth covered with glass and heated to accelerate plant growth
hothouse glass building artificially heated for growing plants; greenhouse
humus organic part of soil resulting from decomposition of plant or animal matter
hydroponics growing of plants without soil in nutrient-rich solutions of moist, inert material
irrigation bringing of water to plant beds, esp. by ditches or channels
landscape gardening practice of arranging lawns, flower beds, and bushes in attractive manner for human use, esp. as a profession
leaching loss of soluble matter from soil due to filtering through of water
leaf mold rich soil composed largely of decayed leaves
lime calcium compound used as soil amendment to enhance crop growth
loam friable mixture of sand and clay
loppers long-handled pruning shears
manure fertilizer of animal excrement
mulch protective ground cover of leaves, straw, and peat moss
n-p-k initials for ingredients in complete fertilizer: nitrogen (n), phosphorus (p), and potassium (chemical symbol k)
nursery place where young trees or plants are raised
organic (*adj*) designating plants grown with animal or vegetable fertilizers only
peat moss mulch of slightly decomposed plant remains
perlite light, porous soil additive composed of volcanic material
pest destructive or troublesome insect, small animal, or weed
photosynthesis production of organic substances from carbon dioxide and water in green plant cells, which chemically transform radiant energy of sunlight
pinching removal of tips of twigs and branches to force bushy growth
pleaching training of plant growth so that plaited branches form hedge or arbor
pollard tree pruned to produce dense, leafy dome
pollination transfer of pollen from stamens to pistils
propagation multiplication of an organism by natural reproduction
prune (*vb*) control growth of plant by trimming at top to increase quality and yield of flowers or fruit
pruner bladed device for cutting back plant growth; brush cutter
rake long-handled, toothed tool for gathering loose material or smoothing surface
root-bound (*adj*) designating potted plant whose roots have no room to grow
scree rocky debris, sometimes re-created as rock garden habitat
shredder compost maker
silt soil composed primarily of sediment that accumulates on bottoms of rivers and bays, with particles smaller than sand but larger than clay
sod carpet of grass; turf
soil upper layer of earth that may be cultivated, and that can support plant growth; this material collected and placed in gardens or pots, consisting of small particles of rock together with humus
soil amendments substances added to improve soil texture and fertility, such as compost, peat moss, perlite, lime, or chemicals
spade digging instrument with blade that is pushed into ground with foot
spading fork spade with forklike tines
sphagnum long-fibered, highly absorbent peat moss
sprinkler device for distributing water evenly over large area of garden
staking providing support for plants with thin strips of wood stuck upright in ground
terrace raised, flat mound of earth with sloping sides, often in series of descending levels
thinning pruning by removing whole branches to create less density; removal of some seedlings to foster growth of others
top-dress (*vb*) apply mulch to protect seeds
topiary pruning of hedges into unique or formal shapes; hedge so pruned
topsoil rich, relatively fertile top layer of soil
transpiration loss of water from plant leaves into air
transplant (*vb*) transfer plant from one home to another
trellis structure of thin strips on which climbing plants are trained
trowel small tool with curved, scooplike blade on handle, used in turning earth and digging
turf sod
weed (*vb*) remove unwanted growth from garden
wheelbarrow shallow, open container on single wheel with handles, used for moving soil and plants
wilting limpness in plant due to lack of water, poor root function, or disease
windbreak plants used as barrier to wind

Plants and Plant Parts

annual plant with life cycle of one year or season
anther part of stamen that produces and releases pollen
bark outside covering of stems and roots of trees and woody plants
biennial plant with two-year life cycle, in which vegetative first-year growth is followed by fruiting and drying during second year
bole tree trunk

bolt (*vb*) prematurely produce flowers and seeds, esp. in hot weather
bonsai potted tree or shrub that has been dwarfed, usu. by pruning roots and pinching
bract leaflike structure growing below or encircling flower cluster or flower
broad-leaved (*adj*) describing a plant having leaves that are not needles
bud small swelling on plant from which shoot, leaf cluster, or flower develops
bulb dormant underground bud stage of some plants
cactus fleshy-stemmed plant with reduced or spinelike leaves, living in dry places and requiring little water
calyx outer whorl of protective leaves of flower
cambium layer of formative cells beneath bark of tree
carpel ovule-bearing leaf or leaflike structure that is primary segment of pistil
climber vine or climbing plant with tendrils
conifer cone-bearing evergreen, usu. with narrow, needlelike or small, scalelike leaves
corm underground stem base that acts as reproductive structure
corolla petals of a flower
cotyledon first leaf or two of seedling
crab grass weedy annual grass that roots and spreads rapidly in lawns and gardens
creeper plant whose stem puts out tendrils or rootlets and that moves along surface as it grows
crown topmost portions of tree's leafy canopy
deciduous (*adj*) designating any plant that sheds all its leaves once each year
evergreen plant that maintains functional green foliage throughout year
exotic plant that is not native to growing area
eye bud of root or tuber
fern nonflowering plant having fronds instead of leaves and reproducing by spores instead of seeds
filament stalk of stamen bearing the anther
flora plants of specific region or time
flower (*n*) seed-producing plant with stem that bears leaflike sepals, colorful petals, and pollen-bearing stamens; plant cultivated for its blossoms; reproductive organ of some plants; bloom; blossom; (*vb*) produce blossoms
foliage groups of leaves, flowers, or branches; greenery
frond fern or palm foliage
fruit mature ovary of flowering plant, usu. edible
go to seed pass to stage of producing seeds at end of growth cycle, used esp. of seasonal crops
grass member of family of flowering plants with long, narrow leaves, used for food and fodder or as lawns
greenery green vegetation; foliage
herb seed-producing plant with little or no woody tissue, valued for its medicinal, aromatic, or savory qualities
kernel grain or seed, esp. inside fruit
latent bud dormant bud in stem or beneath bark
lateral bud bud growing on side of stem
leaf flat, thin structure growing from stem or twig of plant, used in photosynthesis and transpiration
moss any of various small, green plants without true stems, reproducing by spores and growing in velvety clusters in moist areas on rocks, trees, or the ground
orchid perennial epiphyte cultivated for its brightly colored flowers
ornamental plant or shrub grown for its decorative effect
perennial plant that lives two years or more; herbaceous plant that lives beyond its flowering stage
petal one of the circle of flower parts inside the sepals
petiole stem connecting branch to leaf blade
pistil central, seed-bearing part of flower, comprised of one or more carpels, each with style and stigma
plant member of kingdom of living things capable of carrying on photosynthesis in cells, primarily adapted for terrestrial life
pollen fine, dustlike grains containing male sexual cells, produced in anthers or similar structures of seed plants
rhizome creeping horizontal stem lying at or just beneath soil surface, bearing leaves at its tip and roots from its underside
root underground part of plant that functions in absorption, aeration, food storage, and as support system
runner long, slender stem growing from base of some perennials
seed fertilized plant ovule containing embryo and capable of germinating to produce new plant
seedling plant grown from seed rather than cutting; young plant or tree
sepal usu. green, leaflike outer circle of calyx
shoot new growth, sprout, or twig on plant
shrub woody perennial plant with several low-branching stems; bush
spike stem with flowers directly attached to its upper portion
spore reproductive cell in mosses and ferns, capable of producing new adult individual
sprout young growth on plant; new growth from bud, rootstock, or germinating seed
spur projection from rear of flower, arising from sepal or petal
stalk stem or main axis of plant; any slender, supporting or connecting part of plant
stamen pollen-producing part of central flower, comprised of filament and anther
stem main upward-growing axis of plant
stigma free upper tip of flower style on which pollen falls and develops
stolon stem that takes root at intervals along ground, forming new plants; runner
style slender, stalklike part of carpel between stigma and ovary
succulent plant with thick, fleshy tissues that store water
taproot deep, main root from which lateral roots develop

tendril threadlike, often spiral part of climbing plant that clings to or coils around objects
thorn sharp-pointed, leafless branch of plant
tree tall, woody perennial with single stem or trunk and branches usu. beginning at some height above ground
trunk thick, primary stem of tree
truss compact flower cluster at tip of stem
tuber fat, underground stem from which certain plants grow, similar to but shorter and thicker than rhizome
variegated (*adj*) designating plant with patterned or bicolored leaves and petals
vegetable any herbaceous plant all or part of which may be used as food
vine plant that grows along the ground or clings to vertical support by means of twining stems, tendrils, and rootlets
water sprout nonflowering shoot springing from bud of main plant branch
weed undesired, uncultivated plant for which no purpose has been found, often growing in profusion and interfering with growth of desired plants

HOBBIES

Hobby leisure activity, skill, or sport engaged in for enjoyment and enrichment; avocation
angling, antique collecting, antique refinishing, aquarium building, audiophile, avocation
backpacking, ballooning, bingo, birdwatching, board games, bridge
camping, cards, carpentry, ceramics, climbing, coin collecting, collecting, cooking, crafts, crewel embroidery, crocheting, crossword puzzle, customizing, cycling
decoupage, do-it-yourself, drying flowers
embroidery
fabric painting, fiber arts, fishing, fly fishing, folk dancing
gambling, games, gaming, gardening, glass painting
handicrafts, hang gliding, home decorating, hunting
ice-skating, ikebana, in-line skating
jewelry making, jogging
kite flying, knitting
landscaping
macramé, manège, mask making, mobile making, model airplanes, model cars, model trains, mountain climbing, mountaineering
needlecrafts, needlepoint, numismatics
orchid growing, origami
paper flower making, paperworking, papier-mâché, pastime, pets, philately, phillumenism, photography, pottery, pressing flowers, puppetry, puzzles
quilting
recreation, riding, rock climbing, rollerblading, roller-skating
scouting, scrimshaw, scuba diving, sewing, shell carving, skateboarding, skeet shooting, skin diving, skydiving, sledding, snorkeling, spelunking, stained glass, stamp collecting, stenciling, stitchery, surf fishing, surfing
taxidermy, terrarium building, tie-dyeing, toymaking, trapshooting, trapunto
weaving, whittling, windsurfing, woodworking
yachting

GAMES, ACTIVITIES, AND TOYS

Athletic Events and Activities

acrobatics, aerobics, aikido, aquaplaning
backpacking, ballooning, bareback riding, bellyboard riding, body-surfing
caber, calisthenics, canoeing, cartwheels, climbing
fishing, fly-fishing
gliding, gym, gymnastics
handball, handsprings, hang gliding
iceboating, Indian wrestling
judo, jujitsu
karate, kendo, kung fu
martial arts, mountaineering
ninjutsu
racquetball, riding, rock climbing
sailing, sailplaning, sculling, shooting, skateboarding, skating, skeet shooting, skiing, skin diving, skydiving, sledding, snorkeling, snowboarding, somersaulting, squash, surf casting
tae kwon do, tobogganing, trapshooting, tumbling
waterskiing, whitewater rafting, windsurfing, wrestling

Public Contests and Performances

aerobatics, aquacade, aquatics

beauty contest, bullfighting
carousel, cavalletti, cockfighting, contortionism
demolition derby, dog racing, dog show, dressage
equestrian events
funny cars
Grand Prix racing
harness racing
Ice Capades, Ice Follies
jousting
lists
Maypole celebrations
quarterhorse racing, quintain
rodeo, rope walking
Soap Box Derby, stock-car racing, synchronized swimming
thoroughbred racing, tightrope walking, trampoline jumping, trapeze performing, trot racing

Outdoor Games

badminton, bandy, boccie, broomball, bumper cars, bungee jumping
capture the flag, catch, croquet, curling
dodge ball, Dodgem
Frisbee
gliding
hare and hounds, hide-and-seek, hopscotch, horseshoes
jacks, jump rope
keepaway
leapfrog
marbles, merry-go-round, miniature golf, muss
obstacle race
paddleball, paddle tennis, pall-mall, pepper, punchball, pushball
quoits
racquets, ring-a-lievio, ring-around-the-rosey, ring taw, ringtoss, roller-skating
sack racing, shuffleboard
tag, teetertotter, tetherball, three-legged race, tipcat, trapshooting, tug of war

Indoor Games

acrostics, anagrams
bagatelle, billiards, bingo, blindman's buff, bluff, board games, bo-peep
cards, cat's cradle, charades, consequences, crambo, craps, crossword puzzle
darts, dice, dominoes
fan-tan
games of chance, games of skill, ghosts
hazard
jacks, jackstraws
keno
lotto
mumbletypeg, musical chairs
nine ball, Nintendo
pachinko, parlor games, peekaboo, pick-up-sticks, pinball machines, pin the tail on the donkey, pocket billiards, pool, post office, put-and-take, puzzles, pyramids
raffle, reversi, roulette
skittle, slot machine, snooker, spillikins, spin the bottle
tic-tack-toe
video games

Pool and Billiards

billiards game played with hard ivorylike balls that are driven with a cue stick on cloth-covered, rimmed table without pockets
pool game played with fifteen numbered balls and white cue ball that is driven with a cue stick into other balls, the object being to sink balls into pockets at the perimeter of a cloth-covered, rimmed table
backspin, balkline, bank shot, break, bumper
carom, chalk, combination shot, crutch, cue, cue ball, cushion
eight ball, English
massé
nine ball
object ball
pocket
rack, rotation, run
scratch, shot
table scratch, topspin

Card Games

cards any game played with a set of marked pieces of cardboard, usu. in a deck of fifty-two divided into four suits (clubs, diamonds, hearts, and spades), each suit numbered one (ace) through ten plus a jack, queen, and king
all fours
baccarat, beggar-my-neighbor, bezique, blackjack, blind poker, Boston, brag, bridge
canasta, casino, chemin de fer, clubs, concentration, conquian, contract bridge, cooncan, crazy eights, cribbage, cutthroat contract
draw poker, duplicate bridge
Earl of Coventry, euchre
fan-tan, faro, fish, five-card stud, frog
gin, gin rummy, go fish
hearts, high-low
loo, lowball
Michigan, monte
nap
old maid, ombre
pairs, patience, penny ante, pinochle, piquet, poker, Pope Joan, primero
quadrille
rouge et noir, rubber bridge, rummy, Russian bank
seven-up, skat, slapjack, snap, snipsnapsnorum, solitaire, speculation, straight poker,

strip poker, stud poker
tarak, three-card monte, twenty-one
vingt-et-un
war, whist

CARD TERMS

ace, ante
bank, banker, bid, bluff, bug, bullet
call, check, contract, cowboy, crossruff, croupier, cut
deal, dealer, dealing box, deuce, deuces wild, discard, double, draw, draw poker
face card, fill up, flop, flush, four of a kind, full house
hand, hole card, house, hoyle
inside straight, in the hole
joker
lead, limit
major suit, manille, mechanic, meld, misdeal, moriah
nob, no trump
odd trick, one-eyed, overtrick, overtrump
pair, pam, pan, pass, penny ante, picture card, playing card, pot, pot limit, preemptive bid
raise, royal flush, rubber, ruff
singleton, shoe, shoot the moon, shuffle, slough, spadille, straight, straight flush, strong suit, stud poker, suit
three of a kind, trey, trump, two pair
underbid, undertrick
wild card
Yarborough

Board Games

board game game played on flat sheet of wood or cardboard with markings, usu. requiring moving of pieces about the board
acey-deucy
backgammon, Balderdash, Battleship
Candyland, checkers, chess, Chinese checkers, Chutes and Ladders, Clue, Connect Four
draughts
fox-and-geese
go
Life
mah-jongg, merels, Monopoly, morris, Mousetrap
Operation, Othello
Parcheesi, Pictionary
Risk
Scattergories, Scrabble, Scruples, shogi, Sorry!
tiddlywinks, tivoli, trick-track, Trivial Pursuit, Trouble
Uno,
Yahtzee

CHESS

chess game played by two persons, each having sixteen pieces that are moved about a board having sixty-four squares
advance
bishop, black
capture, castle, check, checkmate, chessman
develop, draw
end game, en passant, en prise
fianchetto, fork
gambit, grandmaster
horse
jeopardy
king, knight, kriegspiel
master, mate
opening
passed pawn, pawn, perpetual check, piece
queen
rook
stalemate
white

Electronic and Computer Games

GAME SYSTEMS

Atari
Game Boy
Nintendo
Sega, Sega Genesis, Sega Saturn, Sony PlayStation

GAMES

Asteroids
Carmen Sandiego, Centipede
Dark Forces, Donkey Kong, Doom, Double Dragon
Flight Simulator
King's Quest
Legend of Zelda, Lemmings
Missile Command, Mortal Kombat, Myst
Oregon Trail
Pac Man
Rebel Assault
7th Guest, SimCity, Sonic the Hedgehog, Street Fighter, Super Mario Brothers
Tank Commander, Tetris
Virtua Fighter
Wing Commander, Wolfenstein

Types of Toys

balls, board games
cards
dolls
mechanical toys, models
novelties
playthings, pull toys, puzzles
soldiers, stuffed animals
windup toys

Toys and Playthings

toy usu. small object, often representing something familiar, for children to play with

action figure, air rifle, alphabet blocks, arrows
Barbie doll, Barney, battledore, beachball, beanbag, bell ringers, bells, bicycle, Big Wheels, blocks, bobblehead doll, boomerang, building blocks
Cabbage Patch doll, cap gun, carriage, chemistry set, Chia pet, Chinese puzzle, clockwork toy, cockhorse, coloring book, comic book, counters, crayons
darts, dice, doll carriage, doll clothes, doll furniture, dollhouse, dreidel
Erector set, Etch-a-Sketch, expression blocks
Gumby, gyroscope
hand puppet, historiscope, hobbyhorse, hoop, hula hoop
Irish mail
jack-in-the-box, jack-o'-lantern, Jenga, jigsaw puzzle, jolly jumper, jungle gym
kaleidoscope, Ken doll, kewpie doll, kite
Lego, Linkin' Logs
magic lantern, Magna Doodle, marionette, marbles, Matchbox car, maze, mechanical bank, Mr. Potato Head, model airplane, model railroad, music box, myriopticon
Nerf ball, Nerf gum, nested blocks, ninepins, Noah's ark
pail and shovel, paints, paper doll, pet rock, picture car, Pik-up-Stix, piggy bank, pinball, pinwheel, Play-doh, pogo stick, pop gun, Power Rangers, puppet, puzzle
rag doll, Raggedy Ann doll, rattle, rocking horse, roller skates, rubber ball
scooter, See 'n' Say, seesaw, shoofly, shuttlecock, Silly Putty, skateboard, skatemobile, Sky Dancer, sled, sleigh, slide, slingshot, Slinky, slot car, Smurf, soapbox, space toys, squirt gun, stilts, swing
tangram, teddy bear, teetertotter, tiddlywinks, Tinkertoys, tin rattle, tin soldier, top, toy animal, toy book, toy car, toy drum, toy soldier, toy train, toy truck, trading cards, Transformers, tree house, tricycle, Troll
velocipede
wading pool, wagon, walky-talky, water pistol, wheels, whirligig, whistle, windmill
yo-yo
zoetrope

SMOKING AND TOBACCO

ash powdery burned tobacco, esp. burned portion of a cigar or cigarette
black tobacco dark, strong-tasting cigarette tobacco
bong water pipe
briar pipe carved from root burl of evergreen brier shrub
butt portion remaining after cigarette or cigar has been smoked and stubbed out; *Slang.* cigarette
calumet ornamental, ceremonial pipe of American Indians; peace pipe
canaster coarse pipe tobacco
chain-smoke (*vb*) smoke cigarettes compulsively
chaw *Informal.* plug of chewing tobacco
cheroot cigar cut square at both ends
chew plug of chewing tobacco
chewing tobacco tobacco leaf treated and pressed into small cakes, portions of which are broken off and chewed
chillum part of water pipe containing tobacco
cigar cylindrical roll of cured tobacco encased in tobacco leaf wrapper
cigarette thin tube of finely chopped, cured tobacco encased in thin paper, often with filter at one end
cigarette paper rolling paper
cigarillo small, thin cigar
cinder portion of burned tobacco not yet reduced to ashes
claro light-colored, mild cigar
clay pipe pipe with bowl made of clay
colorado cigar of moderate strength and color
corncob pipe pipe made from dried cob of corn
corona cigar with long, straight sides and roundly blunted, unsealed end
cud individual portion of chewing tobacco
curing process of treating and aging raw tobacco to improve its burn and flavor as smoke
cuspidor open receptacle for expectoration of tobacco juice; spittoon
dottle unburned or partially burned tobacco caked in bowl of pipe
dudeen short, clay tobacco pipe
filter porous substance used to remove impurities from smoke
filter tip cigarette with one end of cellulose or charcoal for filtering smoke
hand rolling making one's own cigarettes from loose tobacco and rolling papers
hard pack cigarette box made of thin cardboard
Havana high-quality Cuban cigar
humidor jar or receptacle for storing tobacco and cigars and maintaining their moistness
lighter device, usu. with flint, wick, and flammable fuel, used to ignite smoking material
maduro cigar with dark brown leaf wrapper
menthol cigarette containing menthol, which has cooling effect on mucous membranes
nicotine chief active ingredient of tobacco
panatela long, slender, flat-sided cigar
passive smoking inhalation of cigarette, cigar, or pipe smoke of others, esp. by nonsmoker in enclosed area
peace pipe calumet
perfecto cigar tapering nearly to a point at each end
pigtail twisted strand of tobacco
pinch small amount of chewing tobacco or snuff
pipe smoking device consisting of hollow stem with bowl-shaped receptacle for tobacco at one end and mouthpiece at other

pipe bowl rounded portion of pipe, open at top and connected to one end of pipestem at bottom, into which smoking tobacco is placed
pipe cleaner flexible wire coated with cotton and inserted through pipe stem to remove tar
pipe tobacco tobacco leaves cut in shreds suitable for smoking in a pipe
plug flat, compressed cake of tobacco
quid plug of chewing tobacco
rappee snuff made of dark, pungent tobacco
rolling paper thin slip of paper, usu. gummed at one edge, for hand rolling cigarettes; cigarette paper
secondhand smoke smoke from someone else's cigarette to which one is exposed secondhand through proximity, as in office or restaurant
shag strong, coarse pipe tobacco cut in fine shreds
smokeout day during which smokers are encouraged to abstain from smoking as part of widespread campaign
smoker railroad car designated for smoking; smoking car; person who smokes regularly
smoking act of inhaling and exhaling fumes of burning tobacco
snort single inhalation of snuff
snuff tobacco preparation to be inhaled, chewed, or placed against gums
snuffbox small, lidded container for holding snuff
soft pack cigarette packet made of folded paper
spittoon cuspidor
stogy cigar, esp. roughly made, inexpensive one
Surgeon General's Report published findings of U.S. government study regarding health dangers of cigarette smoking
tar dark, viscous, bituminous residue present in smoke and containing poisonous by-products
tobacco leaves of cultivated plant of the nightshade family, cured for smoking, chewing, or use as snuff
tobacco juice discolored, brown saliva from chewing tobacco or snuff
tobacconist dealer in tobacco and smoking supplies
tobacco shed long structure in which tobacco is hung for aging, drying, and curing; tobacco barn
twist hand-rolled cigarette
Virginia tobacco tobacco cultivated in eastern United States and cured by heat or dry air, stronger and darker than Burley
water pipe any of various devices in which smoke is cooled by passing through water before being inhaled

DRINKING AND ALCOHOLIC BEVERAGES

Drinking Terms

abstinence total restraint from consumption of alcohol
aging process of maturing liquor by long-term storage
alcohol colorless, inflammable liquid intoxicant in wine, beer, and spirits
ale liquor infusion of malt by fermentation, flavored with hops, and stronger than beer
apéritif drink taken as appetizer before meal
bacchanalia drunken revel, esp. honoring Roman god Bacchus
bathtub gin homemade spirit made from raw alcohol and essential oils
beer alcoholic beverage brewed by slow fermentation from malt and hops; brew; suds
bitters alcoholic liquor flavored with astringent, aromatic, strong-tasting herbs
blue law law restricting alcoholic use, sale, or consumption
bock beer strong dark beer, aged very short time, drunk esp. in spring
bond designation for government-supervised distilled spirits, aged at least four years, and 100 proof
bootlegger one who smuggles or illegally sells liquor
booze *Informal.* liquor; (*vb*) drink alcohol
brewer one who makes beer
brut (*adj*) designating very dry champagne
bubbly *Informal.* champagne
BYOB bring your own booze; designation on party invitation that drinks will not be supplied by host
carding *Informal.* requiring proof of age from customer before selling him or her alcoholic beverage
cask wooden container for aging and storage of alcoholic beverages
cellar stock of wines, usu. stored in cool basement
chaser drink taken immediately after another kind of drink, esp. beer after whiskey
cocktail mixed alcoholic drink
cordial liquor sweetened with fruit
corkage charge by restaurant for opening bottle of wine purchased elsewhere

corn whiskey mash made from eighty percent corn
digestif after-dinner drink, esp. liqueur, that aids digestion
distillation purification of alcoholic liquor by heating, separation, and condensation
distiller one who makes alcoholic liquor by distillation, vaporizing and extracting its essence
double two shots of liquor in one drink
draft amount drunk in one swallow
dram small drink of liquor
drinking consumption of alcoholic beverages, usu. for pleasure; such consumption to excess
dry (*adj*) designating locale or time in which sale and consumption of alcohol is forbidden; describing wine that is opposite of sweet
fifth one-fifth gallon, standard U.S. bottle size for spirits
finger measure indicating drink filled to width of one finger
gill measure equal to four fluid ounces
hangover unpleasant aftereffects of too much drink, esp. headache and nausea, experienced following day
hard liquor liquor with alcoholic content higher than that of wine and beer
highball liquor, esp. whiskey, mixed with soda in a tall glass
hogshead large cask, holding from 63 to 140 gallons (238 to 530 l)
home brew homemade alcoholic drink
jeroboam oversized wine bottle holding approximately 3 liters (3.3 quarts)
jug large, narrow-mouthed, earthenware container, esp. for liquor; contents of jug or alcoholic liquor
keg small barrel, esp. for beer on draught
keg party *Informal.* gathering at which beer is served from keg
libation alcoholic drink, esp. wine, poured as offering to god
liqueur usu. flavored, sweet, thick alcoholic liquor
liquor alcoholic drink, usu. distilled rather than fermented; booze
long neck (*adj*) *Informal.* designating beer bottle with long neck
magnum large wine or champagne bottle holding 2/5 gallon (1.5 l)
malt liquor strong beer made by fermenting malt
maraschino cherry cherry preserved in sweet liqueur distilled from juice of bitter wild cherry, served in certain cocktails
mash crushed malt or meal mixed with hot water and fermented to form beer or whiskey
Mickey *Slang.* alcoholic drink doctored with knockout drug; Mickey Finn
mixer nonalcoholic beverage, often carbonated, combined with spirits in cocktail
moonshine *Informal.* low-quality, illegally distilled or smuggled whiskey, esp. corn liquor
near beer malt liquor with very low alcohol content
neat (*adj*) straight up
nightcap drink taken just before going to bed
nog strong English ale
noggin small quantity of drink, esp. one-fourth pint
off the wagon *Slang.* having drunk an alcoholic beverage after a period of abstinence
one for the road final drink before leaving bar or party
on the wagon *Slang.* denying oneself alcoholic drink; designating a period of abstinence
package store outlet selling alcoholic beverages for consumption elsewhere
prohibition legal forbidding of manufacture and sale of alcoholic drinks
proof arbitrary standard measure of alcoholic strength of beverage, often twice percent of alcohol content
punch mixture of juice, soda, and liquor
punt hollow in exterior bottom of wine bottle
rocks *Informal.* ice cubes
shooter shot of spirits to be drunk in one gulp
single-malt whiskey made entirely from malted barley distilled at a single distillery
sober (*adj*) not drunk, esp. habitually temperate in use of alcohol
sobriety quality of being sober
social drinking moderate drinking at gatherings
soft (*adj*) designating wine and beer, as opposed to hard liquor
soft drink nonalcoholic beverage or mixer
sparkling wine champagne and other effervescent wines
spike (*vb*) *Informal.* add alcohol to drink or increase amount of alcohol contained therein
spirits alcoholic beverages; liquor
split small bottle, esp. of champagne, usu. 6 ounces (177 l)
stiff (*adj*) strong, in describing drink; high in alcoholic content
straight up (*adj*) designating an alcoholic drink without mixer or chilled drink without ice, such as a martini; neat
teetotaler one who does not drink alcohol
temperance moderation or abstinence from alcoholic drink
toast drink taken in honor of person or event, accompanied by words of praise or good wishes, often a standardized phrase
vintage year in which wine grapes were grown
vintner winemaker
wassail riotous drinking and revelry
wet (*adj*) designating locale or time in which consumption of alcoholic drinks is permitted
whiskey distilled liquor made from fermented mash of cereal grain, such as barley, rye, or corn
white lightning *Informal.* moonshine; illegal, low-quality liquor
wine fermented grape juice

Bars, Bar Tools, and Habitués

after-hours (*adj*) designating establishment serving alcohol after normal bar hours
alehouse place where beer and ale are sold
bar place where drinks are served across a long counter; such a counter

bar back busboy who brings supplies and cleans up for bartender
barhop (*vb*) *Informal.* visit and drink at series of bars over course of evening
barkeeper person who owns or tends bar; barkeep
barrelhouse cheap drinking and dancing establishment
bartender preparer and server of alcoholic drinks at bar counter
beer garden outdoor bar serving beer
beer hall large bar primarily or solely serving beer, esp. German
bistro small bar or tavern, esp. European
bottle club often private club serving drinks after normal legal closing hours
bouncer person employed to maintain order in bar, as by removing unruly customers
cabaret club serving food and drink and providing entertainbment
café small, informal barroom or cabaret
cash bar bar at special, often private function that sells drinks to those in attendance
cocktail lounge public room where drinks are served, esp. in hotel or restaurant
corkscrew spiral device with handle for removing cork stopper from wine bottle
cover charge entry charge, usu. for entertainment, in club or bar
dramshop bar or saloon
draught drawing of beer from large container or keg; beer so drawn
happy hour early evening hours, usu. between four and seven p.m., when bar serves drinks at reduced price or with free snacks
honky-tonk cheap, often disreputable bar or club
jigger small glass used to measure one and a half ounces of spirits
last call final chance to order drinks before bar closing
no-host bar bar, usu. at private party, requiring payment for drinks
on tap designating beer stored in keg or barrel and drawn off through tap
on the house designating drink purchased for customer at bar's expense
pony glass short, narrow, stemmed glass for cordials and straight up cocktails
pourer spigot attachment for bottles allowing one serving to pour each time bottle is upended
pub public house; tavern or bar , esp. in Britain
rathskeller restaurant patterned after German beer hall, usu. in basement
roadhouse tavern or nightclub located on main thoroughfare outside city limits
rock glass short, stout glass for straight liquor on ice
round single serving of drinks for all present
saloon public room for sale and consumption of alcoholic drinks
shot small measure of undiluted liquor, usu. one and a half ounces
snifter balloon-shaped, stemmed goblet that narrows at top, esp. for brandy
soda gun bar device with hose and selector for adding nonalcoholic beverages to drinks
sour mix lemon juice and sugar used in mixed drinks
speakeasy saloon or club selling alcohol illegally, esp. during Prohibition
speed rack bartender's device, on runners, with slots that hold bottles of house brands most frequently used
steward supervisor of storage and service of wine in restaurant or large household
swizzle stick long rod, often in spiral shape, used to mix drinks
tab unpaid portion of bill accumulating at bar
tavern place where liquor is sold and consumed; formerly an inn
twist slice of lemon peel curled over and served in certain drinks

Toasts

toast drink taken in honor of person or event, accompanied by words of praise or good wishes, often a standardized phrase
à votre santé
bottoms up
cheerio, cheers, chin chin
down the hatch
gesondheid, gun-bei
health, here's looking at you, here's mud in your eye, here's to you
kam pai
l'chaim
many happy returns
na zdorovye
prosit, prost
salud, sante, skal, skoal
to your health
wassail

Beers

beer alcoholic beverage brewed by slow fermentation from malt and hops
ale
beer, bitter, bock beer
craft-brewed beer
dark beer, dortmunder
ice beer
kumis, kvass
lager, light beer
malt liquor, mead
near beer
pale ale, Pilsner, porter, pulque
stout
weiss, wheat beer

Wines

wine fermented grape juice
Alsace, amontillado, amoroso, apple wine, Asti Spumante
Barbera, Bardolino, Barolo, Beaujolais,

Bergerac, blanc de blancs, blanc de noirs, blush, Bordeaux, Burgundy
Cabernet Sauvignon, Catawba, Chablis, Champagne, Chardonnay, Châteauneuf-du-Pape, Chenin blanc, Chianti, Cinzano, claret, cold duck, concord, Côtes de Nuits, Côtes du Rhone
dandelion wine, dessert wine, Do, Dolcetto, Dom Perignon (trade name), Dubonnet (trade name)
fortified wine, Frascati, Fumé Blanc
Gamay, Gewürztraminer, Graves, Grenache
hard cider, hock
Johannisberg Riesling, jug wine
Lachryma Christi, Lambrusco, Liebfraumilch
Macon, Madeira, Malaga, Margaux, Marsala, Mateus Rose, Médoc, Merlot, Moselle, Muscadet, Muscat
Napa Valley, Navarra
oloroso, oporto, Orvieto
Pauillac, Petite Sirah, Pinot Blanc, Pinot Noir, Pomerol, Pommard, port, Pouilly-Fuissé, Pouilly-Fumé
red wine, Riesling, retsina, Rhine, Rhone, Rioja, rose, ruby port
sack, St. Estephe, St. Julien, sake, Sancerre, Sauterne, Sauvignon Blanc, sherry, Shiraz, soave, Sonoma, sparkling wine, Sylvaner
table wine, tawny port, Tokay
Valdepeas, Valpolicella, vermouth, vinho verde, Vouvray
white cabernet, white wine, white zinfandel
zinfandel

Spirits

spirits alcoholic beverages; liquor
advocaat, American whiskey, applejack, aquavit, Armagnac
bathtub gin, blended whiskey, bourbon, brandy
Campari, Canadian whiskey, Cognac, corn liquor, Courvoisier
Dutch gin
gin, grain alcohol, grappa, grog
Irish whiskey
mao-tai, marc, mash, mescal, Metaxa, moonshine
negra
ouzo
pulque
raki, Rémy Martin, rum, rye
Scotch whisky, single-malt Scotch, slivovitz
tequila
vodka
whiskey

Liqueurs and Cordials

cordial liquor sweetened with fruit
liqueur usu. flavored, sweet, thick, alcoholic liquor
absinthe, alcool blanc, amaretto, anisette, apricot brandy, Asiago
Baily's Irish Cream, B and B, Benedictine, bitters
Calvados, cassis, Chamborel, Chartreuse, Cointreau, crème de bananas, crème de cacao, crème de cassis, crème de fraise, crème de framboise, crème de menthe, crème de violette, curaçao
Drambuie
Frangelico
Galliano, Goldschalger, Grand Marnier
Irish Mist
Kahlua, Kir, kirsch(wasser), kummel
Marachino, Midori, mocha liqueur
pastis, Pernod, Pimm's, poire William
ratafia
Sabra, sambuca, schapps, sloe gin, Southern Comfort, Strega
Tia Maria, triple sec
Vandermint
Yukon Jack

Mixed Drinks

Alabama slammer amaretto, Southern Comfort, sloe gin, and lemon juice
alexander gin, crème de cacao, and light cream
angel's kiss crème de cacao, sloe gin, brandy, and light cream
Bacardi cocktail Bacardi rum, juice of lime, and grenadine
B & B Benedictine and brandy
Bahama mama rum, coconut liqueur, coffee liqueur, pineapple juice, and lemon juice
banshee crème de banana, crème de cacao, light cream
bay breeze vodka, pineapple juice, and cranberry juice
Bellini champagne, peach nectar, lemon juice, and grenadine
between the sheets brandy, triple sec, rum, and a squeeze of lemon
B-52 Kahlua, Irish Mist, Grand Marnier
Black Russian vodka and coffee liqueur
black velvet Guinness stout and champagne
bloody Caesar littleneck clam, vodka, tomato juice, Worcestershire sauce, Tabasco sauce, horse-radish, and dash of salt
Bloody Mary vodka, tomato juice, lemon juice, Worcestershire sauce, Tabasco, and salt and pepper
blue lagoon vodka, blue curaçao, and lemonade
blue margarita tequila, blue curaçao, and lime juice
blue whale vodka, blue curaçao, orange juice, and lemon juice
bocce ball amaretto, orange juice, and soda
brandy alexander crème de cacao, brandy, and heavy cream
Bronx cocktail gin, dry vermouth, sweet vermouth, and orange juice
bullshot vodka, beef bouillon, and salt and pepper
buttered rum hot buttered rum

Cape Codder vodka or rum, cranberry juice, and squeeze of lime
cement mixer Irish cream liqueur and lemon or lime juice, mixed in the mouth
champagne cocktail champagne, sugar, and bitters
champagne cooler brandy, Cointreau, and champagne
chi-chi vodka, pineapple juice, and cream of coconut
clamato cocktail vodka, clam juice, and tomato juice
cobbler wine or liquor, fruit, and shaved ice
collins liquor, squeeze of lemon or lime, soda water, and powdered sugar
cooler wine or other spirits, fruit juice, and carbonated water
Cuba libre rum, cola, and a squeeze of lime
daiquiri rum, squeeze of lemon or lime, and sugar
a day at the beach coconut rum, amaretto, orange juice, and grenadine
depth charge shot of schnapps in a glass of beer
dirty banana Kahlua, banana liqueur, rum, and pineapple juice
eggnog liquor, milk, beaten egg or crème, and sugar
Fifth Avenue crème de cacao, apricot brandy, and light cream
firefly light crème de cacao, cream, and rosemint
fizz liquor, carbonated beverage, citrus juice, and sugar
flip liquor or wine, egg, and sugar
foxy lady amaretto, crème de cacao, and heavy cream
frappé liqueur poured over shaved ice
French connection Cognac and amaretto
fuzzy navel peach schnapps and orange juice
Gibson gin, dry vermouth, and a pearl onion
gimlet gin or vodka, lemon or lime juice, and sugar
gin and tonic gin and quinine water
gin fizz gin, squeeze of lemon, sugar and soda
gin rickey gin, lime juice, and soda
godfather scotch and amaretto
godmother vodka and amaretto
golden Cadillac crème de cacao, Galliano, and light cream
grasshopper crème de cacao, crème de menthe, and light cream
greyhound vodka and grapefruit juice
grog rum and water, served hot with lemon and sugar
Harvey Wallbanger vodka, Galliano, and orange juice
highball liquor and water or carbonated beverage
Hollywood vodka, Chambord, and pineapple juice
hot buttered rum rum, sugar, butter, and hot water; buttered rum
hot toddy toddy
Indian summer apple schnapps and hot apple cider
Irish coffee whiskey, hot coffee, sugar, and whipped cream
Jack Rose apple brandy, lime juice, and grenadine
kamikaze vodka, triple sec, and lime juice
King Alphonse dark crème de cacao and cream
Kir white wine and crème de cassis
Kir royale champagne and crème de cassis
Long Island iced tea rum, gin, vodka, triple sec, lemon juice, and cola
madras vodka, orange juice, and cranberry juice
mai tai rum, curaao, grenadine, lemon and pineapple juice, almond syrup, and sugar
Manhattan whiskey and sweet vermouth
Margarita tequila, triple sec, and lemon or lime juice
martini gin and dry vermouth
melon ball melon liqueur, vodka, and pineapple juice
Mexican coffee coffee liqueur, tequila, coffee, and whipped cream
mimosa champagne and orange juice
mind eraser Kahlua and vodka on ice, topped with club soda
mint julep bourbon, crushed ice, sugar, sprigs of mint, and water
Moscow mule vodka, ginger ale, and a squeeze of lime
mudslide Kahlua, Irish cream liqueur, and vodka, with cream and/or ice cream
negus wine, hot water, sugar, nutmeg, and lemon
nutcracker amaretto, hazelnut cream, and coconut
nutty professor Grand Marnier, hazelnut liqueur, and Irish cream liqueur
old fashioned whiskey, sugar, bitters, and water
orange blossom gin, orange juice, and sugar
passion mimosa champagne and passionfruit juice
peppermint pattie white crème de cacao and white crème de menthe
Pimm's cup Pimm's No. 1 Cup and lemonade or ginger ale
piña colada rum, coconut milk, and crushed pineapple
pink lady gin, grenadine, and egg white
pink squirrel crème de noyeaux, crème de cacao, and light cream
planter's punch rum, squeeze of lime, sugar, and carbonated water
platinum blonde rum, Cointreau, and cream
posset hot milk curdled with ale or wine, sweetened and spiced
pousse café grenadine, yellow chartreuse, crème de cassis, white crème de menthe, green chartreuse, and brandy, served in layers
prairie oyster cognac, vinegar, Worcestershire sauce, catsup, and angostura
presbyterian rye or bourbon, soda, and ginger ale
punch any combination of alcoholic beverages, fruit juices, and other beverages, usu. in a large bowl
quaalude vodka, hazelnut liqueur, coffee liqueur, and milk
Ramos gin fizz gin, egg white, cream, lemon juice, and sugar
red death amaretto, Southern Comfort, sloe gin, Yukon Jack, lemon juice, and lime juice
rickey gin or vodka, soda, and a squeeze of lime

Rob Roy Scotch and sweet vermouth
rum and coke rum and cola
rusty nail Scotch and Drambuie
salty dog gin or vodka, grapefruit juice, and salt
sangre tequila, tomato juice, lemon juice, Worcestershire sause, tobasco, and salt and pepper
sangria red wine, fruit juice, fruit chunks
San Juan cooler rum, lemon juice, and pineapple juice
Scarlett O'Hara Southern Comfort, cranberry juice, and lime juice
Scotch and Soda Scotch whiskey and Soda
screwdriver vodka and orange juice
sea breeze vodka, grapefruit juice and cranberry juice
Seven and Seven Seagram's Seven Canadian Whiskey and 7-UP
sex on the beach vodka, peach-flavored schnapps, orange juice, cranberry juice, and pineapple juice
sidecar brandy, cointreau, and lemon juice
Singapore sling gin, cherry-flavored brandy, sugar, and carbonated water
slam dunk Southern Comfort, orange juice, and cranberry juice
sling liquor, sugar, lemon or lime juice, and water
slippery nipple sambuca and Bailey's Irish Mist
sloe gin fizz sloe gin, squeeze of lemon, and powdered sugar
smash liquor, sugar, sprigs of mint, water, and ice
snake bite Yukon Jack and lime juice
sombrero coffee flavored brandy and milk or light cream
sour liquor, squeeze of lemon or lime, sugar, and sometimes soda water
spritzer white wine and carbonated water
stinger brandy and crème de menthe
syllabub sweetened milk or cream mixed with wine or cider
Tang orange-flavored vodka, orange juice, grapefruit juice, and 7-UP
tequila sunrise tequila, grenadine, and orange juice
toddy rum or other liquor, boiling water, and sugar; hot toddy
Tom and Jerry rum, spices, milk, egg, and sugar
Tom Collins gin, squeeze of lemon or lime, sugar, and carbonated water
velvet hammer vodka, crème de cacao, and light cream
virgin Mary tomato juice, Worcestershire sauce, Tabasco sauce, lemon juice, salt and pepper
vodka and tonic vodka and tonic water
vodka martini vodka and dry vermouth
Wassail spiced ale or wine, sometimes with baked apple
whiskey sour whiskey, squeeze of lemon, and powdered sugar
white lady gin, cream, egg white, and powdered sugar
White Russian vodka, coffee liqueur, and milk or cream
white spider vodka and white crème de menthe
wild thing tequila, cranberry juice, club soda, and lime juice
wine cooler wine and carbonated beverage
wu-wu vodka, peach schnapps, cranberry juice, and grapefruit juice
zombie rum, apricot-flavored brandy, pineapple juice, squeeze of lime, squeeze of orange, and powdered sugar

Chapter Eighteen
Structure and Usage

GRAMMAR, PHONETICS, AND LINGUISTICS

Grammar and Usage
Parts of Speech
Punctuation and Diacritics
Phonetics
Linguistics and Writing Systems

Grammar and Usage

ablative case indicating noun is starting point, means, instrument, or agent
abstract noun noun describing something general or not perceivable by sense
accusative case indicating noun is direct object of verb
active voice verb form indicating that subject is performing action expressed by verb
agreement parallelism, as between subject and verb, in person, number, gender, or case
antecedent substantive that is replaced by pronoun, usu. later in same or subsequent sentence
apodosis clause expressing result in conditional sentence
apposition placing of word or phrase after a substantive to explain or identify it
article modifier "a," "an," or "the" used to signal presence and definiteness or indefiniteness of following noun
aspect verb form indicating nature of action expressed by verb with regard to duration, repetition, beginning, or completion
attributive adjective or noun placed adjacent to noun it modifies
auxiliary verb verb used with main verb to indicate tense, mood, or voice
case role of noun, pronoun, or adjective in relation to rest of sentence, usu. shown by inflection
causative word noting causation
clause group of words containing subject and predicate
collective noun noun that is singular in form but denotes a group
comma fault use of comma between related main clauses in absence of conjunction, usu. considered incorrect in formal usage; comma splice
comma splice comma fault
common noun noun that refers to any or all members of a class of beings or things rather than a particular individual
comparative second degree of comparison of adjectives or adverbs, indicated by ending "-er" or the word "more"
complement word or phrase that completes a grammatical construction in the predicate and describes or is identified with the subject or object
complex sentence sentence containing one independent clause and one or more dependent clauses
compound-complex sentence sentence containing more than one independent clause and one or more dependent clauses
compound sentence sentence composed of two or more simple sentences joined by coordinating conjunctions
compound word word formed by combining two or more existing words
concrete noun noun describing something that can be perceived by sense
conditional (*adj*) designating clause, word, mood, or sentence that expresses a condition or hypothetical state
conjugation inflection of a verb
connective word that joins words, phrases, clauses, and sentences
construction arrangement of two or more words or morphemes in grammatical unit
contraction shortened form of word or phrase, with omitted letters replaced by apostrophe
coordinating conjunction conjunction that connects two words, phrases, or clauses of equal grammatical rank
copula verb that links subject and predicate; linking verb
correlative word used regularly in association with another word, such as the conjunctions "either" and "or"
count noun noun that refers to countable thing and can be used in the singular or plural, such as "bus"
dangling participle participle that appears from its position to modify a word other than the one intended
dative noun case for indirect object in inflected languages
declarative sentence sentence that makes a statement
declension inflection of nouns, pronouns, and adjectives for gender, number, and case; class of nouns or adjectives having similar inflected forms
definite article article "the" that classes modified noun as identified or specific
demonstrative pronoun or adjective that points out the person or thing referred to
dependent clause clause unable to function as complete sentence on its own; subordinate clause
determiner word that modifies or restricts a noun and is placed before any other adjectives
diagram grammatical analysis of sentence in graphic form
direct object word or phrase representing person or thing that receives action denoted by transitive verb
dvandva compound word composed of comparable, nonsubordinate elements, such as "bittersweet"
emphatic (*adj*) designating a form used to add emphasis, such as "do" in "I do like it"
epicene (*adj*) designating a noun or pronoun capable of referring to either sex
exclamatory sentence sentence expressing surprise or strong feeling

exophora use of word or phrase that refers to something outside its linguistic environment, such as "that" in "Look at that"
expletive word used to introduce a subject, esp. "there" or "it" used as introductory word
factitive (*adj*) pertaining to verb expressing process of making or rendering in a certain way
feminine grammatical gender that includes most nouns referring to females, as well as other nouns
first person form of pronoun or verb indicating speaker or group including speaker, as "I" or "am"
function word word that expresses grammatical relationships and has little semantic content
future verb tense indicating action or state in the future
future perfect verb tense indicating action to be completed by or to extend up to specified time in the future
gender grammatical distinction applied to nouns and pronouns, often correlated with sex, but sometimes based on arbitrary assignment
genitive noun case indicating possession or origin
gerund verb form ending in English in "-ing" and functioning as verbal noun
govern (*vb*) require the use of a particular form of another word
grammar study of the way sentences of a language are constructed; these features or constructions themselves; set of rules accounting for these constructions
helping verb auxiliary verb
heteroclite (*adj*) irregular in inflection
historical present present tense used in narrating past event
hypotaxis dependent or subordinate relation or construction
imperative verb mood indicating command or request
imperfect verb tense indicating habitual or incomplete action continuing at some temporal point of reference in past
impersonal (*adj*) being a verb with only third person singular forms and having an unspecified subject
inceptive verb form or aspect expressing beginning of an action; inchoative
indefinite article article "a" or "an" that classes modified noun as singular but unidentified
indefinite pronoun pronoun such as "some" or "any" that does not specify the identity of its referent
independent clause main clause
indicative verb mood indicating statement or question
indirect object word or phrase representing person or thing with reference to which the action of verb is performed
infinitive basic verb form that does not show person, number, or tense and is often preceded by "to"
inflection change in grammatical function of word, as in case, number, or person, esp. by adding affix
intensifier intensive
intensive linguistic element, esp. an adverb, indicating increased emphasis or force; intensifier
interrogative word or construction used in asking a question
intransitive verb verb having no direct object of its action, which is complete
inversion change in usual word order, as in placement of auxiliary verb before subject
irregular (*adj*) not conforming to the usual pattern of inflection in a language
linking verb copula
locative noun case indicating place or position
loose sentence sentence in which subordinate clause or modifiers follow completion of main clause
main clause clause that could stand alone as complete sentence
masculine grammatical gender that includes most nouns referring to males, as well as other nouns
mass noun noun that refers to indefinitely divisible substance or abstract notion, such as "electricity" or "truth"
misplaced modifier word, phrase, or clause erroneously placed in sentence so that it modifies a different noun from that intended
modal auxiliary auxiliary verb used with another verb to express mood, such as "can" or "must"
modifier word or phrase qualifying or describing meaning of another word, esp. adjective and adverb or prepositional phrase
mood indication of condition or manner of verb's action: indicative, imperative, subjunctive, optative
neuter grammatical gender for nouns not classed as masculine or feminine
nominative case usu. indicating that noun is subject of verb
nonrestrictive clause relative clause that describes or supplements modified element but is not essential to its basic meaning
noun phrase grammatical construction that functions as a noun, consisting of a noun and any modifiers or a noun substitute, such as a pronoun
number indication whether noun, verb, etc., refers to one or more than one: singular, plural, dual
object noun or noun substitute that receives or is affected by action of verb; noun or pronoun representing goal of preposition
objective grammatical case used for object of transitive verb or preposition
optative verb mood expressing a wish or desire
paradigm set of all inflected forms of a word
parataxis joining together of clauses or phrases without conjunctions
parse (*vb*) analyze, describe, and grammatically label the parts of a sentence
participle verb form that can be used as adjective or with auxiliary verb to form certain tenses
particle small, usually uninflected word that has grammatical use rather than lexical meaning, esp. a word that does not fit into part of speech categories
part of speech basic class of words in given lan-

guage to which any word can be assigned based on meaning, form, or function in a sentence
passive voice verb form indicating that subject is receiver of action expressed by verb
past verb tense referring to events or states in times gone by
past participle verb form usu. ending in "-ed" or "-en," used as adjective or in forming passive voice or perfect tenses
past perfect verb tense indicating action or state completed before specific time in past
perfect verb tense noting action or state terminated prior to some temporal point of reference
perfect participle past participle
periodic sentence sentence in which completion of main clause is suspended until end
periphrastic (*adj*) using two or more words instead of an inflected word to express a grammatical function
person indication of person speaking, spoken to, or spoken about: first (I, we); second (you); third (he, she, it, they)
personal pronoun any pronoun that distinguishes speaker or one spoken to or about: I, we, you, he, she, it, they
phrasal verb unit consisting of verb and one or more adverbs or prepositions, often having idiomatic meaning
phrase sequence of grammatically related words lacking subject and predicate
pluperfect past perfect
plural form designating more than one
positive first degree of comparison of adjectives or adverbs, being the basic form
possessive form or case indicating ownership or possession
postposition placing of word, particle, or affix after another word to modify it or relate it to other elements of sentence
predicate that which is said about subject of sentence
predicate nominative noun or pronoun that has same referent as subject and is used in predicate with copula
prepositional phrase phrase made up of preposition and its noun or pronoun object with any modifiers
present verb tense indicating action or state occurring or existing now
present participle verb form ending in "-ing" used as modifier or in forming the progressive
present perfect verb tense indicating action completed at present time or continuing from past into present
preterit verb tense indicating action or state, esp. completed action or state, in past
principal parts verb forms from which all other inflected forms can be derived, consisting of infinitive, past tense, and past participle
privative affix indicating negation or absence, such as "a-" in "apolitical"
progressive verb form indicating continuing action
proper noun name of specific person, place, or thing, usu. indicated by capitalization
qualifier adjective or adverb used to qualify or limit meaning of word modified
quantifier modifier that establishes amount or extent of word modified
reduplication doubling of syllable or other element, sometimes in modified form, to generate derivative or inflected form
reflexive verb taking subject and object with same referents; pronoun used as object to refer to subject of verb
regular (*adj*) conforming to usual pattern of inflection in a language
relative clause subordinate clause that modifies antecedent noun or pronoun
relative pronoun pronoun used to introduce relative clause
restrictive clause relative clause that identifies or limits meaning of word modified and is essential to meaning of sentence
run-on sentence sequence of two or more main clauses not separated by semicolon, conjunction, or period
second person form of pronoun or verb used in referring to one or ones addressed, as "you"
sentence grammatically independent unit expressing a statement, question, command, or exclamation, usu. consisting of subject and predicate
sentence fragment phrase or clause written as sentence but lacking subject or verb
serial comma comma used after next to last item and before conjunction in series of three or more items
simple sentence sentence consisting of only one main clause and no dependent clauses
singular form designating just one
split infinitive placing of word or phrase, usu. adverb, between "to" and its verb in infinitive form
strong verb verb that forms past tense and past participle by internal vowel change
subject word or phrase about which something is stated in sentence
subjunctive verb mood indicating doubt, wish, or hypothetical state
subordinate clause dependent clause
subordinating conjunction conjunction joining independent clause and dependent clause
substantive word or group of words functioning as a noun
superlative highest degree of comparison, of adjectives or adverbs, indicated by ending "-est" or the word "most"
suppletive (*adj*) describing inflected form of word entirely different from stem, such as past tense of "go"
tense verb form indicating time of action or state denoted by verb
third person form of pronoun or verb indicating person or thing spoken of, as "he" or "goes"
transitive verb verb indicating action upon direct object and able to form passive voice

verbal word derived from verb and used as noun or adjective: gerund, infinitive, or participle
verb phrase verb and its modifiers, objects, or complements functioning together in a sentence; main verb and auxiliary verbs functioning together as a verb
vocative noun case indicating direct address
voice verb form indicating whether subject acts or is acted upon
volitive (*adj*) pertaining to verb expressing a wish or permission
weak verb verb that forms past tense and past participle by adding suffix

Parts of Speech

adjective word modifying a noun usu. by describing, delimiting, or specifying quantity
adverb word modifying a verb, adjective, other adverb, or clause, usu. by indicating where, when, how, or to what degree
conjunction word connecting words or word groups
interjection word used by itself to express emphatic feeling, such as "hurrah" or "yikes"
noun word naming a person, animal, object, idea, quality, act, or place
preposition word expressing relation between its object and another word or phrase in sentence
pronoun word taking place of a noun or noun phrase
verb word expressing action, state of being, or a relation between things

Punctuation and Diacritics

accent mark mark used to show emphasis on a particular syllable or how a letter is to be pronounced
acute accent ´ short line slanting up to right placed over vowel to show that it has a certain sound quality or has the main stress
ampersand & standing for the word "and"
angle brackets <> used to set off what is enclosed
apostrophe ' used in contractions and possessives
asterisk * placed in printed matter as reference or to indicate omission of material found elsewhere; star
bang *Slang.* exclamation point (Printing and Computers)
braces { }; used to connect words or items to be considered together
brackets [ ] used to enclose and set off matter within text, to indicate aggregation, or as parentheses within parentheses
breve ˘ small, open, U-shaped symbol placed over letter to indicate short vowel or short or unstressed syllable
bullet • large, solid, vertically centered dot placed in printed matter to call attention to particular passage, or used for syllable divisions in dictionaries
caret ‸ used to indicate where something is to be inserted
cedilla ç cedilhooklike mark placed under consonant, usu. "c," to indicate modification of usual phonetic value, as in French "façedilade"
circumflex ^ placed over vowel to show that it is long, pronounced with rise or fall in pitch, or pronounced with particular sound quality
colon : used to direct attention to matter that follows, esp. list, quotation, or explanation, and indicating a nearly full stop
comma , used to set off word, phrase, or clause or to separate items in list, and indicating slight pause
dagger † vertical cross widening at top of upright used as reference mark or to indicate person has died
dash — used to indicate break or shift in thought or sentence, around a parenthetical element, or prior to attribution of quote
diacritic mark placed over, under, or through a letter to indicate pronunciation or stress, or to distinguish words with identical spellings
diacritical mark diacritic
diagonal virgule
dieresis ¨ placed over second of two vowels to show that it is pronounced separately, as in "naïve"
diesis double dagger
ditto mark » placed on next line under word or phrase to indicate repetition
double dagger ‡ vertical cross with two horizontals used as reference mark; diesis
ellipsis ... used to indicate omission of letters or words
exclamation point ! used to replace period for emphasis at end of sentence; exclamation mark
grave accent ` short line slanting up to left placed over vowel to show that it has certain sound quality, has secondary stress, or is pronounced rather than silent
haček ˇ; small V-shaped symbol over consonant, usu. indicating palatalized sound
hamza '; indicating glottal stop in Arabic
hyphen - used to divide or join compound words, to break word between two lines, and in writing out compound numbers
index ☞ stylized hand with one finger extended horizontally and other fingers curled, used to point out important note or paragraph in text
interrobang ‽ question mark overlaid on exclamation point used at end of exclamatory rhetorical question
interrogation mark question mark
macron ¯ horizontal line placed over vowel to indicate it is long or over syllable to indicate long or stressed syllable
paragraph mark ¶ used to indicate beginning of new paragraph
parallels || used as reference mark in printing
parentheses ( ) used to enclose amplifying or explanatory word or phrase or alternative term
period . indicating end of sentence, also used after abbreviations and initials
prime ′; placed after letter or character to

distinguish from another of the same kind, as A, A´;, or to show primary stress
punctuation system of standardized graphic symbols inserted in written matter to clarify meaning and separate structural units
question mark ? used to replace period at end of interrogative sentence
quotation marks " " used to set off and surround spoken or quoted material, some titles, and special or borrowed words; ' ' used to set off and surround a quotation within a quotation
quotes quotation marks
section mark § pair of S's stacked vertically and interlocking, used to indicate beginning of text subdivision or as reference mark
semicolon ; used to separate major elements of sentence, such as independent clauses, and to separate elements of series which themselves contain commas
slash virgule
solidus virgule
square brackets brackets
star asterisk
stress mark mark placed before, over, or after syllable to indicate stress in pronunciation
subscript any symbol written below normal line of letters
superscript any symbol written above normal line of letters
swung dash ~ used in place of word or part of word previously spelled out
tilde ˜ placed over letter "n" in Spanish to indicate palatal sound (ny) or over vowel in Portuguese to indicate nasalization
umlaut ¨ two dots placed above vowel, esp. in German, to indicate modification of its sound, as in "Lübeck"
virgule / placed between words to separate alternatives, indicate "or," "and or," or "per"; diagonal, slash, or solidus
vowel point dot, line, or other mark placed above or below consonant symbol to indicate vowel sound, as in Hebrew

Phonetics

accent variation in pronunciation of words due to regional, class, or cultural factors; emphasis on particular syllable of word or word within phrase
affricate consonant sound involving complete closure in vocal tract gradually released with audible friction
allophone one of the alternate phonetic forms of a phoneme, depending on its environment
alveolar consonant sound made by tongue against bony ridge behind upper front teeth
apheresis loss of one or more sounds or letters at beginning of word
apocope omission of last letter, syllable, or part of word
aspirate sound characterized by audible breath accompanying sound's articulation
assimilation process by which speech sound becomes more like neighboring sound
bilabial consonant sound formed by coming together of both lips
cardinal vowel any of eight primary, sustained vowel sounds used as reference points for describing vowel sounds of a language
click sound formed by suction of air into mouth and sudden plosive or affricate release
close (*adj*) designating vowel produced with tongue close to roof of mouth
closed (*adj*) designating syllable ending with consonant
cluster succession of two or more consonants in a syllable
consonant one of two basic categories of speech sounds, based on closure or near-closure in vocal tract to produce blockage of air or audible friction
dental consonant sound made by pressure of tongue against teeth
digraph pair of letters representing single speech sound, such as "sh" in "show"
diphthong complex vowel sound characterized by gliding change in tone during articulation of single syllable
dissimilation process by which speech sound becomes different from neighboring sound or disappears because of identical sound nearby
disyllable word consisting of two syllables
ejective voiceless stop or fricative produced with air compressed above closed glottis
elision omission of sounds in connected speech
enclitic unstressed word or form closely connected in pronunciation with preceding word and not normally used on its own
epenthesis insertion of extra sound in middle of word
excrescent (*adj*) designating sound inserted in word due to articulation but without grammatical or etymological justification
flap consonant sound produced by rapid flip of tongue against roof of mouth or upper teeth
free variation relationship between speech sounds such that one may occur in place of the other with no change in meaning
fricative consonant sound characterized by audible friction of moving air forced between vocal organs; spirant
geminate doubled consonant sound
glottal stop consonant sound made in larynx by closing glottis or vocal cords
guttural (*adj*) articulated in back of mouth or with tongue against soft palate
implosive consonant sound formed by inward-moving air, closure of mouth, and vocal cord vibration
inflection quality or variation of tone or pitch of voice
International Phonetic Alphabet IPA; symbols used as universal system for transcribing speech sounds of any language
intonation pattern or form of pitch in articulation of words

intrusive (*adj*) designating speech sound inserted in connected speech where it is not present in the spelling
IPA International Phonetic Alphabet
labial speech sound formed by active use of lip or lips
labiodental speech sound formed by lower lip in contact with upper teeth
lambdacism substitution of "l" for "r" or mispronunciation of "l"
liaison linking of words, esp. in French, in which otherwise silent final consonant is pronounced as initial sound of following word that begins with vowel
liquid speech sound, such as "l", pronounced without friction and capable of being prolonged like a vowel
long vowel vowel sound relatively long in duration
metathesis transposition of letters, syllables, or sounds in a word
modulation variation in pitch and loudness of the voice
monophthong vowel retaining same quality throughout its duration
monosyllable word consisting of only one syllable
mouillé (*adj*) pronounced as a palatal or palatized sound, as the sounds spelled "ll" and "ñ" in Spanish
mutation phonetic change in initial consonant of a word under certain conditions, as observed in the Celtic languages; umlaut
nasal speech sound formed by audible passage of air through nose
obstruent speech sound characterized by stoppage or obstruction of exhalation: stop, fricative, or affricate
occlusion brief complete closure in vocal tract, resulting in stoppage of exhalation and ensuing pressure
open (*adj*) designating vowel produced with relatively large opening above the tongue; designating syllable ending with vowel
orthoepy study of pronunciation; standard pronunciation of a language
palatal speech sound formed with tongue close to or touching hard palate
paragoge addition of letter or syllable to end of word without changing meaning
pharyngeal speech sound produced in the pharynx
phone single speech sound
phoneme smallest unit of sound in a language that can distinguish one word from another
phonemics study of phonemes and phonemic systems of languages
phonetic alphabet alphabet having separate symbol for each distinguishable speech sound
phonetics study of speech sounds and their production, transmission, reception, and transcription
phonology study of distribution and patterns of speech sounds in a language or languages
pitch acoustic character of speech based on high or low quality of sound frequency
plosive consonant sound characterized by sudden release of complete closure in vocal tract, with audible expulsion of compressed air
polysyllable word consisting of two or more syllables
primary accent primary stress
primary stress strongest, principle stress of a word; primary accent
proclitic unstressed word or form closely connected in pronunciation with a following word and not normally used on its own
pronunciation act or manner of producing speech sounds; accepted way in which a word, syllable, or letter is sounded in a given language; phonetic transcription of word
prothesis addition of sound or syllable at beginning of word
Received Pronunciation RP; prestigious, regionally neutral pronunciation of British English derived from educated speech of S England, widely used in British broadcasting
resonance amplification of speech sound by vibrations of air in vocal tract
retroflex (*adj*) designating speech sound made with tip of tongue curled up and back toward hard palate
rhotacism excessive use or misarticulation of the sound "r"
RP Received Pronunciation
schwa neutral, unstressed vowel sound made in center of mouth; symbol (ə) for this sound
secondary accent secondary stress
secondary stress stress in word weaker than primary stress but not unstressed; secondary accent
short vowel vowel sound relatively short in duration
sibilant speech sound characterized by "s" or hissing sound
sonant speech sound that is voiced; speech sound that forms syllable by itself
sonorant voiced speech sound made with relatively free passage of air, such as vowel or nasal
spirant fricative
stop consonant sound made with complete closure at some part of vocal tract; plosive
stress degree of force applied in pronouncing sound, syllable, or word, producing relative loudness
suction stop click or implosive
syllable basic uninterrupted unit of pronunciation consisting of vowel sound, vowel sound with one or more consonant sounds, or consonant pronounced alone
synaloepha blending of vowel at end of one word with vowel at beginning of next
syncope dropping of sounds or letters from middle of word
syneresis contraction of two syllables or vowels into one, esp. to form diphthong
synizesis combination of two vowels that do not form diphthong
tonic syllable in an utterance having principal stress, usu. accompanied by change in pitch
transcription writing of speech sounds using phonetic symbols

trigraph three letters representing single speech sound
trill speech sound formed by rapid rolling or tapping motion of tongue or uvula
triphthong monosyllabic speech sound composed of three different vowel qualities
umlaut change in vowel sound in a Germanic language under influence of vowel originally occurring in following syllable
unstressed (*adj*) pronounced without stress or emphasis
unvoiced (*adj*) voiceless
uvular speech sound made by placing back of tongue against fleshy process on soft palate
velar speech sound formed by placing back of tongue against soft palate
vocalic (*adj*) relating to or containing a vowel or vowels
voiced (*adj*) produced with vibration of vocal cords
voiceless (*adj*) produced without vibration of vocal cords; unvoiced
vowel one of two basic categories of speech sounds, based on free passage of air through vocal tract

Linguistics and Writing Systems

abbreviation shortened or contracted form used to represent entire word or phrase
ablaut regular alternation of internal vowel, reflecting change in grammatical function
acronym word formed from initial letters of set series of words
affix morpheme added before, after, or within base word to create new word; prefix, suffix, or infix
Afroasiatic family of languages including Semitic, Egyptian, Berber, Cushitic, and Chadic
agglutination word formation in which distinct morphemes are combined without fusion or change, esp. addition of affixes to base word
allomorph alternate phonological shape of morpheme, such as plural form "-en" in "oxen" and "-s" in "goats"
alphabet letters of a language, arranged in set order; system of symbols or characters representing individual speech sounds of language
alternation variation in form of linguistic unit as it occurs in different environments or under different conditions
amelioration melioration
American Sign Language language consisting of manual signs and gestures, used by deaf people in the U.S. and parts of Canada
analogy process by which words or phrases are created or altered on model of existing language patterns
analytic (*adj*) designating a language that uses function words and changes in word order, rather than inflected forms, to express grammatical relations
Anglo-Saxon Old English
antepenult third syllable from the end in a word
anthropological linguistics study of relationship between language and culture, esp. in preliterate societies
antonym word opposite in meaning to another
applied linguistics use of linguistic theory in teaching, psychology, lexicography, and data processing
Aramaic ancient Semitic language from whose script were derived Hebrew, Arabic, and many other scripts
archaism word, form, or usage no longer in common use
argot special, often secret vocabulary and idiom of one group
artificial language language invented for specialized use, esp. for international communication or computer programming
Austronesian family of languages spoken in Malay Peninsula, Indonesia, Philippines, Vietnam, Madagascar, and Oceania; Malayo-Polynesian
Baltic branch of Indo-European languages including Latvian, Lithuanian, and Old Prussian
Bantu subbranch of Niger-Congo family of languages spoken in central and southern Africa, comprising over two hundred languages including Kikuyu and Swahili
bilingual (*adj*) fluent in two languages
blend word formed from parts of other words, such as "brunch" or "motel"
bound form linguistic form that occurs only in combination with other forms, such as most affixes
boustrophedon ancient form of writing in which lines alternate running right to left and left to right
Braille system of writing using combination of raised dots that are read by touch, for use by the blind
Briticism word or usage characteristic of British English, esp. when employed in American English
cant special language used by underworld group or by members of a profession
Celtic branch of Indo-European languages including Irish, Scottish Gaelic, Welsh, and Breton
citation quotation or excerpt showing particular word or phrase in context
code-switching alternate use of two or more languages or varieties of a language within same conversation or passage
cognate language related to another by descent from same language; word related to another by descent from same root word
coinage newly invented word
collocation regular occurrence of lexical items together, such as "commit crime"
colloquial (*adj*) designating language characteristic of or suitable to familiar, casual conversation
combining form linguistic form that occurs only in combination with other forms
comparative linguistics study of patterns of similarities and differences between languages
computational linguistics study of the applications of computers in processing and analyzing language, as in automatic machine translation
connotation associated or secondary meaning of

word in addition to its explicit or primary meaning
corpus collection of spoken or written utterances taken as representative sample of a given language and used for linguistic analysis
creole pidgin that has developed in complexity over time and has become the native language of a group of speakers
cuneiform system of writing using wedge-shaped characters, used by the ancient Assyrians, Babylonians, and others
cursive (*adj*) designating handwriting or printing in which letters are joined together in flowing style
Cyrillic Greek-based alphabet used in Russian and other Slavic languages
dead language language no longer in use as sole means of oral communication in a community
deep structure (in transformational grammar) underlying semantic or syntactic representation of sentence from which surface structure may be derived
definiendum term to be defined at head of dictionary entry
definiens defining part of dictionary entry
demotic current, everyday form of a language, esp. the Modern Greek vernacular; simplified form of ancient Egyptian hieroglyphic writing
denotation explicit or direct meaning of word
derivation formation of new words by adding affixes or changing shape of base word
descriptive grammar approach to grammar concerned with actual usage of speakers rather than with norms of correctness
descriptive linguistics study of structure of one language without reference to its history or comparison with other languages
diachronic (*adj*) relating to study of a language as it changes over time
dialect regionally or socially distinct variety of a language
dialectology study of dialects
direct discourse exact quotation of speaker's words
discourse analysis study of patterns and rules governing units of connected speech or writing longer than one sentence
doublet either of two different words ultimately deriving from the same source
Dravidian language family of South Asia, spoken mainly in S India
eponym person or mythological figure after whom something is named
Esperanto invented language intended for international use, based on words common to major European languages
etymology study of history and development of form and meaning of words; derivation of a word
etymon linguistic form from which another is historically derived
fingerspelling communication in sign language by means of manual alphabet
fluency ease and proficiency of expression in specific language
folk etymology modification of word based on false assumption about its origin or irrelevant analogy with familiar word
formal (*adj*) referring to language use typical of impersonal and official situations, characterized by complex vocabulary and sentences, careful grammar, and avoidance of colloquial expressions
franglais French spoken with large admixture of English words
free form linguistic form that can be used by itself as an independent word
generative grammar formalized set of rules that can generate all acceptable grammatical sentences of a language to explain tacit understanding native speaker has of that language
Germanic branch of Indo-European languages including German, English, Dutch, and Scandinavian languages
ghost word word that has come into existence through error, as through a misprint
glossary alphabetical listing of specialized terms and their meanings, usu. for one particular field
grapheme smallest distinctive unit of a writing system, esp. one representing a single phoneme
graphology study of writing systems
Grimm's law pattern of consonant correspondence between Germanic and other Indo-European languages demonstrated by Jakob Grimm in 1822, establishing regular process of change in language as basis for future linguistic analysis
hapax legomenon word that appears only once in a text, the works of an author, or the written record of a language
Hellenic branch of Indo-European languages including ancient and modern Greek
heteronym word spelled the same as another but having different sound and meaning, such as "lead" the metal and the verb
hieratic (*adj*) designating simplified form of hieroglyphics used by priests in ancient Egypt
hieroglyphics system of writing, as that of ancient Egypt, that uses pictorial symbols
historical linguistics study of language as it changes over a period of time
Hobson-Jobson alteration of word borrowed from foreign language to fit patterns of borrowing language
holophrase single word functioning as phrase or sentence
homograph word with same spelling but different meaning from another word
homonym word with same pronunciation and spelling but different meaning from another word; homophone
homophone word with same pronunciation but different meaning from another word
hypercorrection use of an inappropriate pronunciation, form, or construction to avoid using a seemingly incorrect form
ideogram written symbol representing idea or thing directly; ideograph
idiolect individual person's distinct manner of speaking

idiom expression having a meaning not predictable from usual meanings of its constituent words; language or style of speech peculiar to a people
illiteracy inability to read and write one's native language
Indic Indo-Aryan
indirect discourse inclusion of speaker's words in altered form in longer sentence
Indo-Aryan subgroup of Indo-Iranian branch of Indo-European languages including Sanskrit, Hindi, and Urdu
Indo-European widespread family of languages spoken primarily in Northern Hemisphere, including Italic, Germanic, Slavic, Baltic, Hellenic, Celtic, and Indo-Iranian branches
Indo-Iranian branch of Indo-European languages including Indic and Iranian subgroups
informal (*adj*) referring to language use suitable to or typical of casual or familiar speech or writing
informant native speaker of language who supplies utterances or other data for someone analyzing or learning the language
interlingual (*adj*) using two or more languages, as some dictionaries
Iranian subgroup of Indo-Iranian branch of Indo-European languages including Persian, Pashto, Avestan, and Kurdish
isogloss line on map marking limits within which particular feature of speech occurs
Italic branch of Indo-European languages including Latin and modern Romance languages such as French, Spanish, and Italian
jargon technical or specialized terminology of group or profession; obscure or unintelligible language
jive special slang jargon, often flippant or misleading
king's (or queen's) English correct, standard speech and usage of educated persons in England
language system using combinations of vocal sounds, written symbols, or gestures with accepted meanings to express thoughts and feelings common to one people of specific region or culture; communication using such a system
language family group of related languages descended from common parent language
language universal property or feature common to all languages
Latin Italic language of ancient Rome that is primary source of Romance languages
lemma form of word or phrase that represents its entire inflectional range, such as the form glossed in a dictionary
letter written symbol representing speech sound in particular alphabet
lexeme smallest distinct lexical unit in language system; item of vocabulary
lexical (*adj*) pertaining to the words or vocabulary of a language
lexicography art and practice of making dictionaries
lexicology study of formation and use of words
lexicon vocabulary; listing of words in a language; total stock of words in a language
lingo language, esp. jargon or slang, of a particular field, group, or individual
lingua franca language used for communication between persons who ordinarily speak different languages
linguist specialist in linguistics; polyglot
linguistic atlas set of maps showing distribution of linguistic features in the speech of an area; dialect atlas
linguistics study of sound, structure, meaning, vocabulary, and development of language, including fields of phonetics, phonology, morphology, syntax, semantics, pragmatics, comparative, and historical linguistics
lipreading understanding of spoken words from movement of speaker's lips without hearing sounds made
literacy ability to read and write
loan translation compound word or phrase formed by translation of each of the elements of a compound from another language
loanword word borrowed from another language
logogram character or symbol that represents entire word
longhand normal handwriting in which words are spelled out in full
Malayo-Polynesian Austronesian
manual alphabet set of finger signals representing letters of alphabet, used in sign language
melioration semantic change in a word over the course of time to a more approved or respectable meaning
metalanguage language used to describe or analyze language
metalinguistics study of relation of language to other culturally determined behavior
Middle English English language of period c1150-1475
Modern English English language since c1475
morpheme smallest distinctive grammatical unit of a language that is meaningful in itself and indivisible
morphology branch of linguistics involving forms and structure of words and patterns of word formation in particular language; these patterns of word formation themselves
mother tongue language first learned by a person
multilingual (*adj*) able to speak several languages
native speaker person speaking particular language learned naturally during childhood
natural language language that is the native language of a group of speakers
neologism new word or existing word with new meaning introduced into language
Niger-Congo large family of African languages
nonce word word invented or formed for particular occasion
nonstandard (*adj*) designating grammar, word choice, etc., used and considered acceptable by most educated native speakers
Old English English language before c1150; Anglo-Saxon
onomastics study of origin and use of proper names

orismology science of defining technical terms of a field of study
orthography representation of language sounds by written symbols or letters; study of letters and spelling; correct or standard spelling
paragraph subdivision of written composition set in block, usu. beginning on indented line, and having some coherence
parlance specified style of speaking, esp. involving choice of words
paronym word derived from same root as another; cognate
patois provincial dialect differing from standard form of the language; jargon
pejoration semantic change in a word over the course of time to a less favorable or less respectable meaning
penult next to the last syllable in a word
philology study of written texts to determine meaning and authenticity; older term for linguistics, esp. historical and comparative linguistics
phonogram symbol representing word, sound, or syllable
phraseogram written symbol that represents phrase, as in shorthand
pictograph pictorial symbol representing idea or thing, as in picture writing
picture writing system using pictures or pictorial symbols to record events or express ideas
pidgin auxiliary language with simplified grammatical structure and vocabulary drawn mostly from one language, used by speakers of two different languages for communication
pinyin system for romanizing Chinese into Latin alphabet
polyglot (*adj*) multilingual; composed of numerous linguistic groups; (*n*) person who knows several languages
polysemous (*adj*) having many meanings
portmanteau word blend
pragmatics branch of linguistics concerned with language in context, including speaker's intent and relation to listener; branch of semiotics concerned with relations between symbols and their users
prefix affix added before base word
prescriptive grammar approach to grammar concerned with establishing norms of correct and incorrect usage or rules based on these norms
protolanguage assumed parent form of language
provincialism word, phrase, or sound distinct to particular region or dialect; regionalism
psycholinguistics study of relationship between language and psychological processes of its users
reconstruction determination of hypothetical earlier form of a language by comparison of data from a later stage of the language
reflex element in a language that has developed from corresponding element in earlier form of the language
reformed spelling simplified spelling that eliminates unpronounced letters, such as "thru" for "through"
regionalism provincialism
romaji system of writing Japanese using letters of Latin alphabet
Roman alphabet Latin alphabet
Romance language one of the group of Indo-European languages descended from Latin, including French, Spanish, Italian, Portuguese, and Romanian
root morpheme that is the basic element of a word, underlying inflected or derived forms
rune character of ancient Germanic alphabet
script distinctive formation of letters by hand; handwriting; any system of writing
semantics branch of linguistics concerned with nature, structure, and development of meaning in language; branch of semiotics concerned with relationship between signs or symbols and what they denote
semiotics study or theory of signs and symbols in language and other communicative behavior
Semitic subfamily of Afroasiatic languages including Akkadian, Aramaic, Arabic, and Hebrew
shorthand rapid writing system using simple strokes and symbols to represent letters, words, and phrases
signed English form of communication using the signs of American Sign Language but using English grammar
sign language system of hand motions and finger configurations representing letters, ideas, and things, used in communication among deaf
Sino-Tibetan family of Asian languages including Mandarin and other Chinese dialects, Burmese, and Tibetan
slang informal, often nonstandard language consisting of newly coined words and extended meanings; specialized vocabulary, jargon, or vernacular
Slavic branch of Indo-European languages including Russian, Polish, Czech, Bulgarian, Serbo-Croatian, and Slovene
sociolect dialect used by particular social group
sociolinguistics study of interactions of language and society
source language original language of text to be translated
spelling standardized arrangement of letters to form specific words
Sprachgefühl sense of established usage and what is linguistically effective or appropriate
standard (*adj*) designating relatively unified, institutionalized form of language accepted as norm to be spoken and taught
stem part of inflected word which remains unchanged, to which inflections are added
structural linguistics study of nature and structure of language as network of coherent systems of formal units
substandard (*adj*) designating colloquial usage differing from standard dialect and deemed incorrect
substratum set of features of a language traceable to influence of earlier language that it has replaced
suffix affix added after base word

Sumerian language of ancient Mesopotamia, attested in pictographic and cuneiform writing
superstratum set of features of a language traceable to influence of a language formerly spoken in the society by a dominant group
surface structure representation of final syntactic form of sentence derived from deep structure in transformational grammar
syllabary system of written symbols each representing a syllable
syncretism merging of two or more different inflected forms into one
synonym word with same or essentially similar meaning as another word
syntactics branch of semiotics dealing with formal properties of symbol systems and relationship of signs to each other
syntagmatic (*adj*) referring to relationship among linguistic elements that occur sequentially
syntax rules for arranging words to form phrases, clauses, and sentences; study of this
synthetic (*adj*) designating language that uses affixes, rather than separate words, to express grammatical relationships
tagmeme grammatical unit based on relationship between a grammatical function and the class of items than can fill that function
target language language into which text is to be translated; language that one is learning
taxeme feature of arrangement of elements in construction, such as selection, order, or phonetic modification
thesaurus book listing words and their synonyms and antonyms
tone language language in which otherwise phonologically identical words are distinguished by different pitches, such as Chinese
toneme phoneme consisting of contrasting tone in tone language
tongue language or dialect
topic portion of sentence containing item about which information will be provided by rest of sentence; theme
transformational grammar system of grammatical analysis, esp. a form of generative grammar, concerned with process by which surface structure is derived from deep structure
translation rendering of passage from one language into another
transliteration representation of letters or words from one language in characters or letters of another language
ultima last syllable of a word
usage actual or customary manner in which language is used in a community; way in which particular word or phrase is used, esp. when choice of words is involved
variant one of two or more different spellings, pronunciations, or forms of the same word
vernacular language or dialect indigenous to place; common spoken language, distinct from formal written language
vocabulary words of a language; body of words known or used by an individual or group; list of words, usu. arranged in alphabetical order and defined or translated
vulgar (*adj*) designating the popular or informal variety of a language, esp. Latin

RHETORIC AND FIGURES OF SPEECH

adage proverb; traditional wise saying
allegory extended metaphor; representation of idea with concrete, structured image
alliteration succession of words or stressed syllables of word group beginning with same consonant sound or with same letter
allocution address; formal speech
allusion reference to famous, historical, or literary person or event
ambiguity expression of idea in words that may be interpreted more than one way
amplification figure of speech that emphasizes ideas through reiteration, embellishment, or elaboration
ana miscellaneous sayings or bits of information on some topic
anacoluthon deliberate failure to complete sentence, followed by shift to another thought or construction
anadiplosis repetition of last word in phrase or sentence, to constitute first word in following phrase or sentence
anagram rearrangement of letters in one word to form another
analogy comparison of things alike in certain respects to establish basis for exposition or argument
anaphora repetition of same word or phrase to begin consecutive sentences or clauses
anastrophe deliberate reversal of usual, logical order of sentence parts for emphasis
anathema formal denunciation
anecdote short narrative or description revealing point of interest about person or event
anonym pseudonym formed by backward spelling of real name
antiphrasis ironical description meant to convey impression opposite that normally conveyed by words used
antithesis use of strongly contrasting words and images
aphorism succinct, memorable statement of a truth; maxim
apophasis statement of assertion while denying intention of mentioning that subject
aposiopesis abrupt interruption that leaves thought incomplete
apostrophe direct form of address aimed at someone or something not present
apothegm tersely worded maxim
appellative descriptive name, designation, or epithet
archaism old, obsolete diction or vocabulary, esp. when used for effect

argumentation form of discourse emphasizing persuasion

assonance juxtaposition of similar word sounds, esp. vowels

asyndeton condensed expression characterized by omission of conjunctions

aureate (*adj*) distinguished by flowery rhetoric

axiom self-evident truth, succinctly stated

banality expression devoid of originality or wit; cliché

bon mot clever remark or comment; witticism

brocard short, proverbial rule

bromide commonplace saying or turn of phrase

buzzword slogan or catchword conjuring popular idea or image

byword proverb; word or phrase associated with a person or thing

cacology poor diction or pronunciation

cadence rhythm and measure of written or spoken language

cant insincere language intended to convey impression of genuine feeling

catachresis wrong use of one word for another that sounds similar to it or has similar meaning

catchword commonly repeated word or phrase; slogan

chestnut old and familiar anecdote or joke

circumlocution roundabout mode of expression; use of unnecessary verbiage

cliché stereotyped expression; trite description; banality; platitude; truism

cognomen distinguishing name or epithet

conceit ingenious idea expressed as elaborate, fanciful metaphor or analogy

connotation shades and variety of meanings attached to word or phrase in addition to specific denotation; implication

conundrum question or riddle whose answer involves a pun

curse invocation of evil upon someone; imprecation; malediction

dead metaphor figure of speech drained of its power of analogy; metaphor grown colorless with overuse

declamation recitation as exercise in oratory or elocution

denotation specific, literal meaning

diatribe abusive, bitter style of speech

diction selection and use of words to convey meaning; quality, style, and sound of an individual's speech relative to prevailing standards

discourse speech; lengthy, formal discussion of subject

dithyramb wildly enthusiastic speech or writing, usu. of irregular form, esp. impassioned poem or chant

double entendre intentionally ambiguous statement, esp. with one possibly indecent meaning

double-talk intentional ambiguity; mixture of sense and nonsense

dysphemism harsh or unpleasant language used as substitute for more direct or neutral expression, opposite of euphemism

echoism onomatopoeia

elaboration development of theme or image

ellipsis omission of words essential to meaning and structure, but easily filled in by reader or listener

elliptical (*adj*) tending to be ambiguous, unclear, or roundabout

elocution practice of oral delivery or public speaking

eloquence artful, persuasive, elegant, or vivid language

endearment affectionate form of address

epigram concise, vivid saying

epilogue concluding remark or statement; last of seven parts of oration in classical rhetoric

epithet descriptive, often disparaging phrase characteristically applied to a person or thing because of its accuracy and color

equivocation use of ambiguity in order to deceive or evade

eulogy formal, extended statement of praise, esp. to honor deceased person; panegyric

euphemism indirect, mild language used as substitute for direct, possibly offensive description; opposite of dysphemism

euphuism florid, affected, artificial style of speech

exclamation sharp, sudden utterance; vehement protest or complaint

exordium introduction to oration; first of seven parts of oration in classical rhetoric

expatiation speaking or writing at great length

expletive emphatic interjection

exposition form of discourse emphasizing explanation

figurative language metaphorical language used outside its usual forms of construction and meaning for purposes of description, persuasion, or originality of expression

figure of speech expressive language construction in which word meaning differs from literal sense of words

forensics art, study, and use of argumentation and debate

glossolalia unintelligible, ecstatic speech; speaking in tongues

harangue bombastic ranting; extended attack or complaint; Philippic

homily morally instructive speech

hyperbole extravagant exaggeration for comic or colorful effect or emphasis

hypocorism pet name; diminutive form imitating baby talk

hypothesis tentative assumption to be tested in argument

imprecation curse

innuendo insinuation; words with an unpleasant connotation

invective abusive language

invocation address to God or higher power

irony figure of speech conveying intent or reality different from, or opposite to, literal meaning of words used; speech employing elements of restraint, humor, sarcasm

lingo strange, obscure language or jargon peculiar to one group

litany prayer or supplication
litotes understatement, such as "not bad," in which affirmative is expressed by negating contrary statement
locution style of expression
logodaedaly arbitrary and capricious coinage of words
malapropism incorrect use of word similar to appropriate word
malediction curse
maxim aphorism, proverb
meiosis understatement, esp. for humorous effect
metaphor identification of one thing by another; trope, or turn of phrase, describing one idea in terms of another idea or image analogous to it
metonymy substitution of name of an object associated with a word for the word itself
motto word or phrase used regularly to characterize something or some group
narration form of discourse emphasizing recounting of event
nutshell brief statement reducing something to its essence
oath any profane expression, esp. one irreverent toward God
obiter dictum *Latin.* lit. saying by the way; incidental, uncalculated remarks
onomatomania obsession with words, their sounds, and meanings
onomatopoeia use of words whose sounds imitate or suggest their meaning; echoism
oration formal speech intended to persuade; in classical rhetoric, a speech divided into seven parts: exordium, narration, exposition, proposition, confirmation, confutation, and epilogue
oxymoron combination of two contradictory terms
palindrome word, phrase, or sentence reading the same backward or forward
panegyric eulogy
pangram sentence or verse containing all letters of the alphabet
parable short story that illustrates a moral attitude or principle
paradox apparently contradictory statement that is actually true
paraphrase restatement of thought to retain meaning while changing form of expression
parenthesis remark made as explanation
password secret word or phrase used to gain admission to restricted area; shibboleth
periphrasis indirect, wordy style of expression
peroration summation of major points and persuasive concluding remarks occurring at end of speech
persiflage banter; light chatter
personification act of verbally endowing animals, objects, or abstractions with human attributes
phatic (*adj*) designating speech used to express goodwill or sociability rather than to impart information
Philippic harangue
platitude trite or commonplace remark; cliché
pleonasm redundancy
polemic argument set forth, esp. on controversial subject
profanity common or vulgar language, esp. characterized by irreverence toward God or sacred things
prolepsis anticipation and response to opponent's argument before it is actually stated
prologue introductory remark or statement
proverb brief popular saying, usu. of unknown origin, expressing a commonplace truth; wise saying succinctly stated; adage; maxim; saw
pun wordplay based on similarity of sound but difference in meaning between words; paronomasia; play on words
punch line concluding phrase or line of joke, pun, or riddle
rebuttal reply to argument
redundancy use of more words than needed to express idea; pleonasm
repartee conversation characterized by wit; clever reply
repetition reiteration of word, phrase, or idea for emphasis
retort sharp, incisive, often retaliatory reply; reply in kind
rhetoric theory and use of clear, persuasive, vivid language in presentation of argument or point of view; principles of oratory; undue use of exaggeration or bombast
rhetorical figure nonstandard usage that does not alter meaning of words
rhetorical question question asked solely for effect, and not to elicit a reply
riposte quick, sharp reply
sarcasm caustic, ironical language intended to wound or belittle another
saw sententious saying; maxim
saying formulation grown familiar through repetition; adage; saw
sesquipedalianism use of very long words
shibboleth phrase characteristic of particular group; password
shop talk jargon or lingo of particular occupation
simile expression showing similarity between two unlike things, generally begun with comparison word "like" or "as"
slogan catchword
slur disparaging remark or characterization
Socratic method question and answer format of discourse; assumption of ignorance in debate for ironical effect
solecism ungrammatical combination of words; error in diction
speaking in tongues utterance of incom-prehensible sounds while in ecstatic state, usu. believed to be words of deity
speech theory and practice of oral communication, esp. before an audience
spoonerism intentional or accidental transposition of initial sounds of two or more words; confusion resulting from such transposition
synecdoche metaphoric form in which a part signifies the whole and less general stands for more general, or vice versa

synthesis dialectic combination of thesis and antithesis to deduce solution or truth
thesis position set forth for argument by speaker or writer
threnody dirge, lamentation
trope figure of speech; turn or twist on ordinary, literal sense of word or words
truism commonplace statement of truth; cliché
understatement form of irony in which something is represented as less than it really is
verbigeration continual repetition of words and phrases
vitriol extremely caustic speech or writing
watchword motto used as sign of recognition within group or as guiding principle for action
wordplay verbal wit; use of rhetorical figures of speech

QUALIFIERS AND CONNECTIVES

Conjunctions
Prepositions
Limitations and Conditions
Reflections and References
Comparisons
Approximations and Generalizations
Emphasizers
Maximizers and Superlatives
Absolutes and Guarantees

Conjunctions

according as, afore, after, against, albeit, also, altho, although, an, and, and also, and/or, as, as far as, as how, as if, as long as, as though, as well as
because, before, being, both, but
considering
directly
either, ere, ergo, except, excepting
for, forasmuch as, fore
gin
how, howbeit, howe'er, however
if, immediately, inasmuch as, insofar as, insomuch as, instantly
lest, like
much as
neither, nor, notwithstanding, now
once, only, or, otherwise
plus, provided, providing
save, saving, seeing, since, sith, so, sobeit, so long as, still, supposing, syne
than, that, then, tho, though, till
unless, unlike, until
well, what, when, whence, whencesoever, whene'er, whenever, whensoever, where, whereabout, whereabouts, whereas, whereat, whereby, where'er, wherefore, wherefrom, wherein, whereinto, whereof, whereon, whereso, wheresoe'er, wheresoever, wherethrough, whereto, whereunder, whereunto, whereupon, wherever, wherewith, whether, while, whiles, whilst, whither, whithersoever, why, without
yet

Prepositions

a, abaft, aboard, about, above, absent, according to, across, adown, afore, after, against, agin, à la, aloft, along, alongside, amid, amidst, among, amongst, an, anent, après, around, as, aside, aslant, as of, as to, astraddle, astride, at, athwart
bar, barring, bating, because, before, behind, below, ben, beneath, beside, besides, between, betwixt, beyond, but, by
chez, circa, concerning, considering, contra, cum
despite, down, during
ere, ex, except, excepting, excluding
failing, for, forby, fore, forth, frae, from
in, including, inside, instead of, into
less, like
maugre, mid, midst, minus, mongst
near, neath, next, next to, nigh, notwithstanding
o', o'er, of, off, on, onto, opposite, or, out, outside, over
pace, past, pending, per, plus
re, regarding, respecting, round
sans, save, saving, since, sith, syne
than, thorough, thro, throughout, thru, thwart, till, times, to, touching, toward
under, underneath, unless, unlike, until, unto, up, upon
versus, via, vice, vis-à-vis
wanting, while, with, withal, within, without, worth

Limitations and Conditions

a bit, a breath, a couple, additionally, admitting, a few, albeit, a little, all but, all the same, all things considered, alone, although, a mite, as far as, as good as, aside from, as is, as it is, as long as, as soon as, as the case may be, as well, at all, at best, at least, at most, a trifle, at worst, au contraire
barely, barring, below, besides, be that as it may, bit by bit, briefly, but, by any chance, by any means, by chance, by degrees, by hook or by crook, by no means, by the same token
catch, circumstantially, conceivably, conditionally, considering, contingent on, cursory
decreasingly, demi-, depending, discounting
else, even, even so, even still, even though, even with, ever less, everything being

equal, except, except for, excepting, except that, excluding, exclusive of, exempting, expressly
faintly, few, for all one knows, for all that, for aught one knows, formerly, for my part, for the most part
God willing, gradually, grain of salt, granting
half, halfway, handful, hardly, hardly ever, hedged, hemi-, hen's teeth, hereby, how, howbeit, however, howsoever
if, if and only if, if and when, if at all, if it so happens, if not, if only, if possible, if then, ill, in, in addition, in any case, in any way, in a way, in brief, in case, infrequently, in no way, in part, insofar as, in some measure, in spite of, in that case, iota, irregardless
just, just in case, just so, just the same
kicker, kind of
latter, least, leastways, leastwise, leaving aside, less, less and less, less than, let alone, like, little by little
maybe, mayhap, mere, merely, midway, might, mildly, mini-, minimus, minus, minutely, mite, moderately, modestly, modicum, momentary, mostly
namely, nary, nay rather, needless, negligible, neither, never, nevertheless, nohow, no less than, nominal, no more than, nonetheless, nor, not hardly, not in the least, not much, not often, notwithstanding, nowhere near, null
occasionally, off, on balance, once, on condition that, only, only if, on the whole, otherwise, overly, overmuch
part by part, partial, partially, partly, partway, passing, pending, pennyworth, perchance, perhaps, personally, picayune, piddling, piecemeal, pittance, possibly, pretty, pretty much, provided, providing, provisionally, purely
qualifying, quasi, quite the contrary
rarely, rather, regardless, relatively, remote, restricting, restrictive
sans, satisfactory, save, saving, scarcely, seldom, semi-, several, short of, slightly, sliver, smattering, smidgen, so as, sobeit, so far, so long as, so many, some, somehow, somehow or other, someway, somewhat, soon, sort of, soupçon, sparely, sparsely, speck, sporadically, spot, step by step, still, still and all, stipulated, strings, subject to, submarginal
tad, temporary, that being said, that being so, that is to say, though, thumbnail, tittle, to, to a certain point, to a degree, token, to some degree, to some extent, trace
under, under par, under the circumstances, unless, upon my word, up to
verge, videlicet, viz
waiving, waning, wee, well, were it not, when, whereof, whichever, whit, with a catch, withal, without, with reservations, with strings, with the proviso, with the stipulation, worse
yet

Reflections and References

according, accordingly, according to, aforementioned, again, against, allowing for, all the same, all things considered, along, along with, amid, amidst, among, amongst, and so, and so forth, and so on, anent, apart, apparently, arguably, around, as, as a result, as being, as far as, as if, as they say, as though, as to, asunder, as well as, attended by, at the same time
because, because of, between, betwixt, by, by and by, by dint of, by the way, by virtue of, by way of
concerning, conjointly, consequently, considering, contrary to, counter to, coupled with
ditto, due to
either, else, elsewise, ergo, etcetera, evidently
finally, for each, for example, for instance, for that reason, for this reason
given
hence, henceforth, henceforward, hereat, hereby, herein, hereinafter, hereinbefore, hereinbelow, hereon, heretofore, hereunder, hereunto, hereupon, herewith, hither, hitherto, how come
ibid, imprimis, in addition to, inasmuch as, incidentally, incidental to, including, in conjunction, indeed, in keeping with, in lieu of, in line with, in other respects, in other words, in passing, in re, in relation to, in return, insofar as, insomuch as, instead, instead of, in the matter of, intro-, in turn, in twain, in two, in view of, irrespective
jointly
loc cit
midst, mongst, much as, much less, mutually
natch, naturally, naturellement
of, of course, on account of, only, on that account, on the other hand, op cit, or, or else, other than, otherwise, outwardly
penultimate, per, peripheral
qua
re, readily, regarding, respecting, respectively
secondary, seeing that, selectively, self-styled, separately, severally, side, since, snap, so, so as, soever, sofar as, so forth, so much, so on, specified, spotty, square, stated, subsidiary, such, supposed, supra, surfeit
tacit, that is to say, then again, thence, there, thereat, thereby, therefore, thereinafter, thereof, thereon, thereto, theretofore, thereunder, thereupon, thus, thus and so, thusly, together with
uncommon, undue, unduly, unusual, unusually, upon
variable, various, variously, veritable, vice, virtual
what for, what if, whence, where, whereat,

wherefor, wherefrom, whereinto, whereon, wheresoever, whereupon, whichever, while, why, with, with regard to, with relation to, with respect to
yet

Comparisons

about, above, à la, alike, all get-out, all that, almost, and then some, another, as, as much as, as well as
beside, better
close to, comparably, comparatively, compared to, complementary
different
either, either-or, enough, equally
farther, further
in comparison, increasingly, in kind, in like manner
just about
like, like so, like that, likewise
mainly, middling, mixed, moiety, more
nearly, near miss, next to, nigh, no less than, nor
opposite, or, over, over against, over and above
premium
rather, relatively
same, second best, second class, second fiddle, second rate, similar, so, somewhat, so-so, sufficient, super, surpassing
tantamount, than, third rate, to-and-fro, to wit
unlike, unparalleled, unprecedented
vice versa, vis-à-vis
well-nigh, what, whereas, whether, while, worse

Approximations and Generalizations

about, a few, after all, again, a little, all in all, a lot, any, anyhow, anyway, apparently, approximately, around, as a rule, as a whole, as it were, as much as, at all events, at any rate, at large, aught
ballpark, before long, belike, be that as it may, borderline, broadly, by and large
circa, close, close to, collectively, commonly, comparatively
en masse, essentially, ever
fairly, for all that, for that matter, for the most part
generally
here and there
in all, in any case, in any event, in a way, in general, in short
just about, just the same
kind of
lately, latterly, like, long and short of it
mainly, mas o menos, mezzo-mezzo, more or less, much
near, neither here nor there, now and then
often, only just, on the whole, overall
possibly, primarily, probably, proportionately
relatively, reputedly, roughly, roundly
say, seeming, seemingly, simply, some, sometimes, somewhat, somewhere, somewhere near, soon, sooner or later, sort of, so-so, so to speak, such and such, sundry
then again, thereabouts, to a degree, to an extent, to the tune of, truth of the matter
virtually
whatever, what have you, whatnot, wherever

Emphasizers

above, after all, again, all, all-around, all of, all told, a lot, also, altogether, and how, as well, awfully
beside, besides, big deal, by far
decidedly
either, especially, even, evermore so, ever so, exceedingly, expressly
far and away, fine, further, furthermore
increasingly, indeed, in detail, in particular, in the main
just, just so
lastly
mainly, mighty, moreover, more than ever, mostly
namely, no matter, notably, not to mention
obviously, on top of, over, over and above
particular, particularly, plus, primarily, pronounced
quite
real, really, resounding, respective, right
simply, singularly, so, specially, specifically, still, strong, such
tall order, telling, terribly, to boot, too, to say nothing of, to say the least
up
very
well, whopper

Maximizers and Superlatives

all, all along, all-embracing, all get-out, all-inclusive, all over, a lot, always, aplenty, a sight, at length
best, bevy
chiefly, chock-full, commonly, considerable, copious
decidedly, doozie
ever, evermore, every, exceedingly, extremely
far, far and away, farthest, first water, foremost
galore
head and shoulders, head over heels, hook, line, and sinker, hyper
ideally
jillion
lickety-split, likely, lots
major, many, maxi-, mighty, more and more, most, much, multiplicity, myriad
nth, numerous
oft, often, oftentimes, oodles
part and parcel, plenteous, plentiful, premium

radically, rattling, real, rife, right, rip-roaring, roaring
scads, slew, smashing, socko, spanking, spate, staggering, stiff, strong, super, super-duper, supreme, surpassing, sweeping
thumping, thundering, tiptop, top
ultra-, unbounded, unbridled, unmitigated, unremitting, unrivaled, untold, up
vast, vaulting, very
walloping, waxing, way, whacking, whopping, wide-ranging, widespread, withering
zillion

Absolutes and Guarantees

above all, absolutely, actually, after all, all, all along, all out, all over, all the while, altogether, always, as a matter of course, as a matter of fact, at any cost, at first, at last, at long last, at that
bar none, by all means
cap-a-pie, certainly, clean, clearly, complete, completely, conclusively
dead on, decidedly, definitely
entirely, even, eventually, exactly, expressly
fare-thee-well, finally, first, first and foremost, firstly, first of all, first things, forever, forever and ever, forevermore, for good, for keeps, forsooth, for sure, full-out, fully
granting
hands down, head to toe
identically, immeasurably, in all respects, in a word, in conclusion, indeed, indubitably, inevitably, in fact, infinitely, in full, in no way, in particular, in point of fact, in reality, in the first place, in the long run, in toto, invariably, irrespective of
just, just so
lastly, literally, literatim, lock, stock, and barrel
minimus
nada, naught, necessarily, needless to say, never, nil, nix, nohow, no ifs, ands, or buts, no more, none, not a bit, not at all, not a whit, now and forever, no way, nowise, null, null and void
of course, once, once for all, one and all, only, out-and-out, outright
paramount, par excellence, perfectly, plain, plenary, plumb, precisely, premier, prime, primo, principal, proper, purely
quite
really, right
same, selfsame, sheer, simply, smack-dab, solely, solid, so much as, squarely, stark, stock-still, stone, supreme, sure, sure enough, surely
thoroughly, through and through, to a tee, top flight, topnotch, total, totally, to the limit, to the utmost, truly
ultimately, unadulterated, unconditional, unconditionally, undeniably, under no circumstances, unlimited, unmistakably, unqualified, unreservedly, uppermost, utmost, utter, utterly, uttermost
verbatim, verily, veritably, versal, void
well, whatever, whatsoever, wherever, whole, whole hog, wholly, wide, without exception, word-for-word, world, worst
zero, zilch

PREFIXES AND SUFFIXES

Prefixes

a- not (*asocial*)
ab- away from (*absent*)
acantho- spine, thorn (*acanthus*)
aceto- vinegar, acetic acid (*acetometer*)
acro- top, tip (*acrophobia*)
actino- ray, beam (*actinometer*)
adeno- gland (*adenovirus*)
aero- air, gas (*aerodynamic*)
agri- farming (*agribusiness*)
agro- field, soil, crop production (*agronomy*)
algo- pain (*algolagnia*)
allo- other (*allotrope*)
alti- high (*altitude*)
ambi- both (*ambidextrous*)
amphi- both, around (*amphibious*)
amylo- starch (*amyloplast*)
an- not, lacking (*anarchy*)
ana- up, against, back (*anabasis*)
andro- male (*androgenous*)
anemo- wind (*anemometer*)
angio- container (*angiosperm*)
aniso- unequal (*anisotropic*)
ante- before (*antebellum*)
antho- flower (*anthophore*)
anthropo- human (*anthropology*)
anti- against (*antibody*)
apo- away, apart (*apogee*)
aqui- water (*aquifer*)
arbori- tree (*arboriculture*)
archeo- ancient, old (*archeology*)
archi- first, most basic (*architrave*)
arterio- artery (*arteriosclerosis*)
arthro- joint (*arthropod*)
asco- sac (*ascomycete*)
astro- star (*astronomy*)
atmo- vapor, gas (*atmosphere*)
audio- hearing, sound reproduction (*audiophile*)
auri- gold (*auriferous*); ear (*auriform*)
auto- self, same (*automatic*)
avi- bird (*aviculture*)
bacterio- bacteria (*bacteriophage*)
baro- weight, pressure (*barometer*)
batho- deep (*bathosphere*)
bene- good (*benevolent*)
biblio- book (*bibliography*)
bio- life (*biography*)

blasto- bud, embryo (*blastosphere*)
brachio- arm (*brachiopod*)
brachy- short (*brachylogy*)
brady- slow (*bradycardia*)
branchio- gills (*branchiopod*)
broncho- throat (*bronchoscope*)
caco- bad (*cacology*)
calci- calcium (*calcify*)
calli- beautiful (*calligraphy*)
cardio- heart (*cardiology*)
carpo- fruit (*carpophore*)
cata- down, against, back (*cataclysm*)
ceno- common (*cenobite*)
centi- hundred (*centigram*)
centri- center (*centrifuge*)
cephalo- head (*cephalothorax*)
cerebro- brain (*cerebrospinal*)
cero- wax (*ceroplastic*)
chalco- copper (*chalcocite*)
cheli- claws (*cheliped*)
chilo- lip (*chiloplasty*)
chiro- hand (*chiropractor*)
chloro- green (*chlorophyll*)
choreo- dance (*choreography*)
chromo- color (*chromolithography*)
chrono- time (*chronometer*)
chryso- gold (*chrysolite*)
circum- around (*circumference*)
cis- near to, on near side of (*cisalpine*)
clado- branch (*cladogenesis*)
clino- slope (*clinometer*)
co- variation of com-, used esp. to form new words (*coworker*)
coel- cavity (*coelenteron*)
com- with, together with (*combine*)
contra- against (*contravene*)
copro- excrement (*coprophilia*)
cortico- cortex (*corticosteroid*)
cosmo- universe (*cosmology*)
costo- rib (*costotomy*)
cranio- skull (*craniotomy*)
cruci- cross (*cruciform*)
cryo- - cold (*cryogenics*)
crypto- hidden (*cryptography*)
cteno- rake, comb (*ctenophore*)
cupri- copper (*cupriferous*)
cysto- bladder (*cystoscope*)
cyto- cell (*cytoplasm*)
dactylo- finger, toe (*dactylomegaly*)
de- negation (*dehumidify*)
deca- ten (*decagon*)
deci- tenth (*decimeter*)
demi- half, lesser (*demitasse*)
demono- devil, demon (*demonolatry*)
dendro- tree (*dendrology*)
denti- tooth (*dentifrice*)
dermato- skin (*dermatology*)
deutero- second (*deuteropathy*)
di- two, double (*dicotyledon*)
dia- thorough, opposed, completely (*diagnosis*)
dicho- in two parts (*dichotomy*)
dino- terrifying (*dinosaur*)
diplo- double (*diplopod*)
dis- apart, asunder, away, or having a general negative or reversing force (*disability, discontent, dislike*)
dodeca- twelve (*dodecahedron*)
dorsi- back of body (*dorsiflexion*)
duo- two (*duologue*)
dyna- force, power (*dynamotor*)
dys- evil, bad, impaired (*dysfunction*)
eco- ecology (*ecosystem*)
ecto- outside, external (*ectoderm*)
electro- electric (*electromagnetic*)
enantio- opposite (*enantiomorph*)
encephalo- brain (*encephalogram*)
endo- within (*endogenous*)
ennea- nine (*enneahedron*)
entero- intestine (*enterology*)
entomo- insect (*entomophagous*)
eo- early, dawn (*eolith*)
epi- on, over, near (*epidermis*)
equi- equal (*equilateral*)
ergo- work (*ergonomic*)
eroto- sexual desire (*erotogenesis*)
erythro- red (*erythrocyte*)
ethno- race, nation (*ethnography*)
eu- good (*eugenics*)
eury- broad, wide (*euryphagous*)
ex- former (*ex-president*); out of, thoroughly (*extract, exhaust*)
exo- outside, external (*exogamous*)
extra- outside, external (*extraterrestrial*)
febri- fever (*febrifuge*)
ferro- iron (*ferromagnet*)
fibro- fiber (*fibroblast*)
fissi- split, cleft (*fissiped*)
flori- flower (*floriculture*)
fluoro- fluoride (*fluorocarbon*)
fructi- fruit (*fructiferous*)
galacto- milk (*galactophorous*)
gameto- mature reproductive cell (*gametogenesis*)
gamo- joined, united (*gamopetalous*)
gastro- stomach (*gastronomy*)
geo- land, earth (*geology*)
geronto- old age (*gerontocracy*)
glosso- tongue (*glossolalia*)
glotto- tongue (*glottochronology*)
glyco- sugar, sweet (*glycogen*)
gono- sexual, reproductive (*gonophore*)
grapho- writing (*graphomotor*)
gymno- naked, nude (*gymnogynous*)
gyneco- woman (*gynecology*)
hagio- holy (*hagiography*)
halo- salt (*halogen*)
haplo- single, simple (*haplology*)
hecto- hundred (*hectoliter*)
helico- spiral (*helicospore*)
helio- sun (*heliotherapy*)
hema- blood (*hemagglutination*)
hemato- blood (*hematocyst*)
hemi- half (*hemisphere*)
hemo- blood (*hemoglobin*)
hendeca- eleven (*hendecagon*)
hepato- liver (*hepatotoxin*)
hepta- seven (*heptagon*)

hetero- different (*heterogeneous*)
hexa- six (*hexagon*)
hiero- sacred (*hierogram*)
histo- tissue (*histology*)
holo- complete, whole (*hologram*)
homeo- similar, like (*homeostasis*)
homo- same (*homogeneous*)
homoio- similar, like (*homoiothermal*)
hyalo- glass (*hyaloplasm*)
hydro- water (*hydrodynamic*)
hyeto- rain (*hyetograph*)
hygro- wet (*hygrometer*)
hylo- matter (*hylotheism*)
hyper- above (*hyperactive*)
hypno- sleep, hypnosis (*hypnotherapy*)
hypo- under (*hypothermia*)
hystero- womb (*hysterectomy*)
iatro- medicine (*iatrogenic*)
ichythyo- fish (*ichthyology*)
icono- image, likeness (*iconology*)
ideo- idea (*ideology*)
idio- peculiar (*idiosyncrasy*)
il- not (*illogical*)
ileo- intestinal ileum (*ileocolitis*)
ilio- ilium portion of hipbone (*iliofemoral*)
im- not (*impartial*)
immuno- immune (*immunology*)
in- not, used to give negative or privative force, esp. to adjectives (*inexpensive*)
inter- between (*interscholastic*)
intra- inside, within, interior (*intracellular*)
ir- not, against (*irreducible*)
irido- rainbow, iris of eye (*iridotomy*)
iso- equal (*isometric*)
jejuno- jejunum portion of intestine (*jejunostomy*)
juxta- close, near, beside (*juxtaposition*)
karyo- cell nucleus (*karyolysis*)
kerato- horn (*keratogenous*)
kineto- movement (*kinetoscope*)
labio- lip (*labiovelar*)
lacto- milk (*lactogenic*)
lamelli- plate, scale (*lamelliform*)
laparo- abdominal wall (*laparoscope*)
laryngo- larynx (*laryngoscope*)
lepido- scale (*lepidopteron*)
lepto- thin, fine (*leptodactylous*)
leuko- white (*leukocyte*)
levo- left (*levorotatory*)
ligni- wood (*ligniform*)
litho- stone (*lithography*)
logo- word, spoken (*logomachy*)
longi- long, length (*longicorn*)
luni- moon (*lunitidal*)
lympho- lymph (*lymphocyte*)
lyso- decomposition, dissolving (*lysosome*)
macro- large (*macrocosm*)
magni- great, large (*magnify*)
male- evil, bad (*malevolent*)
masto- breast (*mastopathy*)
matri- female (*matriarchy*)
mechano- machine (*mechanoreceptor*)
mega- great (*megalopolis*)
megalo- great (*megalomania*)
melano- black (*melanocyte*)
mero- part (*merogony*)
meso- middle (*mesopause*)
meta- after, beyond, changed (*metaphysics*)
metro- measure (*metronome*)
micro- small (*microorganism*)
milli- one thousandth (*millimeter*)
mis- wrong, ill, incorrect (*misprint, mistrust*)
miso- hatred (*misogyny*)
mono- single, one (*monotone*)
morpho- shape (*morphology*)
muco- mucus (*mucopurulent*)
multi- many (*multifaceted*)
musculo- muscle (*musculoskeletal*)
myco- fungus, mold, mushroom (*mycotoxicosis*)
myelo- marrow, spinal cord (*myelocyte*)
myo- muscle (*myocardium*)
myria- ten thousand (*myriagram*)
mytho- myth (*mythology*)
myxo- mucus, slime (*myxovirus*)
nano- one billionth (*nanosecond*)
narco- stupor, drugged state (*narcoanalysis*)
naso- nose (*nasolacrimal*)
necro- dead body (*necrophilia*)
nemato- thread (*nematocyst*)
neo- new (*neologism*)
nepho- cloud (*nephometer*)
nephro- kidney (*nephrology*)
neuro- nerve (*neurology*)
neutro- neutral (*neutrosphere*)
nocti- night (*noctilucent*)
nomo- custom, law (*nomology*)
non- not, freely implying negation or absence of something (*nonprofessional, nonpayment*)
noso- disease (*nosogeography*)
noto- back of body (*notochord*)
nucleo- nucleus (*nucleotide*)
nycto- night (*nyctophobia*)
ob- against (*obverse*)
octa- eight (*octagon*)
oculo- eye (*oculomotor*)
odonto- tooth (*odontogeny*)
oleo- oil (*oleomargarine*)
oligo- few (*oligopoly*)
omni- all (*omnipotent*)
oneiro- dream (*oneiromancy*)
onto- being, existence (*ontology*)
oo- egg (*oocyte*)
ophio- snake (*ophiolatry*)
ophthalmo- eye (*ophthalmology*)
opistho- back, behind (*opisthograph*)
opto- eye (*optometry*)
organo- body organ (*organoleptic*)
ornitho- bird (*ornithology*)
oro- mountain (*orography*); mouth (*oropharynx*)
ortho- straight (*orthopedic*)
ossi- bone (*ossiferous*)
osteo- bone (*osteopath*)
oto- ear (*otolaryngology*)
out- beyond, to an end point, abnormal (*outdoors, outlast, outmoded*)
over- too much, to excess (*overweight*)

ovi- egg (*oviparous*)
oxy- sharp, acute (*oxymoron*)
pachy- thick (*pachyderm*)
paleo- ancient, old (*paleolithic*)
pan- all (*pantheism*)
para- beside, beyond; guard against (*parallel, parachute*)
pari- equal (*paripinnate*)
partheno- without fertilization (*parthenogenesis*)
patho- disease, suffering (*pathological*)
patri- male (*patriarchy*)
pedi- foot (*pedicab*)
pedo- child (*pedophilia*)
penta- five (*pentagon*)
per- through, very (*pervade*)
peri- around, very (*perimeter*)
petro- stone (*petrology*)
phago- eating (*phagocyte*)
pharmaco- drug (*pharmocology*)
pharyngo- pharynx (*pharyngoscope*)
pheno- shining, appearing (*phenotype*)
philo- loving (*philosophy*)
phlebo- vein (*phlebotomy*)
phono- sound (*phonograph*)
photo- light (*photography*)
phreno- brain (*phrenology*)
phyco- seaweed, algae (*phycology*)
phyllo- leaf (*phyllotaxy*)
phylo- race, tribe, species (*phylogeny*)
physio- nature (*physiology*)
phyto- plant (*phytogenesis*)
piezo- pressure (*piezoelectric*)
pinni- web, fin (*pinniped*)
pisci- fish (*pisciculture*)
plagio- oblique (*plagiotropic*)
plano- flat (*planogamete*)
pleo- more (*pleomorphism*)
pleuro- side, lateral (*pleurocarpous*)
pluto- riches, wealth (*plutocracy*)
pluvio- rain (*pluviometer*)
pneumato- air, breath (*pneumatophore*)
pneumo- air, breath (*pneumococcus*)
pod- foot (*podiatry*)
polio- gray matter (*poliomyelitis*)
poly- many (*polygon*)
post- after (*postmortem*)
pre- before (*preproduction*)
preter- beyond (*preternatural*)
primi- first (*primipara*)
pro- before, forward (*prologue*); for, favoring (*proslavery*)
proprio- one's own (*proprioceptive*)
proto- first (*prototype*)
pseudo- false (*pseudonym*)
psycho- mind, spirit, soul (*psychosomatic*)
pterido- fern (*pteridology*)
ptero- wing (*pterodactyl*)
pyelo- pelvis (*pyelonephritis*)
pyo- pus (*pyorrhea*)
pyro- fire (*pyromania*)
quadri- four (*quadrilateral*)
quinque- five (*quinquevalent*)
re- again (*revitalize*)
recti- straight (*rectilinear*)
reni- kidney (*reniform*)
retro- backward (*retroactive*)
rhabdo- rod, wand (*rhabdovirus*)
rheo- flow, current (*rheostat*)
rhino- nose (*rhinoplasty*)
rhizo- root (*rhizogenic*)
rhodo- rose (*rhodolite*)
sacchar- sweet, sugar (*saccharide*)
sangui- blood (*sanguiferous*)
sapro- rotten, decomposed (*saprogenic*)
sarco- flesh (*sarcophagous*)
scato- excrement (*scatology*)
schizo- split (*schizophrenia*)
sclero- hard (*scleroderma*)
seleno- moon (*selenography*)
self- of or by oneself (*self-analysis*); to, with, or toward oneself (*self-abnegating*); independent or automatic (*self-governing, self-operating*)
semi- half, partially, somewhat (*semiweekly, semi-detached*)
septi- seven (*septilateral*)
sero- serum (*serology*)
sesqui- one and a half (*sesquicentennial*)
sex- six (*sexpartite*)
shm- used to form jocular variations as replacement for initial consonant in standard form of word (*fancy shmancy*)
sidero- iron (*siderolite*)
siphono- tube (*siphonostele*)
socio- society (*sociology*)
somato- body (*somatotype*)
somni- sleep (*somnifacient*)
spermato- seed (*spermatozoon*)
spermo- seed, germ (*spermophyte*)
spheno- wedge (*sphenography*)
sphygmo- pulse (*sphygmometer*)
spiro- respiration (*spirograph*); coil, spiral (*spirochete*)
sporo- spore (*sporophyte*)
steato- fat, tallow (*steatopygia*)
stego- cover (*stegosaur*)
stelli- star (*stelliform*)
steno- close, narrow (*stenography*)
stereo- solid (*stereoscope*)
stomato- mouth (*stomatoplasty*)
strati- stratum (*stratification*)
strepto- twisted (*streptococcus*)
stylo- column, pillar (*stylolite*)
sub- below, under (*subarctic*); secondary (*subplot*)
super- above (*supernatural*)
supra- above, beyond (*supraorbital*)
sus- under, beneath, secondary (*suspend*)
syl- with (*syllepsis*)
sym- with (*symmetry*)
syn- with (*synoptic*)
synchro- occurring together (*synchrotron*)
tacho- speed (*tachometer*)
tachy- rapid (*tachycardia*)
tauto- same (*tautology*)
techno- technique, skill (*technology*)
tele- distant (*telekinesis*)
teleo- final (*teleology*)

telo- end (*telophase*)
teno- tendon (*tenotomy*)
tera- trillion (*terabyte*)
terato- monster (*teratology*)
terri- land, earth (*terricolous*)
tetra- four (*tetralogy*)
thanato- death (*thanatology*)
thaumato- miracle, wonder (*thaumatology*)
theo- god (*theology*)
thermo- heat (*thermoplastic*)
thrombo- blood clot, coagulation (*thrombocyte*)
toco- birth, child (*tocopherol*)
tomo- cut, section (*tomography*)
tono- stretching, tension (*tonometer*)
topo- place, local (*topology*)
toti- entire (*totipalmation*)
toxico- poison (*toxicology*)
toxo- poison (*toxoplasmosis*)
tracheo- trachea (*tracheotomy*)
trachy- rough (*trachycarpous*)
trans- across, through, on far side of (*transverse*)
tri- three (*trilateral*)
tribo- friction (*triboluminescence*)
tricho- hair (*trichocyst*)
tropho- nourishment (*trophosome*)
tropo- turn, response, change (*troposphere*)
ultra- beyond (*ultrasonics*)
un- not, freely used to give negative or opposite force to adjectives (*unhappy*); used to reverse action or state of verb (*unfasten*)
under- beneath, below, or lesser in place, grade, or extent (*undersized*)
uni- single, one (*unicycle*)
urino- urine (*urinoscopy*)
uro- urine (*urology*)
vaso- vessel (*vasoconstrictor*)
veno- vein (*venostasis*)
ventro- abdomen (*ventrodorsal*)
vermi- worm (*vermiform*)
vini- wine (*viniculture*)
vitri- glass (*vitriform*)
vivi- living, alive (*vivisection*)
xantho- yellow (*xanthophyll*)
xeno- foreign (*xenophobia*)
xero- dry (*xeroderma*)
xylo- wood (*xylophone*)
zoo- animal (*zoology*)
zygo- yoke, double (*zygomorphic*)

Suffixes

-ability combination of -able and -ity for nouns corresponding to adjectives ending in -able (*capability*)
-able capable of, fit for, tending or given to (*laudable, singable*)
-ably combination of -able and -ly for adverbs corresponding to adjectives ending in -able (*tolerably*)
-acea used in formation of names of zoological classes and orders (*Crustacea*)
-aceae used in formation of names of botanical families (*Rosaceae*)
-aceous resembling, made of (*herbaceous*)
-acious used in formation of adjectives corresponding to nouns ending in -acy or -acity (*fallacious, audacious*)
-acity quality of, having characteristics of (*tenacity*)
-acy ending for nouns of quality, state, or office (*delicacy, papacy*)
-adelphous having stamens growing together in bundles (*monadelphous*)
-agogue leader, bringer of, practitioner (*demagogue*)
-aholic one who has addiction to or obsession with something (*workaholic*)
-al having form or character of, pertaining to (*autumnal, natural*); used to form nouns from verbs (*refusal*)
-ales used in formation of names of botanical orders (*Cycadales*)
-algia pain (*neuralgia*)
-amine variation of amino- in chemical compounds (*chloramine*)
-an used to form adjectives, esp. of place and membership (*American, Elizabethan*)
-ana collection of items (*Americana*)
-ance used to form nouns corresponding to verbs or to adjectives ending in -ant (*brilliance*)
-ancy combination of -ance and -y denoting state or quality (*brilliancy*)
-androus male (*polyandrous*)
-andry used in nouns corresponding to adjectives ending in -androus (*polyandry*)
-ane used in names of hydrocarbons of methane or paraffin series (*propane*)
-anthous having flowers of specified type or number (*monanthous*)
-arama variation of -orama (*foodarama*)
-arch chief, leader, ruler (*matriarch*)
-archy rule, government (*monarchy*)
-arian used to form personal nouns from adjectives or nouns ending in -ary (*librarian*)
-aroo variation of -eroo (*buckaroo*)
-arooni variation of -aroo, diminutive or additionally jocular (*sockarooni*)
-asis used in scientific and medical words from Greek (*psoriasis*)
-ast one connected with or given to (*enthusiast*)
-ate use to form nouns that denote office or function or a person who exercises function (*consulate, magistrate*); used in chemistry to indicate salt of acid ending in -ic (*nitrate*)
-athon used in compound words to indicate event drawn out to unusual length (*danceathon*)
-ation combination of -ate and -ion used to form nouns corresponding to verbs with stem -ate (*separation*)
-ative combination of -ate and -ive to form adjectives corresponding to verbs with stem -ate (*regulative*) or from other stem words (*normative*)
-biosis mode of life (*aerobiosis*)
-blast bud, sprout (*ectoblast*)
-carp part of fruit or fruiting body (*endocarp*)
-carpic used in formation of adjectives from stems ending in -carp (*endocarpic*)
-carpous having fruit (*apocarpous*)

-cele tumor (*variocele*)
-cene variation of -ceno (*Pleistocene*)
-ceno new, recent (*cenogenesis*)
-cephalic variation of -cephalous (*brachycephalic*)
-cephalous having a specific kind of head (*brachycephalous*)
-chroic variation of -chroous (*monochroic*)
-chrome color (*polychrome*)
-chroous having a specific kind of color (*isochroous*)
-cide killer, act of killing (*suicide*)
-clase used in formation of compound words for minerals with specified cleavage (*plagioclase*)
-clasis breaking (*thromboclasis*)
-cle used to form diminutive nouns (*particle*); used to form nouns that denote place appropriate to action of verb from which they are formed (*receptacle*)
-coccus spherical bacterium (*streptococcus*)
-coele cavity (*enterocoele*)
-colous inhabiting specified place or thing (*nidicolous*)
-cracy rule, government (*democracy*)
-crat ruler, supporter of particular form of government (*autocrat*)
-cule variation of -cle (*molecule, ridicule*)
-cyst cyst sac (*statocyst*)
-cyte cell (*leucocyte*)
-dactyl used to form nouns corresponding to adjectives ending in -dactylous (*pterodactyl*)
-dactylous having toes or fingers (*tridactylous*)
-dendron tree (*rhododendron*)
-derm skin (*pachyderm*)
-drome running; racecourse or other large structure (*hippodrome, airdrome*)
-ectomy excision or removal of particular part (*appendectomy*)
-elle used to form diminutive or derivative nouns (*bagatelle, organelle*)
-emia blood condition (*anemia*)
-ence used to form nouns from verbs or from adjectives ending in -ent (*abstinence, difference*)
-ensis pertaining to or originating in, usu. in scientific terms (*carolinensis*)
-eous composed of, resembling (*igneous*); used to form adjectives from nouns, esp. those ending in -ty (*beauteous*)
-er used to form comparative degree of adjectives or adverbs (*smaller, faster*); used in formation of nouns of person from object of occupation, place of origin, or specific characteristic (*hatter, villager, teetotaler*); used to form agent nouns from verbs (*employer*); used to form occupation names (*butcher*)
-ergic activated by, sensitive to, releasing (*allergic*)
-ern used to form adjectives from directions (*northern*)
-eroo used to form familiar, usu. jocular nouns (*switcheroo*)
-ers *Chiefly Brit.* informal variation of noun or adjective (*preggers*)
-ery used to form nouns denoting occupation, condition, place, products, things collectively, actions, or qualities (*archery, bakery, cutlery, trickery*)
-esce used to express beginning of action of verb (*convalesce*)
-escence used to denote nouns of action or process, change, or condition corresponding to verbs ending in -esce or adjectives ending in -escent (*convalescence*)
-escent used in formation of adjectives expressing beginning of action (*convalescent*)
-ese used to form adjectival derivatives of place names, esp. for inhabitants or language of place (*Japanese, Viennese*); used to characterize jargon (*computerese*)
-esis used in nouns of action or process (*genesis*)
-esque indicating style, manner, or distinctive character of adjective or individual (*picturesque, Kafkaesque*)
-ess used to form feminine nouns (*countess*)
-est used to form superlative degree of adjectives or adverbs (*smallest, fastest*); formerly used to form second person singular indicative of verbs (*knowest*)
-eur used to form agent nouns or occasionally adjectives from verbs (*masseur, provocateur*)
-euse used to form feminine nouns corresponding to nouns ending in -eur (*masseuse*)
-ey variation of -y, esp. after words end in "y" (*clayey*); used informally or to denote little one (*Charley*)
-fest assembly of people for common purpose (*songfest*)
-fex maker (*spinifex*)
-fic making, producing, causing (*honorific*)
-fication used to form nouns of action or state corresponding to verbs ending in -fy (*specification*)
-fid split, divided (*bifid*)
-florous having flowers (*uniflorous*)
-fuge that which repels or drives away something specified (*vermifuge*)
-fy make, cause to be, render (*beautify*)
-gamy marriage (*monogamy*)
-gen that which produces (*hydrogen*)
-genesis origin, beginning (*parthenogenesis*)
-genetic used to form adjectives from nouns ending in -genesis (*parthenogenetic*)
-genic producing or causing, produced or caused by, used to form adjectives corresponding to nouns ending in -gen or -geny (*hallucinogenic, cosmogenic*)
-genous giving rise to the thing specified (*androgenous*)
-geny origin (*phylogeny*)
-glot having a tongue or speaking, writing, or written in a language (*polyglot*)
-gnathous having a jaw (*prognathous*)
-gnomy knowledge (*physiognomy*)
-gnosis knowledge (*prognosis*)
-gnostic used to form adjectives from nouns ending in -gnosis (*diagnostic*)
-gon angled (*polygon*)
-gony production, origination (*cosmogony*)
-grade walking or moving in specified manner (*retrograde*)
-gram something written or drawn (*epigram,*

diagram); message, bulletin (*telegram*)
-graph drawn or written, esp. instrument used to produce writing (*telegraph*)
-graphy process, science, or art of drawing, writing, recording, or representing (*biography, photography, choreography*)
-gynous taking an attitude toward women (*misogynous*)
-gyny used to form nouns corresponding to adjectives ending in -gynous (*misogyny*)
-hedral used to form adjectives from nouns ending in -hedron (*polyhedral*)
-hedron figure with faces or sides of specified number (*octahedron*)
-holic variation of -aholic (*chocoholic*)
-ia used in names of diseases, places, Roman feasts, and Latin plurals (*malaria, Romania, Saturnalia, Reptilia*)
-ial variation of -al (*editorial*)
-ian variation of -an, esp. denoting type, engagement in, or practice of (*reptilian, Episcopalian, electrician*)
-iasis disease (*psoriasis*)
-iatrics medicine, treatment (*pediatrics*)
-iatry specific area of healing or medical practice (*psychiatry*)
-ibility variation of -ability when base adjective ends in -ible (*responsibility*)
-ible variation of -able (*horrible*)
-ibly combination of -ible and -ly for adverbs corresponding to adjectives ending in -ible (*visibly*)
-ic used to form adjectives from other parts of speech (*poetic*); having some attribute of, in the style of (*sophomoric, Byronic*); used in chemistry to show higher valence in opposition to -ous (*ferric chloride*)
-ical combination of -ic and -al to form adjectives corresponding to nouns or adjectives ending in -ic (*economical*)
-ician used to form personal nouns denoting occupation (*beautician*)
-ics field of study, body of knowledge or principles, usu. corresponding to adjectives ending in -ic or -ical (*ethics, physics*)
-id descendant of, esp. for names of dynasties (*Abbasid*); name of zoological family or class or adjective pertaining to taxonomic division (*arachnid*); used to form adjectives corresponding to nouns ending in -or (*pallid*)
-idae denoting names of zoological families (*Candiae*)
-ide indicator of chemical compounds (*chloride*)
-idine denoting names of chemical compounds derived from other chemical compounds (*guanidine*)
-idion variation of diminutive -idium (*enchiridion*)
-idium diminutive for scientific terms (*peridium*)
-ie variation of -y or -ey, esp. denoting little one (*birdie*)
-iensis variation of -ensis (*mississippiensis*)
-ier indicating person engaged in trade or occupation (*cashier*); used on loanwords from French, often with loss of final "r" sound (*dossier*)
-iform shaped like (*cruciform*)
-iformes taxonomic names of animals (*Passeriformes*)
-ify variation of -fy used to form verbs from adjectives (*intensify*)
-il variation of -ile (*civil*)
-ile used to form adjectives expressing capability, susceptibility, liability, or aptitude (*agile, docile, fragile, prehensile*)
-ility used to form abstract nouns corresponding to adjectives ending in -le, -ile, or -il (*ability, agility, civility*)
-illion indicating numerals of specified exponential degree (*trillion*)
-ine like, pertaining to, made of (*marine, crystalline*); names of chemical substances (*chlorine*)
-ing used to form nouns that express action, result, or product of verb (*building*) or participial adjective form of verb (*thinking man*); belonging to, descended from (*farthing*)
-ious used to form adjectives corresponding to nouns ending in -ity (*atrocious*)
-isation *Brit.* variation of -ization (*organisation*)
-ise *Brit.* variation of -ize (*specialise*)
-ish used to form adjectives from nouns denoting belonging to, having characteristics of, or inclined to (*British, childish, bookish*); used to form adjectives from adjectives meaning somewhat or rather (*sweetish*)
-ism used to form nouns denoting action, condition, doctrine, or usage (*criticism, barbarism, Darwinism, realism, witticism*)
-ist used to form personal nouns corresponding to verbs ending in -ize or nouns ending in -ism (*apologist, socialist*)
-istic used to form adjectives from nouns ending in -ist or -ism (*socialistic, altruistic*)
-istical combination of -istic and -al to create additional adjectival form (*linguistical*)
-istics combination of -ist and -ics to form collective noun (*linguistics*)
-ite denoting person associated with place, group, belief, or system (*Israelite, laborite*); mineral and fossil names (*anthracite, ammonite*); names of chemical compounds (*sulfite*); used to form adjectives and nouns from adjectives and some verbs (*opposite*)
-itious used to form adjectives from nouns ending in -ition (*ambitious*)
-itis inflammation (*arthritis*); abnormality or excess (*computeritis*)
-itive used in substantives of Latin origin (*transitive*)
-ity used to form abstract nouns expressing state or condition, esp. from adjectives (*insincerity*)
-ium used on nouns borrowed from Latin (*tedium*), certain compound words (*equilibrium*), and associative derivatives of personal nouns (*collegium*)
-ization combination of -ize and -ation (*civilization*)
-ize added to adjectives and nouns to form transitive verbs meaning make, give form to, or subject to some process (*fossilize, dramatize, terrorize*), or to form intransitive verbs denoting change of

state, kind of behavior, or activity (*crystallize, apologize, philosophize*)
-kinesis movement (*telekinesis*)
-lalia abnormal or disordered speech (*glossolalia*)
-latry worship of (*idolatry*)
-lepsy seizure, fit (*epilepsy*)
-less without (*childless*)
-like used to form adjectives denoting similarity, preceded by hyphen if base word ends in double "l" (*childlike, bell-like*)
-ling denoting one concerned with, often pejoratively or diminutively (*hireling, duckling*); used with adverbs to express direction, position, or state (*underling, darkling*)
-lith stone (*paleolith*)
-lithic used in names of archaeological ages (*Neolithic*)
-logue used in names of kinds of discourses or writing (*monologue, travelogue*)
-logy science of, body of knowledge (*biology, theology*)
-ly used to form adverbs from adjectives (*slowly*); added to nouns denoting every time (*hourly*); used to form adjectives meaning like (*cowardly*)
-lysis dissolving, breaking down, decomposing (*electrolysis, analysis, paralysis*)
-lyte something subjected to a process, often where process ends in -lysis (*electrolyte*)
-lyze used in verbs corresponding to nouns ending in -ysis (*analyze*)
-machy battle, fighting (*logomachy*)
-mancy divination (*oneiromancy*)
-mania obsession with, craving for (*pyromania*)
-megalia variation of -megaly (*hepatosplenomegalia*)
-megaly abnormal enlargement of specified part (*cardiomegaly*)
-ment used in nouns denoting action, product, or means (*refinement, fragment, ornament*)
-mer member of particular chemical group (*polymer*)
-merous having parts of specified kind or number (*pentamerous*)
-metric used to form adjectives based on nouns ending in -metry (*geometric*)
-metry process of measurement (*chronometry*)
-morph form or structure (*allomorph*)
-morphic variation of -morphous (*anthropomorphic*)
-morphism used to form nouns corresponding to adjectives ending in -morphous or -morphic (*isomorphism*)
-morphous having specified shape, form, or structure (*polymorphous*)
-mycete fungus, mushroom (*ascomycete*)
-mycetes taxonomic names of fungi, esp. classes (*Myxomycetes*)
-ness used to form abstract nouns denoting quality and state from adjectives and participles (*darkness, preparedness*)
-nomy distribution or arrangement (*economy, taxonomy*)
-oate denoting names of chemical compounds (*benzoate*)
-ock used to form descriptive and diminutive names (*bullock, hillock*)
-odont having or relating to teeth, esp. used as base in combination with -ia or -ics (*orthodontia*)
-odus variation of -odont, used for names of zoological genera (*ceratodus*)
-odynia pain (*pododynia*)
-oid similar to, like (*ovoid*)
-oidea used for names of zoological classes (*Echinoidea*)
-ola used in various commercial coinages and jocular variations of other words (*granola, crapola*)
-oma tumor (*melanoma*)
-onym word, name (*synonym, pseudonym*)
-oon used in formation of nouns from Romance languages (*bassoon*)
-opia eye, sight (*myopia*)
-opic used to form adjectives corresponding to nouns ending in -opia (*myopic*)
-opsia variation of -opia (*hemianopsia*)
-opsis likeness, esp. to named thing (*coreopsis*)
-opsy medical examination (*biopsy*)
-opy variation of -opia (*amblyopy*)
-or denoting condition or property, sometimes in noun form corresponding to adjective ending in -id (*squalor*); used to form animate or inanimate agent nouns, often as variation of -er (*traitor, projector*)
-orama used in compound words, esp. in advertising and journalism (*scoutorama*)
-orial used to form adjectives based on nouns ending in -tor or -tory (*editorial, valedictorial*)
-ory used to form adjectives that imitate words ending in -tory or -sory (*excretory, sensory*); used in nouns denoting place or receptacle (*crematory*)
-ose full of, given to (*verbose*); used in chemical names of sugars and carbohydrates (*fructose, lactose*)
-osis denoting action, condition, or state, esp. abnormal one (*hypnosis, tuberculosis*)
-ota used in plural form of taxonomic names, esp. phyla (*Eukaryota*)
-ote used to form singular nouns from taxonomic names ending in -ota (*eukaryote*)
-otic used to form adjectives denoting relationship to indicated action, process, state, or condition, often based on nouns ending in -osis (*hypnotic*)
-our *Brit.* variation of -or (*honour*)
-ous used to form Anglicized adjectives, generally meaning possessing or full of (*nervous, tremendous*); used in chemistry to show lower valence in opposition to -ic (*ferrous chloride*)
-pagus used in names of malformed conjoined twins (*thoracopagus*)
-parous bearing, producing (*oviparous*)
-pathic used to form adjectives from nouns ending in -pathy (*homeopathic*)
-pathy suffering, feeling, disease, or treatment (*antipathy, sympathy, psychopathy, homeopathy*)
-ped having specified feet (*biped*)
-pede variation of -ped (*centipede*)
-penia lack, deficiency (*leukopenia*)
-phage thing that devours (*bacteriophage*)
-phagia variation of -phage (*hemophagia*)
-phagous eating, feeding on, devouring (*creophagous*)

-phagy eating, devouring (*anthropophagy*)
-phany appearance, manifestation (*epiphany*)
-phasia denoting names of speech disorders (*aphasia*)
-phil variation of -phile (*esosinophil*)
-phile lover of (*bibliophile*)
-philia affinity for or tendency toward, also unnatural attraction (*hemophilia, necrophilia*)
-philiac used to form adjectives from nouns ending in -philia (*hemophiliac*)
-philic used to form adjectives from nouns ending in -phile (*bibliophilic*); affinity for, among class of substances (*acidophilic*)
-philism used to form abstract nouns based on nouns ending in -phile (*bibliophilism*)
-philous liking, having affinity for (*dendrophilous*)
-phily variation of -philia (*hydrophily*)
-phobia fear (*acrophobia*)
-phone speech sound or instrument of sound transmission (*homophone, microphone*)
-phony used to form abstract nouns corresponding to nouns ending in -phone (*telephony*)
-phore bearer of (*gonophore*)
-phorous used to form adjectives corresponding to nouns ending in -phore (*gonophorous*)
-phrenia indicating names of mental disorders (*schizophrenia*)
-phyllous having leaves (*monophyllous*)
-phyte plant (*lithophyte*)
-plasia growth (*hypoplasia*)
-plasm living tissue, cell substance (*ectoplasm*)
-plast cell, living substance (*chloroplast*)
-plasty molding formation or surgical repair (*rhinoplasty*)
-plasy variation of -plasia (*homoplasy*)
-plegia paralysis (*paraplegia*)
-ploid having chromosome sets (*hexaploid*)
-pnea breath (*dyspnea*)
-pod having specified kind or number of feet (*cephalopod*)
-poda having specified feet, used in names of zoological classes (*Cephalopoda*)
-pode variation of -podium (*pseudopode*)
-podium footlike part (*monopodium*)
-podous used to form adjectives from nouns ending in -pod (*cephalopodous*)
-poiesis making, formation (*hematopoiesis*)
-poietic used to form adjectives from nouns ending in -poiesis (*hematopoietic*)
-pterous having wings (*dipterous*)
-rel used in diminutive or pejorative noun (*scoundrel*)
-rhiza variation of -rrhiza (*coleorhiza*)
-rrhagia rupture, profuse flow or discharge (*bronchorrhagia*)
-rrhaphy suture (*herniorrhaphy*)
-rrhea flow, discharge (*diarrhea*)
-rrhexis rupture (*enterorrhexis*)
-rrhiza root (*mycorrhiza*)
-rrhoea variation of -rrhea (*melanorrhoea*)
-saur used in names of extinct reptiles (*dinosaur*)
-saurus variation of -saur (*tyrannosaurus*)
-scope instrument for viewing (*microscope*)
-sepalous having specified sepals (*polysepalous*)
-ski jocular or informal addition derived from Slavic names (*Russki*)
-sky variation of -ski (*buttinsky*)
-some used to form adjectives from verbs and nouns (*burdensome*); meaning body in compounds (*chromosome*); collective used with numerals (*threesome*)
-sophy science of, wisdom (*philosophy*)
-sperm one having specified seeds (*angiosperm*)
-spermal used to form adjectives from nouns ending in -sperm (*gymnospermal*)
-sporous having specified spores (*helicosporous*)
-stichous having specified rows (*distichous*)
-stome organism having a mouth (*cyclostome*)
-stomous having specified mouth (*monostomous*)
-stomy surgical operation involving creation of artificial opening (*colostomy*)
-taxis arrangement or order (*heterotaxis*)
-taxy variation of -taxis (*epitaxy*)
-teen used to form cardinal numerals from 13 to 19 (*fifteen*)
-therm heat (*isotherm*)
-thermy heat, heat generation (*diathermy*)
-tion used to form abstract nouns, esp. from verbs, expressing action, state, or associated meanings (*revolution, relation*)
-tious added to various stems to form adjectives (*facetious, bumptious*)
-tome cutting instrument (*osteotome*)
-tomous cut, divided (*dichotomous*)
-tomy cutting, incision, surgical excision (*appendectomy*)
-ton used to form nouns from adjectives (*simpleton*)
-tonia muscle or nerve tension or personality disorder (*hypertonia, catatonia*)
-tonic used to form adjectives from nouns ending in -tonia (*catatonic*)
-trix used to form feminine, esp. of nouns ending in -tor (*executrix*)
-trope one turned toward (*heliotrope*)
-troph nutrient matter or organism with specified nutritional requirements (*embryotroph, heterotroph*)
-trophic having nutritional requirements, maintaining an activity (*autotrophic, gonadotrophic*)
-trophy used to form nouns meaning feeding or growth (*mycotrophy, hypertrophy*)
-tropic turned toward, having an affinity for (*geotropic, psychotropic*)
-tropism variation of -tropy (*heliotropism*)
-tropous turned, curved (*anatropous*)
-tropy used to form abstract nouns corresponding to adjectives ending in -tropic or -tropous (*psychotropy*)
-tude used in abstract nouns and formation of new nouns (*platitude*)
-ty used in nouns denoting quality or state (*unity*); added to numerals to denote multiples of ten (*twenty*)
-type having a particular characteristic, regarded as a group or class (*prototype, phenotype*)
-urgy technique or art of dealing or working with something (*chemurgy*)

-vore one that eats (*carnivore*)
-vorous eating (*omnivorous*)
-ward used to denote spatial or temporal direction (*backward, afterward*)
-wards variation of -ward (*towards*)
-xion *Brit.* variation of -tion (*connexion*)
-y characterized by, inclined to (*juicy, dreamy*); added to usu. monosyllabic bases to create informal nouns (*granny, cabby*); used to denote little one (*Billy*)
-yer variation of -er in formation of occupational names (*lawyer*)
-zoa used in names of zoological classes (*Protozoa*)
-zoon animal or organism, esp. single member of zoological class name ending in -zoa (*protozoon*)

ABBREVIATIONS

A.B. *Latin.* artium baccalaureus; Bachelor of Arts
abbrev abbreviation
abr abridged
AC alternating current; air conditioning
ack acknowledge, acknowledgment
A.D. *Latin.* anno Domini; in the year of the Lord
adj adjective
admin administration
adv adverb
aeron aeronautics
agcy agency
agric agriculture, agricultural
aka also known as
alt alternate; alternation; altitude
a.m. *Latin.* ante meridiem; morning
AM amplitude modulation
amb ambassador
ammo ammunition
amp ampere; amplifier
anat anatomy
anon anonymous
approx approximate
Apr April
apt. apartment
arch. architecture
arith arithmetic
art. article
ASAP as soon as possible
assoc associated, association
asst assistant
astron astronomy
att attached; attorney
aug augmented
Aug August
aux auxiliary
ave avenue
avg average
AWOL absent without leave
B.A. Bachelor of Arts
bal balance
b and w black and white
bbl barrel
B.C. before Christ
B.C.E. before Christian (common) era
bd board
bet between
bf boldface
bibliog bibliography
biog biography
biol biology
blvd boulevard
bot bottom; botany
bro brother
B.S. Bachelor of Science
bskt basket
BTU British thermal unit
bu bushel
bull. bulletin
bur bureau
BYOB bring your own booze/beer/bottle
C Celsius, centigrade
c cent; century; copyright
ca circa
cal calorie
calc calculate
cap. capitalize
capt captain
cat. catalog
CB Citizens Band
cc cubic centimeter
Cdr Commander
C.E. common era, same as A.D.
cent. century
CEO chief executive officer
cert certificate, certified
cf *Latin.* confer; compare
cg centigram
chap. chapter
chem chemistry
chm chairman
chron chronology
cie *French.* compagnie; company
circ circular
cl centiliter
class. classified, classification
cm centimeter
CNS central nervous system
co company
c/o care of
COD cash on delivery
Col. Colonel
col colony; column
collab collaboration
colloq colloquial
comb. combination, combining
comm commander; commerce; committee
conc concentrated
cond condition
conf conference
confed confederate
Cong Congress
conj conjunction
const construction; constitution
contd continued
contemp contemporary
contr contraction

contrib contributor, contribution
coroll corollary
corp corporation
corr correct; correspondence
CPA certified public accountant
CPI consumer price index
cpl corporal
CPR cardiopulmonary resuscitation
cr credit; crown
crim criminal
crit critical, criticism
CRT cathode-ray tube
ct court
ctr center
cu cubic
cum cumulative
CYA cover your ass
d *Latin.* denarii; penny (Britain); diameter; dime; dollar
DA district attorney
dba doing business as
dbl double; decibel
DC direct current
D.D. Doctor of Divinity
D.D.S. Doctor of Dental Science
Dec December
dec deceased
def definition
deg degree
Dem Democrat
denom denomination
dept department
deriv derivative, derived
dial. dialect
diam diameter
dict dictionary
dim. diminished; dimension
DINK dual income, no kids
dip. diploma
dir director
dist district; distance
div division; divorced
do. ditto
DOA dead on arrival
doc. document
dol dollar
doz dozen
Dr. Doctor
DST daylight-saving time
dt's delirium tremens
dup duplicate
E east, eastern
ea each
eccl ecclesiastical
ecol ecology
econ economics
ed editor
educ education
EEG electroencephalogram
e.g. *Latin.* exempli gratia; for example
EKG electrocardiogram
el elevation
elec electric
elem elementary
elev elevation
enc enclosure, enclosed
encyc encyclopedia
env envelope
eq equal, equalization
equiv equivalent
ERA earned run average
esp. especially
ESP extrasensory perception
Esq. Esquire
est estimated
et al *Latin.* et alia; and others
etc. *Latin.* etcetera; and so forth
et seq *Latin.* et sequens; and the following one
etym etymology
ex. example
exam examination
exc except
exec executive
ex lib *Latin.* ex libris; from the books of
exp expense; express
ext extension; exterior
F Fahrenheit
f feminine; father; feet
fac facsimile
fath fathom
Feb February
fec *Latin.* fecit; he made it
fed federal; federation
fem feminine
ff and following
fid fiduciary
fig figurative
fin. finance; finish
fka formerly known as
FM frequency modulation
fn footnote
f.o.b. freight on board
fol folio; following
foll and the following entry
for. foreign
freq frequent
Fri Friday
frt freight
frwy freeway
Ft. fort
ft foot, feet
fur. furlong
furn furnished
fut future
fwd forward; foreword
fx special effects
FYI for your information
g gram
gal. gallon
gaz gazette
gds goods
gen general
geneal genealogy
geog geography
geol geology
geom geometry

GIGO garbage in, garbage out
gloss. glossary
gm gram
GOP Grand Old Party
Gov. governor
Govt government
gp group
GQ General Quarters
gr gram; gross; grade
grad graduate
gram. grammar
gtd guaranteed
guar guarantee
ha. hectare
hdqrs headquarters
hf half
HMS His (or Her) Majesty's Ship
Hon. Honorable
hor horizontal
hosp hospital
hq headquarters
hr hour
HRH His (or Her) Royal Highness
ht height
hwy highway
ibid *Latin.* ibidem; in the same place
id. *Latin.* idem; the same
i.e. *Latin.* id est; that is
illus illustrated
imper imperative
in. inch
inc incorporated
incl including
incorp incorporated
ind independent; index
indic indicative
inf infinitive
init initially
in loc cit *Latin.* in loco citato; in the place cited
insp inspector
inst institute
instr instructor
int interior; interim
interj interjection
interrog interrogative, interrogation
inv invoice
I/O input/output
IOU I owe you
IQ intelligence quotient
irreg irregular
ISBN International Standard Book Number
isl island
ital italics
Jan January
jct junction
J.D. *Latin.* Jurum Doctor; doctor of law
Jly July
Jn June
jour journal
JP justice of the peace
jr junior
juv juvenile
k kilogram; thousand; karat; kilobyte
kg kilogram
kHz kilohertz
kilo. kilogram
km kilometer
kn knot
KO knockout
Kt knight
kW kilowatt
L *Latin.* libra; pound (Britain)
l liter
lab laboratory
lang language
lat latitude
lb. *Latin.* libra; pound
l.c. lower case
lect lecturer
lex lexicon
lf lightface; left field
lg large
lic license
Lieut lieutenant
ling linguistics
liq liquid
lit. literally
Litt. D. *Latin.* litterarum doctor; doctor of letters
LL.B. *Latin.* legum baccalaureus; bachelor of law
LL.D. *Latin.* legum doctor; doctor of laws
ln lane
loc cit *Latin.* loco citato; in the place cited
long. longitude
LPN licensed practical nurse
Lt. lieutenant
lt light
Ltd limited
m meter; masculine; million
M.A. Master of Arts
mach. machine
mag magazine
Maj. Major
Mar March
masc masculine
math mathematics
max maximum
MC master of ceremonies
M.D. Doctor of Medicine
mdse merchandise
meas measure
mech mechanical, mechanics
med medicine
memo memorandum
met. metropolitan
M.F.A. Master of Fine Arts
mfd manufactured
mfr manufacturer
mg milligram
mgr manager
mi mile
mid middle
milit military
min minimum; minister; minute
misc miscellaneous
ml milliliter
mm millimeter

MO *Latin.* modus operandi, method of operation; money order; mail order
mo. month
mod. moderate
Mon Monday
MP Military Police; Member of Parliament
mph miles per hour
Mr. mister
Mrs. title of respect for a married woman
Ms. title of respect for a woman regardless of marital status
M.S. Master of Science
ms manuscript
MSG monosodium glutamate
Msgr Monsignor
M.S.W. Master of Social Work
Mt. Mount; mountain
mtge mortgage
mtn mountain
muni municipal
N north, northern
n noun; neuter; noon
N/A not applicable
nat national; natural
naut nautical
NB *Latin.* nota bene; note well
NE northeast; northeastern
neg negative
neut neuter
no. *Latin.* numero; number
nom nominative
Nov November
np no pagination
nr near
num numeral
NW northwest; northwestern
OBE Order of the British Empire
obit obituary
obj object; objective
obs obsolete
occas occasional, occasionally
Oct October
off. officer; official
op opus
op cit *Latin.* opere citato; in the work cited
opp. opposite
orch orchestra
org organization
orig. originally, origin
ot overtime
oz. ounce
p page
PA public address (system)
P and L profit and loss
par. paragraph
paren parentheses
Parl Parliament
part. participle
pat. patent
PC personal computer; politically correct
pc parsec
pd paid
PE physical education
per. period; person
perh perhaps
perm permanent
pers personal
pfd preferred
ph phase; phone
pharm pharmacy
Ph.D. Doctor of Philosophy
philos philosophy
photo photograph
phr phrase
phys ed physical education
pk peck
pkg package
pl plural; place
p.m. *Latin.* post meridiem; afternoon
PO post office
poss possessive
POV point of view
pp pages
ppd postpaid; prepaid
pref preface; preferred
prelim preliminary
prep. preposition
pres president
priv private
prod. product
pron pronoun; pronunciation
pronun pronunciation
pro tem *Latin.* pro tempore; for the time being
prov province
P.S. postscript
Ps Psalms
pseud pseudonym
psych psychology
Pt. Point
pt part; pint
p/t part time
pub. publication
pvt private
pwr power
PX post exchange
q quart
QED *Latin.* quod erat demonstrandum; which was to be demonstrated
qt quart
qty quantity
qv *Latin.* quad vide; which see, in reference to
R *Latin.* Rex, Regina; king, queen
R and R rest and recreation/recuperation
rbi run batted in
rd road
rec recipe; receipt
ref reference
refrig refrigerator
reg registered; regulation
rel relative
REM rapid eye movement (sleep)
Rep Republican
res reserve; residence
ret. retired
rev reverse; review; revised
Rev. Reverend

RFD Rural Free Delivery (postal route)
rh relative humidity
rhet rhetoric
RIP rest in peace
riv river
R.N. registered nurse
rnd round
rpm revolutions per minute
RR railroad
RSVP *French.* répondez s'il vous plaît; please answer
rt right
rte route
Rx pharmaceutical prescription
S south, southern
s second
SASE self-addressed stamped envelope
Sat Saturday
S.B. *Latin.* scientiae baccalaureus; bachelor of science
sci science
sd sound
SE southeast; southeastern
secy secretary
Sept September
seq *Latin.* sequens; the following
sgd signed
sing. singular
sm small
S.M. *Latin.* scientiae magister; master of science
soc society; sociology
sol. solution
SOP standard operating procedure
soph sophomore
SOS save our ship, international distress signal
spec special; specification
specif specifically
SPQR *Latin.* senatus populusque romanus; the senate and Roman people
sq square
SS steamship
St. Saint; street
st state
std standard
Ste. Saint (female)
stet *Latin.* it stands; let the original stand
sub. subject; subtract
subj subject; subjunctive
Sun Sunday
supp supplement
supr supreme
supt superintendent
sur surface
surv survey
SW southwest; southwestern
sym symbol
syn synonym
t ton
tba to be announced
tbs tablespoon
TCB take care of business
TD touchdown
tech technical
tel telephone; telegraph; telegram
temp temporary**terr** territory
Test. Testament
TGIF thank God it's Friday
theol theology
therm thermometer
Thurs Thursday
tit. title
TKO technical knockout
tkt ticket
TNT trinitrotoluene (explosive)
tot. total
Tpke turnpike
tr translation; transpose
treas treasury
trib tributary
tsp teaspoon
Tues Tuesday
u.c. upper case
UFO unidentified flying object
ult ultimately
unan unanimous
uncert uncertain
univ universal
u.s. *Latin.* ut supra; as above
usu. usually
util utility
v verb; versus
val value
var variable, variety
vb verb
ver verse
vet veteran
vi intransitive verb
VIP very important person
viz *Latin.* videlicet; that is to say, namely
voc vocative
vocab vocabulary
vol volume; volunteer
VP vice president
vs versus
vt transitive verb
vv verses; *Latin.* vice versa, conversely
W west, western
w week; wide; watt
Wed Wednesday
whsle wholesale
wk week
wt weight
X extra
x cross
Xmas Christmas
yd yard
yr year
z zero; zone
zool zoology

Chapter Nineteen

Action and Sense Words

VERBS OF MOTION

Gaits
Mood and Intent
Directions

Gaits

amble walk at an easy pace or in a leisurely manner
barrel move along rapidly and heavily; roll along
bounce move in a lively manner, as if by sudden leaps
bound move by leaping forward
bustle hurry with a great show of energy and purpose
canter move with a three-beat gait, easier than a gallop, used esp. of horses
caper skip along gaily
clamber climb using both hands and feet
clomp clump
clump walk clumsily and noisily
crawl move slowly or laboriously; move in a prone position without the use of hands or feet
curvet prance or canter, used esp. of horses
dander saunter; stroll at a leisurely pace
dart move suddenly and rapidly
dash move with a sudden burst of speed; flash
dogtrot move at a quick, easy gait, like a dog
drift float smoothly or effortlessly; move in an aimless or casual way
flash dash
flit move swiftly and lightly in irregular motion; skim along
flitter move lightly, like a bird; flutter
flow glide smoothly, as though in fluid
flutter move with quick, irregular, or flapping motions; flitter
fly move very quickly
footslog tramp or march heavily, esp. through mud
frogmarch force a person to walk forward with arms grasped behind the back
gallop bound quickly in a three-beat gait, like a horse
gallumph tromp heavily in clumsy gait
glide move smoothly and effortlessly
goose-step move in high-kicking soldier's march with stiff knees
hobble proceed unevenly or haltingly; walk lamely, with a limp
hop move in short, bounding leaps, like a rabbit
hurdle bound over (obstacles)
hurry go quickly
hurtle rush forward recklessly
inch move slowly, bit by bit
jog run at a moderate pace
jounce move joltingly in an up-and-down manner; bounce
jump spring; leap; bound
leap spring forward through the air
limp walk lamely or jerkily, favoring one leg
lope move in a long, easy, bounding gait
lumber move slowly with heavy feet and drooping shoulders
march move with a regular, measured gait, in step with others; proceed with purpose
maunder move in a dreamy, aimless way
mince walk with short steps in a dainty, affected manner
mosey stroll, amble, or saunter; leave quickly
pace walk with a slow, measured tread, often back and forth
pad walk with dull, muffled footsteps
patter move as though on little feet, making a light noise
plod walk heavily, slowly, or tediously; trudge
prance move by springing forward; strut about in a spirited manner
prowl move about stealthily; pace nervously
ramble roll along in a leisurely, aimless manner
reel walk unsteadily
run spring forward quickly so that both feet are off the ground between each step
sashay glide or move in a nonchalant way
saunter strut or stroll in a leisurely manner
scamper run or dash quickly, lightly, or playfully; scurry; skelter
scrabble scratch and claw; grope and clamber for a foothold
scramble move or climb quickly, using hands and feet
scuff walk without lifting one's feet
scuffle shuffle; scrape one's feet
scurry scamper
scuttle run or move with hasty steps, esp. away from danger
shamble walk in a lazy, awkward manner, dragging one's feet
shuffle drag one's feet; move along rhythmically; scuffle
skelter scamper
skip spring or leap lightly in bounding gait
skitter move quickly and lightly over a surface; skip
slide move easily and smoothly over a surface
slither slip or glide over a surface; slide along smoothly
slog plod heavily; tramp over a difficult path
slosh flounder and splash about in mud, water, or slush
spring leap forward through the air
sprint run at top speed, esp. for a short distance
stagger reel, sway, or totter along unsteadily
stamp proceed by bringing one's feet down firmly with each step
step move by lifting each foot and setting it down in a new position
step lively move lightly, with springy step
stomp stamp; step down hard

straddle walk with legs spread apart
stride move vigorously with long, measured steps
stroll proceed idly, at a leisurely pace
strut walk with vain, pompous, or affected air
stumble walk unsteadily or clumsily; trip over one's own feet
stump walk heavily and clumsily
swagger walk with an arrogant strut
tiptoe walk quietly or cautiously, with weight on one's toes
toddle walk with short, uncertain steps
totter proceed weakly, wobbling with faltering steps
tramp walk, tread, or step heavily; tromp
trample tread heavily and noisily, esp. while crushing things under one's feet
tread step or walk on, along, or over something
trip stumble and fall
tromp tramp
trot move in a quick, steady, bouncy gait between a walk and a run
trudge walk wearily or laboriously; plod
waddle move with slow, short steps, rocking from side to side like a duck
wade walk through water or mud
walk advance at a moderate pace in steady steps; move along by foot
waltz move in a breezy, conspicuous manner; dance along
wamble move in unsteady, shaky, or staggering gait
whisk move lightly and rapidly
wobble proceed with an unsteady rocking motion, esp. clumsily, from side to side
zip move with great speed and vigor
zoom move quickly, esp. with loud hum or buzz

Mood and Intent

accelerate move more rapidly; quicken one's step
ambulate walk easily from place to place
balk hold back or hesitate
barge move forward heedlessly or clumsily, often colliding with things
bestride stand, ride, or walk across
blunder move unsteadily, in confusion
bob move up and down with a short, jerky motion
bop shuffle along as if to music; go quickly
brush touch lightly in passing
buck charge against; spring into the air
budge move slightly; begin to move
caper leap or skip about playfully
careen swerve from side to side while moving forward
career go at full speed
catapult move quickly or forcefully through the air
cavort frolic playfully; romp
charge rush to attack; bear down on
chase pursue hastily
chug move laboriously and noisily
clip move swiftly
coast move forward under acquired momentum
convoy escort for protection
course move swiftly through or along designated path
cover ground move quickly across distance
cower crouch and pull away in fear
creak along move slowly, unsteadily, and squeakily
creep go timidly or cautiously so as to escape notice
cringe shrink in fear or deference
crouch bend low to the ground
crowd press forward; advance by pushing
cruise move at controlled speed; wander about with little purpose
crumple collapse in a heap
dally tarry
dance move lightly in time to music
dawdle loiter; waste time; piddle
decelerate slow down
dillydally loiter
dither move in a trembling, agitated manner
dive plunge headfirst
dodder proceed feebly and unsteadily
dodge move to and fro on irregular course
drag dawdle; proceed laboriously
drift float smoothly or effortlessly; move in aimless or casual way
duck bend over to avoid some object
ease maneuver carefully; move against slight resistance
elude evade skillfully
escape get away from danger or restraint; evade
escort accompany as protection
evade avoid deftly; escape
falter stumble; walk unsteadily
fiddle about putter aimlessly; dally
fidget move nervously or restlessly
flail move or toss about freely, often to no effect
flap flutter; toss about ineffectually
flee run away in haste
flick go or pass abruptly and swiftly
flip leap up and turn over in air
float move gently and lightly, as though suspended in fluid
flock assemble and move together in a group
flounce move with jerky motions or angry impatience
flounder struggle with stumbling movements
flump fall suddenly and heavily
flurry move in an excited, confused manner
frisk jump, skip, or frolic in a playful manner
frolic romp about in a frisky, merry way
gad move about restlessly and to no purpose
gallivant roam frivolously
gambol frolic, jump, or skip playfully
glissade glide down slope in standing or squatting position
grovel crawl in a submissive, facedown position
gush issue forth suddenly, forcibly, or copiously
halt come to a stop
hasten move rapidly; hie
herd assemble and move together in a group
hie hasten
hike walk a great distance for exercise or pleasure

hover hang suspended in place above something
hulk move heavily and clumsily
hunch push forward in bent posture
hustle proceed in aggressive, hurried manner
idle saunter aimlessly; loiter
intrude enter a place uninvited, often by force
jaunt make short journey for fun
jet move very rapidly, in a rush
jostle push or shove one's way forward roughly, esp. through a crowd
journey travel to a set destination; voyage
knife move through something swiftly and easily, like a knife
leapfrog vault over the backs of others
linger remain in place longer than expected
loaf lounge lazily or idly
loiter remain in place for no apparent reason; move slowly and idly; dillydally; idle; loll
loll loiter; lounge; sprawl
lollop bound or leap forward
lounge move idly or lazily; loll
lunge thrust oneself forward suddenly
lurk move furtively to avoid notice; slink; sneak
make way allow another to pass or enter
maneuver change direction or position adroitly for specific purpose
maunder move in a dreamy, aimless way
meander wander aimlessly, without direction; ramble or drift along a winding course
mooch wander about without purpose in a slow, lazy manner
moonwalk *Slang.* slide backward, apparently without lifting one's feet
muddle through work one's way clear of obstacles without planning or direction
nip up spring to one's feet from supine position
obtrude force oneself in where one is not welcome
paddle move through water by flailing one's hands and feet
parade march as if in procession, esp. to show off
patrol move about to observe an area or maintain security
piddle dawdle
plane glide across a surface; fly along effortlessly
play move in a lively, cheerful manner
plow proceed steadily or laboriously; push through
plug away keep moving against one or more obstacles
poke along move slowly, without direction
post move rapidly
potter wander vaguely; putter
promenade take a leisurely public walk, esp. to show off
prowl roam stealthily; pace restlessly
pursue follow intently so as to overtake
pussyfoot tread cautiously or stealthily
putter move aimlessly or idly among objects; potter
quicken one's step accelerate
quickstep make energetic march
ramp rear up and advance menacingly, used esp. of four-legged animals
rampage rush about wildly
range pass across large area
rip rush headlong
ripple flow in small undulations
roam wander without purpose; rove
rock move oneself rhythmically to and fro
romp run in a lively, effortless, energetic manner; cavort
rove roam
rumble move heavily, esp. with a deep, muffled sound
rush move in great haste; dash forward in attack
rush headlong move rapidly and out of control
sail skim across a surface as through propelled by wind
scoot move hastily; dart lightly
seep flow or pass slowly through something
settle become fixed in one position
shadow follow someone secretly, at a distance, for the purpose of observation
shilly-shally dawdle; go indecisively
shimmy shake, vibrate, or wobble with a dance-like motion
shoot move rapidly; pass rapidly over
shoulder push one's way roughly through a crowd
shunt force or turn someone aside or out of the way
skate glide along smoothly, as if crossing ice
ski glide over a surface as if wearing skis on snow
skid slide out of control sideways
skim glide lightly across a surface
skulk sneak or lurk about in a stealthy or cowardly manner; slink
sled slide across a surface as though on runners
slink move stealthily or furtively; lurk
slouch move idly, drooping with hunched back
slump fall or sink suddenly; assume drooping posture
snake make one's way quietly along a winding course
sneak slink; lurk
souse plunge into liquid
speed move rapidly
splash flail or move about noisily in water
sprawl lie back carelessly with limbs outspread
spurt gush forth; rush forward
squirm wriggle or twist about
stalk pursue a quarry or prey; walk stiffly and proudly
stampede flee headlong in panic as a group
steal come or go secretly, unexpectedly, and unobserved
stir begin to move from position of rest
straggle hang back; fall farther behind
streak rush past rapidly
stream issue forth or flow from someplace
surge rise and fall in waves
swarm move in great numbers, hovering like bees
swim propel oneself smoothly as through water
swoop rush down upon suddenly, esp. in attack
swoosh move swiftly with a rustling sound
tarry remain in place; wait for something; dally
tear move with great haste
tool cruise or drive along
toss move restlessly; jerk about

tour range over an area for pleasure or inspection
track follow the footprints or path of
trail follow; come after
traipse tramp about; wander aimlessly without reaching one's destination; proceed haphazardly
trek make slow, difficult progress over long route
trespass enter upon another's property uninvited
trickle move slowly, bit by bit
troop gather together and move in a group
trundle roll along
twinkle flutter lightly about
twitch move erratically or jerkily; fidget
undulate move with a sinuous, wavelike motion
upspring bound up from place
usher lead the way to help others find their place
vamp move in a bewitching manner
visit come or go to see someone or someplace
voyage journey
waft move or float lightly as though through air
wag move jerkily from side to side or up and down
wallow move slowly and with difficulty, as though through mud
wash flow along; run up against
welter toss or heave about
wheel roll along easily and swiftly
whiz move swiftly and effortlessly
whoosh rush past with a sudden hissing noise
wiggle move from side to side with quick, jerky motions
wince shrink back from a blow, recoil
wing fly as if on wings; move swiftly
worm creep along in a devious, stealthy manner
wrench move aside with a violent twist
wrestle move by force
wriggle writhe; squirm from side to side
writhe move in twists and bends

Directions

about-face turn in the opposite direction
advance move forward
angle move indirectly toward or away from a person or object; turn sharply in a new direction
approach draw near
arise move upward from lower position
arrive reach one's destination
ascend move or climb upward
attain arrive at
back off step away from
back-pedal step back rapidly
backtrack return over course already covered
back up move backward
bear down on catch up with; approach rapidly
begone depart
betake oneself cause oneself to go
bolt make sudden, hasty departure or escape
bounce strike a surface and rebound
bowl along move along smoothly and quickly
burst forth issue forth suddenly from spot
bypass circumvent (an obstacle)
carom strike and rebound
cast veer
catch overtake
circle revolve around
circumambulate circle on foot, esp. ceremonially
clear out depart permanently or abruptly
climb ascend; make steady upward progress
close in on begin to overtake
come move toward something; approach; arrive at
come about reverse direction; tack
come back return
come down move from higher to lower position
come forth emerge
come in enter
come out emerge
come up move from lower to higher position
commute travel back and forth regularly between two points
continue keep on same course as before
converge tend or incline toward a single point
crab move sideways, diagonally, or obliquely, esp. with short bursts of speed
crisscross move in many intersecting lines across a given space
cross move or traverse from one side or place to another
cruise be on one's way; travel
cut move abruptly at a sharp angle
debouch march out into open ground from confined place, used esp. of troops
decamp depart from resting place, often quickly or secretly
decline slope downward from straight course
deflect turn from true course or straight line
depart begin a journey; go away; leave; set out
descend move downward
desert depart from someplace, often permanently
deviate turn aside from normal course
diddle move rapidly back and forth or up and down
divagate stray from course
double back return over same course
draw away increase distance from given place
draw near reduce distance from given place; approach
ebb recede, like the tide
eddy move against current; move in a circle
edge advance gradually; move sideways
egress depart
embark set out from a place, esp. on a voyage
emerge rise; appear; come forth from concealment; come out
emigrate leave one's native country and settle elsewhere
enter arrive at; come in
evacuate depart rapidly from an endangered place
exit leave; go out
fade drift away from focus of activity
fall descend freely under force of gravity
fall back lag
fall down collapse to ground
fishtail swerve or slide from side to side out of control while moving forward
flinch pull back in abrupt movement
follow come behind or after, moving in same direction

ford wade across body of water
gain arrive at; follow more closely
gain ground lessen distance between oneself and another so as to follow more closely
get along depart
get going move faster; depart
go move along; proceed; move on a set course, esp. depart from someplace
go away depart
gravitate move toward; tend toward
gyrate revolve around fixed point or on axis
hang back remain at some distance behind
head move forward toward set point; go in certain direction
hunker down squat or stoop on one's haunches
immigrate enter and settle in a foreign country
issue forth pass or come out from enclosed place
jag change direction repeatedly in irregular pattern
jerk move with abrupt, erratic motion
jibe shift suddenly from one side to the other, used esp. of ships
jiggle move with short jerks up and down or back and forth
jink move unexpectedly with abrupt turns and shifts
juke move evasively through obstacles; fake another out of position, esp. in football
lag fail to keep up; fall back
land attain one's destination, esp. from above
lap overtake another in race, increasing lead by one full circuit of course
lead go before others
leave depart
light arrive at and come to rest
list veer to one side
loop move in curves or arcs
lose ground follow less closely; fall farther behind
lunge rush forward with sudden thrust
migrate move from one country to another
mount ascend; climb on top of
move go or pass from one place to another; progress
move along proceed in one direction
navigate set one's course at sea
negotiate maneuver through, around, or over
outpace exceed in speed and pass
outstrip get ahead of; leave behind
overhaul overtake
overtake catch up with and pass; overhaul
pass move; proceed; depart; move past another going in the same direction; come up to, then move beyond
peel off veer sharply aside from group moving in one direction
perambulate travel or walk over or through
peregrinate wander; traverse; travel over on foot
pitch plunge forward, often rising up abruptly afterward
pivot turn in place as if on a shaft
plummet descend rapidly
plunge rush or fall violently, with headlong haste
pounce swoop down upon suddenly
press on move forward despite obstacles
proceed continue forward in same direction
progress move forward, upward, or onward
pull back move away from
put about turn in new direction
quit leave someplace
radiate proceed from or toward a center
rappel descend steep incline by sliding down rope passed around one's body
rear rise up on one's hind legs like a horse
rebound reverse direction; bounce back
recede pull back; withdraw
recoil draw back, esp. in alarm or disgust
reel fall back from a blow; recoil
reenter come in again
regress move backward
repair go; betake oneself
retire withdraw; fall back
retract draw back
retreat draw back from a dangerous situation; flee; turn tail
return come back to a place formerly visited
reverse change direction of one's movement, usu. to opposite direction
revolve turn in a complete circle on an axis in place
ricochet bounce back or off
rise get up or move upward
roll move by turning over and over
rotate turn in circles on central axis in place
run away retreat; move off rapidly
sally forth set out; depart
scale climb over
scatter disperse in all directions
schuss make straight, high-speed downhill run on skis
scrunch crouch; hunker down
scud move or run swiftly, like a ship driven by a gale
seesaw move up and down or back and forth
separate move away from
set foot in enter (new region or place)
set forth begin a journey; leave someplace
set off start moving
set out depart; begin journey
sheer deviate from one's course
shift change place or position
shin draw oneself up by holding fast with hands and legs
show up arrive
shunt travel back and forth
shuttle move or transport to and fro
sidestep step around so as to avoid
sidle move sideways
sink descend slowly toward the bottom
skirt pass around; move along the border of
slalom zigzag between and around obstacles
slant move at an angle
slip away retreat; depart quietly
soar rise up to great height
somersault tumble head over heels
spin revolve rapidly in place
spiral move in circles around axis

squat crouch near ground without sitting
stand forth move forward
start out begin progress; set out
steer direct one's course
steer clear of stay away from; avoid
step out depart at energetic pace
stray wander from set course; roam about
stretch extend over distance in particular direction
strike out set out; depart
sway swing slowly and rhythmically to and fro
sweep move steadily in wide circuit or curve
swerve alter one's course abruptly; turn aside
swing move freely in wide curve; move back and forth
swivel turn as if on pivot
tack change direction, used esp. of ships
tag along come after someone; follow another closely
take off begin to move; depart; rise up into the air
teeter move back and forth, esp. near an edge
topple fall down
travel move or go from one place to another; depart from current location
traverse move along or across, from one side to the other
tumble turn end over end, esp. in flight
turn reverse or alter direction; veer from course; rotate on axis
turn about veer from course
turn back reverse direction; retrace one's steps
twine wind about in twisting course
twirl revolve rapidly in place
twist follow winding course; change direction sharply
vault leap over, esp. with aid of hands or pole
veer change direction; turn to one side; cast
verge move or incline in some direction
waggle move from side to side shakily
wander move without direction or purpose; roam about in irregular course
wave waver
waver sway in place; move to and fro; wave
weave follow zigzag or side-to-side course
wend proceed over long, winding course
whirl spin in a circle; turn rapidly in place; move or be carried along quickly
wind proceed by twists and turns, changing direction constantly
windmill move like a windmill, esp. by rotating one's arms in wide arcs
withdraw pull back; retreat
wobble proceed with unsteady, rocking motion; go clumsily in side-to-side motion
wreathe turn in circles or spirals
yaw deviate from a straight course, used esp. of ships
zag execute sharp turn
zig alter direction sharply
zigzag proceed in zigs and zags, making sharp turns first to one side, then to the other

VERBS OF SIGHT

admire regard with respect or wonder
assay examine and evaluate
avert one's eyes look away to avoid another's glance or some unpleasant sight
bat an eye blink with surprise or emotion
behold gaze upon; see
blear make one's eyes dim or watery
blink look glancingly; close and open one's eyes quickly
browse look over in a casual, leisurely manner
canvass examine carefully; survey entire area
cast about seek by looking around
cast a glance direct one's gaze at something
catch sight of become aware of; distinguish; manage to see
check examine carefully
check out examine and evaluate
command a view of overlook, esp. from strategic position
compare examine two or more items to determine differences or similarities
contemplate view thoughtfully and with steady attention
descry catch sight of; discover
detect note; discover the true nature of; spot
discern come to recognize; perceive by sight
distinguish single out; perceive clearly; recognize differences; spot
draw a bead on focus one's aim at
drop one's eyes lower one's eyes before another person's gaze
envisage visualize in a specific way
envision picture in one's mind
espy catch sight of
examine look over closely; inspect
eye view; gaze at
face look at directly
fix one's eyes on gaze at intently
focus adjust one's eyes to produce a clear image at a particular range
follow watch the movements of
gape gaze dumbly, esp. with mouth open
gawk stare stupidly
gaze look at intently, eagerly, or steadily
give the evil eye stare at with malicious intent
give the once-over scrutinize rapidly in detail, from top to bottom
glance look quickly
glare stare angrily or relentlessly
glaze get a blurred, glassy look in one's eyes
glimpse take or get a brief look at; identify quickly
glint glance briefly; have bright emotion in one's eyes
gloat observe with unpleasant, superior satisfaction
glower stare with brooding, sullen anger
goggle stare with wide, protuberant eyes
identify observe to establish the identity or nature of a person or thing

inspect examine carefully and thoroughly
keep tabs on watch closely or maintain surveillance on
leer cast a lascivious, wanton look; ogle suggestively; make eyes
look use one's power of vision so as to see something
look askance at take a sidelong glance at
look away avert one's eyes; turn one's eyes from object
look daggers glare or glower sullenly and with hostility
look for search
look on observe passively
look out be watchful
look over examine or inspect, usu. briefly
look sideways at glance sidelong at, usu. implying disapproval
look up lift one's eyes toward the sky
look upon view; regard; scrutinize
make eyes at ogle or leer at
make out see and identify, esp. with difficulty
mark take note of
marvel gaze with amazement or curiosity
mind notice; heed attentively
monitor observe over time; check for specific reason
moon gaze at dreamily or longingly
note observe with attention
notice mark with attention; take note of
observe regard with attention, esp. to form judgment
ogle eye amorously or lewdly; make eyes at
overlook gaze down on from above; look past; fail to see
oversee survey, inspect, or supervise (some activity)
overview survey generally
peek look quickly or furtively from a concealed place
peep look cautiously or stealthily, esp. through a small opening
peer gaze searchingly, with difficulty or curiosity
perceive observe so as to understand; become aware of the presence of
pick out distinguish one among many
pick up catch sight of
pore over gaze at or study intently
preview view in advance
pry look at carefully or inquiringly, esp. against another's will
read observe so as to discern the true nature of; scan; study
recognize see to be that which is already known
reconnoiter appraise and examine so as to gain information
regard heed with attention; look attentively
register perceive; take note of
remark observe with attention
review view or examine again, esp. to form judgment
rivet fix the eyes in a steady, intent gaze
roll one's eyes shift gaze continuously; turn eyes up in sockets as sign of disapproval
scan examine or search hastily from point to point
scour pass eyes over in search of something
scout observe to acquire information
scowl contract one's brow and glower in disapproval
screen examine in detail to differentiate
scrutinize inspect closely; look upon
search look over carefully for purpose of discovery; look for
see perceive with one's eyes; examine; recognize; watch
seek search out
set eyes on catch sight of, esp. for first time; look at
sift pass one's eyes over so as to differentiate
sight look carefully in one direction; catch sight of; aim at
size up examine closely to evaluate
skim pass one's eyes over swiftly; give a cursory glance to
skirr search about; glance over rapidly; skim
snoop look into or pry in a sly or intrusive manner
spectate observe passively
spot distinguish; take note of; detect
spy catch sight of; observe in secret, esp. with hostile intent
squint look with one's eyes partly shut
stare gaze fixedly or intently, often with wide eyes
stare down gaze at with fixed stare to force another back down
study consider and examine carefully or in detail
supervise oversee
survey examine overall; inspect and evaluate
take note of observe with particular attention; spot; take notice of
take notice of take note of
take stock of examine and appraise
tend pay close attention to; observe closely
trace follow or examine carefully, in step-by-step detail
view watch attentively; regard in a special light; survey or inspect
visualize see and form a mental image of
watch observe closely; look at; see
watch out be vigilant and watchful
wink close and open one eye quickly, esp. as a signal or hint
witness see by personal presence or perception

VERBS OF SPEECH

Modes and Manners of Expression
Intonation and Inflection
Speech Sounds and Noises
Expressions of Feeling
Reasoning and Informing
Judgments Pro and Con
Questions and Answers

Modes and Manners of Expression

add speak further; go on to say
affect feign; make a pretense to
air express publicly or aloud; ventilate
announce proclaim, esp. publicly; foretell; give notice of; annunciate

annunciate announce
assert declare forcefully as true; postulate
babble talk foolishly, excessively, and unintelligibly
banter address in a playful, joking, or teasing manner
beckon call to; attract attention of
bicker argue incessantly over petty issues
bid command another's action; greet; make an offer
blab reveal indiscreetly; chatter thoughtlessly
blabber blab; speak foolishly
blather talk foolishly
blatter talk noisily and rapidly
blither talk foolishly
blurt utter suddenly and inadvertently
break begin uttering a sound or series of sounds
broach mention for first time
bubble gurgle; speak excitedly
burble babble excitedly; prattle
call command or order; summon or invite
chat talk informally, lightly, and familiarly
chatter talk incessantly and rapidly
chime in insert remark into others' conversation
chitchat chat idly; gossip
chorus speak in unison with others
clam up cease speaking and remain silent
command give an order; direct with authority
comment utter brief opinion or explanation
confab confabulate
confabulate speak at an informal, impromptu conference; confab
confide tell a secret; entrust information
continue add to; resume after interruption
converse hold a dialogue; speak with others
couch phrase in specific language
coze converse informally or familiarly
declaim speak impressively or dramatically
declare state firmly; announce formally and openly
deliver bring forth in words; utter; enunciate
demand request as if by right; insist on
deny say something is untrue or does not exist; refuse to acknowledge; disown
dictate order with force of authority; speak aloud for another to write down
echo repeat another's words exactly
embellish add entertaining details
evoke call up or inspire a particular response
exaggerate overstate; make unfounded claims; speak of something as greater than it is
excuse pardon; justify a fault or error; release from obligation
express put into words; make known; state
falter stammer; speak hesitantly
fib speak dishonestly; lie on unimportant issue
greet receive another in specified way, usu. upon meeting
harangue make lengthy, often pompous and bombastic, speech
harp speak repeatedly and tiresomely about something
hem and haw speak hesitantly and evasively
herald proclaim the approach of
hesitate speak slowly and uncertainly, esp. with pauses
indite put into words; compose
ingeminate repeat
insist declare or demand emphatically
interject interrupt; throw in a remark
interrupt stop a person in the midst of something, esp. by inserting a remark; speak while another is speaking
introduce announce (a speaker); present to another to make acquainted; acquaint with a subject
invoke call upon God in prayer; summon up a spirit by incantation
issue send out; put forth, usu. officially; state
iterate repeat
jabber talk rapidly and unintelligibly
lie tell an untruth; deceive another
maintain assert as true; affirm in agreement
maunder ramble; mumble incoherently
mention speak of briefly; refer to by name
mimic imitate another's speech; repeat words exactly
muster summon; call
narrate give an account of; recount events; tell a story
natter chatter
note remark upon; speak of attentively
observe remark; take note of
orate speak pompously; make a formal speech
order command; ask for
outspeak speak frankly or boldly; excel in speaking
overstate exaggerate
page summon by calling name
palaver chatter idly; talk aimlessly and profusely
parody mimic humorously
parrot mimic or imitate; repeat words mechanically
pass change the subject of conversation
patter speak rapidly and mechanically; employ the glib, rapid speech of salesman or comedian
perorate deliver lengthy, rhetorical speech
persist continue to repeat or press an opinion
phrase express in words or in appropriate terms
pipe up begin talking
pontificate speak pompously, pretentiously, and dogmatically
portray describe in words; represent verbally
prattle chatter childishly
predict forecast or prophesy
present introduce one to another; bring before the public; bring formal charge in court
prevaricate speak evasively; lie
proclaim declare loudly; announce officially
profess claim; pretend
promise declare that one will or will not do something
prompt incite to action; assist with words
prophesy predict with assurance based on mystical knowledge; speak as if divinely inspired; vaticinate
put it state something in particular way
quip utter witty or sarcastic remark
quote repeat exact words of
ramble talk disconnectedly at length; wander from the subject
rattle ramble quickly and obliviously; chatter incessantly

recount narrate story; tell in detail
reel off list rapidly
refer allude to; call attention to
regale entertain with stories
rehash express old material in new form with little change
reiterate say again or repeatedly
relate narrate; tell in detail
remark say; comment on
repeat say again; say something said by another; say over; ingeminate; iterate
require order or oblige to do something; claim by right or authority
say express in words; state opinion or belief; utter or pronounce
sermonize give long, moralizing talk
shoot off one's mouth talk too freely or indiscreetly
shoot the breeze chat casually
simper say with a weak, silly smile
slobber fawn over; speak with spittle running from one's mouth
smatter speak words of a language with little or no knowledge of the language
sneer speak with upper lip curled, usu. contemptuously
soliloquize utter one's thoughts without addressing anyone, esp. in stage performance
sound utter or pronounce
speak utter words to express something; make a public speech; converse politely; use one particular language to communicate
speak out speak loudly, freely, and frankly
spell out name letters of word aloud in order; explain methodically
spit it out say what is on one's mind without delay
squib utter in an offhand manner; speak in brief, satiric bits
state express in words; declare; report particulars of
stretch exaggerate or extend beyond the truth
stumble make blunders in speech; speak haltingly and awkwardly
summon send for; call together; call upon
swear promise on an oath; state emphatically; curse
alk convey or exchange ideas or information with spoken words; express, utter, or discuss in words; have the power of speech; use one particular language to communicate
alk down silence another by speaking loudly and persistently
ell inform; reveal
itle provide a name for
ouch on mention briefly
rifle talk frivolously; toy with; treat casually
urn a phrase speak gracefully and precisely
waddle talk nonsense
witter talk rapidly, in an anxious manner
tter make a sound with the mouth, esp. a word
aticinate prophesy
entilate air
enture dare to utter; suggest
verbalize put into words
vocalize express aloud in words; use one's voice in speech or song
voice express in words; utter aloud; pronounce
vouchsafe grant in gracious or condescending manner
vow promise solemnly
waffle talk vaguely, indecisively, and evasively
warn inform of danger; advise of action to avert danger
warrant guarantee or assure
wrangle argue, quarrel noisily or angrily

Intonation and Inflection

accent stress (a particular sound or syllable)
articulate utter distinctly; give clear expression to
bawl cry loudly
bellow roar; speak in a loud, deep voice
blare utter raucously and noisily
blubber weep noisily
bray cry harshly, like a donkey
breathe whisper; speak softly
buzz hum, like a bee; murmur or whisper; speak dully and continuously
cachinnate laugh loudly or excessively
cackle laugh shrilly, with sound like a hen's
call speak loudly and distinctly, so as to be heard at a distance
cant talk or beg in whining singsong
catcall express disapproval loudly
caterwaul cry out harshly; quarrel noisily
chant recite in monotonous, repetitive tones
cheer encourage or applaud with shouts
chuff make noisy explanations or grunts
clatter talk noisily
croon sing sweetly and softly
cry shout shrilly; call out like an animal
devoice pronounce a formerly voiced sound without vibration of vocal cords
drawl speak slowly, usu. prolonging vowels
drone make sustained murmur or humming sound; utter at length in monotonous tone
enounce pronounce distinctly; articulate
enunciate pronounce words clearly and distinctly
gabble talk quickly and indistinctly
groan make long, deep sound of pain, grief, or disapproval
growl make low, threatening, animal-like sound
grumble make low, unintelligible sounds in throat
hammer make point emphatically and repeatedly
holler shout
hoot cry out in scorn or disapproval with long "o" sound, like an owl
howl utter long, wailing cry, like a dog's, in amusement, pain, or scorn; weep loudly; yowl
incant utter magical words or sounds
inflect alter tone or pitch of speaking voice
intone recite as a chant, esp. in monotone
jabber chatter, like a monkey
keen utter high, wailing tones
lilt speak in light, pleasant rhythm
mince speak affectedly, esp. to appear refined

mispronounce utter word sounds incorrectly
moan emit or speak with low, mournful, inarticulate sound of pain or suffering
modulate vary pitch or tone of voice, esp. to softer level
mouth form words with lips only; declaim with exaggerated distinction
mumble speak indistinctly
murmur speak in low voice with continuous sound
mutter utter subdued grumbles, often in low, unclear tones
nasalize speak with a twang, as though pushing voice through one's nose
proclaim declare loudly
pronounce utter distinctly, correctly, or in a particular way
pule whimper softly and plaintively
raise one's voice speak loudly; shout
rasp speak in rough, grating voice
rhyme speak in words with identical sounds, esp. at end of lines of speech
roar utter long, deep, loud sound, like a lion's; laugh loudly
roll off one's tongue be uttered eloquently, smoothly, and glibly
rumble utter with heavy, deep, rolling sound
scream utter a sudden, sharp, loud cry
screech utter a high, shrill, piercing cry, esp. in terror or pain
shout speak loudly, esp. to attract attention or to express strong emotion; holler; yell
shriek utter a shrill cry or scream
shrill utter in high, thin, piercing tone
sigh utter a long, audible exhalation expressing grief, exhaustion, or relief
sing speak in musical sounds and rhythm, esp. to set melody
slur pronounce indistinctly, running sounds together
snarl growl angrily, esp. with bared teeth, like a beast
sob utter through uneven breaths caused by heavy weeping
speak up speak more loudly
splutter speak rapidly and indistinctly, esp. with rapid series of spitting sounds; sputter
sputter speak in series of quick, explosive sounds; splutter
squeak speak in a high-pitched cry
squeal speak with a long, shrill crying sound, like a pig
stammer speak with a series of involuntary pauses or rapid repetitions of one syllable
stress place accent on particular syllable
stutter suffer involuntary disruption of speech, esp. repeating first consonant sound of words
sustain prolong sound of word
susurrate whisper
tongue produce speech effects with one's tongue; sound certain words
trill speak with vibrating sound in one's voice, like a bird's song
troll sing in carefree, jovial way
trumpet proclaim in bright, rising tone
twang speak with nasal intonation
ululate howl or wail; hoot
wail utter a long, sad cry
warble sing with a gentle trilling sound, like bird's song
whimper make feeble frightened or complaining sounds; whine softly
whine make a long, high, complaining cry
whisper speak softly, using breath but not vocal cords
whoop utter a loud, excited cry; holler
yammer persist in talking loudly; wail; grumble
yell shout
yowl howl

Speech Sounds and Noises

bark cry out sharply and gruffly, like a dog
bay howl; make a prolonged barking noise
bell speak in ringing tones, resembling a bell's
blat make sharp, loud noise
bleat cry pathetically, like a sheep
boo utter a long exclamation of disapproval by sounding the syllable "boo"
boom make prolonged, deep, resonant sound
caw utter harsh, raucous call, like a crow's
cheep utter faint, shrill sound, like a bird's
chirp emit short, sharp sound, like a bird's
chitter twitter
clack chatter; prattle; make abrupt, sharp sound
cluck utter throaty cry or laugh, like a hen's
coo make soft, murmuring sound
cough emit sharp, rasping sound from the chest
crack emit sharp, sudden, explosive sound
croak make deep, hoarse sound, like a frog's
crow make loud, shrill cry, like a crow
gargle make sound like liquid bubbling in throat
gasp speak with sudden, short intakes of breath, esp. out of fear or shock
gibber make meaningless, unintelligible sounds, esp. in fear
giggle laugh in silly, nervous way, often shrilly
gobble speak with guttural sound, like a turkey
grunt make gruff, snorting sound, like a pig
gulp suppress words by swallowing hard; choke or gasp for air; swallow hard in shock or fear
gurgle make low, bubbling sound in throat
hawk clear throat noisily
hem make sound of clearing throat, esp. while searching for words
hiss speak, esp. expressing disapproval, with prolonged "s" sound, like a snake
huff blow or bluster, esp. in annoyance; breathe heavily
hum utter prolonged "m" sound; drone like an insect
lisp speak defectively, with "s" and "z" sounds pronounced as "th"
mew speak weakly, with a cry like a cat's
mewl cry weakly; whimper
moo emit low, deep sound, like a cow

neigh make long, high-pitched cry, like a horse
oink make grunting sound, like a pig
peep make high, weak, chirping sound, like a bird
puff emit short, light exhalations; breathe hard
purr make low, soothing, vibrating sound, like a cat
quack utter harsh cry, like a duck
roll emit deep, prolonged sound, like a drum's
scat improvise nonsense syllables, esp. to jazz
snap make sharp cracking sound
sniffle speak while repeatedly drawing air up into nose
snuffle speak with noisy sniffs through partly blocked nose
squall utter harsh cry or scream, esp. like a baby
squawk utter loud, harsh cry, like a bird
itter giggle with high-pitched sound
twitter make a rapid series of light, chirping sounds, like a bird's; chitter
vheeze speak with audible hoarse whistling sound from the chest
vhinny speak with low, gentle neighing sound, like a horse would make
ap bark shrilly, like a dog
elp utter sharp, shrill cry or bark, like a dog's; yip
ip yelp
odel utter prolonged musical call, with voice alternating between falsetto and normal pitch
ing utter high-pitched, shrill sound

xpressions of Feeling

vow declare openly or assuredly
ait tease; torment maliciously
emoan complain; express regret
ewail express sorrow over; cry about
larney flatter, wheedle, or con
luster boast; talk loudly or boisterously
oast exaggerate oneself; speak with unwarranted ride; vaunt
rabble squabble; argue noisily
urst out express suddenly with feeling
haff tease good-naturedly; banter
heer encourage or applaud with shouts
hortle laugh loudly and gleefully
huckle laugh quietly, half suppressing the laugh-er
amor protest or demand loudly
mplain express dissatisfaction or pain; find ult; protest wrongs; gripe; grouse; squawk
nfess admit to sins, errors, or weaknesses; state ne's attitude reluctantly
ack make a joke; wisecrack
ow express gleeful triumph
y call out in pain or grief; emit a loud, wordless xpression of grief
rse exclaim violently in anger; call evil upon nother; utter oath or obscenity; cuss
thuse express with enthusiasm
claim cry out suddenly from pain, pleasure, or rprise
hort urge on energetically
ult rejoice greatly
me seethe and splutter angrily

gam engage in friendly conversation
gibe jeer or ridicule
giggle laugh in silly, nervous way
greet speak in a friendly or respectful manner, esp. upon meeting
gripe complain
groan make long, deep sound of pain, grief, or disapproval
grouse complain
grumble complain with ill temper; grump
grump grumble
gush talk with extravagant enthusiasm or flattery, esp. in an affected manner
harass attack or annoy repeatedly
heckle interrupt and harass a public speaker
howl utter long, wailing cry in amusement, pain, or scorn; weep loudly
hurl utter vehemently, esp. abuse or curses
hype exaggerate merits of; mislead by sensationalizing
imprecate utter curses; invoke evil
insult speak ill so as to hurt another's feelings or arouse anger; treat with insolence or contempt
jape joke
jeer shout at rudely or scornfully
jest joke, esp. lightly
joke make humorous remarks; poke fun at; make light of; jape; jest
jolly keep another in good humor to win cooperation
josh joke, tease, or kid
kid tease; deceive in fun
lament express great sorrow or regret
lash out attack violently; hurl insults
laugh utter sound of mirth with a smile and expulsion of air
moan emit or speak with low, mournful, inarticulate sound in pain or suffering
needle annoy; provoke intentionally
obsess speak of continuously and at undue length
paint describe in vivid detail
pledge promise solemnly
pour out express freely
preach deliver a public religious address; urge people to adopt certain moral ways, esp. in an obtrusive manner
profess declare openly or affirm, esp. one's belief
promise vow or pledge to do or not do something; declare emphatically
protest express disagreement or disapproval; declare firmly
quip utter clever or witty remark
rage talk angrily or wildly; rave
rail speak loudly or insistently; scold harshly; complain bitterly
rally rouse; urge on
rant speak loudly, violently, and theatrically
rave talk wildly, furiously, and nonsensically; speak about with great admiration; rage
razz tease or ridicule good-naturedly
reassure restore confidence; remove fears of
refuse express unwillingness to do something
regret express sorrow over loss; state disappointment, repentance, or annoyance

renounce reject; refuse to abide by; formally give up claim
repent express regret over one's actions
repine fret; express discontent or longing
repudiate deny; disown utterly; reject
rhapsodize speak of ecstatically
rib tease
ridicule make fun of; laugh at another's weaknesses or faults, esp. in malicious, scornful way
rip tear apart verbally; utter violently; spit out
rouse urge on, awaken, or excite
sass speak rudely or impertinently
scoff express scorn, derision, or contempt
scorn reject as unworthy or contemptible; express contempt
scream utter a sudden, sharp, loud cry; express intense hysteria
share describe something so that others may experience it
sigh utter a long, audible exhalation expressing grief, exhaustion, or relief
simper utter weakly or sadly
slash speak of cuttingly or harshly
slight insult by discourtesy or lack of respect
snap speak with sudden irritation
snarl speak in a bad-tempered manner
sneer express scorn or contempt, esp. with curled upper lip
snicker giggle slyly; laugh at covertly, in a suppressed manner; snigger
snigger snicker
snivel cry miserably; complain with a whine
snub speak unkindly or scornfully to reject or humiliate another
sob utter through uneven breaths caused by heavy weeping
spit utter violently, often while saliva is ejected from mouth
spout gush forth; speak at length
spur urge on, arouse, or incite
squawk complain
squeal protest sharply, esp. in long, loud, high cry
swear promise on an oath; state emphatically; curse; use profanity
talk back reply defiantly
talk down speak condescendingly
taunt try to provoke with scorn or criticism; jeer at
tease try to provoke playfully by jokes, questions, or sarcasm
threaten express intention to punish or harm another
unburden oneself confess to relieve one's conscience
unleash make (unrestrained verbal assault); let loose (a torrent of words)
unload release one's emotions through words
urge encourage; try hard to persuade; recommend strongly
vaunt boast
vent give verbal outlet to, esp. one's feelings
wail utter long, sad cry; lament or complain persistently
weep express sadness or sorrow by shedding tears; cry at length
welcome greet with pleasure or ceremony
whimper make feeble, frightened, complaining sounds; whine softly
whine complain in petty, feeble way
wisecrack make witty, clever remarks
wish express one's desire, aim, or hope
yawn express boredom by inhaling deeply with mouth wide open
yawp squawk noisily; clamor; complain
yowl utter loud, wailing cry; howl

Reasoning and Informing

accent stress or emphasize
advise counsel; warn; recommend
allege assert without proof; give as reason or excuse
allude refer to indirectly
apprise inform; give notice
attest affirm to be true; bear witness or testify
attribute assign cause, characteristic, or origin to
bandy exchange comments, esp. argumentatively
beat around the bush speak evasively; wander from subject to subject
belabor make a point to absurd lengths
break the news make something known
cajole persuade by flattery
cant speak hypocritically
chaffer bargain for; haggle over
chew over discuss at length
clarify explain or make understandable
clear the air speak openly to remove hostility, tension, or confusion
coax persuade gently
collogue confer privately
communicate succeed in conveying information or feelings; transmit; make known
confer discuss with others
confide tell a secret; entrust information
constate assert positively
contend assert or argue a point
contrast compare or appraise differences
convey impart information; communicate
convince persuade by argument; overcome doubts
counsel advise, esp. professionally
decree order based on lawful authority
define state or explain precisely, esp. meaning of word or thing
delineate describe clearly in accurate detail
depict describe
describe set forth the nature of something; depic
disclose reveal or make known
discourse speak extensively on same subject; lecture
discuss talk about with others; examine by mear of argument
divulge reveal something unknown
elucidate clarify; explain
emphasize stress the importance of
enounce state as a proposition
equivocate speak ambiguously to conceal truth or avoid commitment

explain show meaning of, make clear; state reasons for
expound explain in detail
fill in inform more fully; provide additional information
get across make one's point clear
get over get across; convince another
gloss over cover up, esp. a mistake
gossip reveal personal or sensational facts; spread rumors
hash over discuss further, esp. when already settled
hint suggest; refer to indirectly
hold forth speak at length; lecture about
illustrate explain by giving examples
imply suggest indirectly, hint at
import imply; indicate
impute attribute or ascribe
induce persuade
inform provide information
insinuate imply or hint, esp. artfully or unpleasantly
instruct inform; teach another; direct or command
interpret explain meaning of; analyze; translate speech to another language
itemize state in list form
lay down assert, allege; set down, impose
lecture discuss formally and at length, often before a group
limn describe, portray
list state as a series of names or items
name mention specifically; provide the word that designates something
narrate give an account of; tell a story
notify inform; report on; make known
offer propose or suggest; declare oneself ready
open broach subject; declare ceremoniously
outtalk surpass verbally; get the better of in talking
parley discuss or confer, esp. with enemies or to settle dispute
persuade convince by reasoning; induce
philosophize speak thoughtfully on moral issues
pitch attempt to sell by persuasion
plead make an appeal or entreaty; address court as an advocate
postulate state as true as the basis for reasoning
preface introduce; lead up to
prelect discourse formally and publicly; lecture
prescribe lay down a course to follow
proffer propose; offer
propagate transmit or spread widely; publicize
propose offer for consideration; declare as one's plan
proselytize try intensely to convert others to one's point of view
psychologize analyze motives and feelings of oneself or others
read utter written words aloud; interpret
reason discuss calmly and thoughtfully
rebut refute; disprove
recant formally withdraw one's former statement
recap recapitulate
recapitulate state again, esp. main points of discussion; recap
recite state in order, esp. facts; repeat aloud from memory
recount tell in detail; narrate
refute prove a statement wrong
relate narrate; tell in detail
relay pass on a message or information
repeat tell another what one has heard or learned
report give an account of; describe as news
represent describe as; declare to be
resolve settle an issue
restate say again, often in altered form
retell inform of again; narrate again
retract withdraw statement or opinion; unsay
reveal make known; uncover
specify mention or state in detail
spell out explain explicitly; detail unmistakably
stipulate insist on as part of agreement
stress emphasize a point
submit offer or propose for consideration; contend
suggest propose for consideration
summarize list key points of; sum up; synopsize
sum up summarize; state essentials of
sustain confirm; uphold validity of
sway influence
synopsize summarize
take back withdraw or deny earlier statement
talk into persuade to do or think something
talk out of discourage from doing or thinking something
talk over discuss; review
talk sense speak reasonably
tattle reveal another's secrets, esp. misbehavior; gossip
tell inform; reveal
tell all reveal everything, including secret information
testify express personal conviction; attest to; bear witness, esp. in court
transmit convey to another, esp. information
treat deal with some subject; discuss
typify represent in essentials common to a group
understate describe in restrained terms; represent something as less than it is
unsay retract
unswear retract; recant on an oath
unveil disclose or make known publicly
validate confirm truth of
verify check or confirm truth of
voice express a given position or point of view
vouch guarantee certainty or accuracy of
wheedle persuade or obtain by coaxing and flattery
withdraw take back an earlier statement
witness testify or attest to, esp. in court
word phrase carefully; select words that best express something
work in find place for something in conversation

Judgments Pro and Con

acknowledge recognize as valid
affirm validate or confirm; state positively
agree accept; concede as true; assent
animadvert make critical remarks
argue dispute or contend; give reasons pro or con; discuss; give evidence for or against

assent agree
attack criticize with great vigor; denounce
aver assert in pleading; verify
avouch declare as a matter of fact; confirm; acknowledge; confess
backbite say mean or spiteful things
barrage subject to repeated verbal attacks
belittle speak slightingly of; disparage; decry
berate scold vigorously and repeatedly
carp complain about; find fault with
castigate criticize severely, esp. as punishment
comminate denounce
complain express dissatisfaction or disapproval
concur approve; express agreement
confront face boldly; take opposing position
contradict disagree or state opposition, esp. in an arbitrary, impatient manner
criticize comment unfavorably; express judgment on; discuss critically
decry belittle
demur object mildly
denigrate sneer at; blacken the reputation of
denounce speak against; accuse; proclaim publicly to be guilty or evil; comminate
deplore regret deeply; express shock or distaste over
discredit damage reputation of; cause to be disbelieved
disparage belittle
dispute argue, debate; quarrel; question truth of
dissuade persuade against; alter another's opinion
espouse support position or cause
execrate declare to be evil
flatter compliment excessively, esp. to gain favor
fulminate utter with denunciation; issue censure or invective
fuss complain vigorously or pettily
hector intimidate with bullying attacks; bluster
judge state one's considered opinion on, esp. critical opinion
laud praise
lecture address another reprovingly, esp. to correct faults
make fun of ridicule, esp. jokingly
malign say unpleasant and untrue things about; castigate
mock scoff or jeer contemptuously; ridicule by mimicry of speech
moralize speak of right and wrong conduct
nag complain or find fault incessantly
niggle find fault in petty way; fuss over details
object express disfavor; protest or disagree
opine express judgment
poke fun at ridicule or tease
praise speak highly of and express approval; laud
profane speak of irreverently and disrespectfully
promote publicize; speak well of
question express doubt about
quibble raise petty objections
rate scold angrily
rebuke scold sharply; reprove
recommend advise an action; endorse; praise one to another
remonstrate protest; complain
reprehend rebuke; blame
reprimand rebuke, esp. formally
reproach express disapproval of another's fault
reprove condemn for a fault or offense
revile criticize angrily and abusively
ridicule make fun of another's faults, esp. in scorn
salute express respect or admiration for
scandalize slander, defame, or speak maliciously of
scold rebuke or censure severely; find fault with noisily
score berate; denounce
slander utter false statements damaging to another's reputation
slash criticize cuttingly and harshly
slur speak ill of
smirch discredit another's reputation
speak one's mind express opinions frankly; speak one's piece
speak one's piece speak one's mind
speculate express an opinion without knowledge
support state one's approval of; corroborate
talk up discuss favorably; promote
tout praise highly
upbraid reproach; criticize
vilify speak evil about
vindicate clear of blame or suspicion; prove to be valid
vote give formal expression of one's opinion or choice

Questions and Answers

acknowledge admit agreement with
admit concede as true; acknowledge; allow
answer respond to question or accusation; reply
appeal request earnestly; ask for corroboration or vindication
ask call for an answer; put a question to; request; invite
ask about pose question on
badger question persistently
beg ask for earnestly and humbly; evade; sidestep
beseech beg for earnestly; implore
come back respond; answer quickly
concede admit truth of something; admit defeat
confess admit to sins, errors, or weaknesses
consult seek advice or opinion of
cross-examine pose a series of questions, esp. to court witness
demand request as if by right; insist on
deny refuse to acknowledge
divulge reveal something unknown
entreat beg, implore
examine inquire into; ask questions of
explain elaborate on a brief answer
grant admit that something is true
grill question intensely at length
impetrate ask for; entreat
implore request earnestly, beg for
importune request persistently
inquire ask, question; investigate; also, *esp. Brit.*, enquire

interrogate question, esp. formally and at length
investigate inquire systematically in close examination
invite ask another for comments or to do something
offer propose or suggest an answer
pester annoy with frequent requests or questions
petition request earnestly and formally
plead make an appeal or entreaty
pose state a question
pray entreat someone, esp. God
press demand insistently; urge or pressure; beseech
proffer offer, esp. in answer
pry inquire into, often furtively or impertinently
pump question persistently for information
put a question to ask; inquire
query ask a question; express doubt
question ask for information; seek or demand an answer
quiz question or examine briefly or rapidly
react respond to a question
rebut prove false or oppose by evidence or argument
refuse deny request or demand; answer "no"
rejoin reply sharply or critically
reply answer
request ask for something
respond answer, esp. a specific question
retort answer, esp. with quick, witty, or angry reply; riposte
retract change or withdraw statement or opinion; unsay
riddle pose question that is both amusing and puzzling
riposte retort
supplicate ask for humbly; beseech
talk back answer or respond defiantly
temporize evade direct answer, esp. to gain time
testify bear witness, esp. in court
unsay retract, esp. a previous statement

SOUNDS AND NOISES

Sound, Hearing, and Deafness
Actual Sounds
Descriptions of Sounds
Speech Sounds
Comic Sound Effects

Sound, Hearing, and Deafness

acoustics branch of physics that deals with sound and sound waves
attend (*vb*) listen to
audio (*adj*) pertaining to transmission, reception, or reproduction of sound
audiology study of hearing disorders and rehabilitation of those with hearing impairments
audiometer instrument for recording acuity of hearing
auditory (*adj*) pertaining to hearing, sense of hearing, or organs of hearing; perceived through the sense of hearing
aural (*adj*) pertaining to the ear or sense of hearing; auricular
babel confused mixture of sounds or noises
bug hidden, electronic listening device
cacophony harsh discordance of sound; dissonance
clamor loud and continuous noise
closed-captioned (*adj*) designating television program broadcast with captions visible with use of a decoder, intended for the hearing-impaired
consonance harmony of sounds
deaf (*adj*) partially or wholly deprived of sense of hearing
deaf-mute person who is unable to hear or speak
decibel unit of measure used to express differences in power in acoustics, designating degree of loudness
din loud, confused, continuous noise
discord inharmonious or confused combination of sounds; harsh noise; dissonance
dissonance inharmonious or harsh sound; cacophony; discord
dumb (*adj*) mute
earshot distance within which a sound or voice can be heard
eavesdrop (*vb*) listen secretly to a private conversation
euphony agreeableness of sound, esp. harmonious or pleasant-sounding combinations of tones
faint (*adj*) lacking loudness
frequency number of cycles per unit time of a sound wave, determining its pitch
hard-of-hearing (*adj*) hearing-impaired
hearing sense by which sounds are perceived; act of perceiving sound
hearing aid compact electronic amplifier, usu. placed behind one's ear to improve hearing
hearing-impaired (*adj*) having reduced or deficient hearing ability; hard of hearing
hush silence or quiet, esp. after noise; (*vb*) make silent
inaudible (*adj*) incapable of being heard
listen (*vb*) give attention with the ear for purpose of hearing; wait attentively in expectation of perceiving a sound
listen in (*vb*) overhear; eavesdrop
loud (*adj*) designating a sound or tone having exceptional volume; noisy or clamorous
loudness measure of a sound's intensity, independent of its pitch and timbre
lull temporary quiet or stillness; soothing sound
muffle (*vb*) deaden sound, esp. by wrapping that which is producing it
mum (*adj*) silent
mute (*adj*) silent, esp. refraining from speech; not emitting sound; incapable of speech, dumb
noise sound, esp. loud, harsh, or confused one; clamor
otology study and treatment of diseases of the ear
overhear (*vb*) hear, esp. speech, without speaker's

intention or knowledge; eavesdrop; listen in
pitch degree of height or depth of a tone or sound, depending on the relative rapidity of its frequency
quiet (*adj*) making little or no sound or noise; silent
racket loud, disturbing noise or uproar; clamor; din
register tonal range of a voice, instrument, or sound-producing device
resonance prolongation of sound by reflection or reverberation; characteristic quality of a particular voiced sound
resonant (*adj*) deep and full of resonance; sonorous
resonate (*vb*) resound
resound (*vb*) echo or ring with sound; sound loudly; resonate
reverberate (*vb*) reecho, resound; be reflected repeatedly, as sound waves from walls of a confined space
ring (*vb*) give forth a clear, resonant sound; resound or reverberate
sibilation hissing sound
silence absence of sound; stillness
soft (*adj*) designating sound or tone having very little volume; low or subdued in noise level
sonant (*adj*) sounding; having sound
sonic (*adj*) pertaining to sound
sonority condition of being resonant or sonorous
sonorous resonating with sound; loud and deep-toned; rich and full in sound
sound sensation produced by stimulation of organs of hearing by vibrations transmitted through air or other medium; mechanical vibrations transmitted through an elastic medium that produce stimulation of organs of hearing; particular auditory effect thus produced; any noise, vocal utterance, or musical tone; (*vb*) make or emit a sound
soundproof (*adj*) impervious to sound
still (*adj*) free from sound or noise; silent; subdued or hushed in sound
stone-deaf (*adj*) totally deaf
stridor harsh, grating, or creaking sound
timbre characteristic quality of a sound, independent of its pitch and loudness
tone any sound considered with reference to its pitch, strength, timbre, and source; quality of a sound
tone-deaf (*adj*) unable to distinguish differences in pitch in musical tones
ultrasound sound with frequency greater than 20,000 hertz, approximately the upper limit of human hearing
voice sounds uttered through mouth of living creature, esp. human being; such sounds as distinctive to an individual
volume degree of sound intensity or loudness

Actual Sounds

ahh, arf, arp
baa, beep, birr, blap, blat, boing, boo, bow-wow, burp, buzz
caw, cheep, chink, chirp, chirr, chirrup, churr, clang, clank, clap, click, cling, clink, clinkety-clank, clip, clip-clop, clomp, clonk, clop, clop-clop, clunk, coo, cuckoo
ding, ding-a-ling, ding-dong, dong, drivit
eek
fizz
gong, goo
haw, hem, hiccup, hiss, honk, hoo, hum, hurrah
ick
meow, mew, mewl, moo
oink
pat, ping, pit-a-pat, pitter-patter, plink, plonk, plunk, pop, pow, purr
quack
rat-a-tat, ring, ring-a-ling, riprap
splat, splish, squish, swish, swoosh
tantara, tap, tat, tick, ticktock, ting, ting-a-ling, toot, tweet
varoom
whap, whirr, whish, whizz, whomp, whoop, whoopee, whoosh, woof, wow
yahoo, yikes, yip, yo, yoo-hoo, yow
zap, zing

Descriptions of Sounds

baffle, bang, bawl, bay, belch, bell, blare, blast, bleat, bleep, bong, boom, boop, bray, bruit, buffet, bugle, bump, burble
cacophony, catcall, caterwaul, cheer, chime, chip, chuff, chug, chunk, clack, clamor, clangor, clash, clatter, cluck, clump, conk, crack, crackle, crash, creak, crinkle, croak, cronk, crool, croon, crow, crump, crunch
drill, drone, drum
fart, flick, flump, flutter
gag, gaggle, gargle, glop, gnash, gobble, grate, grind, gulp, gurgle, guzzle
hammer, hawk, hoot, howl, huff, hush
jangle, jingle
keck, keen, knell, knock
lap, lisp, low
mash, mizzle
neigh, nip
pad, paradiddle, patter, peal, pestle, pip, pipe, pitter, plash, plop, pound, pule, pummel
racket, rap, rasp, rattle, report, roar, rollick, rumble, rustle
scrape, scratch, screak, scream, screech, shake, shatter, shriek, shrill, shush, sizzle, skirl, slam, slap, slur, slurp, smack, snap, snarl, sneeze, sniff, sniffle, snivel, snore, snort, snuffle, sob, splash, splatter, squall, squawk, squeak, squeal, squib, stertor, stomp, strum, swat
tamp, thill, throstle, thrum, thud, thump, thunder, thunk, thwack, ticktack, tinkle, tintinnabulate, tirl, toll, tootle, tramp, tread, trill, tromp, trumpet, twang
ululate
warble, whack, wham, whang, wheeze, whinny, whistle, whiz, whop, whump, winnow, wolf
yak, yakety-yak, yawp, yelp, yodel
zip, zoom

Speech Sounds

babble, bark, bellow, blab, blabber, blather, blatter, bleat, blither, blubber, blurt, bluster, brattle, bray, bubble, bumble, burble
cackle, caw, chat, chatter, chitter, chuff, cry
gab, gabble, gibber, giggle, groan, growl, grumble, grunt, guffaw
holler, hoot
jabber
murmur, mutter
natter, nicker, noodle
patter, prattle, pribble
quibble
shout, simper, sing, snicker, splutter, sputter, squeal, stammer, stutter, susurrate
tattle, titter, trill, twaddle, twitter
wail, warble, whimper, whine, whisper
yabber, yammer, yap, yell, yelp, yowl

Comic Sound Effects

aaaa, aaargh, aaarrgh, ack, ahchoo, ak
babrom, bada, ba-da-bam, badow, baff, balump, bam, bammm, bang, bash, ba-wrooo, bawww, bdlm, bdlmp, bdmp, beep, bep, bida-bom, biff, bing, blaff, blam, blamma, blang, bl-eech, bleed, bleeed, bllam, bllom, blm, blodom, blog, blom, bloo, blop, blouw, blrashh, blug, bof, boing, bom, bong, bonk, boom, boom-ba-doom, bop, bounce, boyng, bradada, brat, brrrrram, brrt, burble
chomp, chonk, chop, chsh, chugalug, clang, clank, clash, clik, clikety, clrrash, coff, crack, crackle, crak, crash, creak, crunch, cut
dang-a-lang, danglang, dig, ding, dingdong, dinggg, dong, doof, drinnggg, dzzzz, dzzzzz
ech, eeeeeeee, eeeeek, eep, ert
feh, flink, floom, floosh, foomf, fooosh, foosh, froosh, fsst, fwadoom, fweet
gag, gah, gasp, ge-boom, gha, ghaaa, gleh, glig, glk, glook, glub, glug, go, gong, gonng, goo, gop, gring, grinngg, grrr
hack, ha-ho, hf, hmf, hnf, honk, hrf, huf, huh, humph
inng
jab
kaf, kchow, kchunk, klak, klaket, klakkety, klek, klik, klink, klomp, klop, kneek, kortch, kpow, krak, kree, kreet, krk, krr-oomf, kr-rumf, krumf, kruuungg, ktak, kweeg
mf, mff, mhf, nf, nfs, nggg, ngs, nok, nyaaoooo
oof, oop, ooze, oww
paf, piu, plip, ploosh, pok, poof, poom, poot, pop, pow, ptung, ptweeeeng, punt
rap, rat, rat-tat, rattle, ring, room, rowf, rrinngg, r-rip, rrip, rrowr, rrrooaar, runch
schplivartz, scree, screeech, screeee, shmek, skeee, skloorgle, skntch, skramm, skreech, skrotch, skwee, skweee, slam, slap, slap-ap-ap, slash, slep, slosh, smak, smash, smashh, smeeeeeeer, smek, smesh, smooch, snap, snf, snick, snif, snuf, sob, spa-bam, spla-poom, splash, splat, splinter, sploog, sploosh, splow, splush, spong, sponggg, spung, sput, squeee, sreiikk, stomp, swish, swok, swop
tap, tat, thud, thunk, tick, tilt, tinkle, toot, treee, tromp, trompitty, tsk, tsss, tsssboom, twang, twee, tweep, twerp
ugh, ung
vaaaagglum, vash, va-va-voom, voof, voom, vroooom, vrrumm
waa, waaah, waf, wak, wee, weoooeeeoooee, wham, whap, whirr, whom, whomp, whoom, whoosh, whuf, wok, woop, wrraaammmm, wurf
yap, yappa, yatata, yayter, yeaaaaa, yeeeaaaakk, yhaaa, yitti, yoop, yotter, youch, yyp
z, zaaaaa, zap, zetz, zing, zip, zok, zop, zot, zzap, zzip, zzz, zzzzz

SMELLS AND TASTES

Smells

air (*vb*) ventilate by exposure to open air
ambrosia something appealing to smell or taste, orig. food of the gods
anosmic (*adj*) having complete or partial loss of sense of smell
aroma usu. agreeable odor, often arising from spices or plants; bouquet of wine
aromatic (*adj*) having a pleasing scent or odor
bad breath halitosis
balm aromatic fragrance or sweet odor, esp. in resinous, oily substance exuding from certain plants
BO body odor
body odor BO; natural smell of human body, esp. unpleasant odor of perspiration
bouquet distinctive aroma of wines and liqueurs
breath hint or mere suggestion of scent, esp. carried on a light current of air
cologne mildly perfumed toilet water
deodorant any agent used for eliminating odors
deodorize (*vb*) eliminate unpleasant odor
eau de toilette perfumed toilet water; cologne
effluvium slight trace or invisible exhalation of vapor, usu. noxious or disagreeable
emanation breath or issuing forth of vapor
essence perfume or scent; basic or intrinsic smell of something
fetid (*adj*) having a strong, unpleasant smell; olid
foul (*adj*) unpleasant smelling

fragrance sweet or pleasing odor
fulsome (*adj*) sickening or disgusting to the senses
fume usu. vaporous smokelike exhalation, esp. of odorous or harmful nature
fumigation exposure to smoke or vapors, usu. in disinfecting process
funk strong, offensive smell
fust strong, musty, or moldy smell
gamy (*adj*) having the tangy, slightly tainted odor of uncooked game
halitosis condition of having foul-smelling breath
heady (*adj*) intoxicating and exhilarating to the sense of smell
incense aromatic substance that produces sweet odor when burned; any fragrant scent or perfume
malodorous (*adj*) foul-smelling
mephitis any poisonous stench, esp. noxious exhalation from the earth
miasma noxious exhalation, esp. from decomposing organic matter
musk strong odor of substance secreted in gland of male musk deer, or synthesized, used in making perfume; must
nasal (*adj*) pertaining to the nose or nostrils
nidor strong smell, esp. of burning meat or fat
odor sensation perceived by sense of smell, either agreeable or disagreeable
olfaction sense of smell; act of smelling
olfactory (*adj*) pertaining to sense of smell
olid (*adj*) fetid
perfume agreeable scent, odor, or volatile particles emitted by a substance; (*vb*) impart a pleasant fragrance
pomander ball-shaped mixture of aromatic substance
potpourri fragrant mixture of dried flower petals and spices
putrefy (*vb*) cause to rot or decay with offensive odor
putrid (*adj*) in state of foul decay and decomposition with accompanying odor of rot
rancid (*adj*) having an unpleasant, stale smell
rank (*adj*) having an offensive, foul smell or taste
redolent (*adj*) fragrant, having a pleasant odor; smelling of
reek strong, unpleasant smell, esp. vaporous stink; (*vb*) give off strong, unpleasant odor
rot state of putrefaction and decay and its attendant unpleasant odor
sachet small bag or case of perfumed powder, used for scenting clothes or linens
savory (*adj*) agreeable in smell, esp. fragrant
scent distinctive, usu. agreeable odor; perfume; sense of smell; (*vb*) imbue with odor or perfume
smell odor or scent that may be perceived through the nose by the olfactory nerves; (*vb*) perceive by sense of smell or inhale odor of
smelly (*adj*) having or emitting a strong, unpleasant odor
sniff scent or odor perceived; (*vb*) smell something by short inhalations through the nose
snuffle (*vb*) draw air into nose so as to smell something
stench foul or offensive smell
stink (*vb*) emit a strong, offensive smell; (*n*) a strong, offensive smell
stuffy (*adj*) poorly ventilated, stale, lacking fresh air
sweet (*adj*) fragrant, perfumed, or fresh to the smell
trace hint or suggestion of a particular scent; whiff
unscented (*adj*) having no smell; without scent or odor added
vapor visible exhalation of gaseous particles into the air
ventilate (*vb*) provide fresh air to enclosed place
waft faintly perceived odor; trace of scent in the air
whiff slight trace of odor or smell of something

Tastes

acerbic (*adj*) sour or astringent in taste
acidic (*adj*) sharp and biting in flavor
acrid (*adj*) sharp, biting, or bitterly pungent
aftertaste sensation of taste remaining after substance causing it is no longer in mouth
appetizing (*adj*) appealing to the taste
astringent (*adj*) harshly biting, esp. constrictive to taste buds
biting (*adj*) sharp, somewhat acidic, producing harsh taste
bitter (*adj*) having a harsh, disagreeably acrid taste; being one of the four basic taste sensations
brackish (*adj*) having a slightly salty or briny flavor
briny (*adj*) salty in flavor
caustic (*adj*) sharp and acidic
delectable (*adj*) delicious or appetizing
delicious (*adj*) very pleasing to taste
dry (*adj*) of wines, not sweet or fruity
dulcify (*vb*) sweeten
flavor distinctive taste; additive imparting specific taste
flavorful (*adj*) possessing strong flavor; tasty
flavoring something that imparts a particular taste
four basic tastes elemental taste sensations that are mediated by sense organs and form basis of most other tastes: bitter, salt, sour, sweet
fruity (*adj*) tasting of fruit; of wines, sweet
full-bodied (*adj*) at full strength or flavor, esp. of wines
gamy (*adj*) having the tangy, tainted flavor of uncooked game
goût *French.* taste, relish
gustatory (*adj*) pertaining to taste or tasting
honey (*adj*) sweet
hot (*adj*) sharply pungent or peppery
juicy (*adj*) succulent, mouth-watering
mouth-watering (*adj*) appetizing
nip biting or tangy taste
palatable (*adj*) good-tasting
palate sense of taste
peppery (*adj*) hot and pungent, tasting of pepper
pickled (*adj*) preserved in and tasting of brine

piquant (*adj*) pleasingly sharp, biting, or tart
pungent (*adj*) biting or acrid; having a sharp affect on taste organ
rancid (*adj*) having an unpleasant, stale taste
rank (*adj*) having an offensive, foul taste
relish pleasing or appetizing flavor; enjoyment of the taste of something
saccharine (*adj*) very sweet; artificially sweet
saline (*adj*) salty
salt (*adj*) producing that one of the four basic taste sensations that is not sweet, sour, or bitter
salty (*adj*) tasting of salt
sapor flavor; quality of substance affecting sense of taste; savor
saporific (*adj*) imparting or producing flavor
savor quality of substance affecting sense of taste; sapor
savory (*adj*) agreeable to the taste, sometimes piquant
scrumptious (*adj*) delicious
seasoning salt, herbs, or spices that enhance flavor of food
sec (*adj*) of wines, dry, not sweet
sharp (*adj*) strongly pungent or biting
smack taste or flavor, esp. hint of flavor
sour (*adj*) tart, acidic, lemony; being one of the four basic taste sensations
spicy (*adj*) piquant or pungent; seasoned with spices
strong (*adj*) having a powerful, dominant, specific flavor
succulent (*adj*) juicy and full of good flavor**sugary** (*adj*) sweet like sugar
sweet (*adj*) tasting of sugar or honey; being one of the four basic taste sensations
sweet-and-sour (*adj*) combining the tastes of sugar or honey and vinegar or lemon juice
syrupy (*adj*) very sweet, esp. of viscous liquids
tang strong, distinctive taste or flavor
tart (*adj*) sour or acidic, sharp to the taste
taste sense by which flavor or savor of things is perceived and appreciated; (*vb*) perceive or try the flavor of something
taste buds small bodies, primarily on tongue, that are perception organs for sense of taste
tasteless (*adj*) having no distinct flavor
tasting act of perceiving or testing the flavor of something
tasty (*adj*) good-tasting, delicious, savory
tongue movable organ on floor of mouth used in eating and containing taste buds that perceive flavors
toothsome (*adj*) agreeable to the taste, palatable
zest agreeable or piquant flavor imparted to something
zesty (*adj*) agreeably piquant

Chapter Twenty
Common Expressions

EXCLAMATIONS

Grunts, Calls, and Sounds
Interjections
Curses and Oaths

Grunts, Calls, and Sounds

aah, achoo, ack, ah, aha, ahem, ah-ha, aw
baa, bah, blah, boo, bowwow, brrr
cheep
eek, eh
guffaw
hah, ha-ha, harrumph, haw, heehaw, heigh-ho, hem, hi-ho, hmmm, ho, ho-hum, hoo, hoy, huh, humph, hunh, hup, hut
ick
la-di-da, lo
nah
o, oh, oink, oof, ooh, ooh-la-la, oompah, oomph, ooo, ow
peugh, pip-pip, poof, pshaw
rah
shh
ta-da, tut, tut-tut
ugh, uh-huh, uh-oh, umph, unh-unh
varoom
wahoo, wha, whee, wo, wow, wowee
yah, yahoo, yay, yech, yikes, yo, yoikes, yoo-hoo, yow, yuck, yum, yummy, yum-yum
zap

Interjections

alack, alas, alleluia, amen, and how, avast, aw-shucks, aye
banzai, boy, bravo, by jingo
cheerio, cheers, chop-chop
dear, dear me, ditto
egads, eh, what, eureka
fiddlesticks, fore, forsooth
gadzooks, gee, gee whillikers, gee whiz, gesundheit, giddyap, golly, golly gee, golly whillikers, good golly, good gracious, goody, gracious, gracious me
hallelujah, hark, heads up, hear ye, hear ye, heave-ho, heavens, heavens to Betsy, here here, hey, hip-hip, holy cow, holy mackerel, holy moly, holy toledo, hooray, hosanna, hurrah, huzzah
jeepers
lackaday, lo and behold
mama, marry, my gracious, my my, my stars, my word
nah, nay, nerts, nope, nuts
oh boy, oh dear, oh my, okay, okey-doke, okey-dokey, ole, oops, oopsy-daisy, ouch, oy, oyez
peekaboo, phew, pooh, prithee, prosit
rah, rah-rah, roger, rot
salud, scram, shaddup, shucks, shush, skoal
tallyho, ten-four, there, there, timber, touché, tsk tsk, tush, tut-tut
viva, voila
whatever, well, whew, whoa, whoop-de-do, whoopee, whoops, why, woe is me, wowie, wowie-zowie
yea, yeah, yep, yippee, yo mama, yup
zooks, zounds, zut

Curses and Oaths

arse, ass, asshole
bastard, bejesus, blame, blast, bleep, blimey, bosh, brother, bull, bullroar, bullshit, by cracky, by Jove
Christ, cockadoodie, cocksucker, cotton-pickin', crap, crapola, crikey, criminy, cunt
dad-blamed, dadburn it, dad-gummed, dammit, damn, damnation, damn it, dang, darn, dash, dod, doggone, doodie, drat, durn
faugh, feh, fie, for Christ's sake, frig, frigging, fuck, fuckin', fuckin'-A, fucking, fuckin'-hell, fuck it
God, goddamn, goddamnit, gol blame, gol darn, good God, good Lord, gramercy
heck, heckuva, hell, hellacious, hell's bells, helluva, holy gosh
jeez, jeez Louise, Jesus, Jesus Christ, Jesus H. Christ
merde, motherfucker, mother of God, my ass
noogie
Od
phooey, pish, piss, piss off, poop, pox
sacre bleu, Sam Hill, sheesh, shit, shoo, shoot, son of a bitch, son of a gun, sumbitch
tarnation
what the dickens, what the hell, what the Sam Hill

GREETINGS AND FAREWELLS

Greetings
Farewells
Interchangeables

Greetings

ahoy, all hail
bonjour
glad to see you, good to see you, greetings
hail, halloa, have a good one, hello, hello there, hey, hey-ho, hi, hi, there, hi ya, hola, how are you?, how do?, how do you do?, howdy, howdy-do, howdy-doody, how d'ye

do?, how goes it?, how's by you?, how's everything?, how's it going?, how's the world treating you?, how's things?, how you be?, how you been?, how you doing?, hullo
many happy returns
que pasa?
salud, salutations, shake
welcome, what it is?, what's happening?, wie gehts?
yo

Farewells

à bientôt, à demain, adieu, adios, arrivederci, à toute à l'heure, Auf Wiedersehen, au revoir
be good, be seeing you, bless you, bonne nuit, bon voyage, buenas noches, buona notte, bye, bye-bye
catch you later, come again
das vedanya
enjoy
fare thee well, farewell
God be with you, God bless, Godspeed, good-bye, good luck, good night, gute Nacht
happy trails, hasta la vista, hasta luego, hasta maìana, have a good one, have a nice day
later, later on
maìana
over, over and out
peace
regards, roger
sayonara, see ya, see you later, see you later alligator
take care, take it easy, ten-four, toodleoo

Interchangeables

all hail, aloha, ave
bonjour, bon matin, bon soir, buenas tardes, buenos dias, buona sera, buon giorno
check, cheerio, cheers, ciao
good afternoon, good day, good evening, good morning, good to see you, guten Abend, guten Morgen, guten Tag
hail
konbanwa, konichiwa
pip-pip
regards
salaam, shalom

INSULTS, SLURS, AND EPITHETS

Appearance or Style
Intelligence or Aptitude
Behavior or Personality
Morality or Character
Sexuality or Gender
Ethnic Origin, Race, or Religion

Appearance or Style

Amazon, ape, armpit
baboon, bag, bag lady, bear, beggar, behemoth, beldam, biddy, blastie, blimp, blob, bohunk, booger, bruiser, brute, bug, bumpkin, bunny, burrhead, butterball, buzzard
chit, city slicker, clotheshorse, codger, Colonel Blimp, conehead, coot, cootie, cornpone, cow, cripple
dandy, dinosaur, dirt bag, dog, dotard, dwarf
eyesore
fancyass, fatso, fatty, feeb, ferret face, fleabag, fogy, fop, fossil, four-eyes, Frankenstein, freak, frump
geek, geezer, ghost, ghoul, gimp, golem, golliwogg, goon, gorgon, gorilla, grease monkey, greaser, guttersnipe
hag, have-not, hayseed, heifer, hick, hillbilly, hobbledehoy, hobo, ho-dad, hog, homunculus, hoyden
invalid
jarhead
lard, lardass, Little Lord Fauntleroy, longhair, lummox, lump, lunger
malkin, mannequin, measle, meatball, Medusa, monkey, monstrosity, moose, mossback, mug, mutant, mutt
Neanderthal
old bag, ox
peacock, peewee, picklepuss, pig, pilgarlic, pimple, pimpleface, pinhead, pipsqueak, pizzaface, plain Jane, plugugly, porker, preppy, prune, pus bucket, pustule, pygmy
ragabond, ragamuffin, ragtag, relic, reptile, ronyon, rooster, rube, runt
sad sack, scarecrow, scrag, shlump, shorty, shrimp, shriv, skinhead, slattern, slicker, slob, slouch, sloven, small fry, sow, spas, spastic, specter, spud, squirt, stick, string bean, stumblebum, sweat hog, swell
tank, tawpie, Teddy boy, toad, toff, tomboy, troglodyte, troll, tub
ugly duckling
waif, wallflower, wart, weenie, whale, whiffet, white bread, wombat, wraith
yokel
zit

Intelligence or Aptitude

addlebrain, addlehead, addlepate, airhead, ament, April fool, automaton
bananahead, basket case, beefhead, beetlehead, bimbo, birdbrain, blatherskite, blockhead, blubberhead, blunderhead, bonehead, boob, bozo, brain, bubblehead, bufflehead, buffoon, butthead
cabbagehead, chawbacon, chickenbrain, chowderhead, chucklehead, chump, clod, clodhead, clodpate, clodpoll, clot, cluck, conehead, crackbrain, cretin, criticaster, cuckoo
deadhead, dimwit, ding-a-ling, dingbat, dingdong, ditz, dodo, dodo brain, dolt, dolthead, donkey, doofus, dope, dork, dullard, dullhead, dumbbell, dumb bunny, dumb cluck, dumbhead, dumbo, dumdum, dummkopf, dummy, dunce, dunderhead, dunderpate, dupe
asy mark, egghead
athead, fatwit, featherbrain, featherhead, feeb, flathead, flibbertigibbet, fool
aby, gawk, gudgeon
alf-wit, hammerhead, harebrain, highbrow
diot, ignoramus, imbecile
ackass, jiggin, jobbernowl, jolterhead, jughead
lutz, know-nothing, knucklehead
ackwit, lamebrain, lightweight, loggerhead, loon, lowbrow, lumpkin, lunkhead
neatball, meathead, mental midget, mongoloid, moron, muddlehead, mumpsimus, musclehead, mushhead, muttonhead
incompoop, ninny, ninnyhammer, nitwit, no-brainer, noddy, noodlehead, nudnik, numskull
atzer, peabrain, peahead, pinbrain, pinhead, pointyhead, potatohead, puddinghead, puttyhead
attlebrain, rattlehead, retard, rockhead
ap, saphead, scatterbrain, sciolist, shit for brains, silly fool, simp, simpleton, slobbering idiot, slowpoke, softhead, stupe, submoronic twit, sucker
chie, thickhead, thickwit
egetable, void
itling, woodenhead
yo
phead

ehavior or Personality

idhead, agent provocateur, agitator, airyairy, alky, alien, also-ran, amateur, ndroid, animal, annoyance, appendage, pple polisher, archenemy, artiste, artsyrtsy, ass, asshole, ass-kisser
ckbreaker, badass, baggage, bag lady, anana, banshee, barbarian, barfly, bastard, ear, beast, beggar, bellyacher, bête noir, ighead, bigmouth, big shot, bindle stiff, bitch, blabbermouth, black sheep, blatherskite, blellum, blow-hard, Boeotian, boaster, bookworm, boor, bore, botcher, brat, brawler, bruiser, brute, bugbear, bugger, bullshit artist, bullshitter, bully, bullyboy, bungler, buster, busybody, butt, butterfingers, buttinsky, buzzard
carper, chatterbox, chauvinist, cheapo, cheapskate, chicken, chimp, chiseler, chowhound, chuff, chump, churl, cipher, clam, clochard, clod, clodhopper, clown, clunk, clunker, cold fish, Comstocker, copycat, cornball, couch potato, cousin, crab, crackpot, crank, crazy, cream puff, creature, crumb, crybaby, cube, cur, curmudgeon, cuss, cutup
dabbler, deadwood, dick, dickhead, dilettante, dinosaur, dip, dipshit, ditz, dog breath, dog meat, do-gooder, dogsbody, donkey, do-nothing, doofus, doormat, dork, dotard, doubting Thomas, drag, draggletail, dreamer, drifter, drip, drone, dropout, drudge, druggie, drunk, dud, duffer, dweeb
earbender, eightball, enfant terrible, extremist
fart, fat cat, fathead, fawner, featherweight, finagler, firebrand, fish, flake, flamer, flâneur, flash in the pan, flibbertigibbet, floater, flop, flubber, flunky, fogy, fox, fraidy-cat, freak, freebooter, freeloader, fucker, fuckface, fuckhead, fuckup, fuddy-duddy, fumbler, fungus, fussbudget, fusspot
gadfly, galoot, gasbag, gawk, geep, geezer, glutton, goat, goldbrick, golem, goody-goody, goody two shoes, goof, goofball, goof-off, goon, goose, gossipmonger, gourmand, gowk, grease monkey, greenhorn, griper, grobian, grouch, groupie, grump, gull
hack, ham, hambone, hamburger, hangdog, hanger-on, hard case, hardhead, hardnose, harridan, has-been, head, heathen, hedonist, hellion, hellhound, hell-raiser, high-muck-a-muck, hippie, homebody, horse's ass, hot dog, hothead, hotshot, hoyden, hypochondriac, hypocrite
iceberg, icicle, idler, incendiary, incubus, inebriate
jackal, jackanapes, jackass, jack-off, jailbird, jay, jerk, jerk-off, jester, Johnny-come-lately, joker, juicehead, juicer, junkie
kibitzer, killjoy, klutz, knave, knight-errant, know-it-all, know-nothing, kook
lackey, laggard, lamb, lame, lame duck, landlubber, larrikin, layabout, lazybones, lemming, lemon, leper, lightweight, litterbug, loafer, loggerhead, lollygagger, looby, loon, loser, lotus-eater, loudmouth, lounge lizard, lout, lowbrow, lubber, lug, lunatic, lurdan, lush
madman, madwoman, maenad, malcontent, mama's boy, maniac, marshmallow,

Martian, martinet, masher, meanie, meatball, meddler, megalomaniac, mercenary, merry-andrew, meshugene, milksop, milquetoast, mimic, misanthrope, mischief-maker, miscreant, miser, misfit, misogynist, mobster, mole, mollycoddle, Momus, moneybags, monger, mongrel, mooch, mooncalf, mother, motherfucker, motor-mouth, mouse, muck-a-muck, muckraker, mugwump, mule, mutt

nag, namby-pamby, name-dropper, narc, nebbish, nemesis, nerd, nervous Nellie, nibs, niggard, ninny, nit, nitpicker, nobody, nomad, nonentity, nonperson, noodle, no one, Nosy Parker, nothing, nouveau riche, novice, nut, nutter

oaf, oddball, odd man out, old fart, old fogy, outcast, outsider, oyster

pack rat, pain, pain in the ass, pain in the neck, palooka, panhandler, pantywaist, pariah, patch, patsy, pauper, pawn, peasant, peckerwood, pedant, penny pincher, peon, pepper pot, pest, petticoat, pettifogger, pharisee, philistine, pigeon, piker, pill, pinchbeck, pip, pipsqueak, pisher, pisser, playboy, playgirl, plebe, plunderer, poetaster, polecat, Pollyanna, pollywog, poltroon, poop, poseur, prankster, pretender, prima donna, princess, procrastinator, profiteer, provocateur, pseudo, psycho, pub-crawler, puckfist, pug, punching bag, punk, pussy, putty, putz

quicksilver, quidnunc

rabble-rouser, rake, rapscallion, reb, rebel, recluse, redneck, reject, renegade, revisionist, reynard, riffraff, roach, roadhog, robot, roughneck, roundheel, roustabout, rover, rowdy, rube, ruffian, rummy, rumormonger, runabout, runagate

sad sack, sap, sawney, scapegoat, scaramouch, scaredy-cat, scavenger, scofflaw, scrapper, screwball, scrooge, scrounger, scut, seadog, second banana, second fiddle, sheep, shit, shithead, shlemiel, shlep, shlimazel, shlub, shlump, shmegege, shmo, shmuck, shmutz, shnook, showboat, show-off, shrink, shrinking violet, silly ass, sissy, sitting duck, skinflint, skunk, slacker, slasher, slave, slave driver, slowpoke, slug, slugabed, sluggard, slut, sly boots, smart aleck, smarty-pants, smellfungus, snail, snip, snitch, sniveler, snob, snoop, so-and-so, SOB, sob sister, social climber, sod, sodbuster, soft touch, softy, son of a bitch, sop, sorehead, sot, sourball, sourpuss, souse, speedfreak, spendthrift, spider, spoilsport, sprat, spud, spy, square, squealer, squirt, stick, stick-in-the-mud, stickler, stiff, stinkard, stinker, stockjobber, stooge, straight arrow, stranger, stray, street arab, street person, strutter, stuffed shirt, succubus, sucker, swab, swagman, swellhead, swine, sycophant

tagalong, taskmaster, tattletale, tease, tenderfoot, termagant, terror, tightwad, tinhorn, tinker, toad, toady, tomboy, tomfool, tool, toper, tosspot, touch, toughie, tourist, tout, townie, tramp, tramper, transient, trickster, tripe, troublemaker, truant, tumbleweed, turd, turkey, twerp, twit, Typhoid Mary, tyro

ulcer, underling, unperson, upstart

vagabond, vagrant, vandal, varlet, vassal, Venusian, vulture

wacko, waffler, wag, wage slave, Walter Mitty, wangler, wanker, war-horse, washout, weakling, weenie, weirdo, wench, wet blanket, wethead, wheedler, wheeler-dealer, whiffler, whippersnapper, whipping boy, white trash, wildcatter, wild man, wimp, windbag, wino, wiseacre, wise guy, wise-ass, wisenheimer, witch, wolf, workaholic, worm, worrywart, wowser, wreck, wretch, wuss

Xanthippe

yahoo, yardbird, yenta, yes-man, yobbo

zany, zealot, zero, zombie, zonker

Morality or Character

adulterer, Ananias, Antichrist, archfiend, arriviste

Babbitt, backbiter, backstabber, bamboozler, bandit, betrayer, bigamist, bigot, bilker, blackguard, blank, bloodsucker, Bluebeard, bogeyman, bounder, brigand, brown-noser, buccaneer, bum, burglar, butcher

cad, caitiff, cancer, cannibal, cardsharp, car line, cateran, charlatan, cheat, chintz, chiseler, churl, commie, comsymp, con artist, con man, counterfeiter, coward, creep, crook, crud, culprit

dastard, deadbeat, debauchee, deceiver, delator, demagogue, demon, desperado, despot, devil, dictator, dissembler, dodger, dog, double-crosser, double-dealer, dregs, dreck, dross

failure, faitour, faker, fascist, felon, fibber, fiend, finagler, fink, flimflam man, fly-by-night, forger, fraud, freeloader

ganef, goldbrick, gold digger, good-for-nothing, gouger, grafter

heel, heretic, highwayman, hilding, hoaxer, hoodlum, hooligan, huckster, humbug, hypocrite

idolator, impostor, Indian giver, indulger, infidel, informer, ingrate, insurgent, interloper, intruder

jackal, jailbird, jellyfish, JD, judas, juvenile delinquent

kaffir, killer, kleptomaniac, knave

leech, liar, libertine, lily-liver, louse, lout, lowlife

mafioso, malingerer, mammon, miscreant, miser, monster, monstrosity, mountebank

ne'er-do-well, no-account, no-goodnik
ogre, operator, opportunist, outlaw
pagan, pariah, parasite, Peeping Tom, perjurer, pervert, philanderer, philistine, phony, picaro, pickpocket, pimp, pinko, piranha, pirate, pissant, plagiarist, plague, poacher, poltroon, ponce, prevaricator, profligate, psychopath, puke, pusher
uack, quisling, quitter
acketeer, rake, rapist, rat, ratfink, recreant, recusant, red, reprobate, ringleader, robber, robber baron, rodent, rogue, rotter, roué, rustler
aboteur, sadist, saltimbanco, savage, scab, scalawag, scandalmonger, scoundrel, scourge, scum, scumbag, scumsucker, scuzz, scuzzball, serpent, sham, shark, sharp, shill, shirker, Shylock, shyster, sickie, sicko, Simon Legree, sinner, slanderer, slave driver, sleaze, sleazebag, sleazeball, slime, slimebag, slimeball, slime bucket, slumlord, slyboots, snake, snake in the grass, sneak, snipe, snitch, snollygoster, sociopath, sponge, stoolie, stool pigeon, swindler, swine
hief, thug, traitor, transgressor, trash, trickster, troublemaker, turncoat, twotimer, tyrant
surer, usurper
ampire, vermin, vicemonger, villain, viper, ulture
armonger, waster, wastrel, weasel, whoreson, witch, worm, wrongdoer
ellowbelly

exuality or Gender

mazon
wd, bearded clam, bitch, brazen hussy, ugger, bull dyke, butch
strato, cat, chicken, chicken hawk, chippy, loset queen, cock, cocksucker, concubine, oquette, courtesan, cow, cream puff, cuckld, cunt, cyprian
viate, dick, diesel dyke, dildo, dingleberry, ink, dong, douche bag, drag queen, dyke
, faggot, fag hag, fairy, fetishist, flit, oozy, fox, fruit, fruitcake, fucker
golo, gunsel
, harlot, harpy, harridan, heifer, hen, omo, hooker, hussy
le, john
h, lecher, les, lesbo, libertine, lily, Little ord Fauntleroy
ama's boy, masher, meat, minx, mo, mothfucker
nce, nancy, nympho
maid
nsy, pantywaist, pecker, pederast, edophile, Peeping Tom, pervert, philanerer, piece, pimp, playboy, playgirl, ponce, of, poofter, prick, prig, procurer, prong, ostitute, prude, punk, pussy, puta

queen, queer, quim
rosy piglet, rut hostess
satyr, shmuck, shrew, sissy, slattern, slit, slut, snatch, sodomist, spinster, stag, streetwalker, stripper, strumpet, stud, swinger, swish, switch hitter
tail, tart, tomboy, tramp, transvestite, trick, trollop, twat
vamp, virago, vixen, voyeur
wanker, wanton, weenie, wench, whore, wiener, wienie, wolf, woman of the street

Ethnic Origin, Race, or Religion

abo, alien, arkie, Aunt Jemima, Auslander
babu, blackie, bohunk, Brit, buck, burrhead
Charlie Chan, Chinaman, Chink, cockney, coolie, coon, cracker
dago, darky, dink
foreigner, Frenchy, frog
ginzo, gook, goomba, goy, gringo, Guinea
half-breed, Hebe, heinie, high yeller, honky, howley, hun, hymie
immigrant, Injun
Jap, JAP, Jew boy, jig, jigaboo, jungle bunny
kike, kraut
limey
Mick, moke, Mr. Charlie
nigger, niggra, Nip
ofay, okie
pachuco, paddy, paleface, picaroon, Polack
redskin
Russki
sheeny, shegatz, shikse, slant, slant-eye, slope, spade, spic, squaw
Ubangi, Uncle Tom
WASP, wetback, whitey, wog, wop
yid
Zulu

TERMS OF ENDEARMENT AND RESPECT

Pet Names
Friendly or Familiar Address
Titles and Honorifics
Affectionate Reference
Respectful or Admiring Reference

Pet Names

acushla, angel, angel baby
babe, baby, baby doll, baby face, beau, booboo, bubaloo, bubbles, bubehleh, buttercup
calf, candy, cara mia, cherry, chickabiddy, chickadee, cookie, corazon, cupcake, cutie, cutie pie

daddy, daisy, darling, dear, dearest, dear heart, dearie, dimples, doll, dollface, dove, dreamboat, duck, duckie, duckling, ducks, dumpling
goose
hon, honey, honeybunch, honey child
kitten
lamb, lambchop, lambkin, liebschen, loosker, love, lover, luv
mi amore, monkey, monkey face, muffin, my dear, my love, my pet, my sweet
noodles
pet, pigeon, pooch, pooh, poppet, precious, puddin' head, pumpkin, punkin, puss, pussy willow
snooks, snookums, sugar, sugarpie, sugarpie honeybunch, sweetheart, sweetie, sweetie pie, sweetkins, sweetness, sweet patootie, sweet pea, sweet potato, sweets, sweet thing, sweetums
tomato, toots, tootsie, turtledove
valentine

Friendly or Familiar Address

ace, amigo, auntie
big fella
big guy, binky, boyo, brat, bro, brother, bub, bubba, bud, buddy
cap, captain, champ, chap, chief, chuck, chum, cock, cousin, cove, coz, curly
dad, daddy, deadeye, doc, dude
fella, friend
gaffer, gal, gill, girl, girlie, girlie-girl, goofus, gov, governor, gramma, grammy, grampa, gramps, granny, guy
hombre, home, homeboy, homes, hotshot
jack
kid, kiddo
lad, laddie, lady, lass, lassie, little one
ma, ma'am, mac, maestro, mama, master, mate, mio, missy, mom, momileh, mommy, monkey, moose, muchacho, munchkin, my main man, my man
neighbor, nuncle
old bean, old boy, old chap, old fellow, old man, old scout, old thing, old timer, old top padre
pa, pal, pal o' mine, papa, pard, pardner, peewee, pooh-bah, pop, poppa, pops
rascal
sarge, shrimp, sis, sister, scout, skip, skipper, skippy, sleepyhead, slick, slim, slugger, son, sonny, sonny boy, soul brother, speedy, sport, sprout, squirt, stretch
tot
unc, uncle
whippersnapper, whiz, whizzer
youngster

Titles and Honorifics

babu, Brother, bwana
Dame, dean, diva, Dom, don, dona
Eminence, Esquire, Excellency
Father, Frau
grace
Herr, Highness, Holiness, Holy Father, Holy Mother, Honor, Honorable
Imperial Highness, Imperial Majesty
lady, ladyship, liege, lieutenant, lord, lordship
ma'am, madam, madame, mademoiselle, maharishi, majesty, massa, master, memsahib, milady, miss, mister, mistress, monsieur, monsignor, most honorable, most reverend, Mother, Mr., Mrs., Ms., my lady, my liege, my lord
officer
padre
rabbi, reverence, reverend, right honorable, right reverend, rinpoche, Royal Highness, Royal Majesty
sahib, sergeant, seìor, seìora, seìorita, Serene Highness, Serene Majesty, signora, signore, signorina, sir, sire, sirrah, Sister, sister, sri, swami
taipan
worship
yogi, Your Eminence, Your Excellency, Your Grace, Your Highness, Your Holiness, Your Honor, Your Majesty, Your Reverence, Your Worship

Affectionate Reference

alter ego, apple of my eye
beauty, belle, beloved, best friend, best girl, blood brother, boy, boyfriend, brat, brother
calf, candy, card, Casanova, chap, character, charmer, cherub, chick, chit, choice, chum, cohort, colleen, colt, companion, comrade, confidant, confrere, cowpoke, crackerjack, crème de la crème, critter, crony, cub, Cub Scout
damsel, darb, diamond in the rough, dilly, dish, Don Juan, doozer, dream, dreamboa[t], dulcinea, dynamo
eager beaver, eagle, elf, enchantress, enchi[...] lada
familiar, fatso, favorite, fellow, filly, fireball, firecracker, flash, fox
gal, gamine, geezer, gem, girl, girlfriend, g[o-]getter, goose, green thumb, guy
handyman, heartthrob, hepcat, highroller, hombre, honcho, hotshot, humdinger, hunk
idol, imp, inamorata, ingenue
jewel, jim-dandy, junior
kingpin
lad, lady love, lamb, lass, lefty, light, live wire, looker, love, lovebird, lucky devil, lucky stiff, lulu
main squeeze, mensch, minikin, minx, monkey, moose, moppet

eighbor, number one, numero uno, ıymph
d duffer, old geezer, old lady, old man
artner, peach, pearl, pigeon, pip, pippin, ixie, playmate, plum, pollyanna, pooch, ooh-bah, posy, powerhouse, prince, protégé, puck, pud, pup, puppy
conteur, rascal, Romeo, rose
amp, sensation, sharpy, showman, sideick, slim Jim, smoothie, sophisticate, soul rother, spring chicken, sprite, spud, teady, sugar daddy, swan, sylph
ammate, top banana, top dog, tops, tot, reasure, trouper, trump
chin, vamp, Venus
ater nymph, whippersnapper, whiz, hizbang, whiz kid, whizzer, wiz, wonder, rangler
ınkee Doodle dandy, youngster, yours truly

spectful or Admiring Reference

e, adept, aficionado, agha, all-American, l-around girl, all-around guy, all-star, tar boy, Atlas, avatar
hadur, ball of fire, bellwether, big name, g timer, blockbuster, blood brother, blue ood, blue ribbon, boy wonder, Brahman, rownie, buck
ptain, celeb, chief, classic, colleague, lonel, connoisseur, crackerjack
adeye, diva, doyen, dynamo
le scout, elder, elder statesman, expert
hion plate
ius, gentleman, gentlewoman, gourmet, vernor, grand dame, gray beard, guru
dyman, Hercules, hero, heroine, homeming queen, honcho, humanitarian
presario, individual, insider, intellectual, n man
k-of-all-trades, jack rabbit, journeyman, dge
per, king, knockout
, laureate, leader, leading lady, leading ın, leatherneck, liege, lifesaver, lion, minary
donna, maestro, maiden, man about vn, man of God, man of letters, martyr, rvel, master, mastermind, matinée idol, tron, maven, maverick, mentor, millione, muse
ural, nonesuch
hand
rone, paladin, paragon, past master, triot, patron, phenom, phrasemaker, k, pilot, pioneer, poet laureate, pres, sident, pro, prodigy, pundit
en
avis, reformer, Robin Goodfellow, bin Hood, role model
, saint, samaritan, Samson, savant, savseer, select, self-starter, senator, sensei, rpshooter, sleuth, smart cookie, socialite, soldier, solon, somebody, sovereign, spark plug, specimen, spitfire, sponsor, standard bearer, star, statesman, strongman, stud, superman, superstar, superwoman, supremo, swami, swashbuckler
teacher, thoroughbred, titan, torchbearer, trailblazer, trendsetter, troubleshooter, tutor, tycoon
up-and-comer
veteran, VIP, virgin, virtuoso, visionary, volunteer
warrior, watchdog, winner, wise man, wit, wizard, wonder, wonder-worker, workhorse, worldbeater, worthy, wunderkind
yeoman, yogi
zaddik

NONSENSE, CONFUSION, AND TROUBLE

Foolishness, Bunkum, and Trifles
Drivel and Silly Talk
Fusses and Troubles
Confusion
Nonsense Words and Cutesies

Foolishness, Bunkum, and Trifles

airy-fairy
bagatelle, balderdash, ballyhoo, baloney, bauble, bilge, blah, blaha, blatherskite, bluff, blunder, bluster, bogus, bollocks, bosh, braggadocio, bravado, brummagem, buffoonery, bull, bullshit, bunkum, bunk, burlesque
caacaa, cheek, claptrap, cock, cockalorum, cockamamie, codswallop, corn, cow pat, crambo, crap, crock, crud, curliewurly
diddlyshit, diddly-squat, doodad, doodle, doo-doo, doohickey, dreck, dregs, drool, dung
fancy, fanfaronade, farce, fiddlededee, fiddle-faddle, fiddlesticks, fig, flapdoodle, flimflam, flotsam, flubdub, fluff, flumadiddle, flummery, flummox, folderol, foofaraw, foolishness, footle, foozle, fribble, frills, frippery, froth, fudge
gadget, gammon, gas, gewgaw, gibberish, gimcrack, glob, goop, guff, gunk
hambone, hanky-panky, hem and haw, hogwash, hokum, hooey, hoot, horseshit, hot air, humbug, humdinger, humdrum
idiocy, inanity
jabberwocky, jazz, jetsam, jiggery-pokery, jingle, jive, joke, jot, junk
kitsch, kludge, knavery
lampoonery, lip
malarkey, meshuge, mickey mouse, mishe-

gaas, mockery, monkeyshine, muck, mush
nonsense, non sequitur
oddment
pap, piddle, poop, poppycock, puffery, pulp, put-on
quackery
raffle, raillery, rattletrap, razzmatazz, refuse, ribbing, rigmarole, rodomontade, roguery, rot, rubbish, Rube Goldberg
sap, sass, scat, scum, scuttlebutt, send-up, sham, shit, shlock, shtick, skullduggery, slag heap, slapdash, slobber, slop, slurry, slush, sob story, spoof, sport, stuff, swagger, swill
taradiddle, tittle, tomfoolery, tommyrot, tongue-in-cheek, tosh, trangam, trash, trickery, trifle, trinket, tripe, trivia, trumpery
vapors
waggery, wank, waste, whatnot, whigmaleerie, whim, whimsy, white elephant, whoopla, whopper, widget, wind, wisecrack
yuck

Drivel and Silly Talk

babble, badinage, bibble-babble, blabber, blather, blatter, blither
chatter, chitchat, chitter, chitter-chatter, claptrap, cliché
ditty, doggerel, drivel
footle, fribble, fustian
gab, gabble, gibber, gibber-gabber, gibberish, gibble-gabble, gobbledegook, gossip
jabber, japery
logorrhea
natter, nitpicking
palaver, persiflage, piffle, pleasantries, prattle, prittle-prattle
scribblings, silliness, small talk, squiggles, stultiloquence
tittle-tattle, twaddle, twiddle-twaddle, twitter
verbiage
yabber, yak, yakety-yak, yikety-yak

Fusses and Troubles

ado
bear, bickering, billingsgate, blooey, bobbery, boo-boo, boondoggle, bother, brannigan, brawl, broil, brouhaha, bug, bugaboo, bugbear, bummer
callithump, cattawumpus, collywobbles, commotion, conniption, crash
delirium, derring-do, disturbance, dither, donnybrook, doozie
feud, fit, fix, flap, flurry, fluster, foible, foul-up, fracas, fray, free-for-all, frenzy, furor, fuss
glitch
haggle, hash, hassle, hell, helter-skelter, high jinks, hoopla, hubble-bubble, hubbub, hullabaloo, hysteria
imbroglio
jam, jumble
katzenjammer, kibitzing, kink
lather, loggerheads, logjam
madhouse, maelstrom, megillah, melee, mess, mishmash, mix-up, moil, muss
no-no
peeve, pickle, pother, pratfall
quarrel
racket, rage, raise Cain, raise hell, rat's nes rattrap, rhubarb, roughhouse, row, rowdy dow, ruckus, ruffle, rumble, rumpus
scramble, scrap, scrape, screwup, seizure, set-to, shambles, shenanigan, shindig, shindy, short circuit, slam-bang, snafu, snarl, snit, spasm, spat, squabble, stew, stink
tamasha, tiff, tizzy, to-do, trouble, tsimme tsores, tumult, tussle, twitter
unrest, uproar
vendetta
whoop-de-do, whoopee, whoopla, wingding, wormwood, wrangle, wreckag

Confusion

absurdity, addlement, agitation, anarchy, ataxia
bafflement, bewilderment, blooper, bollix boner, boo-boo, botch, bungle
cacophony, catawumpus, chaos, churn, clinker, cloud, cloudland, clutter, confusi
daze, disorder
embranglement, entropy
farblondjet, farmisht, farrago, fartumlt, flutter, fog, folly, fret
gaffe, gallimaufry, goof
haze, higgledy-piggledy, hocus-pocus, hodgepodge, hokey-pokey, hotchpotch
jumble, jungle
ludicrousness
maze, medley, mishmash, mist, mix-up, motley, muddle, mumbo jumbo
olio, olla podrida
pandemonium, pastiche, patchwork
ridiculousness, rummage
scattershot, shambles, slaphappy, swirl, switcheroo
tintamarre, tohubohu, topsy-turvy, Tweedledum and Tweedledee
unset
voodoo, vortex
waffling, whirligig, whirlpool, whirlwinc

Nonsense Words and Cutesies

artsy-craftsy
bleep
caboodle, chichi, comfy, coo, cuckoo, cut
dingus, doodad, doodle, doohickey
gaga, gizmo, gussy up
harum-scarum, heebie-jeebies, ho-hum hoity-toity, hugger-mugger, hunky-dor

hurly-burly, hurry-scurry
itsy-bitsy, itty-bitty
kit'n'caboodle, knickknack
lardy-dardy
mollycoddle
namby-pamby, newfangled, niminy-piminy
okey-dokey, oodles
palsy-walsy, peekaboo, pell-mell, p's and q's
raggle-taggle, razzle-dazzle, rinky-dink
screaming-meemies, shilly-shally, skimble-scamble
teensy, teensy-weensy, thingamabob, thingamajig, thingummy, tidbit, tutti-frutti
whatchamacallit, whatsis, whim-wham, whoosis, willies, willy-nilly, wishy-washy

Chapter Twenty-One

Foreign Expressions

LATIN WORDS AND PHRASES

ab initio from the beginning
ab intra from within, from inside
ab origine from the origin or source
ab urbe condita lit. from the foundation of the city; Roman dating system; AUC
ad astra per aspera to the stars through difficulties
ad extremum to the extreme; at last
ad hoc lit. for this; for this purpose
ad hominem lit. to the man; argument directed at man's character, not his position
ad infinitum to infinity; endlessly
ad interim temporarily
ad libitum at one's pleasure, without restriction; ad lib.
ad nauseam to the point of nausea; repeatedly; endlessly
ad patres lit. to his fathers; deceased
adsum I am here, used in response to a roll call
ad valorem according to value, esp. tax thus imposed
ad verbum lit. to the word; worded exactly as the original
Agnus Dei lamb of God, i.e., Christ
alma mater lit. nourishing mother; one's academic institution
alter ego other self; best friend
alumna female graduate of academic institution
alumnus male graduate of academic institution
amor vincit omnia love conquers all
anno Domini in the year of the Lord
annuit coeptis God favored our undertaking
annus mirabilis notable, remarkable year or event
ante bellum before the war
ante meridiem a.m.; before midday
a posteriori from what comes after; cause deduced from effect
a priori from what comes before; deduced from what is known
ars gratia artis art for art's sake
ars longa, vita brevis art is long, life is short
ave be well; farewell
bona fide in good faith
carpe diem seize the day
caveat emptor let the buyer beware
caveat lector let the reader beware
cave canem beware of the dog
ceteris paribus other things being equal
circa ca; around or about, esp. of time
cogito, ergo sum I think, therefore I am
compos mentis of sound mind
con against, opposite of pro
cornucopia horn of plenty
corpus delicti body of the crime; evidence of crime
cui bono to whose advantage?; legal principle that responsibility for act lies with one gaining by it
cum with
cum grano salis with a grain of salt
cum laude with praise or honors
curriculum vitae lit. course of life; resumé
de facto from fact; in reality
Dei gratia by the grace of God
de jure by right
delirium tremens dt's; advanced, trembling alcoholic delirium
Deo volente God willing
de profundis from depths of despair
desideratum something much wanted or needed
deus ex machina lit. god from a machine; divine intervention
Dominus vobiscum the Lord be with you
dramatis personae cast of a drama
ecce homo lit. behold the man; Christ crowned with thorns
ecce signum lit. behold the sign; behold the proof
editio princeps first edition
emerita female who has served with honor
emeritus one who has served with honor
eo nomine by or under that name
e pluribus unum one out of many, inscribed on U.S. coins
ergo therefore
errare humanum est to err is human
erratum error
et alia and others
et cetera etc.; and the rest; and so on
et sequens and the following
et tu, Brute lit. and you, Brutus; even you are guilty of betrayal
ex cathedra lit. from the chair; with authority
excelsior higher; ever upward
exeunt they go out, esp. leave stage
exit he or she goes out, esp. leaves stage
ex libris from the books or library of
ex nihilo nihil fit from nothing comes nothing
ex officio by virtue of office
ex parte lit. from one side, used esp. of partisan legal communications
ex post facto derived from what was done after
ex tempore lit. out of time; spontaneously, without preparation
factotum person, esp. servant, who does various chores
fiat lux let there be light
gaudeamus igitur therefore let us rejoice
habeas corpus lit. you may have the body; esp. a writ used by defense lawyer to require formal pressing of charges against accused
hic jacet here lies, used on tombstones
homo sapiens lit. rational man; species of modern human beings
homunculus miniature man, thought to reside within humans or in spermatozoon by 16th-century scientists
horribile dictu horrible to relate
humanum est errare to err is human
ibidem ibid.; in the same place, used in bibliographies and footnotes
idem the same; something previously mentioned

id est i.e.; that is
ignoramus lit. we ignore; extremely ignorant person, know-nothing
illuminati persons possessing enlightenment
imprimatur lit. let it be printed; license to print; sanction or approval in general
in absentia in one's absence
incunabula lit. swaddling clothes; origin or earliest stages, esp. of printed books
in excelsis in the highest degree
in extremis at the moment of death
in flagrante delicto while the crime or act is occurring
infra dignitatem beneath one's dignity
in loco citato in loc. cit.; in the place cited, used in bibliographies and footnotes
in loco parentis in place of the parent
in medias res in the middle of things
in memoriam in memory of
in omnia paratus prepared for all things
in re in the matter of; regarding
in situ in place; in its natural or original position
in statu quo in the former or current state
inter alia among other things
inter nos between ourselves
inter se among themselves
in toto in all; entirely
in utero in the womb
in vino veritas in wine lies the truth
in vitro in glass, esp. a test tube
in vivo in that which is living
ipse dixit lit. he himself said it; statement made but not proved
ipso facto by or based on the fact itself
jacta alea est the die is cast
lapsus linguae slip of the tongue
lex talionis law of corresponding retaliation, as an eye for an eye
literati highly educated, literate persons
locus place
lusus naturae freak of nature
magna cum laude with great praise or honors
magnum opus one's great work
mala fide in bad faith
mandamus lit. we demand; writ commanding specific act or duty
margaritas ante porcos pearls before swine
materfamilias female head of household
mea culpa my fault
memento mori lit. remember you must die; reminder of death
mens rea lit. guilty mind; criminal intent
meum et tuum mine and thine
mirabile dictu wonderful to relate
mirabile visu wonderful to behold
mittimus lit. we send; warrant of commitment to prison
modus operandi method of operating
modus vivendi way of living
mons veneris lit. mound of Venus; round protuberance beneath female pubic hair
mutatis mutandis after changing what had to be changed
ne plus ultra lit. not more beyond; highest level of perfection
nolens volens whether unwilling or willing
noli me tangere touch me not
nolo contendere lit. I do not wish to contend; legal plea of no contest to charges
non compos mentis not of sound mind
non possumus lit. we cannot; statement of inability to do something
non sequitur it does not follow
nota bene note well; pay attention
obiter dictum passing remark without legal weight
omnia vincit amor love conquers all
opere citato op. cit.; in the work cited, used in bibliographies and footnotes
opus work, esp. musical composition
passim lit. here and there; repeated in many places
paterfamilias male head of household
paternoster our father
pax peace
pax vobiscum peace be with you
per annum per year; annually
per capita lit. per head; per person
per diem daily
per se in itself; inherently
persona non grata unwelcome person
post meridiem p.m.; after midday
post mortem after death, esp. an examination
postscriptum lit. written after; used to tag addition to a letter
prima facie at first view
primus inter pares first among equals
pro in favor of
pro bono publico for the public benefit
pro et contra for and against
pro forma lit. for form; done perfunctorily, as a formality
pro patria for one's country
pro rata proportionately according to an exact formula
pro tempore for the time being; temporarily
qua lit. who; in the capacity of; as
quid nunc what now?
quid pro quo something given for something; an exchange
quod erat demonstrandum Q.E.D.; which was to be demonstrated
quod erat faciendum which was to be done
quodlibet lit. whom it pleases; philosophical point for disputation
quod vide q.v.; which see, referring to something
quorum lit. of whom; minimum attendance at assembly or meeting
quo vadis where are you going?
rara avis lit. rare bird; anything unusual or rare
re regarding, short for in re
reductio ad absurdum leading logically to an absurd conclusion
redux brought back
regina queen
requiescat in pace rest in peace

res thing; matter; fact
res ipsa loquitur the thing speaks for itself
res publica popular affairs; commonwealth
rex king
rigor mortis stiffness of death
sanctum sanctorum lit. holy of holies; sacred place
saturnalia revelry or uproarious festivities
semper fidelis always faithful
sequitur it follows
sic thus, esp. to note a textual mistake
sic passim thus throughout, used of word or idea found throughout text
sic semper tyrannis thus always to tyrants
sic transit gloria mundi so passes the glory of the world
sine die indefinitely, with no set date in the future
sine qua non lit. not without which; indispensable thing or condition
status quo conditions as they are now
stet lit. it stands; let the original stand, used in proofreading
stupor mundi wonder of the world
subito immediately; suddenly, esp. as a musical direction
sub rosa lit. under the rose; in secret, covertly
sui generis of its own kind; one of a kind
summa cum laude with the highest praise or honors
summum bonum the highest or chief good
tabula rasa clean slate
tempus fugit time flies
terra firma solid ground; dry land
terra incognita unknown ground, uncharted territory
ultra vires exceeding legal authority
ut infra as below
ut supra as above
uxor wife
vade mecum lit. go with me; pocketbook carried for ready reference
veni, vidi, vici I came, I saw, I conquered
verbatim word for word
verbum sap enough said, inferring something left unsaid
versus lit. toward opposite; against or in competition with
via media middle way
vice versa conversely; the opposite way
vide see, used to direct or refer a reader elsewhere
videlicet lit. it is permitted to see; namely
viva voce lit. with the living voice; by word of mouth
vox populi lit. the voice of the people; popular opinion
vox populi, vox Dei the voice of the people is the voice of God

FOREIGN WORDS AND PHRASES

French
Other Romance Languages
German, Greek, and Other Languages

French

à bas down with
à bientôt see you soon
adieu good-bye, farewell
affaire d'amour love affair
agent provocateur outside agitator who incites others to criminal acts or riot
aide de camp senior military officer or confidential adviser
à la carte lit. on the card; priced separately on the menu
à la mode in the fashion
amour love
ancien régime the old or former regime
à propos relative or pertaining to; fitting; to the purpose
au contraire on the contrary
au courant up to date
au fait well-versed, expert
au naturel in its natural state, esp. nude
au revoir good-bye, until we meet again
avant-garde the vanguard, esp. in the arts
à votre santé to your health
beau geste fine gesture, often for effect
beau idéal model or conception of excellence
beau monde fashionable society
beaux arts fine arts
belles lettres serious literature
bête noire pet peeve
billet-doux love note
bon appétit good appetite; enjoy your meal
bonhomie good nature
bonjour hello, good day
bon marché inexpensive
bon mot witty turn of phrase
bonne chance good luck
bon vivant person who lives well and enjoys socializing
bon voyage have a good journey
bric-à-brac trinkets, baubles
cachet sign or expression of approval; superior status
canaille common people, rabble
canard insult or hoax
ça ne fait rien no matter, it is not important
carte blanche unrestricted authority or access
cause célèbre notorious incident
c'est la guerre that's the way of war, used to express resignation
c'est la vie that's life
chacun à son goût each to his own taste
chef-d'oeuvre masterpiece

chez la famille at home with one's family
chez moi at my home
comme ci, comme ça so-so, neither one way nor the other
comme il faut proper, appropriate
contretemps unfortunate mishap or inconvenience
coup d'état usu. violent overthrow of government
coup de grâce final blow
crème de la crème very best or top level, usu. used of people
cul de sac dead end
danse macabre dance of death
déclassé reduced to or having low status
décolletage low-cut neckline on dress
déjà vu lit. already seen; illusory sense of having previously experienced something
demimonde group whose activities are ethically or legally questionable, esp. prostitutes
dénouement resolution or outcome, esp. of story
de rigueur strictly according to the rules
dernier cri the last word
déshabillé state of being poorly or carelessly dressed
désolé heartbroken, disconsolate
double entendre word or expression having two meanings in context
éclat flair, dash
élan vital creative force
embarras de richesses embarrassment of riches
éminence grise person wielding power in the background
en famille just among the family
enfant terrible irresponsible person, esp. incorrigible child
en garde on guard
en masse as a group
en passant in passing
entr'acte intermission
entrée main course of meal
entre nous just between us
esprit de corps spirit of and loyalty to one's group
fait accompli accomplished fact
faute de mieux for lack of something better
faux pas social error
femme fatale dangerous, enticing woman
fin de siècle end of the century, usu. decadent
gaucherie vulgarity, awkwardness
grande dame aristocratic elderly lady
habitué one who frequents some establishment
haute couture high fashion
haute cuisine elegant, often rich food
hauteur snobbish, aloof manner
haut monde high society
hors d'oeuvre appetizer
idée fixe obsession
je ne sais quoi lit. I do not know what; that indescribable something
joie de vivre exuberant high spirits
laissez faire policy of government in which affairs are allowed to run their own course
lèse majesté attack on ruler or established authority
l'état c'est moi I am the state
longeur tedious, dreary passages of language
ma chère my dear, said of females
madame married woman
mademoiselle unmarried woman
maison house
maître d'hôtel chief waiter
manqué having failed
Mardi Gras lit. fat Tuesday; pre-Lenten festival on Shrove Tuesday
mélange mixture
ménage à trois three-way relationship, usu. sexual
merci thank you
merci beaucoup thank you very much
métier vocation or calling
mon cher my dear, said of males
monsieur mister, sir
mot juste word that conveys precise meaning
n'est-ce pas? isn't it so? don't you agree?
noblesse oblige obligations of noble birth
nom de guerre lit. war name; pseudonym, stage name
nom de plume pen name
nouveau riche person who is newly rich
objet d'art work of art
objet trouvé found object, usu. of artistic value
papier-mâché paper and glue mixture used to form sculptures
par example for example
par excellence superior, preeminent
parti pris point of view determined in advance; prejudice
parvenu newcomer, upstart
passé out of date, no longer in fashion
petit bourgeois person who belongs to lower middle class, usu. made up of shopkeepers and clerks
pièce de résistance principal or showpiece object or event
pied-à-terre temporary or part-time residence
plat du jour featured dish of the day
plus ça change, plus c'est la même chose the more things change, the more they remain the same
potpourri medley, usu. of scented herbs and spices
prix fixe set price
protégé person under's one care or tutelage
provocateur one who challenges or agitates others
raconteur storyteller
raison d'être reason for being
recherché esoteric, rare; mannered, affected
répondez s'il vous plaît please respond
risqué indelicate or suggestive
roman à clef novel depicting historical figures under fictional names
sacré bleu exclamation meaning good God
sang-froid composure, self-possession
sans souci without concern or worry
savoir-faire knowledge of what to do or say, esp. in social situation
s'il vous plaît please
soi-disant so-called

son et lumière sound and light show
succès d'estime critical success, esp. for work of art
table d'hôte set meal served at fixed time and place
tant mieux so much the better
tant pis so much the worse
tête-à-tête intimate, private conversation
touché lit. touched; signifying strike in fencing or comment that is on the mark
tour de force display of power, skill, or virtuosity
tout de suite immediately
tout le monde everyone
trompe l'oeil fooling the eye, esp. illusion of perspective in painting
vis-à-vis regarding, relating to
voilà there it is, look at that, it is so
volte-face reversal, turnabout

Other Romance Languages

a cappella *Italian.* sung without instrumental accompaniment
adios *Spanish.* good-bye
aficionado *Spanish.* fan, enthusiast
al dente *Italian.* lit. to the tooth; firm to the bite, said esp. of food
alfresco *Italian.* in the open air
amigo *Spanish.* friend
arrivederci *Italian.* good-bye, until we meet again
auto-da-fé *Portuguese.* lit. act of faith; execution of condemned heretics after public declaration of judgment
bambino *Italian.* baby, child
basta *Italian.* enough! stop it!
bodega *Spanish.* wineshop; small market
buenas dias *Spanish.* hello, good day
caballero *Spanish.* horseman, gentleman, cavalier
campesino *Spanish.* farmer, peasant
cantina *Spanish.* bar, café
caramba *Spanish.* exclamation of amazement, anger, or dismay
che sarà sarà *Italian.* what will be, will be
ciao *Italian.* good-bye, see you later
cognoscenti *Italian.* those in the know, esp. intellectuals
compaìero *Spanish.* male companion or partner
con mucho gusto *Spanish.* with great pleasure
conquistador *Spanish.* conqueror
desperado *Spanish.* bold, reckless bandit or outlaw
diva *Italian.* exalted female singer
dolce far niente *Italian.* sweet inactivity
dolce vita *Italian.* the good life
gaucho *Spanish.* cowboy, mounted herdsman
gracias *Spanish.* thank you
hacienda *Spanish.* ranch
hombre *Spanish.* man, fellow
inamorata *Italian.* female sweetheart or lover
incognito *Italian.* anonymously or in disguise
incommunicado *Spanish.* isolated from any contact with others
junta *Spanish.* usu. military council serving as government
machismo *Spanish.* strong sense of masculinity and virility
maestro *Italian.* master, esp. of music
magnifico *Italian.* great man
maìana *Spanish.* tomorrow
mas o menos *Spanish.* more or less
mucho *Spanish.* much
olé *Spanish.* shout of approval or encouragement
padre *Spanish.* father, esp. clergyman
peccadillo *Spanish.* minor offense, venial sin
pentimento *Italian.* appearance of earlier stages or images, esp. in painting
per favore *Italian.* please
por favor *Spanish.* please
posada *Spanish.* inn
prego *Italian.* please
presto *Italian.* quickly, right away
prima donna *Italian.* principal female, leading lady
pronto *Spanish.* quickly, right away
que pasa? *Spanish.* what's happening?
que será será *Spanish.* whatever will be will be
quién sabe? *Spanish.* who knows?
salud *Spanish.* to your health
selor *Spanish.* sir, mister
seìora *Spanish.* married woman
seìorita *Spanish.* unmarried woman
siesta *Spanish.* afternoon nap or rest
sotto voce *Italian.* softly, under one's voice
toro *Spanish.* bull
vamos *Spanish.* let's go
vaya con Dios *Spanish.* God be with you
vertù *Italian.* love of arts and fine things
virtuoso *Italian.* person skilled in one field, esp. a performer
viva *Spanish.* exclamation of approval

German, Greek, and Other Languages

acedia *Greek.* listlessness, sloth
Achtung *German.* attention
agape *Greek.* non-erotic love
ahimsa *Hindi.* doctrine of nonviolence
aloha *Hawaiian.* hello or good-bye
Angst *German.* anxiety
anomie *Greek.* lawlessness and loss of purpose leading to despair
apocrypha *Greek.* secret, hidden things, esp. in texts
ataxia *Greek.* lack of control or order
auf Wiedersehen *German.* good-bye, until we meet again
babushka *Russian.* grandmother, old woman; head scarf
banzai *Japanese.* lit. 10,000 years; cry of victory or salute
Blitzkrieg *German.* sudden, violent attack
bwana *Swahili.* sir, master, father
catharsis *Greek.* cleansing or purification, esp. from guilt through drama or art
charisma *Greek.* capacity to inspire and lead others
cosmos *Greek.* orderly universe
danke schön *German.* thank you very much
ding hao *Chinese.* very good, excellent

Doppelgänger *German.* phantom double
do svidaniya *Russian.* good-bye, until we meet again
Dummkopf *German.* dummy, blockhead
ersatz *German.* fake, imitation
eureka *Greek.* I've found it; it is real or true
Frau *German.* married woman
Fräulein *German.* unmarried woman
geisha *Japanese.* young woman trained as companion for men
Gemütlichkeit *German.* good-natured, friendly cordiality
Gestalt *German.* unified whole that cannot be inferred from its component parts
Gesundheit *German.* good health to you, used esp. after someone sneezes
glasnost *Russian.* openness, esp. social and political
gnothi seauton *Greek.* know thyself
gulag *Russian.* forced-labor camp
guru *Hindi.* venerable teacher
halcyon *Greek.* lit. kingfisher; calm, peaceful
hara-kiri *Japanese.* ritual suicide by disembowelment
Hausfrau *German.* housewife
hoi polloi *Greek.* common people
hubris *Greek.* excessive pride and arrogance
iota *Greek.* atom; small amount
jawohl *German.* yes, definitely
kamikaze *Japanese.* person on a suicide mission, orig. a pilot; any reckless person
kaputt *German.* finished, ruined, broken
kismet *Turkish.* fate
Kitsch *German.* vulgar, trashy, valueless work
kowtow *Chinese.* fawn, bow low
kudos *Greek.* fame, glory, adulation
l'chaim *Hebrew.* to your health
Lebensraum *German.* additional room needed for expansion
logos *Greek.* rational principle that governs the universe
Lumpenproletariat *German.* vagrants, criminals, and rabble without class consciousness
mazel tov *Hebrew.* congratulations
nabob *Hindi.* man of wealth and power
nirvana *Sanskrit.* extinction of desire and achievement of perfect holiness
pariah *Hindi.* outcast
perestroika *Russian.* policy of Soviet economic and political reform
pogrom *Russian.* massacre or persecution
pundit *Hindi.* authoritative, scholarly commentator
Putsch *German.* insurrection
Rathskeller *German.* basement tavern
sahib *Arabic.* master
salaam *Arabic.* peace
samurai *Japanese.* member of feudal warrior caste
sayonara *Japanese.* good-bye, farewell
Schadenfreude *German.* pleasure derived from another's misfortune
shalom *Hebrew.* peace
skoal *Swedish.* to your health
stasis *Greek.* cessation of movement or circulation
Sturm und Drang *German.* storm and stress
swami *Sanskrit.* master, esp. religious teacher
taboo *Polynesian.* prohibited act
tovarishch *Russian.* comrade
Übermensch *German.* superman
uhuru *Swahili.* freedom
ukase *Russian.* command or edict
verboten *German.* forbidden
Wanderjahr *German.* year of travel
Wanderlust *German.* desire to travel
Weltanschauung *German.* comprehensive world view or outlook
Weltgeist *German.* spirit of the times
Weltschmerz *German.* world-weary sorrow
Wunderkind *German.* prodigy
yogi *Sanskrit.* practitioner of yoga
Zeitgeist *German.* spirit of the time

YIDDISH BORROWINGS

baleboste efficient, competent housewife or hostess
beheyme cow, or big dummy, used esp. of women
bube grandmother
bubele little bube; dear, sweetie
bubkes lit. beans; nothing
chazerei lit. pig food; junk, unpalatable stuff
chutzpah gall, nerve, or brashness
drek *Vulgar.* shit, literally or figuratively
farblondzhet (*adj*) wandering aimlessly; confused or out of it
farmisht (*adj*) confused, mixed up
farshtunkener stinking, nasty one
fartumlt (*adj*) disoriented, confused
feigel lit. bird; *Slang.* homosexual male
futz (*vb*) *Vulgar.* screw around; mess with
gelt money
gevalt lit. violence, force; outcry of alarm, as in "oy gevalt"
golem robot, lifelike creature; clay icon
goy gentile, non-Jew
goyim gentiles, non-Jews
goyish (*adj*) non-Jewlike
haimish (*adj*) homey, cozy
kibitz (*vb*) meddle, offer gratuitous advice
kishke intestine, gut; stuffed derma
kish meyn tokhes *Vulgar.* kiss my ass
klutz dullard; clumsy person
knish lit. stuffed dumpling; *Vulgar slang.* vagina
kosher (*adj*) fit to eat under Jewish dietary laws; proper, legitimate
kreplach lit. triangular dumplings; *Slang.* nothing
kvell be delighted
kvetch (*vb*) complain, whine, nag; (*n*) crotchety person
luftmensch person whose head is in the clouds, dreamer
macher wheeler-dealer, big shot
mamzer lit. illegitimate child; despicable individual; *Slang.* con man
maven expert, connoisseur

megillah long story, rigmarole
mensch admirable human being, person of dignity and integrity
meshugas insanity, nonsense
meshuge (*adj*) crazy, mad, or nuts
meshugene crazy person
mishpoche family, clan
nakhes good feeling, pride and joy; pleasure
nebbish nobody, loser, drip, or hapless one
nogoodnik bum to be avoided at all cost
noodge (*vb*) nag, pick at; (*n*) nagger, badgerer
nosh (*vb*) snack, nibble, or eat a bit; (*n*) tidbit or snack
nosher one who nibbles constantly
nu (*interj*) well? so? so what?
nudnik talkative bore; dummy
ongeblozn (*adj*) puffed up, conceited, or arrogant
oy (*interj*) oh!
parnose livelihood
patsh slap
patshke (*vb*) fiddle about lazily
pisher little squirt; someone of no consequence
plotz (*vb*) burst, explode
punim face
pupik bellybutton
putz *Vulgar.* lit. penis; jerk
schmooze (*vb*) have a heart-to-heart talk; chitchat or gab with one's associates
shadchen marriage broker, matchmaker
shegetz non-Jewish boy or young man; Jewish boy who fails to observe religious practices
shiksa non-Jewish woman, esp. girl or young woman
shlemazel born loser, someone always unlucky
shlemiel fool, social misfit, or failure; awkward person
shlep (*vb*) drag, haul around; trudge; (*n*) slob, bum
shlock shoddy, poorly crafted items
shlong *Vulgar.* penis
shlump slob, drip
shmaltz lit. rendered chicken fat; mawkish over-sentimentality, maudlin mush
shmate rag, cheap dress; shoddy garment or object
shmeer (*vb*) bribe, grease the palm of; (*n*) complete array of things
shmegege buffoon, idiot
shmendrik weak, ineffectual person
shmo boob, dummy
shmuck *Vulgar.* lit. penis; bad person, idiot, fool, or bastard
shmutz garbage, dirt
shnook pathetic but lovable fool, easy mark, or sucker
shnorrer beggar, panhandler; miser, wheedler, or cheapskate
shnoz nose, esp. large one
shpritz (*vb*) lit. spray; inject life into, poke fun at
shtick verbal bit, esp. comic routine; one's special interest or talent
shtunk something that smells unpleasant; louse
shtup (*vb*) stuff; push; *Vulgar.* have sex with
shvitzer someone who sweats a lot; braggart
tchatchkes knickknacks, trinkets
tokhes rear end, buttocks; tush
tsimes fuss, big to-do, or brouhaha
tsores worries, woes, or afflictions
tush toches
vey pain, as in "oy vey"
vitz joke, wisecrack
yenta gossipy person, busybody
yid derogatory term for a Jew
zaftig (*adj*) juicy, plump; voluptuous, sexy
zhlub someone insensitive and boorish

Chapter Twenty-Two

Character and Behavior

PERSONALITY AND BEHAVIOR

Appealing/Unappealing
Warm/Cold
Extroverted/Introverted
Dominant/Submissive
Strong/Weak
Active/Inert
Happy/Sad
Calm/Angry
Moderate/Excessive
Proper/Vulgar
Intelligent/Stupid
Special/Ordinary
Wise/Foolish
Good/Bad
Giving/Demanding
Helpful/Troublesome

Appealing/Unappealing

Appealing, Elegant, Neat, Rich, or Fancy

adorable, affluent, alluring, appealing, aristocratic, arresting, attractive
beautiful, becoming, beguiling, bewitching, breathtaking
caparisoned, captivating, charismatic, charming, chic, Circean, classy, clean, club by, couth, crisp, cuddly
dandy, dapper, dashing, dazzling, dear, debonair, decorous, desirable, devastating, dignified
elegant, enchanting, engaging, enthralling, enticing, entrancing, exquisite
fancy, fashionable, fetching, finished, flowery, flush
galluptious, glamorous, glorious, graceful, gracious
handsome, healthy, highborn, hygienic
immaculate, impeccable, imperial, ingratiating, intoxicating, inviting, irresistible
kempt, kingly
lardy-dardy, lavish, lush, luxuriant, luxurious
magnetic, mellifluous, mod, modish
natty, neat, nifty, nobby, nubile
opulent, ornate
patrician, photogenic, picturesque, plush, plushy, polished, posh, prepossessing, pretty, princely, privileged, prosperous
redolent, refined, regal, resplendent, rich, ritzy, royal
sanitary, sartorial, scrumptious, seductive, select, sexy, silk-stocking, sleek, slick, smart, smooth, snazzy, soigné, sophisticated, spanking, spellbinding, spiffy, splashy, splendid, spotless, spruce, stainless, stately, sterling, striking, stunning, stylish, suave, sumptuous, surefooted, sure-handed, svelte, swank, swanky, swell, swish
tantalizing, tasty, tidy, trendy, trig, trim
ultrachic, ultramodern, ultrarich
voguish
wealthy, well, well-groomed, well-heeled, well-off, winning, winsome
yummy

Unappealing, Shabby, Messy, Poor, or Clumsy

abysmal, accident-prone, all thumbs, angular, askew, awkward, awry
blowsy
cadaverous, chunderous, clumsy, contaminated, crumpled
déclassé, decrepit, derelict, destitute, dingy, disfigured, disgusting, dowdy, down-and-out, drippy, dumpy
fiddle-footed, filthy, frightful, frowzy, funky
gaudy, gawky, geeky, ghastly, gnarly, graceless, grisly, grotesque, gruesome
hard-up, heavy-footed, hideous, homely, horrid, horrific
icky, imperfect, impoverished, impure, incondite, incongruous, indecorous, indigent, inelegant, infelicitous, insolvent
lowborn, lowly
macabre, malodorous, meretricious, messy, monstrous
odious, oily, oleaginous, overdressed
penniless, penurious, plain, poor, putrescent, putrid
ragged, ragtag, rancid, ratty, repellent, repugnant, repulsive, revolting, rough, rugged
scabrous, scandalous, scraggly, scummy, scuzzy, seedy, shabby, shaggy, shocking, shoddy, sickening, simian, slatternly, slavering, sleazy, slimy, slobbery, sloppy, slovenly, slummy, sordid, squalid, stinky, subhuman
tacky, tatty, tawdry, tenth-rate, tousled
ugly, ulcerous, unappealing, unbecoming, unclean, uncoordinated, uncouth, underprivileged, undesirable, undignified, unfashionable, unfit, unhandy, unhealthy, unkempt, unpolished, unsanitary, unsavory, unsightly, untidy, unvarnished, unwashed
weather-beaten, woolly
yucky

Warm/Cold

Warm, Friendly, Sensitive, or Loving

adoring, affable, affectionate, agreeable, amatory, amenable, amiable, amicable, amorous, appreciative, approachable, ardent, avuncular
chummy, companionable, compassionate, congenial, convivial, cordial

devoted, disarming
earthy, empathic
familiar, favorable, fond, forgiving, friendly
genial, good-humored, good-natured, gracious, gregarious
heartwarming, hearty, hospitable
ingratiating, intimate
kind, kindhearted, kindly, kindred
largehearted, likable, lovable, loving
merciful
neighborly
open, open-hearted
pally, palsy-walsy, personable
reverent, romantic
sensitive, sensual, sentimental, sociable, soft, soft-hearted, summery, sympathetic
tender, tender-hearted, touching
warm, warm-hearted, well-disposed, worshipful

COLD, UNFRIENDLY, IRRITABLE, OR CRUEL

abrupt, alien, aloof, arctic, arid, asexual, ashen, astringent, atrabilious, austere
bad-tempered, bilious, bitter, bleak, bloody, blunt, brusque, brutal
callous, cantankerous, catty, cheap, chilly, chintzy, chippy, churlish, closed, cold, cold-blooded, cold-hearted, contemptuous, crabby, cranky, cross, crotchety, cruel, crusty, cryptic, curmudgeonly, cursed, curt, cussed, cutthroat, cynical
dispassionate, distant, domineering, dour, Draconian, dry, dyspeptic
egocentric, empty, envious
forbidding, formidable, freezing, frigid, frosty
gelid, glacial, glowering, gray, greedy, grouchy, grudging, gruff, grumpy
hardened, hardhearted, hateful, haughty, heartless, hollow, huffish, humiliating
icy, ignoble, ill-humored, ill-natured, ill-tempered, impersonal, inconsiderate, indifferent, inhospitable, insensitive, insulting, insusceptible, intolerant, inured, irreconcilable, irritable
jealous
liverish
matter-of-fact, mean, mechanical, merciless, misanthropic, miserly
nasty, niggardly, nippy
ornery
parched, parsimonious, peckish, peevish, penurious, persnickety, petty, piercing, pinchbeck, pitiless, Procrustean, psychopathic
raw, reactionary, remorseless, remote, ruthless
sadistic, salty, self-serving, sere, sexless, sharp-tongued, shrewish, snappish, snarly, snippety, snippy, snitty, snotty, sour, spiteful, spleenful, splenetic, stark, steely, stern, stiff, stingy, stoical, stony, strict, surly, suspicious
testy, tetchy, thick-skinned, tight, tight-fisted, touchy, troglodytic, truculent, tyrannical
uncharitable, uncommunicative, uncongenial, unfeeling, unforgiving, unfriendly, ungrateful, unkind, unkindly, unmerciful, unmoved, unsympathetic
vengeful, venomous, vexatious, vicious, vitriolic
waspish, wintry, withholding, wizened, wooden, wrongheaded

Extroverted/Introverted

EXTROVERTED, OUTGOING, OUTSPOKEN, OR DRAMATIC

ambitious, assertive, atwitter
blatant, bloviating, blustering, boisterous, bold, bombastic, brash, brazen, breathy
chatty, choleric
defiant, dramatic
emphatic, evangelical, excited, exhibitionistic, expansive, expressive, extemporaneous, extroverted, exuberant
flagrant, flamboyant, flashy, flirtatious, forward, freewheeling
garrulous, grandiloquent, gregarious, gushy
high-profile, histrionic
immodest, indiscreet, intrusive
jabbering
lippy, logorrheic, loquacious, loud, loud-mouthed
madcap, malapert, meteoric, militant, multiloquious
noisy
obstreperous, obtrusive, orotund, outgoing, outspoken, overbearing, overt, overweening
pert, petulant, presumptuous, prolix, protrusive, protuberant, public, pugnacious, pushy
rah-rah, raucous, red-hot, rousing
shrill, sonorous, spectacular, splashy, stagestruck, stagy, stentorian, strident, stridulous, swinging, switched-on
talkative, theatrical, throaty, turgid
uninhibited, unreserved, unselfconscious, uproarious
verbose, visible, vitriolic, vocal, vociferous, voluble
wordy

INTROVERTED, RESERVED, ISOLATED, OR MYSTERIOUS

abashed, alien, alienated, alone, aloof, anonymous, antisocial, ascetic, asocial, austere, autonomous, awkward
bashful
chary, clannish, claustral, cloistered, cloistral, concealed, confidential, covert, coy, crafty
delitescent, detached, discreet, distant
elliptical, elusive, enigmatic, eremitic, estranged, evasive

ghostly, guarded
hermitic,
incommunicado, indirect, inhibited, inner-directed, inscrutable, insular, introspective, introverted, invisible, inward, isolated
laconic, latent, lone, lonely, low-profile
misty, misunderstood, modest, monastic, monkish, mum, mute, mysterious
nebulous, nonverbal
oblique, obscure, occult
paradoxical, passive, phantom, private
quiescent, quiet
reclusive, reluctant, remote, repressed, reserved, restrained, reticent, retiring
secluded, secretive, self-absorbed, self-conscious, self-effacing, sensitive, sequestered, shadowy, shamefaced, sheepish, short-spoken, shy, silent, smoky, sneaky, soft-spoken, solitary, solo, spectral, sphinxlike, spooky, standoffish, stay-at-home, stealthy, still, stolid, strange, sub rosa, subterranean, surreptitious, suspicious
taciturn, tactful, tight-lipped, tiptoe
ultracool, unapproachable, unassertive, unassuming, unclear, uncommunicative, undemonstrative, understated, unexpressive, unfathomable, unobtrusive, unsociable
vanishing, veiled, voiceless
wary, watchful, wistful, withdrawn, wordless, wraithlike
xenophobic

Dominant/Submissive

Dominant, Stubborn, Proud, or Confident

abusive, adamant, ascendant, assuming, assured, authoritative, autocratic
bossy, bullheaded, bumptious
certain, cock-a-hoop, cocksure, cocky, commanding, compelling, conclusive, confident, controlling, contumacious
decisive, determined, direct, directed, dogged, dogmatic, dominant, domineering, do-or-die
egoistic, egotistic, emphatic, enduring, entitled, entrenched
firm, fixed, focused, forceful, formidable
grandiose
hard-ass, hard-bitten, hard-boiled, hard-edged, hardened, hardheaded, headstrong, hellbent, high and mighty, high-flown, high-handed, high-powered
immovable, impenetrable, imperative, imperious, impervious, implacable, impregnable, independent, indestructible, indomitable, inexorable, inflated, inflexible, insistent, insuperable, intent, intimidating, intractable, intransigent, invincible, invulnerable, ironbound, ironclad, irresistible
lordly
macho, magisterial, magistral, messianic, mighty, militaristic, mulish
obdurate, obstinate, omnipotent, one-sided, opinionated, orgulous, orotund, ossified, overweening, overwhelming
persistent, persuasive, pertinacious, pervicacious, pigheaded, poised, portentous, possessive, predominant, preponderant, presumptuous, prideful, prodigious, proprietary, proud, purposeful, pushy
ramrod, recalcitrant, redoubtable, refractory, relentless, renitent, resolute, rigid
secure, self-assured, self-confident, self-important, self-involved, self-possessed, self-righteous, self-satisfied, self-seeking, single-minded, smug, stiff, strident, strong-minded, strong-willed, stubborn, sure, swaggering, swashbuckling, swellheaded
take-charge, tenacious, territorial, thick-skinned, turgid
unassailable, unbending, undaunted, unfaltering, unflagging, unflinching, unreceptive, unregenerate, unrelenting, unstinting, unstoppable, unswerving, unwary, unwieldy, unwilling, unyielding
vain, vainglorious, vehement, volitive
whole hog, willful

Submissive, Uncertain, or Tentative

accommodating, acquiescent, adaptable, ambivalent, apologetic, apprehensive, assailable, awkward
balky
caducous, chameleonic, changeable, chary, chivvied, compliant, concessive, conciliatory, culpable, cursory
dainty, deferential, dependent, diffident, doubtful, downtrodden, dubious, ductile
effeminate, equivocal, exposed
fatalistic, fawning, flexible, flimsy
halfhearted, halting, haphazard, harmless, hesitant, humiliated
ill at ease, impalpable, inconclusive, inconstant, incredulous, indecisive, indirect, inoffensive, insecure, irresolute
labile, lambent, loath, lost
malleable, masochistic, mealy-mouthed, meek, mousy, mutable
noncommittal, nude
obedient, obeisant, obsequious
penitent, phlegmatic, plastic, pliable, pliant, prostrate, protean
qualmish, queasy, questioning, quizzical
receptive, reconciled, reluctant, repentant, reserved, resigned, respectful
self-abnegating, self-denying, sequacious, serviceable, servile, shackled, slavish, solicitous, squishy, subdued, submissive, subservient, suggestible, supple, suppliant, susceptible, sycophantic
tentative, tenuous, thin-skinned, timid, tongue-tied, tractable, tremulous
unresisting
vacillating, vague, vulnerable
wavering, wishy-washy
yielding

Strong/Weak

Strong, Bold, or Tough

able-bodied, adventuresome, adventurous, all-powerful, audacious
ballsy, belligerent, bluff, blunt, bold, brash, brave, brawny, burly
clutch, courageous
daring, dauntless, decisive, doughty, durable
effective
fearless, firm, flinty, forbidding, formidable, full-blooded
gritty, gutsy, gutty
hale, hard-ass, hardball, hard-nosed, hardy, heavy, hell-for-leather, hoydenish
indestructible, inexhaustible, intrepid
lionhearted, lusty
manly, massive, mettlesome, mighty, militant, motivated, muscular
nervy
oppressive
physical, plucky, potent, powerful
ready, red-blooded, reliant, resilient, robust, rocky, rough, rugged, ruthless
scrappy, self-made, self-reliant, self-sufficient, self-supporting, self-sustaining, skookum, solid, spartan, spirited, spunky, stalwart, staunch, steadfast, steely, stout, stout-hearted, strapping, street-smart, streetwise, strong, sturdy, substantial
thriving, tough, truculent
unblinking
valiant, valorous, venturesome
warlike
yeomanly

Weak, Fearful, or Anxious

abashed, afraid, ailing, alarmed, anemic, anxious, apprehensive, ashamed, asthmatic
bedridden, bloodless, brittle
candy-ass, clinging, consumptive, cowardly, craven, creaky, cringing
debilitated, decrepit, delicate, desperate, dilute, disconcerted, doddering
effete
faint, fainthearted, faltering, fearful, feckless, feeble, fidgety, fitful, flimsy, fragile, frail, frangible, frightened, futile
gimpy, gutless
hagridden, helpless, horrified, horror-struck, humbled, humiliated, hung-up
ill, impotent, impoverished, impuissant, incapacitated, ineffective, inept, infirm, insecure, insufficient
jittery
lame, lily-livered, limp, limp-wristed
mawkish, meager, milk-livered, mortified
namby-pamby, needy, nervous, neurotic
oversensitive, overwhelmed
pale, pallid, paltry, panicked, panic-stricken, paranoid, pathetic, pavid, petrified, phthisic, pitiful, plaintive, poor-spirited, punchless, puny, pusillanimous
recreant
scared, shaky, sheepish, short-winded, shrinking, sickly, simpering, skimpy, skittish, slight, sniveling, snuffling, spasmodic, spineless, spooked, squeamish, stressed, stressed-out, sulky
terrified, timid, timorous, toothless, tottering, trapped, trembling, tremulous
uncomfortable, undernourished, uneasy, unnerved, unwell, uptight
vertiginous
wan, wary, washed-out, washy, watery, weak, weakhearted, weak-kneed, wet, whining, whiny, white, white-livered, wimpy, wispy, wormy
yellow

Active/Inert

Active, Lively, Awake, or Limber

acrobatic, active, adroit, agile, alert, alive, ambulatory, athletic, attentive, avid, awake
bouncy, breezy, bright-eyed, brisk, bubbly, bustling, busy, buxom
catalytic, chipper, crisp, curious
deft, diligent, dynamic
eager, effervescent, elusive, energetic, energized, enterprising, errant, exhilarated, exuberant
fecund, feisty, fervent, fleet, fleet-footed, fluent, fluid, footloose, free, fresh, frisky, frolicsome
galvanic, go-go, gymnastic
hale, high-spirited, high-strung, hurried
industrious, interested, intrigued, irrepressible, itinerant
jaunty, jingly
kinetic
lambent, liberated, light, limber, lissome, lithe, lively, lyric
mercurial, mobile, motile
nimble, nomadic
operose, outdoorsy
peppy, peripatetic, perky, productive, prolific, prompt
quick, quicksilver
rambunctious, rapid, raring to go, ready, reborn, renascent
saltatory, sassy, saucy, sentient, sinuous, skittish, snappy, speedy, spirited, sprightly, springy, spruce, spry, strenuous, supple, swift, switched-on, sylphlike
tireless
unencumbered, up-and-coming
vibrant, vigilant, vigorous, vital, vivacious, volant, volatile
wakeful, whippy, wide-awake, wide-eyed, willowy
zappy, zestful, zesty, zingy, zippy

INERT, LAZY, TIRED, OR INSENSATE

abstracted, aged, apathetic, asleep, atrophied
barren, beat, benumbed, blank, blasé, bored, bovine, bushed
cadaverous, comatose, complacent
dazed, dead, delitescent, dilatory, disinterested, docile, doltish, dopey, dormant, draggy, dreamy, drooping, droopy, drowsy, drugged, dull, dulled
emotionless, empty, enervated, exhausted
fallow, fatigued, flat, floppy
glassy, glassy-eyed, groggy
haggard, hazy, hoary, hypnotic, hypnotized
idle, immobile, impassive, impervious, inactive, inanimate, inattentive, incapacitated, indifferent, indolent, inert, insensate, insipid
jaded
kaput
lackadaisical, languid, languorous, late, latent, lazy, leaden, lethargic, lifeless, listless, logy, lymphatic
malingering, moribund, mute
numb
otiose, overripe
paralyzed, passive, phlegmatic, placid, pococurante, poky, porcine, punch-drunk, punchy
rusty
sagging, sapped, satiated, sedentary, semicomatose, semiconscious, senseless, shiftless, shot, slack, sleepy, slothful, slow, sluggish, sodden, somnolent, spaced-out, spent, spiritless, stagnant, static, stiff, stuporous, supine
tardy, tepid, tired, torpid, truant
uninterested, unmindful, unmotivated, unresponsive
vacant, vacuous
weary, wizened, world-weary, worn-out
yawning
zombold, zonked

Happy/Sad

HAPPY, PLAYFUL, OPTIMISTIC, OR ELATED

agrin, airy, amazed, amused, amusing, astonished
beatific, bemused, blissful, blithe, bonhomous, buoyant
carefree, cavalier, cheerful, cheery, chipper, content, contented, convivial
delighted, devil-may-care, droll
ebullient, ecstatic, elated, enchanted, enraptured, enthusiastic, espiègle, euphoric, expectant, exuberant, exultant
fanciful, fancy-free, festive, flying, frolicsome, fulfilled, fun-loving, funny
gamesome, gay, gemütlich, giddy, giggly, glad, gleeful, glowing
happy, happy-go-lucky, harmonious, hilarious, hopeful, humorous
impish, infectious
jaunty, jocose, jocular, jocund, jolly, jovial, joyful, joyous, jubilant
laughing, lighthearted, lilting, ludic
merry, mirthful, mischievous
optimistic, overjoyed
perky, playful, pleased, psyched, puckish
radiant, rapturous, ravished, relieved, rhapsodic, riant, risible, roguish, roseate, rosy
sanguine, sated, satisfied, silly, sky-high, spirited, sportive, starry-eyed, stoked, sunny
thankful, triumphant
up
waggish, whimsical, wishful

SAD, SERIOUS, PESSIMISTIC, OR DISCONTENTED

abject, absorbed, abysmal, achy, afflicted, aggrieved, agonizing, anguished
beleaguered, bereaved, bereft, bleak, blue, brokenhearted, brooding, bummed, bummed out
chagrined, cheerless, contrite, crestfallen, crushed
dark, dejected, demure, depressed, deprived, desolate, despondent, disconsolate, discontented, discouraged, disenchanted, disgusted, disillusioned, dismal, dissatisfied, distraught, distressed, disturbed, doleful, dolorous, doomed, dour, down, down-at-heel, downbeat, downcast
elegiac, embittered
fatalistic, forlorn, fretful, funereal
gloomy, glum, grave, grief-stricken, grieving, grim, grouchy, grum, grumpy, guilt-ridden, guilty
hapless, harried, heartbroken, heavy-hearted, homesick, hopeless, humorless, hurt
inconsolable, indisposed, injured
joyless
lachrymose, languishing, lonely, lonesome, lovesick, lugubrious
maudlin, melancholy, miserable, misty-eyed, moody, mopey, morbid, morose, mournful
nostalgic
oppressed, out-of-sorts, owlish
pained, pathetic, pensive, perturbed, pessimistic, pining, pitiable, pitiful, plaintive, plangent, poignant, pouty, pungent
regretful, remorseful, repentant, rueful, ruthful
sad, saturnine, serious, severe, sighing, sober, solemn, somber, soppy, sorrowful, sorry, stern, stricken, Stygian, subdued, suffering, suicidal, sulky, sullen, surly
teary, teary-eyed, tortured, tragic, tristful, troubled
unfortunate, unfulfilled, unhappy, unlucky
wailful, weepy, wistful, woebegone, woeful, wounded, wrecked, wretched, wronged

Calm/Angry

CALM, GENTLE, OR EASYGOING

apollonian

calm, casual, composed, constrained, cool, cool-headed
dégagé, demure, dewy, dispassionate, dry-eyed
easygoing, emollient, even-tempered
gentle
imperturbable
laconic, laid-back, lenient, levelheaded, low-key, low-pressure
matutinal, meditative, mellow, mild, muted
neutral, nonchalant, nonviolent
objective
pacific, pacifistic, passive, patient, peaceful, poised
quiet
relaxed, restrained, reticent
sedate, self-disciplined, self-possessed, serene, soft, steady, stoical, subdued
taciturn, tame, temperate, tempered, tranquil
unbothered, unemotional, unflappable, unforced, unhassled, unhurried, unruffled, unstirred, untroubled

ANGRY, EMOTIONAL, AGGRESSIVE, OR PASSIONATE

aggravated, aggressive, aghast, agitated, amorous, angered, angry, animated, annoyed, antsy, appetent, argumentative, avid
bellicose, belligerent, blooming, brash, breathless
choleric, combative, competitive, contentious
dedicated, defiant, dramatic
edgy, effusive, emotional, engagé, enthusiastic, excitable, excited, explosive
ferocious, feverish, fierce, fiery, fire-eating, flighty, flustered, frazzled, free-swinging, frenzied, fuming, furious
harried, hassled, henpecked, hepped-up, het up, high-keyed, high-pressure, high-strung, hostile, hot, hot-blooded, hotheaded, huffy, hungry, hyper, hysterical
impassioned, impetuous, impulsive, incensed, indignant, inflammatory, intemperate, intensive, intent, irascible, irate, irrepressible
jealous
livid, lusty
mad, manic, miffed, militant, militaristic
overwrought, overzealous
passionate, peeved, peppery, perfervid, piqued, pissed, pissed off, pugnacious, pushy
quarrelsome
rabid, raddled, raging, rambunctious, rash, resentful, restive, restless, ruffled, rumbustious
scrappy, seething, self-indulgent, sensuous, short, short-tempered, sick and tired, snappish, sore, soulful, spontaneous, steaming, stewing, sthenic, stir-crazy, stirred up, stormy, strained, subjective, sulfurous, sultry
temperamental, tempestuous, tense, testy, ticked, ticked-off, ticklish, torrid, touchy, trigger-happy, troubled, truculent, tumultuous, turbulent, turned-on
unglued, unreasonable, unreconciled, unremitting, unrestrained, unsettled, unstable, upset
vehement, Vesuvian, vexed, violent, visceral, volcanic
warm-blooded, white-hot, worked-up, wound-up, wrathful, wrought-up, wroth
zealous

Moderate/Excessive

MODERATE, SANE, CONSERVATIVE, OR OLD-FASHIONED

abstemious, abstinent, adjusted, assiduous
balanced, businesslike, buttoned-down
careful, cautious, celibate, chary, circumspect, clocklike, closemouthed, collected, composed, concise, concrete, conscientious, conservative, consistent, constant, controlled, conventional, cool-headed
diplomatic, down-to-earth
equitable
factual, frugal
gingerly, gradual
inveterate
laconic, levelheaded
matter-of-fact, middle-of-the-road, mild, moderate, modest
no-nonsense
objective, obsolete, old-fashioned, orderly, orthodox, ossified, outdated, outmoded
passé, penny-wise, pious, practical, pragmatic, prudent
rational, reasonable, regimented, regular
safe, sane, sensible, sober, sound, sparing, square, stable, standardized, standpat, steady, stick-in-the-mud, sticky, stodgy, strait-laced, stringent, studied, superannuated
tactful, temperate, thrifty, tough-minded
ultraconservative, utilitarian
workmanlike

EXCESSIVE, MAD, INSANE, OR RADICAL

aberrant, abnormal, addictive, alcoholic, amok, anarchic, anarchistic, apoplectic, avaricious
berserk, brash
chaotic, crazed, crazy
daffy, daft, delirious, demoniacal, deranged, deviant, dizzy, dotty, dysfunctional
eldritch, epicurean, erratic, esurient, excessive, extravagant, extreme
fanatic, fanatical, febrile, fey, flagrant, flaky, florid, frantic, freakish, frenetic, frenzied
gonzo, greedy
headlong, hedonistic, heedless, hog-wild, homicidal, hyper, hysterical

immodest, incendiary, inordinate, insane, insatiable, irrational
kamikaze, kooky
loco, lunatic
mad, madcap, maniacal, monomaniacal
nihilistic
obsessive, odd, off, off-the-wall, overwrought
perfervid, phrenetic, pinko, pixilated, potty, prodigal, profuse, psycho, psychotic, punk
quirky
rabid, radical, raging, rakish, rapacious, rash, ravening, raving, reckless
screwy, spasmodic, strange, streaky, surreal, sybaritic
temerarious
ultra, ultraist, unbalanced, unbridled, unconventional, uncurbed, unfettered, unhinged, unrestrained
voracious
wacky, warped, wasteful, way-out, weird, wiggy, wild-eyed, wired
zany, zooey

Proper/Vulgar

PROPER, COURTEOUS, REFINED, OR PURITANICAL

aesthetic, appropriate, auspicious
ceremonious, chaste, citified, civil, civilized, classical, clubby, conforming, conventional, correct, courteous, courtly, couth, cultivated, cultured
decent, decorous, delicate, demure, dignified, diplomatic, discreet
effete, elitist, established, esthetic, ethical
fastidious, felicitous, finicky, formal, fussy
gallant, genteel, gentlemanly, gracious
hoity-toity, holier-than-thou, honorable
ingratiating, irreproachable, Ivy League
kosher
law-abiding, legitimate
maidenly, mannered, matronly, modern, modest, moral, moralistic
obedient, official, orthodox
pietistic, polite, pompous, precious, presentable, priggish, prim, prissy, pristine, professional, proper, prudent, prudish, pudibund, punctilious, punctual, puritanical
refined, religious, reputable, respectable, respectful, rhetorical, righteous, right-thinking, rigid
safe, sanctimonious, seemly, self-righteous, smooth, smug, snobbish, snooty, soapy, sporting, sportsmanlike, squeamish, stable, staid, starchy, stiff, stilted, straight, straight-arrow, strict, stuffy, suave, suitable
tactful, tasteful, taut, tight-assed, too-too, traditional, tweedy
U, unflappable, upright, uptight, urbane
Victorian
well-behaved, well-bred, well-mannered, white, white-bread

VULGAR, RUDE, DEGENERATE, OR WILD

abandoned, aberrant, abnormal, abominable, aboriginal, abusive, animalistic, anomalous, atavistic
barbaric, base, bawdy, beastly, bibulous, bizarre, blasphemous, blooey, blunt, boorish, brash, brazen, brutish
caddish, cannibalistic, carnal, cheap, cheeky, coarse, common, concupiscent, coquettish, crass, crude
debauched, decadent, degenerate, depraved, deviant, dirty, dirty-minded, discourteous, disobedient, disorderly, disreputable, dissipated, dissolute
egregious, erotic
farouche, feral, flatulent, flip, flippant, flooey, foul, fresh
garish, gauche, gross
heathenish, heteroclite, heterodox, hoggish, hokey
ill-bred, illicit, ill-mannered, immoderate, immoral, impertinent, impolite, impolitic, improper, impudent, inappropriate, incestuous, incongruous, indecent, indecorous, indelicate, inexcusable, informal, insolent, intoxicated, irregular, irreverent
kinky, knockabout
lascivious, lawless, lecherous, lewd, libertine, libidinous, licentious, loose, loud, low, lowbrow, lubricious, lustful
mannerless, meretricious
native, naughty, non-U
obscene, obstreperous, offbeat, offhand, opprobrious, outlandish, outrageous, outré, overdressed
perverted, plebeian, pornographic, primitive, profane, profligate, promiscuous, prurient, prying, purple
queer
Rabelaisian, racy, raffish, rakish, rambunctious, randy, rank, raucous, raunchy, raw, rebellious, recherché, refractory, revolutionary, ribald, riotous, ripped, rip-roaring, risqué, roily, rough, rough-and-tumble, rough-hewn, rowdy, rowdydowdy, rude, rumbustious, rustic, ruttish
salacious, sassy, savage, scabrous, scandalous, scurrilous, self-abandoned, shameless, showy, slutty, smutty, steamy, swinish
tactless, tasteless, tawdry, tipsy, trashy
unbecoming, unblushing, uncivil, uncivilized, uncontrollable, unconventional, uncool, uncouth, uncultured, undiplomatic, ungracious, unmanageable, unmannered, unmannerly, unnatural, unrefined, unruly, unseemly, unsportsmanlike, untamed, untoward
vulgar
wanton, weird, whorish, wild

Intelligent/Stupid

Intelligent, Informed, Clever, or Articulate

abreast, accurate, acute, analytical, apt, argute, articulate, astute, au fait, authoritative
bookish, bright, brilliant, broad ranging
canny, cerebral, clear, clearheaded, clear-sighted, clever, cogent, cognizant, coherent, comprehensive, concise, conscious, conversant, cunning
discerning, donnish, droll
educated, erudite, expert
facile, fluent
glib, heads-up, heady, highbrow, high-minded, hip
imaginative, incisive, informed, ingenious, innovative, inquiring, inquisitive, insightful, intellectual, intelligent, interpretive, inventive
keen, knowing, knowledgeable
learned, limpid, literate, logical, lucid, luminous
mental
observant, omnilegent, omniscient, organized
pawky, pedagogic, penetrating, perceptive, percipient, perspicacious, piercing, pithy, precocious, prescient, proficient, profound
quick-witted
rational, recondite, reflective, retentive, right, ruminant
savvy, serious-minded, sharp, sharp-witted, shrewd, silver-tongued, smart, smooth-tongued, subtle, succinct
terse, trenchant, tuned-in
ultrasmart, uncanny, understanding, unerring, urbane
versed
well-advised, well-informed, well-read, well-rounded, well-spoken, with-it, witty, worldly, worldly-wise

Stupid, Ignorant, or Confused

absent-minded, abstracted, addlebrained, addled, agog, amnesiac
backward, baffled, befogged, befuddled, benighted, besotted, bewildered, blithering, bovine
confounded, confused, cretinous
dense, dim, dimwitted, disorganized, disoriented, doltish, dull, dumb, dumbfounded, duncical
empty-headed, erroneous
fallible, fatuous, fat-witted, feeble-minded, foggy, fuzzy
hazy
idiotic, ignorant, illiterate, imbecilic, inarticulate, incognizant, incoherent, incompetent, inconscient
lumpish
maundering, mindless, mixed-up, moronic, muddled, muddleheaded, myopic, mystified
nescient, numb
oblivious, obtuse, opaque
perplexed, preoccupied, purblind, puzzled
rambling, rattled, retarded
scatterbrained, senile, simple, simpleminded, slaphappy, slow, slow-witted, sophomoric, spaced, spaced-out, spacey, speechless, stunned, stunted, stupefied, stupid, stuporous, subliterate, subnormal
thick, thickheaded, thick-witted, turbid
unclear, unconscious, undiscerning, unfocused, uninformed, unknowing, unlearned, unlettered, unorganized, unread, unschooled, unskilled, untutored, unversed
vacant, vacuous
witless, woodenheaded, woozy, wrong
zoned out, zonked out

Special/Ordinary

Special, Bright, Skillful, or Unusual

ablaze, able, acclaimed, accomplished, adept, adequate, admirable, admired, ageless, aglow, all-around, amazing, ambidextrous, anointed, artful, artistic, arty, atypical, auspicious, avant-garde
bedazzling, blessed, bodacious, breathtaking, bright, brilliant
capable, celebrated, charismatic, colorful, competent, conspicuous, consummate, controversial, coordinated, corking, creative, creditable
dazzling, different, distinct, distinctive, distinguished, divine
eccentric, efficient, effulgent, eminent, esteemed, estimable, excellent, exceptional, exclusive, exemplary, exotic, extraordinary
famous, fascinating, favored, fine, first-class, first-rate, flashing, foremost, fortunate
glimmering, glittering, glorious, glossy, glowing, grand, great
handy, heavenly, hip, honored
iconoclastic, idiosyncratic, illuminated, illustrious, imaginative, imperial, important, imposing, impressive, incandescent, incomparable, incredible, individual, indubitable, inimitable, inspiring, invaluable, inviolate, iridescent
jazzy
light, lucky, luminous, lustrous
magical, magnificent, majestic, major, marquee, marvelous, masterful, matchless
nonpareil, notable, noted, noteworthy, novel
original, otherworldly, outstanding
peculiar, peerless, perfect, phenomenal, praiseworthy, preeminent, prepared, prestigious, priceless, primary, Promethean, prominent, protean, proverbial
quaint, qualified, quality
radiant, rare, refulgent, remarkable, renowned, resourceful, respected, resplendent, reverential, ripe

sacred, saintly, scintillating, select, sensational, serendipitous, sexy, shining, signal, significant, singular, skillful, sole, sovereign, sparkling, special, spicy, splendid, startling, stellar, storied, stupendous, sublime, successful, super, superb, superhuman, superior, superlative, supernatural, supreme, surefooted, sure-handed
talented, terrific, tiptop, titled, together, top, topflight, topnotch, top-of-the-line, tops, towering, transfigured
uncommon, unconventional, unequaled, unexcelled, unique, unmatched, unorthodox, unprecedented, unusual, unwonted, utopian
valuable, valued, varied, vast, versatile, victorious, vintage, vivid
well-known, well-spoken, well-thought-of, whiz-bang, wonderful, wondrous, worthwhile, worthy

ORDINARY, DULL, PLAIN, OR BANAL

automatic, average
banal, bland, blank, boring, bourgeois
characterless, colorless, common, commonplace, conventional, cursory, customary
dated, derivative, dim, dingy, dismal, down-to-earth, drab, dreary, dull
empty, everyday, expressionless
faded, fair, fallible, familiar, faulty, flat
garden-variety, glib, gratuitous
habitual, hackneyed, homespun, humble, humdrum
imitative, inartistic, inconclusive, inconspicuous, indifferent, inefficient, inept, inferior, inglorious, innocuous, insignificant, insipid
jejune
lackluster, lifeless, low-class, lowly, low-quality, lukewarm, lusterless
matter-of-fact, mediocre, menial, middling, mild, minor, modest, mortal, mundane, musty
negligible, nondescript, normal
obvious, okay, one-dimensional, ordinary
passable, pedestrian, perfunctory, petit bourgeois, plain, plain-spoken, plastic, plebeian, proletarian, prosaic, prototypical
regular, repetitive, rinky-dink, run-of-the-mill
secondary, second-class, second-rate, shoddy, simple, small-time, soggy, soporific, spare, stagnant, stale, standard, stereotypical, sterile, stock, stripped-down, subordinate, superficial, superfluous
tarnished, tasteless, tedious, tepid, terrestrial, timeworn, tiresome, tolerable, trite, typical
unadorned, unassuming, undistinctive, undistinguished, unexceptional, unexciting, unhip, unimaginative, uninspiring, uninteresting, unprepared, unpretentious, unqualified, unsung, untalented, untitled, useless, usual
vapid
workaday, working-class, would-be

Wise/Foolish

WISE, MATURE, OR EXPERIENCED

actualized, adult, all-knowing, all-seeing, august, aware, awesome
balanced, broad, broad-minded
centered, clear, clear-sighted, cogent, coherent, complex, contemplative
deep, discriminating, disinterested, dispassionate
eloquent, enlightened, ethereal, exalted, experienced
farseeing, farsighted, focused
grand, grown-up
immortal, impartial, infallible, infinite, influential, integrated
judicious, just
large-minded, levelheaded, lofty, lucid
magisterial, majestic, mantic, masterful, masterly, mature, metaphysical, mystical
noble
old, Olympian, omnipresent, omniscient, open-minded, orbicular, oriented
patriarchal, perfect, philosophical, practiced, prescient, profound, prophetic, psychic
realized, resonant
sacred, sacrosanct, sagacious, sage, sapient, serene, sophisticated, spiritual, sublime, supernal, supreme, sybilline
telepathic
unassailable, unbiased, understanding, universal
vatic, venerable, veteran, visionary
weathered, weighty, wise, wizardly

FOOLISH, IMMATURE, BIGOTED, OR TRIVIAL

abstract, absurd, adolescent, affected, amateurish, anthropocentric, anti-intellectual, artless, artsy, asinine, awe-struck
balmy, barmy, bathetic, bedazzled, biased, bigoted, blind, bumbling
callow, capricious, careless, childish, chumpish, clownish, comical, corny, cretinous, cute, cutesy
daffy, daft, distracted, dopey
ethnocentric
farcical, flabbergasted, flatulent, flighty, foolhardy, foolish, foppish, frivolous, frothy
garrulous, gibbering, giddy, goofy
half-assed, half-baked, half-cocked, harebrained, harum-scarum, hasty, highfalutin, homophobic
idiotic, ill-advised, imbecilic, immature, impetuous, impractical, imprudent, inane, indiscreet, inexperienced, infantile, injudicious, in the clouds, irrational
juvenile

kooky
la-di-da, laughable, lightheaded, long-winded, loquacious, ludicrous
melodramatic, mincing, minor, misanthropic, misogynous, moronic, mushyheaded, muzzy
naif, naive, narrow, narrow-minded, nattering, nerdy, nonplussed, nutty
parochial, pedantic, petty, picayune, piddling, pinchbeck, prejudiced, preposterous, pretentious, prolix, provincial, pubescent, puerile
quixotic, quizzical
rash, rattlebrained, redundant, repetitious, ridiculous
sappy, sectarian, sententious, shallow, shortsighted, sightless, silly, singsong, skin-deep, small-minded, small-time, soft-headed, sophistic, speechless, spoony, superficial, superstitious
trifling, trivial
unfledged, ungrounded, unrealistic, unwise, unworldly
verdant
waggish, wide-eyed, windy, woolly-headed
yeasty, youthful
zany

Good/Bad

Good, Sincere, Honest, or Just

aboveboard, angelic, authentic
benevolent, bona fide
candid, capital, choice, conscientious, constant
dear, decent, deserving, devout, direct
earnest, ethical
fair, fair-minded, fine, first-rate, forthcoming, forthright, foursquare, frank, free
genuine, God-fearing, good, guileless
harmonious, high-minded, holy, honest, honorable, humane
idealistic, impartial, incorruptible, irreproachable
judicious, just
loving, loyal
magnanimous, moral
natural, noble
organic
prelapsarian, principled, pure
real, reliable, reverent, righteous, right-minded
scrupulous, selfless, seraphic, simon-pure, sincere, straightforward, sublime
true, true-blue, truthful
unimpeachable, up-and-up, up-front, upright, upstanding
veracious, veridical, vestal, virtuous
wholehearted, wholesome, worthy

Bad, False, Evil, Insincere, or Dishonest

accursed, adulterous, affected, amoral, apocryphal, apostate, arch, artificial, awful
backhanded, bad, baleful, baneful, barefaced, base, bent, bloodthirsty, bogus
calumnious, canting, casuistic, contemptible, corrupt, counterfeit, crafty, crooked, cunning, cursed
damned, debased, deceitful, deceptive, delusive, demoniacal, despicable, detestable, devilish, devious, diabolical, disgraced, dishonest, disingenuous, disloyal, dissembling, duplicitous
egregious, ersatz, evasive, evil, execrable
fake, fallen, false, fatuous, feigned, fell, fiendish, flagitious, flagrant, foul, foxy, fraudulent, fulsome, furtive
guileful
hangdog, heinous, heretical, hexed, high-sounding, hollow, horrid, hypocritical
ignoble, ignominious, infamous, infernal, insidious, insincere, irredeemable
Janus-faced, jive
loathsome, lowdown
malefic, malevolent, malignant, mealy-mouthed, mendacious, miscreant, misleading, mock, monstrous, moralistic, murderous
nefarious
odious, ostentatious
perfidious, pernicious, perverse, pharisaic, phony, piacular, predatory, pretentious, pseudo, purulent
recreant, reprobate, rotten
sanctimonious, scurvy, selfish, serpentine, shady, sham, shameful, shifty, sinful, sinister, slanderous, slippery, sly, smarmy, sneaky, sophistic, sorcerous, specious, spurious, stealthy, synthetic
tainted, terrible, traitorous, treacherous, two-faced
unashamed, unconscionable, unctuous, underhanded, unfair, ungodly, unholy, unjust, unpardonable, unprincipled, unscrupulous, untruthful, unworthy
vain, venal, venomous, vile, villainous, viperous, virtueless, vulpine
wicked, wily, worthless

Giving/Demanding

Giving, Trusting, Innocent, or Generous

accessible, accommodating, adaptable, approving, artless
beatific, believing
candid, careless, childlike, complaisant, compliant, credulous
democratic, dewy-eyed, doting, dulcet
easy
faithful, frank, free
game, generous, giving, good-natured, gracious, grateful, guileless, gullible

hopeful, humble
impressionable, inconsistent, indiscriminate, indulgent, ingenuous, innocent, insouciant, instinctive, intuitive
lax, liberal
naive, natural
obliging, open
permissive
rapt, reciprocating
saccharine, selfless, simple, sugary, sweet, syrupy
tender, tolerant, transparent, trustful, trusting
ultraliberal, unabashed, uncritical, understanding, undesigning, unguarded, unquestioning, unsophisticated, unsparing, unsullied, unsuspecting, unwitting
virginal
young

Demanding, Critical, Calculating, or Selfish

abrasive, accusatory, acerbic, acidic, acquisitive, admonishing, agnostic, anal, aporetic, arbitrary, arrogant, assiduous, assumptive, atheistic, attentive
biting, blameful, bumptious
cagey, calculating, captious, carping, categorical, caustic, caviling, censorious, challenging, cheap, chiding, choosy, clinical, compulsive, conceited, condescending, constipated, contemptuous, contradictory, contrary, costive, covetous, crafty, critical, cryptic, cutting
definite, deliberate, demanding, deprecatory, derogatory, dictatorial, didactic, disabused, disapproving, disbelieving, disciplined, discriminating, disdainful, disparaging, distrustful, doctrinaire, dogmatic
edacious, egocentric, exacting, exigent
facetious, fastidious, fault-finding, fussy
gluttonous, grabby, greedy, guarded
hard, harsh, high-and-mighty, hubristic, huffy, hypercritical
impatient, incisive, insistent, ironic
judgmental
logical
materialistic, measured, methodical, meticulous, mocking, mordacious, mordant
narcissistic, niggling
obsessive, omnivorous, opinionated, opportunistic
painstaking, particular, patronizing, pejorative, peremptory, perseverant, persistent, pertinacious, picky, pointed, political, precise, procacious
querulous
ravenous, rebuking, reproving, Rhadamanthine, rigorous
sanctimonious, sarcastic, sardonic, satiric, satirical, scolding, scornful, scrimping, scrupulous, sedulous, selective, self-centered, selfish, self-serving, self-willed, set, sharp, sharp-edged, skeptical, slashing, specific, supercilious, superior, systematic
tactical, tendentious, thorough, tireless, trenchant
ultracritical, unbelieving, ungenerous, unrelenting, unstinting, uppish, uppity, usurious
vain, vituperative, voracious
withholding, wolfish, wry

Helpful/Troublesome

Helpful, Positive, Responsible, or Nice

accessory, accommodating, aggrandizing, altruistic, amenable, amicable, attached, avuncular
beneficent, benevolent, benign, big-hearted, brotherly
caring, charitable, chivalrous, civic-minded, clement, compassionate, concerned, conciliatory, conscientious, considerate, constructive, cooperative
dutiful
eager, equable, equitable
faithful, fatherly, felicitous, fortunate, fraternal
good-hearted
helpful, heroic, humane, humanitarian, hunky-dory
indulgent, instructive, intimate
large, lenient, loving, loyal
magnanimous, maternal, merciful, motherly, munificent
neighborly, nice
obliging
paternal, patriotic, philanthropic, pleasant, positive, progressive, propitiatory, propitious, protective, provident
reliable, responsible, responsive
selfless, self-sacrificing, sensitive, sharing, sisterly, social, social-minded, solicitous, soothing, sunny, supportive, sympathetic
tender, thoughtful, tonic, tried-and-true, trustworthy, trusty
unfailing, unselfish, upbeat, useful
valuable, voluntary
well-intentioned, well-meaning, wholesome, worthwhile

Troublesome, Negative, Irresponsible, or Unpleasant

abrasive, abusive, acrid, acrimonious, annoying, antagonistic, arch, argumentative, avaricious, averse
balky, baneful, bilious, bitter, bothersome, bullying
cagey, capricious, carking, cloying, comminatory, complaining, covetous, crafty, crappy, creepy, crotchety, crummy, cutthroat
dangerous, designing, destructive, difficult, discontented, disquieting, disturbing, divisive, dour, downbeat

envious
fearsome, feral, fickle, fierce, foxy, fractious
harsh, horrendous, horrible, horrid, horrific
importunate, incompatible, infamous, inhumane, invidious, irksome, irreconcilable, irresponsible
jackleg, jangly, jaundiced
libelous, lousy, lupine
maddening, maladjusted, manipulative, mean, meddlesome, menacing, minatory
nagging, nauseating, negative, negligent, nerve-racking, nettlesome, nihilistic, nosy, notorious, noxious
objectionable, obnoxious, odious, offensive, officious, ominous, onerous, oppressive
parlous, pernicious, pesky, pestilent, pesty, petulant, polypragmatic, pompous, prankish, preachy, prickly, provocative, pugnacious
querulous
rancid, rancorous, rapacious, rascally, remorseless, renitent, reprehensible, restrictive, rivalrous, roguish
sacrilegious, savage, scary, scathing, scurrilous, seditious, self-destructive, severe, sharp, sick, slanderous, slashing, slinking, sly, small, smirking, snide, sniffish, sniffy, snobbish, snoopy, snotty, sordid, sour, spiteful, spleenful, sticky, stroppy, stuck-up, subversive
terrifying, thorny, thoughtless, toxic, treacly, tricky, troublesome, truculent, trying
unconcerned, undependable, unfaithful, ungrateful, unpleasant, unsympathetic, useless
venomous, vicious, vindictive, virulent, vitriolic, vituperative, vulpine

SEX, LOVE, AND ROMANCE

Love and Romance
Flirtation, Dating, and Courting
Sexuality and Libido
Homosexuality
Anatomy and Physiology of Sex
Contraception and Fertility
Sex Acts
Perversions, Fetishes, and Titillations
Pornography and Prostitution

Love and Romance

amative (*adj*) inclined to love and lust
amatory (*adj*) pertaining to love and lovemaking
amorist lover, devotee of love
amour love affair, esp. illicit one
ardor enthusiasm in love
carry a torch endure unrequited love
celibacy state of being unmarried; abstention from sexual love
cheat (*vb*) deceive one's lover with another, secret lover
chemistry animal attraction; sympathetic understanding; rapport
chivalry courageous, honorable, supportive attitude toward women
cohabit (*vb*) live together
concubine mistress, kept woman; secondary wife of polygamous male, usu. of inferior rank
conjugal love affection and relations between married couple
courtly love polite, formal, old-fashioned love
cuckold husband of woman who is having sex with another man
Dear John *Informal.* letter from woman telling her lover she is ending the relationship
devotion faithful, enduring love
dote on (*vb*) care for excessively or foolishly
ecstasy sexual bliss
enamor (*vb*) charm, fill with love or desire
fair sex women collectively, sometimes considered offensive
fancy (*vb*) be attracted to or fond of
favor token of love
inamorata woman who loves or is loved
inamorato man who loves or is loved
intimacy special, deep closeness growing from mutual love
love strong emotional attachment to another person; sexual passion or desire based on such feelings; intense affection or caring for another
lovelorn (*adj*) heartsick, rejected, or unhappy in love
lover person who is in love with another, esp. one having a sexual or romantic relationship with another; person with whom one is having an extramarital affair
lovesick (*adj*) anxious or emotionally unbalanced from love
moonstruck (*adj*) dreamily romantic; in love
mush overly sentimental affection
paramour married person's lover
philander (*vb*) engage in love affair without willingness to marry
pine (*vb*) long for one's lover
platonic love nonsexual love
rapture ecstasy of love
reconciliation settlement of differences with one's lover and resumption of romantic relationship, as after a separation
romance close emotional and physical relationship; love affair
seduction enticement of another into having sex
stardust naively romantic quality
sugar daddy *Informal.* man using his wealth to attract young woman as his lover
swoon (*vb*) faint with love
toy with (*vb*) play at love with no commitment
turtledoves sweethearts, lovers
unrequited love love for someone who does not love in return
yen craving for someone or for love

Flirtation, Dating, and Courting

advances overtures made in hopes of starting a relationship or sexual encounter
affair temporary romantic relationship
assignation lovers' arrangement to meet
beau male suitor; boyfriend
bewitch (*vb*) charm or delight with feelings of love
billet-doux love letter
bird-dog (*vb*) *Slang.* steal or attempt to steal another person's date
blade dashing, jaunty young man
blind date arranged meeting between previously unacquainted people
boy toy *Derogatory slang.* young man who serves as sexual plaything, esp. to a famous or wealthy person
buss (*vb*) kiss
caress (*vb*) fondle gently
come-hither (*adj*) beckoning in a flirtatious manner
computer dating service that matches couples based on personal information put into computer
coo (*vb*) speak gently, lovingly
coquetry flirtation
cosset (*vb*) fondle as one would a pet
courtship act and process of seeking to become another's lover; wooing of one person by another
cruise (*vb*) *Informal.* travel about in search of sexual companionship
dalliance flirtation; fondling, amorous foreplay
date arrangement to meet for pleasant or romantic activity; romantic partner; (*vb*) see a romantic partner on regular basis
Dutch treat date on which each person pays his or her own costs
endearment word or term of affection; pet name
femme fatale irresistibly attractive woman
fling inconsequential love affair
flirt (*vb*) court playfully; (*n*) person who tempts others through playful courting
fondle (*vb*) caress, stroke gently
forbidden fruit attractive but unavailable love interest
French kiss deep kiss with tongue inserted in partner's mouth
gallivant (*vb*) run around in search of sexual companionship
hanky-panky *Informal.* questionable sexual conduct
indiscretion coy or ill-advised reference to sexual encounter
jilt (*vb*) abandon one's sweetheart
ladies' man extremely flirtatious, sexually interested male
lady-killer *Informal.* devastatingly attractive man who fascinates women
liaison sexual encounter or affair
liberties impertinent or unwarranted sexual actions
necking prolonged kissing and fondling
ogling closely eyeing the object of one's affection
one-night stand *Informal.* casual, unrepeated sexual encounter
osculation kiss
parietal (*adj*) having to do with rules governing contact between sexes and dating hours, esp. at institution
pass *Informal.* approach to another with intimated offer of sex
personals classified advertisements for sexual partners
pet name affectionate term of address
pin (*vb*) formalize steady dating arrangement with girl by giving her one's fraternity pin
reconcile (*vb*) resolve differences and renew affection
rendezvous meeting between lovers, sometimes in secret
soul kiss passionate, open-mouthed kiss with tongue of one partner in mouth of the other; French kiss
spoon (*vb*) *Informal.* court by caressing and kissing, esp. in a sentimental manner
squire (*vb*) escort woman to social gathering, esp. in a proper manner
string along (*vb*) *Informal.* encourage suitor with no intention of responding
suitor man courting a woman; swain
swain suitor
tease (*vb*) engage in coy, playful flirtation; (*n*) flirt, coquette
temptress female who entices or allures
tryst romantic meeting, rendezvous
wolf whistle man's whistle of appreciation for woman's appearance

Sexuality and Libido

age of consent age when one may legally engage in sex
animal magnetism erotic attraction
aphrodisiac substance that increases sexual desire and performance
asexual (*adj*) having no sexual orientation
birds and bees euphemism for basic information about sexuality and reproduction
bisexual (*adj*) attracted to both males and females
carnal (*adj*) relating to physical desire
chastity virginity, sexual innocence
Circean (*adj*) dangerously or fatally attractive
concupiscence strong sexual desire
conjugal rights sexual rights of husband and wife
continence total abstinence from sexual activity
easy (*adj*) available for indiscriminate sex
emasculate (*vb*) deprive male of his power and sexuality, literally by castration or figuratively
epicene (*adj*) with characteristics of both sexes; sexless, neither male nor female
erotic (*adj*) pertaining to sexual love; strongly sexual
erotica art and literature with erotic content
facts of life basic information about sexuality and reproduction
fast (*adj*) easily available for sex
free love uninhibited sexual behavior, generally

without expectation of conventional social contracts such as marriage
frigid (*adj*) sexually unresponsive, said esp. of women
heterosexual one attracted to opposite sex
homosexual one attracted to same sex
impotent (*adj*) unable to achieve erection for sexual intercourse
Kinsey scale sevenfold numerical scale of sexual orientation, devised by Alfred Kinsey, in which zero is exclusive heterosexuality and six is exclusive homosexuality
lascivious (*adj*) lustful, lewd
lechery lewdness, lustfulness
letch *Slang.* lecherous individual
liberated (*adj*) without sexual inhibition
libertine one who indulges freely in sex
libido sexual desire and energy
love potion magic substance that creates desire; aphrodisiac
lust strong sexual desire, esp. without deep affection
machismo exaggerated, showy claims of virility
macho (*adj*) overly assertive, virile, and domineering
magnetism fundamental sexual attractiveness
misogyny hatred of women
neuter (*adj*) having no sex
nubile (*adj*) ready for marriage, said esp. of young women
nymphet sexually precocious girl in early teens
philter magic substance that arouses passion; love potion
potency virility, sexual ability
promiscuity indiscriminate, casual, frequent sexual activity
prudery extreme modesty, sexual restraint
prurience lewd, lascivious desire or thought
salacious (*adj*) lewd, lascivious
scabrous (*adj*) risqué; obscene
sensuality fondness for and indulgence in sensory pleasure; lasciviousness
sexuality state of being or feeling sexual
sybarite sensualist, voluptuary
transsexual (*adj*) sexually oriented as if one's body were of the opposite sex
trollop promiscuous woman
vamp wily, seductive woman
vestal virgin chaste woman
voluptuary person given over to sensual gratification

Homosexuality

AC/DC (*adj*) *Slang.* bisexual
age-differentiated (*adj*) designating homosexuality involving usu. bisexual adult male and sexually passive young boy prized for his androgynous qualities, predominant in Islamic world, ancient Greece, and pre-industrial Europe
androphilia homosexuality involving two adults, both of whom self-identify as males, predominant in 20th-century United States and Europe
bisexual (*adj*) attracted to and sexually active with both males and females; (*n*) such a person
camp something involving self-conscious and extravagant humor, irony, or amusement, often with playful inversion of values; (*vb*) behave in an extravagantly theatrical and stereotypically effeminate manner
catamite boy or youth in homosexual relationship with man; gunsel
come out (*vb*) declare one's homosexuality to family and friends or publicly; enter gay subculture
drag clothing worn by one sex that is characteristic of the other sex
drag queen male transvestite
effeminate (*adj*) not masculine in appearance or behavior, said esp. of homosexuals
gay (*adj*) homosexual, either male or female, sometimes restricted to males only
gay liberation sociopolitical movement to combat legal and social discrimination against homosexuals, begun in late 1960's
gay pride communally nurtured sense of self-esteem and self-assertion among homosexuals
gender-differentiated (*adj*) designating homosexuality involving fixed sexual roles in which one partner is passive and the other active-penetrative
heterosexism prejudicial discrimination against nonheterosexual practices based on tacit belief in universality of heterosexual norms
homoeroticism sexual arousal caused by member of same sex
homophile one who is homosexual; (*adj*) supportive of gay rights and interests
homophobia irrational fear of or aversion to homosexuals
homosexual person sexually attracted to and usu. sexually active with members of the same sex
in the closet secretly homosexual
latent (*adj*) in popular usage, designating one who appears heterosexual while repressing unconscious homosexual tendencies
lesbian female homosexual
outing public exposure of another's homosexuality against his or her will
out of the closet having revealed one's homosexuality
pederasty sexual relations between a man and an boy, usu. under sixteen
queer bashing physical and verbal assault on gays, usu. by young homophobic males who self-identify as heterosexual
situational (*adj*) designating homosexuality that occurs in sex-segregated situations, such as prisons, ships, or boarding schools, where heterosexuals are deprived of contact with the opposite sex, usu. temporary and without homosexual self-identity
transvestite person who dresses in clothing of opposite sex, esp. drag queen

Anatomy and Physiology of Sex

AIDS acquired immune deficiency syndrome; fatal disease characterized by inability of body to fight various infections due to HIV virus, which attacks immune system, transmitted by direct contact of body fluids

androgynous (*adj*) having both male and female characteristics
ARC AIDS-related complex; various diseases and infections to which AIDS sufferers are susceptible
areola pigmented area around nipple
arousal condition in which there are physiological signs of sexual stimulation, such as erection
bosom woman's breast
breast woman's mammary gland
bust woman's breasts
buxom (*adj*) describing woman having large breasts and full body
callipygian (*adj*) having shapely buttocks
castration removal of man's testicles
cervix neck of uterus
chlamydia gonorrhealike venereal disease caused by parasite
cleavage area between woman's breasts
climax orgasm
clitoris small, sensitive, erectile protuberance at upper end of female vulva
conception fertilization of egg by sperm
crabs pubic lice
cramps pain caused by menstrual period
crotch genital area
cryptorchidism undescended testicles
ejaculation male orgasm with emission of sperm
erection stiffening of blood-filled penis due to sexual arousal
erogenous (*adj*) designating areas of body that are sensitive to sexual stimulation; erotogenic
erotogenic (*adj*) erogenous
estrous cycle period of increased sexual interest and activity
eunuch castrated male
fallopian tube female internal tube that carries eggs from ovaries to uterus
foreskin fleshy covering of head of penis
genitalia genitals
genitals external sexual organs, male or female; genitalia
gonad organ producing eggs or sperm
gonorrhea infectious venereal disease characterized by inflammation of and discharge from mucous membrane
G spot extremely sensitive and erogenous spot in front wall of vagina, instrumental in orgasm
gynandrous (*adj*) having physical characteristics of both sexes
hermaphrodite person with physical characteristics of both male and female
herpes simplex recurrent, incurable venereal disease affecting mouth or genitals with sores
hymen membrane that partly closes vagina of virgin; maidenhead
labia majora outer folds at vaginal opening
labia minora inner folds at vaginal opening
maidenhead hymen
mammary (*adj*) pertaining to woman's breasts
mons veneris female pubic mound
multiply (*vb*) have sexual intercourse, conceive, and bear children
nipple dark, sensitive, protuberant opening of breast through which milk flows
orgasm convulsive climax of intercourse
ovary egg-producing organ of female
ovulation monthly dropping of egg from ovary to uterus
ovum egg produced by female
penis male erectile organ of copulation and bonding, used esp. by heterosexuals for insertion of sperm into uterus
period monthly menstruation
phallic (*adj*) pertaining to the penis
phallus penis; object that represents or symbolizes penis
PMS premenstrual syndrome
premenstrual syndrome PMS; physical and emotional changes associated with hormonal fluctuations prior to menstruation
prepuce foreskin
priapic (*adj*) pertaining to the penis
priapism abnormal, persistent erection without accompanying sexual desire
private parts external sexual organs; genitals
procreate (*vb*) have sexual intercourse resulting in childbirth
prostate gland gland at base of urethra in males
puberty onset of sexual maturity
pubescence arrival at puberty
pubic (*adj*) pertaining to or situated in area of pubis
pubic lice small parasitic insects living in pubic hair and transmitted by sexual contact
pubis lower abdomen, covered with hair and forming bony protuberance above genitals
pudenda external female genitals
reproduction sexual process of conception, pregnancy, and birth of young
safe sex use of condom during intercourse as protection against disease; practice of oral sex or mutual masturbation for same purpose
scrotum sack holding testicles
semen male ejaculate containing sperm
sex basic division of a species into male and female, for purpose of reproduction; sexual activity; instinct or attraction drawing one sex toward another; sexual intercourse; genitals
sex change operation surgical reconstruction of one's sexual organs as those of the opposite sex
sexually transmitted disease any of various infections acquired through contact of sexual organs, including AIDS, ARC, chlamydia, crabs, gonorrhea, herpes simplex, pubic lice, syphilis, trichomoniasis, venereal disease, and yeast infection; venereal disease
smegma sebaceous matter secreted around penis or clitoris; cheese
social disease venereal disease
spado castrated man
sperm spermatozoon, male seed in semen
sterile (*adj*) barren, incapable of procreating
syphilis infectious degenerative venereal disease acquired through sexual contact or congenitally
testicle sperm-producing gland at base of penis; testis

testis testicle; *pl.* testes
trichomoniasis parasitic infestation of vagina causing heavy discharge
tumescence stiffening and engorging of penis
uterus organ of conception and nurturance of fetus; womb
vagina canal from vulva to uterus
vas deferens tube carrying sperm from testicle to penis
venereal disease disease transmitted by sexual contact with infected person; sexually transmitted disease; social disease
vulva external female genitals
yeast infection fungus living in vagina

Contraception and Fertility

abortion induced expulsion of fetus from mother's womb
artificial insemination insemination of woman for purposes of conception through medical procedure rather than intercourse
barren (*adj*) infertile; unable to conceive
bilateral tubal ligation BTL; surgical sterilization of female
birth control prevention of conception by chemical or mechanical means; contraception
birth-control pill contraceptive hormone, usu. estrogen and progesterone, taken daily in tablet form by women, that causes temporary infertility
BTL bilateral tubal ligation
cervical cap diaphragmlike device used with spermicidal jelly to prevent sperm from entering uterus
climacteric period of major physiological change, such as menopause
coil intrauterine contraceptive device
coitus interruptus contraception through withdrawal of penis before ejaculation
condom usu. rubber sheath worn on penis to capture semen during intercourse and thus prevent conception
contraception prevention of pregnancy
contraceptive sponge absorbent material containing spermicide placed on cervix for contraception
diaphragm rubber disk worn on cervix during intercourse for contraception by preventing sperm from entering uterus
douche water or cleansing agent used for washing semen from vagina after intercourse, considered ineffective contraceptive method
false pregnancy symptoms of pregnancy without having actual embryo in womb
fertility ability to conceive or impregnate
fertility drug hormonal substance used to induce ovulation and produce pregnancy
foam spermicidal substance placed in vagina for contraceptive purposes
gravid (*adj*) pregnant
hysterectomy surgical removal of uterus
impregnate (*vb*) make (a female) pregnant; cause (an egg) to be fertilized
infertility inability to conceive or impregnate; barrenness; sterility
intrauterine device IUD; contraceptive device worn continuously for up to several years inside uterus to prevent fertilization or implantation
in utero (*adj*) in the womb or uterus
in vitro (*adj*) *Latin.* lit. in glass; artificially inseminated and maintained, as in a test tube
IUD intrauterine device
loop type of IUD
menarche first menstruation, at beginning of fertility
menopause end of menstruation and fertility
menses monthly menstruation
menstruation monthly discharge of blood from uterus when conception has not occurred
morning-after pill contraceptive chemical taken after intercourse to prevent implantation of embryo
pessary contraceptive device worn in vagina
pill birth-control pill
pregnant (*adj*) carrying fetus inside womb; with child
prophylactic device something that prevents conception and venereal disease, esp. a condom
rhythm method contraceptive method that gauges likelihood of fertility during woman's menstrual cycle
salpingectomy surgical severing of fallopian tubes to sterilize a woman
spermicide substance that kills sperm
sterility inability to produce living offspring
sterilization surgical procedure that prevents conception
tubal ligation sterilization of female by sealing off of fallopian tubes to prevent ovum from reaching uterus
tying one's tubes *Slang.* tubal ligation
vasectomy surgical procedure for sterilizing men by cutting vas deferens

Sex Acts

action *Slang.* sexual activity
act of love intercourse
adultery sex act by married person with someone other than spouse
astride (*adj*) taking a dominant position during penetration
autoeroticism self-stimulation, masturbation
bed (*vb*) take to bed for sexual activity
blow job oral penile sex, fellatio
bundling cuddling in bed without undressing
coition coitus
coitus sexual intercourse; coition
congress sexual intercourse
consummation sexual intercourse, esp. on wedding night
copulation sexual intercourse
cunnilingus oral vaginal sex
deflower (*vb*) have sexual intercourse with a virgin
ejaculate (*vb*) emit sperm at orgasm

fellatio oral penile sex

foreplay fondling and caressing before actual intercourse

fornication sexual intercourse, esp. between unmarried persons

inseminate (*vb*) ejaculate into (vagina); impregnate (a female)

intercourse copulation between male and female

in the saddle having mounted one's usu. female partner

irrumation oral penile sex, esp. involving active thrusting of penis; fellatio

know (*vb*) have sexual intercourse with (biblical)

lie with (*vb*) have sexual intercourse with

lovemaking sexual relations

make love have sexual intercourse

masturbation self-stimulation of one's sexual organs

mate (*vb*) have sexual relations

ménage à trois sex act among three people

missionary position sexual intercourse with man on top and woman underneath lying face to face

mount (*vb*) position oneself atop female

onanism masturbation; uncompleted intercourse

penetration entry of male into female

premarital sex sexual relations before marriage

quickie *Informal.* brief, often secretive sex act

ravish (*vb*) force someone to have sexual relations

relations sexual intercourse

seduce (*vb*) entice unwilling or doubtful person into sex

sexual intercourse copulation between male and female

sexual relations intercourse and related sexual activities

sleep around (*vb*) *Informal.* have casual sex with numerous partners

sleep with (*vb*) have sexual intercourse with, make love to

statutory rape sex with person under legal age of consent

suck (*vb*) pull gently with mouth, esp. on partner's genitals

union sexual intercourse

venery gratification of sexual desire

Perversions, Fetishes, and Titillations

lgolagnia pleasure and gratification derived from inflicting or suffering pain; sadism

estiality sexual activity with animals

ondage sex involving forcible restraint or tying up of partner

reather person excited by telephoning someone, often unknown, and breathing heavily over phone

hild abuse sexual molestation of child by adult

rime against nature sexual perversion

ate rape rape inflicted by person with whom victim is socializing voluntarily

efile (*vb*) humiliate or brutalize sexually

eviance behavior that is socially disapproved of and considered unnatural or abnormal

ominance sex in which one partner humiliates, degrades, or intimidates the other for sexual stimulation

exhibitionism exposing oneself to others for sexual stimulation

exploitation degradation, victimization, or profit making from sexual activity

fetish sexual obsession with a specific object or usu. nonerogenous body part

flagellation sexual stimulation by whipping or beating

flashing sudden public exposure of one's nudity for sexual stimulation

frottage practice of deriving stimulation by rubbing up against another person, as in a crowded place

golden shower urination that causes sexual stimulation

homeovestism dressing oneself as a sexual object, esp. among women, to derive sexual excitement

incest sexual relations among family members

incubus evil male spirit who has sex with women in their sleep

indecent exposure public nudity

kinky (*adj*) perverse, decadent, or unusual in one's sexual habits

masochism derivation of sexual pleasure from undergoing pain, abuse, or cruelty

molestation sexual assault, esp. of defenseless person or child

mooning *Slang.* exposing one's bare buttocks in public

necrophilia sexual stimulation from corpses

nymphomania insatiable sexual craving in women

off-color (*adj*) somewhat offensive, indecent

orgy group sexual relations

panty raid college prank involving males' theft of females' underwear

paraphilia mental disorder characterized by preference for unusual sexual practices and perversions

pedophilia sexual desire in an adult for children

Peeping Tom voyeur

perversion deviance or sexual maladjustment; such an act; paraphilia

rape forcible sexual relations

sadism derivation of sexual pleasure from inflicting pain on others

sadomasochism derivation of sexual pleasure from inflicting and undergoing pain or cruelty; S and M

S and M sado masochism

scopophilia sexual pleasure derived by looking at nude bodies or erotic photographs

sexual assault rape or molestation

sodomy anal intercourse; intercourse with animals

streaking running naked through public place as form of exhibitionism

submission allowing oneself to be dominated to derive sexual stimulation

succubus female demon who has sex with men in their sleep

swinging *Slang.* exchanging partners with another couple

taboo (*adj*) forbidden due to indecency or bad taste
telephone sex stimulation through verbal sexual fantasies heard over telephone
titillation erotic stimulation
transsexuality predisposition to identify with opposite sex, often accompanied by sex change operation
transvestism practice of dressing in attire of opposite sex, esp. among men
unnatural act sexual practice considered abnormal
urolagnia deriving sexual stimulation from urination, esp. drinking of urine
vice immoral or illegal sexual practice
voyeurism watching others disrobe or engage in sex for purposes of sexual stimulation
vulgarity coarse sexual behavior and language

Pornography and Prostitution

bagnio brothel
bawd female procurer, madam
beefcake *Informal.* photographs of nude or nearly nude young men in magazines, posed to display their muscles or genitals
bordello brothel, whorehouse
brothel whorehouse; bagnio
camp follower prostitute on military base
centerfold photo of nude woman or man featured in magazine
cheesecake *Informal.* photographs of nude or scantily clad women posed suggestively
concubine woman serving as mistress or member of harem
courtesan prostitute for upper classes of society
demimondaine female prostitute
demimonde society of female prostitutes
escort service service providing call girls under guise of being public dates
geisha professional hostess for men's parties, often mistakenly thought to be prostitute (Japan)
gigolo man supported by women in return for sex
groupie *Informal.* female who pursues celebrities, esp. rock musicians, for sex
hard-core (*adj*) graphic and explicit in pornographic content
harem group of wives or concubines belonging to polygamous male
harlot prostitute
madam woman managing whorehouse
massage parlor business usu. providing sexual services for sale in addition to nonsexual massage
obscenity indecent, offensive sexual behavior or content
odalisque female slave, harem concubine
pander (*vb*) solicit customers for prostitutes
peep show lewd entertainment featuring nude women
pimp procurer
pinup girl usu. naked or scantily clad woman posing seductively for photographs
pornography writing or pictures portraying sexual activity and intending to arouse
procurer man who solicits customers for prostitute; pimp
prostitute person who sells sexual acts to strangers
prostitution sexual intercourse or acts for payment
red-light district area of city with whorehouses and prostitutes
smut pornography
soft-core (*adj*) having borderline pornographic content
solicit (*vb*) offer sexual services for hire
streetwalker prostitute doing business on public streets, usu. cheaper than call girl
stripper person doing striptease dance
striptease lewd entertainment featuring woman or man removing clothes in time to music
strumpet prostitute
tart prostitute
tramp prostitute
trollop prostitute
white slavery prostitution ring using young, often rural girls kidnapped into bondage
whore prostitute
X-rated (*adj*) pornographic, used esp. of a book or film

STRATEGY, INTRIGUE, AND DECEPTION

Strategy and Tactics

about-face sudden reversal of position
aggrandizement actions intended to increase power or wealth
angle secret motive; (*vb*) attempt to gain advantage, often by improper or illicit means
approach preliminary steps taken in setting about task or problem
arm-twisting application of direct, personal pressure to achieve desired result
arrangement informal, often secret agreement or plan
artfulness skill and cunning in adapting means to ends
artifice clever, artful stratagem
baffle (*vb*) confuse, perplex
bait (*vb*) tease or torment with persistent, malicious attacks to generate desired response
bedevil (*vb*) utterly confuse and harass so as to take advantage of
befuddle (*vb*) confuse, perplex
bewilder (*vb*) utterly confuse or puzzle by numbe

or complexity of considerations
bind situation in which one is obstructed or held in check; predicament
blow hot and cold change from favorable to opposing view and back again
blueprint detailed plan
brinkmanship pushing a risky situation to the limit of safety
buttonhole (*vb*) detain in conversation as if by physical restraint
buy off (*vb*) persuade to action or restraint by payment or other inducement
cagey (*adj*) shrewd, esp. cautious not be entrapped
calculated (*adj*) carefully thought out to accomplish an end
call one's bluff confront and expose another's empty threat or pretense
canny (*adj*) clever, calculating, or shrewd
captious (*adj*) designed to confuse or ensnare, esp. in argument
capture (*vb*) take or attain domination of by stratagem or guile
carrot something used as a lure or incentive
cash in on (*vb*) obtain advantage or profit from
cat and mouse act of teasing and playing with something before destroying it
catch concealed drawback, complication, or means of entrapment
Catch-22 paradoxical problem whose solution is made impossible by circumstances inherent in it; senseless and self-contradictory policy or bureaucratic regulation
change of heart reversal of opinion or point of view
chart (*vb*) carefully plan out (a course of action)
circuitous (*adj*) indirect or evasive in deeds or language
clout predominant influence within particular circle
coax (*vb*) persuade or influence by flattery; manipulate to desired end by prolonged effort and adroit handling
coercion use of force or intimidation to obtain compliance
competition rivalry between two or more parties to secure the favor of a third party
complicate (*vb*) make more difficult or complex than necessary
compromise (*vb*) make mutual concessions to achieve overall end or reach agreement
concession act of yielding on or acknowledgement of disputed point
concoction scheme or plan that has been devised; fabrication
conduit person who serves as means of transmitting or distributing information or goods
confound (*vb*) perplex, baffle, or throw into confusion
confrontation face-to-face encounter with adversary
contrivance artificial arrangement or scheme
convoluted (*adj*) tortuously involved, complex, or confusing
corner (*vb*) drive into a position without escape; entrap
countermine (*vb*) devise stratagem or counterplot, esp. for halting enemy attack
coup swift, cunning, and successful action
craft skill or cunning in achieving ends or deceiving others
cross (*vb*) oppose, contradict, or thwart
cunning ingenuity, craftiness, and subtle skill, often used for deception
curve deceptive or misleading maneuver
dare (*vb*) meet boldly or defiantly; challenge another to prove himself or herself
deploy (*vb*) spread out, place, use, or arrange strategically
design specific purpose; plans and schemes formed to achieve some purpose
device stratagem or trick, esp. method of deception
diagram detailed plan or outline in graphic form
disown (*vb*) refuse to acknowledge as pertaining to oneself; deny responsibility for
distraction something intended to divert attention away from something else
diversion pretense or feint that draws attention away from one's true purpose or primary action
dodge clever expedient or contrivance, used to evade or gain advantage
embarrass (*vb*) involve in public shame or difficulty; place in doubt; impede by obstacles or difficulties
encroach (*vb*) advance gradually or stealthily beyond proper limits; trespass into another's territory
engineer (*vb*) manage by skillful contrivance
enticement temptation that leads on or excites false hopes
entrap (*vb*) place in position from which there is no escape; corner
evasion elusion or escape by trickery or clever stratagem; avoidance of one's obligations
fabrication concoction
feather one's nest take advantage of opportunities for gain, esp. at another's expense
feint attack aimed at one point as a distraction from the real point of attack
fence (*vb*) parry arguments by avoiding direct answers
finesse (*vb*) handle situation with skill and adroitness
flip-flop *Informal.* abrupt, often repeated, change of position
foil (*vb*) keep from succeeding; thwart
forestall (*vb*) obstruct or thwart by prior action
freeload (*vb*) *Informal.* take advantage of another's generosity
gambit maneuver calculated to gain an advantage, esp. at the outset
gamble venture of uncertain outcome or involving risk
game stratagem, often tricky or illegal
game plan carefully thought out, long-range strategy or course of action toward a specific end

gamesmanship use of ethically dubious or improper but not strictly illegal means and expedients to achieve an objective
gimmick ingenious scheme or device; hidden feature
hatch (*vb*) invent, fabricate, or initiate
hedge intentionally evasive, vague statement; line of retreat left open in order to avoid commitment
hogtie (*vb*) make helpless so as to hamper or thwart
hook something that entices or attracts others
horse trading crafty negotiating or self-serving compromise
house of cards scheme or plan that is delicately balanced and vulnerable to imminent collapse
hucksterism use of aggressive or flashy methods to influence others, esp. to make a sale
impede (*vb*) hinder or retard in progress by means of obstacles
instigate (*vb*) incite or provoke to action
interlope (*vb*) intrude upon another's rights or territory
inveigle (*vb*) obtain, persuade, or entice by flattery and artful talk
jockey (*vb*) maneuver cleverly for position of advantage
juggling act process of skillfully managing several elements at once
jury-rig (*vb*) construct or arrange temporarily in haphazard manner
knack clever method or stratagem
labyrinth complex, sometimes devious arrangement or maze
lead on (*vb*) induce to follow unwise course; draw into trap
live by one's wits achieve one's goals through cunning, guile, and mental quickness
loophole means of escape, esp. through an ambiguity or omission in a document permitting an evasion or misconstruction of its intent
low blow unscrupulous or unfair attack
lull (*vb*) cause to feel a false sense of security, esp. prior to attack
lure (*vb*) attract or entice into danger by false promise or decoy
Machiavellian (*adj*) devious, cunning, or unscrupulous
machination scheme or crafty design with evil purpose
maneuver (*vb*) employ clever stratagems or schemes to achieve an end; skillfully manipulate a person or situation to one's advantage
manipulate (*vb*) manage skillfully, esp. control by cunning or insidious means to one's advantage
map out (*vb*) envision and plan beforehand
mastermind (*vb*) provide skillful direction and supervision for (an important activity)
meddle (*vb*) interfere with or involve oneself in another's activity without right or invitation
nepotism favoritism shown toward one's relations
nickel-and-dime (*vb*) defeat by small, gradual incursions
obviate (*vb*) eliminate (a difficulty) before it arises
on the make seeking to improve one's position by any means necessary
opportunism unscrupulous or unprincipled exploitation of opportunities
orchestrate (*vb*) arrange so as to achieve best result
outflank (*vb*) bypass (one's adversary)
outfox (*vb*) outwit
outguess (*vb*) outwit by anticipating others' actions
outmaneuver (*vb*) outdo or defeat by skillful planning
outreach (*vb*) take advantage of through deception
outsmart (*vb*) outwit
outwit (*vb*) use superior cunning or ingenuity to get the better of; outfox; outsmart
parlay (*vb*) use (one's assets) to achieve greater success or wealth
parry (*vb*) evade or adroitly ward off
pass the buck shift one's responsibility to another
pawn person used or manipulated to further another's purposes
perpetrate (*vb*) execute or commit (an act, esp. a crime)
perplex (*vb*) hamper with complications or confusion
pitch *Informal.* persuasive line of reasoning
pitfall trap or hidden danger
play both ends against the middle maneuver opposing groups against each other to one's own advantage
play possum gain advantage of someone by feigning sleep or death
ploy maneuver or stratagem, esp. used to frustrate adversary
ply (*vb*) supply or offer something so as to gain advantage
posture viewpoint or attitude regarding specific condition
provoke (*vb*) stir up intentionally
pull strings exercise covert influence or control
put up to (*vb*) incite or instigate
raid surprise attack; daring escapade, esp. against adversary; sudden incursion by legal authorities
ransack (*vb*) search thoroughly, esp. during a robbery
retrench (*vb*) reduce, diminish, or curtail to economize or shift emphasis of plans
revenge (*vb*) inflict injury in return for
sandbag (*vb*) *Informal.* coerce by threat or force; treat harshly; thwart
scenario description of possible outcome based on projected actions
scheme cunning, usu. secret plan of action
scuttle (*vb*) abandon, withdraw from, or eliminate (prior plans or resources)
shrewd (*adj*) astute, keen, clever
smooth operator one who maneuvers and manipulates with deft cunning
song and dance long, misleading or irrelevant statement, often used as distraction
stratagem clever trick or device for outwitting or gaining advantage over adversary or attaining objective

strategy careful, cleverly devised plan or series of maneuvers for attaining a specific goal or result
string along (*vb*) *Informal.* draw into a circumstance and keep in an unresolved state
subtlety astute perception in handling others
tactics system or method for achieving success or advantage by use of one's means and resources
tease (*vb*) tempt, tantalize, or taunt, esp. with persistently petty annoyances
temptation something that entices another to do wrong
throw off (*vb*) mislead or distract
thwart (*vb*) successfully frustrate (another's purpose)
toy with (*vb*) amuse oneself at another's expense
trip up (*vb*) detect in a fault or mistake; expose
trump card *Informal.* final, conclusive factor that gives advantage to one group or person
twist clever and unexpected device or development
undermine (*vb*) subvert and weaken in degrees by insidious, often secret actions
use (*vb*) manipulate; take advantage of
vacillate (*vb*) alter one's opinion or position frequently; hesitate in one's decisions
vex (*vb*) puzzle or confound
volte-face *French.* about-face; reversal of position
vulpine (*adj*) foxy, cunning or sly
waiting game delaying of an action in hopes of a better opportunity to come
weave (*vb*) contrive by an elaborate combination of elements
wheel and deal *Informal.* pursue one's goals without restraint by using personal power
wild card unpredictable person or element with determining impact
window of opportunity most advantageous moment for doing something or implementing a plan
wrangle (*vb*) obtain by petty, persistent argument
wrinkle innovative device, trick, strategy, or aspect

Intrigues, Plots, and Corruption

agent provocateur one who associates with and incites suspected persons to incriminating acts
agitator one who stirs up public feeling, esp. inciting unlawful acts
baksheesh tip or bribe
bane curse; source of harm
bookmaking determining odds and accepting illegal bets
bribe something given secretly to influence opinion, esp. money; payoff
cabal plot, esp. persons secretly united against their government
cloak-and-dagger (*adj*) pertaining to melodrama, intrigue, and espionage
collusion secret agreement to cooperate for deceitful purpose
complicity taking part in or having knowledge of another's illicit activity
conspiracy secret agreement or scheme among several parties to perform wrongful act
contract secret arrangement for hired assassin to commit murder
corruption inducement to or engagement in improper or wrongful acts
coup d'état secret plot by small group to overthrow existing government in sudden, decisive action
covin conspiracy to defraud or harm others
cult secret organization intensely devoted to promotion of specific goals, individuals, or beliefs
depose (*vb*) remove from office
dethrone (*vb*) remove from power, esp. from royal throne
fix (*vb*) illegally predetermine or prearrange outcome of something, usu. for profit
gang group secretly organized to perform illegal acts; ring
gerrymandering inequitable division of political territory
guerrilla one engaged in sabotage, terrorism, and irregular warfare
henchman unscrupulous, often violent, subordinate
inside information details or plans known only to select individuals and held in confidence
insurgency often disorganized and sporadic revolt against a government
insurrection organized, open rebellion against a government
intrigue secret scheme or plot; underhanded or deceitful stratagem, often very intricate
jobbery unscrupulous conduct by public officials for private gain
kickback reimbursement of funds based on secret collusion, usu. to defraud another
load (*vb*) alter balance of dice to make them predictable
mole double agent whose cover is established before spying begins
mutiny organized opposition to authority, esp. on ship
patronage awarding of official jobs to gain political advantage
payoff *Informal.* bribe
payola *Informal.* secret payments for promotion or service, esp. to radio disc jockeys by record companies
plot secret plan, usu. for evil or unlawful end; intrigue
power play maneuver or strategy in which concentrated power is used to control a situation or rival
propaganda information and ideas spread deliberately to further one's goals or hinder those of one's adversary
putsch secret plot to overthrow a government, usu. relying on a sudden and swift uprising
rebellion defiance of or resistance to established authority
revolt organized uprising against a government
sabotage destruction of property or interference with the operation of a business or government so as to undermine it

scandal disgraceful or discreditable action or circumstance; public slander
sedition incitement of public disorder or insurrection against legal authority
sinecure office providing income for little or no work
slush fund money used for buying influence and corrupt political favors
snitch (*vb*) *Informal.* inform; (*n*) informer
stack (*vb*) prearrange secretly for purpose of cheating, esp. a deck of cards
subversion systematic efforts to undermine an organization by working secretly within it
terrorism coercion by use of systematic, random violence and intimidation
tokenism practice of making only insignificant, symbolic actions to satisfy demands
treason violation of allegiance to one's government, esp. an attempt to overthrow it or kill its leader
Trojan Horse something with a deceptive appearance, intended to undermine an adversary from within
underground secret organization plotting disruptions of civil order and concealing fugitives
uprising popular, often regional acts of opposition to authority
usurpation taking of another's office without right
vendetta prolonged, bitter feud involving revenge killings
vice corruption, esp. habitual moral failing

Secrecy and Concealment

abscond (*vb*) depart secretly
alias assumed name
ambush trap in which persons lie concealed and attack by surprise
backdoor (*adj*) indirect, concealed, or devious
beard decoy or disguise in social situation
behind-the-scenes (*adj*) working in secret
black market illicit trade in regulated goods
blind activity or organization used to conceal another, often illicit, purpose
booby trap bomb or mine concealed from the unwary in an apparently harmless object; any hidden trap set for an unsuspecting person
bug concealed device for eavesdropping
bury (*vb*) conceal by covering from view
bushwhack ambush, esp. by those hiding out in the woods
camouflage deception or concealment by disguise and artifice
cipher message in code; method of altering a text to conceal its meaning
clandestine (*adj*) done in secret; surreptitious
classified (*adj*) designating information not to be revealed publicly, esp. for reasons of national security
code system of arbitrary symbols with assigned meanings, used to communicate in secret
concealment means, place, state, or act of concealing or being concealed
confidence secret communication
contraband smuggling or illegal trafficking in prohibited goods
cover disguise; something that conceals or obscures the truth
covert (*adj*) secret or veiled; undercover
coverup stratagem for concealing, esp. conspiracy to prevent public disclosure of illegal or unethical act
cryptic (*adj*) intentionally obscure; used to conceal
cryptography writing and analyzing of messages written in secret code or cipher
disguise clothing and makeup used to conceal one's identity; misrepresentation of how something really is; masquerade
dissemble (*vb*) conceal facts or true motives by some pretense; give or put on a false appearance; dissimulate
fine print something deliberately obscure, esp. limitations of agreement
foxhole hiding place
fugitive one who runs away, hides, or assumes a disguise to evade capture
hole up (*vb*) take refuge, as from pursuers; hide
hugger-mugger (*adj*) secret; muddled or confused
hush-hush (*adj*) highly secret
incognito (*adj*) having one's identity concealed
inside information true or essential facts about something, often not widely known
intelligence information gathered covertly about enemy activities
lie low (*vb*) remain in hiding or out of sight for a period of time
low-profile (*adj*) in a deliberately inconspicuous or anonymous manner; without attracting attention
mask part of a disguise; something that conceals the truth
masquerade false or misleading appearance; disguise
obscurantism deliberate withholding of knowledge to gain advantage
on the lam escaping or hiding from authorities, esp. as a fugitive
palimpsest writing material erased and written over
password secret word or phrase, usu. used to gain entry to something
pig in a poke something offered with its true value concealed
recess partly concealed area
safe house haven where one may hide or safely engage in secret activities
screen something that shelters, protects, or conceals
secrecy state or condition of being secret or concealed; ability to keep secrets; habit of being secretive
shadow (*vb*) observe another over time from a distance without being noticed; (*n*) one who does this
smoke screen something intended to obscure or mislead
Star Chamber secret, arbitrary, unfair tribunal

stonewall (*vb*) *Informal.* act in an evasive, obstructive manner; refuse to cooperate, esp. with official inquiry
stowaway someone concealed on a vehicle so as to obtain transport
sub rosa (*adv*) covertly or secretly
subterfuge deceptive artifice or stratagem, esp. to conceal or evade
subterranean (*adj*) operating secretly outside normal society
suppress (*vb*) keep hidden or withhold from the public
surreptitious (*adj*) stealthy and underhanded; clandestine
surveillance concealed observation, esp. of an adversary
tail (*vb*) secretly observe or follow; (*n*) one who does this
tap (*vb*) cut in on (electric circuit or telephone line), usu. to eavesdrop
top-secret (*adj*) designating secret information, the revelation of which would pose grave danger to authority or security
track (*vb*) follow traces of and observe secretly; trail
ulterior (*adj*) beyond what is shown or avowed; intentionally kept concealed
undercover (*adj*) acting in secret; engaged in spying; covert
underhanded (*adj*) secretive or deceptive; sly; dishonest
under-the-counter (*adj*) clandestine, usu. involving illicit transaction or merchandise
under-the-table (*adj*) secret, underhanded; as a bribe
under wraps *Informal.* hidden away; kept concealed
up one's sleeve kept hidden, esp. for last-minute use, as a trick
veil something that serves to conceal or obscure
waylay (*vb*) ambush; attack by surprise
wiretap device attached to telephone line in order to eavesdrop

Pranks and Tricks

antic attention-grabbing, playful prank
caper frivolous prank; illegal or questionable act
caprice impulsive, unpredictable change or action
chicanery deception by cunning artifice or trickery
dido mischievous antic; prank
fourberie trickery, esp. underhanded maneuvers
hocus-pocus nonsense, sleight of hand, or trickery used to conceal deception
legerdemain sleight of hand; trickery
monkeyshine prank
practical joke prank intended to cause minor harm or embarrassment
prank mildly mischievous act or playful trick; dido; monkeyshine
prestidigitation sleight of hand
ruse trick or subterfuge
shenanigan *Informal.* mischievous trick or nonsense
skulduggery unscrupulous activity; devious tricks
sleight of hand cleverly executed, deceptive tricks or conjuring, usu. requiring manual dexterity; legerdemain; prestidigitation
trick clever and deceptive maneuver; mischievous prank; delusive appearance
waggery mischief; inclination to play practical jokes
wild-goose chase futile pursuit, esp. one intentionally induced by someone
wile trickery, guile, or ensnaring stratagem

Falsehood, Pretense, and Exaggeration

adulterate (*vb*) alter so as to make less pure or less valuable
affected (*adj*) not genuine in manner
apocrypha writings or statements of doubtful authenticity
apostasy total departure from one's beliefs
audacity bold, arrogant disregard for conventional thought or restrictions
backhanded (*adj*) indirect and devious
baloney *Slang.* trivial lies and exaggeration
belie (*vb*) give false impression of
bill of goods *Informal.* something intentionally misrepresented
bogus (*adj*) not genuine; counterfeit
brown-nose (*vb*) *Slang.* ingratiate oneself; seek favor
bum steer *Informal.* intentionally bad advice or misdirection
butter up (*vb*) *Informal.* gain favor of through lavish flattery
cajole (*vb*) persuade by flattery or false promises
calumny misrepresentations that injure another's reputation
canard false, fabricated, or exaggerated story or report
cant insincere statements; private language of some group, esp. the underworld
charade deceptive act; pretense
chimerical (*adj*) wildly improbable and imaginative
cock-and-bull story outrageous fabrication related as truth
contrive (*vb*) fabricate or invent, esp. in crafty manner
cook the books manipulate financial records to give a false impression
cop out (*vb*) *Informal.* back down on agreement or back out of unwanted responsibility
counterfeit (*vb*) make imitation of with intent to deceive; feign; (*adj*) bogus; fake; imitation; phony
cozen (*vb*) win over or influence by shrewd trickery and artful persuasion
crocodile tears hypocritical sorrow; false tears
cry wolf (*vb*) give false or needless alarm
defamation injury to another's reputation by libel or slander
dirt *Informal.* malicious gossip
dirty pool *Informal.* underhanded behavior; misconduct
distortion lacking, or altered from, a true sense or proportion

doctor (*vb*) tamper with or falsify, as a document
double-talk deliberately ambiguous or contradictory language with the appearance of sense, intended to deceive or confound
duplicity dishonesty about one's true motives or meaning
elusion skillful evasion of an adversary or difficulty
embellish (*vb*) add to or adorn for effect; exaggerate
equivocation use of ambiguous statements in order to mislead others or evade the truth
exaggeration enlarging on truth or reality; overemphasis; baloney; fish story; hokum; tall talk
exorbitant (*adj*) exceeding the bounds of what is proper or customary
extravagance excessive, unrestrained behavior or notion
fabricate (*vb*) invent, esp. concoct so as to deceive
facade false appearance; false front
facsimile exact copy or forgery
fairy tale exaggerated, implausible story
fake impostor, charlatan; worthless imitation of something; (*adj*) counterfeit
fallacy deceptive or delusive appearance; mistaken idea
false (*adj*) intentionally untrue; treacherous or disloyal; counterfeit
false front facade
falsehood dishonesty, lies; extreme exaggeration; untruth
falsify (*vb*) misrepresent; make false by alteration; fudge
fast and loose (*adv*) in a cunning and deceptive manner
fast-talk (*vb*) influence or deceive by glib, deceitful speech
feign (*vb*) give false appearance of; pretend
fish story *Informal.* tall tale; exaggeration of true facts
fishy (*adj*) questionable or suspicious
flannelmouthed (*adj*) speaking in a shifty, ingratiating way
fob off (*vb*) pass off (inferior substitute) as genuine
foist (*vb*) assert surreptitiously, by stealth or deceit; pass off as genuine
fool's paradise condition of imaginary satisfaction
forgery fabricating or altering of a document for purpose of fraud; document so produced
frame (*vb*) incriminate (an innocent person) by prearranged trick
fudge (*vb*) fail to meet responsibilities or commitments; welsh; exaggerate or falsify
gilding making things appear better than they are
glad hand *Informal.* insincere, ingratiating greeting
gloss deceptively appealing appearance
goldbrick one who malingers or shirks duties
guise false appearance; pretext
half-truth statement that mixes truth with falsehoods in order to deceive
hokum silly, nonsensical exaggeration and lies
hook something intended to attract and entrap
huckster one who employs showy methods or extravagant claims to promote and peddle merchandise or ideas
humbug something intended to deceive or mislead; someone pretending to be what he or she is not; gammon
hype (*vb*) promote by extravagant, often misleading propaganda; (*n*) such propaganda and exaggerated claims
hyperbole extreme exaggeration for effect
hypocrisy false appearance or pretense of virtues and beliefs one does not hold
illusion state of being intellectually deceived; misleading image
imitation (*adj*) counterfeit
impersonation disguising oneself or pretending to be another
impostor someone assuming false character or name for purpose of deception; fake
indirect (*adj*) tending to evade or misrepresent what really is; backhanded
jive false, misleading, or insincere and deceptive talk
lay it on (*vb*) exaggerate in order to impress or persuade
libel written or published defamation of another's reputation
line *Informal.* dishonest, evasive, or misleading statement
lip service insincere statement of devotion or support
lowball (*vb*) state deceptively low price or estimate
make believe (*vb*) pretend or feign
malinger (*vb*) pretend illness in order to avoid duties
mealy-mouthed (*adj*) inclined to use indirect or devious language
mendacity deception; dishonesty
mirage something that appears other than it is or seems to exist when it does not
mislead (*vb*) deceive; give false impression or advice to
misrepresent (*vb*) provide false information about or mistaken impression of
pass off (*vb*) offer or sell with intent to deceive; misrepresent
perjury dishonest statement under oath in court of law
phantom (*adj*) fictitious or illusory
phony (*adj*) false; counterfeit; (*n*) insincere or deceitful person
piracy unauthorized appropriation or use of another's property, esp. in copyright infringement
plagiarize (*vb*) represent (another's work) as one's own
pose attitude or appearance assumed for effect
pretense false, professed, or make-believe act or intent; charade
pretext assumed appearance or purpose used to conceal true intent
prevaricate (*vb*) equivocate; veer from truth
prodigal (*adj*) reckless, extravagant, or excessive
pseudo (*adj*) false or spurious
pull someone's leg trick or deceive another playfully
put on (*vb*) mislead deliberately; feign
put something over on deceive
quasi (*adj*) resembling or seeming

questionable (*adj*) doubtful or suspicious; likely to be false
recreant one who deserts friends or betrays beliefs
red herring distraction or false clue
ringer impostor, esp. one entering competition under false pretense
roorback defamatory, published political lies
scalp (*vb*) *Informal.* buy and resell at greatly increased price
shady deal arrangement of dubious merit and authenticity
shifty (*adj*) given to deception, evasion, and fraud
shuffle (*vb*) act in shifty, evasive manner
simulation act or object that is counterfeit or feigned
slander false oral statements that defame another's reputation
snare something deceptively appealing; trap
so-called (*adj*) misrepresented as such
sophistry false though apparently valid argument used to deceive
spoof good-natured hoax, esp. parody
spurious (*adj*) superficially similar but innately false
stretch (*vb*) amplify or exaggerate beyond the norm for one's own advantage
suborn (*vb*) induce another to lie or commit perjury
sweet talk *Informal.* insincere flattery
synthetic (*adj*) contrived as a substitute for the real thing
tall tale extremely fanciful or highly exaggerated story; yarn
tampering altering of something so as to falsify it; engaging in secret improprieties
tergiversation equivocation or evasion
tortuous (*adj*) characterized by indirect tactics; tricky, crooked, or devious
traduce (*vb*) betray with falsehoods and thus defame
trifle (*vb*) deal lightly or in a mocking manner
trump up (*vb*) concoct or invent for purpose of deception
two-time (*vb*) *Informal.* jilt or betray, esp. one's lover
untruth lie or falsehood
veneer superficial, deceptively pleasing appearance
whole cloth total and utter fabrication
whopper extravagant lie or deception
window dressing misrepresentation intended to give favorable impression of something
yarn highly embellished story; tall tale

Fraud, Treachery, and Deception

backslide (*vb*) fail to live up to one's beliefs or moral values
barefaced (*adj*) unscrupulous; not concealing one's vices
baseness lack of noble qualities of mind or spirit; villainy
betrayal disloyalty in time of need, esp. treacherous exposure to an enemy
bilk (*vb*) cheat by evading payment due
blackmail extortion through intimidation or by threat of public revelation or exposure
bluff (*vb*) deceive or frighten by pretense of strength
bounce (*vb*) draw (check) on insufficient funds
bunko *Informal.* swindle or scheme that takes advantage of another's ignorance
burn (*vb*) *Slang.* deceive or cheat in transaction, esp. by overpricing or failing to deliver goods
cardsharp one who habitually and successfully cheats at cards
cat's-paw person used to serve the purposes of another; dupe; tool
charlatan person making extravagant pretense of knowledge or skill; fraud; mountebank; quack
con *Informal.* confidence game; swindle
confidence game appropriation of funds by making false promises of quick profits, usu. from unethical investment; con; sting; swindle
deception act of deceiving; that which deceives
decoy someone or something used to lure an unsuspecting victim into danger or distract attention from some other action
defraud (*vb*) cheat out of something by deception
dirty trick *Informal.* fraudulent or unscrupulous secret act
discredit (*vb*) injure the reputation of; cast aspersions on the authenticity of
dodge clever expedient or contrivance used to evade, trick, or deceive
double-cross (*vb*) *Informal.* betray by treachery; cheat by acting contrary to expectations
double-dealing (*adj*) marked by duplicity; deceitful
dupe one easily deceived or fooled; object of a swindle; cat's-paw; chump; easy mark; fool; gull; mark; patsy; pigeon; pushover; sap; sucker; tool
easy mark one highly susceptible to fraud or swindle; dupe
embezzle (*vb*) steal or appropriate to one's own use, as funds entrusted to one's care; peculate
extort (*vb*) obtain from another by intimidation, misused power, or ingenuity
finagle (*vb*) get by using trickery or deception; swindle, cheat, or trick
fleece (*vb*) defraud or extort money from; gaff; overcharge
flimflam *Informal.* deception or fraud, esp. one involving misleading talk
fraud deception and trickery, esp. a breach of confidence to gain an advantage, or an inducement to part with something of value; impostor; one who practices trickery and deception
front one who serves as a cover for illegal activity, or induces victims to engage in scheme perpetrated by another
gouge (*vb*) extort from or overcharge
graft use of dishonest or illegal means for gain or profit
greenhorn naive person who may easily be swindled or tricked
grift methods used to obtain illicit profits, esp. from confidence game

highway robbery *Informal.* exorbitant profit or gain derived from business transaction
hoax act intended to deceive or trick, esp. into accepting as real that which is not; mischievous deception
illicit (*adj*) prohibited by law or custom; not permitted or authorized
infidelity lack of faith; betrayal, esp. of one's spouse
kangaroo court court that disregards legal principles and justice, esp. so as to make fair trial impossible
launder (*vb*) *Informal.* disguise source of (illicit funds) so that they appear legitimate
loan shark *Informal.* person charging excessive interest on loans
milk (*vb*) exploit illicitly or excessively for advantage; drain someone or something of resources
monte gambling card game, usu. a swindle
peculate (*vb*) embezzle
perfidy treachery, esp. disloyalty or betrayal
Ponzi investment swindle in which early investors receive return from money of later ones, who never see return
profiteering making exorbitant profit, esp. on scarce or rationed articles
pyramid (*vb*) speculate in securities by using paper profits as margin for additional trading
quisling traitor who betrays his or her country to an invading enemy
racket organized illegal scheme or activity; swindle
racketeer one engaged in organized illegal activities, esp. extortion through intimidation
robber baron businessman profiting by exploitation of unscrupulous but legal activity
runner smuggler or distributor of illicit goods
scam fraudulent operation or swindle
setup arrangement that draws unsuspecting party into swindle
shaft (*vb*) *Informal.* treat poorly by taking advantage of or betraying
shake down (*vb*) extort money from
sham deceptive trick or hoax; spurious imitation or counterfeit object; impostor
shark shrewd individual preying upon others through extortion and trickery
shell game fraud involving sleight-of-hand substitution of valueless item for one of value; thimblerig, using walnut shells instead of balls
shill *Slang.* decoy for pitchman, gambler, or con game; capper
shortchange (*vb*) cheat by returning less than correct change
shyster *Informal.* one unscrupulous in professional duties, esp. a lawyer
skim (*vb*) *Slang.* fraudulently conceal or underestimate (profits, as from gambling), esp. to avoid paying taxes
skin game swindle or con game
sponge (*vb*) acquire without paying for or by taking advantage of another's generosity
squeeze (*vb*) pressure so as to obtain or extort something
steal (*vb*) vengefully take (something that belongs to another), esp. in secret or by force; pilfer; pinch; swipe; walk off with
sting *Slang.* apparent swindle used by authorities in investigation of fraud or racket; confidence game
swindle (*vb*) obtain (another's assets or money) by fraud or deceit; (*n*) action or scheme intended to defraud or deceive; con; confidence game; racket; skin game
thimblerig sleight-of-hand swindle involving small ball that must be found under one of three cups, similar to three-card monte
three-card monte sleight-of-hand swindle in which mark must identify one of three cards that have been moved around facedown by dealer
traitor one who betrays his or her country or another person or reneges on responsibilities
treachery failure of faith or trust; act of perfidy or treason
turncoat one who betrays a cause or supports an enemy
two-faced (*adj*) double-dealing; inconstant in allegiance; hypocritical
unconscionable (*adj*) unscrupulous; done without conscience
unscrupulous (*adj*) lacking principles; willing to do anything to achieve one's goal
victimize (*vb*) defraud, cheat, or take advantage of
wangle (*vb*) obtain by underhanded methods; manipulate for fraudulent ends
welsh (*vb*) *Informal.* renege on one's obligation or debt, esp. a bet
wildcat (*adj*) financially reckless and conducted in violation of normal business practices

Chapter Twenty-Three
Cognition

TIME PERCEPTION

Fixed Times
Periods of Time
Relative Time

Fixed Times

anniversary commemoration of each full year's passage since original event
annual (*adj*) yearly, once a year
autumnal equinox September 22 in Northern Hemisphere
biannual (*adj*) occurring twice a year; occuring every two years; semiannual
bicentennial (*adj*) occurring every 200 years; (*n*) 200th anniversary
biennial (*adj*) occurring every two years; (*n*) two-year anniversary; event that occurs once in two years
bimensal (*adj*) bimonthly
bimonthly (*adj*) occurring every two months; twice a month; bimensal; semimonthly
bissextile day February 29, occurring every fourth year
biweekly (*adj*) occurring every two weeks; twice a week; semiweekly
canonical hour any of certain times of the day set apart for prayer and devotion
centenary observation of hundred-year anniversary
centennial hundredth anniversary; (*adj*) occurring every hundred years
curfew time designated by authority to retire or stay indoors for the night
decennial (*adj*) occurring every ten years
diurnal (*adj*) daily
duodecennial (*adj*) occurring every twelve years
eleventh hour last possible moment for some action
equinox moment in year when center of sun is in line with equator and day and night are of equal length: about March 21 and September 22
harvest moon full moon nearest autumnal equinox
hebdomadal (*adj*) weekly, every seven days
high noon exactly twelve o'clock noon
ides fifteenth or thirteenth day of each month in ancient Roman calendar
last-minute (*adj*) done when time is running out
midday noon, middle of day, when a.m. turns to p.m.
midnight middle of night; twelve o'clock at night, when p.m. turns to a.m.
millennial thousandth anniversary; (*adj*) occurring every thousand years
noon twelve o'clock midday, when a.m. turns to p.m.; noontime
perennial occurring year after year
quadrennial (*adj*) occurring every four years; lasting four years
quadricentennial 400th anniversary; (*adj*) occurring every 400 years
quarterly (*adj*) occurring four times per year
quincentennial 500th anniversary; (*adj*) occurring every 500 years
quinquennial (*adj*) occurring every five years
quotidian (*adj*) daily, everyday
semiannual (*adj*) occurring every half year or twice a year
semicentennial (*adj*) occurring every fifty years
semidiurnal (*adj*) occurring every half day or twice a day
semiweekly (*adj*) occurring every half week or twice a week
septennial (*adj*) occurring every seven years
small hours extremely late at night; hours after midnight and before dawn
solstice time in year when sun is farthest north or south of celestial equator, in Northern Hemisphere about June 21 or December 21, respectively; longest or shortest period of sunshine during year
summer solstice June 21 in Northern Hemisphere
time dimension of reality characterized by flow of events and phenomena through irreversible procession of moments; systematized demarcation of the passage of such moments into units of seconds, minutes, hours, days, and years; period or point in time; fourth dimension in space-time continuum
tricennial (*adj*) occurring every thirty years
tricentennial 300th anniversary; (*adj*) occurring every 300 years
triennial (*adj*) occurring every three years; continuing or persisting for three years
trimonthly (*adj*) occurring every three months
triweekly (*adj*) occurring every three weeks; occurring three times a week
twilight period of dimming light just after sunset
vernal equinox March 21 in Northern Hemisphere
vespers prayer said at evening; sixth canonical hour
vicennial twentieth anniversary; (*adj*) occurring every twenty years
winter solstice December 21 in Northern Hemisphere

Periods of Time

aeon eon
age period of time corresponding to life of object or individual; period in Earth's history
April fourth month of year, containing 30 days, following March, preceding May
August eighth month of year, containing 31 days, following July, preceding September
autumn season of shortening days ending in winter solstice, extending from September 22 to December 20; fall
blue moon long period of time
calendar year 365 days, beginning January 1 and ending December 31; 366 days in leap years
century 100 years

circadian (*adj*) occurring in twenty-four-hour cycles
cycle regular, recurring interval of time; set period of days or years
day period of twenty-four hours; sunrise to sunset
decade period of ten years
December twelfth and last month of year, containing 31 days, following November, preceding January, including first day of winter
elapsed time time measured from beginning to end of event
eon extremely long period of time; aeon
epoch significant time period marked by historical events; geologic time division smaller than period
era significant period of time marked by historical events; major geologic time division including periods
eternity forever, time without end; immeasurable time
fall autumn
February second month of year, containing 28 days or 29 days every fourth year, following January, preceding March
fiscal year twelve-month-period, used in business and accounting, usu. beginning July 1 or October 1
fortnight period of two weeks
Friday sixth day of week, following Thursday, preceding Saturday; last day of regular workweek in United States
hiatus break or gap in continuity
historical year year beginning with January 1
immemorial (*adj*) extending beyond memory
infinity boundless, limitless time
interim interval of time
interlude short time intervening between events or dramatic acts
interregnum period of vacancy of throne or royal office; period of time when there is lapse in normal government functions
January first month of year, containing 31 days, following December, preceding February
July seventh month of year, containing 31 days, following June, preceding August
June sixth month of year, containing 30 days, following May, preceding July, including first day of summer
leap year 366-day year, occurring every fourth year, in which February has 29 days
life span period of life from birth to death
longevity length of a life span
lustrum period of five years
March third month of year, containing 31 days, following February, preceding April, including first day of spring
May fifth month of year, containing 31 days, following April, preceding June
Metonic cycle period of nearly 19 years, after which phases of moon return to some calendar date, used in Gregorian calendar
Monday second day of week, following Sunday, preceding Tuesday; first day of regular workweek in United States
month period of approximately thirty days, based on time required for one complete revolution of the moon; one of twelve divisions of year
Neolithic (*adj*) designating period of cultural development from about 10,000 to 3000 B.C.
November eleventh month of year, containing 30 days, following October, preceding December
October tenth month of year, containing 31 days, following September, preceding November
olympiad period of four years
period duration or division of time; geologic division within era including epochs
perpetual day period at North and South poles when sun does not set
perpetual night period at North and South poles when sun does not rise
prehistoric (*adj*) pertaining to period before written history
Saturday seventh and last day of week, following Friday, preceding Sunday; first day of weekend; Jewish Sabbath
season period of time characterized by particular weather, events, and holidays, one of four major divisions of year
second one sixtieth of a minute; fundamental unit of time equal to 9,192,631,770 emission cycles of cesium-133
September ninth month of year, containing 30 days, following August, preceding October, including first day of autumn
sidereal day time taken for one complete rotation of Earth
spring season of lengthening days ending in summer solstice, extending from March 21 to June 20
stint limited period of time, esp. for accomplishment of some task
summer season of shortening days ending in autumnal equinox, extending from June 21 to September 21
Sunday first day of week, following Saturday, preceding Monday; last day of weekend; Christian Sabbath
term fixed period of time in which an activity, office, tenure, or agreement is valid and ongoing
Thursday fifth day of week, following Wednesday, preceding Friday
time frame period of time designated for completion of something; timespan
time immemorial time before recorded history or beyond memory; time out of mind
time-out cessation of activity for specified duration, esp. in athletic contest
Tuesday third day of week, following Monday, preceding Wednesday
Wednesday fourth day of week, following Tuesday, preceding Thursday; midweek
winter season of lengthening days ending in vernal equinox, extending from December 21 to March 20
year period of 365 days, during which Earth makes one full revolution around sun; twelve months

Relative Time

after, aftertime, afterward, again, ago, ahead of time, already, anachronism, ancient, anew, anon, ante-, antiquated, antique, anymore, anytime, aperiodic, aprés, archaic, asynchronous, atemporal, at once, at the drop of a hat, at times, auld lang syne
before, belated, betimes, betweentimes, borrowed time, brief, by-and-by, by turns
chronic, chronological, circa, coeval, conclusion, concurrent, constant, contemporaneous, contemporary, continual, continuous, current
dated, delay, directly, during
early, ephemeral, ere, erelong, erenow, erewhile, erst, erstwhile, eve, eventually, ever
first, fore, forenoon, former, formerly, for the time being, frequent, from time to time, fugitive
henceforth, hereafter, heretofore
immediate, imminent, impermanent, impromptu, in a flash, in a moment, in a trice, in a twinkling, in a wink, infrequent, in good time, in no time, instantaneous, interim, intermediate, in the meantime, in the offing, in time, in turn, isochronal
last, late, lickety-split, long ago, long since
meantime, meanwhile, meta-
ne'er, never, never again, nevermore, new, nonce, nowadays, now and then
occasional, occasionally, off and on, off-peak, off-season, often, ofttimes, old, on again, off again, ongoing
parachronism, part-time, permanent, post-, postdate, posthaste, pre-, precedence, preceeding, precursor, predate, preliminary, preprandial, presently, presto, previous, primeval, prior, procrastination, prolong, promptly, pronto, proximo
rare, rarely, recent, recurrent, remote, repeatedly, respite, retrospective, right away
seldom, semipermanent, simultaneous, someday, sometime, sometimes, soon, sooner or later, sporadic, spur-of-the-moment, straightaway, straight off, subsequent, successive, sudden, summary
tardy, temp, temporal, temporary, tempus fugit, terminal, then, thence, thenceforth, thereafter, theretofore, thereupon, therewith, time after time, time and again, time-consuming, time-honored, timeless, timely, time of life, timesaver, time-tested, time warp, transience, transitory
unceasing, until, untimely, upcoming, upon, up-to-the-minute, urgent
vestigial, vintage
well-timed, when, whenever, whensoever, while
yesteryear, yestreen, yet, yore

SPATIAL POSITIONS AND RELATIONS

Fixed Positions and Points
Dimensions and Directions
Relative Positions

Fixed Positions and Points

acme highest point
aloft (*adv*) high in the air
angle point at which two lines converge
apex highest point
apogee highest or most distant point
attitude position in space determined by relationship of object's axis and a reference point
balanced (*adj*) in equilibrium due to even distribution of weight on all sides
base bottom point or position
beginning origin; point at which something starts
benchmark point of reference for making measurements
blind spot area that cannot be seen
capsheaf highest point, acme
center middle, esp. point around which circle is drawn
circumcenter center of circumscribed circle
corner point where converging lines, edges, or sides meet
crest highest point
crown highest point
dorsal (*adj*) near or on the back
dorsolateral (*adj*) on both the back and sides
edge line at which area begins or ends; border
end point marking most extreme extent; part lying at limit
endpoint either of two points at ends of line segment
epicenter exact center, esp. Earth's surface beneath focus of earthquake
extremity farthest point
fix charted position or bearings
focal point focus
focus point at which lines or rays come together, cross, or diverge; focal point; hub
fork point of branching
hindmost (*adj*) nearest the rear position
hub focus
inverted (*adj*) with top and bottom parts reversed
metacenter intersection of lines through centers of buoyancy of a floating body at rest and when tipped to one side
midpoint point at or near the center or middle
nadir lowest point, esp. opposite zenith in celestial sphere
navel central point, middle
node point at which parts begin or focus; point at which curve crosses itself at different tangents
omphalos center or navel

perigee point in orbit of heavenly body at which it is nearest to Earth
perihelion point in orbit of celestial body at which it is nearest to sun
plumb (*adj*) perpendicular; exactly vertical
point definite, unique position on scale; geometric element positioned by ordered set of coordinates
position space occupied by an object at a given moment
prone (*adj*) having front surface facing downward
prostrate (*adj*) lying facedown on the ground
quadrant one of four parts into which an area is divided by two perpendicular lines
quincunx arrangement of five items around a square or rectangle with one at each corner and one in the center
reclining (*adj*) leaning backward from vertical position
recumbent (*adj*) lying down, reclining; leaning
section distinct part of something, esp. solid cut by plane
sector portion of circle bounded by two radii
segment portion of larger figure, esp. circle, cut off by one or more lines or planes
square (*adj*) exactly aligned; straight, level
stationary (*adj*) fixed in position
summit highest point
supine (*adj*) on back with front surface facing upward
terminus end of a line
top highest point
transverse (*adj*) reaching across, esp. at right angles to front-back axis of object
ultimate (*adj*) farthest, esp. most remote; last in series
ultima Thule *Latin.* lit. ultimate Thule; farthest point or limit of a journey, esp. point farthest north
ventral (*adj*) situated on the front side of a body
vertex highest point; point opposite and farthest from base; termination of line; intersection of two or more lines
zenith highest point, esp. point in celestial sphere opposite nadir

Dimensions and Directions

aligned (*adj*) arranged in a straight line; set in order
area extent of space or surface bounded by fixed lines
ascending (*adj*) moving upward from lower to higher level
askew (*adv*) to one side
aslant (*adv*) obliquely, at a slant
asymmetrical (*adj*) lacking symmetry, irregular; unsymmetrical
azimuth arc of horizon measured clockwise from fixed point at north or south
backward (*adv*) in reverse of normal direction; with back foremost; toward the rear
bearing horizontal direction of one point measured in degrees from another point
beeline direct course, straight line
bidirectional (*adj*) capable of moving in two, usu. opposite, directions
breadth dimension from side to side; width
bulk three-dimensional magnitude
centrifugal (*adj*) moving away from center or axis
centripetal (*adj*) moving toward center or axis
circuitous (*adj*) following an indirect path
circumference outer boundary, esp. perimeter of circle
clockwise (*adj*) in direction in which clock hands rotate
counterclockwise (*adj*) in direction opposite that in which clock hands rotate; backward
depth dimension downward from top, horizontally inward, or from back to front
descending (*adj*) moving downward from higher to lower position
dextral (*adj*) on or leaning to the right
diagonal (*adj*) running in an oblique direction from a reference line
diameter straight line from one side of circle to the other through center point
dimension magnitude measured in one direction, esp. width, length, or thickness that determines a position in space
direction line along which something is pointing, facing, or moving
distance extent of space between two points, lines, surfaces, or objects, usu. along shortest path
east direction of sunrise; direction to one's right when facing north
elevation distance upward from fixed surface
elongation condition of being stretched or lengthened
encircling (*adj*) running completely around in a circle
equiangular (*adj*) having all angles equal
equilateral (*adj*) having all sides equal
extent maximum space across or through which something stretches out or reaches
falling (*adj*) descending freely, usu. straight downward
field region covered by a feature or through which a force acts
forward (*adv*) moving toward a point in front
fourth dimension time dimension used as coordinate with length, depth, and breadth in space-time continuum
frontal (*adj*) located at or moving against the front
geocentric (*adj*) having Earth as center
geodesic (*adj*) pertaining to the geometry of curved surfaces
grade degree of inclination of slope
heading specific direction, esp. compass point toward which something is moving
height distance from bottom to top; extent upward above surface; highest part or point
horizontal (*adj*) parallel to the horizon or level ground; level; at right angles to vertical
incline grade, slant, or deviation from vertical or horizontal position

inward (*adv*) toward or at the inside or center
isometric (*adj*) having equality of measure
isosceles (*adj*) having two sides equal and non-parallel
latitudinal (*adj*) having side-to-side extent, esp. as measure of distance from Earth's equator
left (*adj*) located toward the west when facing north
length longest linear extent or dimension of object
lengthwise (*adv*) longitudinally, in direction of length; lengthways
level (*adj*) flat; horizontal; having all parts at equal height
linear (*adj*) consisting of or moving in a straight line; having a single dimension
longitudinal (*adj*) placed or moving lengthwise; having top-to-bottom extent
north cardinal point of a compass in direction of north terrestrial pole, to the left of a person facing the rising sun and directly opposite south
oblique (*adj*) neither perpendicular nor parallel to another surface; slanting or sloping
obtuse (*adj*) designating an angle greater than 90 but less than 180 degrees
outward (*adj*) directed away from the center; situated on the outside
parallax apparent displacement of moving object as viewed from two different points
patulous (*adj*) spreading widely from the center
perimeter boundary of closed plane figure
plane flat or level surface; two-dimensional body
prolate (*adj*) extended in line joining the poles
protracted (*adj*) extended in space, esp. forward or outward
radial (*adj*) extending from a center; moving along a radius
radiating (*adj*) extending in a direct line away from or toward a center
radius line extending from center of circle to its boundary
range maximum extent outward
rectilinear (*adj*) moving in or forming a straight line
retroflex (*adj*) turned sharply backward
retrograde (*adj*) directed or moving backward, against the general direction
reverse (*adj*) moving opposite to the regular direction; having backside forward
right (*adj*) located toward the east when facing north
rotary (*adj*) turning on an axis
sinistral (*adj*) on or leaning to the left
slope slant, oblique course; measure of upward or downward inclination
south cardinal point of a compass in direction of south terrestrial pole and directly opposite north
space particular extent in one, two, or three dimensions; distance between two or more objects
space-time four-dimensional continuum having three spatial coordinates with which to locate an event or object
straight (*adj*) moving or extending continuously in one direction without turning
straightforward (*adj*) moving in a direct line
stratified (*adj*) forming layers in a graded series
symmetrical (*adj*) corresponding in size, form, and relative position on opposite sides of line, plane, point, or axis
tabular (*adj*) arranged in vertical and horizontal rows
tangential (*adj*) digressing suddenly from one course and turning to another
three-dimensional (*adj*) having height, width, and depth
trajectory curve followed by body projected through space
triangulation technique for determining location through bearings from two fixed points at a given distance
two-dimensional (*adj*) having height and width only
unidirectional (*adj*) moving in one direction only
unsymmetrical (*adj*) asymmetrical
vector line segment with both magnitude and direction in space
vertical (*adj*) perpendicular to horizon or level surface; upright; designating an extent to the highest point; at right angles to horizontal
west direction of sunset; direction to one's left when facing north
width extent from side to side, at right angles to length

Relative Positions

abeam, about, above, abutting, across, adaxial, adjacent, adjoining, advance, afar, afield, after, against, ahead, alongside, ambit, amid, amidst, among, anent, anterior, antipodal, apart, apposed, around, aside, astraddle, astride, at, at hand, athwart, atop, away, axial
back, back-to-back, before, behind, below, beneath, beside, between, betwixt, beyond, bordering, bottom, by
cater-corner, caudal, central, centric, close, coaxial, coextensive, coincident, colinear, collateral, collinear, concentric, configuration, confocal, consecutive, conterminous, contiguous, convenient, converse, coplanar, coterminous, covering
decussate, deep, detached, discontinuous, discrete, distal, distant, distinct, down
elsewhere, encircling, enclosed, enclosing, encompassing, enveloping, equidistant, even, exterior, external
face-to-face, facing, far, far and away, farther, flanking, flush, foot, fore, fore and aft, forth, forward, fringe, from, front, fronting, further
halfway, hard by, hence, hereabout, here and there, hither, hithermost
immediate, indoors, inferior, infra-, inner, inside, interior, intermediate, interposed,

intersecting, interspersed, interstice, intervening
kitty-corner
lateral, leeward, levitated, long-distance, lower
maximum, mean, medial, median, mid, midair, middle, midline, midst, midway
near, nearby, next, next to, nigh, nip and tuck, not far
obverse, off, on, onward, opposite, out, outdoors, outer, outside, over, overlying
parallel, peripheral, perpendicular, point-blank, port, position, posterior, propinquity, proximal, proximate, proximity
rear, remote, retral, retro-
separate, side by side, spatial relation, starboard, sub-, successive, super-, superior, superjacent, supra-, surrounding
thence, thenceforth, thereabout, therefrom, therein, thither, through, toward, trans-, traverse, 'tween, 'twixt
ulterior, under, underneath, up, upside down, upward
via, vicinity
whence, where, whereto, whither, windward, within, within an inch, without
yon, yonder

SHAPES

acicular (*adj*) needle-shaped
acuminate (*adj*) tapering to a slender point
acute (*adj*) of an angle of less than ninety degrees
amygdaloid (*adj*) almond-shaped
anchor object that has a broad, hooklike arm
angular (*adj*) sharp-cornered; having points from which two lines diverge
annular (*adj*) ring-shaped
apical (*adj*) narrowing to a pointed tip
arc unbroken segment of a curved line
arcuate (*adj*) curved like a bow
asymmetrical (*adj*) lacking balance; not the same on both sides of central axis
attenuated (*adj*) tapering to long, slender point
awry (*adj*) turned or twisted from a central axis
bacillary (*adj*) rod-shaped
ball round or spherical shape
bell hollow, curved shape with open, circular base and surface curving to a central apex
biconcave (*adj*) concave on both sides
biconvex (*adj*) convex on both sides
bifurcate (*adj*) divided into two branches
bilateral (*adj*) two-sided; symmetrical on both sides of an axis
biradial (*adj*) having both bilateral and radial symmetry
block cube
bolus lumpy, rounded mass
botryoidal (*adj*) formed like a bunch of grapes
bowl concave hemisphere opening upward
box rectangle with upright sides; cube
branching (*adj*) forming subdivisions like a tree
brick rectangular solid longer than it is wide
bulbous (*adj*) round like a bulb
bump swelling or lump in flat surface
bursiform (*adj*) pouch-shaped
campanulate (*adj*) bell-shaped
capitate (*adj*) enlarged at the head and spherical; forming a head
catenary curve formed by flexible, nonelastic cord hanging freely between two points
catenulate (*adj*) chainlike in shape
chevron V or inverted V
circinate (*adj*) rolled up on the axis at the apex; ring-shaped
circle curved line every point of which is equidistant from a fixed center
circular (*adj*) circle-shaped
clavate (*adj*) club-shaped and thicker at one end; claviform
claviform (*adj*) club shaped; clavate
clothoid (*adj*) tear-shaped loop
cloverleaf figure formed by four leaves on one stem
club stylized cloverleaf figure on playing cards
coil series of loops, spiral
columnar (*adj*) arranged in vertical rows
compass (*adj*) curved; forming a curve or an arc
concave (*adj*) hollowed, rounded, or curved inward
concavo-convex (*adj*) concave on one side and convex on the other, esp. with greater curvature on concave side; convexo-concave
cone solid with circular base and vertical surface of line segments that join every point of base circumference to common vertex
conical (*adj*) cone-shaped
conoid (*adj*) conelike or nearly conelike
contour outline of curving, irregular figure
convex (*adj*) curved or rounded outward, as with exterior of sphere or circle
convexo-concave (*adj*) concavo-convex, esp. with greater curvature on convex side
convoluted (*adj*) twisted; coiled
cordate (*adj*) heart-shaped; cordiform
cordiform (*adj*) heart-shaped; cordate
crenate (*adj*) having margin or surface cut into scallops or notches
crenulate (*adj*) having irregularly wavy or serrate outline
crescent shape bounded by convex and concave edges of less than half a hemisphere
crook bent or hooked form
cross two lines intersecting, esp. at right angles; X-shaped figure
cruciform (*adj*) cross-shaped; (*n*) cross
cube regular solid of six equal square sides
cubical (*adj*) cube-shaped
cucullate (*adj*) hooded; hood-shaped
cuneal (*adj*) wedge-shaped
cuneate (*adj*) triangular at base and tapering

toward a point; cuneal
curlicue figure with multiple, nonduplicating curves and spirals
curvature amount or state of being curved
curve path of a point not moving in a straight line
cusp point or apex; tip of crescent
cuspidate (*adj*) terminating in a point
cycle circular or spiral arrangement
cycloid curve generated by point on circumference of circle as it rolls along a straight line
cylinder straight tube joining two equal, parallel, circular bases
cylindrical (*adj*) cylinder-shaped
decagon ten-sided polygon
decahedron ten-faced polyhedron
decurved (*adj*) curved or bent downward
decussate (*adj*) X-shaped
deltoid (*adj*) triangular
dendriform (*adj*) resembling a tree; dendroid
dendroid (*adj*) tree-shaped; dendriform
dentiform (*adj*) tooth-shaped
diamond four-sided figure with long diagonal vertical; lozenge
discoid (*adj*) disk-shaped
disk flattened, circular object, sometimes thicker at center than at edge
dodecagon twelve-sided polygon
dodecahedron twelve-faced polyhedron
dogleg course that takes a sharp bend or abrupt turn
dome convex hemisphere, usu. opening downward and attached at base
donut doughnut
double helix pair of intertwined helixes
doughnut ring-shaped solid; donut
egg oval
elbow otherwise straight shape that is bent, esp. at ninety- degree angle near its center
ellipse elongated closed circle, oval
elliptic (*adj*) ellipse-shaped; elliptical
elliptical (*adj*) elliptic
elongate (*adj*) stretched out
ensiform (*adj*) sword-shaped
falcate (*adj*) hooked or curved like a sickle; falciform
falciform (*adj*) sickle-shaped; falcate
fastigiate (*adj*) narrowing toward the top; having upright clustered branches
foliate (*adj*) branching, esp. into leaves
frustum part of solid cone or pyramid left by cutting off top portion by plane parallel to base
fungiform (*adj*) mushroom-shaped
fungoid (*adj*) funguslike in form
funnel hollow cone with tube extending from base
globe sphere, esp. the Earth
globose (*adj*) globular
globular (*adj*) globe-shaped, spherical; globose
gurge spiral, whirlpool
hastate (*adj*) triangular or arrow-shaped with two spreading lobes at base
heart standardized representation of heart as matching curves joined at vertical axis and tilted upward to form V-notch at top
helical (*adj*) spiral, helix-shaped
helicoid (*adj*) forming or arranged in a flat coil or flattened spiral
helix spiral; curve traced on cylinder or cone by point moving at constant oblique angle across right sections
hemihedral (*adj*) having half the number of planes required by symmetry
hemisphere half a sphere
heptagon seven-sided polygon
heptagonal (*adj*) having seven angles and seven sides
hexagon six-sided polygon
hexagonal (*adj*) having six angles and six sides
hexagram figure formed by completing externally an equilateral triangle on each side of a regular hexagon
horn curved ends of a crescent
hump rounded, protruding, often irregular lump
hyperbola plane curve generated by a point moving so that the difference of its distances from two fixed points is constant
icosahedron twenty-faced polyhedron
infundibuliform (*adj*) funnel- or cone-shaped
involute (*adj*) curled or spiraling inward
knot interlacing or tying of strands
lanceolate (*adj*) narrow and tapering at one end, like the head of a lance
ligulate (*adj*) strap-shaped
linear (*adj*) narrow and elongated
lobate (*adj*) having roundish projections or divisions
loop curving or doubling of line to form closed or partly open curve within itself
lozenge diamond
lump often irregular bump, hump, or knob
lunette crescent or half-moon shape
meniscus crescent; concave or convex upper surface of column of liquid
moline (*adj*) having the end of each arm forked and recurved
moniliform (*adj*) resembling a string of beads
napiform (*adj*) globular at top and tapering off gradually; parsnip- or carrot-shaped
nodular (*adj*) in shape of rounded or irregular mass
nodule small, rounded lump or irregular mass
nonagon nine-sided polygon
notched (*adj*) having V-shaped or rounded indentation, esp. at edge
obcordate (*adj*) heart-shaped with notch at apex
oblate (*adj*) flattened or depressed at poles
oblique (*adj*) inclined; neither parallel nor perpendicular; having no right angle
oblong square, circle, or sphere elongated in one dimension
obovate (*adj*) ovate with narrower end at base
obovoid (*adj*) ovoid with broad end toward apex
obtuse (*adj*) being an angle of more than 90 but less than 180 degrees
obverse (*adj*) having base narrower than top
octagon eight-sided polygon
octagonal (*adj*) having eight angles and eight sides

octahedron eight-faced polyhedron
ogee pointed arch with reversed curve near each side of apex
ogival (*adj*) ogee or ogive-shaped
ogive pointed arch
ophidiform (*adj*) resembling snakes
orb circle; spherical body
orbicular (*adj*) spherical, circular
oval (*adj*) broadly elliptical; egg-shaped
ovate (*adj*) shaped like longitudinal section of an egg with basal end broader
ovoid (*adj*) egg-shaped; ovate
palmate (*adj*) resembling a hand with fingers spread
parabola plane curve that is the path of a moving point whose distance from a fixed point remains equal to its distance from a fixed line
parabolic (*adj*) parabola-shaped; bowl-shaped
parallelepiped prism with six faces that are parallelograms
parallelogram quadrilateral with opposite sides parallel and equal
parted (*adj*) divided into distinct portions by deep, lengthwise cuts
peaked (*adj*) coming to a point at top
peltate (*adj*) shield-shaped
pentacle pentagram
pentagon five-sided polygon
pentagonal (*adj*) having five angles and five sides
pentagram five-pointed star with alternate points connected by a continuous line; pentacle
pentahedron five-faced polyhedron
pentangle pentagram
pinnate (*adj*) resembling a feather, with similar parts arranged on opposite sides of an axis
plane flat, two-dimensional surface; (*adj*) two dimensional
plano-concave (*adj*) flat on one side, concave on the other
plano-convex (*adj*) flat on one side, convex on the other
polygon closed plane figure bounded by three or more straight lines
polygonal (*adj*) shaped like a plane bounded by three or more straight lines
polyhedral (*adj*) having the shape of a polyhedron
polyhedron solid figure having many faces
pretzel shape that resembles a loosely tied knot
prism polyhedron with two polygonal faces lying in parallel planes and other faces being parallelograms
prismatoid (*adj*) polyhedral with all vertices in two parallel planes
prismoid (*adj*) prismatoid with parallel bases having the same number of sides
prolate (*adj*) elongated in direction of a line joining poles
pyramid polyhedron with polygonal base and triangular sides with common vertex
pyriform (*adj*) pear-shaped
quadrangle quadrilateral
quadrangular (*adj*) quadrilateral-shaped
quadrilateral four-sided polygon; quadrangle
rectangle parallelogram all of whose angles are right angles, usu. with adjacent sides of unequal length
rectangular (*adj*) rectangle-shaped
rectilinear (*adj*) forming a straight line
reniform (*adj*) kidney-shaped
retroflex (*adj*) turned or bent abruptly inward
retuse (*adj*) having apex that is rounded or obtuse with a slight notch
rhomboid (*adj*) rhombus-shaped
rhombus equilateral parallelogram having oblique angles
right angle angle bounded by two lines perpendicular to each other
right triangle three-sided polygon with two sides meeting at right angle
ring circular shape
rondure circle or sphere; graceful curving roundness
round (*adj*) circular; ring- or ball-shaped
sagittate (*adj*) shaped like an arrowhead
scalloped (*adj*) having a border formed by a continuous series of circle segments or angular projections
scroll spiral, rolled, or convoluted form
scutate (*adj*) shield-shaped
semicircle half a circle
serrate (*adj*) notched or toothed along edge
shape specific external surface or outline of an object having a distinct form
shell upright concave shape, usu. hemispherical, often open horizontally
sickle curve in a half circle
sigmoid (*adj*) curved like the letter C; curved in two directions like the letter S
solid three-dimensional shape; (*adj*) three-dimensional
spade stylized spearhead shape used on playing cards
spatulate (*adj*) thin and flat like a spatula
sphere solid bounded by a surface on which all points are equidistant from a fixed central point; ball
spherical (*adj*) sphere-shaped
spicate (*adj*) arranged in the form of a spike
spiral three-dimensional curve generated by a point moving in one or more turns about an axis; (*adj*) winding around a fixed line in a series of planes; coiling around a center while receding from or approaching it; helical
square parallelogram with four equal sides and four right angles; (*adj*) having four equal sides and four right angles in plane figure
star figure with five or more points formed by overlapping triangles with common center
stellate (*adj*) star-shaped
straight line series of points arranged without angles; direct line between two points
styliform (*adj*) bristle-shaped
switchback zigzag arrangement
tapering (*adj*) becoming narrower at one end than the other
terete (*adj*) cylindrical or slightly tapering

ternate (*adj*) arranged in threes
tetartohedral (*adj*) having one-fourth the number of planes needed for symmetry
tetrahedron four-faced polyhedron
toothed (*adj*) having series of notches resembling teeth
toroid surface generated by a closed plane curve rotated about a line lying in the same plane as the curve but not crossing it
toroidal (*adj*) torus-shaped
torus doughnut-shaped surface
trapezium four-sided plane having no two sides parallel
trapezoid four-sided plane having two parallel sides
trapezoidal (*adj*) having the form of a trapezoid
triangle three-sided plane figure with three angles
triangular (*adj*) three-sided and plane
trifoliate (*adj*) having three lobes
trifurcate (*adj*) branching into three
trihedral (*adj*) having three faces
trilateral (*adj*) having three sides
trochoid curve generated by a point on the radius of a circle as the circle rolls on a fixed straight line
truncated (*adj*) having the end square or even
tube hollow, elongated cylinder, often flexible
tubular (*adj*) tube-shaped
turtleback raised, convexly arched surface
unciform (*adj*) hook-shaped
uncinate (*adj*) bent at the tip like a hook
V two equal line segments diverging upward at an acute angle from a point
vermiculate (*adj*) having irregular, thin, wavy lines like the trail of a worm
villiform (*adj*) closely set and resembling bristles or velvet pile
virgate (*adj*) shaped like a rod or wand
volute (*adj*) spiral- or scroll-shaped
wheel round, circular form
whorl something that whirls, coils, or spirals
winding (*adj*) describing a line that is curved, sinuous, or irregular
worm irregular spiral or tube; vermiculate; zigzag
X two crossed line segments, usu. of equal length
zigzag series of sharp, angular turns; switchback

COLORS

White
Gray
Black
Brown
Reddish Brown
Red
Pink
Orange
Yellow
Green
Blue
Purple

White

alabaster, argent
blond, bone
chalk, Chinese white, columbine
dove
eggshell
flake white
gauze
ivory
milk-white
nacre
off-white, oyster
pearl, platinum, pure white, putty
silver, snow
white
zinc white

Gray

ash
battleship
charcoal, cinder, cinereous, cloud
dark gray, dove
flint
granite, gray, greige
iron
lead, light gray
merle, moleskin, mouse, mushroom
neutral
obsidian
pale gray, pelican, plumbago
salt-and-pepper, silver gray, slate, smoke, steel
taupe

Black

black, blue-black, Brunswick black
carbon
ebony
ink
jet

lampblack
pitch, pure black
raven
sable, soot

Brown

acorn, amber, anthracene, autumn leaf
beige, biscuit, bistre, brindle, bronze, brown, brunet, brunette, buff, burnt almond, burnt umber, butternut
café au lait, camel, Cologne brown
dark brown, doeskin, Dresden, dun
earth, ecru
fallow, fawn, fox
hazel
khaki
leather, light brown
manila, maple sugar, Mars brown, mink, mocha
negro, nougat, nutria
otter
peppercorn, pongee, putty
raffia, raw sienna, raw umber
sandalwood, seal
tan, tanaura, tawny, toast, topaz
umber
Vandyke brown
walnut

Reddish Brown

auburn
baize, bay, brick, burgundy, burnt ocher, burnt sienna
caramel, Castilian brown, chestnut, chocolate, cinnamon, cocoa, cordovan
fulvous
ginger
henna
ight red-brown, liver
mahogany
nutmeg
ocher, oxblood
piccolopasso
reddish brown, roan, russet
sand, sedge, sepia, sienna, sorrel
erra cotta, titian
Venetian red

Red

lizarin crimson, alpenglow, annatto
lood-red, bois de rose, bougainvillea, Bourdeaux, brick red, brownish red
admium red, cardinal, carioca, carmine, carnelian, Castilian red, cerise, cherry, Chinese red, cinnabar, claret, cochineal, cranberry, crimson, crimson lake
amask, dark red
aded rose, fire-engine red
arnet, geranium, grenadine, gules
ndian red, iron red
ckey
light red, lobster
madder lake, maroon, Mars red, murrey
orange-red
paprika, peach, Persian red, pinkish red, ponceau, poppy, Prussian red, puce
red, rhodamine, rose madder, ruby, rust
scarlet, stammel, strawberry
tile red
Venetian red, vermilion
wild cherry, wine

Pink

begonia, blush
cameo, carnation, casino pink, coral
deep pink
fiesta, flamingo
hot pink
incarnadine
livid pink
mallow pink, melon, moonlight
nymph
ombre, orchid rose
pale pink, peach, petal pink, pink
reddish pink, rose, royal pink
salmon, shell pink, shocking pink
tea rose

Orange

apricot, aurora
burnt Roman ocher
cadmium orange, carotene, carrot, chrome orange, copper
dark orange
helianthin, hyacinth
mandarin, marigold, mikado
ocher, orange
pale orange, pumpkin
realgar, red orange, Rubens' madder
Spanish ocher
tangerine, terra cotta
yellow-orange

Yellow

amber, auramine, aureolin, azo yellow
barium yellow, blond, brass, brazen, brazilin, buff, butter
cadmium yellow, calendula, canary, Cassel yellow, chalcedony, chamois, champagne, chrome yellow, citron, corn, cream, crocus
dandelion
flax
gamboge, gold, goldenrod, green-yellow
honey
Indian yellow
jonquil
lemon, linen
maize, mustard
Naples yellow
orange-yellow, orpiment

pale yellow, palomino, pear, primrose, purree
quince
reed
saffron, safranine, sallow, sand, snapdragon, straw, sulphur, sunflower
wheaten
yellow, yellow ocher, yolk

Green

absinthe, aqua, avocado
bay, beryl, bice, blue-green, brewster, Brunswick green
cadmium green, celadon, chartreuse, chrome green, clair de lune, corbeau, cucumber, cypress
dark green, drake
emerald
fir green, flagstone, forest green
grass, gray-green, green, gunpowder
holly
jade
kelly green, Kendal green
leaf, light green, lime, Lincoln green, lizard, loden, lotus
malachite, marine, mint, moss, myrtle
Niagara green, Nile green
olive
pale green, parrot, patina, pea green, pistachio green
reseda
sea green, serpentine, shamrock, spruce
teal, terre verte, tourmaline, turquoise
verdigris, viridian
willow green
yellow-green, yew

Blue

aquamarine, azure
baby blue, blue, blueberry, bluebonnet
calamine blue, cerulean, cobalt blue, Copenhagen blue, cornflower, cyan
Delft blue, Dresden blue
flag blue
gentian, greenish blue
Havana lake, Helvetia blue, huckleberry, hydrangea
ice blue, Indanthrene, indigo
jouvence
lapis lazuli, light blue, lucerne, lupine
marine, midnight blue, milori
Napoleon blue, navy blue
pale blue, peacock blue, powder blue, Prussian blue, purple-blue
reddish blue, royal blue
saxe blue, sea blue, sky blue, smalt, steel blue
teal blue
ultramarine
Venetian blue
water blue, Wedgwood blue, wisteria, woad
zaffer

Purple

amaranth, amethyst, Argyle, aubergine
blue-violet, bluish purple, bokhara
campanula, clematis
dahlia, damson, deep purple
fuchsia
grape, gridelin
heliotrope, hyacinth
imperial purple
lavender, light purple, lilac
magenta, mauve, monsignor, mulberry
orchid
pale purple, pansy, periwinkle, phlox, plum, prune, purple
raisin, raspberry, reddish purple, royal purple, rubine
solferino
tulip, Tyrian purple
violet, violetta

VERBS OF THOUGHT

Thinking, Judgment, and Consideration
Reasoning and Examination
Learning and Memory
Knowledge and Understanding
Belief and Conception

Thinking, Judgment, and Consideration

appraise estimate the nature or merit of
assess appraise, judge
assume suppose to be true
attend consider, give heed to
attitudinize form opinion
brainstorm (*n*) sudden idea; exchange ideas with others to stimulate creative thinking
brood meditate quietly; ponder moodily, think persistently about
browse consider casually
chew over mull, think over at length
cogitate meditate, ponder hard
concentrate focus one's thoughts
conceptualize think about, interpret
conjecture conclude or suppose from scant evidence; surmise, guess
consider think about carefully
contemplate meditate on, consider thoroughly with deep attention
count consider
decide arrive at conclusion or solution
dwell on linger over in thought
engross occupy the mind or attention completely
entertain take into consideration
esteem consider or believe to be of a certain value; regard highly
estimate guess extent of, conjecture about

figure regard, consider
fret worry, brood
gather conclude from observation or hints
gauge estimate, judge
grope search for answer or comprehension
guess arrive at a conclusion by intuition and without sufficient evidence; surmise; conjecture about accurately
hazard guess, estimate
heed pay attention to, mind
interpret construe in a certain way, conceive; explain the meaning of
judge form an opinion of, esp. by weighing evidence
look into consider, explore
meditate think contemplatively; center one's thoughts; muse, reflect
mind heed closely
mull ponder at length
muse reflect on something from all sides, often inconclusively
note give careful attention to
occupy one's thoughts totally engage one's mind
occur come to mind
opine form an opinion about
outfox outsmart
outguess anticipate another's plans or motives
outsmart get the better of by thinking; outfox; outthink; outwit
outthink excel in thinking; get the better of by thinking
outwit get the better of by superior ingenuity and clever thinking; outsmart
percolate penetrate; brood over
perpend reflect on carefully
ponder meditate on; consider quietly, deeply, and thoroughly
predetermine decide on beforehand
prejudge form an opinion prematurely
premeditate consider or plan out before acting
preoccupy engross to the exclusion of all else
rack one's brain strain for solution
read make out the significance of
reappraise evaluate again
reckon estimate; figure, assume
reconsider consider again with a view toward change of decision or action
reevaluate reconsider; appraise again
reflect consider quietly
regard take into account or consideration
rethink consider again
revise reconsider, change one's opinion
revolve in one's mind mull over, consider at length
ruminate ponder, muse; go over in one's mind repeatedly and slowly
second-guess use hindsight to criticize or correct; predict
select choose one over another
simmer be in initial stages of consideration
sink become deeply absorbed, as in thought
size up appraise, evaluate, judge
sleep on consider overnight
speculate reflect or meditate on some subject; indulge in idle conjecture; guess, surmise
surmise guess; infer without strong evidence
tackle think seriously about some problem
take into account consider
theorize speculate
think employ one's powers of judgment or reason; consider; remember; ponder; occupy one's mind in reflection on
think about consider
turn over consider; revolve in one's mind
view examine, survey, consider
weigh consider carefully, evaluate
wonder think or speculate curiously or doubtfully; ponder over
worry fret; experience concern over
wrestle with occupy oneself in serious thought about; consider all sides of; debate internally

Reasoning and Examination

abstract determine and summarize essentials; consider as general instance apart from specific examples
adduce offer as evidence
analyze subject to careful scrutiny
arrive at conclude by reasoning
attribute regard as based on or having specific meaning
belabor apply unreasonable scrunity
calculate consider logically and dispassionately
canvass examine carefully in detail
cast about contrive, plan
cerebrate use reason, think about
check test validity by examining closely
check out examine and approve; consider carefully
clarify make intelligible; free from confusion
clear up explain so as to eliminate confusion; clarify
compare examine for differences or similarities
conclude determine or decide by reasoning
construe analyze and explain
contrast compare with something else
convince prove by argument
correlate determine and establish an orderly connection between two or more things
crack puzzle out and resolve
debate consider from all sides
deduce infer or conclude by reasoning from something known or assumed
deliberate consider carefully and thoroughly
derive infer, deduce
diagnose analyze to determine the cause of
dissect examine minutely in all component parts; analyze
educe deduce from something undeveloped
establish determine, prove
evaluate study and determine value or amount of
examine inspect or investigate carefully
explore analyze, study, investigate
figure calculate; conclude
figure out solve, determine

find out discover truth of by study or observation
follow keep one's mind on, attend to
hypothesize make an assumption as premise in an argument
infer derive a logical conclusion from premise or evidence; guess, surmise
inspect examine critically
integrate bring together and unite information and thoughts into a coherent whole
intellectualize consider the rational content or form of
interpolate estimate unknown from known
interpret explain the meaning of; construe or conceive in a specific way
investigate examine closely and systematically
metagrobolize tackle a difficult or puzzling problem
observe examine carefully; consider from all sides
penetrate discover the true nature of by careful examination
place estimate the nature of; determine proper order or position of
plumb examine deeply, closely, and critically
pore over study attentively; meditate on intently
probe investigate thoroughly
prove establish the truth or accuracy of
puzzle exercise one's mind to understand something mysterious; attempt a solution by guesswork
question analyze, examine; doubt, dispute
rationalize consider logically; invent plausible reasons for
reason think logically so as to reach a conclusion
redefine clarify meaning; reexamine
reduce comprehend something complex by analyzing its component parts
research investigate thoroughly
review evaluate critically; examine or study again
scrutinize examine very closely
search look into carefully in an effort to find something hidden; examine
sift through separate and examine various possibilities
solve determine the answer to a problem
sort out examine and place in order
strategize plan carefully toward a specific end
study investigate carefully and in detail; think deeply, reflect on
surmise imagine; infer from scant information
survey inspect or consider comprehensively
syllogize reason by means of premises that support a logical conclusion; deduce
synthesize combine elements to reach a conclusion
think over evaluate from all sides for possible action
think through consider thoroughly and reach a conclusion
trace follow logically from beginning to end
work out devise or arrange by careful calculation
work over consider at length; examine thoroughly

Learning and Memory

absorb take in, learn
acquaint oneself with become familiar with, furnish oneself with knowledge about
ascertain discover, learn with assurance
assimilate absorb and comprehend
bear in mind remember, consider
bethink oneself think, consider; remind oneself; remember
call to mind remember
catch on grasp mentally, understand
commit to memory memorize
digest assimilate information; arrange methodically in the mind
discover gain knowledge of for the first time; realize
evoke call up or produce memories
fix in one's mind remember; settle on
glean gather information slowly and patiently
inquire into investigate, seek information about
learn acquire information, knowledge, or understanding
master become adept through understanding and study
memorize learn exactly by rote; commit to memory
pick up learn; acquire understanding of through light study
recall remember
recollect remember
remember call back to the level of consciousness; think of again; retain in one's memory; recall; recollect
reminisce think about past experiences, often wistfully
retain hold in one's mind or memory
sink in have something penetrate one's mind
soak up absorb and fill one's mind with
study apply one's mental faculties so as to acquire knowledge
summon up recall, evoke
take in grasp the meaning of, comprehend; absorb

Knowledge and Understanding

appreciate be fully aware of nature or value of
apprehend understand, perceive
collect one's thoughts organize one's thinking
comprehend understand
crystallize give one's thoughts a definite form
dawn on begin to be perceived
determine resolve conclusively
discern recognize or understand, esp. as distinct or different
distill determine the essence of
distinguish separate mentally; recognize as different
familiarize make known to oneself
fathom penetrate and understand thoroughly
get at penetrate, determine the truth of
grasp comprehend
identify determine the particular nature or identity of; recognize
know perceive clearly with certainty; recognize, be acquainted with; understand the nature of; be convinced of
make out decipher meaning of, comprehend
perceive become aware of; gain understanding of

pierce see into and understand against resistance
prehend apprehend
realize understand clearly or fully, apprehend
recognize perceive clearly, realize to be real or true; identify from past experience
resolve reach conclusion or solution
see perceive, comprehend
see through recognize the true nature of
sense become aware of; comprehend, grasp
understand grasp the idea or meaning of; comprehend

Belief and Conception

believe have confidence in the truth of without proof; hold an opinion
conceive originate, imagine
concoct originate, fabricate, conceive
conjure up imagine or contrive as if by magic
contrive fabricate, invent
create conceive, originate; imagine
daresay believe or assume to be probable
deem believe; hold as an opinion
divine discover or perceive intuitively, not by reason
dream fantasize or imagine; consider as a remote possibility
dream up conceive or devise an idea or plan
envisage have a mental picture of
envision imagine, picture to oneself
evoke re-create from memory or imagination; conjure up
expect imagine; suppose
fabricate conceive, create, concoct
fancy form a conception of; believe without assurance
fantasize imagine; dream
feel believe, think
find feel; discover
foresee know beforehand, esp. by intuition
harbor maintain a thought or feeling about
hatch conceive or concoct an idea or plan
have a hunch guess, intuit
hold believe, have an opinion
ideate form an idea or thought; conceive
imagine form mental image or notion of; guess or conjecture; create
incline lean toward one view or plan of action
incubate hatch; give form to an idea
intuit understand or know without rational thought; feel
invent imagine, contrive
make up conceive, imagine, devise
moon indulge in dreams over
opine hold an opinion on; suppose
originate conceive, create
picture envision in one's mind, imagine
preconceive form an opinion in advance without real knowledge
prefigure picture or imagine beforehand
presume assume or suppose to be true as a matter of fact
realize become fully aware of; conceive of
reify ascribe concrete qualities to an abstraction
rely on believe, trust
suppose assume, often for the sake of argument
suspect believe to be true or likely
take it assume, imagine
tend pay heed to; exhibit disposition toward
think up imagine, contrive, devise
trust believe
visualize envision or form a mental image of
weave form by elaborate combining of elements into a connected whole

REASONING AND INTUITION

Reason and Rationale
Order, Hierarchy, and Systems
Intuition and Imagination

Reason and Rationale

adduce (*vb*) bring forward, cite, allege
analogy inference derived from likeness between two or more things
analysis systematic separation and examination of parts
antithesis contrast or opposition, esp. of ideas or argument in dialectic process
apologia reasoned defense or justification
apprehension understanding
argument chain or sequence of reasons leading to conclusion
assumption statement accepted as true before being proved
axiom generally accepted truth or principle
biconditional (*adj*) pertaining to the relation between two statements that is valid only when both are true or false
brainstorm (*vb*) engage in a session of energetic thinking, often in a group; (*n*) sudden valuable idea
circumscribe (*vb*) define clearly
clarification something that reduces confusion or makes an issue understandable
clincher final, irrefutable statement that wins an argument
cogent (*adj*) compelling, persuasive; relevant
cogitation deep thinking
cognition process of knowing or gaining knowledge, esp. intellectual process
cognitive (*adj*) involving the acquisition of knowledge
coherent (*adj*) logically clear and consistent
comprehension intellectual understanding, mental grasp
conception ability and process of forming ideas
confutation refutation of an argument
conjecture inference, guess
construe (*vb*) explain, interpret; understand
contend (*vb*) argue, contest
contest (*vb*) challenge, attempt to refute

contradiction assertion of contrary statement; opposition
contradistinction distinction by contrast or opposition
contraposition antithesis, opposition
controvert (*vb*) dispute, deny, contradict, contest
convention general agreement in principle
convince (*vb*) prevail in argument, persuade
correct (*vb*) remove errors, rectify; (*adj*) factual, true
counterexample example that refutes another statement
counterproposal alternative proposal made after rejecting initial proposal
criterion measure or standard of judgment
crux central or decisive point in argument
cumulative (*adj*) increasing by successive additions; tending to lead to the same conclusion
cut-and-dried (*adj*) done according to routine, formula, or set plan
data facts or information; material providing grounds for discussion
datum given fact on which argument or premise is based or from which conclusion may be drawn
debate (*vb*) dispute, deliberate; examine question or issue verbally; (*n*) formal argument or discussion of opposing views
deduction reasoning process that proceeds from general to particular
define (*vb*) determine or describe in specific terms
definition formal statement or explanation of meaning
definitive (*adj*) conclusive; most reliable or complete
delimit (*vb*) set boundaries or limits
demystify (*vb*) explain clearly so as to remove confusion
determine (*vb*) define, settle, fix, ascertain, limit
dialectic art or practice of logical discussion, esp. in investigating truth of a theory or opinion
didactic (*adj*) instructive, pertaining to teaching
differentiate (*vb*) distinguish; mark or perceive differences
discursive reasoning reasoning that draws inferences from logical thought patterns
disjunction separation into elements
disprove (*vb*) refute
dispute (*vb*) contend, argue
disquisition formal inquiry or discourse
dissect (*vb*) analyze
dissertation disquisition, discussion; essay
epistemic (*adj*) concerning knowledge
esemplastic (*adj*) capable of shaping diverse elements into a unified whole
examination thorough, detailed investigation or study
excogitate (*vb*) think out, contrive
explicate (*vb*) interpret, explain
expostulate (*vb*) reason earnestly, usu. against something
extrapolate (*vb*) infer an unknown from something that is known
fact something known to be true or real
facultative (*adj*) relating to mental activity or capacity
fallacy false idea, error in reasoning
forensic (*adj*) pertaining to argumentation
forethought premeditation
generalization general inference derived from particular
gist essential point of argument or story
grasp comprehension
hypothesis unproved assumption for debate or discussion; proposition
idea concept, mental impression, or notion
ideation process of forming ideas or images
implausible (*adj*) not particularly believable
implication something implied or suggested as naturally inferred or understood
induction reasoning process that proceeds from particular to general
inference logical conclusion drawn from premise
information knowledge, data
intellect mental faculty for knowing, judging, perceiving, and reasoning
intellection intellectual activity
intellectualize (*vb*) seek or consider rational content or form of; apply reason and ignore emotional or psychological significance of
interpretation explanation of meaning
irrelevant (*adj*) not pertinent, immaterial
ken (*vb*) *Scottish.* know, discern
last word conclusive point in discussion
logic method of sound reasoning that relates sequence of facts, events, or notions
lucid (*adj*) clearly expressed
middle ground reasonable position between extremes
moot (*adj*) open to discussion or debate; irrelevant to an issue in debate
notion idea, proposition, theory
nub point, gist
perception capacity for comprehension; keen mental faculty or observation
perspicacious (*adj*) endowed with keen mental perception
perspicuous (*adj*) presented in clear and precise manner
pertinence relevance to the matter at hand
polemic controversial argument; person who argues in opposition to another
position point of view; statement of proposition or thesis
postulate hypothesis assumed as basis for line of reasoning
prehension mental understanding
premise something assumed as basis for argument or position
proposition anything stated for consideration or discussion or to be proved
proviso conditional stipulation
ratiocination process of careful, precise reasoning
rational (*adj*) conforming to reason
rationale fundamental reason, basis, or explanation
reason power to form logical conclusions and sound judgments
reasoning orderly use of mental faculties to reach conclusions and draw inferences
reductionism simplification of a complex con-

cept, phenomenon, or issue, esp. oversimplification or distortion

reflection careful consideration of something

refutation use of evidence to prove something false

relation connection between things that belong or function together

riddle cleverly puzzling or confounding question

rumination extended meditation; going over of something in one's mind

sophistry deceptive or fallacious reasoning

sound reasoning valid thinking

specious (*adj*) unsound though appearing to be true

speculation assumption of truth based on insufficient evidence

standard criterion for judgment; established rule or measure

statement proposition, presentation of point

stipulation specific, essential condition or accepted point

syncretism reconciliation of conflicting beliefs or forms

synthesis combining of disparate elements into a whole

tangent sudden change or digression in reasoning process

tenable (*adj*) defensible; reasonable

theorem proposition that can be drawn from premises or is part of general theory

theory coherent series of plausible propositions that serve as explanation for something

thesis position or proposition set forth for proof or argument

thought act or process of thinking; cogitation; reasoning power

thought-out (*adj*) derived by careful mental consideration

thrust essential element or principal goal of argument

treatise systematic exposition of essentials of argument and its conclusion

unilateral (*adj*) one-sided, imbalanced

viable (*adj*) having likely chance of working

watertight (*adj*) flawless; having no possibility of evasion or misunderstanding

well-founded (*adj*) based on sound or valid reasoning

well-grounded (*adj*) having a sound basis or foundation

well-taken (*adj*) justified, based in truth or fact

wit mental soundness or ability, esp. facility for making unusual connections and brief, clever expressions

Order, Hierarchy, and Systems

agenda outline or list of things to be considered

antecedent conditional element in proposition

aperçu *French.* brief outline or summary

breakdown classification into categories

canon system of rules or laws; body of criteria and standards

case history recorded details and past, used for analysis

catalog list, register of items arranged systematically

category specific division within classification system

catena chain or sequence of linked things, events

chain sequence of connected things, events

class large, inclusive set sharing common characteristics

classification systematic arrangement into classes, groups, or categories with specific characteristics

codify (*vb*) organize systematically

collate (*vb*) place in order; compare critically

columniation organization of material into rows and columns

compartmentalize (*vb*) separate into distinct categories

compendium collection of information; brief summary of larger work

component element or facet

comprise (*vb*) constitute; include within scope; be made up of

concatenation connected series or chain

consecutive (*adj*) in order

construct something organized or structured by mental activity

continuum consistent series or whole, esp. sequence progressing by small gradations

corollary one proposition that is proved incidentally by another

correlative (*adj*) related as reciprocal proofs

course usual procedure; progression in steps

delineate (*vb*) outline; set forth in precise detail

dichotomy division into two mutually exclusive or contradictory parts

division distinct group forming portion of larger group

domino effect cumulative effect that results when one action initiates a series of events

flow chart diagram using symbols to display step-by-step procedure or system

framework basic underlying structure or plan

full circle series of developments that return to source, original position, or opposite position

gradation arrangement in levels or stages; single level within such a series

grade level within hierarchy

grid network of evenly spaced horizontals and perpendiculars; any system so organized

hierarchy organization into a branching or ranked structure

increment something added, esp. very small amount or series of regular successive additions

index list of specific data or items, usu. arranged alphabetically

infrastructure basic, underlying framework or feature of an organizational system

interface point at which independent systems meet and interact

juxtapose (*vb*) place side by side

level grade or rank within structure

linear (*adj*) proceeding logically or sequentially in a straight line

list meaningful sequence of items

logistics detailed planning, implementation, and

coordination of an operation, esp. military
matrix arrangement of elements into rows and columns
method systematic procedure or mode of inquiry in a field or discipline
nomenclature system of terms and symbols for describing something
offshoot collateral branch; secondary element
order arrangement or sequence of things or events; category, class, rank, or level
organization act or process of arranging systematically into logical or consistent form
outline hierarchical organization of material; summary; plan
partition division into constituent elements
plan design; detailed program; orderly arrangement of parts
position order or place within structure or hierarchy
precedent established standard or rule
précis concise summary of essential points or facts
prerequisite something required before proceeding to the next level
principium *Latin.* lit. that which is first; fundamental principle
principle comprehensive, fundamental law or assumption
rank (*vb*) organize into hierarchy of relative positions; (*n*) position in such a hierarchy
reticulate (*vb*) divide, arrange, or mark into network
rudiment basic principle or element
section separate part or portion
sector distinctive portion of larger system, esp. one bounded by specific lines
sequence continuous, connected series
set number of things with common characteristics classed together
skeleton structural framework
spectrum continuous sequence or range
step one stage in process; grade or rank in scale
step-by-step (*adj*) taken in proper sequence, one at a time
strategy detailed plan or method for obtaining specific goal
structure defined organizational pattern or arrangement
subcategory division of category within structure
subdivision smaller set within larger set forming division of whole
subset set each of whose components is part of a larger, inclusive set
subsidiary secondary part ranked lower in hierarchy
succession sequence; process of following in order
sui generis *Latin.* lit. of his, her, or its own kind; constituting a class unto itself
summary concise, general description of larger argument or system
superstructure overlying framework or extension built on top of or added to basic structure
syntax connected, organized system; harmonious placement of parts, esp. linguistic
system interacting or interdependent combination of things forming unified whole
systemic (*adj*) relating to or common to a particular system
template model or pattern for duplicating existing object or system
tree branching hierarchical structure
vicious circle chain of events in which each response generates a new problem

Intuition and Imagination

aperçu *French.* sudden intuitive insight
caprice sudden, unpredictable, apparently unmotivated idea
chimerical (*adj*) imaginary; visionary; wildly fanciful
clairvoyance ability to perceive matters beyond one's senses; precognition; second sight
collective unconscious genetically determined part of unconscious common to all members of one race or people
common sense sound practical judgment not based on reasoning or special knowledge
conation impulse or tendency to act with resolution
conceit fanciful idea or thought
conception inception and understanding of ideas and abstractions
concoction fabrication, fanciful creation
conjecture guess; speculation
conjuring imagining or contriving ideas
creation act of making, imagining, or inventing something new
creativity ability to imagine and make new or original forms, ideas, or things, esp. by transcending traditional thinking
daydream wishful product of one's imagination
delirium hallucinatory, visionary mental disturbance
dream visionary product of one's unconscious imagination
enchantment state of imaginative rapture
ESP extrasensory perception
extrasensory perception ESP; ability to perceive another's thoughts or things beyond one's normal senses
fabrication creation, invention, or construction
fabulous (*adj*) being the product of imagination
fancy whim, notion
fantastical (*adj*) conceived by unrestrained imagination
fantasy creation of unrealistic images and dreams; caprice
feeling intuitive sense separate from rational process
fiction creation or invention of the imagination
figment something invented or contrived
flash sudden intuitive perception
flight of fancy extravagant indulgence in whim and imagination
guess opinion not based on specific evidence
hallucination fantastic, unrealistic vision or impression

humor sudden, inexplicable whim or notion
hunch strong intuitive feeling about future
idea newly formulated or original thought or notion
idealization overestimation of something in its ultimate, perfected form
illusion misapprehension, hallucination, or misleading image
image mental representation of something not present
imagination creative faculty to produce mental images of things not present, previously unknown, or suggestive of something stored in memory
implicit (*adj*) unexpressed but essential to nature of something
impression distinct image of something; reaction
impulse sudden, spontaneous inclination or idea
ingenuity skill and cleverness in conception or design
innovation new way of doing or viewing something
insight clear, deep perception
inspiration power of arousing intellect or emotions, esp. to receive or conceive new insights or ideas; such a new insight or idea
instinct perceptions or impulses coming from below the conscious mental level; natural aptitude or faculty
intimation indirect or subtle communication of idea
intuition direct knowledge or insight independent of any reasoning process
invention creation, fabrication, contrivance
make-believe fancy, daydream, illusion
mind's eye inner eye that provides the ability to conceive of or remember imaginary scenes
myth fanciful, usu. traditional, imaginary tale serving as basis for commonly held belief
notion one's opinion or view of something, often fanciful or vague; personal theory, whim, or inclination
novelty innovation, fresh idea
passing fancy notion or whim held briefly
perception awareness of one's environment, esp. recognition by intuition or senses
phantasm fantasy, illusion, figment of imagination
phantasmagoria constantly shifting, hallucinatory succession of images
precognition clairvoyance
premonition intuitive anticipation of an event without reason; presentiment
presentiment premonition
pretend (*adj*) make-believe or imagined
psychic sense sensitivity to immaterial or supernatural powers and influences
quixotism capricious, impractical devotion to ideals and dreams
rapture powerful experience involving heightened perception and sensations, as of another sphere of existence
reverie daydream; state of being lost in thought
second sight clairvoyance
sixth sense extraordinary intuitive power of perception beyond the five senses; intuition
spark something that ignites one's imagination or thoughts
speculation conjectural consideration of a matter; guess; surmise
telepathy extrasensory communication from one mind to another, as by ESP
theory imaginative but unverifiable speculation serving as explanation for something
visile (*adj*) denoting one who draws primarily on visual data and input
vision perception with one's imagination; extraordinary or vivid discernment or insight; supernatural appearance that provides insight
visualization ability to imagine or conceive
whim sudden, unusual, or capricious notion or thought
whimsy imaginative, playful, and fantastic creation; whim or caprice
wishful thinking unrealistic dream; ascribing reality to one's hopes and wishes

JUDGMENT AND CRITICISM

Judgments and Critiques

analysis critical evaluation of whole or parts
appraise (*vb*) estimate value, worth, or significance
arbitration act of hearing and determining the outcome of a controversy by a mediator
argue (*vb*) give reasons pro and con
auto-da-fé pronouncement of judgment
candor forthrightness; lack of prejudice
censor supervisor of morals and conduct; official who passes judgment on material
commentary explanation and evaluation, usu. written
consensus general or unanimous agreement; majority of opinion
criticism act of passing judgment as to the merits of anything; faultfinding; analysis and evaluation of a literary or artistic work or performance; critique
critique critical evaluation; usu. written; review
discretion personal choice or judgment; ability to form free and responsible decisions

editorial expression of opinion on some subject, esp. in newspaper
estimation opinion, judgment
evaluate (*vb*) assess, form opinion on
free will exercise of free or voluntary choice or decision
hairsplitting making overly fine distinctions; quibbling
inclination disposition, esp. favorable; slant
intercede (*vb*) intervene to reconcile conflict
judge (*vb*) form an opinion through careful deliberation
judgment pronouncement of one's opinion; process or capacity for forming opinions
judicious (*adj*) having or exercising sound judgment
misjudge (*vb*) form an unjust or mistaken opinion
misread (*vb*) misinterpret, judge incorrectly
notice critical review
opine (*vb*) form, hold, or express opinion
opinion point of view, appraisal of particular matter
option power or freedom to choose or make independent judgment
outlook point of view, opinion
overlook (*vb*) inspect and examine so as to reach judgment on
partiality bias, predisposition
parti pris *French.* preconceived prejudice or bias
partisan adherent to cause, supporter of point of view
pass (*vb*) render favorable judgment or verdict
pass judgment express firm, irrevocable opinion
peremptory (*adj*) allowing no contradiction, precluding all debate
point of view opinion; position from or manner in which something is considered or appraised; viewpoint
position firm point of view or opinion on something
preconception opinion formed without knowledge or experience
predisposed (*adj*) inclined in advance, pro or con
prepossession prejudice or opinion formed beforehand, esp. favorable one
rank (*vb*) determine relative value or position of
rate (*vb*) set value of; assign rank to
reconsider (*vb*) assess previous judgment and form new opinion
referee (*vb*) arbitrate as judge; (n) one who so arbitrates
review (*vb*) provide critical analysis, esp. written or broadcast
second thoughts reservations about previous position or judgment
sentence formal judgment arrived at by deliberation, esp. in court of law and specifying punishment
sentiment judgment based on feeling; opinion
speculate (*vb*) form or express opinion without knowledge of subject
surmise (*vb*) infer on scant grounds; conjecture
think better of reconsider
two cents worth opinion offered on topic being discussed
umpire (*vb*) wield authority to resolve disputes; (*n*) one who has such authority
unbiased (*adj*) fair, free from prejudice
vacillate (*vb*) hesitate or waver in opinions
value judgment opinion as to worth of something
vantage point point of view, position
verdict opinion based on evidence
vet (*vb*) appraise, verify, or check
view opinion or judgment on something
viewpoint position from which or basis on which judgment is made; point of view
vote (*vb*) state one's opinion, esp. express formal opinion in political process
will disposition, inclination

Approval, Respect, and Recognition

accept (*vb*) approve of, admit to; recognize as true
acknowledge (*vb*) recognize as rightful or genuine; state agreement with
admire (*vb*) regard with approval and respect
appreciate (*vb*) recognize value of; hold in high esteem
approbation approval, esp. formal approval
approval ratification; favorable opinion
approve (*vb*) express favorable opinion; give formal consent
begrudge (*vb*) view with reluctant approval
bow (*vb*) incline head or body in respect
carte blanche full discretionary power; unconditional authority
cite (*vb*) give credit to
coddle (*vb*) treat with extreme care
commemorate (*vb*) honor memory by ceremony or observance
compassion sympathetic awareness and concern for others' distress
condone (*vb*) pardon, excuse
consideration esteem, regard; opinion based on matters taken into account
cotton to (*vb*) *Informal.* take a liking to
countenance (*vb*) extend approval, sanction
credence mental acceptance as true
credibility capacity for belief; ability to instill or evoke belief
credit (*vb*) consider favorably as source of action or possessor of trait
cup of tea something one likes or is well-suited to
curtsy slight dip of body and bending of knees as show of respect by women
deference respect for another's wishes
deserving (*adj*) deemed worthy
dignify (*vb*) give distinction to, show respect for
esteem high regard
estimation esteem, honor
exemplary (*adj*) commendable, deserving imitation
fancy (*vb*) take a liking to, often capriciously
favor (*vb*) support, view positively, prefer; (*n*) partiality, warm regard
favorable (*adj*) expressing approval or partiality
favoritism partiality, showing of special favor
genuflect (*vb*) touch knee to floor as show of respect or reverence

grant (*vb*) accord another his or her due
gratuity something given freely as show of recognition for service or favor
high opinion esteem, respect or regard for
honor (*vb*) hold in high regard, show recognition of
idealize (*vb*) hold in excessively high regard, esp. as model for imitation
imprimatur formal approval, sanction
inclination liking, disposition toward
indulge (*vb*) take pleasure in; treat with excessive consideration
kowtow (*vb*) show servile deference; touch forehead to ground as sign of deep respect
laurels honors
like (*vb*) approve, feel inclined toward, prefer
love (*vb*) feel strong or active affection, admiration, and respect for; enjoy greatly
obeisance gesture of respect
oblige (*vb*) perform a favor; put another in one's debt by doing favors
opt (*vb*) decide in favor of
pardon (*vb*) forgive; excuse; tolerate another's fault
partiality favorable bias or predisposition
pass muster obtain approval or acceptance
pay respects express esteem and regard for
pet one favored with great kindness or consideration
popular (*adj*) widely approved of or preferred
predilection favorable opinion or bias
preference special choice; favorable view
prize (*vb*) value highly, hold in esteem
proclivity inclination, predisposition toward
propensity strong inclination or tendency
prostrate (*vb*) lie facedown on ground as show of submission and respect
ratify (*vb*) formally approve, usu. by vote
recognition acknowledgment; special attention
red carpet show of exceptional courtesy
regard esteem, respect
relish (*vb*) appreciate, be pleased by
reputation one's place in public esteem, overall character as judged by others
repute condition of being known, esp. in positive light
respect (*vb*) consider worthy of high regard and esteem
reward something given in return for service or merit
rubber-stamp (*vb*) approve routinely or automatically
salaam ceremonial salutation and show of respect made by bowing with right palm on forehead
salute (*vb*) express respect and admiration; make any of various gestures of respect; (*n*) gesture of respect, esp. with right palm at forehead
sanction authoritative approval or permission
satisfaction state of contentment or gratification; confident acceptance of something as good or true
save face maintain dignity, prestige, or reputation
say-so authoritative approval
seal of approval official indication or mark of approval
select (*vb*) choose, express preference, discriminate
self-pride sense of satisfaction at one's own character and achievements
self-regard consideration for oneself
self-respect proper regard for oneself and one's dignity and value as a person
smile on (*vb*) look favorably on
superiority quality or state of having higher status or worth
take kindly to develop a partiality toward
take to respond favorably to
testimonial expression of appreciation; recommendation
think better of improve one's opinion of
thumbs-up *Informal.* act or gesture of approval or assent
tribute show of respect, gratitude, or affection
untouchable (*adj*) above criticism
valuation assessment of worth
value (*vb*) place high relative worth on
vote of confidence expression of support or approval
vouchsafe (*vb*) grant as privilege or special favor, esp. in condescending manner
well-disposed (*adj*) favorably inclined
wow (*vb*) elicit enthusiastic approval or delight from

Support, Encouragement, and Agreement

adopt (*vb*) accept formally
advocate (*vb*) plead a cause; (*n*) one who pleads a cause
aegis support, esp. formal guidance and protection
affirm (*vb*) declare as valid or confirmed
agree (*vb*) settle by mutual consent; concur
appoint (*vb*) select officially
assent (*vb*) agree
assist (*vb*) help, support
aver (*vb*) assert; verify
avouch (*vb*) guarantee as factual or provable; affirm
beau geste *French.* fine but often empty gesture
beneficent (*adj*) resulting in good; kindly or charitable
beneficial (*adj*) conducive to well-being; producing an advantage
benefit (*vb*) produce well-being or an advantage
bonhomie geniality
boon timely benefit, blessing
boost (*vb*) assist, promote
booster enthusiastic supporter
buck up (*vb*) raise morale of; become more cheerful
buoy (*vb*) support or sustain; raise spirits of
champion (*vb*) actively support or defend
choice act of selecting; best part; one selected
cold comfort limited sympathy or encouragement
comfort consolation in time of affliction; feeling of encouragement
commiserate (*vb*) express sympathy or condolences
concur (*vb*) agree
condolence expression of sympathy

confirm (*vb*) ratify, sanction; establish the validity of
congratulate (*vb*) salute another's success or good fortune
console (*vb*) comfort another in distress or sorrow
corroborate (*vb*) support with evidence; confirm
embrace (*vb*) accept readily, gladly
encourage (*vb*) inspire with courage or confidence; give assistance to
encouragement support, inspiration, aid
endorse (*vb*) express definite, public approval
espouse (*vb*) embrace or adopt a cause
exculpate (*vb*) clear of alleged fault
exhort (*vb*) urge strongly
exonerate (*vb*) relieve of obligation or duty; free from blame
find for (*vb*) decide in favor of
hold up (*vb*) bring to notice for support
hold with (*vb*) agree, concur with
hortatory (*adj*) giving encouragement, urging on
humor (*vb*) accommodate another by indulgence
indulgence act of great consideration
ingratiate (*vb*) gain favor or acceptance by a deliberate act
mollify (*vb*) appease, soften in temper or feeling
name (*vb*) decide on, choose
nod indication of one's support or assent
nominate (*vb*) designate, propose for honor or office
nurture (*vb*) further the development of through kind support
OK informal expression of support or approval; (*adj*) all right; (*vb*) express or give one's support or approval to
okay OK
on behalf of on the side of, in support of
palliate (*vb*) excuse; mitigate gravity of
partisan adherent to a cause; supporter of point of view
pass (*vb*) approve formally, as by a legislative body
pep talk brief, emotional talk calculated to arouse support or foster determination
persuade (*vb*) prevail on by argument or entreaty
placate (*vb*) appease, calm by concessions
please (*vb*) give pleasure or satisfaction to
prelation promotion to higher status, grade, or rank
preselect (*vb*) choose in advance
pro (*adv*) favoring or supporting; (*n*) argument in affirmation; proponent of an issue
promo *Informal.* something devised to advertise or promote
promote (*vb*) encourage or advance a person or thing through one's support
prop up (*vb*) support or sustain
proponent supporter, advocate
proselytize (*vb*) attempt to convert others to one's opinion
protestation solemn declaration or affirmation
pump up (*vb*) fill with enthusiasm and excitement
recommend (*vb*) support or represent as worthy
reinforce (*vb*) strengthen by support or assistance
relent (*vb*) become less severe, give in
second (*vb*) give support or encouragement; endorse a motion
see eye to eye agree in all ways
side with agree with, support
single out (*vb*) select, distinguish from group
soothe (*vb*) appease by attention or concern
suit (*vb*) be agreeable, satisfactory, or appropriate to
support (*vb*) uphold, advocate; aid, help; corroborate
swallow (*vb*) accept without opposition
unanimous (*adj*) having the agreement and consent of all
uphold (*vb*) support
validate (*vb*) give official approval or confirmation of; support, corroborate
vindicate (*vb*) relieve of blame; justify; defend, support
vouch for (*vb*) attest, guarantee; supply supporting evidence for
whitewash (*vb*) cover up the faults of, protect from blame
win over (*vb*) convince of one's opinion
witness (*vb*) affirm, support
yea (*interj*) expression of affirmative response or vote
yea-say (*vb*) agree, affirm something
yes-man one who always agrees with a superior

Praise, Exaltation, Flattery, and Applause

acclaim shouted approval or praise
acclamation approval loudly expressed, esp. by applause, cheers, or shouts
accolade expression of praise; award or honor
adore (*vb*) esteem, worship, or honor
adulate (*vb*) flatter or admire excessively or servilely
aggrandize (*vb*) make great or greater in power, wealth, or honor
apotheosize (*vb*) elevate to divine status, deify
applause display of public approval, esp. hand clapping
awe fearful reverence, admiration, or submission
belaud (*vb*) praise excessively
bepraise (*vb*) praise
blandish (*vb*) cajole with gentle flattery
blarney clever, often coaxing flattery; cajolery
bless (*vb*) speak kindly of; wish well; extol
boast (*vb*) brag, praise oneself
bow and scrape submit oneself before a superior
brag (*vb*) boast, indulge in self-glorifying talk
bravo (*interj*) shout of praise
butter up (*vb*) *Informal.* charm with flattery or praise to gain favor
cajole (*vb*) persuade with clever flattery
canonize (*vb*) sanction by authority, esp. ecclesiastical
celebrate (*vb*) honor; present for widespread public notice and praise
cheer (*vb*) comfort, restore hope to; encourage or salute with shouts; (*n*) shout of encouragement or praise
commend (*vb*) praise; present as worthy of confidence
compliment (*vb*) express respect, affection, or

admiration for; flatter; praise
court (*vb*) seek to attract or win over by flattery and attention
crown (*vb*) bestow favor on as a mark of honor
curry favor seek advancement through flattery and fawning attention
dote (*vb*) bestow lavish, excessive fondness
elevate (*vb*) exalt in rank or status
encomium glowing, enthusiastic praise
encore demand, as by audience, for reappearance or additional performance as expression of approval for performer
eulogize (*vb*) speak or write high praise for
eulogy formal commendation or high praise, esp. for deceased person
exalt (*vb*) glorify or elevate by praise
extol (*vb*) praise highly, glorify
fawn (*vb*) show excessive affection, esp. by servile flattery
flatter (*vb*) praise excessively or insincerely
flattery insincere or excessive praise
glorify (*vb*) extol, elevate
grace (*vb*) confer favor or honor on
hail (*vb*) acclaim, greet with approval
hallow (*vb*) respect highly, venerate
hand outburst or round of applause
here-here (*interj*) *Chiefly Brit.* expression of support or encouragement
hip-hip hooray (*interj*) signal for applause or intensifier of cheers
homage reverential regard, respect, or tribute
hooray (*interj*) expression of appreciation or encouragement; hurrah
hosanna (*interj*) shout of praise or acclamation
hurrah (*interj*) hooray
huzzah (*interj*) hurrah
hype extravagant promotion; excessive praise
idolatry excessive or blind devotion or reverence
idolize (*vb*) admire to excess; worship
immortalize (*vb*) confer undying fame on
inflate (*vb*) expand or puff up, esp. unjustifiably
kudos honor, praise
laud (*vb*) praise, acclaim
lionize (*vb*) treat as person of importance
merit (*vb*) possess praiseworthy qualities and virtues
olé (*interj*) shout of approval; bravo
ovation prolonged, enthusiastic applause
paean song of praise or tribute
panegyric formal, elaborate written or oral praise
plaudits enthusiastic expression of approval; round of applause
plug (*vb*) *Informal.* promote insistently; praise highly
praise (*vb*) express approval; commend
put on a pedestal elevate, exalt
rave extravagantly enthusiastic appraisal or review
resound (*vb*) be celebrated
revere (*vb*) regard with high esteem or awe
root for (*vb*) wish success; applaud noisily
salvo round of cheers or applause
self-congratulation uncritical satisfaction with one's own accomplishments
self-flattery exaggeration of one's strengths along with denial of one's weaknesses
self-glorification boastful exaggeration of one's strengths
set up (*vb*) extol as model
stroke (*vb*) *Informal.* flatter, promote feelings of self-approval in
sweet-talk (*vb*) *Informal.* coax or persuade by flattery and cajolery
talk up (*vb*) praise, extol
tout (*vb*) flatter loudly or extravagantly
venerate (*vb*) regard with reverence and deference
viva (*interj*) *Spanish, Italian.* exclamation of approval
worship (*vb*) regard with high honor and reverence

Disapproval, Disrespect, and Denial

adverse (*adj*) unfavorable; opposed to one's interest
animosity feeling of strong dislike or enmity, esp. when displayed in action
animus strong dislike, often prejudiced and hostile; animosity
antipathy aversion, dislike
askance (*adv*) with disapproval, suspicion, or mistrust
aversion repugnance coupled with a strong desire to avoid; dislike
avoid (*vb*) shun or keep away from as indication of distaste
bias prejudice
brush-off *Informal.* curt, rude dismissal
censorious (*adj*) given to censure
chasten (*vb*) discipline by inflicting suffering on so as to improve or purify
cold shoulder intentionally unsympathetic and disrespectful treatment
confound (*vb*) refute or contradict
contradict (*vb*) assert the contrary, imply the opposite; deny directly
correct (*vb*) point out another's errors; punish with a view to improving
correction rectification of errors
critical (*adj*) inclined to find fault
criticism unfavorable observations or comments
cross out (*vb*) eliminate from consideration; x out
debase (*vb*) lower another in status or esteem
decry (*vb*) express strong disapproval of
deflate (*vb*) reduce in size or importance
denial refusal to recognize or acknowledge something; disavowal or disowning of
deny (*vb*) refuse to recognize or acknowledge; disavow, disown
deprecate (*vb*) express earnest disapproval of; belittle
detest (*vb*) dislike intensely, loathe
detract from (*vb*) take away a part from
dim view skeptical or unfavorable attitude
disapproval unfavorable judgment or condemnation
disapprove (*vb*) express unfavorable judgment on
disavow (*vb*) deny knowledge of

discard (*vb*) reject as useless
disclaim (*vb*) deny interest in or connection with; disavow
discommend (*vb*) cause to be viewed unfavorably; disapprove of
discontent dissatisfaction with
discount (*vb*) view with doubt; underestimate importance of
discountenance (*vb*) treat or view with disfavor
discredit (*vb*) deprive of good repute; destroy confidence in accuracy of
discriminate (*vb*) treat unfavorably without justification
disenchantment state of freedom from illusion, esp. from overoptimism
disesteem disfavor, low regard
disfavor disapproval, dislike
disgruntled (*adj*) discontented; having ill humor
dishonor (*vb*) bring shame on, deprive of honor or prestige; treat in degrading manner
disillusionment condition of being free of illusions
dislike (*vb*) regard with displeasure
dismiss (*vb*) put aside from serious consideration, make light of
disown (*vb*) repudiate, refuse to acknowledge
displease (*vb*) incur disapproval or dislike
disqualify (*vb*) deprive of right or privilege; render unfit
disregard (*vb*) treat as worthless by ignoring
disrepute state of being held in low regard
disrespect lack of consideration; low regard
dissatisfaction condition of displeasure or discontent
distaste dislike, aversion
downgrade (*vb*) minimize or depreciate in quality or importance
embarrass (*vb*) place in state of confusion or self-conscious discomfort
enmity feeling of ill will or extreme dislike and animosity
eschew (*vb*) abstain from or avoid on moral or practical grounds
fair game deserving of or susceptible to criticism
frown on (*vb*) express disapproval of or displeasure toward
harp on (*vb*) dwell on persistently, esp. by voicing criticisms
hate (*vb*) dislike intensely
hiss sibilant sound made as expression of disapproval
hoot cry or shout of derision or objection
hypercritical (*adj*) excessively critical, censorious
ignore (*vb*) refuse to notice; deem unworthy of consideration
inconsequential (*adj*) unimportant, insignificant
inexcusable (*adj*) incapable of being justified
inferiority sense or state of having low status or worth
in the dog house *Slang.* in a state of disfavor
judgmental (*adj*) tending to pass moral judgment and view others as inferior to oneself; quick to judge
knock (*vb*) *Informal.* find fault with, esp. with trivial criticisms
libel unjustly damaging or unfavorable opinion expressed in written or printed form; anything defamatory
lose face be deprived of one's dignity, prestige, or reputation
low opinion lack of regard or respect for
make light of (*vb*) treat as object of little importance
muckrake (*vb*) search for and expose misconduct, esp. of officials
nay (*interj*) expression of negative reply or vote; denial or dissent
naysay (*vb*) deny; reject; express negative opinion
neglect (*vb*) disregard, ignore
one-upmanship art or practice of maintaining an advantageous position over others
ostracize (*vb*) exclude from group by common consent
pass up (*vb*) neglect to take advantage of; decline, reject
pejorative (*adj*) tending to disparage or devalue
pet peeve frequent subject of complaint
pharisaism hypocritical and judgmental self-righteousness
pick apart (*vb*) find fault with all aspects of
pick at (*vb*) criticize repeatedly, esp. for minor faults
pick on (*vb*) single out for undeserved criticism and harassment
play down (*vb*) understate merits or significance of
pooh-pooh (*vb*) express disdain for; dismiss lightly
potshot random or aimless critical remark
prejudice preconceived judgment or opinion, esp. unfavorable
question (*vb*) express doubt about
reduce (*vb*) downgrade, demote
reject (*vb*) refuse to accept or consider; rebuff; turn down
reprehend (*vb*) voice disapproval or censure
reproach (*vb*) express disappointment or displeasure
reproof expression of censure or criticism
reprove (*vb*) scold or correct gently; express disapproval of
repudiate (*vb*) disown, refuse to accept, reject with denial or condemnation
riot act firm reprimand or warning
segregate (*vb*) distinguish and separate from others
serve one right treat as one deserves, esp. criticize or punish justly
shun (*vb*) deliberately avoid or look down on
skepticism attitude of doubt
slight (*vb*) treat with disdain or indifference
slough over (*vb*) treat as slight or unimportant
snobbishness air of superiority coupled with rebuffing of those deemed inferior to oneself
snooty (*adj*) showing disdain and snobbishness
snub (*vb*) slight, disregard, or insult
spank (*vb*) strike on buttocks with open hand as expression of disapproval

stereotype oversimplified characterization; unjustified generalization
stigma mark of shame or discredit; stain on reproach
stigmatize (*vb*) bring disgrace or infamy on
stricture adverse criticism
stuck-up (*adj*) *Informal.* self-important, snobbish
stultify (*vb*) cause to appear stupid, foolish, or irresponsible
supercilious (*adj*) patronizing and haughtily disdainful of others
ake to task criticize for shortcomings
alk down (*vb*) deprecate, criticize
arget (*vb*) set as object, esp. for criticism
ease (*vb*) disturb or provoke by persistent irritating remarks and distractions
humbs-down gesture of disapproval
oy (*vb*) act with indifference; trifle
urn down (*vb*) reject, show disfavor toward
ncomplimentary (*adj*) unfavorable, derogatory
nderrated (*adj*) valued at less than true worth
ndervalue (*vb*) depreciate, treat as though of little worth
ndeserving (*adj*) not worthy of consideration, respect, or assistance
nfavorable (*adj*) adverse, contrary; not propitious
nflattering (*adj*) unfavorable, derogatory
npopular (*adj*) disapproved of or disliked in general or by a particular group
npromising (*adj*) appearing unlikely to succeed
nsatisfactory (*adj*) inadequate; worthy of disapproval or rebuke
nsung (*adj*) insufficiently praised
nworthy (*adj*) lacking in value, undeserving
to (*vb*) refuse to approve; reject or prohibit mphatically
tiate (*vb*) debase or corrupt; make ineffective or veak
rite off (*vb*) depreciate; regard as lost or worthless
rong (*vb*) treat unfairly or disrespectfully
out (*vb*) cross out

pposition, Disagreement, and Attack

jure (*vb*) repudiate or renounce firmly and olemnly
monish (*vb*) express warning or disapproval, sp. gently
versary person or group that opposes or tacks; opponent
flict (*vb*) assault or attack repeatedly
gue (*vb*) dispute, contend
sail (*vb*) attack violently with ridicule or abuse
sault (*vb*) attack violently
odds (*adj*) of opposing viewpoints
ack (*vb*) direct unfriendly words or unfavorable iticism against; set upon in hostile manner
n censure, condemnation
nish (*vb*) remove by authority or force; exile
ckball (*vb*) vote against; ostracize or exclude cially
st (*vb*) attack vigorously with vehement words
o (*interj*) sound exclaimed as disapproving shout
brand (*vb*) stigmatize, mark with disapproval
bring to terms compel to agree or submit
buck (*vb*) *Informal.* oppose, resist
carp (*vb*) find fault, complain unreasonably
cavil (*vb*) raise trivial objections
challenge (*vb*) dispute, call in question
chuck (*vb*) discard or set aside as unwanted
combat (*vb*) oppose
complain (*vb*) express displeasure
con (*adv*) in opposition, against
confront (*vb*) oppose or challenge directly
contest (*vb*) dispute, challenge
contumacious (*adj*) obstinately disobedient or rebellious
counter (*vb*) act in opposition
cow (*vb*) intimidate with threats
cross (*vb*) oppose, run counter to, contradict
damage (*vb*) do harm or injury to
daunt (*vb*) lessen the courage of
debunk (*vb*) expose and strip of falseness
decline (*vb*) withhold consent
demur (*vb*) object or hesitate based on one's scruples
differ (*vb*) disagree in opinion or belief; be at variance
disagree (*vb*) differ in opinion; fail to agree; dissent
discourage (*vb*) hinder by disfavoring
dispute (*vb*) argue, debate, quarrel with
dissent (*vb*) speak out against; differ in opinion, esp. with the majority (n) expression of disagreement
dissidence disagreement
dissuade (*vb*) deter through advice or persuasion
division separation by disagreement or difference of opinion
exclude (*vb*) bar from consideration or inclusion
excommunicate (*vb*) exclude from membership, esp. from church group
exile expulsion from one's native land
fight (*vb*) oppose
find against (*vb*) decide for opposite view or side
flak annoying criticism or opposition
forbid (*vb*) prohibit, rule against
gainsay (*vb*) deny, dispute; contradict, oppose
harass (*vb*) annoy, attack, or impede repeatedly
heckle (*vb*) harass with questions or gibes
hostile (*adj*) critical, antagonistic toward, opposed
hostility enmity or antagonism; opposition or resistance to an idea or project
hound (*vb*) harass or attack without respite
impeach (*vb*) accuse of misconduct in office; challenge the credibility of
impugn (*vb*) oppose or assail as false or without integrity
lash out (*vb*) make severe verbal attack, esp. reproach
niggle (*vb*) find fault constantly in petty way
nitpick (*vb*) engage in petty, unjustified criticism
object (*vb*) oppose firmly; express distaste for
obstruct (*vb*) hinder, impede by blocking
offend (*vb*) cause dislike, anger, or resentment
offense assault, attack; something that insults, displeases, or outrages
onslaught furious attack or assault

opponent person who is on the opposing side; adversary
oppose (*vb*) take contrary view; resist, combat
opposed (*adj*) contrary; set in contrast to
oppugn (*vb*) assail by criticism; dispute
plaint lamentation, protest, complaint
polemic controversial refutation of another's opinion; person who makes such a refutation
press (*vb*) assail, harass, afflict
protest complaint, objection, expression of dissent
quibble (*vb*) equivocate, hedge; cavil, carp
rebut (*vb*) contradict or oppose by argument
recriminate (*vb*) retort bitterly, make retaliatory accusation
redbait (*vb*) attack as communistic
renounce (*vb*) withdraw or abandon one's previous support; repudiate
reprobation condemnation or rejection as unworthy or evil
repudiate (*vb*) reject as untrue
resist (*vb*) exert force against
resistance opposition by one to another
run counter to oppose, be contrary to
squelch (*vb*) put down with crushing force
stymie (*vb*) hinder or block
taboo (*adj*) forbidden; banned as evil; (n) prohibition
take issue with oppose, form contrary opinion
take on (*vb*) contend against
take sides state opinion in opposition to another
tear into (*vb*) attack without restraint
tee off (*vb*) *Slang.* make angry denunciation
torment (*vb*) afflict, cause severe distress
variance disagreement, dispute, or quarrel
verboten (*adj*) forbidden; prohibited by law
withstand (*vb*) resist or oppose with determination, esp. successfully
write down (*vb*) depreciate or disparage in writing
wrong (*adj*) incorrect, judged to be false

Blame, Censure, Ridicule, and Contempt

abuse (*vb*) attack verbally, revile; maltreat
accursed (*adj*) under a curse, damned
accuse (*vb*) find fault with, blame
affront (*vb*) insult
allegation assertion, esp. of culpability, made with little or no proof
anathema something detested; ban or curse, esp. by ecclesiastical authority
animadversion unfavorable or censorious comment or criticism
arrogance feeling of superiority over others, esp. offensive display of superiority
aspersion derogatory remark or malicious charge
backbite (*vb*) slander, speak ill of
backstab (*vb*) attempt to discredit by underhanded means
bad-mouth (*vb*) *Slang.* criticize severely; speak disloyally of
barb pointed or biting and openly unpleasant remark
baste (*vb*) scold soundly; denounce vigorously
bawl out (*vb*) *Informal.* reprimand severely
belittle (*vb*) portray as little or less than might seem; mock; disparage
beneath contempt at the lowest possible level of respect; utterly degraded
berate (*vb*) condemn vehemently at length
besmirch (*vb*) tarnish or detract from another's honor
blacken (*vb*) defame, sully, ruin the reputation of
blame (*vb*) find fault with; hold responsible
blasphemy insult to, contempt for, or irreverence toward something sacred
blot mark of reproach, stain of infamy
booby prize prize given in good-natured acknowledgment of poor performance or achievement
brickbat uncomplimentary or unkind comment
bring to account reprimand
Bronx cheer raspberry
burlesque (*vb*) imitate derisively or mock, esp. by caricature
butt victim of abuse or ridicule
calumniate (*vb*) malign with false statements or misrepresentations
calumny false and malicious statements damaging to another's reputation
caricature distortion or exaggeration to make someone or something appear ludicrous
castigate (*vb*) punish or criticize severely; chastise
censure (*vb*) find fault with in a harsh or vehement manner; (*n*) vehement expression of condemnation
chaff (*vb*) ridicule in a good-natured, teasing manner
charge (*vb*) accuse of wrongdoing; blame
chastise (*vb*) criticize severely
chew out (*vb*) *Slang.* reprimand, scold harshly
chide (*vb*) voice disapproval; reproach, rebuke
comeuppance *Informal.* deserved rebuke or penalty
commination denunciation
condemn (*vb*) express strong disapproval or adverse judgment; pronounce guilty; declare to be wrong
contemn (*vb*) scorn, treat with contempt
contempt disdain, lack of respect; disgrace
contumely insulting or humiliating behavior based on contempt
correction punishment, rebuke
criticize (*vb*) find fault with; censure
crucify (*vb*) persecute or treat cruelly with gross injustice
culpable (*adj*) deserving condemnation or blame
curse (*vb*) invoke evil or harm upon; revile profanely
cuss (*vb*) *Informal.* curse
damn (*vb*) condemn harshly as a failure
debase (*vb*) reduce in status or value
defamation calumny, disgrace, or harm done to another's reputation
defame (*vb*) use malicious statements to disgrace or harm another's reputation
degrade (*vb*) bring into contempt or low esteem
demean (*vb*) degrade; lower in status or dignity
denigrate (*vb*) defame, cast aspersions on
denounce (*vb*) condemn publicly as evil or blameworthy

depreciate (*vb*) disparage, represent as of little value
derision bitter, contemptuous ridicule
derogate (*vb*) express low opinion of
desecrate (*vb*) treat irreverently or contemptuously; profane that which is sacred
despise (*vb*) look down upon with contempt; regard as worthless
detest (*vb*) dislike intensely
diatribe bitter, abusive, sarcastic criticism
disdain (*vb*) view scornfully, treat with contempt
disgrace (*vb*) humiliate; cause to lose favor; bring shame upon
disgust marked aversion, total repugnance
disparage (*vb*) degrade, speak slightingly of
dress down (*vb*) censure severely
dump on (*vb*) *Informal.* belittle; bad-mouth
effigy crude figure representing and ridiculing a hated person
epithet descriptive word or phrase, esp. one that is disparaging or abusive
excoriate (*vb*) censure severely; scathe
execrate (*vb*) detest utterly; denounce as evil
fault (*vb*) criticize, blame
find fault criticize
flay (*vb*) criticize harshly
fleer (*vb*) sneer or laugh at derisively; mock
flout (*vb*) scorn, treat with contemptuous disregard
fulminate (*vb*) utter denunciations and invective
castigate (*vb*) criticize harshly
gibe (*vb*) deride, taunt; (*n*) mocking, sarcastic remark
gloat (*vb*) view with triumphant and often malicious satisfaction, esp. another's misfortune
goat one who takes blame for something, often undeservedly; victim
going-over severe scolding
grill (*vb*) question intensely; torment
harangue passionate, critical, or scalding speech; tirade or vehement attack
hatchet job forceful, malicious critique
high horse contemptuous, superior attitude or manner
humble (*vb*) destroy another's prestige, spirit, dignity, or power
humble pie embarrassing humiliation and submission under pressure
humiliate (*vb*) cause another a painful loss of dignity or self-respect
implicate (*vb*) show incriminating connection; blame
imprecate (*vb*) curse, invoke evil upon
impute (*vb*) lay blame on; discredit
incriminate (*vb*) charge with or show evidence of involvement in wrongdoing
indict (*vb*) formally charge with wrongdoing; criticize, accuse
infamy bad public reputation or reproach received for evil ways
insolence insulting and contemptuous behavior or attitude
insult (*vb*) treat or speak of with contempt or indignity; affront

irreverence lack of proper or accustomed respect
irrision derision
jape (*vb*) make mocking fun of
jeer (*vb*) taunt, mock, or speak of with derision
lambaste (*vb*) *Informal.* berate harshly; censure
lampoon (*vb*) ridicule harshly with satire
laugh at (*vb*) express scorn or derision for by laughter; make fun of
laughingstock object of ridicule
loathe (*vb*) feel intense contempt and aversion for; abhor
make fun of ridicule, mock; make sport of
make sport of make fun of
malediction curse
malign (*vb*) speak evil of; utter injurious, often false, statement; defame, slander
mock (*vb*) treat with contempt or ridicule
Momus god of censure and mockery (ancient Greece); carping critic
moralize (*vb*) express opinion on right and wrong conduct; chastise others for misconduct
mortify (*vb*) subject to severe embarrassment and shame
mud *Informal.* abusive, malicious remarks
mudslinging using offensive epithets and false attacks to discredit one's opponent
name-calling using offensive terms to humiliate and induce condemnation of another
needle (*vb*) *Informal.* tease, torment, or goad repeatedly
objurgate (*vb*) denounce or berate harshly; castigate
obloquy abusive, condemnatory language, esp. by numerous persons
odium intense loathing and contempt
onus disagreeable burden or blame
opprobrium disgrace or reproach due to shameful conduct; cause or object of infamy
pan (*vb*) *Informal.* criticize severely, esp. in review of a performance
Philippic speech full of bitter condemnation
piece of one's mind *Informal.* severe scolding or rebuke
pillory (*vb*) expose to public ridicule
pink (*vb*) wound by piercing criticism or ridicule
poison-pen (*adj*) written with malice, usu. anonymously
poke fun at ridicule
pollute (*vb*) debase, defile, make impure
pox curse, evil; expression of distaste or aversion
profane (*vb*) desecrate or defile with abuse or irreverence
put down (*vb*) *Informal.* disparage, belittle; criticize, esp. contemptuously
put to shame expose faults of, censure, or humiliate
rag (*vb*) *Informal.* scold; subject to prolonged torment; tease
rail (*vb*) revile; denounce vehemently and bitterly
rap (*vb*) *Slang.* rebuke, criticize sharply
raspberry *Informal.* expression of disapproval, esp. contemptuous sound made through compressed lips; Bronx cheer
razz (*vb*) *Slang.* heckle, deride, tease
rebuff (*vb*) snub or reject peremptorily

rebuke (*vb*) reprimand; express strong disapproval to
reprimand (*vb*) reprove or censure sharply, esp. from position of authority
revile (*vb*) subject to verbal abuse
revulsion strong sense of distaste and repugnance
ridicule (*vb*) make fun of, mock, deride
roast (*vb*) *Informal.* criticize mercilessly, often in public
roorback defamatory falsehood published for political effect
rub it in *Informal.* emphasize something unpleasant to tease or annoy
sacrilege gross irreverence toward sacred person or thing
sarcasm sharply ironical utterance or cutting remark
satirize (*vb*) censure or ridicule by ironic description of human vices and follies
scald (*vb*) subject to heated criticism or censure
scapegoat one who bears blame for others
scathe (*vb*) assail with severe denunciation
scoff (*vb*) mock; express scorn or derision
scold (*vb*) censure severely or find fault with, esp. from position of authority
scorch (*vb*) censure, attack harshly
score (*vb*) berate, censure, denounce
scorn (*vb*) reject or dismiss disdainfully as unworthy; deride
self-criticism harsh assessment of oneself
self-flagellation extreme criticism of oneself
self-incrimination act of incriminating oneself, esp. by giving evidence
shame (*vb*) cause to feel guilt or humiliation
shoot down (*vb*) *Informal.* deflate, ridicule, discredit
show up (*vb*) embarrass, discredit, expose faults of
silent treatment aloof expression of disapproval made by completely ignoring another
slam (*vb*) *Informal.* criticize harshly
slander (*vb*) damage another's reputation by uttering falsehoods
slap down (*vb*) assault verbally, insult
slash (*vb*) criticize viciously
slur (*vb*) insult, disparage
smear (*vb*) maliciously attack another's reputation; vilify
smirch (*vb*) discredit, disgrace
sneer at (*vb*) laugh at scornfully; jeer and mock
soil (*vb*) damage or disgrace another's reputation
purn (*vb*) scorn, reject disdainfully
stain (*vb*) bring dishonor or blame on; blemish
sully (*vb*) defile, tarnish
supercilious (*adj*) patronizing; haughtily disdainful
swipe *Informal.* sharp, critical remark
taint (*vb*) contaminate morally, corrupt; tarnish
talking-to reprimand, scolding
tarnish (*vb*) bring disgrace on; sully
taunt (*vb*) reproach or challenge in a mocking or insulting manner
tear down (*vb*) vilify, denigrate
tell off (*vb*) *Informal.* reprimand, scold
thumb one's nose *Informal.* express contempt, esp. through rejection
thunderbolt sudden, severe attack
tick off (*vb*) *Chiefly Brit.* scold severely; rebuke
tirade prolonged outburst of verbal abuse
tongue-lashing harsh verbal criticism or scolding
traduce (*vb*) speak maliciously or falsely of, slander
trash (*vb*) *Informal.* censure, revile; utterly destroy by criticism; dismiss as worthless
travesty grotesque or debased imitation
twit (*vb*) subject to light ridicule or reproach
umbrage vague feeling of resentment over perceived insult
upbraid (*vb*) find fault with; criticize harshly, scold vehemently
vilify (*vb*) defame or slander with abusive statements
vilipend (*vb*) regard with low opinion; disparage, depreciate
vituperate (*vb*) censure severely, revile harshly
walk all over treat contemptuously and without regard
whispering campaign systematic dissemination of derogatory rumors
wig (*vb*) *Brit. informal.* scold severely, rebuke
wipe one's boots on treat contemptuously with no regard

Chapter Twenty-Four
The Dark Side

DRUG ABUSE AND ALCOHOLISM

Drug Names and Forms
Drunkenness, Drunkards, and Alcoholism
Paraphernalia and Behavior
Users and Abusers

Drug Names and Forms

acid *Slang.* LSD
addictive drug substance inducing physical or psychological dependence
amphetamine central nervous system stimulant; amphetamine sulphate
amyl nitrite pharmaceutical drug that dilates blood vessels, producing brief exhilaration
anabolic steroid muscle-building hormonal substance with dangerous side effects
analgesic painkilling drug
angel dust *Slang.* PCP
antidepressant pharmaceutical treatment for depression or apathy
aphrodisiac drug that increases sexual arousal
ataraxic drug tranquilizer
atropine antispasmodic drug
balloon small measure of heroin stored in toy balloon
barbital addictive hypnotic sedative taken as white powder
barbiturate pharmaceutical central nervous system depressant and muscle relaxer
belladonna psychoactive depressant derived from deadly nightshade
bindle paper in which drugs are wrapped
black beauty *Slang.* Biphetamine in black capsule
blow *Slang.* cocaine
body drug physically addictive substance
brick *Slang.* block of pressed marijuana, usu. one kilo
bud marijuana, esp. the resinous flower of the female plant
caffeine mild stimulant in coffee and tea
cantharides supposed aphrodisiac Spanish fly
cephalotropic drug drug that changes physiological functions of the brain
chloral hydrate crystalline compound used as sedative
coca plant with stimulant alkaloids from which cocaine is derived
cocaine addictive central nervous system stimulant derived from coca leaf; *Slang:* Bernice, blow, blowzeen, bouncing powder, candy, Cecil, coke, crack, flake, girl, lady snow, nose candy, Peruvian perfume, snow, toot, white girl
codeine painkilling depressant
coke *Slang.* cocaine
cola caffeine-containing seeds or nuts of African tree
controlled substance any behavior-altering or addictive drug whose possession and use are restricted by law
crack extremely powerful and addictive form of smokable cocaine
crank *Slang.* methamphetamine
crystal meth *Slang.* methamphetamine in crystalline form
datura plant with strong hallucinogenic and intoxicant effects; jimson weed; locoweed
desoxyn pharmaceutical amphetamine
DET diethyltryptamine
diet pill drug taken to reduce appetite, esp. amphetamine
diethyltryptamine DET; synthetic derivative of tryptamine hallucinogenic effects
dime bag *Slang.* small container of heroin or other drug sold for $10
dimethyltryptamine DMT; intensely hallucinogenic synthetic drug
DMT dimethyltryptamine
doobie *Slang.* marijuana cigarette
dope *Slang.* any drug or narcotic, esp. heroin or marijuana
dose amount of drug to be taken by one person at one time
downer *Informal.* any depressant or sedative-hypnotic drug
drug any habit-forming, behavior-altering, or damaging illicit substance, esp. narcotic
dust *Slang.* PCP
ecstasy *Slang.* mild hallucinogen
freebase *Slang.* ether-purified cocaine
ganja *Slang.* marijuana
grass *Slang.* marijuana
H *Slang.* heroin
hallucinogen any drug producing intense visual and sensory distortion
hard drugs physically addictive substances, esp. heroin, morphine, and cocaine
hash *Informal.* hashish
hashish concentrated form of marijuana resin; hash; resin
hash oil oil derived from hashish
head drug *Informal.* psychologically addictive substance, esp. hallucinogen
hemp *Cannabis sativa* plant, source of marijuana
heroin addictive narcotic opium derivative produced by treating morphine with acetic acid; *Slang:* boy, dope, gow, H, horse, junk, noise, poison, scag, skag, smack, tecata
homegrown (*adj*) locally grown or nonimported, as of marijuana
hypnotic sleep-inducing drug
ibogaine plant-derived stimulant
jimson weed datura
joint *Slang.* hand-rolled marijuana cigarette
junk *Slang.* heroin
laudanum opium in solution
laughing gas nitrous oxide
line *Slang.* small amount of chopped cocaine, arranged in a strip for inhalation
locoweed datura

LSD lysergic acid diethylamide; powerful, psychedelic, synthetic hallucinogen
lysergic acid LSD
mandrake narcotic herb
mannite milk sugar for cutting heroin
marijuana dried *Cannabis sativa* or *Cannabis indica* leaves and flowers, smoked or eaten as mild hallucinogen; *Slang:* banji, bhang, boo, bush, dagga, gage, gangster, ganja, grass, hay, herb, hooch, kif, killer weed, M, marahoochie, Mary Jane, mezz, mota, muggle, pot, reefer, shit, smoke, tea, 13-m, viper's weed, weed, yerba
MDA methyldiamphetamine, a stimulant
meperidine crystalline narcotic used as sedative and painkiller
meprobamate nonbarbiturate sedative; Miltown
mescal small succulent with hallucinogenic, buttonlike tops
mescaline hallucinogen derived from succulent mescal plant or peyote cactus
meth *Informal.* methamphetamine
methadone synthetic opiate used to replace heroin in treatment of addicts
methamphetamine amphetamine, esp. street drug in powder form; crank
methaqualone nonbarbiturate sedative-hypnotic substance used to induce sleep; Quaalude
milk sugar white lactose crystals for cutting cocaine or heroin
MMDA amphetamine with hallucinogenic properties
morning glory seeds mildly hallucinogenic plant seeds
morphine painkilling opium alkaloid narcotic; *Slang:* Aunt Emma, M, unkie, white nurse
narcotic painkilling or sleep-inducing substance, esp. opiate or pharmaceutical hypnotic, usu. addictive
neuroleptic drug antipsychotic drug that reduces anxiety and tension; tranquilizer
nicotine poisonous alkaloid present in tobacco leaves
nitrous oxide inhaled anesthetic with hallucinogenic properties; laughing gas
nonbarbiturate sedative pharmaceutical depressant that affects the central nervous system
nutmeg mildly hallucinogenic plant seed
opiate narcotic derived from or containing opium
opium narcotic derived from poppy plant; *Slang:* black, blackstuff, Chinese molasses, gow, hop, poppy
paper *Informal.* folded paper containing dose of drugs
paregoric soothing opium extract
PCP phencyclidine; addictive drug orig. used as animal tranquilizer, acting as depressant, anesthetic, stimulant, convulsant, and hallucinogen; angel dust
pep pill stimulant
peyote hallucinogenic cactus, chewed or used as source of mescaline; top
pharmaceutical drug manufactured legally by company but acquired without prescription
phencyclidine PCP
popper vial of amyl nitrite
psilocin substance produced after ingesting psilocybin
psilocybin hallucinogen derived from *Psilocybe mexicana* mushroom
psychedelic intensely mind-altering substance that produces heightened awareness and hallucinations, esp. LSD, psilocybin, and mescaline
psychoactive drug depressant, stimulant, or hallucinogen that affects central nervous system
psychotropic drug substance affecting mood or behavior, without central nervous system stimulation or depression, esp. tranquilizers, antidepressants, marijuana, and hashish
quinine substance used in cutting heroin
reefer *Slang.* marijuana cigarette; marijuana
sedative-hypnotic drug that depresses central nervous system
shot hypodermic injection of a drug
sleeping pill pill or capsule containing a barbiturate for inducing sleep
smack *Slang.* heroin
soft drug nonaddictive or psychologically addictive substance
soma legendary hallucinogen made from intoxicating plant
soporific hypnotic or sleep-inducing drug
Spanish fly preparation of powdered blister beetles, used as an aphrodisiac; cantharides
speedball *Slang.* injected mixture of cocaine or amphetamine and heroin
spliff *Slang.* large marijuana cigarette, esp. of Jamaican ganja
stimulant any drug that increases central nervous system activity; upper
sugar cube *Slang.* form of liquid LSD dropped on cube of sugar
synthetics narcotics produced in laboratory
tab single drug dose in form of compressed powder
taste minute quantity of a drug, often offered to entice buyer
tetrahydrocannabinol THC; active substance in marijuana and hashish
THC tetrahydrocannabinol
tranquilizer pharmaceutical drug that alleviates anxiety; trank
upper *Informal.* stimulant
weed *Slang.* marijuana

Drunkenness, Drunkards, and Alcoholism

AA Alcoholics Anonymous
alcoholic one suffering from alcoholism; beverage containing alcohol; boozer; chronic drunk; drunkard
Alcoholics Anonymous AA; organization that helps alcoholics to stop drinking by following twelve-step program
alcoholism condition of uncontrollable continual or sporadic heavy drinking of alcohol
bender prolonged period of drunkenness
bibulous (*adj*) inclined or addicted to drink
binge drinking spree

boozer *Informal.* one who drinks to excess; alcoholic
debauchery indulgence in excessive drinking or other immoral pleasures
delirium tremens dt's; violent hallucinations and seizures induced by prolonged alcohol abuse
dipsomania uncontrollable craving for alcohol
drunk (*adj*) intoxicated by alcoholic drink; temporarily impaired, excited, or stupefied by alcoholic drink; *Slang:* addled, besotted, blasted, blind drunk, blotto, bombed, canned, cockeyed, crispy, crocked, fried, high, inebriated, in one's cups, lit up, loaded, muzzy, oiled, pickled, pie-eyed, pissed, plastered, polluted, potted, ripped, shitfaced, shnockered, skunk drunk, sloshed, smashed, sotted, soused, sozzled, squiffed, stewed, stinking, stinko, stoned, swacked, tanked, tiddly, tight, tipsy, wasted, wiped out, woozy, wrecked, zonked
drunkard person often or habitually drunk
dt's delirium tremens
ebriosity habitual intoxication
fantods jitters; delirium tremens
hair of the dog *Informal.* drink of liquor supposed to relieve a hangover
hangover severe headache, nausea, or other unpleasant aftereffects of too much drink
hung over (*adj*) feeling unpleasant aftereffects of too much drink
immoderation excessive drinking
indulgence act of drinking, esp. to excess
in one's cups *Slang.* drunk
intemperance excessive drinking of alcohol
intoxication loss of control, excitement, or stupefaction due to consumption of alcohol
juicer *Slang.* drunkard
lush one who drinks to excess; alcoholic
morning after period upon awakening when aftereffects of night of drinking are felt
oenophile one who loves or is a connoisseur of wine
off the wagon *Slang.* having returned to drinking after period of temperance
pass out (*vb*) become unconscious from drunkenness
problem drinker alcoholic, one who cannot control drinking
sleep it off overcome aftereffects of drink by sleep
sober up (*vb*) take action or pass time to end a state of drunkenness
sot chronic drunkard
tank up (*vb*) take drink; become inebriated
tippler one habitually drunk
tipsy (*adj*) slightly intoxicated
twelve steps step-by-step program for recovery from addiction, originated by Alcoholics Anonymous
under the influence inebriated, esp. while driving a car
under the table so intoxicated as to be lying on floor; outdrunk by another
wino *Informal.* one chronically addicted to drink, esp. cheap wine
woozy (*adj*) intoxicated; slightly dizzy

Paraphernalia and Behavior

abuse (*vb*) use any drug to excess; (*n*) excessive use of drug
addiction physical or psychological dependence on drug
bad trip *Slang.* negative response, including panic, fear, and psychosis, due to hallucinogenic drug
black market covert, illegal sale of drugs
bust *Slang.* arrest for possession or sale of drugs
buzz *Slang.* initial mild effect of drug
cap gelatin capsule for holding drug dose; (*vb*) insert drug into capsules
clean (*adj*) *Slang.* not in possession of drugs; (*vb*) remove stems and seeds from marijuana
cold turkey *Informal.* sudden withdrawal from addictive drug use
come down (*vb*) feel drug high depart, return to normal state
contact high mildly altered state caused by proximity to marijuana smoke or smokers
crack house building used as crack distribution center, usu. in poor urban area
crack pipe small glass pipe used for smoking crack cocaine
crash (*vb*) *Slang.* fall asleep or come down from effect of drug
crutch device for holding butt of marijuana cigarette
cut (*vb*) dilute a drug, esp. heroin or cocaine, with adulterating inactive substance
dependency physical or psychological addiction to drugs
detoxification period of treatment and counseling during which addict overcomes drug dependency
dropper medicine dropper used as homemade drug injection equipment
drug abuse excessive use of any drug or narcotic
drug testing examination and analysis, usu. of blood or urine, to determine presence of drugs, usu. conducted by government or employer
freebase (*vb*) *Slang.* process cocaine with ether and heat to intensify its effects; smoke freebased cocaine
get off (*vb*) experience effects of drugs, esp. by injection
glue sniffing breathing glue fumes for hallucinogenic or euphoric drug effect
habit physical dependence on addictive drug; amount required each day to satisfy dependency
hassle (*vb*) *Informal.* buy drugs, bargain for drugs
high (*adj*) euphorically under the influence of drugs; (*n*) *Slang.* such a state
hit *Slang.* (*vb*) inject drugs; (*n*) single drug injection; one drag on a marijuana cigarette
hookah water-cooled pipe for smoking marijuana or hashish
hypo *Informal.* hypodermic syringe
hypodermic syringe small glass syringe used to inject drugs; hypo
jag state of intense, protracted drug stimulation
methadone maintenance program of legally administered methadone provided to prevent recidivism of former heroin addicts
miss drug injection that misses vein

narcoterrorism terrorist tactics employed by drug dealers against government agents
narghile type of water pipe
needle hypodermic needle used for drug injections
nod out (*vb*) *Slang.* be under the influence of narcotics; doze off into drug stupor
OD overdose
outfit equipment for injecting drugs
overdose OD; intake of quantity of drugs above one's tolerance, producing debilitation or death
panic bad reaction to drug; heroin shortage
paraphernalia implements and objects used in preparing and ingesting drugs
physical dependence physiological addiction to drug
pipe device for smoking marijuana, hashish, or crack cocaine; *Slang.* easy-to-inject vein
pop (*vb*) *Slang.* inject heroin under skin, not into vein
possession having drugs on one's person or property
potentiate (*vb*) cause drug to act more powerfully by action or use of another drug
psychological dependence drug craving based on desire for pleasure, not physical addiction
reverse tolerance increased sensitivity to smaller doses of drug the more it is taken, as with marijuana
rig equipment for injecting drugs
setting environment and mental state of person preparing for hallucinogenic drug experience
sick (*adj*) suffering from drug withdrawal
spaced-out (*adj*) *Slang.* feeling floating sensation or numbing effects of drug use
stash hiding place for drugs; hidden supply of drugs
stem *Slang.* glass pipe for smoking crack or ice
straight (*adj*) *Informal.* not using illicit drugs
straw thin tube used for sniffing drugs in powdered form, esp. cut-off straw
substance abuse long-term addiction to or excessive use of narcotics or controlled substances
tie off (*vb*) wrap cord or strap around upper arm to force veins into prominence for injection
toke *Slang.* single puff on marijuana cigarette
tolerance resistance to the effects of a drug, resulting in the need to use increasingly large doses of that drug for the same effect
toot *Slang.* a snort of a drug, esp. cocaine
tracks *Slang.* needle marks from repeated drug injections
trip *Slang.* (*n*) hallucinogenic drug experience; (*vb*) take a hallucinogen, esp. LSD
using (*adj*) *Slang.* taking drugs; addicted to drugs
water pipe device in which marijuana smoke is cooled by passing through water before entering hose leading to smoker's mouth
withdrawal cessation of use of addictive drug with painful or unpleasant symptoms

Users and Abusers

acid freak *Slang.* LSD user
acid-head *Slang.* habitual user of LSD
addict person who is physically or psychologically dependent on some drug; junkie
bagman *Slang.* drug seller
burnout person who is apathetic and disoriented from prolonged drug use, esp. from marijuana smoking
candy man *Slang.* drug seller
connection *Slang.* drug seller; supplier of drugs
cook *Slang.* chemist in illicit drug laboratory
croaker *Slang.* doctor supplying narcotics to addicts
dealer *Slang.* drug seller
dope fiend *Slang.* drug addict
dopehead *Slang.* drug addict
dope pusher *Slang.* drug seller
doper *Slang.* regular drug user, esp. marijuana smoker
drug seller person who buys and sells drugs illegally; *Slang:* bagman, candy man, connection, dealer, man, pusher, source
flower children youthful psychedelic drug users in the 1960's, esp. in San Francisco's Haight-Ashbury district
freak *Slang.* person using particular kind of drug on frequent basis, such as a speed freak
guide person experienced in LSD use who guides another's LSD trip.
head *Slang.* drug user or addict, esp. one using a particular drug, such as a pothead
hustler *Slang.* drug addict forced into stealing or prostitution to support habit
junkie *Informal.* heroin addict; drug addict
narc *Slang.* police officer on narcotics detail
pillhead *Slang.* habitual amphetamine or barbiturate user
pothead *Slang.* regular marijuana user
pusher *Slang.* drug seller
shmecker *Slang.* heroin user
source one's drug supplier; dealer
speed freak *Slang.* regular user of amphetamines
straight *Slang.* person not using drugs
tea head *Slang.* marijuana user
trafficker large-scale drug seller or importer
vice squad narcotics division of police

MENTAL DISTURBANCES

Insanity
Mental Institutions
Agitation, Abnormality, and Instability

Insanity

amok (*adj*) in a murderous frenzy; raging violently
balmy (*adj*) *Informal.* crazy
batty (*adj*) crazy; demented
bent (*adj*) abnormal, esp. somewhat crazed or perverse
berserk (*adj*) frenzied; crazed
crackpot *Informal.* one given to eccentric or lunatic notions
crazed (*adj*) distracted, overexcited, slightly nuts
crazy (*adj*) mentally deranged or demented; insane; (*n*) *Slang.* one who acts or is insane

criminally insane prone to criminal acts or threats; dangerous
demented (*adj*) perversely insane; mad
dementia insanity, esp. severe mental impairment due to brain damage
demoniac (*adj*) behaving as though possessed by the devil
deranged (*adj*) insane
feeble-minded (*adj*) mentally deficient; moronic
frenzied (*adj*) marked by violent agitation; berserk
frenzy temporary madness; intense agitation and compulsive activity
go mad become insane; suffer a breakdown
gone (*adj*) *Informal.* lost in madness, outside reality
go to pieces break down, suffer an emotional collapse
have a screw loose be crazy
homicidal (*adj*) having murderous intent or making threats
idiot one who is severely mentally deficient
insane (*adj*) mentally disordered or deranged; suffering from insanity; *Slang:* around the bend, balmy, bananas, barmy, batty, bonkers, cracked, crazy, deranged, loco, loony, nuts, off one's rocker, out of one's tree, psycho, wacko
insanity various deranged states of mind, mental disorders, conditions, and incapacity; dementia; lunacy; madness
lather *Informal.* agitated or overwrought state
loony *Informal.* (*n*) lunatic; (*adj*) crazy; insane
lose one's mind go insane
lunacy insanity
lunatic insane person
mad (*adj*) mentally disturbed or deranged; insane; completely senseless or disordered
madman insane person; lunatic
madness insanity
maniac one who is totally, often dangerously, insane
mental (*adj*) affected with a disorder of the mind
moonstruck (*adj*) mentally deranged
moron one of very low mental capacity
moronic (*adj*) feeble-minded
nut mildly crazy or eccentric person, usu. harmless; fruitcake
oddball *Informal.* eccentric or abnormal individual
off one's head crazy
out of one's head crazy
out of one's mind crazy
over the edge gone crazy
possessed (*adj*) behaving as though controlled by supernatural power or powerful subconscious impulse
psycho (*adj*) psychopathic; insane; (*n*) psychopathic person
psychopathic (*adj*) exhibiting amoral and antisocial behavior, including the inability to tell right from wrong
psychosis major, severe form of mental disorder
psychotic one afflicted with severe mental disorder; insane person
rabid (*adj*) frenzied, raging uncontrollably
raving (*adj*) speakingwildly, deliriously
schizoid (*adj*) suffering from schizophrenia or multiple personality; schizy
screaming-meemies *Informal.* extreme terror or nervous hysteria
sick (*adj*) mentally ill
sociopath psychopathic personality with extremely asocial or antisocial behavior
touched (*adj*) unbalanced or slightly crazy
unbalanced (*adj*) mentally disordered, deranged
unhinged highly distraught or unsettled
weirdo *Informal.* extraordinarily strange individual
zany (*adj*) eccentric or mildly abnormal in behavior

Mental Institutions

asylum institution for the relief and care of the mentally ill
commit (*vb*) place someone in mental hospital
committed (*adj*) required to enter and remain in mental hospital
halfway house residence for formerly institutionalized patients that helps to facilitate their readjustment to normal life
home mental hospital
insane asylum institution for the care and treatment of the mentally ill; booby hatch; bughouse
institution mental hospital
lunatic asylum mental hospital
madhouse mental hospital
mental home low-security mental hospital
mental hospital institution for the care and treatment of the mentally ill; funny farm; home; institution; loony bin; lunatic asylum; madhouse; nut house; snake pit
mental ward section of hospital reserved for mentally ill
padded cell heavily padded, individual holding room for confinement of psychotic patient
psychiatric ward section of regular hospital reserved for the mentally ill; psycho ward
sanatorium sanitarium
sanitarium hospital for the treatment of the mentally ill; sanatorium

Agitation, Abnormality, and Instability

abandon freedom from normal restraints in behavior
aberrant (*adj*) departing substantially from standard behavior
abnormality deviation from normal, accepted behavior
agita *Informal.* anxiety; agitation
agitated (*adj*) overly excited or anxious
agitation mental excitement or disquiet; perturbation
agony intense mental pain or tortured state of mind
amentia mental deficiency, esp. low intellectual capacity
analgesia insensibility to pain while conscious
angst feeling of anxiety, apprehension, and insecurity
anguish extreme mental distress
anomaly any abnormality or deviation from the norm

anxiety distress, uneasines, apprehension, and psychic tension caused by fear of impending or imagined danger or misfortune
at loose ends distracted, unsettled, uncertain
at sea confused, dazed, or disoriented
attack fit of disorder; active episode of recurrent illness
at wit's end perplexed, esp. having exhausted one's mental resources
baffled (*adj*) confused; confounded
bewildered (*adj*) extremely confused and disoriented
bizarre (*adj*) odd, extravagant, or eccentric in behavior
black out (*vb*) undergo temporary loss of consciousness, vision, or memory
brainsick (*adj*) mentally disordered
breakdown physical, mental, or nervous collapse; nervous breakdown
breaking point point at which one succumbs to stress
broken (*adj*) completely crushed in mind and spirit
brooding (*adj*) depressed, moody
bugaboo imaginary object of fear, causing disproportionate anxiety
bundle of nerves extremely anxious individual
butterflies *Informal.* queasy feeling due to nervousness or agitation
cabin fever restless irritability from isolation or prolonged confinement
catatonic (*adj*) marked by stupor, rigidity, muteness, and bizarre or purposeless activity; (*n*) one suffering from catatonia
cold sweat concurrent chills and perspiration from fear or shock
collapse nervous breakdown or extreme depression
comatose (*adj*) in a state of prolonged unconsciousness
come to (*vb*) awaken from unconsciousness
compulsive (*adj*) unable to control an irrational impulse to do something
confounded (*adj*) baffled or confused
confused (*adj*) unable to differentiate reality; disturbed in mind or purpose; muddled
conniption fit of hysteria, rage, or alarm
consternation amazement or dismay causing confusion
crack up (*vb*) *Informal.* suffer a breakdown; go insane
crisis turning point in mental disorder
crumble (*vb*) suffer emotional collapse; go to pieces
death wish conscious or unconscious desire to die
delirious (*adj*) suffering from delirium
delirium state of confusion, disordered speech, hallucination, and frenzy
delusion persistent false belief regarding self or others
depression condition of general despondency, dejection, and withdrawel
despair utter loss of hope and confidence
deviant (*adj*) straying from normal behavior; (*n*) one who so strays
diabolical (*adj*) perverse, as though possessed by devil
disorientation displacement from a normal sense of time, place, and identity
distracted (*adj*) confused, unfocused, at loose ends
distraught (*adj*) extremely agitated
distress mental pain or suffering
disturbed (*adj*) showing symptoms of emotional illness and distress
dither nervous, disoriented, or indecisive state
dizzy (*adj*) mentally confused
doldrums spell of inactivity or depression
dotty *Informal.* mentally unbalanced; amiably eccentric
eccentric one who behaves abnormally; oddball
eccentricity bizarre or abnormal, but harmless, activity
erratic (*adj*) peculiar, inconsistent, or unpredictable in behavior
euphoria feeling of extreme elation
fanatic (*adj*) marked by excessive behavior
fantasy delusive view or idea
fantods emotional outburst or fit
fazed (*adj*) disturbed or disconcerted
fit sudden, violent emotional reaction or outburst
flustered (*adj*) confused, anxious, or agitated
frantic (*adj*) mentally deranged, out of control, or very nervous
frazzled (*adj*) in state of extreme nervous fatigue
freak out (*vb*) *Slang.* behave irrationally
hallucination perception of objects not really there
hysteria uncontrollable, irrational outburst of emotion or intense anxiety
hysterics fit of hysteria
imbalanced (*adj*) mentally disturbed or abnormal
instability tendency to behave in an unpredictable or erratic manner
insufficiency lack of mental fitness
jangled (*adj*) tense, irritated, nervous
Jekyll and Hyde person marked by dual personality, one good and one evil
jitters extreme sense of panic and nervousness; heebie-jeebies; screaming-meemies; willies
kamikaze (*adj*) recklessly self-destructive
lobotomized (*adj*) sluggish, dull-witted, or calmed due to lobotomy
maladjusted (*adj*) poorly adapted to normal society; eccentric
malcontent one rebelliously opposed to societal norms
manic (*adj*) hyperactive; excessively excited or agitated
mental (*adj*) *Informal.* affected with a disorder of the mind
mental illness disorder of the mind
mixed-up (*adj*) completely confused or emotionally unstable
muddled (*adj*) confused
nervous breakdown breakdown
neurotic (*adj*) excessively anxious or indecisive
non compos mentis *Latin.* lit. not of sound mind; mentally incompetent or unsound

obsessive (*adj*) unable to escape some persistent idea or need
off-the-wall (*adj*) *Informal.* extreme terror or nervous hysteria; jitters
on pins and needles experiencing nervous anxiety or anticipation
on tenterhooks in a state of uneasy suspense or anxiety
overwrought (*adj*) extremely anxious or agitated
paroxysm sudden emotional outburst
peculiar (*adj*) odd or eccentric in behavior
perturbation agitation
perverse (*adj*) obstinately unreasonable, willful, or evil
phobic (*adj*) suffering from exaggerated, illogical fears
pixilated (*adj*) slightly unbalanced
prostration state of overwhelming exhaustion or helplessness
queer (*adj*) peculiar or eccentric in behavior
rage uncontrollable anger directed at any available target
rattled (*adj*) confused, disconcerted, and anxious
retarded (*adj*) severely mentally deficient
rocky (*adj*) *Informal.* unstable, upset, or unsteady
shaken-up (*adj*) disoriented or confused
shattered (*adj*) in a state of mental, emotional, or nervous collapse or disintegration
shock sudden, violent emotional disturbance, usu. caused by traumatic event or injury
slough of despond state of extreme depression
spell period of mental distress
state abnormal condition of mind
stressed-out (*adj*) *Informal.* exhausted or extremely anxious
strung-out (*adj*) *Slang.* addicted to a drug; in an extreme state of nervous exhaustion
stupor state of extreme apathy or torpor from stress or shock
tangled (*adj*) disoriented or bewildered
tantrum uncontrollable fit of rage or hysteria
trance sleeplike state of suspended animation
trauma disordered psychic state due to emotional stress or physical injury
turmoil state of extreme agitation and confusion
turn *Informal.* nervous shock, as from fright
twitter state of anxiety, agitation, or extreme upset
unsound (*adj*) abnormal or disordered, as in the mind
unstable (*adj*) unable to control one's emotions or behave within accepted norms
up the wall extremely anxious or agitated
worked-up (*adj*) agitated, unable to contain emotions
zoned (*adj*) *Slang.* dazed, disoriented, or confused

CRIME

Crimes
Criminals
Police Procedures and Detection
Legal Procedures and Trials
Prison and Punishment

Crimes

abduction carrying off of person by force, esp. for sex or prostitution or as hostage
adultery engaging in extramarital sex
aggravated assault severe physical attack
air piracy skyjacking
arson intentionally setting fire to property
assassination murder of public figure
assault personal physical attack or threat of violence
assault and battery assault with actual physical contact or violence upon other person
battery physical violence upon another person, esp. beating
bigamy marrying while already legally married
blackmail demand for payment based on threat of embarrassment, exposure, or harm; extortion
bootlegging illegal production, distribution, or sale of something already owned or copyrighted, or something unregistered or outlawed; piracy
break-in illegal entry of another's property
breaking and entering entry into another's property, forcibly or with criminal intent
bribery offering payment for favors or corrupt behavior, esp. involving a public official
bunko confidence game or swindle that takes advantage of victim's ignorance
burglary breaking into and entering private property for purpose of crime, usu. theft
capital crime crime punishable by death
chop shop *Informal.* garage where stolen cars are dismantled so that their parts can be sold separately
collusion action by two or more persons to commit crime, esp. fraud
confidence game fraud or swindle involving misleading trickery; bunko
conspiracy secret plan among two or more persons to commit unlawful act
contempt of court willful disrespect for rules and orders of a court
counterfeiting manufacture of fake money
crime illegal act against person or property for which offender is liable to punishment
crime against humanity sinful act of monstrous proportions, such as genocide, directed against a group because of race, religion, or national origin
crime of commission illegal act involving specific violation of law
crime of omission illegal act involving failure to perform specific requirement of law

crime of passion illegal act committed in heat of anger or jealousy
defalcation failure to meet promise; act of embezzlement
defamation injury to person's character; spoken slander or written libel
disorderly conduct any of various activities that disturb public peace
drive-by shooting usu. gang-related shooting by unseen assailant in passing car
embezzlement theft of money or appropriation of property entrusted to one's care
extortion demand for payment based on threat of embarrassment, exposure, or harm; blackmail
felony serious crime, punishable by imprisonment
forgery fraudulent imitation of documents or signatures
frame (*vb*) falsely accuse or incriminate an innocent party
fraud deception or trickery for illegal gain
graft bribery, esp. of public officials
grand larceny theft of personal property exceeding specified value
gunrunning smuggling of firearms
hijacking takeover of public vehicle by violent means
hit-and-run (*adj*) guilty of leaving the scene of an auto accident to avoid responsibility for injuries and damage caused
holdup armed robbery
homicide taking of human life, usu. intentionally
hot (*adj*) *Slang.* stolen
infraction violation of a law
involuntary manslaughter taking of human life through criminal negligence
job *Slang.* crime
justifiable homicide killing person for defensible reason
kidnapping holding person, esp. child, captive in exchange for ransom
larceny theft of personal property
libel publication of statement damaging to another's reputation
lift (*vb*) *Informal.* steal
looting stealing from locations left unprotected after violent event or natural catastrophe
malfeasance wrongdoing or misconduct, esp. an act in violation of public trust committed by a public official
malicious mischief intentional or reckless harm or damage to property of another
manslaughter taking of human life by accident or negligence
mayhem willfully inflicting bodily injury on another person; deliberate violence or damage; state of rowdy disorder
misconduct intentionally improper behavior by a public official, esp. malfeasance
misdemeanor illegal act less serious than a felony, usu. punishable by fine or probation
mugging robbery, esp. in public place
murder taking of human life for no defensible reason
mutiny rebellion against authority, esp. military
nuisance use of one's property to damage or inconvenience another
numbers racket illegal lottery run by organized crime syndicate
obstruction of justice act that hinders or prevents completion of legal process
offense breach of criminal laws
organized crime network of criminals acting systematically in illegal activities; syndicate
peculation embezzlement of public funds
perjury lying while under oath, esp. giving false testimony in court
petty larceny theft of personal property of less than a specified value
pickpocketing theft from unsuspecting victim's person, esp. from a pocket
pilferage theft of small amounts of goods done over time to avoid detection
piracy bootlegging
plunder robbery by force, esp. in wartime; taking of property by force or fraud
poaching taking of fish or game from private property or protected reserve
premeditated crime crime planned and committed with malice aforethought
prostitution sexual intercourse for payment
purse snatching forceful theft of woman's handbag from her arm
pyramid scheme confidence game in which first investors are paid off with investment of later ones, who never see a return
racketeering operation of a business characterized by systematically dishonest practices
rackets *Informal.* often the rackets; businesses controlled by racketeering
rape forcible sexual intercourse without consent, esp. committed by a man against a woman
reckless endangerment action that could result in injury to another though it may not have
resisting arrest attempt to evade or physically prevent arrest
robbery theft aggravated by force or threat of assault
roll (*vb*) *Slang.* rob a helpless person, esp. an insensible drunk
rustling *Informal.* stealing, usu. cattle or horses (U.S. Old West)
safecracking forcible entry into locked safe to steal its contents
sedition incitement to rebellion against government
shanghaiing kidnapping a person into service aboard ship, esp. by drugging
shoplifting theft from store by person posing as customer
skyjacking forcible, violent seizure of aircraft; air piracy
slander making of false and malicious verbal statements damaging to another's reputation
smuggling import or export of goods that are outlawed or in avoidance of customs duty
sodomy performance of unnatural sex acts, usu. anal sex or sex with an animal
soliciting seeking clients for prostitute

stealing wrongfully taking another's property; theft
subornation inducing another to commit an illegal act, esp. perjury
swindling performing fraudulent business transactions
syndicate organized crime
terrorism use of intimidation and random violence, esp. as a political weapon
theft stealing
tong war violence between Chinese secret societies seeking to control organized crime
treason betrayal of one's country or government
trespass illegal use or occupation of another's property, esp. entry upon another's land
vagrancy wandering idly in a public place without home or money
vandalism defacing or damaging of another's property, often random and purposeless
voluntary manslaughter taking of human life with mitigating circumstances
white-collar crime illegal acts by professionals or office workers against institutions, government, or businesses
white-slave trade organized recruitment or abduction of victims, usu. women, into prostitution
wilding *Slang.* wanton, random assault and vandalism

Criminals

accessory person who, though absent, assists another to commit a crime or evade capture
accomplice criminal's active partner in crime
arsonist person who intentionally sets a fire
bandit robber, esp. one who attacks victims in public places
bluebeard any man who allegedly murders a series of women he has married
bookie person accepting illegal bets
bootlegger seller of illegal items; smuggler
brigand bandit, esp. member of gang operating in forest or mountains
burglar thief
call girl high-class prostitute reached by telephone
career criminal one who habitually engages in crime
cat burglar one skilled at breaking into buildings, even those secured against theft, by climbing through upstairs windows or across roofs
con artist confidence man
confidence man swindler or instigator of fraudulent business schemes; con artist; con man
con man confidence man
Cosa Nostra *Italian.* lit. our affair; Mafia
criminal person engaging in illegal acts; crook
crook criminal
delinquent person who violates the law
family *Slang.* Mafia
felon person guilty of a felony
fence receiver of stolen property
first offender person guilty of crime for first time
fugitive person fleeing arrest or imprisonment
gang organization of street criminals, usu. young
gangster person working in criminal organization; highbinder
gun moll *Slang.* gangster's girlfriend; female criminal
gunslinger *Informal.* violent criminal who wore gun on hip (U.S. Old West)
hardened criminal habitual criminal committed to life of crime
highwayman person who stops travelers to rob them
hit man *Slang.* hired assassin
hoodlum violent young ruffian; member of organized crime syndicate
hooker *Slang.* prostitute
hooligan violent young ruffian; street gang member
juvenile delinquent criminal under age of legal majority
kleptomaniac person unable to stop stealing
loan shark *Informal.* lender charging illegally high interest rates
Mafia organized crime syndicate, orig. Sicilian; Cosa Nostra
mafioso member of Mafia
mass murderer killer of many people
mob gang of criminals; organized crime syndicate
mugger person attacking and robbing others on street
murderer person who willfully takes another's life; killer
Peeping Tom person who spies on sexual or private activities of others
peterman *Slang.* safecracker
pickpocket person who steals money or valuables from victim's pocket, esp. in crowded place; cannon; hook
pimp person soliciting for prostitutes
poacher person who steals fish or game from another's land or protected reserve
point *Informal.* person who occupies lookout position during illegal activity or crime
prostitute person engaging in sex for pay
prowler person entering another's home for purpose of robbery or violence
public enemy dangerous criminal widely sought by law enforcement agencies
racketeer person involved in rackets, organized crime, or illegal business operations
safecracker robber specializing in forcing open safes; peterman
scofflaw person who violates the law with contempt, esp. one who fails to pay fines owed
second-story man burglar specializing in entering buildings through upstairs windows
serial killer mentally unbalanced person who kills one victim after another
smuggler transporter of illegal goods, esp. across borders; bootlegger
squatter person illegally occupying another's vacant property
streetwalker prostitute who solicits on the streets
thief one who steals; burglar
thug brutal, petty criminal; professional strangler
tong member of secret Chinese gang

underworld segment of society engaged in crime as profession
vandal person engaged in wanton violence to property, usu. not motivated by theft

Police Procedures and Detection

AKA also known as; prefix before alias
alias false name used by criminal
all-points bulletin APB; description of wanted criminal issued to all police in area
APB all-points bulletin
apprehend (*vb*) catch suspect or criminal
arrest (*vb*) lawfully detain suspect; (*n*) act of apprehending and detaining suspect; bust
arrestee person arrested on suspicion of crime
at large describing a criminal who is free, having evaded arrest
badge *Informal.* policeman
ballistics study of firearms and bullets, used in detection and identification of weapons used in crimes
beat police officer's assigned area of duty
Bertillon system fingerprinting and identification system
billy club policeman's heavy wooden stick or baton; night stick
blotter book in station house in which arrests are recorded as they occur
bobby *Brit. informal.* policeman
book (*vb*) register arrestee at jail or place of detention
bounty payment offered for capture of criminal at large
break piece of luck that helps to solve a crime
bust *Slang.* arrest
canary *Slang.* person confessing a crime or offering information to police
case unsolved crime or one being tried
citizen's arrest arrest made not by police but by person whose authority rests on fact of citizenship
clamp down (*vb*) increase police activity, usu. on specific problem
clue piece of information leading toward arrest of criminal
collar (*vb*) *Informal.* arrest
comb (*vb*) thoroughly inspect scene of crime; search intensely for clues
confession admission of guilt
cop *Informal.* policeman
copper *Informal.* policeman
coroner public officer investigating deaths likely to be due to criminal acts
crack (*vb*) solve a case
crackdown intensification of police efforts to control crime
crime lab laboratory in which evidence is examined scientifically to aid in apprehension of suspects
criminology study of crime, its causes, detection, correction, and prevention
custody arrest and detention of suspect or criminal
dactyloscopy method of studying fingerprints to establish identification
delator professional informer
detection art and practice of finding solutions to crimes
detective police officer or private individual skilled at acquiring information about crimes and tracking down suspected criminals; dick; hawkshaw; shamus
detention holding of suspect or criminal in custody to await charges, trial, or sentencing
DNA fingerprinting identification of criminal suspect by matching genes in known segment of labeled DNA with those in forensic sample, as blood or hair, obtained from suspect
dragnet systematic police search for criminal
evidence facts or objects leading to apprehension of suspect or solution of crime
facial identification system FIS; computerized method of identifying suspects
false arrest improper arrest without legal cause or due process
FBI Federal Bureau of Investigation
Federal Bureau of Investigation FBI; U.S. national police and investigative agency
finger (*vb*) *Slang.* identify someone as a suspect; inform on someone
fingerprints inked impression of lines on tips of fingers, used in identification of suspect
first degree designation for police procedure involving initial arrest of suspect
FIS facial identification system
forensics investigative procedures used in deciding legal matters; scientific examination of evidence for use in criminal case
frisk police search of person believed to be carrying concealed weapon or stolen or illegal goods, usu. by patting suspect's clothing
fuzz *Slang.* police
G-man government man; law enforcement officer
handcuffs metal bands that lock around wrists, used to restrain hands of prisoner or suspect
hawkshaw detective
heat *Slang.* police
informer person giving information on crime to police; fink; stool pigeon
K-9 corps dogs used in law enforcement
lead clue aiding in apprehension of suspect
lie detector polygraph
lineup technique in which victim or witness is asked to identify suspect from several people standing in line
manhunt intense police search for suspect or fugitive
marshal federal judicial officer who performs duties of sheriff; police officer
Miranda rule law requiring that police inform persons being detained or interrogated of their constitutional rights
MO modus operandi
modus operandi *Latin.* mode of operating; characteristic procedure followed by habitual criminal, useful in detection; MO
most wanted list FBI's roster of criminals with highest priority for arrest

MP military police
nab *Informal.* catch and arrest suspect
night stick policeman's billy club
paddy wagon *Informal.* police van for transporting arrestees
police governmental organization concerned with maintaining public order and safety, enforcing laws, and apprehending criminal suspects
policeman member of a police force, esp. male; *Slang* or *Informal:* badge, bobby, cop, fuzz, heat, the man
polygraph machine registering biological stress signals when subject is questioned about suspected activities; lie detector
posse group empowered by law to pursue and apprehend criminal suspect
precinct police headquarters for section of city
private detective investigator for hire, with no legal authority to make arrests; private eye
private eye *Slang.* private detective
rap *Slang.* criminal charge; (*vb*) arrest, detain
rap sheet *Slang.* record kept by law-enforcement officials of a person's arrests and convictions
roll over on (*vb*) inform on one's accomplice to help police make arrest
run in (*vb*) *Slang.* arrest suspect and bring to jail
Scotland Yard metropolitan London police
search and seizure search of person or premises by police with probable cause warrant
search warrant legal document empowering police to search premises for evidence of illegal activity
second degree designation for police procedure involving transport of suspect to jail or detention
sheriff law-enforcement officer of county or other civil subdivision of state
snitch *Informal.* informer
stakeout waiting in hiding for suspect to appear or illegal act to occur
suspect person suspected of committing crime but not yet convicted by legal due process
sweep movement of large number of police across area where suspected crimes are occurring or criminals hiding
third degree designation for police procedure involving interrogation of suspect; brutal or unethical methods of police questioning
vice squad police unit enforcing laws against immoral acts, esp. prostitution and drugs
vigilante individual or group attempting to enforce law and punish offenders without legal authority
voiceprint method of coding human voice into electronic pattern, used for identification of suspects
warrant legal document authorizing police action
wired (*adj*) carrying a concealed microphone or recording device in order to collect evidence

Legal Procedures and Trials

acquittal act of relieving accused from charge of alleged crime; not-guilty verdict
alibi excuse intended to avert blame, esp. one in which accused person claims to have been elsewhere at time crime was committed
arraignment appearance in court for indictment on charges
bail money or security deposit paid to court for release of person awaiting trial, guaranteeing defendant will appear for trial or forfeit bail money
chambers judge's private office adjoining courtroom
charges crimes of which suspect is accused
circumstantial evidence evidence that implies one fact by proving other events or circumstances suggesting it
complicity association or participation in crime
confession suspect's admission of guilt
conviction legal establishment of guilt in committing crime, usu. after trial
cop a plea *Informal.* plead guilty to lesser crime than the one that is charged
custody charge and control over suspect, exercised by court and esp. by police
defendant suspect on trial in court of law
detainer writ or order for further detention of a person already in custody, sometimes from another jurisdiction
entrapment illegal method of enticing suspect into committing or revealing crime
evidence legally admissible facts or objects that help to establish guilt or innocence of defendant
exonerate (*vb*) clear of all charges or guilt
extradition transfer of criminal suspect from place of apprehension to location of legal jurisdiction
eyewitness person who actually saw a crime committed
frame (*vb*) set up innocent person to appear guilty of crime
grand jury jury with power to indict only
guilty (*adj*) justly charged with and convicted of the commission of a crime
hearsay evidence testimony given as secondhand information rather than by eyewitness
incrimination showing evidence or proof of involvement in crime
indictment formal charging with commission of crime
insanity plea seeking exoneration on basis of temporary insanity or lack of responsibility for actions
jump bail fail to appear in court after bail bond has been posted
misconduct improper behavior by attorney or judge
penal code body of law dealing with punishment of crime
plaintiff filer of legal complaint against defendant
plea formal declaration of guilt or innocence by defendant
plea bargaining reduction of criminal charges in exchange for guilty plea to lesser offense
preventive detention holding a prisoner without bail or on very high bail
probable cause reasonable grounds for assuming validity of criminal charge
probation suspension of sentence, allowing convicted offender freedom based on accountability to authorities

prosecutor government official responsible for presenting case against accused
protective custody detention of person solely for his or her safety
public defender government official appointed by court to defend accused person unable to afford attorney
remand (*vb*) return accused to custody pending further action
self-defense defense of criminal act by claiming danger to accused existed at time of commission
sentence punishment handed down by judge on convicted offender
sequester (*vb*) isolate jury in private place for discussion or to pass judgment
state's evidence testimony of accomplice in crime, who becomes voluntary witness for the prosecution in return for reduced sentence
subpoena writ commanding a person to appear in court or face penalty
substantiate (*vb*) verify another's testimony; give proof
summation attorney's concluding remarks to jury
summons written notice requiring appearance in court
suspended sentence court's permission for convicted offender not to serve prison sentence
testify (*vb*) provide sworn statement in court
testimony statements by witness under oath during trial
trial legal procedure for hearing testimony, weighing evidence, deciding guilt or innocence of criminal suspect, and setting sentence
verdict decision of jury as to suspect's guilt or innocence
warrant writ issued by court, esp. to make arrest
witness person giving evidence at trial
Witness Protection Program program of U.S. government designed to insure safety or anonymity of witnesses, esp. informers
writ formal legal document or instrument

Prison and Punishment

administrative segregation placement in solitary confinement of prisoner not accused of any disciplinary infraction
amnesty pardon handed down to group or class of offenders
bastinado punishment by beating soles of feet with stick
behind bars *Informal.* imprisoned or in jail
big house *Slang.* penitentiary or prison
bilboes shackles attached to long iron bar for prisoner's feet
black hole any wretched place of imprisonment or confinement
break escape from jail or prison
brig naval prison, esp. on ship
capital punishment sentence of death; death penalty
cell small room in which prisoner is held or lives
cellblock prison unit consisting of a number of cells
chain gang group of convicts chained together, esp. when doing manual labor outside
chair *Informal.* electric chair
clemency mercy shown to prisoner by authorities
commitment sentencing of criminal to prison term
commute (*vb*) reduce sentence
con *Informal.* convict
concentration camp enforced labor and execution center, esp. one run by Nazis in World War II
condemned (*adj*) sentenced, esp. to death
conjugal visit private visitation privilege extended to prisoner for exercise of conjugal rights with his or her spouse
convict person found guilty of crime serving time in prison; con
cooler *Slang.* jail
correctional institution prison or penal colony for long-term incarceration
county jail local center for short-term incarceration of persons awaiting trial or sentencing or convicted of minor offenses
death penalty capital punishment
death row area in prison housing convicts sentenced to death
debtor's prison prison in which debtors were formerly held until able to pay debts
detention facility jail, camp, or hall for inmates awaiting trial or sentencing and for aliens awaiting deportation
do time *Slang.* serve a sentence
drunk tank *Informal.* city jail cell in which persons arrested for public drunkenness, and other arrestees, are held overnight
dungeon prison, esp. dark and forbidding one
electric chair seat in which condemned prisoner is strapped for electrocution
electrocution execution by electric charge
ex-con *Informal.* former convict, now released from prison
execution putting to death of person convicted of crime, usu. by electrocution, gas chamber, firing squad, hanging, injection, or guillotine
executioner prison officer charged with carrying out execution
false imprisonment illegal confinement of someone against his or her will and without cause
firing squad group of soldiers who execute prisoners by simultaneously shooting them
flogging whipping as punishment
gas chamber airtight prison room in which execution by poison gas takes place
gibbet upright post with projecting arm at top for hanging bodies of executed criminals as warning
guillotine instrument for execution by beheading, in which a heavy blade is dropped between two grooved uprights
hanging execution by strangulation or breaking of neck, usu. by suspending prisoner from rope tied around his or her neck
holding cell prisoners' temporary place of confinement
hole solitary confinement

house arrest confinement under guard in one's normal living quarters instead of prison
house of correction place of confinement and reform for criminals convicted of minor offenses
house of detention place of confinement for alleged criminals awaiting trial, and sometimes for witnesses
incarceration imprisonment
injection execution by injection of toxic substance
inmate prisoner
jail building for short-term confinement of prisoners and those accused of crimes; county jail; *Slang*: calaboose, can, city hotel, clink, cooler, jug, poky; also, *esp. Brit.*, gaol
jailbird inmate, esp. longtime or repeat inmate
jailer official overseeing jail operations and guarding prisoners; turnkey; warder
jailhouse lawyer prisoner who does legal research and writing for others while serving time
joint *Slang.* usu. the joint; prison
keeper jailer, prison guard
knout (*vb*) flog
lam *Slang.* escape from prison or flight to evade authorities
life sentence prison term lasting for entire life span
lockdown confinement of all prisoners to their cells
lynching illegal execution of suspect, usu. hanging by mob
maximum-security prison heavily guarded prison housing prisoners with long sentences and dangerous or hardened criminals
medium-security prison prison with moderate security, less than maximum and more than minimum
minimum-security prison moderately guarded or unguarded prison, such as a work farm, housing white-collar and less serious offenders and those serving short sentences or nearing release
mittimus warrant of commitment to prison
pardon official cancellation of sentence or punishment for crime
parole release from prison before full sentence has been served
parolee prisoner who has been set free but must maintain contact with authorities
pen *Informal.* penitentiary
penal (*adj*) pertaining to or constituting legal punishment
penal colony prison, esp. one in isolated area
penal institution jail, reformatory, or prison
penitentiary maximum-security prison, esp. one maintained by a state or the U.S. government for serious offenders
pillory wood frame used to restrain head and hands as punishment
political prisoner person deemed politically dangerous by state and falsely imprisoned for supposed crimes
population prisoners who are not in segregation and are allowed to mix with others
POW prisoner of war
prison state or federal institution for long-term confinement of convicts, usu. felons; *Slang*: big house, can, clink, coop, joint, slammer, stir
prisoner person accused or convicted of crime and held in jail or prison; captive; inmate
prisoner of war POW; person held captive by enemy during wartime
prison riot violent outburst by prisoners against prison conditions
probation suspension of prison sentence on guarantee of good behavior and regular reporting to authorities
protective custody administrative segregation of prisoner deemed in danger if allowed to mix with other prisoners
punishment penalty imposed by legal system on convicted offender
rack torture device in which victim's body is bound to frame and stretched
rat *Slang.* (n) informer; (vb) inform on
recidivism repetition of, or chronic engagement in, criminal acts; return to confinement for any reason, including technical parole violations
reformatory penal institution for reform and rehabilitation of young offenders, esp. minors; reform school
reform school reformatory
rehabilitation preparation of prisoners for reentry into society by eliminating criminal impulses
reprieve delay in execution of sentence
segregation locked-down housing apart from other prisoners, usu. in solitary, either disciplinary or administrative
sentence punishment determined by law
serve time pass time of sentence in prison
shakedown search of prisoner or prison cell, undertaken by guards, esp. for contraband or weapons
slammer *Slang.* prison
solitary confinement holding of prisoner alone in isolated cell for extended period
stockade military prison
stocks heavy wooden frame with holes for confining ankles and wrists, formerly used for punishment
time prison sentence
torture cruel and unusual punishment, esp. infliction of extreme pain
trusty well-behaved and trustworthy prisoner given special privileges and responsibilities, often having power over other prisoners
turnkey jailer
up the river *Slang.* serving time in prison
violate (*vb*) *Slang.* return to incarceration as a parole violator
warden prison administrator
warder jailer
ward of the state minor or incompetent person under protection or custody of court
water torture punishment in which water is dripped slowly onto victim's forehead
whipping punishment by flogging with whip
work camp work farm

work farm minimum-security prison in which inmates are allowed out of their cells to work, esp. outdoors; work camp
yard enclosed outdoor area for exercise of inmates, where prisoners can mingle
yardbird *Slang.* convict or prisoner

VIOLENCE

Violent Events
Fights
Attacks
Violent Actions
Violent Persons

Violent Events

annihilation total destruction; extinction
atrocity cruel, inhumane act
barbarity brutal or inhuman conduct; cruelty
bastinado beating with stick or cudgel
bedlam place or occasion of uproar and commotion
bloodbath violently gory conflict
bloodshed slaughter; taking of life, as in war or murder
brouhaha uproar
brutality savagery; cruel or harsh treatment
butchery brutal, heartless killing
carnage large-scale destruction of life
collision violent meeting of opposites; striking or crashing together
commotion agitated or disturbed activity; fray; tumult
conflagration extensive, extremely destructive fire
contest conflict, fight, or struggle for victory over opponent; altercation
coup de grâce *French.* lit. blow of mercy; deathblow; final, decisive stroke
deathblow coup de grâce
decimation large-scale destruction
demolition act of destruction
despoilment forceful, violent deprivation or destruction of goods or property
destruction tearing down or totally eliminating something
devastation total destruction; laying waste
disturbance outbreak of public disorder; disruption of the peace
explosion sudden, violent expansion or outburst, esp. involving combustion and loud noise, as with explosive material
extinction annihilation
fight physical conflict between opponents
furor rage or frenzy of activity or feeling
fury anger, rage, or wrath
fuss tumult, or small disturbance; a quarrel over something trivial
havoc ruinous destruction or devastation; chaos
holocaust destruction or sacrifice, esp. of human life on grand scale
inferno hellishly violent conflagration
internecine (*adj*) mutually destructive, esp. due to conflict within a group
massacre indiscriminate mass killing; widespread butchery
mass murder large-scale killing; slaughter
mayhem maiming or disfiguring of another person; random or deliberate violence
monstrosity very large-scale, severe, shocking event
outbreak sudden instance of violence
outburst sudden expression of violent emotion or action
outrage instance of violent brutality
paroxysm convulsive and uncontrollable seizure; fit of violent action or emotion
rage intense, uncontrollable anger
reign of terror period of violence and fear; situation of ruthless oppression
revolt violent attempt to overthrow established authority
riot violent disruption of public order or peace; uproar
ruin destruction by defeat or decay
savagery barbarity or cruelty
shambles place of slaughter or wreckage
slaughter ruthless killing, esp. in large numbers
spoliation robbery and plunder, esp. during war
Sunday punch knockout punch; one's most powerful blow
tumult violent and noisy disturbance; commotion
upheaval widespread social unrest or agitation
uproar disturbance or tumult; outbreak of chaos; brouhaha
violence exertion of rough physical force to injure or abuse
war organized, armed conflict between nations
wrack and ruin state of destruction or wreckage
wreckage remains of something after a violent event resulting in extensive damage to it

Fights

altercation dispute; contest
argument dispute between proponents of opposing views
battle conflict between soldiers or armies
battle royal battle distinguished by great valor and bloodshed
brawl noisy fight or quarrel
broil quarrel, dispute, noisy argument or fight
clash hostile meeting of opponents; conflict
combat fight, esp. armed military encounter; fray
conflict fight or struggle between enemies
contention struggling or striving together in a contest; rivalry
contest conflict, fight; struggle for victory over an opponent; altercation
contretemps inopportune occurrence; dispute
dispute combat or controversy over a difference of opinion; altercation; contretemps; quarrel
dogfight rough physical fight

donnybrook riotous event with uncontrolled fighting
duel fight between two persons, esp. with witnesses and rules of conduct
duke it out fight, esp. with fists; do battle
feud protracted hostility between two parties, with alternate strikes against each other
fight physical conflict between opponents
fisticuffs striking with the fists
flap noisy argument
fracas noisy fight or brawl
fray combat, fight; commotion; contest
free-for-all wild and uncontrolled fight with many participants
go to the mat engage in physical struggle, as in wrestling
gunfight fight between opponents armed with pistols or rifles; shootout
hammer and tongs vigorously, with great violence or force
horseplay playful fighting
infighting battle at close quarters
joust contest between knights mounted on horseback and armed with lances
knock-down-drag-out (*adj*) describing esp. violent and prolonged fight
melee confusing crush of battling opponents
mix-up fight or brawl
quarrel angry disagreement; dispute
roughhouse (*vb*) engage in playful, boisterous fighting
row noisy quarrel; abusive, quarrelsome dispute
ruckus noisy commotion; fracas; rumpus
rumpus noisy disturbance; ruckus
run-in unexpected, violent encounter
scrap *Informal.* fight, usu. casual or brief
scrape fight or quarrel
scuffle confused, disordered fight; tussle
set-to brief, sharp fight or argument
shootout gunfight
shoving match fight conducted by rough pushing
skirmish light, brief conflict
spat petty quarrel
squabble noisy dispute or brawl
strife contest; fight
struggle difficult, exhausting fight, often prolonged
tiff small, angry outburst; petty quarrel; spat
tussle physical contest between opponents
vendetta prolonged feud involving killing for revenge
war sustained, widespread conflict, esp. between nations or peoples, with heavily armed and equipped soldiers

Attacks

accost (*vb*) approach in challenging manner
aggravated assault severe attack
ambush surprise attack by concealed force
assail (*vb*) attack vigorously or violently; assault
assault sudden attack or invasion; physical attack on a person; (*vb*) assail; attack
attack (*vb*) set upon in a forceful, aggressive, violent manner; begin hostilities against; (*n*) hostile and aggressive action; assault
battery physical beating of a person
blitz lightning quick, all-out attack
blow sudden, hard stroke with hand or weapon
bombard (*vb*) attack with projectiles or bombs
breathe down someone's neck chase menacingly and begin to overtake
charge (*vb*) rush at or advance aggressively
cheap shot attack from blind side or at weakest point
close in on (*vb*) surround; gain ground on
crowd (*vb*) close in on or press against
foray raid, esp. for booty in war
go at (*vb*) advance aggressively on an opponent
harass (*vb*) badger or persecute repeatedly
harry (*vb*) raid, invade, harass, or torment
have at (*vb*) make hostile advance upon
intrusion entry without permission or invitation; invasion
inundate (*vb*) overcome by superior force
invasion forceful or hostile intrusion, infringement, or entry, esp. by an army
lash out (*vb*) strike or kick suddenly and aggressively
light into (*vb*) *Informal.* attack suddenly and vigorously
lunge (*vb*) thrust or plunge forward
onrush strong forward rush or movement
onslaught vigorous, powerful attack
pay back (*vb*) retaliate against or punish
pillage robbery or plunder, usu. in war; rapine
raid sudden invasion, esp. by surprise
rapine pillage
sneak attack surprise attack, esp. by hidden forces
start something *Informal.* pick a fight
storm (*vb*) attack with overwhelming force
strafe (*vb*) attack with machine-gun fire from the air
strike (*vb*) hit with force; (*n*) sudden attack
swing at (*vb*) aim blow at an opponent
thrust at (*vb*) move aggressively toward an opponent
tilt (*vb*) charge at an opponent

Violent Actions

abuse do wrongful harm to someone; maltreat
accost approach forcibly
act up behave uncontrollably and unpleasantly
afflict inflict injury or distress
annihilate destroy completely, make extinct
annoy harass repeatedly in quick attacks
antagonize provoke; act in hostile manner
avenge exact satisfaction for a wrong
batter beat repeatedly
beat up strike forcefully with hands or weapon
belt hit, often with a belt or strap
blast ruin, destroy; afflict with blight
blight ruin; cause to wither or decay
blow off steam *Informal.* forcefully vent strong feelings

blow one's top *Informal.* explode with anger
blow up *Informal.* lose one's temper
bludgeon hit with a clublike weapon
boil over lose one's temper
bomb drop bombs on; bombard; shell
bombard bomb
bother purposefully annoy or irritate
brandish wave a weapon menacingly
brawl argue noisily
break smash or split violently into pieces
broadside hit from side
browbeat intimidate
brutalize treat cruelly
buffet hit with hand or fist; cuff repeatedly
bulldoze overpower with intimidating force
bully intimidate
burn set fire to; incinerate
burst break apart with sudden violence
bust *Informal.* hit or break
butcher chop up or kill brutally
butt strike with head
cane strike with thin stick
chafe rub against so as to wear away
choke strangle by applying pressure around neck
chop cut up with knife
churn shake violently, stir up
clap hit across back
claw strike or tear with something sharp or pointed, esp. fingernails
clobber strike hard blow
clout strike
club hit with heavy weapon
coerce compel by force
collar seize by neck
come to blows engage in physical fight
commandeer seize arbitrarily, often for military or public use
confront face an enemy; provoke hostile encounter
conquer take by force, defeat opponent
consume destroy completely, esp. by fire
countervail exert equal force against
crack strike so as to break open
crash collide violently, shatter or break in pieces
cream *Slang.* defeat decisively in a fight
crucify execute by crucifixion; defeat utterly
crunch grind or press with crunching sound; step on
crush squeeze or press until damaged or destroyed; oppress
cudgel beat with heavy stick
cuff strike with one's hand; slap
cut penetrate, divide, or detach with a sharp-edged instrument
cut up damage or injure, esp. by lacerations; slice into pieces
damage cause injury to; impair
dash hurl or throw forcefully
decimate destroy a significant portion of, orig. every tenth person
deck *Informal.* strike forcefully to the ground
defeat overcome, esp. in battle
defile pollute
demolish destroy, ruin, or take apart
dent make a depression or hollow in something
depopulate destroy or reduce the number of inhabitants of
deracinate uproot from home or native culture
desecrate treat without respect
despoil plunder or ravage
destroy ruin, demolish, or exterminate; reduce to fragments or useless form
devastate lay waste; destroy utterly
devour destroy by consuming
disembowel eviscerate
dismantle take apart
dismember cut limb from limb
do mischief commit intentional harm
drill bore a hole in; hit dead on
drum hit repeatedly
embroil engage in battle
eradicate wipe out
erupt burst out, break into rage or anger
eviscerate remove innards of; disembowel; gut
explode burst violently
expunge obliterate
exterminate destroy completely, annihilate
extirpate root out, eradicate, or expel
fell cause to fall, knock down; kill
fire cause to burn; shoot a gun
flail beat, esp. with free-swinging stick attached to handle
flay skin, strip off surface
flog whip
fly at rush, attack
force coerce, impose, or take violently
fracture break, crack
fragment break into parts
gash cut deeply
gnash grind
gouge force or scoop out, esp. an eye
grapple fight closely; seize and hold opponent in physical contest
graze strike glancing blow upon
grind wear down to powder or fragments; gnash
gut eviscerate
hack chop up, mangle
hammer strike or beat heavily
have it out engage in a fight
hew cut or strike forcibly with ax
hit strike, knock, or deliver blow to
horsewhip flog with whip
hurt wound, cause pain or injury
impair damage, harm, or injure
impale pierce with sharp stick or rod
impinge collide with or strike
implode burst inward
incinerate burn
infect contaminate or pollute with disease
injure harm or damage
intimidate frighten with threats of harm; browbeat; bully
invade make an assault on; enter forcefully and with hostility
irritate provoke, annoy; attack sore spot
irrupt violently burst or break in

jab poke, punch
jar conflict or clash; shake
jolt shake roughly, knock
jump on leap upon in attack
kick strike with foot
kill take another's life by violence
knee jab with knee
knife strike or attack with blade
knock hit; make a striking blow
knock out KO; strike hard to render unconscious
knuckle press or strike with knuckles or fists
KO knock out
lacerate tear or cut
lash strike suddenly, esp. with a whip
lay low knock down, beat
level demolish completely, raze to the ground
lick hit repeatedly, defeat in fight
liquidate eliminate opponents, esp. by killing
loot rob, plunder
lop off cut off
maim disfigure, mutilate
maltreat abuse
mangle mutilate, injure
manhandle treat roughly
mar injure, damage
maraud plunder, raid
mash smash, reduce to pulp
maul beat up, injure
mess up dishevel, disarrange
mistreat abuse
mob attack in group
molest bother, intrude on, or interfere with; attack sexually
mug attack and rob in public place
mutilate damage, esp. by cutting off a body part
nab *Informal.* seize
nettle irritate, sting, or provoke
nip sever, bite off, or snap at
nuke *Informal.* obliterate with or as if by nuclear weapon
obliterate destroy completely, erase; expunge
off *Slang.* kill
oppress master by superior force; control through intimidation or by force
oust forcibly eject, drive out
overpower overcome by superior force
overrun trample, run over, or overwhelm
overwhelm oppress or overpower
paw *Informal.* handle roughly
pelt strike repeatedly
pepper assault or hit repeatedly with small blows
persecute harass, oppress
pestle grind or pulverize
pick a fight incite another into conflict
pierce penetrate sharply, as if by stabbing
pillage plunder or rob
pinch squeeze or compress tightly and painfully
pistol-whip strike repeatedly with gun
plague torment; infest
plaster *Informal.* strike hard; defeat decisively
plow under force out of existence; overpower
plunk *Informal.* strike; hit with a ball or other object
poison harm or kill with poisonous substance
poke thrust, intrude
pollute poison, taint, or make foul
pound batter or hammer
powder beat into small pieces; pulverize
prod jab or poke, with or as if with pointed object
pulverize reduce to fragments
pummel beat or pound
pump strike rapidly and repeatedly
punch strike with fist; sock
puncture pierce with pointed object
punish injure in retaliation; do severe harm to
push thrust or press forcefully
push around shove from place; bully
quash suppress, subdue
rabbit punch (*n*) quick, sharp blow to neck or base of skull
rack torture or torment; stretch body of another on rack
rage show or proceed with violent anger
raid invade or attack suddenly
ram batter; strike with great force
rampage act wildly and recklessly
ransack plunder, search for booty
rap hit with sharp blow
rape seize or plunder; assault sexually
ravage devastate, plunder
raven seize violently; devour
raze tear down or demolish
ream *Informal.* batter, esp. by stretching apart
rend tear apart, split; rive
retaliate injure someone in return for injury inflicted
riddle attack repeatedly, esp. with bullets
riot disturb the peace or public order
rip tear, cut
rive rend
rock knock backwards with a blow
rough up abuse; handle harshly
rout set to flight, drive from place
rub abrade
ruin destroy, wreck
run amok behave wildly, with uncontrollable violence
rupture tear apart, break open
rush assault
sack plunder or loot
sail into *Informal.* assault vigorously
savage attack in a ferocious, barbarous way
scald burn, esp. with boiling liquid
scalp cut or pull skin from skull of
scar cut and disfigure; wound permanently
scathe damage or harm as if by scorching
scorch parch or shrivel with heat
screw twist into strained position; abuse
sear burn or char surface of
seize grasp forcefully, confiscate; nab; nail
set upon attack suddenly
shatter break into fragments; destroy violently
shed blood engage in savage, bloody fighting
shell bomb
shoot hit with a bullet or arrow
shove push roughly

shred tear into strips
sic attack (used esp. to incite dog upon victim)
sideswipe strike along side with glancing blow
sink destroy by submerging
skewer pierce with sharp object
slam strike or shove forcefully
slap strike with open hand; cuff
slash cut or gash, esp. with sharp blade
slay destroy, esp. kill by violence
slice cut
slit cut to strips; make long, narrow slice in
slug *Informal.* hit hard with fist
smack strike with loud sound
smash crush, shatter, or break up
smite strike hard with hand or weapon; strike down or slay
smother stifle; suffocate
snip cut to bits, clip
snipe shoot at from a distance
spank beat on buttocks
spike pierce with pointed object
spill blood fight so as to cause bleeding
splinter break or split into long, narrow pieces
split tear apart, divide forcefully
squash mash or crush; suppress
squeeze apply pressure to
squelch crush down; suppress or stamp out
squish squash or squeeze
stab puncture with knife or sharp object
stamp beat upon with foot; crush or pound
stave break a hole in; splinter or smash
steamroller flatten in a fight; roll over an opponent with superior force
stick pierce with pointed object
sting pierce or wound with poison
stomp stamp or step on heavily
stone hit repeatedly with rocks, esp. to kill
storm attack suddenly with superior force
strafe attack with machine-gun fire from the air
strangle suffocate or choke by squeezing around neck
strike hit with one's fist or an object; clout
strong-arm use violence or intimidation to persuade
stun daze or deaden with blow
subdue beat into submission
subject bring under domination, force to submit
suffocate (*n*) choke; smother
sunder rend, split, or break apart
swamp overwhelm by submerging; sink
swat strike or hit
take on oppose (another); entice (someone) to fight
tap hit lightly
tear rip, split, or pull apart
thrash beat or flog
thresh thrash, beat, or cut up
throttle choke or strangle
thump beat or pound; *Informal.* thrash severely
thwack strike or hit with something flat
tilt cause to fall over; upset the balance of
torment torture
torture cause extreme pain to, inflict suffering on; torment
trample crush under one's feet
trash *Informal.* lay waste, ruin, or vandalize
trim *Informal.* administer beating to
trounce beat soundly
tussle scuffle; struggle at close range
tweak pinch and pull with a twist or jerk
twist wrench and turn with rotary motion
tyrannize oppress, intimidate
vandalize destroy or desecrate property with malicious intent
vanquish conquer or defeat in battle
violate ravish, rape; mistreat
wallop beat soundly; *Informal.* hit hard
waste devastate or totally demolish; *Slang.* murder
whack strike with solid blow
whale strike soundly; beat on repeatedly
wham hit hard
whip strike with a lash, flog; defeat decisively
whomp *Informal.* inflict loud, heavy blow or slap
whop *Informal.* strike forcibly
whump thump
whup regional variation of *whip*; beat or defeat decisively
work evil cause damage or injury, esp. by immoral or wicked means
work over *Informal.* beat up; hit repeatedly
wrack wreck, destroy
wreak inflict or exact punishment, injury, or vengeance
wreak havoc cause destruction or chaos
wreck ruin, destroy
wrench twist or pull sharply
wrest wrench or seize violently
wring twist (another's neck) with the hands
yank pull sharply
zap *Informal.* strike or stun with sharp blow
zonk *Slang.* knock out; strike soundly

Violent Persons

aggressor initiator of unprovoked attack
agitator one who incites others to violence; firebrand
anarchist one who resists all authority, esp. by terrorism
animal brutish person
annihilator one who utterly destroys
arsonist one who sets things on fire; incendiary
assailant attacker
assassin murderer, esp. the fanatical or hired killer of a politically prominent person
attacker one who uses force to harm others or start a fight; assailant
barbarian cruel, uncivilized brute; Goth
beast brutal, animallike person
berserker frenzied and ferocious warrior of Norse legend
bomber one who sets off explosions
brute savage, cruel, unfeeling person
bully blustering, overbearing person who terrorizes weaker people
butcher brutal or indiscriminate killer
cannibal person who eats human flesh

cutthroat merciless murderer, esp. one who cuts throats
destroyer one who crushes, kills, and totally wipes out opponents; exterminator
devil cruel, evil, remorseless person
exterminator destroyer
fiend cunningly evil person; hellhound
firebrand agitator
fire-eater angry person always ready to attack others
fury raging, vengeful person
goon *Informal.* hoodlum or thug, esp. one hired to attack others
Goth barbarian
hard-nose *Slang.* tough, obstinate person
hellhound fiend
hellion *Informal.* mischievous troublemaker
hell-raiser *Informal.* one who stirs up trouble
henchman person hired to perform violent acts for another
hijacker terrorist who commandeers planes and other vehicles
holy terror *Informal.* uncontrollable troublemaker
hoodlum tough, young street ruffian, esp. member of lawless gang; hooligan
hooligan hoodlum
hothead person easily aroused to anger or attack; hotspur
hotspur hothead
Hun savage barbarian
incendiary arsonist
invader one who attacks another's territory
killer murderer
knave unprincipled, untrustworthy, or dishonest person; rascal
maniac wildly insane person
monster cruel, vicious person
mugger one who assaults others with intent to rob
murderer one who takes another's life; killer
predator one who lives by plunder and robbery
raider one who suddenly attacks or invades
rapist one who forces another to have sexual intercourse
rascal mischievous troublemaker; knave; rogue
rogue rascal; scoundrel
roughneck crude, rowdy person
rowdy rough, disorderly, quarrelsome person
ruffian brutal, lawless person, esp. hoodlum; rough; tough
savage ferocious, brutal, beastly person; rogue
scoundrel wicked, disreputable person; rogue
she-wolf evil, vicious, predatory woman
slasher one who attacks with knife or blade
spitfire easily-angered person, esp. woman
terminator cold-blooded killer, esp. one for hire
terror *Informal.* wildly uncontrollable person
terrorist one who uses force, often random, to intimidate or gain political ends
thug brutal hoodlum, thief, or murderer, esp. gang member
tiger fiercely belligerent person
tigress ferocious woman
tinderbox highly excitable or inflammable person
who is potential source of widespread violence
tough ruffian
troublemaker one who agitates or incites others to quarrel
vandal malicious, destructive person
villain wicked person, criminal
virago quarrelsome, foul-tempered woman
vixen ill-tempered, evil woman
warrior person with fighting spirit
witch evil, devilish person, esp. a woman, who professes to have supernatural powers
wolf fierce, cruel person

DEATH

Dead or Dying

asleep (*adj*) dead; into the state of death
at peace (*adj*) dead
bite the dust die
buy the farm *Slang.* die or be killed
cash in one's chips *Slang.* die
casualty person killed in war or accident
dead (*adj*) no longer living; (*n*) the dead; dead persons collectively
death act of dying; total and permanent cessation of life
deceased (*adj*) dead
demise death
departed (*adj*) dead
die (*vb*) experience death; cease living
DOA dead on arrival; term used to indicate person was dead on arrival at hospital
done for *Informal.* dead or close to death
done in *Informal.* dead, esp. from unnatural causes
drop dead *Informal.* die suddenly
dying (*adj*) about to die; approaching death
eclipsed (*adj*) having died
eighty-sixed (*adj*) *Slang.* dead, esp. killed
elapsed (*adj*) having died
end death
expire (*vb*) die, esp. after prolonged disease
extinct (*adj*) no longer living, esp. of a species
fatality person who has died, esp. in accident, war, or crime
final rest death
final sleep death
goner *Informal.* one who is dead or about to die
have one foot in the grave be dying
in extremis (*adj*) at the point of death
kick the bucket *Slang.* die

late (*adj*) recently deceased, used as reference with person's name
lost (*adj*) dead
meet one's Maker die
moribund (*adj*) dying, about to die
mortal living being who must eventually die; (*adj*) causing or liable to cause death
pass away (*vb*) die
pass on (*vb*) die
perish (*vb*) die, esp. in violent or untimely manner
rest state of death
six feet under *Slang.* dead and buried
succumb (*vb*) die, esp. from disease
terminal (*adj*) dying, esp. from fatal illness
waste away (*vb*) die slowly from disease
wither and die degenerate from disease until death

Unnatural Deaths

asphyxiation death by lack of oxygen or from breathing obstruction; smothering; suffocation
beheading executive by decapitation
Black Death bubonic plague
brain death cessation of brain activity, indicated by flat EEG reading
buried alive asphyxiated beneath the ground
choking windpipe obstruction by physical pressure or due to breathing of poisoned air
crucifixion nailing of hands and feet to cross
decapitation removal of head from neck
disease fatal wasting or impairment of body function
electrocution death by electric shock
evisceration death by disembowelment
execution putting to death as legal punishment for crime
fatal illness disease that results in death
firing squad execution by several rifles fired at once
gallows structure for hanging by the neck
guillotine structure with large blade for decapitation
hanging execution by strangulation or breaking of neck in suspended noose wrapped around neck
immolation death by fire
murder unlawful taking of another's life with malicious intent
natural causes old age, infirmity, or general debility
OD overdose
old age general infirmity resulting from aging
overdose OD; ingestion of toxic amount of drug
pestilence devastating epidemic of contagious disease
poisoning ingestion of a toxic substance
sacrifice being offered to deity as victim
smothering being deprived of air or overcome by smoke or fumes; asphyxiation
stake wood post to which person is tied and burned
starvation total deprivation of food
stoning being beaten by thrown stones
strangulation stoppage of breath by compression of throat
suffocation being deprived of oxygen or prevented from breathing; asphyxiation
suicide taking of one's own life
vaporization dissipation into small particles due to pressure or molecular disturbance

Murder and Suicide

assassination murder of a public figure
bloodshed taking of life; slaughter
blow away (*vb*) *Slang.* murder
bump off (*vb*) *Slang.* murder
butcher (*vb*) slaughter or kill in a barbarous or indiscriminate manner
carnage bloody slaughter of large numbers of people; massacre
-cide suffix meaning killer or killing of
contract *Slang.* agreement to commit murder for payment
disembowelment evisceration; removal of the bowels or entrails
dispatch (*vb*) murder deftly; eliminate quickly
dispose of (*vb*) murder or eliminate
do away with (*vb*) murder
do in (*vb*) *Informal.* murder
dust (*vb*) *Slang.* murder
euthanasia merciful, painless killing of hopelessly sick person; mercy killing
extermination complete and immediate elimination by killing
fratricide killing one's brother
genocide killing of entire race or nation
hara-kiri ritual suicide by disembowelment; seppuku (Japan)
holocaust genocide, esp. of Jews by Nazis in World War II
homicide taking another's life with malicious intent; murder
infanticide killing a baby
kill (*vb*) take another person's life by violence
liquidate (*vb*) eliminate by killing
lynching execution, usu. hanging, by mob without legal sanction
manslaughter accidental murder without malicious intent
martyrdom self-sacrifice for the sake of some principle or cause
massacre indiscriminate, ruthless killing of numerous, often helpless persons
mass murder murder of numerous individuals, usu. by one person
matricide killing one's mother
mercy killing euthanasia
murder unlawful taking of another's life with malicious intent; (*vb*) commit an act of murder; *Slang:* blow away, bump off, chill, dispatch, dispose of, do away with, do in, dust, grease, knock off, off, rub out, snuff out, stretch out, whack, waste, wax, zap
parricide killing one's parent or close relative
patricide killing one's father
pogrom organized massacre of a minority people, esp. Jews
poisoning secret administering of toxic substance to cause another's death

purge elimination of undesirable elements in group or society
regicide killing one's king or queen
ritual murder killing by group in ceremonial rite
ritual suicide killing oneself in a prescribed manner
rub out (*vb*) *Slang.* murder, often by organized crime
sacrifice taking victim's life as religious offering
self-immolation burning oneself to death
self-slaughter suicide
seppuku hara-kiri
serial killing murder of one victim after another over time by same killer
shooting killing by gunshot
slaughter brutal or violent killing of single person or large numbers of people
slay (*vb*) murder
snuff out (*vb*) *Informal.* murder
strangulation killing by choking or cutting off air supply
suffocation killing by smothering or strangulation
suicide taking one's own life; self-slaughter
suicide pact agreement between two people to commit suicide simultaneously
waste (*vb*) *Slang.* murder

Dead Bodies

bones dead body, esp. one decomposed
cadaver dead body, esp. one prepared for dissection
carrion dead body left out for animals and birds to eat
corpse dead body
dead body remains of a person who has died
dead man corpse
deceased polite or formal term for one who is dead
decomposition natural decay of dead body
dust one who is dead and decomposed into dust
dust and ashes one who is dead and decomposed into dust
loved one overly polite euphemism for dead person
mortal remains corpse
remains corpse
rigor mortis temporary stiffening of body shortly after death
skeleton bones of body after decomposition of flesh
stiff *Slang.* corpse

Burial and Funerals

autopsy examination and dissection of corpse to determine cause of death; necropsy; postmortem
barrow mound of earth and stones over grave
bereaved family and friends of deceased
bier stand or pedestal for a coffin or the coffin itself
body snatcher graverobber
boneyard *Slang.* cemetery
burial interment of dead body in grave
burial ground cemetery, esp. tract of land set aside for primitive cemetery
burial mound mound built over burial ground or grave
cairn heap of stones set up as memorial to the deceased
casket elaborate coffin
catacomb underground cemetery consisting of tunnels with recesses for tombs
catafalque ornamental bier on which body lies in state
cemetery area set aside for burying the dead in graves or tombs; boneyard; burial ground; graveyard; necropolis
cenotaph honorary tomb for person buried elsewhere
cerecloth waxed cloth for wrapping corpse
cerement waxed shroud or graveclothes
charnel house repository for bodies and bones of the dead
cinerarium vessel, esp. urn, used to receive ashes of the cremated dead
coffin box or case for burying corpse; pall
columbarium vaulted structure with recesses for cinerary urns
coroner public official who investigates deaths not due to natural causes
cortege funeral procession
cremains ashes of cremated body
cremation reduction of body to ashes for interment
crematorium crematory
crematory place, such as funeral establishment, at which cremation is done; furnace for cremation; crematorium
cromlech circle of stone monoliths on burial mound
crypt underground vault or burial chamber
death march funeral procession
death watch vigil kept over dead or dying person
deep six burial at sea
dirge song of lamentation at funeral
dolmen prehistoric tomb, usu. consisting of two upright stone slabs supporting one horizontal slab (Britain and France)
elegy funeral song or poem of lamentation for the dead
embalming treatment of corpse to prevent decay
entomb (*vb*) place corpse in burial tomb
epitaph memorial inscription on tomb or grave
eulogy praise for the deceased at funeral service
exequies funeral rites or ceremonies
exequy funeral procession
exhumation digging up of corpse from grave
extreme unction anointment of dying person with oil and prayer for recovery, administered by priest; final Catholic sacrament before death; last rites
funeral observance held for dead person before interment
funeral director manager of funeral home
funeral home establishment for embalming and preparation of dead for burial or cremation
funerary (*adj*) associated with burial
grave excavation in ground for burial of body
gravedigger person who digs graves
graverobber person who steals corpses after

burial, as for medical dissection or profit; body snatcher
gravestone monument marking burial site
graveyard cemetery
hearse large automobile used to convey corpse to burial place
in dust and ashes mourning
inhume (*vb*) bury, inter
in memoriam in memory of, written in epitaph
inter (*vb*) perform interment; bury
interment disposition of dead body in earth or tomb, or by cremation
inurn (*vb*) place ashes in a burial urn
Kaddish Jewish prayer of mourning
keen loud, wailing lamentation for the dead
knell bell tolled to signal death or funeral
kurgan burial mound (Eastern Europe and Siberia)
lamentation mourning aloud for the dead
last rites extreme unction
lay out (*vb*) prepare corpse for viewing prior to interment
lay to rest bury corpse
lich gate roofed gateway at entrance to churchyard under which coffin rests at beginning of burial service
lie in state be laid out on public display in official recognition of one's stature in life
mausoleum large building for aboveground entombment
memorial service in honor of the deceased after burial or interment
monument tombstone or other grave marker
morgue storage place for dead bodies pending identification and burial
mortician undertaker
mortuary building for storing dead bodies and preparing them for burial
mourning customary show of grief for deceased person
mummy body embalmed and wrapped in cloth for burial (ancient Egypt)
necropolis cemetery
necropsy autopsy
obsequy funeral rite or ceremony
pall coffin; cloth draped over coffin, bier, or tomb
pallbearer one of several persons carrying coffin to grave
plot individual burial site in cemetery
postmortem autopsy
pyre combustible heap for burning dead body as part of funeral rite
Requiem Mass Catholic Mass and liturgy celebrated for the repose of the dead
requiescat prayer for the repose of the dead
rest in peace RIP; standard acknowledgment of death; wish or prayer for the deceased
RIP rest in peace
sarcophagus coffin, esp. one of stone
sepulcher tomb or other place of burial
shrine tomb or other receptacle for the dead
shroud cloth or sheet in which corpse is wrapped for burial; cerecloth; cerement; winding sheet
taps bugle call at military funerals
threnody elegy or song of lamentation, esp. for the dead
tomb place of interment; excavation for a grave; burial vault or chamber
tombstone stone marker placed on or over burial site
tumulus ancient grave; artificial mound over burial site
undertaker one who prepares the dead for burial and manages funerals; mortician
urn ornamental vessel containing ashes of cremated dead person
vault underground burial chamber or tomb
vigil long, prayerful watch over dead or dying person
wake often festive vigil held over body of dead person prior to burial
winding sheet shroud

Beyond the Grave

abyss bottomless pit, gulf of nonexistence after death
afterlife existence of the soul in heaven; great beyond
damnation condemnation of soul to hell
devil, the ruling spirit of hell; Satan
Final Judgment determination of soul's fate by God
ghost soul of deceased returning in bodily likeness; specter; wraith
ghoul evil being that robs graves and feeds on corpses
Grim Reaper personification of death as cloaked skeleton holding scythe
Hades mythological underworld (ancient Greece)
heaven dwelling place of God and joyful abode of the souls of the dead
hell dwelling place of the devil and abode of the condemned souls of the dead
hellfire fire in hell
hereafter life after death or beyond mortal existence
infernal (*adj*) relating to or inhabiting the eternal inferno of hell
nether world hell
purgatory in Roman Catholic belief, intermediate state after death in which the souls of sinners become fit for heaven
resurrection act of rising from the dead, esp. for Final Judgment
revenant one who returns from death
rise from the dead achieve resurrection; return as a ghost
saint one of the dead entered into heaven, esp. the canonized or holy dead
Satan the devil
soul nonbodily spirit of deceased that exists after death
specter visible yet incorporeal spirit or ghost; wraith
spirit soul of deceased, esp. malevolent being or ghost
Styx principal underworld river in myth (ancient Greece)

transmigration passage of soul at death from body of one being to another
underworld hell
vampire reanimated corpse that returns at night to drink blood of living people
wraith apparition of living person in exact likeness, seen just before death; ghost, specter

Language of Death

antemortem (*adj*) preceding death
black humor morbid comedy, esp. relating to death
body bag large receptacle made of heavy material, used to transport corpse from battlefield or death scene
cryonics freezing of recently deceased people in hopes of resuscitation when cure exists for their fatal disease
deathbed bed on which someone dies
death instinct self-destructive impulse based on desire to achieve state of harmonious nonexistence in death; Thanatos
death rate number of deaths per thousand in specific group or at given place and time
death rattle gurgle of air passing through mucus in throat of dying person
death toll number of casualties from particular incident
intestate (*adj*) without a valid will at time of death
morbidity dwelling on gloomy thoughts of death
mortality being subject to death; death in large numbers; proportion of deaths in population due to specific cause
necrology list of those who have died within a given period; obituary
necrophilia achieving erotic stimulation from corpses
obit *Informal.* obituary
obituary biographical notice of person's death published in newspaper; necrology
posthumous (*adj*) occurring after one's death
post-obit (*adj*) effective after particular person's death
predecease (*vb*) die first; die before another person or event
quietus removal from activity, as in death
skull and crossbones emblem of death depicting skull and two crossed skeleton bones, esp. on pirate flag or as warning sign for poisons
stillbirth birth of dead child
stillborn (*adj*) dead at birth
swan song farewell appearance or last act, sometimes before death
testate (*adj*) having made and left a valid will
Thanatos primal, instinctual desire for death; personification of death (ancient Greece)
vital signs index of essential body functions, including pulse, breathing, and body temperature, that indicate life
widow surviving wife of dead husband
widower surviving husband of dead wife

Chapter Twenty-Five
Faith

RELIGION

World Religions

Baha'i modern religion developed in Iran in 1863 by Baha'Allah, emphasizing universal brotherhood, social equality, and the unification of all religions

Brahmanism pantheistic religious system of highest Hindu caste, based on the Brahmanas and Upanishads text commentaries on the Vedas, source of pre-Hindu religion introduced in 2nd millennium B.C.

Buddhism religion and philosophic system founded in India in 6th c. B.C. by Siddhartha Gautama, the Buddha, teaching that meditation and the Eightfold Path enable one to escape suffering and achieve Nirvana

Byzantine Church Orthodox Eastern Church

Catholicism Roman Catholicism

Christianity doctrine, faith, and monotheistic religious practice based on belief in Jesus Christ as Messiah and Son of God and on Old and New Testaments of Bible

Christian Science Christian religious movement and system of healing through prayer founded in 19th c. America by Mary Baker Eddy

Church of Jesus Christ of the Latter-day Saints Mormon Church

Church of Rome Roman Catholicism

Confucianism ethical and social teachings based on sayings of Confucius in China in 6th c. B.C., later incorporated into Taoist and Buddhist religions

Druze independent religious sect founded in 11th c. and containing elements of Islam, Christianity, and Judaism, believing in transmigration of souls, now practiced chiefly in Syria, Lebanon, and Israel

Eastern Orthodox Church Orthodox Eastern Church

Gnosticism esoteric salvational system from 2nd c., based on secret knowledge combining elements of mythology, ancient religions, and Christianity

Hinduism religion and social system of Hindus of Indian subcontinent, recognizing authority of Vedas and other sacred texts, emphasizing karma and reincarnation and worship of various deities, based on four goals and four stages in human life and socially rooted in four castes

Islam doctrine, faith, and practice of monotheistic Muslim religion in which Allah is supreme deity and Koran is sacred revelation, devoted to worship of Allah through Five Pillars, founded by prophet Muhammad in 7th c. Arabia; Muhammadanism

Jainism ancient monastic religion of India, influential on Hinduism, founded by Mahavira in 6th c. B.C., emphasizing asceticism, reverence for all living things, and cycles of rebirth

Judaism doctrine, faith, and practice of ancient monotheistic Israelite religion based on written Torah (first five books of Hebrew Bible or Old Testament) and teachings of the Talmud, which view religion as part of everyday family life, founded around 2000 B.C.

Lamaism form of Mahayana Buddhism and Tibetan Bonism, with elaborate ritual and strong hierarchy under Dalai Lama, practiced in Tibet, Nepal, and Mongolia

Latter-day Saints Mormon Church

Mazdaism Zoroastrianism

Mormon Church Christian religion founded in United States in 1830 by Joseph Smith and now centered in Utah, based on Book of Mormon accounts of ancient American peoples who were to found Zion, emphasizing revelation and proselytizing; Church of Jesus Christ of the Latter-day Saints

Muhammadanism Islam

Orthodox Eastern Church Christian church comprising local and national churches in southwest Asia and eastern Europe that split from Western church in 5th c. because of its rejection of the Roman pope and communion with patriarch of Constantinople, marked by elaborate ritual and iconography: includes Albanian, Bulgarian, Greek, Rumanian, Russian, Serbian, Syrian, and Ukrainian Orthodox churches; Byzantine Church; Eastern Orthodox Church

Protestantism any of various Christian denominations established during or following the Reformation against papal authority and Roman Catholicism in 16th c.

Roman Catholicism highly ritualistic, dogmatic Christian doctrine and faith based on Scripture and tradition, with hierarchy of celibate clergy under an infallible pope claiming direct historical line from apostle Peter, formal sacraments and Mass, and veneration of saints and Virgin Mary; Catholicism; Church of Rome

Shinto polytheistic, highly ceremonial, native religion of Japan, influenced by Confucianism and Buddhism, emphasizing worship of nature and ancestors and formerly divinity of emperor

Sikhism institutional mixture of Hinduism and Islam, founded by Nanak in northern India in 16th c., that rejects caste system

Taoism Chinese religion and philosophy based on 6th c. B.C. teachings of Lao-tzu, advocating simplicity and selflessness in following the Tao or path to enlightenment through balance of yin and yang

Theosophical Society eclectic belief system founded by Madame Blavatsky in 1875, based largely on Brahmanic and Buddhist teachings

Vedanta Society nondualistic Hindu philosophical system in fulfillment of the sacred Vedas and Upanishads

Zen variety of Mahayana Buddhism seeking intuitive illumination of satori through simplicity, meditation, and instruction from masters, practiced esp. in Japan and Korea

Zoroastrianism religious system of Persia prior to founding of Islam, established by Zoroaster in 6th c. B.C. and based on Avesta as holy scripture, emphasizing continuous apocalyptic struggle between good and evil; Mazdaism

Christian Denominations and Sects

Amish strict Mennonite community distinguished by self-sufficient living style that rejects technology, inspired by 18th c. Swiss bishop Jacob Amman

Anabaptist Protestant sect important in 16th c. advocating adult baptism and separation of church and state, precursor to Mennonites and Baptists

Anglican Church Protestant denomination developed after Henry VIII of England separated from Roman Catholic Church in 1534 and consolidated in reign of Elizabeth I, retaining many theological and hierarchical elements of Catholicism; Church of England

Armenian Apostolic Church Monophysite Christian church organized in United States in 1899

Assemblies of God largest of Pentecostal churches founded in early 20th c., practicing faith healing, speaking in tongues in enthusiastic services, and believing in second coming of Christ

Baptist Church Christian Protestant denomination whose evangelical beliefs include religious liberty with no creeds or hierarchy, priesthood of all believers, and adult baptism by total immersion, founded by John Smyth in 1609

Calvinism religious doctrine, based on beliefs of 16th c. Reformation leader John Calvin, advocating austere morality, predestination and election, and piety

Christian Science Christian religious sect and system of healing founded in 19th c. by Mary Baker Eddy; Church of Christ, Scientist

Church of Christ offshoot of Presbyterian Church founded in 1804, emphasizing literal interpretation of New Testament

Church of Christ, Scientist Christian Science

Church of England Anglican Church

Church of God any of various Christian denominations that emphasize personal conversion, imminent return of Christ, and sometimes speaking in tongues

Church of the Brethren Dunkers

Church of the New Jerusalem Swedenborgians

Congregational Church Christian church organization, developed from 16th c. separatist revolt in England, in which each local congregation is independent in governance and recognizes only Christ as its head

Coptic Church Christian Egyptian and Ethiopian Monophysite Church recognizing St. Mark the Evangelist as its founder and using Arabic in its services, known as Coptic Orthodox since 19th c.

Dunkers Christian denomination founded in 1708 in Germany that practices trine immersion and opposes taking of oaths and military service; Church of the Brethren

Episcopal Church Christian denomination that evolved from Church of England within Anglican communion, developed in United States in 1784, with worship based on Book of Common Prayer

Friends Quakers

Greek Orthodox Church autonomous branch of Eastern Orthodox Church that consists of Church of Greece, patriarchate of Constantinople, and churches using Greek in the liturgy and Byzantine rite

Huguenots French Protestant denomination of 16th and 17th c. comprised of followers of John Calvin

Jehovah's Witnesses evangelical Christian sect, founded in United States in 19th c. by Charles Russell, that refuses to participate with the government, actively proselytizes, and believes in imminent second coming of Christ

Lutheran Church conservative Protestant denomination based on teachings of Martin Luther, 16th c. German leader of Reformation, emphasizing authority of Scripture with justification and salvation by faith alone

Mennonites evangelical Protestant denomination, descended from Anabaptists, named after 16th c. Dutch religious reformer Menno Simons, that emphasizes simplicity and separation from worldly things, including military service, and adult baptism

Methodist Church Christian Protestant denomination, founded as 18th c. evangelical movement by Anglican John Wesley, emphasizing God's grace, individual responsibility, and study of the Bible as interpreted by reason and tradition

Metropolitan Community Church Christian congregation of gay men and lesbians

Millenial Church Shakers

Moravians Christian denomination descended from Bohemian Brethren, holding Scriptures to be only rule of faith and practice

Presbyterian Church Christian Protestant denomination founded by John Knox in Scotland in 1557 as British form of Calvinism, governed by its ministry and congregationally elected elders

Puritans Protestant group in England and American colonies in 16th and 17th c. that wanted to reduce Roman Catholic elements of Church of England, characterized by strict religious and moral discipline, influenced by John Calvin

Quakers Christian religion founded in 17th c. England by George Fox, emphasizing individual's spiritual inner light and rejecting sacraments and ordained ministry, associated with pacifism and social activism; Friends; Religious Society of Friends

Reformed Church Christian Protestant denomination governed by its ministry and congregationally elected elders and serving as continental European form of Calvinism

Rosicrucians occult group founded in 1868 by R.W. Little, claiming descent from ancient brotherhood said to be founded by 15th c. Christian Rosenkruez

Russian Orthodox Church autocephalous branch of Eastern Orthodox Church whose liturgy is in Old Church Slavonic, headed by patriarch of Moscow in communion with patriarch of Constantinople

Seventh Day Adventists Christian denomination whose evangelical doctrine anticipates the imminent return of Christ to Earth and observes Saturday as Sabbath, founded in United States in 1863

Shakers religion founded in England in 1747, led by Ann Lee, advocating celibacy, communal property, and simple way of life; Millenial Church; United Society of Believers in Christ's Second Appearing

Swedenborgians religious sect founded in 18th c., influenced by Emanuel Swedenborg, a Swedish mystic who claimed to receive divine revelations; Church of the New Jerusalem

Uniates Eastern Orthodox church that is in union with Roman Catholic Church, acknowledges the Roman pope, but maintains its own liturgy, discipline, and rites

Unitarianism Christian denomination that arose during the Reformation that rejects doctrine of the Trinity, posits universal salvation, emphasizes religious tolerance and congregational autonomy, and incorporates humanism and nontheistic thought

Unitarian-Universalism American liberal religious denomination in Christian tradition, formed by merger of Unitarians and Universalists in 1961

United Church of Christ American Protestant denomination formed by merger of Evangelical and Reformed churches and Congregational Christian Church in 1957, with simple services and governing synod

United Society of Believers in Christ's Second Appearing Shakers

Universalism liberal Christian denomination founded in 1779, emphasizing universal fatherhood of God and final salvation of all souls

Zwinglianism religious system following doctrines of Ulrich Zwingli, 16th c. Swiss Protestant reformer, maintaining that Eucharist is merely symbolic and not literally the body of Christ and that church should model itself on ancient Christianity

Christianity

Abel second son of Adam and Eve, killed by his brother Cain

Adam first human, father by Eve of Cain and Abel

Advent period of prayer and fasting beginning four Sundays before Christmas

agape divine love of God or Christ for humankind

Agnus Dei liturgical prayer to Christ the Savior

Agony Christ's suffering in garden of Gethsemane

agrapha sayings of Jesus other than those in Gospels

Annunciation announcement of Christ's coming birth, made by archangel Gabriel to Mary

Antichrist principal opponent of Christ; Satan

apostolic succession unbroken chain of succession from apostles, perpetuated through pope and other bishops by laying on of hands in ordination of clergy in Catholic, Orthodox, and Anglican churches

Ascension Christ's bodily ascent into heaven following Resurrection

Assumption the bodily taking up of the Virgin Mary to heaven

Ave Maria Roman Catholic prayer to the Virgin Mary; Hail Mary

beatification official papal recognition of dead person as blessed, often prior to canonization

beatitudes blessings spoken by Jesus in Sermon on the Mount

Beelzebub chief devil, Satan

Cain eldest son of Adam and Eve, murderer of his brother Abel

Calvary place where Christ was crucified

canonical hours periods of day designated for prayer and devotion: matins and lauds, prime, tierce, sext, nones, vespers, and compline

canonization official recognition by Roman Catholic Church of dead person as a saint

canticle liturgical song based on Biblical text

catechism formal religious instruction in form of questions and answers

christen (*vb*) bring into the church by baptism

Christendom Christian church and its congregation throughout world

Christmas celebration of birth of Christ on December 25 among Western Christians and on January 6 in Eastern Orthodox Church

Christology study of nature of and deeds of Jesus Christ

church lit. members of the body of Christ, used to designate Christian house of worship

communion Holy Communion

compline final canonical hour, following vespers

confession Catholic sacrament received on admitting one's sins to priest and receiving absolution and doing penance

confirmation Catholic sacrament received at and Protestant rite performed at ceremony of acceptance of membership into church at time of adolescence

consubstantiation actual presence of Christ, embodied in bread and wine of the sacrament of the Eucharist

Counter Reformation movement in Catholic Church in response to Protestant Reformation

credo statement of beliefs recited in unison at Mass
cross symbol of Christianity, Christ's Crucifixion and death, and the redemption of humankind
crown of thorns wreath placed on Christ's head before Crucifixion
crucifix representation of Christ crucified on cross
Crucifixion Christ's death on the cross
Crusades Christian wars of Middle Ages to reclaim Jerusalem from Islam
denomination religious body with particular name and practices, esp. one of various Protestant sects
Doxology words of praise for God beginning ""Praise God from whom all blessings flow"
Easter celebration of Resurrection of Christ
ecumenism Christian movement toward unity that transcends denominational distinctions
Eden paradise in which Adam and Eve resided before the Fall
encyclical letter from pope to all bishops on religious or civil matters
Epiphany commemoration of manifestation of Christ to the Magi
eschatology doctrine of last things; second coming of Christ and Judgment Day
Eucharist sacrament of Holy Communion; sacrifice of the Mass; Lord's Supper
evangelical counsels vows taken by members of religious order, including poverty, chastity, and obedience
Eve first woman, wife of Adam, mother of Cain and Abel
ex cathedra *Latin.* lit. from the chair; from seat of authority, applied to infallible pronouncements of pope
excommunication expulsion from Catholic Church
Fall, the lapse of humans into state of sinfulness through sins of Adam and Eve
Father one of three-part aspect of God
fundamentalism beliefs and practices based on literal interpretation of Bible, esp. among Protestants
genuflection bending of knee and crossing of oneself in reverence
golden rule Christ's maxim that we should do unto others as we would have them do unto us
gospel good news message of salvation and kingdom of God, esp. as announced to world by Christ; story of Christ's life and teachings
Hail Mary Catholic prayer repeated as atonement for sins; Ave Maria;
halo radiant light surrounding head of Jesus, Mary, or any saint
heaven dwelling place of God and resting place of souls of the faithful dead
hell dwelling place of Satan and place of eternal torture for souls of the damned
High Mass Catholic Mass in which celebrant and choir sing specified parts
Holy Communion sacrament in which one eats body and drinks blood of Jesus Christ; communion; Eucharist
Holy Grail cup or platter used by Christ at Last Supper
Holy Mother Virgin Mary
Holy Spirit one of three-part aspect of God
holy water water blessed by Catholic priest
host wafer representing flesh of Christ in communion
Immaculate Conception Catholic dogma that Mary was conceived without sin and that Christ was born to Virgin Mary through miraculous agency of God
indulgence removal of punishment for sin based on penance or on certain prayer practices; writ of forgiveness sold at one time by Catholic Church, protested by Martin Luther in 95 Theses
infallibility principle of papal immunity from liability to error and pontiff's unfailingly correct judgment in matters of faith
Inquisition medieval tribunal of Catholic Church intent on persecution of nonbelievers and those seen as heretics
Jesuits largest Roman Catholic order of men, founded by Ignatius Loyola in 1540, which played a role in Counter Reformation and later in missionary work; Society of Jesus
Jesus 1st century Jewish prophet from Nazareth and founder of Christianity
John the Baptist Nazarite prophet who baptized Jesus, later executed by Herod Antipas
Judas Iscariot one of Christ's twelve apostles, who betrayed him to Romans
Kyrie eleison short Greek liturgical prayer used in Mass
Last Supper Passover meal eaten by Jesus and his disciples on the eve of his Crucifixion
Latin language of Roman Catholic liturgy and Mass
lauds canonical hour in early morning, accompanied by psalms of praise, usu. recited with matins
Lent forty-day period of penitence prior to Easter
Lord's Prayer prayer beginning ""Our Father" that Jesus taught his disciples; Paternoster
Lord's Supper Eucharist; Holy Communion
Madonna Virgin Mary
Mary Virgin Mary
Mary Magdalene follower of Christ who witnessed his Crucifixion and was first to see him resurrected
Mass central religious rite of Roman Catholic Church, which reenacts Christ's Last Supper in celebration of Eucharist
matins first canonical hour of day, designated for morning prayer and psalms of praise
miracle event deviating from laws of nature and being sign of God's power or presence
Mother of God Virgin Mary
Nativity birth of Christ, esp. as depicted in art
Nicene Creed statement of Christian faith in 325A.D. stipulating that Jesus is only begotten Son of God and of one substance with the Father
Ninety-Five Theses document written by Martin Luther in 1517, protesting sale of indulgences, which began Protestant Reformation
nones fifth canonical hour, orig. midafternoon

novena Roman Catholic devotion consisting of nine separate days of prayer or services
obsecration prayer of supplication
Our Lady Virgin Mary
passion sufferings of Christ between night of the Last Supper and his death
Paternoster Lord's Prayer
patristics study of writings of church fathers
Pentecost festival celebrating descent of Holy Spirit on apostles
Peter chief among Christ's twelve apostles, founder of church in Rome and first pope
Prince of Darkness Satan
Protestant any of various Christian churches outside Roman Catholic Church
Protestant Reformation Christian schism within Catholic Church in 16th c. that resulted in Protestantism; Reformation
purgatory place where penitent souls are purified for ascent to heaven
Rastafarianism religious sect, orig. Jamaican, holding Haile Selassie to be the Messiah and Ethiopia to be Eden, and anticipating eventual return of blacks to Africa
Reformation Protestant Reformation
Requiem Mass Catholic funeral Mass
requiescat prayer for repose of the dead
Resurrection rising of Jesus from the dead after his Crucifixion and burial, an essential event in Christian belief
Roman Catholicism Christian church headed by pope as bishop of Rome
Sabbath holy day consecrated to worship of God, Sunday for Christians
Salvation Army evangelical and social service organization founded in England in 1865 by William Booth
Satan supreme evil spirit residing in hell
Second Coming Christ's promised return after Ascension
Society of Jesus Jesuits
Son Jesus Christ, Son of God
stations of the cross images representing fourteen stages of Christ's passion
stigmata bodily marks resembling wounds of crucified Christ that appear supernaturally on bodies of certain inspired persons
synod ecclesiastical council
transubstantiation change during consecration of bread and wine of Eucharist into Christ's body and blood
Trinity three aspects of God, as Father, Son, and Holy Spirit
Vatican see of bishop of Rome; city-state serving as headquarters of Roman Catholic Church
vespers evening religious service
virgin birth conception of Jesus by Virgin Mary through miraculous agency of God
Virgin Mary Mary, mother of Jesus by virgin birth; Holy Mother; Madonna; Our Lady
wafer thin piece of unleavened bread used in Eucharist; host

Judaism

Abraham patriarch and founder of ancient Hebrew nation
Aggadah nonlegal, narrative material in Talmud and Midrash containing parables and illustrative anecdotes
ark sacred gilded wood chest containing stone tablets bearing the Covenant; enclosure for Torah in synagogue
Ashkenazim German and Eastern European Jewry
bar mitzvah ceremony marking boy's reaching age of religious responsibility and maturity
bas mitzvah bat mitzvah
bat mitzvah ceremony marking girl's reaching age of religious responsibility and maturity; bas mitzvah
bris brith milah
brith milah rite of circumcision for male infant performed on eighth day after birth; bris
cabala mystical interpretation of Scriptures, with emphasis on secret meanings in text, by medieval Jews; kabala
Canaan ancient land promised by God to Abraham, occupying region that is now Israel; Holy Land
Chanukah Hanukkah
Chasidim Hasidim
Chosen People the Israelites, according to the Old Testament
Conservative form of the practice of Judaism, adapting ritual and traditional forms to modern life, less strict than Orthodox practice in adherence to rituals
covenant God's agreement to protect the faithful of Israel, as revealed in the Torah
daven (*vb*) recite Jewish prayers, esp. with nodding motion of upper body
David second king of Israel, who unified Jewish tribes and established capital at Jerusalem circa 1000 B.C.
Decalogue Ten Commandments
Diaspora historical exile of Jews from Israel to Babylonia in 6th c. B.C., when Judaism became distinguishable in modern form
Essenes Palestinian sect of Roman period characterized by ascetic practices and apocalyptic theology
Exodus flight of Israelites from Egypt led by Moses, forming second book of Pentateuch
First Temple Solomon's Temple at Jerusalem, destroyed by the Babylonians in 6th c. B.C.
Flood great deluge that covered Earth, described in Genesis
Gabriel archangel of Hebrew tradition, serving as divine messenger
Haggadah book containing liturgy and songs for Seder service at Passover
Halakhah body of Jewish law contained in the Bible, Talmud, and oral tradition
Hanukkah festival of lights celebrating victory of the Maccabees over the Syrians, observed for eight

days to commemorate miracle of oil lamp in temple at Jerusalem; Chanukah
Hasidim followers of form of Jewish mysticism that emphasizes strict rituals and religious zeal, originating in Eastern Europe in 18th c.; Chasidim
Hebrew classical language of Judaism; in modern form, an official language of Israel
Hebrews Semitic people of Palestine traditionally descended from Jacob and considered ancestors of modern Jewry; Israelites
Herod king of Judea from 37 to 4 B.C., builder of Second Temple at Jerusalem
High Holy Day Rosh Hashanah (New Year) and Yom Kippur (Day of Atonement)
Holy Land Canaan; Palestine
holy of holies innermost part of tabernacle
Israel northern kingdom of the Hebrews traditionally descended from Jacob, including ten of the Twelve Tribes; modern Jewish state founded in 1948; chosen people of God; name given to Jacob
Israelites Hebrews descended from Jacob and inhabiting ancient kingdom of Israel
Jacob second son of Isaac and father of patriarchs of twelve tribes, forefather of Hebrew people
Jewish calendar lunisolar calendar reckoned from 3761B.C., containing twelve months and 353 to 355 days, adjusted every nineteen years to match solar cycle, used to determine religious holidays
Jewry Jewish people
Judah southern kingdoms of the Hebrews, including the tribes of Judah and Benjamin; fourth son of Jacob or the tribe descended from him
Judeo-Christian tradition Western religion, culture, and heritage based on both Judaism and Christianity
kabalah cabala
Kaddish Hebrew prayer for the dead
Kol Nidre opening prayer of Yom Kippur
kosher (*adj*) following dietary and ceremonial laws governing what is fit to eat by Jews
Maccabees Jewish family led by Judas Maccabaeus, who regained Jerusalem from the Syrians in 164 B.C., as commemorated by Hanukkah, and lost it to Rome in 63 B.C.
Magen David Star of David
manna miraculous food supplied to Israelites during their journey through the wilderness
Masada mountaintop fortress overlooking Dead Sea that was site of Zealots' last stand against Romans circa 70 A.D.
Midrash rabbinic explanation and exegesis of Jewish Scripture focusing on nonliteral meaning of text
mikvah *Hebrew.* ritual bath of purification
minyan *Hebrew.* quorum of ten men needed for Jewish worship
Mishnah formal code of Jewish law, finalized in 3rd c.
mitzvah act that fulfills a commandment or injunction; in modern usage, any kindness
Moses prophet who led Israelites out of slavery and received God's law on Sinai
Noah tenth descendant of Adam, chosen by God to survive the Flood with sons and animals in ark
Orthodox form of Judaism strictly conforming to rituals and traditions of Torah and Talmud
Passover commemoration of deliverance of Israelites from slavery; Pesach
Pesach *Hebrew.* Passover
Pharisee member of ancient Jewish sect who strictly adhered to oral laws and traditions, distinguished from the Sadducees
Purim festival in which costumes and masks are worn in celebration of Jews' deliverance by Esther from massacre in Persia
Rabbinical Judaism form of Jewish practice founded after destruction of Second Temple in 70 A.D.
Reform modern practice of Judaism that does not require observance of rituals and emphasizes ethical aspects and rational thought
Rosh Hashanah Jewish New Year
Sabbath holy day consecrated to worship of God, Saturday for Jews
Sadducee member of ancient Jewish sect, composed chiefly of priests and aristocrats, who opposed the Pharisees
Sarah wife of Abraham
Saul first king of Israel
Second Temple Herod's temple at Jerusalem, destroyed by Romans in 70 A.D. except for Western Wall
Seder Passover service that recounts story of Exodus from Egypt through Haggadah
Sephardim medieval Spanish and Portuguese Jews who emigrated to North Africa, Turkey, and Palestine to escape the Inquisition; their descendants
shalom *Hebrew.* peace, used as a greeting or farewell
Shavuoth holiday commemorating revelation of Ten Commandments to Moses on Mount Sinai
Shema liturgical prayer recited daily expressing love of God
shul *Yiddish.* synagogue
Star of David six-pointed star that is symbol of Judaism, formed from two equilateral triangles; Magen David
Sukkoth Jewish holiday celebrating the fall harvest and commemorating shelters of Hebrews during Exodus
synagogue Jewish house of worship; shul
Ten Commandments fundamental rules for life, given by God to Moses; Decalogue
Twelve Tribes original groups of Hebrews descended from Jacob, who settled kingdoms of Israel and Judah
Wailing Wall Western Wall
Western Wall holy stone wall remaining from Second Temple, destroyed in 70 A.D., used as site of Jewish prayer in Jerusalem; Wailing Wall
yeshiva all-day school of religious and secular learning
Yiddish Germanic language with mixture of Hebrew words, written in Hebrew letters, used primarily by Ashkenazim of Eastern Europe
Yom Kippur day of atonement and repentance

following Rosh Hashanah, observed by fasting and prayer
Zealots Jewish sect of Roman period, characterized by revolutionary political ideology, that violently resisted Roman rule
Zion Palestine as Jewish homeland and symbol of Judaism, orig. hill in Jerusalem on which temples were built
Zionism worldwide Jewish movement, begun in late 19th century, that resulted in establishment of state of Israel

Islam

adhan call to prayer five times daily
Allah God; Supreme Being
Allah akbar God is great; rallying cry and call to faith of Islam
Ash-Shaytān Satan; the devil
ayatollah teacher, judge, and leader of Shi'ite sect
azan call to prayer made five times a day by the muezzin
baqa in Sufism, the pure spiritual state remaining after extinction of the self
Black Muslims Nation of Islam
caliph spiritual leader claiming succession from Muhammad
dervish mystic, esp. Sufi, engaging in ecstatic whirling and dancing
fana in Sufism, annihilation of the self and union with the Divine
Fatiha first chapter of the Koran, recited at beginning of each of the five daily prayers
fatwa authoritative opinion or judgment in Islamic law
Five Pillars of Faith five requirements of faith in Islam: profession, worship, alms-giving, pilgrimage to Mecca, and fasting during Ramadan
giaour person outside Islamic faith, esp. an infidel
hadith tradition, esp. relating to sayings and deeds of Muhammad and his followers
hafiz title of respect for a Muslim who knows the Koran by heart
hajj pilgrimage to Mecca
hajji Muslim who has made pilgrimage to Mecca
Hegira Muhammad's exodus from Mecca to Medina in 622A.D.
'Id al-Adha major four-day festival in last month of calendar
ihram white robes worn by male Muslims on their pilgrimage to Mecca
imam Muslim religious leader
iman act of faith in God
jihad holy war or crusade undertaken as Islamic duty
Ka'ba shrine in Great Mosque at Mecca that is objective of Muslim pilgrimage, regarded as House of God
kafir infidel or unbeliever
kamal perfection of Allah
kashf revelation
Koran Allah's revelation to Muhammad, arranged in written form as sacred Islamic text; Qur'an
Mahdi Muslim messiah who will establish reign of righteousness throughout world
Mahomet Muhammad
marabout hermit or holy man, esp. in North Africa
maulvi term of respect for expert in Islamic law in India
Mawlid celebration of birthday of Muhammad
Mecca holy city of Islam and birthplace of Muhammad, in what is now Saudi Arabia, toward which Muslims bow in prayer
Mohammed Muhammad
Moharram Islamic new year festival, in first month of lunar calendar
mosque Islamic house of worship
muezzin caller of faithful to prayer
mufti jurist who explains Islamic law
Muhajirun people who accompanied Muhammad on the Hegira
Muhammad 6th-7th c. A.D. Arab prophet and founder of Islam; Mahomet; Mohammed
mujtahid Shi'ite teacher with authority to interpret Islamic law and religion
mullah teacher of religious law; 'ulama
Muslim follow of Islam
nabi prophet
namaz ritual prayer
Nation of Islam organization of African-Americans advocating teaching of Islam and racial separatism
qadi Islamic scholar and judge in primarily religious court with civil authority
Qiyama last judgment
Qur'an Koran
Ramadan sacred month of fasting from sunrise to sunset during ninth month of lunar calendar
sayyid title of teacher descended from prophet Muhammad
shari'ah religious law and practical ordinances based on the Koran
sherif governor of Mecca, claiming descent from Muhammad
Shi'ah Shi'ite
Shi'ite member of the smaller of two major Islamic sects, given to fundamentalism, led by succession of imams; Shi'ah
Sufi follower of Sufism
Sufism mystical Islamic sect and system that seeks union with God through ecstatic trance, associated esp. with Iran
Sunni member of the larger of two major Islamic sects, based on orthodox law and theology of Koran and other works
sura any one of the 114 chapters of the Koran
tariqah spiritual path of Sufism
'ulama teacher and doctor of Muslim law and religion; mullah; Muslim religious teachers collectively
ummah people of the Muslim world
Wahhabi member of conservative Muslim group, found mainly in Saudi Arabia, practicing strict interpretation of Koran
wali saint

zahid ascetic
zuhd asceticism

Eastern Religions

ahimsa principle of nonviolence to living things (Hinduism, Jainism)
amrita beverage of immortality (Hinduism)
ananda perfect bliss (Hinduism)
anatta doctrine of nonexistence of personal soul (Buddhism)
anekantavada seeing issues from more than one side (Jainism)
anicca doctrine of impermanence through cycle of birth, growth, decay, and death (Buddhism)
atman individual self; principle of life (Hinduism)
Atman World Soul, from which individual souls derive
bardo plane of intermediate existence between death and rebirth, basis of Tibetan *Book of the Dead* (Vajrayana Buddhism)
bhakti devotional acts (Hinduism)
Bhakti religious movement centered around worship of gods (Hinduism)
bhikshu monk, esp. disciple of Buddha (Buddhism)
bodhi supreme knowledge and Enlightenment (Buddhism)
Bodhisattva enlightened person who postpones Nirvana in order to help others attain enlightenment (Buddhism)
bo tree sacred fig tree, under which the Buddha is believed to have attained enlightenment
Brahman ultimate reality, characterized as pure being, consciousness, and bliss (Hinduism)
Buddha 6th c. B.C. Indian, Siddhartha Gautama, whose teachings are basis of Buddhism; first of three Tisarana, or sources of refuge
bushido spiritual path of samurai class (Japan)
caste one of many subdivisions of the four religious and social classes of Hinduism: Brahman or priest, warrior, merchant/farmer, artist; varna
chakra one of seven sources of spiritual energy within body, tapped by yoga, lying at the intersection of cosmic order and human order (Hinduism)
cit pure consciousness (Hinduism)
Confucius Chinese philosopher of 6th-5th c. B.C. whose *Analects* and sayings form basis of Confucianism
dagoba shrine housing sacred relics
Dhamma teachings of the Buddha; truth; second of three Tisarana, or sources of refuge (Buddhism)
dharma cosmic law; everyday duty; spiritual doctrine (Hinduism)
dhyana meditation (Hinduism, Buddhism)
Diwali festival of lights in October (Hinduism)
dukkha first noble truth of Buddhism, that life is suffering caused by craving and attachment (Hinduism)
Eightfold Path eight pursuits leading to Enlightenment: understanding, motives, speech, action, livelihood, effort, intellectual activity, and contemplation (Buddhism)
Enlightenment spiritual awakening; awareness that releases one from cycle of dependent origination (Buddhism)
Ganges sacred river in northern India in which Hindus bathe
Golden Temple principal site of Sikh worship in India
guna three aspects of nature: passion, inertia, and purity (Hinduism)
Hare Krishna Vedic sect whose members engage in group chanting of Krishna's name, founded in United States in 1966
hatha yoga physical discipline using postures and breathing to effect changes in awareness (Hinduism)
Hinayana Theravada
jiva individual soul or ego self taken as manifestation of Atman (Hinduism)
jnana wisdom acquired through meditation and study (Hinduism)
karma action and results of action; moral cause and effect (Hinduism, Buddhism, Jainism, Sikhism)
karma yoga yoga of action (Hinduism)
koan baffling aphorism that inspires awakened mental state or disrupts discursive thought (Zen Buddhism)
lama monk or priest (Mahayana Buddhism)
Lao-tzu Chinese teacher of 6th c. whose *Tao Te Ching* forms basis of Taoism
Lingayat sect of southern India that does not recognize caste distinctions (Hinduism)
lotus symbolic water lily (Buddhism)
Mahavira last of Tirthankara and consolidator of Jainism in 5th c. B.C.
Mahayana later of Buddhism's two main branches, predominant in China, Japan, Korea, Tibet, and Vietnam, encompassing Vajrayana
mandala complex design of circle surrounding square, with symbolic and ritual power, used in temple design and as art form (Hinduism, Buddhism)
mantra holy word or sound used in meditation (Hinduism)
maya illusion; phenomenal world seen without awareness (Buddhism, Hinduism)
Middle Path middle way of life, between asceticism and luxury (Buddhism)
moksha liberation, release from cycle of ordinary experience and reincarnation of samsara (Buddhism, Hinduism, Jainism)
mudra sacred hand gesture (Hinduism, Buddhism)
Nanak founder of Sikhism in 16th c. India, who combined elements of Islam and Hinduism
naos ancient temple or shrine
neti neti *Sanskrit.* lit. neither this nor that; ineffable and undifferentiated nature of Brahman (Hinduism)
Nirvana release from endless cycle of rebirth into state of cosmic bliss (Buddhism)
Om mantric sound that is complete expression of

Brahman (Hinduism); also used in Vajrayana Buddhism
panth community of Sikhs
parinirvana Nirvana achieved at death of physical body
prajna knowledge, wisdom, spiritual insight, and enlightenment (Hinduism, Buddhism)
prana breath, sacred life force (Hinduism)
rahit ritual and ethical code enumerating five signs of faith: uncut hair, dagger, breeches, comb, and bracelet (Sikhism)
raja yoga yoga of kingly discipline and spirituality (Hinduism)
samadhi union of meditator with object of meditation; transcendence (Hinduism, Buddhism)
samsara cycle of rebirth and transmigration of souls (Hinduism); rebecoming and reexistence (Buddhism)
Sangha greater community of Buddhist practitioners; monastic order founded by the Buddha; third of three Tisarana, or sources of refuge
Sankhya yoga one of six leading systems of Hindu philosophy, stressing duality and reality of spirit and matter
sat realm of existence or being (Hinduism)
Satcitananda reality, combining sat (being), cit (consciousness), and ananda (bliss), seen through qualities of Brahman (Hinduism)
satori enlightenment, awakening (Zen Buddhism)
stupa memorial mound that may contain relics of saint (Buddhism)
Sunyata that which exists absolutely and without predication (Buddhism)
t'ai chi ch'uan neo-Confucian concept of single, ultimate principle and source of all things; stylized meditation exercise based on this concept (China)
Tantra tradition incorporating secret ritual with mystical practices rooted in harmony of masculine and feminine aspects of cosmos, often expressed in sexual ritual (Hinduism, Buddhism)
tantrayana Vajrayana (Hinduism)
Tao the way or path to self-realization and enlightenment (Taoism)
tapas yoga techniques of breath control and bodily conditioning for greatest creative power (Hinduism)
Theravada earlier of Buddhism's two main branches, predominant in Sri Lanka, Burma, and Southeast Asia; Hinayana
Tirthankara twenty-four chronologically sequential Jain sages, last of whom is Mahavira, consolidator of Jainism
Tisarana three levels or sources of refuge: Buddha, Dhamma, and Sangha (Buddhism)
tope shrine or stupa (Buddhism)
Trimurti divinity in three aspects of Brahma, Vishnu, and Shiva (Hinduism)
upaya instructional device such as koan (Buddhism)
Vaishnava Bhakti sect devoted to worship of Vishnu (Hinduism)
Vajrayana tantric Buddhism, with mystical aspects, emphasizing male and female symbolism and deities, predominant in northern India, Tibet, and Nepal; tantrayana
varna caste (Hinduism)
Vedanta classical philosophy in fulfillment of Vedas, dealing with nature of Brahman in dualistic (Dvaita) and nondualistic (Advaita) doctrines (Hinduism)
vinaya monastic code of discipline (Buddhism)
Way, the Tao (Taoism)
yang cosmic force of masculine, active, light, warm, contracting, creative energy of heaven (Taoism)
yantra diagram for meditation (Hinduism)
yin cosmic force of feminine, passive, dark, cold, expansive, material energy of earth (Taoism)
yin and yang two modes of cosmic energy that form dynamic Tao, or way of the universe, and combine in various proportions in all things
yoga spiritual discipline and practice involving meditation, physical postures, breathing exercises, and devotional acts: hatha (physical), jnana (wisdom and intellect), karma (action), raja (kingly spirituality), and sankhya (philosophic) (Hinduism)
zazen cross-legged meditation practice (Zen Buddhism)
zendo retreat for meditation; monastery (Zen Buddhism)

God and Divinity

Adonai *Hebrew.* the Lord, God
Agnus Dei figure of a lamb as representation of Jesus Christ
Ahura Mazda Supreme Being, representing forces of good and evil (Zoroastrianism)
Allah God, Supreme Being (Islam)
All-Knowing God the omniscient (Christianity)
Almighty God the omnipotent (Christianity)
Atman soul, self (Hinduism)
Brahma god of creation, mediating between Vishnu and Shiva (Hinduism)
Buddha enlightened being (Buddhism)
Christ anointed Jesus Christ, Savior and Son of God, second element of Trinity (Christianity)
Creator Supreme Being, God
deity supreme being, god, divine being
demigod half divine being, born of union of god and mortal
deva a god or divinity (Buddhism, Hinduism); one of an order of evil spirits (Zoroastrianism)
Divine Mind Supreme Being (Christian Science)
divinity deity, god, divine being
earth mother great mother, goddess
Father God, first element of the Trinity (Christianity)
First Cause Supreme Being as creator of universe
god immortal being or personification of natural or psychic force
God Supreme Being (Christianity)
goddess female god or deity

Godhead essence of God, Supreme Being; Holy Trinity
God the Father Christian God in aspect of creator of universe and humankind
God the Son Jesus Christ
Good Lord usu. the Good Lord; God (Christianity)
Good Shepherd Jesus Christ
Great Mother ancient nature goddess (pre-Hellenic Europe, Near East)
Holy Ghost Holy Spirit
Holy Spirit spirit of God, third element of the Trinity; Holy Ghost; Spirit
Holy Trinity tripartite nature of God: Father, Son, and Holy Spirit; Godhead (Christianity)
idol image or representation of deity, or object made into god
Immanuel *Hebrew.* lit. God is with us; name attributed to Christ by Christians
Indra sky, storm god (Hinduism)
Jahweh Yahweh
Jehovah Yahweh, God (Judaism)
Jesu Jesus
Jesus Christ Son of God and Savior of humankind, both fully human and fully divine
kami gods, spirits of the divine (Shinto)
King of Heaven God (Christianity)
King of kings Jesus Christ
Krishna avatar of Vishnu (Hinduism)
Lamb of God Jesus Christ
living Christ Christ as present through the Eucharist
Lord Supreme Being, God; Christ
Lord of hosts Jehovah, God
Lord of lords Jesus Christ
Mahdi expected restorer of Islam
Maker God
Messiah Jesus Christ; expected deliverer of Jewish people
Nazarene Jesus Christ
numen divine spirit
Omnipotent (*adj*) all-powerful: attribute of God (Christianity)
Omnipresent (*adj*) all-present: attribute of God (Christianity)
Omniscient (*adj*) all-knowing: attribute of God (Christianity)
pantheon group of gods
Paraclete Holy Spirit
Prince of Peace Jesus Christ
Rama incarnation of Vishnu (Hinduism)
Redeemer Jesus Christ
Sat Guru God (Sikhism)
Savior Jesus Christ
Shaddai *Hebrew.* God
Shiva god of destruction (Hinduism); Siva
Siva Shiva
Son of God Jesus Christ
Son of Man Jesus Christ
Spirit Holy Spirit
Supreme Being God; deity responsible for creation
Tathagata Buddha's name for himself
Trimurti triad of gods Brahma, Vishnu, and Siva (Hinduism)
Trinity god in three aspects: Father, Son, and Holy Spirit (Christianity); creator/mediator, preserver, and destroyer (Hinduism); Holy Trinity
Vishnu god the preserver (Hinduism)
Yahweh *Hebrew.* God in Old Testament; Jahweh
Yama god of the dead (Hinduism)

Practice and Doctrine

ablution ritual bathing of body or washing of object or person
absolution forgiveness for sins
agnosticism belief that God's existence is unknowable; nescience
amen solemn ratification of faith used at end of prayer by Christians and Jews
anathema curse, ban, or excommunication pronounced by religious authority; offering consecrated to deity
animism belief that natural objects and phenomena have souls
antinomianism belief in Christian faith alone as necessary for salvation, without necessity of moral law
apotheosis deification, esp. by elevating mortal to god
asceticism religious practice of strict discipline and self-denial
atheism nonbelief in God
atonement reconciliation with God through forgiveness of sins; suffering and death of Jesus for human sins Christ
autocephalous (*adj*) having its own chief bishop but in communion with other Orthodox churches
benediction blessing
benison benediction or blessing
blasphemy sacrilege; intentional offense to God
blessing act of consecrating or wishing God's favor upon; benediction; benison
canon religious code or doctrine; canon law, authoritative texts
celibacy abstention from marriage and sexual relations, as by priest
chastity abstention from sexual activity
commandment one of Biblical Ten Commandments
conclave meeting of Roman Catholic cardinals to select pope
concordat ecclesiastical agreement between pope and sovereign
confession disclosure of sins to achieve absolution
consecration dedication of person or object to sacred use
conventicle assembly for worship, esp. secret or unsanctioned one
conversion formal change from one religion to another
Creation formation of Earth and beginnings of humanity as told of in sacred texts, esp. fundamentalist view that God created world in seven days as in Genesis

creationism doctrine that matter and all its forms were created by an omnipotent God, esp. literal belief in story of Creation in Genesis
creed formal statement or system of religious beliefs, esp. for specific denomination
cult particular system of religious practice or religious group, usu. unorthodox or deviating from major faith and practicing in an absolute, oppressive, or obsessive way, often under the direction of a charismatic leader
deadly sins seven sins held to be fatal to spiritual progress: pride, covetousness, lust, anger, gluttony, envy, and sloth
deism belief in transcendent God as creator without further intervention in human affairs
devotions religious practices, esp. prayers
dispensation God's ordering of affairs of the world; exemption from practices authorized by religious authority
ditheism belief in two equally powerful gods; belief in existence of antagonistic forces for good and evil, as in Zoroastrianism
doctrine religious teaching
dogma religious teaching formally stated as creed or article of faith
dualism doctrine of two independent eternal principles; distinction between conventional and ultimate reality in Hinduism
ecclesiastical (*adj*) relating to church as formal and established institution
ecumenical (*adj*) pertaining to whole Christian church, esp. promoting its unity
ethics fundamental moral principles that guide one's behavior toward others and world at large
evangelize (*vb*) spread the gospel
Evensong evening prayer
exegesis analysis and interpretation of Scripture
expiation atonement for one's sins
extreme unction Christian sacrament of anointing one who is near death; sacrament of the sick
faith emotional belief in divine order as ultimate reality, usu. involving existence of God and practice of specific religious doctrine, not requiring proof
faith healing miraculous healing by power of God
fast abstention from food, usu. as religious discipline
fideism exclusive reliance on faith and exclusion of science and philosophy in religious matters
grace undeserved love and mercy of God toward humankind; sanctifying energy mediated by God's word in Protestantism and through sacraments in Catholicism
hagiography writings and critical studies of saints
hagiology literature or biography dealing with lives of saints
hajj pilgrimage to Mecca (Islam)
hallelujah expression of praise for God
healing curing of physical affliction through faith and prayer
henotheism allegiance to one god while allowing worship of any of several other gods by family or tribe
heresy unorthodox or dissenting religious belief
hermeneutics science of theological interpretation
heterodoxy unorthodox theological views
holy orders Christian sacrament of ordination as priest or deacon
hosanna cry of love for God
hymn sacred song in praise of God
idolatry worship of physical image of deity
indigenous religion religion limited to a particular region
interdenominational (*adj*) common to or involving different religious denominations
invocation act of calling upon deity, usu. in prayer
isagogics branch of theology introductory to Bible study and exegesis
kenosis doctrine that Christ gave up His divine attributes to experience human suffering
laying on of hands rite in which cleric places hands on head of person being confirmed or ordained, also used in faith healing
libation pouring out of wine to honor deity
libertinism indulgence of flesh as religious expression
litany prayer in form of call and response, usu. between minister and congregation
literalism literal interpretation of Bible
liturgy rites of religious worship
love feast meal of fellowship and charity taken as rite
mantra holy word or sound used in meditation (Hinduism)
matrimony Christian sacrament of marriage before God
meditation spiritual and mental discipline or exercise involving contemplation and awakened state of awareness
monasticism system and way of life of monks
monotheism belief in a single God
morals specific attitudes and behaviors derived from broad ethical principles and beliefs
mortal sin serious, willful transgression against law of God that deprives soul of divine grace until absolution and possibly results in eternal damnation
nescience agnosticism
nondualism lack of distinction between conventional and ultimate realities (Hinduism)
oblation offering to God of bread and wine in Eucharist
observance recognition and celebration of religious rite
offertory offering of bread and wine before consecration at Eucharist service; period for collection during worship service
ordination Christian sacrament received upon joining priesthood
original sin sin or evil innate in humankind, stemming from Adam's sin
orthodoxy correct religious belief according to specific doctrine
orthopraxy correct religious behavior and rituals according to specific doctrine

paganism belief in god other than Christian, Jewish, or Muslim God
pantheism belief that God is manifested by and throughout the universe; worship of eclectic body of deities
penance specific act of repentance for sins; Catholic sacrament
Pentecostalism belief in and practice of revivalism, baptism, speaking in tongues, and faith healing, with emphasis on activity of Holy Spirit (Christianity)
pilgrimage journey to sacred place to reaffirm religious faith
polytheism belief in and worship of more than one god
prayer address, petition, or offering to God or deity
preach (*vb*) deliver a sermon proclaiming the gospel or stating religious and moral truths
predestination notion that salvation of human soul is preordained by God
preterition Calvinist doctrine that God passes over those not elected to salvation
proselytize (*vb*) attempt to convert others to one's beliefs or religion
psalm any sacred song or hymn from Bible's Book of Psalms used in worship
purification ceremonial cleansing of spiritual pollution
redemption salvation and deliverance from evil, esp. through Christ's act of mercy toward humankind
reincarnation rebirth of soul in another body (Hinduism)
repentance contrition for sins
retreat period of seclusion for religious exercises and meditation
revival evangelistic rekindling of religious fervor
rite solemn ceremonial practice following specific form
ritual specified form, manner, and language of religious ceremony
sacrament religious act or practice symbolizing conferment of divine grace; Catholic sacraments are baptism, confirmation, Eucharist, penance, extreme unction, holy orders, and matrimony; Protestants include only baptism and communion
sacrament of the sick extreme unction
sacrifice religious offering made to deity
sacrilege act or statement that degrades the sacred
salvation deliverance from damnation, liberation from sin and its punishment; redemption and reconciliation to God
schism split or division over orthodoxy in religious group, esp. Great Schism, as between Roman and Eastern churches in 9th c. and during period of rival popes in 14th to 15th c.
scholasticism philosophical system of 11th to 15th c. that attempted intellectual analysis of religious doctrine, based on teachings of St. Thomas Aquinas and St. Augustine
scripturalism detailed, often literal, analysis of the Bible
sect religious group deviating from orthodox faith, usu. having specific practices prescribed by its leader
secularism system or philosophy that rejects religious necessity or interpretation
sermon religious discourse delivered by clergyman as part of service
sign of the cross cross formed in the air by moving hand rapidly from head to chest and shoulder to shoulder as sign of prayer
solemn vow irrevocable public vow taken by clergy and members of religious orders in Catholic Church committing them to observe rule of an order, often against ownership of property and marriage
supplication earnest prayer of petition
syncretism attempted reconciliation of elements from two or more religions to create new religion
tent meeting camp meeting
theism belief in God; belief in gods
theology systematic study of God and religious faith and practices
theonomy state of individual or society that regards its own nature as being in accord with divine nature
theurgy working of divine or supernatural agency in human affairs
tithing paying one-tenth of one's income to support church
total immersion baptism in which candidate's entire body is immersed in water
tradition source of authority, doctrines, practices, and institutions of religion, such as Mosaic law in Judaism, teachings of Christ in Christianity, and Koranic revelation in Islam
trine immersion baptism in which candidate is immersed three times, once for each part of Trinity
unction anointing with oil as consecration
unfrock (*vb*) deprive priest of right to exercise office
venial sin sin that does not deprive soul of sanctifying grace, unlike mortal sin
viaticum Eucharist given to person near death
virtues seven natural and cardinal virtues: faith, hope, charity, prudence, justice, temperance, and fortitude
worship showing honor and devotion to a deity

Individuals and Titles

abbé member of secular clergy, esp. in France
abbot superior of monastery
acolyte altar server; member of highest-ranking of four minor orders in Catholic Church
agnostic one who does not know whether God exists
altar boy boy assisting celebrant in liturgical service but not formally inducted as acolyte
altar girl girl who performs functions of altar boy
anchorite religious hermit or extreme ascetic
angel divine being, esp. messenger of God
apostate deserter of religious faith

apostle messenger or preacher of religious principles, esp. one of twelve original followers of Jesus
archangel chief angel; one of seven chief angels in Bible
archbishop chief bishop (Christianity)
archdeacon chief deacon, ranking below bishop (Christianity)
archpriest chief priest
Arhat one who has attained Nirvana through ascetic practices (Buddhism)
atheist nonbeliever in God
avatar deity in physical form on Earth (Hinduism)
ayatollah teacher, judge, or leader of Shi'ite sect, with superior training in theology and law (Islam)
believer person with faith, esp. in specific religion
bhikshu monk observing rules of his order, such as vows of poverty (Buddhism)
bishop high-ranking ecclesiastical officer with authority over diocese and its clergy (Christianity)
Bodhisattva enlightened person who postpones Nirvana in order to help others attain Enlightenment (Buddhism)
bonze monk (Buddhism)
brother fellow member of religious order (Christianity)
buddha enlightened being with fully realized awareness of true nature of existence; statue of the Buddha used as symbol in Buddhism
caliph spiritual leader claiming succession from Muhammad
cantor singer or leader of choir (Judaism)
cardinal ecclesiastical officer ranking above bishop, usu. an archbishop; member of Roman Catholic Church's College of Cardinals
celebrant person performing rite, esp. priest officiating at Eucharist
cenobite member of religious order living in convent or monastery
chaplain person conducting religious services and performing sacraments in place other than church, as in military field or hospital, or for an organization
chela disciple of a guru (Hinduism)
cherub one of second order of angels, represented as winged child
clergy ordained priests, ministers, and rabbis, as distinct from laity; clerics
cleric member of the clergy
colporteur person who travels about to sell Bibles
communicant church member entitled to receive the Eucharist
congregation gathering of people as religious community, esp. for specific services in church
convert person adopting or changing religion
convocation consultative assembly of Christian clergy
council assembly of bishops
crucifer carrier of cross at head of procession
crusader participant in medieval expeditions to Holy Land to reclaim it from Muslims
curate clergyman
curé parish priest in France
Dalai Lama chief lama of Tibetan Buddhism
deacon minister or layman assisting priest (Christianity)
dean Roman Catholic priest supervising one district of diocese; head of chapter of cathedral church
dervish Islamic mystic, esp. Sufi, engaging in ecstatic whirling and dancing
devil's advocate official of Catholic Church who examines evidence given in demand for canonization
dewal priest (Hinduism)
disciple follower of religious teacher or leader
ecclesiastic member of clergy or religious order
elder minister or esteemed congregation member
Eminence title of honor applied to cardinals of Catholic Church
eparch bishop or metropolitan of administrative subdivision of Orthodox Eastern Church
eremite member of religious order living as hermit or recluse
evangelist itinerant or special preacher of Protestant denomination
Evangelist any of the writers of the four Gospels
exarch bishop of Orthodox Eastern Church, ranking below patriarch and above metropolitan
fakir monk or wandering mendicant believed to possess magical powers (Hinduism, Islam)
father form of address for priest
father confessor priest who administers sacrament of confession
friar member of mendicant order
gentile person who is not Jewish
giaour person outside Islamic faith, esp. infidel
guru spiritual master, esp. Hindu
hajji Muslim who has made pilgrimage to Mecca
heathen pagan, esp. nonbeliever in Christian, Hebrew, or Muslim God
heavenly host angels and others dwelling with God in heaven
hegumen head of Orthodox Eastern monastery
heretic person rejecting orthodox or accepted religious beliefs
hermit religious recluse
high priest chief priest; primary priest of ancient Jewish Levitical priesthood
Holy Roller derogatory description of member of Pentecostal sect, based on frenetic quality of services
illuminati person claiming spiritual grace or enlightenment
imam leader (Islam)
infidel disbeliever in specific religious doctrine, esp. that of Islam
Jesus freak *Informal.* member of fundamentalist group, usu. comprised of young people, that emphasizes intense personal devotion to Jesus Christ
kaffir infidel or nonbeliever in Islamic faith
laity congregation of people ministered to by clergy
lama priest (Tibetan Buddhism, Lamaism)
magi priests (ancient Persia)
maharishi great teacher or wise man (Hinduism)
mahatma great soul, sage (Hinduism)
manciple steward of a monastery

martyr person put to death for defending religious principles
mendicant member of religious order living by alms or charity
Messiah expected deliverer of Jewish people; Jesus Christ
metropolitan bishop of diocese of Orthodox Eastern Church, ranking below exarch
minister clergyman or -woman, esp. Protestant one
ministry all ministers of a specific religion
missionary Christian proselytizer in non-Christian region
mohel *Hebrew.* person who performs brith milah, or rite of circumcision
monk man living in religious order, either Christian or Buddhist
Monophysite person who believes that Christ has one nature, partly divine and partly human
Monsignor title conferred on certain Catholic prelates
Mother Superior head nun of convent
muezzin caller of faithful to prayer (Islam)
mufti jurist who explains Islamic law
mullah teacher of religious law (Islam)
neophyte recent convert to a faith
novice person undergoing probationary period before taking vows of religious order
nullifidian person without religious faith, esp. skeptic
nun woman living in cloistered religious order, either Christian or Buddhist
padre father or priest; chaplain in military service
pagan heathen, nonbeliever in Christian, Hebrew, or Muslim God; formerly, follower of ancient Roman religion
palmer pilgrim returning from Holy Land carrying a palm branch, esp. in Middle Ages
Pariah member of lowest caste in India or Burma (Hinduism)
parishioner member or inhabitant of parish
parson rector; Protestant clergyman
pastor priest, minister, or spiritual shepherd of congregation; shepherd
patriarch bishop of Eastern Orthodox Church; Roman Catholic bishop next in rank to pope; church father
penitent person who confesses sin and seeks repentance
pilgrim person traveling to sacred place as affirmation of devotion, usu. Christian to Holy Land or Muslim to Mecca
pillar saint stylite
pontiff pope
pope bishop of Rome and head of Roman Catholic Church
preacher member of clergy, esp. Christian one; predicant
precentor person, sometimes of the clergy, who leads church choir or conducts choral service
precisian strict adherent to moral or religious standards, esp. Puritan of 16th or 17th c.
predicant preacher
prelate ecclesiastic of high order, such as bishop or archbishop
preterite those passed over by God; those not elected for salvation
priest ordained member of clergy, official minister
primate archbishop or bishop ranking first among the bishops of a province or country
prior superior ranking next to abbot in monastery
prophet messenger of God, esp. one revealing judgment of God
proselyte new convert to a religion
provost chief dignitary of a cathedral
pundit learned, religious man (Hinduism)
qadi Islamic judge, scholar, and religious teacher
rabbi leader of a Jewish congregation; title of respect for Jewish scholar or teacher
rabbinate office of a rabbi; all rabbis collectively
Reb *Yiddish.* form of address or title for rabbi
recreant one who renounces faith
rector member or clergy in charge of parish
reprobate one who is damned
Reverend form of address for member of clergy
rishi religious sage (Hinduism)
sadhu holy man (Hinduism)
sage wise, pious person
saint holy person consecrated by religious body
sannyasi wandering beggar and ascetic (Hinduism)
sayyid title given to teacher descended from prophet Muhammad (Islam)
seminarian person studying to become member of the clergy
sensei spiritual teacher (Japan)
seraph one of the highest order of angels, usu. pictured as six-winged
sexton person who watches over church property and usu. rings bells for services
shaman person with spiritual insight and authority, empowered to conduct religious rites in nativist religions
shepherd pastor
sister member of woman's religious order; form of address for nun
starets religious teacher or counselor
stylite ascetic saint living atop pillar; pillar saint
subdeacon cleric ranking below deacon
swami religious teacher, holy man (Hinduism)
televangelist evangelist who preaches over television
tertiary lay member of religious order, usu. living in its community
theologian person who has studied religious faith and practices
tulku reincarnation of holy man (Tibetan Buddhism)
twice-born (*adj*) pertaining to a person of Brahman caste; pertaining to a person who has undergone reincarnation (Hinduism)
vicar member of Episcopal clergy in charge of mission chapel; representative of Anglican prelate with broad pastoral duties
votary person bound by religious vows
wali saint (Islam)
yogi practitioner of yoga philosophy and discipline (Hinduism)
zahid ascetic (Islam)

Zealot member of militant Jewish sect that flourished between 100 B.C. and 100 A.D.

Structures and Institutions

abbey monastery
altar raised platform where sacrifices and offerings are made to God
apse recessed, vaulted niche at end of choir in church
archdiocese area of jurisdiction of archbishop
basilica early Catholic church
bema sanctuary of Orthodox Eastern Church; altar in Jewish synagogue
benefice ecclesiastical office guaranteeing fixed income
bethel church for seamen
cathedral church that is diocesan seat of bishop or archbishop, often large and elaborately decorated
chancel area near altar reserved for clergy and choir
chancery office of diocese
chapel small house of worship associated with larger church
cloister monastery, esp. area within monastery restricted to its members
College of Cardinals chief ecclesiastical body of Roman Catholic Church, advisory to pope and including all cardinals
confessional stall in which Catholics make confession of their sins to unseen priest
convent residence for nuns or sisters of religious order; nunnery
curia the papal court
dagoba shrine housing sacred relics of Buddha
diocese territorial jurisdiction of bishop
divinity school Protestant seminary
Holy See See of Rome; Vatican
house of worship church, synagogue, or temple
jube screen separating chancel from nave, often supporting a rood
mandira Hindu temple
mihrab prayer niche in Islamic mosque
misericord room in monastery set aside for monks permitted relaxation of monastic rules
mission local church or parish supported by larger religious organization, usu. in effort to convert nonbelievers
monastery home for persons of particular religious order, esp. monks; abbey
mosque Islamic house of worship
naos ancient temple or shrine
nave main axis of church or cathedral
nunnery convent
order community of monks or nuns following specific rules; major Catholic orders include Benedictine, Dominican, Franciscan, Jesuit, Marist, Paulist, and Trappist
pagoda Buddhist or Shinto temple
pantheon temple dedicated to all gods
papacy institution and office of the pope
parish local church or ecclesiastical district
parsonage house provided by church for Protestant clergyman, such as parson
pew bench or seat on which several persons sit in church
priory religious house governed by prior or prioress, usu. part of an abbey
pulpit lectern from which preacher conducts religious service, esp. interpreting the Bible as God's word
rectory residence of rector or parish priest
sacristy room in church for storage of sacred vessels and for clergy's preparation for services
sanctuary sacred portion of church surrounding altar
sanctum any sacred or hallowed place
see seat of bishop's office and authority
See of Rome seat of power of the pope, who has jurisdiction over Catholic churches throughout world; Holy See; Vatican
seminary institution providing training for ministry or esp. for priesthood
shrine place of devotion to saint or deity
shul *Yiddish.* synagogue
stupa memorial mound that may contain relics of saint (Buddhism)
Sunday school place of religious instruction on Sundays for children, esp. Christian
synagogue Jewish house of worship; shul; temple
synod church council
tabernacle house of worship, esp. large tent for evangelical services; portable sanctuary in which Ark of the Covenant was carried by Israelites after the Exodus
temple edifice for religious services; Jewish synagogue; shrine to specific deity or saint; primary locus for a religion
tope dome-shaped Buddhist monument for relics
Vatican Holy See of the pope; city-state serving as headquarters of Roman Catholic Church
vestry room in church for storage of vestments

Sacred Texts and Objects

Abhidhamma Pitaka third section of Pali Canon, consisting of abstract philosophical treatises (Buddhism)
Adigranth Granth (Sikhism)
American Standard Version American version of Bible, published in 1901
Analects text of teachings of Confucius
Angas sacred texts of Jainism
Apocrypha writings originally within the Bible, but judged unsuitable for inclusion by rabbinical or church authorities
aspergillum brush or small perforated container for sprinkling holy water (Catholicism)
aspersorium vessel for holding holy water (Catholicism)
Atharva-Veda one of ancient Aryan Vedic sacred texts (Hinduism)
Avesta book of sacred writings of Zoroastrianism
Bhagavad-Gita part of Indian epic poem the Mahabharata, written between 200 B.C. and 200A.D., in form of dialogue between hero and

avatar Krishna (Hinduism)
Bible sacred texts of Old and New Testaments, source of teachings and religious authority for Judaism and Christianity; Christian Bible
Book of Common Prayer official book of services and prayers for Anglican communion
Book of Mormon sacred book of Mormon church, revealed by Joseph Smith
Book of the Dead book of prayers and charms for use of soul in afterworld (ancient Egypt)
Brahmana ritual text of Vedic period (Hinduism)
breviary book of prayers, hymns, and psalms used by priests in daily office
butsu representation or figure of the Buddha
censer ornamental container in which incense is burned; thurible
chalice Eucharistic cup
chrism consecrated oil used in baptism and other sacraments
chrisom white cloth or robe worn by person during baptism
ciborium vessel containing Eucharistic bread or host
cloth attire worn by clergy
crosier bishop's or abbot's staff
Dead Sea Scrolls scrolls dating from Essene period, containing partial texts of Hebrew Bible or Old Testament and some non-Biblical scrolls, in Hebrew and Aramaic
Dhammapada text containing essential teachings of the Buddha
Epistle extract from Epistles of New Testament, usu. attributed to Paul, used in Eucharistic service
Five Classics basic ethical texts of Confucianism, attributed to Confucius, including I Ching, Book of Rites, Book of History, Book of Songs, and Spring and Autumn Annals
font vessel for holy water, often of stone
Gospels story of life and teachings of Christ in first four books of New Testament
Granth sacred scripture of Sikhism; Adigranth
habit attire worn by clergy and members of religious orders
Hagiographa third part of Hebrew Bible containing the Psalms, Proverbs, Job, Ruth, Esther, and other books besides the Pentateuch and Prophets; Ketuvim; the Writings
Hebrew Bible Old Testament: Torah, Prophets, and Hagiographa
Holy Scriptures sacred writings of Old or New Testament or both together
hymnal book of Christian hymns
I Ching Book of Changes, one of Five Classics of Chinese Confucian canon, dealing esp. with divination through trigrams that reflect yin and yang
icon powerful image of sacred personage, usu. painted on wooden panel (Orthodox Eastern Church)
Jataka stories and fables concerning previous lives of the Buddha
Kama Sutra teachings of Hindu god of erotic love Kama
Ketuvim *Hebrew.* Hagiographa
King James Bible edition of Christian Bible published during reign of King James I of England circa 1610
Koran Islamic holy book, composed of 114 chapters or suras, believed to have been revealed to Muhammad by Allah; Qur'an
Law, the Pentateuch; Torah
lectionary book listing selections of sacred texts to be read in divine service
Mahabharata epic containing Hindu religious text Bhagavad-Gita
megillah *Hebrew.* scroll of Biblical books, esp. Book of Esther, read on Purim
menorah candelabrum, esp. one with nine branches, used at Hanukkah (Judaism)
mezuzah scroll with words from Deuteronomy, placed in small container affixed to doorjamb (Judaism)
missal large book of prayers and authorized readings for celebration of Catholic Mass
Nevi'im *Hebrew.* Prophets
New Testament portion of Bible that describes life and teachings of Christ and his followers, through Gospels and Epistles, written circa 100 A.D.
Old Testament portion of Bible that describes God's covenant with the Israelites, made up of the Torah or Pentateuch, Prophets, and Hagiographa, compiled between 1000 B.C. and 100 B.C.; Christian name for Hebrew Bible
Oral Law Talmud
Pali Canon ancient Buddhist sacred texts, orig. recorded from oral traditions in 1st c. B.C., consisting of sermons, rules of monastic order, and philosophical treatises; Tripitaka
Pentateuch first five books of Hebrew Bible; Torah
phylactery either of two small leather containers holding scriptural passages, worn on left arm and forehead during prayers by Jewish men; both phylacteries comprise the tefillin
Pitaka any of the three divisions of the Pali Canon: Abhidhamma Pitaka (philosophy), Sutta Pitaka (sermons), and Vinaya Pitaka (rules of monastic order) (Buddhism)
prayer book formal book of prayers, esp. Book of Common Prayer
Prophets second part of Hebrew Bible, containing books by prophets such as Isaiah, Jeremiah, and Ezekiel; Nevi'im
Psalter book of Psalms
pseudepigrapha Christian and Jewish sacred texts not recognized in the canon and considered possibly spurious
Qur'an Koran
Ramayana second great Hindu epic, containing story of Prince Rama
reliquary container or shrine for sacred relics
Revelation book of New Testament describing Apocalypse
Rig Veda oldest of ancient Aryan Vedic sacred texts (Hinduism)
rosary string of beads used by Roman Catholics, Hindus, and Buddhists for counting prayers or mantras
rubric directions for conducting religious service

sacred text writings that are source of authority and legitimacy for a religion
Sama-Veda one of ancient Aryan Vedic sacred texts (Hinduism)
Scripture sacred text
Septuagint oldest Greek version of Old Testament
shofar ram's horn sounded on Rosh Hashanah (Judaism)
stoup basin for holy water, usu. located near entrance of church (Christianity)
sutra religious text, esp. collection of aphorisms on any of various aspects of life (Hinduism, Jainism); any of the Buddha's sermons (Buddhism)
Sutta Pitaka second section of Pali Canon, consisting of sermons of the Buddha and stories about him (Buddhism)
Synoptic Gospels first three gospels in New Testament: Matthew, Mark, and Luke
tallith fringed prayer shawl (Judaism)
Talmud text of canon and civil law and rabbinical teachings, incorporating the non-Scriptural oral law, compiled in 6th c., codified in Jerusalem and Babylon; Oral Law (Judaism)
Tantra any of several books of esoteric doctrine regarding rituals and meditation (Hinduism)
Tao Te Ching teachings of Lao-tzu, basic text of Taoism, composed of eighty-one brief chapters describing the way of the Tao
tefillin both phylacteries (Judaism)
thurible censer
Torah first five books of Hebrew Bible, containing entire written body of Jewish law and wisdom sealed for all time in the form of holy scrolls; the Law; Pentateuch
Tripitaka Pali Canon (Buddhism)
Upanishads philosophical commentaries forming final portion of Vedic texts, written beginning circa 900 B.C.
Vedas ancient, sacred Hindu scriptures composed of Atharva-Veda, Rig-Veda, Sama-Veda, and Yajur-Veda, compiled between 1000 B.C. and 500 B.C.
vestment ceremonial garment worn by clergy during religious rite
Vinaya Pitaka first section of Pali Canon, consisting of the rules of the monastic order (Buddhism)
Vulgate Latin version of Christian Scriptures
Word usu. **the Word**; the Word of God; the Bible
Writings, the Hagiographa
Yajur-Veda one of ancient Aryan Vedic sacred texts (Hinduism)
yarmulke skullcap worn by Jewish males, esp. during prayer and religious study
Zend-Avesta Zoroastrian sacred texts
Zohar definitive text of the cabala, consisting chiefly of interpretations of the Pentateuch (Judaism)

Books of the Bible

Old Testament

Genesis, Exodus, Leviticus, Numbers, Deuteronomy, Joshua, Judges, Ruth, I Samuel, II Samuel, I Kings, II Kings, I Chronicles, II Chronicles, Ezra, Nehemiah, Esther, Job, Psalms, Proverbs, Ecclesiastes, Song of Solomon (also Song of Songs, Canticle of Canticles), Isaiah, Jeremiah, Lamentations, Ezekiel, Daniel, Hosea, Joel, Amos, Obadiah, Jonah, Micah, Nabum, Habakkuk, Zephaniah, Haggai, Zechariah, Malachi

Apocrypha

I Esdras, II Esdras, Tobit, Judith, (additional parts of Esther), Wisdom of Solomon, Ecclesiasticus, Baruch, (additional parts of Daniel), Prayer of Manasses, I Maccabees, II Maccabees

New Testament

Matthew, Mark, Luke, John, The Acts (of the Apostles), Romans, I Corinthians, II Corinthians, Galatians, Ephesians, Philippians, Colossians, I Thessalonians, II Thessalonians, I Timothy, II Timothy, Titus, Philemon, Hebrews, James, I Peter, II Peter, I John, II John, III John, Jude, Revelation (also Apocalypse)

Religious States and Experiences

acroamatic (*adj*) esoteric and revealed only to chosen disciples orally
adoration worship of a divine being
afflatus inspiration, divine bestowing of knowledge
afterlife state of existence following physical death
antediluvian (*adj*) before the Flood
apostasy abandonment of one's faith
astral plane subtle dimension more refined than physical reality
beatitude blessedness, bliss
blessed (*adj*) consecrated, holy, enjoying bliss; state prior to sainthood
bliss perfect, heavenly joy
born-again (*adj*) designating person who has experienced spiritual awakening and new religious commitment to Christ as personal savior; reborn; saved
calling in ancient use, God's selection of individual; now spiritual impulse toward religious vocation
canonization elevation to sainthood
charity love for one's fellow man and acts conveying such goodwill
damnation condemnation to eternity of suffering in hell
divinity state of being godlike
ecstasy state of absorption in the divine, with loss of awareness of body or outside world
enlightenment state of spiritual awakening
enthusiasm extreme religious devotion, usu.

associated with intense emotionalism
epiphany direct manifestation of God or deity to a person
exaltation state of heightened spiritual awareness
glossolalia speaking in tongues while in state of religious ecstasy
God-fearing (*adj*) deeply fearful or respectful of God
godliness piety, devotion to one's faith
grace state of being in divine favor; effect of God's mercy
hallowed (*adj*) blessed, made or kept holy
immanence inherent presence of God or divinity in Creation and daily life
immortality unending life without death
impiety lack of reverence for God
inspiration sudden spiritual awakening resulting from divine influence
irreverence disrespect for and discounting of divinity, Creation, and religion
manna divinely supplied spiritual nourishment
martyrdom self-sacrifice to point of death in service of others or for maintenance of one's faith
metanoia profound transformation or conversion
metempsychosis rebirth, reincarnation
Molinism quietism
mystical (*adj*) involving direct communion with God or the divine
numinous (*adj*) inspiring awe and fascination, pertaining to mysterious aspect of divine power and religious experience
piety devotion to religious duty and practice; piousness
piousness piety
profane (*adj*) irreverent, unholy; defiling what is sacred
quietism type of religious mysticism marked by attainment of perfection through systematic contemplation; Molinism
rebirth reincarnation; transmigration of soul
reborn (*adj*) born-again
receive Christ (*vb*) be reborn, accept Christ as one's personal savior
recreant (*adj*) failing to keep faith
redemption salvation, deliverance from sin or evil
reprobation rejection by God and exclusion from salvation
revelation disclosure of God's will to humankind
reverence respect and awe for divinity, Creation, and religion
righteousness freedom from sin, sanctity
sacred (*adj*) consecrated, holy
sacrosanct (*adj*) extremely sacred or holy
saintliness charity, piety, holiness of spirit and action
salvation deliverance from sin, evil, and punishment; redemption
sanctity state of being sacred or holy
saved (*adj*) having accepted Christ as one's personal savior; born-again
spirituality conviction in one's experience of the mysterious aspect of divine power
transcendence state of God's nature or highest principle as above and apart from immanent Creation
transformation experience in which adherent to religion moves from one state to another, as by conversion, leap of faith, or following a path
transmigration of soul rebirth, reincarnation
unholy (*adj*) lacking in purity
venerable (*adj*) blessed, honorable; state prior to sainthood
veneration reverential love and adoration
zeal intensely passionate religious fervor

MYTHOLOGY AND FOLKLORE

Mythological and Folkloric Beings
Gods and Divinities
Myths, Legends, and Fables
Utopia

Mythological and Folkloric Beings

Abominable Snowman legendary creature living in high Himalayas; yeti
Achilles greatest Greek hero of Trojan War, invulnerable to weapons except for one heel
Adonis beautiful young man loved by Aphrodite, who symbolized the death of nature in fall and rebirth the following spring (Greece)
Aeneas son of Aphrodite who led survivors of Troy west to found Rome
Aesculapius son of Apollo and the nymph Coronis, the first physician (Greece)
Agamemnon leader of the Greeks during siege of Troy
Aladdin poor boy in *Arabian Nights' Entertainments* who possessed magic lamp with jinn that would do his bidding
Ali Baba poor woodcutter and hero of *Arabian Nights' Entertainments* who opened a door by saying ""open sesame" and found hidden treasure of the Forty Thieves
Amazons single-breasted Scythian women warriors
Argus hundred-eyed being who guarded Io, and whose eyes were transferred to peacock's tail after death (Rome)
Arthur semilegendary British king of Camelot during 6th century
Atlas Titan bearing Earth and firmament on his shoulders (Greece and Rome)
Atropos one of the Fates (Greece)
Babe the Blue Ox legendary blue ox belonging to Paul Bunyan (United States)
banshee female spirit who warns of death by wailing (Ireland and Scotland)
barghest legendary doglike goblin that portends death or misfortune

basilisk serpent with deadly breath and glance; cockatrice
behemoth any creature of monstrous size and power
Beowulf hero of medieval epic poem (Britain, 8th c.)
bogeyman frightening, demonic figure of popular folklore
brownie tiny, fanciful brown elf who does household chores at night
bugbear goblin that devours disobedient children
Calliope chief muse; muse of epic heroic poetry (Greece)
Callisto nymph loved by Zeus, changed into she-bear by Hera and then into Great Bear constellation (Greece)
Calypso daughter of Atlas who held Odysseus captive on her island (Greece)
Cassandra priestess daughter of King Priam of Troy whose prophecies were never believed (Greece)
Castor and Pollux twin brothers of Helen who protect seagoers (Greece)
centaur half-horse, half-human monster
Chaos representative of the void prior to creation of Earth (Greece)
Charybdis woman turned into whirlpool by Zeus; companion to Scylla (Greece)
Chimera flame-belching monster, part goat, part lion, and part dragon
Cinderella fairytale heroine who escapes mistreatment by stepmother and stepsisters to marry prince (Europe)
Circe evil woman who turned humans into swine (Greece)
Clio muse of history (Greece)
Clotho one of the Fates (Greece)
Cyclops member of a family of one-eyed cannibal giants (Greece)
daemon supernatural force, spirit for good or evil, in popular folklore
Daphne nymph loved by Apollo and turned into laurel tree, whose branch Apollo wore on his head (Greece)
Delphic oracle oracle of Apollo whose answers were enigmatic and ambiguous (Greece)
Don Juan legendary, dissolute Spanish nobleman famous for his many seductions
dragon reptilian monster, often with breath of fire
Dryad forest nymph who protects trees (Greece)
dwarf small, usu. misshapen and ugly creature with magic powers
dybbuk dead person's evil spirit that invades living person (Jewish folklore)
Eight Immortals holy men who have attained immortality (Taoism)
elf mountain fairy, seen by moonlight
Eumenides the Furies (Greece)
Euterpe muse of music (Greece)
fairy small, supernatural being with magic powers; fay
Fates three sisters who spin, weave, and cut the thread of life: Atropos, Clotho, and Lachesis (Greece and Rome)
faun sylvan demigod (Rome)
Faust character in medieval legend who sold his soul to the devil for knowledge and power
Furies three snake-haired female torturers of the damned (Greece and Rome)
Galahad noblest and purest of knights of the Round Table, who gained the Holy Grail
Ganymede cupbearer of Zeus (Greece)
genie spirit in human form summoned to carry out one's wishes
genius tutelary spirit attending a person throughout life; (*pl.*) genii
giant huge and monstrously formed creature, enemy of gods and people (Scandinavia and Greece)
Gigantes huge monsters, children of Gaea, who were defeated by Olympian gods (Greece)
Gilgamesh hero of Sumerian and Babylonian epics
gnome dwarfish creature who lives underground
goblin demon of popular folklore in the form of a grotesque, often malicious sprite
golem figure artificially constructed in human form and endowed with life (Jewish folklore)
Gorgons three hideous monsters in the form of winged sisters with power to turn person viewing them to stone (Greece)
Graces three daughters of Zeus attendant on Aphrodite, embodying beauty and charm (Greece)
gremlin type of elf, usu. mischievous troublemaker said to be responsible for minor malfunctions
Grendel half-human monster slain by Beowulf
griffin monster that is half eagle and half lion
Guinevere King Arthur's wife
Harpy winged, ravenous, half-woman monster that robs its victims of food (Greece)
Helen Greek queen whose abduction instigated the Trojan War
Herakles Hercules (Greece)
Hercules son of Jupiter and greatest hero, who performed twelve labors (Rome)
Hermaphroditus son of Hermes and Aphrodite, united with a nymph to form one body with sexual characteristics of both genders (Greece)
hero mythic person whose story is told in epic tale of adventure or struggle
hippocampus creature who is half horse and half dolphin
hobbit small, furry creature who lives in burrow in the earth
hobgoblin mischievous goblin or sprite, esp. Puck
Houyhnhnm one of a race of horses endowed with reason in Jonathan Swift's *Gulliver's Travels*
Hydra nine-headed serpent whose heads grew back as they were cut off, slain by Hercules (Greece)
Hyperion one of the Titans, son of Uranus and father of Helios, Selene, and Eos
Icarus son of Daedalus who flew too near the sun, melting his wax and feather wings and causing him to fall into the sea (Greece)
incubus evil demon that has sex with women while they sleep
Iris messenger of God in multihued robe representing rainbow (Greece)

Jack Frost personification of cold and frost (U.S.)
Jason leader of the Argonauts who retrieved the Golden Fleece (Greece)
John Henry legendary black railroad worker who outdrove steam drill (U.S., 19th c.)
kelpie horse-shaped water spirit (Scotland)
Kraken legendary monster of northern seas (Scandinavia)
Kriss Kringle Santa Claus
Lachesis one of the Fates (Greece)
Lancelot greatest knight of King Arthur's round table and lover of Queen Guinevere
Lares household gods who are spirits of ancestors (Rome)
lemures spirits of the dead (Rome)
leprechaun dwarf or sprite; fairy and beneficent spirit (Ireland)
Leviathan huge Biblical sea monster, either reptile or whale
Lilith woman or phantom said to be former wife of Adam in Jewish folklore
little people leprechauns, fairies, elves
Loch Ness monster dinosaurlike creature reportedly seen emerging from waters of Loch Ness (Scotland)
Lorelei siren or river spirit with fatal charm (Teutonic folkore)
loup-garou *French* werewolf
maenads frenzied female followers of Bacchus or Dionysus (Greece and Rome)
manes spirits of dead (Rome)
manitou spirit that controls nature and is source of natural and supernatural power (Algonquian Indians)
Medusa snake-haired woman monster beheaded by Perseus; one of the Gorgons (Greece)
Merlin magician and seer of Arthurian legend
mermaid creature with fatal charm who is half woman and half fish
Midas legendary Phrygian king whose touch turned objects to gold (Greece)
Midgard serpent monster that grew to surround the entire world (Scandinavia)
Minotaur bull-headed, human-torsoed, flesh-eating monster slain by Theseus (Greece)
Mnemosyne mother of the muses and goddess of memory
Moirai Fates (Greece)
monster any of various legendary, mythical creatures, usu. hybrid of animal forms
Muses nine daughters of Zeus and Mnemosyne who inspire artists: Calliope (heroic poetry), Clio (history), Erato (love poetry), Euterpe (music and lyric poetry), Melpomene (tragedy), Polyhymnia (eloquence and sacred poetry), Terpsichore (dance), Thalia (comedy), Urania (astronomy)
naiad freshwater nymph (Greece)
Narcissus youth who loved his own reflection and was turned into a flower (Rome)
Nereid sea nymph; Oceanid (Greece)
Nibelungs race of dwarfs who possessed a treasure of Rhine gold that was captured by Siegfried (Teutonic)
Niobe bereaved daughter of Tantalus who wept for her slain children even after being turned to stone (Greece)
nix water spirit that lures its victims into its underwater home (German folklore)
nymph semidivine spirit of natural region such as water, forest, mountains, or valleys (Greece)
Oceanid Nereid
Oedipus king who unwittingly killed his father and married his mother after solving Sphinx's riddle (Greece)
ogre hideous giant cannibal
oracle intermediary between gods and man who answered questions at shrine (Greece)
orc monster similar to an ogre
Orpheus lyre-playing musician who tried unsuccessfully to rescue his wife from Hades (Greece)
Pandora original woman who opened forbidden box, bringing woes and evils to humanity (Greece)
Parsifal knight who sought Holy Grail (Teutonic)
Paul Bunyan giant lumberjack with a pet blue ox named Babe, reputed to have shaped the Rocky Mountains (U.S., 19th c.)
Pecos Bill legendary cowboy who dug the Rio Grande River (U.S., 19th c.)
Pegasus winged horse born of Medusa's blood (Greece)
Penates gods who serve as family household guardians (Rome)
Perseus hero who slew Medusa (Greece)
Peter Pan boy who never grew up in Sir James Barrie's play
phantom specter or apparition
phoenix immortal bird that cremates itself every 500 years, then emerges reborn from ashes (Greece)
Pied Piper legendary folk hero who led people by entrancing them by playing his flute (Germany)
pixie fairy, said to be spirit of dead child
poltergeist noisy ghost
Polyhymnia muse of eloquence (Greece)
preta wandering or disturbed ghost (India)
Prometheus hero who stole fire from gods for mankind and was punished by Zeus (Greece)
Proteus sea god who assumed different shapes (Greece)
Psyche beautiful mortal loved by Eros (Greece)
Puck mischievous sprite of English folklore; Robin Goodfellow
Python dragon who guarded chasm at Delphi, slain by Apollo (Greece)
Rama hero of the epic tale Ramayana and perfect, devoted Hindu (India)
Remus twin brother of Romulus (Rome)
Rip Van Winkle man who slept twenty years and awakened to a changed world, from story by Washington Irving (U.S., 19th c.)
Robin Goodfellow Puck
Robin Hood legendary, benevolent folk hero outlaw (Britain)
roc bird of enormous size and strength (Arabia)
Romulus one of twin brothers raised by a wolf, founder of Rome

Rudra father of storm gods who controls powers of nature (Vedic)
Rumpelstiltskin dwarf who spins flax into gold in German folktale
sandman folkloric character who puts sand in the eyes of children to make them sleepy
Santa Claus benevolent purveyor or gifts to children on Christmas Eve; Kriss Kringle
satyr goat-footed demigod of forest and field, noted for lasciviousness
scapegoat goat let loose on Yom Kippur after sins are laid on its head
Scheherezade in *Arabian Nights' Entertainments*, wife of sultan of India, who spared her life because she told such wondrous tales each night
Scylla sea nymph who was transformed into sea monster, companion of Charybdis (Greece)
sibyl any woman who served as mouth piece of the gods in delivering prophecies and oracles
Siegfried hero of the *Nibelungenlied* (Teutonic)
Sigurd hero of the *Volsunga Saga*; counterpart of Siegfried in the *Nibelungenlied* (Scandinavia)
Silenus forest spirit, sometimes called oldest of satyrs (Greece)
Sinbad sea-voyaging adventurer of *Arabian Nights' Entertainments*
Siren singing sea nymph who charms sailors to their deaths (Greece)
Sisyphus crafty murderer and thief condemned by Zeus to roll a stone up a slope so that each time he approached the top the stone escaped him and rolled down again (Greece)
Sleeping Beauty fairy tale princess awakened from a prolonged, charmed sleep by the kiss of her true love
Sphinx human-headed, winged lion and poser of enigmatic riddles (Greece)
spirit supernatural being
sprite spirit, esp. mischievous elf
stork bird that is symbolic deliverer of new babies
succubus female demon who has sex with men while they sleep
sylph air spirit
Syrinx mountain nymph who was transformed into the reed from which Pan made his panpipe
Tantalus son of Zeus condemned in Tartarus to forever reach for unattainable fruit and water
Termagant mythical deity in form of violent, dominating personage, believed by Medieval Christians to be worshipped by Muslims
Terpsichore muse of dance (Greece)
Thalia muse of comic and lyric poetry (Greece)
Theseus hero who slew Minotaur (Greece)
Titan one of a race of giant deities, children of Uranus who held power under Cronus and were overthrown by the Olympian gods (Greece)
Tom Thumb tiny hero of folk tales
tooth fairy fairy who exchanges gift for baby tooth placed under pillow of child
Triton half fish, half man and son of Poseidon with power over waves (Greece)
troll misshapen, woodland-dwelling dwarf or giant of limited intelligence (Scandinavia)
undine female water spirit
unicorn creature with horse's body, lion's tail, and single horn, representing purity and supernatural powers
Urania muse of astronomy (Greece)
Valkyries maidens who escort warriors to Valhalla (Teutonic and Norse folklore)
vampire reanimated corpse who exists on blood of sleeping victims
vestal virgin one of the virgins tending sacred fire of Vesta (Rome)
water nymph semidivine marine creature
werewolf man capable of transmogrifying into shape of a wolf who preys on human victims; wolfman
William Tell rebellious hero of Swiss legend forced to shoot arrow through apple on his son's head
windigo evil spirit, cannibal demon (Native American folklore)
wolfman werewolf
wood nymph semidivine forest creature
yeti Abominable Snowman
Ymir first living creature and progenitor of giants, whose corpse formed earth, water, and heavens (Scandinavia)
zombie reanimated corpse under spell of demon or deity

Gods and Divinities

Aeolus god of winds (Greece)
Agni god of fire (India)
Amphitrite goddess of the sea, wife of Poseidon (Greece)
Amun-Ra supreme national god (Egypt, 18th dynasty)
Anshar father of Anu, Ea, and Enlil (Mesopotamia)
Anu supreme sky god (Mesopotamia)
Anubis jackel-headed god of the underworld, death, and judgment of soul (Egypt)
Aphrodite goddess of love and beauty (Greece)
Apollo god of arts, intellect, and prophecy (Rome)
Apollon god of arts, sciences, reason, and inspiration (Greece)
Ares god of war (Greece)
Artemis goddess of hunting (Greece)
Ashur winged national god of battle (Assyria)
Astarte goddess of fertility and love (Phoenicia)
Athena goddess of wisdom and crafts (Greece)
Aurora goddess of dawn (Rome)
Baal god of fertility (Phoenicia)
Bacchus god of wine; Liber (Rome)
Balder god of sunlight personifying goodness, son of Frigg (Scandinavia)
Bel goddess and wife of Anu (Mesopotamia)
Benten goddess of love and the arts (Japan)
Brahma creator god in Trimurti (India)
Ceres goddess of fertility and agriculture (Rome)
Chloris goddess of flowers (Greece)
Comus god of revelry and feasting (Greece and Rome)

Cronos leader of the Titans and son of Uranus who castrated his father and fathered Zeus and other Olympian gods by his sister Rhea; Kronos (Greece)
Cupid god of love (Rome)
Cybele great mother goddess (Phrygia)
Daikoku god of wealth (Japan)
Demeter goddess of agriculture and fertility (Greece)
Diana goddess of the moon and forest (Rome)
Dionysus god of ecstasy and wine (Greece)
Dis god of the underworld and the dead (Rome)
Ea god of freshwater and wisdom (Mesopotamia)
Emma-O ruler of hell (Japan)
Enlil god of air and king of the gods (Mesopotamia)
Eos goddess of dawn (Greece)
Eris goddess of strife and discord (Greece)
Eros god of love (Greece)
Faunus god of fields and shepherds (Rome)
Flora goddess of flowers (Rome)
Frey fertility god (Scandinavia)
Freya goddess of beauty and love (Scandinavia)
Frigg mother goddess, consort of Odin (Scandinavia)
Fu-hsing god of happiness (China)
Gaea goddess of earth, mother and wife of Uranus (Greece)
Ganesha god of wisdom (India)
Geb earth god, father of Osiris (Egypt)
Gula goddess of healing (Mesopotamia)
Hades god of the dead and underworld (Greece)
Hanuman monkey god (India)
Hathor goddess of love and joy (Egypt)
Hebe goddess of youth (Greece)
Hecate goddess of magic and dark powers (Greece)
Helios sun god (Greece)
Hephaestus god of the forge and crafts (Greece)
Hera goddess of women and childbirth, consort of Zeus (Greece)
Hermes messenger of gods (Greece)
Hestia goddess of hearth and home (Greece)
Horus solar god, son of Isis and Osiris who ruled earth after avenging his father's murder (Egypt)
Huitzilopochtli god of war and the sun (Aztec)
Hygeia goddess of health (Greece)
Hymen god of marriage (Greece)
Hypnus god of sleep (Greece)
Indra rain god (India)
Inti personification of the sun (Inca)
Ishtar mother goddess of fertility and love, daughter of Anu (Mesopotamia)
Isis goddess of maternity, wife of Osiris (Egypt)
Janus god of beginnings and doorways (Rome)
Jove Jupiter (Rome)
Juno goddess of women and maternity, consort of Jupiter (Rome)
Jupiter sky god and chief god; Jove (Rome)
Juventas goddess of youth (Rome)
Kali goddess of motherhood and death, consort of Shiva (India)
Kore Persephone
Krishna god of love (India)
Kronos Cronus
Kuan Yin goddess of compassion (Chinese Buddhism)
Kubera god of riches (India)
Lakshmi lotus goddess of prosperity, wife of Vishnu (India)
Liber god of ecstasy and wine; Bacchus (Rome)
Loki trickster god of evil (Scandinavia)
Lug sun god (Celtic)
Luna moon goddess (Rome)
Mahakala god of wealth (India)
Marduk chief god (Babylonia)
Mars god of war (Rome)
Maui trickster god (Oceania)
Mercury messenger of the gods; god of communication (Rome)
Minerva goddess of wisdom and the arts (Rome)
Mnemosyne goddess of memory, mother of Muses (Greece)
Morpheus god of dreams (Greece)
Mors god of death (Rome)
Mot god of sterility (Phoenicia)
Nemesis goddess of punishment and reward (Greece)
Neptune sea god (Rome)
Nike goddess of victory (Greece)
Njord god of winds and prosperity (Scandinavia)
Nox goddess of night (Rome)
Nut sky goddess, wife of Geb (Egypt)
Nyx goddess of night (Greece)
Odin god of wisdom, magic, and death; chief god (Scandinavia)
Orcus god of the underworld, identified with Pluto (Rome)
Osiris god of the Nile, vegetation, and the dead (Egypt)
Pallas Athena bright Athena (Greece)
Pan shepherd god (Greece)
Pauguk personification of death (North American Indians)
Persephone daughter of Demeter, wife of Hades; Kore (Greece)
Phoebus Apollo shining Apollo (Greece)
Picus god of divination (Rome)
Pluto god of the underworld (Rome)
Plutus god of wealth (Greece)
Pomona goddess of orchards and gardens (Rome)
Poseidon sea god (Greece)
Priapus god of fertility (Greece)
Proserpina daughter of Ceres, wife of Pluto (Rome)
Psyche goddess of the soul, unified with Cupid (Rome)
Ptah creator of the universe, depicted as upright mummified man (Egypt)
Quetzalcoatl feathered serpent god of creation (Aztec and Toltec)
Ra sun god (Egypt)
Rahu mischievous, four-armed deity of natural disasters (India)
Rhea great mother goddess, wife and sister of Cronus and mother of Zeus (Greece)

Rhiannon goddess associated with horses (Wales)
Salacia goddess of oceans (Rome)
Sarasvati goddess of learning and wisdom (India)
Saturn agriculture god, father of Jupiter (Rome)
Selene moon goddess (Greece)
Seth brother and enemy of Osiris and god of evil (Egypt)
Shiva destroyer god in Trimurti (India)
Sin moon god (Mesopotamia)
Sol one of two sun gods (Rome)
Somnus god of sleep (Rome)
Surya sun god (India)
Svetovid god of fertility and war (Eastern Europe)
Tammuz vegetation god (Mesopotamia)
Thanatos god of death (Greece)
Themis goddess of law and justice (Greece)
Thor god of thunder and war (Scandinavia)
Thoth god of wisdom, arts and sciences, and magic; scribe of the gods (Egypt)
Thunderbird culture god (North American Indians)
Tlaloc rain god (Aztec)
Tuatha Dé Danann ancient gods (Ireland)
Tyche goddess of fate (Greece)
Uranus original god of heaven and father of the Titans, including Cronus (Greece)
Venus goddess of love and beauty (Rome)
Vesta goddess of the hearth (Rome)
Victoria goddess of victory (Rome)
Vishnu preserver god in Trimurti (India)
Vulcan god of the forge and fire (Rome)
Wotan chief god (Germany)
Xipe god of vegetation (Aztec)
Xochipilli god of flowers and pleasure (Aztec)
Yama ruler of hell and lord of the dead (India)
Zephyrus god of the west wind (Greece)
Zeus chief god and ruler of heaven; god of thunder and lightning (Greece)

Myths, Legends, and Fables

Aegis shield of Zeus with head of Medusa at its center, borne by Athena on missions (Greece)
Aesir pantheon of the gods (Scandinavia)
Aesop's Fables collected animal fables attributed to Phrygian slave Aesop
ages of humankind major, significant eras in mythological history of humankind: golden age, silver age, bronze age, iron age
amaranth purple flower that never fades or dies
ambrosia food of the gods, conferring immortality
amrita elixir of immortality (India)
anthropomorphism practice of endowing natural world with human attributes
Arabian Nights ancient Oriental tales told by Scheherazade
Argonauts fifty Greek heroes who sailed with Jason to retrieve the Golden Fleece
Atlantis legendary continental island that disappeared into Atlantic Ocean during ancient or prehistoric times
Bifrost rainbow bridge between heaven and Earth (Scandinavia)
Book of the Dead texts placed as protection in tombs of the dead (Egypt)
Camelot site of King Arthur's palace and court (Britain)
cautionary tale traditional story with moral lesson
charm amulet or object that brings luck or wards off evil
cosmic egg mythic image of creation
cosmogony creation myth
creation myth mythic explanation of formation of universe; cosmogonic myth
Deluge, the great flood of various legends
etiological myth myth explaining creation of the universe
Excaliber King Arthur's sword
fable story with fantastic events and creatures having allegorical meaning; legend
fairyland home of fairies; enchanted place
fairy tales universal stories about fairies or other imaginary and magical creatures, esp. for children, usu. based on oral tradition
Flood universal deluge that is subject of myth and legend in many cultures, including Mesopotamian and Judeo-Christian
folklore traditional beliefs, narratives, and superstitions of a culture
fountain of youth legendary spring whose waters restore health and youth to anyone who drinks them
Gilgamesh major epic text of Mesopotamia
golden apples treasure of Garden of the Hesperides, retrieved by Herakles (Greece)
Golden Fleece magical treasure retrieved from Colchis by Jason (Greece)
Gordian knot intricate knot whose untier would rule Asia, supposedly cut by Alexander the Great with sword
Great Turtle upholder of world (Native American)
Grimm's fairy tales folklore collection compiled by the Grimm brothers, including Snow White, Rumpelstiltskin, Tom Thumb, and Hansel and Gretel
Hesperides legendary garden at western extremity of world, where golden apples grow (Greece)
Holy Grail cup that was object of mystical quest by Arthurian knights
land of Nod mythical land of sleep
legend traditional story or narration
lore folk knowledge, body of information
lotus legendary fruit that induces state of dreamy forgetfulness (Greece)
motif recurrent theme in myth or legend
myth tale or traditional narrative that describes adventures of gods and legendary heroes, and reveals human behavior and natural phenomena through its symbolism
mythology collected body of myths of one people or culture
nectar wine conferring immortality (Greece)

Olympus mountain home of the gods, ruled by Zeus (Greece)
Oz magical or otherworldly land described in Oz books of L. Frank Baum
Palladium statue of Pallas Athena, believed to provide protection for city of Troy (Greece)
parable short allegorical story with a moral
Ragnarok end of the world and destruction of the gods and humankind in a final battle with evil powers (Scandinavia)
saga legendary narrative about heroic adventures
scarab representation of a beetle, esp. as symbol of sun or cyclical cosmic pattern (Egypt)
soteriological myth myth describing hero as bringer of salvation
sun disk symbolic representation of sun or sun god, as in Egyptian, Babylonia, and Aztec mythology
tale legendary, fictitious, traditional story told dramatically
Yggdrasil giant tree that supported the world (Norse)

Utopia

Agapemone communistic, free love establishment founded in 1849 at Spaxton, England
Arcadia region of innocence and simplicity
Atlantis legendary island in Atlantic Ocean with highly developed, utopian society, said to have sunk beneath the sea
Avalon island home of Morgan Le Fay, represented as earthly paradise, to which King Arthur was taken after his death
Big Rock Candy Mountain place of refuge in children's song
brave new world futuristic society described in novel by Aldous Huxley
Brook Farm egalitarian utopian farming community founded in 1841 in Massachusetts
Cockaigne imaginary land of idleness and luxury
El Dorado place of fabulous wealth and abundance sought by 16th-century explorers
Erewhon utopia in Samuel Butler's novel of same name
Fountain of Youth magical fountain providing eternal youth, held by Spanish explorers to lie somewhere in Americas
Goshen land of plenty, esp. land assigned to Israelites in Egypt
Happy Valley utopia in writings of Samuel Johnson
heaven on earth earthly dwelling place as peaceful and perfect as heaven
Hesperides garden at western extremity of world that produces golden apples (Greek mythology)
land of milk and honey land of plenty; Canaan, as envisioned by the ancient Hebrews
land of plenty earthly dwelling place that provides for all of humanity's physical and spiritual needs
Laputa utopia in writings of Jonathan Swift
lotus land legendary Greek land of dreamy idleness
lubberland imaginary land of idleness and leisure amid plenty
Modern Utopia utopia as described in book by H.G. Wells
Nephelococcygia utopia in plays of Aristophanes
never-never land illusory, ideal land or condition
New Atlantis utopia in writings of Sir Francis Bacon
New Harmony socialistic colony, founded in Indiana in 1825, that established first kindergarten, free public school, and free library in United States
Oneida Community utopian settlement in New York State, founded on theory that sin can be eliminated by social reform
pie in the sky state of perfect happiness or utopia, esp. when illusory
pipe dream illusory or fantastic plan or way of life
Seven Cities of Cibola utopian legend
Shangri-la remote, imaginary paradise on earth and land of eternal youth, after fictional Himalayan land described by James Hilton in *The Lost Horizon*
utopia any ideal place or state, esp. in its laws and social conditions; any visionary, sometimes impractical scheme for social improvement
Utopia imaginary island with ideal government, from 16th-century book by Sir Thomas More
Xanadu legendary city of opulence and pleasure, home of Kublai Khan

MAGIC AND THE OCCULT

Belief Systems and Theories
Rites, Practices, Spells, and Symbols
Occult States and Experiences
Individuals and Objects

Belief Systems and Theories

alchemy medieval chemistry and speculative philosophy aimed at transforming base metals into gold and prolonging life
ancestor worship adoration of ancestors, whose spirits are believed to have power to intervene in affairs of the living
animal magnetism mysterious natural force used by Franz Mesmer to hypnotize and cure patients; mesmerism (France, 18th c.)
animism belief in existence of spirits separate from bodies; attribution of conscious life to objects in nature
astrology divination according to positions of stars and planets
black magic magic used for evil or diabolical purposes

cabalism belief in the esoteric, the occult, or mysticism
Chaldean (*adj*) belonging to ancient Semitic sect of Babylonia, versed in occult arts and astrology
chiromancy palmistry
diabolism devil worship
Gnosticism early Christian heresies stressing esoteric knowledge of spiritual truth, practiced by secret, self-styled elite sect
hermetics Gnostic teachings of Hermes Trismegistus, characterized by abstruse occultism
macumba Brazilian voodoo
mesmerism animal magnetism
Mithraism men's Persian mystery cult of late Roman Empire
mysticism belief in acquisition of spiritual truth, power, and communion with ultimate reality through intuition, insight, or application of specific secret rites, sometimes expressed in romantic love of the divine
numerology divination through numbers and study of their occult significance and interrelationships
obeah sorcery and magic among blacks of the Caribbean, Africa, and southeastern United States
oneiromancy divination through dreams
palmistry divination by analysis of creases in palm of hand; chiromancy
panpsychism belief that every physical event has a psychic aspect
parapsychology branch of psychology concerned with investigation of paranormal phenomena such as clairvoyance and telepathy
phrenology analysis of character based on size and shape of skull
santeria Afro-Caribbean belief system that includes animal sacrifices and uses Catholic saints as representations of the spirit world
Satanism devil worship
shamanism animistic belief in unseen world of gods, demons, and ancestral spirits responsive only to shamans (northern Asia)
sorcery use of evil power for divination or manipulation of the natural world for specific ends
tarot any of a set of twenty-two specially marked cards that symbolize archetypal personalities and situations, used for fortunetelling
telepathy communication between minds by paranormal means
voodoo West Indian religion derived from African ancestor worship, characterized by rites, trances, animistic deities, spells, and hexes
white magic magic practiced with intent to do good or benefit others
wicca witch theology based on empowerment of women who care for Earth and cosmos
witchcraft sorcery and magic acquired through communication with devil
zombiism belief in voodoo cult of the zombie

Rites, Practices, Spells, and Symbols

abracadabra magical incantation, often rapid and nonsensical
aleuromancy use of flour for divination
arcanum mystery or rite known only to initiates
ascendant zodiacal sign rising at eastern horizon at moment of one's birth
aspect relative position of planets and stars having astrological influence on human affairs
astral house position of planets in connection with influence on specific aspects of life
astral traveling leaving one's body and venturing forth as a spirit
augury divination by omens and signs
auspice prophetic sign
black art magic practiced by witches, conjurers, and diabolists
Black Mass perversion of Catholic Mass by worshiping Satan
cabala esoteric, occult, or secret doctrine; orig. medieval Jewish mystical theosophy and thaumaturgy
call up spirits summon mystical forces by incantation
cargo cult Pacific Islands religious cult believing in acquisition of material goods through intervention of spirits
cast a chart calculate, diagram, and analyze all zodiacal positions at time of person's birth
cast a spell impose magic power over; conjure
conjure (*vb*) summon by incantation; affect by magic
conundrum riddle whose answer involves a pun; mystery
coven assembly of witches or diabolists, esp. thirteen such
crystal gazing divining by looking into a crystal ball
curse invocation of harm on another; (vb) wish or invoke calamity or injury upon
cusp period of transition from one zodiacal sign to next
dowsing art of finding water, oil, or metals by means of magic rod
enigma obscure occurrence; riddle or mystery
ephemeris table of positions of celestial bodies at stated times, used in divination
esotericism doctrine and practice of arcane or secret rites
ether rarefied element; medium in which spirits appear; intoxicating gas
exorcism rite or spell that casts out evil spirit from possessed person or object
faith healing miraculous curing of disease or injury through belief in God and his servants
Fata Morgana mirage consisting of multiple images that resemble castles
fetish superstitious belief in object's magical or supernatural powers; object of such belief
folk medicine primitive healing based on nature or ritual, not medical technology and science
fortunetelling divining and predicting future events, esp. concerning an individual's life
grigri African amulet or fetish; gris-gris

gris-gris grigri
haruspication divination by examination of entrails or liver of slaughtered animal
haunting habitual reappearance of ghost or specter
hex curse, jinx, evil spell
hocus-pocus nonsense and sleight of hand used to cloak deception in magic rites
hoodoo voodoo, bad luck
horoscope prediction based on astrological chart
house one of twelve equal sectors of celestial sphere in astrology
hypnosis sleeplike state induced by repetitious speech or movement, marked by heightened suggestibility
idolatry worship of physical object or living person
incantation verbal spell or charm used in magical rites and sorcery
initiation ceremony admitting new member to secret cult, brotherhood, or belief system
jinx spell bringing bad luck; curse
levitation phenomenon of floating on air in apparent defiance of laws of gravity
lifeline long crease in hand consulted for divination in palmistry
lycanthropy delusion that one has become a wolf
magic use of illusion, sleight of hand, ritual, and incantations for divination, enchantment, or to invoke a curse
malison curse, invocation of harm
medicine show show offering supposed cures through sale of patent medicines
mental telepathy reception or transmission of thoughts without words
mind reading ability to perceive another's thoughts through preternatural power
mirage illusion or appearance of something that does not really exist
mumbo jumbo verbal nonsense and sleight of hand associated with rites, spells, or magic
nympholepsy demoniac frenzy induced by nymphs
occult (*adj*) pertaining to magic or any system claiming use or knowledge of secret or supernatural powers or agencies
oddity inexplicable, magical occurrence
omen event or phenomenon said to portend future
open sesame magical incantation that causes desired result
Ouija *Trademark.* board with alphabet and signs for reception of telepathic messages
patent medicine packaged nonprescription drug with incompletely described ingredients; quack remedy; harmless potion sold as cure-all
phase particular stage in regular cycle of moon, used in astrology
portent omen of future event, usu. an unfortunate one
potion usu. secret mixture of liquids with magic powers
precognition clairvoyance relating to future events
prediction foretelling of future events
prophecy prediction of the future
psychokinesis movement of objects through mental processes, without use of physical means; telekinesis
rainmaking rites, esp. dances, intended to bring rain
riddle mystifying or misleading question posed as problem to be solved
rite prescribed ceremony or liturgy for specific purpose
scrying crystal gazing; divination by crystals
seance session or meeting to receive spirit communications
shamrock trifoliate plant considered symbol of good luck, esp. by Irish
sigil sign, word, or device of occult power
sign one of twelve divisions of zodiac
soothsaying prophecy, divination
sortilege divination by lots
spell words with magic powers; state of enchantment
spellbind (*vb*) bind or hold by spells
spirit rapping communicating with spirits of dead by rapping on table
spirit writing writing of medium under supposed influence of spirits
stargazing practicing divination through astrology
summons spiritual calling
sun dance ceremony consisting of dancing, symbolic rites, and often self-torture (North American Indians of the Plains)
superstition belief or practice resulting from fear of unknown, trust in magic, or false concept of causation
taboo often ritualized fear or prohibition of specific object or practice
telekinesis psychokinesis
telepathy extrasensory communication between minds
thaumaturgy working of magic or miracles
time machine theoretical device for traveling forward or backward in time
transubstantiation change of one substance into another, esp. Eucharistic transformation of bread and wine
vaticination prediction, prophecy
vortex gateway into another dimension
Walpurgis Night eve of May Day, when witches congregate and ride
wanga voodoo charm or spell
whammy *Informal.* magic curse or spell that brings bad luck
wish invocation of good or evil on someone or something
wizardry practice of sorcery; magical power of transformation
zodiac imaginary belt in heavens encompassing paths of planets, divided into twelve astrological signs

Occult States and Experiences

adumbrative (*adj*) vaguely foreshadowed, with sketchy sense of future
apocalyptic (*adj*) forecasting or suggesting end of world
aura luminous radiation surrounding object or individual
bliss serenity, inner peace, complete happiness
chimerical (*adj*) visionary and improbable; existing only in fantastic imagination
clairaudience power of hearing something not audible to the ordinary ear
clairvoyance ability to discern objects not present to the senses; perception beyond normal range; precognition
déjà vu uncomfortable sense of familiarity with new experience; sense of having been in a situation before; paramnesia
devoid (*adj*) empty, blank, lacking sensibility
disbelief incredulity or difficulty in accepting reality of what has been experienced
disembodiment separation of spirit or mind from physical body
dread heightened fear, esp. of the unknown
ecstasy complete, rapturous delight; trancelike, often prophetic state beyond self-control
eerie (*adj*) spooky, filling one with dread of the unknown
entrancement supersensible, nonrational, trancelike state
extrasensory (*adj*) beyond realm of senses
extraterrestrial something or someone from outer space
fatidic (*adj*) prophetic
foresight ability to see and predict future; vision
fourth dimension something outside range of ordinary experience as measured in length, breadth, and depth, usu. time
glossolalia pseudolanguage of ecstasy or possession; speaking in tongues
hallucination visual or auditory perception of objects without reality, often experienced in trancelike state
hermetic (*adj*) recondite, characterized by occultism or Gnosticism
hypnotic (*adj*) suggesting hypnosis, trance, or detachment from consciousness
manifestation physical evidence of phenomena
materialization physical manifestation of nonmaterial phenomenon or spirit
nepenthe forgetfulness of sorrow, orig. a potion used to induce such forgetfulness
obsession persistent, usu. disturbing, preoccupation with one idea, feeling, person, place, or thing
occult (*adj*) beyond ordinary knowledge or understanding; mysterious or supernatural
out-of-body experience sensation of perceiving oneself from external viewpoint as though mind or soul had left body
paramnesia déjà vu
paranormal (*adj*) supernatural, scientifically inexplicable
phantasmagoria rapidly fluctuating, dreamlike scene or imagery
possession domination by evil spirit or passion; replacement of one's normal personality by another's
precognition clairvoyance
prescience foreknowledge of events; divine omniscience
preternatural (*adj*) extraordinary, existing outside nature
psi extrasensory perception; psychic phenomena in general
psychedelic (*adj*) describing abnormal psychic state of heightened awareness, often produced by drugs and accompanied by hallucinations
psychic (*adj*) sensitive to nonphysical, supernatural forces
second sight clairvoyance, precognition
sixth sense keen, intuitive power of perception beyond that of the five senses
somnambulism sleepwalking
supernatural extraordinary phenomena inexplicable by science or senses
surrealistic (*adj*) having bizarre, dreamlike quality
touched (*adj*) having received divine revelation, inspiration, or supersensible powers
trance state of profound abstraction, deep hypnosis, or suspended animation
transcendental (*adj*) beyond limits of ordinary experience, reality, and comprehension; supernatural
vibration characteristic aura or spiritual emanation that infuses individual or body, sensed intuitively
vision supernatural, often revelatory appearance in dream, trance, or ecstasy
xenoglossia magical knowledge of a language one has never learned

Individuals and Objects

adept trained practitioner
alkahest universal solvent in alchemy
anchorite one living in seclusion for religious reasons
ankh cross with loop at top, used as symbol of enduring life (ancient Egypt)
apparition unusual phenomenon or vision, esp. ghostly figure
archimage great wizard or magician
astrologer practitioner of astrology and stargazing
azoth mercury, regarded as first principle of all metals by alchemists
barsom bundle of sacred twigs
botanica store in which plants and other materials are purchased for use in rituals, esp. in santeria
channel individual through whom spirits make contact
charm amulet worn to ward off evil and bring good fortune
chiromancer palm reader
conjurer magician, wizard

crystal ball glass orb used for divination
dervish member of Muslim order known for frenzied, whirling devotional practice
doomsayer soothsayer who predicts apocalypse
Doppelgänger ghostly double of living person
Dracula deranged, possessed individual, orig. a Transylvanian count, who draws strength by drinking blood of others; vampire
Druid ancient Celtic priest, magician, or wizard
effigy crude physical representation or image, esp. of hated person
fakir Hindu or Muslim ascetic or wonder-worker; dervish
flying saucer unidentified moving object in air reputed to be from another planet or solar system; UFO
fortune cookie folded Chinese dessert cookie with written prophetic message or advice enclosed on slip of paper
fortuneteller individual claiming ability to prophesize future
glyph symbolic figure carved in relief
gnosis essential esoteric and spiritual knowledge held to be achieved through faith by Gnostics
hag ugly female demon or witch
haruspex minor priest who practiced divination, esp. from entrails of animal killed in sacrifice (ancient Rome)
hei-tiki Maori charm worn around neck
hobgoblin mischievous goblin; bogy
icon idol, symbol, or object of devotion
illuminati persons claiming superior religious enlightenment
initiate new convert to belief system
joss Chinese idol; cult image
juju African magical fetish or charm
kachina doll representing deified ancestral spirit of Hopi Indians
magician practitioner of illusion, sleight of hand, and incantation for prophecy
magus wise man, sorcerer, or magician
marabout Muslim hermit
mascot person, animal, or object adopted by group as symbolic good luck figure
medicine man shaman, sorcerer, or priest healer, esp. among American Indians; witch doctor
medium individual serving as channel for communications with spirits
megalith very large, rough stone, esp. used for primitive religious monuments
menat amulet used to secure divine protection (ancient Egypt)
mind reader person who can discern thoughts of others through supernatural means
moly mythical herb with magical powers
monolith single great stone, obelisk, or column, often built as symbolic religious monument
mystagogue one who initiates another into mystery cult
neophyte novice, recent convert
nightrider member of secret society who rides masked at night to perform acts of terrorism, esp. member of Ku Klux Klan
omen occurrence or phenomenon portending future event
oracle person or shrine through which deity reveals secret or divine purpose
palm reader one who divines by examining creases in person's palm; chiromancer
panpsychist advocate of belief that every physical event has psychic aspect
phantasm ghost, specter, figment of imagination
philosophers' stone stone believed to have power to convert base metals to gold, sought by alchemists
philter potion, charm, or drug with power to cause person to fall in love
planchette small, triangular or heart-shaped board on casters with suspended pointer, used to produce automatic writing, esp. on Ouija board
precursor incident or phenomenon that portends future event
premie recent initiate to cult
prophet person who predicts future events
psychic individual sensitive to supernatural and spiritual forces; medium
pythoness female practitioner of divination, esp. priestess of Apollo
querent person who asks questions or seeks information, esp. through medium
rabbit's foot foot of rabbit carried for good luck
revenant person who returns as ghost or specter
scarab stone beetle used as talisman and symbol of destruction (ancient Egypt)
seer person with power to foretell events
sensitive medium, psychic
shaman priest who uses magic for cures, divination, and sorcery, esp. among tribal peoples; witch doctor
sign omen; one of twelve divisions of zodiac
soothsayer person who practices divination
sorcerer wizard, shaman, practitioner of sorcery
specter ghost, phantasm, visible disembodied spirit
spellbinder person who casts spells
talisman charm or object held to bring good luck and avert evil
tea leaves leaves from emptied cup of tea whose arrangement is used in divination and prophecy
teleplasm emanation from body of medium that serves as means for telekinesis
thaumaturge magician, performer of miracles
third eye spot in forehead receptive to occult or mystical knowledge or perception; intuition
tiki Polynesian wood or stone image of supernatural power
totem pole carved, painted pillar with series of American Indian symbolic images
UFO unidentified flying object believed to be from outer space; flying saucer
visionary mystic, prophet, or psychic
wand slender rod used by conjurers and magicians
warlock sorcerer; man who practices black magic
werewolf person transformed into wolf or who assumes shape of wolf; wolfman

wicca witch in wicca doctrine
witch woman practicing white or black magic or sorcery, said by Christians to be possessed by the devil
witch doctor medicine man; shaman
wizard male sorcerer or magician
wraith apparition of living person seen just before death; ghost, specter

ESCHATOLOGY

Fate
Heaven and Paradise
Hell

Fate

apocalypse prophetic revelation of cataclysm that results in forces of good defeating forces of evil
apocalyptic number 666, number of the beast in Revelations
appointed lot one's predetermined worldly fate or fortune
Armageddon final battle between forces of good and evil
balance determination of one's fate
bane source of ruin or destruction
cataclysm violent upheaval, usu. at end of the world
coup de grâce *French.* decisive act or event; deathblow
crack of doom signal that indicates moment at which one's fate is decided; doomsday
curse ill fate or misfortune, esp. due to external intervention
damnation condemnation to hell or ill fate
deserts one's deserved reward or punishment
destiny inevitable and predetermined course of one's life
doom unhappy destiny; ruin or death
doomsday day of Last Judgment at end of the world
eschatology study of or religious doctrine concerning the end of time, judgment day, death, resurrection, and immortality
fatality something established by fate; disaster that results in death
fate inevitable outcome of one's life; prescribed order of things or predetermined cause of events
Fates three sisters who determine man's fate; weird sisters (Greek mythology)
finality irrevocable end toward which life moves
Final Judgment final determination of mankind's ultimate fate at end of the world
fortune destiny or fate, esp. favorable; hypothetical force that unpredictably determines events
inevitable that which is predetermined and cannot be avoided
infinity doomsday, day of Final Judgment
Judgment Day day of God's judgment at end of the world, determining fate of mankind
karma force generated by a person's actions, determining his or her destiny in future existence (Eastern religions)
kismet fate
Last Judgment final judgment of mankind
Last Things end of history and final fate of individuals and humankind
lot one's worldly fate or fortune; that which comes one's way in life
millennium period of Christ's Second Coming and His reign of holiness on Earth
moira individual destiny or fate (ancient Greece)
Moirai Greek Fates
odds likelihood or chance of particular event or fate
omen portent or indication of one's fortune
oubliette oblivion, finality, or death
predestination God's foreordination of all events; fate or destiny; predetermination
reincarnation rebirth of soul in another body (Hinduism)
retribution reward or punishment, esp. in hereafter
Revelations last book of Bible, in which apocalypse is described
samsara indefinitely repeated karmic cycle of birth, misery, death, and rebirth or rebecoming (Hinduism and Buddhism)
stars celestial bodies said in astrology to determine one's destiny; luck
twist of fate unexpected development, reversal of one's fortune; wild card
weird sisters Fates; Moirai
wild card twist of fate
writing on the wall portent of one's fate or destiny
zero hour time at which Final Judgment occurs or one's fate is determined

Heaven and Paradise

Abraham's bosom heaven
afterlife life after death; great beyond
afterworld place of life after death
Alfardaws Muslim paradise
Assama Muslim paradise
Canaan promised land of rest and refuge (Judaism)
Celestial City heavenly Jerusalem in Bunyan's *Pilgrim's Progress*
City of God heaven, paradise
Civitas Dei *Latin.* city of God, esp. in Catholicism
Eden original paradise recorded in Book of Genesis in Old Testament; Garden of Eden; paradise
Elysian fields Elysium
Elysium heaven of Greek and Roman mythology
empyrean highest paradise; visible heavens
eternal life immortal life of soul after death of body
eternal reward eternal life of the soul in heaven as reward for living a good life
eternity timeless state into which soul passes

after death
everlasting afterlife, eternity
Fiddler's Green heaven reserved for sailors and soldiers
Garden of Eden Eden
Garden of Irem fabled Islamic garden of paradise
great beyond usu. the great beyond; afterlife
happy hunting ground paradise of hunting and feasting for warriors after death (Native American)
heaven realm of bliss and eternal happiness after death; abode for souls of the dead at God's side
hereafter afterlife, eternity
Kingdom of God heaven (Christianity)
Kingdom of Heaven heaven (Christianity)
Land of Beulah quiet paradise for those waiting to enter Celestial City in Bunyan's *Pilgrim's Progress*
Land of the Leal heaven (Scotland)
New Jerusalem heaven
Nirvana freedom from rebirth (Buddhism)
Olympus heavenly dwelling place of ancient Greek gods
paradise realm of eternal goodness and happiness after death; Eden; reward
Pearly Gates entrance to heaven
Promised Land heaven
purgatory place of temporary suffering and punishment where souls are purified of sin prior to entry into heaven (Christianity)
reward paradise
salvation redemption or deliverance from sin
seventh heaven highest heavenly realm (Islam)
Valhalla heavenly hall and dwelling place of Norse gods and deceased heroes
welkin vault of heaven
Zion heaven as gathering place of true believers

Hell

abyss hell, bottomless infernal regions
Amenti region of the dead (ancient Egyptian mythology)
Arallu region of the dead (ancient Babylonian mythology)
Avernus hell
brimstone fire and sulfur of hell
damnation eternity in hell
Erebus place in underworld that dead pass through to reach Hades (Greek mythology)
eternal punishment banishment of soul into hell for infinity
Gehenna place of suffering and torture; hell where dead are punished after death (Judaism)
Hades realm of the dead (Greek mythology); hell
hell region or condition of punishment for wicked persons after death; abode of evil spirits, esp. the devil
hellfire fire of hell
inferno hell in form of fiery region of torture
limbo region adjacent to hell for souls forbidden from heaven
Naraka region of punishment after death (Hinduism)
Nastrond dark, noxious hall of punishment (Norse mythology)
nether world hell
Nifleheim place of eternal cold, darkness, and fog that is abode of those who die of illness or old age (Scandinavian mythology)
Pandemonium hell, demonic region; capital of hell in Milton's *Paradise Lost*
perdition hell; place of utter damnation
Sheol abode of the dead; hell (Judaism)
Styx principal river of the underworld (Greek mythology)
Tartarus infernal regions below Hades (Greek mythology)
Tophet hellish place of punishment after death in the Bible
underworld underground region for the dead; hell
void abyss; dark, unknown regions beyond life

TRUTH, WISDOM, AND SPIRITUAL ATTAINMENT

Mystical States and Experiences
Practice, Discipline, and Belief
New Age
Enlightenment, Truth, and the Unknowable

Mystical States and Experiences

afflatus divine inspiration or communication of wisdom and power
awakening becoming aware of spiritual life and one's true self
beatitude consummate bliss, transcendent happiness; state of being blessed
dark night of the soul negativity and dissatisfaction that precede spiritual enlightenment
deliverance liberation, state of being freed, esp. from darkness or bondage
disembodied (*adj*) lacking substance or reality normally present; having spirit separated from corporeal substance
divine revelation enlightenment or perception of truth through act or intervention of God
ecstasy complete, rapturous delight; trancelike state of receptivity to enlightenment
epiphany revelation or manifestation of God or the divine; sudden intuitive perception of something's essential meaning
euphoria feeling of supreme well-being or elation
extrasensory (*adj*) beyond one's normal sense perceptions
inner light divine presence in soul that provides

spiritual enlightenment and moral guidance
mystical (*adj*) possessing spiritual reality separate from senses and intellect; involving direct communion with God or spirits
nirvana highest state of enlightenment, salvation, harmony, and transcendence
oneness harmony, integrity, and wholeness of spirit
perfection condition of fullness or completion; attainment of highest state; flawless state or condition
purity perfection of spirit; absence of flaws or disharmony
quietism passive, withdrawn posture toward worldly matters
rapture spiritual ecstasy and exaltation due to knowledge of divine things
revelation divine or supernatural communication of spiritual truth
saint one distinguished by piety, virtue, and benevolence, without regard for self; spirit of departed person canonized by church to serve as guide for spiritual growth
salvation deliverance from spiritual estrangement and attachment to material world into state of religious fulfillment and recognition of ultimate reality
sanctity holiness, saintliness of life and character
totality state of being complete, comprehensive, and unified
touched (*adj*) having received divine revelation, inspiration, or supersensible powers
transcendence state of being beyond limits of everyday experience, reality, or comprehension; supernatural, unified, or spiritual realm
vision supernatural, revelatory appearance in dream, trance, or meditative state

Practice, Discipline, and Belief

anagogic (*adj*) having spiritual meaning or sense; arising from or striving toward lofty ideals
anthroposophy mystical religious system similar to that of theosophy
antinomian one who holds that divine grace is sufficient for salvation and moral law is unnecessary
ark place that provides protection and security through divine presence
asceticism strict self-denial and austerity as measure and means of spiritual discipline
ashram religious retreat for sage and disciples
astral (*adj*) relating to the stars; denoting a supersensible substance held in theosophy to pervade all space and survive the individual after death
astral traveler spiritual guide; one who makes spiritual, out-of-body journey
augur (*vb*) predict future by omens
blessing something conducive to spiritual attainment; consecration by divine care or intervention
chakra in yoga, any of seven body points that are sources of psychic energy and spiritual power
channel (*vb*) convey information from spiritual world
communion contact and communication with God or spirits
contemplation deep thought; silent meditation on spiritual matters
cornerstone that which is essential, basic, or indispensable to all that follows or is built upon it
élan vital life force, vital principle of life
embodiment physical incarnation of noncorporeal thing
empyrean true and ultimate heavenly sphere; transcendentally exalted source of noble ideas or feelings
eudemonics art or method of attaining happiness
fasting prolonged abstention from food for purification and spiritual insight
forgiveness act or state of ceasing to feel resentment or seek retribution over wrong committed by another
grace beneficence or generosity, esp. of God toward humankind; disposition to kindness and compassion
guru master, teacher, spiritual guide
healing removal of negative energy, making one sound and whole; restoring spiritual integrity
higher law guiding principles of divine or moral law
hylozoism doctrine that all matter is inseparable from life
indwell (*vb*) exist within as guiding spirit or motivating force
key something serving to reveal or solve a mystery or provide an entrance to spiritual enlightenment
leap attainment of enlightenment through sudden awareness or revelation
life, the occupation with and devotion to spiritual matters, esp. to the exclusion of material concerns; the way
lotus position erect sitting posture in yoga, with each foot resting on thigh of the opposite leg with sole upturned
mandala graphic, mystic representation of universe used as meditation aid, esp. concentric geometric shape such as square within a circle
manifestation perceptible outward expression of something, esp. form or guise of spirit or divinity
manna divine or spiritual nourishment
mantra ritualistic incantation used in meditation
master wise individual, learned in spiritual discipline and inspiring devotion among disciples
material (*adj*) corporeal or bodily, the opposite of spiritual
meditation private devotion; spiritual exercise of deep contemplation or sustained introspection, esp. silent repetition of mantra
medium individual believed to be capable of channeling information from spirit world
meridian flow lines of energy movement through body
miracle inexplicable, extraordinary event suggesting divine intervention or spiritual guidance
moral (*adj*) ethically good, principled; conforming to or acting on inner conviction of what is right
music of the spheres ethereal harmony supposed to be produced by movements of spheres of heavenly bodies
mysteries secret initiation rites for supposed bet-

terment of worshipers
nimbus shining cloud around divine being
numen divine spirit inhabiting natural object or phenomenon; dynamic, creative force; human need for and capacity to have spiritual life
odyssey long, adventurous journey, esp. in search of enlightenment
omni- prefix meaning all
one way life devoted to spiritual attainment
panacea universal remedy for all ills
past life previous physical existence of spirit, esp. as basis of one's karma
path spiritual direction, one way; attainment of enlightenment through systematic spiritual discipline
perseverance steadfast persistence in pursuit of spiritual grace, esp. until succeeded by state of glory
pietism intensity of devotional experience and practice
pundit learned wise man
purging self-purification by expulsion of harmful substances
purification cleansing of sin; moral or spiritual purgation
querent one who consults a spiritual guide
realization act or process of becoming real, taking form, or achieving potential
rebirth spiritual regeneration or revival
reflection meditation; consideration of something with view to understanding
reflexology massage of foot or hand to promote generalized healing and relieve stress
rejuvenation regeneration of youthful vigor
renunciation ascetic self-denial; rejection of one's previous values or lifestyle
sacrifice self-denial, loss, or abstinence from something to promote spiritual growth
seeker one who devotes life to search for enlightenment and salvation
spirit essence of deity serving as invisible activating power; soul; noncorporeal essence and animating principle of life
swami master, teacher, wise man
theosophy religious beliefs held to be based on special mystical insight into divine nature
TM transcendental meditation
transcendence quality of being beyond what is experienced and perceived in material world
transcendental meditation TM; simple Hindu technique of two daily twenty-minute meditations with chanted mantra, now popular in the West
transfiguration act or process of undergoing ennobling spiritual change
visionary one who sees beyond common experience or perception
visitation special administration of divine favor, affliction, or revelation
votary devotee living by vows
way, the path to spiritual attainment and harmony; the life
Word usu. the Word; divine guidance and inspiration
zazen meditation practice in cross-legged position
Zen practice of self-discipline and meditation to achieve direct spiritual enlightenment

New Age

affirmation positive thought consciously used to create a desired result
akashic records universal memory of nature and all souls; the book of life
All That Is God; Creative Forces; Divine Mind
altered state of consciousness any shift of primary focus to levels of reality other than the physical plane; trance or hypnotic state
ambient sound soothing, environmental background music; New Age music
amulet bag small protective pouch for carrying items of personal sacred significance, such as crystals
Aquarian Age two-thousand year astrological World Age beginning around 2000A.D., in which humanity is expected to evolve towards peace, spiritual enlightenment, global community, and renewal of the Earth
aromatherapy use of essential oils for relaxation and healing, usu. in conjunction with massage and acupuncture
astral body inner body composed of electromagnetic energy that links the soul with the physical body; energy body
Atlantis lost, legendary island civilization in Atlantic Ocean between Europe and North America, said to have sunk beneath the sea in ancient times
aura magnetic energy field; luminous quality radiating from a person
belief system primary ideas or attitudes about life that shape one's relationship to reality
biomagnetics study of magnetic energy as it effects human health
bodywork any of various psycho-physical, hands on healing techniques utilizing massage, movement, and seeking to balance the energy and emotional bodies
catalyst guide or teacher who functions as facilitator to speed one's psychic or spiritual growth
chakra system major channels through which life force flows into physical body; mediating channels between astral and physical bodies associated with major glands and acupuncture points
channeling receiving energy and information from other levels of reality ranging from discarnate beings to the Divine Mind or collective unconscious
core belief idea or attitude ingrained in one's mental patterns as truth
core tone vibrational essence of the individual soul carried within each incarnation
Creative Forces God; All That Is; Divine Mind; life force
creative visualization technique using mental imagery and affirmations to produce positive energy and conditions conducive to harmony and positive changes in life
crystal transparent, usu. quartz crystalline structure that vibrates at high frequency, used in conjunction with gemstones for healing and meditation
discarnate being incorporeal being or spirit
Divine Mind God; All That Is; Creative Forces

Earth plane physical world of external reality
emotional body octave or level of body that vibrates with all unresolved emotions from any incarnation
energy body astral body; level of body containing chakra system
feeling tone vibration of being, emanating from emotional body, that resonates from core tone
Great Year in astrology, cosmic cycle of twelve World Ages, occurring once every 26,000 years; Aquarian Age marks beginning of next Great Year
guiding spirit source of channeled information, usu. spirit of deceased person
hands-on healing channeling life-force energy through hands to remove negative energy, make oneself whole, and restore spiritual integrity
Harmonic Convergence shift point at end of Mayan Great Cycle, occurring in August, 1987, when a synchronized global meditation coincided with passage of a galactic beam through Earth and the sun in expectation of 5000 years of peace and harmony
harmonizing bringing something or someone into accord and balance
healer person who is a channel for the life force with intent to be of service to others
higher mind level of mind fueled by soul rather than ego and capable of accessing broader perspective
higher self one's essence or eternal nature; soul
holistic (*adj*) emphasizing organic or functional relation between parts and whole
incarnate (*adj*) in a physical form; within a body
inner child part of emotional body that holds unfinished childhood business as well as the capacity to be eternally childlike
inner guide spiritual guide; inner voice; part of greater being that is not presently incarnate
karmic bond deep connection of two souls from past incarnations that is carried into present lifetimes
karmic debt good deeds owed in present life to balance or complete a past incarnation
Lemuria legendary pre-Atlantean civilization located on lost subcontinent in Pacific Ocean whose people were known as the Mu
light positive energy; the source
light being spirit guide; discarnate being; saint
magnet body that produces magnetic field capable of attracting iron, influencing personal vibrations, and healing
mindfulness meditation technique in which full awareness is focused on the present moment
negative energy energy that is toxic or draining to the life force and counter to affirmation of life
New Age evolution of human consciousness and spiritual movement toward the light of the Aquarian Age; spiritual healing based on various techniques and methods such as astrology and crystal interpretation
New Age music ambient or environmental acoustic jazz that is spiritually soothing or uplifting, often using a blend of ancient and modern instruments
octave harmonic interval or level of consciousness
organic (*adj*) forming an inherent vital part; composed of, using, or grown only with animal or vegetable matter
oversoul supreme reality or mind; spiritual unity of all being
past-life therapy technique of releasing karmic blocks through a regression process in order to access one's full potential
peak experience glimpse of enlightenment
pendulum suspended body swinging freely from fixed point, used as simple means of receiving channeled information
primal body level of the body that contains the cellular memory of humanity's animal heritage and the dark side of nature from one's past lives
psychic person who can access energy and information from nonphysical realms; sensitive, medium, or channel
psychic therapy spiritually based therapy that utilizes altered states to experience and integrate the soul level of consciousness
pyramid structure in the form of a square base with triangular walls meeting at apex that concentrates and transmits energy for meditation and regeneration
regeneration spiritual renewal or rebirth, esp. a radical transformation of one's life
self-actualization fulfillment of one's potential; attainment of peace of mind and harmony
soul consciousness eternal perspective and link between the ego/mind and the Divine Mind
soul mates two or more souls originally split off from the same or larger oversoul
third eye sixth chakra at center of forehead, connected with pineal gland, through which soul sees into physical plane; energy center through which psychic sense of vision operates
vibration velocity of movement of energy or life force through a body; characteristic aura, derived from this movement of energy, that one senses intuitively from an individual or body

Enlightenment, Truth, and the Unknowable

attainment accomplishment or acquisition of enlightenment
clear (*adj*) free of mundane, worldly matters, enabling one to see the spiritual essence of things as they are; at the highest state of enlightenment
compassion consciousness of other people's suffering and selfless tenderness toward it
empathy capacity for vicarious experiencing of another's thoughts or feelings and understanding based on it
enlightenment state of being in harmony with laws of the universe; realization of ultimate universal truth and absence of desire
entelechy realization or actuality, as opposed to potential
humility freedom from pride and arrogance;

modesty of spirit and ability to view others and oneself realistically
illumination spiritual enlightenment
infinity boundless space, energy, knowledge, or capacity
innominate (*adj*) unnamed or of unknown name; unnamable
insight apprehension of inner nature of things; intuitive understanding of others and oneself
intuition revelation by insight or innate knowledge, without reasoning
light, the spiritual illumination, enlightenment, ultimate truth
mastery great skill or knowledge in some discipline
nobility superiority and righteousness of character or mind
omniscience infinite knowledge and understanding
perspective capacity to view things in their true relationships
profundity depth of insight; spiritual awareness
quietude tranquility, peace, inner harmony
quintessence purest, most concentrated form or part, esp. of immaterial thing
realized (*adj*) spiritually enlightened, in harmony with oneself
recognition discovery of true nature of something or someone
revealed (*adj*) pertaining to truths based on intuition or divine inspiration
sagacity wisdom, keenness of discernment, understanding
seeing enlightenment
sense of self understanding and acceptance of one's true nature
Tao eternal order of the universe and source of reality; right way of life, virtuous conduct
truth fundamental, spiritual reality that lies beyond perceived reality and experience
uncharted territory mysterious regions beyond what has been explored, observed, or experienced
universal (*adj*) present in all spheres of human life; (*n*) an ultimate truth
unknowable ultimate reality lying beyond human perception and experience, understood only through spirituality
unknown that which has yet to be discovered, identified, revealed, understood, or explained
verity state of being eternally and fundamentally true or necessary; something that is true, as a principle, belief, or idea
window revelation of truth, esp. moment or point of such revelation
wisdom understanding of spiritual truth; enlightenment; capacity to discern the essence of the ways of human beings and the universe

Index

This index provides an alphabetical list of entries in the book that have definitions.

son et lumière, 491, 585

table d'hôte, 282, 585